Black Sea
Samsun
Ankara
Sivas
Erzurum
Mt Ararat
TURKEY
Kayseri
Lake Van
Tabriz
Caspian Sea
Adana
Mosul
Aleppo
Nicosia
CYPRUS
Limassol
Famagusta
Larnaca
SYRIA
Homs
Tripoli
LEBANON
Beirut
Damascus
Kirkuk
Haifa
ISRAEL
Nablus
Tel Aviv (Jaffa)
Gaza
Port Said
JORDAN
Amman
Jerusalem
Hebron
Isma'iliyya
Suez
Ma'an
Sinai
'Aqaba
Jauf
Baghdad
Tigris
IRAQ
Karbala
Najaf
Euphrates
Basra
Khorramshahr
Abadan
KUWAIT
Kuwait
Elburz Mountains
Kazvin
Tehran
Dasht-i-kavir
Mashad
Hamadan
Qom
Kermanshah
Zagros Mountains
IRAN
Isfahan
Yazd
Kerman
Shiraz
Bushire
Zahedan
Bandar Abbas
Mazar-i-Sharif
Hindu Kush Mountains
Herat
AFGHANISTAN
Kabul
Shindand
Ghazni
Kandahar
Nafud
Ha'il
Najd
Hijaz
Nile
Wejh
Luxor
Aswan
The Gulf
Jubail
Dammam
Dhahran
Al Khobar
BAHRAIN
Manama
Doha
QATAR
Dubai
Abu Dhabi
UNITED ARAB EMIRATES
Medina
Yanbu'
Riyadh
SAUDI ARABIA
Muscat
Nizwa
Red Sea
Jidda
Mecca
OMAN
Arabian Sea
Bisha
Rub' al-Khali
Port Sudan
Suakin
Merowe
Atbara
Abha
Najran
Sad'a
Marib
NORTH YEMEN
San'a
SOUTH YEMEN
Shibam
Salala
Mukalla
Omdurman
Khartoum
Kassala
Hudayda
Ta'iz
Aden
Gulf of Aden
White Nile
Blue Nile
DJIBOUTI
Berbera
Hargeisa
SOMALIA
Indian Ocean
Juba
Mogadishu
Kismayu

THE CAMBRIDGE ENCYCLOPEDIA OF THE MIDDLE EAST AND NORTH AFRICA

The Cambridge Encyclopedia of THE MIDDLE EAST AND NORTH AFRICA

Executive Editor
Trevor Mostyn

Advisory Editor
Albert Hourani

CAMBRIDGE UNIVERSITY PRESS
Cambridge
New York New Rochelle Melbourne Sydney

Published by the Press Syndicate of the University of Cambridge
The Pitt Building, Trumpington Street, Cambridge CB2 1RP
32 East 57th Street, New York, NY 10022, USA
10 Stamford Road, Oakleigh, Melbourne 3166, Australia

First published 1988

British Library Cataloguing in Publication Data

The Cambridge encyclopedia of the Middle
East and North Africa.
1. Middle East 2. North Africa
I. Mostyn, Trevor II. Hourani, Albert,
1915–
956′.052

Library of Congress Cataloging in Publication Data

The Cambridge encyclopedia of the Middle East and North Africa
executive editor, Trevor Mostyn, advisory editor, Albert Hourani,
p. cm.
Includes index.
ISBN 0 521 32190 5
1. Middle East. I. Mostyn, Trevor. II. Hourani, Albert Habib.
DS44.C37 1988
956 –dc19 88–10866 CIP

ISBN 0 521 32190 5

Printed in Great Britain by Cowells

Contributors

AA	**Ayad Abou Chakra** *Al-Sharq al-Awsat* newspaper, London
MA	**Maureen Ali** Writer and film-maker, London
JAA	**Dr J. A. Allen** School of Oriental and African Studies, University of London
JA	**Dr Julia Ashtiany** Specialist in Arabic literature, Oxford
MAs	**Mohsen Ashtiany** Specialist in Persian literature, Oxford
JB	**Professor John Baines** University of Oxford
KBB	**Professor Kevork B. Bardakjian** Harvard University
CB	**Carole Berger** Journalist, Cairo
MB	**Dr Michael Brett** School of Oriental and African Studies, University of London
AB	**Alison Brown**
KB	**Professor Kathleen R. F. Burrill** Columbia University, New York
DB	**David Butter** *Middle East Economic Digest*, London
HC	**Helena Cobban** University of Maryland
DC	**Dr Dominique Collon** British Museum, London
SSD	**S. Samar Damluji** Royal College of Art, London
MSD	**Dr Margaret S. Drower** University College, London
AD	**Professor Alasdair Drysdale** University of New Hampshire
SE	**Sonia Ewart** Antiquarian Books, London
MF	**Michael Field** *Financial Times*, London
CF	**Professor Clive Foss** University of Massachusetts, Boston
DGi	**David Gilmour** Writer and journalist, East Lothian, Scotland
PG	**Pandeli M. Glavanis** University of Durham
DG	The late **David Goldstein** British Library, London
SG-B	**Sarah Graham-Brown** Writer and journalist, London
CG	**Charles Gurdon** Writer and journalist, London
FH	**Professor F. Halliday** London School of Economics and Political Science
SNH	**S. Nomanul Haq** Harvard University

CJH **Dr Colin J. Heywood**
School of Oriental and African Studies, University of London

NH **Nadia Hijab**
Writer and journalist, London

DRH **Dr Donald R. Hill**
Honorary Research Fellow of the Department of History and Philosophy of Science, University College London

RH **Dr Robert Hillenbrand**
University of Edinburgh

MH **Dr Martin Hinds**
Trinity Hall, Cambridge

DH **Dr Derek Hopwood**
St Antony's College, Oxford

AHH **Albert Hourani**
St Antony's College, Oxford

IH **Dr Ian K. A. Howard**
University of Edinburgh

AH **Anthony Hyman**
Writer and journalist, London

RI **Robert Irwin**
Writer, London

CI **Professor Charles Issawi**
Princeton University

GJ **George Joffe**
Economist Publications, London

TK **Profesor Tarif Khalidi**
American University of Beirut

AK **Alexander Knapp**
Wolfson College, Cambridge

OL **Dr Oliver Leaman**
Liverpool Polytechnic

SNCL **Dr Samuel N. C. Lieu**
University of Warwick

SL **Simon Louvish**
Novelist and film lecturer, London

NL **Dr Noah Lucas**
University of Sheffield

AM **Dr Andrew Mango**
Encyclopedia Britannica, Turkish edition

PM **Peter Mansfield**
Writer and journalist, London

DM'd **David McDowall**
Writer, London

KM **Dr Keith McLachlan**
School of Oriental and African Studies, University of London

VM **Vladimir Mirodan**
Director and lecturer in drama, London

MBM **Baqer Moin**
British Broadcasting Corporation, London

DM **Dr David O. Morgan**
School of Oriental and African Studies, University of London

TM **Trevor Mostyn**
Writer and journalist, London

BM **Dr Basim Musallam**
University of Cambridge

TO **Tony Odone**
Middle East Economic Digest, London

TP **Dr Tudor Parfitt**
School of Oriental and African Studies, University of London

VP **Vahe Petrosian**
Middle East Economic Digest, London

JP **Dr James Piscatori**
School of Advanced International Studies, Washington

AJR **Professor A. Jihad Racy**
University of California, Los Angeles

BTR **Barbara T. Racy**
University of California, Los Angeles

HR **Dr Hugh Roberts**
University of East Anglia

PRo **Philip Robins**
Royal Institute of International Affairs, London

MHR **Malise Ruthven**
Writer, London

MR **Miriam Ryan**
Writer on medical affairs, London

PR **Peter Ryan**
Writer on science, London

NS **Naomi Sakr**
Economist Publications, London

NAS **Nabil Anis Saleh**
Law Consultant for the Middle East, London

GS **Professor George Saliba**
Columbia University, New York

IS **Dr Ian J. Seccombe**
University of Durham

PS **Dr Peter Sluglett**
University of Durham

PAS **Pamela Ann Smith**
Writer and journalist, London

PJS **Dr Paul Stevens**
University of Surrey

NSt **Professor Norman A. Stillman**
State University of New York, Binghamton

RS **Richard Synge**
Africa Economic Digest, London

ST **Susannah Tarbush**
Middle East Economic Digest, London

MT **Dr Mina Toksoz**
Economist Publications, London

HK **Dr Hilary Waardenburg-Kilpatrick**
Catholic University of Nijmegen, The Netherlands

DW **Dr David Waines**
University of Lancaster

CJW **Christopher Walker**
Writer, London

RW **Dr Rodney J. A. Wilson**
University of Durham

OW **Dr Owen Wright**
School of Oriental and African Studies, University of London

ABZ **Dr A. B. Zahlan**
Consultant on science policy, London

Contents

PART V THE COUNTRIES

PART VI INTER-STATE RELATIONS

Maps

Preface

The editors are extremely grateful to Brenda Christie who gave them her constant and conscientious assistance throughout the project.

Thanks are also due to the following who kindly read various articles or provided material for them: Professor John Baines, Dr Sebastian Brock, Professor Geoffrey Lewis, Professor Wilferd Madelung, Peter Mansfield, Dr David Morgan, Dr Amikam Nachmani, Dr Farhan Nizami and Dr R. Navabpour.

They are also particularly grateful to Helen Finney for her help in selecting photographs, Margaret Owen for advising on the transliteration, Margaret Sharman for sub-editing the text, and to Robin Rees and Elinor Cole at Cambridge Reference.

Note on cross-referencing within the text

An asterisk against a name or word in the text indicates that there is an entry on this subject, or substantial further reference to it, which can be found elsewhere in the book by looking it up in the Index.

Transliteration

In principle, the editors have tried to follow the system of transliteration used by the *Encyclopaedia Judaica* for Hebrew words and names; for those in Arabic, Persian and Turkish, they have adopted the system used in the *International Journal of Middle East Studies* in a simplified form (no diacriticals [ʿ] for the letter ʻ*ayn*; [ʾ] for *hamza* in the middle of a word only).

It has not been possible to be wholly consistent, however. Some words and names have a familiar English or French form, which may be used not only by foreign writers but by members of the indigenous population; some are common to Arabic, Persian and Turkish but pronounced differently in each of them, and may therefore have to be transliterated differently according to the context; it has sometimes seemed best to spell a word as it is pronounced locally, rather than in accordance with its form in literary Arabic.

Acknowledgements

The publishers gratefully acknowledge the assistance of Frank Spooner Pictures and Middle East Archive in the collection of illustrations for this book.

Note In the photographic acknowledgements the following abbreviations have been used: FSP, Frank Spooner Pictures; MEA, Middle East Archive.

9 © Alistair Duncan, MEA; 12, 13 © Richard Turpin, FSP; 15 © Jill Brown, FSP; 19 © Anthony Hyman; 20 Turkish Tourist Office: 23 *tl* © Trevor Mostyn; *tr* © Alistair Duncan, MEA; 24 © Trevor Mostyn; 29 © Alistair Duncan, MEA; 35 © Anthony Hyman; 38 © Alistair Duncan, MEA; 39 © Anthony Hutt, FSP; 41 By courtesy of the Trustees of the British Museum; 45 © K. Eddy; 52 © Jill Brown, FSP; 57 © H. Shehadeh, FSP; 64 © Alistair Duncan, MEA; 69 © Anthony Hutt, FSP; 72 © FSP; 76 © Ronald Sheridan, Ancient Art & Architecture Collection; 77 © Richard Turpin, FSP; 84 © Royal Geographical Society; 86 © Photo-Dérounian-Alep; 87 Turkish Tourist Office; 89 © D. G. McDowall, FSP; 90 © Peter Ryan, FSP; 93 © Trevor Mostyn; 95 © Michael Beazley, FSP, Masstock Saudia Ltd.; 97 © R. Roxburgh, FSP; 100 © John Lawrence, FSP; 101 © Trevor Mostyn; 105 © Jill Brown, FSP; 106 © Peter Ryan, FSP; 109 Iraq Petroleum Co.; 111 © Jill Brown, FSP; 121 © Kim Naylor, FSP; 123 © Claudia Al-Rashoud, FSP; 124 © Jill Brown, FSP; 126 © H. Shehadeh, FSP; 128 © Christine Osborne, FSP; 129 © M. Sparrow, FSP; 130 © Trevor Mostyn; 134 © Claudia Al-Rashoud, FSP; 138 © Christine Osborne, FSP; 157 © Gamma-FSP; 159 © Anthony Hutt, FSP; 161 © Abbas-Gamma, FSP; 162 © Peter Maxey, FSP; 163 © Vahe Petrossian; 165 © Alistair Duncan, MEA; 169 © Helen Tann, FSP; 176 © Trevor Mostyn; 177 © T. Goltz, FSP; 182 © Liz Thurgood; 183 © Iverson-Gamma, FSP; 184, 187 © David Harris, Israeli Government Tourist Office; 193, 194, 195 © Alistair Duncan, MEA; 196 © R. Harding, W.I.F.T.; 206 © Peter Maxey, FSP; 208 © Anthony Hutt, FSP; 211 © Alistair Duncan, MEA; 213 Fogg Art Museum, The Bridgeman Art Library; 214 Courtesy of Paramount Pictures Corporation © 1921, 1948 by Paramount Pictures Corporation. All Rights Reserved; 216 *bl* © Christine Osborne, FSP; *tr* © Alistair Duncan, MEA; 217, 218 *bl*, *tr* By courtesy of the Trustees of the British Museum; 221 *bl* © P. Ryan, FSP; *tr* © Bill Lyons, FSP; 223 © Christine Osborne, FSP; 224 © Alistair Duncan, MEA; 225 © W.I.F.T.; 229 © Alistair Duncan, MEA; 233 © G. Adams, FSP; 234 © S. S. Dambuji; 236 The Aga Khan Award for Architecture; 237 © Anthony Hutt, FSP; 240 © Christine Osborne, FSP; 241 © Claudia Al-Rashoud, FSP; 243 © Barbara T. Racy; 247 © Alistair Duncan, MEA; 249 © Barbara T. Racy; 251 © Alistair Duncan, MEA; 257 Artificial Eye Film Company; 265 © Ronald Sheridan, The Ancient Art & Architecture Collection; 268 © W.I.F.T., MEA; 273 Bodleian Library; 276 © Alistair Duncan, MEA; 278 © Transworld, Gamma, FSP; 282 © Gamma, FSP; 285 United Nations; 289 © Abbas-Gamma, FSP; 290 © Mingam-Gamma, FSP; 294 © Novosti-Gamma, FSP; 297 *tl*, *br*, 298 *tl* © Anthony Hyman; 299 © A. Diamond, Anthony Hyman; 302 *tl* © Eds. Photo-Africaines; *tr* © Eds. La Cicogne; 303, 305 © Gamma, FSP; 307 © Trevor Mostyn; 309 © D. G. McDowall, FSP; 311 © John Lawrence, FSP; 313, 314 Cypriot Tourist Office; 321 © Alistair Duncan, MEA; 322 © Gamma, FSP; 327, 329 © Abbas-Gamma, FSP; 331 © Liz Thurgood; 332 *l*, *tr*, *cr* © Abbas-Gamma, FSP; *br* © Mingam-Gamma, FSP; 334 © Islamic Republic News Agency; 338 © Anthony Hyman; 339 © Islamic Republic News Agency; 343 © Jill Brown, FSP; 346 © Abbas-Gamma, FSP; 348 © Jill Brown, FSP; 351, 353, 354, 357 BIPAC; 359 © Alistair Duncan, MEA; 360 © Bill Lyons, FSP; 361 © Trevor Mostyn; 362 © G. Nehmeh, UNRWA; 367 © G. Ferrari, FSP; 370 © Alistair Duncan, MEA; 372 © Associated Press Ltd.; 375 © UNRWA; 376 © Jill Brown, FSP; 382 © Gamma, FSP; 384 © Jill Brown, FSP; 389 © R. Turpin, FSP; 396 © John Lawrence, FSP; 397 © D. Chappell, FSP; 398 © John Lawrence, FSP; 404 © G. Adams, FSP; 406 Saudi Press Agency; 408 Courtesy of Robert Maxwell; 411 © FSP; 416, 418 © N. Worrall, FSP; 419 © Kim Naylor, FSP; 420 © N. Worrall, FSP; 421 © Christine Osborne, FSP; 422 © K. Eddy, FSP; 425 © Gamma, FSP; 426 © Trevor Mostyn; 429, 435 © J. Brown, FSP; 440 © K. Eddy; 442 Burmah Oil Co.; 443 Abu Dhabi Petroleum Co.; 444 United Arab Emirates Information Office; 445 © Christine Osborne, FSP; 446 © S. Smith, FSP; 449 © UNRWA/FSP; 455 © FSP; 457 © Trevor Mostyn; 459 © D. Shirreff, FSP; 466 © Abbas-Gamma, FSP; 469 © UNRWA; 470 © G. Nehmeh, UNRWA; 474 BIPAC; 476 © Gamma, FSP; 478 © Peter Maxey, FSP; 489 © M. Winter Chaumeny, UNRWA; 491, 493 © Islamic Republic News Agency; 495 © Jill Brown, FSP.

Part I

LANDS AND PEOPLES

Sunset across the Nile, Cairo

The physical environment

Situation of the area in the world

The region known as the Middle East and Maghrib (North Africa) has a number of common environmental characteristics arising from its geology and climate. The region comprises a major part of the ancient geological blocks of Africa and Asia. These ancient blocks originated in the Precambrian and Palaeozoic eras of the geological past 200 million or more years ago and are normally referred to as plates. The movement of these plates at various times in the past largely explains the present terrain and landforms of the Middle East and North Africa. Climatically, the region also has some uniform characteristics in that much of it is influenced by the Mediterranean regime with a pattern of cool moist winters and hot dry summers, but with the additional feature that the Mediterranean influence, dominant in the north of the region, becomes progressively weaker towards the south. In the south and especially

Structural elements of the Middle East

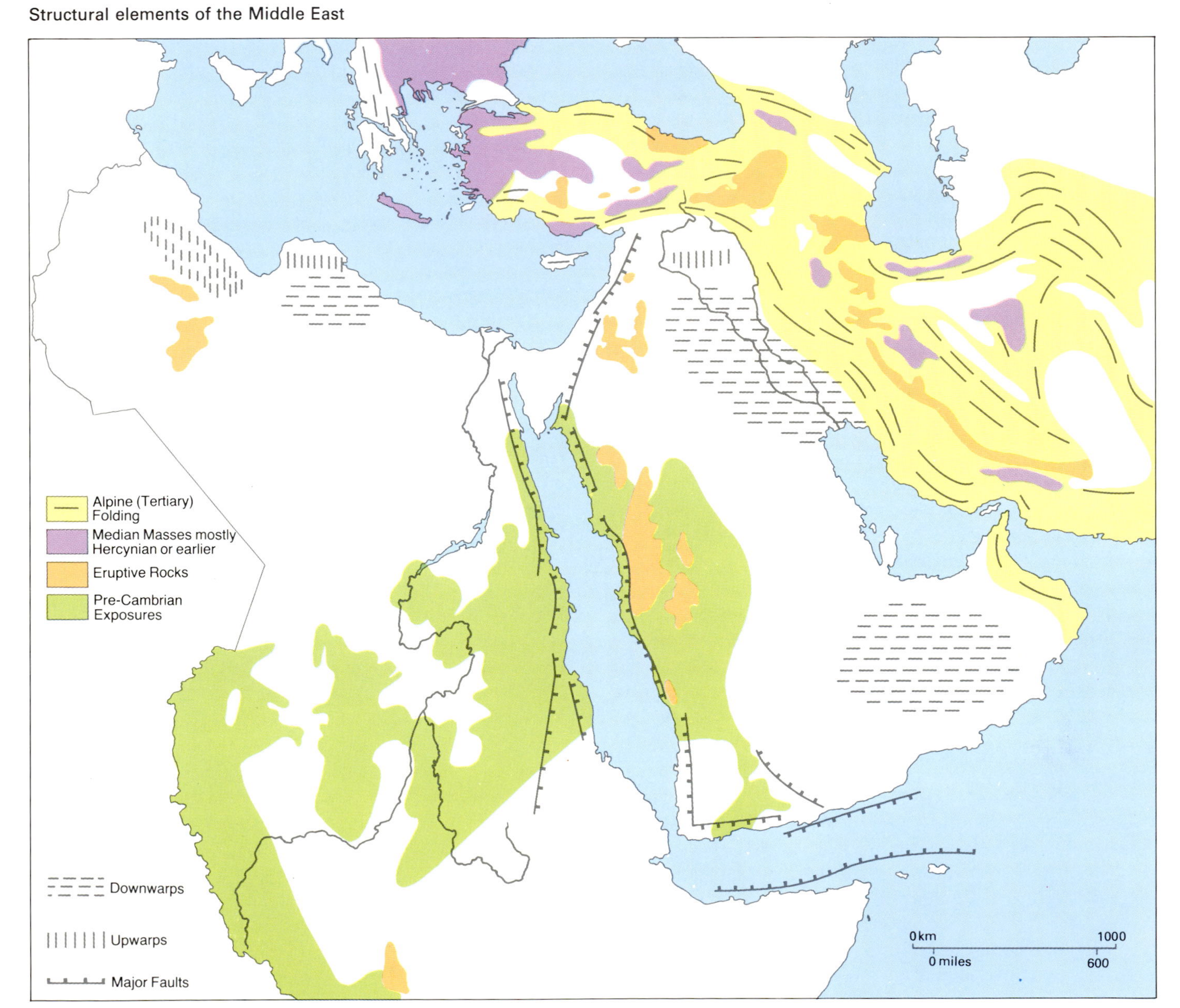

in the desert interiors the climate is uniformly arid throughout the year. The southern part of Arabia is anomalous in that it is affected by a local monsoon bringing modest summer rainfall.

The presence of the ancient blocks has determined the low and generally uniform relief of the southern part of the region. The basement rocks are occasionally exposed, for example in the western part of Saudi Arabia and in the central Sahara, but their main influence on the region and especially on its topographical uniformity is in providing the stable basement to the whole of the southern three-quarters of the region. The basement rocks of the Precambrian era are overlain in places by Palaeozoic deposits and by sediments laid down in the relatively recent Jurassic and Cretaceous periods of the Secondary era when the region was beneath an ancient sea known as the Tethys Sea. The Secondary rocks are mainly undisturbed and cover large tracts of Libya, Egypt and the Arabian peninsula, as well as Jordan, Syria and Iraq.

The position of the ancient blocks and especially their movements have also determined the location of the major mountains of the region and the trend and severity of the remarkable fault structures of the Jordan Valley, the Gulf of ʿAqaba and the Red Sea. The ancient blocks of Africa and Eurasia were originally consolidated with those of the Americas, the Indian subcontinent and Australasia in a major plate known as Gondwanaland. The various elements have for the most part moved apart and some, such as the Americas, are still moving away from Eurasia and Africa. But it is the relationship of Africa and Eurasia which has been important for the Middle East. During the Secondary era there was a tendency for the two plates to move apart and it was during this era that the depression covered by the waters of the Tethys Sea extended over what is now the Middle East. In the Tethys depression the very important Jurassic and Cretaceous strata were laid down. They were important for two reasons. First, it was these rocks which were crumpled and folded during the Alpine earth movements of the Tertiary era, when the African Plate moved northwards against the Eurasian Plate. The resulting mountains, the Atlas Mountains of the Maghrib, the Taurus Mountains of Turkey and the Elburz and Zagros Mountains of Iran have considerably affected the direction taken by communications, especially in the past. The major significance of the Jurassic and Cretaceous rocks is, however, in the crude petroleum deposits which were accumulated during their deposition. The shifts of the African Plate together with the contiguous Arabian peninsula during the Tertiary created shocks which resulted not only in the major folds of the mountain ranges of the north of the region but, more important as far as the contemporary economies of the region are concerned, they also created the minor folds characteristic of parts of Iraq and Iran, as well as onshore and offshore tracts of the Gulf and the Sirte Basin of Libya. These gentle folds trapped countless reservoirs of crude oil which have proved to be the richest deposits in the world. These reservoirs lie only in those areas where the Jurassic and Cretaceous sediments have been slightly disturbed; where the Alpine folds are severe the petroleum deposits have not accumulated. In addition, they have not been trapped in the very extensive tracts where the Secondary sediments have not been disturbed. Here they lie on particularly stable elements of the plates, far from zones of crumpling or other tectonic disturbance, for example in north-west Egypt or in central Arabia.

The other major terrain features of the region, the major fault structures of the Jordan Valley, the Gulf of ʿAqaba and the Red Sea, also owe their location and scale to shifts in the ancient blocks. When the African Plate shifted there was a western as well as a northern component in the movement as the whole African system moved around a focus located in that particularly complex zone of the Aegean and western Turkey. The strains created by these shifts brought about the down-faulted features of the Jordan Valley and the even wider rift zones of the Gulf of ʿAqaba and the Red Sea.

The tectonic background to the region is important in one further matter. The Middle East and North Africa are areas of the world often disturbed by earthquakes and an understanding of the plate tectonics of the region is useful in comprehending and explaining the areas affected by such problems. The zones of relatively recent mountain building, the Alpine fold areas of the Atlas, Taurus, Elburz and Zagros Mountains are still unstable and almost every year there is a report of a major earthquake in Turkey or in the northern part of Iran. The major fault systems of the region are also regions of instability; in addition there are some well-known ancient lines of stress in the plates themselves which occasionally cause local instability in northern Africa and Arabia.

Relief

The mountainous north of the region includes terrain which rises to over 4000 m in the Taurus of southern Turkey, and to over 3000 m in the mountains which skirt the southern edge of the Black Sea. In Iran the highest point, Mount Damavand, just north of Tehran, rises to over 2600 m and the highest point in the Zagros Mountains is over 4600 m. The more extreme tectonic character of the folded mountainous areas in the geological past is evidenced by the presence of extinct volcanoes, such as the dramatic cone of Mount Ararat in northern Turkey, and also by the frequent earthquakes which occur in northern Turkey, Iran and the Maghrib. The Atlas Mountains of the Maghrib are arranged in two major folded systems of the Atlas and the Anti-Atlas. In parts of the Maghrib, and especially in Algeria, the zone between the two folded elements is a high plateau with its own internal drainage system creating the *chotts* (*shatts*) or salt-flats associated with low-lying areas.

The desert areas have little amplitude of relief and are characterized by low-lying rocky terrain and by sand seas. The sand seas

Ouarzazate and the High Atlas Mountains, Morocco

are very extensive and cover about one-third of northern Africa and the Arabian peninsula. The dune features of the sand seas are active in that their surface is constantly modified by the wind, but they take up characteristic profiles which are repeated in crescent (*barkhan*) and linear (*seif*) forms. Some of these linear features can cover distances of over 100 km in the deserts of the Sahara and Arabia. The extensive low-lying desert terrain, although easy to traverse, has, nevertheless, imposed serious impediments to movement. Traders and armies have avoided the large deserts and generally have found routes round them. Where water is available well-established routes have emerged, but for the most part the record shows that the deserts have been regarded as barriers to cultural and economic exchange throughout history.

The mountains of the north of the region have also imposed constraints on mobility for thousands of years. Trading and military activities have been accomplished through gaps dictated by the relief of these uplands. The valleys in the Zagros as well as the lower terrain in the eastern part of Iran have guided conquering armies moving both east and west throughout history. Relief has not often been the basis for the definition of international boundaries because many of them were drawn as a result of the disruptive phases following the First World War (involving Turkey, Iran, Iraq, Syria, Lebanon, Transjordan and Palestine) and after the Second World War (involving Israel and Jordan). One longstanding boundary which accords largely with relief is that between the Arab and the Persian (Iranian) worlds. It lies at the foot of the Zagros Mountains. Unhappily for the Kurds*, the belief that the line between the Arab and the Persian tradition should follow this relief has led to the boundary between modern Iraq and Iran being drawn through the Kurds' traditional and mainly upland homeland.

Outside the mountainous north of the region, uplands occur only round the faulted Jordan Valley and Sinai and in the extreme south, in Yemen and Oman. The uplands of Yemen, which reach over 4000 m, are associated with the faulting of the Red Sea, while the uplands of Oman owe their broken nature to Alpine folding, associated volcanic activity and extensive lava flows.

The Gulf (known variously as Persian or Arabian Gulf)

The Gulf is a shallow warm-water sea and an active area of deposition into which one of the two most important river systems of the region, the Tigris-Euphrates, drains. The Gulf is just the sort of environment, albeit on a very much smaller scale, which geologists believe existed in the period of the much more extensive Tethys Sea of the Secondary era. The area is underlain by gently disturbed Secondary sediments which have formed small domes ideal for the entrapment of saline water and crude oil. The oil is trapped between the saline water on which it floats and impervious strata which cap the domes. Oil resources are exploited on both the Arabian and the Iranian shores of the Gulf and there are substantial resources beneath the Gulf itself. These offshore deposits will be easy to exploit with existing technology should the market for oil justify the necessary investment.

The Red Sea

The Red Sea is a major relief feature of the Middle East region. It is part of the major rift system which extends from the Jordan Valley to the East African Rift Valley. Like most down-faulted geological systems, the flanks of the rift are fractured with numerous parallel faults, some of them marked by sharp breaks of slope such as the 2000-m scarps which flank the coastal plain of the south-western corner of the Arabian peninsula. The Red Sea is both a divide and an important linking feature in that it separates the continent of Africa from that of Asia; and since the respective shores are dry and inhospitable, movement across the Red Sea has never been significant. At the same time the Red Sea has provided access to the heart of the region from the south and this has been of great importance as technologies of transportation have evolved in the past two centuries.

Climate: temperature, rainfall and winds

The northern part of the Middle East and North Africa lies in the latitudes characterized by the Mediterranean regime, a seasonal system in which the rainfall maximum occurs in the winter along with minimum temperatures. The mechanism which drives the climate of the region is the same which affects all regions of the world, namely the seasonal shift of the elevation of the sun. These motions cause the high temperatures throughout the northern hemisphere in the summer. Mediterranean latitudes are special, however, in that they lie between the temperate humid regime to the north and the tropical arid regime to the south. This seasonal shift means that one season enjoys temperate humid conditions and the other tropical, arid conditions. The northern Middle East especially experiences the changeable cyclonic pattern of rain-bearing depressions of temperate latitudes in the winter while in the summer high-pressure rainless conditions dominate the whole of the region.

No part of the region is well endowed with rainfall except the small tract of land on the northern flanks of the Elburz Mountains in Iran and the coastal plain on the south of the Caspian Sea, which enjoys an annual rainfall of over 2000 mm. Other areas which attract rainfall of over 1500 mm lie mainly in the upland areas of northern

Dune formation, North Africa

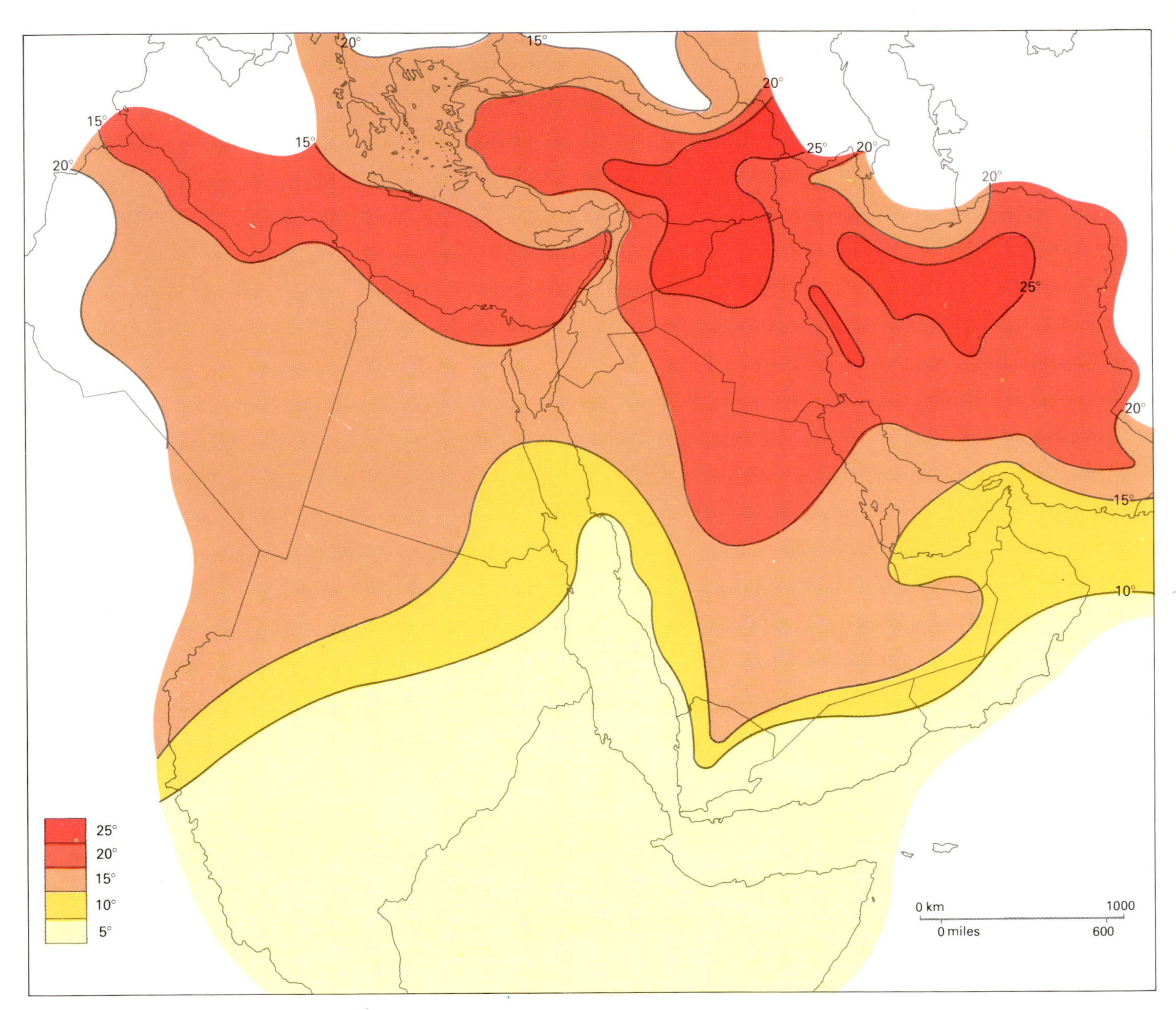

Annual temperature range in degrees centigrade

Turkey and parts of the High Atlas of Algeria. The only accessible Mediterranean tract which has over 1000 mm lies on the southern coast of Turkey, and the only region in the heartland of the Middle East which enjoys reliable rainfall of over 600 mm is the coastal tract and uplands of western Syria, Lebanon and Israel. This favoured region has been greatly preferred for settlement throughout the history of the region and one is tempted in any discussion of the Middle East to draw attention to the very close relationship between levels of rainfall and the location of human settlement. Succeeding civilizations have sought areas where the water supply is secure and have built their agricultural and urban infrastructures either in the well-favoured eastern coast of the Mediterranean or in the river valleys of the Nile and the Tigris-Euphrates.

The pressure systems which dominate in the summer and winter determine the direction of prevailing winds. In the winter westerly systems dominate, especially in the north of the region. In the summer, and especially in the early summer, it is common for winds to come from the south, bringing arid conditions to regions which have previously enjoyed the cooler and more humid influences of the Atlantic. One anomaly is the extreme south of Arabia where the meagre rainfall of the coastal region arrives in the summer as a consequence of the monsoon effect caused by the heating of the Arabian peninsula during the summer. Some of the precipitation of the relatively well-endowed mountains of North and South Yemen (600 mm per year) is explained as an effect of the same monsoon.

A very important feature of the rainfall of the Middle East is its unreliability, which is extreme in areas of low precipitation. Only those limited areas with over 1500 mm have reliable rains, while the very substantial marginal tracts with between 200 and 300 mm have a very unreliable precipitation, which may vary by 50 per cent above or below the annual average. At the same time the water balance in the Middle East is dominated by very high levels of evapo-transpiration. In the high rainfall regions of Turkey and parts of north-west Iran the annual evaporation is between 500 and 600 mm, only about one-third to one-quarter of annual precipitation. Outside this favoured northern region the annual evaporation is always above 1000 mm per year and much of northern Africa and Arabia endures the much higher annual levels of 2000 mm. The highest rates in the world are experienced in the area of Aswan in southern Egypt where three metres a year evaporate from open water surfaces.

Water resources

The water resources deriving from precipitation falling within the region are meagre. Only small tracts of cultivable land, less than 3 per cent of the region, receive agriculturally useful levels of rainfall above 300 mm per year. Fortunately, very important volumes of water are imported from outside the region via the Nile tributaries; Sudan uses most of its annual allocation of 18.5 km^3, some 30 per cent of which comes from the White Nile flowing from East Africa, and the rest from the Blue Nile, the Atbara and the Sobat, fed from Ethiopia's summer monsoon. The Tigris-Euphrates system derives all its waters from within the region but the majority of the river-flow crosses the borders of the countries in which the source precipitation falls. A substantial proportion of the 56 km^3 of the system is used by the downstream states of Syria and Iraq.

Groundwater has for long been an important source of water and its potential contribution to rural, urban and industrial activity has been transformed by new technologies for lifting and distributing it. In the past accessible coastal groundwater was important and this water has supported settlements along the coasts of northern Africa, the Levant, Turkey and the Gulf. The use of such water is unlikely to have exceeded more than 1 km^3 for the whole region until recently. With the development of new water-handling technologies, however, governments, and especially oil-rich governments, have turned to groundwater which is often located in the Secondary and even Palaeozoic sediments of the central Sahara and the Arabian peninsula. By the late 1980s Saudi Arabia was annually using more than 1 km^3 of groundwater for agricultural purposes; Libya was using 0.2 km^3 of fossil water, and was planning to move each year 2 and ultimately 3 km of fossil groundwater 900 kilometres from the south to the coast. All such water is a relic of the period when rainfall was higher in the Sahara and in Arabia. Some fossil groundwater is 30,000 years old and associated with the last phase of the Ice Age, while some is 6000 years old and associated with the more pluvial conditions which prevailed at some periods in the past. As a finite resource it will have to be managed in accordance with conditions prevailing in the international market for agricultural commodities and with the considerations of national food security which preoccupy governments in the region.

Washing clothes in the river at Wadi Sha'ab, Oman

Soil

Climate is an important soil-forming factor and the dominant aridity thus affects the characteristics of the soil. Low rainfall and high temperatures ensure that the upward movement of water in the profile dominates in soils of the Middle East with consequent accumulations of salt, gypsum and calcium carbonate nodules, none of which are conducive to productive farming. Much of the soil of the region is also sandy, since its provenance is the sandy material derived from the silica-rich parent material of much of the area. Elsewhere, where limestone is the parent material, as it is in large and accessible tracts of northern Africa and the countries of the eastern Mediterranean, the relict deposit of *terra rossa* accumulates after millennia of the dissolving of limestone sediments.

Where river systems have brought silt, for example from Ethiopia in the case of the Nile and from Turkey and Iran in the case of the Tigris-Euphrates, soil profiles associated with fluvial areas with

Soil type distribution

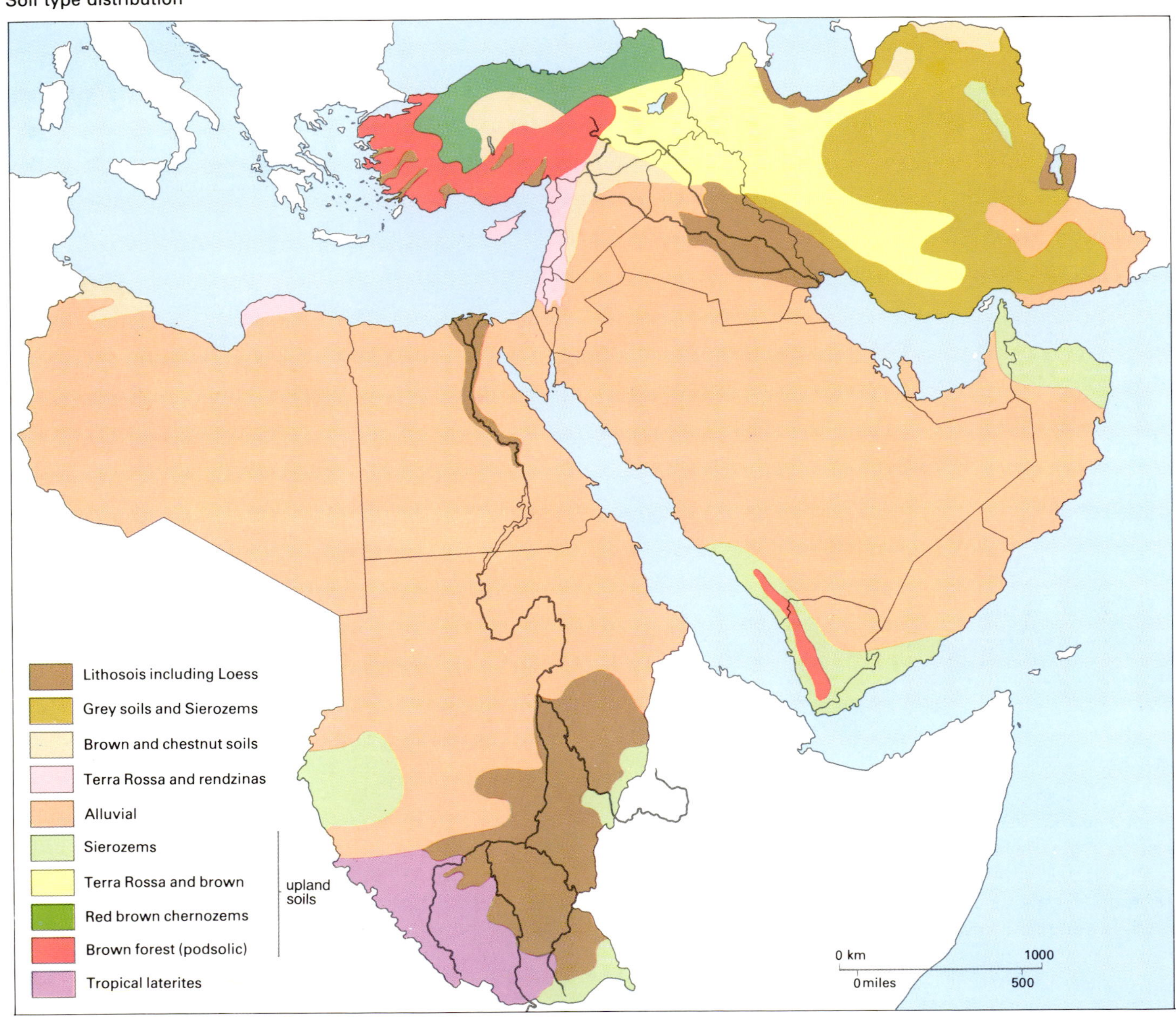

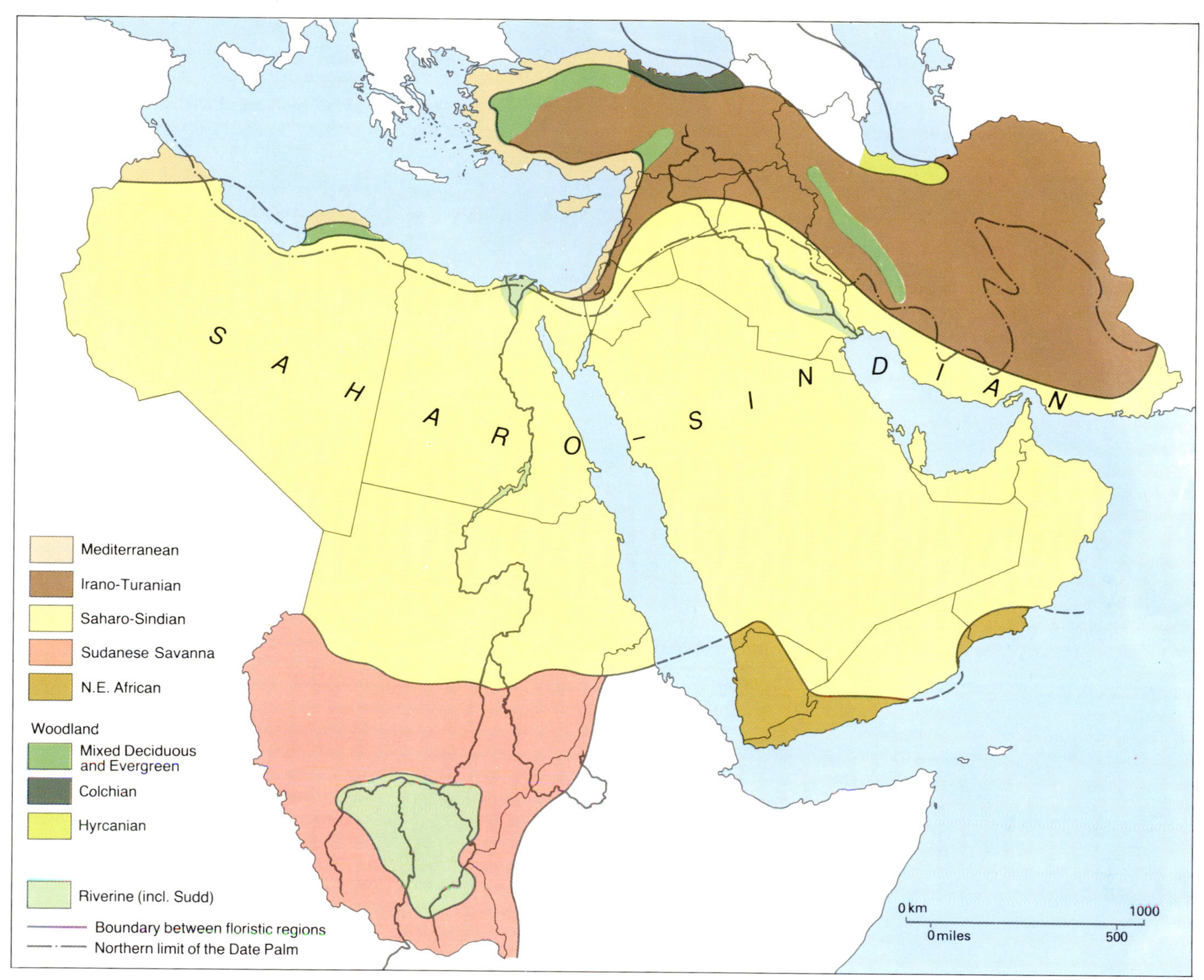

Natural vegetation

generally high water tables are encountered. Since high summer temperatures are still dominant even in these areas it is only when continuous cultivation takes place throughout the year that a high nutrient status can be developed and maintained.

The silt soils of the Nile lowlands and delta remain fertile and productive and the tendency towards salinity is being kept at bay by further investment in drainage. This has become necessary in order to counteract the effects of the greater volumes of water available since the middle 1960s, following the control of the total flow of the river by the dam at Aswan. The riverine lowlands of Iraq and Syria are very seriously affected by salinity and alkalinity and the productiveness of these alluvial soils is poor by international and regional standards.

Vegetation and fauna

The forest, shrub and herb vegetation of the Middle East and North Africa reflects the availability of soil moisture deriving from rainfall and the intensity of use. The region is marked by the tendency to use its vegetation resources very heavily. This tendency is a natural consequence of the overpopulation of the Middle East and the need

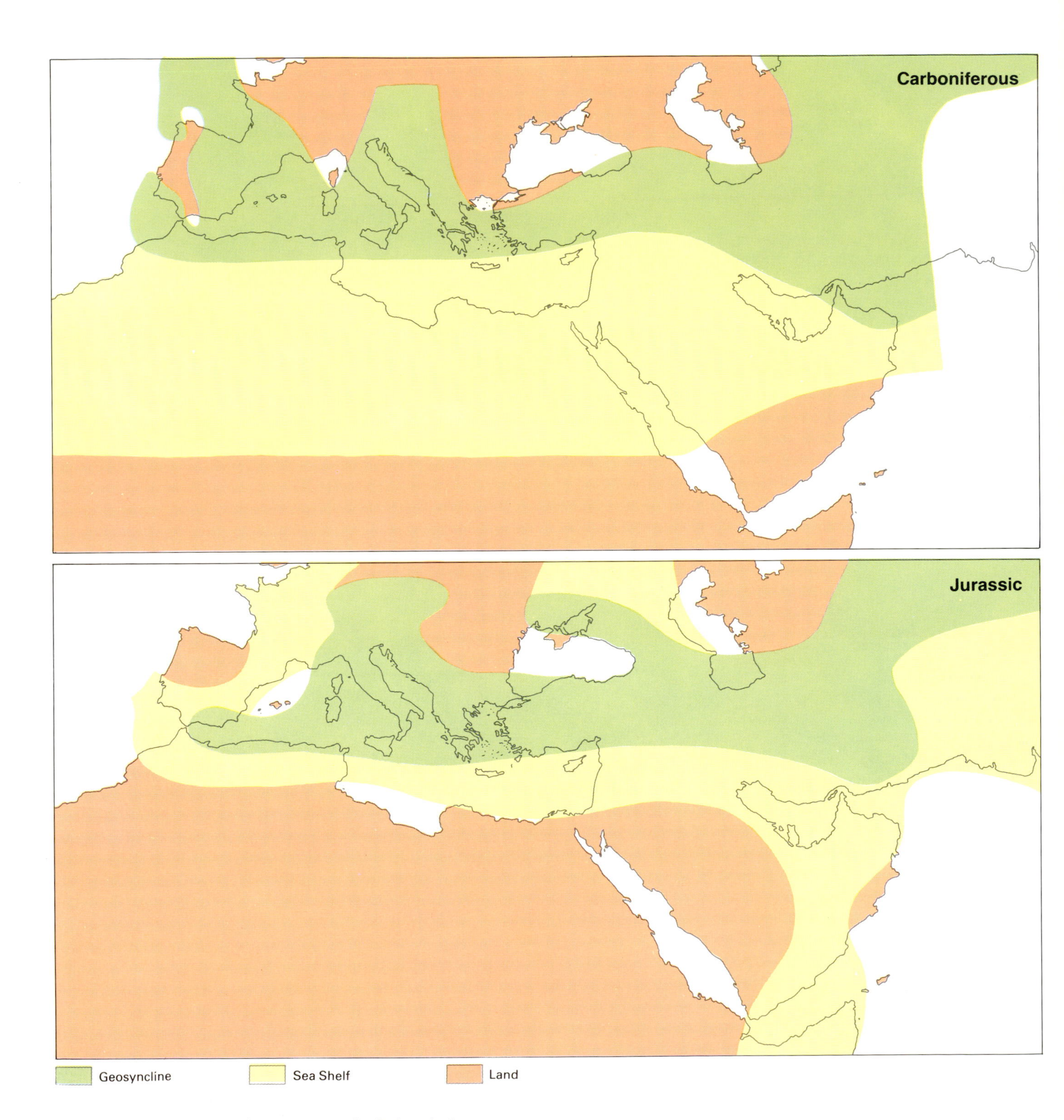

Gondwanaland and the Tethys at two geological periods

to produce animal products at the maximum possible level. Meanwhile, the demand for animal products has been progressively increased since the 1960s by the rising purchasing power of the oil-enriched economies. It is difficult, therefore, to find natural stands of forest or shrub. These are often degraded by the selective feeding of livestock on the preferred species; herbage never survives more than a few days after it appears because of heavy pressure on grazing. Only Turkey has vegetation which is not seriously degraded, in particular because Turkey enjoys a relatively high rainfall, sometimes exceeding 1000 mm per year in the uplands.

Wildlife has been reduced in much the same way and special measures have been necessary to preserve and in some cases restock rare species such as the oryx. Livestock levels are beyond the carrying capacity of the vegetation resources everywhere except Turkey, and the largest livestock populations are those of sheep and goats followed by cattle. The camel has for millennia been an important multi-purpose animal, being useful for transportation as well as for providing meat, but its numbers are falling. Livestock is not only reared on the semi-natural rangelands of the region but also in the cultivated tracts. Cattle, for example, are an integral part of the farming systems of the river lowlands, where they are used for water lifting and ploughing as well as for providing livestock products such as milk and meat. At the same time flocks of sheep and goats, which spend the winter season on the rainfed rangelands marginal to the dryland cultivation areas, are brought on to the stubble of the harvested rainfed grain fields in summer and some herdsmen have arrangements with farmers in the irrigated river lowlands for the same purpose.

Mineral resources

The major mineral resource of the region is petroleum. It is found in the Secondary deposits of the lowlands of Iraq and Iran and of the areas which lie beneath and which flank the Gulf. Oil is also found in Sinai and in the eastern region of Libya as well as offshore of Libya and Tunisia. Algeria has oil near the border with Libya. The second important mineral after oil is phosphates. Morocco is the world's leading producer and a significant proportion of Jordan's and Tunisia's foreign exchange is derived from phosphate exports, although the amount varies sharply as a result of the fluctuations in world demand and the level of prices. Iran and Turkey are rich in a variety of minerals, notably copper, and coal is also produced in Turkey. Iron ore is found in many countries and in large quantities in southern Libya. Uranium is believed to be present in the southern part of Libya.

The main regions

Iran and Afghanistan

Apart from the lowlands of Iran, which lie to the south of the Caspian Sea, and in Khuzestan in the south, both Iran* and Afghanistan* are mainly high plateaus. The complex terrain of these two countries derives from the elements of the ancient blocks which have been caught up in the tectonic events of the Tertiary. These blocks form the basement of the major interior basins of Iran, the Dasht-i-Lut (the Barren Plain) and the Dasht-i-Kavir (the Salt Plain), which are surrounded by the major folded structures of the Elburz and the Zagros Mountains and also the mountains of Khorasan and Baluchistan. Afghanistan is a high plateau lying mostly above 1000 m in the west and 2000 m in the east. In the north-west of the country the mountains rise to over 6000 m as the western part of the Hindu Kush.

Both Iran and Afghanistan receive very little rainfall except in the coastal lowlands of the Caspian Sea and the uplands of the Zagros Mountains. Temperatures are everywhere high in the summer. Some rainfed crop-production is feasible in the better-watered regions but for the most part cultivation is carried out with the assistance of irrigation on very limited tracts. Both countries are heavily overgrazed.

Anatolia

Like Iran, Turkey* consists of an inner core formed by two elements of the ancient blocks caught in the tectonic events of the Tertiary. These two nuclei lie in central Anatolia and beneath the

Buzkashi, the national game of Afghanistan

Menderes lowlands in the extreme west of the country. The central plateau is flanked in the north and the south by folded mountains. These are known as the Pontic Fold System in the north and the Taurus Fold System in the south. In the east of Turkey the folded structures merge into the uplands of western Iran and northern Iraq. On the basis of these underlying structures Anatolia can be divided into five sub-regions, the Black Sea coastlands extending from the Soviet border in the east to the Bosphorus in the west, the Aegean–Marmara lowlands, the Mediterranean coastlands of south Turkey, the central plateau and finally the eastern highlands.

The uplands of Turkey enjoy rainfall of between 1000 and 2000 mm a year, some of which falls as snow, especially in the east of the country which experiences great extremes of temperature and precipitation. The plateau area is also characterized by extremes, with winter temperatures averaging −1°C, and a hundred days of frost being recorded each year. Summers are warm with high day temperatures and cool nights. The coastal lowlands enjoy much more equable conditions with little or no frost, comfortable temperatures even in the winter and good growing temperatures throughout the year, provided that water can be led to the fields. Rainfall is generally over 500 mm throughout the coastal areas and in the east of the Black Sea lowlands it rises to the region's extreme of 2450 mm per year at Rize.

The plains below Mount Agri, Turkey

The Fertile Crescent and Cyprus

The Fertile Crescent takes its name from its curved shape and the fact that it is a relatively well-watered region. It includes the coastal lowlands and hills of Israel*, the West Bank*, Lebanon*, Syria* and the lowlands of the Tigris-Euphrates. It is better watered because the coastal hills of the eastern Mediterranean catch the moisture from the easterly moving depressions in winter, providing up to 600 mm in northern Israel, Lebanon and southern Syria. Rainfall in the northern parts of Syria and Iraq is generally over 200 mm and the respective farming communities attempt to produce rainfed crops on a high proportion of these marginal lands. Where crops are not raised, the rangeland resource is heavily grazed.

The structure of the coastal ranges of the eastern Mediterranean is important in determining relief. Extensive down-faulted grabens characterize the region, and the remarkable Jordan Valley system extends southwards from the Lebanon to the Dead Sea, which lies 400 m below sea level. Parallel heavily faulted and folded uplands flank the down-faulted areas, forming the beautiful limestone hills of the West Bank and the grand scenery on the east side of the River Jordan. Further north the mountains of the Lebanon and the Anti-Lebanon Mountains flank the down-faulted area of the Bekaa Valley.

The lowlands of the Tigris-Euphrates enjoy the second largest flow of surface water in the Middle East and major cultivation is sustained by their flow. Such is the nature of the soils of these lowlands, and especially the high levels of groundwater, that saline and alkaline conditions are common in both Syria and Iraq despite the huge investments made in water control and drainage. Because of the difficulties and expense of maintaining soil fertility, it has been proved impossible to halt the deteriorating trend.

The Arabian peninsula

The basement of the peninsula is part of the ancient block which was separated from the African Block by the downfaulting of the Red Sea. Related tectonic movements formed the very deep rifts of the Dead Sea and Jordan Valley and of the Gulf of Suez. The basement is overlain by Secondary, relatively little disturbed, geological deposits which lie saucer-like one on the other with their lowest points situated beneath the Gulf area. The importance of the arrangement of the geology is in the way it determines the location and existence of the potentially very important non-renewable resources of oil and water. Both the oil and the water have moved down the west to east-sloping strata so that there are important oilfields and sources of groundwater trapped in useful and accessible domes and aquifers in the eastern part of the peninsula.

The only high ground in the peninsula is in the mountains of Yemen in the south west and those of the Jabal al-Akhdar in Oman in the east. Rainfall is significant in Yemen at over 800 mm annually in the highest tracts and is sufficient to support an important agricultural sector. The rains of the Jabal al-Akhdar are much less reliable and lower but they do have significance in the surrounding areas as the alluvial fans which flank the mountains are periodically recharged with storm water enabling oases to exist often fed by open and subterranean channels like the *qanat* of Iran but in Oman called *falaj*.

The Nile Valley

The Nile Valley includes two Middle East countries, Egypt* and Sudan*. The Nile catchment includes vast tracts of these countries but as scarcely any precipitation falls within these tracts active fluvial processes occur only in the very confined river lowlands. The Nile has two sources of water, first the highlands of East Africa from which the White Nile comes and secondly the mountains of Ethiopia from which flow the Blue Nile and other important tributaries such as the Atbara and the Sobat. The White Nile contributes two-sevenths of the water in the Nile system and the Ethiopian tributaries five-sevenths. The flow of the White Nile is steady throughout the year, partly reflecting the even annual rainfall regime of the highlands in the east of Africa and the effect of the saturated Sudd region in southern Sudan through which the White Nile flows. On the other hand the Blue Nile and the other tributaries which flood each August from the Ethiopian mountains are fed by summer monsoon rains.

For millennia the Ethiopian flood carried tonnes of silt and the heavily charged water bore its rich burden throughout the length of the system as far as the delta at the Mediterranean. Farming practices were adjusted to make use of the flood and spread the fertile silt in basins which could be cultivated for one season in high summer temperatures ideal for crop germination and growth. With the improved engineering practices available from the early part of the nineteenth century the control of the river began first with the barrage built just north of Cairo by the ruler of Egypt, Muhammad ʿAli*. Further control works were constructed further up the river in Egypt and beginning in 1906 installations were constructed and extended at Aswan to enable the perennial irrigation of progressively larger proportions of the Nile lowlands. With the construction of the High Dam at Aswan* in the late 1950s and early 1960s three times the annual flow of the Nile was able to be stored in Lake Nasser (see Irrigation). The dam made it possible to use perennial irrigation on all of the irrigated land of the country and also to attempt the reclamation of additional sandy tracts on the flanks of the valley, especially on the western edge of the delta. Attempts were also made in the 1960s to bring into cultivation the difficult and often saline low-lying tracts at the northern edge of the delta.

Water control works were also constructed at various points on the Blue and White Niles in Sudan. It was argued by British engineers in the early part of the twentieth century that such works would be better sited in Sudan as the structures could be built more economically and they would have the double advantage of serving the farmers of both Sudan and Egypt. Thus dams were built at Roseires on the Blue Nile and at Jabal Aulia on the White Nile. The Egyptian government was, however, understandably intent on securing a reliable supply of water and wanted to construct works which would be under its own control and not subject to the intervention of any other political interest. By the terms of the Nile Waters Agreement of 1959, Egypt was allocated 55.5 km^3 of the estimated 84 km^3 at Aswan, and 18.5 km^3 was allocated to Sudan. It was estimated that the loss by evaporation and seepage at the lake would be 10 km^3. Sudan was still not using all of its allocation by the late 1980s, to the benefit of Egypt. However, as both governments are aware that the supply of water will not be sufficient to meet the demands of the 1990s, they are actively seeking to enhance the supply by works such as the Jonglei Canal, which is designed to improve the flow by 4 km^3 in its first phase, half of which would go to each country. Both governments will need to gain water from their existing systems and Egypt is intent on securing about 8 km^3 from the management of its surface systems and from the use of groundwater, especially in the delta. Egypt's use of Nile water is very intensive and successful and the acquisition of new water would enable the irrigation of half a million hectares of new land. In Egypt, high priority is given by the government to the reclamation of new land.

The Maghrib

The Maghrib* includes two major geographical regions, the Tertiary fold mountains and plateaus of the Atlas Mountains in the north, and the deserts of the Sahara in the south. These major regions are different both in their geology and in their climate. As well as being mountainous, the northern regions are affected by the Mediterranean climatic regime with cool moist winters and hot dry summers. The winter rains are enhanced by the effect of the high relief of the Atlas Mountains, and large upland tracts of all three countries of the region receive rainfall of over 1000 mm a year. The three countries of the Maghrib all include the two zones of the Mediterranean uplands and of the arid Sahara, although the size of the desert zone varies, affecting only about a half of Tunisia* but over 80 per cent of Algeria*.

The northern zone can be further subdivided according to its geological structure and relief. The strains of the mountain-building period are very evident, especially in Morocco*, and there are a number of major folded elements with high plateaus between them. The structure of Algeria is less complicated, with two major folded zones, the Atlas Mountains and the Anti-Atlas to the south. The

Atlas Mountains abut the Mediterranean coast in many places, or are divided from it by only a narrow coastal plain. The high plateau between the two folded tracts is characterized by internal drainage systems and semi-arid conditions with sufficient rainfall for dryland farming in the north.

Ways of life

Because of the arid conditions which prevail over the 71 per cent of the Middle East which receives less than 200 mm of rainfall a year, only two types of land-management practice are possible over this very large rainless area. These are irrigated farming and pastoralism. The first is a technological and engineering solution to the problem posed by the absence of sufficient rainfall annually and/or seasonally to enable cultivation and crop-production. Irrigated farming is an intensive activity in that it requires high inputs of water and labour and to be most effective it also requires ancillary inputs of seeds, fertilizers and pesticides. Pastoralism, on the other hand, and especially the practice of nomadic pastoralism, is the ultimate adaptation of Man to the low productive potential of tracts with rainfall of less than 200 mm per year. Pastoralism is an extreme low input and low output strategy. No reliable crop-production is possible in areas with such low rainfall not only because it is, on average, insufficient to sustain crops, even crops such as hardy varieties of barley or the undemanding olive, but also because it is subject to great variation. There is a one-in-five chance that the rainfall will be only 60 per cent of the average 200 mm. Moreover, the variation is proportionately more extreme the lower the average rainfall.

In the remaining 29 per cent of the region the third system of subsistence, that of rainfed farming, can be pursued. The method is sometimes referred to as dryland farming. Such farming is possible only in those areas with more than 200 mm of reliable rainfall. Of this area only about 20 per cent is suitable for cultivation, the rest being too high or too irregular in terrain for crop-production. Rainfed farming is possible in only about 6 per cent of the total Middle East and North African region and irrigated farming in just over 1 per cent of the total region. Livestock-rearing by various types of pastoralism is sustainable in about 20 per cent of the total region and is most secure in upland areas where rainfall is relatively reliable. This is the only system which can make use of the very low vegetation sustaining environments with rainfall levels falling as low as 50 mm per year.

Nomadic pastoralism

Nomadic pastoralism is important in the relatively well-watered but very broken terrain of the northern countries, Turkey and Iran, as well as in the northern parts of Iraq and Syria. The uplands of the Maghrib are also grazed by nomadic pastoralists. Where the practice involves the regular seasonal movement of the community and its livestock, for example in the Zagros Mountains of Iran, where the upland pastures are used in the summer and those of the lowlands in the winter, it is known as transhumance. Similar seasonal transhumant movements enable the economic use of extremely marginal environments in Libya*. In the north-east of the country the pastoralists take advantage of the southerly shift in winter of the cooler and humid Mediterranean conditions to graze land which is without vegetation in summer. In all the countries of the Maghrib pastoral communities use the marginal tracts on the edge of the desert in the milder and moister winter and retreat to the better-watered areas and uplands in the summer.

True nomadism, where there is no regular movement and no element of settled life, exists amongst some pastoralists in the Middle East, such as those of the Arabian peninsula and parts of the Sahara. The practice utilizes the poorest tracts of all, where shrubs and herbs cover less than 10 per cent of the surface. Economic use can only be made of such cover through the mobility of the livestock and their orderly supervision by small communities of shepherds or herders, who are prepared to move their tents according to the availability of feed. Sheep and goats are the main types of stock raised but camels have also long been reared in the same way; as they are able to survive on the most marginal environments of all they have always had a special place in the complex complementarities which exist within the pastoral communities and between pastoralists and settled communities.

Cultivation in the plains and the river valleys

Cultivation can be sustained where there is more than 200 mm of reliable rainfall per year, or where water can be led to farmland from surface flows or from groundwater. Only 6 per cent of the region has level terrain and access to sufficient water to sustain cultivation, and of this less than half could be considered to lie in the important river lowlands. In Egypt, for instance, the cultivated area lying in the fertile valley of the Nile comprises only 2.5 per cent of the total land area of the country.

Only the river valleys of Turkey and the Caspian area of Iran receive sufficient water for rainfed farming. Elsewhere cultivation has always depended on irrigation water; indeed the earliest recorded cultivation by irrigation occurred in the river valleys of the Tigris-Euphrates and the Nile. The systems of water-spreading and so-called basin irrigation which developed seven thousand years ago served the farmers of the region well for millennia, and it is only in

An irrigation canal in the Nile Delta, Egypt

the past hundred years that new technologies for storing and distributing water have begun to change farming in the river lowlands. Both the Nile and the Tigris-Euphrates and their tributaries have been dammed to store water. The biggest installations are at Aswan where the lake stores three times the annual flow of the river. In the past two decades methods for the utilization of water have changed with an increase in the use of sprinkler systems and most recently in the use of trickle systems. These methods can cut the use of water from the 1.5 m depth of water per year commonly used for flood irrigation to half that level for selected tree and row crops.

Cultivation in the mountains and uplands

The Middle East and North Africa have not only extensive mountains but also some large and important plateaus. Much of Turkey falls into this category, as well as substantial tracts of Iran, Iraq and the Maghrib. In the most broken of the uplands only grazing is possible but, where soils are favourable, communities engage in rainfed crop production. A substantial proportion of the grain production of Turkey comes from its central plateau area and on the foothills and plateaus of northern Iraq grain is also grown. The plateau areas of central and eastern Iran are for the most part too dry for crop production, but on favourable soils in the Zagros, especially in the central and north regions, grain and other crops are raised. In the Maghrib the farmland of the central plateau area is a major source of the agricultural resources of Algeria and, to a lesser extent, those of Morocco.

Urban life

Urban settlements have been part of the life of the Middle East and North Africa for over 7000 years. Damascus is considered to be the oldest continuously occupied city in the world and the archaeological heritage of the Nile and Tigris-Euphrates is a testament to the economic success of the past civilizations of the region. The surpluses accumulated mainly from rural activity enabled the construction of settlements and cities as well as the bureaucratic infrastructures to supervise irrigation, agriculture, trade and national security. It has been argued that the imperatives of organizing the distribution of water stimulated the regulation of other features of the economy and government and it is for this reason that the civilizations of the Middle East are often referred to as 'hydraulic civilizations'.

The River Jordan flowing through the Zarqa Valley, Jordan

In the past the proportion of people living in cities rarely exceeded 10 per cent of total population and the proportional contribution of agriculture and rural activities to the economies of the region was of the same order. Since 1900 population* has risen steadily and since 1950 at rates of over 3 per cent in many countries. The rapid increases of the recent past have also been associated with very rapid growth in the size and populations of cities. Cairo's population has increased from 1 million to 14 million in fifty years and there are other massive cities such as Istanbul, with over 4 million, and Tehran with over 6 million. The rate of urbanization, that is, the increase in the proportion of the total population living in cities, has also been rapid, with less than 20 per cent urbanization being common as recently as 1940 compared with over 50 per cent recorded currently in populous countries such as Egypt. In the oil economies, where there are special distortions, the rates of urbanization since 1960 have been phrenetic, with shifts from a low level of 20 per cent in 1960 to over 70 per cent by the 1980s in countries such as Libya.

Systems of authority

It has been customary to describe the economic, political and cultural life of the region in terms of the dominance of one of these three ways of life: pastoral, agricultural and urban. This is too simple a description. A better model is one which takes into account the mobility of individuals and groups between the different modes of life, even in a single lifetime.

The physical environment does, however, strongly affect the ways in which people organize themselves. Arid tracts have limited carrying capacities, and the mobility of nomadic pastoral life requires an annual pattern of decision-making about directions of movement, places of encampment, and ways of maintaining the solidarity of the group. In these circumstances clear systems of authority emerge. Since groups attempting to sustain themselves in arid areas are small, the basic 'political' organization is that of the 'fraction'; authority lies with a leader (shaykh) or leading family, whose power is restrained, however, by the collective experience of the group preserved by its older members, or heads of families. Such fractions tend to be linked by intermarriage, or at least to believe that they have common ancestors, and they might therefore be called clans; their unity finds expression in a sense of collective honour, to be defended against that of other groups.

Fractions amalgamate and split up because of the rise or fall of respected leaders, or because of natural events. A more or less permanent amalgamation can become a 'tribe', which may include many thousands of people scattered over a wide area. A tribe can develop and maintain a solidarity of its own, and its leading family can exercise considerable authority. By the nature of the environment, however, it cannot be as permanent or as closely united as a clan or fraction, or act collectively so often or so effectively. However its membership varies, it still tends to express its solidarity in terms of real or imagined common ancestry, and a tribal name can survive for centuries, even when the human group which uses it may have changed.

In regions of settled agriculture, particularly in those which are isolated, in secluded mountain valleys or on the edge of deserts, a rather similar organization into 'tribes' can exist. Because the population is sedentary, however, the authority of leading families may be stronger, and their control over the land more secure than in the desert. A tribe of this kind may have grown up around a family with military or religious prestige, but here too the idea of common ancestry is important. Such sedentary groups tend to be permanent: in parts of the Middle East and North Africa there are tribes, or at least tribal names, which have existed in the same place for a very long time.

Whether nomadic or sedentary, it is a common feature of societies organized tribally that they should think of themselves as existing in opposition to other such groups standing on the same level, and that conflicts should break out between them from time to time on questions of honour, or on rights of cultivation or grazing. It would not be correct, however, to draw from this a general conclusion about the necesary and eternal opposition of 'the desert and the sown'. In a condition of equilibrium, the tribes of the desert and its margins have interacted among themselves, coming together and

A Targi nomad, Tamanrasset, Algeria

splitting up without affecting the settled farming communities in the river valleys or other favoured lowlands. When the desert ecosystem fails them, or when there is a protracted drought, pastoral communities may be forced into conflict with settled farmers. On the other hand tension has been generated throughout history when settled farmers have expanded their cultivation at the expense of nomadic pastoral communities. This has happened particularly during the present century, not only because of an increase in the settled population but also because changes in methods of transportation have destroyed the economic basis of the life of tribes which rear camels in the high desert (although not necessarily of those which raise sheep).

Another and more lasting tension is that which sets 'tribal' authorities against another kind of authority rooted in the cities. Urban populations carrying on a complex life of manufacture and trade need to regulate their lives in a different way from pastoral and agricultural groups. Their governments have to be organized bureaucratically, and to possess the means of enforcing decisions or laws. In order to pay their officials and soldiers, the rulers of the cities have to take part of the surplus production of the countryside, by means of taxation or in other ways, and as far as their strength allows they must extend their authority over the rural hinterland by means of garrisons, tax-collectors, or those whom they recognize as landowners. There is here an inevitable opposition with the independent power of the 'tribal' authorities created by rural processes, although some of them may be drawn into the city-based system of officials, tax-collectors and landowners. In recent generations the authority of governments has been expanding, and that of 'tribal' leaders diminishing, in a process which is perhaps irreversible, given modern changes in methods of production and distribution, and also of administration and control.

Landownership

The tensions between different kinds of society and authority are shown clearly in different ideas about who owns the land. Pastoral tribes regard themselves as collective owners of their areas of habitual grazing. Villages living outside the range of direct urban authority may also think of the land they cultivate as belonging to the village as a whole; in some places it has been common for the use of the land to be redistributed, annually or less frequently, among the different families in the village (the *musha'* system). Urban governments, however, basing themselves on Islamic law* or tradition, tended in the past to think of agricultural land as belonging to the ruler as head of the community; he levied taxes on its produce (and also, when he could, on the livestock of the nomad), and those who cultivated it had no more than a more or less permanent usufruct. Freehold land (*mulk*) existed mainly in the town. Some property was constituted by its owners into *waqf*, an endowment of which the income was to be used in perpetuity for religious or charitable purposes. From at least the tenth century onwards, the custom grew up of the ruler giving soldiers or officials the right to collect and keep the tax on a certain area of land in return for military or state service, or instead of a salary or pension. Later, under the Ottomans*, the task of collecting the tax was given to tax-farmers, who took a commission and were supposed to transfer the rest to the government. In these and other ways a class of virtual landowners grew up.

Those who cultivated the land for its owners were not always or necessarily landless labourers. There were many kinds of contract between owner and cultivator, who could obtain some security of tenure. The most widespread form of agreement was that for 'share-cropping', by which those who contributed land, seed, animals and labour (and, on irrigated land, water) would each take a portion of the produce or the profit.

During the nineteenth century the system of tenure was regulated and changed in a number of countries. In Algeria under French rule, laws on the French model were introduced, and much of the land passed into the hands of European settlers. In Egypt, successive laws created a system of full landownership, and large estates grew up. In the Ottoman Empire, the Land Law of 1858 defined the various categories of landholding and provided for the issue of title deeds, giving holders of *miri* land a perpetual right to its usufruct, and therefore virtual ownership of it. The effect of this, too, was to create large estates.

From the 1950s onwards the system of tenure has been once more changed by new laws, which have limited the size of landholdings and distributed land to smallholders linked by cooperatives. The first such reform took place in Egypt after the revolution of 1952, and similar measures were taken in Iran, Syria and Iraq. In North Africa, land taken from European settlers after the end of French rule was also distributed; similarly in Israel, much land which formerly belonged to Arab owners or cultivators has been taken over by the state and redistributed to Jewish settlements.

JAA

Further reading

P. Beaumont, G. H. Blake and J. M. Wagstaff, *The Middle East: a geographical study* (London, 1976)
P. Beaumont and K. S. McLachlan, *Agricultural Development in the Middle East* (Chichester, 1985)
M. Clawson, H. H. Landsberg and L. T. Alexander, *The Agricultural Potential of the Middle East* (New York, 1971)
W. B. Fisher, *The Middle East* (London, 1971)
C. C. Gischler, *Water Resources of the Middle East and North Africa* (London, 1978)
J. M. Wagstaff, *The Evolution of Middle East Landscapes* (London, 1985)

Languages and peoples

The Middle East lacks the extreme linguistic diversity of neighbouring Europe, South Asia, and sub-Saharan Africa. Nevertheless, the variety of languages in the region, particularly in its northern portions, is greater than sometimes supposed. Whereas almost all of Europe's many languages have a common ancestry and belong to the Indo-European family, those of the Middle East are divided among three quite different language families: the Hamito-Semitic, the Indo-European and the Altaic. To a large extent, this diversity reflects the Middle East's location at the confluence of three continents, where cultural interaction has historically been intense. The Middle East has been one of the world's great human junctions, exposed to cultural influences from several directions.

The spread of languages

Languages spread geographically through a process of diffusion. A distinction may be made between expansion diffusion and relocation diffusion. In the former, the language spreads throughout a

Language distribution

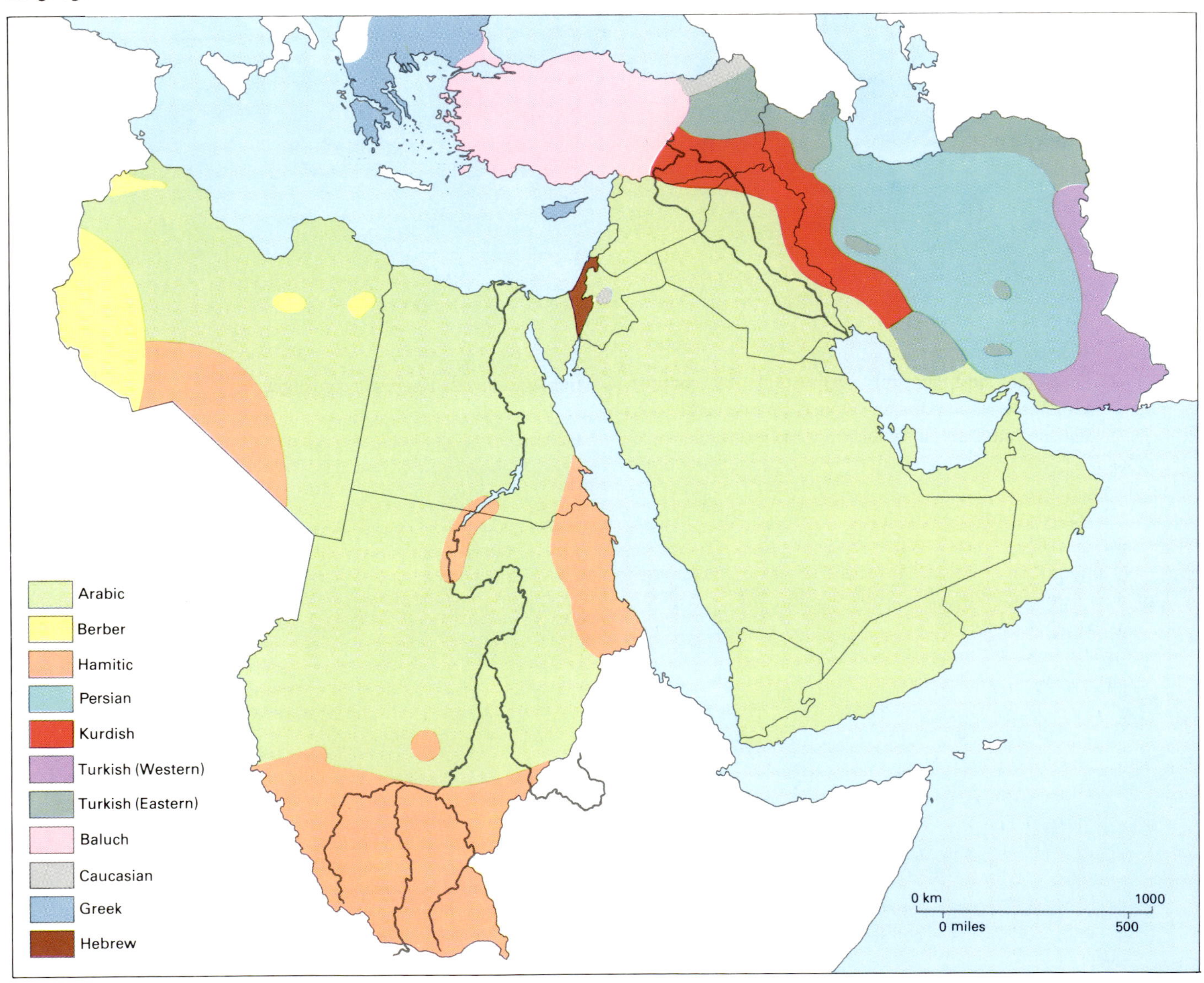

population, from region to region, so that the number of speakers and the area where the language is spoken both grow. In relocation diffusion, speakers of the language themselves move bodily from one location to another, thereby carrying it into a new region. Typically, a language will also be transmitted hierarchically from one urban centre to another or among elite social groups before being adopted in rural areas or by the masses. In practice, these processes have often occurred together in the Middle East. Frequently, Middle Eastern languages spread as a result of imperial expansion and conquest (Persian, Turkish and Arabic, for example). Certain languages were diffused in conjunction with a religion or were closely tied to one (Arabic and Hebrew). Economic factors also helped to change the cultural map. Language often migrated along established transportation and trade routes or spread as commercial lingua francas. Conversely, physical and cultural barriers often retarded the rate of language diffusion and deflected it in a new direction. Mountain ranges, because they hinder migration, frequently coincide with stable language boundaries. The northward spread of Arabic, for instance, was halted to some degree by the Zagros and Taurus Mountains (which nonetheless were sufficiently permeable to permit the spread of an idea: Islam*). For the same reason, many mountainous zones in the Middle East are refuge areas for language (and religious) minorities and are characterized by a high degree of linguistic fragmentation. Kurdish, Berber, and several other minority languages have survived in these relatively inaccessible settings, which historically have been better able to resist outside control and cultural assimilation. By contrast, language boundaries on lowland plains, which have generally been more homogeneous culturally, have tended to be less stable.

Language is one of the primary ways the peoples of the Middle East differentiate themselves and define their national identities and political allegiances. However, linguistic divisions do not coincide with racial or physical differences, which are highly complex, extremely blurred as a result of centuries of miscegenation and cultural interaction, and of little or no sociological significance. Any attempt to classify the peoples of the Middle East according to racial type is confronted with almost insuperable definitional and measurement problems and runs the risk of constructing aggregates that have no cultural validity, no precise boundaries, and no discrete geographic expression. Nevertheless, the exaggerated claims of nationalists in certain Middle Eastern countries that their populations are racially unique have some popular support. Many Iranians, for example, take pride in their Aryan ancestry, minimizing the extent to which the population has been infused with Turkic, Mongol, and Arab elements.

Where, then, did the main languages of the Middle East originate, how did they spread, and how are they now distributed geographically?

Arabic

Arabic belongs to the South Semitic group of the Semitic subdivision of the Hamito-Semitic language family. This subdivision includes Assyro-Babylonian, Aramaic, Hebrew, Phoenician, South Arabian and Ethiopic. The original home of the Hamito-Semites may have been North Africa and the original Semites are thought to have crossed into Arabia through Yemen by the Bab al-Mandab.

A distinction must be made between written and colloquial Arabic. Written Arabic, the religious and modern literary language, does not vary throughout the Arab world and serves as a bond between all Arabs. All books and newspapers are written in this standard Arabic, which is universally understood by literate Arabs. In addition, the spoken form of standard Arabic serves as a lingua franca (it is used, for example, in news broadcasts, political speeches and, to a lesser degree, in the cinema and theatre). Everyday spoken Arabic, by contrast, varies significantly from place to place. Differences exist within countries and between them. At the regional level, a number of dialects can be identified: Maghribi, Egyptian, Syrian, Iraqi and Arabian peninsular. Each of these, in turn, has numerous subdivisions. In some instances differences are sufficiently great to preclude communication unless the classical form is used. Eastern Arabs have difficulty understanding colloquial Moroccan or Algerian Arabic, for example. However, the spread of mass media, dramatically increased spatial interaction in the form of tourism and labour migration, and the expansion of literacy have familiarized Arabs with one another's dialects (particularly Egyptian) and favour linguistic convergence.

Origins and expansion of Arabic

Arabic originated within the Arabian peninsula and remained largely confined there until the seventh and eighth centuries, when conquering Arab armies spread Islam and elements of Arab culture within a remarkably short time to the Fertile Crescent, North Africa, Spain, Persia, Afghanistan, and even farther afield (see History). Before these conquests, the languages of North Africa and Iran were not Semitic and those of the Fertile Crescent, although Semitic, were not Arabic. Gradual Arabization, to the extent that it occurred, generally followed Islamization, which offered certain financial and social advantages. Conversion to Islam entailed learning Arabic prayers and some familiarity with the Arabic text of the Qur'an. However, in numerous instances conversion to Islam occurred without Arabization (among the Persians, Turks, Kurds and Berbers, for example), while in other cases people retained their faith but adopted Arabic after it emerged as the leading language of commerce and government (most notably many Jews, the Egyptian Copts, and numerous other Levantine Christian communities). Thus, Arabs and Muslims cannot in any sense be equated. Although most Arabs are Muslim most Muslims are not Arab.

The term 'Arab' was applied originally by the Arabs themselves only to tribes who lived in the Arabian peninsula before the diffusion of Islam or to those who claimed a relationship with such tribes. As Arabization progressed, increasing numbers of people who spoke Arabic had no such links. Initially, they did not regard themselves and were not considered as Arabs. The term 'Arab' today encompasses all those who speak Arabic. As a result, it includes people whose physical appearance and culture, in certain aspects, differ greatly from those of the original Arabs of the Arabian peninsula. The Arabs do not constitute a homogenous racial group. On the contrary, they are as varied as the peoples of Europe: some have black hair, others blond; some have dark skins, others fair; some are indistinguishable from southern Europeans, others could be taken for West Africans.

Areas that underwent Arabization retained elements of their pre-Arab culture: Berber in the Maghrib, Pharaonic and Coptic in Egypt, and Aramaic in the Fertile Crescent. Arab culture changed, but was also changed by, the cultures with which it came in contact. Consequently, although the Arab world's high culture exhibits remarkable unity from Morocco to Oman, there are important differences in the everyday, popular culture of individual Arab countries, many of which have distinctive cultural patterns and personalities and have been shaped by unique historical experiences. The tension within the Arab world between centripetal, integrating forces and centrifugal, differentiating ones has been the principal obstacle to achieving a greater measure of political unification. Nevertheless, pan-Arabism – the belief that the Arabs can surmount the artificial political boundaries that separate them – retains its ideological appeal within the region. The prospect of Arab unity tantalizes all Arabs to some degree, regardless of regional and other differences among them.

Arabic is spoken by more people than any other language in the Middle East and predominates throughout North Africa, the Fertile Crescent and the Arabian peninsula. The eighteen countries in which it is the chief language measure over 8m square kilometres – larger than every country except the Soviet Union – and encompass over 180m people, of whom perhaps 160m are Arab. Arabic-speaking communities are also found beyond the political boundaries of this zone in parts of Turkey, Iran, coastal East Africa, and the interior of several West and Central African countries. In addition, nineteenth- and twentieth-century migrations have carried over 3m Arabs to Europe, the Americas and Australia.

Globally, Arabic is the sixth most common first language. However, this understates its importance, because Arabic has a special significance to all Muslims, regardless of their mother tongue. God transmitted his message through an Arab, Muhammad*, so Arabic is revered as the language of Revelation. To Muslims, God's words are perfect and immutable, so translations of the Qur'an* are not acceptable substitutes for the original Arabic version, even among non-Arabs, except as guides to meaning. Many non-Arab Muslims recite the Qur'an and say their prayers in Arabic without fully knowing the language. Arabic words have also entered many other languages through Islam or as a result of commercial and political interaction. In addition, the Arabic script is the basis for the Persian, Pushtu, Urdu, and several other scripts.

Armenian

Armenian belongs to the Thraco-Phrygian subfamily of the Indo-European language family. Most of the world's 5.7m Armenians* currently live outside the Middle East. This was not always the case, however. The historic Armenian homeland includes north-eastern Turkey, north-western Iran, and parts of the Soviet Union. Armenians have occupied parts of this region continuously for almost 2½ millennia. The Armenians are believed to have entered eastern Anatolia in the eighth century BC. According to tradition, their first kingdom was established in the region of Lake Van. By the sixth century BC Greek sources referred to 'Armina' and described the distinctive people living there. Christianity was introduced at an early date, and Armenia is thought to have been the earliest Christian kingdom. For most of its history Armenia did not enjoy independence, however, and lay within the Ottoman, Persian, Russian, or other empires.

During the latter part of nineteenth century, the disintegration of the Ottoman Empire, the growing influence of Europe and the spread of nationalistic ideas resulted in a considerable displacement of Armenians and other populations.

Berber

Little is known for certain about the origins of the Berber language although it appears to have been spoken by the early Libyans and to have linguistic links with Ancient Egyptian. It belongs to the Hamitic subfamily of the Hamito-Semitic language group.

The peoples of north-west Africa conquered by the Carthaginian warrior Hanno were Berber-speaking and by the time of the Vandal invasions of the fifth century AD Berber was beginning to supplant Latin in areas where Latin had previously gained ground from Berber and Punic. When waves of Muslim Arabs arrived in the seventh and eleventh centuries AD, the population of the Maghrib was overwhelmingly Berber. The greatest of the Berber dynasties of the Islamic era was that of the Almoravids*. Berber identity has flourished because Arabization was less complete and rapid in this area than elsewhere in the Middle East after the expansion of Islam. As a result, Berbers continue to be a major component of the population in several North African countries today. Very generally, lowland areas, which were most exposed to new cultural influences and assimilation, are Arab while the mountains remain heavily Berber.

In Morocco*, Berbers, who are thought to number approximately 10m or 40 per cent of the total population, are found throughout the country but particularly in the Rif and Middle Atlas Mountains. Algeria's 7m Berbers, who are concentrated in the Kabylie and Aurès Mountains, account for roughly 30 per cent of the population. Other countries with Berber populations include Niger (10 per cent or 650,000), Mali (6 per cent or 450,000), Libya (5 per cent or 150,000), and Tunisia (3 per cent or 200,000).

Differences between Arabs and Berbers are complex and subtle. Numerous ties cut across the ethnic divide. Physically, the two groups are more or less indistinguishable because most Moroccans and Algerians are of Berber stock, regardless of the language they speak. In addition, Arabic is the official language of all the Maghribi countries and the language of status and culture. Consequently, most Berbers are bilingual and some 85 to 90 per cent of all Moroccans and Algerians speak Arabic. Berbers, who lack a written language of their own, also use the Arabic script.

Berbers have little sense of cultural cohesion and remain politically fragmented. They speak a variety of distinct, mutually unintelligible dialects. In fact, there is no common Berber language. Berbers use the term 'Imazighen' rather than 'Berber' to describe themselves. Their identifications and communal allegiances are primarily tribal and parochial. In Morocco's Rif region, for example, there are some thirty Berber tribes, the most important being the Ait Waryaghar. Other large Berber groups in Morocco include the Berraber, who speak a dialect of Tamazight, and the Shluh, who speak several dialects of Tashilhait. Black Haratin Berbers are found in the drier steppe zones. The main groups in Algeria are the Kabyles and Mzabis. Another important Berber subgroup is the Tuareg, who are found in southern Algeria, Niger, Mali, and parts of Libya. The spoken form of Tuareg is called Tamarshak, the written form Tifinagh. Partly because of these many divisions, no serious transnational Berber nationalist movement has emerged or is likely to do so.

Greek

Greek is an Indo-European language with documents going back to the fourteenth century BC. Greek developed through various phases, an ancient phase comprising the Mycenaean, Archaic and Classical periods, a Hellenistic and Roman phase, a Byzantine phase and a Modern phase.

The conquests of Alexander the Great*, which began in 323 BC,

Illuminated pages of a sixteenth-century Greek gospel

initiated a millennium of Hellenization and Greek colonization in Asia Minor, the Fertile Crescent, and other parts of the Middle East. Greek became an international language and was spoken for many centuries throughout the eastern Mediterranean and parts of Asia Minor and Africa. In the Fertile Crescent, it was the dominant language of the wealthy and educated, although Aramaic remained the language of the masses. Greek was used to write much of the New Testament and was the principal language of the Byzantine Empire until its defeat by the Turks in 1453.

There are relatively few Greek speakers in the Middle East today. At the beginning of the twentieth century, the largest concentration outside Greece was in western Asia Minor. As a result of an agreement in 1923, however, some 1.5m Greeks living in Turkey were repatriated to Greece and 800,000 Turks from Greece resettled in Turkey. Turkey's Greek population currently numbers fewer than 70,000. The main concentration of Greeks in the Middle East today is in Cyprus, where 80.7 per cent of the population is Greek (the rest being mainly Turkish). Elsewhere in the Middle East, Greek is used liturgically along with Arabic by Greek Orthodox Christians in Lebanon, Syria and Jordan. It must be emphasized that members of this denomination are Arab, not Greek.

Hebrew

Hebrew is part of the north-west Semitic group of the Semitic subfamily of the Hamito-Semitic language family. It shares many grammatical, syntactical and lexical similarities with Arabic, a sister tongue. The script, written from right to left, is derived from Square Hebrew, which evolved from Aramaic.

Hebrew is both an old language and a new one. It was used by the Jews in biblical times, and much of the Old Testament was written in it. However, Aramaic began to replace it in everyday use after the Babylonians defeated the Jews in the sixth century BC. After the Romans expelled them from Palestine between AD 64 and 135, the Jews adopted the languages of the lands into which they had been scattered: Arabic, Spanish, German, and numerous others. For almost 2000 years, however, Hebrew continued to be used in religious services and literature and there were always Jews who spoke it. With the birth in the late nineteenth century of modern political Zionism, which aimed to reverse the diaspora and create a Jewish state in Arab Palestine, efforts were made to revive the language as a Jewish lingua franca and symbol of national reawakening. When Israel* was born in 1948, this modernized, secularized Hebrew was made the principal official state language as well as the chief instrument for integrating Jewish immigrants from Europe, Africa and Asia, all of whom had their own vernacular languages. Even today, Arabic, German, Russian, English, Yiddish and other languages are spoken as well as Hebrew.

Kurdish

Kurdish is part of the Iranian subfamily of the Indo-European language family and a close relative of Persian. It is divided into two major, mutually understandable dialects: Kermanji, which is spoken in northern and western Kurdistan, and Kurdi (Sorani), which is used in the south and south-west.

Despite their linguistic homogeneity, the Kurds* are divided among many tribes. The precise number of Kurdish-speakers is not known, and estimates should be interpreted cautiously. Censuses in the Middle East generally do not provide information about ethnic affiliation because governments, anxious always to preserve national unity, fear such information may draw attention to divisions they wish to downplay or even give legitimacy to separatist claims. For political reasons, therefore, countries where Kurds live consistently underestimate their number (when they provide estimates at all). Kurdish nationalists are inclined to do the opposite, with the result that the overall size of the Kurdish population in the Middle East may be as small as 10m or as large as 20m. Either way, the Kurds are among the largest linguistic groups in the Middle East and certainly the largest without a state of their own. On numerous occasions in the twentieth century Kurds have risen in revolt against central governments seeking to impose their authority over them. Their desire for autonomy remains strong.

The heart of Kurdistan, the Kurdish homeland, extends between the Taurus Mountains of south-eastern Turkey and the Zagros Mountains of northern Iraq and western Iran. Smaller Kurdish-speaking communities are also found in Syria and the Soviet Union. Kurdistan's political fragmentation and Kurdish tribal divisions have made it difficult to mount a successful transnational rebellion. Conversely, because Kurds straddle the boundaries of five states and inhabit relatively inaccessible mountainous areas governments have had difficulty extinguishing rebellions within individual countries once they start.

Persian

Persian belongs to the Iranian group of the Indo-Iranian subfamily of the Indo-European language family. Thus, it has completely different origins from Arabic and Turkish. Indo-European tribes began arriving in Iran from the plains of Eurasia via the Caucasus early in the third millennium BC. Iran gets its name from these Aryan tribes, which included the Medes, Persians, Parthians and Scythians, among others. The Achaemenid clan, under Cyrus the Great, established the first great Persian Empire, which encompassed much of the Middle East between the sixth and fourth centuries BC. Written records begin with the inscriptions of Darius the Great on the rocks of Behistun near Kermanshah. Old Persian, with its cuneiform script, dates from this period. Its descendant, Middle Persian, which was written in the Aramaic and Pahlavi scripts, prevailed during the Sasanid era between the third and seventh centuries AD. Modern standard Persian, or Farsi, evolved directly from Middle Persian. After the Muslim Arab invasion in the seventh century, Persian experienced considerable structural change and many Arabic words were introduced. Since the tenth century Persian has remained essentially the same. Modern Persian is written in a modified Arabic script.

Persian is the third most widely spoken language in the Middle East after Arabic and Turkish. The overwhelming majority of all Persian-speakers are located in Iran*, but some 750,000 are also found in western Afghanistan*, where they are locally known as Farsiwan or Parsiwan. Other small Persian communities are found around the Persian Gulf, particularly in Bahrain. Persians account for roughly 50 per cent only of Iran's population, which is by far the most linguistically heterogenous of any Middle Eastern country. Generally, the Persians are concentrated in the central plateau region, whereas the minorities are distributed around the periphery of the country. Nevertheless, Persian is unquestionably the predominant language of Iran as well as its official language; it is used in government administration, education, mass media and literature, and all educated Iranians (although few Arab, Turkish or Kurdish peasants) can speak and read it. In addition, Persian (along with Shiʿi* Islam) is a major component of Iran's distinctive national identity and helps to differentiate the country from its neighbours.

Pashto

Pashto is part of the Indo-Iranian subfamily of the Indo-European language family and thus is related to, but distinct from, Persian. The dialect spoken in Afghanistan* differs from that spoken in Pakistan*, although all Pashto dialects are mutually understandable. The mostly semi-nomadic Pushtun tribes have historically resisted outside control, acquiring a reputation as fierce fighters in the process. Pashto-speakers, who are variously known as Pushtuns, Pukhtuns, Pakhtuns and Pathans, are found in roughly equal numbers in Afghanistan and Pakistan. Many Pushtuns regard Pashto and Afghan as synonymous.

Somali

Somali, a Cushitic language belonging to the Hamitic subfamily of the Hamito-Semitic family, is spoken by perhaps 7m people in north-eastern Africa. Racially, Somalis possess some Negroid features and some Caucasian ones. All are Sunni* Muslim. Political boundaries drawn by the colonial powers left the Somalis, like many other peoples in Africa, split among several states. The largest concentration, some 4m people, are located in the Somali Democratic Republic (Somalia*), where they comprise over 90 per cent of the population. Historically, Arab cultural influences, transmitted through Mogadishu and other coastal trading cities established by Arabs between the seventh and tenth centuries, have been considerable; as a result, although Somali is the main language, Arabic is also used officially. Elsewhere, approximately 2m Somalis live in the Ogaden region of Ethiopia, 500,000 in northern Kenya, 100,000 in Djibouti*, and several thousand in the Arabian peninsula (notably in Aden*).

Syriac and Aramaic

Aramaic belongs to the north-west group of the Semitic subfamily of the Hamito-Semitic language family and is related to Arabic and Hebrew, both of whose alphabets show Aramaic influences. The Arameans introduced their language to Syria when they settled there during the second millennium BC. By the seventh century BC, Aramaic was a lingua franca within the Fertile Crescent and widely used in commerce. The Persians gave it official status in their Empire. Throughout the Greek and Roman eras it remained the principal vernacular language in Greater Syria. It was spoken by the Jews and was the language of Jesus. Not until after the rise and spread of Islam in the seventh century did Arabic almost completely supplant it. Modern forms of Aramaic, such as Syriac, are spoken by very few people in the Middle East today, but this does not convey the historical importance of the language within the region. Syriac-Aramaic is now mainly used liturgically among certain small Christian communities in Lebanon, Syria and Iraq and has practically disappeared as a living language.

Turkish

The Turkic group of languages belong to the Altaic family. A distinction can be made between western and eastern branches. Turkish languages found in the Middle East belong to the Ogüz* (Oghuz) group, one of four in the western branch. The Ogüz are believed to have entered Central Asia in the eighth century AD. Some of the Ogüz from the south-west, called Seljuks*, subsequently migrated into Asia Minor and the Middle East. Modern-day Turkish, as spoken in Turkey*, Cyprus* and parts of the Balkans, and Azeri, which is spoken in Iran*, evolved from this line.

Globally, some 90m people speak Turkish languages. Turks constitute a majority of the population in Turkey and parts of Cyprus, Iran, Afghanistan, China and the Soviet Union. Spatially, they are distributed over an area extending from south-eastern Europe to north-eastern Siberia. However, these Turks differ in race, religion, nationality, ecological adaptation and social structure. The languages they speak are not necessarily mutually intelligible and are written in a variety of scripts. What they have in common is that they are descended from one parent language, Proto-Turkic, which is believed to have originated in eastern Eurasia. Four major waves of migration by the Huns, Ogüz Turks, Kipchaks and Mongols carried Turkic peoples far beyond this hearth into Central Asia, the Middle East and Europe.

Turkey, with over 40m Turkish-speakers, is the sole country in which Turkish is the predominant language and the only state constituted to give expression to Turkish nationalism. In 1928, Kemal Atatürk*, the father of the modern Turkish Republic, decreed that Turkish, which had been written using the Arabic script, would henceforth be written in a modified Roman alphabet. In addition, an attempt was made to 'purify' Turkish by ridding it of Arabic and Persian accretions.

Azeri Turks, or Azerbaijanis, are found in both Iran, where they number over 3m, and in the Soviet Union, where there are roughly 4.5m. This division dates from the early 1800s. Azeri is similar to the Turkish of Anatolia, but written in the Arabic script in Iran and in Cyrillic in the USSR. Iran's Azeris are concentrated in the country's north-west, particularly in the important grain-producing regions of Qazvin, Kermanshah, Reza'iyeh, and Tabriz. Despite their linguistic similarities with the Anatolian Turks, Iran's Azeris have not harboured separatist sentiments. On the contrary, they have played a leading political and commercial role within Iran and like most Iranians (but unlike most other Turks) are Shiʿi Muslim. The Soviet Union's Azeris are largely concentrated in the Soviet Socialist Republic of Azerbaijan. The Russians twice tried to unite the Azeris under their control during their occupation of north-western Iran in 1909–14 and 1941–6. In the most recent attempt, they created a puppet Azeri state, but this had little popular support and collapsed after the Russians withdrew. Iranian and Soviet Azeris have shown little interest in trying to bring about their reunification.

Turkoman, which resembles Azeri and Anatolian Turkish, is another member of the Ogüz group. Most of the 3m or so Turkomans (also spelled Turkman and Turkmen) live in a politically fragmented region to the east of the Caspian Sea. The majority, some 2m, live in the Soviet Union, with most of the rest roughly equally divided between Iran and Afghanistan. The artificial boundaries that separate them have been impermeable for only half a century, although they were demarcated long before that. Syria, Iraq and Turkey also have small and increasingly assimilated Turkoman communities as a result of past migrations.

AD

Further reading

H. Arfa, *The Kurds: an historical and political study* (London, 1966)
G. Baer, *Population and Society in the Arab East* (London, 1964)
C. Coon, *Caravan: the story of the Middle East* (Huntington, NY, 1976 edn.)
R. Cottam, *Nationalism in Iran* (Pittsburgh, 1979, rev. edn.)
A. Hourani, *Minorities in the Arab World* (London, 1947)
M. Rodinson, *The Arabs* (Chicago, 1981)
R. V. Weekes ed., *Muslim Peoples: a world ethnographic survey* (Westport, CT, 1978)

Religions

The ancient Near East

During the past century, the discovery by archaeologists of buildings, paintings, sculptures, inscriptions, tablets and papyri has added greatly to the knowledge of the religions of the ancient Near East derived from the Old Testament and Greek, Latin, Syriac and Arabic literature. With many local variations, the earliest known systems of belief contained a multiplicity of gods, associated with natural or other forces which affect human life; rituals of petition or propitiation were performed in special places, often by men or women set apart for the purpose, and there was a concern for the fate of individuals after death.

In ancient Egypt*, this multiplicity was ordered into hierarchies of gods: Re, the sun-god and supreme deity; Osiris, the god of the dead who became closely linked to Re; Isis, the wife of Osiris and queen of the gods. Horus, the son of Re and Isis, was regarded as being embodied in the King of Egypt (the Pharaoh). The gods were worshipped in temples containing their images in human or animal form, by rituals performed by priests. The idea of life after death led to the creation of elaborate tombs for kings and members of the elite, where their bodies, perserved by mummification, were surrounded by a wealth of grave goods for life in the other world. Side by side with the state religion there were popular cults, the practices of which were designed to invoke a wide range of supernatural powers which could affect the natural order.

In Syria* and Palestine*, there was no such stable political order which could give unity to the array of local gods; each city and its hinterland had its own gods, but there was some similarity between them. Some gods were thought of as being more important than others: El the creator of the universe, Baal-Hadad the god of storms, Dagan the god of fertility. The ritual of worship involved the sacrifice of animals in temples, but there were also rural shrines, sacred springs or stones regarded as the dwelling-places of gods. The best-known of the local cults is that of the Canaanites; it was carried by their successors, the Phoenicians*, to the coast of North Africa.

So far as it is known, the religion of ancient Arabia was not dissimilar to this. In Yemen* in the south-west, a triad of gods, with the moon god as supreme, was worshipped by priests in temples; further north, the cult of El and other gods was carried on in sanctuaries to which pilgrimages were made and where sacrifices were offered.

In Mesopotamia, from the time of the Sumerians onwards there was a hierarchy of gods expressing the forces of nature: An the god of heaven, Enlil the chief god of the pantheon, and others. Each city was patronized by a major deity who was worshipped in a large temple. The will of the gods was divined by examining the entrails of animals and studying the movements and combinations of heavenly bodies. Beliefs about the life of the gods and the creation and destiny of human beings were embodied in myths. In Iran*, too, the religion taught and practised by the priests, or Magi, so far as it is known, was that of a number of gods formed into a hierarchy.

Judaism and Mazdaism (Zoroastrianism)

During the first millennium BC, in more than one place the religion of public rituals in honour of a hierarchy of gods was modified in the direction of sole worship of a supreme god, and of individual piety. In Palestine*, one of the peoples who lived there, the Hebrews or Jews*, came to believe in the existence of a single God, Yahweh, creator of the universe, who had made a covenant with the Hebrews and expressed his will through the prophet Moses; the revealed will of God was embodied in a holy scripture, the Torah, and was binding on individuals as well as on the people as a whole. Their main place of worship was the Temple in Jerusalem, but at some time in this millennium a group split off from the main body and worshipped elsewhere in Palestine; these were the Samaritans.

In Iran too there grew up the worship of a supreme god, Ahura Mazda (the 'Wise Lord'), beneath whom there were a 'Holy Spirit' and 'Evil Spirit' in opposition to each other. The rites of worship were performed by priests ('Magi'), and there was a body of scriptures, the Avesta, the earliest part of which was formed of hymns attributed to a religious teacher, Zoroaster (hence the name Zoroastrianism* often used for this religion).

In this millennium the greater part of the region felt the impact of the spread of Greek religion, because of the conquests of Alexander the Great* and the foundation of Greek cities. There took place a process of mutual assimilation of the Greek gods with local ones. In Iran, in particular, the cult of the ancient gods, and the religious teaching of Zoroaster, were temporarily submerged. Among those who were touched by Greek culture, the religious ideas of the philosophers also spread.

The rise of Christianity

After the Mediterranean world was incorporated in the Roman Empire, a new impulse was given to the tendency towards monotheism and individual piety by the appearance of Christianity* and its adoption as the official religion of the Empire in the fourth century AD. The ancient religions were gradually extinguished, although vestiges of them remained in different forms, in the survival of local shrines, centres of pilgrimage and petition; Christain churches were built within the temple complexes of the Egyptian gods. Christianity was a divisive as well as a unifying force. Its revealed holy book added to those of the Jews (regarded as the Old Testament) a New Testament which recorded the life and teachings of Jesus Christ and of his apostles. For those who wished to give the new religion a rational form, it posed problems about the nature of Christ and his relationship with the God whom he called his Father. The controversies about the nature of Christ split the Church of his followers. The main body of the Church, that which was supported by the Emperor, accepted that Christ had both a divine and a human nature, fully united in one person; this was the doctrine supported by the Emperor and his government, and its adherents were known, in Near Eastern countries, as Melkites* (from the word for 'king' in various Semitic languages). The Nestorians*, however, who were mainly outside the Roman Empire, maintained a sharper division between the two natures and spoke of the word of God dwelling from conception in the man Jesus; at the other end of the spectrum, the Monophysites* held that the incarnate Christ had only a single nature, composed out of two natures. Thus, while the Nestorians rejected any phrase which imputed suffering to God, the Monophysites, and many Melkites, were willing to use such language. A compromise which was later advanced was that of the Monotheletes, who asserted that Christ had two natures, divine and human, but only one will, a divine one.

Each of these theological positions was reinforced by ethnic and local loyalties. The official doctrine of the imperial government was supported by most Greeks; that of the Nestorians by a large part of the Syriac-speaking population of Syria and Mesopotamia; that of the Monophysites by other Syriac-speaking Christians, the Armenians, and most Egyptian Christians. The Syrian Monophysites were popularly known as Jacobites*, after their most important thinker, the Armenians as Gregorians after the apostle of Armenia, and the Egyptians as Copts (a word derived from the ancient name for Egypt).

In parts of North Africa, another theological controversy served in a similar way as a means of expression of hostility to imperial authority. A large part of the population were Donatists, holding that the Church should be a body uncorrupted by the world, only priests who were in a state of grace could administer valid sacraments, and the government should not interfere in the affairs of the Church.

Within the main body of the Church, that supported by the imperial government, there later appeared a schism between the eastern and western parts, partly over a question of doctrine, but mainly over that of ecclesiastical authority; the western or Roman Catholic part accepted the supreme doctrinal authority of the pope, the bishop of Rome, while the Eastern Orthodox part was a group of autocephalous churches under a number of patriarchs and other authorities.

Although most subjects of the Emperor sooner or later became Christians, the Jews remained faithful to their own religion, Judaism, which moved into a new phase after the destruction of the

Temple in Jerusalem by the Romans during the first century AD. The communal worship of God by priests could only take place in the Temple; in its absence, authority in the community began to be exercised by lay teachers and preachers (rabbis) in synagogues or places of teaching. The study by rabbis of the Torah and the oral laws which had developed over the centuries gave rise to a body of discussions and interpretations which was formalized in the Talmud, compiled in the two main centres of Jewish religious life, Palestine and Babylon, and which was to serve henceforward as the basis of a system of laws of ideal individual and social behaviour. Those who accepted this version of Judaism came later to be known as Rabbanites.

Both Judaism and Christianity (mainly in its Nestorian form) spread eastwards into Iran, but here they had to contend with other religious movements. Under the Sasanians* (third–seventh centuries) there was a revival and further development of Mazdaism, in a more dualistic form, with Ahura Mazda being identified with the 'Holy Spirit'. There was also the challenge of a new religion, Manichaeism. This was named after its founder, Mani, a religious teacher who taught that man was embedded in the world but should strive to be liberated from its evils by coming to a new knowledge of his true self, through an inner illumination; in liberating himself he would also help to restore the true nature of the universe by defeating the principle of evil which was at war with God. For a time Manichaeism spread far beyond Iran, westwards throughout the Roman world, eastwards into inner Asia and as far as China.

The coming of Islam

A new period in the religious history of the region began with the rise of Islam* in the seventh century, and the formation of the Empire of the Caliphs, stretching from Spain and Morocco to central Asia. In course of time, most inhabitants of the countries ruled by the Caliphs became Muslims, adherents of the religion of Islam; this happened both by the gradual conversion of indigenous peoples and by the expansion of peoples already converted, Arabs in Syria, Iraq, Iran and North Africa, and much later Turks in Anatolia. Once more, however, older forms of worship and ideas of the divine continued to exist in new guise.

Islam, like Christianity, divided as well as united. Muslims believed that God, who had revealed himself through history to a succession of prophets that included Moses and Jesus, had given His final revelation to the prophet Muhammad* in the form of the Qur'an, the full expression of the divine will for human life. Questions soon arose, however, about the way in which the revelation should be interpreted, and about the nature of authority in the Muslim community, once the Prophet Muhammad was no longer alive. The main body of Muslims, who came to be called Sunnis*, believed that the Qur'an should be supplemented, as a guide to God's will and human action, by the traditions of what the Prophet and his companions had said and done; they believed, also, that the temporal authority of the Prophet over the community had been transmitted to a line of Caliphs.

Conflict very soon arose, however, about the line of transmission. Almost thirty years after the Prophet's death, the position of the fourth Caliph, ʿAli*, the cousin and son-in-law of Muhammad, was challenged by the governor of Syria, Muʿawiya*. ʿAli agreed to a process of arbitration, and one group of his supporters therefore withdrew from his camp, maintaining that a holder of legitimate authority should not be willing to submit the will of God to a human judgement. They were known as Kharijis* (after the Arabic word for 'going out' or 'withdrawing'). A number of later groups claimed affiliation with them, the most lasting and widespread being the Ibadis*.

In the event, ʿAli was murdered and the Caliphate passed to Muʿawiya and his family, the Umayyads*; but there remained many who continued to support ʿAli's claim, and who were known as 'partisans of ʿAli', (*Shiʿat ʿAli*, Shiʿa* or Shiʿis). There gradually developed among them the doctrine that ʿAli was not only the rightful temporal ruler of the community; he was the Imam, the only authoritative interpreter of the Qur'an, without error or sin, and the office of Imam passed by designation to other members of his and the Prophet's family (his wife, Fatima, was Muhammad's daughter).

The Shiʿa differed among themselves, however, about the line of transmission of the Imamate. The Zaydis* believed that any worthy descendant of the Prophet could become Imam. Those who are usually known as 'Twelvers'*, or simply as Shiʿis*, believed that the line had culminated in the twelfth Imam, who had disappeared, but would return at the end of time to usher in the reign of justice. A third group, the 'Seveners' or Ismaʿilis*, differed from the Twelvers in their view of who the legitimate seventh Imam was, and believed that it was his son who would return in the fullness of time.

Some Shiʿi groups, and in particular the Ismaʿilis, developed a cosmology of their own. They believed that the universe had been created by God by means of successive emanations. The human world ruled by the Imam would in due course ascend to God by way of inner illumination or gnosis, and history would culminate in the return of the Imam. This doctrine, they held, was the real meaning of the Qur'an lying beneath its apparent meaning, and it could only be communicated to those who were ready for it.

Ismaʿili beliefs spread with the coming to power, in Tunisia and then in Egypt, of the Fatimid* dynasty which claimed descent from ʿAli and Fatima. Once more there arose divisions between those who accepted different interpretations of the faith. Under the Fatimids, official Ismaʿili teaching was changed so as to recognize the Fatimid rulers themselves as Imams. Towards the end of the

The shrine of Imam Riza at Mashad, Iran

dynasty, a conflict broke out between supporters of two claimants to the throne, and the Isma'ili community split into different groups, including the Nizaris*, who held that the line of Imams was still continuing, and the Tayyibis, for whom the Imam was in concealment.

The esoteric teaching of the Isma'ilis had many variations, and gave rise to a number of sects which developed in a different way from the main body of Islam. Among them were the Druzes*, who believed that the one God, immediately present to human beings, had embodied himself in a sequence of emanations, the last of whom was one of the Fatimid rulers of Egypt, al-Hakim; the Nusayris or 'Alawis*, for whom God was inexpressible; and the Ahl-i Haqq, who believed in successive manifestations of God.

During the early Islamic period the Jewish community also divided over questions of doctrine and law. In the eighth century there emerged a group, the Karaites, who differed from other Jews on the question of the sources of religious law. They held that the Torah was the only source of law, and that every scholar should study it for himself; in due course, however, they developed their own traditions of interpretation.

The modern age

New kinds of division appeared with the forging of links between the Middle East and Western Europe from the sixteenth century onwards. The work of Catholic missionaries had an impact on all the Eastern churches. Already in the twelfth century, at the time of the Crusades, the Maronites* had given up their Monothelete doctrine and accepted Catholic teaching and the primacy of the pope, while retaining their own liturgy and eclesiastical hierarchy. From the seventeenth century onwards, Churches with a similar position – usually called 'Uniates' – emerged from the other Eastern Churches. From the Nestorian Church there arose the Chaldaean Catholics; from the three Monophysite churches, the Armenian, Coptic and Syrian Catholics; from the Eastern Orthodox Church, the Greek Catholics (for whom, rather than for the Orthodox, the term 'Melkite' came to be commonly used).

Later still, in the nineteenth century, the activities of European and American Protestant missions led to the creation of Episcopalian, Presbyterian and other Protestant Churches, mainly by conversion of members of Eastern Churches; few Jews or Muslims were converted.

In the Jewish communities of Western Europe and North America the reception of Protestant and secular ideas led also to the creation of separate 'reform' or 'liberal' Jewish communities, which abandoned much of the ritual and legal observances of the orthodox.

The opening to the modern Western world may also have played a part in the emergence of a new religion out of Shi'i Islam in the nineteenth century. It began as a dissident movement in Iran, where a religious teacher, Mirza 'Ali Muhammad, was recognized by his followers as the Bab, the gate or forerunner of the twelfth Imam who was expected to return, or even as himself the Imam. His adherents were known as Babis and most of them recognized as his successor Baha Allah, through whose writings, and those of his son, Baha'ism became a distinct religion, teaching that God has revealed his will through a succession of messengers, that in the end all religions are one, and mankind should be united.

The present situation

The religions of the ancient Near East only continue to exist as a substratum in popular Islam, Christianity and Judaism; Manichaeism has wholly vanished; the Donatists, and members of other Christian groups in North Africa, ceased to exist when North African Christianity disappeared after the spread of Islam; Monothelete Christianity also vanished when the Maronites accepted Roman Catholic doctrine. Apart from these, however, all the religious systems mentioned here still have adherents in the Middle East or North Africa.

To say this may be to give the impression that the region is a mosaic of small, closed and antagonistic religious communities. In a sense, this would be a misleading impression. Some of the communities are very small indeed. The vast majority of Muslims are either Sunnis or Shi'i Muslims of the 'Twelver' branch; the greater number of Jews are Rabbanites; only the Christians are split into a number of Churches, no one of which is predominant. The tradition of Middle Eastern society, however, is one in which religious identity serves as the point around which historical memories, social customs and political loyalties tend to cluster. This tradition has been strengthened by the practice of Muslim governments of giving formal recognition to a number of communities. Any survey of the region should therefore draw attention to the existence and whereabouts even of the smaller communities.

Muslims

Islam in its Sunni form is the most widespread of all the religions. Sunni Muslims form almost the entire population of North Africa. They are a majority in Egypt, the northern part of the Sudan, Turkey, Afghanistan, Syria, Jordan, Saudi Arabia, most of the Gulf states and South Yemen, and are present in all the other countries of the region. In matters of religious law Sunnis follow a number of different legal schools. Most North Africans accept the Maliki* school, Turks are Hanafis*, in Saudi Arabia the dominant school is the Hanbali*, and the Shafi'i* school is widespread in the Arab countries. The differences between these schools, however, are not so great as to divide their followers into different sects.

Shi'ism in its 'Twelver' form is the religion of most Iranians and a majority in Iraq, and is also widespread in the Gulf, Saudi Arabia, eastern Turkey, and southern and eastern Lebanon. Zaydi Shiʿism is widespread in North Yemen.

Of the Ismaʿili groups and offshoots, Nizari Ismaʿilis live in small communities in northern Syria, and Tayyibis in North Yemen. Druzes are to be found in Lebanon, southern Syria, and northern Israel. The main body of Nusayris live in coastal Syria, the Ahl-i Haqq in western Iran.

Ibadis form the main religious group in Oman in south-eastern Arabia, and there are smaller numbers of them in Libya and Tunisia, and the desert fringe of Algeria.

Christians

Adherents of the Eastern Orthodox Church form the majority of the population in Cyprus, and are to be found also in Lebanon, Syria, Jordan, Israel and some other countries. They are often known as 'Greek' Orthodox, but this term is misleading, as most of those in Arab countries are Arabic-speaking.

The Nestorian Church survives among the so-called Assyrians*, in northern Iraq, Iran and some other countries. Of the Churches marked by the Monophysite controversy, Armenians* are to be found mainly in Syria, Lebanon and Iran, with smaller communities elsewhere; the Armenian community in Turkey, which was formerly large, almost disappeared after the disturbances and massacres of the earlier part of this century. The Copts live almost entirely in Egypt, where they form the largest minority. The Syrian Orthodox live mainly in Syria and southern Turkey.

Of the Uniate communities, the largest Maronite* community is in northern Lebanon, but they live also in Syria, Israel and other countries. The other Uniates are to be found wherever the Eastern Churches from which they separated exist: Coptic Catholics in Egypt, Greek Catholics in Lebanon, Syria, Jordan and Israel, Chaldaean Catholics in Iraq and Iran, Syrian Catholics in Syria and elsewhere, Armenian Catholics in Lebanon and elsewhere. In most countries there are few members of the western Catholic Church (known locally as 'Latins'), but in southern Sudan Catholic missionary work has led to the creation of Catholic communities from among those who formally adhered to indigenous religions.

Protestant missions, too, have created Churches in the southern Sudan, and Protestants are also to be found in the other countries where there are Christian communities.

Jews

The position of the Jews in the region, like that of the Armenians, has been changed by political events during the present century. The largest Jewish community in the Middle East is now concentrated in Israel, where it forms a majority of the population. Most members of the former Jewish communities in the Middle East and North Africa have now emigrated, either to Israel or elsewhere. Of those which still exist, the communities in Morocco, Turkey, and Iran are the largest.

Almost all the Jews are Rabbanites. As in all communities which have been deeply touched by modern Western culture, there is a wide spectrum of attitudes, from virtually complete secularism to strict orthodoxy. Among the orthodox, there are differences of liturgy, practice and custom between Ashkenazis, mainly coming from western, central and eastern Europe, and Sephardis, from Mediterranean or Middle Eastern countries. There is a small Karaite community in Israel, and an even smaller Samaritan one mainly in the occupied West Bank.

Others

There are small communities of Zoroastrians in various parts of Iran. Babis and Baha'is* also exist in Iran, although their numbers are shrinking under the present regime, which does not recognize Baha'ism as a separate religion. There are also some Baha'is in other countries.

Finally, there are two other communities besides these which cannot be classified as Muslims, Christians or Jews. In northern Iraq, and also in Turkey and Iran, there are Yazidis. Their religion seems to include elements drawn from Christianity and Islam. In their belief, God created the world, but it is sustained by a hierarchy of angels or subordinate beings, the chief among them being symbolized by a peacock. They deny the existence of evil or the devil; human beings, they maintain, will be gradually purified and perfected through a succession of lives.

The Mandaeans live in southern Iraq, and also in Iran. Ancient indigenous religious traditions survive among them. They believe in the ascent of the soul, by way of an inner illumination, to reunion with the supreme being; baptism, a process of purification, forms an important part of their ritual.

AHH

Further reading

A. J. Arberry, ed., *Religion in the Middle East* (Cambridge, 1969), 2 vols.
R. B. Betts, *Christians in the Arab East* (London, 1979)
H. A. R. Gibb, *Islam* (Oxford, 1975)
E. Kedourie, ed., *The Jewish World* (London, 1979)
R. C. Zaehner, ed., *A Concise Encyclopedia of Living Faiths* (London, 3rd edn., 1977)

Part II
HISTORY

Interior view of the Dome of the Rock, Jerusalem

Ancient history of the Near East

The past of the Middle East has been illuminated in modern times by the study of the buildings, tombs, artefacts and inscriptions on stone, papyrus and clay revealed by archaeological excavation. Agricultural settlements were established very early in the fertile parts of Syria* and Palestine*, Anatolia* and Iran*, while urban life, regular government, organized religion and literate cultures developed later in the valleys of the Nile, Tigris and Euphrates. Although the different regions were linked by trade and cultural contacts, and at time by conflict and conquest, it will be convenient to treat them separately.

Ancient Egypt

Herodotus is often quoted as saying that Egypt is the gift of the Nile. The Nile creates a narrow band of cultivable land bordered by desert, some 470 km long and never more than a few kilometres wide except in the north, where it widens into the Delta area of Lower Egypt. Until the building of the Aswan High Dam*, the floods, which took place in about August, caused the waters to rise between 6 and 9 m and a layer of rich, black alluvial mud was deposited which made the country exceptionally fertile. If one of the world's earliest civilizations grew up along the Nile Valley it is precisely because the ancient Egyptians had to take maximum advantage of these inundations, had to organize their agriculture accordingly and had to cooperate. The Nile also united the country

Relief from the tomb of Ramose at Luxor

in another way: it was the main highway, and the prevailing wind from the north meant that it was possible to sail upstream and to use the current for travel downstream.

In about 300 BC Manetho, an Egyptian writing in Greek, divided the history of his country into thirty-one dynasties, and this division is still in general use. Before the dynastic period, however, there was a proto-dynastic one, from about 4000 BC. This can be divided into a number of phases, named after archaeological sites which are typical of them: Badarian (including Tasian), Naqada I (Amratian), and Naqada II (Gerzean). Slate palettes and ivory handles dating from this period testify to contacts with south-western Iran. Regional divisions ('nomes') seem to have corresponded roughly with later ones, but politically the country was divided into Upper and Lower Egypt, each with a King; the King of Upper Egypt wore a white crown and the King of Lower Egypt a red crown, and they ruled from Hierakonpolis and Buto respectively.

The early dynasties

The country was united under Menes, generally identified with Narmer, whose palette shows him wearing both crowns (the 'double crown'), and with this union there begins the Early Dynastic Period (*c.*3100–2686 BC), a time of considerable administrative reorganization and the establishment of a new capital at Memphis. The tombs of Abydos and Saqqara which date from this period give evidence of trade with western Asia and military expeditions eastwards into Sinai. The Third Dynasty marks the beginning of the Old Kingdom (2686–2181 BC), a period of expansion; one of the Kings, Djoser, may have fixed the southern boundary of his Kingdom at the First Cataract on the Nile. It was also a period of centralized rule by Kings (Pharaohs), who are now known mainly by their pyramids on the edge of the Nile Valley at Giza. During the Sixth Dynasty Pepi I and his successors sent expeditions to Punt (Ethiopia), Nubia, Libya, Sinai and western Asia, but the increasing power of the nobles resulted in a decentralized administration and ultimately in political fragmentation. There followed a time of political chaos and anarchy known as the First Intermediate Period (*c.*2181–2050), and its history is obscure. In about 2160, however, the local governor (nomarch) of Heracleopolis established the Ninth Dynasty and gained control of Middle Egypt, while the nomarchs of Thebes seized power in the south and eventually reunited the whole country under the Eleventh Dynasty.

With this dynasty began the Middle Kingdom (*c.*2050–1786 BC). During the earlier part of the period a single administration was re-established and steps were taken to curb the power of the nomarchs. New foreign expeditions were launched, and in the reigns of Pharaohs of the Twelfth Dynasty such as Sesostris I and III and Amenemes IV there were extensive contacts with Syria by way of the port of Byblos on the Syrian coast. In the south, lower Nubia* was annexed to Egypt, forts were built between the First and Second Cataracts, and there is evidence of penetration even further to the south.

The Hyksos and later

The end of the Twelfth Dynasty was followed by the Second Intermediate Period (*c.*1786–1567); once more there was a decline of central authority, but there does not seem to have been the same political or cultural disruption as in the First Intermediate Period. There may have been a period when different dynasties ruled Upper and Lower Egypt. In part of Lower Egypt, rulers from Asia, known as the Hyksos, formed the Fifteenth and Sixteenth Dynasties. Their capital was Avaris in the eastern Delta, but their rule extended far beyond that, and their influence reached as far as the Sudan* and Palestine; artefacts bearing names connected with them have been found even further afield. In later ages the Hyksos were regarded as oppressors and attempts were made to erase all trace of them, but the evidence which survives points to a period of stable rule.

Hyksos power ended when they came into conflict with the rulers of Thebes in Upper Egypt, belonging to the Seventeenth Dynasty. One of the rulers, Amosis I, captured the Hyksos capital of Avaris and established the Eighteenth Dynasty, whose Pharaohs ruled a reunited Egypt. This marks the beginning of the New Kingdom (*c.*1567–1085 BC). It was a period of territorial expansion; Amosis captured a Hyksos fort in southern Palestine, and under later Kings such as Tuthmosis I, III and IV and Amenophis I and II, Palestine and parts of Syria were annexed and Egyptian armies reached the Euphrates. In the south the Kingdom eventually extended beyond the Fourth Cataract, while in the west there were successful campaigns against the Libyans.

The new prosperity of the Kingdom and its increasing foreign contacts led to an upsurge of artistic activity, particularly during the reigns of Amenophis III and IV. The latter Pharaoh changed his name to Akhenaten and moved his capital from Thebes to Akhetaten (of which the modern name is El-Amarna); he initiated a new religious cult, that of Aten, and what is called the Amarna Age. His successor Tutankhamun, however, returned to the older cult, that of Amun. He died young, and it is his magnificent tomb which was discovered in 1923. The famous Amarna letters, found by peasants, date from this period; they are correspondence with the kings of western Asia and with petty Syrian and Palestinian rulers and show that Egypt's foreign power diminished in this period.

Eventually, however, a general called Horemheb became Pharaoh and reasserted Egyptian power. His period marks the transition to the Nineteenth Dynasty, founded by Ramesses I. Under Ramesses II there was a war with the Hittites from Anatolia; both sides claimed victory in the famous battle of Qadesh in Syria (*c.*1285 BC), but a dynastic marriage eventually led to peace. There followed a period of foreign incursions into the Delta, but Ramesses III revived Egyptian fortunes, established the Twentieth Dynasty and defeated a massed sea and land attack by the 'Sea Peoples' from the Aegean and Anatolia in *c.*1195. Thereafter there was a decline in prosperity and political stability; Egypt lost its Asiatic Empire, and the country was again divided.

This division and weakness lasted throughout much of the Late Dynastic Period (1085–332 BC). The Twenty-first Dynasty Pharaohs ruled from their capital at Tanis in the Delta, but Upper Egypt was controlled by the high priests of Thebes. Under the next dynasty, of Libyan origin, the Pharaohs appointed their sons as high priests of Thebes in an unsuccessful attempt to unite the country; later, a little-known line of Pharaohs of the Twenty-third Dynasty ruled concurrently with them in the Delta. There followed a period of further disintegration; Egyptianized rulers from the Sudan gained control of the whole country and founded the Twenty-fifth dynasty (*c.*715 AD). But the Assyrians invaded Egypt, occupying Memphis in 671, and later even reached Thebes. Their vassal, Psammetichus I, gained control of the whole country and finally broke the ties with Assyria; he ruled from Sais and the period is therefore known as the Saite.

During the dynasty which he founded, the Twenty-sixth, foreign trading colonies were established in Egypt, notably by the Greeks at Naucratis, and there was a diminution of Egyptian power; an Egyptian army was defeated by the Babylonians in Syria, control over Nubia was lost to local dynasts, and in the west, too, the Egyptians suffered a severe reverse. Finally, Psammetichus III was defeated by Cambyses of the Persian Achaemenid Dynasty and Egypt became a satrapy of the Persian Empire. In due course the Persians were expelled, but the succeeding dynasties had to struggle against them, often with Greek help. Finally, in 343, the Persians recovered Egypt, and ruled there until it was conquered by Alexander the Great* in 332.

Egyptian religion

Before the unification of Egypt each regional centre worshipped its own gods, which were often associated with animals. This accounts for the large number of deities attested in later times, and the prominence achieved by some, at one period or another, is due to the greater political importance of the city of which they were the tutelary deity. At the time of the unification of Egypt, the falcon god Horus of Hierakonpolis emerged as the principal god and became identified with the King during his lifetime. Other gods who rose to prominence at this time were Seth of Ombos – the god of storms and violence, Thoth of Hermopolis – the ibis-headed inventor of writing, Ptah – the creator god of Memphis, and Re – the sun god of Heliopolis, who was later assimilated to Amun – the great god of the Eighteenth Dynasty Pharaohs of Thebes. Important goddesses were cow-headed Hathor, hippopotamus-headed Thoeris, and Bastet – the cat-headed goddess of Bubastis.

Despite political fluctuations, the local deities, who were varied both in form and character, continued to be worshipped and were incorporated into the Egyptian pantheon and mythology. In certain ceremonies, often based on the agricultural calendar, they would visit each other by boat. The *Sed* festival took place at Memphis, after the King had reigned for thirty years, and confirmed him as ruler of Upper and Lower Egypt, but it was the daily temple ritual of Heliopolis which formed the basis of official religion, with the King, or a priest as his representative, acting as Horus and as high-priest of the god Re in all the temples of the land. By the end of the third millennium BC the cult of Osiris had become inextricably linked with this ritual. According to myths Osiris, a King of Lower Egypt, was killed by his brother Seth who dismembered him. His widow Isis travelled throughout Egypt collecting the separate pieces and reconstituted Osiris by whom she had the child Horus. This belief in life after death led to elaborate mummification and burial rites presided over by the jackal-headed god Anubis.

Egyptian writing

The language of the ancient Egyptians was related to both the Semitic and Hamitic groups. Before 3000 BC contact with Sumer and Elam (southern Iraq and south-western Iran) led to the development of the system of writing which we know as hieroglyphic. As in

The Rosetta Stone, British Museum, London

Sumerian, a picture-sign represented an actual object, or a word, or part of a word with the same sound, and 'determinative' signs were added to indicate the sense. However, whereas Sumerian pictographs developed into cuneiform, Egypt retained its picture signs for some 3500 years. The hieroglyphic script could be written in either direction and in vertical columns. Hieratic and demotic, which were written from right to left, were cursive forms developed from hieroglyphs for writing in ink on papyrus, the one at an early period and the other much later in Egyptian history. The famous Rosetta Stone, in the British Museum since 1802, bears a trilingual inscription in hieroglyphic, demotic and Greek scripts and this finally provided the key to the decipherment of hieroglyphs.

Further reading

J. Baines and J. Malek, *Atlas of Ancient Egypt* (Oxford, 1982)
T. G. H. James, *An Introduction to Ancient Egypt* (London, 1979)

Mesopotamia

The first inhabitants of Mesopotamia seem to have lived on the wooded slopes of the Zagros, where traces of them have been found in caves and later at the village site of Jarmo (*c.*10,000–6000 BC). With the development of agriculture and animal husbandry settlers moved into the fertile plains of northern Mesopotamia where the rainfall was adequate for the raising of crops and where game was abundant. In southern Mesopotamia, the advent of irrigation agriculture, first attested at Choga Mami in the foothills of the Zagros, led to the settlement of the valleys of the Tigris and the Euphrates, but much evidence is buried under the alluvium. At Eridu a sequence of temples was recovered going back to before 5000 BC. The use of irrigation and the need for trade, due to the absence of raw materials, led to the development of organized societies. At the site of Uruk, in the mid-fourth millennium BC, wheel-made pottery, monumental architecture and sculpture, cuneiform writing and urban administration developed, centred on the temples which carried on trade with south-western Iran (Susa), Syria (Habuba Kabira) and Anatolia (Samsat and Arslan Tepe/Malatya). In the north the site of Tepe Gawra demonstrates independent development but there is evidence of links with the south.

In the first half of the third millennium BC city-states grew up and the temples lost some of their power to dynasties of rulers. At Ur the famous 'Royal Cemetery' dates to *c.* 2650 BC. The texts of the period are written on clay tablets in Sumerian. We do not know whether the Sumerians were the indigenous inhabitants of southern Mesopotamia; their language is not related to any known group. These texts attest close links with cities on the Euphrates (Mari) and in Syria (Ebla), where cuneiform was adapted for writing Semitic dialects. Abundant lapis lazuli from Afghanistan and chlorite vessels from southern Iran are evidence of trade with the east.

In 2334 BC Sargon united the warring city-states to form the Akkadian Empire. This included northern Mesopotamia, and Sargon and his successors went further afield, into Syria, Iran, and possibly Anatolia*; there is evidence also of trade with the Indus Valley. Sargon's new capital, Akkad, has not yet been located, but it was probably near Babylon. This was the centre of a flourishing art; cuneiform writing was used for the language of the Empire, which was Akkadian, a Semitic language. What has been called 'the world's first Empire' was short-lived, however. The Gutians from the east invaded it, and there was a period of political instability from which some Sumerian city-states re-emerged: Lagash under Gudea, and Ur under Kings of the Third Dynasty (Ur III). This neo-Sumerian period came to an end *c.*2000 BC, under the combined attack of Elamites from the east and the Semitic Amorites from the west.

During the next two centuries these nomadic Amorites settled throughout Mesopotamia and created small independent Kingdoms. The south was governed in succession by the rulers of Isin and Larsa, while in the north the city of Assur established a flourishing and well-documented trade with central Anatolia; one of its rulers, Shamsi-Adad (1813–1781 BC) gained control of northern Mesopotamia, but his successors were overcome by the ruler of Babylon, Hammurabi (1792–1750 BC), who had extended his power over the south. Hammurabi is best known for his law code, now in the Louvre in Paris.

The First Dynasty of Babylon was in its turn overthrown by the Hittites from Anatolia in 1595 BC. There followed a period of rule by the Kassites. Opinions differ as to whether they came from further east or from the middle Euphrates to the north-west; their personal names betray their foreign origins, but they adopted the language and culture of the Babylonians, and provided stable government for several centuries, until they were overthrown by the Elamites in 1171 BC.

In the meantime, Hurrians from eastern Anatolia had been settling peacefully in northern Syria and Mesopotamia since the late third millennium BC, and in the sixteenth century BC they established the Mitannian Empire under an aristocracy using an Indo-Aryan language. Business archives found at Nuzi provide evidence for them in the fifteenth century BC. In the next century their Kings corresponded with the Amarna Pharaohs in Egypt, as did those of Babylon and Assyria. The Assyrians were the vassals of Mitanni, but gradually gained power, and when dynastic conflicts led to the collapse of the Mitannian Empire, Ashur-uballit of Assyria (1365–1330 BC) seized control of its territory in the east.

Assyrian power grew from this time, and eventually an Empire was founded by Ashurnasipal II and Shalmaneser III. Later Kings

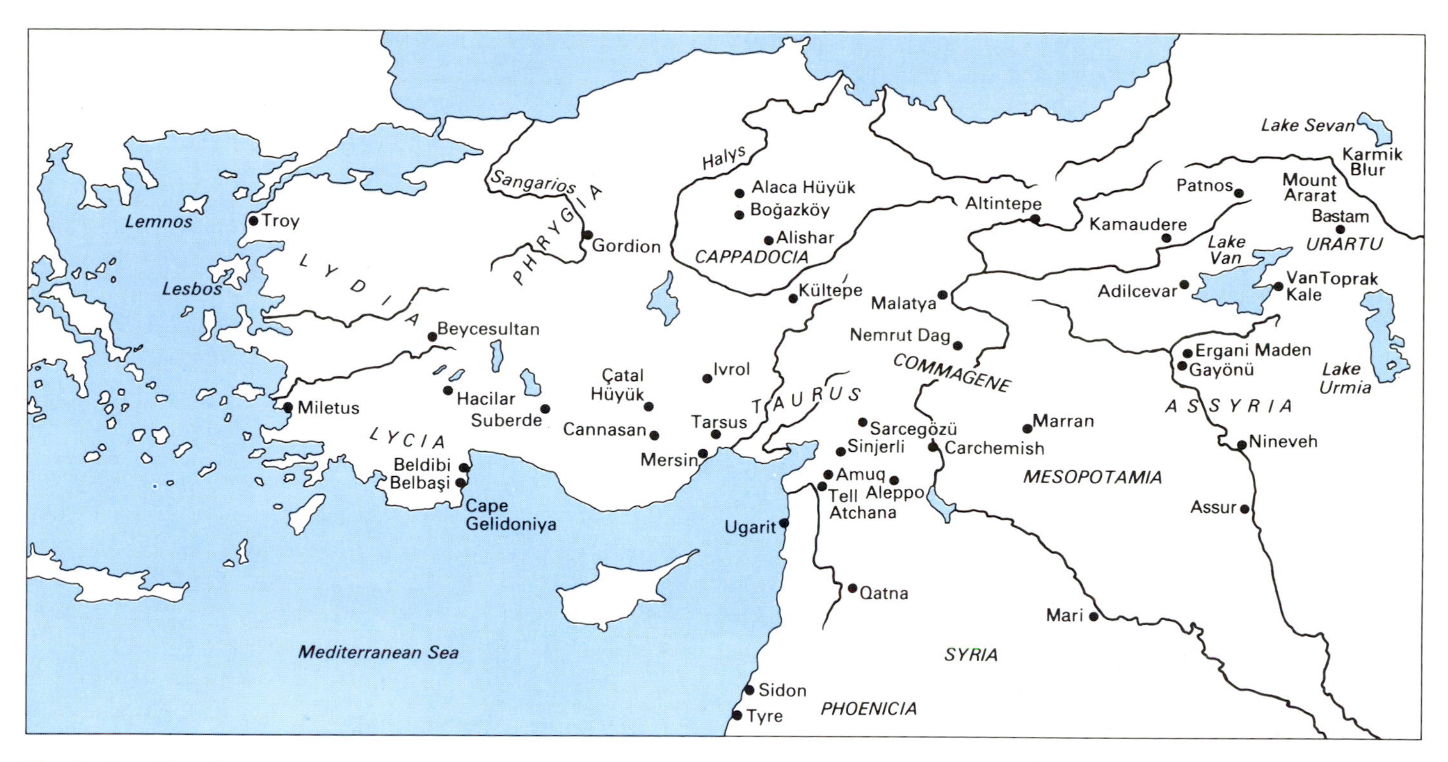

The Ancient Near East

such as Tiglath Pileser III, Sargon II, Sennacherib, Easarhaddon and Ashurbanipal carried Assyrian arms into Urartu in the north, Iran in the east, Babylonia in the south, and Syria, Palestine and Egypt in the west. In the seventh century BC Ashurbanipal collected a huge library of cuneiform texts, which have survived because they were written on clay tablets (they are now in the British Museum). Together with tablets taken from other sites they have enabled a detailed and reasonably sure chronology of Mesopotamian history to be drawn up. (There are some uncertainties about dates before the sixteenth century BC, and it is the 'middle chronology' which has been used here.)

The last few years of the Assyrian Empire are obscure, but it is known that it collapsed in 612 BC before a concerted attack by the Medes from the east and the Babylonians from the south. Once again the centre of power shifted southwards, to Babylon under Chaldaean Kings such as Nebuchadnezzar II (602–562 BC). The last King, Nabonidus, was overthrown in 539 BC by the Persian Achaemenid King Cyrus the Great. The fall of this neo-Babylonian dynasty marked the end of the political independence of Mesopotamia. Thereafter the country was ruled by a succession of foreign dynasties: first the Persians from the east (until 331 BC), then the Greek Macedonians and Seleucids from the west (until 247), then the Parthians or Arsacids, once more from the east (until AD 228), and then the Sasanians until the Islamic conquest* in the seventh century AD.

Mesopotamian religion

It seems that the Sumerians worshipped chthonic deities representing fertility (Inanna and Dumuzi), subterranean water (Enki/Ea) and air (Enlil), presided over by a heavenly god, Anu. The Semitic Akkadians worshipped astral deities: the sun (Shamash), the moon (Sin), Venus (Ishtar) and the storm (Adad). It became necessary to amalgamate the two series of deities and Ishtar, for instance, acquired the attributes of Inanna and became, in addition, a warrior goddess. Furthermore, different aspects of basically the same deity were worshipped under different titles in the various city-states and the process of synchretism is found here also. Tribal and national gods, such as Amurru (the god of the Amorites), Assur (the god of the Assyrians) and Marduk (the god of Babylon, also known as Bel) were assimilated into the system. At the end of the third and beginning of the second millennia BC some kings were deified in their lifetime. The most important festival of the year was the Akitu or New Year festival. Myths and legends were woven around these deities, for instance Inanna's descent to the underworld in search of

Dumuzi, or the *Epic of Gilgamesh* which includes the Babylonian version of the biblical flood. Many omen texts have also survived.

Mesopotamian writing

Mesopotamia is responsible for the invention of writing. The extensive trade networks established in the second half of the fourth millennium BC led to the need for an efficient recording and accounting system. At first, it seems, small clay tokens representing goods were enclosed in sealed clay balls. Since the balls had to be broken for the contents to be visible, the shapes and numbers of the tokens were indicated by signs impressed on the clay ball. It soon became apparent that signs on a tablet-shaped piece of clay would be a sufficient record and so the first inscribed tablets appear. The early signs are pictures or symbols, representing numerals and merchandise, and cannot be read as consecutive texts, but the potential of this discovery was rapidly exploited. Sumerian words are largely monosyllabic so that the sign depicting the head, *sag*, for instance, could also be used for the sound *-sag-* in longer words. Later, when the system became adapted for writing Semitic Akkadian it acquired the reading *resh*, which could also be used as a word or a syllable, and the process was repeated for other languages. Determinatives were added which indicated how a word should be read and to what class it belonged. For some reason it was found easier to turn the tablet through 90°, a phenomenon which is found in many systems of writing, and since it was easier to impress signs into clay with a stylus than it was to draw them, the original pictograms rapidly became linear and simplified. The resulting script, which was written from left to right, is known as cuneiform (from Latin: *cuneus*, wedge) because of the nail-shaped wedges which make up the signs. The system of writing spread to all parts of the Near East and was even, during the Amarna period, used in international correspondence with Egypt. Since clay tablets are not as easily destroyed as papyrus, parchment and wood, many hundreds of thousands of texts have survived, including the library of the Assyrian kings at Nineveh, now in the British Museum. A trilingual inscription in Old Persian, Babylonian and Elamite, carved in *c.*520 BC by the Achaemenid King Darius, led to the decipherment of cuneiform in the first half of the last century.

Further reading

S. Lloyd, *The Archaeology of Mesopotamia* (London, 1978)
G. Roux, *Ancient Iraq* (London, 1964)

Anatolia

Anatolia forms a land-bridge between regions lying all around it, and it also has important mineral resources; for both these reasons, it has been linked with its neighbours by invasion or trade throughout history. All that is known of its early history has had to be reconstructed from the results of archaeological excavation; this has shown that some of the earliest pre-pottery cultures in the ancient Near East developed in central Anatolia, at sites such as Çatal Hüyük (before 6500 BC), probably under the impetus of trade in obsidian. Another site, Çayönü in the east, was situated close to copper mines, and copper was used for beads even before the development of metal technology made possible other uses of it. Trade in such materials extended to the Aegean, where it was handled by the city of Troy in the west, and also to Cilicia and beyond.

We know little about the indigenous population in the third millennium BC, but in the second half of the millennium Indo-European peoples, the Luwians and Hittites, began moving in, and by the next millennium they were firmly established. By this time too there were commercial relations with Mesopotamia. There may have been Akkadian merchant colonies in central Anatolia by the third quarter of the third millennium BC, and they are better attested during the early centuries of the second millennium, when merchants from Assur settled outside some of the major towns such as Kültepe and Boğazköy. They used the cuneiform script of Mesopotamia, and wrote on clay tablets which have survived, and it is now that Anatolia emerges clearly into history. In this period the Hittite Old Kingdom was established, with its capital at Hattusas (Boğazköy). By the second half of the seventeenth century BC the King was able to raid into Syria, and in 1595 Mursilis II led his army south as far as Babylon and brought about the fall of Hammurabi's dynasty; but he did not follow up his success.

After a period which is somewhat obscure, we find that the Kingdom has grown into an Empire. Its expansion into northern Syria brought the Hittites* into conflict with the Egyptians. In the reigns of the Hittite Muwatallis and the Egyptian Ramesses II the two powers fought in one of the great battles of antiquity, at Qadesh near Homs in Syria (*c.*1285 BC). Within a century, however, Hittite power had disappeared. Shortly after 1200 the 'Sea Peoples' swept through Anatolia and Syria, destroying cities as they went; they seem to have consisted of Aegeans and Anatolians, some of them known from Egyptian sources as mercenaries, who were forced to move by economic and political pressures. The Trojan War, which took place at this time, was one manifestation of this movement of peoples.

Little is known of what happened in the next few centuries, but when the picture clears once more we find the successors of the Hittites established on the borders of Syria and Anatolia, notably at Carchemish: they used a hieroglyphic script for a language which is closer to Luwian than to Hittite. In the ninth century BC these neo-Hittite Kingdoms came into conflict with the expanding power of Assyria; it is they who are the 'Hittites' mentioned in the Old

The stone heads on Mount Nemrut, Turkey

Testament. Other Kingdoms were established elsewhere in Anatolia at this time. To the north and east, the Urartians of the highlands united to resist the threat from Assyria*, and set up a Kingdom centred on Lake Van. Further to the north and west, the Phrygians (a people with Thracian affinities) had a Kingdom with its capital at Gordion; one of their Kings, Midas (*c.*700 BC), lost his life when the Cimmerians from south Russia invaded Anatolia, and it is possibly his tomb which has been excavated at Gordion. The legend of the wealth of King Croesus of Lydia was based on that country's invention of coinage. In 546, however, Lydian power was destroyed by the expansion of the Achaemenids of Persia westwards into Anatolia.

On the coast, the Myceneans had been setting up colonies since the late second millennium. In the fifth century BC they came into conflict with the Persians, and this led to the wars between Greeks and Persians (490–449 BC). In the next century, Achaemenid domination of Anatolia came to an end when Alexander the Great* crossed the Hellespont in 334 BC and finally destroyed the Achaemenid Empire.

Anatolian religion

Lack of texts for the earlier periods is a severe drawback but the fertility goddesses depicted at Çatal Hüyük and Hacilar are already associated with leopards – a feature still found in Hellenistic times, while the male god is associated with a bull and survives as the storm god of the Hittites and later as Zeus Dolichaios. Springs also seem to have had a particular sanctity. The picture clears to some extent in the second half of the second millennium BC when the Hittites adopted the cuneiform script: the sun goddess of Arinna was the patron deity of the Hittite Kings and her consort was the Hittite storm god. Later both deities were assimilated with their Hurrian counterparts Hepat and Teshub, who were carved with other deities in the rock-cut shrine of Yazılıkaya near the Hittite capital. These deities continued to be worshipped in the first millennium BC. The chief god of Urartu was Khaldi, while Phrygians worshipped Cybele and Attis. These latter were absorbed into Greek and Roman religion together with many Anatolian and eastern deities, and the famous monument at Nemrut Dağ depicts synchretic deities such as Zeus-Oromazdes and Apollo-Mithras.

Writing in Anatolia

It seems probable that the Anatolians developed their own pictographic writing but there is no evidence for literacy until they adopted the use of Mesopotamian cuneiform when Assyrian merchants established trading colonies in Cappadocia at the beginning of the second millennium BC. The Hittites adapted cuneiform for writing their Indo-European language and thanks to this we can decipher their hieroglyphic inscriptions. This script first appears in about 1500 BC and survives the fall of the Hittite Empire to reappear in the neo-Hittite cities on the borders with Syria, where it is used to write Luwian, a language related to Hittite. The Karatepe bilingual inscription with Phoenician has considerably assisted in its decipherment. Further east the Urartians also adapted cuneiform for writing their language while to the west the Phrygians and Lydians used an early form of the Greek alphabet.

Further reading

O. R. Gurney, *The Hittites* (London, 1981)
S. Lloyd, *Highland Peoples of Anatolia* (London, 1964)

Syria–Palestine

The major trade-routes along the Euphrates and Khabur valleys linked them historically and culturally to Mesopotamia. The Uruk culture flourished at Tell Brak and Habuba Kabira in the fourth millennium BC and the Early Dynastic period is well represented at Mari and Ebla, whose cuneiform archives are related to those of Sumer in the third millennium BC. Ebla was destroyed by the Akkadians who also built a palace at Brak. In the earlier part of the second millennium the whole region formed part of the kingdom of Shamshi-Adad: archives found at Mari and other sites throw light on the history of the period and continue into the reign of Zimri-Lim, until the latter was overthrown by Hammurabi of Babylon in 1759 BC. The archives of Alalakh (Tell Atchana), on the Syrian–Turkish border, enable us to reconstruct the history of the kings of Yamhad (Aleppo) from *c.* 1720 BC until the kingdom collapsed when invaded by the Hittites from Anatolia in the second half of the next century. When the Mitannians founded their northern Syro-Mesopotamian kingdom *c.* 1500 BC, Alalakh became part of it, as further archives demonstrate, but the Mitannian capital has not been found.

The Levant coast belonged to a different north–south trade network and there is evidence at Jericho for obsidian trade with Anatolia from the tenth millennium BC onwards. When the area emerges into history it is populated by Semitic Canaanites who had major ports at Ras Shamra (Ugarit) and at Byblos and major cities at Hazor and Megiddo. In the south, Ajjul and Lachish were probably frequently under Egyptian domination. In the fourteenth century BC the Egyptians controlled most of the Levant and came into conflict with the Hittites, whose territorial ambitions had led them into north Syria. The Amarna Letters, found in Egypt, give us much information concerning these troubled times and in *c.* 1285 the two powers met at the inconclusive battle of Qadesh near Homs in Syria. Further inland the population consisted largely of pastoralists who were often semi-nomadic: the rock-cut burials found at numerous sites testify to changes in population but it is rarely possible to relate them to specific ethnic groups. One such group was, however, to assume a major place in history: in the thirteenth century BC the Israelites settled in the hills and in Transjordan. They were soon to come into conflict with the Philistines, one of the Sea Peoples who destroyed many of the major coastal towns of the Levant before their defeat by the Egyptians, after which they settled in Ashdod, Askelon and Gaza, and introduced iron technology. By *c.* 1000 BC the Israelites had founded a kingdom; David established his capital in Jerusalem where Solomon built his temple. Cities with elaborate water systems were constructed. By the end of the tenth century the kingdom had divided (Israel and Judah).

Along the coast to the north, the Phoenicians were engaged in trade and had invented the alphabet in order more easily to conduct their business. Later they set up Punic trading colonies in Cyprus, North Africa and Spain. Their wealth attracted the unwelcome attentions of the Assyrians from the ninth century onwards and the latter also extended their conquests into Israel and Judah. Later the neo-Babylonians under Nebuchadnezzar captured Jerusalem and carried the Israelites into exile in 587 BC. When Babylon fell to the Persians in 539 BC, the Israelites were allowed to return but many stayed in the East. Syria–Palestine became part of the Achaemenid Empire, but when conquered by Alexander the Great* in 333 BC it was absorbed into the Hellinistic world.

The religion of Syria–Palestine

As we should expect, the religion of eastern Syria was strongly influenced by Mesopotamia, and late fourth-millennium temples at Brak, Habuba Kabira and Jebel Aruda have similar ground plans. The deities worshipped at Mari in the third and second millennia are also those of Mesopotamia, with the addition of West Semitic gods such as Dagan and Lim. The Hurrians, who settled in north Syria and Mesopotamia in the second millennium BC may have come from eastern Anatolia; their main deities were Hepat, Kumbaba, Shaushka and the storm god Teshub. The religion of the Canaanites, who lived along the Levant coast, is well known thanks to literary texts recording myths, which were found at Ugarit, and to biblical references. El was the father of the gods and Asherah was his consort, but Baal and his virgin sister Anath or Astarte, as fertility deities, play a greater part in the myths. Baal wins kingship by overcoming the powers of chaos typified by the sea god Yamm but is in turn defeated by Mot (death). Anath, however, succeeds in securing his revival. Fertility rites are inveighed against in the Bible but the numerous clay female figurines found in excavation show that fertility cults were widespread (see also Genesis 31:19–35). Sacred groves and high places are also often referred to. Human sacrifice of the first-born may have been a feature of early Canaanite religion which was later replaced by animal sacrifice. However, by the first millennium BC it had been revived and spread to the Phoenician colonies in the west where its occurrence at Carthage is well documented.

Writing in Syria–Palestine

Although Mesopotamian trade extended up the Euphrates into Syria, and sealed clay balls and bullae are found, there is no evidence, so far, of writing except at Brak where two small tablets bear the summary drawings of animals. The use of Mesopotamian cuneiform writing spread to Syria in the third millennium BC. There are inscriptions on the statues from Mari and the script was adapted for writing the West Semitic dialect of Ebla. Akkadian tablets have been found at Brak and cuneiform was adapted for writing Hurrian at the end of the third millennium BC. During the eighteenth and most of the seventeenth centuries BC the use of cuneiform was widespread throughout northern Syria. In the fourteenth century BC Akkadian became the lingua franca for the whole of the Near East, and the vassal governors of the Canaanite city-states used it to write repeatedly to their Egyptian overlord, asking for his military support; this correspondence has been found at El-Amarna. Cuneiform was also adapted for writing the Semitic language of Ugarit, on the coast, and some texts are written in a cuneiform alphabet. The alphabet was a major contribution to civilization. The Levant merchants were caught between four unwieldy scripts, each requiring several hundred signs. To the north and south were the Hittites with their different hieroglyphic scripts, to the east there was cuneiform and to the west the Minoan–Mycenaean Linear B script. An alphabet uses fewer than thirty letters and since sounds are represented rather than syllables and words it is far easier to adapt to different languages. During the second millennium there were several attempts at creating alphabets, including the Ugaritic. The Phoenician alphabet finally developed at the beginning of the first millennium BC. It depicted only consonants (like present-day Arabic and Hebrew), but the Greeks changed the value of some signs, added others, turned some around and passed it on to the Romans. The Phoenician script is, therefore, the ancestor of all subsequent alphabets, including our own, and the word 'alphabet' is based on the first two letters of the second millennium BC Canaanite prototypes: 'a' for *aleph* (bull), 'b' for *beth* (house), represented by simple pictures of a bull (inverted but still recognizable today) and a house.

Further reading

J. Gray, *The Canaanites* (London, 1964)
D. Harden, *The Phoenicians* (London, 1962)
P. R. S. Moorey, *The Making of the Past: Biblical lands* (Oxford, 1975)

Iran (Persia)

The early history of Iran* has had to be reconstructed mainly from the excavation of ancient sites. These show that, because of geographical conditions, several cultures, which can be distinguished by their painted pottery, grew up in isolation from each other. One of them emerged in Susiana (the area around Susa) in south-western Iran. Geographically this area is an extension of the southern Mesopotamian plain, but it has always been inhabited by people of different ethnic origins from those of Mesopotamia, and the two areas have had complementary histories. At times the balance of power between them was even, but when one area grew conspicuously weaker the other would try to dominate it.

In the second half of the fourth millennium BC, the Uruk culture flourished in southern Mesopotamia (Sumer), and the two areas seem to have been economically interdependent and to have carried on a lively trade. Writing on clay tablets developed almost at the same time in both areas, but whereas the Sumerian cuneiform system was to survive for over 3000 years and spread to other countries of the Middle East, including Iran, the Proto-Elamite script of south-western Iran was destined to be relatively short-lived, although it is attested at a number of sites which were linked with Susa by trade (for instance Malyan, Sialk and Yahya). The evidence of the cylindrically shaped seals which were used for sealing consignments of goods shows that there was greater emphasis on agriculture and grain storage in Susiana, as against animal husbandry in Sumer. Susa also seems to have been linked by trade with Egypt* at this time, and the presence of lapis lazuli artefacts here and at Uruk points to the existence of some trade with Afghanistan*.

During the earlier part of the third millennium BC, Susiana continued to have a strong and distinctive culture independent of that of Mesopotamia, and known as Proto-Elamite. Later, however,

Ancient Iran

Charmakli Depe

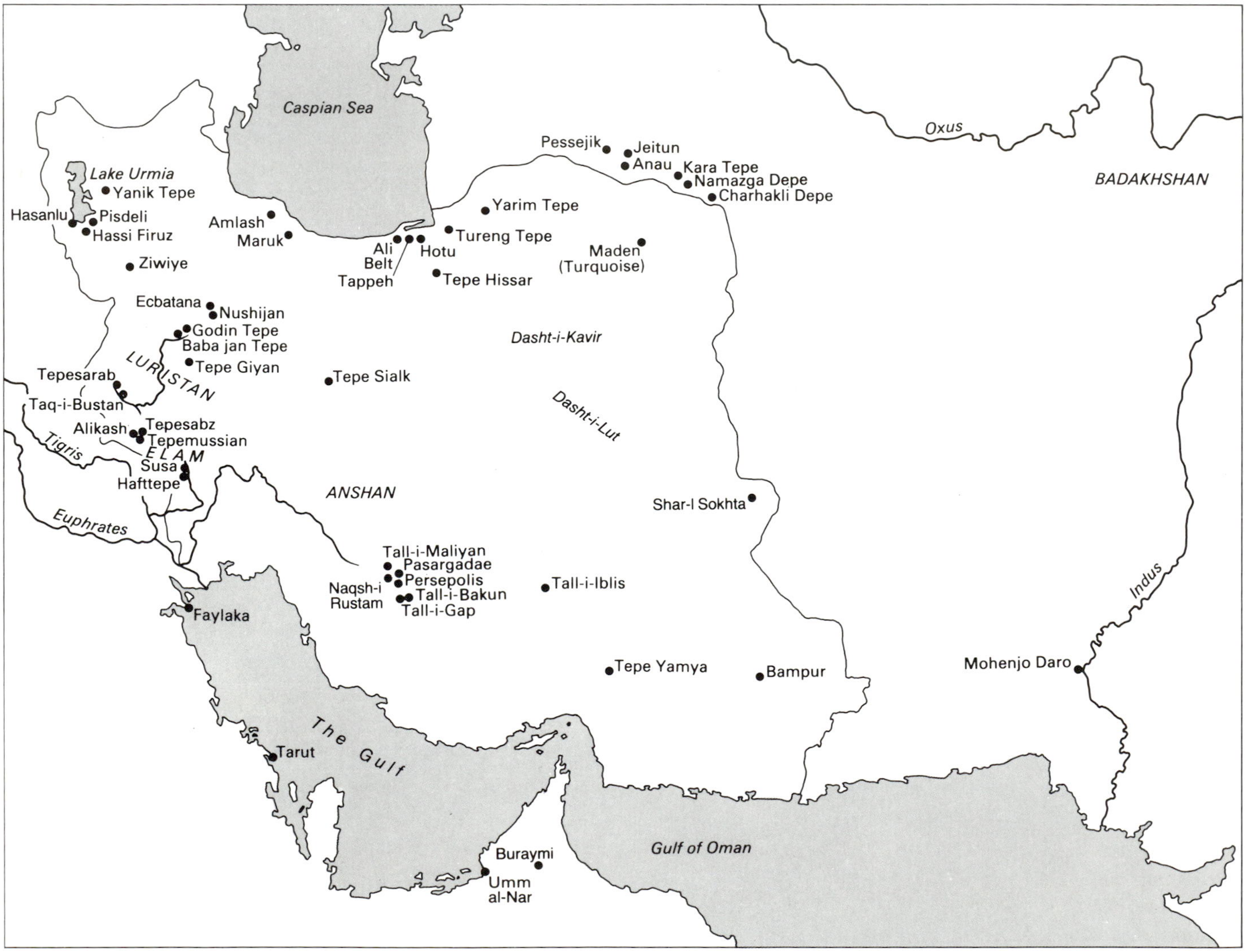

it seems to have become a province of Sumer, at least culturally. Literary compositions indicate that early dynastic rulers of Sumer organized their own trading ventures through Susiana, and archaeological discoveries have thrown light on these: at Shar-i Sokhta in eastern Iran lapis lazuli was processed before being sent further west (a gaming board has been found there similar to one at Ur in Sumer), and at Tepe Yahya, south of the central desert of Iran, chlorite bowls produced for the Mesopotamian and Syrian markets have been found.

In the third quarter of the third millennium southern Mesopotamia was dominant, and the Akkadian and Ur III rulers (see Mesopotamia) were able to appoint governors in Susa, but both dynasties were brought to an end by incursions from the highlands of Gutians and Elamites respectively; Susa was then able to establish its own line of Elamite rulers, while other states grew up along the Zagros borders with Mesopotamia.

During the second millennium Susa remained independent, and in the thirteenth century BC its power expanded under dynamic rulers. One of the places within its power was Choga Zanbil, where huge temples and a ziggurat* have been found. In 1171 the Elamites once more invaded Mesopotamia and brought about the downfall of the Kassites, who may have originated in the Zagros and had held power since the beginning of the sixteenth century.

In the second half of the second millennium, the history of Iran was transformed by the movement of Indo-Aryan tribes from the north. They brought with them a new language, a new type of pottery, new ways of handling horses (including the use of the bit), and improved metal technology and iron-working techniques. The main excavated sites which have thrown light on this process are Marlik, Sialk and Giyan. The most important of the tribes were the Manaeans, Medes and Persians.

In the early part of the first millennium, north-eastern Iran was exposed to pressure from the expanding Assyrian power in northern Mesopotamia; the Manaean stronghold of Hasanlu, south of Lake Urmia, was destroyed by the Assyrians *c*.800 BC. Later, however, the Medes united with the Babylonians and were able to bring about the downfall of the Assyrians in 612 BC. After a period of rivalry, the Medes and Persians formed a dynastic alliance, but in the end Media was drawn into the Persian Empire of the Achaemenids (549–331 BC), created by Cyrus the Great with its capital at Pasargadae. Cyrus extended his rule beyond Iran: he defeated Croesus in Anatolia, captured Babylon, and died campaigning in the east. His son, Cambyses, conquered Egypt, and then under Darius the Great the Empire extended from the Danube and the Nile to the Oxus and the Indus. Darius moved the capital to Persepolis and also had a palace at Ecbatana (Hamadan); it was his trilingual rock-cut inscription at Behistun near Kermanshah which enabled scholars to decipher the cuneiform script in the last century.

The territorial expansion and ambitions of Darius the Great led to wars with the Greek city-states (490–449). A century later the balance of power was reversed, when Alexander the Great conquered the Empire and burnt Persepolis in 331 BC. For a time Iran became part of the Seleucid Empire, which succeeded that of Alexander, but in 250 BC the Parthians of north-eastern Iran, led by Arsaces, established an Empire which extended as far as the Euphrates and came into conflict with the Romans. Their rule continued until AD 226, when they were replaced by another Iranian dynasty, the Sasanians, who ruled until the coming of Islam.

Iranian religion

We know little of the religions of ancient Iran due to a lack of written sources. The Proto-Elamite script of south-western Iran has not been deciphered but animals are frequently depicted in sculpture and on seals in the attitude of humans, and seals depict deities standing, sitting and kneeling on attribute animals, often snakes. The names of some deities are known from cuneiform inscriptions, notably In-Shushinak, the patron of Susa, and Choga Zanbil. It seems that nature gods were worshipped and, later, Indo-Iranian gods such as Mithras, the god of the contract. There is some debate as to when Zoroaster lived but by Achaemenid times Zoroastrianism was widespread, with its conflict between good and evil, light (Ahura-Mazda) and darkness (Ahriman), priests or Magi, fire-altars and towers of silence, and its holy writings – the *Avesta*.

Writing in Iran

Writing developed in south-western Iran in the second half of the fourth millennium BC, at the same time as it did in Mesopotamia, but the script, which was also written on clay and is known as Proto-Elamite, has not been deciphered. Its use was not restricted to Elam, however, and the distribution of the tablets indicates a widespread trade network. Proto-Elamite lasted for several centuries but was finally replaced by the cuneiform script of Mesopotamia. The inscriptions are few, however, and there was probably another script in use, written on perishable materials. The famous Behistun rock relief, depicting Darius the Great's victory over his enemies in 520 BC, is inscribed in cuneiform in the three languages of the Achaemenid Empire: Indo-European Old Persian, Semitic Babylonian and Elamite which is not related to any known linguistic group; this inscription provided the key to the decipherment of cuneiform.

DC

Further reading

M. A. R. College, *The Parthians* (London, 1967)
W. Culican, *The Medes and Persians* (London, 1965)
S. A. Matheson, *Persia, an Archaeological Guide* (London, 1979, 2nd edn.)

From Alexander to the coming of Islam

The Near East in the classical and early Byzantine periods

'There are four great empires in this world: the first is the empire of the Babylonians and the Persians, the second is that of the Romans, the third is that of the Axoumites [the Ethiopians] and the fourth is that of the Silis [or Sinis, i.e. the Chinese].' This enumeration of empires by Mani, a third-century Mesopotamian gnostic teacher, is a reflection of the geopolitics of the Eurasian land-mass and adjacent Africa for much of the classical period. The Islamic conquest would reintroduce a Near Eastern Empire on a scale which the classical world had not seen since the destruction of the Persian Empire of the Achaemenids by Alexander the Great* in the third century BC.

In the time of Darius I (521–486 BC) and Xerxes I (486–65 BC), Persian power ranged from Thrace in Europe to the Hindu Kush and from the Caspian to the Egyptian desert. This first great Eurasian Empire confined Greek civilization to the fringes of the Mediterranean and forced the Greeks, in Socrates' words, to live 'round the sea – like frogs round a pond'.

This constraint was decisively broken by the victories of Alexander the Great (356–23 BC) over the forces of Darius III (*c*.380–30), culminating in the battle of Gaugamela (331) east of the Tigris, which opened the way for penetration of Greek influence into the heartland of Iran and into western Central Asia. Alexander's untimely death eight years later without a strong heir, however, led to a prolonged period of strife amongst his chief lieutenants (the *diadochoi*) and the subsequent division of what had been the largest Empire in the history of the Near East. Ptolemy, the son of Lagus and friend of Alexander, inaugurated in 304 a Greek dynasty bearing his name in Egypt, to which Alexander had appointed him as Satrap. Demetrius, the son of another former officer of Alexander, Antigonus Monophthalmus, secured the throne of Macedonia in 294 after many vicissitudes and his descendants, called the Antigonids, remained the chief military power in Greece until its conquest by the Romans in the second century BC. More significant for the history of the Near East was the founding in 312 by Seleucus I Nicator of a Greek dynasty in Babylon which came to rule over the eastern parts of Alexander's Empire from the Syrian coast to the foothills of the Pamirs and became the harbinger and defender of Greek culture in the Near East for the next two centuries.

The Legacy of Alexander

A characteristic feature of Greek civilization was the city (*polis*) and it was through the establishment of urban settlements with their autonomous and democratic institutions that the Greeks had earlier colonized Sicily and South Italy. A new wave of colonization came in the wake of Alexander's victories. In this Alexander played a leading role and the most famous and magnificent of his foundations, Alexandria in Egypt, still bears his name to this day. Alexandria was not merely founded as a trading post or military colony but a true Greek city in the fullest sense of the word. Local sources show that it had its own code of laws, modelled substantially on those of Athens, and an elaborate system of laws and jury courts, again modelled on the Athenian system. Its Greek inhabitants were even organized into *demes*, a system of local administration which was peculiar to Athens.

The Seleucid kings continued Alexander's policy of founding colonies and cities and pursued it even more vigorously. Their motives were more political than ideological. Seleucus had always hoped to return to his native land as sovereign. However, he was operating a long way from home and had no power base in the European mainland. Experience had shown that the Iranians under his rule would not readily support him on a campaign which involved fighting far away from the Asiatic homeland. He and his immediate successors therefore had to base their military power almost entirely on the Greek elements of their Empire, especially their personal friends, the remnants of Alexander's army and the Greek mercenaries who had joined their ranks. In order to prevent them from being absorbed by the native population it was important that they should live in separate communities with their distinct way of life. A considerable number of new cities were founded by the Seleucids in Syria and Mesopotamia: they included Antioch-on-the-Orontes (modern Antakya), named after Antiochus, the father of Seleucus; Seleucia in Pieriea after Seleucus himself; Apamea (modern Dinar) after his wife and Laodicea (modern Latakia) after his sister. Most of the sites were well chosen and the cities founded upon them would continue to be important centres of population well into the Islamic period. Near modern Salahiyya on the Euphrates the remains of the Hellenistic circuit wall of Dura-Europos, a sizeable Macedonian military colony founded either by Seleucus or one of his generals, can still be seen. We learn from documents recovered from the excavation that the surrounding territory was divided into allotments (*kleroi*), which were distributed among the Macedonian settlers and provided their owners with crops of cereals, grapes and fruits.

Some of the ancient cities in Syria and Mesopotamia were also refounded and given new names: Aleppo became Beroea, Hama became Epiphania, Carchemish became Europas, Harran became Carrhae and Nasipina became Antioch in Mygdonia, although it was better known throughout the classical period by the Hellenized form of its name, Nisibis. Urhai was first given the name of Edessa after the old Macedonian royal city which shared with it the same tendency to flooding. Its name was later changed to Antioch on the Beautiful Waters by Antiochus IV Epiphanes (*c.*215–163 BC), but reverted to Edessa after his reign. A medieval Syriac source embodying earlier material shows how an ancient Assyrian city (near modern Kirkuk, Iraq) had its circuit walls rebuilt by Seleucus and the urban area enlarged. The additional territory was then divided up by streets into districts each devoted to a particular trade or profession and Seleucus brought in new settlers, especially artisans from surrounding territories to augment the population. Babylon was given the status of a Greek city by Antiochus IV but this once great city was completely overshadowed by Seleucia, a new capital city on the Tigris founded by Seleucus about 24 km south-east of modern Baghdad. Its population grew to over half a million, augmented by periodic forcible transfers of population from Babylon. It was a predominantly Greek city and acted as a major focus of Hellenizing influence in Mesopotamia. As the eastern capital of the Seleucid Empire, it was the seat of the governor-general of the East, an office which was held usually by the Crown Prince. Commanding the most convenient lines of communication between the two halves of the Empire, it was a thriving river-port and its inhabitants, especially the aristocrats and merchants, derived considerable wealth from trade.

Greek rule in the Near East

Syria and Mesopotamia enjoyed two centuries of peace and prosperity under Greek rule. The only restive element within the Seleucid Empire were the Jews in Palestine, who resisted Antiochus IV's attempts at Hellenization. A popular revolt led by Judas Maccabaeus led eventually to the establishment of an independent Jewish state under the rule of the hereditary Hasmonean High Priests. In the east, however, the Seleucids lost control of the Central Asian Satrapies *c.*250 BC when Diodotus, the Satrap of Bactria, revolted and assumed the title of King. Emboldened by this, the Parthians, an Iranian people living in Hyrcania, also rebelled against their Greek overlords. Led by a succession of outstanding Kings beginning with Arsaces (*c.*250–30 BC), the Parthians gradually displaced the Seleucids from Iran. A major counter-offensive was launched by Antiochus III ('the Great') (*c.*242–187 BC) in 209, which saw the recovery of much of the eastern half of Alexander's Empire. However, Antiochus' expansionist policy was ruined by his failure to recognize the advent of Rome as a new superpower in the Mediterranean. He allied himself with Philip V of Macedon and briefly invaded Greece, where he was defeated by the Romans near Thermopylae (191). The Romans followed him into Asia and a year later defeated him once more at Magnesia. By the Treaty of Apamea in 198, the Seleucids handed over virtually all their Mediterranean possessions to Rome, though theoretically they remained a major power in Asia. With the accession of Mithridates I to the Parthian throne in 171, however, the Seleucids were forced onto the defensive. By the time of his death in 138/7 BC, the Parthian Empire comprised the whole of the Iranian plateau, the regions around the Caspian, and Babylonia. What was left of the Seleucid Empire in Syria and Palestine eventually fell victim to internal strife and Roman expansionism. However, Roman fortunes in the East suffered a temporary setback in 88 BC when Mithridates of Pontus, one of the last great Hellenistic dynasts, invaded the Roman province of Asia where he was greeted as a liberator by the Greek population. Tigranes, the equally ambitious king of Armenia, formed an alliance with him and swiftly occupied much of Syria and northern Mesopotamia. Both however were later decisively defeated by Pompey, who made Syria a Roman province in 64 BC. The Nabataean Arabs took advantage of the political vacuum created by the decline of Seleucid power and raided as far north as Damascus and even laid siege to Jerusalem. Aramaic-speaking Arab kingdoms were also established around the cities of Palmyra (Tadmur), Edessa and Hatra.

The power of Rome

By then Rome had also consolidated her control over the western half of the Mediterranean through her famous wars with Carthage, culminating in the destruction of the ancient Punic city in 146. Utica (modern Utique), her neighbour and rival which had given support to the Romans in the last stages of the conflict, was rewarded with lands of the fallen city. A strong Roman commercial presence was soon felt in former Carthaginian territories. Although Rome originally decreed that neither house nor crop should rise again on Carthaginian soil, the city-site was colonized by Julius Caesar (100–44 BC) and land-hungry settlers from Italy landed on the North African littoral in ever-increasing numbers in the last years of the Republic. Administered at first by a minor Roman official based at Utica, the Roman territories in North Africa were reorganized by Augustus (63 BC – AD 14) to reflect the increasing importance of the region. The province of Africa, which extended from the Ampsaga (Oued Kebir) to the borders of Cyrene, corresponding roughly to the province of Ifriqiyya in Islamic times, was governed by a proconsul with his administrative headquarters at Carthage, now officially a Roman colony. At first the governor held both civil and military powers, but this was altered by Emperor Caligula (AD 12–41) in AD 39 when an imperial legate was placed in charge of Numidia and south Tunisia, where the main Roman forces were stationed. As Roman power extended westwards along the foothills

Mosaic figure in Aphrodite's house, Bulla Regia, Tunisia

of the Atlas Mountains, two new provinces, Mauretania Caesariensis and Mauretania Tingitana, corresponding roughly to modern Morocco, were created by Claudius (10 BC – AD 54) before AD 44. To the east, Cyrene, together with Crete, became a regular senatorial province under Augustus and later under Septimius Severus (reigned 193–211), while Numidia was finally separated from Africa Proconsularis and given provincial status. Unlike the eastern provinces where the Parthians and later the Sasanians posed a constant military threat and necessitated the deployment of large numbers of troops for frontier defence, Roman North Africa suffered only from occasional nuisance raids by tribes living on the fringes of the desert. The Aurès Mountains, penetrated in the second century AD, were defended by a sole legion stationed at Lambaesis with help from a nearby veteran colony at Timgad. Under the *Pax Romana*, the Maghrib enjoyed four centuries of uninterrupted peace and prosperity. It was much exploited for its wealth in raw materials, especially agricultural products such as cereals and olive oil. The increasing demand for the latter would lead to the gradual extension of agriculture and urban settlement on the Numidian plateau and the interior of Cyrenaica. The Maghrib also produced a rich crop of men of letters in the Latin tongue, and many distinguished jurists and imperial officials. This reflects the high degree of urbanization and the quality of city life in the African provinces, where more than 500 communities were founded, many enjoying Roman municipal or colonial status. Carthage became the most important city in the western Empire after Rome, and boasted of a fine university at which Augustine of Hippo was once a pupil and later a teacher. There was a marked concentration of settlements on the coast and the fertile river valleys. In the areas around Carthage, some cities were only a few miles apart. All the cities, whatever their status, enjoyed a high degree of autonomy in the day-to-day administration of municipal affairs. Some of the Berbers* who had lived on the periphery of the Carthaginian civilization became settled farmers on large estates during the Roman period, but some continued their nomadic existence. (This survival of the Berbers as a distinct cultural group in the Roman period was to be of importance, as they were among the first to be Islamicized. The invading Islamic forces, with an increasing Berber component, began to establish garrison towns to guard their lines of communication. This led to a new process of urbanization and the gradual and systematic replacement of the Roman settlers.)

Roman annexation of Egypt

Rome completed the process of transforming the Mediterranean into a Roman lake by the annexation of Egypt in 30 BC. Unlike North Africa, where the Romans had virtually destroyed the infrastructure of the Carthaginian Empire, Rome took over a highly centralized administration from the Ptolemies, which was in good working order, and simply adapted it to her needs. Rome and many other cities in Italy had grown reliant on imported corn from Egypt and the latter's special importance was clearly recognized by Augustus who administered the province directly through a prefect of the Equestrian Order. No senator was appointed to this position or even allowed to enter the country. The basic administrative unit in Egypt was not the *polis* but the nome, a relic of Pharaonic times. The nomes were subdivided into toparchies and these again into villages. In the capital of the nome, the metropolis, resided the provincial officials. This hierarchical structure left little room for local autonomy and at the time of Roman annexation there were only four exceptions: Naucratis (a Greek emporium of considerable antiquity), Alexandria, Ptolemais and Paraetonium, the last three all being Hellenistic foundations. To these were later added Antinoöpolis (Shaykh Abadeh), founded as a Greek city by the Emperor Hadrian in memory of his favourite Antinous who was drowned in the Nile in AD 130. It possessed a city council but no adjacent territory. The other metropoli received their councils under Septimius Severus and in the fourth century, the administration of Egypt was brought more into line with the other provinces. (This was the system which would later be inherited by the Arabs. Though the term 'nome' survived in Arabic, in the early centuries of Arab rule the administrative divisions of Egypt, which corresponded very closely with Byzantine cities, were styled *kura*, the translation of the Greek *xōra*, territory (of a city), and not nome.)

Like North Africa, Egypt was exploited by Rome for its agricultural resources but, unlike North Africa, its communities seem to have derived little from this one-sided trade. Alexandria, through which nearly all trade with Rome flowed, was the only city which counted in Egypt, and ports like Berenice, which handled the Red Sea trade, were never in the same league as Palmyra, Edessa or Damascus as centres of trade and commerce. A large and influential Jewish community had been settled in Alexandria and Cyrene since Ptolemaic times. The Jews collaborated with the Roman conquerors and received special privileges in return, leading to friction with Greek Alexandrians and frequent communal riots. The most serious of these broke out in 115 and was followed by similar revolts in Cyprus, Palestine and Mesopotamia. Newly discovered documents speak of a small number of wealthy and influential Greeks using other people, including their own slaves, as cat's paws to organize arson and murder in Alexandria. The revolt was brutally suppressed. The extent of the damage could be judged by the number of inscriptions recording the repair of buildings during 'the Jewish disturbances'. The centre of Cyrene was completely wrecked and much of Alexandria had to be rebuilt by Hadrian.

With the acquisition of Syria, Palestine and Egypt in the last century of the Republic, Rome now had a major presence in the Near East, which inevitably involved her in military confrontation with the Parthians. The first clashes resulted in the destruction of a major Roman force under Crassus near Carrhae (53 BC) and the severe mauling of Mark Antony's legions in Armenia (36 BC). In the early Empire, Roman policy towards Parthia centred on a strong mobile army in Syria and diplomatic efforts to secure the neutrality of frontier kingdoms like Armenia and Osrhoene, which were regarded as vassals by both superpowers. Armenia in particular was the object of much intrigue and military action under the Julio-Claudians. A compromise was reached in 66 BC by which a pro-Parthian candidate was accepted for the throne of Armenia, but he received his diadem personally from Nero. The balance was completely upset by Trajan, who annexed both Armenia and the Nabataean Kingdoms and launched a major offensive against Parthian-held Mesopotamia (AD 105–16). He was the first Roman Emperor to have seen the Persian Gulf (at the head of a triumphant army) but this major expansion of Roman power was short-lived as revolts in his rear forced Trajan to withdraw, and after his death in the following year most of the newly conquered territories were abandoned by his successor Hadrian, who was the first Emperor to pursue a systematic defensive policy along all Rome's frontiers. A limited return to expansion was carried out by the Antonine and Severan Emperors, and by the beginning of the third century Rome controlled most of northern Mesopotamia, giving the Romans a choice of invasion routes. Frontier cities like Edessa and Nisibis were also fully drawn into the Roman orbit; Dura-Europos was occupied by the Romans in AD 165 and became an important frontier post.

The flames of Hellenism in the east, however, were not extinguished overnight by the coming of new masters. The metropolis of Seleucia was spared the ravages of war and enjoyed a high degree of autonomy well into the first century AD. The Parthians were unashamed in their admiration of Greek culture, especially in art and architecture. They styled themselves 'philhellenes', and documents and inscriptions of this period found in Dura-Europos, Avroman and Susa show that Greek continued to be used as one of the main administrative languages; in the case of Susa, the city still possessed a distinctively Greek form of municipal government well into the first century AD. The Parthians founded a new capital at Ctesiphon, across the river from Seleucia, and from there they were able to reap the harvest of Hellenic culture as exemplified by the former Seleucid capital. Ctesiphon housed academies in metaphysics, astronomy, natural history, geography and medicine, and we even hear of philosophers from Greece establishing their schools in Babylonia. In Roman Syria, the cities founded or refounded by the Macedonians were given a new lease of life and became extremely prosperous. Their culture was predominantly Greek and produced such fine writers as Libanius and John Chrysostom in the fourth century. Latin was used primarily as an administrative language and for legal learning. There was much chauvinism with regard to the primacy of Greek. Libanius, for instance, was anxious to deny that one of his ancestors was from Italy, in spite of the fact that he was fluent in Latin. This Hellenism was limited to the cities and a babel of native languages was used in the countryside. In the Mesopotamian cities, while some of their aristocrats would regard a Graeco-Roman education as important for advancement, native Syriac culture was predominant in all sectors of the population.

Trade routes

Trans-continental trade via Parthian-held territories flourished in the first two centuries AD as the Roman Empire grew in wealth. The famous Silk Road from China descended from the Pamirs to Media and thence to Babylonia where it converged with another stream of commerce from Arabia and the Red Sea at Seleucia. This trade then passed northwards through the Assyrian plains to Mesopotamian and Armenian cities like Edessa, Nisibis and Artaxata or via the Syrian desert to cities like Damascus and Antioch. Seleucia was one of the main beneficiaries of this trade. However, a major change in the course of the Tigris towards the end of the first century deprived the city of its river frontage and henceforth its importance as a centre of transit trade was eclipsed by Vologesias, a river port founded a few decades earlier by the Parthians. Seleucia went into an irreversible decline and was largely in ruins by the time of Trajan's invasion (AD 115–16). The trans-desert trade brought prosperity to the Nabataean Arabs and also to Palmyra. The latter was made a free city by Hadrian, who visited it in AD 130, and a Roman colony by the Severans. The many dedicatory inscriptions on its extant and still magnificent buildings show that merchants and caravans were at the heart of its economic and civic life. The merchants were organized into companies based in a number of Parthian cities, all major trading centres in their own right, and the city furnished them with caravan leaders and its own desert police to protect them against the elusive beduin marauders. One of the inscriptions speaks of a Palmyrene merchant who build and dedicated at Vologesias a temple of the Augusti, which goes some way to show the priority given by the Parthians to this cross-frontier commerce.

The advent of Christianity

The first two centuries AD also saw the emergence of Christianity from an obscure offshoot of Judaism to a major religious and cultural force in the Roman East. Antioch, where the Christians first received the name of their sect, was a major centre of the religion before the end of the first century. The religion also diffused eastwards across the Euphrates into the Parthian Empire. Although the Parthians were Zoroastrians, they were highly tolerant in matters of religion. Pagan semitic cults flourished in Mesopotamian cities and Babylonia also housed one of the largest Jewish communities outside Palestine. Jewish communities also existed in many Mesopotamian cities, which undoubtedly helped to prepare the ground for the introduction of Christianity. Recently discovered texts show that Jewish Christians opposed to the teaching of Paul also found refuge in south Babylonia in the Parthian period. A harmony of the gospels compiled by Tatian, a Christian from Assyria, was available in Syriac by the middle of the second century and enjoyed a wide circulation in the East. By the time of Constantine's conversion, Christianity was already firmly established in Edessa, Nisibis and Seleucia-Ctesiphon.

The Sasanian dynasty

A major change of hegemony took place in AD 226, when the Parthian King Artabanus V was defeated and killed by Ardashir, a prince of Fars, at the battle of Hormizdagan. The coming of the new dynasty, that of the Sasanians, marked a major renaissance of Iranian fortunes. The Sasanians considered themselves rightful heirs to the Achaemenids and regarded the Parthian period as an interregnum and their Kings as essentially usurpers. Militarily they were far superior to the Parthians and provided Rome with a much more formidable enemy. In three campaigns launched between 244 and 260, Shapur I (241–72), Ardashir's successor, defeated three major Roman armies and raided as far north as Cilicia, capturing Antioch on probably more than one occasion. The Romans in desperation sought help from Septimius Odaenathus, the Arab King of Palmyra. He struck at Shapur's rear and succeeded in capturing Ctesiphon in 259, forcing Shapur to withdraw from Roman territory. Shortly after his victory, Odaenathus was murdered at the instigation of his wife Zenobia, who took over the reins of government. Capitalizing on Rome's weakness in the East, she extended Palmyrene power into Egypt in 269 in an attempt to revive the dynasty of the Ptolemies. Her success was short-lived, as Rome had finally realized the need for stronger men at the helm. She was defeated and captured by Aurelian (270–5), the first of a series of soldier emperors who would restore army discipline and revive Roman fortunes in the face of her foreign adversaries. In 297, Caesar Galerius won a major victory over the Persians in Armenia. With his harem in Roman hands, the Shahanshah Narses (293–303) was forced in the ensuing treaty signed at Nisibis in 298 to make large territorial concessions to the Romans.

Roman defences

The victory of Galerius gave Diocletian (293–301), his senior partner, the opportunity of thoroughly overhauling Rome's defences in the East. The system which gradually emerged was not a continuous barrier like the Great Wall of China or Hadrian's Wall in England. The Roman *limes* in the East was a deep zone consisting of forts and strongly defended cities linked together by a network of military roads. The fulcrum of the system was at Antioch, with advanced bases at Edessa and Nisibis. Diocletian was responsible for establishing a redoubt at Circesium where the Khabur joins the Euphrates, and linking it by a new road (the Strata Diocletiana) to Palmyra and Busra to the west and south and by other roads to Singara to the east and Sura to the north. This defence line made use of low hills wherever possible to enable the defenders to see further. The roads usually ran straight and forts were built at intervals of about thirty Roman miles. Light auxiliary cavalry were extensively used to patrol the frontier posts. Their main duty was to foil sudden raids by marauding beduin and to act as a trip-wire and a scouting force in the case of a full-scale Persian invasion. The system was weakest at its southern end; the lack of good communications in the Hawran and Transjordan was to prove a fatal weakness in the defence of Palestine and Syria against Islamic forces. Considerable use was made by both the Romans and Sasanians of friendly Arab tribes to protect this exposed southern flank and act as guides and auxiliaries in their campaigns. They were highly effective in their role as desert policemen, and in paying them large annual subsidies both the Romans and Sasanians hoped not only to secure their loyalty but also to make them subject to attack by poorer tribes who lived further into the desert. Two important confederations of Arab tribes would eventually emerge, the Ghassanids who were vassals of Byzantium and the Lakhmids, centred on the oasis city of Hira, who were allied to the Sasanians. Both would play a significant role in Romano-Persian relations and were frequently mentioned in accounts of military operations along the frontier.

The Roman defence system as strengthened by Diocletian proved its worth under Constantius II (324–61), when Shapur II (309–79) made repeated attacks at certain strong points, especially Nisibis. Although he finally made some piecemeal gains, he suffered heavy losses. This defensive strategy, however, was abandoned by the more venturesome Julian 'the Apostate' (361–3), who launched an all-out attack down the Euphrates, wishing to repeat the successes of Trajan. He failed to capture Ctesiphon, however, and was killed by an Arab in a skirmish during the withdrawal. With the Roman army still trapped in Persian territory, his successor Jovian was forced to conclude a humiliating peace with Shapur II, which saw the return of all the territories gained in 298 as well as the strategic fortresses of Nisibis and Singara. Though intermittent war continued between the two states, their relationship remained stable until the sixth century when the Romans, in order to make good their loss of Nisibis, constructed a new fortress at Dara which embodied all the latest in defence technology. This provoked the Persians to a full-scale renewal of hostilities, and under Chosroes Anushirwan (531–79) they captured Antioch, killing or deporting most of its inhabitants. A 'city of captivity' was constructed south of Ctesiphon to settle them. It was primarily a transplanted Roman city and much of its building material and decorations were either plundered or imported from Syria. Known to the Arabs as al-Rumiya, this Roman colony must undoubtedly have played a major role in the transmission of Greek learning to the Persians via Syriac and later to the Arabs through the same Semitic intermediary. The same Chosroes also crushed the Empire of the White Huns (Hephthalites) in Central Asia with the help of the Turks who lived on the borders of China. By this he secured the eastern frontiers of the Persian Empire and acquired valuable experience in waging long-distance campaigns to the detriment of the Byzantines. Justinian (527–65), anxious to divert Persian attention away from the Byzantine Empire, despatched an embassy in 531 to the Christian Kingdom of Axum in present-day Ethiopia, which at that time was in control of what was once the Himyarite Empire in southern Arabia. He offered to buy silk from them instead of the Persians in return for a military alliance against the Persians. The embassy was a failure and the Axumites were eventually expelled from the Himyarite Kingdom by the Persians. The removal of a Christian power from the Arabian peninsula created a political vacuum which undoubtedly facilitated the expansion of Islam in the next century.

The spread of Christianity and the schisms

The conversion of Constantine (306–37) to Christianity added an important new dimension to Romano-Persian relations. The number of Christians in Persia had increased considerably with the settlement there of Roman captives from the wars of Shapur I. The religion at that time was persecuted in the Roman Empire and the Christian deportees were able to worship freely in Persia under the genuinely tolerant Shapur. From Bahram (273–6) onwards, however, priests of the ancient Zoroastrian religion, now being revived in a new form, gained ascendancy at court and there were sporadic persecutions of Jews, Christians and Manichaeans (followers of the gnostic teacher Mani). Constantine, who saw himself as protector of Christians both inside and outside the Roman Empire, intervened on behalf of the Christians in Persia. This merely caused them to be seen as a potential fifth column and when Simeon the Catholicos refused to collect a double tax from his flock in order to support the war effort against Rome, Shapur II had him and his closest companions executed. The Persian Church survived the persecutions, but in the fifth century a great doctrinal controversy in the Roman Church over the person of Christ would irretrievably alter her fortunes. The Council of Chalcedon (451) condemned both the position of the Monophysites* (who believed that Christ had only one nature, and that divine) and that of the Dyophysites or Nestorians*, who put greater emphasis on the separation between the divine and human natures of Christ than on their unity. The council in turn asserted that in Christ the two separate natures were held without fusion. This compromise formula was unacceptable to the more extreme participants of the controversy and caused a major schism in the Church. The teaching of Nestorius, which had already found support in Persia before Chalcedon, was accepted as orthodox by Persian Christians at the Council of Seleucia-Ctesiphon in 486. At the same time Monophysitism gained widespread support in Roman Syria, Mesopotamia and Egypt. Its missionaries, such as Ahoudemmeh and Jacob Baradaeus (after whom the Monophysites are sometimes known as Jacobites), won converts to their creed among the Ghassanid Arabs and among the inhabitants of Najran, in south-western

Arabia. Within both the Monophysite and Nestorian spheres of influence were significant pockets of Christians who came to be known as Melkites* because of their loyalty to the Chalcedonian formula. In Roman Mesopotamia and Egypt, the position of their bishops often had to be defended by secular authorities. The Emperor in Constantinople came to be seen by many in these provinces as a heretic, and this led to the growing estrangement of these strategically important areas. It is not surprising, therefore, to find that in Egypt the chief organizer of Roman resistance to the Arab invasion was the Melkite bishop of Alexandria. In Persia, the Church, now shorn of the odium of being an outpost of the 'religion of the Caesars', entered into a phase of rapid growth and expansion. By the time of the Islamic conquest, Christians could be found holding important positions and their churches were established in far-flung reaches of Iran and Khorasan as well as Mesopotamia. It fell to the Nestorian Bishop of Merv to bury Yazdgerd III, the last Shahanshah of Persia (632–51), who was murdered while fleeing into Central Asia after his decisive defeat by Arab forces at Nahawand.

The Vandals

The unity of the Mediterranean under Roman rule suffered a major setback when in 429, the Vandals, under King Gaeseric, crossed into Africa from Andalusia where they had been temporarily settled. First allocated Numidia and Mauretania, they were in almost complete control of the Maghrib by 442. Before long, Sicily and Italy became subject to the frequent and devastating raids of their armed merchant fleets. This resulted in a marked cessation of trade and shattered the fragile economic unity of the western Mediterranean. The agricultural system of Roman Africa was little altered by the invasion but the replacement of Roman landlords by Vandal grandees had a serious effect on the prosperity of the cities. The Catholic Church had come to play a major political role in North Africa as a consequence of the Donatist schism which had its origins in the great persecution of the early fourth century. Consequently it became a rallying point of resistance to the Vandals, who were heretical Aryans and suffered periodic persecution. The Maghrib was recovered by Belisarius in 533 on behalf of the Byzantine Emperor Justinian. It received substantial economic aid from the East and had recovered sufficiently by the beginning of the next century to be the power base of the Byzantine general Heraclius in his bid to overthrow the unpopular Phocas who had usurped the throne in Constantinople in 610.

The advent of Islam

The struggle between Byzantium and Persia for the hegemony of the Near East reached a new level of intensity in 603 when the Shahanshah Chosroes Parwez (590–628) launched an all-out attack against the eastern Roman Empire to avenge the murder of the Emperor Maurice (582–602), who had earlier helped him to regain the Persian throne against his rival Bahram Chobin (590–1). The Roman defences suddenly fell apart and Persian forces met with success on all fronts. For twenty-five years they ravaged and laid waste, almost unopposed, upper Mesopotamia, Syria, Palestine and Asia Minor. Jerusalem was captured in 614 and the Holy Lance taken as booty to Ctesiphon. Egypt fell in 616 and only the defences of Constantinople stood between Chosroes and the recreation of the Empire of the Achaemenids. Though the Persians were now encamped at Chalcedon and were surveying the defences of Constantinople, the Byzantines still had as a major weapon their navy, which had not yet been significantly challenged or deployed. In 622, a few months before the arrival of Muhammad at Medina, Heraclius sailed with a picked force from Constantinople and struck at the over-extended Persian communication lines in Cilicia. The next year, he sailed into the Black Sea and, after landing at Trebizond, headed inland and wintered in Mesopotamia, again cutting the vulnerable Persian supply lines into shreds. In December 627, Heraclius won a decisive victory over the Persians near the ruins of Nineveh. He also secured the surrender of the main Persian army in Asia Minor by strategem, relieving the pressure on Constantinople. The defeated Chosroes Parwez was murdered by his supporters and the Persian Empire lapsed into anarchy. By then the Ghassanids had fallen out of favour with the Byzantine Emperors because of their devotion to Monophysitism, and the Lakhmids had been dealt a severe blow by Chosroes Parwez, who in 602 deposed their King and occupied Hira. Thus, when the Islamic forces emerged from Arabia, they found both superpowers thoroughly exhausted by their latest titanic struggle and both without their Arab allies, who were their only effective defence against their brethren from Hijaz.

SNCL

Further reading

M. Boyce, *Zoroastrians* (London, 1979)
P. Brown, *The World of Late Antiquity* (London, 1971)
The Cambridge History of Iran, Vols. 2 and 3 (Cambridge, 1983–5)
N. C. Debevoisse, *A Political History of Parthia* (Chicago, 1938)
A. H. M. Jones, *The Greek City from Alexander to Justinian* (Oxford, 1940)
A. H. M. Jones, *Cities of the Eastern Roman Provinces* (Oxford, 1971, 2nd edn.)
S. N. C. Lieu, *Manichaeism in the Later Roman Empire and Medieval China* (Manchester, 1985)
D. Oates, *Studies in the Ancient History of Northern Iraq* (Oxford, 1968)
J. B. Segal, *Edessa the Blessed City* (Oxford, 1970)

Early Islamic history: 7th–10th centuries

The Middle East at the beginning of the seventh century

At the beginning of the seventh century, the great powers in what we now call the Middle East were the Sasanian and Byzantine Empires, the former ruling Iran from the metropolitan province of Iraq, the latter including among its provinces Syria, Egypt and coastal North Africa. Such at least was the state of affairs at the turn of the seventh century; but the early 610s witnessed the beginning of a Sasanian westward offensive and over fifteen years of war with the Byzantines, in the course of which Sasanian forces occupied both Syria and Egypt before finally being repulsed by Emperor Heraclius in 629. The debilitating effects of this prolonged period of war are generally supposed to have assisted the success shortly thereafter of invading elements from where successful invasion might least have been expected: Arabia.

Little is as yet known with any certainty about Arabia on the eve of Islam, and such is likely to remain the case until serious and extensive archaeology has been carried out there. There was a Sasanian presence in eastern and part of north-central Arabia, as well as in Oman, and from *c.*575 the Sasanians extended their reach to Yemen and the southern entrance to the Red Sea. This posed a threat to Christian Axum on the opposite shore in present-day Ethiopia, putting a stop to Axumite ambitions in Arabia, and limiting Egyptian-based maritime interests in the southern Red Sea and beyond. In the north, the Arab client kingdoms of the Ghassanids and the Lakhmids had been brought to an end by the Byzantines in 584 and the Sasanians in 602 respectively. In short, most of what little we know about the Arabian peninsula at this time relates to its peripheral areas. Of the interior, almost nothing can be said: at Najran in northern Yemen there was a Christian community with its own bishop, and further north, at Yathrib in the Hijaz, Jewish elements were to be found. But most of the rest of the population is conventionally dismissed as having been pagan in one manner or another; the social organization of these people, whether nomadic or settled, was tribal; their simple economy revolved around stock-rearing, small-scale agriculture and basic handicrafts.

The beginnings of Islam

In the early part of the seventh century an Arab Prophet emerged in western Arabia. Muhammad* is believed to have been born in about 570, to have belonged to the tribe of Quraysh living in Mecca, and to have received his 'call' to prophethood in about 610. His message – or rather a cumulation of messages, believed by Muslims to have been mediated to him by God over time through the Archangel Gabriel – came to achieve the status of scriptural revelation in the form of the Qur'an*; in it Muhammad's own role is represented as that of 'herald' (or 'bringer of good tidings') and 'warner', as one of coming to his people in the manner of the prophets who had preceded him, urging the overriding importance of worshipping and obeying the One God, and spelling out the dire consequences of failure to do so. The God in question was the Abrahamic God, and the religion was the religion of Abraham: we have here the beginnings of a monotheism which would in due course underpin a sense of Arab ethnicity.

The Kaʿba and the Great Mosque, Mecca

There were, however, obstacles. According to Muslim accounts, Muhammad met with opposition to his prophetic endeavours from some of the more influential of his fellow-Meccans, to a point where it became necessary for him to sever his Meccan ties and emigrate with his adherents to Yathrib, further north in the Hijaz, where he might function more effectively. This move, the so-called *hijra* of 622, was to mark the starting point of the Muslim calendar; and Yathrib came to be known as Medina* ('Al-Madina', the city [of the Prophet]). From there the Prophet spread his message throughout the Arabian peninsula, by means of raids as well as by more peaceful means, and in less than ten years he achieved the submission even of the Meccans. By the time of his death in 632, there prevailed in Arabia a Medinan hegemony supported by the new religion brought by the Prophet and Messenger of God, Muhammad.

The early Arab conquests and the first civil war

The death of the Prophet posed the problem of how this Medinan hegemony was to be maintained. The resolution of this dilemma became urgent because of the 'apostasy' of a number of important tribal leaders in the peninsula, who had accepted the leading role of the Prophet in Medina, but were disinclined to accept the leadership of a Medina which now lacked the Prophet. The matter was dealt with forcibly, in the form of the 'wars of the apostasy': armies were mobilized under Medinan auspices and the dissidents were suppressed. The initiative for this is credited to Abu Bakr*, an elderly Qurashi adherent of the Prophet who, after Muhammad's death, had been accorded the leading role in Medina. He is held by Sunni Muslims to have been the first Caliph*, though later his legitimacy came to be challenged by those who championed the Shiʿi cause. The term 'Caliph' (Arabic *Khalifa*) signifies 'deputy' or 'successor'. The mainstream Muslim view of the role of Abu Bakr as Caliph is that he was the successor of the Messenger of God in temporal matters, but not of course in religious matters, since he was not himself a prophet; indeed, Muhammad had been the 'seal of the prophets'.

The suppression of the 'apostasy' and the restoration of Medinan hegemony in the peninsula under the aegis of the new religion were preconditions for the conquests that followed. Thus unified on an unprecedented scale, the Arabs formed armies which conquered Syria, Iraq and northern Mesopotamia in rapid order. By 640, in the Caliphate of ʿUmar ibn al-Khattab* (634–44), the Arabs controlled the whole of the Fertile Crescent: Byzantine control of Syria had come to an end, and the Sasanian Empire was in disarray, with its metropolitan province gone. In the following year, an Arab army effected the conquest of Egypt, which thereafter became a base for operations further west. In the north, the Arabs had by the mid-640s pressed into Armenia and into Azerbaijan as far as the Araxes River. In the east, most of the rest of what had been the Sasanian Empire had been mopped up by 650, in the Caliphate of ʿUthman ibn ʿAffan* (644–56), when Arab forces entered Khorasan; by the mid-650s, an Arab army was campaigning as far away as Sistan (in modern Afghanistan and eastern Iran).

At this point the first civil war erupted. It was a five-year-long affair that began in 656 with the murder in Medina of the Caliph ʿUthman (who was from the Qurashi clan of Umayya) by rebellious provincial Arab elements, and ended in 661 with general acceptance of another Umayyad Caliph, Muʿawiya ibn Abi Sufyan, who was (and remained) based in Syria. The unsuccessful contender with Muʿawiya in the power-struggle that followed the death of ʿUthman was ʿAli ibn Abi Talib, one of the Prophet's kinsmen (generally believed to have been the son of the brother of the Prophet's father) and hence a fellow-member of the Qurashi clan of Hashim; he was in addition the son-in-law of the Prophet, having married his daughter Fatima, who had borne him two sons, Hasan and Husayn. ʿAli had sought to gain power on the basis of an Iraqi coalition, but this fell apart in the face of Muʿawiya's intransigence and the strength of his Syrian army. The political origins of Shiʿism lie in the hard core of ʿAlid loyalists, the Shiʿa or 'party [of ʿAli]'.

The Orthodox or Rightly-Guided Caliphs (the Rashidun)

632	Abu Bakr
634	ʿUmar ibn al-Khattab
644	ʿUthman ibn ʿAffan
656–61	ʿAli ibn Abi Talib

C. E. Bosworth, *The Islamic Dynasties* (Edinburgh, 1966)

The Umayyad Caliphate

The Caliphate of Muʿawiya marked the end of the era of the Medina-based Caliphs (who came in due course to be regarded as the Rightly-Guided Caliphs*) and the beginning of a Syrian-based Umayyad dynastic rule that would last until 750. What can be said of the nature of this Arab rule? Obviously, at the time of Muʿawiya's accession to the Caliphate it was in an extremely early state of evolution: the Prophet had been dead for just thirty years, during which time the Arabs had conquered most of what we now think of as the Middle East. They had taken their first steps towards attempting to run themselves and their large subject populations in these remarkable new circumstances, only to find themselves plunged into civil war when the Caliph ʿUthman was murdered in Medina. Seen from Muʿawiya's perspective, the issue was clear: the caliphal role had to be backed by a mailed fist in a velvet glove, the glove being manifest in his assiduous winning over of the Arab tribal nobility of the various provinces, notably Iraq, while the fist (which he never had to use) was the Syrian army. But matters did not remain so for very long after the death of Muʿawiya in 680: a further civil war involving Iraqi support for a Hijazi anti-Caliph to replace

Some Muslim dynasties

Note: some of the dates are approximate; it is not always easy to know when a dynasty began or ceased to reign. Names of countries indicate main centres of power of dynasties; they are used in a loose geographical sense, without exact reference to modern frontiers.

'Abbasids 749–1258. Caliphs, claiming universal authority; main capital Baghdad.
Aghlabids 800–909. Tunisia, eastern Algeria, Sicily.
'Alawis 1668–today. Morocco.
Almohads (al-Muwahhidun) 1130–1269. Maghrib, Spain.
Almoravids (al-Murabitun) 1056–1147. Maghrib, Spain.
Aq Qoyunlu 1378–1508. Eastern Turkey, north-western Iran.
Ayyubids 1169–1260. Egypt, Syria.
Barakzay 1819–1973. Afghanistan.
Buyids (Buwayhids) 932–1062. Iran, Iraq.
Durranis 1747–1819. Afghanistan.
Fatimids 909–1171. Maghrib, Egypt, Syria. Claimed to be Caliphs.
Ghaznavids 977–1186. North-eastern Iran, Afghanistan, northern India.
Hafsids 1228–1574. Tunisia, eastern Algeria.
Hashimites of Iraq 1921–1958. Iraq.
Hashimites of Jordan 1923–today. Transjordan, part of Palestine.
Idrisids 789–926. Morocco.
Ilkhanids 1256–1353. Iran.
Mamluks 1250–1517. Egypt, Syria.
Marinids 1196–1464. Morocco.
Mughals 1526–1858. India.
Muhammad 'Ali and successors 1805–1953. Egypt.
Muluk al-tawa'if (ta'ifa, 'party kings'). 11th century. Spain.
Nasrids 1230–1492. Southern Spain.
Ottomans 1281–1922. Turkey, Syria, Iraq, Egypt, Cyprus, Tunisia, Algeria, western Arabia.
Pehlevis 1924–1979. Iran.
Qajars 1779–1924. Iran.
Qara Qoyunlu 1380–1468. North-western Iran, Iraq.
Rassids 9th to 13th centuries, end of 16th century–1962. Zaydi Imams of Yemen.
Rasulids 1229–1454. Yemen.
Sa'dids 1511–1649. Morocco.
Safavids 1501–1732. Iran.
Saffarids 867–end of 15th century. Eastern Iran.
Samanids 819–1005. North-eastern Iran, central Asia.
Sa'udis 1746–today. Central, then western Arabia.
Seljuks 1038–1194. Iran, Iraq.
Seljuks of Rum. 1077–1307. Central and eastern Turkey.
Timurids 1370–1560. Central Asia, Iran.
Tulunids 868–905. Egypt, Syria.
Umayyads 661–750. Caliphs, claiming universal authority: capital Damascus.
Umayyads of Spain 756–1031. Claimed to be Caliphs.

the Caliph in Syria resulted in the victory of the Umayyad 'Abd al-Malik ibn Marwan in the mid-690s. An important consequence of this was that the tribal nobility of Iraq ceased to play their earlier central role in the running of their province. The fist was beginning to show through the glove. The Caliph 'Abd al-Malik (685–705) and his viceroy of the East, al-Hajjaj ibn Yusuf, no longer felt the need for an unreliable tribal nobility when they could use a reliable Syrian army; and the quasi-tribal system of provincial organization gave way to a system of military faction controlled from Syria.

What of the state of the new Arab religion at this point? Over sixty years had now passed since the death of the Prophet who brought the religion which had first sustained, and then been sustained by, the Arab conquests. Like the Arab political order, it too had evolved during those years, although the details of the stages of that

The Umayyad Caliphs

661	Mu'awiya I ibn Abi Sufyan
680	Yazid I
683	Mu'awiya II
684	Marwan I ibn al-Hakam
685	'Abd al-Malik
705	al-Walid I
715	Sulayman
717	'Umar ibn 'Abd al-'Aziz
720	Yazid II
724	Hisham
743	al-Walid II
744	Yazid III
744	Ibrahim
744–50	Marwan II al-Himar

C. E. Bosworth, *The Islamic Dynasties* (Edinburgh, 1966)

evolution are not very clear. It would appear, however, that each Umayyad Caliph regarded himself as the religious guide of the Arab community as well as its temporal leader, and was widely recognized as such. This historical truth was gradually discarded by later generations, as religious authority passed into the hands of religious scholars who elaborated the theory that the only true Caliphate had been that of the 'Rightly-Guided Caliphs'; but that merely tells us how they wished to view the Umayyad Caliphate, not how it was viewed in its own time. In the Umayyad perception, God had earlier used prophets in order to communicate His wishes to mankind, and He now used Caliphs. The Caliphs were God's deputies on earth; and in God's opinion, as the inscription (dated 72 AH = AD 691–2) on ʿAbd al-Malik's Dome of the Rock in Jerusalem informs us (as does the Qur'an), 'the [true] religion . . . is *al-islam*'. Clearly, if the Caliphs were God's deputies on earth, they were also his deputies over Islam.

Leaving aside the Qur'anic evidence, this inscription constitutes the earliest indication we have of 'Islam' as the name of the new religion. The same inscription also provides the earliest known major public proclamation of Muhammad as the Servant of God and his Messenger; Jesus is accorded the same role, but trinitarian Christianity is specifically attacked. In other words, the inscription seeks both to identify Muhammad as the founding figure of Islam and to establish the credentials of Islam over other faiths (notably Christianity). In so doing it can be viewed as one of a number of manifestations of rapid state maturation in the time of ʿAbd al-Malik and his son al-Walid (705–15), as well as of further expansion, westwards through the Maghrib and into Spain, and eastwards to north-western India and the fringes of China. Islam was the best of religions, being that professed by the ethnic minority of Arab conquerors, whose leader in all things, both temporal and religious, was the Caliph; but the Jews, Christians and others who made up the subject populations were free to hold to their faiths and manage their own affairs as long as they caused no trouble and paid their taxes to the Caliph and his representatives.

Not all Muslims, however, concurred with the Umayyad vision of the caliphal role. Members of the conquering community of Arabs were increasingly finding themselves reduced to the role of subjects without any say in public affairs, while non-Arabs began to convert to the faith of the conquerors and join their society through the institution of clientage. The resultant proliferation of interests within the Islamic confession and the erosion of its strictly Arab character became increasingly apparent in the course of Umayyad rule. From an early stage, hard-line puritan opponents of any form of governmental control had emerged as Kharijites*, although they were too extreme and peripheral to survive for long in any significant form; and partisans of the Prophet's kinsman ʿAli, and of various descendants of his (notably his son Husayn, martyred at Karbala in 680), constituted a Shiʿi opposition (primarily in Iraq), which espoused egalitarian principles and claimed not that government as such was bad, but that it was in the wrong hands. In the course of the third civil war (744–50), the Umayyad family in Syria itself became caught up in, and divided by, the system of military faction on which its rule was based. The rebels from Khorasan, who moved west and took over, opted for a Caliph from the Prophet's clan of Hashim (albeit a descendant of the Prophet's uncle al-ʿAbbas rather than of ʿAli). What has justly been called 'the Arab Kingdom' gave way to the ʿAbbasid Caliphate.

The ʿAbbasid Empire

The ʿAbbasid Caliphate based in Iraq (at Baghdad for the most part) lasted just over five centuries, from 749 to 1258; but it lost most of its temporal and religious authority in the course of the first hundred years. This change was accompanied by two main developments: a proliferation of power centres in what had earlier been provinces of a centralized ʿAbbasid Empire, and the emergence of Sunni Islam.

The Arab Kingdom left by the Umayyads stretched from Central Asia in the east to the Iberian peninsula in the west. In basing themselves in Iraq, the early ʿAbbasids proved to be indifferent to taking on resurgent Byzantine sea-power in the Mediterranean, with the result that they did not aspire to control territories any further west than present-day Tunisia. The Muslim rulers of those territories were accordingly on their own, and in the Muslim parts of Spain (Al-Andalus) none other than a branch of the Umayyad family was able to establish an independent state. For the rest, however, the early ʿAbbasids and their bureaucrats constructed a sophisticated and highly centralized administration based on Baghdad, this being in marked contrast with the Umayyad system, which had been centralized only at the provincial level. This administration took shape under the second ʿAbbasid Caliph, al-Mansur (754–75), and reached its apogee under his grandson, the fifth ʿAbbasid Caliph, Harun al-Rashid (786–809); its principal architects were members of the Barmakid family (Muslim descendants of the guardian of a Buddhist temple near Balkh). Within three years of the death of al-Rashid, a fourth civil war was under way, between two of his sons, the Caliph al-Amin based in Baghdad, and the heir apparent al-Ma'mun, based at Merv in Khorasan; after a prolonged siege of Baghdad, Amin was killed in 813 and al-Ma'mun's administrators moved into Iraq, but the war dragged on and it was not until 819 that al-Ma'mun himself returned to Baghdad. By this time the imperial administration was barely a shadow of what it had been and the work of restoring control over no more than Syria and Egypt required a further six years. In the meantime (in 821) al-Ma'mun hived off all of his eastern domains to one of his generals, Tahir ibn al-Husayn, whose tenure of office resulted in the ninth-century dynasty of the Tahirids of Khorasan (821–73); they were succeeded

The ʿAbbasid Caliphs

749	as-Saffah
754	al-Mansur
775	al-Mahdi
785	al-Hadi
786	Harun al-Rashid
809	al-Amin
813	al-Ma'mun
817–19	Ibrahim ibn al-Mahdi
833	al-Muʿtasim
842	al-Wathiq
847	al-Mutawakkil
861	al-Muntasir
862	al-Mustaʿin
866	al-Muʿtazz
869	al-Muhtadi
870	al-Muʿtamid
892	al-Muʿtadid
902	al-Muktafi
908	al-Muqtadir
932	al-Qahir
934	al-Radi
940	al-Muttaqi
944	al-Mustakfi
946	al-Mutiʿ
974	al-Ta'iʿ
991	al-Qadir
1031	al-Qa'im
1075	al-Muqtadi
1094	al-Mustazhir
1118	al-Mustarshid
1135	al-Rashid
1136	al-Muqtafi
1160	al-Mustanjid
1170	al-Mustadi'
1180	al-Nasir
1225	al-Zahir
1226	al-Mustansir
1242–58	al-Mustaʿsim
	Mongol sack of Baghdad

C. E. Bosworth, The Islamic Dynasties (Edinburgh, 1966)

there first by the Saffarids and then the Samanids (900–1005). Similar developments occurred in the course of the ninth and tenth centuries through most of the rest of what had been the centralized ʿAbbasid Empire: in the west, based at their capital of Qayrawan in present-day Tunisia, the Aghlabids achieved effective autonomy from 800, forming a dynasty that lasted until 909, when it was brought to an end by the Shiʿi Fatimids; in Egypt and Syria, the Tulunids ruled from 864 to 905, to be followed by the Ikhshidids (935–69), who were in turn replaced by the Fatimids (969–1171); and so on. Even Baghdad was not spared: from the middle of the tenth century a Daylamite Buyid dynasty (945–1055) established itself there. In short, what was going on in the Muslim world of the ninth and tenth centuries was a proliferation of political power (and thus too of high culture and elegant court life) in a number of local centres. With the notable exception of the Umayyads in Spain who assumed the Caliphate in 928, and of the Fatimids who also proclaimed themselves Caliphs, these dynasties, while effectively autonomous, were nominally loyal to the ʿAbbasid Caliphs; but the caliphal role had clearly become little more than symbolic by the middle of the tenth century.

This caliphal loss of temporal power to the generals was accompanied by the loss of religious authority to the religious scholars; and here the crucial issue was the kind of Islamic law that was in the making. Jurisprudence in the Umayyad period appears to have been concerned with establishing and maintaining laws which were in line with the available holy scripture, generally agreed normative practice (*sunna*), and the dictates of straightforward commonsense. A strong case can be made for the view that the Umayyad Caliphs themselves occupied a central position in the making of law, as might be expected in view of what has already been said about them above; but this is played down in the received wisdom, which instead focuses on the so-called 'ancient schools' of law (Kufan, Basran, Medinan and Syrian), consisting of scholar-jurists who probably had no official status and for whom *sunna* simply meant good local practice. It was only in the early ninth century that scholar-jurists began to elaborate what was to become the 'classical theory' of Islamic law; and the crucial point in that theory was that *sunna*/normative practice, as a source of law, was thenceforward regarded as uniquely and wholly the *sunna* of the Prophet, as documented in the growing tradition (*hadith*) literature of his sayings and actions. This initiative, which is linked with the name of Shafiʿi (d.820), proved to be the most important single development in the shaping of Sunni Islam. For one thing, normative practice of the present was replaced by what now had to be represented as normative practice of the past (and of a single individual in early seventh-century Medina at that); the messenger of the Qur'an was being turned also into its interpreter, the actions and sayings attributed to him being as much a source of law as the Qur'an itself was. For another, this was a development which seriously restricted the role of the Caliph as a maker of Islamic law: it was now no longer open to him to determine for legal purposes what normative practice was or should be, since such normative practice was now that of the Prophet. While the Caliph could of course still use his functional authority to mete out punishment, he could no longer act as the exponent of God's law, save in his capacity as one of many scholar-jurists.

In view of this, it might be concluded that the early ʿAbbasid Caliphs were remarkably slow to perceive the implications of what was going on. But to arrive at this conclusion would be to forget that they had come to power as Hashimites, kinsmen of the Prophet. The Umayyads had conveniently lacked such a relationship and could regard prophetic practice in the most nebulous of ways, seeing themselves as the ultimate arbiters of what was valid law in the eyes of God. The ʿAbbasids were in a more difficult position; and the fact that none of the first six ʿAbbasid Caliphs claimed to have ultimate control of the law as such is perhaps indicative both of their retrospective dislike of Umayyad claims to that effect, and of the extent to which local schools of law had by that time become entrenched. The seventh ʿAbbasid Caliph, al-Ma'mun, did claim as much, sought to correct the mistaken beliefs of the 'vulgar masses', and initiated an inquisition (*mihna*) in order to test the suitability or otherwise of the views of judges, scholar-jurists, and exponents of *hadith*; but he died too soon to see it through, his immediate successors lacked his will and drive, and the inquisition was soon shelved. This marked the decisive end of any notion of a caliphal role in the definition of Islam and it permitted the unchecked development of what would in due course become recognizable as Sunnism. The '*hadith* people' and their hero, Ahmad ibn Hanbal, won through, and populist sentiments and what passed as prophetic *hadith* were the order of the day. It was now unquestionably the religious scholars, rather than the Caliphs (for all that these latter were still on occasion styled 'God's deputies'), who were the 'legatees of the prophets'; and henceforward it would be they who, armed with this religious authority, and at a distance from those who held temporal power, would elaborate classical Sunni Islam.

The development of an Islamic society and culture

By the early tenth century, Islamic society and culture had moved a long way from the simple organization and world-view of the Arab tribesmen who had effected their astonishing conquests three hundred years earlier. Initially, real or assumed Arab ethnicity and kinship were central to the social organization of the Arab conquerors; at the same time, while by no means all of them settled in towns, there is no significant evidence of the Arab tribal aristocracy having become consolidated on the land with a dependent peasantry beneath it, as was the case with the Germanic conquerors of Europe. The direction to be taken by Islamic society was accordingly determined in the first instance rather by what went on in the towns. There, what had started off as clan and tribal groupings came to be reshaped by military and administrative exigencies, by absorption of clients, and by divisions of wealth; groups came to be defined by more than blood ties. With the foundation of Baghdad in 756, and with increasing non-Arab conversion to Islam, the transformation of kinship groups into neighbourhood communal groups began to move a stage further; by the ninth century sectarian affiliation was assuming an increasingly important role as an organizing principle for such groups in the metropolis. By the tenth century, this was demonstrably true of the other towns and cities making up the urban network of the Islamic world: thus the Palestinian geographer Maqdisi, writing in about 985, draws attention to the striking shift by his own time toward the use of sectarian labels (notably as between Sunna and Shiʿa) for the designation of local factional alignments. In other words, as Islam developed from being the ethnic religion of the Arabs toward realizing its potential as a universal religion, sectarian identities became no less socially important than ethnic identities.

This does not of course mean that the Arab component was unimportant on the cultural level: on the contrary, the Arabs had brought their language and their poetry, and Arabic served as the lingua sacra of Islam, being underpinned in that capacity by the Arabic Qur'an and in due course by the Arabic *hadith* literature, documenting the model behaviour of the Arab Prophet in early seventh-century Arabia. But what the Arabs had originally brought with them from the peninsula had been reshaped and added to by the new circumstances in which the conquerors found themselves and by exposure to non-Arab cultural influences. This process was not very conspicuous in Umayyad Syria, where the Arab conquerors were still relatively cohesive and the indigenous cultural resources were somewhat fragmented; but in Iraq the cultural resources were stronger and, with the establishment of an ʿAbbasid Caliphate based in Iraq, and that at a time when in social terms the singular Arabness of Islam was already being eroded, the circumstances became particularly conducive to indigenous cultural input into what the Arabs had brought, so forming the synthesis that became classical Islam.

This happened in two main ways. First, pre-existent law surfaced in piecemeal fashion and Islamic guise, now identified and authenticated not as pre-existent law of the Fertile Crescent but as prophetic *hadith* rooted in Arabia; the ninth century witnessed the formation of vast compilations of *hadith*, numbering hundreds of thousands of items which, along with the Qur'an, would henceforward serve the learned laity of Muslim religious scholars as the major source of Islamic law. Secondly, there was a tension which was never resolved between two different conceptions of social order: one was the Sunni conception of a community living under a law which emanated from the will of God; the other was the ancient Persian conception, still surviving in an Islamic form, of a king designated by God to regulate the life of society by statecraft. This duality provided the foundation for the classical Islamic combination of a temporal power which was in the hands of the Sultan/Amir and a religious authority (above all legal) which resided with the religious scholars.

MH

Further reading

M. Cook, *Muhammad* (Oxford, 1983)
P. Crone and M. Hinds, *God's Caliph: religious authority in the first centuries of Islam* (Cambridge, 1986)
F. M. Donner, *The Early Islamic Conquests* (Princeton, 1981)
G. R. Hawting, *The First Dynasty of Islam* (London, 1986)
H. Kennedy, *The Prophet and the Age of the Caliphates* (London, 1986)

Islamic history: 1000 to 1500

For almost two centuries, the formal authority of the ʿAbbasid Caliphs in Baghdad was scarcely challenged in the region stretching from Iran to Tunisia, although local centres of government became increasingly autonomous. In the middle of the tenth century, however, there arose a movement of a new kind which questioned the very basis of ʿAbbasid sovereignty.

The Fatimids

The Fatimid movement began in Ifriqiyya (Tunisia) in the early tenth century. The Fatimid version of Ismaʿili* Shiʿism was a dynastic cause which asserted the superior right of the descendants of Fatima's children to leadership of the Islamic community over that of the Caliphs of Baghdad. But it was also a proselytizing esoteric doctrine. Once Egypt had been taken from the Ikhshidids in 969, the city of Cairo, founded in that year, became the centre for the diffusion of Ismaʿili doctrine, and the al-Azhar Mosque (a Fatimid foundation) housed the Daʿwa or propaganda bureau. Ismaʿili preaching was chiefly directed beyond the territories of the Fatimid Caliphate. Within Egypt, Ismaʿili doctrine seems to have been the preserve of a court and esoteric elite. There was little or no pressure on the predominantly Sunni* Muslim and Coptic Christian* population of Egypt to convert, and Sunni Muslims, Christians and Jews were able to hold office even at the highest levels of the administration. Ismaʿili doctrine was syncretistic, and the speculative tolerance of the elite encouraged a cultural efflorescence in Egypt.

Ismaʿili preachers chiefly directed their efforts at the subjects of the ʿAbbasid Caliphate and the Sunni Muslim and Twelver* Shiʿi regimes in the eastern Islamic world generally. The late tenth and the eleventh century were peculiarly the age of Shiʿi regimes in the Middle East, among them the Hamdanid Arab Emirs of Aleppo and the Mirdasids who succeeded them, the ʿUqaylids who ruled over both Mosul and Aleppo and the Banu ʿAmmar in Tripoli. The holy places in Arabia were controlled by radical Carmathian Shiʿis. Even the ʿAbbasid Caliphs in Baghdad were 'protected' from 945 to 1055 by the Buyids, who, however vaguely, professed a form of twelver Shiʿism. *Daʿis* (Ismaʿili preachers) spread esoteric and revolutionary doctrines in these lands. Many of the preachers were able to travel in the guise of merchants, for Fatimid Egypt traded extensively with the Muslim world, as well as with India, Java and East Africa.

Fatimid Caliphs and their often domineering *wazirs* also used armies to pursue their aims by territorial conquest. Early Fatimid armies were predominantly Berber and Arab. In the eleventh century, Arab, Berber, Nubian, Turkish and Armenian regiments vied for power in the Fatimid lands. Fatimid troops occupied most of Syria, and Fatimid overlordship was established over the holy cities of the Hijaz. At one point, in 1059, the Caliphs in Cairo were even able to claim a brief and indirect lordship over Baghdad. But the decline of the revolutionary messianic impetus provoked first the breakaway of the Druze* movement in the 1020s and then the formation of the Assassin* sect in Syria and Iran in the 1090s. In the west, the loss of direct control over Tunis, where the Zirid governors acted increasingly as autonomous agents, and the naval threat posed by the Norman occupation of Sicily (1071) severely affected the regime's income from commerce; for in the eleventh century the commerce of the Fatimid Empire was centred not on Egypt, but on Tunisia. Catastrophic failures of the Nile to rise in some years and recurrent plague epidemics certainly also contributed to the financial problems. The shortfalls in fiscal revenue explain the feuding for diminished revenues between the ethnically divided regiments. In the 970s the Fatimids had had to defend Syria and Palestine from revived Byzantine ambitions. From the 1060s onwards the entry of Turkish war bands and then of Seljuk armies into Syria posed an even stronger threat to Fatimid control.

In the eleventh century the Oghuz Turks led, or in some areas followed, by their dominant clan the Seljuks, moved across the Middle East. The numbers taking part in this tribal migration were probably quite small, but Turks had been extensively employed throughout the Islamic lands as administrators, mercenaries, and *mamluks* (slave soldiers) before the eleventh century. A more general feature of the central Middle Ages in the Islamic lands was the ascendancy of alien military corps – Turkish, Kurdish, Armenian or Daylami, over predominantly Arab populations. The great days of the Arabs were effectively over. The ʿAbbasid Caliphs were the distinguished prisoners of the Buyids, military aristocrats

Prayers in Al-Azhar Mosque, Cairo

from Daylam (a mountainous province south of the Caspian Sea). Though the Buyids were Shiʿis, they nevertheless claimed to rule in the name of the Sunni Caliphs.

Even where the ruling dynasties remained Arab, the dominant dynasties were confessionally estranged from their subjects and, as we have seen, in many areas Shiʿi rulers presided over predominantly Sunni populations. Previously the distinction between Sunni and Shiʿa was not well marked (see Islam), but in this century anti-Shiʿi polemic initiated by Hanbali lawyers and theologians intensified. The development of a conscious Sunni identity was reinforced by the Sunnism of most of the eleventh-century Turkish elite. The Oghuz Turks moved from Central Asia into Transoxiana and Khorasan. In 1055 the first Seljuk Sultan, Toghril, took control of Baghdad, but the Seljuk capital was for a long time in Isfahan. The Seljuks, like the Buyids they replaced, claimed to act in the name of the Caliph.

The Seljuks

In the reign of Sultan Malik Shah (1072–92), his chief minister Nizam al-Mulk sketched out, in the *Siyasat-Name*, an elaborate court protocol and administrative structure which drew on Sasanian and ʿAbbasid precedents. But, precedent and pretension apart, the Seljuk Sultans were never really the autocrats of their Empire (with its foggy boundaries). They never wholly succeeded in emancipating themselves from their role as tribal leaders, nor did they establish clear rules of succession. Rather, rule tended to be shared within the clan. As a result the Seljuk regime was weakened by the creation of apanages for princes of the blood and by damaging civil wars. Moreover, even in Nizam al-Mulk's blueprint for imperial government, there were two institutions which made for decentralization. The first was the *atabeg* (which might be translated as military tutor). These protectors of young princes often usurped their wards' inheritances. The second was the *iqtaʿ* – a word with many meanings, but usually referring to a grant made to a soldier, courtier or administrator of fiscal revenue on a designated source of revenue, usually land. The *muqtiʿ*, or grantee, collected the revenue for himself and in principle enjoyed no other rights over the assignment. But the system was obviously open to abuse and, under the Seljuks and other regimes, *iqtaʿ* assignments sometimes became hereditary estates. *Iqtaʿ* was a Buyid innovation, but its use spread under the Seljuks and more widely yet under the Zangids, Ayyubids and Mamluks. Like the *iqtaʿ*, the formation of a Sunni identity (mentioned above) preceded the coming of the Seljuks. The *madrasa* or teaching college, devoted particularly to the teaching of Sunni religion and law, also existed earlier in the Ghaznavid Sultanate, but it was taken up and diffused under the Seljuks and it, too, had a major role in shaping Sunnism.

Nomadic Oghuz Turks continued their quest for pastureland, moving across northern Iran and into Anatolia. This tribal drift prepared the way for the subsequent establishment of a cadet branch of the Seljuks as Sultans in Anatolia. Though the Anatolian Seljuks supplemented their tribal levies with *mamluks* and mercenaries, they were never very securely in control of the mass of the Turkoman migrants into Anatolia, and the raiding of frontier tribesmen, *ghazis* or warriors for the faith, drew the unwilling Sultan Alp Arslan into conflict with Byzantium and in the end to a surprise victory over Emperor Romanus Diogenes at Manzikart in 1071. After 1071 the Turkish colonization of Asia Minor intensified and the Seljuks briefly established their capital at Nicaea. Byzantium's growing difficulties led in turn to an appeal to the West by Emperor Alexius Comnenus and the coming of the First Crusade (1097–9).

In Syria, Seljuks were never very strongly established. Most of the coastal cities either remained under Fatimid control or were governed by independent dynasties, while the highlands of Syria and Lebanon tended to remain the preserve of Shiʿi schismatics and Christians. Moreover, Turkish tribal leaders and warlords were only erratically responsive to the directions of the Seljuk Sultan. Even in the years of crisis, the Fatimids managed to retain their bases in southern Palestine. The financial and regimental problems faced by the Fatimid regime from the 1060s onwards were partially resolved by one of their generals, Badr al-Jamali, in the years 1073–7.

As has been noted, some of the Fatimid troubles were due to the loss of their African and Italian provinces and the concomitant decline in maritime power. In the tenth and early eleventh centuries, the Zirids governed in Tunisia on behalf of the Fatimids. In 1041 the Zirid Emir, Muʿizz, openly seceded. The Umayyad Caliphate in Spain had, like its Fatimid rival in North Africa, long been plagued by rivalries between officers and regiments of different races – Arab, Berber and European converts to Islam. But these rivalries were contained and, under the leadership of al-Mansur, the general who effectively controlled the caliphs from *c.*1080 until his death in 1108, the Caliphate of Cordoba seemed more of a menace to the Christian powers in the north than ever. After his death, the Caliphate fell apart with mysterious suddenness. The formerly united territory was split into principalities and city states, the Taʿifa, or 'Party' kingdoms, and the divisions between their rulers mirrored the earlier racial rivalries within the Caliphate. The abolition of the Caliphate by the citizens of Cordoba in 1031 was a belated acknowledgement of the fact that the institution had outlived its usefulness by a couple of decades. Culture and commerce continued to flourish in the Taʿifa states established at Saragossa, Seville, Toledo and elsewhere, but even before the Christian offensive which culminated in the capture of Toledo in 1081, many of these principalities had been paying their Christian neighbours tribute or protection money. The loss of Toledo provoked the Almoravids* to come to the rescue of their co-religionists and cross over into Spain in 1086. But in the long run the Almoravids were more successful in absorbing the Ta'ifa principalities into their Empire than they were in stemming the Christian advance.

The Crusades

There are many signs of a revival of Christian power in the Near East and the Mediterranean region generally during the twelfth century. Most obviously, the First Crusade established a series of crusader principalities along the Syro-Palestinian coast. In the wake of the First Crusade, the Comneni Byzantine Emperors were able to reconquer much of Anatolia, and a Christian Armenian Kingdom was established in Cilicia. Armenians were also influential in the Fatimid politico-military establishment. The Christian Kingdom of Georgia, in its heyday, profited from the disorganization of the Great Seljuks. Christian, especially Italian, shipping dominated the Mediterranean. The Normans based in Sicily harassed Zirid Ifriqiyya and briefly occupied Mahdiyya, Jerba and Tripoli, and in Spain, even as early as the 1090s, the forces of the *Reconquista* were making gains from the Almoravids.

Saladin

Muslim opinion was slow to respond to the crusader menace. Shi'i preachers were, at first, prominent in urging a united front against the crusader states, but in the long run this *jihad* was a Sunni-organized and dominated movement. Zengi, a Turkish *atabeg* in Mosul, was the first effectively to canalize public opinion to Islam's and his own advantage. Zengi's son, Nur al-Din, continued the war against the crusader states, but the Zengids gained more territory from their Muslim neighbours than they did from the crusader states. Zengid success in battle was assisted by the addition of Kurdish warrior elites to their predominantly Turkish armies. When, during the 1160s, Nur al-Din began to intervene in Egypt to pre-empt crusader ambitions there, he sent a force under Kurdish generals, and it was one of these Kurds, Saladin (Salah al-Din), who declared the suppression of the Fatimid Caliphate in 1169. After Nur al-Din's death in 1174, Saladin worked hard to acquire both Nur al-Din's territories in Syria and his mantle as leader of the *jihad* (see Islam). Like the Zengids, Saladin was a patron of the *madrasa* and a sporadic persecutor of Shi'is. Like the Zengids too, he and his kinsmen had ambitions in upper Iraq. Because of Saladin's eastern ambitions, his relations with the 'Abbasid Caliph al-Nasir (1180–1225) were only formally friendly.

The last Great Seljuk Sultan Toghril's defeat at the hands of the eastern Khwarizm Turks at the battle of Rayy in 1194 allowed a partial revival of 'Abbasid power, in Iraq at least. In the west, the Almohads* (al-Muwahhidun), another Berber puritan revivalist movement which had replaced the Almoravids in Spain and North Africa (*c.*1120–47), were similarly jealous of Saladin's pre-eminence in the Muslim world. Saladin's victory over the army of the Kingdom of Jerusalem at Hattin in 1187 confirmed his reputation, but it provoked the Third Crusade (1189–92); and Richard the Lionheart's campaigning in Palestine severely strained the resources of the recently formed Ayyubid Empire and its still rudimentary administrative and military structure. It was perhaps fear of future similar responses from Europe that led Saladin's Ayyubid successors in the thirteenth century to prosecute the war against what was left of the crusader principalities less energetically.

Saladin's Empire was never really a unity, even in his own lifetime. It was a confederacy in which the chief principalities were shared out among the leading members of the ruling Ayyubid clan. After Saladin's death these princes were as much at war with one another as they were with the crusading principalities or other Muslim neighbours. In the first decades of the thirteenth century, the Muslim world presented a strikingly fragmented appearance. At different times there were rival centres of Ayyubid government in Cairo, Damascus, Aleppo, Hama, Homs and Kerak. To the north, the Seljuk Sultans of Konya exercised an increasingly uncertain authority over Turkoman tribesmen. To the east, in upper Iraq, authority was parcelled out among a number of warlords and minor dynasties, of which that of Mosul was perhaps the most important. In lower Iraq, the 'Abbasid revival initiated by Caliph al-Nasir continued, though his attempt to use youth groups as well as Sufis and Shi'is to extend his authority yet further came to nothing. The Assassins still held on to their fortresses in Persia and Syria. Further east, in Iran, Afghanistan and Transoxiana, the Empire of the Khwarizm Turks with its huge territories and its (largely Kipchak Turkish) cavalry armies, seemed more impressive than it actually was. The Almohads still governed Morocco but, after their defeat by a Christian army at Las Navas de Tolosa in 1212, they were to leave the defence of Muslim Spain to less powerful dynasties.

The Islamic world was as fragmented in the early thirteenth century as it had been at the end of the eleventh. However, there were forces making for unity across the frontiers – trade, the pilgrimage, the peripatetic nature of scholarship and Sufism, popular commitment to *jihad*, and the widespread respect or at least lip-service paid to the Caliph. In the course of the next two and a half centuries most of the little dynasties and adventurers' principalities were absorbed into great territorial empires. These empires made increased use of slave soldiers and administrators, of highly trained horse archers and, from *c.*1350 onwards, of artillery. The empires were formed as a response to or in the wake of the Mongol invasion of the Near East.

The Mongols

The Mongols first appear as a tribal confederacy formed on the northern frontiers of China under the leadership of Chinggis (Genghis) Khan (1206–27). Their armies created a world Empire. The elite forces were Turco-Mongol cavalry archers but, as they moved west into the Near East and Europe, their armies were swollen by confederates and tributaries. In 1219–23 they destroyed the Khwarizm Empire. In 1256 they destroyed the Assassin centre at Alamut. In 1258 they captured Baghdad and killed its Caliph. The Mongol prince Hülagü ruled as the first Ilkhan of Iran and Iraq (1256–65). There are many indications of urban and rural decay in these regions prior to the coming of the Mongols, but the settlement of tens of thousands of Mongol pastoralists in Azerbaijan must have accelerated their decline. It certainly drove displaced Turkoman tribesmen into Syria and Anatolia.

As Mongol armies began to penetrate not only the Near East but also the Caucasus and the Russian steppes, the disasters of war brought more slaves onto the market. Particularly large numbers of Kipchak Turks, originating from the Russian steppes, were bought by al-Salih Ayyub, the Ayyubid ruler of Egypt and Damascus (1240–9). They were known as Bahri *mamluks* from the location of their barracks on an island in the Nile. The death of al-Salih Ayyub in the midst of a crisis brought about by Louis IX's Crusade against Egypt in 1249, the impressive performance of the Bahris against the crusaders in the Delta, and the subsequent murder of the last Ayyubid, Turanshah, allowed a junta of these *mamluks* to acquire some control over affairs in Egypt. But rule over Egypt and Syria did not pass completely into their hands until their prestige was further confirmed by their defence of Syria against Mongol invasion and their first victory over the Mongols at ʿAyn Jalut in Palestine in 1260. Qutuz, a *mamluk* who had usurped the Sultanate of Egypt, led the *mamluks* to victory, but it was another *mamluk*, Baybars, who reaped its benefits. In assassinating Qutuz he initiated a pattern which was to be repeated many times in the next two and a half centuries of Mamluk rule, for the Mamluk Sultanate was a despotism exacerbated by assassination.

In fact the Mongol hordes were never very numerous and they owed their victories over most Muslim armies to superior training and logistics. But they met their match at the hands of the similarly disciplined Bahri *mamluks* and, though the Mongols attempted repeatedly to conquer Syria in the next half-century, Damascus was only occupied by them for a few months in 1300. After 1260 Mongol Ilkhans based themselves in the pasturelands of Azerbaijan, loosely controlled most of Iran and all of Iraq, and acted as overlords of the Anatolian Seljuks and the Cilician Armenians. For half a century the frontiers between Iraq and Syria were closed to all save spies, beduin raiders and refugees.

The two regimes were not so very dissimilar and in some respects they seem to have consciously imitated one another. During the reigns of three vigorous Sultans, Baybars (1260–77), Qala'un (1279–90), and al-Ashraf Khalil (1290–3), the Mamluk regime was consolidated. Not only were the Mongols held in check but all the Ismaʿili castles in Syria were taken by Baybars, and the three Sultans waged a successful war of attrition against the remnants of the crusader states. Acre and the other remaining fragments of the crusader principalities were finally occupied by Khalil in 1291. Baybars and his successors also made unsuccessful attempts to intervene in Anatolia. The Seljuk Sultan of Anatolia had submitted to the Mongols after the battle of Köse Dagh (1243) and the greater part of Anatolia remained under Mongol hegemony, however loose, until approximately the 1340s. However, increasingly large areas were effectively dominated by Turkoman tribal confederacies, such as that of the Qaramans.

The Mamluks

Mamluk prestige rested not only on its success in waging the *jihad*, but also on Baybars's establishment of a new line of puppet ʿAbbasids as Caliphs in Cairo, and on his success in getting the sharifs* of Mecca and Medina to recognize at least a nominal Mamluk suzerainty over the holy places of the Hijaz. Under the Mamluks*, Egypt and Syria also developed an administration of unparalleled sophistication. The Mamluk Sultans inherited from their predecessors in Egypt an elaborate fiscal administration, organized around *diwans* (offices). This they extended to Syria. The royal chancery also expanded vastly. Above all the civilian Arab administrators were now shadowed and supervised by trained and usually literate *mamluks*. The growth of the administration was made possible by the success of both the *madrasas** and the barracks in providing men with administrative skills. A parallel development can be detected in Morocco in the Marinid use of the *huffaz* (lit. memorizers) as an elite corps trained in both military and administrative skills. Peace between Mongol and Mamluk was only agreed in 1322, when the frontiers were once more open to trade and diplomacy. The renewed commerce, much of it coming up from the Gulf and the Euphrates and across to Aleppo and the Mediterranean, does much to explain the prosperity of the Mamluk lands during the remarkably peaceful third reign of al-Nasir Muhammad ibn Qala'un (1310–40). But much was also due to the initiatives undertaken by the Sultan and his ministers in such areas as irrigation, sheep-farming, horse-breeding, building works and state-controlled commercial and industrial enterprises.

From the 1340s onwards things took a turn for the worse. The Black Death spread through Egypt and Iraq in 1347 and then through Syria, Arabia and North Africa in 1348. The Black Death and later frequently occurring outbreaks of pneumonic plague undoubtedly caused severe problems to most Muslim regimes. The most obvious of these were rural labour shortage and declining sources of recruitment for slave soldiers. In the Mediterranean, however, the economic damage brought about by the epidemics was to a considerable extent compensated for by the growth of European markets for Eastern spices and other commodities, which in turn was assisted by the expansion of Italian, Spanish and southern French commercial fleets. The Hafsids of Tunis and the Turkish princes who controlled the ports on the south coast of Asia Minor benefited as much from this commerce as the Mamluk lands did.

In Iran, the Ilkhani ruler Ghazan and his chief minister, Rashid al-Din, attempted sweeping reforms in the 1290s and after, but the Mongols were not really successful in soldering Mongol tribal practice onto the Persian tradition of settled government. Moreover, the absence of any agreed theory of succession to the throne led to frequent civil wars. After the death of the Ilkhan Abu Saʿid in 1335, the Ilkhanate broke up into a number of Mongol and Turkish principalities. By this time, many of the originally shamanist Turco-Mongol elite had converted to Sunni Islam. In the late fourteenth century, a Turco-Mongol warlord, Timur, created an extensive empire. He took control of the Mongol Chaghatayid lands in Transoxiana and from his capital in Samarkand mounted a series of remarkably successful capaigns in India, Russia and the Near East. Timur's interest in the profitable control of international commerce led him into war with the emergent Ottoman power. At the battle of Ankara (1402) he crushed the Ottomans and re-established principalities hostile to them in Anatolia. His earlier brief occupation of Mamluk Damascus in 1401 was of less consequence. Timur died in 1405. His successors could not match his military successes, though they continued to rule much of what is now Afghanistan and eastern Iran until the late fifteenth century.

In this period, the Maghrib was Islam's Wild West: the interior a prey to tribal warfare, much of the coast a base for pirates. In Algeria in the 1370s, the philosopher historian, Ibn Khaldun, worked on a scheme of history (the *Muqaddima*), based on the cyclical decline of settled government and its periodic conquest by vigorous nomads, whose regimes in turn declined as they become sedentarized. Ironically, he wrote in a period when this was ceasing to be applicable. There were to be no further tribal and revivalist movements like those of the Almoravids and Almohads. The Marinid rulers of Morocco and the Hafsid rulers of Tunis made only sporadic attempts to aid their co-religionists within the shrinking frontiers of Andalusia, the Muslim part of Spain. The last foothold, Nasirid Granada, was lost to the Christians in 1492.

At the same time as the volume of Near Eastern trade with Europe grew, so too did its commerce with the rest of Asia. There was even a brief period in the 1420s when Chinese junks brought goods to ports in the Hijaz. This stimulated the assertion of more direct control over the Hijaz by the Mamluk Sultan Barsbay (1422–37). It was in his reign, too, that Muslim fleets made a strong showing in the eastern Mediterranean for the first time since the heyday of the Fatimids. Successful raids were mounted against Cyprus, culminating in the invasion of 1426. Later Sultans sent expeditions against Rhodes and other bases for Christian sea-raiders. At the same time the Ottoman fleet began to threaten the Venetian and Genoese thalassocracies in the Mediterranean, and the Hafsids and Marinids sponsored corsairs.

In the fifteenth century, extravagance and splendour existed side by side with acute shortages of resources in the Mamluk lands (wealth and poverty were, so to speak, compartmentalized). Cairo was a (probably *the*) centre of Islamic scholarship. At the same time, the culture of the court and military elite increasingly came to resemble that of the courts of the Ottomans and the Turkoman principalities, so that from *c.*1450 onwards one can speak of an international court culture. Though the military elite seem to have been less able to deal with internal disorder, particularly on the part of beduin and Turkomans, nevertheless the Mamluk Empire was now larger than ever. In particular it had expanded into southern and eastern Turkey. The Mamluks fought a series of largely successful wars to retain their influence there and also to defend the Euphrates frontier. In this century, eastern Anatolia, north-west Iran and the southern Caucasus became one great war zone. As the Timurid Empire broke up, the zone was fought over by the Turkish Dhulgadirid and Qaraman principalities and by the confederacies of Black and White Sheep Turkomans. From the beginning of the sixteenth century onwards, the Safavids, the Mamluks and the Ottomans fought over eastern Anatolia. Competition here eventually provoked the Ottoman Sultan Selim's invasion of Syria in 1516. Some Mamluk resources had been previously diverted to deal with the menace of a Portuguese blockade in the Red Sea. The defeat and death of the Mamluk Sultan Qansawh al-Ghawri at the battle of Marj Dabiq led Selim on into Egypt in 1517, and victory at Raydaniyya in 1517 gave him control of the Mamluk lands. Thereafter, two great power blocks faced one another in the Near East, the Ottomans and the Safavids.

RI

Further reading

J. M. Abun-Nasr, *A History of the Maghrib* (Cambridge, 1975, 2nd edn.)

The Cambridge History of Iran, Vol. 5. *The Saljuq and Mongol Periods*, ed. J. A. Boyle (Cambridge, 1968)

S. D. Goitein, *A Mediterranean Society: The Jewish communities of the Arab world as portrayed in the documents of the Cairo Geniza.* 4 vols. (Berkeley and Los Angeles, 1967–83)

M. G. S. Hodgson, *The Venture of Islam*, Vol. 2. *The Expansion of Islam in the Middle Periods* (Chicago, 1974)

P. M. Holt, *The Age of the Crusades: the Near East from the eleventh century to 1517* (London, 1986)
R. G. Irwin, *The Middle East in the Middle Ages: the early Mamluk Sultanate 1250–1382* (Beckenham, Kent, 1986)

The Safavids and their successors

The rise of the Safavids

The Safavid dynasty had its origin in a long-established Sufi order which had flourished in Azerbaijan, in north-west Persia (modern Iran) since the early fourteenth century. The founder-head of the order, Shaykh Safi al-Din (d.1334), after whom it is named, established his headquarters in the town of Ardabil, where his shrine remains to this day. The history of Safi's own family can be traced back for two centuries, and it appears to have been of Kurdish descent.

Safi al-Din and his immediate successors built up a powerful position for the order in Azerbaijan, acquiring both followers and, as surviving records show, very considerable quantities of landed property. At this time and for long after, the Safavids were of the Sunni persuasion, though this fact was so inconvenient to the first Shahs of the Shiʿi Safavid dynasty that the historical record was as far as possible doctored so as to show that Shaykh Safi, too, was a Shiʿi and indeed laid claim to the status of *sayyid*, representing his descent from the Prophet Muhammad.

The highly successful, peaceful and essentially 'apolitical' evolution of the Safavid order continued for a century and a half. The great change occurred when Junayd (d.1460) was at its head. Junayd had been expelled from Ardabil and replaced by his uncle, Jaʿfar. So he went on his travels, going to Syria and to eastern Anatolia, where he gained many recruits from among the Turkoman tribes. The order now became a militant political movement, and there was a shift away from respectable Sunni Islam towards

The Masjid-e-Shah Mosque, Isfahan

extremist notions that are very hard to define. Both Junayd and his son and successor Haydar were killed fighting in the Caucasus, where they had marched in the hope of waging *ghaza*, holy war, against the Christians. Both had married into the family of Uzun Hasan Aq-Qoyunlu, the Turkoman who had become the dominant ruler in Persia and Iraq. Ultimately, however, the Aq-Qoyunlu concluded, correctly, that the power of the Safavid order had become a danger to them.

It was the collapse and factional struggling of the Aq-Qoyunlu after 1490 that gave the Safavids their chance. In 1499 Isma'il, the young head of the order, emerged from hiding, gathered support and defeated the Aq-Qoyunlu at Sharur (1501). In the same year he occupied Tabriz, the Aq-Qoyunlu capital, and made it his own. Persia had a new dynasty.

Safavid Persia, 1501–1722

Not for some years did it become clear precisely what kind of state Shah Isma'il was to create. His main military support had been from Turkoman tribes, called Qizilbash, red-heads, after the twelve-gored hat they wore in honour of the twelve Shi'i imams. These came from Anatolia, Syria and north-west Persia. With such followers, and having fixed his capital at Tabriz, the traditional Mongol-Turkish centre, Shah Isma'il may well have been thinking in terms of a basically Turkoman state consisting of eastern Anatolia, Azerbaijan, western Persia and Iraq. The events of the first half of his reign, however, produced a state of a quite different geographical shape: essentially the same as, though rather larger than, the modern state of Iran.

The new frontiers were the result of conflict. In the east, matters on the whole went the Safavid way. The Uzbeks took control of Transoxiana, but they were unable permanently to prevent the rest of the former Timurid lands in eastern Persia and western Afghanistan from falling within the Safavid sphere. In the west, though much of Iraq for the time being came under Safavid rule, eastern Anatolia, where a large proportion of the Safavid order's most fervent supporters had originated, was lost to the Ottomans. The present Turko-Persian frontier, which had no reality before the sixteenth century, now came into being and proved durable, if accidental in origin. Tabriz, as a capital, was hazardously close to a hostile frontier, and Shah Isma'il's successors in due course moved further towards the centre of their kingdom: Shah Tahmasp I (1524–76) to Qazvin, and Shah 'Abbas I (1587–1629) to Isfahan.

The newly established Safavid state based its power on three foundations. Initially, the dynasty had seized power with the backing of the fanatically devoted Qizilbash tribesmen, for whom (and perhaps for himself as well, to judge from his Turkish poetry) Shah Isma'il was in some sense divine. Gods are not usually expected to lose battles, however, and it has often been thought that

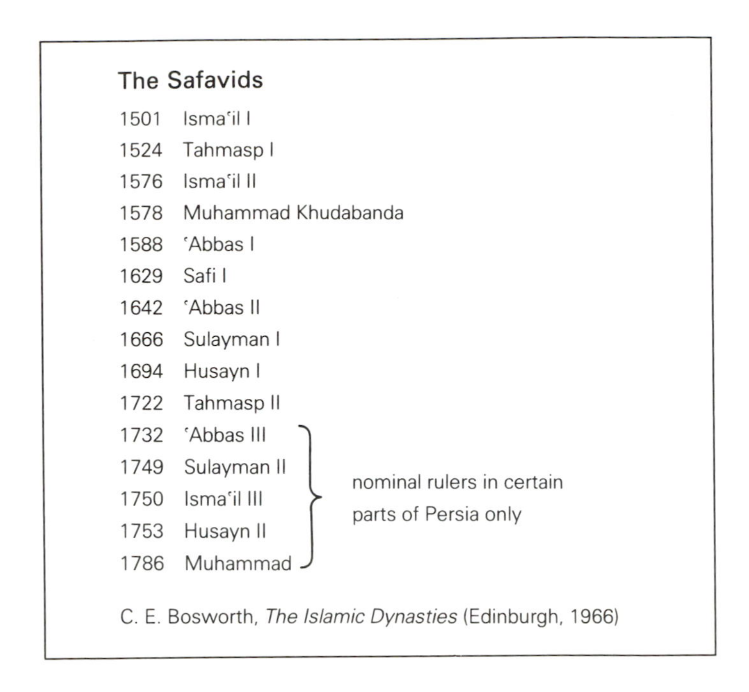
The Safavids

1501	Isma'il I	
1524	Tahmasp I	
1576	Isma'il II	
1578	Muhammad Khudabanda	
1588	'Abbas I	
1629	Safi I	
1642	'Abbas II	
1666	Sulayman I	
1694	Husayn I	
1722	Tahmasp II	
1732	'Abbas III	nominal rulers in certain parts of Persia only
1749	Sulayman II	
1750	Isma'il III	
1753	Husayn II	
1786	Muhammad	

C. E. Bosworth, *The Islamic Dynasties* (Edinburgh, 1966)

Isma'il's position in the eyes of the Qizilbash suffered irretrievable damage as a result of his defeat at the hands of the Ottomans at Chaldiran (1514). The factional struggles among the Qizilbash after Isma'il's death in 1524 certainly suggest a lack of reverence for the divinity of the Shah, but the change in attitudes ought not to be exaggerated: there continued to be plenty of life in the old ways.

Nevertheless, if the Safavid Empire had been a purely tribal Turkoman state it would probably not have survived the troubles that befell it at the beginning of Tahmasp's reign and after his death. It endured because it had two other foundations: the new state religion, Twelver Shi'ism*, and the support of the Persian bureaucracy.

The population of Persia in 1500 was largely Sunni. On his accession, however, Shah Isma'il declared Twelver Shi'ism* to be the required faith, and proceeded to enforce it, brutally where necessary. The religion of the Safavid order before 1501 has generally been described as Shi'ism, but whatever it was, it was certainly not the respectable Twelver variety. When the Safavids in fact became Shi'i has been much, if inconclusively, debated. One recent and persuasive view is that Isma'il himself was the first demonstrably Shi'i Safavid. Shi'ism had been so much a minority faith in Persia that the new religious establishment had to be staffed by means of a brain drain from the Arab lands: Shi'i *'ulama* were imported, especially from Bahrain and from Jabal 'Amil in Lebanon. It is impossible to say at what stage the allegiance of the Persian people as a whole was given actually, as well as officially, to the newly imposed faith. But in due course this did happen, and it may be that Twelver Shiʿism played some part in defining Persia, as a political and cultural entity, as against the Arab lands and the Ottoman Empire to the west and the Uzbeks and the Mughals to the east, since all these were officially Sunni.

All previous Turco-Mongol rulers of Persia had speedily found that, as the Chinese say, while the Empire could be conquered from horseback, it had to be governed in a different fashion. The Safavids were no exception. The Persian bureaucracy, always a body capable of recognizing political realities, rallied to the new rulers, and government went on virtually without a break. Indeed, the administrative framework in the Safavid period was still, in its essentials, that laid down under the Seljuks. This strong thread of institutional continuity helped to give stability to the regime.

While the new state appeared to have been firmly established and consolidated, both internally and externally, during the first two Safavid reigns (1501–76), the decade of weak rule, Qizilbash faction and foreign incursions which followed the death of Tahmasp might have seemed to herald the break-up of the Empire. In fact it was the surprising prelude to the period that marked the height of Safavid power and achievement: the reign of Shah ʿAbbas I.

During the years before 1587, much of the west and north-west of the Safavid Empire had been lost to the Ottomans, and parts of the east to the Uzbeks. Turning first on the Uzbeks, ʿAbbas managed to stabilize Persia's eastern frontier. War with the Ottomans then followed, until ultimately the territory lost to them had for the most part been recovered.

In the meantime ʿAbbas had moved to lessen the dynasty's dependence on the military support of the Qizilbash tribes, which had twice resulted in internal chaos. He formed corps of soldiers, especially cavalry and artillerymen, of Caucasian – Georgian, Armenian and Circassian – origin. Whereas the Qizilbash were maintained by the revenues of the provinces they received as assignments (*tiyul*) in return for providing a fixed number of troops, the new forces were paid directly from the royal treasury. Gradually, more provinces were resumed as crown lands (*khassa*), in order to produce the necessary revenue. Hence the Shah's direct control over his kingdom increased. In due course, leading members of the new military class began to be appointed to some of the great offices of state in place of Qizilbash chiefs. ʿAbbas also moved groups of Qizilbash about the country in order to weaken their tribal links. ʿAbbas's reign witnessed a cultural as well as a political efflorescence in Persia. Of this the most notable monument is the city of Isfahan, still essentially the creation of Shah ʿAbbas. Much of our information about his court there derives from the accounts of European visitors; the period saw a great increase in contacts, diplomatic and commercial, between Persia and Europe.

Shah ʿAbbas is remembered as a King who was just in his dealings with his subjects. This benevolence did not, however, extend to his leading followers or to his own family, who were often treated harshly and arbitrarily. One of ʿAbbas's unfortunate legacies to his dynasty was his decision to incarcerate the royal princes in the harem. This reduced the risk of revolt which had existed when princes were allowed to act as provincial governors, but it also meant that ʿAbbas's successors lacked experience of government, or indeed of the world in general, when they came to the throne; and they tended to remain under the influence of eunuchs and the women of the court.

The decline of the Safavids is conventionally dated from Shah ʿAbbas's death in 1629. It must be said, however, that a decline that did not result in fall for nearly a century is a curious phenomenon. It is certainly true that none of Shah ʿAbbas's successors were of his calibre, though his namesake ʿAbbas II (1642–66) was an able ruler by any other standards, perhaps partly because he was too young when he ascended the throne to have spent long in the harem. But while the personal qualities of the Shah were crucial for a polity in which so much depended on the man at the top, the fact that the Safavid Empire survived for so long, despite a succession of inadequate rulers, is an eloquent testimony to the strength and durability of the structures set up by Ismaʿil I, Tahmasp I and ʿAbbas I.

Effective government deteriorated so badly under the last Safavid, Sultan Husayn (1694–1722), that the regime was overthrown by a small and ill-organized force of rebel Afghans. Safavid pretenders and tame Safavid figureheads still lingered on the scene, but the dynasty had in reality collapsed.

The Safavids' successors, 1722–1796

Afghan rule in Persia was short-lived. Power soon fell to Nadir Shah, a member of the Afshar Qizilbash tribe, who embarked on a career of military conquests which extended as far as Bukhara and Delhi. Nadir re-established the territorial integrity of Persia but impoverished it in the process. He attempted, unsuccessfully, to shift the state Shiʿism of Persia in the direction of Sunnism; but Twelver Shiʿism was by now too deeply rooted for this to prove acceptable.

After Nadir's assassination in 1747 by his own terrified tribesmen, the Afshars continued to hold north-east Persia (Khorasan) till 1796. Most of the rest of the country fell to Karim Khan Zand, who ruled with the title of Vakil (deputy), rather than Shah, from his capital at Shiraz. Karim Khan provided Persia with a welcome interlude of benevolent rule. He reversed Nadir's anti-Shiʿi policy; and the eighteenth century, chaotic enough politically, was for Persian Shiʿism a period in which foundations were laid which have endured to the present. The Shiʿi *ʿulama* built up a formidable position, to a considerable extent independent of state control.

Persian Princess meets the daughter of the Emperor of China

Karim Khan failed, on his death in 1779, to provide for the succession. A further time of anarchy was resolved by Agha Muhammad Khan Qajar, who set up a dynasty which ruled Persia until 1925.

DM

Further reading

W. Blunt and W. Swaan, *Isfahan, Pearl of Persia* (London, 1966)
P. Jackson and L. Lockhart eds., *The Cambridge History of Iran*, Vol. 6, *The Timurid and Safavid Periods* (Cambridge, 1986)
V. Minorsky ed. and tr., *Tadhkirat al-Muluk* (London, 1943)
J. R. Perry, *Karim Khan Zand* (Chicago and London, 1979)
R. M. Savory, *Iran under the Safavids* (Cambridge, 1980)
J. B. Woods, *The Aq-Qoyunlu: clan, confederation and Empire* (Minneapolis and Chicago, 1976)

The Ottoman Empire to 1800

The Ottoman Empire was the most enduring political creation to emerge from the last stages of the *Völkerwanderung* of the western (Oghuz) Turks from Central Asia to Anatolia and the Balkans, and their concomitant partial Islamization. The first wave of this complex process of conquest, conversion and settlement had washed into Anatolia in the second half of the eleventh century and the resulting settlement of the east and centre of the peninsula by Turkish pastoralists was accompanied politically by the foundation of the Seljuk Sultanate of Rum. Established at Konya as a long-lived (1098–1308) cadet branch of the Great Seljuk Sultanate in Iran, it was destabilized in the mid-thirteenth century by the Mongol invasion of western Asia. This upheaval not only reduced to vassalage and political desuetude the Rum Sultanate but precipitated a second wave of westward migration across Anatolia. This brought into the former Seljuk–Byzantine borderlands (*uj*) of western Anatolia a *mélange* of detribalized Turkomans and dispossessed urban elements from Muslim Anatolia and even further east. It was thus as a border principality (*beylik*) that the Ottoman state came into existence in north-west Anatolia *c.*1300, one of a congeries of otherwise mainly ephemeral principalities linked tenuously to the moribund Rum Sultanate and its Ilkhanid overlords.

The long-accepted view of the foundation of the Ottoman state, which perceived it to be the work of a nomadic tribe of Turks of Central Asian origin, who had fled before the Mongols, was a powerful political myth. First propagated by late-fifteenth-century court chroniclers (e.g. Neshri, fl. 1480–1500), it was reflected by post-Byzantine Greek historians (e.g. Chalcocondylas, fl. *c.*1475) and was received from both genres into the canon of western accounts of Ottoman history (e.g. von Hammer). While the historicity of Osman, the eponymous founder of the state, is not altogether open to question, neither the ethnic nor the tribal (Kayi/Oghuz) origins argued by Turkish historians, nor the equally all-embracing '*ghazi*' theory propounded by Wittek can be regarded as entirely tenable. The combination of the obscurity of its origins, and the later universality of its claims to rule and its political longevity, however, made the Ottoman state a unique phenomenon. It was not only the sole Islamic universal state to survive politically (if not institutionally) into the twentieth century, but the only one (at least since the overthrow of the Umayyad Caliphate) to have its political centre of gravity within the Mediterranean world as the successor – in geographical terms – of Rome and Byzantium. It was not, however, Byzantine, but rather Mongol–Ilkhanid institutions, superimposed on earlier Perso-Islamic (ultimately ʿAbbasid) bureaucratic forms, that came to constitute the dominant elements in the developed Ottoman state.

For the period preceding the conquest of Constantinople (1453), Ottoman history must be reconstructed on the basis of indigenous or external literary sources of often doubtful reliability. Out of the mists of the fourteenth century, and with its chronology still in part a matter of discussion, emerges a picture of steady territorial expansion on the part of a principality in which political and social tensions between the centre (ruler; court; *ʿulama*; bureaucracy; standing *mamluk-kul* troops) and the periphery (marcher lords and their followers; Turkoman elements; dervishes), together with the imposition of a concept of sovereignty adhering to the descendants of Osman, are both reminiscent of earlier Turco-Islamic military regimes and a constant theme in Ottoman history until the resolution of the conflict in favour of the former group in the early sixteenth century. The picture offered by recent scholarship of the nascent Ottoman state under Osman and his successors (Orkhan, 1326–62; Murad I, 1362–89; Bayazid I, 1389–1403), committed to a policy of vigorous expansion fuelled by devotion to the idea of holy war (*ghaza*) against Byzantium and its Christian neighbours, can be further qualified. The objective role played in Ottoman expansion by, for example, a population pressure gradient leading from Anatolia into the Balkans (a regime of settlement, not occupation), or by economic forces (such as the profitable relationship, from the reign of Orkhan, with Genoa, or the role of the slave trade), must be weighed against the proximity of Constantinople or Ottoman ideological hostility to Byzantium as factors in the process prior to 1453.

The first expansion of Ottoman territory under Osman at the expense of Byzantium culminated in the capture of Bursa (1326). Bursa, rapidly transformed into an Islamic *polis* as the main residence of the ruler, served as the base from which the remaining Byzantine strongholds in Bithynia were overrun (Nicaea/Iznik, 1331; Nicomedia/Iznikmid, 1335). The absorption of the neighbouring *beylik* of Karasi (1345) took the Ottomans into the Troad, from whence, having already participated as mercenaries in the Byzantine civil wars in Thrace, they were well placed to cross the Dardanelles (1352), to seize Gallipoli (1354), and, under the leadership of Orkhan's son Süleyman Pasha (d. 1357), to begin a massive process of conquest and settlement in the new Islamic marchland of Rumeli (Rum Eli – 'Greek Country'). Early in the reign of Murad I the conquest of Edirne (Adrianople) effectively severed the links between Constantinople and its hinterland and gave the Ottomans control of the main south-east–north-west communication axis across the Balkans as well as the routes from Constantinople to the Aegean littoral and the Adriatic, and to the lower Danube.

The framework for empire

Edirne soon became the main seat of government and a secure base for further conquest. With the emergence of a rudimentary provincial organization (Hudavendigar – 'the Sovereign's [province]', around Bursa; Pasha Eli– 'the Pasha's [i.e. Süleyman's] country' in Thrace), and the parcelling out of the conquered lands as grants of land (*timar*) made by the ruler in return for the rendering of military service, the framework of the future Empire began to be laid down. Politically, the rulers of Bulgaria, Serbia and Byzantium became unwilling Ottoman vassals, while a process of 'Ottomanization' of the conquered territories converted large tracts into either the personal estates (*has*) of the ruler or revenue-yielding holdings of land (*timar*) granted in exchange for military service – a form of tenure not analogous to the Western fief but having possible antecedents or parallels in the *iqtaʿ* of earlier Islamic regimes or in the Byzantine system of *pronoia*. Indeed, apart from the much-disputed institution of the *devshirme* (tribute levy originating in the late fourteenth century of the male children of (mainly) Slav and Albanian Christian peasantry of the Balkans), together with those of the Janissary corps, for which it provided the recruits, virtually every aspect of the Ottoman system of government and statecraft has antecedents in earlier Perso-Islamic or Perso-Mongol polities, or in the practices and legalities of orthodox Sunni Islam. Where the Ottoman state differed from its predecessors was in the durability of its institutions and in the far greater role in the life of its subjects played by the state as such. Islamic law, for example, was incorporated into the state structure via the bureaucratization of the office of the cadi (*qadi*) and formed the lynchpin of Ottoman administration and government. The law of the Empire consisted of the *sharīʿa* plus customary law and the dispensations of the ruler, codified in a series of imperial and provincial legal codes. These last were generally prefixed to the great series of provincial cadastral surveys, which were drawn up, probably also from the end of the fourteenth century, following the incorporation of a territory into the Empire, and continued to be made thereafter at irregular intervals until the last decades of the sixteenth century. In this institution, as in a number of other Ottoman bureaucratic and chancery practices, we can now trace antecedent influences which were mainly Perso-Islamic but by extension Mongol and even Chinese.

It was, perhaps, these elements, already to some degree present in the state by *c.* 1400, that preserved it following the invasion of Anatolia by the Central Asian conqueror Timur, the defeat of Bayezid I and his Balkan auxiliaries at Ankara (1402), and the Sultan's death in captivity in the following year. In the ensuing period of social and political chaos (1403–13) the Ottoman state, nominally a Timurid vassal, and reduced territorially by the restoration of several of the annexed Anatolian *beylik*s, was partitioned between several of the sons of Bayezid (Süleyman and Musa in Rumeli; Mehmed, ultimately victorious, at Amasya and Bursa).

The state, ravaged by social and religious conflict, survived largely due to its structural strength and the astute diplomacy and statecraft of Mehmed I (1413–21), who succeeded both in neutralizing Christian and Muslim coalitions, and in defusing the social tensions inherent in incidents such as the revolt of Shaykh Badr al-Din (1415–16). After 1425 Murad II (1421–51) was able to revive the old policies of expansion, wresting Thessaloniki from Venice in 1430, reducing Serbia and Byzantium once more to tributary status, and launching raids by the border freebooters (*akinji*) north of the Danube. A vigorous but ill-coordinated and ultimately fruitless Christian counter-offensive led by the Hungarian magnate Janos Hunyadi ended in the crusaders' defeat at Varna, 1444. It demonstrated however, both the vulnerability of Ottoman rule in the Balkans as long as Constantinople remained untaken and the fragility and the significance of the personal factor in Ottoman statecraft, in the rulership crisis between Murad II and his son and designated successor, Mehmed, which the Crusade had precipitated.

The fall of Constantinople

The conquest of Constantinople, the first major achievement of the new sultan Mehmed II (1451–81), and the resulting political extinction of Byzantium, mark the final transformation of the Ottoman state from a peripheral, if remarkably successful, border principality to an Islamic *imperium* in the full sense of the term. Nonetheless it continued to manifest a number of the characteristics of a mixed, 'colonial' polity in a direct line of descent from the Seljuk Sultanate of Rum. The use, for example, of Greek, Slavonic and Italian, as well as Turkish, as the language of formal documents issued by the Sultan's chancery, or the excess of non-Muslims over Muslims in the population of (at least) Rumeli, or the growing ascendancy of the *kul/ghulam* system, which provided the ruler not only with a quasi-praetorian guard (the Janissary corps) but a ruling elite drawn largely from *internal* non-Muslim elements, all point to such a conclusion.

The external history of the reign of Mehmed II is one of unremitting – and generally successful – expansion. Failure to take Belgrade from Hungary (1456) did not prevent the final reduction of Serbia (1459), which was followed by conquests in Bosnia (1463), the Morea (1460, 1464), and, following the death in 1468 of Iskender Beg (Scanderbeg), Albania. The same years witnessed in Anatolia the conquest of the last Christian state in the East, the Empire of Trebizond (1461) and of the last significant successor-state of the Rum Seljuks, the Emirate of Qaraman (1468). Mehmed continued in the following decade to further his imperial ambitions, but with less success, and in the face of a hostile coalition (1471–9) linking Venice and the east Anatolian Turkoman confederacy of the Aq-Qoyunlu, which under Uzun Hasan (d.1478) constituted the sole serious opponent of the Ottomans in the East. The last years of the Conqueror, with both ruler and state exhausted by unremitting warfare, were less successful. The extension of Ottoman rule into the Crimea (1475) was to leave a legacy of not always profitable involvement in the affairs of the Giray Khans and a permanent downturn in the external trade of the Black Sea littoral with the Mediterranean. Attempts in the last year of Mehmed's life to establish a bridgehead in southern Italy (occupation of Otranto, 1480–1), and to wrest Rhodes from the Knights of St John, were abandoned at his death. A bitter struggle for the throne followed between his sons Bayezid and Jem (1481–2). The flight of the latter (d.1495) to exile in Rhodes, France and, ultimately, Rome, when coupled with the pietism of the new Sultan and a general reaction to the events of the previous reign, effectively braked the headlong pace of expansion. More important than the limited wars with Poland (1497–9) and Venice (1499–1503) in this period was the supplanting of Aq-Qoyunlu rule in Iran and eastern Anatolia by the militantly Shiʿi dynasty of the Safavids with the accession of Shah Ismaʿil in 1501. The Safavids* found their main support from among the disaffected Turkoman tribes of Anatolia. Out of a severe crisis compounded of the Safavid invasion, the Turkoman insurrection (revolt of Shah Kuli, 1511) and the enforced abdication of Bayazid II (1512), Selim II (1512–20) moved swiftly, eradicating Safavid support in Anatolia and taking the offensive against Shah Ismaʿil in the Chaldiran campaign. This led to the temporary Ottoman occupation of Tabriz in 1514, and the initiation of a century and a half of conflict between the two Islamic polities. The final act in the political and religious polarization of the Middle East and the shift of the political centres of gravity of the region back to the Bosphorus and the Iranian plateau was achieved by Selim's invasion and destruction of the Mamluk Sultanate (the battle of Marj Dabiq and the occupation of Syria in 1516; the battle of Raydaniyya and the occupation of Cairo in 1517). This not only gave the Ottomans control over the Red Sea and access to the rich revenues and resources of Egypt, but it also gave them sovereignty over the holy places of Islam and the immense prestige which this brought them.

Süleyman the Magnificent

It was the economic and political impetus furnished by the developments in Selim I's reign which largely furnished the continuing policies of territorial expansion and increased religious orthodoxy under his son and successor Süleyman I, known in the West as 'the Magnificent' and to his subjects as 'Kanuni', the Lawgiver. The first act of Süleyman's reign – the conquest of Belgrade (1521) – opened up Hungary to Ottoman penetration. The piecemeal destruction of the Hungarian kingdom (the battle of Mohács, 1526; the occupation of Buda, 1529; incorporation as a *beglerbeglik*, 1541) brought the Ottomans face to face with Habsburgs by land, just as a vigorous Ottoman Mediterranean policy (the conquest of Rhodes, 1522; the tacit alliance with France, 1526; incorporation of the North African 'regencies' into the Ottoman sphere) opened up half a century of naval confrontation with Spain. By the middle years of Süleyman's reign the Ottoman Empire extended territorially from the middle Danube to Aden and Eritrea, and from the headwaters of the Euphrates and the southern littoral of the Crimea to Algiers. A military presence had reached into the Indian Ocean and, briefly, as far as Sumatra, while in Europe the Habsburg rulers in Vienna might legitimately be regarded in Ottoman eyes as tribute-paying vassals only one rung above the tributary princes of Moldavia, Wallachia and Transylvania.

In political terms the Ottoman Empire was a world power; in economic terms, however, its status was open to question. Apart from the silk trade, which was in any case largely a transit trade, and with the East Indian spice trade via the Red Sea vulnerable to European interlopers, the state possessed neither the major economic resources of the Spanish New World nor an entrepreneurial class sufficiently liberated from the trammels of Islamic legalism or its own *dhimmi** status to fuel any trend towards nascent capitalism. The trade in slaves, both from the wars in Europe and from sub-Saharan Africa, which might have been significant in this context, remained an undeveloped asset. The possession of a largely docile *re'aya* class removed any stimulus to develop a capitalistically profitable plantation economy, as perhaps also did the diversion of the profits of war and taxation into magnificent but economically questionable imperial building projects or subsidies to the religious establishment. The Ottoman state was not alone, in the mid-sixteenth century, in consisting of an economically backward Empire of soldiers, clerics and administrators resting on an immobile, tax-paying, peasant base. Like Spain and Ming China, the Ottoman state at the time of its greatest brilliance was both magnificent and anachronistic.

The sixteenth century and decline

To adduce a single cause for the political, social, economic and military crisis which overtook the Ottoman Empire in the last third of the sixteenth century is unrealistic. Portents – the military stalemate in Hungary after 1541, or the political murder of Prince Mustafa – were as much symptoms as causes of a deep crisis within the fabric of the Ottoman state. Decline in the ability of the Sultans themselves (Selim II, 1566–74; Murad III, 1574–95; Mehmed III, 1593–1603; Ahmed I, 1603–17) was to some extent masked by the continuing high calibre of the leading pashas and generals who had emerged under Süleyman I (for instance, the Grand Vezir Mehmed Sokollu, 1565–79). Long and unprofitable wars against the Safavids (1578–90: temporary conquest of much of the Caucasus and north-west Iran) and the Habsburgs (1593–1606: Treaty of Zsitvatorok) overtaxed the strength of an economy already weakened by inflation (from 1584: possibly fuelled by an influx of New World silver, as part of the general economic crisis of the late sixteenth century). Social discontent, possibly compounded by overpopulation, which brought about unprecedented demands on the state by seekers after office, from Janissary to Grand Vezir, and by changes in the nature of warfare which rendered obsolete the whole *sipahi* (military) 'establishment', together with changes in the pattern of world trade, which reduced the Red Sea and the eastern Mediterranean to an economic backwater, compounded the problem. Thus both the stability and job security of the entire *kul* apparatus, and the economic bases and *raison d'état* of the *sipahi* class were shattered and within a matter of decades the 'classical' institutions of the Empire, while continuing to exist, had become economically or militarily redundant.

It is in this context that the much-discussed phenomenon of Ottoman 'decline' – rather, a painful readjustment to new realities – should be considered. The virtual abandonment of the *devshirme*, the emergence of new foci of political and economic power in the households of the leading politico-military dignitaries, and the emergence of a more entrepreneurial system of tax-farming and proprietorial land tenure (*iltizam*; *malikane*) erected on the ruins of the *timar* system, in the years after 1600, mark the end of the 'classical' Ottoman system. In one sense the Ottoman Empire, like, for example, that other monolithic Empire, Spain, weathered the storm. An apparent *renovatio imperii* under the direction of the capable ministerial family of Köprülü, members or clients of which held the Grand Vezirate for half a century from 1656, witnessed the successful conquest of Crete (1645–69) and Podolia (1676), together with small territorial gains in north-west Hungary against the Habsburgs (Treaty of Vasvár, 1664). A second unsuccessful attempt to take Vienna (1683), however, brought into the field a Habsburg-inspired coalition of Austria, Venice, Poland and Hungary. Within a few years Hungary was lost for ever (fall of Buda, 1686), and by the terms of the Treaties of Karlowitz (1699: concluded under Anglo-Dutch mediation) the Ottomans were obliged to cede territory to all the allies.

Ottoman history thereafter, until the end of the eighteenth century, is (at least externally) largely the record of a partially successful holding operation against Austria and, in particular, Russia. Internally, the period is marked by further erosion in the power of the Sultanate and a progressive increase in local autonomies (*a'yan*; *derebeyis*). The slight degree of receptivity to external cultural influences (such as the introduction of printing in Arabic script or the appearance of baroque motifs in Ottoman architecture) has perhaps been overemphasized by historians. In essence, by the eighteenth century the Ottoman state and its culture had become

The Sultan Ahmad as a young man (Ottoman painting, 1620–30)

both moribund and incapable of either renewal or supersession within its traditional forms. A combination of profitable conservatism, embedded deep within the religious establishment, the bureaucracy and the military, and economic peripheralization (increasing engrossment of long-distance trade by either *dhimmi* elements – mainly Greek – or outsiders operating under the provisions of the Capitulations*), conspired to render merely quaint and backward what had once been a powerful and a unique state. It is significant that the Wahhabi* movement, the first manifestation of radical reform in modern Islam, should have appeared in the late eighteenth century, not within the boundaries of the empire, but in the remote fastnesses of central Najd. It might be regarded, nonetheless, as surprising that of the three options for survival open to the Ottoman Sultanate at the end of the eighteenth century – a renovation of traditional forms, as under the Köprülü a century earlier; a revivifying return to radical Islam; and the adoption of a non-traditional dynastic absolutism – it should have been the last of these which, under Selim III (1789–1807) and his successors, secured the existence of the dynasty and the state until the third decade of the twentieth century.

CJH

Further reading

M. A. Cook ed., *A History of the Ottoman Empire to 1730* (Cambridge, 1976)

S. Faroqhi, *Towns and Townsmen of Ottoman Anatolia* (Cambridge, 1984)

H. Inalcik, *The Ottoman Empire: The Classical Age, 1300–1600* (London, 1973)

B. McGowan, *Economic Life in Ottoman Europe: taxation, trade and the struggle for land, 1600–1800* (Cambridge, 1981)

T. Naff and R. Owen, ed., *Studies in Eighteenth Century Islamic History* (Illinois, 1977)

V. J. Parry,'La manière de combattre', in V. J. Parry and M. E. Yapp, eds. *War, Technology and Society in the Middle East* (London, 1975)

The Kingdom of Morocco

Morocco takes its name from Marrakush (Marrakesh), founded by the Almoravids (al-Murabitun)* about 1070 as the capital of their Moroccan Empire. This Empire, which for the first time united the whole of Morocco in a single state, was taken over by the Almohads (al-Muwahhidun)* in 1147, under whom it reached its maximum extent, from Tripolitania to Muslim Spain. When that Empire disintegrated in the middle of the thirteenth century, the Moroccan portion fell to the Merinids of Fez. For over a hundred years theirs was still the greatest state in the Muslim west, but by the fifteenth century they had lost control of Marrakesh and the southern half of the country. Their last Sultan was executed by the citizens of Fez in 1465; their cousins and successors the Wattasids remained confined to the northern region. Meanwhile in 1415 the Portuguese occupied Ceuta, and by 1520 had acquired a string of *fronteiras* or fortified harbours on the Atlantic coast as far as Agadir. From the Canaries, the Spaniards endeavoured to establish themselves still further south, while in 1497 they took Melilla as the first in a line of *presidios* along the Mediterranean coast as far as Tripoli.

The Bou Jeloud Gate, Fez

The reasons for this political weakness at home and abroad lay in the failure of the medieval Moroccan state both to create a central government proof against succession disputes and palace intrigues and to keep a predominantly tribal population permanently in subjection. By the beginning of the sixteenth century, however, new, non-tribal elements were beginning to fill the political vacuum. Sufi* saints were attracting popular followings; marabouts or local holy men were becoming influential over the tribes, and the notion of sharifianism*, of a class of born leaders descended from the Prophet, was spreading outside Fez. The Portuguese presence in the south polarized the tribes into allies and enemies of the Christians; in these circumstances, a *sharif* from the borders of the Sahara was chosen in 1511 to lead the holy war upon them. In the hands of his two sons, the holy war turned into a long campaign for the throne which ended in 1554, when the younger brother, Muhammad al-Shaykh, finally took possession of Fez to found the so-called Saʿdian dynasty. Firearms gave him victory and the power to rule, but left him militarily inferior to the Ottomans at Algiers, by whom he was murdered in 1557. To ward off the Turks, he and his successors turned to Spain, only to be threatened by Christian imperialism. Impending disaster, however, turned to triumph at the battle of Alcazarquivir in 1578, when the invading King of Portugal was killed. The following twenty-five years of the reign of Ahmad al-Mansur al-Dhahabi, 'the Victorious, the Golden', were the climax of the dynasty, distinguished by the conquest of the western Sudan in 1591.

Such an achievement, rivalling that of the Spanish conquistadors, was made possible by imitation of the Ottomans. Ahmad claimed the Caliphate, and thus the leadership of the Muslim community. Whether in splendour at Marrakesh or in a vast tent-palace on the road, he presided over a formal administration conducted by a wazir in council. The janissary element was provided by a large force of musketeers, many of them Spanish renegades. For the first time since the mid-fourteenth century, Morocco was governed by a regular 'army' of secretaries, soldiers and judges. But this orderly regime broke down on Ahmad's death in 1603 in disputes over the succession which swiftly reduced the Saʿdians to mere rulers of Marrakesh. Their musketeers took service with the great marabouts of the Atlas, of whom the most powerful and prestigious, shaykhs of the *zawiya* of Dila in the Middle Atlas, almost became the new Sultans. They were forestalled and overthrown, however, by an adventurous *sharif* from the Tafilelt in south-eastern Morocco, the founder of the present ʿAlawite dynasty. Taking Fez as his capital in 1666, Maulay ('My Lord') Rashid reunited Morocco before his death in 1672, when he was succeeded by his brother, Maulay Ismaʿil.

Maulay Ismaʿil

During his immensely long reign, 1672–1727, Ismaʿil recreated a central government at Meknès, the new palace city he built to rival Versailles. It was a central government, however, which largely dispensed with central administration. For the Ottoman model adopted by Ahmad al-Mansur, Ismaʿil substituted his prestige as a *sharif* and Commander of the Faithful, backed by his tribal cavalry, the Udaya, and his famous black slave army (*ʿabid*). He simply expected to be served by subordinates who met their own expenses, and his, out of local revenues – a wholly informal fiscal feudalism applying to his vast household, his troops and his provincial governors. It was a system both oppressive and repressive, but through patronage broadly based; moreover, unlike that of the Saʿdians, it survived the succession crisis on Ismaʿil's death. The state was nevertheless weakened, and when his grandson Sidi Muhammad came to the throne in 1757 he felt obliged to reopen

Morocco's trade with Europe, creating the port of Essaouira (Mogador) for the purpose; it was the beginning of a return to centralized administration.

Essaouira marked a major change in both foreign and religious policy. *Jihad** against the Christians, who in the sixteenth century had occupied the Moroccan coast, was the principal duty of the Sultan, his chief claim to the *bayʿa* or oath of allegiance from his subjects. The duty was discharged by Muhammad himself in 1769, when he evicted the Portuguese from Mazagan, leaving only Ceuta and Melilla in the hands of Spain. This defence of Islam was in turn a defiance of the Ottomans, against whose representatives at Algiers Ismaʿil had waged a long and unsuccessful war. To justify the breach of the long-standing embargo on trade with the infidel, Muhammad turned to the Law; but whereas Maulay Ismaʿil had simply demanded the necessary *fatwa* from the *ʿulama*, Muhammad invoked his authority as Commander of the Faithful to prescribe the texts they should follow. After his death in 1790, such legalism almost provoked a revolution under his son Sulayman (1792–1822), but continued to sustain the twin policies of administrative reform and trade with Europe that dominated the nineteenth century.

MB

Further reading

J. M. Abun-Nasr, *A History of the Maghrib* (Cambridge, 1985, 3rd edn.)
M. Brett, 'Morocco and the Ottomans: the sixteenth century in North Africa', *Journal of African History*, XXV (1984), 331–41
C.-A. Julien, *History of North Africa: from the Arab conquest to 1830*, Eng. tr. of 2nd edn. by R. Le Tourneau, ed. (Paris, 1952; London 1970)
Patricia Mercer, 'Palace and Jihād in the Early ʿAlawī State in Morocco', *Journal of African History*, XVIII (1977), 531–53

The Middle East and North Africa: 1800–1939

European expansion and the need for reform

Between 1800 and 1939 most of the Middle East and North Africa came under varying types and degrees of European colonial control, with far-reaching political and economic consequences for its populations. In 1800, European penetration had barely begun, with Napoleon's expedition to Egypt* in 1798. By 1939, the whole of the area between Morocco* and Afghanistan*, except for Saudi Arabia*, Yemen*, Iran*, the Turkish Republic* (established in 1923) and Afghanistan itself, was ruled or controlled by Britain, France or Italy, and the three Empires of the Ottomans, the Qajars and the Sharifians of Morocco, had either disappeared or (in the case of the Sharifians) been relegated to purely decorative functions. In 1800, apart from those engaged in long-distance trade, the mass of the population was engaged in subsistence activities and was thus only tangentially affected by or indirectly participating in the world economy; by 1939 market relations had penetrated to the remotest settlements in the Sahara and to the most inaccessible villages in the Kurdish mountains. Between 1800 and 1939 the combined population of Anatolia and the Arab Middle East including Egypt but excluding the Arabian peninsula (for which no estimates are available) quadrupled, from about 11m to over 43m; the population of the Maghrib* rose less dramatically, from about 10.75m in 1800 to about 17m in 1936, while that of Iran rose from between 5m and 6m in 1800 to over 16m in 1937.

In broad terms, the expansion of the European economies which followed the Industrial Revolution was accompanied by demands for raw materials for the factories of Europe and for new markets for their products. The Middle East and North Africa could satisfy both needs, as suppliers of primary products, and also of cotton (Egypt and Syria), silk (Lebanon) and tobacco (Anatolia and Iran); and, because of the Europeans' power to insist on tariffs which favoured their own commercial interests and also of the generally underdeveloped state of industry in the area, as major consumers of European manufactured goods. As will be described, the pace and nature of European penetration was not uniform over the area, and local reactions to it varied substantially. Nevertheless, certain patterns tended to repeat themselves in the course of the nineteenth century.

In the first place, it was only in the late eighteenth and early nineteenth centuries that the educated and ruling classes in the Middle East began to become aware of how far the area as a whole had fallen behind Europe, both in a material and technological sense, and in the less tangible spheres of intellectual and political development. Rulers like the Ottoman Sultans Mahmud II (1808–39) and ʿAbd al-Majid I (1839–61); and Muhammad ʿAli*, originally an Ottoman soldier sent to restore the authority of Istanbul in Egypt, who rapidly established himself as *de facto* independent governor (1805–48), aided by a few bureaucrats and intellectuals who had some contact with Europe and European thought, began to institute wide-ranging reforms. In general, they wanted to modernize their governments and, particularly in the case of the Ottomans, to assert or reassert the control of the central administration over the provinces and to extract taxes from them more regularly and efficiently. These efforts required a major overhaul of the administrative, legal and educational apparatuses, and, as the Islamic *ʿulama* had always controlled the two latter institutions, the state's imposition of what were essentially European legal codes and educational syllabuses aroused some opposition from that quarter.

Another area where rulers considered the need for reform to be particularly acute was the armed forces. In the wake of the Treaty of Kucuk Kaynarja, concluded after a major defeat of the Ottomans by the Russians in 1774, and the wars with Austria and Russia between 1787 and 1792, Sultan Selim III (1789–1807) had attempted to set up an army corps on European lines, the Nizam-i Cedid, with the help of French instructors. However, this new model army could only be established alongside, rather than instead of, the existing Janissary corps, and in fact it was to be the Janissaries' opposition to this and other innovations that forced Selim to abdicate in 1807. His cousin and successor Mahmud II, whom he greatly influenced, was evidently determined to push ahead with similar reforms, but it was not until May 1826 that he was able to announce the establishment of a new force, which he proclaimed to be 'a restoration of the military order of Süleyman the Magnificent'. The Janissaries rose in revolt again a few days later, but they were defeated by troops loyal to Mahmud, and formally disbanded on 17 June. In a similar episode in Cairo in 1811, Muhammad ʿAli had massacred most of the Mamluks, whose control of land and the military establishment had prevented him from gaining absolute mastery over Egypt.

The *tanzimat*

Both in Egypt and the Ottoman Empire the destruction of the traditional military order was essential in order to avoid the possibility of effective opposition to the reforms. In general, the various legal, educational and administrative measures known collectively as the *tanzimat*, which were introduced into the Ottoman Empire between 1840 and 1876, remained in force until the Empire's demise after the First World War, and indeed frequently formed the basis of similar institutions in the Empire's successor states: for example, until the land reforms of the 1950s and 1960s, land tenure in much of the Fertile Crescent rested essentially on the Ottoman Land Code of 1858. Thus the nineteenth century was a period of very considerable ferment, although this important fact was frequently unperceived or ignored by colonial administrative officials in the Middle East after the First World War, who cherished notions of an 'unchanging East' which had little foundation.

In many ways the effect of the reforms fell far short of the ambitions of those who were trying to implement them. As well as attempting to reassert the authority of the state and inculcate 'Ottoman' civic loyalties in the hearts and minds of its subjects, the Ottoman reformers were anxious to give the European powers as few pretexts as possible to intervene in the internal affairs of the Empire. Thus in the first major document of the *tanzimat*, the Hatt-i Sharif of Gulhane, issued in 1839, basic civil liberties and an equitable system of taxation were promised to 'all our subjects, of whatever religion or sect they may be'. It was also hoped that by this means the territorial integrity of the Empire would be preserved. Neither objective was realized; the powers insisted on their right to 'protect' the groups with which they had traditional links, notably the French on behalf of the Lebanese Maronites and other Catholics (mostly converts from the Greek or Syrian Orthodox communities) and the Russians on behalf of the Orthodox, and the Empire continued to contract in size throughout the nineteenth century as a result of foreign invasions and successful independence struggles. This process had of course started well before the *tanzimat* with the successful national movements in Serbia (1817, 1833) and Greece (1821–32) and the gradual conquest of Algeria by the French after 1830.

Reforms of education, land tenure, the military establishment, and the legal system similar to those introduced in the Ottoman Empire were inaugurated in Egypt by Muhammad ʿAli and his successors Saʿid (1854–63) and Ismaʿil (1863–79), in Tunisia by Ahmad Bey (1837–55) and Muhammad al-Sadiq Bey (1859–82), and in a less comprehensive manner by Maulay Hasan of Morocco (1873–94). Forms of representative government were introduced in Tunisia in 1861 and in Egypt in 1866. In both countries constitutional movements were stifled by foreign occupation. In the Ottoman Empire, in the face of considerable opposition, a constitution was enacted in 1876, but the Ottoman parliament was suspended almost immediately (in 1878) by the autocratic ʿAbd al-Hamid II (1876–1909) until 1908–9; in Egypt these developments did not take place until 1922–3, since the constitutional movement was smothered by the British occupation in 1882.

Iran: autocracy and the constitution

In contrast, Anglo-Russian interference and rivalry in nineteenth-century Iran had effectively prevented the central state from acting as an engine of 'modernization'. No body of reforms comparable to the *tanzimat* was introduced; there was no major reorganization of the army. However, there was widespread public concern at Nasir al-Din Shah's (1848–96) apparent readiness to sell off substantial economic concessions to foreigners, which manifested itself particularly in country-wide protests in 1891–2 organized by the *ʿulama* against the granting of a monopoly to a British subject for the sale and purchase of tobacco. The success of this protest movement encouraged the growth of an opposition alignment of clergy, merchants and intellectuals whose aim was to limit the power of the Qajar Shahs and inaugurate a constitution and an elected assembly. Their efforts were partly successful after the struggles during the period between 1905 and 1911, known as the Constitutional Revolution, but although a constitution was drafted and accepted in 1907, the Qajars were generally able to ignore both it and the *majlis* (parliament) with the support of their Tsarist Russian allies until the demise of the latter in the Russian Revolution. In the chaos that followed the end of the First World War, Riza Khan*, the leader of the Cossack brigade, the only organized military force left in the country, managed to seize power in 1921 and after crushing tribal opposition and deposing the last of the Qajar Shahs had himself proclaimed Shah in 1925, the founder of a new dynasty, the Pahlavis, whose name stressed Iran's pre-Islamic past.

Economic penetration

Three major consequences of the reforms and the desire to 'catch up with Europe' in the Middle East and North Africa should also be mentioned. One of these, the spread of education* and the resulting heightening of political awareness, has already been hinted at, since this new atmosphere was largely responsible for the growing pressures for constitutional government and representative assemblies, which produced the movements whose limited gains have been described. The wider implications of this new consciousness will be discussed more fully below, together with another important facet of it, the belief which was coming to be held increasingly among concerned Muslim intellectuals that the challenge posed by an advancing and aggressive Europe could only be met by a revitalized Islam, either reinterpreted in ways more in tune with the world of the nineteenth century, or restored to the pristine purity exemplified by the rule of the Prophet and the Rightly-Guided Caliphs*.

However, before tracing the progress of these new political, intellectual and religious ideologies in the nineteenth and early twentieth centuries, a very different consequence of the reforms must be mentioned. Although the introduction of the new measures originated partly from a desire on the part of those who framed them to bring greater efficiency and more centralized control to the government of their own domains, they were encouraged in these aims by the local representatives of the European powers, who perceived, correctly, that the institution of European-style legal codes, the extension of peace and 'order' to the rural areas and other improvements such as greater security of tenure for landlords would also have the effect of facilitating European economic penetration.

During the nineteenth century the value of European trade with the Arab Middle East increased from less than £10m a year to over £100m, a process which created a new class of agents, importers and exporters, many of whom either came from the minority Christian and Jewish communities, or, particularly in Egypt and North Africa, were Europeans. The rise of this comprador bourgeoisie was accompanied by the impoverishment and the decline in status of those craftsmen and artisans who did not manage to change from traditional methods of production to cope with new consumer demands. Thus while the port cities of Beirut and Alexandria, through which most of the 'new' imports and exports passed, increased their populations about tenfold, first between the beginning and the middle of the nineteenth century, and then again between the 1850s and the mid-1870s, the numbers of artisans in the inland cities of Syria either remained constant, in the case of Aleppo, or declined sharply, in the case of Damascus. Although recent research has emphasized the ability of some groups of workers (such as those who found employment in the Lebanese silk industry after the 1860s) to adjust to the new economic circumstances, and in particular to take advantage of the increased economic activity which resulted from the expansion of the domestic market, the migration of some hundreds of thousands from Syria and Mount Lebanon to the Americas alone between 1860 and 1914 suggests that fairly substantial numbers were simply unable to adapt.

Two other general economic tendencies can also be observed in most parts of the region. First, the value of imports into the area from Europe greatly exceeded the value of exports, with the result that the value of the local currencies gradually declined, thus contributing to a constant and growing crisis in the balance of payments. Between 1844 and 1873, for example, the value of the Moroccan currency fell by about 90 per cent. Secondly, at various times in the nineteenth century, and for purposes which were generally but not always financially sound, the governments of Morocco, Tunisia, Egypt, the Ottoman Empire and Iran all began to borrow on the European money markets and, except for Iran, all eventually went bankrupt as a result. Although there were obvious extravagances on the part of individual rulers, most of the debts were incurred by governments attempting to modernize their armies and bureaucracies along European lines or inaugurating ambitious programmes of public works, building railways, roads and harbours, or setting up irrigation schemes, projects which they had often been encouraged to undertake by their European advisers. The cost of these efforts to modernize far exceeded the sums available from ordinary taxation, and even the increases in revenue obtained from more efficient collection and the wider cultivation of cash crops for export could not keep up with the continuous rise in government expenditure.

As these states' financial situation deteriorated, their creditworthiness, and thus the terms on which they were able to borrow, also declined. In consequence, although deemed to have borrowed specific sums, they often actually received less than half the full amount, but were nevertheless forced to pay back the fictitious principal at rates as high as 10 or 12 per cent. Thus, between 1854 and 1879, four years after it had been declared bankrupt, the Ottoman state borrowed £T256m, of which it had actually received only £139m; between 1862 and 1873 the Egyptian government had borrowed £68.4m, of which it had received £46.6m. In similar circumstances the Tunisian state owed about 137m francs in 1869, and was also forced to declare itself bankrupt; the Moroccan state had already been bankrupted by the indemnity it had been forced to pay Spain to compensate the latter for withdrawing its army of invasion from Tetouan in 1860. These bankruptcies were almost invariably followed by the installation in the local treasuries of European financial controllers, whose task was to ensure that the state's revenues were used to pay off the national debt. The austerity programmes and the tax increases on which the European controllers insisted often aroused strong local opposition, which crystallized into the first manifestations of national feeling in the form of more or less organized acts of resistance. In Tunisia, Egypt and Morocco these acts of defiance were themselves followed by European invasion, ostensibly to 'protect' the rulers from their rebellious subjects, but which were the prelude to long periods of direct or indirect foreign rule.

Intellectual influences from Europe

As well as leading to subordination to European economic and strategic interests, the 'rediscovery of Europe' had a number of other consequences for the inhabitants of the Middle East and North Africa. Under Selim III the Ottoman Empire began to send its diplomats to reside in the capitals of the European states to which they were accredited, and under Mehmed II and Muhammad ʿAli and their successors, students were regularly sent to Europe both to study European languages and to attend educational institutions, particularly in France. A printing press was opened in Istanbul in 1784, and a translation bureau established there in 1833; in Egypt a government press was set up at Bulaq in 1822, and a translation bureau opened in 1841, under Rifaʿa al-Tahtawi*, whose account of his travels and studies in Europe was widely read by his contemporaries. In the course of the nineteenth century large numbers of European technical and scientific textbooks, as well as major literary works, were translated into Arabic and Turkish, and the study of foreign languages became more widespread.

Such developments naturally had a profound effect on the intellectual climate of the time, since European philosophical and political ideas, as well as scientific discoveries, now began to spread throughout the area. This process was further assisted by reorganization of the educational systems of Egypt (after 1837) and the Ottoman Empire (after 1846). In Greater Syria the foundation of schools and other educational establishments in the 1830s by European and American missionaries contributed considerably to the revival and revitalization of the Arabic language, whose importance both as an official and as a literary language had declined sharply during the centuries of Ottoman rule. Although the missionaries' contribution to the *nahda*, the Arabic linguistic and literary renaissance of the nineteenth century, has sometimes been overemphasized, the fact that Protestant writing placed Christianity firmly within the vernacular meant that it was necessary for the American and British missionaries to learn Arabic and also to commission textbooks in Arabic for use in their schools. In 1866 the American missionaries founded the Syrian Protestant College, now the American University of Beirut, which soon developed into one of the leading educational institutions in the area. A number of local Christian scholars, notably Nasif and Ibrahim al-Yaziji*, and Butrus al-Bustani*, who were associated with the work of the missionaries, also pursued research into classical Arabic literature, and in 1847 Yaziji and Bustani founded Jamʿiyyat al-adab wa'l-ʿulum (The Literary and Scientific Society), the first literary society in the Arab world.

Although an important aspect of the early *tanzimat* reforms had been the projection of the Ottoman Empire as a multi-confessional (and implicitly a multi-ethnic) society and the fostering of *osmanlilik* (Ottomanism) as a focus of loyalty for all Ottoman citizens, these objectives were only very partially realized. The secularization of the legal and educational systems did not greatly affect the Empire's role as the heartland of the Islamic world, a state (*dawla*) ruled over by a Sultan/Caliph who was in some not quite explicit sense the successor of the Prophet Muhammad, in which the non-Muslim monotheistic communities lived as protected but essentially second-class citizens. In this state, religion rather than language or ethnicity was the primary focus and indeed the only 'official' means of identity, but the highest administrative posts in the Empire were generally reserved for Muslims of Ottoman Turkish culture.

In the late 1870s, at the beginning of the reign of ʿAbd al-Hamid II, the general atmosphere of cautious liberalization and secularization which had been characteristic of the previous decades was abruptly replaced by a more repressive political order. The suspension of the constitution and the indefinite prorogation of the Ottoman parliament in 1878 was accompanied by ʿAbd al-Hamid's emphasis on his own role as Caliph of all the Muslims, and his embrace of the pan-Islamic movement. In these circumstances, both the non-Muslim and the non-Turkish communities within the Empire were made increasingly aware of their inferior status, and, inspired by European notions of equality and national identity, began to seek to change this situation in their favour. In the Arab provinces of the Empire, particularly in Greater Syria, this process was facilitated both by the *nahda*, which made Arab intellectuals, both Muslims and Christians, increasingly conscious of their common cultural and ethno-linguistic heritage, and by the movement for Islamic reform associated with Muhammad ʿAbduh* and his pupils, one wing of which laid stress on the importance of the Arab contribution to Islam.

Islamic reform and Arab nationalism

In one sense, the earliest manifestation of 'Arab nationalism' was the

Wahhabi* movement which began in the Arabian peninsula in the eighteenth century. On his journeys through the Arab regions of the Ottoman Empire, Muhammad ibn ʿAbd al-Wahhab (1703–91), who was born in ʿUyayna in the Najd, observed what he considered to be deviations from true Islam and believed it his mission to lead Muslims back to orthodoxy. In 1744 he married into the house of Saʿud, a family based in al-Dirʿiyya near Riyadh, and with the support of his father-in-law began a movement to restore Islam to the pristine purity of the Rightly-Guided Caliphs*. The movement flourished during the late eighteenth and early nineteenth centuries, and its adherents sacked Karbala in 1802, and occupied Mecca in 1803 and Medina in 1805. It was only checked by expeditions under Muhammad ʿAli and his sons in 1811–15 and 1816–18, and even then Saʿudi/Wahhabi power revived later in the century. A century later, Rashid Rida, one of Muhammad ʿAbduh's most distinguished pupils, developed some of the themes of the Islamic Modernism of his teacher in the direction of Islamic fundamentalism, and identified himself with the House of Saʿud, which was at that stage gradually taking over the greater part of the Arabian peninsula.

Jamal al-Din al-Afghani* (1839–97) and Muhammad ʿAbduh (1849–1905) were the founders of Islamic Modernism. Both wished to reform and revitalize Islam, in order to enable the Muslims to stand up effectively to the challenge of Europe. Afghani considered that the most effective method of doing this was to incorporate European ideas of the nation into a new vision of the Islamic *umma*, while ʿAbduh's main concern was to promote a progressive interpretation of the *sharīʿa* by stressing individual interpretation based on reason, an approach which enables Muslims to accept all modern science and technology as being part of God's revelation. In fact, if taken to its logical conclusion (as ʿAli ʿAbd al-Raziq was to do in the 1920s) this approach seems to lead to the separation of religion from politics and thus a major departure from traditional Islamic practice.

The earliest figure to combine Islamic Modernism and an embryonic form of Arab nationalism was ʿAbd al-Rahman al-Kawakibi (1849–1902), a Syrian from Aleppo who was forced into exile in Egypt to escape the attentions of ʿAbdül Hamid's secret police. The main theme of Kawakibi's work was that the Caliphate had fallen into disrepute under the Ottomans, and it could only be reformed by being returned to Quraysh, the Prophet Muhammad's tribe. In this connection it is interesting to record that a British consular report from Aleppo in 1858 mentions that the 'Mussulman population of northern Syria hopes for a separation from the Ottoman Empire and the formation of a new Arabian state under the sovereignty of the Shareefs of Mecca'. Kawakibi wanted the Caliph to be elected for a three-year period, and his 'temporal' powers to be strictly limited. Again, the logical consequence of this line of thinking is a separation of the temporal from the spiritual, although Kawakibi himself remained an orthodox Muslim and does not seem to have been aware of these implications.

Although what became the Arab national movement continued to gain momentum in the 1880s and 1890s, with some of its more active representatives being obliged to take refuge in Egypt or in Europe, many Arabs were prepared to take part in the wider movement of opposition to ʿAbdül Hamid, and to join one of the groups making up the loose coalition known generically as the Young Turks. Thus the most important of these groups, a society consisting largely of army officers called the Committee of Union and Progress, founded in 1887, had a number of Arab members, perhaps most notably the Egyptian ʿAziz ʿAli al-Misri and the Iraqi Mahmud Shawkat. Nevertheless, when the committee succeeded in seizing power in July 1908, and eventually in forcing the abdication of ʿAbdül Hamid ten months later, it gradually became clear that although its aims were not 'Islamic' its principal concern was once more to foster and promote the position of the *Turkish* element in the Empire, and that there was to be no place in the new order for ideas of provincial autonomy and decentralization. At this point, in the crucial years between 1909 and the outbreak of the First World War, many intellectuals and political activists in the Arab provinces began to come round to the view that the cultural and political aspirations of their fellow countrymen would be best served by the separation of the Arab provinces from the Ottoman Empire, and, some felt, by the creation of an Arab state under an Arab king. A few of these individuals were also aware that the achievement of these aims would not be entirely unwelcome to the European powers, particularly Britain.

French rule in Algeria and Tunisia

Developments in Arab North Africa were very different, since the territories which now form the modern states of Morocco, Algeria, Tunisia, Libya and Egypt were subjected to various different forms of direct colonial rule. Thus France invaded Algeria* in 1830, and carried out a particularly ruthless campaign of conquest against the indigenous population, killing large numbers of those who resisted and confiscating huge areas for occupation by European settlers, of whom there were already nearly 110,000 in 1847 and some 553,000 in 1901. The Algerians were driven off their lands and forced to cultivate the more marginal areas; they were subjected to numerous forms of discrimination, paying taxes for services enjoyed almost exclusively by the *colons*, who were given the right to elect six members to the Chamber of Deputies in Paris in 1870. Such educational facilities as had previously existed were run down, and the Algerians were not encouraged to attend French schools; similarly, as part of a general attack on Islamic institutions, the rural *zawiyas* (lodges of the Sufi orders) were closed down as 'hotbeds of fanaticism'. A rising in Kabylia in 1871 was the last major act of resistance until the war of 1954; more than 2.5m hectares were confiscated from the tribes which had taken part, and nearly 11m francs were taken in collective fines. By the last quarter of the nineteenth century, as far as the French population was concerned, Algeria had become part of Metropolitan France, although the Muslim population was subject to a mass of discriminatory laws and regulations.

In Tunisia*, the indebtedness of the government and the presence of a small but influential settler community served as the principal levers for French intervention. In theory, Tunisia had been part of the Ottoman Empire since 1574, but had been ruled by a locally based dynasty, the Husaynis, since 1705. Tunisia was relatively highly urbanized in the eighteenth century, had a well-integrated economy which included acting as a major entrepôt for the trans-Saharan trade, and enjoyed a fair measure of political stability, factors which recent research has stressed as assisting its emergence as a national entity. In the 1830s the Ottomans, who had invaded Tripolitania to reimpose their authority there, were clearly prepared to launch a similar attack on Tunisia, and were only prevented by the presence of French warships off the coast. Under Ahmad Bey reforms similar to those of the Ottoman *tanzimat* were introduced, and, not without considerable resistance from Muhammad al-Sadiq Bey, a constitution in 1861, largely as a result of pressure from the statesman and political philosopher Khayr al-Din (*c.*1823–90). However, at this point the reforms were suspended because of opposition from those close to the court; at the same time, British, French and Italian interests were becoming increasingly involved in the Tunisian economy, and initiated a number of speculative ventures which in their turn forced the Bey to seek assistance from European banks. Khayr al-Din was recalled from the political wilderness to head the international debt commission in 1869, and became prime minister between 1873 and 1877, when he was removed because of his obstructive attitude towards French attempts to play a more active political role in Tunisia. However, at the Congress of Berlin in 1878, Britain hinted that she would not oppose any overt expression of France's colonial designs, and in 1881 a minor incident on the border with Algeria was a convenient pretext for a French invasion and the imposition of a protectorate, a form of colonization in which the indigenous institutions (particularly the office and some of the functions of the Bey) were supposedly left intact, with a parallel French administration headed by a resident-general.

In contrast to the situation in Algeria, where the traditional social and political leadership was almost completely destroyed in the course of the nineteenth century, an embryonic Tunisian national movement, the Young Tunisians, had developed by 1900. Their objective was more that of reform than of national independence, a prelude to the main internal disagreement between those who sought assimilation into the French community and those who wanted complete independence. By 1934 the defeat of the assimilationists had been formalized by the creation of the Neo-Destour Party under Habib Bourguiba*, working closely with the powerful Confédération Générale des Travailleurs Tunisiens, founded in 1924.

The British in Egypt

In Egypt, the early national movement was directed both against the constraints and austerities imposed by the European financial controllers, and against the virtual monopoly of political power enjoyed by the circle around the ruling family, which was largely composed of Turco-Circassians, the descendants of Muhammad ʿAli and those who had accompanied him in 1805. In February 1879 Ahmad ʿUrabi organized a demonstration of native Egyptian officers in the army, ostensibly in protest against the arbitrary barrier imposed on their promotion above the rank of colonel. Over the next two years, especially after the deposition of Khedive Ismaʿil by the Ottoman Sultan in response to pressures from the Powers, and his replacement by the more pliant Tawfiq in June 1879, this developed into a political movement with nationalist overtones. In July 1882, having previously sought, but failed to obtain, French support, the British government sent a force to Egypt to 'restore the authority of the khedive', which defeated the Egyptian army at Tall al-Kabir in September. ʿUrabi and six of his associates were tried and exiled to Ceylon (Sri Lanka) a few months later.

Although Britain did not officially declare a protectorate over Egypt until the outbreak of the First World War in 1914, the regime imposed after 1882 had most of the features generally associated with such arrangements. Between 1883 and his retirement in 1907, Egypt was ruled by the British agent and consul-general, Lord Cromer, a member of a well-known British banking family. He established a balanced budget by 1886, and encouraged the expansion of the irrigated area, particularly by repairing the barrage on the Nile north of Cairo constructed under Muhammad ʿAli, and building the Aswan Dam. However, these developments were accompanied by an increasing pauperization of the peasantry on the one hand and the concentration of landholdings on the other; in 1930, 44 per cent of the cultivated area was held by 12,000 landowners, with the remaining 56 per cent divided among some 2.2m small owners, out of a rural population of 11.5m (1937 census).

The national movement had been virtually stifled after the occupation, and did not make itself felt again until 1900. Led by the journalist and lawyer Mustafa Kamil (1878–1908), one of its main themes was the restoration of links with the Ottomans, a factor which explains the lack of coordination between the opposition groups in Egypt and those in the Fertile Crescent, where the main objective was either to obtain greater autonomy from Istanbul, or, after 1909, separation from the Ottoman Empire. Thus Kamil saw pan-Islamism as the means of freeing Egypt from British colonial rule, but, like Afghani, he regarded pan-Islamism more as an expression of anti-colonial solidarity than as an irredentist movement. Also, since he concentrated much of his efforts on trying to convince political circles in France to intervene against Britain on Egypt's behalf, he was deeply disappointed at the establishment of the Entente Cordiale between Britain and France in 1904, under which the two Powers acknowledged each other's pre-eminence in Egypt and Morocco respectively.

Between Kamil's death and the First World War, opposition politics became dominated by less radical nationalists, who generally believed in liberal constitutionalism and a more gradual evolution towards reform under the aegis of Britain. By November 1918, however, the national movement had gained new impetus; Egypt had been a vital base for the British army during the Middle East campaigns, and had contributed substantially to the war effort in terms of requisitions and compulsory labour service. Sa'd Zaghlul (*c.*1859–1927), a lawyer of provincial origin who had been minister of education between 1907 and 1913, became the principal figure in a group of politicians who wished to send an Egyptian delegation (*wafd*) to the Paris Peace Conference. When this request was refused there were widespread anti-British demonstrations in Egypt, which greatly increased in intensity after Zaghlul's deportation to Malta in March 1919. Later in the year a commission of enquiry under Lord Milner was sent to Egypt, with which Zaghlul was eventually persuaded to cooperate, but further concessions were required and Zaghlul was deported again before Britain was persuaded to issue the Declaration of Egyptian Independence in February 1922.

Even under this agreement four matters were 'absolutely reserved to the discretion' of the British government: the security of the communications of the British Empire, the defence of Egypt, the protection of minorities and foreign interests and matters relating to the Sudan. Although a constitution was promulgated in 1923, and elections held in January 1924 in which the Wafd won an overwhelming victory, the Egyptians chafed at the limited nature of their independence. In addition, the period between 1924 and 1936 was marked by a struggle between the Wafd, the palace under King Fu'ad (1917–36) and the British Residency, each vying for authority against each other. The treaty of 1936, which was concluded shortly after Fu'ad's death, marked a victory for Britain on all but the third of the reserved points and provided for a 20-year military alliance between the two countries. 'Real' independence for Egypt was only achieved sixteen years later, after Nasser's seizure of power in 1952.

Moroccan Spahis, 1937

France's 'civilizing mission' in Morocco

The destiny of Morocco* had been linked closely with that of Algeria since the 1840s, when Amir ʿAbd al-Qadir, the principal leader of the Algerian resistance to the French, was forced to retreat there. The French forced the Moroccans not to give him assistance, so that he and his troops were actually attacked by the Sharifian army in 1846. For the rest of the nineteenth century the Moroccan Sultans, with the assistance of the British diplomatic representatives, succeeded in postponing French colonial penetration, but Spain, which had been in continuous occupation of Ceuta, Melilla and Alhucemas since the sixteenth century, sought to extend her influence further into the Rif. As we have seen, a *casus belli* was established, and the Spanish laid siege to Tetouan in 1859, only evacuating the town after a huge indemnity had been paid.

During the reign of the capable Hasan I (1873–94) a number of reforms were made, but as well as causing economic chaos the new arrangements were widely criticized as being impious and un-Islamic. An attempt to establish a new tax in 1901 was also vigorously resisted for the same reason. Between 1901 and 1912 there were frequent outbursts of rural dissidence, directed both against increasing French penetration (especially after the Entente of 1904) and the Sultans' apparent inability to withstand it. Eventually, the siege of Fez by tribal forces forced ʿAbd al-Hafiz (1908–12) to make desperate appeals for French intervention; the raising of the siege signalled the beginning of full-scale French occupation, and indeed of the Protectorate, enshrined in the Treaty of Fez of March 1912, followed a few months later by an agreement between France and Spain to a division of the territory which gave the administration of the northern part of the country to Spain.

As in Tunisia, the government of Morocco was carried on by the French around or alongside the traditional political structures, with the French attempting to make the old elites into the new ruling class. Another cornerstone of French policy, especially under the governorship of Lyautey (1912–25) and his immediate successors, was the notion, which had little foundation in fact, that 'Arabs' and 'Berbers' were discrete entities and could be treated separately. The idea was to prise the Berbers away from the 'Arab/Muslim yoke' of the traditional Moroccan state, teach them French and associate them closely with the machinery of the Protectorate. This policy failed almost entirely, especially after riots and demonstrations following the promulgation of a decree known as the Berber *dahir* in 1930, which marked an important stage in the national movement.

It took the French more than twenty years to 'pacify' Morocco, in the face of vigorous resistance from the tribes; at one point in the Rif War (1921–6) some 700,000 Spanish and French troops were involved. Urban protest and resistance developed more slowly, but by the 1930s the Comité d'Action Marocaine had been formed, with ʿAllal al-Fasi (1907–74) as the principal figure in the movement. The group presented a plan of reforms to the Sultan, the resident-general and the French prime minister in 1934. The hopes of the nationalists were raised briefly with the election of the Popular Front government in France in June 1936, but it fell a year later: the Comité was disbanded and al-Fasi sent into nine years' exile in Gabon. By 1939 these blows had caused the national movement to lose much of its impetus, and it was not until 1944, with the formation of the Istiqlal (Independence) Party, that opposition political activity began again.

Italy and the Sanusi in Libya

Between 1835 and 1843 the Ottomans took Tripolitania from the Qaramanlis*, and created provincial headquarters in Tripoli and Benghazi. The reconquest was highly unpopular, and in many ways resembled a colonial invasion, since the tribes in the remoter regions put up fierce resistance to the Ottomans, one group holding out in the Jabal Nafusa for twenty-three years. In 1843 Muhammad al-Sanusi, an Algerian who had founded the order that bears his name in Mecca a few years earlier, opened the first Sufi *zawiya* in al-Bayda in Cyrenaica. Some ten years later he moved his headquarters to Jaghbub near the frontier with Egypt, and the order continued to expand its activities and open more branches in what is now southern Libya, Niger and Chad long after his death in 1859. The order preached Islamic reform, the desirability of modelling its communities on that of the Prophet at Medina, and the defence of the territory of Islam against European encroachment, although this does not seem to have extended to responding to requests for support from other protest movements, such as those of ʿUrabi and the Sudanese Mahdi. However, by the end of the century European colonial expansion had begun to affect Libya as well, spearheaded by Italy, where the colonial lobby was smarting for what was perceived as France's insult to Italian aspirations in Tunisia. In 1911 the Italians invaded, and met with fierce resistance from Ottoman troops, aided by Sanusi and other tribal forces. Although Ottoman forces withdrew, and the Italians occupied most of the coastal towns by 1913, the struggle for control of the interior only ended in 1931 with the capture and execution of the Sanusi's representative, ʿUmar al-Mukhtar. The Italian occupation ended with the arrival of the British armies in 1942, and the country became formally independent in 1951.

The First World War and the peace settlement

By the First World War, therefore, all of North Africa was under some form of European control, and the Ottoman Empire was reduced to Arab Asia, Anatolia, and some of the Aegean islands, having lost all its remaining European territories (except eastern Thrace, still part of modern Turkey) as a result of the Balkan Wars of 1912–13. Instead of remaining neutral in 1914, as the British had hoped, the Ottomans allied with the Central Powers at the end of October, and before the end of the year British Indian troops had landed in the Shatt al-ʿArab*. The Ottomans proved more tenacious than the British had expected; imperial troops sustained heavy losses in Mesopotamia in 1915–16 and particularly in the ill-fated Dardanelles expedition of 1915. On the other side of the Fertile Crescent, the British had repelled a Turkish attempt to cross the Suez Canal in 1915. A counter-offensive force entered Palestine in 1916 and by 1918 had occupied the whole of Syria. Here they were assisted by the British-sponsored Arab revolt, led by the sons of the Sharif of Mecca, which broke out in June 1916.

In the course of the war, Britain, France, Italy and Russia made a series of secret arrangements to divide the Ottoman Empire in the event of an Allied victory. The best-known of these, the Sykes–Picot Agreement*, internationalized Palestine, gave Istanbul and the Straits and large parts of Armenia and Kurdistan to Russia, control of Mesopotamia and the ports of Haifa and Acre to Britain, and Syria and Lebanon to France. At the same time, the British were negotiating with Sharif Husayn, promising him, with certain explicit and rather more implicit exceptions, an independent Arab state. Finally, the Balfour Declaration* (2 November 1917) stated that the British government favoured 'the establishment in

Palestine of a National Home for the Jewish people' (see Israel and the Arab–Israeli problem).

There is still considerable controversy over, in particular, precisely how aware Sharif Husayn was of the general principles of Sykes–Picot when he entered into his own agreement with Britain, but the settlement which emerged as a result of the Paris Peace Conference and the Treaty of Lausanne (1923) certainly fell very far short of local aspirations. The Fertile Crescent was divided into separate political units called Mandates*, which were assigned to Britain and France under the aegis of the League of Nations, France obtaining control of Lebanon and Syria, and Britain obtaining Palestine, (Trans-)Jordan and Iraq. All that was left of Sharif Husayn's 'independent Arab state' was the short-lived Kingdom of the Hijaz which was absorbed into the Kingdom of Hijaz, Najd and its Dependencies (now Saudi Arabia) under the rule of ʿAbd al-ʿAziz ibn ʿAbd al-Rahman al-Saʿud* in December 1925.

The creation of Saudi Arabia

The Saʿud family's control over Najd, and its wider ambitions to take over other parts of the Arabian peninsula, had been checked first by Muhammad ʿAli's* campaigns on behalf of the Ottoman government between 1811 and 1840, and subsequently by the family's local rivals, the Rashids of Ha'il. In 1891, the Rashids, with the encouragement of the Ottomans, succeeded in capturing the Saʿudi capital, Riyadh, and the head of the Saʿud family, ʿAbd al-Rahman, was forced into exile in Kuwait with his son ʿAbd al-ʿAziz. In 1902 the latter made a daring and successful raid on Riyadh, and over the next twelve years managed to drive Ottoman forces out of northern and eastern Arabia. While recognizing the reality of the situation, the Ottomans attempted to retain their own suzerainty by giving ʿAbd al-ʿAziz the title of governor of Najd.

The young King ʿAbd al-ʿAziz of Saudi Arabia

By 1913, ʿAbd al-ʿAziz, or Ibn Saʿud as he is usually known, aided by his newly established army of *ikhwan*, composed of units of fanatical Wahhabi* soldiery, had seized the oasis of Hasa on the Gulf coast from the Ottomans, and thus came to control territory which abutted on Britain's traditional sphere of influence. During the First World War the British succeeded in persuading him not to assist the Ottomans, partly by means of a monthly subsidy, but the authorities in Iraq and India were unwilling to consider mounting a campaign on the eastern side of the Arabian peninsula which would involve the use of local forces along the lines being negotiated by the authorities in Cairo with Sharif Husayn, and in consequence Ibn Saʿud played no major part in the fighting.

However, even before the war ended, the *ikhwan* launched an attack against the Sharifs of Mecca of the Hashimite family in the Hijaz, whom they considered infidels, and were only prevented from advancing further by British pressure. In 1920, Ibn Saʿud occupied part of ʿAsir, to the south of the Hijaz, and added the area around Ha'il to his kingdom a year later. By this time the *ikhwan* were attacking the Hijaz once more, and also making raids into the British mandated territories of Iraq and Transjordan (now ruled, under British auspices, by Sharif Husayn's two sons Faysal and ʿAbd Allah), which, since Ibn Saʿud was still receiving money from Britain, were something of an embarrassment. As far as the Hijaz was concerned, the situation was eventually resolved largely by the growing unpopularity of Sharif Husayn's rule, especially after his unilateral assumption of the Caliphate* after its abolition by Atatürk in March 1924. Less than two years later, Wahhabi forces entered Jidda, and Ibn Saʿud was proclaimed King of the Hijaz in January 1926. By the end of the 1920s both the Saʿudi/Iraqi and the Saʿudi/Transjordanian frontiers had been agreed upon, and the Saʿudi state reached its present extent with the annexation of ʿAsir in 1934. In view of the immense wealth of Saudi Arabia in the 1970s and 1980s, it is useful to remember how extremely poor it was until comparatively recently; before the Second World War the state's sole revenues were derived from pilgrim dues and the Hijaz customs, which, in 1938, five years after the first oil concession (for £50,000, to Standard Oil), produced a total of £1,300,000.

Kemal Atatürk

The reforms of Atatürk

In 1918 the Ottoman Empire faced an armistice whose terms were humiliating in the extreme; the Arab provinces had fallen to the Allies before the fighting ended, and in August 1920 the Treaty of Sèvres, accepted by the Ottoman government, stipulated the demilitarization of the Straits and the division of western Anatolia between Greece, Italy and France. However, the nationalists, led by Mustafa Kemal, a leading general in the Ottoman army, were determined to resist these terms. With the support of the Grand National Assembly, Kemal led a successful campaign against the Greek occupation forces which ended in their withdrawal in 1922 and ultimately in the international recognition of Turkey within virtually all her present frontiers under the Treaty of Lausanne in July 1923. (The boundaries between Turkey and Iraq and between Turkey and Syria were settled in 1926 and 1939 respectively.)

Almost immediately, Mustafa Kemal*, later known as Atatürk, the father of the Turks, began a sweeping programme of reforms whose general aim was to turn Turkey into a modern secular state on Western lines. Turkey became a republic under his presidency in 1923; the capital was moved from Istanbul to Ankara, and the Caliphate was abolished in March 1924. By the end of the 1920s the educational system had been secularized, the fez forbidden and replaced by European caps and hats, the Gregorian calendar made compulsory, the Islamic legal system abandoned, and the Latin alphabet substituted for Arabic. Needless to say, these and other innovations were often vigorously resisted, especially by religious conservatives. Atatürk also created the Republican People's Party, which functioned both as a national rally and as a means of control; no official opposition was allowed until 1946, and manifestations of dissent were vigorously resisted. In particular, the government pursued consistently repressive policies against the Kurdish* population of the south-east, which amounted to a virtual denial of its separate ethnic or linguistic identity.

Nevertheless, Atatürk's achievements in a mere fifteen years (he died in 1938) were impressive. In addition to his legal, social and political reforms, he presided over a major revitalization of the economy, creating mixed state and private banks, and encouraging the protection of domestic industry. Faced with the world economic depression of the 1930s, the government embarked on a new policy, known as étatism, based on the principle that the state, rather than individual entrepreneurs, should take responsibility for major industrial investment, although no major nationalizations of existing private concerns took place. Partly under Soviet influence, a five-year plan was inaugurated in 1934, whose main aim was to create self-sufficiency in key spheres of manufacturing industry. The government also assisted the agricultural sector by subsidizing domestic wheat production by making purchases at guaranteed prices. By the end of the Second World War (in which Turkey remained neutral until March 1945) the basis of a modern secular state with a relatively stable mixed economy had been firmly established.

The reforms of Riza Shah

During the same period, similar policies were being pursued in a less systematic way in Iran* by Atatürk's contemporary, Riza Shah*. Iran had not undergone an earlier era of reform comparable to the *tanzimat** in the Ottoman Empire, with the result that Riza Shah's efforts at 'modernization' faced perhaps even more daunting obstacles than those confronting Atatürk; in particular, the authority of the central government was by no means universally recognized in the rest of the country, and there was no standing army, civil service, or national system of taxation. However, post-war Iranian governments were able to benefit from income from the oil concessions signed with the Anglo-Persian Oil Company and Standard Oil; until 1933, Iran produced over 90 per cent of all Middle Eastern oil, and was in fact only overtaken as the region's largest producer by Saudi Arabia in the early 1970s.

Riza Shah's rule was essentially a military dictatorship, and, like Atatürk, he permitted no opposition or dissent. The limited democratic gains of the Constitutional Revolution (1905–11) were laid aside, and the *majlis* reduced to rubber-stamping the Shah's decrees. In the course of the 1920s conscription was introduced, a civil service established and the educational and legal systems reorganized on Western secular lines. As in the Ottoman Empire in the nineteenth century, a land code was introduced which facilitated the accumulation of large estates by those who were best placed to register landed property in their own names. At the same time the nomads were largely disarmed and settled, often suffering impoverishment in the process, since their economy depended on regular transhumance between summer and winter pastures.

Riza Shah encouraged the building of roads and railways, most notably the Trans-Iranian railway connecting the north and south of the country, which was completed in 1936. Industry and industrial investment were encouraged along the lines being pursued in Turkey, but Riza Shah's policies ensured that the Iranian economy remained fundamentally dependent upon the West, partly because of the weakness and over-centralization of the domestic market. In fact, his reforms benefited only a very small minority of the population. In particular, agriculture remained extremely backward; in the middle 1930s over 95 per cent of the rural population were landless share-croppers, and landlords were not inclined to invest when labour was so cheap and plentiful. Thus, while Riza Shah created much of the infrastructure of a modern state, the economic position of many, if not most, Iranians actually declined in the course of his reign. His political inclinations led him to become an enthusiastic supporter of the German Reich in the 1930s, and his pro-Nazi sympathies prompted the British and Russians to force his abdication after the entry of Allied forces into Iran in August 1941.

The Mandates

In the inter-war period, the political order established by France and Britain was widely contested in the Arab Middle East. The Mandate* regimes were highly unpopular, especially in Syria and Palestine; in Iraq, having succeeded in setting up a government which was entirely dependent on the British connection, the British felt able to make a formal withdrawal in 1932, although real independence was not obtained until 1958. In Palestine* there was mounting tension between the Arab population and the Jewish settlers, who formed 11 per cent of the population in 1922 and 29 per cent by 1936. Until the rebellion of 1936–8, the Arab leadership appeared weak and internally divided; by 1939, the British had announced that Jewish immigration would be allowed to reach a certain ceiling and must then cease, which was seen as criminally generous by the Arabs and criminally restrictive by the Zionists.

The report of the Peel Commission in July 1937 had recommended that Palestine be partitioned. This involved the absorption of Galilee into the proposed Jewish state. Jerusalem, Bethlehem and a corridor to the sea would remain under the Mandate while the rest of Palestine would be united with Transjordan (see Israel and The Arab–Israeli Problem).

In Syria and Lebanon, the French presence was welcomed by the Maronites* and the other Uniate Catholic communities, mostly in Lebanon, but by few others. Lebanon was enlarged at the expense of Syria, amid great hostility in Syria; there was a major national rising in Syria in 1925–7 in which a victory for French arms was not always quite certain. The unpopularity of the Mandate regime was evident throughout the period, although, as in Morocco, expectations were raised with the election of the Popular Front government in France in 1936, and negotiations on a treaty took place between 1936 and 1939; independence was finally granted in 1946.

PS

Further reading

P. W. Avery, *Modern Iran* (London, 1967)
P. M. Holt, *Egypt and the Fertile Crescent 1516–1922* (London, 1966)
A. Hourani, *Arabic Thought in the Liberal Age 1798–1962* (London, 1962 and reprints)
Nikki R. Keddie, *Roots of Revolution; an interpretive history of modern Iran* (New Haven, 1981)
B. Lewis, *The Emergence of Modern Turkey* (London, 2nd edn, 1968)
Magali Morsy, *North Africa 1800–1900; a survey from the Nile Valley to the Atlantic* (London, 1984)
Roger Owen, *The Middle East in the World Economy 1800–1914* (London, 1981)

Part III
SOCIETIES AND ECONOMIES

The commercial centre of Bahrain's capital, Manama, by night

Growth and development

Perhaps the best definition of the distinction between growth and development is the one quoted by Lord Acton about a hundred years ago: 'We must carefully distinguish development from mere increase; it is the acquiring, not of greater bulk, but of new forms and structures which are adapted to higher conditions of existence.' This point is echoed in a recent thoughtful article by R. A. Flammang: 'a large number of economists distinguish growth and development in terms of the degree of structural change involved. Development, in particular, is seen as involving such changes. Words like "transformation" are common in such definitions, and most stress that structural changes include social and political, as well as economic, elements. Some consider development to include growth – that is, development is structured change plus increases in output.'

A quick look at the history of Egypt, Turkey, the Fertile Crescent and Iran up to the First World War (see Modern History) shows much growth but little development. Between 1830 and 1914 their populations rose from about 20 to 45 million, foreign trade from about £10m to £130m and railway mileage from nil to 9700 km. Numerous ports had been built, the area under cultivation had been greatly extended, a rudimentary banking system had been established and the main cities had been provided with modern amenities. But except for the expansion of certain cash crops – notably cotton in Egypt, which necessitated an elaborate irrigation system – no transformation of the structure of production took place. In particular, the region's traditional handicrafts declined and were not replaced by factories, so that its economy was even more agricultural than in the past; its human resources were left untapped, as witnessed by a literacy rate of well under 10 per cent; and almost all the modern sectors of its economy were owned and run by foreigners. In addition, it had accumulated a huge foreign debt.

Apart from the spectacular development of the oil industry* and the recent large-scale indebtedness of most countries, the main feature of the region's history since then has been the attempt to transform the structure of its economy. This was greatly facilitated by the achievement of, first, political independence and then fiscal and financial autonomy through the abolition of the Capitulations* and lapse of various international commercial treaties in the inter-war period; and the severing, after the Second World War, of the links between most currencies and sterling or the franc. These measures, plus the massive nationalizations and sequestrations of the last twenty-five years, have transferred control of the economy from foreign to national hands.

Industrialization

The economic objective that has been most consistently pursued has been industrialization*, which has appealed to the governments for many reasons. It is regarded as the most dynamic sector of the economy. It is expected to provide employment for a large part of the rapidly growing urban population. It is hoped that it will reduce dependence on imports and, in particular, on outside sources of arms. No less important, it is looked upon as the main channel for introducing the modern technology the region needs so badly. Hence manufacturing and mining have received every kind of protection and encouragement and, together with energy, have been allocated some 30–40 per cent of total investment. Manufacturing output has risen correspondingly, by around 10 per cent a year in most countries, and output of electricity has multiplied many times over. The share of manufacturing in Gross Domestic Product, which in the 1950s stood at a little over 10 per cent, is now over 20 per cent in the more advanced countries. However, almost everywhere, industry is highly overmanned, non-competitive and still greatly dependent on imports of machinery, spares and raw materials.

Transport has also received much attention, and by now the region has adequate railways, roads and airports. It has also established a network of national banks, insurance companies and other institutions which, together with a few foreign establishments, meet its main credit and other financial needs.

Agriculture* has received much less attention, and has made correspondingly less progress, although it still accounts for 25–30 per cent of GDP and employs half of the population. Agrarian reforms have greatly improved the land tenure system and given the farmers greater incentive. Huge dams and canals have extended the irrigated areas, notably in Iraq and Syria. Mechanization has

Offloading goods at Jordan's port of ʿAqaba

expanded, especially in Turkey. Diversification of crops has slightly increased, and cash crops now occupy a larger share of the cultivated area. Perhaps most significant, use of fertilizers has greatly increased. But investment in agriculture is still too small and the low prices set by the governments, which wish to keep down the cost of living in the towns or increase their profit on exports of certain crops, have discouraged farmers. In few countries has food output matched population growth – much less demand – and all except Turkey have become heavy importers.

Human resources have been greatly developed. Life expectancy has doubled since 1945 – from about thirty to sixty years – literacy has risen to 50 per cent or over and there are now tens of thousands of the scientists, physicians, engineers, agronomists, statisticians, economists and other technicians needed for development. However, death rates are still high and birth rates and rates of natural increase are among the highest in the world. The Middle East ranks very low in the scale of the Physical Quality of Life Indices and most of it suffers from severe population pressure.

The level of living of the masses has risen somewhat in the last three decades, mainly because of economic growth and foreign aid and also because of measures taken by the governments to provide water, electricity, housing and social services in the urban, and to a certain extent the rural, areas. The great degree of inequality of wealth and income formerly prevailing has also been reduced, in most countries, by nationalization, sequestrations, and progressive taxation.

Lastly, an aim proclaimed by all Arab governments has been economic unification between countries. However, political differences have so far prevented effective regional integration and the scope of the Arab Common Market is still strictly limited. Several joint projects have been implemented. More important has been the economic aid – amounting to many tens of billions of dollars – extended by the oil-rich countries to others. In addition, there is the spontaneous integration effected by the movement of millions of Arab and Turkish workers to the oil countries and the flow of their remittances home – a few billion dollars each year (see Population and Migration).

In most respects the course of development in Israel has been different. That state started with a relatively large industry, a technically advanced agriculture, a good infrastructure and human resources that were much more developed than those of its neighbours. Since then there has been progress in all these fields, with the establishment of numerous high-skill industries, the introduction of new crops such as cotton and early ripening fruits and vegetables and the founding of several institutions for technological and scientific education.

Many problems remain, including some not mentioned here, such as urban hypertrophy, the burden of armaments and the stifling effects of bureaucracy. But there is no doubt that the Middle East is more developed than it was in 1914 and better adapted to present conditions of existence.

CI

Further reading

Jahangir Amuzegar and W. Ali Fekrat, *Iran: economic development under dualistic conditions* (Chicago, 1971)
Flammang, R. A. 'Economic Growth and Development: counterparts or competitors?', *Economic Development and Cultural Change*, October 1979
B. Hansen and G. A. Marzouk, *Development and Economic Policy in the UAR* (Amsterdam, 1965)
A. O. Krueger, *Foreign Trade Regimes and Economic Development: Turkey* (New York, 1974)
R. Mabro, *The Egyptian Economy, 1952–1972* (Oxford, 1974)
M. W. Thornburg et al., *Turkey: an economic appraisal* (New York, 1949)

The government as an economic factor

For nearly two centuries the economic role of the government in the Middle East has steadily expanded. In the last few years a reversal has occurred and it is possible, though improbable, that this new trend will be carried further.

Compared to European mercantilist states, the economic and social functions of the traditional Muslim (Mamluk*, Ottoman*, Safavid*) state were restricted, but a little wider than those of European medieval states. Social needs, in education, health and welfare, were met by private charity, usually by providing endowments (*waqf**) to mosques, schools, hospitals, public fountains, caravanserais, and so on. The chief economic functions of the state were to ensure law and order and to collect taxes, mainly tithes on agricultural produce and customs duties on foreign and internal trade. Other activities included the provisioning of cities with food and the raw materials needed by craftsmen, the supervision of markets, the regulation of prices and the control of guilds formed by craftsmen and traders. In Egypt, the government supervised irrigation works and in Turkey and Iran some roads of military importance were built. The minting of coins was also a public function, but Muslim states showed much less interest in maintaining the stability of the currency than did contemporary European states – for example, the Ottoman currency was steadily debased from around 1450 on, and the Iranian from not much later. In foreign trade Muslim states – moved by considerations of provisioning and revenue, not mercantilism – had a liberal import policy, subjecting goods to a light duty (3 to 5 per cent), but prohibiting or taxing certain exports. These duties became fixed through the Capitulations concluded with European powers. Hence, to raise additional revenue, the rulers increasingly granted monopolies, covering internal or external trade, to favoured subjects.

During the nineteenth century Muhammad ʿAli* (1805–48) attempted a transformation of Egypt's economy and society through rigid state ownership and control, but this failed owing to internal weaknesses and external opposition. Elsewhere, the role of the state changed significantly. On the one hand because of foreign pressure, acting through the Anglo-Turkish Commercial Treaty of 1838 and similar instruments, government control over tariffs and price-fixing was abandoned, monopolies were dismantled and markets were freed and opened to foreign activity. On the other hand, the state took on many new functions. It built much infrastructure, mainly railways, ports, irrigation works and roads. It opened many technical and general schools, it promoted such cash crops as cotton, silk and tobacco and it provided growers with improved seeds, credit and other facilities. Lastly, it built and operated a few industries. However, the bulk of economic activity was left to private enterprise, with very little government regulation or encouragement.

In the inter-war period the government's role expanded greatly. The lapse of the commercial treaties and the abolition of the Capitulations* gave the Middle Eastern states full tariff and fiscal autonomy. This was used to promote industrial and agricultural development, increase revenue and introduce new taxes, such as income tax and death duties. Central banks* were established and development banks, such as the Sumer and Eti Banks in Turkey and Misr Bank in Egypt, were founded. There was further investment in infrastructure. Lastly, the governments used their power to transfer control over large sectors of the economy from foreign to national hands.

Increasing government control

During the Second World War the government's role greatly increased, through rationing, price control, exchange control, sequestration of Axis property, and so on. In the 1950s and 60s there was a further large expansion. In the oil-producing countries this came about because of the huge increase in oil revenues, which made the government by far the greatest source of investment. The large foreign aid received by most countries had a similar effect. In others – notably Egypt, Syria, Iraq, South Yemen, Sudan and, since the revolution, Iran – there was a wave of nationalizations: the government took over banks, insurance companies and other financial institutions. It also took over almost all large-scale industry and thus came to account for 60–90 per cent of industrial output. It nationalized sea and river transport and those railway and tram systems that were still in private hands. It established full control over foreign trade. Except in Lebanon, Israel, Jordan, some of the smaller oil countries and, to a lesser extent, Turkey, private enterprise remained dominant only in agriculture (which, however, was subjected to land reform in the main countries), housing, contracting and various services. By the mid-1970s in almost all countries, government investment exceeded private, and in countries such as Egypt and South Yemen it accounted for 90 per cent of the total. Government consumption ranged from a quarter to a half of the total. Planning became universal. Naturally, the bureaucracy expanded, in Iran from 60,000 in 1940 to 500,000 in the mid-1970s and in Egypt from 240,000 to 1,250,000, with another 1,000,000 in public enterprises.

Revival of the private sector

This sudden extension of the public sector has produced many disruptions: inefficiency, misallocations, shortages, delays and corruption. Most observers believe that productivity has sharply dropped in enterprises that were nationalized and compare public enterprises unfavourably with the remaining private ones. Hence, in the last ten years or so, nationalization has stopped and some attempts have been made to revive the private sector. In Egypt*, Sadat inaugurated the *infitah* (opening up) policy which gave both foreign and private capital important concessions and established duty-free zones for industry. In Turkey, Prime Minister Ozal has vigorously sought to limit government interference and plans to sell off some state enterprises. In Syria, President Asad has looked much more favourably on private enterprise than his predecessors and has allowed the emergence in agriculture of entrepreneurs, *al-mustathmirun*, who lease small plots from beneficiaries of land reform and farm them in large units using tractors, pumps and other machinery. In both Iraq and Iran the exigencies of war have forced the government to relax its anti-capitalist measures and have

Note on *infitah*

Under Law 43 of 1974 for Arab and Foreign Investment, modified by Law 32 of 1977, approved investments, even if a public sector firm had a majority share, were considered part of the private sector and therefore exempt from the regulations laid on public sector firms. Extraterritorial enclaves were set up in the main cities; foreign capital could be moved freely to and from them, they were exempt from Egyptian taxes and could export to Egypt on payment of the usual customs duties. Foreign firms established in other parts of the country were granted tax remission and special facilities for capital movement. These laws, and other concessions, attracted a fair amount of capital to banking and tourism but relatively little to industry. Industry has been hurt by the loosening of restrictions on imports, designed to provide a greater amount of goods to consumers.

fostered a large number of private businesses in industry and trade. These measures were among the factors that raised the growth rate and produced a greater abundance of goods in Egypt, Syria and Turkey, but they also aroused strong criticism centred on increasing inequality, ostentatious consumption, rapidly rising prices and greater foreign economic penetration. Managers and workers in nationalized industries, and the government bureaucracy in general, fear both private and foreign competition. Traditional and Muslim circles resent the increasing foreign presence and the contagion of Western mores and consumption patterns. More generally, there is deep opposition to capitalism, which is seen as part of the former Western domination and present Western threat and which is believed to have exploited the region's resources for the benefit of foreigners and minority groups. Basically, profits and interest are regarded as illegitimate sources of wealth (see Islamic Banking). Government ownership, on the other hand, seems to many to be the proper instrument for carrying out the main objectives sought by the Middle Eastern peoples. These are, first, nationalism, the determination to be masters in their own house; secondly, socialism, defined as state control over the means of production, and the absence of large inequalities of wealth; thirdly, the application of the basic injunctions of Islam such as aiding the poor and avoiding ostentation. Moreover, there is no traditional awareness of the dangers of an overgrown state and of the need to fight its expansion. In these circumstances, and in the absence of a cohesive and powerful group of producers and intellectuals working for the extension of private enterprise, it seems unlikely that government control over the economy will show any significant diminution in the near future.

CI

Further reading

J. Bharier, *Economic Development in Iran* (London, 1971)
Z. Y. Hershlag, *Turkey: the challenge of growth* (Leiden, 1968)
Z. Y. Hershlag, *The Economic Structure of the Middle East* (Leiden, 1975)
C. Issawi, *The Economic History of the Middle East* (Chicago, 1966)
C. Issawi, *The Economic History of Iran* (Chicago, 1971)
C. Issawi, *The Economic History of Turkey* (Chicago, 1980)
C. Issawi, *An Economic History of the Middle East and North Africa* (New York, 1981)
C. Issawi, *The Fertile Crescent, a Documentary Economic History* (forthcoming)
R. Owen, *The Middle East in the World Economy* (London, 1981)
R. Owen, *Cotton in the Egyptian Economy* (Oxford, 1969)
Edith Penrose, *Iraq* (London, 1978)
John Waterbury, *The Egypt of Nasser and Sadat* (Princeton, 1983)

Nomads in the Algerian Sahara

The decline of nomadism

Nomadism in all its various forms has suffered rapid decline over the past 150 years. In many ways the passing of pastoral nomadism from a position of dominance to one of minor importance in this period was the most dramatic single change in the rural and political landscape of the Middle East and North Africa. Statistics are imprecise but it is estimated that on average nomads comprised 10 per cent of the population of the region in the mid-1960s, although in Afghanistan the figure was as high as 16 per cent. Twenty years later the nomads made up a mere one per cent of the regional total.

Governments, with few exceptions, were eager to enforce the settlement of their nomads, particularly in the wake of the Ottoman land codes of the mid-nineteenth century, which provided for an end to communal ownership of land as practised by the nomadic pastoralists. In Syria and Iraq during the last century, in Iran during the 1930s, and in Saudi Arabia after 1925, the state reduced the mobility and power of the pastoral nomads. Systematic detribalization was also attempted as part of the same process. In recent decades further assaults were made on the nomads to force them within the organization of the state for purposes of taxation, conscription and political control.

Economic change in the oil era was the ultimate cause of the decline of nomadism and its moral values. Oil* revenues created new forms of wealth and new opportunities for employment. Oil exploration and development gave the nomads the chance to act as labourers, drivers and guides; rapid expansion of construction as a result of oil wealth created urban employment for them; and rapidly expanding government agencies recruited nomads as policemen, guards and soldiers. Land settlement projects such as the Al-Faysal beduin scheme in Saudi Arabia* and well-drilling programmes made further incentives for nomads to settle, since permanent supplies of water enabled cultivation throughout the year and the ability to grow fodder for the families' herds. Not all sedentarization projects were successful. Nomads kept their new lands but leased them to tenant farmers, as in the Khashm al-Girba project in Sudan*. Expensively reclaimed lands were occasionally abandoned. But there were many examples of great agricultural enterprise by nomad settlers, of which the tractor farmers of the Egyptian Western Desert and the Turkoman cotton growers of the Dasht-i Gorgan area of northern Iran are instances.

Economic influences

The growing gap between the incomes of those engaged in nomadic pastoralism and those working in other areas of the economy was made dramatically wider as a consequence of rapidly rising oil revenues during the 1970s. The attraction of wages, living conditions and health facilities that were overwhelmingly better than those offered by livestock-herding ensured a decanting of all but the most determined from nomadism to sedentary life in the oil-rich states in that period.

Decline

The particular problems for nomads in North Africa in the post-colonial period were twofold. In Algeria and Libya the rapid pace of economic change stimulated by exploration for and production of oil and gas provided paid work for the nomads in and around the oilfield areas. Within a comparatively short time the economic foundations of the pastoral nomadic groups had been eroded away. Concentration of government agencies and development activity in the urban areas of the north attracted population away from the tribal territories of nomadic and semi-nomadic groups on a large scale. Improved living conditions in the southern towns led to nomadic settlement such as that by the Tuaregs in the Saharan oasis of Ghadames during the 1960s. Pastoral nomadic tribes in the better-watered areas of the Jabal al-Akhdar in Libya were affected by the gradual loss of pasture through land enclosure for arable farming. By the 1970s there were only 1372 Libyan nomadic households and 11,068 semi-nomadic families, or less than 4 per cent of total households. Economic development in both Tunisia and Morocco had similar if less dramatic effects.

Secondly, hand-in-hand with the growing economic attractions of urban employment, the problems of desertification on the desert peripheries made survival for pastoralists increasingly difficult. Persistent drought through the 1970s and 1980s reduced livestock numbers universally through the North African Saharan fringe and accelerated the already high rate of losses among the nomadic communities as families were unable to survive on the output of their much diminished herds.

In Saudi Arabia those who stayed in the nomadic herding economy were faced with a new difficulty, that of deterioration of rangeland. Livestock was concentrated near government-provided wells, around which pasture was overgrazed, leading to a rapid fall in its carrying capacity. New and augmented consumer demand for livestock products was answered in many cases by imports. Lamb and mutton were substituted for camel meat, depriving nomadic camel-herders in Saudi Arabia, especially, of their market. Elsewhere, locally raised sheep were in considerable demand, and herders with fatstock made a good living providing animals for feast days, albeit not on a scale adequate to save the nomadic way of life. The pattern established in the oil-exporting states was adopted by their neighbours. Only Afghanistan*, and to an extent Sudan, remained aloof from this process.

The universal decline in nomadism from the beduin heartland of the Arabian peninsula to the Tuareg* areas of southern Algeria created two quite separate crises. First, the great virtue of the nomads was their ability to make use of lands deep in the desert or high in the mountains that were of no value to arable farmers. Even where nomadism survived those economic and political pressures aligned against it, the more distant and difficult regions were abandoned, leaving vast areas unused and politically vulnerable to external encroachments. Second, tribal populations of nomadic pastoralists were among the mainsprings of cultural and religious strength throughout the Middle East and North Africa. Elimination or weakening of these important roots resulted in a serious deterioration in the artistic, moral and linguistic traditions of the Turkish, Persian and Arab communities, though most notably among the last, since they were affected in so concentrated a period of economic and social revolution – 1950 to the present day.

KM

Further reading

J. A. Allan, K. S. McLachlan, and E. T. Penrose, *Libya* (London, 1968)
Fredrik Barth, *Nomads of South Persia* (London, 1964)
J. I. Clarke and W. B. Fisher, *Populations of the Middle East and North Africa* (London, 1972)
Government of Libya, *Statistical Yearbook* (Tripoli, 1978)
D. L. Johnson, *The Nature of Nomadism* (Chicago, 1969)
Shirley Kay, *The Beduin* (Newton Abbot, 1978)
Richard Tapper, ed., *The Conflict of Tribe and State in Iran and Afghanistan* (London, 1983)
Wilfred Thesiger, *Arabian Sands* (Harmondsworth, 1965)

Agricultural change

The agricultural scene in the Middle East today encompasses an enormous variety of farming systems and methods, ranging from subsistence farming little changed for millennia to some of the most technologically advanced techniques in use anywhere in the world. In the Tihama coastal plain of North Yemen*, for example, traditional wadi agriculture exists only a few kilometres from a large mechanized Soviet-style state farm in one direction and from new private estates using modern Western machinery and bio-technology in the other.

Agricultural change in the Middle East gathered momentum in the 1950s, and was given a major stimulus by the surge of oil wealth in the 1970s, which had repercussions on economies throughout the region. There have been large increases in agricultural production: cereal production, for example, grew from 25.2m tonnes in the early 1950s to 59.2m tonnes in 1982. The use of inputs such as machinery, fertilizer and improved seeds has pushed up yields and helped extend the cultivated area.

The oil states in particular have seen some dramatic agricultural achievements in recent years, notably Saudi Arabia's attainment of self-sufficiency in wheat. Yet, despite the apparent progress in the past three decades, there is growing anxiety in the region over agricultural performance, and planners are placing increased emphasis on this sector. Many countries had previously seen industry as the key to rapid economic development, and had directed the main thrust of their development effort accordingly. But the process of industrialization has been fraught with difficulties, and the results have seldom lived up to expectations.

At the same time, concern has grown in the Middle East over the enormous growth in the region's feed imports, which have made it the part of the world with the most rapidly increasing food deficit. The Gulf countries have perhaps been the most vocal in lamenting the region's lack of food security. But it is some of the poorer countries, such as Morocco, Tunisia, Egypt and Sudan, that have seen popular discontent over food policies, in particular prices, erupt into riots that have taken on a wider political dimension. In addition, governments have become alarmed at the constant exodus of people from rural areas to the slum belts of already overcrowded cities such as Cairo, Tehran and Casablanca, where they may become alienated, hopeless and politically volatile.

Investment in agriculture

Throughout the Middle East, government officials now at least pay lip-service to the need to revitalize the agricultural sector. Since 1984, the Arab Fund for Economic and Social Development (AFESD) has channelled half its lending into agriculture, and government development plans allocate increased resources to agriculture. In this, the Middle East is following the general trend in development thinking – the World Bank, for example, has in the past few years stressed the link between a country's agricultural development and its overall growth. The famine in Sudan in 1985 served as a warning that even a country with great agricultural potential can be plunged into disaster when years of bad management and weak planning are followed by adverse climatic conditions. Some voices warn that unless decisive measures are taken to deal with the weaknesses of Middle Eastern agriculture, the tragedy of Sudan could be repeated in other parts of the region before the end of the century.

Combine harvesters threshing wheat in Saudi Arabia

Despite the processes of industrialization* and urbanization*, a significant proportion of the labour force in the Middle East is still employed in agriculture, although in most countries the proportion has declined significantly since 1965. In 1981, agriculture employed four-fifths of the Afghan and three-quarters of the North Yemeni labour force. Around half the labour force in Egypt*, Morocco* and Turkey*, 40 per cent in Iran and Iraq and a third in Syria and Tunisia were to be found in agriculture. Even in Saudi Arabia*, 61 per cent of the labour force was classified as working in agriculture.

But agriculture's contribution to GDP has been much smaller than its role as an employer, and the agricultural efficiency ratio– that is the ratio of agriculture's contribution to GDP to its share of the labour force – is low. In 1981, it was 0.71 in Israel*, 0.58 in Syria*, 0.42 in Egypt, 0.43 in Turkey and 0.27 in Morocco.

Some countries did manage to achieve significant increases in agricultural growth in the 1970s, notably Syria, where agriculture grew by 8.2 per cent a year in 1973–83 compared with a decline of 0.7 per cent in 1965–73. But only a handful of countries, including

Iran*, Turkey, Syria, Jordan* and Iraq*, increased food production per capita between the mid-1970s and early 1980s, and there was a decrease in Egypt, North Yemen, Tunisia*, Israel, Algeria and Morocco.

In the 1970s, Egypt, Morocco, Iraq and Syria changed from being net exporters of grain to being net importers, and only Turkey was able to switch from being an importer to an exporter. Middle East food imports jumped from $1700m in 1970 to $27,000m in 1984, and by 1980 Egypt was importing 40–45 per cent of its food needs, Jordan more than 50 per cent and Saudi Arabia 75 per cent. One reason for the rapid growth in food imports was the growth in population, with some Middle Eastern countries having population growth rates which are among the highest in the world. In the oil states, the influx of huge numbers of foreign workers further pushed up demand (see Population and Migration) and introduced new types of food into the region. As incomes have risen, tastes have shifted away from traditional cereal and vegetable-based diets (which tend to be seen as the food of the poor) towards relative luxuries such as meat, eggs, butter, poultry and milk. The rapidly swelling demand for livestock-related products has triggered a rise in imports of coarse grains – barley and sorghum – used for animal feed. The heavy subsidies on food in many Middle Eastern countries have also encouraged consumption and sometimes waste: in Egypt, subsidized loaves are used to wipe tables or as animal feed.

Environmental problems

Agriculture in the Middle East operates within serious environmental constraints. Rainfed farming requires a minimum of 200 mm of rainfall a year, appropriately distributed. Only Lebanon* and Turkey receive this minimum over their total surface areas. Even within those areas of the Middle East where rainfed farming is theoretically possible, a large part of the terrain may be unsuitable for cultivation. In an effort to lessen their dependence on rainfall and the wild fluctuations in production between years of high and low precipitation, governments have introduced irrigation schemes using surface and groundwater. Many of these schemes have run into serious difficulties, however, including increases in salinity, the depletion of aquifers and poor maintenance of structures.

There is now a renewal of interest in areas of low (200–300 mm) and medium (300–400 mm) rainfall, which cover about 60 per cent of the cultivable land in the Middle East. In the past, these areas had been neglected in favour of prestige projects in high-rainfall and irrigated areas. At the International Centre for Agricultural Research in the Dry Areas (Icarda) in Aleppo, researchers are looking at ways of making the delicately balanced barley–livestock system in areas of low rainfall less vulnerable to drought. Such work is seen as vital in trying to prevent soil degradation, desertification and the abandonment of large areas.

Some countries are suffering from agricultural labour shortages as a result of migration to the cities or abroad, often to the oil states. In North Yemen, migration to Saudi Arabia has contributed to the loss of terraces in the highlands, and to steep rises in labour costs. Mechanization is being encouraged and the role of women in agriculture is at last being given due recognition. Some countries are now using foreign workers to fill agricultural labour shortages. Moroccans, Egyptians and Sudanese are working in Iraq, Egyptians and Pakistanis in Jordan and a variety of nationalities in Libya.

The land tenure* system in a number of countries is seen as an obstacle to agricultural development. In Morocco, 75 per cent of farming families hold five hectares or less, and own 25 per cent of agricultural land. In some countries, tenant farmers resist paying for improved inputs when they know they will be obliged to share the increased production with their landlords. The widespread fragmentation of holdings also creates difficulties in, for example, introducing mechanization. Nor has land reform generally had the desired effect. In some cases the reform has been half-hearted, and the powerful landowners have been able to regain their former position. In others, private farmers have been discouraged from cultivation and have left the land.

Much criticism has been levelled at government policies towards agriculture. In their eagerness to quell potential discontent in urban areas, governments have discriminated against the relatively less powerful rural areas. Price policies, and paying farmers less than international prices, discriminate against the rural sector. But the question of food subsidies is extremely sensitive, and on several occasions in recent years governments in the Middle East have been forced by popular reaction to rescind increases in the price of basic foods.

Research

Some agricultural experts argue that the Middle East achieved its major increases in yields in the 1970s, and that no spectacular breakthroughs can be expected in the future, certainly not a Green Revolution. But scientists at Icarda and other research institutions claim to have some of the answers to the region's food-production problems, if governments are ready to take notice. Icarda is working on the region's basic food crops – barley, wheat, faba beans, chickpeas, lentils and forage – to find seeds and techniques that will improve yields and provide stability of production, so that years of poor rainfall need not lead to total crop failure.

In 1985 two new research bodies were formed – the Rainfed Agriculture Information Network (Rain) and the Association of Agricultural Research Institutions in the Near East and North Africa (Aarinena). It is hoped that, rather than being mere talking shops, these two bodies will have an influence on the ground. If the fruits of research are to make their maximum impact in the field, the

Middle East's extension services will have to be greatly improved. Extension workers play an important role in conveying improved seeds, and new practices to farmers, yet they have a lowly status and are poorly paid. Extension services tend to be starved of funds and are rarely provided with sufficient vehicles and other necessities.

Even under optimal conditions, few countries in the Middle East could expect to become self-sufficient in food. Some analysts argue that this does not really matter; what is important is that a country has food security, rather than being self-sufficient, and this could be attained through assured food imports. But governments hardly relish the thought of ever-growing food import bills, and although the battle between major grain exporters such as the US and Europe for Middle East markets may lead to cheaper grain imports, this could in turn further discourage domestic production. It has been estimated that from 269m in 1983, the population of the Middle East will rise to 421m by 2000. Middle Eastern agriculture faces a major challenge if food production is to keep pace with population growth, let alone enable a higher degree of self-sufficiency to be realized.

ST

Further reading

P. Beaumont and K. McLachlan, eds., *Agricultural Development in the Middle East* (London, 1985)
J. I. Clarke and H. Bowen-Jones, eds., *Change and Development in the Middle East* (London, 1981)
M. G. Weinbaum, *Food, Development, and Politics in the Middle East* (London, 1982)

Irrigation

Irrigation in the Middle East is as old as civilization itself. The region's two great river systems, the Nile and the Euphrates–Tigris, sustained well-organized and relatively advanced networks of irrigation over thousands of years. The Ma'rib Dam in Yemen*, first built in around 1000 BC, played a vital part in generating Yemen's ancient wealth. The ingenious systems of underground canals known as *qanawat* (sing. *qanat*) or *aflaj* (sing. *falaj*) were developed long ago to tap underground water sources in several countries, including Iran*, Afghanistan*, the United Arab Emirates (UAE)* and Oman*, and are still in use today.

The modern development of irrigation in the Middle East attempts both to improve and in some cases rehabilitate systems in the region's traditional irrigated areas, and to extend irrigation to new areas. In some cases, modernization basically consists of updating the farmers' traditional methods: this is the case in the wadis of North Yemen*. In others, entirely new technology has been introduced. Of the 100m hectares of arable and permanent cropped land in the Middle East in 1981, only 17.4 per cent was irrigated. But irrigation plays a role out of all proportion to this relatively modest percentage, and some 60 per cent of the region's food production comes from irrigated areas.

Irrigation reduces dramatically the risk of crop failure, and allows yields sometimes three times as high as those in rainfed areas. It also permits cropping intensity to be increased to two or three crops a year. There is tremendous variation in the degree to which countries in the Middle East depend on irrigation for agriculture. Of the 17.4m hectares of irrigated land in the Middle East in 1981, Iran had by far the greatest amount with 5.9m hectares, and with 37 per cent of its cultivated land irrigated. Egypt, with 2.9m hectares, depended totally on irrigation for agriculture, as did Kuwait*. Turkey* had 2.1m hectares of irrigated land, Sudan* had 1.9m and Iraq* 1.8m, accounting for 7.3, 14.9 and 32.1 per cent of arable land respectively.

The Kenana irrigation canal, Sudan

Since 1960, the total irrigated area in the Middle East has increased by about 37 per cent. Whereas the traditional areas of irrigation contain fertile alluvial soils, the recent expansion has often been onto sandy and highly calcareous soils. Egypt experienced considerable difficulties in irrigating sandy soils, but in the past decade much progress has been made in various countries in matching such soils to appropriate technology. The major source of water for irrigation in the region are surface water and groundwater. Because of the high cost of production, desalinated water has found only limited application in agriculture in the Gulf states. Treated sewage effluent seems to have much potential as an irrigation medium, however, and is being used increasingly in the Gulf. There has for some years been talk of transporting water for irrigation to the Gulf or Libya* in oil tankers, but despite a number of academic studies and conferences on the feasibility of the idea, it has yet to find an application.

In the past twenty-five years there has been much development of irrigation associated with the region's rivers, whether the dominant Nile and Euphrates–Tigris systems, or smaller rivers such as the Orontes in Syria*, and the Jordan* (whose exploitation for irrigation has caused much friction between Israel and Jordan over the years).

Egypt's High Dam

The controversy over the High Dam at Aswan* in Egypt, the construction of which was completed in 1968, is likely to continue for years to come. The dam's planned benefits included expanding the cultivated area by 1.2m feddans, converting 850,000 feddans from basin to perennial irrigation, allowing multiple cropping and the cultivation of different crops, and generating 10bn kWh of electricity. These benefits must be set against a number of undesirable effects however, including the loss of a large amount of water through evaporation from Lake Nasser, the trapping of silt which formerly fertilized the Nile Valley and delta, the increasing salinity of the water, the erosion of the coastline, an upset in the ecology of the eastern Mediterranean and an increase in bilharzia and malaria. It is also feared the dam may be vulnerable to earthquakes. Neither have the expected benefits materialized to the extent planned.

Sudan's Gezira project

In 1959 Sudan* and Egypt* signed an agreement on the use of the waters of the Nile, which allocated Sudan 18,500m cubic metres a year, and Egypt 55,500m cubic metres. The general malaise that afflicted the Sudanese economy for some years before the overthrow of Nimeiri* in 1985 did not spare the country's irrigation schemes – indeed, shortly after the president's overthrow the country's engineers presented a petition to the new government demanding that the Gezira rehabilitation project be suspended.

Gezira is the country's most important irrigation scheme, producing export crops such as cotton, groundnuts and sorghum. After a drastic fall in yields in the 1970s, a rehabilitation scheme backed by the World Bank was introduced. But the engineers argued that by concentrating on repairing machinery, clearing canals and improving irrigation systems, the project ignored the fact that the level of the Blue Nile has been falling in recent years. The engineers wanted the storage capacity at the Sennar and Roseires Dams to be increased, and criticized the water-sharing agreement with Egypt for failing to recognize Sudan's needs. There was concern in Egypt over the sharing of the waters in the aftermath of the 1985 coup in Sudan, and the case of the Nile highlights an increasingly important factor in Middle Eastern river-based irrigation projects – the need for riparian states to reach an accord on water use.

Projects for the Euphrates

In the mid-1970s, following the building of the dam at Tabqa in Syria, there was a crisis between Syria* and Iraq over the sharing of the waters of the Euphrates. With the three Euphrates riparian states – Turkey, Syria and Iraq – carrying out major irrigation schemes using the river's waters, an agreement on allocation is needed if future disagreements are to be avoided. Turkey's Keban Dam on the Euphrates was completed in 1983, and Syria has expressed nervousness in recent years over the likely effects of the Atatürk Dam being built on the Euphrates in south-east Turkey. Due to be completed in 1993, the dam will irrigate 726,000 hectares and will feed the longest irrigation system in the world.

Syria has pinned much of its hope for future economic development on its Euphrates irrigation scheme, which is intended to irrigate 640,000 hectares. Work has been progressing much more slowly than planned, and by 1981 only 60,000 hectares had been irrigated by the Tabqa project. Gypsum deposits in the soil have caused technical diffculties involving the collapse of canals, and these have greatly increased the cost of the project.

Iraq has embarked on a programme to build a number of giant dams, with the Saddam (Mosul) Dam on the Tigris and the Qadisiyya (Haditha) Dam on the Euphrates due to be completed in 1986. Three more large dams are planned for the Tigris. Waterlogging and salinity have bedevilled Iraq's irrigation scheme, and a 300-km main outfall drain nicknamed 'the third river' has been built to collect saline water from a number of large irrigation projects.

In some countries in the region with no permanent rivers, seasonal floods in the wadis are an important source of surface water. In the western Tihama coastal plain of North Yemen, farmers have traditionally used materials such as stones, tree trunks, brush and sand to construct deflectors and barrages, so as to divert spring and summer floods which rush from the highlands towards the Red Sea, using the water in spate irrigation. The area's seven major wadis are now being developed in turn, with the installation of permanent diversion structures and a network of canals.

In the east of Yemen, the UAE president Shaykh Zayid laid the foundation stone for the new Ma'rib Dam in October 1984. This will harness the waters of Wadi Dhana to irrigate initially 10,000 and later 20,000 hectares, and is a project of considerable emotive significance given the historical associations. Groundwater occurs either in shallow alluvial aquifers which are constantly recharged or in deeper aquifers containing 'fossil' water* many thousands of years old. Libya*, Saudi Arabia* and Egypt have enormous deep aquifer systems, and Libya and Saudi Arabia have spent large sums in the past decade on irrigation systems using their water. Libya's ambitious centre-pivot schemes in its southern desert have not been a great success, however, and the government subsequently decided to transport the aquifer water from the desert to the coast in the vast Great Man-made River project.

There has been much debate about the wisdom of countries 'mining' their fossil water, and disagreement over whether recharge of aquifers occurs and, if so, how quickly. In the latter part of the 1970s and early 1980s, Saudi Arabia imported large numbers of centre-pivot irrigation systems to tap its aquifers. The government has since admitted that agricultural water used in the third plan (1980–5) was four times the planned level. As a result of excessive water use, the water table has fallen markedly in some areas. In fact, the introduction of electric and diesel water pumps has led to a fall in the water table throughout the region in recent years. When this occurs in coastal areas, it can lead to the intrusion of sea water into the aquifer, as has happened in Libya and some Gulf states.

Irrigation methods

Several methods of applying irrigation water are used in the Middle East. The oldest system is basin irrigation, in which water is flooded onto the fields, and held in by field bunds. This method can be developed into furrow irrigation, although in this case land must be levelled, which can be expensive. One problem with basin irrigation is the uneven distribution of water, which tends to lead to overwatering.

It is often claimed that sprinkler irrigation is the most efficient method for the Middle East, particularly on light sandy soils. The reasons why it has not been more widely adopted include the high capital cost and the need for constant maintenance. Sprinkler systems include centre-pivots rotating arms capable of irrigating up to 100 hectares, and travelling irrigators bearing rain-guns or conventional sprinklers. Rain-guns can be very bad for desert soils, however, causing erosion and carrying away fine seeds. One drawback of sprinkler systems is their relatively high evaporation rates.

Trickle or drip irrigation was pioneered in forestry projects in Abu Dhabi in the 1970s. It is a very precise method, delivering water to individual plants through emitters inserted into plastic tubes. The method is suited to large-spaced trees such as citrus or avocado, or row crops, rather than to grain or fodder crops. Fertilizers may be added to the water, and are thereby distributed very efficiently. As water is supplied only to the plants, weed growth is not a problem. But the capital costs are high, and the emitters are easily blocked by particles of sand, chemical deposits or algae. Drip irrigation has been extensively used in the Jordan Valley* in vegetable production, but it probably accounts for only one per cent of irrigated land in the Middle East as a whole. Its use will probably increase, however, as treated sewage effluent schemes become more widespread. Special precautions must be taken in using treated waste water because of the risks associated with disease-carrying organisms, and drip irrigation is safer in this respect than sprinklers.

In Kuwait and Abu Dhabi, in particular, there has been research into the use of new hydroponic techniques. In the nutrient film method, roots are placed in plastic troughs without soil, with a thin film of nutrient trickling down the channel.

In the next few years, there is likely to be increasing emphasis on rehabilitating existing irrigation schemes, and on ensuring that operations and maintenance are fully taken into account in designing new projects. One particularly serious problem in irrigation schemes in a number of countries is salinity, often combined with waterlogging. Iraq has been particularly badly affected, with large areas abandoned as a result. Efforts are being made to counteract this difficulty, and to ensure that future irrigation schemes are properly equipped with drainage systems.

ST

Further reading

P. Beaumont and K. McLachlan, eds., *Agricultural Development in the Middle East* (London, 1985)
H. Bowen-Jones and R. Dutten, *Agriculture in the Arabian Peninsula*. The Economist Intelligence Unit Special Report No. 145 (London, 1983)
J. I. Clarke and H. Bowen-Jones, eds., *Change and Development in the Middle East* (London, 1981)
R. G. Khouri, *The Jordan Valley, Life and society below sea level* (London and New York, 1981)
T. Naff and R. C. Matson, eds., *Water in the Middle East, Conflict or Cooperation?* (London, 1984)

Desalination

A major problem that faces Middle Eastern and North African states is access to sufficient water for domestic, industrial and agricultural use. Although major river systems do exist – the Euphrates–Tigris system, the Nile with a catchment area covering one tenth of the continent of Africa, the rivers of the Levant and those in North Africa – much of the region lies outside their scope. Rainfall is also a major problem, since much of the area is classified as arid or semi-arid, receiving less than 150 mm of rainfall per year. Only the Levant littoral, Turkey, the uplands of North Yemen and the coastal regions of North Africa receive adequate rainfall for efficient agriculture, quite apart from domestic and industrial needs.

The problem is worsened by the rapid population* growth rates in the region and the ever-increasing rate of urban drift which has led to serious pressure on urban water supply. Industrialization*, particularly when it has involved heavy industry, has made further demands on available water resources. In Saudi Arabia, for example, urban and industrial water use rose from 502m m^3 in 1979 to 823m m^3 in 1985 and was expected to rise to 2279m m^3 in 2000; while agricultural and rural use only rose from 1859m m^3 in 1979 to 1901m m^3 in 1985, although new agricultural schemes are to raise this to 3258m m^3 by 2000.

However, if large areas of the Middle East do not have access to adequate rainfall or groundwater resources, as is particularly the case in the Arabian peninsula and in Libya, only two other possibilities exist. One is the use of subterranean fossil water that may or may not be recharged by rainfall. This has been used, both in Saudi Arabia and in Libya and to a lesser extent through the *qanat* or *falaj* traditionally in use in Iran, Oman and Morocco. However, modern methods of extraction can easily endanger what is, in effect, a fragile resource. Either the water table sinks or water raised proves to be saline and brackish. The alternative is to use a desalination system, whereby contaminated water is purified to make it potable or useable for agricultural purposes.

The Dubai Aluminium Company's desalination plant

Desalination has proved particularly appropriate in areas close to the coast, where sea water provides an inexhaustible supply. It has also been used for aquifer sources which are too saline for normal use without purification. It has been calculated that if only 5 per cent of the world's desert coastlines – 1500 km in length – were provided with desalinated water for agricultural and potable purposes to a depth from the coast of only 32 km, sufficient food could be provided for one billion people. The limiting factor – apart from indigenous technological skills with intensive irrigation systems – is cost, for desalination is usually a highly costly way of producing water. In 1964, for example, a desalination plant delivering one million gallons of desalinated water per day was estimated to operate at a cost of \$0.33 per m^3; although this cost had fallen to \$0.07 per m^3 by 1974, largely as a result of economies of scale, for modern plants are far larger. External energy costs have limited this reduction in recent years.

The cost arises from the fact that all systems of desalination require considerable energy input, usually as heat, and unless such energy is available as a byproduct of other processes the energy cost is inevitably a limiting factor on the applicability of such techniques. This has meant first of all, that the states that have considered large-scale desalination systems have all been oil-rich states – Saudi Arabia, the Gulf states and Libya – and secondly that such systems have either been built in conjunction with thermal power stations (to use the waste energy) or have made use of flared waste natural gas.

The typical large-scale desalination plants constructed during the 1970s were distillation plants, usually using multi-stage flash distillation techniques. Other systems used vapour compression technology or freezing processes. In Sudan, where waste energy was extremely sparse, solar distillation systems have been tried with considerable success – although that country's severe economic problems at the end of the 1970s and in the early 1980s have restricted development.

Two other approaches have now been developed to reduce costs – the generation of cheap energy through nuclear power and the development of reverse osmosis purification systems, whereby pure water from contaminated water is forced through an osmotic membrane under pressure. An alternative membrane process is electro-analysis. Both systems have the advantage that energy input is low and thus production costs are also low. However, osmotic systems do not produce water as pure as distillation systems – typically 500 parts per million of dissolved salts as against 100 parts per million.

Despite the costs, desalinated water production is undoubtedly going to play a significant role in the Arabian peninsula in years to come. In Saudi Arabia, for example, desalinated water production has grown from 63m m^3 out of total water provision of 4658m m^3 in 1979 to 605m m^3 out of total provision of 5340m m^3, in 1985, and is expected to grow to 1198m m^3 out of a total of 6523m m^3 in the year 2000 – a 1900 per cent increase in twenty years, compared with only a 140 per cent increase as far as total water provision is concerned over the same period.

Kuwait depends on desalination for urban and industrial supply, generating 169.5m m^3 in 1980. The UAE in 1980 generated 2m m^3 out of total need of 362m m^3, while additional desalination capacity is to be provided at the Tawila power plant. In Bahrain, desalination provided 35.6m gallons per day (60.5m m^3 per year) in 1985, out of a total requirement of 53m gallons per day (88m m^3 per year). Of this total, 10m gallons per day come from reverse osmosis. In the case of Qatar, desalination in 1985 provided most of the industrial and urban water supply, at 59.5m gallons per day (98.7m m^3 per year), a figure which will rise to 159.5m gallons per day by the early 1990s. In 1986, Oman generated 24m gallons per day (39.8m m^3 per year) for the capital. Libya, which was expected to invest heavily in desalination, has instead chosen to exploit its fossil water reserves through the Great Man-made River Project. Despite this, in the Gulf at least, desalination will continue to be a vital component of demographic, industrial and agricultural survival for the long-term future of the region.

GJ

The growth of modern industry

Since achieving independence, virtually every country in the Middle East and North Africa has ensured that the development of a modern industrial centre should play a major role in its economic planning. This decision has been imposed upon these countries both by the pressure of demographic growth and by a conscious preference for industrial development over development in other sectors of their economies. Rapid demographic growth, a consideration that has dominated all Middle Eastern and North African countries over the past four decades, has brought with it its seemingly inevitable concomitant, urbanization, thus creating an employment demand which, in theory, industrialization* should satisfy. Meanwhile, a preference for industrial development has, in many cases, been engendered by a desire for national economic autarky and a belief in the developmental efficacy of import substitution.

The Union Cement Company at Ra's al-Khayma, UAE

At the same time, the underlying natures of the economies of the Middle East and North Africa have played a significant role in determining patterns of industrialization. The oil producers of the Gulf, together with Libya* and Algeria*, have sought to capitalize on their valuable hydrocarbon assets – particularly since 1973 – to develop export oriented refining and petrochemical industries. The non-oil-producers, or those with only limited amounts of oil, such as Syria*, Egypt* and Tunisia*, have been forced into a greater degree of diversification in industrial development. Iran* and Iraq* fall into a separate category. Both countries had, early on, aimed for considerable industrial diversification, given their relatively large resource bases and population levels. Now, however, they have been forced by the pressures of the Gulf War and rising oil prices in the late 1970s into petroleum-dependent development. Even though the war has adversely affected industrial development in both countries, it is evident that, once hostilities subside, it will be the petroleum sector that will dominate and that diversification will lose much of its significance – except as a political catchword.

Basic development amongst non-oil-producers has emphasized industrialization designed to process national resources – agricultural products, textiles and leather or minerals. Morocco*, for example, the third largest producer of phosphate in the world, generates around 20m tons of phosphate rock each year, much of which is processed into phosphoric acid or fertilizer. Tunisia produces olive oil in large quantities. Oman* has developed a copper-processing industry based on local resources, while Turkey* has a highly productive agricultural sector. Turkey in this context is an interesting case, since it is virtually the only Middle Eastern state to have developed a relatively diversified industrial sector.

Indeed, this concentration on indigenous resources underlines a further aspect of industrialization in the region – one that is common both to oil-producers and non-oil-producers. All are concerned over their ability to earn foreign exchange and increasingly look to their industrial sectors to help in this respect. Initially, exports reflect a natural resource base of agricultural products and minerals – oil for the oil-producers, vegetables and citrus for Morocco*, Tunisia and Jordan* (as well as phosphate ores in varying quantities), potatoes and oil for Egypt, hides and dates for Iraq, pistachio nuts for Iran. Early industrial activity also tends to reflect such resources – fruit juices, preserves, olive oil, phosphate-based fertilizers and phosphoric acid – but soon moves into labour-intensive production, such as textiles (an area that has become particularly important in North Africa as a result of the growing European market, although Iran's carpet industry is also significant). Then come consumer durable assembly and industrial servicing, such as automobile repair and maintenance.

Export markets tend to reflect colonial economic patterns, just as the pattern of industrialization reflects a prior European and Middle Eastern experience. Egypt, after all, founded its initial industrialization programme in the 1830s. It was based on textile production from cotton which had been introduced as an industrial crop – an example that was toyed with, but never taken up, by the then Qaramanli ruler of Tripolitania, Yusuf Pasha. The wealth thus created was used to support Muhammad ʿAli's* military ambitions – while the army itself engendered further demand for industrialization. Tunisia followed this example in the 1840s, while the Ottoman Empire* embarked on a much more elaborate industrialization campaign in the 1870s. In all cases, the inspiration for industrialization came from the European example as exemplified in Britain and, later, in France and Germany – largely as a move to prevent imperialist encroachment into the area – and in all cases it led to financial ruin as economies ill-suited to the process of capital formation collapsed under the weight of industrialization programmes designed primarily to meet military ends.

In the colonial period industrialization began again – only this time along patterns designed to satisfy European demand for cheap produce either in the metropolitan countries or for settler populations in the colonies created in the region, particularly in North Africa. Inevitably, such industries reflected the natural resource bases and thus concentrated on the processing of agricultural and mineral materials. Only in Turkey – as a result of the étatist policies introduced by Kemal Atatürk* after the First World War – was a more balanced industrialization programme undertaken, creating the elements of primary and secondary, as well as consumer, industry. Iran*, too, under the Pahlavi dynasty, attempted a similar pattern of development but with little success. The Second World War provided a further spur to industrialization, particularly in Egypt, the Levant and Iran, where the Allied armies required local industrial facilities as part of their logistical base. Immediately after the war, an attempt was made to industrialize in the hope of prolonging the colonial presence, as occurred in Algeria, with the Constantine Plan of the early 1950s.

Post-independence development

With the advent of independence, however, new national governments seized on the opportunity to reform and rationalize their nascent industrial sectors, bringing in light industry and developing the construction sector to substitute for imports in satisfying local consumer demand, then moving on to assembly industries for consumer durables and, in a few cases, expanding into heavy industry, usually iron and steel production – as in Egypt, Algeria, Tunisia and Iran. The problem has been a lack of continuing capital investment in such developments and this has meant that the desire for import substitution has been buttressed by a growing realization that foreign currency to provide the necessary investment can only be earned through exports – in which industry must play a growing role, because of the added value it imparts to those materials that it processes.

Europe is still an absolutely crucial market for the majority of Near Eastern and Maghribi states. Not only does it take primary produce but it also provides the only viable destination for industrial goods. Furthermore, it is the essential source for the capital goods needed for development. Thus, erstwhile colonies and colonizers are bound together in an ever-closer embrace – which no amount of rhetoric over the opportunities and obligations of the Third World can alter – in which primary commodity exports and consumer industrial goods earn the foreign exchange to pay for the essential capital equipment which enables the industrialization process to continue.

Israeli industry has developed along a somewhat different path. Before independence, industry was largely devoted to satisfying internal demand and was segregated according to the confessional divide. Since 1948, however, industry has developed within the economy and now represents around 29 per cent of GDP – whereas the average within the Arab world is between 8 and 14 per cent. The main emphasis has been on the creation of export orientated industry directed towards European and US markets; three main sectors have been developed – food processing, light engineering and consumer durables, and high technology. One particular specialization has been arms production as a result of the continuing state of hostilities between Israel and its Arab neighbours. Israel exports small arms and has also begun the production of heavy arms such as tanks. The latest development has been the production of fighter aircraft – partly through access to US technology.

One striking aspect of Israeli industry – and one that sets it apart from the industry of the Arab world – is that, in addition to the state and private sectors, there is a trade union* controlled sector. The trade union federation, the Histadrut, controls much of the large-scale industrial development and the construction sector through a holding company, Hevrat Ovdim. It is also engaged in partnership arrangements with private investors. A further peculiarity is that much of the food-processing sector is controlled by agricultural cooperatives – the *kibbutzim*. It should also be noted that the high general levels of education and skills amongst the Israeli population, together with the access to cheap labour reserves in the occupied territories since 1973, has aided industrial development and unit costs.

Israeli industry has also made great efforts to gain access to modern technology through link-ups with foreign companies in Europe and the USA. This has been stimulated, particularly in the high-technology sector, by preferential access to the US market, where Israel now has a free trade agreement. Several Israeli companies are also quoted on the US stock exchanges and are increasingly concentrating their activities there. Other companies, particularly in the construction sector, have looked for contracts in the Third World in recent years. Here the increasing improvement in the diplomatic climate, particularly in Africa, has stimulated such developments. However, Israeli industry also depends on its access to investment through a relatively highly developed financial sector – a feature which is only now becoming available in the Arab world.

A crucial factor generally throughout the Middle East has been access to foreign investment for development, particularly when indigenous investment sources are inadequate. This has been especially important for non-oil producers and for states where there are few alternative primary products to generate export revenue. Indeed, apart from oil and agricultural produce, the Middle East and North Africa are regions deficient in raw materials. The only other significant raw material is phosphate. The problem has often been, however, that such investment is difficult to obtain, unless, like Israel, there is a political imperative to stimulate it. Furthermore, indigenous technical capacity is also often inadequate, despite the massive educational programmes that have been undertaken in every Middle Eastern country since independence, and this has restricted industrial development.

Effect of oil prices

Amongst major oil producers (see The Oil Industry), the pattern of industrial development has been somewhat different. Here the interest of European and US based multinational oil companies, from the 1920s in Iraq and Iran and in the late 1930s in the Gulf, as well as during the 1950s and 1960s in North Africa, has meant an initial concentration on petroleum exploration and extraction – a trend that continued until the oil majors lost control of Middle Eastern and North African oil industries in the mid-1970s. As oil prices and national revenues rose after 1975, however, many oil-producing states decided to capitalize on this natural hydrocarbon asset by improving their financial returns through processing. As a result, countries such as Iraq, Saudi Arabia*, some of the smaller Gulf states (notably Kuwait*), Algeria and Libya constructed oil refineries designed solely for export to Europe, the USA and particularly the growing markets in the Far East. In addition, certain countries began to construct petrochemical plants – Iran, Saudi Arabia, Iraq, the Gulf states – designed generally to produce 'building block' petrochemicals. Libya took a similar path. Kuwait, however, also branched out in another direction by buying into petroleum processing plant and distribution networks in Europe and the USA during the early 1980s, thus creating the first truly vertically integrated petroleum industry in the Middle East. The new petrochemical plant has begun to come onstream during the mid-1980s, unfortunately at a time of general economic recession and in an environment of massive overcapacity in the developed world, especially in petrochemicals. The result has been that considerable tensions have developed between Middle East producer states and their anticipated markets in Europe and the USA, particularly between Saudi Arabia and the other Gulf states in the Gulf Cooperation Council* on the one hand and the European Economic Community (EEC) on the other.

Oil wealth and industrial diversification

These problems in the industrial sectors of oil-producing states – which have also diversified into other areas, particularly heavy industry such as iron, steel and aluminium production and processing and ship repair – are mirrored by problems that have developed amongst non-oil-producers. The sad fact is that industry has not fulfilled the hopes based upon it. Despite large-scale investment, the sector rarely contributes more than 10 to 15 per cent to Gross Domestic Product in any Middle Eastern country today. Furthermore, much plant has proved to be inappropriate and incapable of proper use. Frequently heavy industrial plant has been too small to benefit from economies of scale, and unit production costs have compared unfavourably with those in Europe and Japan, thus making exports difficult unless supported by state subsidy. In addition, lack of the appropriate technological skills and of local demand has often led to serious underuse. Trends in world market prices have also been misjudged, with the result that opportunities that were anticipated for exports have not materialized. Furthermore, after an initial 'exuberant' phase of output, inefficient, inappropriate and authoritarian management techniques, usually as the result of the dominant role of the state, have often led to declines in industrial growth rates. This is usually accompanied by a failure to sustain investment under the provisions of economic development plans. In Nasserist Egypt during 1965 for example, the stagnation of the industrial sector as the Second Plan was being introduced led to bureaucratic reforms. During the 1980s Syria has taken similar steps. In Algeria, the sixty-five state companies of the Boumedienne* era have been broken up into some 300 autonomous units, while, at the same time, the role of the private sector is being increased, in a search for greater economic efficiency which began in 1979.

Challenges from the recession and the oil glut

A further stage of developmental retrenchment, particularly in industry, is now under way. Countries like Morocco and Tunisia and, to a lesser extent, Egypt, which sought to develop industry through multinational investment for export processing during the 1970s, have discovered that such short cuts to a diversified industrial base are subject to the vagaries of the international economy. Other states have seen their export opportunities being severely cut back. As a result – and in consequence of the deterioration in their balance-of-payments positions (Morocco has a $16bn foreign debt, Algeria's debt abroad now approaches $17bn, while Egypt is moving towards a total external debt of $30bn) – countries such as these have begun to turn to the private sector to bear the brunt of industrial development. Under the prodding of the World Bank and the International Monetary Fund (IMF), trade regimes have been liberalized – thus vitiating the original dream of industrialization as a device for import substitution, usually behind protective tariff barriers – and the private sector, rather than the state, is being obliged to generate the necessary investment for future industrialization. It is difficult to see quite what effect this will have, although the social, economic and political effects of such readjustments amongst the populations involved are clearly going to be severe, as riots in Tunisia and Morocco in January 1984 and in Egypt in February 1986 have shown. Nevertheless, these developments, when coupled with the tensions recently created in petroleum and petrochemical sectors as a result of oil-price falls and rising tariff barriers, mean that modern industry in the Middle East and North Africa is undergoing radical change and adjustment in this, the second stage, of its evolution since independence.

GJ

Further reading

Industrialisation in the Arab World. Economist Intelligence Unit (London, 1986)
Country Studies (EIU, various years)

Islamic banking

Although the concept of Arab banking is rooted in the Qur'an*, the *hadith** and the early period of Islam, its restatement as a practical, modern system was originally discussed in the 1950s by a few Islamic academics, notably an Egyptian professor, Ahmad al-Naggar. The value of financial intermediation was perceived, and devout Muslims increasingly needed to use the services which commercial banks provided. At the same time it was recognized that there was a basic conflict between the operational practices of commercial banks and the principles of Islamic finance. It was felt that this conflict would be resolved if a new type of financial institution could be established which used modern methods, but functioned in accordance with the provisions of the *shari'a* (Islamic law*).

In the Qur'an, *riba** (usury) is explicitly forbidden, and many Muslim scholars regard all interest payments as *riba*. The objection is partly on redistributive grounds. Borrowers are thought to be more in need than lenders, which is why they seek credit, yet interest penalizes those in need and rewards those with financial surpluses. Interest is also believed to be inefficient by modern Islamic economists. Entrepreneurs with new ideas are forced to take all the risk, while banks funding their endeavours get a fixed interest return. This acts as a deterrent to business enterprise. The possibility of a guaranteed income makes those with surplus funds reluctant to provide venture capital.

Interest charges are often unfair on individual borrowers. Government economic policy may affect interest rates, with rates increased because of balance-of-payments worries or other reasons. Yet this penalizes the borrower with an overdraft or a loan subject to the market rate of interest. Similarly, interest rates often rise when inflation worsens, but this may penalize borrowers just when they are being hurt through rising costs.

Islamic economists such as Ahmad al-Naggar believed that altruism would not be sufficient to ensure that savings were harnessed for productive investments in a modern Islamic society. The supplier of funds would expect some return, especially in an economy where commercial banks offered competitive interest rates. Islamic law makes provision for a reward for investors through *mudaraba*, *musharaka*, *ijara* and *murabaha* contracts.

Mudaraba is an agreement between two or more persons whereby one provides finance and the other the entrepreneurial skills or management for the business venture. Financial losses are assumed by the financier. Unless he makes a financial investment, which is unusual, the manager risks his time and effort but no financial loss. In contrast, under *musharaka*, where money is the main investment, a partnership is formed in which all parties provide some finance and share profits and losses, usually in accordance with their initial subscription. Under both schemes, business risks are shared and the investor can identify with his or her fellow Muslims who are involved in the venture. Community solidarity develops and the participant will feel a greater identity with the Islamic *umma* (community of believers – see Islam).

Ijara is a lease contract as well as a hire contract. *Ijara wa iqtina* is the type of hire purchase described by the Islamic financial institutions as 'lease-purchasing financing'. *Murabaha* is a kind of resale agreement whereby the seller purchases the goods wanted by the buyer, and resells them at an agreed mark-up. Such arrangements cover short-term stock finance. Islamic banks usually provide both long-term and short-term contracts, with the depositor sharing in the bank's profit. These, in turn, are determined by the returns on the bank's advances through *mudaraba*, *musharaka* and the other contracts.

The first Islamic bank

The first institution describing itself as an Islamic bank to be established in the Middle East was the Mit Cham Savings Bank, which Ahmad al-Naggar helped found in 1963. Its operations were confined to a few Egyptian villages in the Nile Delta but it enjoyed modest success and attracted deposits from many rural landowners who had never used a bank before. In 1972 the bank was reconstituted as the Nasser Social Bank, and it started to advance funds to a wide range of small businesses, including trading establishments and handicraft enterprises. Its paid-up capital by 1985 exceeded $18m, a small fraction of the capital of Egypt's big four state-owned commercial banks, but nevertheless enough to constitute a significant financial institution.

Boom in Islamic banking

The oil revenue boom of the mid-1970s resulted in the rapid development of Islamic banking in the Arabian peninsula. The Dubai Islamic Bank was founded in 1975 by a group of wealthy merchants from the UAE, and in 1977 the Kuwait Finance House commenced business. Further Islamic banks were opened in Bahrain in 1981 and Qatar in 1983. Prince Muhammad ibn Faysal of Saudi Arabia was one of the main backers of the Islamic banking movement, and he helped found the Faysal Islamic Banks of Egypt and Sudan in 1977, and in 1985 the Faysal Islamic Bank of Turkey. The prince is also the chairman of Dar al-Mal al-Islami, a Geneva-based international Islamic bank, which attracts its many deposits from the Gulf states.

Two other Saudi Arabian-based financial groups have emerged to challenge the position of Faysal's group as the leading international force in Islamic banking. They are the Al-Baraka group, backed by Shaykh Salih Kamil, and the Al-Rajhi Company for Currency,

The Dubai Islamic Bank, UAE

Exchange and Commerce, the long-established Saudi Arabian money-changers. The Al-Baraka group has established an Islamic investment bank in Bahrain and a finance house in Turkey, and was the first Islamic bank to be permitted to operate as a licensed deposit-taker in the United Kingdom. The Al-Rajhi group has also opened a London office, but its main business is within Saudi Arabia, where it is the third largest financial institution after the National Commercial and Riyad Banks.

Some Islamic scholars, notably those in Iran, are openly critical of the Arab Islamic banks, regarding them as capitalistic institutions. According to these critics, merely avoiding interest payments represents little more than a token gesture, especially in economies where commercial banks are still permitted to operate along Western lines. What is required is a fundamental restructuring of the whole financial system. The Tehran government attempted such a restructuring when it Islamized all Iran's banks in 1984. It is too early to assess the results of this experiment, but many Arab Islamic bankers are watching developments in Iran with considerable interest.

RW

Further reading

M. ʿUmer Chapra, *Towards a Just Monetary System* (Leicester, 1985)
S. Hamoud, *Islamic Banking* (London, 1985)
R. Wilson, *Islamic Business: theory and practice* (London, 1985, 2nd edn.)

The oil and gas industry

The creation of the operating companies

The period before the Second World War can be regarded as the 'setting-up time' in which the institutional context which was crucial to determine the subsequent developments of the industry in the region was created. The main developments were the signing of the concession agreements and the creation of the operating companies. While the governments of the region wanted to develop their oil potential, they lacked the finance and skills to do so. However, the oil companies were able to provide these and concession agreements had to be set up to govern the basis of the relationship. The first effective concession was granted in Iran in 1901, followed by Bahrain (1924), Iraq (1928), Saudi Arabia (1933), Kuwait (1934) and Qatar (1935). Concessions in other countries of the region came in the 1950s.

These concessions led to the creation of the operating companies which were to dominate the industry during the 1950s and 1960s – the Anglo Persian Oil Company (APOC), the Iraq Petroleum Company (IPC), the Arabian American Oil Company (Aramco) and the Kuwait Oil Company (KOC). The companies were (or became) jointly owned by various combinations of major international oil companies. This joint ownership occurred for two reasons. First, the US and French governments both exerted significant pressure on the British government to allow their oil companies similar access to that of British oil companies obtained by virtue of Britain's mandate or treaty relations. Secondly, it reflected an attempt to accommodate large finds of oil in an already glutted market.

These developments in effect created a bargaining environment in which the terms of the concessions and the nature of the companies' operations became the subject of increasing dissatisfaction from the governments in the region. Although the terms of the concessions differed between the countries, there were four broad areas of dissatisfaction. First, the large area covered by the concession (an average 88 per cent of territory), coupled with the general lack of any compulsion on the companies to relinquish acreage, effectively placed the control of the country's resources in the hands of only one company. Secondly, the long life of the concessions (an average of 82 years) also became onerous since there was no provision for renegotiation. Thirdly, the fiscal terms of the agreement (a fixed royalty per ton) also generated dissatisfaction. Finally, and most importantly, by virtue of the agreement the government lacked any managerial control over the companies. Operating and pricing decisions were entirely at the discretion of the companies. These characteristics, created prior to the Second World War, were to set the scene for the conflict which continued through the post-war period.

Laying the Jubayl-Yanbuʿ pipeline north of Medina, Saudi Arabia

Operations and conflict – revenue

The period of the 1950s and 1960s was dominated by two issues – government revenue and control. The revenue issue concerned both price and volume. In the late 1940s, following the example set by Venezuela, governments of the Middle East switched from a royalty basis to a 50-50 profits tax in order to secure revenue. This created something of a problem because the vertically integrated structure of the industry (the same firm was involved in production, transport, refining and distribution) meant that there was little or no market for crude oil. No market meant no price and therefore no means of computing profits. To get round this the companies introduced the idea of posted price as a tax reference price which was intended to reflect the market value of the crude.

Oil prices in the region in the three decades before 1950 had, via the Gulf (of Mexico) basing point system, been determined by the US domestic price. During the fifties the companies tried to maintain that link but because of the very low production costs associated with Middle East crude this became impossible. Twice, therefore, the companies cut the posted price and hence the host governments' revenues without consultation. In response to this the major producers of the region together with Venezuela set up in 1960 the Organization of Petroleum Exporting Countries (OPEC)* with the specific intention of restoring the cuts in price. This prevented any further fall in the posted price for the rest of the decade despite the fact that the realized market price of crude was falling under the growing pressure of excess supply.

The other element in the revenue equation was volume. The joint ownership of the producing capacity in the region effectively turned the area into the world's stockpile of crude. Thus the companies orchestrated supply between their various sources in order to match worldwide supply with demand and protect the price structure. The result was that the countries experienced wildly fluctuating production levels and, hence, revenues. This was made even more pronounced when Iran's production effectively stopped between 1951 and 1954, and later as new sources of crude came onstream in the region. Older producing areas had to cut back to accommodate the new sources – Algeria (1958), Libya (1961) and Abu Dhabi (1962). Attempts by the governments to persuade the companies to increase lifting (and hence revenue) were very common but had limited success. Relations were especially bad in Iraq following Law 80 of 1960, when the government effectively took over all the non-producing areas of the IPC concession. These bad relations enabled the companies to hold back Iraqi production more than that of the other producers.

Operations and conflict – control

In general, despite these various problems, aspects of the agreements (such as royalty expensing) were renegotiated, acreage was relinquished and revenues to the governments rose throughout the period, generating increasing dependence on oil revenues. There was limited flexibility in the system although the second issue of the period – control – remained an intractable problem.

Some of the original concession-holders had given indications of allowing some local participation in the operating companies, but the owning companies refused to implement this participation. Local governments wanted control for three reasons. First there was national prestige, the need of governments to have some say over their nations' main resource. As political competition in the region grew, so too did the need to be seen somehow to 'control' the oil companies which were popularly perceived as being agents of imperialism. Secondly, there was the belief that decisions over pricing and production (and hence revenue) should take government wishes into account. Finally, there was a genuine desire to see the oil sector used as a vehicle to promote general economic development by maximizing the linkages. For example, throughout this period the flaring of associated gas was a point of contention. The companies argued that it had no economic value while the governments argued that it represented a valuable national resource.

As outlined above, some renegotiation of the concession terms did take place but the companies would not give way on the issue of control. This led to increasing popular pressure in the region for nationalization. In 1951, Iran had nationalized the Iran National Oil Company but the companies had successfully blocked oil sales and the government of Dr Musaddiq* was eventually overthrown in a coup engineered by Britain and the United States. For the most part, despite the clamour for action, the governments of the region were against nationalization. This was partly because of the memory of Dr Musaddiq and partly because the declining price of crude oil made the prospects of becoming a crude seller unappetizing. However, it was necessary to provide an alternative with which to assuage national pride. Shaykh Yamani, the Saudi Arabian minister of oil in 1967, developed the idea of participation in which the governments of the region would take an equity share not only in the crude producing companies but also their downstream affiliates. In effect he was advocating an alliance of governments and major oil companies to offset the perceived negative effects of the so-called independent oil companies on the price structure.

The ten golden years – revenue

The 1950s and 1960s had set the scene for what was to be the pinnacle of power for the oil producers of the Middle East and North Africa. The decade of the 1970s saw an acceleration in the pace of change in the regional industry which was to have an impact far beyond the region. Three issues dominated – prices, government takeovers and moves downstream. Each will be dealt with separately despite the obvious links between them.

The winter of 1969 saw some increase in product prices in Europe, which fed through to company profitability. This led to a demand from the producing governments for an increase in posted prices, the stated *raison d'être* for OPEC's creation. Here Libya played the key role. Since the first posted price had been set in Libya in 1961 it had been a point of contention. In 1969 the old regime was swept away by a group of young army officers. It was this new group who demanded negotiations with the companies for an increase in price in January 1970. The companies refused negotiations on the grounds that it was their prerogative unilaterally to determine posted prices. However, unlike many of the other producers in the region, there were a number of companies operating in Libya, many of whom were dependent upon access to Libyan crude. By a process of divide and rule, Libya managed to force the smaller oil companies to accept an increase in price. Thus for the first time the posted price was altered as a result of company-to-government negotiations. The Gulf producers immediately demanded parity and a series of negotiations led in 1971 to the Tehran and Tripoli agreements, which were to be five-year agreements on price. This new, relative bargaining power appeared to be swinging strongly towards the governments.

Following these pricing agreements, the market continued to strengthen and by 1973 market prices were above posted prices. At this point OPEC demanded a price renegotiation. The companies stalled, and in October the Gulf producers unilaterally increased the posted price and at the same time announced an Arab oil embargo against countries supplying to Israel as a weapon after the 1973 Arab–Israeli war*. The governments' unilateral action and the explicit intrusion of Arab politics into the supply decision threw the market into turmoil and prices rose sharply. In December, OPEC met in Tehran and announced yet another price increase despite some reluctance from Saudi Arabia. Within months the price of crude had increased nearly four times to generate the first oil shock.

The ten golden years – control

Meanwhile, as the pricing context changed so too did the situation of control. Yamani's ideas on participation gained widespread favour and, after a series of preliminary skirmishes, serious negotiations began in 1972. These were general negotiations between the governments and the companies to hammer out a broad agreement which would form the basis for specific negotiations. The agreement was duly signed in October 1972 by Saudi Arabia, Kuwait (which did not ratify it), Abu Dhabi and Qatar. However, other changes were afoot which were to undermine the participation agreement. In 1971 Algeria nationalized its oil companies as did Iraq in 1972. In 1973 Iran took over the Consortium which was created in 1954 as part of the nationalization 'settlement', and Libya announced its own participation deal on much more favourable terms. As a consequence, the participation agreement looked increasingly unfavourable. Kuwait was the first to demand better terms, followed rapidly by the other signatories to the October agreement. By 1976, all the major operating companies in the region had been taken over *de jure* by the governments.

This now gave to the Middle Eastern and North African producers the power to determine their own production level. However, the loss by the companies of the joint ownership of the operating companies meant that this means of controlling supply to protect prices had disappeared. At this point Saudi Arabia effectively adopted the role of swing producer to restore market stability. Thus the orchestration of supply jointly undertaken by the companies was now replaced by Saudi Arabia alone, although guided from the companies as to what the market could bear. In addition, the companies also retained some elements of a *de facto* controlling role in that, despite the takeover, they continued to market the crude oil on behalf of many of the new government owners.

By the mid-1970s the countries appeared to have achieved their two aims, which had emerged in the 1950s – control and high revenues. The next stage was the development of a refining and petrochemical capacity. The high revenue meant that investment in such plant could be made and the control gave the governments, as disposers of the crude, the choice of where to refine. It also gave them the power to stop flaring the associated gas and gather it for use as a petrochemical feedstock. The motives for the moves downstream were numerous and varied between countries. They ranged from a desire to promote development to a desire to diversify away from dependence on crude oil. Other motives included a desire to make profits and to extend control in the international oil industry. The first half of the 1970s saw the emergence of grandiose plans for export refineries, basic petrochemical plants and gas liquefaction

Table 1. Crude oil production – million barrels per day

	1930	1940	1950	1960	1970	1975	1980	1984
Algeria	—	—	—	0.18	1.03	0.98	1.02	0.70
Iran	0.13	0.18	0.66	1.07	3.83	5.35	1.47	2.03
Iraq	—	0.06	0.14	0.97	1.55	2.26	2.65	1.22
Kuwait	—	—	0.34	1.69	2.99	2.08	1.66	1.05
Libya	—	—	—	—	3.32	1.48	1.83	1.08
Qatar	—	—	0.03	0.17	0.36	0.44	0.47	0.32
Saudi Arabia	—	0.01	0.55	1.31	3.80	7.07	9.90	4.08
UAE	—	—	—	—	0.78	1.66	1.70	1.07
Egypt	—	0.02	0.06	0.07	0.33	0.22	0.56	0.86
Oman	—	—	—	—	0.33	0.34	0.29	0.42
Syria	—	—	—	—	0.08	0.18	0.16	0.17

Sources: OPEC Annual Statistical Bulletin, 1984; OAPEC Annual Statistical Reports – various years; BP Statistical Review of World Energy, 1986.

Table 2. Marketed production of natural gas (million cubic metres)

	1964	1970	1975	1980	1984
Algeria	721	2 599	7 516	11 647	35 039
Iran	1 205	12 881	20 282	7 138	13 500
Iraq	761	784	1 299	1 281	590
Kuwait	1 699	2 037	3 212	4 071	4 114
Libya	—	294	4 635	5 170	4 600
Qatar	79	1 005	2 003	4 741	5 930
Saudi Arabia	647	1 230	3 772	11 431	7 150
UAE	—	756	1 090	6 863	9 760

Source: OPEC Annual Statistical Bulletin, 1984.

Table 3. Oil and gas reserves – life at end 1985 (years at 1985 production)

	Oil	Gas
Algeria	26	86
Iran	59	*
Iraq	84	*
Kuwait	*	*
Libya	54	*
Qatar	30	*
Saudi Arabia	*	*
UAE	99	90
Egypt	12	44
Oman	22	N/A
Syria	22	N/A

Note: *Over 100 years
Source: BP Statistical Review of World Energy, 1986.

Oil process plants – Units 11 and 12 – by night at Kirkuk, Iraq, 1964

facilities. These plans had two characteristics: they were uncoordinated and they involved no market studies. The result was that, in a world already suffering gross over-capacity in such activities, the plans were untenable and a great many were quietly dropped although some (notably in Saudi Arabia*) did reach fruition.

In the meantime, the producers of the region attempted to spend their newly acquired fortunes. At the risk of over-generalization and over-simplification, one must admit that these attempts were badly carried out. They involved enormous waste and introduced severe distortions into the working of the non-oil economy. Although it is true that the welfare of the populations did materially improve, the sustainability of this improvement remains a moot point. The oil bought growth but it is debatable if it bought development.

Saudi Arabia – control and crisis

Between 1974 and 1979, Saudi Arabia, by virtue of its swing role position, retained its predominant place among the region's oil producers, although there were numerous contenders also seeking that position. There were some minor adjustments to price but in general the real price of oil declined from its peak of December 1974. The next major change started with the Iranian oil workers' strike of October 1978, followed by the overthrow of the Shah* and by the Iranian revolution*. The result was that the price of oil rose from $12.70 to $34 per barrel in October 1981, having risen at times much higher in the interim. Trying to make any sense out of the second oil shock is extremely difficult because it was a crisis of perception and expectations in a context of general panic. Most of the region's producers played a very passive role and simply charged whatever they thought the market could bear. Any semblance of an orderly price structure disappeared. The exception was Saudi Arabia which, while trying to restrain the rising prices, at the same time added significantly to the uncertainties by virtue of its continually changing position over production. First, in company with Kuwait and Abu Dhabi, it increased production. It then reduced production because of technical problems, increased it and then reduced it again in protest against the Camp David Accords*.

When the crisis, aggravated by the outbreak of the Iran–Iraq War* in September 1980, had settled down, a number of key changes had occurred in the region's oil industry which were to set the pattern for the 1980s. During the crisis, the governments had taken over the marketing of crude oil. This had two consequences. First it meant that the oil companies had lost much of their vertical integration and henceforth their downstream profitability depended upon the market price of crude. Secondly, there was a widespread loss of information about the global supply-and-demand picture. In addition, because of the prevalence of *force majeure* to cancel crude sales contracts, long-term contracts in the region had become discredited: increasingly oil was being traded on short-term contracts or on a spot market basis (one transaction at a time). A final aspect of the regional situation which, although not immediately related to oil politics, was to influence the price of oil, was the growing fragmentation caused by the Camp David Accords and by the Gulf War. More than ever the region seemed divided into a multitude of conflicting camps.

Defence of the price structure

In the oil and gas sector during the 1980s the key issue so far has been the defence of the price structure. Following the second oil shock, oil demand began to fall. This was due partly to the immediate response of the consumers to the higher prices created by the shock, but it was also due to the lagged response to the first oil shock which was feeding its way through the system. Because of the short-term nature of the supply contracts, the fall in demand began visibly to translate itself into a downward pressure on prices. As before, the key role was now taken by Saudi Arabia. Despite its concern to protect its market and to prevent oil prices rising too much, in the aftermath of the second oil shock the Saudis made a basic policy decision to defend the structure of the now much higher prices. Thus when the price structure showed signs of weakening, Saudi Arabia immediately resumed its swing role. However, this time it was not enough. Not only was demand falling but new sources of crude oil, prompted by the first oil shock, were now coming into production. The result was that some other mechanism to orchestrate supply was needed. Thus in March 1982, for the first time since the mid-1960s, OPEC began to try and set a production level for its members in order to offset the downward pressure on prices.

This move created several problems. First, the loss of information meant that no-one could be sure at what level to set supply. Secondly, there were severe problems in distributing the quotas between the OPEC members, an element greatly aggravated by the regional frictions already alluded to. However, even given the distribution of quotas there was no mechanism to detect or deter cheating on the agreements. Furthermore there were strong pressures to cheat. All the OPEC members had become locked into a high-spending regime and attempts to reduce government spending were proving to be politically problematical. In addition, since many of the plans for utilization of associated gas had gone ahead, low oil production caused acute gas shortages, which affected public utility supplies as well as the capacity operation of the downstream plants.

However, as long as Saudi Arabia was willing to retain the swing role, cheating and error could be brought under control. In March 1983, after the failure of the previous year's agreement on production, OPEC met in London and after a long and arduous session agreed on a $5 per barrel cut and an overall quota of 17.5 million barrels per day. What then followed was effectively a series of holding actions as OPEC tried to adjust price and output to cope with the changing market situation and the internal cheating. In essence the leading OPEC people believed the fall in oil demand was only temporary as a result of world recession and therefore it was only necessary to hold on a little longer when the equation would right itself. Gradually, the realization began to grow that this was a mistaken view and that the fall in oil demand was concerned with a fundamental shift away from oil via a process of conservation and fuel switching. Meanwhile, Saudi Arabian production was dropping and revenue pressures were beginning to bite. Within Saudi Arabia itself many were arguing that the high price strategy was a mistake and was causing a decline in the importance of oil which would reflect eventually upon Saudi Arabia's standing regionally and internationally.

The low point was reached in the summer of 1985 when Saudi Arabia's production dropped to less than 2 million b/d. September then saw a major policy switch backed by Kuwait. The OPEC pricing structure was to be abandoned and the oil priced on a market-related formula. Saudi Arabia also announced that it would now produce according to its quota level. In December 1985, OPEC met and agreed to seek its 'fair market share'. The market interpreted that as a declaration of a price war and the oil price collapsed within weeks to below $10. Such a rapid collapse caused considerable dismay among the producers, although there were those who saw this low price route as the, albeit painful, way to eventual salvation via an increase in demand and a cutting-off of much producing capacity. In the event, pressures were brought to bear; Shaykh Yamani was sacked at the end of October 1986 and replaced by Hisham Nazer. The fair-share policy was ditched and a return to a fixed price system was announced by King Fahd starting with a target of $18. The OPEC meeting in December produced an

Organization of Arab Petroleum Exporting Countries (OAPEC)

OAPEC was formed in 1968 by Saudi Arabia, Kuwait and Libya. Its purpose was to provide the three conservative oil-producing states with a counter-balance to the pressures growing within the Arab League* to use oil as a weapon in the struggle against Israel. The 1969 Libyan revolution effectively destroyed its original purpose, which was to provide the 'traditional' states with a bulwark against the 'radical' states – mainly Algeria and Egypt. However, in its place was developed an organization with an expanded membership and significant potential for policy coordination. By 1972, all the Arab oil producers had joined the organization, and in 1973 Dr ʿAli Attiga was appointed secretary-general. He, in turn, began to collect together in the Kuwait headquarters an impressive collection of Arab oil talent.

As OAPEC developed it deliberately avoided involvement in pricing or production decisions, preferring to leave these to OPEC. Unfortunately, the October 1973 price increase was assumed by many to be the result of an OAPEC decision. This was reinforced by a silly advertisement placed in the Western press by the Arab League. The assumption is, however, quite mistaken and detracts from OAPEC's real achievements.

During the 1970s, the Arab oil producers began a whole series of projects related to oil and gas production and processing. Initially there was virtually no coordination and OAPEC provided a forum in which some of the excessive duplication could be avoided. This led to a number of joint projects in a variety of energy-related fields. The scope for such cooperation was unlimited and the prospects seemed good, particularly as the Secretariat was quite deliberately not aiming for unrealistic goals. Unfortunately, the early promise and potential failed in the 1980s for two reasons. First, the divisions in the Arab world created by the Camp David Accords spilled over into the decision-making process for OAPEC. Secondly, the fall in oil revenues significantly reduced the member governments' willingness to provide funds, a factor reinforced by the rise of the Gulf Cooperation Council (GCC)*. Thus, short of funds in a depressed market for oil and oil-related projects, OAPEC lost much of its impetus, and gradually the excellent team gathered during the 1970s began to disperse.

agreement on prices and production. The market responded and the price moved to its target. Many remain sceptical about future prospects, and only time will show for how long the agreement holds.

PJS

Further reading
M. A. Adelman, *The World Petroleum Market* (Baltimore, 1972)
A. M. El-Mokadem, D. Hawdon, C. Robinson and P. J. Stevens, *OPEC and the World Oil Market 1973–1983* (London, 1984)
A. Sampson, *The Seven Sisters* (London, 1975)
I. Seymour, *OPEC, Instrument of Change* (London, 1980)
G. W. Stocking, *Middle East Oil* (Nashville, 1970)

Solar energy

The Middle East and North Africa together form the most insolated region in the world, with all regions except Anatolia receiving above 160 gram calories per square centimetre of sunlight per year. Indeed, apart from the Mediterranean littoral regions of Turkey and North Africa, the region as a whole receives between 180 and 200 gram calories per square centimetre of solar energy each year. The significance of this energy source can be appreciated once it is realized that the solar energy falling on Saudia Arabia each year is equivalent to the total proved fossil energy reserves of the world. It is clear, therefore, that Middle Eastern and North African states would be well advised to tap this inexhaustible and renewable resource.

The problem about exploitation has, however, been twofold. First of all, until relatively recently there was no effective and efficient technology available for exploiting solar energy. As a result, initial attempts were inevitably small-scale and did little to address the real energy needs of Middle Eastern and North African states. Now, however, photovoltaic systems for converting solar energy directly to electricity have been developed and the growing efficiency of such systems – particularly after development work in Japan in 1983, which has meant that it is now possible to produce photovoltaic cells in bulk from amorphous silicon – has made it possible to consider large-scale projects for energy conversion based on the photovoltaic effect. Such developments are still hampered, however, by the fact that those states which are the most insolated are also those with the most abundant oil and gas reserves which are amongst the cheapest in the world to exploit. This has meant that, inevitably, petroleum reserves have provided the easiest and most immediate access to satisfy energy needs and the development of solar-energy resources has suffered as a result.

Consequently developments in solar energy have been limited, although there has been an acceleration in the past three years.

Solar energy project of the Kuwait Institute for Scientific Research

However, for many governments in the region the issue remains one of pious hope rather than one of active development. Nonetheless, progress has been made. Saudi Arabia, for example, has been linked with the USA in the Soleras project which, since 1981, has used a stand-alone photovoltaic generator to provide 350-kw worth of electricity for three desert villages. Some 7000 persons are involved and receive sufficient power for lighting and domestic power, irrigation and water supply from the project.

More importantly, solar-electricity generating costs have fallen since 1975 from $30 per watt to $6–$7 per watt in 1983 as a result of technological development – a development that automatically makes solar energy a more attractive option, even though costs are still very high in comparison with conventional generating costs. The result has been that solar energy is widely used in small-scale applications throughout the Gulf. Dubai has introduced solar street lighting; small-scale reverse osmosis desalination* units powered by solar energy have been created in Saudi Arabia and Qatar; while Oman has a solar-powered telecommunications system. As prices fall still further and as applications become technologically more refined – as with air conditioning, for example – so the use of solar power throughout the Gulf region will expand, even though oil-generated electricity and other forms of power are likely to remain cheaper alternatives, particularly after the recent fall in oil prices.

Outside the Gulf region, solar power has a significance as a genuine alternative to oil- or coal-generated energy and here considerations of relative cost are extremely important. Syria, for instance, is actively pursuing solar-energy alternatives, but lack of investment resources has made any significant progress difficult. Jordan, on the other hand, has developed an integrated energy programme in which the Ministry of Energy and Mineral Resources, created at the end of 1984, has been pursuing a $68m programme with World Bank aid of $30m for the development of solar energy alongside oil. Israel has for many years experimented with solar energy, and has a full-scale pilot solar-energy plant on the shore of the Dead Sea, but so far has not significantly extended its application. Tunisia is engaged in solar-energy research, while Algeria commissioned a Belgian firm in May 1983 to build a 30-kw solar-energy generator designed to supply 300 households in the Adrar region at Melouka. Other projects are under way around Tamanrasset, where French consultants have estimated the total available power at 5200 gwh per year. Morocco has recently commissioned a pilot project at Beni Oukil, in Oujda province. This is designed to pump water at a rate of 27,000 litres per hour, drawing energy from 30 m^2 of photovoltaic panels.

Indeed, the Beni Oukil project may well signal the immediate future for solar energy in the Middle East and North Africa – small-scale local projects satisfying local needs in electrical energy in regions where national systems can only reach with difficulty. Such an approach would minimize the still considerable cost disadvantage of solar energy by setting it against the heavy capital investment costs of conventional systems. At the same time, more traditional uses of solar energy should not be forgotten – hydro-solar schemes to extract salts from saline or sea water or solar distillation as developed for small-scale desalination systems in Sudan. It is clear that solar energy now has an essential role as a complement to conventional energy provision systems in the short term, while the long-term future will depend on the technologist's success in reducing energy production costs to those comparable with conventional techniques.

GJ

Nuclear energy

Although the Middle East and North Africa is conventionally seen as an energy exporting area, it is also a region of rapid population growth and development. Furthermore, not all states in the region are plentifully endowed with energy resources. Only eight of the thirteen OPEC* states are in the Middle East or North Africa, while OAPEC only involves eleven of the twenty-two countries that are conventionally seen as making up the Middle East and North Africa. Thus about half of the states of the region depend heavily on imported energy to satisfy their rapidly growing energy demand. This demand is fuelled by demographic growth (between 2.3 and 3 per cent throughout the region), urbanization (as all states see urban populations grow more rapidly than population overall) and industrialization (as development leads to industrial growth rates of up to 10 per cent per year).

Energy-poor states must, therefore, rely on indigenous sources – small amounts of oil and gas, wood, hydro-electric power or solar energy – or import. However, given the rapid nominal growths in crude prices after 1973–4 when prices increased fourfold, and again in 1979–80 when they doubled again, energy crude imports have become an increasingly heavy burden for many states. Even though oil prices collapsed by 40 per cent at the start of 1986 and are expected to remain at levels of 30 per cent below the official OPEC price in mid-1985 of $27 per barrel, the burden of energy import costs will remain and has led several states to consider alternatives.

The obvious alternative has been nuclear power and, during the 1970s, several oil states considered the creation of a nuclear power sector to supplement the rapidly expanding thermal electrical and hydro-electric generation sectors that had already been developed. Oil states necessarily began the process because of the heavy investment involved, one which non-oil states could not permit themselves to contemplate in the short term. Nonetheless, the growing recurrent cost of imported energy and the drain of this on national balances of payments have increasingly persuaded the richer non-oil states, such as Turkey and Egypt, to consider the nuclear path.

Iran led the way, with ambitious projects for nuclear power generation under the provisions of the five-year plan, involving as many as five nuclear stations and technical help from the USA, UK, France and Germany. The Islamic Revolution then intervened and the plans were all shelved. Since 1984, however, cautious moves have begun to resuscitate the plans for the partly finished plant at Bushehr, where Kraftwerk Union has been considering construction of two 1200 mw units at a cost of about $2bn. This has created considerable tension both inside and outside the country – abroad because of fears that the nuclear power claim is merely a cover for more nefarious purposes involving the production of nuclear weapons, and at home because such plans seem to suggest a return to the grandiose ambitions of the Pahlavi dynasty.

Indeed, the fears that programmes for nuclear power may be a cover for other less desirable aims have seriously hindered both the ability of Middle Eastern states to gain access to nuclear technology and, often, their willingness to take the risks. There is always the warning of the Israeli raid on the Iraqi research nuclear reactor Tammouz in 1981. Nonetheless, despite the experience of the Israeli raid, Iraq has pushed ahead with studies for a nuclear power programme and the USSR has proposed two stations, to be built by Atomexport, within its $2bn development aid programme for Iraq. Originally, Saudi Arabia had agreed to finance the rebuilding of the Tammouz complex, but this now seems to have been put into abeyance. Indeed, all Middle Eastern states except Israel, Mauritania, Oman, Somalia and the two states of South and North Yemen are members of the International Energy Authority and have therefore adhered to the Nuclear Non-Proliferation Treaty. Several of them, therefore, are actively pursuing the nuclear power option.

Libya, for instance, has been anxious to acquire nuclear technology for a decade and already has a small 10 kw research reactor at Tarhuna. In 1981, it created a nuclear energy secretariat, attached to the heavy industry secretariat. In 1984, Libya invited Belgonucléaire, a semi-state Belgian company, to provide a nuclear power station on the Gulf of Sirte with the USSR providing two 440-mw power sets and reactor cores. However, Israeli and US pressure forced the Belgian government to withdraw in December 1984. By December 1985, the USSR had promised Libya that it would build the power station alone. Fuel for the station will come from Libya's own reserves and from the Libyan-controlled Tibesti massif in the Aozou Strip – the disputed portion of territory along the Libyan–Chadian border. It remains to be seen whether Israel will permit a state which it considers to be a fundamental danger to its own survival to proceed with these plans for nuclear power production.

Algeria, Morocco and Tunisia all have plans for a nuclear power industry over the next two decades. Algeria, which has 50,000 tons of proved uranium reserves in the Adrar region – 128m tons of oil equivalent, or three to four years' worth of oil exports – began to export uranium ore to France in 1984 through Sonarem, which received enriched uranium in return. This is to be used in an ambitious nuclear power programme which should provide 10 per cent of the country's electricity by the end of the century. In May 1985, Algeria purchased a RA-6 research reactor from Argentina as part of the development process involved. Tunisia also hopes to have a nuclear power station by 2000 and has sought Soviet help in this respect. Morocco has plans for four 600 mw nuclear units, with one being constructed by the mid-1990s, probably with French help. A research centre was founded in 1983 and Morocco expects to extract uranium from its phosphate production – about 21m tons annually.

Only three other states in the region have plans for nuclear power at present – Syria, Turkey and Egypt. Syria has proposed a long-term plan for the construction of a 600-mw unit. Egypt, with a recently discovered deposit of uranium 500 km south-west of the capital, Cairo, has proposed a 20-year nuclear power plant programme in which the first stage will involve five 1000-mw stations. The intention has been to commission the first unit – probably to be built by a West German company – by 1991, but Egypt has had considerable difficulty in finding the right financial mix to enable building to begin. Turkey, which has 8.6m tons of oil equivalent of uranium ore, has planned to build a 600-mw power station at Akkuya on the Mediterranean coast. The contractors, AECL of Canada and Price Brothers of Britain, will construct and operate the plant at their own cost for the first fifteen years and will then hand it over to Turkey. However, financing problems have delayed the start of the project.

It is clear that the Middle East is poised on the verge of a major move into nuclear power generation, particularly amongst the oil-poor states of the region. Oil producers, except for Iran, Algeria and Iraq, have shown little interest so far in this energy option because of their ample supplies of oil and because, in many cases, the economic operating size of modern nuclear power stations – usually about 2000 mw of installed capacity – is too large for their needs, being roughly the average installed capacity anticipated for the Gulf Cooperation Council states (Kuwait, the UAE, Qatar, Bahrain and Oman, together with Saudi Arabia).

The one area where such states may find a nuclear power capacity useful is where there is a renewed interest in the construction of small and medium power reactors generating between 150 and 500 mw. These would be used for purposes other than direct power generation – desalination or local industrial energy provision for heating or other purposes. The International Atomic Energy Authority considers that there could be a world market of up to fifteen such plants by the end of the century and that five states in the Middle East and North Africa – Iraq, Libya, Morocco, Syria and Tunisia – might be interested.

Israel's nuclear research centre at Dimona, in the Negev, is furnished with a French nuclear reactor and is engaged on a variety of research programmes, including nuclear power. There have always been rumours, however, that the centre has also been involved in research for military purposes. During 1986 newspaper allegations backed up with considerable detail suggested that Israel has now created a stockpile of about a hundred nuclear warheads. The uranium ore required for this was said to have come from a shipment of 200 tons of yellowcake that had disappeared during the 1970s. Although the evidence appears persuasive, it must be emphasized that there is, as yet, no independent evidence to confirm the accusation. Israel is not a signatory to the Nuclear Non-Proliferation Treaty, although it is a member of the International Atomic Energy Authority.

GJ

Population and migration

Population

In the mid-1980s the twenty-six countries of the Middle East and North Africa had a combined population of almost 310 million, some 6.5 per cent of the world population. The enormous range of population size within the region is shown on Table 4. Turkey*, Iran* and Egypt* are among the twenty largest populations in the world, ranking 17th, 19th and 20th respectively. At the same time three countries, Qatar*, Djibouti* and Bahrain* have populations of less than 500,000. The seven largest countries (Turkey, Iran, Egypt, Morocco*, Sudan*, Algeria*, Afghanistan*) have a combined population of 228 million and account for almost three-quarters of the region's total population. The two largest countries, Turkey and Iran, which have about one-third of the population total, are both non-Arab. Overall, slightly more than one half of the region's population is non-Arab.

The largest Arab countries (Egypt, Morocco and Algeria) are in North Africa, rather than the Fertile Crescent or the Arabian Peninsula. Overall, North Africa accounts for 32.9 per cent of the region's population compared with 10.2 per cent in the Fertile Crescent (Iraq*, Syria*, Lebanon*, Jordan*) and 5.3 per cent in the Arabian Peninsula.

Crude birth rates are generally high throughout the region (Table 5), with eight countries having a crude birth rate in excess of 45 births per thousand population. In the smaller Gulf states (Bahrain, Qatar, Kuwait* and the UAE*) crude birth rates are biased downwards by their large migrant worker populations. Taking nationals alone, birth rates in these countries are also above 45 per thousand. These countries have generally pro-natalist population policies, paying substantial family allowances and providing free education and health services.

In most countries birth rates have fallen only marginally, if at all, over the last 25 years. The persistence of high birth rates can be attributed in large part to the prevalence of early and universal marriage, the limited availability of family planning advice and contraceptives, and the cultural acceptance of large families as the norm. Significantly, those countries with the lowest crude birth rates (Egypt, Israel*, Lebanon) have substantial non-Muslim populations, and a high degree of educational attainment and workforce participation amongst women.

Crude death rates range widely in the region (Table 5), from 3.7 deaths per thousand population in Kuwait to 22.3 in Afghanistan*. The highest crude death rates are found in the poorer countries, particularly those with a large and dispersed rural population. These range from over 21 per thousand in Afghanistan, North

Table 4.

Country	Number	%Total	Growth rate
Turkey	50,664,550	16.3	1.9
Iran	49,728,000	16.1	3.1
Egypt	46,637,980	15.1	2.7
Morocco	22,280,960	7.2	2.6
Sudan	21,521,200	6.9	2.8
Algeria	20,203,660	6.5	3.1
Afghanistan	16,797,660	5.4	2.3
Iraq	15,620,780	5.0	3.5
Saudi Arabia	11,215,480	3.6	3.8
Syria	10,452,520	3.4	3.7
North Yemen (YAR)	9,274,170	3.0	3.0
Tunisia	7,174,150	2.3	2.5
Somalia	4,651,480	1.5	3.0
Israel	4,198,400	1.4	1.9
Libya	3,779,350	1.2	4.3
Lebanon	2,699,520	0.9	1.9
Jordan	2,689,570	0.9	5.2
South Yemen (PDRY)	2,174,380	0.7	2.6
Mauritania	1,880,600	0.6	2.6
Kuwait	1,697,300	0.6	4.5
UAE	1,600,000	0.5	7.6
Oman	1,218,800	0.4	4.7
Cyprus	667,900	0.2	1.2
Bahrain	427,300	0.1	4.2
Djibouti	362,200	0.1	2.9
Qatar	294,900	0.1	5.1
Total	309,912,810	100.0	

Sources: HRD base, *Socio-demographic Profiles of Key Arab Countries* (Newcastle upon Tyne, 1987); World Bank, *World Development Report 1986* (Washington DC, 1987); UNESCWA, *Demographic and Related Socio-economic Data Sheets, 1984* (Baghdad, 1985).

Table 5.

Country	Infant mortality per '000	Crude deaths per '000	Crude births per '000
Mauritania	187.0	20.9	50.1
Yemen AR	164.0	22.1	49.6
Yemen PDR	137.0	18.7	49.3
Afghanistan	181.6	22.3	48.1
Oman	116.5	15.3	47.5
Somalia	143.0	21.3	46.5
Sudan	93.6	17.4	45.9
Libya	91.0	11.0	45.0
Iraq	81.8	7.9	43.8
Syria	60.0	8.3	43.0
Djibouti	nk	7.6	42.0
Saudi Arabia	110.0	12.6	41.8
Jordan	63.1	6.7	41.5
Morocco	98.0	14.0	40.0
Iran	100.0	10.0	40.0
Algeria	107.0	8.9	39.5
Egypt	104.5	10.9	37.4
Bahrain	44.1	5.9	36.8
UAE	42.2	3.8	34.9
Tunisia	83.0	9.0	33.0
Kuwait	23.8	3.7	32.9
Turkey	82.0	9.0	31.0
Qatar	46.6	6.6	30.2
Lebanon	44.4	8.8	29.8
Israel	14.0	7.0	24.0
Cyprus	17.0	8.2	19.7

Sources: as Table 4.

Yemen, Somalia and Mauritania, to 17 per thousand in the Sudan and 19 per thousand in South Yemen.

The lowest crude death rates are in the largely urban, oil-rich Gulf states whose better housing and sanitation combine with higher disposable incomes and greater access to medical services. These rates are also biased down by the presence of large migrant worker populations with their age distribution eased towards the 20–49 age bracket.

Over the last 25 years mortality rates have fallen substantially in all except the poorest countries of the region. In Jordan, for example, crude death rates have fallen from 18 per thousand in 1965 to 8 per thousand in 1985. Over the same period the crude death rate in Afghanistan has fallen by less than 3 per cent.

The reduction in mortality is primarily a result of falling infant deaths. These tend to mirror crude death rates, being lowest in the urbanized Gulf states, and highest in the poorer countries with minimal access to health services. Infant mortality rates (deaths in the first year of life per thousand live births) are exceedingly high in Mauritania* (187), Afghanistan (182), North Yemen* (164), Somalia* (143) and SouthYemen* (137).

The decline in death rates has been the chief cause of rapid population increase in the region. Given the room for further improvements in the mortality figures, population growth rates are likely to remain high. Between 1950 and 1960 the average annual increase was 2.5 per cent; since the 1970s it has averaged 2.8 per cent a year. Natural increase ranges from under 2 per cent a year in Turkey to 3.6 per cent in Iraq. High rates of immigration into the oil-producing Gulf states have resulted in rates of population growth ranging from 3.8 per cent a year in Saudi Arabia to 7.6 per cent in the UAE.

Rapid population growth will inevitably mean that the proportion of the population aged under 15 years, already 49 per cent in countries such as Oman and Kuwait, is likely to grow further. Higher natural increase and stronger, rural-to-urban migration also point to a burgeoning in the urban population of the region, already over 40 per cent compared to 35 per cent in 1970.

Early migration to the Americas

International labour migration has had a pervasive and growing effect on socio-economic conditions and demographic structures in many of the countries of the Middle East and North Africa. Today, the region hosts more than 4.5m migrant workers. However, prior to the 1970s it was predominantly a region of net population outflow. In the late nineteenth and early twentieth centuries thousands of emigrants from the Ottoman-ruled Levant joined the great wave of European migration to the 'New World' and in particular to the USA. Recorded Arab immigration into the USA rose from a few hundreds in the 1880s to around 4000 in the late 1890s and to over 9000 in 1913. This wave of emigration, which was initially dominated by the outflow of Christians from the Mount Lebanon area, was largely stimulated by the economic emaciation and political insecurity which characterized the terminal decades of Ottoman rule. Immigration restrictions introduced in the mid-1920s, the world depression and the Second World War largely curtailed immigration after 1925. Nevertheless, by 1940 there were more than 206,000 Americans of 'Syrian' origin or parentage. Similarly, in Latin America large Arabic-speaking communities had been established in Brazil (135,000), Argentina (90,000) and Mexico (20,000). For the most part these early 'Syrian' immigrants earned their living through peddling, an occupation which hastened their acculturation.

Further emigration to the New World began in 1948 and accelerated in the wake of the June 1967 Arab-Israeli War* when some 142,000 Arabs entered the USA, a large proportion of them of Palestinian origin. In the post-war period Australia also became an important destination for Arab immigrants. In 1978, for example, there were more than 146,000 first- and second-generation persons originating from Arab countries, the two main contributors being Lebanon and Egypt.

Influx from North Africa

In terms of sheer volume, however, the period from the late 1950s up to the early 1970s was dominated by temporary emigration for employment from the three Maghrib states (Algeria, Morocco, Tunisia*) and from Turkey to Western Europe. This new pattern of migration was fuelled by Europe's growing demand for access to a cheap and essentially temporary labour force at a time of rapid economic expansion.

The growth of Maghribi emigration to Europe began from Algeria during the French colonial period. For example, in the First World War thousands of Algerians were brought across to France to work in transportation, mining and the munitions factories. By 1962, the eve of Algerian independence, the Algerian population in France had reached some 350,484. After independence the Algerian government continued the policy of exporting labour and a series of agreements were made with France to regulate the flow of workers. After 1965 Algeria's development strategy was based on a programme of heavy industrialization*, which created relatively few jobs and largely neglected the traditional agricultural sector. Labour exports were seen as a vital safety valve for the relief of social pressures created by growing unemployment and underemployment. By 1972 the Algerian community in France, now the largest foreign group, had grown to 798,690.

The independent Moroccan and Tunisian governments also placed considerable emphasis on emigration to Europe as a solution to the problems of unemployment. Both countries signed bilateral agreements in the 1960s to facilitate labour transfers with France and other European labour importers. Nevertheless, France was to remain the most important destination for Maghribi emigrants. By 1972 the Moroccan community in France had grown to 218,146, while the number of Tunisians had increased from 47,000 (1964) to 119,546 (1972).

Turkish guest-workers

During the 1960s Turkey also became a major source of labour for Western Europe and in particular for West Germany. A bilateral agreement on labour exports was signed in October 1961 in an attempt to direct labour emigration through official channels. In 1963 the number of Turkish *gastarbeiter* working in West Germany was 22,065; by 1973 that number had grown to 615,827, some 78 per cent of all Turks working abroad. Like the North Africans, the majority of Turks were employed in low-paid and unskilled occupations in the manufacturing, construction and service sectors.

Turn-about in immigration policies

In the early 1970s the economic conditions which had brought about the massive growth in labour inflows came to an abrupt end. In September 1973 Algeria unilaterally terminated all new emigration to France in protest against growing racial unrest and in order to pre-empt anticipated French restrictions on immigration. In the face of deepening recession Germany banned the entry of non-EEC migrant workers in November 1973, while France and most other European countries followed suit in 1974. With rising domestic unemployment, policies aimed at inducing immigrant workers to return home were soon introduced. These policies have been less than successful and continued family regroupment and natural increase have largely compensated for those workers returning home. For example, the Moroccan community in France had grown to over 421,000 by the 1982 French census. In 1982 more than 3.5m Turks and North Africans were living in Western Europe, of whom 1.5m were economically active.

Trans-migration within the region

The oil-price increases of 1973–4 had a dramatic effect on the scale and pattern of international labour migration in the Middle East and North Africa. While employment opportunities in Western Europe were declining, new demands for expatriate manpower were

Table 6. Migrant workers by country of origin and employment, 1980 (thousands)

Country of origin	Saudi Arabia	Libya	UAE	Kuwait	Iraq	Oman	Qatar	Bahrain	Jordan (East Bank)	North Yemen (YAR)	Total	Per cent share
Egypt	155	250	18	82	223	5	6	3	56	4	803	26.7
North Yemen (YAR)	325	—	5	3	—	—	2	1	—	—	336	11.2
Jordan/Palestine	140	15	19	54	10	1	8	2	—	2	251	8.3
South Yemen (PDRY)	65	—	7	10	—	—	2	1	—	—	89	3.0
Syria	25	15	6	35	5	—	1	—	4	1	89	3.0
Lebanon	33	6	7	8	5	1	1	—	1	1	62	2.1
Sudan	56	21	2	6	—	2	1	1	1	1	90	3.0
Maghrib	1	65	—	—	—	—	—	—	1	—	66	2.2
Oman	10	—	19	2	—	—	2	1	1	—	34	1.1
Iraq	3	—	1	40	—	—	—	—	1	—	44	1.5
Somalia	8	5	5	1	—	—	—	—	1	1	20	0.7
All Arabs	821	377	89	241	243	9	23	9	66	10	1884	(62.8)
Pakistan	30	65	137	34	8	32	21	26	2	3	358	11.9
India	29	26	110	45	2	85	12	12	4	2	327	10.9
Other Asian	94	27	21	10	6	12	5	11	8	1	195	6.5
All Asians	153	118	268	89	16	129	38	49	14	6	880	(29.3)
OECD and Europe	30	15	12	5	3	4	1	6	3	1	80	2.7
Africa and other	6	10	1	1	2	1	1	1	1	1	26	0.9
Turkey	2	26	—	1	2	—	—	—	—	—	31	1.0
Iran	11	—	41	39	—	—	18	3	—	—	112	3.7
Subtotal	49	51	54	46	7	5	20	10	4	2	249	(8.3)
Total	1023	546	411	376	267	143	81	68	84	18	3013	100.4
Per cent share	34.0	18.1	13.7	12.5	8.9	4.8	2.7	2.3	2.7	0.6	100.0	

Source: J. S. Birks, *et al.* 'Who is Migrating Where? An Overview of International Migration in the Arab World', in A. Richards and P. Martin, *Migration, Mechanization and Agricultural Labour Markets in Egypt* (Boulder, 1983), pp. 103–16.

stimulated within the region itself. Tunisian and Turkish emigration, for example, turned increasingly to Libya. This redirection of labour migration reached a peak in 1981 when more than 55,000 Turks were placed in Arab countries, primarily in Libya (30,700), Saudi Arabia (14,300) and Iraq (10,500). The increased oil revenues which accrued to the main oil-exporting countries of the region (Bahrain, Iraq*, Kuwait, Libya*, Oman, Qatar, Saudi Arabia*, UAE) effectively removed the financial constraints to economic growth. Accelerated economic growth and the implementation of spectacular development programmes were, in view of the limited supply and skill content of indigenous manpower, inevitably dependent on the availability of expatriate labour. The supply of labour was facilitated by the laissez-faire attitudes towards labour emigration which prevailed throughout the labour-surplus and capital-poor economies of the region. In addition to the small size and youthful age structures of the population in the oil-exporting states (for example, in 1974 some 49 per cent of Saudi Arabia's population was aged under 15), the domestic labour force is limited by social constraints on women's participation.

The number of immigrant workers in the Arab oil-exporting states grew from about 0.8m in 1972 to 1.60m in 1975 and an estimated 3m in 1980. The accompanying table shows one estimate of migrant stocks in 1980. However, it is difficult to be precise about numbers since there is considerable clandestine immigration and employment. Estimates for 1985 suggest that the immigrant labour force is now probably in excess of 4.3m, some 28 per cent of the total workforce.

Unlike the Maghribi and Turkish workers in Europe, immigrants in the oil-rich Arab states are employed at all skill levels, from professional and technical staff to unskilled labourers. A significant proportion of professional and technical workers are drawn from North America and Western Europe. Overall the largest proportion of immigrant workers (around 56 per cent) are employed in the construction sector.

Although Saudi Arabia (34 per cent) and Libya (18.1 per cent) account for over half of all migrant workers in the region, the level of dependence on immigrant labour is greatest in the smaller Gulf states, notably the UAE where an estimated 251,000 migrants accounted for 85 per cent of total employment in 1975. The respective percentages for Qatar and Kuwait were 81.8 and 69.4; by 1980 these had risen to 82.5 and 79.9 per cent respectively.

During the mid-1970s non-oil-exporting Arab states provided 65.6 per cent of the migrant workers in the region. Egypt (34.78 per cent), North Yemen (30.8 per cent) and Jordan (13.5 per cent) accounted for over half the expatriate workers. Included with the Jordanians are the many thousands of Palestinians* who began migrating to the Gulf after the June 1967 Arab-Israeli* War. Considerable numbers of school-teachers and civil servants are working abroad on a secondment basis, for example Egypt had over 120,000 government employees on secondment in the early 1980s. For the most part, however, migration is arranged by individuals through informal methods and contacts.

Since the mid-1970s the pattern of migrant origins has changed significantly with the Arab share of labour inflows falling from 65 per cent in 1975 to only 48 per cent in 1985. Arab immigrants have been increasingly outnumbered by the growth in Asian immigration. The stock of Asian migrant workers in the Middle East is currently estimated at up to 2.6 million. In the late 1970s South-East and East Asian countries, including the Republic of Korea, Philippines and Thailand, joined the initial flows from Pakistan and India. In contrast to the informal Arab response to labour demands in the oil-exporting countries, Asian labour migration has been characterized by a high degree of organization and has been closely associated with the successful penetration of contracting companies from these countries into the Middle East construction market. These companies undertake to provide a self-contained workforce, accommodated on a work-camp basis, which is repatriated on completion of the contract. For example, over 98 per cent of Korean workers in the Middle East in 1980 were employed by Korean construction firms. While providing a more cost-effective labour force, the controlled supply of Asian manpower also reduces the social and political implications associated with hosting a large Arab immigrant workforce and community.

The growth of the non-national workforce in the oil-rich states has been paralleled by the development of significant immigrant communities, as dependants rejoin migrant workers in the host country. In 1975 the 1.6m migrant workers in the region were accompanied by 1.7m dependants, while by 1985 the number of dependants may have exceeded 6 million. The development of these immigrant communities poses important questions for the host countries, where in many cases immigrants now outnumber the indigenous population. For example, by 1985 Kuwaiti nationals represented only 40.1 per cent of the state's total population, while their share of employment had declined to only 23 per cent. As well as adding to the cost of infrastructure and service provision, growing immigrant communities are increasingly seen to pose a threat to national culture and identity. Moreover, rising political aspirations, particularly among Arab expatriates, may pose a threat to the political stability of their conservative hosts.

Oil states cut back on immigration

As a result of the downturn in world oil prices in the early 1980s and falling capital expenditure in the oil-rich states, immigration and employment policies have begun to be re-evaluated. The volume of new labour immigration has begun to decline: for example, the number of new work permits issued in Kuwait in 1985 was 54 per cent down on the 86,000 issued in 1983, while there is growing evidence of return migration from the Gulf. The outflow of unskilled labour is likely to increase if one of the key aims of the 1985–90 Saudi development plan, to reduce the foreign labour force by 600,000, is even partially achieved.

The Arab labour-supplying countries initially saw labour outflows as an expedient means of reducing high rates of underemployment and unemployment, and of increasing foreign exchange earnings. However, the disproportionate loss of high-level manpower has been a major disadvantage which has led to domestic skilled labour shortages and wage inflation. Labour shortages have been particularly prevalent in Jordan, which by 1975 had up to 40 per cent of its manpower abroad. In response, Jordan has itself become a significant labour importer, employing more than 130,000 immigrant workers (mainly Egyptians) by 1982. Emigration has also had a sometimes disruptive effect on traditional economic sectors, for example labour withdrawal has led to the deterioration of farm terraces in North Yemen* and to falling production of labour-intensive export crops such as cotton and coffee. Although remittance earnings have been a major source of foreign exchange (in North Yemen, for example, remittances in 1982 stood at YR 4000m compared to domestic export earnings of only YR 22m), accounting for 13 per cent of GDP in Egypt, 31 per cent in Jordan, 35 per cent in South Yemen*, their potential as a source of savings and investment capital has been far from realized. Remittances have been largely consumed on the purchase of land, housing and consumer durable goods (often with a high import content), without adding to the productive base of the economy. The extent of this lost opportunity will become increasingly apparent as the Arab labour suppliers face up to the prospect of growing unemployment as a result of falling labour outflows, increasing return migration and shrinking remittance income. Clearly international labour migration and its consequences will remain a major influence on economic development in the Middle East and North Africa for many years to come.

IS

Further reading

N. Abadan-Unat, ed., *Turkish Workers in Europe* (Leiden, 1976)
S. Y. Abraham and N. Abraham, eds., *Arabs in the New World* (Detroit, 1983)
S. Adler, *International Migration and Dependence: the case of France and Algeria* (Farnborough, 1977)
J. S. Birks and C. A. Sinclair, *Arab Manpower: the crisis of development* (London, 1980)
A. R. al-Moosa and K. McLachlan, *Immigrant Labour in Kuwait* (London, 1985)
R. Owen, *Migrant Workers in the Gulf* (London, 1985)

Urbanization

During the last quarter of a century the Middle East and North Africa have become one of the most urbanized regions in the world, one in every two people living in cities by 1985. Yet only a few years previously the ratio had been one city-dweller for every two or three rural-dwellers. The degree of change has varied throughout the area. Oil-exporting states such as Kuwait, Saudi Arabia and the UAE showed very rapid expansion of their towns and cities, and 80 to 90 per cent of their populations became urban-based by the mid-1980s. Kuwait exhibited the most extreme urbanization, with 92 per cent of its population in towns. Urban areas were affected by rising birth rates among their populations, often exceeding 4 per cent annually, migration of rural people from their villages (adding 2 per cent annually), and the arrival of large but regionally variable numbers of foreign emigrants, particularly in countries such as Kuwait (see Population and Migration).

Urbanization meant the rapid concentration of people into a few primate centres, of which Cairo, Tehran, Kuwait and Tripoli (Libya) are examples. The smaller regional towns only expanded slightly. Capital cities such as Beirut or old-established centres such as Istanbul dominated the distribution of population. Many of the primate cities grew up very quickly. Kuwait, a dusty fortress town in 1950, has become a large city.

Threats to the old towns

The cost of rapid growth of cities was the destruction of the traditional walled *madinas*, *suqs* and bazaars (Iran and Afghanistan). Their rigorous apportionment of land-use placed prestigious crafts close to the central mosque, castle and square while the lowly occupations were consigned to the edges of the town. Few of the main cities of the region retain their walls, although there are exceptions among the great centres of Morocco such as Marrakesh and Fez, where the internal strengths of urban culture and a thriving tourist industry assisted the preservation of the traditional core areas. In Kuwait the only important surviving element of the old town is the ruler's palace. Modernization in Iran in the 1930s and 1970s was accompanied by the bulldozing of new straight highways and boulevards through old towns such as the magnificent city of Kerman.

Elsewhere, in old settlements as far apart as Riyadh in Saudi Arabia and Tripoli in Libya, the old towns were allowed to decay gradually as their former inhabitants, now removed to new European-inspired suburbs, were replaced by poor immigrants. The Muslim quarters and Jewish *haras* alike were abandoned. In general, the craft *suqs* and bazaars maintained themselves against the tide of modernization with great difficulty. Even in the strongest of commercial centres such as the Tehran bazaar, modern imported manufactures and plastic goods replaced the products of many traditional manufacturing enterprises.

Urban growth in recent decades has brought about great change in employment patterns. Agricultural and rural crafts have ceased to be the main occupations and have been replaced by service and industrial employment. In the oil-rich economies, construction and work with central government agencies is the main sector of expansion, much of it in the capital cities. New central business districts have been created by the colonization of new lands surrounding older settlements.

Development of new urban areas has taken on a variety of forms. Many new towns are clustered around established centres in the shape of 'European' quarters, such as those built by the French in Fez or by the Italians in the Garden City of Tripoli. In the period before independence such structures indicated the segregation of the native inhabitants in the old town from the colonists in the new. In more recent years the 'European quarters' were taken over by the more prosperous local Arab families. Segregation still occurred, though now between indigenous and foreign peoples as the former attempted to protect themselves against larger immigrant communities. In Kuwait, for example, the old town was taken over by foreigners while the nearby district of Dasma remained an exclusively Kuwaiti preserve.

Table 8. Levels of urbanization (%)

Year	1950	1960	1970	1980	1983
Kuwait	58	72	56	88	92
Israel	—	77	—	89	90
UAE	25	—	52	60	79
Bahrain	71	—	64	—	78
Lebanon	—	44	—	76	78
Jordan	—	43	—	56	72
Saudi Arabia	10	30	24	67	71
Iraq	—	43	—	72	69
Libya	—	23	—	88	61
Qatar	50	—	68	—	58
Tunisia	—	36	—	52	54
Iran	—	34	—	50	53
Syria	—	37	—	50	48
Algeria	—	30	—	44	46
Egypt	—	38	—	45	45
Turkey	—	30	—	47	45
Morocco	—	29	—	41	43
South Yemen (PDRY)	—	28	—	37	37
Oman	—	—	—	4	25
Afghanistan	—	—	12	19	20
North Yemen (YAR)	—	3	—	10	18

Sources: IBRD, *World Development Report* (various years); N. C. Grill, *Urbanisation in the Arabian Peninsula* (Durham, 1984), p. 2.

Table 7. Population in largest city at last census (million persons)

City	Population at most recent estimate
Cairo/Giza	13000
Tehran	5734
Baghdad	3400
Istanbul	2772
Alexandria	2708
Casablanca	2437
Algiers	2200
Ankara	1878
Jidda	1500
Beirut	1500
Riyadh	1308
Damascus	1178
Mashhad	1119
Aleppo	1109
Kabul	973
Isfahan	926
Basra	915

Source: Britannica Book of the Year 1985 (Chicago, 1985)

Table 9. Urban population between 1965 and 1983

	% Population in urban areas		% Growth in urban populations		% in main city	
Country	1965	1983	1965–73	1973–83		
Afghanistan	13	20	6.3	5.5	30	31
Algeria	38	46	2.5	5.4	27	12
Egypt	41	45	3.0	2.9	38	39
Iran	37	53	5.4	5.1	26	28
Iraq	50	69	5.7	5.3	35	55
Israel	81	90	3.8	2.7	46	35
Jordan	47	72	4.7	4.8	31	37
Kuwait	75	92	9.3	7.8	75	30
Lebanon	50	78	6.2	1.6	64	79
Libya	29	61	8.9	8.1	57	64
Morocco	32	43	4.0	4.2	16	26
Oman	4	25	10.8	17.6	—	—
Saudi Arabia	39	71	8.4	7.4	15	18
Syria	40	48	4.8	4.2	35	33
Tunisia	40	54	4.1	3.7	40	30
Turkey	31	45	4.9	3.7	18	24
UAE	56	79	16.7	11.2	—	—
South Yemen (PDRY)	30	37	3.4	3.5	61	45
North Yemen (YAR)	6	18	9.7	8.8	—	25

Source: World Bank, *World Development Report* (Oxford, 1985), pp. 216–17.

Over-rapid expansion of the urban sector has brought serious economic and social problems. Unplanned housing development created both poor-quality suburbs and shanty towns in all but a few favoured cities in the region. Water, electricity and road systems often failed to keep up with the creation of new housing areas. The great *bidonvilles* of Casablanca and the *gecekondus* (illegal shanties) of Istanbul, for instance, were notorious for their lack of all but the most primitive of sanitation or other services. Within the shanty towns there was considerable social organization, with concentrations of families from a common rural origin in the same sector and subjected to a complex hierarchy of wealth and status.

Many entirely new towns have been set up in the recent past. The towns of Dammam in Saudi Arabia, Al-Ahmadi in Kuwait, Agha Jari in Iran and Marsa Breqa in Libya were all examples of modern settlements planned to support the oil industry as oil terminal or residential centres. All were well laid out and generously serviced modern towns in the Western rather than the Middle Eastern urban tradition.

New towns did not fare entirely well anywhere. The more than fifty new towns in Israel, for example, were often built in haste and there were several failures, especially in the north where populations of the towns were in the 6000 to 12,000-person range. With small numbers of people involved in these regional centres, they were not attractive to the more enterprising Israelis, and tended to house immigrants with limited skills and aspirations. The most successful of Israeli new towns were sited in the south. Ber Sheva, at the centre of a planning region of some half a million population and with more than 50,000 people living in the town, was, with some five or six other new towns, of a size adequate to prosper.

Recent urban development has tended to bring further polarization to a region already known for its great diversity of peoples and climate. Growing alienation between town and country, disparity between a rich urban elite and shanty dwellers, and discrimination between local people and immigrants contain the seeds of continuing internal urban tension throughout the region.

KM

Further reading

G. Blake, J. I. Clarke and W. B. Fisher, eds., *Populations of the Middle East and North Africa* (London, 1972)
J. I. Clarke, 'Contemporary Urban Growth in the Middle East', in J. I. Clarke and Howard Bowen-Jones, eds., *Change and Development in the Middle East* (London, 1981)
V. F. Costello, *Urbanization in the Middle East* (Cambridge, 1977)
N. C. Grill, *Urbanisation in the Arabian Peninsula*, Occasional Papers Series No. 25, Durham University (Durham, 1984)
R. B. Serjeant, ed., *The Islamic City* (Paris, 1980)

Social change and class formation

The Middle East has experienced unusually rapid social change over the past thirty years. The most obvious reason has been the dramatic rise in oil* revenues, but although the effects of oil wealth are important in understanding social formations today, other factors have contributed to the present distribution of political power, wealth and status. Chief among these has been the political and economic influence of the major Western powers from the early nineteenth century onwards; the nationalist reaction against imperialism and colonialism and the creation of nation states which are politically independent but economically enmeshed in the world market economy; and the development of new social phenomena such as mass education and complex patterns of migration.

More difficult to characterize with any accuracy are the new social classes and strata which have emerged over the past hundred years. Like social formations in other post-colonial societies, Middle Eastern societies do not fit the class categories developed by Marx and others in relation to Western industrial capitalism. This is not least because the economies of Middle Eastern states have not developed along the same lines as those of the West. Certainly most analysts would argue that these Europe-centred categories need amendment when applied to the dynamics of Middle Eastern societies. Perhaps more important, however, is to understand the processes through which social change has occurred.

Impact of the West

The impact of European imperialism on the Middle East was arguably the most crucial determinant of social change in the late nineteenth and early twentieth centuries. Although its impact varied widely from one part of the Middle East to another, certain general trends were evident. The intensification of trade relations with the industrialized West altered or destroyed older patterns of trade and undermined local craft industries. Cities such as Damascus, formerly a centre of overland trade and artisan production, had become something of a backwater by the beginning of the twentieth century, eclipsed by Mediterranean ports such as Beirut, which benefited from closer connections, through sea trade, with Europe. The urban merchant and artisan classes in Damascus lost economic influence while a new stratum of merchants in the coastal cities emerged, dependent on relationships with European traders and consuls.

Relationships between town and countryside also changed as, to varying degrees, international market relations penetrated agricultural production. This was most dramatically evident in Egypt*, where cotton-production for the international market dominated

A young woman travelling on the 'Lézard Rouge' train, Tunisia

agriculture from the 1860s until the end of the Second World War. It consolidated the power of a class of large landowners and merchants who were also influential in urban political circles. Increasing commercialization of agriculture generally led to greater competition for land and growing landlessness among the peasantry, who still made up the majority of the population in much of the region.

Virtual colonial rule – in Algeria under the French from 1830, in Egypt under the British from 1882, and under the League of Nations Mandate system in Syria, Lebanon, Palestine and Transjordan, and Iraq from 1921 – drew new national boundaries and increased the centralization of power in capital cities, replacing the looser, more decentralized structures of the Ottoman Empire (see Modern History). At one level this had the effect of creating more clearly defined social and political hierarchies among landowners and peasants, urban merchants, artisans and petty traders. But, at the same time, the colonial powers often manipulated and promoted tribal, regional and sectarian allegiances for their own purposes, sharpening ethnic and religious divisions and encouraging people to define themselves by sectarian rather than class criteria. French support for the Maronites* in Lebanon and the ʿAlawis* in Syria, and the British imposition of Sunni, Hashimite rulers on predominantly Shiʿi Iraq are examples of this process.

A further effect of the imposition of national boundaries was the decline in the power of pastoral-based tribal society. While nomadism survived at reduced levels, the power of the great tribal confederations of Syria and Iraq was eroded, although some tribal leaders became settled landowners and continued to wield their influence in urban politics. Only in the Arabian peninsula did the desert tribes retain much of their influence.

The influence of nationalism

Nationalism, the widespread reaction to colonial and imperial domination, became the leading political force in the Arab world from the 1930s onwards. Nationalist movements varied in their social composition but generally represented an alliance of classes and strata which had not benefited from colonial rule or international trade. Prominent among these was an emergent national bourgeoisie which, unlike the comprador merchants and landowners who depended on the international market, wanted an economy free from foreign domination. Also in the forefront of nationalist politics was the growing body of professionals – lawyers, doctors and administrators – excluded from positions of influence under colonial or semi-colonial administrations. Popular support came from urban traders and artisans and, in countries like Egypt, from a small organized working class. These were joined sporadically by sections of the land-hungry peasantry.

After independence, the populist ideologies of Nasser* in Egypt, the Baʿth* parties of Syria and Iraq and the Front de Libération Nationale (FLN*) in Algeria shared a certain common rhetoric, stressing national unity as against class divisions, promising social equality and calling for the mobilization of the people for the development of the country. State and party in these countries took a major role in economic affairs, stepping in to mobilize resources when private capitalism failed to do so. The state also engaged in various forms of social engineering: the creation of mass education and health services and the redistribution of wealth through land reform and other measures.

Failures to restructure

However, with the partial exception of Iraq, where oil revenues have enhanced the state's ability to define the direction of social change, these efforts at reshaping society have fallen far short of what was intended. The main reason for this has been the failure to create independent and flourishing local economies. Mass education has certainly altered the lives of many, but lack of resources, financial and human, have limited the value and scope of both the health and education services.

In the rural areas the power of the old landowning classes was broken, but the substitution of a state-sponsored class of middle-income peasants has not resolved the problems of landlessness and poverty. These problems have been exacerbated by the fact that in most Middle Eastern countries the urban-based national leadership has given low priority to agriculture in economic planning.

One of the results is that, both in countries where the state has attempted a radical reshaping of rural class-relations and in those where only minor adjustments have been made, neglect of rural needs has led to a massive drift of population to the cities. Thus Cairo, Amman, Algiers and Casablanca now have vast shanty towns and slums, housing largely impoverished migrants scraping a living on the margins of society.

In the cities too, the role taken by the state, especially in Iraq, Egypt, Syria and Algeria has led to an enormous expansion in public sector employment in the civil service and state corporations. This has also been, in part, a consequence of the political need to offer employment to those newly emerged from high school and university education. These graduates now form part of a vast army of underpaid and mostly underemployed bureaucrats. In these countries the governments of the last ten years have backed away from their commitment to state intervention and a protectionist economy. The most obvious example has been Egypt* under Presidents Sadat* and Mubarak*, where the policy of *infitah** ('opening up' to international capital) has brought a dramatic restoration in the fortunes of the urban entrepreneurial class, based mainly on real estate speculation and a construction boom, and demand for luxury imported goods. Yet these policies have not led to any significant slimming of the state bureaucracy. The present trend in countries such as Egypt, Algeria and Syria is towards a growing inter-relationship between state and private sectors. Private capitalists use their connections in the upper echelons of the bureaucracy to acquire contracts or permits, while senior bureaucrats use their positions to engage in private business.

At the lower levels of the bureaucracy, civil servants are generally very badly paid and frequently take second and even third jobs in the private sector to supplement their incomes. Thus it is becoming increasingly difficult to view the bureaucracy as a separate social class or series of strata as the line between state and private capital in the economy becomes increasingly blurred.

In states such as Jordan* or Morocco*, ruled by conservative monarchies, the priority has been less state-led social and economic change than a concern to shore up the position of the monarchy and to maintain the influence of classes – and institutions such as the army – which support it. On the whole this has left the power of the landowning/merchant class more or less intact. But in these countries, too, the drift into the cities of the rural poor has altered the urban socio-economic structure and brought sporadic political pressures on the regimes. Pressure has also come from a growing professional stratum. In Jordan, especially in the 1960s, the pressure was compounded by the fact that this stratum consisted mainly of Palestinians* concerned not so much about their class position as about their national rights.

The Gulf: the influence of wealth

In the Gulf states and Saudi Arabia*, social structures have been reshaped by the sudden access of wealth to previously poor tribal societies with a modest mercantile economy in the few cities. The power of the present ruling families rests on the state's ability to command the economy through control of oil revenues and to maintain the allegiance of the small indigenous populations through provision of a high standard of living and services. In Kuwait*, for instance, the merchant class, in the past often at loggerheads with the ruling family, has now generally associated itself with ruler and

Kuwaiti women admiring clothing in the boutiques of Salmiya High Street and the Salhia Complex, Kuwait's most exclusive shopping mall

state in order to share the fruits of prosperity. But affluence has been spread to the wider society, to private entrepreneurs and professionals who find guaranteed employment in the civil service and public sector companies. In Saudi Arabia, where similar trends prevail, it is generally argued that this process has yet to lead to the emergence of clear class structures from tribal and family allegiances. But the sharpest distinctions in Gulf societies are not class divisions among citizens, but divisions between nationals and migrants.

Migration and remittances

From the Arab world, migrants have come mainly from Egypt, Lebanon, Jordan and Syria and included a large proportion of uprooted Palestinians living in the Diaspora. While the social position of these migrants varies from manual worker to professional, their status as non-citizens has generally prevented them from becoming part of Gulf society, and most still view themselves as part of their home society rather than that of the host country. Political participation has also been actively discouraged by governments fearful of their disruptive influence. Mass emigration, from rural to urban areas, to the Gulf and to Europe has been one of the most significant phenomena in the Middle East since the Second World War, yet its impact on society so far seems ambiguous (see Population and Migration). Migrants from rural areas tend to maintain strong family and economic ties with their home village, with family income depending on migrant remittances to maintain it economically even if agriculture still plays a part in its subsistence. Remittances do not necessarily lead to upward mobility – sometimes they are simply used to pay debts or contribute to maintaining a standard of living. Even where they are invested, it is usually in housing, education and consumer goods rather than in production, either urban or rural. The indications are that the migrant boom to the Gulf and to Europe is coming to an end, and it is as yet unclear what long-term social effects it has had, beyond, in some instances, contributing to individual social mobility. However, it is clear that if the majority of migrants are forced to return home, this could cause a serious socio-economic, and possibly political, crisis in a number of countries.

The impact of education

The impact of mass education* is equally hard to assess. Access to education, however inadequate, has certainly increased social mobility and led to some dramatic changes in social status in the course of one or two generations. This has perhaps been most marked among deracinated Palestinians*, for whom education has represented the only portable asset available. Yet for many, the expectations created by education far outstrip the prospects open to them and the mediocrity of most state education systems means that those with money and influence send their children to private schools and to universities abroad, thus perpetuating differentiation and privilege.

Class politics

While the glaring discrepancies between wealth and poverty which still exist in many Middle Eastern societies have led from time to time to riots and other expressions of popular discontent, organized class-based politics (as opposed to the expression of political interests through politics) is rarely in evidence. This is partly explained by the lack of organized forces in society which could sustain such politics. Coherent political organization has largely been confined to political parties based on national rather than class consciousness, or on 'national' institutions such as the army. Disillusionment with secular nationalism has not led to class-based politics in most cases, but to another form of populism based on religious fundamentalism.

The smallness of the organized urban working class has meant that most leftist parties with a rhetoric of class politics are dominated by the intelligentsia rather than by the working class. Trade unionism is consequently not an important political force, and in most countries trade unions* are strictly controlled by government or ruling party.

There are also numerous socio-political factors which cut across class divisions. Sectarian and ethnic cleavages which were utilized by Ottoman and colonial rulers have persisted and play an important part in the politics of a number of countries, of which Lebanon* is the most obvious example. But while communal ties may weld together different social classes in the kind of patronage networks exemplified by the Maronite* community in Lebanon, it is also the case that one of the driving forces behind the Maronite political stance is the defence of entrenched privileges for its business and political establishment. Equally, religious or communal loyalties may galvanize people in a struggle for economic or political power against the elite of their own community as well as against society in general, as has been the case of the Shiʿis in southern Lebanon. In Syria, the ʿAlawi* community, by gaining a dominant position in the Baʿth* party and the state apparatus have transformed themselves from an underprivileged community into a dominant elite.

Thus class and communal factors intertwine, both in defending the status quo and in promoting social change. But this variety of cross-cutting allegiances makes it difficult to predict how far existing social formations will remain intact. Reminders of their fragility are frequent and their stability does not depend solely on the internal dynamics of each society, but on a wide variety of regional and international pressures which have already played a major part in shaping Middle Eastern societies today.

SG-B

Further reading

H. Batatu, *The Old Social Classes and the Revolutionary Movements of Iraq: a study of Iraq's old landed and commercial classes and of its Communists, Baʿathists and Free Officers* (Princeton, 1978)

R. Owen and T. Asad, eds., *The Middle East* (The Sociology of Developing Societies Series) (London, 1983)

M. Rodinson, *Islam and Capitalism*, tr. Brian Pierce (London, 1974)

P. A. Smith, *Palestine and the Palestinians 1876–1983* (London, 1984)

The changing role of women

Education has played the major part in changing women's roles in the region (see Education). Calls for women's education began to be made by liberal reformists in the nineteenth century. In Beirut, Butrus al-Bustani* is said to have given a speech as early as 1849 calling for the education of women. In Cairo, some years later, Rifa'a al-Tahtawi* wrote about the importance of universal primary education for both boys and girls. Women's education and emancipation were among the reforms called for by the Young Turks*. However, writers of the nineteenth and early twentieth century, men and women alike, generally emphasized that a woman's role was within the family; women should be educated so that they might better educate the new generation.

Women at work on washing machine motors in a small factory in Latakia, Syria

Muhammad ʿAli* opened a training school for midwives in Egypt in 1832, and Christian missionaries opened a sprinkling of schools in the 1840s and 1850s in various parts of the Ottoman empire*, but schools for both sexes remained few and far between until this century. Still, several women, mostly from well-to-do families, had received an education by the end of the last century. This is indicated by the number of women's magazines that began to appear at the time. The first Arab women's magazine was *al-Fatat* (The Young Woman), which was published in Alexandria in 1892 by a Syrian woman, Hind Nawfal, and was intended to be a 'scientific, historical, literary magazine' with no political ambitions. By 1909, there were at least thirteen monthly and fortnightly women's magazines appearing in Cairo and Alexandria. In Turkey a women's magazine entitled *Progress* is said to have appeared in 1869; and a weekly called *The World and Women* was published some years later.

The 'father' of feminism in the Arab world is widely considered to be the Egyptian Qasim Amin, a disciple of the great Muslim reformist Muhammad ʿAbduh*, who, along with Jamal al-Din al-Afghani, was a major force in the Arab liberal tradition that sought to reconcile the spirit of Islam with the demands of the modern age.

Qasim Amin's books, *Tahrir al-mar'a* (Liberation of Women, 1899), and *al-Mar'a al-jadida* (New Woman, 1900) caused an uproar among conservatives. Amin called for women's education (though not as advanced as that of men), freedom and equality (except in the matter of polygamy), as well as their right to work to guarantee their freedom. Amin wrote his second book to answer the criticism aroused by the first, and had clearly become more radical along the way. In the first, he had based his arguments on the Qur'an* and the *shari'a**; in the second, he turned to reason rather than to a liberal interpretation of religion.

From the earliest days of the call for change in the position of women in the region, there have been two conflicting trends within nationalist ranks. On the one hand, liberal reformists believed that European powers had been able to dominate the Middle East not just because they had developed modern technology, but also because they had overcome tyranny in their own societies and developed democracy and social institutions. Europeans were free to express themselves and to be creative, and their women seemed to enjoy equality and freedom by contrast with local women. Therefore, the way to shake off domination was to take what was good from the West and add it to what was good in the East. The reformists did not want to relegate religion to a secondary position, as some Europeans had done, but to cleanse Islam of false interpretations incorporated into the people's way of life over the centuries.

By contrast, conservative nationalists believed that European powers planned to strengthen and propagate their domination of the East by subverting its social structures. They therefore looked with great suspicion upon Western ideological imports that were likely to loosen social ties or weaken religious faith. They were particularly suspicious of feminism, which they saw as a direct attack upon the family, the strongest social unit. The way to shake off foreign domination, they believed, was to reinforce tradition and resist attempts at social change, particularly in the position of women.

Conflict between nationalism and tradition

These two trends are still very powerful today. For example, conservative nationalism was a major force in the Algerian Revolution*, and the reason why women, though they played an active part in the revolution, did not come to enjoy personal freedom until well after independence in 1962. Conservative nationalists gained the upper hand in Iran following the 1979 revolution, leading to forced readoption of the veil and resegregation in education and work. Conservative nationalism is also present in varying degrees throughout the Arab world and Turkey. It is one indication of a belief by the people of the region that they continue to be dominated by the West, if not by its armed forces (except in the case of the Israeli occupation of Palestine, the Syrian Golan Heights and southern Lebanon), then by Western economic power and support for unpopular regimes.

In the early twentieth century, women were galvanized into action by the struggle for independence from foreign powers, and agitation for women's rights was one of the results of their participation. In Egypt*, there were frequent protests against the British occupation* which began in 1882, but perhaps some of the most dramatic were the demonstrations by veiled women marching through the streets of Cairo during the 1919 nationalist uprising. The leading female figure of the time was Huda Sha'rawi, who is said to have marched against the wishes of her husband.

The women of Palestine* also organized themselves in an attempt to fight off the threat of Zionist colonization of their country and to protest against the British Mandate*. The first Arab Women's Congress of Palestine was held on 26 October 1929, and was attended by some 200 women from all over the country. The conference resolutions considered British acts in Palestine to be a deliberate violation of all the pledges Britain had given to the Arabs, and called on its members to make every possible effort to abrogate the Balfour Declaration* of 1917 in which Britain promised to help create a Jewish national home in Palestine.

In Iran*, women took part in the constitutional revolution and organized demonstrations in 1905 against the Shah and exploitation of the country by foreign – British and Russian – interests. They formed committees and began to call for women's education. In Turkey, women were active in Atatürk's ranks and one of the most visible figures of the revolution was a woman writer and orator, Halide Edib Adivar.

By the 1920s, more and more women in the region began to feel they were entitled to civic and political rights, although their demands remained less radical than those of women in Europe and the United States. An Egyptian reformist who helped set up the Educational Union of Women in March 1914, Malak Hifni Nasif, remarked that Western women seeking the right to vote were suffering from 'indigestion' as a result of too much progress. However, even though the ten-point plan to improve the status of women that she presented to the first Egyptian Congress of 1911 was quite moderate, it was rejected.

Discarding the veil

In Egypt, Huda Sha'rawi was responsible for another dramatic gesture, one which is looked upon as launching the movement for women's liberation in the Arab world. On her return from the International Conference of Women in Rome in 1923, she took off her veil on arriving at Cairo railway station. The veil has always been considered, particularly by women outside the region, as a symbol of the life of seclusion and total obedience that Muslim women are believed to lead. It should be pointed out here that only the wealthy could afford to keep their women in seclusion and to maintain the establishment of the *harim* (literally, 'forbidden' or 'off-limits'). The majority of women worked as part of the natural course of things, and, as in other pre-industrial societies, they tended to work longer and harder than men. In the fields, women helped their husbands in weeding and sowing, and were largely responsible for breeding the family livestock and poultry and for food processing. Beduin women, too, were responsible for a variety of tasks, including weaving and crafts. Lower-class women in the towns had to work, sometimes outside the home, to make ends meet, either in newly developing industries (often in appalling conditions) or in domestic service or other informal sectors.

These women generally covered their hair but did not veil their faces, and their activities took them outside the boundaries of the home. Given that their work was indispensable for the survival of the family unit, they were able to stake a claim in the decision-making process, their power growing with the size of their family and, as advancing years allowed, even more freedom of movement. Wealthier city women tended both to envy and to romanticize the greater freedom their sisters in the countryside enjoyed. In turn, country women envied the more leisured lives of the wealthy city woman.

In Algeria*, too, the veil took on a special significance during the War of Independence (1956–62) where it became both a symbol of Islamic identity for Muslim women and a cover for freedom fighters. Women played a prominent role in the war. Jamila Bouhaired, who was accused of carrying out attacks on several cafés in Algiers and who was sentenced to death by the French (the sentence was later commuted), is the best known. Others, such as her tragic accomplice Jamila Boupasha who died shortly after the war, and Zoulaika Boujema'a, who smuggled arms through the dreaded Maurice line between Tunisia and Algeria, played positive roles in the fight for liberation. However, many such women were disappointed after the war to find that the equality for which they had fought was not to be respected.

Women in public life

The 'official' history of the women's movement in the Arab world is considered to have begun with Huda Sha'rawi's public rejection of the veil, and with the establishment of the first major Arab women's union by Sha'rawi and her colleagues, the Egyptian Women's Union, in 1923. The Union undertook a great many charitable activities in the fields of health and education, and helped orphans

Traditional and modern women reflect the generation gap in Marrakesh, Morocco

or repudiated women to find shelter and train for suitable work. To this day, state-sponsored and most other women's groups in the region concentrate on literacy campaigns, schools, orphanages and other areas of social welfare. The state is now held to be responsible for most of these services but in the early days these public-minded women were tackling areas of concern that were neglected largely because modern nation states had not yet been established. By so doing, they helped to alleviate the grim conditions of their day.

The Union also worked for women's rights, calling for equality, free access to all levels of education for girls, and reforms in Islamic family laws relating to marriage and divorce, particularly polygamy and repudiation (the man's ability to cast off his wife at will). The slowness of the process of social change is apparent when one seeks to assess how many of these aims have been achieved.

In those countries of the region where there are constitutions, the equality of all citizens is trumpeted, and in all the states where there are parliaments, except the Gulf state of Kuwait*, women have achieved the right to vote and to be elected. Ironically, the Kuwaiti Constitution guarantees equal rights to all citizens of the state; however, the electoral law restricts voting and standing for election to male citizens over twenty-one. The unconstitutionality of the electoral law is often raised by the articulate women's groups in Kuwait seeking the right to vote. These groups lost several battles over the issue in the 1970s and 1980s. In 1986 the whole question was rendered academic by the dissolution of the Kuwaiti parliament.

In the countries where women do vote and stand for election, there are few women deputies, as indeed is the case in most parliaments around the world. Lebanon's women activists have often voiced their disappointment that only one woman has been elected to parliament in the first Arab country to give women the vote, in 1953. In Turkey, women were given the right to vote in 1930.

Most cabinets in the region have included at least (and usually at most) one female minister. The first Arab woman minister was appointed in Iraq in 1959. The women ministers are usually responsible for social welfare, education or health. Jordan had a woman Minister for Social Development, Mrs Inʿam al-Mufti, and broke further with tradition when Layla Sharaf was appointed in 1984 as Minister for Information, a post with some power; she subsequently resigned. In Tunisia in 1983 two women were appointed to the cabinet for the first time. In some of the Gulf countries (Kuwait and the UAE), women have reached the level of under-secretary.

Major developments through education

The most impressive strides in the region have been in the field of education*. There was an explosion in educational facilities in the post-independence era, although demand continues to be greater than supply. According to United Nations figures for 1980, there were some 18.5m male and 12m female students at all levels in the Arab world, 5m male and 3.5m female students in Turkey, and 5.5m male and 3.5m female students in Iran.

Drop-out rates are high for boys in the secondary cycle, as poorer parents need them to start earning a living, and even higher for girls whose parents want to see them safely married (there is a minimum age of marriage, usually 16 for girls and 18 for boys, in most countries in the region; early marriage is still a widespread, though decreasing, practice).

As these figures show, a substantial gap remains between male and female enrolment. Similarly, while there has been a determined effort to tackle illiteracy, it is still high, and women, as elsewhere in the Third World, continue to show much higher rates of illiteracy than men. Part of the reason for the slowness of change is the traditional view of women's roles, but even more important are the financial pressures on parents, who, if they are only able to continue the education of some of their children, will choose the boys as the ones certain to be breadwinners.

Low workforce participation

Economic pressures like inflation, along with education, have led to a change of attitude in the traditional view of women's roles. Surveys on attitudes to education in the region reveal a growing belief that women should be educated to find work. According to studies of the region, in the 1970s Middle Eastern women showed the lowest labour-force participation rates in the Third World. Women in the workforce accounted for 11.4 per cent of the female population in the Middle East compared to 26.8 per cent in Latin America, 42.9 per cent in Asia and 45.8 per cent in Africa. However, the Middle East region also showed the largest proportionate increase since the 1960s (53 per cent).

The increasing participation by Middle Eastern women in the wage labour-force indicates a loosening of family ties, although these remain stronger than they are in the West. The extended family offers its members not only warmth and moral support in difficult situations – even if not all members of a family live under the same roof, they still maintain strong ties – but is also a social security centre, caring for the ill, the aged and disabled, and a job-hunting centre responsible for using its contacts to find its members suitable employment. Within the family, women are to be protected and financially supported by their male relatives if they do not marry or in cases of divorce.

Labour laws in the region are on the whole egalitarian, and maternity leave ranges from adequate to generous. However, these laws are more likely to be applied in the public sector than in the private sectors. In countries with small populations like Iraq or

Jordan, the governments actively encourage the entry of women in the workforce. However, in oil-rich countries which import foreign manpower, like Saudi Arabia, Qatar, the United Arab Emirates and Kuwait, and where a determined effort to make use of womanpower could cut down on the numbers of foreign workers, there is reluctance to offend the powerful traditional religious establishment. These governments try to guarantee each graduate, male or female, a job and many women work in education and health care, or as administrators. However, the process is left to the individual and in Saudi Arabia* has to be accomplished within a policy of segregation at the workplace. Interestingly, change is slowest largely in those countries that can afford to hold it up. In countries like Egypt*, by contrast, women working outside the home are a fact that has been accepted for decades.

While more women are earning their own money, the extent to which this has gained them more personal freedom is less clear. It is still rare throughout the region for a woman to live on her own. Both men and women are expected to remain with the family until they marry; in particular women bear the brunt of protecting the family honour and are expected to remain pure in fact and in reputation until marriage.

Moreover, while economic need is pushing women to work, their ability to find work is not guaranteed. The economic situation in the heavily populated countries – Egypt, Morocco, Algeria, Sudan, Iran and Turkey – is so dire that unemployment is unacceptably high. Even the less densely populated states – Syria, Jordan, Tunisia, Lebanon – are all feeling the pinch of the recession that struck in the 1980s, as are the oil-producers themselves. Both oil exporters and importers in the region were able to stave off the effects of unsuccessful economic policies and corruption in the 1970s because of the massive revenues brought by the increase in the price of oil, which trickled down to poor Arab and Muslim neighbours. In the 1980s, however, the economic situation worsened, leading to turmoil and an unwillingness to see women take jobs away from men.

An area where women have made strong headway has been in the professions. There are substantial numbers of professional women, and they are often able to reach the top of the ladder remarkably quickly. Newspaper and magazine headlines greet each new success, like that of the first woman pilot in Jordan, of women judges in Morocco, Turkey and Iraq, of a woman dean of the Faculty of Law and Islamic Law at Kuwait University, of women television producers, radio announcers, marine biologists, computer scientists, film makers or economists.

Personal rights

There has been least change at the level of personal rights. With the exception of Turkey, rights within the family are governed by personal status laws drawn from the *shariʿa* or by direct application of *shariʿa* law. In Turkey, Kemal Atatürk* was determined that women should have equal rights with men. He began by appointing a committee in 1923 to review Islamic family law. When the committee's work was held up by traditional views, he declared Turkey a secular state. In 1926 it acquired a family code based on the Swiss civil code. (Interestingly, the Swiss were among the last Western nations to revise their family code to make it more equitable to women; the provisions decreeing the man the head of the family, which have been similar throughout the world, were only revised in 1985). However, it is one thing to pass laws, and another for people to accept them. In spite of the fact that polygamy was made illegal and only the children of a secular marriage were considered legitimate, the Turkish authorities had to grant legal status to some 8 million children by 1950.

Tunisia has the most progressive personal status code, passed in 1956, of the Arab states and is the only one to have abolished polygamy (although others have restricted it). The code was passed immediately after independence in 1956 as a result of President Habib Bourguiba's* determination. Although it was based on a liberal interpretation of the *shariʿa**, criticism by conservatives had to be fought off. The code provided for a minimum marriage age and the consent of both partners was required; women had equal rights of divorce with men, and the man's unilateral right to

Members of the Iraqi Women's Federation

repudiate the wife was ended; custody of the children (which in other countries becomes the right of the father after a certain age) was also made more egalitarian and took into account the children's interest. Some Tunisian feminists complain that inheritance continues to be applied according to Qur'anic stipulations, with a woman receiving half a man's share, and that the father is considered to be the head of the family. Again, people, particularly in the rural areas, were slow to realize that a new law existed, and what rights they had under the law.

The subjects raised in personal status codes are the most sensitive in the region. In Algeria, for example, efforts to tackle family laws, apart from fixing a minimum age for marriage, foundered several times because of public outcry. In 1981, a working group was formed to formulate a family code; it worked in strict secrecy and there was no consultation with women. Former resistance fighters and other women activists took to the streets in protest. In 1982 the code was sent to parliament; by this time there was a sharp public debate between liberals and conservatives. Emotions were running so high that the draft was withdrawn. Another commission, which included women deputies, was set up to redraft the bill (and a woman minister was appointed to the cabinet for the first time). The code was finally adopted in 1984, a compromise between tradition and modernity. Polygamy was restricted, women were given the right to divorce on certain grounds, and had first right to custody in cases of divorce.

In Egypt, President Sadat* passed a family code that became known as 'Jihan's law' (after his wife). Egyptian feminists welcomed the improvements as a step along the right path. Women now had the right to keep the house after divorce (a significant gain in overpopulated Egypt). The 1979 law was challenged as unconstitutional in 1985, on the grounds that Sadat had issued it by decree and not through parliament; the court ruled in favour of the challengers. This led to a heated public debate. Many men and women argued that Islam had given women full equality and thus they should have equal rights, while others argued that Islam had allotted to each their rights and duties, and that women had naturally to be protected and maintained. A new law was passed a few months later that kept most of the provisions of the 1979 law. This was hailed as a victory by Egyptian feminists, although the law was not yet egalitarian.

An Arab woman trying out lipstick in a Riyadh cosmetics shop

Referring back to the Islamic ideal

All the debates on the rights of women, whether for political equality as in Kuwait, or over the personal status codes, still take place by and large within an Islamic context and liberals argue furiously with conservatives that it is possible to achieve full equality for women by correctly applying Islamic law, and that women were downtrodden before Islam came to liberate them in the seventh century (for instance, female babies were often killed at birth, a practice Islam forbade). To take the case of polygamy, liberals point out that the Qur'an restricted polygamy by limiting men to four wives, and that this was only meant to be practised in certain situations – when large numbers of men are lost through war or when the first wife is sterile. Moreover, the Qur'an insisted that the wives be treated with absolute fairness, adding that this would prove impossible. Thus, the liberals argue, polygamy is effectively banned.

Both liberals and conservatives point out that the Qur'an gave women their economic rights long before these were achieved in the West. Women could inherit and bequeath property, and hold it in their own names, with no obligation to spend their wealth on their families (the explanation given as to why men receive twice the share of women in inheritance). In the case of divorce, liberals note that the Qur'an urges that women be treated with fairness and kindness. Under Islamic law women can request a divorce if their husbands are impotent, or no longer support them, or mistreat them; however, whether they are successful in their suit or not often depends on the judge hearing the case. Moreover, since the marriage contract is an agreement between two parties, women can stipulate in the contract that they can have the right to divorce, although most are too embarrassed to ask for this at the time of marriage. Conservatives argue that the Qur'an has specified that men are 'a degree above women'; women who are not obedient are to be chastised.

As regards seclusion, liberals note that the Qur'an mentions this only for the wives of the Prophet Muhammad; otherwise both men and women are enjoined to behave chastely. Conservatives argue that the behaviour of the wives of the Prophet is exemplary and should be emulated. Liberals argue that women should have full political rights since a group of women went out to pledge their allegiance to the Prophet, and he accepted their oath. Both liberals and conservatives draw upon examples from the lives of the women at the time of the Prophet to support their arguments: his first wife Khadija, a successful merchant who employed the Prophet before their marriage, another of his wives, ʿA'isha, who played an important political role and was a key reference for the *hadith*, and his daughter Fatima*.

Current threats of reversal of change

To sum up, change in the region has been uneven and in many cases superficial. Slow changes have come through education and as a result of economic necessity, not because of reforms or laws passed by the state. Thus a reversal is possible in any of these countries, even in secular Turkey, and such a reversal has happened in Iran. The reasons for the strength of conservative trends in the region are many and complex. They include a reaction against the rapidity of change and a desire to re-establish the ideal society believed to have existed in the early days of Islam. Thus the loosening of family and community ties by modernization and urbanization could be countered, it is believed, by recreating the Islamic *umma**, as can political and economic domination by the West.

Moreover, conservative Muslim groups are encouraged by several governments to offset leftist movements and to gain legitimacy in the eyes of the people. With the money they receive, some fundamentalist groups give bonuses as incentives to those who wear Islamic dress. With few democratic outlets – parliaments and political parties are carefully controlled – many people turn to religious expression.

Within the Islamic current there is a growing body of 'enlightened Islamists' who, as in the late nineteenth and early twentieth century, seek to combine modern liberalism with the spirit of the religion. The conservatives are currently more powerful than the enlightened Islamists, and they seek resegregation of the sexes, limiting a woman's activities in the public sphere and concentrating her efforts on the home and children.

Female circumcision

Working in women's favour, however, and in favour of the process of democratization in the region, is an increasing willingness to participate in changing their situation through the formation of networks and lobbies. This significant new approach to political and social issues can be illustrated by the present attitude of women activists to female circumcision. Until the 1970s, circumcision was a subject indigenous intellectuals preferred to ignore, largely because it was so often written about or filmed by Western visitors to the

March-past of an Iranian regiment in Tehran as a young woman muses on the future shortly before the revolution in January 1979

exclusion of other subjects. This was seen as part of an effort to make the natives look barbaric.

Female circumcision involves removing a small part or, in extreme cases, all of the clitoris and labia in the belief that this makes women more fertile, more attractive to men and guarantees fidelity. Apart from the loss of sexual response, the operation can result in infection, lasting injury and even death. The practice, which is not Islamic, has been a centuries-old tradition in several African and Afro-Arab countries, dating back to pharaonic times. Now, far from ignoring the subject (while still resenting Western attempts to 'save their darker sisters') there are groups of men and women doctors, health and social workers campaigning to stop the practice.

There is certainly more awareness of women's issues in the region, part of the worldwide awareness generated by the United Nations 1975–85 decade for women. Thousands of words are written on the subject, with more now published by local scholars and writers. Conferences are held on integrating women in development – a favourite catchphrase of governments – and on issues like employment, health, education and personal rights.

Perhaps the most interesting development is the increasing awareness that the struggle to attain equality for women must be imposed on the national agenda, and that women cannot expect automatically to receive their rights once independence is won, but must work for both independence and equality. Having learnt the lesson from the disappointed Algerian women, certain groups of Palestinian women in the occupied West Bank are organizing on different lines. They are working both for independence and social change; otherwise, as one Palestinian activist put it, 'after independence we'll have to start at square one'.

NH

Further reading

L. Beck and N. Keddie, eds., *Women in the Muslim World* (Harvard, 1978)
E. W. Fernea, ed., *Women and the Family in the Middle East: new voices of change* (Austin, Texas, 1985)
E. W. Fernea and B. Q. Bezirgan, eds., *Middle Eastern Women Speak* (Austin, Texas, 1977)
V. Maher, *Women and Property in Morocco: their changing relation to the process of social stratification in the Middle Atlas* (Cambridge, 1974)
C. Makhlouf, *Changing Veils: women and modernisation in North Yemen* (Austin, Texas, 1979)
F. Mernissi, *Behind the Veil* (London, 1985)
N. Saadawi, *The Hidden Face of Eve* (London, 1980)
J. Tucker, *Women in Nineteenth-Century Egypt* (Cambridge, 1985)
N. H. Youssef, *Women and Work in Developing Societies* (Berkeley, California, 1974)
The publications of the Institute for Women's Studies in the Arab World, Beirut University College (New York)

Legal systems

The area loosely called the Middle East is composed of a number of independent countries with legal systems which are far from uniform, but they have certain basic factors in common which have helped in the past and still help to form legal thought and structures, although they do not manifest themselves in the same way in all countries.

Three of these factors are worth mentioning. First, the majority of the population of the area is Muslim, and most of them accept Sunni* Islam. Secondly, most countries of the Middle East and North Africa formed part of the Ottoman Empire*, which became a world power in the sixteenth century and finally expired after the First World War. Thirdly, at one time or other from the nineteenth century onwards nearly all countries were under direct or indirect rule by one or other of the European powers.

Shari'a as the basic legal system

Modern European scholarship has cast doubt on the traditional Muslim explanation of the way in which the Islamic legal system developed, but it is that version which will be given here, because it helps to clarify the concepts and methods of Islamic legal thought.

For Muslims, the *shari'a** is the body of commandments, religious and legal, given by God to mankind through the Prophet Muhammad*. God's will has been revealed in a sacred book, the Qur'an*, in the traditions of what the Prophet said and did (*hadith**), by a consensus of opinion in the community (*ijma'**), and by analogical reasoning (*qiyas**). These are called 'the authoritative sources of jurisprudence' (*usul al-fiqh**).

Only some eighty verses of the Qur'an deal with legal topics regarding secular matters, and even fewer verses give specific legal precepts, such as the injunction to believers to fulfil their contracts (sura 5:1), the recommendation to make use of a pledge when no scribe was available to write a loan agreement and no witness was at hand (2:282), and the prohibition of *riba** or unlawful gain (30:39, 4:161; 3:130; 2:275, 276, 278, 279). The law of inheritance is expounded more fully in the Qur'an, but there are still a number of details which are not dealt with. These lacunae, and other worldly problems for which the Sacred Book does not prescribe, had to be regulated by laws of divine inspiration. As long as Muhammad was alive he was the person to whom adherents looked to settle disputes; after his death an attempt was made to recover and record his deeds, utterances, and even unspoken approval, as directly reported by his Companions, and even as related by succeeding generations of those who had received them from the Companions (*hadith*). Later Muslim scholars accepted that many of these traditions were falsely ascribed to the Prophet, but many of them were undoubtedly genuine.

The circumstances of the community made it necessary to regulate matters which lay altogether outside the purview of the provisions contained in the Qur'an and *hadith*. Consensus of opinion in the community (*ijma*ʿ) was believed by the Sunnis to be the safest way of ascertaining the law. This was justified by an interpretation of certain verses of the Qur'an, and by sayings of the Prophet to the effect that 'there can be no consensus of error or misguided behaviour among my people'. In the process of interpretation and reaching consensus, resort was inevitably made to reasoning by analogy (*qiyas*), in order not to go beyond the limits of the sacred law; a rule of law in the Qur'an or *hadith* was applied by analogy to cases not directly covered by it.

The legal schools

In the course of time legal scholars formed schools of legal thought. There were four main schools among the Sunnis: the Hanafi*, Shafiʿi*, Maliki* and Hanbali* schools, while the Shiʿi, Ibadi* and Zaydi* scholars had their own principles and methods. These schools differ on the relative weight to be given to the various sources of jurisprudence: for example, the Hanafis use *qiyas* extensively, whereas Hanbalis use it only when Qur'an, *ijma*ʿ and even doubtful *hadith* are not available. They differ also in their recognition and use of various subsidiary sources in addition to the four main ones. The Hanafi concept of 'preference' (*istihsan*) and the Maliki concept of 'public interest' (*masalih mursala*) are two among many such subsidiary sources.

In the early tenth century, the point was reached where the exploration of the divine will was exhausted. Sunni jurists and theologians concerned themselves from now onwards with imitating their predecessors and commenting on their treatises. These now began the new era in which 'the door of *ijtihad*'* (the exercise of human reason to ascertain a rule of *shariʿa* law) was closed. The claim of Sunni jurists and theologians to have reached an immutable state initiated a divorce between theory and practice. In practice, rulers and their local governors administered a kind of justice, particularly in criminal matters, and the judges (*qadi**) who administered the *shariʿa* may have exercised a certain discretion, but legal scholars concerned themselves with what ought to be rather than what is. Islamic jurisprudence remained in an ideal world, more or less unchallenged so long as it was protected from alien scrutiny.

Western influences upon law in the Ottoman Empire and North Africa

Serious challenges began in the early nineteenth century, when exchanges between the Ottoman Empire and Europe grew more frequent; it was not only the traffic of commodities and transit of people which increased, but also new ideas which found their way into the minds of a Westernized Ottoman intelligentsia. The system of Capitulations, under which citizens of Western states resident in the Middle East were governed by their own law, attracted the attention of those who were in a position to reform local laws.

These reforms (*tanzimat**) began in the legal sphere in 1850, when the Ottoman government promulgated a commercial code which was an exact replica of the French commercial code of the time. In 1858 a penal code, a mere translation of the French code, was promulgated, and other statutes inspired by the French legal system followed. Between 1869 and 1876 a compilation of Hanafi teaching in regard to obligations was undertaken, and it produced the *Majalla*, which contains provisions in regard to such things as sales, leases, pledges, trusts, mandates, gifts, associations and rules of evidence.

From 1875 onwards, Egypt went even further in the adoption of a legal system based on French law; among other things, it enacted a civil code based on the French one instead of making use of the *Majalla*. Meanwhile Algeria, conquered by the French from 1830 onwards, was subjected some twenty years later to the French criminal, commercial and civil codes. Tunisia and Morocco, which came under French control in 1881 and 1912 respectively, gradually adopted codes based on their French counterparts.

Even in most of these countries, the *shariʿa* continued to regulate matters of personal status (marriage, divorce, testaments). Places more distant from the Ottoman central power, in most of the Arabian peninsula, remained broadly speaking untouched by the Ottoman reforms, and preserved the *shariʿa* intact.

Legal systems in contemporary states

From the end of the Second World War onwards, those countries of the Middle East and North Africa which were under European rule achieved full independence. Most of them adopted new legal systems, and it is now possible to distinguish four different types of system; but it should be remembered that a country in one class may move into another over time, owing to the incessant flux which disturbs most legal systems in the region.

Countries with a wholly secular legal system

Under the firm rule of Kemal Atatürk*, Turkey embarked on a policy of secularism, a course maintained by the state until today. The reform of the legal system in that direction started in 1926 with the adoption of a civil code which reproduces the Swiss code, and includes not only the law of contracts and torts but also personal and family law. A penal code based on the Italian criminal code of 1889 was also enacted in 1926, to be followed by other European-inspired pieces of legislation, such as the commercial code of 1956.

Since the Turkish experiment there has been no other attempt at outright secularism, apart from the rather exceptional case of South Yemen*, which, beginning in 1970, took several steps towards 'scientific socialism' by reforming and codifying its local laws and customs, including family law; the provisions of Islamic law were set aside when the government, under the influence of its form of socialism, felt it to be necessary to do so.

Countries where the shariʿa is still dominant

The legal systems of Saudi Arabia, Oman and North Yemen* still rely heavily on the *shariʿa*, although in different forms: Saudi Arabia follows the Hanbali school, while Ibadism is prevalent in Oman, and the Zaydi and Shafiʿi schools in Yemen. Each of these countries, however, has adopted a substantial number of statutes derived mainly from French and other European legal systems through the intermediary of Egyptian and Lebanese draftsmen, and these limit the *shariʿa* to a certain extent. Thus the operations of commercial companies in these three countries are kept outside the scope of the *shariʿa*, and are regulated respectively by the Saudi Companies Regulation of 1965, the Omani Commercial Companies Law of 1974, and the Yemeni Commercial Companies Law of 1976. By contrast, the *shariʿa* is the civil code of Saudi Arabia and Oman; neither country has produced a contemporary civil code, but North Yemen enacted one in 1976, described as a compendium of Islamic principles and rules. Of the three countries, only Oman has adopted a secular criminal code, that of 1974, which met with opposition from conservative quarters at first, but was later accepted.

Countries with fully established national legal systems

In Egypt, Iraq, Syria, Lebanon, Jordan, Tunisia, Algeria and Morocco there are national legal systems which have certain common characteristics: for example, their commercial and penal codes are practically unrelated to the *shariʿa*, modelled as they are on European counterparts and administered by secular courts, whereas family laws and laws of inheritance continue to be derived from the *shariʿa* and administered by religious courts. By exception, in Tunisia and Egypt the religious courts were disbanded in the mid-1950s and the application of religious laws was entrusted to secular courts. Tunisia is also exceptional because a law of personal status, which was remarkably radical when compared with traditional teaching of the *shariʿa*, was promulgated in 1956, brought into effect in 1957 and substantially supplemented in 1959.

Common influences have not generated a single legal system; on the contrary, there are numerous differences, as a survey of the various civil codes will show. In Lebanon*, the existence of a strong Christian community and the control of France exercised under the Mandate combined to produce in 1932 a code of obligations and contracts drafted by a French jurist and reflecting French law as it existed at that time. Syria* was under the same French Mandate*, but no attempt was made to give it a similar code, although it shared with Lebanon many regulations and statutes introduced by the French. Curiously, the French did not try to give Syria a code of obligations and contracts similar to the Tunisian code of 1906, which contained a number of Islamic principles: it was only in 1949 that it acquired a civil code modelled on that of Egypt*.

This Egyptian code, enacted in 1948 and put into force in 1949, represents a novel attitude towards the reception of foreign laws. It did not adopt them indiscriminately, but selected some of them, either because they did not conflict with the principles of the *shariʿa* or because they blended with those principles; this at least was the claim of the architect of the code, ʿAbd al-Razzaq Sanhuri, but it is in fact an overstatement, because the 1949 code introduced few new *shariʿa* principles into the Egyptian legal system. This explains why Iraq* did not blindly adopt the Egyptian code, although Sanhuri himself was the most prominent member of the committee entrusted with the drafting of an Iraqi civil code; this was enacted in 1951, and it included a number of provisions derived from Islamic law. Even more Islamic is the Jordanian* civil code of 1976, brought into effect in 1977; in it, Islamic principles are included, but sometimes modified almost beyond recognition so as to suit contemporary ideas and requirements.

Of the North African countries ruled by France, Algeria*, which paid the highest price for its independence, was expected to reject the system of law inherited from its French rulers. It did not do so, however, for various reasons, not the least of which was that the system had been in use for more than a century. Instead, a progressive reform of the law was carried out; if not revolutionary, it was deemed more suitable for an independent country. Thus a penal code was enacted in 1966, followed in 1972 by a code of criminal procedure and one of civil procedure. In 1975 a code of commerce and a civil code were published; the civil code is still largely modelled upon the French civil code, although it contains a few principles taken from Arab and Eastern European laws. The most substantial change lies in the fact that matters pertaining to family law, personal status and inheritance are no longer part of the civil code, but instead form the subject matter of the family code published in 1984, which expressly refers to precepts of the *shariʿa*.

Countries with national legal systems in process of development

Two legal systems coexisted in the Gulf from the time of the British penetration of the area, which took place gradually in the course of the nineteenth century and ended with the independence of Kuwait in 1961 and that of Bahrain, Qatar and the seven emirates which today constitute the United Arab Emirates* (Abu Dhabi, Dubai, Sharja, Ras al-Khayma, ʿAjman and Umm al-Qaywayn) in 1971. Natives of these countries were subjected to *shariʿa* law administered by *sharīʿa* courts and occasionally by the ruler himself, whereas all other persons present in the territories were subject to British extra-territorial jurisdiction exercised by foreign secular judges.

After independence, the principles of English common law were not retained by the states, as a way of developing their legal systems. The main reason for this was that there was no consistent British legal legacy, apart from a few orders and codifications, such as the penal code put into force in Bahrain in 1955 (later repealed and replaced by a penal code on an Egyptian model in 1976), and in Dubai in 1970, and a law of contracts brought into effect in Bahrain (1970), Dubai (1971), and then in Sharja, ʿAjman and Ras al-Khayma.

On the other hand, the rule of the *sharīʿa* was not extended in these states, once they became independent, beyond the realm of family and personal matters where it was not disputed, and thus it did not become an all-embracing legal system. The Constitutions of Kuwait (article 2), Bahrain (article 2) and the UAE (article 7) show that the *sharīʿa* is not to have an exclusive role in making law, for they all maintain, in nearly identical terms, that the *sharīʿa* is a primary source of law rather than the only source. It is true that the Constitution of Qatar (article 1) asserts that the *sharīʿa* is the main source, but this was to prove more of a pious statement than a principle to be applied fully.

There are several reasons for the failure to extend the scope of the *sharīʿa*. First, it was commonly assumed in the 1960s that the *sharīʿa* cannot provide for matters of commercial law; many Muslims felt it was more reverent not to distort the teaching of the *sharīʿa* through adaptation and adjustments, but to keep its purity and integrity unimpaired. Secondly, nearly all Middle Eastern Arab countries, once they became independent, adopted commercial statutes, and in some cases civil codes, derived principally from Egyptian laws which themselves had been strongly influenced by French and, to a lesser extent, by other European systems. Egyptian laws were already available in Arabic, and were familiar to members of the legal profession who were to staff the courts of the newly independent states. Thirdly, there is a diversity of Islamic sects and schools of law; to choose one school at the expense of the others might have created problems between Shiʿis and Sunnis in Kuwait and Bahrain, or between adherents of the Sunni schools in the UAE.

Thus Kuwait*, even before independence, turned quite naturally to Egypt for the elaboration of its legal system. A companies law (1960), a commercial code (1961) and a penal code (1960) were among the main pieces of legislation enacted on the pattern of Egyptian law; the *Majalla* continued to act as a civil code, while matters of obligation were dealt with under the provisions of book 2 of the commercial code of 1961. Since then, Kuwait's legal system has undergone further development; new civil and commercial

Corridor of Kuwait's new law courts' complex

codes, both based on Egyptian models, were enacted in 1980 and took effect in 1981, while the companies law of 1960 is now being redrafted.

Qatar, Bahrain and the UAE followed Kuwait's example. Qatar's civil and commercial law of 1971 and the commercial companies law of 1981 follow the Egyptian system. In Bahrain, a draft commercial law which owes many of its provisions to the Kuwaiti and Iraqi codes of commerce awaits promulgation. As for the UAE, there is an increased effort towards achieving uniformity by the enactment of federal laws intended for all the emirates. A federal company law was issued in 1984, but its implementation was suspended for one year by decision of the federal government in December 1985. A federal code for civil transactions, closely based on Jordan's 1977 civil code, was promulgated in 1985 and took effect on 1 April 1986. A draft commercial code inspired by Egypt, as well as other less important drafts, are under study.

Current trends

Until the mid-1970s it was generally assumed that established legal systems would remain reassuringly constant, and legal systems in the course of development would evolve according to the Egyptian/continental-European pattern. It was also assumed that the position of the *sharīʿa* in Saudi Arabia, Oman and North Yemen would continue to be eroded by modern enactments. These assumptions, however, have been challenged by such recent events as the coming of unexpected wealth to the oil-exporting countries, the decline in the power and status of the Western powers in the region, and the

Iranian Revolution, which brought hopes as well as fears, and raised political issues which led to conflicts of interest with Western powers and a deeper distrust of the USSR.

Taken together, such factors have helped to create a more acute sense of an original Islamic identity, and a collective feeling that the *shariʿa* should guide and govern the lives of Muslims from the cradle to the grave, and not be confined to personal and family matters. As a result, there is a growing impetus for a fresh evaluation and new interpretation of the original principles of the *shariʿa*, with the aim of reasserting the *shariʿa* as a valid and reasonable corpus of commercial and civil laws.

As is inevitable when changes of heart and mind of such magnitude take place, fundamentalist movements have acquired a greater momentum in some Islamic states; such movements preach a return to the basic values and sources of Islam as taught in the golden past, and reject the need for a fresh evaluation and interpretation which will take account of modern exigencies.

The changes which have taken place in the Iranian legal system since the revolution of 1978–9 have shown the determination of the advocates of the *shariʿa*. Under the Constitution of 1979, the teaching of the Shiʿi school of law was proclaimed to be the primary source of law. Criminal law was fundamentally changed in line with Islamic precepts, and secular legislation which conflicted with Islamic norms was declared to be no longer enforceable; courts were strongly advised to rely on the legal opinions (*fatwa*) of the Ayatollah Khomeini.

Whether under the influence of more moderate currents of thought or under the pressure of the more extreme ones, the *shariʿa* today claims a more prominent role in the legal systems of the region. Whatever the extent of that role will eventually be, it is likely that the division between Western-inspired statutes and *shariʿa* jurisprudence (the two components of nearly all Middle Eastern legal systems) will grow deeper. One result to be expected from this process is that concepts borrowed from Western laws will be given a different interpretation in the ambience of the *shariʿa* into which they have been transplanted. To take an example: freedom of contract and sanctity of contract, which are the products of the Western school of natural law (with the important role given to *voluntas*) and of canon law (with its tenet that the non-fulfilment of an obligation is a sin) were, for many decades, given the same significance in Middle Eastern countries as in the West. In other words, it was accepted that the mere accord of the two persons' wills could freely create their own contractual terms and conditions. A God-given law, however, necessarily has its own requisites, abhorrences and moral principles which cannot easily be defeated by the agreement of two contracting parties. Freedom and sanctity of contract are recognized concepts of Islamic law, but have a dimension different from that which they have in the West.

The legal system based on the *shariʿa* is *sui generis* and cannot be confused with other existing systems. Similarities necessarily exist between legal systems, and *shariʿa* rules and positive laws can be reconciled when it comes to secular problems more frequently than might be supposed; but it is a perilous and sterile exercise systematically to emphasize the resemblances and ignore the differences.

NAS

Further reading

S. H. Amin, *Middle East Legal Systems* (Glasgow, 1985)
J. N. D. Anderson, *Law Reform in the Muslim World* (London, 1976)
W. H. Ballantyne, *Commercial Law in the Arab Middle East: the Gulf States* (London, 1986)
N. J. Coulson, *History of Islamic Law* (Edinburgh, 1971)
N. J. Coulson, *Commercial Law in the Gulf States* (London, 1984)
H. Liebesny, *The Law of the Near and Middle East* (New York, 1975)
J. Schacht, *An Introduction to Islamic Law* (Oxford, 1964)

Trade unions

In general, trade unions in the Middle East and North Africa have tended to be a minor element within the institutional structures of most states in the region. This is because the industrial sectors in their economies – traditionally the crucial support base for trade union organizations – are generally small in terms of labour demand. Agriculture, usually the largest employment sector, is predominantly based on peasant systems of land exploitation and, as such, is rarely institutionalized through labour organizations, although cooperative organizations are not uncommon. Trade sectors are dominated by self-employment and construction is often based on seasonal employment, while governments rarely tolerate trade union organization within the administration of the state. Indeed, political attitudes towards trade unions are perhaps as important as the relatively small size of the labour force in industrial sectors in ensuring that their role is generally so insignificant.

In most Middle Eastern and North African states the concept of a trade union is either felt to be irrelevant or considered to be an extension of the integrating force of the state. It is rare indeed that independent trade unions, with the sole purpose of concentrating on workers' rights, exist either within the state or in the private sectors. Insofar as they do have a meaningful existence, trade unions are considered to be an element designed to integrate the nascent working class within the structure of the state rather than to protect particularistic interests inside society overall – interests which, moreover, might be considered to be antagonistic to the overriding national imperative.

Government pressures

In some cases, the danger of such a conflict is considered so profound that trade unions are simply not permitted. This is true of Libya*, where the *jamahiri* system of government expressly prevents the existence of organizations that represent the interests of segments of Libyan society. Furthermore, since Libyan industry is organized on the basis of workers' cooperatives – which actually own the industries concerned as a social good – and the operation of industry is, in theory, based on popular committees chosen from the workers themselves, trade unions would serve no purpose. Interestingly enough, however, there are still vestigial remnants of the original trade unions in Libya, which were active up to 1969 and even during the first years of the revolution. The Secretariat of the General People's Congress, the supreme sovereign organ in Libya, still has a secretary in charge, *inter alia*, of trade union affairs. In the Islamic Republic of Iran there are also no trade unions in the usually accepted sense, for these are construed as anti-Islamic. Instead, the function of workers' protection is taken on by workers' confederations, which are designed to operate within an Islamic context of consensus. Saudi Arabia has also forbidden the creation of a trade union movement on similar grounds, although spontaneous organization of workers in the oilfields has in the past been used to bring pressure to bear on foreign companies operating there.

The more usual Middle Eastern practice has been either to harness trade union activity to the interest of government or to place unions under close governmental control, so as to prevent the development of activity that would be considered inimical to government interest. Typical of the former situation was Nasserist Egypt*, where the trade union organization (a confederation) was virtually an extension of the Arab Socialist Union. In the post-Nasser era, however, this has been reversed and there are now several trade unions in Egypt which are actively concerned with the welfare of their members, even at the risk of government displeasure. A confederal structure still exists, although its main function appears to be to publish a bulletin, *The Worker*, in which an attempt is made to recover the pre-Nasserite history of trade unionism in Egypt, particularly the strikes in 1951 and 1952 at Kafr al-Dawar, in which union leaders were executed by the new Nasserite military leadership. The trade union movement in Egypt also has to struggle against the increasing Islamist trend in public life which has already captured most of the professional union organizations.

The more typical structure is one in which the government forces centralization on the union movement through a confederal system, and then applies restrictive and paternalistic legislation to the workplace, thus depriving trade unionism of its essential purpose. This has been the practice in Baʿthist Syria and Iraq. In Iraq*, for instance, unions are under the control of the Ministry of Labour and Social Affairs and, in the public sector (which dominates the economy) there is special employee protection legislation. In the Gulf states, where the working class has traditionally been opposed to government, this technique has been used with considerable success. In Bahrain*, for instance, only Bahraini nationals are permitted to enjoy trade union rights but these are limited and expressed through the General Committee for Bahraini Workers. This is to avoid the problems of the 1960s, when Bahraini workers were a vociferous anti-government element which the authorities suspected were connected with the general workers' movement in the Gulf against existing authority. In Lebanon*, too (at least, before the civil war), workers' interests were catered for through a confederal system under government control, the Confédération Générale des Travailleurs du Liban. The same is true in Jordan*, where the appropriate body is the Trade Union Federation, involving around 77,000 workers who are obliged to accept a statutory 30-day cooling-off period in all disputes.

A variant on this pattern is to permit the existence of a confederal trade union movement as an extension of the single officially tolerated political party. This is the case in South Yemen*, where trade unions, grouped within the General Union of Workers, are an element within the single-party state but completely subordinated to the Yemeni Socialist Party. It thus falls within the same organizational structure as other portmanteau organizations, such as the student movement, the peasants' organization or the women's movement. The same is true in Algeria*, where the Union Générale des Travailleurs Algériens is effectively an extension of the FLN, as is the Union Nationale des Paysans Algériens, the Union Nationale de la Jeunesse Algérienne, or the Union Nationale des Femmes Algériennes.

An alternative structure in this respect is provided in Tunisia*, where the Union Générale des Travailleurs Tunisiens (UGTT) had an honourable history as a partner with the Destourian Socialist Party (DSP) in the struggle for independence. Since 1956, however, it has been increasingly subordinated to the DSP and the government. Every attempt at independent expression has met with severe repression, as occurred in January 1978 during demonstrations over wage demands which turned into riots, and the imprisonment of leading union officials, including the UGTT's secretary-general, Habib Ashur. This pattern was repeated in 1985, partly because of government fears that the union movement might put itself forward as a political alternative to the DSP, and the union movement has now been chastened and brought back under government control.

Independent unions

Independent trade unions do exist in the Middle East, however. The Histadrut* trade union federation in Israel*, although allied with the Labour Party, is clearly independent from it. After all, in the economic crisis that faced Israel in 1985, the Histadrut opposed government austerity policies initially, even though that government was dominated by the Labour Party. Histadrut is, however, unique in one respect, in that it is both a representative of labour demands and a major employer of labour – a position that must, on occasion, cause ideological difficulties. Turkey also has a long tradition of independent trade union organizations – at least, up to the 1983 military coup. Trade union activity is now picking up again, although public sector employees – 35 per cent of the total – are not permitted to belong to a union. In Morocco, the three trade union organizations – the Confédération Démocratique du Travail (CDT), the Union Générale des Travailleurs Marocains (UGTM) and the Union Marocaine du Travail (UMT) – are extensions of specific political parties: the Union Socialiste des Forces Populaires (USFP), Istiqlal, and the now virtually defunct Union Nationale des Forces Populaires (UNFP) respectively. They are also independent of government, and confrontations between the authorities and trade unionists tend to articulate with considerable effect the frustrations felt by Moroccan workers. In Sudan, the trade union movement is also enjoying a rebirth in the aftermath of the end of the Nimeiri* regime, which it, together with the professional organizations, helped to bring down. Sudanese trade unions have a tradition of independence from government and of alliance with political parties, particularly the Sudanese Communist Party, although this link is weakening today.

Arab trade unions are gathered together inside the Arab League* through the Arab Labour Organization. However, the underlying reality they face is in a national, not a regional, context. It is difficult to imagine that the stresses of the Arab world will permit the creation of a generalized trade union movement dedicated to the interests of Arab workers with no reference to the national political context in the near future. Nonetheless, the very fact that trade unionism receives recognition – even if only lip service – from virtually every state in the region provides a basis for future development. It may be a long time, however, before the trade union structures typical of the West emerge there. Indeed, the different cultural environment may make such a development irrelevant to the very real needs of the region. If this is not the case, there are already indigenous examples to follow and there is certainly the will to make them succeed.

GJ

Further reading

Arab Affairs, Arab League (London)
EIU Country Profile Series, *The Economist* Intelligence Unit (London)
D. Hiro, *Inside the Middle East* (London, 1982)

Health

Infant mortality

One generally accepted indicator in assessing the relative health of populations is the mortality rate among infants under the age of 12 months. As might be expected in a region so diverse in tradition and custom, size and wealth, these rates vary enormously, from a high of one death in five live births in Afghanistan*, to one death in a hundred in Israel* (excluding the occupied territories, where the figure ranges between four and ten per hundred).

The biggest killers of young lives from Morocco* to the Yemens* are diarrhoeal diseases and their sequelae, dehydration and malnutrition. Where countries have adopted active primary health care programmes, focusing on preventive health education, low medical technology and maternal and child care at the local community level, as well as investing in clean water supplies, infant mortality rates (IMR) have more than halved since the early 1960s. The middle- and upper-income countries have made the biggest impression on their IMRs, with the least developed economies still facing an uphill struggle. However, among the Arab countries Libya* is alone in ensuring access to drinking water to almost 100 per cent of both its rural and urban populations. In recent years, under the guidance of the World Health Organization and the United Nations Children's Fund programme of immunization against the six childhood diseases (poliomyelitis, diphtheria, pertussis, measles, tetanus and tuberculosis) and use of oral rehydration salts to treat diarrhoeal diseases, many countries have achieved major successes in reducing infant and child mortality rates. This is especially true of Egypt*, Turkey* and Saudi Arabia*.

Advanced health care in the Gulf

While there has been a continual improvement in the health care infrastructure in almost all countries of the region, the most dramatic has been seen in the oil-rich countries of the Arabian Gulf and peninsula. Here, more than a decade of high per capita spending on health has resulted in a rapid expansion of both curative, and latterly preventive services. Kuwait*, Qatar*, the UAE* and Bahrain* can all now boast health facilities and medical manning levels almost equivalent to those of Europe and North America. The health profile of these countries is also changing, as they succeed in controlling and eradicating the traditional infectious and parasitic diseases associated with developing countries, such as tuberculosis, malaria, schistosomiasis and trachoma – many of which are still endemic in many other parts of the region. However, new problems are emerging as traditional ones wane. Rapid changes in lifestyle, brought about by oil wealth, have in turn resulted in health conditions more commonly associated with industrialized countries, such as hypertension, cardio-vascular disease, lung cancer, obesity (often the primary nutritional disorder in industrialized countries) and diabetes. Traffic accidents are now a leading cause of mortality and disablement in many Gulf countries.

Saudi Arabia: sophisticated infrastructure but new health challenges

A similar transformation has occurred in health service availability in Saudi Arabia also, but whereas the populations of the Gulf are small and urbanized, health care delivery in Saudi Arabia has proved more difficult. The kingdom's health profile conforms to two distinct models. The industrialized country model is characterized in urban areas by a low prevalence of communicable diseases, but a high prevalence of hazards such as cancer, cardio-vascular disorders, traffic accidents and mental disorders. But the developing country model also remains true, with a significant incidence of tuberculosis, trachoma, malaria and intestinal infections in the rural population. With curative services now well established throughout the country, nationwide campaigns have been launched to curb the transmission of communicable diseases.

Although many traditional practices and attitudes towards sickness and disease have been altered in recent decades in the Arabian peninsula by the widespread availability of high-quality care, others remain which may be a threat to health. Cases of rickets among children have been attributed to the traditional practice of wrapping children from head to toe, rather than exposing them to sunlight. Also, the genetic disorders which can result from first-cousin marriages, of which there is a high frequency in many Muslim countries, represent an important ever-present problem which has yet to be addressed by the majority of countries in the region. Genetic disorders, such as the blood diseases sickle-cell anaemia and thalassaemia major, and certain enzyme deficiencies are common throughout the Middle East and Mediterranean.

High rates of thalassaemia

Whereas in Cyprus a national genetic counselling service, together with antenatal testing during the first trimester of pregnancy, has significantly reduced the hereditary transmission of thalassaemia major, most other countries of the region are still trying to identify the extent of the problem. Certain population groups appear to be at particular risk – a local epidemiological study carried out in Saudi Arabia's Eastern Province revealed at least 50 per cent of the Shiʿi* population to be thalassaemic trait carriers, representing one of the highest incidences encountered in any population.

Antenatal care

Another traditional practice which continues to pose health risks in many countries of the region is the home delivery of pregnant women by largely untrained village *dayat* or midwives. In rural areas throughout Afghanistan, North Africa, Turkey and many parts of the Middle East, pregnant women do not seek antenatal care, and complicated births often result in maternal as well as infant deaths. There are government programmes to upgrade the skills of the *dayat* in many countries, including South Yemen, Oman, North Yemen, Egypt and Sudan, and others such as Saudi Arabia and the Gulf countries have set up special maternal health units to encourage women to seek antenatal care and hospitalization during delivery.

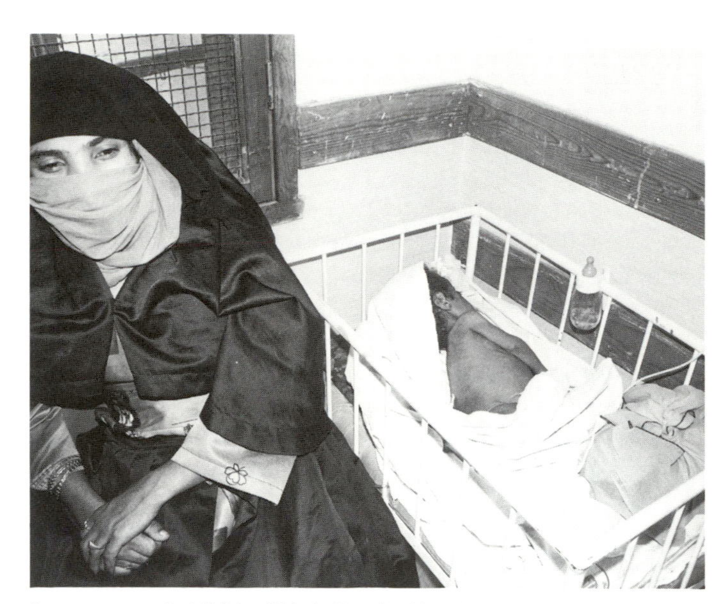

A woman and child in Jibla's Baptist Hospital, North Yemen

Fertility, however, remains a major factor in determining women's status throughout the region and, with the exception of Israel and Lebanon, fertility rates are high. Active family planning or birth-spacing programmes operate in these two and six other countries only – Egypt, Tunisia, Algeria, South Yemen, Turkey and Morocco. With the exception of a few countries – Cyprus, Israel, Lebanon, Kuwait, Bahrain, Jordan and Qatar – literacy rates among women ranged between 2 and 50 per cent by 1983, and cultural attitudes in many of the countries of the region prevent women from joining the labour force. Contrary to the normal patterns, in many of the oil-rich countries fertility rates have tended to increase as incomes rise. However, frequent pregnancies, particularly where IMRs are still high, have a severely detrimental effect on women's health, and in the least developed economies child marriages and multiple pregnancies remain the norm. Nutritional anaemia is widespread among women in these countries and this, together with an absence of care during pregnancy, is in part responsible for high maternal mortality figures.

Table 10. The condition of children in the Middle East and North Africa

Country	Infant mortality rate**		Total pop. (m)	Life exp. at birth (yrs)	Total fertility rate††	Percentage of pop. with access to drinking water		
	1983	1960	1983	1983	1983	Total	Urban	Rural
Qatar	38	160	0.3	71	—	—	—	—
Bahrain	32	150	0.4	68	—	—	—	—
Cyprus	17	31	0.7	74	—	—	—	—
Afghanistan	195	220	14.2	37	6.9	10	28	8
N. Yemen	135	220	6.2	44	6.8	20*	50*	17*
S. Yemen	135	220	2.0	46	6.9	44	85	25
Oman	115	220	1.1	50	7.1	—	—	—
Egypt	100	185	9.2	48	5.2	75	88	64
Libya	95	170	3.3	58	7.2	98	100	90
Morocco	95	170	22.1	58	6.4	—	—	—
Algeria	90	175	20.6	58	7.0	77	—	—
Turkey	90	205	47.7	63	4.4	63*	63*	63*
Tunisia	85	165	6.9	61	4.9	58*	86*	27*
Iraq	75	150	14.7	59	6.7	73*	97*	22*
Saudi Arabia	65	180	10.4	56	7.1	—	73†	34†
Syria	60	145	9.8	67	7.2	71	98	54
Jordan	55	145	3.2	64	7.4	89	100	65
Lebanon	48	75	2.6	65	3.8	92	95	85
UAE	38	160	1.2	71	5.9	93	95	81
Kuwait	23	100	1.6	71	6.1	84	100	17
Israel	14	36	4.1	74	3.1	—	—	—
Iran	115	175	20.4	48	5.6	—	—	—

* UNICEF field office source † WHO Review of National baseline data 1984
** Annual number of deaths of infants under one year of age per 1000 live births.
†† The number of children that would be born per woman, if she were to live to the end of her child-bearing years and bear children at each age in accordance with prevailing age-specific fertility rates.
Source: The State of the World's Children (United Nations Children's Fund (UNICEF), 1986)

Although a comprehensive infrastructure of public and private health care has now been established in many countries of the region and standards of health care delivery have been transformed within a couple of decades, gaps still remain. Few countries, with the exception of Israel and Cyprus, have adequate blood-banking and laboratory analysis facilities, medical equipment maintenance back-up or indigenous drug and medicinal product manufacture. Many of the Gulf countries together with Libya and Saudi Arabia are also very dependent on foreign medical manpower to operate and administer their health care facilities, despite major efforts to encourage local talent. However, given the strong political commitment to continued improvements in public health in the middle- and upper-income countries, the prospects for achieving, at least in part, the World Health Organization's goal of 'Health for All by the Year 2000', look promising.

MR

Education

Traditional education

From early times, Muslim societies developed a system of schools designed both to give a large number of Muslims a knowledge of their faith and of the revealed book on which it was based, and to train a learned class able to preserve and transmit the sciences of religion, and in particular the *shari'a*★, the ideal system of social morality and law which was necessary to maintain the fabric of ordered and civilized society. In elementary schools (*kuttab*, *maktab*), young boys learned to read Arabic and memorize the Qur'an★. At a higher level, Qur'an, *hadith*★, theology (*kalam*) and jurisprudence (*fiqh*) were expounded in the main mosques of a city, and in schools (*madrasa*), primarily for the study of law, which spread from the eleventh century onwards. These were foundations endowed by rulers or by rich and powerful individuals, in which students were lodged and taught by holders of established chairs. The normal method of study was by way of a teacher reading and commenting upon an authoritative text to a circle of students gathered around him; when a student had, in the teacher's opinion, reached an adequate standard of knowledge and understanding of a book or subject, he would be given an *ijaza* or licence to teach it.

Most mosques and schools had a local clientele, but some of them attracted students from far afield because of the fame of a city as a centre of pilgrimage, the reputation of its teachers, the size of its endowments and the prospects it offered to a successful student. Such were the schools of Medina, site of the Prophet's tomb, the Azhar Mosque in Cairo, the Zaytuna in Tunis, the Qarawiyyin in

Fez, and the Shiʿi* schools in cities where lay the shrines of Imams or those associated with them – Najaf and Karbala in Iraq, Qum and Mashhad in Iran. In the Ottoman* period, great schools founded by successive Sultans in Istanbul trained those who aspired to high rank in the judicial and religious service of the Empire.

An analogous system of education existed in the Jewish communities: after study of Hebrew and the Pentateuch, boys would go on to study the Talmud*, the body of discussions and commentaries on Jewish law, in higher schools – in the great academies of Baghdad and Palestine in earlier Islamic times, and later in the *yeshivot* of the main centres of Jewish population. Some of the monasteries of the eastern Christian Churches played a similar role of forming an educated priesthood.

Such schools of religious doctrine and law did not provide all the education which was available. Philosophy and other rational sciences were transmitted in more informal study-circles; the convents (*zawiya*) of the Sufi* orders taught the esoteric interpretation of religion and the path by which the devotee could move towards experiential knowledge of God. In the great Shiʿi schools, however, philosophy and mysticism were studied. Medicine* and other practical skills were handed on by apprenticeship; the relation of master and apprentice formed a close personal link which bound together the generations of Islamic history. Some women seem to have been given a literary and religious education within their homes.

The eighteenth and nineteenth centuries

Schools of a new kind began to appear from the sixteenth century onwards as the relationship between the Middle East and the societies of Western Europe gradually grew closer. Colleges were established in Rome for training priests of the eastern Uniate Churches; Catholic missionaries (French, Spanish and Italian) opened schools in places where there were important Christian communities. Knowledge of a new kind came in through the European languages which were taught in these schools, and through the beginnings of printing among Christians and Jews. In the Greek and Armenian merchant communities with wide contacts, young men went to study in Italy, at the University of Padua and elsewhere; the Armenian Catholic monks of the Mekhitarist order created an important school at Venice in 1715, and later in the century the Greek Society of the Friends of the Muses opened schools in which the main emphasis was upon Greek classical culture.

In the nineteenth century, changes in methods of communication and the growth of European influence made possible an extension of activity by missionaries. Catholics (mainly French) and Protestants (mainly American) created networks of schools to which, by the end of the century, some Muslims as well as Christians were sending their sons. Some of these schools were of a high level: the French Jesuit Université S. Joseph in Beirut (1875), the American Syrian Protestant College, also in Beirut (1866), and the American Robert College in Istanbul (1863). The Russian Imperial Orthodox Society opened schools for Orthodox students, and the Alliance Israélite, founded by French Jews, had a network of schools for Jewish communities from Morocco to Iran.

Some of these schools were intended for girls; by the end of the century the woman school-teacher was becoming a familiar figure. Muslim as well as Christian and Jewish families might entrust their daughters to the care of Catholic nuns or American or British teachers; rich families would have them educated at home by French or British governesses.

More important in the development of modern Middle Eastern societies were the modern schools created by indigenous governments which wished to strengthen themselves in the face of European power by reforming their armies and administrative systems. The Ottoman government created new schools on the European model for army officers, civil servants and doctors in Istanbul; later in the century it opened elementary and secondary schools in provincial centres, and the University of Istanbul in 1900. In Egypt a similar system of professional schools was created in the first half of the century, and a larger system of schools later; the system was maintained by the British after their occupation of Egypt in 1882 but scarcely expanded, and the Egyptian University was established by local initiative in 1908. In Iran, a technical school, Dar al-Funun, was created in 1851. In Tunisia, a reforming government opened the Sadiqiyya College, the first modern school (1875); after the French occupation* of 1881, a number of Franco-Arab schools were established. In Algeria, the French administration created a number of *madrasas* on somewhat modernized lines, but most schools, and the University of Algiers, were intended primarily for European colonists. Throughout the century an increasing number of students went to Europe to obtain a higher education, some going privately and others sent by their governments.

Both in government schools and still more in those maintained by foreign missions, emphasis was placed upon the learning of European languages; in the course of the century, French replaced Italian as the language most widely used. The older Islamic schools did not offer the languages and other subjects which provided the key to understanding the modern world, employment in government service or the new kind of international trade. Except in the Arabian peninsula, which had not yet been touched by the winds of change, their social position declined; but attempts were made to reform al-Azhar, and its graduates could still hope for positions as teachers of Arabic or judges in the religious courts.

The age of empires

The years between 1918 and 1945 were those of the greatest extension of European power in the Middle East and North Africa. Apart from the states of the Arabian peninsula, only Turkey and Iran were free to pursue independent policies in matters of major concern, and in both of them there was a sustained attempt to expand the system of education and use it in order to create modern societies on the European model. In Turkey, under the rule of Kemal Atatürk*, the national system of schools was expanded at all levels, and it was developed in new directions. The system was secular, and the qualities which were thought to create a strong, unified and modern nation were emphasized. The education of girls was encouraged, as a step towards the social emancipation of women. The reform of the Turkish language – the replacement of the Arabic by Latin script, and of Arabic and Persian words by original Turkish or European words – posed special problems. Under Riza Shah*, Iran followed a similar path, rather less rapidly and successfully; the University of Tehran was opened in 1934. In Egypt, which had greater freedom of action in internal affairs after 1922, the university, founded in 1908, was taken over by the state and enlarged in 1925.

In the countries controlled by European empires, the aim of governments was not so much to create nations as to produce the officials and professional men needed to serve a modern administration, and to do so within limits, so as not to give rise to an unemployed and discontented nationalist educated class. Government schools were expanded, but not as fast as nationalists would have wished. Foreign mission schools, and those established by local communities, were allowed to operate freely. The Syrian Protestant College became the American University of Beirut, and an American university was opened also in Cairo. The Hebrew University of Jerusalem was created in order to serve the growing Jewish community in Palestine (1925). The establishment of foreign control increased the flow of students going to Europe and, on an increasing scale, to the United States.

Both in the independent countries and in those dominated by European power, the result of this generation of effort was to create national elites claiming the right and capacity to run their own affairs; such elites included lawyers, doctors and teachers as well as government officials, but fewer scientists and engineers. A striking feature was the expansion of the education of girls, although they still had few opportunities for employment outside the school systems.

Beyond the elites of the great cities, the new schools scarcely touched the masses; cultivators and nomads, and the unskilled population of the growing cities, remained mainly uneducated and illiterate.

The age of nation-states

In the quarter-century after the end of the Second World War, all the states of the Middle East became fully independent, and all, including those in the Arabian peninsula, were fully exposed to the forces which were creating a world-society unified at least on the level of techniques and economic activity. For all of them, national education was an urgent task; it was needed in order to create a unified nation, with the technical skills which were essential for survival in the modern world, and to mobilize the strength of the nation in support of whatever the dominant groups in society considered to be the main purposes of national policy. The urgency was increased by the vast and rapid increase of population everywhere; throughout the area those under twenty-one form more than half of the total population.

Since independence, all governments have devoted a large proportion of their expenditure, ranging from 10 per cent to 25 per cent, to education (Table 11). In some countries, it comes second only to the amount spent on national defence. The aim of all of them is to give at least primary schooling to all boys and girls of appropriate age, and enable a growing proportion of them to go on to secondary and higher education. Some countries are not far from achieving these aims; virtually all their children are in primary schools, or will be soon (Tables 12 and 13). Even where the support of a government is not present, the expansion of schools has been rapid: among the Palestinian refugees, the efforts of UNRWA* and other agencies have succeeded in creating a mainly literate population, and in giving a large proportion of them the opportunity to escape from the life of refugee camps into productive activity.

Some countries have well-developed schemes for reducing adult illiteracy. One of the first was that started by UNESCO at Sirs al-Layyan in the Egyptian Delta; in Iran, a literacy corps was created in 1963; in Israel, compulsory service in the army is used as a means of adult education. Almost the whole population of Israel is literate; in Turkey, the percentage of illiterate men dropped from 35.5 in 1965 to 14.1 in 1985, and that of women from 72.6 to 37.5 (Table 14).

At the higher level, the number of universities has increased very rapidly. In 1939 there were fewer than a dozen in the whole of the Middle East and North Africa, but by the early 1980s there were approximately a hundred, of various kinds and sizes, in addition to technical schools and teachers' training colleges. A rapidly increasing proportion of men and women of the appropriate ages are receiving some kind of higher education or training: 30 per cent in Israel, 33 per cent in Lebanon, 26 per cent in Jordan, 16 per cent in Syria, 14 per cent in Egypt. In most countries universities are open equally to men and women, although in Saudi Arabia women students have special colleges.

Table 11. Expenditure on education as a percentage of total government expenditure

Country	Year	%
Algeria	1980	24.3
Cyprus	1983	11.9
Egypt	1983	8.9
Iran	1983	15.5
Israel	1981	6.8
Jordan	1983	12.5
Kuwait	1983	14.1
Morocco	1983	22.0
Saudi Arabia	1983	10.5
Syria	1983	12.1
Tunisia	1982	14.2
Turkey	1980	10.5
UAE	1983	9.8
N. Yemen	1980	13.7
S. Yemen	1980	16.9

Source: UNESCO, *Statistical Year-Book*, 1985

Table 12. Boys and girls in primary education as a proportion of all boys and girls of appropriate age

		% in school	
Country	Year	Boys	Girls
Afghanistan	1982	19	9
Algeria	1982	106	81
Bahrain	1982	107	93
Egypt	1982	101	76
Iran	1983	113	88
Iraq	1983	113	99
Israel	1983	95	97
Jordan	1982	101	98
Kuwait	1983	96	94
Lebanon	1982	115	105
Mauritania	1982	45	29
Morocco	1983	97	61
Oman	1984	94	72
Qatar	1983	105	101
Saudi Arabia	1983	81	56
Somalia	1983	28	15
Sudan	1982	59	42
Syria	1983	114	96
Tunisia	1983	125	102
Turkey	1983	116	107
UAE	1983	94	95
N. Yemen	1983	107	21
S. Yemen	1983	97	36

Note: the figures for children in school include some who are beyond the appropriate age; thus in countries with almost universal education, the enrolment ratio may exceed 100 per cent.
Source: UNESCO, *Statistical Year-Book*, 1985.

Table 13. Boys and girls in secondary education as a proportion of all boys and girls of appropriate age

		% in school	
Country	Year	Boys	Girls
Afghanistan	1982	11	5
Algeria	1983	50	35
Bahrain	1982	83	70
Egypt	1982	67	45
Iran	1983	47	33
Iraq	1983	67	37
Israel	1983	72	82
Jordan	1982	79	77
Kuwait	1983	86	79
Lebanon	1982	61	63
Mauritania	1982	19	6
Morocco	1983	35	24
Oman	1984	38	19
Qatar	1983	66	78
Saudi Arabia	1983	42	28
Somalia	1983	19	10
Sudan	1982	21	15
Syria	1983	67	44
Tunisia	1983	40	26
Turkey	1983	47	28
UAE	1983	49	61
N. Yemen	1983	16	2
S. Yemen	1983	26	11

See note to Table 12.
Source: UNESCO, *Statistical Year-Book*, 1985

In addition, there are many thousands of Iranians, Turks, Arabs, Israelis and others finishing their education in the United States, Western and Eastern Europe and the USSR, in proportions which depend partly on the political orientation of different countries. One estimate gives the total as a quarter of a million.

Problems of national education

In spite of such impressive figures, few of the products of the new systems of education and few observers would regard the situation in most countries as satisfactory. There is a general opinion that quantity has been increased at the expense of quality: classes are too large, the supply of trained teachers is too small; the training of teachers will take time and is all the more difficult because the profession of school-teaching does not carry high prestige or salaries. One result is the persistence of an older tradition of learning by memorizing facts or texts.

In most countries, the system of education produces more graduates than can be absorbed into government service, and too few with vocational or technical training. Some attempts have been made to change this situation. In Israel, education at all levels is oriented towards the sciences up to the highest level of the universities and the Technion in Haifa. Turkey has the Middle East Technical

Table 14. Percentage of illiteracy among men and women

Country	Year	Men	Women	Total
Afghanistan	1985	61.1	92.2	76.3
Algeria	1985	37.0	63.1	50.4
Bahrain	1985	20.7	35.9	27.3
Egypt	1985	41.4	69.8	55.5
Iran	1985	37.7	61.0	49.2
Iraq	1985	9.8	12.5	10.7
Israel	1985	3.3	6.6	4.9
Jordan	1985	13.4	36.9	25.0
Kuwait	1985	24.3	36.7	30.0
Lebanon	1985	14.3	31.1	23.0
Libya	1985	18.6	50.2	33.1
Morocco	1985	55.2	78.3	66.9
Somalia	1985	81.6	93.5	88.4
Syria	1985	24.1	56.7	40.0
Tunisia	1985	32.2	59.4	45.8
Turkey	1984	14.1	37.5	25.8
N. Yemen	1985	73.1	96.9	86.3

Source: UNESCO, *Statistical Year-Book*, 1985.

University at Ankara, and in countries possessing important oil industries* which have been nationalized, like Algeria, Saudi Arabia and Egypt, there are schools of petroleum technology. Many of the students who go to the United States or Europe study medicine, engineering or technology at a high level, but a large proportion of them join the 'brain-drain', and are absorbed into the economies of the industrialized countries.

To many observers it appears that schools and universities are too strictly controlled by governments and used as media through which the official version of national history, international relations, and economic and social organization can be taught. In most countries, private schools, and in particular foreign ones, have been abolished or are closely supervised. Robert College has become a part, although a distinctive one, of the Turkish state system; but in Beirut the foreign universities continue to work, and there and in some other countries foreign schools and those of minority communities still exist. In some countries universities have boards of governors designed to protect them against direct intervention by the government, but all governments are too aware of the political dangers posed by student movements to leave universities without close supervision. In the West Bank, universities have become centres of Palestinian national feeling and are closely controlled; but the situation is not very different in most other countries.

Connected with the question of foreign schools is that of the teaching of foreign languages. Some of the foreign schools have been accused of weakening national consciousness by neglecting the teaching of the national language. In state schools the main emphasis is naturally on the national language. This helps to serve the essential purpose of creating a unified national consciousness; in Israel, for example, the teaching of Hebrew* is one of the means by which Jews of different ethnic origins are formed into a nation. Problems arise, however, in countries which have more than one language. In Israel the Arab minority are taught in their own language and therefore face an obstacle when they wish to go on to higher education; in Turkey the language of the Kurdish* minority is ignored; in Algeria the attempt to strengthen teaching in Arabic, after the long period of French rule when Arabic and its culture were neglected, arouses the opposition of the Berber-speaking* population, whose language is not officially recognized. Foreign languages are taught, of course, at secondary and higher level; English has replaced French as the language most widely studied, and in Turkey, Iran and Israel Arabic is taught to an increasing extent.

An important problem in all countries is that of the place of religion in education. In most countries the traditional religious schools have lost their importance. The *kuttabs* have been replaced by elementary schools and the higher schools have closed or been absorbed into the university system. The Zaytuna has become the Faculty of Theology and Religious Sciences of the University of Tunis; the Azhar Mosque has become part of al-Azhar University, modern and controlled by the state; but the great Shiʿi schools with their tradition of independent preservation of the Shiʿi faith still continue to exist. There is a strong demand, however, that religion should be taught in state schools. In Israel, the problem is solved by having two systems of state schools: one secular, where the emphasis is upon Jewish history and culture rather than the observances and laws of the faith, and the other religious. Elsewhere, in countries where the bulk of the population is Muslim, some elements of religion are taught in the schools; even Turkey abandoned its formal secularism after 1950.

On the whole, the kind of religion which is taught is that which sees it as an element in the national heritage and a system of social ethics, but there is now a tendency to revive the teaching of the traditional sciences of religion. The Iranian Revolution of 1979 may have far-reaching consequences for the system of education there and elsewhere; already mixed schools have been abolished, although men and women still sit in the same classes in universities, Islamic doctrine and law are emphasized, and the traditional schools have gained in prestige.

AHH

Further reading

G. Makdisi, *The Rise of Colleges: institutions of learning in Islam and the West* (Edinburgh, 1981)
B. G. Massialas and S. A. Jarrar, *Education in the Arab World* (New York, 1983)
J. Szyliowicz, *Education and Modernization in the Middle East* (Ithaca, 1971)
A. L. Tibawi, *Islamic Education: its tradition and modernization into the Arab national systems* (London, 1972)
UNESCO, *Statistical Year-Book* (Paris, annual)
The World of Learning (London, annual)

Scientific and technical education

The development of scientific and technical education

Scientific and technical education has long been seen as a key to national progress. The region was exposed to European technological progress at an early date, and as early as the sixteenth century the Ottoman Sultans had established a palace advisory group. By the nineteenth century, technical and vocational education was already well established in several countries of the region, particularly in Turkey, Syria and Egypt. The first major educational establishment was a medical school established in 1823 by Muhmmad ʿAli* of Egypt to train medical personnel for his armed forces. Since then, a major concern for professional education in medicine*, engineering*, administration and law* has come to characterize many of the educational systems in the region.

Late nineteenth-century interest in Western thought (for instance, the debate on Darwinism engaged by Shibli Shummayyil, Isma'il Mazhar and others) had little to do with science or technology, and did not lead to research in the biological sciences.

Since the end of the Second World War, all governments in the region have embarked on major programmes to develop technical education. These programmes have attempted to develop secondary schools as well as systems of higher education, and at the secondary school level there have been attempts to expand vocational education. A large number of universities have been established, which offer programmes in the sciences, engineering, medical sciences and agriculture*. With the exception of Israel, teaching of the sciences is generally weak.

Professional technical education in the applied sciences (medicine, engineering and agriculture) has been strongly favoured by public policy. The increasing supply of university graduates in these fields of specialization has benefited health services, civil engineering and some services connected with agriculture. The educational systems that have evolved, however, are not strongly related either to worldwide progress in science and technology or to the requirements of the modern industrial and technological activities occurring in the region. For example, the medical schools in all these countries (excluding Israel) have not been active in molecular biology; by the same token, the schools of engineering are not participants in the current advances in robotics, information sciences, new engineering materials or aerospace.

The extensive technological projects that have been implemented by the governments have not utilized the services of local manpower; international consulting and contracting firms were responsible for much of the design and implementation. To date, the educational systems have not established effective relationships with the labour market.

In the absence of strong cultural, scientific and technological associations and institutions, planning in the educational field became the sole responsibility of government bureaucracies.

The brain drain

The poor articulation between the systems of higher education and the demand for manpower has led to a considerable brain drain, that amongst the graduates of national medical and engineering schools being the most significant. Medical schools have generally adopted the Western model of hospital-based medical treatment. The high cost of such medical services has limited the number of hospitals, and consequently of job opportunities for specialized medical professionals. This imbalance between education and job opportunities has led to a substantial brain drain of medical professionals. Foreign study in Europe, North America and the Comecon countries in all advanced disciplines is on a large scale; moreover, a large proportion of those who acquire scientific education and advanced technological specialization abroad do not return. Highly qualified scientific and technical manpower is in high demand. Most industrial countries have adopted immigration laws to facilitate the flow of the brain drain into their markets.

Many of the problems that beset educational policies have been the subject of extensive public debate, but few countries have so far attempted to redesign their educational programmes according to local opportunities. This rigidity in addressing educational and employment problems prevails in most of the countries under consideration.

Statistical picture

Scientific and vocational education depends on a literate society. In 1980, nearly all children of primary school age in the countries of the region were enrolled in schools. The exceptions were: Afghanistan (30 per cent enrolled), Cyprus (84 per cent), Egypt (70 per cent), Mauritania (33 per cent), Morocco (82 per cent), Oman (62 per cent), Saudi Arabia (64 per cent), Somalia (30 per cent), Sudan (51 per cent), North Yemen (YAR) (47 per cent), and South Yemen (PDRY) (72 per cent). Secondary school enrolment – as a percentage of the 12 to 17 age group – was highest in Jordan (79), followed by Kuwait (75), Israel (72), Libya (67), Cyprus (66), Qatar (64), Lebanon (58), Iraq (57) and Egypt (52). All other countries were below 50 per cent. North Yemen had the lowest enrolment rate (5 per cent) followed by Afghanistan (8 per cent). Israel and Mauritania had the highest percentage of their secondary school enrolment in vocational education (41 per cent). The percentage of secondary school enrolment in vocational schools was: Tunisia (27), Egypt and Turkey (both at 22), followed by Jordan (13), Cyprus (12) and Lebanon (11). In all other countries, the range of enrolment was between 0 per cent and 9 per cent. Vocational education in the Arab world is still limited. In the early 1980s, total enrolment did not exceed 200,000 in 321 vocational schools. Eighty-eight per cent of the students were in seven countries: Jordan, Tunisia, Algeria, Syria, Iraq, Egypt and Morocco.

On the whole the countries of the region (excluding Israel) are evolving at different velocities to provide mass primary and secondary education*. It is most likely that, at current rates of growth, all countries, with the exception of the poorest of them, will attain 100 per cent enrolment in primary schools and above 50 per cent in secondary schools by the end of the century.

Higher education in the region has witnessed rapid and significant growth. The growth in the number of enrolled students (excluding those in Israel) since 1950 has been exponential, with a

Table 15. Education in Middle Eastern countries (percentage of population)

Country	20–24 age group	Distribution by field of study		
		Humanities	Social sciences	Applied and pure sciences
Afghanistan (1982)	1.3	8.1	36.2	55.7
Algeria (1980)	4.9	10.9	31.3	57.8
Bahrain (1980)	5.3	nd	58.4	41.6
Cyprus (1982)	nd	nd	45.2	54.8
Egypt (1980)	14.7	15.1	48.9	35.1
Iran (1982)	3.7	11.5	35.9	52.6
Israel (1982)	30.4	31.1	31.2	37.7
Jordan (1980)	26.6	11.9	60.2	27.9
Kuwait (1982)	15.4	11.2	58.9	29.9
Lebanon (1980)	33.6	nd	nd	nd
Morocco (1980)	5.8	38.3	39.3	22.4
Qatar (1982)	16.5	21.8	64.4	13.8
Saudi Arabia (1980)	7.8	44.3	32.9	22.7
Syria (1980)	16.6	23.2	28.6	48.1
Tunisia (1982)	5.1	19.1	35.5	45.4
Turkey (1982)	5.9	7.8	52	40.2
UAE (1982)	6.8	25.4	49.4	25.2
North Yemen (YAR) (1980)	1.2	7.6	86.5	5.9
South Yemen (PDRY) (1980)	2.4	nd	65.1	34.9

Source: UNESCO, *Statistical Yearbook*, for 1984 and 1985, Paris. The following countries had no entries: Djibouti, Iraq, Libya, Mauritania, Oman, Somalia and Sudan.

doubling time of about seven years. Table 15 shows the ratio of students in higher education as a proportion of those in the 20 to 24 age group. In the same table the proportion of all students in all scientific and technical subjects is shown.

Most countries still depend either exclusively or heavily on foreign study for post-graduate education. Post-graduate studies (for example in Egypt and Turkey) are not rooted in professors who are actively engaged in research work, though again Israel is an exception. The number of students from the region enrolled in universities of industrial countries may be around 250,000; a high proportion of these are enrolled in scientific and technical programmes on the post-graduate level. Statistics on foreign study are poor, but there is little doubt that the numbers are large and growing.

Current trends

The main issue facing the systems of education in the region is their relationship to government and society. This relationship encompasses a host of still unresolved problems ranging from the size of financial allocations, the contents of courses and academic freedom to Research and Development (R&D) funding.

The current phase of rationalization of the system of relationships appears to have begun in the 1970s. The Israeli Planning and Grants Committee was established in 1974, since when it has assumed a dominant role in the allocation of grants concerned with research and in academic and manpower planning. In 1981, Turkey enacted the Reform Law which led to a number of improvements, but much remains to be done. Iran is still undergoing a cultural revolution, with major implications to its system of scientific and technical education.

In Egypt the economic expectations to be derived from higher education have been rapidly eroded. G. Psacharopoulos and B. Sanyal report that the mean age of university graduates in Egypt is 33 years; the mean waiting time to secure employment is ten months.

Continuing concern with the performance of the system of scientific and technical education is widespread and of long standing. It is expected that the rate of change of the educational systems throughout the region will accelerate during the coming decades.

ABZ

Further reading

R. Murphy, 'The Ottoman Attitude Towards the Adoption of Western Technology: the role of the Efrenci technicians in civil and military applications', in J. L. Bacque-Grammout and Paul Dumont, eds., *Contributions a l'histoire économique et sociale de l'Empire Ottoman* (Louvain, 1983)

G. Psacharopoulos and B. Sanyal, 'Student Expectations and Graduate Market Performance in Egypt', *Higher Education*, 11 (1982), 27–49

M. Zadok, 'The Israeli Planning and Grants Committee at the Crossroads: from shock absorber to steering wheel', *Higher Education, 13* (1984), 535–44

A. A. Ziadat, *Western Science in the Arab World: the impact of Darwinism, 1860–1930* (London, in prep.)

Scientific research

Science and technology have been recognized by all the governments of the region as important instruments for development. During the past three decades, considerable investments have been made in the establishment of research programmes in universities and in research centres. In general the Ministries of Agriculture and Health operate some of the largest research centres outside the universities.

Research activities at the universities are generally a product of the interests of the professors. At centres of applied research, practical and applied problems are the topics under consideration. A large number and variety of research problems confront every developmental activity. But the available manpower and financial resources devoted to Research and Development (R&D) are generally limited.

During the past four decades, much progress has been achieved in developing the manpower capabilities and institutional facilities for the undertaking of scientific research. There has been an increase by two or three orders of magnitude in the level of R&D activity throughout the region. The region as a whole has a level of activity little different from that of other regions of the Third World. In Israel the level of activity is similar to that of industrial countries.

The governments in the region have given some attention to the planning and management of policies in science and technology. Responsibility for science policy is often undertaken by the Ministry for Higher Education. Public sector organizations have been generally responsible for the major development projects. These, however, have had little to do with science policy or measures that could enhance the transfer and acquisition of science and technology. Public and private projects have been generally planned, designed and implemented through the agency of foreign firms.

Here, then, is a brief description of the present level of activities in the Arab world, Iran, Israel and Turkey.

The Arab world

In the period between 1970 and 1986, interest in science and technology has grown on the national, regional and international levels in the Arab world. On the national level, this has been illustrated in a number of trends and measures, the most important of which are:

(a) the establishment of national policy-making bodies in those countries which had lacked such institutions; or the reform and development of existing ones.

(b) the establishment of research and development institutes or units, and of scientific supporting services.

(c) the establishment of an increasing number of universities and other higher educational and training institutes.

(d) the allocation of public funds for R&D.

(e) the appearance of chapters on science and technology in some national development plans.

(f) the growth of national scientific and technological communities and the increasing awareness of their social function.

(g) inter-Arab and international cooperation.

Scientific research in the Arab world, although on a small scale, is of long standing. Research activity is undertaken in 77 universities and in the 500 research centres in existence. In 1983, some 407 Arab institutions contributed one or more scientific publications. There had only been 289 such institutions in 1977. Seven Arab institutions contributed 100 or more scientific publications during 1983. These were: Cairo University (203), University of Alexandria (163), The National Research Centre, Cairo (123), University of Petroleum and Minerals, Dhahran (121), Kuwait University (119), King Saʿud University (107), ʿAin Shams University, Cairo (101). Twelve Arab institutions published 48 per cent of the total output of the Arab world.

The output of scientific publications from the Arab world increased from about 470 in 1967 to 2616 in 1983. This reflected an annual rate of growth of 10 per cent.

The patterns of growth have varied considerably from country to country. The output from Egypt, Sudan, Jordan and Lebanon is by nationals, while those from the oil-producing countries have generally been by expatriates – Arab and non-Arab – attracted to their academic and research institutions.

Egypt has increased its output by 360 per cent over the 17-year period from 1967 to 1983; yet its share of total Arab output decreased from 63 per cent (1967) to 40 per cent (1983). The share of five major oil-producing countries (Algeria, Kuwait, Libya, Iraq and Saudi Arabia) increased from 14 per cent (1967) to 19 per cent (1977); and then to 31 per cent (1983). The major growth areas during this period were Jordan, Kuwait and Saudi Arabia.

The graph shows the dynamics of change in three major areas of scientific activity: Egypt; the Gulf Cooperation Council (GCC) countries; and Algeria, Libya and Iraq. Egypt appears to be slowly moving towards a 25 per cent share of total Arab output, and it is expected that by 1993 Egypt's share of output will be equal to its share of Arab population. The GCC countries, with about 5 per cent of the population of the Arab world, already produce 27 per cent of output. The trend here is for a continuing expansion.

Kuwaiti and Saudi institutions began a rapid programme of mobilizing professional expatriates in the mid-1970s. At that time research activities in both countries were on a limited scale, but in less than one decade they were able to expand their research output dramatically. Saudi Arabia moved from seventh position in 1967 to second position in 1983. In 1977 it had reached Sudan's level and held third place. The ratio of Egyptian to Saudi publications fell from 37:1 (1967) to 23:1 (1983). Lebanon held second place in 1974 but fell to sixth place in 1983. Libya, Lebanon and Iraq registered decline in output. Nevertheless, it is surprising that Lebanon is still holding the sixth place after eleven years of civil war.

In Table 16 is shown the distribution of some 60,000 scientific professionals and 35,000 technicians who were employed in R&D activities in eleven Arab states. It is likely that the figures for the entire Arab world in 1986 exceed 100,000 scientific personnel.

Table 16. R&D manpower: scientific and technical

Country	Scientific manpower	Number of technicians
Algeria (1982)	2 000	4 000
Bahrain (1982)	2 111	1 022
Egypt (1982)	39 919	12 261
Iraq (1980)	7 454	6 223
Jordan (1982)	1 241	547
Kuwait (1977)	606	161
Lebanon (1983)	280	300
Libya (1983)	1 100	1 500
Mauritania (1982)	30	60
Morocco (1980)	1 100	4 500
Sudan (1982)	4 266	4 270

Source: UNESCO, based on National Reports prepared for CASTARAB II.

Table 17 shows that by 1980–2, nine Arab states were already spending some $930m on R&D. The figures for 1986 are no doubt substantially higher. According to UNESCO (1985) estimates, total R&D expenditures in the Arab states increased from $115m (0.31% of GNP) in 1970 to $1027m (0.27% of GNP) in 1980.

Table 17. Expenditure on R&D

Country	US$ m
Algeria (1982)	230
Egypt (1982)	49
Iraq (1980)	274
Jordan (1979)	25
Kuwait (1977)	22
Lebanon (1980)	6.4
Libya (1980)	77
Saudi Arabia (1979)	233
Sudan (1978)	13.6

Sources: UNESCO, based on National Reports prepared for CASTARAB II.

Iran

The expansion of the system of higher education in Iran during the 1960s and 1970s paralleled the patterns pursued in the neighbouring Arab states. In 1979, the year of the Islamic Revolution, scientists in Iran had contributed some 404 research papers. Eighty-two institutions contributed one or more publications. By 1983 the number of contributions had fallen to 103; they were the product of research workers in twenty-eight institutions, half being contributions from the Universities of Shiraz and Tehran.

The Islamic Revolution has initiated reforms in the entire educational system. New science policies are being formulated. UNESCO statistical publications on R&D contain no recent information on Iran. It is known, however, that in 1980 there were 2,132 scientists and engineers; and that R&D expenditures in 1984 totalled Rial 21.5m.

Israel

The motivation for science and technology in Israel derives from the critical function it assumed in the creation and continuation of the state, as well as in the exercise of its regional and international power. The efficiency with which Israel creates, processes and applies science and technology is on the same level as that of OECD countries.

One can distinguish three phases in the evolution of Israeli science and technology: the period up to 1948; the period from 1948 to 1967; and the period from 1967 to the present.

During the Ottoman period, the Zionist movement focused on 'the return to the land', and thus there was much concern with establishing agricultural settlements. The immigrating Zionists came generally from urban European backgrounds and needed much training and technical advice in the agricultural sciences. A strong relationship between R&D and the agricultural sector took root, and became intensified with time.

The medical sciences were the second area of early local development. The number of immigrant physicians and surgeons was so high that until recently Israel did not need a medical school; yet useful research in the medical sciences continued to be carried out. Until 1948, all fields of scientific activity, other than the agricultural and medical, were on a relatively small scale. Israel's success in agricultural production is well established.

Three major institutions were founded during this period: the Hebrew University of Jerusalem (1925); the Institute of Technology in Haifa (1925); and the Weizmann Institute in Rehovot (1934). During the period between 1948 and 1967, a rapid expansion in the scope of activities of existing institutions took place, and two additional institutions were established: Tel Aviv University in 1954, and Bar-Ilan University in 1955. By the mid-1960s, total enrolment at Israeli universities had reached 27,000 students.

During this second phase, from 1948 to 1967, research in the basic sciences expanded freely, and substantial military R&D programmes were started. The Nuclear Weapons Programme of the Ministry of Defence began to take shape in 1948.

By the mid-1960s, Israel had built an impressive scientific and technological infrastructure. It ranked 16th among the nations of the world in research output. It had more publishing scientists than all of Latin America, and 50 per cent more than all of Africa. Israeli scientists and technologists published three times more than all researchers in the Arab world. Israel's largest scientific city, Jerusalem, was similar in size to Rome, Manchester, Vienna or Edinburgh. Haifa alone had more publishing scientists than either Mexico or Greece.

By 1967, Israeli science and technology had grown in stature, scale and experience. The recognition of Israeli scientists and technologists was worldwide. Science and technology were not yet institutionalized, however, to the point where they could be effectively managed by policy. This brings us to the third and current phase.

By the mid-1960s, it became clear to Israeli leaders that scientific capabilities were not adequately harnessed by the economy to be translatable into marketable exports. Furthermore, Israel's main exports were still citrus fruit, textiles and diamonds, and the first two of these were threatened by competing producers with lower costs. In order to secure a continued supply of exportable products, it was found necessary to increase the technological or scientific contents of either the products or the means of production. The Katchalsky Committee for the organization and administration of government research was established to examine the necessary reforms. The committee's recommendations were: to establish the functions of chief scientists in ministries (such as Commerce and Industry) in order to coordinate and stimulate research activity; to reorganize the governmental research institute into three separate authorities, each headed by the chief scientist of the Ministries of Agriculture, Commerce and Industry, and Development; and to reorganize the National Council for Research and Development in order to plan national science policy with reference to scientific manpower.

The most significant product of the committee's recommendations was the establishment of the Industrial Research Fund of the Ministry of Commerce and Industry. This fund provided a 50 per cent subsidy for all approved research projects. The ultimate objective of the new technology was to increase exports; the *modus operandi* of the fund was to support 50 per cent of the R&D of industrial firms which were willing to bear market risks. The fund had a dramatic impact on the increase of the exports of industrial products. It also led to the rapid development of the military–industrial complex.

In 1983, 4661 publications were produced by scientists in 292 institutions. The Hebrew University ranks as the leading publishing institution with 709 contributions by its faculty in 1983. The total number of R&D workers exceeded 12,600 in 1980.

Israel is the only country in the region that has evolved effective R&D activities together with the capability to manage its R&D establishments. Israeli science and technology is integrated into European and US activities, from which it has received considerable financial support. The US government has also subsidized and supported Israeli military R&D.

Turkey

The Ottoman* (and later the Turkish) government has long been conscious of the importance of technology in the civilian and military spheres. Science planning is undertaken today by the Science Policy Unit of the Scientific and Technical Research Council of Turkey (Tubitak), in collaboration with the State Planning Organization and the major ministries. The stated objectives of the various organizations are to secure relevant technologies, and to strengthen the ability of the national economy for creating, absorbing and adopting technology. Tubitak is active in the fields of industrial research, basic sciences, engineering, medicine, veterinary medicine, agriculture and construction technology.

The level of R&D support in Turkey is the lowest among the OECD countries. In 1979, funding for R&D was at $5 per capita compared with $132 (USA), $97 (Germany), $117 (Sweden) and $9 (Spain).

In 1982, R&D expenditures totalled 27m lira. The number of scientific publications from Turkey in 1983 was 406, where in 1979 it had been 315. Sixty-nine institutions contributed one or more publications during 1983. Professors of the Middle East Technical University contributed 86 of the 406 publications in 1983. There were 13,050 R&D scientists and engineers in 1982.

The Arab world, Iran and Turkey are roughly at the same level of activity. None of these countries has reached the critical mass of activity necessary to support the national economy on a systematic basis.

ABZ

Further reading

OECD, *Science and Technology Indicators* (Paris, 1984), p. 35
UNESCO, *Statistics on Science and Technology* (Paris, 1985)
A. B. Zahlan, *Science and Science Policy in the Arab World* (London, 1978)

Note: All information on the number of publications is derived from: *Current Bibliographic Directory of the Arts and Sciences*, published annually by the Institute for Scientific Information, Philadelphia, USA.

The media of communication

Book publishing, journalism, radio and television

The evolution of publishing in the Middle East

The world's first wood-block printing presses are thought to have been set up in China in the eighth century AD and thence exported to Central Asia where they were used by the Uigur Turks. Later there seems to have been some block-printing in Arabic in the Middle East. However, Islam's sensitivity to the aesthetics of writing militated against the development of the printing industry and its early development in the region was short-lived. Most manuscripts were first printed abroad. In 1514 the *Book of Hours* (*Kitab salat al-sawa'i*) was printed in Fano in Italy and in the late sixteenth century Rome's Medici Press published books in Arabic, such as Idrisi's *Kitab nuzhat al-mushtaq*. Other European countries followed the lead given by Italy. In 1727, in belated response, the Ottoman* Sultan allowed books to be printed in Ottoman Turkish and a press was established by Ibrahim Müteferrika. However, most books within the Empire continued to be published in languages such as Greek, Hebrew and Armenian, while books in Arabic continued to be exported to the region by the Medici Press.

Some of the earliest publishing in the region was by Lebanese. The type-designer and printer of the Medici Press, for example, was Ya'qub ibn Hilal, who worked under the name of Jacques Luna. A printing press was established in Qazhayya in Lebanon in the late sixteenth century, in Shwayr in 1726 and in Beirut in 1751. By the nineteenth century both Arabic and Turkish books were being published in Istanbul. Egypt's first Arabic press was brought by Napoleon* in 1798 but ceased to operate after he left in 1801. Some years later, however, Muhammad Ali* set up a press in Bulaq whose first published work was an Italian–Arabic dictionary. From then on the Bulaq Press published texts on every conceivable subject. From 1825 to 1842 British missionaries published books in Arabic for a publishing house in Malta, for whom the Maronite*, Faris al-Shidyaq (1804–87), wrote. In 1834 American Protestant missionaries brought a printing house to Beirut, where they were to publish books by Lebanese writers such as Shaykh Nasif al-Yaziji (1800–71) and Butrus al-Bustani (1819–83).

In 1857 Khalil al-Khuri founded the Syrian Press and in 1874 'Abd al-Qadir Qabbani launched the first Islamic printing press in Lebanon, where were published many of the newspapers and periodicals that were to be the hallmark of Arab thought during this searching age. An Arabic printing press was set up in Jerusalem in 1846, in Damascus in 1855 and in Mosul in 1856. In 1869 the Ottoman liberal official Midhat Pasha set up an important printing press in Baghdad. Printing presses were launched at the same time in North Africa. Fez started lithographic printing in 1845, Constantine in 1846 and Tunis in 1860. The same development was to take place in the Arabian peninsula, where Yemen started lithographic printing in 1877, Mecca in 1883 and Medina in 1885. Khartoum had its first printing press in 1881.

The press as a vehicle for liberal thought

Until the 1860s virtually the only newspapers in the Ottoman Empire in Arabic and Turkish were official government gazettes published in Cairo and Istanbul. Otherwise, there was virtually nothing published in Arabic, although a few newspapers existed in French, Greek and Armenian. However, the increase in printing presses after 1860 and of writers in Arabic, as well as the new liberalism of the Ottoman regime in Asia Minor and Egypt, made possible the creation of private newspapers and periodicals. Until the end of the century these were mainly run by Lebanese Christians and were published in Beirut, Cairo and Istanbul. They were either independent political newspapers or literary and scientific journals which both introduced Western progress to the Arab world and tried to show how it could be discussed in Arabic.

Between 1870 and 1900 some forty periodical publications and fifteen newspapers were founded in Beirut. Of these, *Lisan al-Hal* (1877) and the learned Jesuit journal *Al-Mashriq* (1898) were widely read. Newspapers were founded by groups of Young Turks* from 1860, both within the Ottoman Empire and in Western Europe, such as that of Sinasi, Ziya Pasha and Namik Kemal, which was published under the patronage of Mustafa Fazil Pasha, a member of the Egyptian khedival family. When this group was exiled to Paris it founded a new journal there but the journal was dissolved in 1871, when its members were allowed to return to Istanbul.

The first important name in newspapers was the Maronite Lebanese Ahmed Faris al-Shidyaq who, after a time working on a translation of the New Testament, went to Istanbul in 1860 and launched there the Arabic *Al-Jawa'ib*, whose early issues discussed current topics such as the significance of the Franco-Prussian War and the 1870 Eastern Crisis. An equally important figure was Butrus al-Bustani, who worked for the British and American consulates in Beirut and taught in American missionary schools. In 1870 he founded the Arabic periodical *Al-Jinan* which was largely written by his son Salim. However, the Sultan's clamp-down on press freedom led to its closure in 1886 and from this date the centre of Lebanese journalism moved from Beirut to Cairo. The most famous of these Lebanese–Egyptian periodicals was *Al-Muqtataf*, founded in 1876 by Ya'qub Sarruf and Faris Nimr, two teachers from the Syrian Protestant College who moved to Cairo in 1885. *Al-Muqtataf* was to remain in circulation for some fifty years. Adib Ishaq (1856–

85), another Syrian Christian, also moved from Syria to Egypt where he was to edit *Misr*, first in Alexandria and later, under a different title, in France.

Reflecting the search for scientific knowledge, *Al-Muqtataf* would probe subjects ranging from microbes in the air to the different roles of men and women. In 1892 *Al-Hilal* was founded in Cairo by Jurji Zaydan (1861–1914). *Al-Hilal* was less scientific than *Al-Muqtataf*, paying more attention to literature and language, archaeology and history.

Publishing and the media in Egypt

Egypt's modern press dates from 1875 when Salim Taqla, a Greek Catholic from Kafarshima near Beirut, migrated to Egypt where he founded the weekly *Al-Ahram*. In 1889 Sarruf and Nimr launched the newspaper *Al-Muqattam*, which was to become the main rival of *Al-Ahram*. *Al-Ahram* was later to be published daily and is Egypt's most important newspaper by far, with a present-day circulation of 900,000 copies on week-days and 1.1 million on Fridays. In 1984 the publishers launched an international edition in London and in January 1987 a North American edition from Long Island. Thanks to satellite communications* all three editions are published simultaneously. With the demise of Lebanon as a major publishing centre after the civil war, Egypt has today once again become the most important publishing centre in the Middle East. Today Cairo has eleven dailies, of which six are in Arabic, one, the *Egyptian Gazette*, in English, two in French, one in Greek and one in Armenian. Cairo also publishes some forty-two weekly or monthly periodicals. Alexandria publishes six dailies and seventeen weekly or monthly periodicals. Although the press is subject to the control of the Supreme Press Council set up by President Sadat* in 1975, Egypt's four main publishing houses, Al-Ahram, Dar al-Hilal, Dar Akhbar al-Yawm and Dar al-Jumhuriyya (who control most of the press), all compete with each other commercially as independent units.

A press law of 1980 attempted to liberalize the organization of Egypt's principal newspapers by transferring 51 per cent of their ownership from the defunct Arab Socialist Union to the newly formed Shura Council. In June 1984 the Shura Council, in a further attempt to open up the press, approved a proposal by the Supreme Press Council that the posts of chairman and editor-in-chief be held by separate people. Today the newly encouraged opposition press has become increasingly outspoken, with *Al-Ahali* representing left-wing and often satirical views and *Al-Ahrar* (named after the party of that name) the liberals. Economic views are expressed by *Al-Ahram al-Iqtisadi* ('Al-Ahram Economist'). The New Wafd* Party, which won some seats in the 1984 elections, founded its own newspaper, the *Wafd*, in March 1984. The opposition press is avidly read by Egyptians seeking a balanced view of affairs, although the accuracy of its reports is sometimes questioned.

Today Egypt is by far the biggest publisher of books in the Arab world, with over fifty publishing houses in Cairo and seven in Alexandria. Overall responsibility for the industry is the General Egyptian Book Organization (GEBO), a government organization responsible for the distribution of textbooks to schools and for organizing Cairo's book-fair held in January in Nasr City. Given Egypt's critically low cost of living, book piracy has been a major problem since the open-door policy (*infitah*)* of the early 1970s. This piracy began at the University of Alexandria, and was run by the Islamic Students' Organization as a service to provide cheaper books to students. The main sales outlet for pirated medical books has been the Qasr al-ʿAini Hospital in Cairo, where 75 per cent of the books pirated are in English.

Publishing and the media in Lebanon

In Lebanon, the birthplace of newspapers in the Middle East, meanwhile, the 1975–6 civil war* and its unended aftermath saw the end of Beirut as the centre for Middle Eastern journalism and the base for most foreign correspondents. Beirut and Cairo have been the traditional centres for book publishing in the Arab world, although the Lebanese civil war has meant that this honour is now restricted to Cairo whose international book-fair in January is the most important in the Middle East, the new Bahrain book-fair having failed to supplant it. Ironically, although some publishers have evacuated West Beirut, there are still as many publishing houses in the capital as there were before the civil war began. Lebanon is also notoriously responsible for book piracy in the region with Lebanese-produced books in Arabic, English and French appearing in neighbouring countries such as Jordan.

When the civil war broke out in 1975 Lebanon's most important daily newspapers, with the highest circulations, were *Al-Anwar* and *An-Nahar*, the English-language *Daily Star*, *Al-Jarida* and *L'Orient le Jour*, Lebanon's principal French-language newspaper. However, there are still an astonishing thirty-eight dailies and twenty-eight weeklies published in Beirut and even during the heart of the civil war some twenty-five newspapers and periodicals, reflecting every angle of political opinion, appeared. Today, *Al-Anwar* has a circulation of over 75,000, *Al-Nahar* 85,000 and *Al-Jarida* nearly 23,000. The foremost newspaper in French, a language widely spoken in Lebanon, is *L'Orient le Jour* with a circulation of 23,000. The second French-language daily, *Le Soir*, has a circulation of almost 17,000. The last English-language daily, the *Daily Star*, closed down in August 1985. New press censorship in January 1977 forced some Arabic newspapers to close down although this may be only a temporary factor.

The media in Kuwait

The reputation for the freest press in the Arabian Gulf states is held by Kuwait, which has for long enjoyed a reputation for greater political freedom than any other Gulf state. Its increasing pre-eminence reflects generous government subsidies and the declining influence of other regional press centres. The deterioration of Beirut as a media centre and the decline of Egypt's influence after the 1978 Camp David Accords* with Israel saw the migration of many Egyptian and Palestinian journalists to Kuwait where they were offered attractive salaries and comparative freedom of expression. Although personal attacks are prohibited, criticism of the authorities is allowed to a limited extent. In Kuwait there is no pre-publication censorship and the government has often used the press to test public responses to its policies. During the Suq al-Manakh* financial crisis the press led an often angry debate. However, it has had to work within fairly strict limits and is, moreover, dependent on the Industrial Bank of Kuwait for part-financing of its new plant and equipment purchases. High technology equipment and satellite communications* have helped promote Kuwait as an education and literary press centre in the region.

The first periodical in Kuwait, a monthly literary and religious magazine called *Al-Kuwait*, was founded in 1928 by a Kuwaiti historian, ʿAbd al-ʿAziz al-Rashid. The magazine was printed in Egypt and disappeared after two years but was replaced by another, *Al-Kuwait wa'l-ʿIraq* (Kuwait and Iraq). In 1946 a magazine called *Al-Baʿtha* (The Mission) was launched by the current minister of state for cabinet affairs, ʿAbd al-ʿAziz Husayn. After the discovery of oil in the 1950s many other magazines followed, among them the present-day official gazette, *al-Kuwayt al-Yawm*, published by the Ministry of Information, and the Ministry's *Al-ʿArabi*, which today has a circulation of 250,000. Following independence in 1961 *Al-Ra'y al-ʿAm*, initially a weekly, became the first Arabic-language daily, and in the following year the English-language daily, *The Kuwait Times*, was launched. 1965 saw the publication of Kuwait's principal Arabic daily, *Al-Siyasa*. Today the Al-Siyasa Publishing House publishes three Arabic dailies including *Al-Siyasa*, two weeklies, one monthly magazine and the English-language *Arab Times*. Of the existing five dailies in Kuwait, *Al-Watan* and *Al-Anba* were set up in the boom years of the 1970s. In 1972 the Kuwait Oil Company launched the *Kuwait Digest*, an English-language monthly. Today there are well over eighty newspapers and magazines published in Kuwait.

Publishing and the media in Saudi Arabia

When Crown Prince Faysal* became prime minister of Saudi Arabia in 1962 its few newspapers and radio stations were concentrated in the Hijaz. Although the first newspapers were launched in 1908 in the Hijaz they were written by Ottoman Turks, Syrians and other Arabs. The Ottomans founded *Al-Hijaz* in March 1908. The first newspaper to be launched by Hijazis was Hidda's *Barid al-Hijaz* in 1924, although it closed down the following year. In the same year the Saudi government launched a hand-printed weekly, *Umm al-Qura*, in Mecca although even this was edited by Syrians at first. Its first editor was Shaykh Yusuf Yasin, an adviser to King ʿAbd-al-ʿAziz. This newspaper, devoted to religious and literary articles, was almost the only publication extant in the Kingdom from 1925 to 1932.

Publications that emerged in the 1930s in the Hijaz included *Sawt al-Hijaz* (1932) and *Al-Nida al-Islami* (1937) in Mecca and *Al-Manhal* (1937) and *Al-Madina al-Munawwara* (1937) in Medina. *Sawt al-Hijaz*, which was suspended with other newspapers in 1941, reappeared a year after the war had ended under the name of *Al-Bilad al-Saʿudiyya* and by 1953 it had been transformed from a literary and religious periodical into the Kingdom's first newspaper. Similarly, *Al-Madina al-Munawwara* became a daily newspaper as *Al-Madina* in the 1950s.

Although Saudi Arabia enjoys the same extremely high technology (including satellite* technology) as Kuwait, the press today is covered by strict legal restrictions which affect the coverage of news. In 1962 many of the Kingdom's journalists were Egyptians with sympathies for Nasserite republicanism and some went on strike in support of Nasser* during the civil war in Yemen. Faysal 'advised our friends of the press' to avoid discussing socialism out of anxiety to 'maintain friendly and brotherly relations' with Egypt. The new press code of 1964 gave the government more power to intervene to control the views of the media. The small private companies that had traditionally owned the various newspapers handed over to big press organizations which are administered by boards of directors who have full autonomous powers in accordance with the press law. Today all newspapers and periodicals are controlled by eight large publishing houses.

The most popular Arabic daily today is *Al-Riyadh*, with a circulation of 90,000. There are eleven key dailies of which eight are in Arabic. The two main English-language newspapers, *Arab News* and the *Saudi Gazette*, were both launched in 1975. Saudi Arabia's two weekly business magazines, *Saudi Business* and the *Saudi Economic Survey*, the former published in 1975 and the latter in 1967, are major sources of economic information for foreign businessmen.

Publishing and the media in Iran

By the time of the revolution in 1979 the number of books published in Iran was in heavy decline. According to the *Echo in Iran*'s Almanac only 3200 titles were published in 1976, of which only 1580 were new titles. Of these new books 36 per cent were literary books and 18 per cent were religious. However, the great increase in publishing costs was only part of the story. The heavy fines and threats of closure for an 'error' and the problems of censorship and increasing restrictions demoralized the publishing companies. Moreover, authors critical of the regime were reluctant to allow their books to be published if this suggested association with it. Pressure was, for example, placed upon writers to join the Shah's new party, the Rastakhiz.

Since 1976 the Iran's Writers Association had been struggling to register and acquire legal status so that it could hold official meetings. Writers faced the dangers of arrest and imprisonment and even Iran's most celebrated historian and former ambassador to India, Fereidun Ademeyat, served prison sentences. Ademeyat was among forty artists and intellectuals who had sent a letter in June 1977 to the prime minister, Amir ʿAbbas Huvayda (Hoveida), calling for more freedom. To some extent the regime tried to control the printing presses with three of its own, the Bunghai tarjuma va nashri-i Kitab, the 25th Shahrivar Printing House and the Danesh Now Printing and Publishing Company, all owned by the Pahlavi Foundation.

The press had been heavily controlled under Riza Shah* but enjoyed more freedom after 1941. In a move to curtail press freedom in 1949 one- to three-year prison sentences were imposed on editors and journalists who insulted the Shah or the royal family. The Shah himself made considerable use of the press and was quoted as saying: 'My voice is heard everywhere; heard through the radio, seen through the TV. The contact is there.' Until the revolution the press was codified by the press law of 1955 as modified by amendments in 1963. Under this law newspapers could not be banned with a court order unless they criticized the Shah or religion. Newspapers with a circulation of less than 3000 and magazines with one of less than 5000 were illegal. All communist publications were banned. The 1965 Reporters' Code of Journalism required all journalists to be licensed by the Ministry of Information. The press was dominated by large family concerns such as the *Ittilaʿat* group, the *Kayhan* group and the *Echo of Iran* group. However, readership was restricted, and in 1978 of 820,000 copies of newspapers printed daily only 200,000 were read outside Tehran, which contained some 72 per cent of Iran's printing presses. The Shah's party newspaper, the *Rastakhiz*, which claimed a circulation of 150,000, was regarded by many as the government's official organ. There were sixteen principal dailies, of which the *Echo of Iran*, *Kayhan International* and the *Tehran Journal* were in English and the *Iran Presse* and *Le Journal de Teheran* were in French. Many of these have ceased to function or else have changed their names. The *Tehran Times*, for example, was founded in 1979 to replace the *Tehran Journal*, while Kayhan produced two new Persian language weeklies, *Kayhan Bacheha* (Children's Kayhan) and *Kayhan Varzeshi* (Kayhan Sport). The post-revolution radical daily, *Azadegan*, was closed down by Iran's prosecutor-general in June 1985, to reappear as *Abrar* (Rightly-guided), because of its criticism of conservative members of the Majlis.

Radical demands for a free press as enshrined in Article 19 of 1906 were reiterated in May 1979 when the Iran Republican Party and the government prepared a new press law that was published in August 1979. Penalties of up to three years' imprisonment were imposed for insulting clergymen. According to Principal 24 of the Islamic Constitution, 'Publications and the press are free to present all matters except those that are detrimental to the fundamental principles of Islam and the rights of the public.' Shortly after the new press laws were announced the government banned forty-one opposition newspapers, including the publications of the NDF, the Tudeh* Party, the Fedaʾi and the Mujahidin*. The new Mustazafin Foundation took over Tehran's popular afternoon dailies, *Ittilaʿat* and *Kayhan*, which each claimed circulations of 100,000.

The media and publishing in Afghanistan

Publishing developed slowly and unevenly in Afghanistan's highly conservative society. Literacy was and remains rare outside the cities, limiting the demand for newspapers and books. There was rivalry between Afghanistan's two main languages, Persian and Pushtu. Persian and Arabic books were usually imported from Iran and India. The influential bi-monthly paper *Seraj-ul-Akhbar* was published in 1911–19, under royal patronage by the Afghan nationalist Mahmud Beg Tarzi, while a small state publishing enterprise was run from Kabul. After the Second World War independent newspapers began to circulate. Despite tiny sales restricted to the cities, these promoted democratic ideas among the small intellectual elite. A press law in 1965 allowed a considerable degree of press freedom, encouraging some competition from liberal, nationalist and left-wing circles, with the government-controlled dailies published in Kabul. Most of the weeklies proved ephemeral but a few had undeniable influence. It is noteworthy that two left-wing weeklies, *Parcham* and *Khalq*, remained the names of the two rival factions of the Communist Party (PDPA) which seized power in a coup in 1978.

Radio and television

The Egyptian Radio and Television Corporation was established in 1928. Today Cairo Radio is no longer the propaganda machine that it was in Nasser's day but it is just as formidable, with daily broadcasts on its home service in nine languages, and twenty-nine languages in its foreign service. In 1964 a commercial radio station called Middle East Radio was launched. Egypt began broadcasting on television in 1960 and today its three channels broadcast 22.5 hours a day.

In July 1953 Egypt's President Nasser had launched a radio station called Sawt al-ʿArab (Voice of the Arabs), which was destined to become one of the most potent weapons in his struggle to spread socialism and pan-Arabism. In 1954 the station increased its transmission by four hours. Throughout the period leading up to the Suez crisis of 1956 this station was to carry on a passionate campaign against imperialism. By 1963 Cairo's propaganda machine was working full blast, with Cairo Radio broadcasting in twenty-four languages and its rate of transmission to the Arab world reaching an extraordinary 755 hours each week. By 1970 Egypt was broadcasting in thirty-four languages and had become the world's fifth country in terms of transmission hours.

Equally important in spreading an ideological message, in this case a conservative and religious one diametrically opposed to that of Egypt, was the development of radio and television in Saudi Arabia. King ʿAbd al-ʿAziz was to fight Wahhabi* (Unitarian) opposition to the installation of the wireless just as King Faysal was later to have to defend the inauguration of Saudi television. When the diehards complained in 1963 that a woman's voice had been heard on Mecca Radio, King Faysal snapped back, 'You'll soon be seeing their faces on television.' King ʿAbd al-ʿAziz had launched his own private radio network, installed by Marconi through the good offices of ʿAbd Allah (St John) Philby in 1932, principally so that his offices throughout the Kingdom could keep him abreast of events. It was all at a cost, with the religious diehards sending emissaries to the radio station to try to prove it satanic. ʿAbd al-ʿAziz responded by explaining that his radio could carry the word of God in the Qur'an. Despite resistance, television was launched in 1965 although great care was taken not to offend Wahhabi sensibilities. Programmes were carefully censored and even Mickey Mouse could not be shown giving his wife an affectionate kiss. An attack by extremists led by the King's grandson, Khalid ibn Musaʿid, on Riyadh's new television station in 1965 led to the death of the prince.

The expansion of broadcasting coincided with the reign of King Faysal, by the end of which radio receivers had expanded from 200,000 with half a million listeners to one million receivers and two and a half million listeners. In 1964 King Faysal's government signed an agreement with the National Broadcasting Company (NBC) International of the US to build a national television network and the first test transmissions began in Jidda and Riyadh in 1965. Within two years a modestly dressed Saudi woman compèred a children's programme despite opposition, and in 1968 a religious scholar, Shaykh Tantawi, launched a programme in which he answered viewers' letters, using Qur'anic teachings to respond to their personal problems. This was intended as a slow move towards liberalization and away from an obsessive concentration on dry Qur'anic readings.

If Egypt and Saudi Arabia exploited their broadcasting services to spread a message, Lebanon developed a broadcasting service which was to be comparatively free from political control. The foreign service of the Lebanese Broadcasting Station, founded in 1937, broadcasts today in six languages. Since the start of the civil war the number of radio receivers has almost doubled to 1.5m, probably reflecting people's desperate need for daily information of 'events'. Before the civil war Beirut had two television companies, the Compagnie Libanaise de Television, founded in 1959, and Tele Orient, founded in the following year. In August 1985 the 'Lebanese forces' Christian militia launched the Lebanese Broadcasting Corporation which today relays on a single channel.

Jordan was a forerunner for television in the Arab world. Its first black-and-white transmission was on 10 July 1968 and on 10 July 1972 it became the first station in the Arab world to broadcast on two channels. It was also the first television station in the Middle East to produce colour television, the first transmission being on 27 April 1974, and to make extensive use of satellite communications. Today its channels cover the whole of Jordan and Palestine/Israel as far as the Mediterranean. Many technicians from Saudi Arabia and the Gulf states train in Jordan before returning home. Bahrain introduced colour television in 1973, the first Gulf state to do so.

Most of the broadcasting on Kuwait's two main radio stations is in Arabic, one concentrating on a local audience, the other appealing to a wider Arab audience. Kuwaiti soap serials, such as 'Ahlam saghira' (Small dreams), which analyse the state's fast changing society, are popular. Kuwait also broadcasts in English, Urdu and Persian and has an FM music station. It has two television channels, one in Arabic and one in English, both of which show the popular educational programe 'Iftah ya Simsim' (Open Sesame – the Kuwaiti equivalent of Sesame Street). Both channels also show various religious programmes such as 'Hadith al-Usbuʿ' (Sermon of the week), presented by the popular Shaykh ʿAli Jassar. Apart from educational, health and scientific programmes, Kuwaiti television shows serials such as 'Darb al-Zuluq' (Slippery path), which shows Kuwaitis trying to adapt to the new life of affluence.

Audio cassettes and the question of piracy

The market for audio cassettes in the region is massive, while the ability of governments to control piracy is extremely limited. In 1986 a report published by the British Publishers Association and the International Federation of Phonogram and Videogram Producers indicted Saudi Arabia as one of the world's biggest importers of pirated sound recording, videos, computer software and, to a lesser extent, of books. The report estimated that 50m pre-recorded pirate cassettes, mostly imported from Singapore and Indonesia, were sold in 1986 as well as 40m blank tapes for in-store taping. Many of these cassettes are re-exported from Saudi Arabia to North Yemen, Somalia, Sudan and Egypt. The Saudi government is considering imposing copyright legislation largely on censorship and religious grounds. It is also believed that the UAE is one of the main distribution centres for Indonesian music pirates. Egypt and Lebanon are major producers of cassette recordings but many of the blank tapes used are imported pirate tapes.

TM

Further reading

A. Dawisha, *Egypt in the Arab World* (London, 1976)
D. Holden and R. Johns, *The House of Saud* (London, 1982)
A. Hourani, *Arabic Thought in the Liberal Age* (Cambridge, 1983)
The Middle East and North Africa 1987, Europa (London, 1986)
W. Rugh, *King Faisal and the Modernisation of Saudi Arabia* (London, 1980)

Satellite communications

Arabsat

Arabsat (Arab Satellite Communications Organization) is a space-based pan-Arab communications network, linking all twenty-two member nations of the Arab League*.

Arabsat 1A and 1B

Each satellite can relay 8000 telephone calls and seven one-way television transmissions between broadcasting studios, or their

First mooted in the early 1970s, Arabsat was brought into formal being by the Arab League in 1976. It became operational in 1985 with the launch of two communications satellites, Arabsat 1A and Arabsat 1B, into Clarke orbits above Zaire from where they are in permanent view of the nations they serve.

equivalent in other forms of telecommunication: radio programmes, telex, electronic mail, facsimile (FAX) and slow-scan picture transmissions, links between computers such as those used in banking, or for booking airline seats, as well as between the complex package of relays required for teleconferencing.

By 1987 Arabsat was in a position to relay domestic television programming nationally and internationally within the Arab world and to enable newspaper publishers to distribute edited pages for simultaneous printing throughout the Middle East. Two space-age facilities are already being made use of by broadcasters and editors in the more developed Arab countries by virtue of their membership of the 109-nation Intelsat (International Telecommunications Satellite Organization) set up in 1969.

Arabsat satellites are controlled by encryted commands, transmitted to them via large steerable dish antennae from the primary ground station at Dirhab near Riyadh in Saudi Arabia, or from the back-up station in Tunis.

Similar dish antennae linked to equipment to receive and transmit Arabsat telecommunications signals are being installed throughout the Arab world. As well as being able to provide regular links between fixed ground stations, Arabsat satellites are equipped to provide temporary communications via small mobile ground stations in a regional emergency, such as the aftermath of an earthquake.

The Arabsat organization chose the French aerospace company Aerospatiale as prime contractor for the development and manufacture of its satellites. Aerospatiale sought help from the US corporation Ford Aerospace which built the successful Indian domestic satellite, Insat, and assistance from other spacecraft builders in the United States and Europe.

The space division of the Japanese NEC Corporation built the ground control stations in Saudi Arabia and Tunisia. For the first few years of network operation, these were manned by ground controllers provided by Aerospatiale.

Aerospatiale built three spacecraft. Two were launched in 1985; the third was being kept as a spare. At launch, each satellite weighed around 1200 kilograms, half of this weight being the fuel needed to position the spacecraft in the desired orbit and keep it there. By current communications satellite standards, Arabsat are medium-size spacecraft and can therefore be launched piggy-back with other payloads. Thus on 8 February 1985 the first to be orbited, Arabsat 1A, shared its ride into space with a Brazilian domestic communications satellite.

Arabsat 1A's night-time launch from the Korou space centre in French Guyana, aboard a European Ariane rocket, was witnessed by Arabsat's then Iraqi director-general, ʿAli al-Mashat, and ʿAlawi Darwish Kayyal, minister of posts, telegraph and telecommunications of Arabsat's principal shareholder, Saudi Arabia. In 1986, an Algerian, Abdul Qadir Baeeri, replaced al-Mashat as Arabsat's director-general.

The second satellite, Arabsat 1B, was taken aboard an American space shuttle and was launched from low-earth orbit to its work station 35,900 km above Africa on 18 June 1985. It shared the shuttle's cargo bay with two other domestic communications satellites: one for Mexico, the other for the United States. However, Arabsat 1B's more noteworthy companion aboard the shuttle was Saudi Arabia's Prince Sultan al-Saʿud, the Arab world's first astronaut.

The Arabsat organization's wisdom in choosing to have two small satellites instead of one larger spacecraft enabled the network to survive the initial failure of Arabsat 1A to keep proper station in orbit. The second satellite, Arabsat 1B, then became the primary 'on-line' spacecraft. Its errant partner was subsequently brought under control but demoted to a back-up role.

The Arabsat network is used to relay live television coverage of regional interest, ranging from prayer-time from the grand mosques of Mecca and Medina to inter-Arab football matches. The network is also used for regional television news exchanges, giving participant national broadcasters daily access to news-gathering on a pan-Arab scale. The same broadcasters can also receive, via Intelsat, the 24-hour global television network news services of the London-based agencies Visnews and Worldwide Television News (WTN), and the Atlanta-based Cable Network News (CNN) service.

By combining the expertise of Arabsat's national news teams with the longer-term experience of the sixteen members of the Federation of Arab News Agencies (FANA), some of which – the Kuwait National News Agency (KUNA) and the Saudi Press Agency (SPA), for example – being already worldwide distributors of printed news, these broadcasters have the means to provide the Arab element of a global television news service.

Broadcasters were less successful with their first attempts to use Arabsat to provide live pan-Arab entertainment. Some of the more exuberant material came up against the sensibilities of conservative broadcasting authorities. Ironically, the same authorities were those with audiences exposed to widely available and far from carefully controlled videotaped entertainment.

The Arabsat network has an enormous potential to serve the region's educational needs. As well as being able to relay television programmes between broadcasting studios, each satellite is also equipped to beam a powerful transmission to a 3 m-diameter receive-only dish antenna for 'community television', bringing to small settlements programmes concerned with primary health care, literacy and the development of professional skills.

Arabsat television transmissions could also be used in 'distance learning' projects, and in support of regional 'open universities' to cope with the growing imbalance between the number of well-educated school leavers and the number of traditional university places open to them.

In hindsight, the creation of the Arabsat communications network will be seen as a fine example of high-technology transfer to a developing region of the globe, and in turn provides the means for transferring its benefits from the well-developed to the less-developed parts of the region.

PR

Clarke orbit

A Clarke orbit, widely used for communications satellites, is named after the science writer Arthur C. Clarke, who first proposed its use in 1945. It is also called a 'geosynchronous equatorial orbit': a satellite in such an orbit remains 'stationary' with respect to the ground beneath it. This convenient arrangement is made possible by natural laws governing the motion of celestial bodies – the discovery of which was advanced by Arab astronomers* between the ninth and fifteenth centuries – whereby the speed of a satellite in a 35,900 km-high orbit above the equator exactly matches the rotation of the earth beneath it.

An Arabsat communications satellite consists of a box-shaped, approximately 2.3 × 1.6 × 1.5 m body, housing propulsion systems and instruments. To this central core are attached two small dish antennae to receive and send signals. Power is provided by a pair of solar-cell panel arrays with a wingspan of 20.7 m. They are folded for launch. The contours on the map show the relative strength of the ground-received signal around the 'footprint' of an Arabsat transmitter directed at the Arab world.

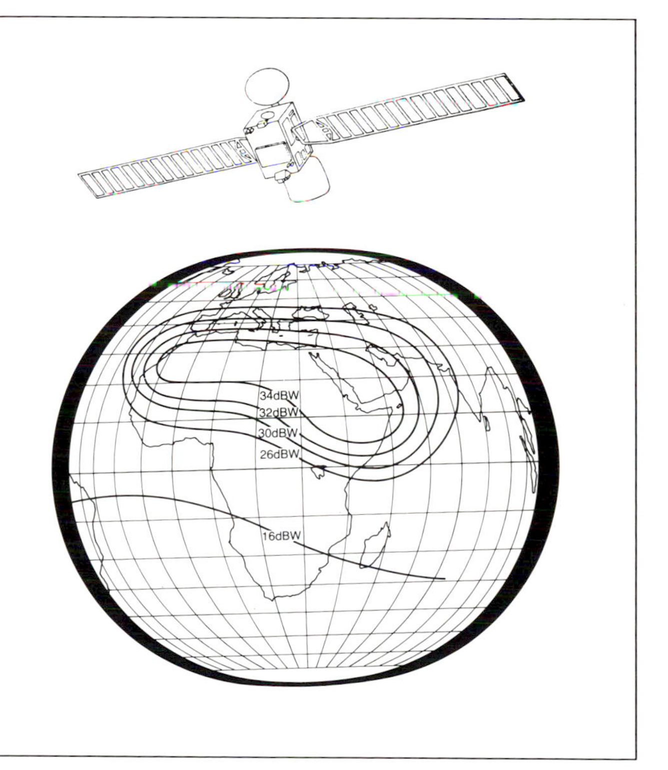

Sport

The historical background

Historically, the Middle East has produced many great legends of heroes with exceptional physical prowess, legends which survive in the folk traditions of Syria, Egypt, the Arabian peninsula, Persia (Iran), Anatolia and North Africa. Among the most famous are those of David and Goliath and Samson and Delilah in Hebrew history and ʿAntara ibn Shaddad and the Saʿalik ('Brigand poets') and Sayf ibn dhi Yazan in the pre-Islamic (Jahiliyya) history of Arabia. Although sport was already well-established in the region, Islam contributed to its importance by encouraging the concept of 'soundness' of body and mind and by harnessing, through the Islamic conquests, the energy of warriors motivated by faith and the search for martyrdom.

Recorded in one *hadith** are the words 'teach your children swimming, archery and horse-riding'. Historical books on the conquests contain endless lists of great swordsmen, archers and riders who still occupy a venerated position in the Islamic ethos. By the time of the Umayyads*, hunting and archery scenes were frequent themes in painting. A fresco of a hunting cavalier in the Qasr al-Hayr al-Gharbi in Syria shows a young man on horseback, in full gallop, pursuing gazelles, one of which lies on the ground mortally wounded while the other looks back at him as he aims an arrow at it.

Persian texts are copiously illustrated with hunting scenes. In a *Shah-Name* dated 1370 in Istanbul's Topkapi Sarayı Library is a brilliant painting of Zal shooting a waterbird before the Turkish maids of Princess Rudaba. A miniature of 1526 in Tabriz shows Iskandar shooting duck from a boat, while a hunting scene from the *Zafar-Name* in 1529 shows salukis, gazelles, lions, panthers and even elephants being hunted by archers in glittering armour. Animals and people are all in a state of thrilling movement.

Another traditional sport in the region, but particularly among the Arabian beduin, was falconry – the training and flying of falcons at wild quarry. The ruling families of Abu Dhabi and Dubai, the Al-Nahyan and the Al-Maktum, have produced generations of able falconers. Indeed, throughout Arabia falconry remains the most important sport. Originally it was the beduins' only method – apart from coursing hares with salukis – of getting fresh meat. Today the techniques of falconry have changed very little since the time of the Jahiliyya.

Among the Arabian tribes, raiding (*ghazw*) the flocks of fellow tribes was essentially regarded as a sport since such raids followed strict conventions. Quick coups involving cunning were favoured and bloodshed was avoided as far as was possible. Even in 1946 J. C. Crowfoot could write: 'Arabs are now raiding each other in Fords and Chevrolets', but today government control has put an end to traditional *ghazws*.

Sport in the modern world: the Olympic era

The late nineteenth century saw a new era in the field of sport in the Middle East. The modern Olympic movement emerged from the Sorbonne Conference, chaired by Baron de Coubertin, in Paris in 1894. A landmark in Middle Eastern sport was the 1924 Paris Olympics, when Egypt's footballers defeated the powerful Hungarians and finished in fifth place, ahead of Italy, France and Ireland. Egyptian athletes, meanwhile, were well placed in the wrestling and weight-lifting competitions. More was to come. In the 1928 Amsterdam Olympics the first Arab Olympic champions emerged. Egypt's Sayyid Nusayr won the gold medal in the light heavyweight category of the weight-lifting competitions and the Algerian-born Bou-Gherra al-Ouafi won the Marathon gold for France. Turkey, today considered a world leader in wrestling, also claimed several victories.

Among the most significant successes in the Olympics that followed were those of the Egyptians in Graeco-Roman wrestling and weight-lifting between 1928 and 1948 and the Marathon victories of Alain Mimoun (the Algerian-born ʿAli Maymun Okasha) for France in Helsinki and Melbourne (1952 and 1956). Lebanon won four Olympic medals between the Helsinki games in 1952 and those in Moscow in 1980. The wrestler Zakariyya Shihab, who won a Graeco-Roman silver in Helsinki in 1952, is an uncle of Muhammad Khayr al-Tarabulsi who won a silver in weight-lifting in Munich in 1972. Tunisia's Muhammad al-Gammudi won the 10,000 m silver at the 1954 Tokyo Olympics, the 5000 m gold as well as the 10,000 m bronze in Mexico in 1968 and then rounded up his career by winning the 5000 m silver in Munich in 1972.

Morocco's al-Radi ibn ʿAbd al-Salam finished second only to the legendary Abebe Bikila in the 1960 Rome Olympic Marathon and at the 1984 Los Angeles Olympics both Nawal al-Mutawakkil and Saʿid Aouita won gold medals. Syria and Algeria won one silver and two bronze medals respectively at the Los Angeles Olympics. Other successes went to great Turkish wrestlers such as Kaplan, Atli, Erkan, Ayik and Ayvaz, and Iran's wrestlers and weight-lifters led by the brilliant Muhammad Nasiri.

Long-distance swimming

Lack of Middle Eastern success in Olympic swimming has been compensated, surprisingly, by success in long-distance swimming, which is not an Olympic sport. Egypt and Syria established themselves among the world's top nations during the 1950s, 1960s and 1970s, especially with the English Channel crossing and the Capri–Naples race.

Football

Association football remains the 'bread and butter' of sports fans and media in the Middle East and North Africa. Traditional local rivalries have created deeply rooted loyalties and dramatic cult followings in the region. Among the most famous teams are al-Ahli (the National) and al-Zamalek in Egypt, al-Hilal and al-Marrikh in Sudan, Espérance-Africain in Tunisia and Fenerbahce–Galatasaray in Turkey. Since the 1924 and 1934 World Cup the Egyptian national team reached the semi-finals in the 1964 Tokyo Olympics and won the African Cup in 1957, 1959 and 1986. The Egyptians' fortunes, however, slumped from the early 1960s, leaving the limelight to the formidable Moroccan, Tunisian and Algerian teams until their latest victory in the African Nations Cup.

The Egyptian club sides, in fact, have established themselves at the top of Africa's two club competitions. Al-Ahli, al-Zamalek and Arab Contractors (*al-muqawwilun al-ʿarab*) won both Africa's Champions' Cup and the African Cup Winners' Cup, making these cups an almost Egyptian domain. Al-Ahli and al-Zamalek have each won the former, while the latter has been in the hands of the Egyptians ever since Arab Contractors won it in 1983 and retained it the following year, only to lose it to al-Ahli in 1985.

In Egypt, football, like most other sports, is played in 'big' omni-sports clubs like those of al-Ahli, al-Zamalek and al-Ittihad of Alexandria. Several of the well-known Arab sports clubs today, especially in the Gulf, North Africa and Sudan are modelled after these old institutions. The Gulf region owes its success to its financial surplus and the interest of the rulers. Today, Saudi Arabia is the Asian Nations' champion. Its former club champion, al-Ittifaq, won the Gulf and the Arab Champions' Cups in 1984–5. Kuwait and Algeria made the headlines in the World Cup finals in Spain in 1982 after success in the Asian Nations' Championship and the Moscow Olympics. Qatar, too, once reached the final match in the World Youth Cup and later appeared alongside Iraq, Saudi Arabia, Morocco and Egypt in the Los Angeles Olympics football competitions. The significance of these achievements is best considered in the light of the fact that their football federations and most other sporting organizations were founded only about 25 years ago. Today the top omni-sports clubs in the region have some of the best complexes and facilities.

The Shuwaykh Secondary School field, for a long time Kuwait's principal ground, is now only a memory. Today each of the big clubs owns a ground with a minimum capacity of 25,000 spectators equipped with up-to-date facilities. The most famous are the Kazma Club Stadium, the Ahmad al-Hamad Stadium of the al-Qadisiyya Club and the Sabah al-Salim Stadium of the al-ʿArabi Club.

Some of Saudi Arabia's most ambitious plans are reaching fruition. The General Presidency of Youth and Sports is responsible for planning, building and equipping sports complexes for regional clubs and pays an annual contribution to them. All major clubs run their own complexes. The most extensive are those of the al-Ittihad and al-Ahli clubs in Jidda, the al-Hilal, al-Nasr and al-Shabab clubs in Riyadh, and the al-Ittifaq, al-Nahda and al-Qadisiyya clubs in the Eastern Province. The Saudi Football Federation had 154 clubs under its banner in 1986; the Athletics Federation controls and administers athletics at 132 clubs; and the Saudi Volleyball Federation also comprises 132 clubs. In addition to club facilities, several stadiums and regional grounds have been built during the last ten years. The largest and newest is the King Fahd Stadium in Riyadh with a capacity of about 68,000.

Kuwait and Czechoslovakia fight for the 1982 World Cup in Spain

The Gulf has also been a leader in regular competitions. The Gulf Football Tournament in 1986 started a new full round in Bahrain where it was inaugurated in 1970. This is the Arab world's leading tournament and has helped to popularize the game. Kuwait has been the most successful competitor, winning the cup six times in eight competitions in 1970, 1972, 1974, 1976, 1982 and 1986, with Iraq winning in 1979 and 1984.

The national federations of Turkey and Cyprus are part of the European Football Federation (UEFA). However, these two countries have been well below the European standard, especially since the beginning of the 1980s when Turkish football went through a barren patch, both on club and national team levels. The period witnessed the meteoric rise of Trabzonspur, a regional side from eastern Turkey, at the expense of the 'old troika' of Istanbul's Fenerbahce, Galatasaray and Beşiktaş, three omni-sports clubs. In Cyprus, Omonia overtook old rivals Apoel but both remain insignificant in comparison with the leading West European sides.

Given the humble status of competitive team sport in Asia, Iranian club teams have rarely had the chance to prove their real metal. Even in Asia's Football Champions' Cup the achievements of the Taj Club team, which had been the champions in 1970, were hardly appreciated, since top Arab club teams withdrew from any competition in which they had to play Israeli teams. In spite of the hollow victories of Taj, Iranian football had its moments of glory in the World Cup finals in Argentina in 1978, where the team competed bravely. The star defender, Iskandarian, went on to play with New York Cosmos, the top American club. Hishmat Mohajerani, the successful coach, enjoyed equal success on his coaching career in the Gulf states, particularly in the UAE.

Israel

Many Israeli sports organizations were founded before the creation of the state of Israel itself in 1948. Before that year Jewish and Arab clubs and associations existed side by side. However, most of the latter, such as Shabab al-ʿArab (Arab Youth) and al-Nadi al-Orthodoxi (Greek Orthodox Club) of Jaffa and Haifa respectively, have since been disbanded or have died out. The Jewish clubs and associations, on the other hand, have flourished under the new state. Central to Israel's sports and youth organizations are two names: Maccabi and Ha Poel.

The Maccabi World Union was founded in 1895 by a group of athletic clubs set up by Jewish communities in Europe and the Ottoman Empire during the last two decades of the nineteenth century. Most of these clubs chose the name 'Maccabi' after Judas Maccabeus, a Hebrew zealot noted for physical prowess and fighting skills. Others took names like 'Hakoah' (Strength), the best-known of which were successful in sporting events in Austria, Egypt and Australia.

By 1914 more than a hundred Maccabi-style clubs were active in Europe alone. In 1929 a Russian settler in Palestine, Yosef Yakutieli, was Palestine's only delegate to the Maccabi World Congress. The Congress unanimously approved his suggestion that Jewish athletes take part in a convocation in Palestine, and the date set was 1932.

Athletes from twenty-two countries took part in the first Maccabiah Games (sometimes described as the Jewish Olympics) in 1932, and since then the games have become the most important events in the Israeli sports calendar. Since 1957 the Games – currently recognized by the International Olympic Committee – have been held once every four years (one year after the Olympics), and have continued to attract leading Jewish athletes, mainly from the United States, Canada, South Africa, Western Europe and Australia. Among the most famous of the competitors in recent Games is the legendary American Olympic swimmer Mark Spitz, who competed in 1965, and won two gold medals in the Mexico Olympics of 1968, and seven gold medals in Munich in 1972.

The Ha Poel ('Worker') sports organization is the sports and youth organ of the Israel Labour Union, Histadrut. The first branch of Ha Poel was established in 1924, and by the 1970s it had around 90,000 members. Today Ha Poel clubs, like Maccabi, are active in various fields of sport, and among the most successful is Ha Poel Tel Aviv.

Israel has never achieved any significant Olympic successes. While Israel was still an active member of Asian sports federations, some considered its achievements hollow because of the continuous refusal of Arab teams to compete with Israeli teams. Still, Israel's football team, which benefited from the Arab boycott, did reasonably well in the football World Cup Finals in 1970 (Mexico), drawing with Sweden and Italy before going out in the first round.

In the Asian Champion Clubs' football championship, Israeli teams made the most of the Arab boycott by winning the tournament three times: in 1967 (Ha Poel Tel Aviv), 1969 and 1971 (Maccabi Tel Aviv). Moreover, several Israeli players became known outside the state. Mordechai Speigler and Gora Speigel played in France, Samuel Rosenthal in West Germany, Avi Cohen and Moshe Gariani in England. Ironically, two of the leading stars of the national team at present are Arabs: Rifʿat Turk and Zahi Armeli.

Football, however, is not Israel's most popular or prosperous sport. This honour is reserved for basketball, where some teams have established themselves among Europe's elite. Maccabi Tel Aviv were winners of the European Cup (League Championship Cup) twice. Maccabi is considered along with Spain's Real Madrid, Italy's Varese, Cantú and Milano, and USSR's CSKA and Jalghiris Kaunas as one of Europe's top teams.

AA

Further reading

A. Abou Chakra, 'Sports in the Arab States: past and present', in *Sports and Leisure in the Arab Countries* (London. Arab–British Chamber of Commerce, July 1985)

Lord Killanin and I. Rodda, eds., *The Olympic Games* (London, 1979)

K. Radnedge, ed., *World Cup Football Directory* (London, 1985, 2nd edn.)

P. Soar, M. Tyler and R. Widda, *Encyclopedia of World Football* (London)

D. Wallechinsky, *Book of the Olympics* (London, 1984)

Part IV
CULTURE

The gardens of the Alhambra at Granada, southern Spain

Islam

Islam, the Arabic word for 'submission', is the name of the religion which was propagated by the Prophet Muhammad* in Arabia during the seventh century AD. Those who accept Islam are known as Muslims, a word derived from the same root. Islam is the third of the great monotheistic religions to appear in the Near East. It regards itself very much as part of that tradition, seeing Abraham as the first Muslim and itself as an extension of Judaism and Christianity, as a reaffirmation, correction and consummation of the earlier religions. The basic principles of Islam are that there is one God and He must be worshipped by men, and that Muhammad is the 'seal of the prophets'. The main sources of the religion and its religious life are the Qur'an, the revelation which Muhammad received during his life, and Muhammad's own practice (*sunna**), as he is regarded as the ultimate messenger of God's wishes for mankind.

The Qur'an

The Qur'an* is regarded by Muslims as the Word of God revealed piecemeal to Muhammad by the Angel Gabriel from the time of his first revelation in Mecca when he was some forty years of age in AD 610 until he died in Medina in 632. The earliest revelations are in the style of a pre-Islamic soothsayer (*kahin*). The Medinan revelations, in particular, lay down much more detailed regulations for the conduct of Muslims, as would accord with Muhammad's position as ruler in Medina.

Doctrinally, the Qur'an emphasizes that God (Arabic *Allah*) is one without any partners. He is the Creator of everything and has absolute power over His creation. The duty of men is to show their gratitude to God by obedience and worship, for men will be judged by God on the Day of Resurrection; those who have sinned against God and have failed to repent will receive eternal punishment in the fires of hell while those who have obeyed his commandments will be rewarded by dwelling for ever in the delights of paradise. The imagery used to describe heaven and hell is of a very physical nature. In order to provide the guidance necessary to attain eternal reward, God sent a succession of prophets from the time of His first creation of mankind.

The Qur'an and the Bible

The Qur'anic account of creation is very close to the accounts in the Bible. The succession of prophets to mankind very much accords with the biblical tradition, including Abraham, Noah, Moses, Aaron and others; but among them are Salih and Hud, who belong to Arab tradition. Many of the stories of these prophets in the Qur'an seem to belong to the Meccan period when Muhammad's message was rejected by most of his fellow-citizens; they illustrate the way in which God's messengers brought His commands to the people, and when the people ignored them they were punished. Muhammad is 'the seal of prophets' and his message is the Qur'an. Jesus is regarded as a prophet and the virgin birth is affirmed, but the Qur'an does not accept the crucifixion as having taken place.

The general moral teaching of the Qur'an urges men to be generous and care for the poor, the weak and orphans in society. It calls for fairness and justice in commercial transactions and forbids hoarding. It contains fairly detailed stipulations on marriage, divorce and inheritance and the various religious duties.

Framework of the Qur'an

The Qur'an is divided into 114 chapters which are called *suras*. These *suras* are divided into verses (*ayat*, literally meaning 'signs'). The *suras* vary in length and, although each is called by a name, the name of the *sura* does not generally seem to reflect its particular theme. The first *sura* (*al-fatiha*, the opening) is a prayer which is frequently recited by Muslims. After that the *suras* are in approximate order of length, with the longest coming first and the shortest at the end. They are not in chronological order; in fact many of them are composite, with passages coming from different periods of Muhammad's career. Many are written in rhyming prose.

According to traditional Islamic belief, the Qur'an itself is the word of God which has existed for all time. Hence the Qur'an is inimitable. This is a claim which it makes for itself when it challenges unbelievers to produce its like. Thus the Qur'an is the miracle which Muhammad presented to the world to demonstrate his prophethood. Each verse is a sign from God. Further emphasizing the miraculous nature of the Qur'an, Muslims traditionally regard Muhammad as unable to read and write, the Qur'an having been taken down by scribes as he recited it.

Variants quickly began to enter the text. The third Caliph, 'Uthman* (d.656), is said to have ordered a group of scholars to produce a canonical text. Copies of that text were sent to all the major cities and other versions were ordered to be burnt. Nevertheless there are seven legitimate readings (*ahruf*) allowed of the Qur'an. The justification for this is the claim that the Qur'an was revealed to the Prophet in these seven readings. The differences in these readings are, in fact, slight. Most of them are not used today.

Tafsir (interpretation) of the Qur'an

Not all the verses of the Qur'an, nor all the words, are clear. Indeed, the Qur'an itself declares that it has clear verses (*muhkam*) and some which are obscure (*mutashabih*). There are cases where the Qur'an seems to contradict itself. As a result an elaborate literature of interpretation, known as *tafsir*, developed. Among the solutions which it gave to these problems was the doctrine of the abrogating (*nasikh*) and abrogated (*mansukh*): a particular revelation was revealed for a specific time or event and it was abrogated by a later revelation. This required Muslim scholars to try to establish the time and the reasons for particular revelations. Among the main exponents of *tafsir* were al-Tabari* (d.923), al-Zamakhshari (1075–1143), al-Razi* (1149–1209) and al-Baydawi (d.1286).

The *hadith* or Traditions of the Prophet

The Qur'an provided an outline of the beliefs and practices necessary for a Muslim but it did not give all the details and interpretations of these. For these, most Muslims looked to the example and habitual practice (*sunna*) of the Prophet, and his words and actions. Although the Prophet does not seem to have claimed any infallibility outside the revelation of the Qur'an, the fact that he had been chosen by God to deliver His message, according to the Muslims, soon led them to believe that his authentic words and actions were infallible. These words and actions were preserved by those who had known him, and transmitted in the form of reports (*hadith**) which were handed down by Muslims. Hence they are commonly termed 'Traditions' in English.

Muslims seem to have started to collect these Traditions from a very early time. Although, in the early days of Islam, there were injunctions not to write them down in order that they should not become confused with the Qur'an, some Muslims do appear to have kept collections of Traditions. As time went by, and with the injunction not to write them down becoming less relevant as the text of the Qur'an was firmly established, scholars of *hadith* began to produce collections of them. The first collections were categorized according to the names of the original transmitter of the Tradition from the Prophet. The term used for collections was *musnad* (collection based on the chain of transmission, *isnad*). The largest and most comprehensive of these which is extant today is the *musnad* of Ahmad ibn Hanbal (d.855), an important and influential traditionist of the third century who gave his name to a school of law. However, the *musnad* is a very cumbersome instrument if one is

The largest demonstration in Tehran since the revolution took place during the feast of Ashura, while the nearby US embassy remained under occupation

looking for guidance from the Traditions on a specific topic. To meet such a demand, collections of Traditions began to be compiled under specific topics (*sanf*). The term for these collections was *musannaf* and most of the collections, including all the authoritative ones, are of this kind.

These collections are the product of attempts to distinguish reliable traditions from others. It was clear to Muslim scholars that many of the reports of the Prophet's words and acts were not authentic; stories gathered around him as they do around all great men, and some of those who handed them on fabricated or exaggerated them. Thus a science of *hadith* criticism was essential. A *hadith* contained two elements: the content (*matn*), what the Prophet was claimed to have said and done, and the chain of transmission back to the Companion of the Prophet who had seen or heard it (*isnad*). The scholars were concerned primarily with the *isnad*: whether it was continuous back to the Prophet, whether the transmitters were reliable, and so on. (For this purpose, it was necessary to know something about the transmitters, hence the compilation of the biographical dictionaries* which are a distinctive feature of Arabic literature.) On the basis of this study, it was possible to classify *hadiths* on a scale ranging from those which were sound (*sahih*) to those which should be rejected. Six major collections were made in the third century of the Islamic era. Two of them in particular are regarded as containing only sound traditions and having an authority second only to the Qur'an: they are the collections of al-Bukhari (d.870) and Muslim (d.875).

Modern western scholars have gone further than medieval Muslim scholars in their criticism of *hadith*. The generally accepted view among them is that the invention of *hadiths* was extensive, and took place by a gradual process: the *matn* of many of them grew up in order to support positions taken in the political and religious controversies of the first Islamic centuries, and the *isnads* going back to the Prophet were also developed during these centuries. Most scholars, however, would accept that there remains a body of genuine Traditions.

The 'pillars of Islam'

These are the basic religious duties of every Muslim, derived from the Qur'an and set out in the Traditions.

(1) The shahada or testimony

This is the twofold assertion: 'I testify that there is no god but God, and that Muhammad is the Messenger of God.'

This is the basic declaration of faith asserting the unity of God and the truth of the message (the Qur'an) brought by His messenger Muhammad. When this formula is said by a person with sincerity, he becomes a Muslim. The first formula, 'there is no god but God', is found in the Qur'an and the meaning of the second formula is also clearly stated there.

(2) Salat or formal prayer

A Muslim must perform the *salat* five times a day. The Qur'an clearly enjoins the duty of performing the *salat* but it does not describe how the *salat* should be performed, nor does it say clearly the number of times that the prayer should be performed. The times of prayer are: dawn (*fajr*), midday (*zuhr*), mid-afternoon (*'asr*), sunset (*maghrib*) and evening (*'isha*). This information is given in the Traditions of the Prophet.

The imam leading the Korban Bayram prayers at a mosque in Kütahya, Turkey

The Fatima Ma'sumah shrine and the 'Azam Mosque (with scaffolding) in Qom

Ritual purity
Before performing the *salat*, a Muslim must be in a state of ritual purity (*tahara*), because only then will his *salat* be acceptable to God. Impurity is removed by total immersion in water, or by a lesser ablution (*wudu*), which is outlined in detail by the Qur'an and consists of washing the face, hands and feet and rubbing the head. Later Islamic writers have interpreted ritual purification as a symbolic cleansing of the limbs from evil in which they have been involved.

The adhan *or call to prayer*
Before the prayer, the faithful are summoned by the muezzin (Arabic *mu'adhdhin*, 'the one who calls') to come to prayer. The formulas for this call to prayer are fixed but the number of times each is repeated tends to vary with different schools of law.

The use of words in the call to prayer is claimed by the Tradition to have been introduced as an alternative to the horn of the Jews and the wooden clappers of the Christians.

The performance of the salat
Muslims may perform the *salat* alone, or in any place they wish; prayer in a mosque (*masjid*) is recommended, and there they face the niche (*mihrab*) which indicates the direction of Mecca (*qibla*). Early in the Prophet's period in Medina the *qibla* had been in the direction of Jerusalem, the holy place also for Christians and Jews, but it was later changed to Mecca. One of the faithful comes to the front and leads them in the *salat*. He is known as the *imam*. During the Prophet's time, he usually took this office himself, and after him the leaders in the area took the responsibility. Now the *imam* is usually an employed functionary of the mosque, but in theory his role can

be taken by any Muslim who knows his religion adequately.

The actions of the prayer are performed in a cycle (*rakʿa*, literally a bowing). The cycle consists of standing with hands slightly raised, bowing, prostrating, sitting on one's haunches and prostrating again. During the cycle, verses of the Qur'an are recited, particularly the opening *sura (al-fatiha)*. The cycle is repeated twice for the dawn prayer, four times for the noon prayer, the afternoon prayer and the night prayer, and three times for the sunset prayer. At the end of the prayer, the worshippers greet each other with the wish for peace to be with them.

The Friday prayer

The noon prayer on Fridays is a special congregational prayer when all the able-bodied men in the area are supposed to attend a mosque (*jamiʿ*) which has a pulpit (*minbar*). Then the number of cycles of prayer is reduced to two and a sermon (*khutba*) is given. This *khutba* is used for religious and political edification. It includes a mention of the legitimate ruler, and this has traditionally been regarded as one of the signs of legitimacy. If the mosque is controlled by the government, it is often used to endorse the government's policy. If, however, it is not controlled by the government, the *khutba* may be used as a means for inciting the believers against the government.

Personal prayer or duʿa

As can be seen, the *salat* is a formal act of worship which gives little scope for personal prayer, although, according to some of the schools of law, the *imam* may occasionally, at a certain point in some of the prayers, make an intercession with God. Ordinarily, when a Muslim wishes to make personal intercession with God, this is not considered as part of the *salat* and is called *duʿa*.

(3) Zakat or alms-tax

A Muslim who is able to do so should pay from his wealth a certain amount for specified purposes. *Zakat* means 'purification', and the payment of *zakat* is regarded as primarily an act of worship of God, for the favour He has granted. Only secondarily is it concerned with the recipients. The uses of *zakat* are laid down in the Qur'an: it is for the poor, those who collect the tax, those whose hearts need to be reconciled, the freeing of slaves, those who are burdened with debts, the wayfarers and in the cause of God.

(4) Fasting in the month of Ramadan

The Qur'an requires all mature Muslims to fast during the month of Ramadan, the eighth month of the Islamic year*, which is a lunar year. The fast is from dawn to dusk; during that time a Muslim should not eat, drink, smoke or have any sexual relationship. As far as possible he should remain in a state of ritual purity. Those who are ill or travelling need not fast, but any day's fasting missed should be made up after Ramadan is over. The fast lasts from the day after the new moon, which indicates the beginning of the month of Ramadan, to the time that the new moon for the ninth month, Shawwal, is seen.

Ramadan is a particularly sacred month in Islam. It is the month in which the Traditions report that Muhammad received the first revelation. It is also the month traditionally regarded as that in which the Qur'an was sent down from the seventh heaven to the lowest heaven to be revealed to Muhammad. During Ramadan there occurs the 'night of fate', an especially sacred night mentioned in the Qur'an. It is traditionally believed that on that night the fates of people are decided for the coming year. While fasting, a Muslim is supposed to pay special attention to his relationship with God by reading the Qur'an. In the evenings special prayers and recitations of the Qur'an are carried out in the mosque.

At the end of Ramadan there is a special festival (*ʿid al-fitr*). On this occasion Muslims are supposed to pay a special *zakat* to the poor so that they too can enjoy the celebration.

(5) The hajj or pilgrimage

Mecca had been regarded as a sacred place by the pagan Arabs, who had visited it and made pilgrimages there before the time of Muhammad. The principal source of Mecca's sacredness was the Kaʿba, a square stone structure incorporating a black stone which was treated with special reverence. As a result Mecca was a sanctuary where the taking of life was forbidden. The form of worship associated with this was to circumambulate (*tawaf*) the Kaʿba seven times and then kiss the black stone. Other rites were also practised in Mecca, including the worship of statues on the hills of Safa and Marwa. A visitor to Mecca would worship at the Kaʿba and then run in a ritual style seven times between those hills, finishing with a sacrifice if he could afford it; this was during the seventh month, Rajab. This pilgrimage was known as the lesser pilgrimage (*ʿumra*). The *hajj* or greater pilgrimage took place in the twelfth month of the year. Before Islam, it involved more than merely a Meccan ritual.

After the rise of Islam, some of these elements were continued in the Islamic ritual. Muslims may perform the *ʿumra* at any time of the year, but the great pilgrimage takes place in the last month of the Islamic year, Dhu al-Hijja. When the pilgrims begin their pilgrimage, on reaching certain points in the vicinity of Mecca they enter into a state of consecration, and put on special garments which are two strips of unsewn cotton cloth. For the rest of the time of the pilgrimage they remain in that state of consecration and must not commit any action which would involve a state of major ritual impurity, nor must they cut their nails or hair. While in the state of consecration, they repeatedly utter the formula known as the *talbiya*, 'Here I am at your service, O Lord.' The pilgrims circumambulate the Kaʿba, which is in the precinct of the great mosque (the *haram*), when they arrive in Mecca. Then they go to the well of Zamzam to collect water. They then go out beyond the sanctuary to ʿArafat on the ninth day, which they spend listening to sermons and in prayer. At dusk they move together into the sanctuary and spend the night in prayer at Muzdalifa, where they gather seven pebbles. At dawn they set out for a suburb of Mecca, Mina, where, after stoning three piles of stones, a sacrifice is performed. The pilgrims then have their heads shaved, although today their hair is usually only trimmed. After that they go back to the Kaʿba and perform the sevenfold circumambulation. They then cease to be in a consecrated state and spend the next three days at Mina in celebration. Every Muslim who has the means is supposed to make the pilgrimage at least once in his life.

Islam has interpreted these rituals somewhat differently from Western non-Muslim scholars. According to the Islamic interpretation the Kaʿba was built at the behest of God by Abraham and his son Ishmael. The circumambulation of the Kaʿba is an act of worship, emulating the angels who circumambulate the throne of God. The running between Safa and Marwa commemorates the frantic running in search of water by Hagar, Abraham's slave wife and the mother of Ishmael, when he had taken them to Mecca and left them there. The well of Zamzam is the well which Ishmael discovered when he struck his staff into the ground. Throwing pebbles at the piles of stones is a symbol for stoning the devil. The sacrifice at Mina is a commemoration of the sacrifice which Abraham made when, at the behest of God, he was going to sacrifice his first-born but God relented and gave him a ram to sacrifice in his place. (Muslims mostly hold that the victim was to have been Ishmael, not Isaac.) The clothes symbolize the equality of all before God.

The *shariʿa* or Islamic law

Shariʿa in Arabic literally means 'a path to water'. As used in Islam it is a way for a Muslim to reach heaven. It is the sacred law of Islam and embraces all aspects of life, not just religious practices; it could be described as the Islamic way of life.

Aerial view of the Great Mosque at Mecca

According to the classical theory of the *shariʿa*, it has four sources:
1. The Qur'an. As the Word of God, this is the fundamental source of Islamic law.
2. The *sunna*. This is the practice as laid down by the Prophet. The *sunna* is established by the Traditions.
3. Consensus or *ijmaʿ*. This may be concerned with the establishment of the meaning of a requirement of the Qur'an or *sunna*. Its support is found in a Tradition ascribed to the Prophet, 'My Community will not agree on error'. This consensus originally referred to the scholars of Islam but was eventually applied to the whole community. In practice it was still the scholars who determined consensus.
4. Analogy or *qiyas*. When a problem of law arises whose solution is not found in either the Qur'an or *sunna*, the Islamic jurist takes a parallel case from either of these. He deduces the cause for the known case and applies that cause to the new case. If the cause is common to both, he works out the appropriate law from that. An example is the case of alcohol: the Qur'an specifically forbids the drinking of wine but it does not mention other alcoholic drinks. However, the cause of the prohibition of wine was its intoxicating effect. Therefore the prohibition by analogy can be applied to other drinks which have the same effect. The validity of *qiyas* was disputed by some schools of law.

The use of reasoning (ijtihad) in establishing laws
Although the classical theory of the sources of law seems to limit the use of reasoning to analogy, other forms of reasoning were sometimes allowed, although carefully defined and limited by the different schools of law, until the nineteenth-century modernists began to extend their use. In particular, laws might be decided and interpreted in terms of their benefit (*maslaha*) for society.

The task of using reason to determine the laws was limited to those Islamic jurists who had had rigorous training and displayed great ability. Such a jurist was called a *mujtahid*. He was an expert in the most important of Islamic sciences, the principles of jurisprudence (*usul al-fiqh*). It was the duty of other Muslims to follow (*taqlid*) the laws laid down by these jurists.

The jurists have evolved five categories for the different laws: *wajib*, that which is obligatory; *mustahabb*, recommended; *mubah*, permitted; *makruh*, disapproved of; and *haram*, forbidden. The obligatory is divided into individual duty (*fard ʿayn*) and collective duty (*fard kifaya*), where some individuals perform it and as long as they do it is not necessary for the rest.

The schools of law
Soon after the Prophet died, Muslims became anxious to know what was the correct Islamic practice. Schools of law emerged in the different cities in the expanding Islamic Empire. Eventually certain teachers or their followers extended their influence beyond the limits of their own areas. Although there were many different schools of law in early times, there are now four principal ones. Sunni Muslims usually now belong to these schools by virtue of the area in which a particular school has become prevalent. Although the differences between the schools are generally fairly small, there are some matters on which they may be greater. A tendency has emerged in recent times to encourage Muslims and Muslim rulers to adopt the legal practice of individual schools according to the appropriateness of their teaching on specific issues, and not to follow one school rigidly. The schools of law are:

Hanafi
This school emerged at Kufa during the second century of the Islamic era. The Hanafis* are followers of Abu Hanifa (d.767). This school tended to emphasize the use of reasoning, but over the course of the years its teaching became fairly static. Today it is the prevailing school among the Sunnis in Iraq, Syria, Turkey, central Asia and India.

Maliki
The founder of the Maliki* school was Malik ibn Anas (d.795), who taught in Medina. Although there was some scope for reasoning in its teaching, it laid great emphasis on the practice of Medina as a guarantee of the interpretation of the Prophet's practice. At the present time it is almost universal in North Africa, and widespread in Central and West Africa.

Shafiʿi
The Shafiʿi* school follows the teaching of the great scholar Muhammad ibn Idris al-Shafiʿi (d.820). He was instrumental in establishing the authority of the Traditions in Islamic law over the practice of a particular school. Despite this, the school did in fact allow some role for the use of reasoning in determining the law. The followers of the school are now mainly in northern Egypt, the Hijaz, South Arabia, East Africa and South East Asia.

Hanbali
The Hanbali* school of law arose among the followers of Ahmad ibn Hanbal (d.855). He was really a Traditionist above all else. He taught a literalist interpretation of the basic sources, Qur'an and *sunna*. It has become the official school of Saudi Arabia.

The development of the shariʿa
The classical theory is concerned essentially with the logical structure of legal thought. Modern Western scholarship has been more concerned with another question, that of the way in which the *shariʿa* developed. Most non-Muslim scholars would now accept, at

least in principle, the version given by J. Schacht. In the first phases of Islamic history, he suggested, disputes were settled and cases decided by the Caliph or his officials or judges in accordance with existing customs and practices (*sunna*), interpreted by rational opinion (*ra'y*) and gradually modified in the light of the Qur'an and the memory of what the Prophet and his companions had said and done; in the conquered provinces, the practices followed were influenced by older systems of law, civil or religious, and by the administrative regulations of previous governments. At the same time there grew up in the main cities of the Caliphate (Mecca, Medina, Kufa, Basra, and the Syrian cities) groups of pious scholars who gradually evolved the idea of what has been called a 'normative' *sunna*, a record not simply of what the community had practised, but of what it ought to practise in order to be truly Islamic; the various groups differed in their view of what this *sunna* was. It was in the course of developing their theories, Schacht suggests, that most of the *hadiths* which have a legal content emerged, and in order to give them legitimacy their *isnads* were gradually prolonged backwards to the Prophet.

The decisive step, in this view, was taken in the second century of the Islamic era, when Muhammad al-Shafi'i (d.820) declared that the *sunna* of the Prophet rather than that of the community should be the basis of the law, together with the Qur'an. He laid emphasis upon the *ijma'* of the community rather than of scholars as the guarantor of the interpretation of the Qur'an and Tradition, and limited the use of reasoning to strict analogy. His general principles of jurisprudence came to be accepted, with modifications, by all the main schools of law.

The content of the shari'a

The *shari'a* embraces every aspect of life in Islam. Apart from those acts of worship already mentioned, prayer, alms-tax, fasting and pilgrimage, it also lays down rules concerned with areas that would be covered by law in the Western sense of the word as well as others. These include:

Jihad

The term *jihad* can be used to refer to individual effort towards moral or spiritual goals but it has commonly been used to signify fighting for the sake of Islam. This is regarded as a religious duty and could therefore be considered as an act of worship. Islamic jurists divided the world into the domain of Islam (*dar al-islam*) and the domain of war (*dar al-harb*); between the two there could be truces but not real and permanent peace. It is the duty of an able-bodied Muslim to defend the domain of Islam from aggression. Although sometimes conceived of as a positive attempt to extend Islam, it is usually interpreted by modern Islamic jurists as a defensive measure against hostile forces. It is one of those duties which some Muslims can perform on behalf of others (*fard kifaya*).

Non-Muslims

The *shari'a* regarded those who lived in *dar al-islam* and adhered to a revealed religion other than Islam – Jews, Christians and the so-called Sabians – as being 'people of the book' (*ahl al-kitab*) or people living under a covenant of protection (*ahl al-dhimma*, *dhimmis*). In practice this protection was extended to Zoroastrians and others, and later to Hindus. Traditionally the system was linked to the agreements believed to have been concluded by the Muslim conquerors with those who surrendered to them, in particular the 'Pact of 'Umar' made with the people of Jerusalem. Non-Muslims in this position were accorded freedom and toleration in return for acceptance of the authority of the Muslim community and ruler. They had to pay a special poll-tax (*jizya*) and in principle were not allowed to bear arms, wear certain colours, or build or repair their places of worship; in practice, such restrictions were not always strictly applied. Non-Muslim men could not marry Muslim women, although Muslim men could marry non-Muslim women; conversion from Islam to other religions was forbidden.

Marriage

The Qur'an allows a male Muslim to be married to four wives at the same time provided that he can treat all of them equally. This provision is interpreted by different Muslims in different ways. The contract of marriage is made by the guardian (*wali*) of the bride and the bridegroom with two witnesses. In the case of a virgin, the guardian has an absolute right to marry her to whom he wishes, except among the Hanafis who require her consent. Where a woman who has previously been married is concerned, her consent to the marriage is required by all the schools. The bridegroom makes a nuptial gift (*mahr*) to the bride or her guardian. Normally only part of the nuptial gift is paid when the marriage takes place, the rest becoming liable if one of the spouses dies or there is a divorce. The *shari'a* recognizes the property rights of married women. Marriage is not allowed between partners with specific degrees of relationship.

Divorce

Divorce is accomplished by a threefold declaration of repudiation by the husband. If a woman wants a divorce, she has to obtain the consent of her husband, but in certain circumstances she can ask the judge (*qadi**) to dissolve the marriage. After every dissolution of a marriage, the divorced wife has to wait for a period (*'idda*) before she can remarry. The sons stay with the mother until they are seven or nine, the girls until they come of age. The Qur'an urges reconciliation rather than divorce.

Inheritance
The Qur'an requires fixed shares of the dead person's estate to be paid to stipulated heirs related to the deceased, these being spouses, children, parents, grandparents, brothers and sisters; a daughter inherits half the amount of a son. The testator may also leave up to one-third of his possessions to people who are not his stipulated heirs.

Women and the shariʿa
It is clear that in some important respects the legal position of women* is less favourable than that of men. According to the *shariʿa*, a girl can be married without her consent; a man is allowed to take up to four wives if he can treat them equally; he can repudiate a wife easily; a divorced wife may lose custody of her children after a certain age. A daughter inherits half as much as a son, and the testimony of a woman in a law-suit has only half the value of that of a man. Orthodox tradition enjoined the seclusion and veiling of women, on the basis of a Qur'anic injunction and the example of the Prophet. On the other hand, women have the same property rights as men, and more generally it is possible to interpret the letter of the law in the light of the injunction to justice and kindness: 'be good in your behaviour towards them'.

It should be emphasized too that the strict letter of the law has never regulated the whole of society. The customs and conditions of specific communities have affected the ways in which the *shariʿa* is interpreted, or even caused it to be set aside; in the steppe and countryside, for example, the veiling and seclusion of women have not been common.

Penal law
Islam leaves the punishments of murder and bodily harm to private retaliation but encourages forgiveness. There are, in addition, certain specific crimes for which a revealed punishment (*hadd* – restrictive ordinance) is enjoined in the Qur'an or *sunna*. These offences are: unlawful intercourse, false accusation of unlawful intercourse, drinking wine, theft and highway robbery. The punishment for unlawful intercourse is death by stoning. The punishment for false accusation is a hundred lashes and for drinking wine eighty lashes. For theft the punishment is the cutting off of a hand or foot. In the case of highway robbery, if homicide is involved, then the punishment is death; if there is no homicide involved, then the punishment is the same as for theft.

*Commercial law**
Islamic laws concerned with commercial transactions are designed to prevent usury and gambling, both of which are absolutely forbidden. Thus Islamic law tends to prohibit all transactions in which there is a great deal of uncertainty. In order to circumscribe these, medieval Islamic jurists evolved a complicated series of devices which enabled traders to carry on more speculative business and yet remain at least nominally within the law. In recent times Muslims have been evolving schemes so that banking* and mortgages can be operated without interest being involved.

Under the provisions of the law, a Muslim man or woman can dedicate the income from a property (normally real estate) to a religious or charitable purpose, such as the building and upkeep of mosques, schools, hospitals, and public fountains, or the relief of the needy. This is called *waqf* (*pl. awqaf*; in the Maghrib: *hubs*, *pl. ahbas*). The endowment is placed in charge of an administrator (*nazir*, *mutawalli*) and ultimately under the control of the *qadi*. By an extension of the system, it was possible for the income to be used for the family of the benefactor, provided it was to go ultimately to a religious purpose, once the family died out.

Slavery
Islam does not prohibit slavery. According to legal theory, those who are captured in war, or who – by extension – are imported from the 'domain of war', can be enslaved. Free-born Muslims cannot be enslaved but the children of slave-parents are themselves slaves. Islam does encourage the freeing of slaves. The law also provides means by which a slave can gain his freedom. The punishments of slaves are generally less severe than those for free Muslims. A Muslim male has the right to have sexual intercourse with those of his female slaves who are not married.

Food taboos and ritual slaughter
As already mentioned, the drinking of alcohol is forbidden by the Qur'an. Muslims are also forbidden to eat pork or any animal that has not been ritually slaughtered by having its throat cut and being dedicated to God as its blood flows. Although Muslims are allowed to eat the flesh of animals slain by Christians and Jews, since the blood would not have been dedicated to any pagan god, they still insist that all animals for meat must be ritually slaughtered.

The application of the shariʿa
The system of law, and the principles of jurisprudence on which it was based, were preserved, developed and transmitted by scholars, particularly in mosques and *madrasas*, schools endowed by rulers or men of wealth. Muslim legal scholars regarded the *shariʿa* as a code of law and social morality which should be obeyed by every Muslim if he wished to avoid divine punishment and receive divine reward. Until modern times, it formed the only recognized code of law in Muslim states. It was administered by *qadis*, judges, appointed by the rulers and giving decisions which had the power of the state behind them. The laws of procedure laid it down that the evidence

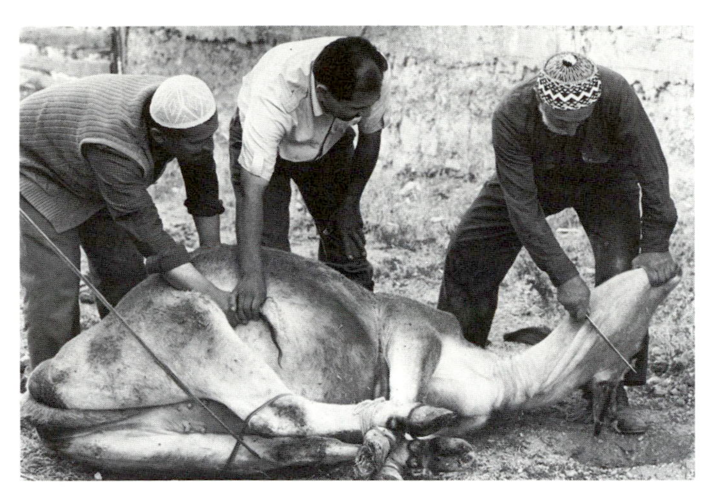

Slaughtering a cow for the Korban Bayram feast at Kütahya, Turkey

The Islamic calendar

Months	Days	Months	Days
1 Muharram	30	7 Rajab	30
2 Safar	29	8 Sha'ban	29
3 Rabi' al-awwal	30	9 Ramadan	30
4 Rabi' al-thani	29	10 Shawwal	29
5 Jumada al-ula	30	11 Dhu al-Qa'da	30
6 Jumada al-akhira	29	12 Dhu al-Hijja	29 or 30

Special days in the Islamic world

Islamic year	1405	1406	1407
New Year	27 Sept. 1984	16 Sept. 1985	6 Sept. 1986
'Ashura	6 Oct. 1984	25 Sept. 1985	15 Sept. 1986
Mawlid al-Nabi	6 Dec. 1984	25 Nov. 1985	15 Nov. 1986
Ramadan begins	21 May 1985	10 May 1986	30 April 1987
'Id al-Fitr	20 June 1985	9 June 1986	30 May 1987
'Id al-Adha	27 Aug. 1985	16 Aug. 1986	6 Aug. 1987

Local dates may vary by one day from those given here.

of two reliable witnesses was required, except in cases of unlawful intercourse, where four witnesses of the act itself were needed; the testimony of two female witnesses was regarded as equivalent to that of one male. In addition to the *qadis*, there were legal experts (*muftis*) who would give rulings on points of law referred to them; these also were appointed by the ruler, at least in later periods. Teachers, judges, *muftis* and other specialists were collectively known as *'ulama*, men of religious piety and learning.

The *shari'a* covered a broad area of human actions in society; it was most specific on matters of personal status (marriage, divorce, inheritance), less so on commercial matters, least on criminal cases and public law. Some of its provisions were generally regarded as theoretical only, and not observed. During most periods, some cases were brought not to the *qadi* but to the ruler or his officials. This was particularly true of criminal cases involving the security of the state; some dynasties had special courts (*mazalim*) to inquire into the abuse of delegated power by their officials. Such matters were decided in the light of natural justice, the interests of the ruler, or established custom. In the early centuries of Ottoman rule, there were even codes of law (*kanun*) for fiscal and criminal matters. These were justified by the right which the *shari'a* itself gave to the ruler to administer the affairs of the community and make regulations within the bounds of the *shari'a*.

In the countryside and desert, the affairs of village and tribe were normally regulated, before the expansion of modern administrative systems, by local custom (*'urf*, *'ada*) preserved by heads of families or the elders of the community. In course of time, however, such customs were often modified by the penetration of Islamic norms.

Political thought: the Caliphate

When Islamic legal scholars thought about the ideal form of the Islamic community and government, they took as their model Medina in the time of the Prophet. The majority of Muslims believed that after that time they had no leader directly inspired by God, and for guidance they looked to the practices of those who succeeded Muhammad as heads of the community, the first four Caliphs*, the 'Rightly-Guided ones' (*al-khulafa al-rashidun*).

The basic assumption of the legal theory was that Muslims formed a single community (*umma*) which had been instituted by God and should be governed in accordance with His Will by a single ruler, the Caliph. A question discussed by theorists was whether the necessity of the Caliphate could be proved by reason or depended upon revelation; eventually the supporters of the view that it depended upon revelation prevailed.

The Caliph (or Imam, as jurists and theologians usually referred to him) should be descended from the tribe to which the Prophet had belonged, the Quraysh*; he should be sound in mind and body and capable of exercising legal reasoning (*ijtihad*). In principle he should be either appointed by his predecessor or chosen by a council (*shura*). In practice, after the first Caliphs, hereditary succession prevailed, although a ceremony of public acceptance (*bay'a*) still took place; in modern times, some Muslim thinkers have regarded the *shura* as a kind of parliamentary democracy. The Caliph's duties were to defend the domain of Islam and maintain the *shari'a*, the only formally recognized system of law; he had executive and administrative power, but not legislative. The *umma* owed him obedience.

The necessity of the Caliphate was accepted by almost all thinkers within the legal tradition, but new problems were posed when the unity of the ʿAbbasid Caliphate began to break up, and smaller, virtually independent states emerged. Al-Mawardi (d.1058) and later thinkers put forward the idea that legitimate authority still belonged to the Caliph, but he could delegate the exercise of it to others; even those who had seized power could be regarded as holding it by a 'delegation of necessity', provided they used it within the bounds of the *shariʿa*.

The ʿAbbasid Caliphate virtually came to an end when the Mongols occupied Baghdad in 1258, although a member of the ʿAbbasid family was still recognized as Caliph by the Mamluks in Cairo. The title of Caliph was sometimes claimed by later rulers of powerful Muslim states, in particular by the Ottoman Sultan in the nineteenth century, until the formal abolition of the Ottoman Caliphate in 1924. In this later period of Islamic history, the attention of Muslim thinkers was directed towards the question of whether those who ruled by seizure of power, commonly called sultans, could be regarded as legitimate rulers. The view put forward by Ibn Taymiyya (d.1328) was that the overriding need was the maintenance of a community under Islamic law. The Sultan's power was necessary because order was better than anarchy. His task was to maintain the *shariʿa*, the basis of social order and justice, and for this purpose he should act in accordance with the *ʿulama*, the men of piety and religious learning. The community should obey him unless he went directly against the *shariʿa*.

These were the political ideas of the jurists, but a different tradition of political thought existed among those who wrote manuals for officials or guides for princes, the so-called 'mirrors for princes' of which the most famous was the *Siyasat-nama* of Nizam al-Mulk (d.1092). These works express an ancient Persian tradition of statecraft in an Islamized form. The ruler was raised up by God for the welfare of human society, he ruled by power, but the purpose of his rule should be to maintain justice, and to preserve the harmony of the world by regulating the different orders of society. From the time of the Seljuks onwards, this idea was combined with that of the jurists to provide rulers with a claim to legitimate authority.

Yet another kind of theory was that put forward by some of the Muslim philosophers who inherited the tradition of Greek ethical and political thought. Al-Farabi (d.950) in particular suggested in his book *al-Madina al-fadila* ('The Virtuous City') that the best of societies was that which was ruled by one who was both philosopher and prophet, knowing the truth through both intellect and imagination, and able to express it directly through ideas to those capable of understanding them, and through symbols to the mass of people. Beneath this ideal political society there was a scale of others which were defective in one way or another.

Sectarianism

So far we have been dealing with the beliefs and practices of the majority of Muslims, those who hold that their lives should be regulated by the Qur'an and the *sunna* of the Prophet as recorded in *hadith*, that the consensus of the community is the only guarantee of truth, and that the successors of the Prophet as heads of the community were the 'rightly-guided Caliphs'. These are known as Sunnis, but there are other groups of Muslims who differ from them in some of their beliefs and practices.

The Kharijis

The first sectarian movements in Islam arose in the context of the political disputes in the early years of Islam after the death of the Prophet. One of them was that of the Kharijis. After the murder of the third Caliph, ʿUthman (d.656), his cousin, Muʿawiya ibn Abi Sufyan, led a rebellion against ʿAli ibn Abi Talib, the fourth Caliph, demanding vengeance for ʿUthman. ʿAli was forced to accept that an arbitration should take place on the matter. A number of his supporters, including some of those who had been associated with ʿUthman's murder, objected after the terms of the arbitration were announced, declaring that judgement belonged only to God. Thus they seem to have emphasized that only the words of God, that is, the Qur'an, should be used to determine a Muslim's behaviour. They withdrew from the community (hence their name of 'Kharijis', from an Arabic word which means 'to go out'), alleging that in countenancing these things Muslims had ceased to be Muslims. For the next fifty years they were responsible for numerous rebellions against the Muslim authorities until they were eventually suppressed.

The Ibadis

The Ibadis are a group of moderate Kharijis who were founded by ʿAbd Allah ibn Ibad in Basra. Although they followed the principal doctrines of the Kharijis, they were prepared, if conditions were not favourable for rebellion, to live in harmony alongside the other Muslims. They are to be found today in North Africa and Oman. In elaborating the law, they allow more scope for Traditions, giving particular prominence to the Traditions reported by early traditionists who were of their persuasion.

The Shiʿa

Shiʿa means 'party', and the Shiʿa are the party or group who claim that leadership of the community (the Imamate) belonged to ʿAli ibn Abi Talib, the cousin of the Prophet and the father of the Prophet's only grandchildren through his daughter Fatima. Although there are many groups of Shiʿis, the name is particularly applied to the Ithna ʿashari, who are the most numerous.

The Ithna ʿashari (Twelver) Shiʿa

They believe that a line of Imams belonging to the family of the Prophet (*ahl al-bayt*) was designated by God to succeed him as leaders of the community, in religion as well as the affairs of the world. In their view, the Prophet publicly designated ʿAli ibn Abi Talib, his cousin and the husband of his daughter Fatima, as his successor, and in not accepting him the community committed an act of infidelity. Each Imam, they affirm, designated his successor until the last known and visible one, the twelfth of the line; hence their name of 'Twelvers'.

The claim that ʿAli was publicly designated by the Prophet was not accepted by most Muslims, but from the beginning there was a group who held that he was the one most fully entitled to succeed Muhammad, and they drew strength from the general respect for the Prophet's family. ʿAli did eventually succeed to political authority in the community, and is regarded by all modern Sunnis as the fourth Caliph, although his power was challenged by Muʿawiya, founder of the Umayyad line of Caliphs. After his death in 661 he was followed for a brief period by his son al-Hasan, who renounced his power by agreement with Muʿawiya, but is regarded by Shiʿis as the second Imam (d. *c.* 669). Shiʿis recognize as the third Imam his brother al-Husayn, who led a revolt against the Umayyads in 681 as a result of the first Umayyad Caliph Muʿawiya ibn Abi Sufyan appointing his son Yazid to succeed him. Al-Husayn had been summoned by his supporters in Kufa in Iraq to come and lead them. He left Mecca with most of his family, expecting strong support in Kufa. News of the proposed revolt reached Yazid and he despatched a strong governor to take control of Kufa. Al-Husayn and his small band were intercepted and almost totally annihilated on the banks of the Euphrates at Karbala. To this day the Shiʿa remember the death of al-Husayn at Karbala and commemorate it as one of their principal religious ceremonies of the year. It has given Shiʿi Islam a concept of the suffering Imam, and redemption through his suffering.

Lineage of the Shiʿi Imams

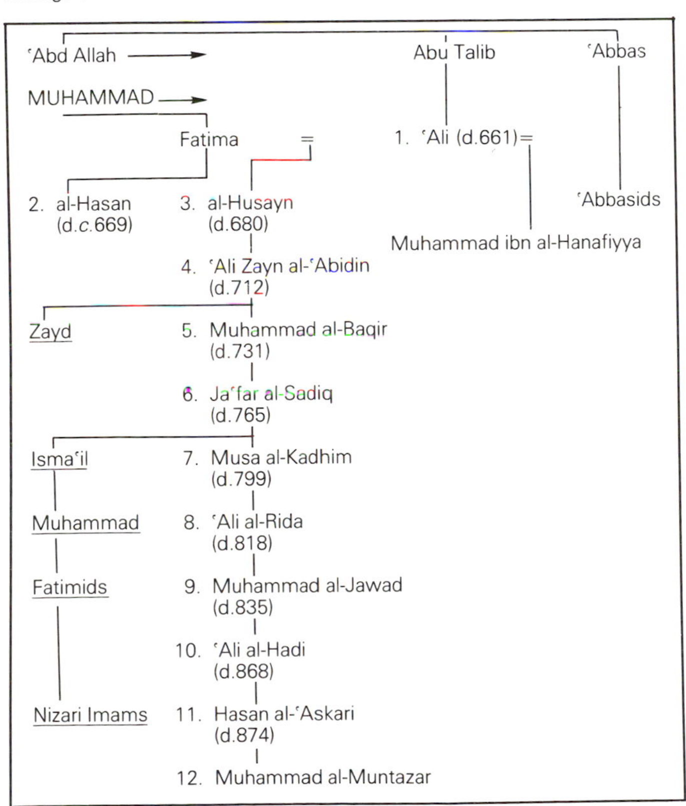

Note: Numbers indicate the line of succession recognized by the 'Twelver' Shiʿis. Names underlined indicate those whom other groups of Shiʿis regard as legitimate Imams.

Development of the Imamate

Some of the party of ʿAli held that the Imamate had passed to his son by another woman, Muhammad ibn al-Hanafiyya, who handed it on to his son Abu Hashim, who in turn passed it to the ʿAbbasids; this group helped to bring about the ʿAbbasid revolution. The Ithna ʿasharis, however, maintain that the Imamate went after the death of al-Husayn to his son ʿAli, known as Zayn al-ʿAbidin (d.712), and then to ʿAli's son Muhammad al-Baqir (d.731). After al-Baqir's death there was another split in the movement. Muhammad's brother Zayd claimed the Imamate and led an unsuccessful revolt in 740; this is the origin of the Zaydi form of Shiʿism (see below). The Ithna ʿasharis, however, accept Muhammad al-Baqir's son, Jaʿfar al-Sadiq, as sixth Imam (d.765).

It was probably the fifth and sixth Imams, Muhammad al-Baqir and Jaʿfar al-Sadiq, who elaborated the doctrines of the Shiʿa. According to these doctrines the Imam was the infallible guide of the community in all matters. He was endowed with knowledge of all things. Only he could interpret and explain the Qur'an, as its inner meaning was hidden from ordinary men. He was the source of law. Although revelation had ceased with the death of the Prophet, the Imam was guided by God. He was God's proof (*hujja*) to the world.

Later came the development of the doctrine of the divine light, or the light of Muhammad. One version of this is that God created Muhammad and ʿAli from one and the same light before the creation of Adam. When Adam was created, this light was placed in his backbone. The light was passed on through succeeding generations of prophets until it was split into two in ʿAbd al-Muttalib, grandfather of Muhammad and ʿAli, so that one light went to Muhammad and the other to ʿAli. Therefore there was in Muhammad the quality of prophethood and in ʿAli the quality of the Imamate.

An elaborate organization was built up with a chain of command leading back to the Imam. Money was collected and distributed by the Imams. The ʿAbbasid authorities began to be very wary of this organization, particularly as there was the firm belief that from the Imams would arise the *mahdi* who would lead a revolution to establish a golden age of justice.

There was some disagreement among the Shiʿa over the succession to Jaʿfar al-Sadiq. Some believed that he had appointed his son Ismaʿil as his successor; as Ismaʿil had died before Jaʿfar, then his son Muhammad ibn Ismaʿil was the Imam. These members of the Shiʿa split from the rest and became the Ismaʿilis. The rest accepted another son of Jaʿfar, Musa, as the Imam. Musa died in prison in 799. He was succeeded by his son ʿAli al-Rida (d.803). This Imam and the following three, Muhammad al-Jawad (d.835), ʿAli al-Hadi (d.868) and al-Hasan al-ʿAskari (d.874), were all kept under close supervision by the ʿAbbasids.

The hidden Imam

The Twelver Shiʿa claim that a son, Muhammad, was born to Hasan and smuggled out of the palace where his father was in detention and that he was the twelfth Imam. He grew up in hiding, communicating with his followers through a series of four emissaries, who alone had direct contact with him. This is known as the lesser occultation. As the fourth of these emissaries was on his death-bed in 941, he informed the Shiʿi adherents that the twelfth Imam had announced that he was going into a period when he would be in greater occultation. He would be in the world and present with his Shiʿa, but would make no contact with them until the time of his return as *mahdi* to bring about the golden age. The Shiʿa are still awaiting the return of the twelfth Imam.

With the disappearance of the twelfth Imam, the Shiʿa were no longer able to refer to him for guidance. It was now the organization itself which guided the Shiʿa, with the scholars taking a leading role. During the period immediately following the disappearance of the twelfth Imam, the Shiʿa in Iraq came under the protection of the Buyids (932–1066). There was then a great flourishing of their theological and polemical works. Gradually a distinctive Shiʿi system of theology, jurisprudence and law was developed. Twelver Shiʿism is widespread in Iran, southern Iraq, southern Lebanon, eastern Arabia, India and Pakistan.

The Zaydis

This was a rival group of the Shiʿa initiated by Zayd ibn ʿAli, the brother of Muhammad al-Baqir. He offered a more vigorously revolutionary policy than did his nephew, Jaʿfar al-Sadiq. As a result many former adherents of his brother left Jaʿfar and followed him. The later Zaydis maintained that the Imam, who must be from the family of ʿAli through the line of Hasan or Husayn, could only become Imam by coming forward and claiming his Imamate, by force of arms if necessary. Later the idea was expanded to include the possibility of Imams from the line of al-Hasan. Although the Prophet had designated ʿAli to be his successor, the designation was not a public one, but had been made privately so that it was hidden from many of the community. This excused the community from committing an act of infidelity by appointing Abu Bakr, ʿUmar and ʿUthman before ʿAli. As ʿAli, who was the most excellent one for the Imamate, had not come forward to claim it by arms, some early Zaydis hold that there could be an Imamate of the less excellent. In this way the Caliphates of Abu Bakr, ʿUmar and ʿUthman were made legitimate. While this doctrine won Zayd some support among traditionalists in Iraq, it was unacceptable to many adherents of the Shiʿa. Their movement spread and there were a number of unsuccessful revolts. Eventually Zaydi dynasties were founded in Tabaristan in 864 and in Yemen in 893. Zaydi Imams ruled Yemen or parts of it until they were overthrown in 1962. Zaydi ritual and law still prevail in North Yemen.

Fatimid Ismaʿilis

During the time of Jaʿfar al-Sadiq, a group of his followers maintained that he had nominated his son Ismaʿil as his successor and, although the latter was believed to have died before Jaʿfar, some declared that Ismaʿil had not really died. Others recognized Ismaʿil's son Muhammad as their Imam. From that time until the middle of the ninth century, the movement continued, but in secret, so little is known of it. It seems that they believed that Muhammad was the seventh Imam who would reappear as the *mahdi*, bringing about a golden age. This movement appears on the historical scene in the form of the revolutionary Qarmatians during the middle of the ninth century. Then in 899, the first Fatimid Caliph, ʿUbayd Allah al-Mahdi, who had established himself in North Africa, claimed that he was the descendant of Muhammad ibn Ismaʿil and that he was the Imam. As the Fatimids gained more power in North Africa, they eventually established themselves in Egypt under their fourth Caliph, al-Muʿizz, who founded Cairo in 969.

Under their rule, Cairo became the centre of widespread Ismaʿili missionary work, putting forward a system of religious doctrines. At the basis of it was a distinction between the exterior teaching of religion (*zahir*) and the inner truth which lay behind it (*batin*). The *zahir* changed with each prophet; the Ismaʿili view of history was of a succession of cycles, in each of which a Prophet was followed by a number of Imams. The inner truth was that of a God who is beyond all human knowledge, and from whom there proceeds a series of emanations through which the human world has been created. (Analogous ideas of emanation were also put forward by Muslim philosophers and Sufi thinkers – see below.)

During the reign of the sixth Fatimid Caliph, al-Hakim (996–

1021), extremist Isma'ilis proclaimed that this Caliph was a manifestation of the Divinity. Although the general organization of the Fatimids rejected this claim, al-Hakim does seem to have given them encouragement. After al-Hakim's death, his followers were wiped out in Cairo but succeeded in consolidating themselves in the mountains of Syria and are known as the Druze (see below).

The 'Assassins'

The Isma'ili movement outside Egypt was strengthened with the conversion of Hasan-i Sabbah. He seized the fortress of Alamut in the mountains of Daylam in northern Iran in 1090. From its security he was able to launch campaigns and propaganda in favour of Isma'ilism, together with political assassinations aimed at intimidating his enemies. His followers were known as addicts of hashish (*hashishiyyun*), a word which entered European usage as 'Assassins'.

After the death of the ninth Fatimid Caliph, al-Mustansir, a split took place. He had nominated his eldest son Nizar as his successor but a palace coup brought about the succession of al-Musta'li, who was recognized by the majority of Isma'ilis in Egypt and outside it. Hasan-i Sabbah refused to recognize al-Musta'li and upheld the Imamate of Nizar. In the absence of Nizar he took upon himself leadership of those who had supported Nizar and claimed the rank of *hujja*.

The son and successor of al-Musta'li, al-Amir, was assassinated by a Nizari supporter in 1130. It is claimed that al-Amir left behind a son, al-Tayyib, who was only two years old. However, the Caliphate was taken over by al-Amir's cousin who took the name of al-Hafiz. Some Isma'ilis claimed that the real Imam was al-Tayyib who had gone into concealment. The last four Isma'ili Caliphs, including al-Hafiz, were not recognized by them. When the Fatimid Caliphate was overthrown in 1171, the supporters of those last four Caliphs, and of the continuity of the Imamate through them, eventually disappeared. Supporters of the claims of Nizar (Nizaris) and of al-Tayyib (Tayyibis) continued to exist, however.

Tayyibi Isma'ilis (the Bohras)

Those Isma'ilis who maintain the concealment of Tayyib live mainly in India and Yemen. They believe that there has been no revealed Imam since 1130, but there has always been an Imam in concealment, since al-Tayyib and his descendants have continued up to the present day. In the meantime absolute authority is given to the *da'i mutlaq*, who is the personal representative of the concealed Imam. The succession of the *da'i mutlaq* is a matter of designation. The residence of the *da'i mutlaq* was in Yemen but the great majority of the faithful were from the Indian subcontinent. (Hence the word 'Bohra', which is thought to come from the Gujarati word *vohoro*, to trade, as the first converts were traders.) Eventually those Isma'ilis who were in Yemen came under severe persecution and the residence of the *da'i mutlaq* was moved to India. With the death of the twenty-sixth *da'i*, there was a dispute for the succession, and the result was a split between two groups, the Daudi Bohras and the Sulaymani Bohras. The *da'i* of the Daudis lives in India. The main body of Sulaymanis live in Najran in Saudi Arabia, and their *da'i mutlaq* resided there until recently.

Nizari Ismailis

Hasan-i Sabbah was succeeded by a companion, and the latter by his son Muhammad, whose own son, Hasan, came to be recognized as a descendant of Nizar. Although the Nizaris had so far adhered strictly to their form of the *shari'a*, Hasan now proclaimed the 'Great Resurrection', with a dispensation from the rules of the *shari'a*. He was eventually murdered. Although his son Muhammad continued the doctrines of his father, there was subsequently a restoration of the *shari'a* this time in its Shafi'i form. The rule of the Imams of Alamut soon came to an end, however. In 1256 the Mongols attacked and destroyed Alamut.

The Agha Khan and the Khojas

By various means, the movement was able to escape total destruction. It is said that the last of the Imams of Alamut, fearing danger, had sent his son to a place of safety. It seems that he settled in Azerbaijan and that for the next two hundred years the Imamate had its centre there. Eventually the Imamate became less covert and in 1840 the then Imam, Hasan 'Ali Shah, who had taken the title Agha Khan, went to India, where there were already a number of his adherents known as Khojas. (The name 'Khoja' is believed to be the equivalent of *khawaja*, master or lord, and was used for the Indian merchants in Sind who were converted.)

The line of Agha Khans has continued until to-day. The present holder has emphasized that he is not to be identified with God. The Khojas are mainly located in Gujarat, Bombay and East Africa but there are small numbers scattered throughout the world. There is a small population of Nizari Isma'ilis who acknowledge the Agha Khan based at Salamiyya in Syria.

The Druze

The faith originated in the closing years of the Fatimid Caliph al-Hakim (996–1021). A number of extremist Isma'ilis regarded him as a manifestation of the Divinity. Although the sect derives its name from al-Darazi, one of its early adherents, the real founder of the movement was another adherent of al-Hakim, Hamza ibn 'Ali. Hamza regarded himself as the Imam and al-Hakim as the embodiment of the ultimate Godhead. Thus the one deity was eternally present; hence the Druze refer to themselves as the unitarians (*al-muwahhidun*). In 1021 when al-Hakim disappeared, Hamza claimed that he had withdrawn to test his adherents and would soon return to reveal his true power. Shortly afterwards Hamza himself disappeared, and was regarded as being in concealment. The movement was then led by al-Muqtana. Letters attributed to him, together with certain writings by Hamza, have since served as the Druze scripture and are called the *Rasa'il al-hikma* (the Epistles of Wisdom). The Druze expect the return of al-Hakim and Hamza. The movement quickly came to an end in Egypt but survives in parts of Lebanon, Syria and Israel. They have become a closed community, discouraging any conversion.

The Nusayris or ʿAlawis

Among the followers of the twelve Imams of the Ithna ʿashari Shiʿa were extremists whose doctrines were rejected by the majority of the supporters of the Imams and the Imams themselves. Muhammad ibn Nusayr al-Numayri was one such extremist. In 859, during the time of the tenth Imam ʿAli al-Hadi, he claimed that he was the *bab*, the 'gateway' to the Imam. Although he was rejected by the Ithna ʿashari Shiʿa organization, he did gain some adherents.

A later successor of Muhammad ibn Nusayr, al-Husayn ibn Hamdan al-Khasibi (d.957), elaborated the doctrines of the sect. They believe that immediately below the ineffable deity there is a spirit from which there are emanations to the physical world in a hierarchical order. When these emanations appear, their task is to lead back to heaven the fallen beings in the physical world, who are imprisoned in their bodies. All the outward forms of Islam have been reinterpreted allegorically. The Qur'an is regarded as an initiation to devotion to ʿAli. As a result of their devotion to ʿAli, this sect is now usually referred to as the ʿAlawis. The majority of the ʿAlawis live in northern Syria and on the borders of Turkey and Syria. In recent times there has been a tendency to stress their common Shiʿi heritage at the expense of their more extreme doctrines.

Islamic theology

Early theological formulations arose in Islam as a result of attempts to justify political positions by reference to religion, and also through contact with scholars from other faiths, particularly Christianity. The early Khariji* movement had emphasized the Qur'an as the only real source of religious, and therefore political, authority. The Kharijis then set about justifying the killing of the Caliph ʿUthman in terms of the Qur'an, for it clearly states that it is forbidden for a believer to kill another believer. They argued that ʿUthman had committed grave sins against religion and had therefore ceased to be a believer, and it was not only permissible to take his life but a duty. The Sunni response to this as formulated by an early group called the Murji'a – whose doctrines had much influence on the Hanafi legal school – was that faith merely involved the public avowal by a person that he was a Muslim. As for grave sins causing a person to cease being a Muslim, that was a matter that only God could decide, and it was not right for Muslims to deny the Islam of others because they disapproved of their actions.

The Muʿtazila

From the early second century of the Islamic era (the eighth century AD), a school of theology emerged that developed a systematic approach to the subject. Greek philosophical works had begun to be translated into Arabic from both Greek and Syriac, and discussion on theological subjects had been taking place with Christian and Jewish scholars. There were also debates on the political questions that had helped form the earlier theological doctrines. Out of all this there arose a school of theology known as the Muʿtazila. Its adherents elaborated five principles of theology. The first was that of the unity of God. This was of course accepted by all Muslims, but the Muʿtazilis defined it in a way which had certain implications: that His attributes were inseparable from His essence, and could not be thought of in any way which made them analogous to human attributes; and that the Qur'an was not one of His attributes, but was created. The second principle was that of God's justice. This too had an implication, that human beings were free, since it would not be just for God to judge them for actions for which they were not responsible. The third principle, that of 'the promise and the threat', was linked to the second: sins without repentance would be punished and good deeds rewarded. The fourth concerned the status of Muslims who believed but sinned; they were in an intermediate position, between faith and infidelity. Finally, emphasis was placed upon the obligation laid by the Qur'an upon believers to enjoin what is good and prohibit what is bad.

Some Muʿtazili ideas had an influence on the ʿAbbasid Caliph al-Ma'mun (813–33) and his successors al-Muʿtasim (833–42) and al-Wathiq (842–6). They used their power to compel Muslims, at least those in public office, to accept the doctrine of the created nature of the Qur'an. A large body of Muslim scholars, however, opposed this, and their opposition found a hero in Ahmad ibn Hanbal (d.855), the traditionist. He refused to accept the doctrine of the created Qur'an and suffered imprisonment. When al-Mutawakkil became Caliph (846–61) he reversed the policy of his predecessors. Muʿtazilism lost its influence with the government, but continued to be an important theological school for some centuries; it was to have a lasting influence on Shiʿi theology.

Al-Ashʿari

The intellectual reaction to the Muʿtazili beliefs was led by al-Ashʿari (d.935). He had been a Muʿtazili but, it was alleged, after a dream in which the Prophet appeared to him, he gave up his former doctrines and adopted the teachings of Ahmad ibn Hanbal. As a result of his intellectual background, he was able to restate these within a more theological framework. The main thrust of his argument was that God is beyond human reason, and to try to limit Him by human logic is an error. Thus the literalist interpretation of the Qur'an's description of God must be upheld. Similarly he upheld the view that the attributes of God are eternal, though he did accept some aspects of the distinction between attributes of God's essence and attributes of God's acts. The Qur'an was eternal and uncreated. As the restrictions imposed on God by His own justice were no longer applicable, the idea of God's determining events was reasserted. No human act could take place without God creating it. On this point, al-Ashʿari did attempt to give some scope for man's responsibility for his actions by elaborating the doctrine of acquisition (*kasb*), by which man acquires responsibility for the action at the moment of its performance. The school of theology that followed al-Ashʿari became the dominant element in Islamic theology and most later theologians were Ashʿaris. The usual term for this kind of theology is *kalam*; those who practised it were called *mutakallimun*.

Avicenna

Although philosophy* was always an interest among only a minority of Muslims, philosophical ideas did exert some influence upon the development of theology. During the third and fourth centuries of the Islamic era (ninth and tenth centuries AD), the teachings of the neo-Platonists were developed among certain scholars. The most notable of these was Ibn Sina (d.1037) (known in Europe as Avicenna*). Among the doctrines that the philosophers put forward that had some influence on theology was the view that matter was eternal. They explained the relationship between God and matter as one in which God was logically prior to matter but in fact both had existed from eternity. Matter was a divine emanation which could only be described as created in the sense that God was logically prior to it, but this emanation had existed and would continue to exist for all time.

At the same period there was also a contribution in terms of moral philosophy that was more acceptable to orthodox thinkers. Miskawayh (d.1030) wrote several works in which he sought to reconcile Platonic and Aristotelian systems of morals with Islam.

al-Ghazali

The Ashʿari response to the materialism of the philosophers was put forward by one of the greatest Islamic thinkers, al-Ghazali* (d.1111), who, in a work entitled *Refutation of the Philosophers*, sought to demonstrate that the metaphysical speculations of the philosophers could not provide the certainty of proof. For a time he had similar doubts about *kalam*, and abandoned his career as a jurist and theologian. His *Refutation* was itself refuted by another distinguished Islamic thinker and philosopher, Ibn Rushd (Averroes*, d.1198).

Ibn Taymiyya

In the course of time, Ashʿari theology became considerably modified from its original form. Although the major doctrines were still upheld, there was much more scope for interpretative analysis of the Qur'an and the *sunna*. A reaction to the methods being followed by the Ashʿaris is to be found in the work of Ibn Taymiyya (d.1328). He vigorously opposed developments in theology and mysticism and endeavoured to restate the faith in the manner of the early Muslims (*salaf*). He emphasized the Hanbali literalist approach and opposed all attempts at providing interpretations of the literal statements of the Qur'an. He was subjected to much persecution in his life, but his theology has proved enormously influential. It was his writing that influenced the founding of the Wahhabi* movement, which in turn was the driving force for the religious approach of the emerging Saudi* state. Ibn Taymiyya has become an important source for many of the modern fundamentalist movements.

Although the term 'orthodox theology' has been used, it should be borne in mind that Sunni Islam, unlike Shiʿi Islam, is not a teaching Church that lays down theological beliefs for its adherents. There was, in fact, no theology that presented a set of theological doctrines which had to be believed; ʿAshari *kalam* was more limited, a science of defending revealed truths by rational arguments. It may be because of this lack of doctrinal authority within Sunni Islam that theology has never attained the importance which it holds in Christianity.

Sufism or mysticism

A prophet who receives revelations from God must be something of a mystic, and there were in Muhammad's life many examples of that inner spirituality which is associated with mysticism. Similarly there are verses in the Qur'an which have a mystical connotation and were used by later mystics as aids and supports to their beliefs. In fact the devotions of the early Muslim community, who spent nights in recitation, prayer and contemplation, could be likened in many respects to those of a mystical cult. The responsibilities of government in Medina moved the religious emphasis much more towards the external aspects of the religious requirements of Muslims, but nonetheless that spiritual aspect of early Islam was not lost.

For early devout Muslims, two matters stood out above all others: first, their own belief in the imminence of the end of the world and the need to escape God's wrath on the Day of Resurrection; and secondly their dismay at the vast wealth that was suddenly brought to Muslims by the early conquests. Such pious Muslims devoted themselves to lives of asceticism and the meticulous performance of their religious duties. The emphasis in their religious practice was on the fulfilment of duties to God rather than an attempt to become closer to God by mystical contemplation. This meant that in their lives the *shariʿa* was all-important. Such a legalistic approach to

Sufis performing the dhikr near Omduram, Sudan

religion could not satisfy the spiritual needs of many devout believers among both intellectual Muslims and the common people.

The popular search for an intimate God

There was a need in Islamic society to provide religious education for ordinary people and religious stimulation to others. During the course of the end of the first century and during the second century of the Islamic era (seventh and eighth centuries AD), a group of religious story-tellers emerged. They went around the towns telling the people stories about their religion. Many of these stories were borrowed from Christianity, Judaism and the Eastern religions; as a result of the expansion of the Islamic world, Muslims had been brought into contact with the mystical traditions of Christianity and the East. These story-tellers began to wear special clothes made of wool (*suf*) which identified them; hence the term 'Sufism' by which Islamic mysticism is commonly known.

Some Muslims began to be concerned about a more personal relationship with God. They found that the observance of the rules of the *shariʿa* was not sufficient to bring them into closer contact with the deity. Contemplation of God led some Muslims to perceive God in more intimate terms. This relationship could be described as a relationship of love born out of contemplation of God's goodness, kindness and concern for men. It is exemplified in the poetry of the famous woman saint Rabiʿa al-ʿAdawiyya (d.801). In her poems she uses the imagery of lover and beloved to describe her relationship with God.

As such mystics approached God with this kind of conception, so the desire to attain the ultimate expression of love, the unity of lover and beloved, began to gain a hold on their thinking. Mystics referred to union with God, the losing of oneself in the ultimate reality of the Divinity. To achieve such union with God, it was necessary for devotees to concentrate on God. As an aid to such concentration, a variety of techniques were evolved. These techniques were known as *dhikr* (remembrance or mentioning of God). Groups would meet together and recite litanies of God's names or sing hymns in praise of God. Special forms of breathing accompanied such litanies, and by these people attained ecstatic states in which some actually felt that they had attained union with God. Dancing was also used to help in bringing about this state (the whirling dervishes).

Al-Hallaj and al-Ghazali

The more strictly orthodox had long been worried by the heterodox trends within this form of religious life, whose exponents seemed to set themselves outside the ordinary sphere of Islamic practice, with their special forms of worship in addition to *salat*. Apart from this, an independent theology or theosophy had been introduced whereby they taught of the annihilation (*fana*) of self to attain subsistence (*baqa*) in the Divinity, and of an elaborate system of stations (*maqamat*) and states (*ahwal*). The stations were more permanent stages along this path; they would begin with such stations as asceticism and lead to total reliance upon God. The states, on the other hand, were more transitory, and the ultimate state that could be achieved in this world was union with God, at least momentarily. Under the guidance of a master, a Sufi novice would pursue a path which led towards this goal.

The disquiet of the orthodox found expression in a famous incident when al-Hallaj was accused of heresy for having declared, after attaining a state of ecstasy, that he was God, and was executed in Baghdad (922). Despite this attempt to stem the tide of Sufism, it continued to expand and increase. Borrowing ideas from neo-Platonism, gnosticism and Shiʿism, it developed its own hierarchical structure. According to this, the world continued to exist by virtue of an invisible network of saints at whose head was the pivotal saint (*qutb*) around whom the whole universe revolved.

Not all Sufis went this far and there were many who tried to combine orthodox and Sufi practices. The most famous exponent of this synthesis was al-Ghazali. He found in Sufism that certainty of God that he had failed to find through his studies of theology and the law. He came back from his Sufi retirement and presented to the Islamic world his great work of reconciliation between Sufism and orthodoxy, *The Revival of the Religious Sciences (Ihya ʿulum al-din)*; in it, he explained the significance of the acts enjoined by the *shariʿa*, and the spirit in which Muslims should perform them. Eventually it came about that most Islamic scholars combined some kind of Sufi practice with their studies in law and theology.

Ibn al-ʿArabi

However, this fact did not prevent esoteric thinkers from continuing to present views that were unacceptable to the majority of Islamic scholars. One important thinker of that kind was Suhrawardi, executed in Aleppo in 1191, who founded the theosophy of illumination. This work was developed further by Ibn al-ʿArabi (d.1240), who regarded himself as the seal of the saints. He elaborated the doctrine of unity of being (*wahdat al-wujud*). In this doctrine Ibn al-ʿArabi held that Absolute Reality is transcendent and its only attribute is self-existence. Ibn al-ʿArabi's thought still exercises considerable influence among followers of Sufism in East and West.

Later the theosophy of illumination was to be further developed in Iran by the great thinker Sadr al-Din al-Shirazi (d.1640). His influence on current theologians and philosophers can still be seen in Iran.

The reaction to this kind of theosophical speculation is best represented by Ibn Taymiyya, who carried vigorous denunciations of the doctrines of Ibn al-ʿArabi. These denunciations by Ibn Taymiyya are widely used in modern fundamentalist criticisms of Sufism.

Sufi orders

As Sufism developed around certain teachers, so their methods were preserved by their followers, and orders of Sufis began to emerge. The term for such an order was *tariqa*, a path towards experiential knowledge of God. These orders had their own houses (*ribat* or *khanqa*), where some Sufis would reside and where the rituals associated with the particular order were carried out. They had elaborate ceremonials of initiation for a novice, who received a cloak (*khirqa*) when he attained full entry into the order. The orders received endowments from rulers and rich citizens to maintain themselves, and the ordinary people were ready to provide them with support. It was the Sufis and their orders that helped the spread of Islam in Africa and the East. Although in the Islamic heartlands in the Middle East Sufism and the orders have become much less significant in modern times, they still hold great sway in areas of Africa and India.

With a few exceptions the orders were not centralized, and local groups could become virtually separate orders. There were therefore a large number of them. Among the most important were the Qadiriyya (spread throughout most of the Muslim world), Mawlawiyya (the 'whirling dervishes', Turkey), Rifaʿiyya (Syria, Egypt), Naqshbandiyya (Turkey, Syria, further east), Khalwatiyya (Turkey, Egypt) and Shadhiliyya (Maghrib). Among orders of modern foundation are the Sanusiyya in Libya and Tijaniyya in the Maghrib and West Africa.

Popular religion and Sufism

The Sufi saints with their ritual *dhikr* held great attractions for ordinary people, who would come and attend sessions of the *dhikr*. They held the Sufi saints in great awe and believed in their ability to perform miracles. When a saint died, his tomb would become a place of visitation and pilgrimage for ordinary people, who hoped by these pilgrimages to gain the intercession of the saint on their behalf. In time, ancient local practices, whether those of animistic Africans or Hindu Indians, were incorporated into popular forms of devotion. Such practices were denounced by Ibn Taymiyya and others, who saw them as contrary to the true Islamic beliefs of the early Muslims.

IH

Further reading

A. J. Arberry, *The Koran Interpreted* (London, 1980)
A. J. Arberry, *Sufism: an account of the mystics of Islam* (London, 1950)
I. Goldziher, *Introduction to Islamic Theology and Law* (Princeton, 1981)
G. E. von Grunebaum, *Muhammadan Festivals* (London, 1976)
T. Khalidi, *Classical Arab Islam* (Princeton, 1985)
M. Momen, *An Introduction to Shiʿi Islam* (London, 1985)
F. Rahman, *Islam* (Chicago, 1979, 2nd edn.)
J. Schacht, *Introduction to Islamic Law* (Oxford, 1964)
W. M. Watt, *Bell's Introduction to the Qur'an* (Edinburgh, 1970)
W. M. Watt, *Islamic Philosophy and Theology* (Edinburgh, 1985, 2nd edn.)

Sufis performing the dhikr in Cairo's Northern Cemetery (City of the Dead)

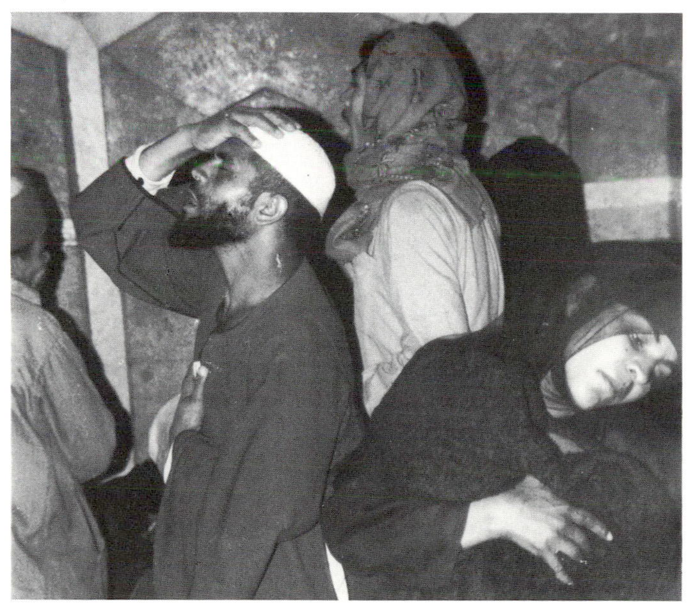

Modern trends in Islam

The appearance of a radical Islamic political movement which came to power in Iran* in 1979 and was manifest among the urban youth of most Middle East countries in the 1970s and 1980s may be traced back to the nineteenth century, when leading Muslim intellectuals first began to grapple with the problem of European domination. The failure of successive *jihads** against the colonial powers convinced the more urbane spirits that Christian power would remain unbeatable until Islam and its institutions were thoroughly reformed from within.

Islam in the modern world

Common to all the reformist or modernizing movements was a return to creative interpretation (*ijtihad**) of the Qur'an and the *sunna* in accordance with modern conditions. In law*, the principal means by which Islam had for centuries achieved its social expression, this meant reforming the superstructure of *fiqh** (jurisprudence) erected by generations of jurists (*'ulama**) according to the principle of blind imitation (*taqlid**) of the earliest authorities and applying it to modern society. The impact of reformists or modernists, however, varied according to the political and cultural context in which they operated. Where European power was virtually unchallengeable, as in British-ruled India after the 'Mutiny' (1857), reformers would appear to be modernizing Islam in order to accommodate non-Islamic rule. Where European power and cultural influence seemed less permanently entrenched – as in Egypt, which remained a nominal part of the Ottoman Empire until the First World War – the modernists would at first appear as reformers bent on strengthening Islam the better to resist Western encroachments. There are no internal criteria, in terms of a fixed scale of 'radicalism' which could be used to distinguish 'modernists' from 'reformists': this may perhaps explain why the great reformers could equally plausibly be seen by subsequent generations as having 'sold' Islam out to the infidel by reducing it to acceptable, non-political dimensions; or as having been stalwart defenders of the faith, determined to resist further colonial or cultural encroachments.

Sayyid Ahmad Khan

The first modernist thinker to have a major impact was Sir Sayyid Ahmad Khan (1817–98), founder of the Muhammadan Anglo-Oriental College at Aligarh in India, where European arts and sciences were taught, in English, alongside traditional Islamic studies. His aim was to produce an educated elite of Muslims able to compete successfully with Hindus for jobs in the Indian civil service. Convinced that the teachings of Islam must be harmonized with modern science, he was strongly influenced by the speculative rationalism of early Muslim thinkers like the Mu'tazilis* and the Brethren of Purity (*ikhwan al-safa*), who responded successfully to the challenge of Greek philosophy. Basing his personal *ijtihad* on a firm foundation of the Qur'an's Arabic idiom, he made a fundamental distinction between the details of revelation (*furu'*) referring to specific historic situations, and the general principles (*usul*) underlying them. Seeing that God's laws must be identical to those of nature, he believed that the *shari'a** must in principle be rooted in natural law. But in practice it reflected the experience of the first generation of Muslims. Using critical methods very similar to those later adopted by such Western orientalists as Goldziher and Schacht, he cast doubt on many traditions (*hadith**), and declared such traditional institutions as polygamy, slavery and concubinage to be forbidden. All laws, he stated, were subject to change according to circumstances, excepting the *'ibadat*, or purely religious duties.

Afghani and 'Abduh

Ahmad Khan's ideas came under fierce attack from some of the Indian *'ulama*, whom he placated by putting them in charge of Islamic studies at Aligarh, thus opening the way to the cultural division between European and Islamic education that would have dire consequences for the future. But the most outspoken attack on him came from a man of similarly progressive views, Jamal al-Din Afghani* (1839–97), celebrated champion of pan-Islamism. Afghani accused Ahmad Khan of being a materialist, which is manifestly untrue; the motive for his attack was political rather than theological. A strong advocate of political resistance to European power on the part of Islam's remaining independent rulers, the Shah of Persia and the Ottoman Sultan, Afghani polemically represented Ahmad Khan's well-known collaboration with the British as the result of religious turpitude. Afghani's chief disciple, Muhammad 'Abduh* (1849–1905), the most influential Arab reformer, faced a similar dilemma to that of Ahmad Khan. In order to gain the opportunity of introducing the far-reaching reforms he regarded as essential, he was obliged to collaborate with British power in Egypt – an attitude which set him against both his former master and the traditionalist *'ulama*. 'Abduh, like Afghani, believed that the truths of science must be harmonized with those of religion: he could not accept the possibility that God's truth, as spoken in the Qur'an, could contradict His truth as revealed in nature. The purpose of revelation was to help human reason, with its fallibility, determine what was good or bad in terms of utilitarian principles, not, as the traditionalist *'ulama* maintained, arbitrarily to endow certain acts with the character of good or bad. In his legal rulings (he rose to the office of Grand Mufti of Egypt) 'Abduh adapted the Maliki* principle of *maslaha** (public interest) in order to allow *shari'a* laws to be adapted to modern requirements. He also introduced the principle of *talfiq* ('piecing together'), whereby rulings could be arrived at by systematically comparing the four legal schools and going behind them to the Qur'an, the *hadith* and the principles of the *salaf al-salih* (pious forbears) or first generation of Muslims. For this he is regarded as the founder of the Salafiyya movement, the term sometimes translated into English as 'fundamentalism'.

Despite his collaboration with the British, ʿAbduh's ideas would prove immensely influential among nationalist circles increasingly conscious of the need for reform. The Salafiyya movement in North Africa, a leading current in the struggle against the French, dates from ʿAbduh's visit to Algiers in 1903. His ideas spread as far as Indonesia, where disciples founded the Muhammadiyya, a reformist movement that played an influential part in generating national resistance to Dutch colonial rule. Like Ahmad Khan, however, ʿAbduh failed in his ultimate aim of reforming traditionalist Islam from within. His ideas were resisted by the citadel of orthodoxy, al-Azhar University, where *ʿulama* trained in time-honoured practices and disciplines held sway. The lack of a centralized religious institution or 'Church' in Sunni Islam militated powerfully against comprehensive reform; instead, the reformist or *salafi* movements tended to develop their own structures parallel to the traditionalist institutions. The latter included al-Azhar, the mosques and pious foundations (*waqf**) which were brought under state control, and the semi-autonomous Sufi orders. The leadership of none of these bodies was up to the intellectual challenge of producing a new *ʿilm al-kalam** which would reconcile modern learning with the Islamic vision of a universe ordered by God. ʿAbduh's followers became divided into two eventually hostile camps: the secularists, who adapted reformist ideas to largely nationalist aims, effectively reducing Islam to a personal religion comparable to Western Christianity; and the radicals who sought to reintegrate society into an Islamic framework from beyond the margins of the state.

ʿAbd al-Raziq

Of the former the most outspoken advocate was Shaykh ʿAli ʿAbd al-Raziq, a graduate of al-Azhar who argued that a distinction must be made between the role of Muhammad as Prophet and his worldly career as a statesman. It was not part of his divine mission, ʿAbd al-Raziq argued, to found a state, but to reveal divine truth. The original *umma** which came into existence under his authority, therefore, had no essential relationship with any particular territory or form of government. The latter was subject to the dictates of human reason, rather than the divine will. ʿAbd al-Raziq's reasoning, though vigorously attacked by al-Azhar (which revoked his diploma), nevertheless provided a theological justification for what in fact was taking place, not just in Egypt but in other states emerging from colonialism. The new constitution adopted in 1923 declared Egypt a sovereign state, free and independent, under a constitutional monarch. Modelled on that of Belgium, it conflicted with traditional Islamic concepts of government on several points. By granting Egyptians equal rights before the law regardless of religious affiliation, it abolished the old distinction between Muslims and *dhimmis**; parliament was given full powers of legislation untrammelled by the *shariʿa*, which was reduced to regulating questions of personal status.

Rashid Rida

The inspiration of the more conservative or 'fundamentalist' radicals was ʿAbduh's closest disciple, the Syrian Rashid Rida, the first important Arab advocate of a modernized Islamic state. Rida formulated his views during the crisis surrounding the abolition of the Ottoman Caliphate by Kemal Atatürk and the Turkish National Assembly. Though originally a supporter of the Ottoman Caliphate, Rida came to accept its demise as a symptom of Muslim decadence; and while no advocate of secularism, he regarded the Assembly as a genuine example of the Islamic principle of consultation (*shura**). The ideal Caliph, according to Rida, was a supreme interpreter of the law (*mujtahid**), who would work in consultation with the *ʿulama*, 'those with the power to bind and loose'. In the absence of a suitable candidate for the Caliphate, and of *ʿulama* versed in the modern sciences (for Rida regarded the contemporary *ʿulama* as generally ignorant, corrupt and subservient to the state), the best alternative was an Islamic state ruled by a disinterested, enlightened elite in consultation with the people, able both to interpret the *shariʿa* and legislate where necessary.

The Muslim Brotherhood

Many of Rida's ideas were taken up by the most influential of the reform movements in Arab lands during the inter-war years, the Muslim Brotherhood. Founded by an Egyptian school-teacher, Hasan al-Banna, in 1928, the Brotherhood's original aims were moral rather than political. It sought to reform society by purging it of both Western influences and decadent medieval accretions, rather than by capturing the state directly. Members met for prayer and were encouraged to observe their religious duties (*ʿibadat*) assiduously, and to abstain from the evils of gambling, alcohol, usury and fornication. However, in the mounting crisis over Palestine during and after the Second World War, the Brotherhood became radicalized. Some of its members took to terrorism, including the murder of Prime Minister Nuqrashi Pasha in 1948 – for which Banna, in a retaliatory assassination organized by the security services, paid with his life the following year. After the overthrow of the monarchy in 1952, in which the Brotherhood played a leading part, it came into increasing conflict with the secular nationalism adopted by Jamal ʿAbd al-Nasir (Nasser)*, and ran foul of his law abolishing the old political parties. In 1954, after an attempt on Nasser's life by a former Brotherhood member, the movement was suppressed, its members imprisoned, exiled or driven underground.

It was mainly during this period that the Muslim Brotherhood became internationalized, with affiliated movements springing up in many other Sunni Muslim countries, notably Jordan, Syria, Sudan, Pakistan, Indonesia and Malaysia. In Saudi Arabia, under the new and vigorous leadership of Amir (later King) Faysal ibn ʿAbd al-ʿAziz*, the Brotherhood found refuge and political support, with funds for the Egyptian underground and salaried posts for exiled intellectuals. In the sharpening conflict with Nasser (whose military focus was the civil war in Yemen), Faysal determined to play the 'Islamic card' for all it was worth.

Iqbal

On the ideological front, a new injection of radical ideas came from Indo-Pakistan, where intellectuals had devised a more systematic reformulation of the problems facing Islam in the modern world than had their Arab counterparts. The seminal thinker of Indian Islam in the twentieth century was Muhammad Iqbal, poet, mystic, philosopher and moving spirit behind the founding of Pakistan. Drawing on insights derived from Western philosophy as well as classical and Persian Islam, he began to develop the first genuinely modernist theology capable of emancipating Islamic thought from the shackles of historicism. The ideal Islamic state, Iqbal argued, must not be confused with that of the four orthodox (or 'Rightly-Guided') Caliphs* as held by most modernists: this state, which had never been realized, was still dormant in the conscience of men. Political activity must, therefore, be directed not at the restoration of an idealized past, but towards a future in which the Caliphate, or man's 'vice-regency' under God, would be equated with the service of mankind.

Maududi

Despite his liberal outlook, Iqbal's most influential follower was an ultra-conservative, Sayyid Abu'l-ʿAla Maududi (1903–79), the most potent intellectual force among modern Sunni radicals. Unlike ʿAbduh and other liberal reformers, Maududi included much of the traditional *fiqh* in his definition of what constitutes *shariʿa* law – for example, he advocated strict purdah (seclusion) for women. In many respects his outlook was indistinguishable from that of the traditionalist *ʿulama* in India and Pakistan. But he also shared Iqbal's vision of the *shariʿa* as a dynamic system of law which could be continually added to by the exercise of *ijtihad*. In effect he wanted to extend the intricate and detailed structure of traditionalist *fiqh* to include every aspect of modern life.

Two of Maududi's doctrines, in particular, were to have a major impact on Islamic radicals in the Middle East. One was the idea, adapted from Iqbal, that the struggle for Islam is not for the restoration of an ideal past, but for a principle – the vice-regency of man under God's sovereignty – vital to the here and now. The *jihad* is therefore not simply a defensive war for the protection of Dar al-Islam*: it may be waged offensively against the forces which threaten to destroy it. The other doctrine, a corollary of Maududi's position on *jihad*, is that the *jahiliyya**, or 'state of ignorance' against which the Prophet Muhammad struggled throughout his career (see Islam), is not confined to the historical period before the coming of Islam. It is part of the current scene affecting Muslim countries, against which true Muslims are duty-bound to struggle.

Sayyid-Qutb

The leading transmitter of Maududi's doctrines in the Arab world was Sayyid Qutb, the Muslim Brotherhood theorist and militant executed in 1966 for allegedly plotting against the Nasser regime. During his many years in Nasser's prisons, Qutb – who had been educated in the United States – had written a comprehensive account of the modern *jahiliyya* in a book called *Signposts along the Road*:

> Nowadays, the entire world lives in a state of *jahiliyya* . . . The principle on which it is based is opposition to God's rule over the earth and to the major characteristic of the Divinity, namely sovereignty . . . The degradation of Man in general in the collectivist regimes, the injustice suffered by individuals and peoples dominated by capital and colonialism, are the consequence of this opposition to the rule of God, the negation of the dignity that God bestowed upon man.

Qutb's suggested solution for this problem was the creation of a new elite or vanguard among Muslim youth which would fight the new *jahiliyya* as the Prophet had fought the *jahiliyya* of old. Like the Prophet, it must choose when to withdraw from the *jahiliyya*, and when to seek contact with it. Qutb's ideas set the agenda for the radicals in Egypt. The most extreme group, calling itself the 'Society of Muslims', led by Shukri Mustafa, opted for the strategy of 'withdrawal': members refused to pray in '*jahili*' mosques (usually those under government control); they refused to serve in the army under an 'infidel' government; they married amongst themselves, and generally created a semi-autonomous religious counter-culture in Egypt's major cities, living mainly off earnings sent by sympathizers working abroad. The Egyptian press dubbed them 'Takfir wa Hijra' – literally, 'declaration of infidelity and *hijra*', indicating that they first declared their fellow-Muslims infidels, and then withdrew from society. The religious establishment pronounced them to be Khariji* heretics, and indeed their strategy had been very similar to these early 'seceders' from the first Islamic community. (They were disbanded after they kidnapped and murdered their leading Islamic detractor, the former Minister for Religious Endowments, Shaykh Muhammad al-Dhahabi.) Another group, led by ʿAbd al-Salam Farraj, emphasized the *jihad*ist aspect of Qutb's thinking. Drawing on a legal ruling advanced by the thirteenth-century legist Ibn Taymiyya* (d.1328), Farraj justified the assassination of President Sadat* on the ground that he was failing to apply the *shariʿa*. (The action was duly carried out by Lieutenant Khalid Islambuli in full view of the world's television cameras on 6 October 1981.) Other Sunni extremists who followed the Qutb line in attempting to seize power directly included the Muslim Brotherhood group in northern Syria whose rebellion in the city of Hama* was suppressed at the cost of an estimated 10,000 lives; and the Islamic Liberation Party which attempted to seize the Military Academy at Heliopolis in Egypt in 1974. The same group was accused of plotting against the Tunisian government in two major trials in 1983 and 1985.

Developments in Iran

Although Qutb's writings have been a major influence on Islamic radicals in Egypt and other Sunni countries, providing a 'liberation theology' argued in both classical and modernist terms, a major inspiration has come from the Islamic Republic of Iran. The developments in ideas and Islamic discourse which led up to the Islamic Revolution, however, occurred almost entirely in terms of the Twelver Shiʿi tradition (see Islam). So while the actions of the Iranian militants, as well as the successes and failures of the Islamic Republic, have exercised a powerful impact on Islamic movements throughout the region, the ideas which gave rise to it have been largely confined to Iran.

During the nineteenth century Iranian clerics (known as *mujtahids* because of their right to act as 'sources of imitation' in interpreting religious texts) enjoyed considerably more political independence and social power than their Sunni counterparts. In theological matters the rationalist (Muʿtazili) tradition they inherited, confirmed by the victory of the *ʿusulis* over the *akhbaris* during the Qajar* period, also made them considerably more responsive to new ideas. Inspired by Afghani (actually a Persian from Asadabad near Hamadan who concealed his Shiʿi origins in order to avoid arousing Sunni prejudices), the *mujtahids* were instrumental in mobilizing a vigorous and successful national protest against the tobacco monopoly granted to an Englishman, Major Talbot, during the 1890s. The 'Tobacco Agitation' turned out to be the dress-rehearsal for the Constitutional Revolution of 1905–6, when a section of the *ʿulama* joined with liberal bourgeois elements in forcing the Shah to grant a Constituent Assembly. They justified their position by arguing that, during the absence of the hidden Imam, it was important to impose constitutional checks on the arbitrary power of the monarch.

Khomeini: the turban and the crown

Sayyid Ruhallah Khomeini, a *mujtahid* from Qum, was thus acting within a well-established tradition of clerical protest when he took the lead in the 1963 agitation against Shah Muhammad Riza Pahlavi's 'White Revolution', a collection of agrarian and social reforms which threatened the interests of the religious establishment (see Iran). The prestige which Khomeini subsequently gained, however, was partly the Shah's own doing: by exiling him to Najaf in neighbouring, and hostile, Iraq, the Iranian monarch effectively freed him to make unbridled attacks on his government with the support of his Iraqi hosts.

Khomeini's radicalism lay in the departure from Shiʿi traditions implied in the doctrine of *Vilayet-i-faqih** (the jurisconsult's trusteeship). In lectures delivered to his students at Najaf, he urged that government be directly entrusted to the *ʿulama*:

> The slogan of the separation of religion and politics and the demand that Islamic scholars should not intervene in social or political affairs have been formulated and propagated by the imperialists; it is only the irreligious who repeat them. Were religion and politics separate at the time of the Prophet . . .?

However, Khomeini's insistence that government should be placed under the overall charge of the *ʿulama* was only part of the radical Shiʿi doctrine that was to come to fruition in the Islamic Revolution. There had been an equally radical departure from tradition on the left of Iranian politics. During the late 1960s and early 1970s student activists were turning increasingly to Islam, with or without an admixture of Marxist ideas, as an activist ideology capable of mobilizing opposition to local tyranny and corruption and Western imperialism.

ʿAli Shariʾʿati

The leading exponent of this version of Shiʿism was Dr ʿAli Shariʾʿati (d.1977), a historian and sociologist who had been partially educated in Paris. Though without a *mujtahid*'s formal training, he came from a religious family. In his writings he drew eclectically on the traditional repertory of Persian Islam, including both the Qur'an and the works of mystics-cum-philosophers like Mulla Sadra and Ibn al-ʿArabi, as well as on Marxist and existential writers like Sartre, Fanon and Camus. The result is a highly individualistic synthesis of Islamic and leftist ideas, in which God is virtually identified with the People, justifying revolutionary action in the name of Islam. A strident critic of the clergy who acquiesced in the Shah's tyranny, Shariʾʿati drew an important distinction between the official Shiʿism of the Safavids and what he regarded as the revolutionary Islam of Imams ʿAli and Husayn and Abu Dharr al-Ghifari (a Companion of the Prophet much celebrated in leftist Islamic mythology). Shariʿati's ideas, disseminated through photocopies of his writings and recordings of his lectures, became immensely popular with the student left. This provided the vital link between the activist vanguard and the more traditionalist majority in the coalition which eventually brought down the Shah. However, after the fall of Shariʿati's disciple Abu'l-Hasan Bani Sadr and the triumph of the official clergy in the Islamic Republican Party, Shariʿati's reputation, and ideas, fell into eclipse.

Qadhafi and the Libyan experiment

Another Islamic eclectic whose ideas have been influential (though they are less well formulated than Shariʿati's) is Muʿammar Qadhafi*, self-styled 'revolutionary leader' of the Libyan People's Jamahiriyya*. In recent years Qadhafi has offended the official *ʿulama* both in Libya and abroad by claiming the right of personal *ijtihad*, relying exclusively on the Qur'an and rejecting the *sunna* as a source of authority. While most people would regard his approach to Islam as highly idiosyncratic and lacking in scholarship, his view that Islam is the 'natural' religion of mankind which should be integrated organically into the social order is shared by many other,

The Ayatollah Khomeini in exile in the village of Neauphile-le-Château near Paris

Khaled al-Islambouli, leader of the assassins of President Sadat, waving a Qur'an during the start of his trial, 1981

more orthodox thinkers. It is unquestionably derived from the Qur'an, although some scholars have detected a strong flavour of Rousseau in his theories. His principle ideological treatise, the *Green Book*, makes no explicit reference to Islamic scripture, attacking in the manner of Shari'ʿati all forms of institutional religion.

Conclusion

Throughout the 1970s and 1980s radicalism (or 'fundamentalism' to give it its popular, but inappropriate name) remained the prevailing current in Islam, not only in the Middle East but throughout most of the Islamic world. Various causes have been given for this resurgence of Islam's activist traditions. The most significant is the failure of nationalist governments to live up to the expectations aroused at the time of independence. Left-wing or Marxist ideas have generally found little favour outside a small Westernized elite. In any case, many of these ideas have been discredited since they were adopted by nationalist regimes, notably in Egypt, Syria, Iraq and Algeria. However, the impact of Islamic radicalism has generally extended far beyond the range of politics. Behind the slogans demanding a return to the *shariʿa* – common ground among all activist currents – lies a more pervasive desire for cultural assertion and cultural reintegration. Modernity is not rejected as such, but Islamic pride demands that modernity should appear in Islamic guise; there is a desire to use the instruments of the West without adopting its life-style. Hence the considerable emphasis attached to formal manifestations of Islam, such as the adoption of Qur'anic punishments, segregation of the sexes and 'religious' dress for women. As many scholars have noted, the standard-bearers of this movement have tended to come from the most Westernized sectors of society – especially among scientists or engineers who have felt that their studies alienated them from their Islamic heritage.

Within the movement at large, especially among former left-wing radicals, one should not dismiss the possibility of political opportunism: as the Iranian Revolution testifies, the slogans of Islam have a far greater potential for mobilizing popular support against government than the secular or Marxist variety. A positive result of the movement could be the lessening of the culture-gap between traditionalist Muslim societies and those which have become more Westernized, and a lessening of gross inequalities of wealth which continue to be accentuated by Western economic penetration. The radical trend seems likely to remain in the ascendant, until economic conditions change sufficiently to allow a more even distribution of wealth. At the same time, the Iranian example does not suggest that Islam has any final answers to economic questions that would command universal assent. Although experiments in interest-free banking* offer interesting possibilities, Islamic modernists have yet to formulate a coherent body of economic thought that could make it possible for the radicals to succeed in their aim of challenging East and West alike.

MHR

Further reading

Hamid Enayat, *Modern Islamic Political Thought* (London, 1982)
Albert Hourani, *Arabic Thought in the Liberal Age* (Oxford, 1962)
Gilles Kepel, *The Prophet and Pharaoh: Muslim extremism in Egypt*, tr. Jon Rothschild (London, 1985)
Edward Mortimer, *Faith and Power: the politics of Islam* (London, 1982)
E. I. J. Rosenthal, *Islam in the Modern National State* (Cambridge, 1965)
Malise Ruthven, *Islam in the World* (Harmondsworth and New York, 1984)
Emmanuel Sivan, *Radical Islam: medieval theology and modern politics* (New Haven and London, 1985)
W. Cantwell Smith, *Islam in Modern History* (Princeton, 1957)

Judaism in the Islamic period

Throughout much of the Middle Ages, the majority of the Jewish people lived in the Islamic world. Many of the Jewish communities there had roots in antiquity, going back long before the Arab conquests of the seventh and eighth centuries and the subsequent Arabization and Islamization of the Middle East, North Africa and Spain. Not only were the demographic centres of world Jewry located in the Muslim lands, but during certain periods, such as the heyday of medieval Islamic civilization in the ninth to thirteenth centuries, the so-called Golden Age of Spain of the late tenth to twelfth centuries, and the Ottoman revival of the Middle East during the fifteenth and sixteenth centuries, the creative centres of Jewish life were to be found in the domain of Islam rather than in Christendom.

Judaism and the birth of Islam

Jewish communities were to be found throughout Arabia when Muhammad* was born in about AD 571. Although insignificant in themselves in the scheme of Jewish history, they seem to have played an important role in the early history of Islam. Arabian Jews were concentrated in the oases of the northern Hijaz, in the Yemen, and to a lesser extent on the eastern coast of the peninsula. They spoke Arabic and in general appear to have adopted the social organization and many of the cultural values of their non-Jewish neighbours. The poetry of the pre-Islamic Jewish poet al-Samaw'al ibn ʿAdiya celebrates the same rugged desert ethos as do the odes of other Jahili* poets. Though assimilated into Arabian society in many respects, the Jews nevertheless stood apart as a separate group because of their religion and its distinctive practices. As elsewhere in the Diaspora, they spoke among themselves a confessional dialect that included Hebrew and Aramaic expressions for religious and ethical terms. Some of these words and concepts gradually passed into more general Arabic usage. The Christian communities of Arabia, it may be added, played a similar role.

Prior to his prophetic calling, Muhammad met many Jews and Christians in his early career as a merchant. Through such contacts, he probably absorbed many basic monotheistic ideas and some familiarity with religious lore. It has long been debated by Western scholars whether Muhammad's principal monotheistic informants were Jews or Christians, and cogent arguments have been advanced for both positions. Be that as it may, it is clear that in the early years of Muhammad's preaching in Mecca, he had a positive attitude toward Jews and Christians as the recipients of earlier divine revelations. All of this changed in 622 when Muhammad emigrated to Medina to lay the foundations of the nascent Islamic state and there came into contact with a large organized Jewish community.

The Jews of Medina had played no part in inviting Muhammad and showed no enthusiasm for him or his religion. Their opposition proved particularly irksome because they attacked him on the all-important revelationary level. The Qur'anic verses revealed to Muhammad during this period take cognizance of the Jews' bitter opposition, and the Jews now came to be considered the primary opponents of the early Muslim community, along with the pagans who until then had been the sole enemy. An adversarial relationship was enshrined in holy writ and was later amplified in the hagiographic literature on the life of the Prophet.

Once the Jews of Medina were eliminated through the expulsion of two tribes and the extermination of a third, a more tolerant attitude mitigated the full force of the negative theological image. For, despite the fact that Muhammad at a certain point in his prophetic career decided that the Jews (and thereafter the Christians) had in some degree corrupted their scriptures, he never questioned the basic validity of their religion. The original recognition accorded them in the Meccan period was never abrogated. Like the Jews of the oases of the northern Hijaz, they were to be fought only until they submitted as humble tribute-bearers in accordance with the clear Qur'anic injunction of *Sura* 9:29.

The Jews under the Caliphate

The great Arab conquests that took place during the century following Muhammad's death united the majority of world Jewry within a single state. Having already been a subject people for more than half a millennium, the Jews were psychologically and economically better prepared to adapt to the restrictions and fiscal impositions on non-Muslims (the so-called 'Pact of ʿUmar'*) than were either the Christians or Zoroastrians. The rabbis had given them a concept of Jewishness that was independent of physical territory or

Torah rolls: (from left to right) European, Indian and Persian

political sovereignty. They also possessed a communal organization moulded in the Graeco-Roman civil tradition. Under the Muslim system of rule these organizations were accorded not only official recognition as legitimate communal bodies but a considerable degree of internal autonomy.

Over the first century and a half of Islamic rule, the Jews adopted the Arabic language which had taken the place of Greek and Aramaic as the lingua franca of the new *oikoumene*, now extended over a greater area than ever before. The Jewish masses also gradually changed over from the agrarian way of life depicted in the Talmud to a more cosmopolitan one in the wake of the Islamic wave of urbanization, especially in Iraq which had a large Jewish population.

The establishment of the ʿAbbasid* capital at Baghdad had profound consequences for all the Jews in the Caliphate. Iraq, still called Babylonia in the Jewish tradition, was the single most important demographic and scholarly centre of world Jewry. It was there that the Babylonian Talmud had been redacted, and it was there that the great academies (*yeshivot*) of Sura and Pumbeditha were located. Some time during the first half of the ninth century, the *ge'onim*, or heads of the academies, came to be recognized as the authoritative leaders of much of world Jewry. The *ge'onim* were the principal propagators and expounders of the Babylonian Talmud which eventually became the constitutional foundation for all medieval Judaism. The pre-eminence of the *ge'onim* was based upon the contention that they were the sole possessors of the living tradition that went back to the ancient rabbis and ultimately to Moses himself. The Jewish communities of the wider Islamic Diaspora sent donations as well as queries (*she'elot*) on legal, ritual and textual matters to the academies, and the *ge'onim* in turn exerted their authority through the responsa (*teshuvot*) they sent back. The documents of the Cairo Geniza show that an enormous network of representatives of the academies in the major cities of the Islamic world facilitated the flow of correspondence and donations back and forth. Not infrequently, these representatives were merchants who had studied at the academies, or whose forebears had done so, and had moved into the Mediterranean basin with the population movements of the ninth to eleventh centuries.

In addition to the academies and the *ge'onim*, Iraq was the seat of the exilarch (*resh galuta*), who was recognized as a descendant of the Davidic royal house. Under the Sasanians, the holder of this office had served as governor of the Jews in the Persian Empire. The exilarch's authority was recognized and reconfirmed at the time of the Arab conquest and took on increased significance with the ʿAbbasid takeover. The exilarch became the leading Jewish representative at the caliphal court. Although his actual authority did not exceed that of the *ge'onim*, he was an important figurehead and a source of immense pride for all Jews, who considered him a living fulfilment of the biblical prophecy that 'the sceptre shall not depart from Judah' (Genesis 49:10).

The pre-eminent position of Babylonian Jewry under the ʿAbbasids was strengthened by the rise of a vigorous mercantile elite that was closely allied with the religious leadership. Jewish merchants from the Radhan district (later called Jukha) around Baghdad conducted an international trade in early ʿAbbasid times that extended from China to Spain. During the late eighth century the gaonate of Pumbeditha was in fact occupied by Radhanites. Jewish *jahbadhs*, or government bankers, such as the Banu Netira and the Banu Aaron, came to wield such influence at the caliphal court and such power in Jewish communal affairs that they could even impose and depose an exilarch.

The revival of Hellenistic science and philosophy in Baghdad during the ninth century and the intellectual and spiritual ferment it engendered had a profound impact upon Jews as well as Muslims. For a few brief centuries a laissez-faire economic and intellectual atmosphere prevailed, first in Baghdad and later in other parts of the Empire, that permitted non-Muslims to take an active part in the general cultural life.

In an interesting parallel with the development of Islam, Judaism evolved and crystallized in many respects during this period into the religious civilization it is today. The synagogue service and ritual in general became more standardized through the prayer books of Rav ʿAmram (*c.*AD 860) and Saadya Gaon (*c.*936). Jewish theologians adopted the dialectical tools of the *mutakallimun** to answer their own pressing matters of faith. Saadya, for example, shows great indebtedness to the Mu'tazili* school in the terminology and methodology of the *Kitab al-amanat wa'l-iʿtiqadat* (Book of Beliefs and Opinions), the first systematic work of Jewish philosophy. Over the next two and a half centuries, the study of philosophy came to be viewed throughout the major Jewish intellectual circles of the Muslim world as an integral part of the study of the Torah.

The Jews of the Islamic Mediterranean

The first new Jewish centre to appear outside Iraq was in Ifriqiyya* (later Tunisia). Under the Fatimids*, who were relatively more tolerant to their non-Muslim subjects than most Muslim rulers, Ifriqiyya became a crossroad of Mediterranean caravan and sea lanes and a major station on the greater Spain-to-India trade route. The prominent role played by Jewish merchants from Qayrawan and other Tunisian cities is richly documented in the Cairo Geniza. In addition to its commercial importance, Qayrawan became the major spiritual and intellectual Jewish centre outside Iraq. In Hebrew literature the 'Sages of Qayrawan', who included the physician and neo-Platonic philosopher Isaac Israeli and the talmudic commentators R. Nissim and R. Hananel, were noted for both their religious and secular scholarship. The Jews of Qayrawan maintained ties with both the Babylonian academies and the venerable academy of Palestine.

The Jewish community of Qayrawan possessed a strong hierarchical organization which may have been modelled in part on that of Baghdad. The head of Qayrawanese Jewry was also the leading figure of the wider North African Jewish community. This individual, who was usually a court Jew, was originally known as the Head of the Congregations, but from 1015 bore the princely title of *nagid*. The primacy of court Jews in communal affairs remained an outstanding feature of Maghribi Jewish social organization until modern times.

The Jews of Andalusia

Shortly after the Jewish community of Ifriqiyya began asserting itself, another major independent Jewish centre started to emerge in Islamic Spain. During the tenth to twelfth centuries, Andalusian Jewry enjoyed a brilliant period of material, cultural and political achievement unparalleled in the history of the Jews under Islam. This sudden efflorescence was intimately linked to the rise of Hasday ben Shaprut (d.975), a Jewish physician, diplomat and statesman at the court of Caliphs ʿAbd al-Rahman III and al-Hakam II in Cordoba. Hasday embarked upon an ambitious programme to make Spain a leading seat of world Jewry. He patronized Jewish scholars and poets, such as the innovative Dunash Ben Labrat, who pioneered the adaptation of Arabic metrics and secular themes to Hebrew poetry. He imported Jewish books on a grand scale, and he loosened Spanish Jewry's dependence upon the Babylonian academies by appointing an Italian rabbi, Moses ibn Hanokh, as chief scholar and head of an independent *yeshiva* in Cordoba.

The period of political, ethnic and social fragmentation under the *muluk al-tawa'if* (party kings)* offered Jews an extraordinary opportunity for government service, and there arose a significant Jewish courtier class. These grandees held offices that went far beyond the positions of petty bureaucrats, physicians and purveyors usually held by Jews in other Muslim countries. Among the Andalusian court Jews were high-ranking administrators such as Yequtiel ibn Hasan (d.1039) in Saragossa, Abraham ibn Muhajir (d. *c.*1100) in Seville, and the powerful Samuel ibn Nagrela, known as ha-Nagid, who between 1030 and 1056 was wazir and military commander of the Zirid Kingdom of Granada. The Andalusian Jewish courtiers possessed a distinctive group ethos whose principal characteristics included a strong sense of elitism with regard to other Jews, a harmonious synthesis of Arabic secular culture and Judaism, and a desire for attaining social and political power.

The so-called Golden Age of Spain came to an abrupt end with the Almohad* conquest and forced conversions in the mid-twelfth century. However, aspects of Andalusian Jewish culture continued to survive in Christian Spain, Provence, the late medieval Maghrib, and eventually throughout the lands of the Sephardi Diaspora. The greatest intellectual figure of Andalusian (and indeed of all medieval) Jewry, Moses Maimonides (Musa ibn Maymun), produced all his important juridical and philosophical work in Ayyubid* Egypt, where he had found refuge from the Almohad persecutions.

The Jews under late medieval Islam

The spiritual, social and economic climate of the Islamic world was radically transformed during the course of the thirteenth century. Islamic civilization came under tremendous pressures from within and without. The humanistic tendencies of Hellenism all but disappeared, while at the same time the Islamic religious element in its most rigid form took a dominant place in society. The general cultural level and socio-economic condition of Islamic Jewry stagnated and declined with the decay of the Muslim world. The Jews of the Middle East and North Africa were left spiritually and numerically impoverished in the wake of periodic persecution, general oppression, and such disasters as war and plague. The discriminatory laws for *dhimmis** were enforced with greater consistency and stringency than in earlier times.

The Ottoman conquest of much of the Middle East and North Africa during the sixteenth century brought about a general amelioration of Jewish life for a brief period. This was coupled with the arrival of large numbers of Spanish, Portuguese and Sicilian Jews who had been expelled from their native lands. These refugees, many of whom were educated and talented, brought with them among other things the first Hebrew printing presses* to the Middle East and the Maghrib. Their cultural superiority over the native Jewish communities ensured the dominance of Sephardi Judaism in Turkey, the Levant, Egypt and North Africa.

Impelled in part by a general air of messianic expectation, the Jewish population of Palestine* swelled to approximately 10,000 during the first half-century of Ottoman rule. Bold development projects for reviving the Holy Land were conceived by Jewish courtiers in Constantinople, such as Dona Gracia Mendes and Don Joseph Nasi. Jerusalem, Tiberias, and above all Safad, became centres of Jewish spiritual and commercial activity. The Kabbalist mystics of Safad, such as R. Isaac Luria, the 'Holy Lion of God', left their lasting imprint not only on the Judaism of the Islamic world, but through the Hasidic movement in Eastern Europe on Ashkenazi Judaism as well. Messianic ardour reached almost hysterical proportions among Middle Eastern Jewry and was only checked by the disappointment caused by the Sabbatian disaster of 1665–6.

Many of the gains achieved by Islamic Jewry during the sixteenth century were lost over the next two hundred years as the general trend of decline which had only been temporarily interrupted continued, and as Ottoman rule became more inefficient, corrupt and religiously conservative.

NSt

Further reading
E. Ashtor, *The Jews of Moslem Spain*, 3 vols. (Philadelphia, 1973–1984)
S. D. Goitein, *Jews and Arabs* (New York, 1974, 3rd edn.)
S. D. Goitein, *A Mediterranean Society*, 5 vols. (Berkeley, 1967–86)
B. Lewis, *The Jews of Islam* (London, 1984)
N. A. Stillman, *The Jews of Arab Lands* (Philadelphia, 1979)

Modern movements in Judaism

At the beginning of the nineteenth century, the Jews of Central and Eastern Europe were in many important respects not dissimilar to their co-religionists in Arab and other Middle Eastern lands. They shared with them religious texts in Hebrew and Aramaic which played a predominant part in their intellectual life; they shared an educational system where the study of these texts was all-important; and they shared a certain religious and legal autonomy *vis-à-vis* the states in which they lived. Partly as a result of Gentile prejudice, and partly as a result of their own desire to remain apart, European Jews, for the most part, had not been touched by the revolution in knowledge represented by the European Renaissance and later developments, any more than had their Middle Eastern brethren.

During the nineteenth century, however, a number of revolutionary movements were to engulf western Jewry. All of these movements were, to some extent, assimilationist, in the sense that they were expressive of a growing tendency among Jews to abandon (or modify) what was in many ways an oriental culture in favour of a Western one. For whereas in the Middle Ages the Jews could justifiably regard themselves as a culturally superior and impressively literate elite by comparison with their Christian neighbours, they now began to perceive that during the centuries of their cultural isolation Western European society had forged ahead. Modern Jewish movements can thus be seen as Jewry's attempts to come to terms with Western developments.

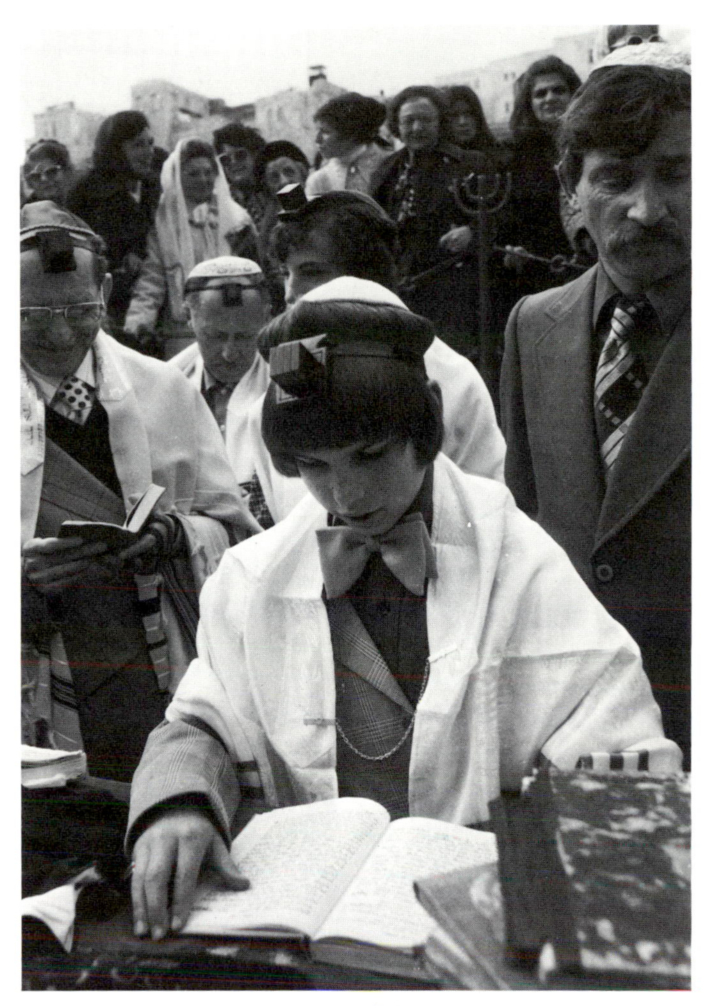
Bar-Mitzva ceremony at Jerusalem's Western Wall

The *Haskalah* in Germany

The *Haskalah** was the first such movement. It started in Germany, particularly in Berlin and Königsberg, in the second half of the eighteenth century and its early years were dominated by the figure of the philosopher Moses Mendelssohn (1729–86). Its chief purpose was to adapt the German *Aufklärung* for Jewish consumption while adapting Jewish social and religious practices to facilitate the absorption of these Western ideas. The most important vehicle for the *Haskalah* in its early phase was a Hebrew periodical *Ha-Meassef* (The Collector) which was published in Königsberg intermittently between 1784 and 1811. In 1783 Mendelssohn finished his famous *Biur*, the translation of the Pentateuch from Hebrew into German written in Hebrew characters with a Hebrew commentary. This translation may have achieved something of its desired effect of creating a fusion of Hebrew and German culture. But its most immediate effect was to teach German Jews, whose spoken language was Yiddish, the German language and to introduce them to the convenience of reading German. It was not long before Hebrew and Yiddish were abandoned. With the acquisition first of the German language and later German culture, the hitherto unassimilated German Jews became thoroughly Westernized, so much so that many, including eight of Mendelssohn's nine grandchildren, left Judaism entirely.

The Reform Movement

The Reform Movement in Germany can be seen as an extension of the German *Haskalah*. Its chief interest was to bring Jewish religious practice into line with 'civilized' norms. In effect, this meant that Judaism was to be made to look as much like Lutheran Christianity as possible. The first efforts of the movement were to make synagogue worship less disorderly and more aesthetic. The liturgy was shortened, the sermon was to be delivered in German, choirs and organ music were introduced and the rabbinate took to dressing themselves in a costume not unlike that worn by the Lutheran clergy. Of much greater significance was the somewhat later development which tended to suppress those elements of the liturgy which expressed the traditional Jewish yearning for Zion and the re-establishment of Jerusalem as the centre of the ancient Israelite cult.

The most influential leader of the reform movement was Abraham Geiger (1810–74), who argued for a de-nationalized Judaism while urging the legitimacy of change – a concept quite foreign to Judaism in its orthodox manifestation. Reform has taken root most firmly in the United States where it has enabled Jewish immigrants from Europe to participate effectively and energetically in American society and culture without losing their identity as Jews. The earlier tendency to eliminate Zion from the prayerbook has been reversed, and now reform Jews are as fervent in their support of the State of Israel as conservative or orthodox Jews and frequently more so. Indeed for many reform Jews, political and financial support for Israel* constitute two of the more important elements of their practice as Jews.

The *Haskalah* in Eastern Europe

If, in Germany, the *Haskalah* led to wholesale assimilation and the formulation of a Westernized form of Judaism, its effects in Eastern Europe where the mass of European Jewry lived were quite different. Jews did not feel themselves to be at any great cultural disadvantage *vis-à-vis* the Gentile populations of Russia and Poland. The traditional languages of Eastern European Jewry were Hebrew* and Yiddish and there were no glittering prizes to be won by the acquisition of Polish or Russian. Hebrew, the written language of the *Haskalah*, therefore had a much better chance of being accepted as the language of enlightenment. Indeed, for a hundred years, at least, Hebrew was to be the chief vehicle whereby Western ideas and modern disciplines were relayed to the Jews of Eastern Europe. The *Haskalah* radiated out from centres in Galicia, Lithuania, Belorussia, Warsaw and Odessa.

Zionism and its antecedents

Orthodox Judaism, of course, sees itself both as a religion and as a nationality. But the transformation of this religious–national identification into a national identification with all the ramifications and aspirations of a modern national movement came about only in the nineteenth century and as a result, partly, of the attempt on the part of the *Haskalah* to graft Western values on to Judaism. Jews started to aspire to the same sort of nationhood as that enjoyed by the nation states among whom they lived. The process of change from one identification to the other was facilitated by the *Haskalah*, which created a new national culture that was both modern and secular; it was expressed in a language (Hebrew) which during the nineteenth century acquired many features of a modern language.

During the first half of the nineteenth century, when the forces of nationalism could be felt throughout Europe and particularly in the Balkans, Jewish thinkers increasingly began to see nationalist solutions to the Jewish predicament. Yehudah Alkalai (1798–1878) a Bosnian Rabbi, was one of the first to adapt traditional Jewish messianism to something akin to a modern practical nationalism. He urged the establishment of a world organization of Jewry which would among other things encourage the settlement of Jews in Palestine. Zvi Hirsch Kalischer (1795–1874) put forward similar ideas. Their proposals, however, had little short-term impact because the active periods of both men coincided with an upsurge of liberalism in Central and Eastern Europe, during which time it was widely believed by 'enlightened' Jews that eventually Jews would be happily integrated into European society. But the ideas of Alkalai and Kalischer influenced the social atmosphere out of which both the Hibbat Tziyyon (Love of Zion) movement and political Zionism itself were to develop.

Hibbat Tziyyon was a loosely organized, largely middle-class and East European movement concerned both with the national cultural renaissance of the Jews and their settlement in Palestine. Although ideologues of the movement like Peretz Smolenskin (1842–85) and Eliezer Ben Yehudah (1857–1922) started formulating the ideology of the movement in the late 1870s, Hibbat Tziyyon received its main stimulus from the pogroms which followed the assassination of Tsar Alexander II in 1881. The wave of irrational Jew-hatred which ensued led many of the proponents of *Haskalah* to turn to the ideology of Hibbat Tziyyon and to abandon the notion that by becoming more and more 'enlightened' (which is to say more and more European) they could become integrated into Western society. The Bilu group, a student organization within Hibbat Tziyyon, was founded in 1881 with the aim of fostering 'the national–spiritual revival of the Jewish people in Syria and the land of Israel'. The first 'Zionist' settlers in Palestine belonged to the Bilu group. With an able ideologue in Leon Pinsker (1821–91), the author of the influential pamphlet *Autoemancipation* (1882) and a network of cells throughout Eastern Europe, Hibbat Tziyyon spread rapidly and was able to establish a number of agricultural 'colonies' in Palestine, none of which would have survived, however, without the financial support of Baron Edmond de Rothschild.

Jewish nationalism, with its roots in Jewish messianism, was particularly sensitive to utopian ideologies in its formative period. Tolstoyan socialism, the Russian *Narodniki* and Marxism all influenced its development. The pioneering ethos (*hehalutz*) which was created can be seen as a fusion of traditional Jewish values and nineteenth-century socialist ones. Not only did these tendencies establish enduring institutions of which the *kibbutz** and the *moshav* are the most obvious, but they also played a vital role in the ultimate success of Zionism in establishing a state.

Political Zionism

Theodor Herzl (1860–1904), a Viennese journalist and playwright, gave charismatic leadership to the awakening national aspirations of the Jews. In the 1890s Herzl was working in Paris where he was horrified by the implications of the Dreyfus Affair and French anti-semitism generally. He came to the conclusion that the Jewish problem could only be solved by the creation of a Jewish state. When Herzl published his treatise *Der Judenstaat* (The Jewish State) in 1896, young 'enlightened' Jews and members of Hibbat Tziyyon (a movement of whose existence Herzl was ignorant) acclaimed the book with such enthusiasm that Herzl found himself the head of a political movement, which he called the Zionist Movement. The policies of this movement were publicly expressed at the first Zionist Congress of 1897 which was evocatively billed as the 'National Assembly of the Jewish People'.

Until his death Herzl attempted by diplomatic means to secure a homeland for the Jews and to build up the financial and political resources of the Zionist Organization*. Although Ahad ha-Am (1856–1927), the most penetrating philosopher of the Jewish national movement, had warned in 1891 that the Arabs of Palestine* were both aware of and opposed to Jewish political designs on their territory, Herzl seems to have been ignorant of this and referred to Palestine as 'a land without a people for a people without a land'. But for Herzl the important thing was not that Palestine should be secured but rather that a homeland somewhere should be achieved, and as quickly as possible. This led him into conflict with the old Hibbat Tziyyon Zionists of Eastern Europe for whom it was unthinkable that the Jewish national home could be anywhere but the land of Israel. Various proposals to establish Jewish homelands in Cyprus, the Sinai and East Africa created serious divisions in the movement. Even before Herzl's death it was decided to concentrate exclusively on the acquisition of territory in Palestine. Within the first decade of its life Zionism had divided into three main tendencies: political Zionism, which maintained that the homeland would have to receive international sanction before large-scale colonization could take place; practical Zionism, which argued that immigration and the development of the land would encourage the community of nations to give the necessary support; and spiritual Zionism, as propounded by Ahad ha-Am, which saw the chief importance of the national home as a cultural centre which would act as a cultural and spiritual focus for the entire Diaspora. The creation of Mizrahi, the organization of orthodox religious Zionists, and Poalei Tziyyon (Workers of Zion), the first Socialist Zionist group, brought further diversity to the movement. Two of the early Zionist leaders, Chaim Weizmann* (1874–1952) and Nahum Sokolow (1859–1936), played an important role in persuading the British government to issue the Balfour Declaration* (1917), which promised the establishment of a Jewish national home in Palestine. Immediately after the First World War the Zionist Movement grew rapidly, although in 1917 the movement's largest single constituency – Russian Jewry – was effectively prevented from participating.

Oriental Jewry

There have been no indigenous movements parallel to the *Haskalah*, the Reform Movement and Zionism among the Jews of the Middle East. But from 1840 when a blood libel levelled at the Jews of Damascus (the 'Damascus Affair') brought the plight of Middle Eastern Jewry to the attention of Jews elsewhere, there were enhanced contacts and channels of communication linking eastern and western Jewries, through which flowed some of the ideas prevalent among Jews in Europe. Many scholars trace the origins of modern political Jewish nationalism to the attempts made by western Jews to bring assistance to their Syrian co-religionists in 1840. In 1860 the Alliance Israélite Universelle was founded in Paris. Its main brief was to provide assistance of all sorts to Jews living particularly in Asian and African countries. The alliance was responsible for establishing a network of schools throughout the Middle East and North Africa which brought a secular education and elements of French culture to generations of Jewish students. The acquisition of a secular education led some Jews to embrace Western concepts of nationalism. Thus small numbers of Jews in Algeria, Tunis and Egypt participated in local Zionist (as well as Arab nationalist) organizations. But the adoption of French culture by the Jewish educated classes led them increasingly to identify with the French and eventually after 1948 many of them preferred to settle in France rather than to emigrate to Israel with their less educated brethren.

TP

Further reading

M. Peli, *The Age of Haskalah* (Leiden, 1979)
D. Philipson, *The Reform Movement in Judaism* (New York, 1967)
J. S. Raisin, *The Haskalah Movement in Russia* (Philadelphia, 1913)
D. Vital, *The Origins of Zionism* (Oxford, 1975)

Christians in Muslim societies

The early centuries

When the religion of Islam first appeared, western Arabia had already been touched by Christianity in its Nestorian and Monophysite forms. On the north-eastern and north-western frontiers of the peninsula there were small states ruled by Arab dynasties which had become Christian; there were Christian merchants in Mecca; further south, in Yemen, there was an important Christian community in Najran which, after being persecuted by a ruler converted to Judaism, had had its position restored to some extent by the occupation of the country by the Christian King of Ethiopia (Axum).

The expansion of the new religion took place in countries where a majority of the inhabitants, or at least a large part of them, were Christians. In the Byzantine Empire* the Orthodox Church was supported by the imperial government, but most of the people of the provinces conquered by the Muslim armies belonged to churches which did not accept the teaching or authority of the Orthodox Church: Monophysite Copts in Egypt, Monophysites* or Nestorians* in Syria. In the Sasanid* Empire, which was incorporated as a whole into the Muslim caliphate, there was a large Christian population, much of it Nestorian. The liturgies and religious literature of these churches were expressed in the Coptic language in Egypt, in Syriac in Syria and further east.

In its first period, then, the Caliphate* was an Empire in which a small Muslim elite ruled a largely Christian population. The Christians in Arabia itself were either converted or obliged to leave, but elsewhere Christians had a status which was gradually formalized, on the basis of charters of protection such as that which the Caliph ʿUmar* was supposed to have given to the Patriarch of Jerusalem. Christians (and also Jews and Zoroastrians) were treated as 'protected people' (*ahl al-dhimma**); they were allowed to worship in their own way, and regulate their affairs through the authority of their own religious leaders, on condition of obedience to the Muslim rulers, and subject to payment of a special tax (*jizya**) and certain disabilities. In some ways, the position of most Christians may have improved, as Nestorians and Monophysites were now treated by the ruler as being on a level of equality with the Orthodox; the Nestorian Patriarch, indeed, was an important personage in the capital of the ʿAbbasid* Caliphs. In the early centuries, it took time for Islam to acquire a culture of its own, and the role of educated Christians was important. They served as officials of the Caliph's government; one of the great theologians of the Orthodox Church, St John of Damascus, belonged to a family which held office at the court of the Umayyads. Christian doctors were important both for their medical skill and because some of them translated works of Greek science and philosophy into Arabic during the period of reception of classical culture. Eastern Christian monasticism may have helped in the development of Islamic spirituality.

There was, however, a gradual process of conversion to Islam. The Caliphs appear on the whole to have upheld the system of protection, and so did the *ʿulama**, the scholars and legal specialists who created and preserved the fabric of Islamic thought and law; there must, however, have been local and temporary pressures and persecution. There were other reasons for conversion: attraction to the monotheism of Islam, or the desire to avoid paying the *jizya*, or to belong in the full sense to the community of the powerful and flourishing Muslim Empire. By the end of the eleventh century, the Christianity of North Africa seems to have disappeared completely; elsewhere, the proportion of Muslims in the population increased throughout the first centuries. Formal conversion was only a first step; it was linked with the adoption of Arabic (at least in the countries west of Iran), and led to the acceptance of Islamic culture.

From majority to minority

By the eleventh or twelfth century, Christians were becoming a minority in countries ruled by Muslims, and the process of conversion and expansion continued. The Christianity of Nubia in the upper valley of the Nile seems to have disappeared by the end of the fifteenth century. The extension of Turkish Muslim rule in Anatolia, first by the Seljuks* and then by the Ottomans*, led to the migration of Turks on a large scale, and also the conversion of many of the Greeks. Conversion may have been made easier by the spread of syncretist versions of Islam which might appeal to country-dwellers; down to modern times, shrines and religious lore common to Muslims and Christians continued to exist. Other Greeks remained under Turkish rule; so too did the Armenians*, after their Muslim conquerors absorbed their two kingdoms, that in north-eastern Anatolia* and that of Cilicia in the south.

There were other places where Christian and Muslim states were in conflict. In the far west of the Muslim world, the period of Almohad* rule in the twelfth century was one of pressure upon non-Muslims; later, the Christian reconquest of Spain affected the position of Muslims there, and they were finally expelled in the early seventeenth century. The formation of the Crusading states in Palestine and Syria at the end of the eleventh century had some impact upon the relationship of local Muslims and Christians; the Catholic ruling elite was not particularly favourable to Christians of the eastern Churches, but their position nevertheless improved, and one Christian community, the Maronites* in Lebanon, established relations with the papacy at this time, and accepted papal supremacy and Roman Catholic doctrine.

The establishment of a strong Sunni Muslim state in Egypt and Syria, first under the Ayyubids* and then under the Mamluks*, meant that from now onwards Muslim rule was unchallenged in countries where there was a large Christian population; there were episodes of pressure and violence, and Christians, their numbers shrinking, became more marginal to society. Further east, there was a moment when it seemed possible that the Ilkhanids*, the Mongol dynasty who seized power in Iran and southern Iraq in the thirteenth century, might be converted to Christianity, but by the beginning of the fourteenth they had chosen Islam.

In spite of difficulties, Christian spirituality and religious culture were still maintained, in particular in the great monasteries, such as the Syrian Orthodox monasteries of Dayr Zaʿfaran and Mar Matta. There were some considerable theologians, for example Michael the Syrian (1126–99), in the Syrian Orthodox Church. The Nestorian Church was still widespread in inner Asia and as far as China, until it was nearly destroyed by the conqueror Timurlane* in the fourteenth century. As time went on, however, the tradition of religious culture weakened, and this was linked with the disappearance of languages associated with eastern Christianity. Greek and Armenian continued to be used, but Coptic died out, both as a spoken language and as one of theology, and was used for liturgical purposes only; the last important literary work in Coptic was produced in the fourteenth century. Syriac dialects lingered on in southern Anatolia and northern Mesopotamia, but Syriac religious literature was greatly diminished, and was replaced by Arabic; the Syrian Orthodox historian Bar Hebraeus (1226–86) wrote with equal ability in both languages.

The Ottoman Empire

In 1453, the expansion of the Ottoman* Turks in Anatolia culminated in the occupation of Constantinople, which became their capital as Istanbul*; in 1516–17 they defeated the Mamluks and occupied Syria and Egypt; in 1571 they conquered Cyprus. Apart from Iran, all the countries of the Middle East where there were Christian communities were now under Ottoman rule. In some ways this brought a change for the better in the position of Christians. The Ottoman state was a Muslim state, but also one of mixed religions and nationalities. It maintained the protection of *ahl al-dhimma** which it had inherited from earlier Muslim dynasties, and which was enshrined in Islamic law, and it dealt with the Christian communities through their own religious authorities. The idea that, after the conquest of Constantinople, the Sultan organized the non-Muslims into communities coterminous with the Empire, and each under a single head, has been shown to be untrue. This did not take place until much later. The Orthodox patriarch of Constantinople and the Armenian archbishop of the city (who also took the title of patriarch later) had considerable authority because they were close to the Sultan and his government, but other patriarchs living in other places were also given formal recognition.

In some other respects the position of the Christians, or at least of some Christians, improved. The Empire was a large trading area, and this helped local manufacture of textiles and other goods, in some of which Christian craftsmen played a part. Maritime trade also increased between the Ottoman ports and those of southern and western Europe, and much of it was conducted by Greek merchants and shipowners. Syrian Christians also played an increasing role in trade between Syria and Egypt, and Armenian bankers provided financial services. To the east, in Iran, Armenians from the Caucasus, who were settled in Julfa, a suburb of Isfahan, by the Safavid* Shahs, had a dominant part in the export of Persian silk along a chain of market towns running through Anatolia to the Mediterranean ports.

One result of the growing contact with Europe was the revival of education in the Greek community. At the beginning of Ottoman rule it was at a low ebb: the only centres of high education were the Patriarchal Academy in Constantinople, a few local colleges, and a few of the monasteries of Mount Athos. In the seventeenth century, the ideas of the Reformation and Counter-Reformation found echoes among the Greeks. One of the patriarchs, Kyril Loukaris (1572–1638), was virtually a Calvinist. His activities precipitated a crisis in the Church, which led to his execution, and a series of councils which condemned his ideas and formulated the teaching of the Church, in a confession of faith to which was attached the name of Dositheos, patriarch of Jerusalem (1641–1707).

In the seventeenth century, some of the rich Greek merchant families living in the Phanar district of Istanbul began to send their sons to receive a new kind of education in Italian universities, particularly that of Padua in the Venetian Republic. They acquired a knowledge of medicine, and of Western European languages and conditions, which was valuable to the Sultan. In 1669 one of them became chief dragoman of the government, that is to say, interpreter and intermediary between the Sultan's ministers and the European ambassadors. Other important and lucrative posts later came into the hands of Greeks of the Phanar: those of dragoman of the navy, and governors of the two tributary provinces of Moldavia and Wallachia in what is now Rumania.

The consequences were far-reaching. The great Greek families became powerful in the Empire, and their influence enabled the patriarch of Constantinople to establish control over the other patriarchates of the Orthodox Church: those in the Balkans fell into abeyance, those of Antioch, Jerusalem and Alexandria became dependent on Constantinople. Greek influence also led to the issue, by the Ottoman Sultans in 1757, of a decree defining the rights of the various Churches in the Holy Places of Palestine; this has remained the basis of the *status quo* until today. An analogous process took place in the Armenian Church. The patriarch of Constantinople extended his power in the community; spiritual authority, however, lay with the two patriarchs of Echmiadzin and Sis, who had the title of 'Catholicos', while a fourth patriarch, in Jerusalem, had a place of honour.

Another important process was the extension of the influence of the Roman Catholic Church. After the end of the Crusades*, links between Rome and the Eastern churches grew weaker, although there were Dominican missions to the Nestorians and Armenians, and the Franciscans were recognized by the Mamluk Sultans as custodians of Christian Holy Places in Jerusalem. A serious attempt to re-establish contact began with the Counter-Reformation. Colleges were created in Rome to train priests of the Eastern churches: Greek, Armenian and Maronite colleges, and the college of the Congregation for the Propagation of the Faith. In the seventeenth century, the Jesuits, Dominicans and others joined the Franciscans in their presence among Eastern Christians.

One result of this activity was to create a class of priests knowing European languages as well as their own, and among them were some distinguished scholars, in particular the Maronite scholars of the Assemani family, who played an important part in the development of oriental scholarship in Europe. A further consequence was the emergence, within the various Eastern churches, of groups who recognized the authority of the pope, and who in the end were to break away and form separate Uniate Churches: Chaldaean, Greek, Armenian, Syrian, and Coptic Catholics.

With the spread of missions there came a development of monasticism on the Western European model. In the mountains of Lebanon*, where the authority of the Sultan* scarcely interfered with the rule of local families, some of them Christian, there were founded Greek and Armenian Catholic monasteries and those of Maronite monastic orders; the tradition of spiritual life and theological study was renewed in them. In the Armenian Church, an order of monks following the Benedictine rule was founded by Mekhitar (1676–1749). Driven out of the Empire by the hostility of the Armenian Orthodox, the Mekhitarists found refuge in Europe, where their great monasteries at Venice and Vienna became centres of Armenian scholarship, literature and printing.

The age of European expansion

The growth of Catholic missions was one of the signs of an expansion of the influence of European nations. From the seventeenth century onwards, the King of France was putting forward a claim to protect Christians in the Ottoman Empire, and by the end of the eighteenth century Russia had a similar claim to intervene in favour of the Orthodox. By the early nineteenth century the navies of Europe dominated the Mediterranean Sea, European ambassadors and consuls had a growing influence over the Sultan and his governors, and European manufactured goods were entering the Middle Eastern market on a large scale. The effects upon the position of the Christians were complex and far-reaching.

There was, first of all, a change in their legal position. Moved partly by European pressure, but also by their own view of what it was to be a strong, civilized state in the modern world, Ottoman Sultans and their ministers removed the legal disabilities from which non-Muslims had suffered. They were to have the same rights as Muslims in law, and in access to state education and positions; in practice their political and social inferiority was never wholly removed, but Christians did become ministers, high officials, and members of the Ottoman parliament when it was created in 1876. Their special status as communities (*millets*) was also recognized and regulated. In 1861 one part of the Empire which had a Christian majority, Lebanon, was given a privileged position, with a Christian governor. Similar changes took place in Egypt*, which, although remaining part of the Empire, was virtually autonomous under its own ruling family, and then under British control from 1882 onwards. Christians entered government service on a large scale, and two of them, the Armenian Boghos Nubar (1825–99) and the Copt Butrus Ghali (1846–1910), became prime ministers.

The changes in commerce and finance also worked in favour of some of the Christian communities. Those who had contact with European merchants and had acquired a knowledge of European languages were able to win positions as traders and financiers, either on their own account or as intermediaries between European companies and the markets of the interior. The great centres of international trade – Alexandria, Beirut, Izmir, Istanbul – were largely dominated by Europeans and by local Christian and Jewish merchants and bankers, living in a European fashion. Many of the local Christians were able to obtain European nationality, or at least protection by European consuls.

Linked with this change in economic life was a change in culture. Western religious missionaries were able to move more freely, and open schools: Catholic ones, using French as a language of instruction, Protestant, mainly English and American, and Russian Orthodox. The French Jesuit Université S. Joseph in Beirut and the American colleges in Istanbul and Beirut were centres of higher education. The Ottoman and Egyptian governments created networks of schools, in the first instance in order to train officials and officers, and so too did local religious communities; this was the period when the Coptic Church began to open itself to currents of change.

The effects were felt beyond the priesthood. A modern educated laity was created, and this included women as well as men, because the missionaries founded girls' schools. Modern education offered

Shafts of sunlight illuminating the Armenian cathedral of St James in Jerusalem

Greek Patriarch on his throne at the Patriarchate in Jerusalem

new opportunities for teachers, business men, doctors, lawyers and journalists. For a generation or more, Syrian and Lebanese Christian journalists and writers, both in Beirut and Cairo, were to play an important part in introducing to the Arabic-reading public some of the ideas and inventions of modern Europe and America. Butrus al-Bustani* (1819–83) and his family published the first Arabic encyclopedia, a compendium of what was known and thought by educated people in the Middle East in the late nineteenth century. Among the Armenians too there developed a secular literature, influenced by that of Europe and expressed in the modern language.

Among the dominant ideas of the nineteenth century was that of nationalism*: of states drawing their strength from a common consciousness and using it for national interests. This idea was to have more than one effect upon the Middle Eastern peoples. On the one hand, the reforming statesmen of the Ottoman Empire tried to propagate the idea of an 'Ottoman' nation which included all races and religious communities equally. On the other, some of the Christians were more deeply moved by the idea of a revival of their own communities, as separate nations in their own states, and of the culture bound up with their languages and churches. This idea was by no means universally held; it was opposed by many of the leaders of the communities, who wished to preserve the Empire, and by some of the religious authorities. It was strong enough, however, to give rise to movements aiming at national independence, with all their fateful consequences.

In 1821 there broke out a Greek national revolt which ended in the creation of an independent Greece. A large part of the Greek population remained in Istanbul and other parts of the Empire, but the symbiosis between Ottomans and Greeks had been shaken, and later events broke it. After the First World War, the attempt by the Greek government to rule part of Anatolia led to a Graeco-Turkish war which ended with a Turkish victory and an exchange of populations; thousands of years of Greek settlement in Anatolia came to an end, although the Orthodox patriarchate still remained in Istanbul.

The symbiosis between Turks and Armenians also broke down. Although Armenians of Istanbul had a strong position in the Ottoman Empire, violent action by Armenian nationalists towards the end of the nineteenth century led to a strong Ottoman reaction and a lasting hostility which culminated, during the First World War, in the widespread deportation and killing of Armenians, and the virtual end of Armenian life in Anatolia. The main Armenian communities in the Middle East were henceforth those of Lebanon, Syria and Iran.

The age of nation-states

After the disintegration of the Ottoman Empire at the end of the First World War, the Middle East entered a new phase of its political history, with control by Britain and France and the rise of movements to create national states. Both these factors affected the position of Christian communities. In the new state of Turkey, the small Greek, Armenian and other Christian groups which remained were marginal to the national community. In Iran too the Armenian and Nestorian Christians played little part in national life, but had a comparatively favourable position under Riza Shah* and his successor, with their tendency towards secularism. In some of the Arab countries, however, the role of Christians was more significant.

In Egypt, Coptic Christians formed some 10 per cent of the population; they included large landowners and merchants, government officials, and professional men and women. Copts were important in the main nationalist party, the Wafd*, which stood for national unity without religious distinctions; one of the most important of the leaders of the Wafd was a Copt, Makram ʿUbayd. The smaller Christian communities, mainly Syrian by origin, played little part in public life, but had a position of prosperity and high culture, until their numbers were diminished under the impact of a new kind of nationalism and a new economic order after the revolution of 1952.

In Syria, too, the Christians formed a considerable part of the population (some 10 per cent). The most important community was the Eastern Orthodox; although most of them were Arabic-speaking, the patriarch of Antioch, with his seat in Damascus, had been a Greek, until an Arab was appointed in the 1890s, partly because of Russian intervention with the Ottoman government. The Orthodox were fully a part of the national community, and some of them played a part in the nationalist movement, which took the form not so much of local territorial nationalism as of a movement for the creation of a united Arab nation. This posed a problem of identity for Arab Christians, since the idea of an Arab nation was linked with memories of what the Arabs had done in history, the creation of a Muslim society and culture; Christian nationalist thinkers advocated the creation of a secular Arab nation in which all could regard the Islamic past as having created their common cultural heritage.

In Palestine, the Christians, who formed some 12 per cent of the Arab population, were comparatively favoured during the period of the British Mandate*, but faced, together with Muslim Arabs, the danger posed by the growth of the Jewish population wishing to create a Jewish national state. The most prominent interpreter of Palestinian Arab nationalism to the English-speaking world, George Antonius (1891–1942), was a Christian. After the partition of Palestine in 1948, some Christians were prominent in the Palestinian national movement, but most of the educated professional and commercial class established themselves in Lebanon or the enlarged Kingdom of Jordan, where they formed an integral part of the national community. Those who remained in Israel*, or in the West Bank* under Israeli occupation after 1967, could not form part of a national community which was defined in Jewish national or religious terms. In Iraq, too, the position of the small Christian groups was somewhat marginal; in the 1930s there was a crisis of suspicion which led to the killing of some of the Assyrian Christians in the north.

There were two countries in which an attempt was made to create a symbiosis between Christian and Muslim communities. When Cyprus* became independent in 1960, the constitution provided that the president would belong to the Greek Orthodox community, which was in a majority, while the vice-president would be drawn from the Turkish Muslim minority, and the two communities would be represented in parliament and government positions. In Lebanon, the special regime which had existed since 1861 was developed under the French Mandate; Lebanon became a Republic with enlarged frontiers, and with a generally accepted political convention that the president should be a Christian from the largest community, the Maronites, while the prime minister should be a Sunni Muslim, and other political and administrative posts were distributed among the various communities. So long as the Mandate continued, the Christians, and particularly the Maronites and other Uniates, were in a favoured position. Links with France and the papacy were close, and some of the patriarchs of the eastern Uniate Churches became cardinals.

Foot washing ceremony of the Greek Orthodox Church, Jerusalem

After Lebanon became independent, the symbiosis continued for a generation, but in 1975 it broke down and civil war began; the reasons were more political and social than religious, but the conflict acquired religious overtones and geographical separation took place, although the leaders of the different communities continued to adhere formally to the idea of a multi-confessional state. In Cyprus, too, agreement between Greeks and Turks was ended when a military coup in 1974 led to an attempt to unite Cyprus with Greece; the Turkish army occupied the northern part of the island, and a separate Turkish Cypriot Republic was created *de facto*, although it had little international recognition. Here too, however, leaders of the two groups were formally committed to trying to restore a symbiosis on new bases.

In the 1970s the legal and social position of Christians came under threat from movements aiming to restore the domination of Islamic law. The Iranian Revolution* of 1979 changed the position of Christians in that country for the worse, and had repercussions in Lebanon, where Iranian help strengthened the religious element among the Shiʿis*, who had by now become the largest community in the country. In Egypt and Syria, the movement of the Muslim Brothers* was strong, and held out for Christians the prospect of returning once more to the position of a 'protected people'. In Sudan*, an attempt by the government to impose Islamic law on the whole country was one of the factors leading to a revival of armed opposition in the south, where the population was not Muslim, and much of it had been converted to Christianity by Catholic and Protestant missionaries.

AHH

Further reading

A. S. Atiya, *A History of Eastern Christianity* (London, 1968)
R. B. Betts, *Christians in the Arab East* (London, 1979)
B. Braude and B. Lewis, eds., *Christians and Jews in the Ottoman Empire*, 2 vols. (New York, 1982)
R. W. Bulliet, *Conversion to Islam in the Medieval Period* (Cambridge, Mass., 1979)
S. Runciman, *The Great Church in Captivity* (Cambridge, 1968)
C. J. Walker, *Armenia: the survival of a nation* (London, 1980)

Classical Arabic literature

Pre-Islamic literature

Poetry forms by far the largest body of so-called 'pre-Islamic'* literature, which has survived only in the compilations of medieval scholars and is therefore difficult to date and authenticate. Traditionally the poems were thought to span a period from about the sixth century AD to the first century of Islam and to have been composed orally and memorized verbatim through several generations. The objection that the poems may not be the product of the pagan beduin milieu but the work of medieval forgers and at best are unlikely to be the exact words of the poets, such as Imru'l-Qays, Labid or Shanfara to whom they are ascribed, has been countered by the argument that they should be seen as late specimens of an archaic poetic tradition which survived into the Islamic era. This theory does not solve the problem of how the poems were composed and by whom, of how far they reflect their environment, and of whether they represent the evolution or merely the fossilization of older poetic forms.

However, for the medieval urban men of letters who regarded beduin poetry as their classical heritage, its importance lay less in its precise date than in the values it embodied. It was thought to reflect a heroic age and to be written in the pure spoken Arabic of the peninsula (in fact its language is an artificial literary idiom); and it established a number of basic themes that were felt to be both quintessentially Arab and symbolic of all human experience. These were constantly referred to by later poets: love and nostalgia (the poet weeps over lost lovers and the deserted encampments that evoke them); resolve and endurance (he dismisses softer feelings and rides off on an arduous journey); manly exercises (war, revenge, the hunt, drinking and feasting); pride (the poet extols himself, his tribe or patron), chivalry, wisdom, the balance between man, nature and fate. The links between these themes or a selection of them as they occur in the longer, polythematic poems (*qasida*, pl. *qasa'id*) are often no more than implied: the poet, writing in the first person, does not tell a story, but juxtaposes complementary or contrasting episodes which depict a synthesis of exemplary experiences rather than individual experience. Archaic poetry is vividly descriptive, often containing bravura extended similes; it is concrete and non-introspective, but within these limits pieces range in compass from the primitive to the sophisticated. The main genres are the *qasida*, satire, and elegy, in which female poets excelled. The basic rhythmic structure of the metres is simple but capable of varied effects; the longest poems rarely exceed some eighty lines and most are much shorter. These technical features, together with the use of monorhyme, were carried over into later poetry, as was the important structural feature of substituting juxtaposition and association for expository narrative.

Early Islamic literature: poetry

Poetry cast in the archaic mould or with archaic features continued to be produced in the Umayyad period by poets such as Jarir and Farazdaq (both d. *c.*AD 728); but the seventh century also saw the rise of new types of poetry, the most important of which was a development of the 'love and nostalgia' motif, the love-lyric (*ghazal*); this, like the *qasida*, was to become a major source of themes and techniques for later poets. The two chief trends are that initiated by 'courtly' love-poets such as the semi-legendary Jamil (d.701), and the ironic variations on courtly themes produced by ʿUmar ibn Abi Rabiʿa (d. end seventh century). The development of *ghazal* seems to be closely linked to that of musical genres, and technical innovations common to both poets are the use of quick rhythms, the abandonment of word-painting as found in the *qasida*, and recourse to melodic patterning to underline or propel the argument of the poem. Jamil popularized the motif of the lovers physically sundered but spiritually united by fate, while ʿUmar subverts courtly conventions to serve the poetic persona of a philanderer; his condensed style relies on the hearer's ability to follow rapid transitions between a range of familiar poetic registers. Both poets accentuated the interplay between formal and thematic elements and so helped to lay the foundations of a new kind of verse which, as developed by early ʿAbbasid poets, was able to make increasing intellectual demands on its readers.

Development of prose

The end of the Umayyad period (mid-eighth century) also saw seminal developments in the field of prose. Though a native Arab tradition of oratory probably survived little altered into the Islamic era, the bureaucrats of the new Empire at first continued to use their own local languages, which left their mark on the earliest surviving works of Umayyad prose; these are 'courtesy books', which adapt the existing resources of Arab oratory to the needs of analytical exposition but take their subject-matter from the political wisdom-literature of the Near East and India. The authors of these didactic epistles, ʿAbd al-Hamid al-Katib (d. *c.*750) and Ibn al-Muqaffaʿ (d. *c.*756), the first a Syrian or Persian, the second of Persian extraction, both writing for political masters, were typical of the new civilization to which their own literary achievement contributed. From this period literary Arabic became the medium of a complex cosmopolitan culture, and 'Arabic' must accordingly be understood as a linguistic, not an ethnic, label, while 'literature' is to be taken in a broad sense. Writing now embraced a multitude of functions of which aesthetic gratification was sometimes a determinant and sometimes a byproduct. *Adab* ('polite literature') was the term often generally applied to all works of whatever form in which moral, political and cultural issues were addressed, whether by way of compilation or analysis and original thought and expression; its use corresponded to the belief that civilization (*adab* also has the sense of manners, decency) is incremental, that humane values can only be developed if they are first preserved and propagated in writing, and that all scholarly and creative endeavour pursues this end. The task which writers of the eighth to tenth centuries especially saw as their business was that of integrating Arab-Muslim civilization into world civilization and of defining its distinctive features by the scholarly process of recovering the Arab past, its poetry and lore, and setting it against the non-Arab heritage, and by an exploration of the intrinsic limits of Muslim doctrine through the medium of legal, historical, exegetic, philosophical and mystical research.

The background against which this task was undertaken was a succession of radical political changes and religious reorientations, vicissitudes which creative and scholarly writing both mirror and attempt to compensate for, and under whose stimulus imaginative and analytical processes received equal impetus. Frequently the two processes are not only coexistent but indistinguishable; thus, in format, most of the works of the two greatest ʿAbbasid prose writers, Jahiz (d.868–9) and Tawhidi (d.1023), are analytical compilations of general cultural material from secondary sources; yet both authors – Jahiz the ironic but unruffled rationalist, Tawhidi the complex yet naive and baffled seeker after religious and intellectual serenity – are unmistakable originals. A further example of the deceptiveness of medieval literary forms and motifs can be seen in the way an apparently non-committal juxtaposition of sources by the historian and exegete Tabari (d.923) masks his interpretative thrust, while the reworking of the same sources by devotional writers transforms them into homiletic fables made colourful by expansion of their fantastic elements, and affecting by a combination of the techniques of popular preaching and orthodox spiritual exercises. This interpenetration of literary and popular narrative is the basis of a new literary form, the *maqama*. As initiated by Hamadhani (d.1008), the genre consists of a sequence of picaresque episodes linked only by the recurrence of a protean rogue-hero and his stooge. Some of the episodes are scenes from everyday life, others are fantastic, and sometimes the two modes are combined in a single episode; the medium in which they are related is *sajʿ*, the pompous rhyming chancellery prose which evolved out of the style of the Umayyad epistolographers. Hamadhani's *maqamat* parody existing narrative modes and the assumptions that underlie them; they are stories without a moral, in which character is presented as the meeting-place of transient relationships and style and matter are in deliberate conflict; they unite a gusto for human foibles reminiscent of Jahiz with a nihilism unprecedented in prose and only paralleled in some of the poetry of the period.

Early ʿAbbasid poetry

A number of early ʿAbbasid poets had turned their backs on the beduin heritage and broached new themes, using techniques foreshadowed by Umayyad lyric poets. Abu al-ʿAtahiya (d. *c.*825) wrote devotional verse (*zuhd*) which marries the negativity of contemporary ascetic themes to the emotive melodic devices of *ghazal*; Abu Nuwas's (d. *c.*815) wine-poetry (*khamriyya*) initiates an absurdist trend, using ironic shifts of register to pose the dilemma of man come of age and equally unable to find fulfilment in conformism or the exercise of free will; his verse derives its dialectic from the tension between the precision of its formulation and the irresolution of its message. Another poetic development of the period was mannerism (*badiʿ*). In an age of eclectic culture, the tug of classical ideals was nonetheless strong; by casting the now unreal clichés of the *qasida* – now consecrated to panegyric and the professional poet's chief breadwinner – into language replete with tropes and startling metaphors, Abu Tammam (d.845) did more than give heroic epithets an up-to-date ring; he also pushed the exploration of the relationship between the 'truth' of a poet's vision and the manner of its expression to extreme limits – and thereby more than any other poet stimulated the development of analytical literary criticism. The wider structural possibilities of a rhetoric based on paradox were exploited by Mutanabbi (d.965); where critics had condemned Abu Tammam as unduly cerebral, they fully acknowledged the emotional force – though not, perhaps, the pessimism – of Mutanabbi's verse, and his prestige confirmed the now irreversible identification of poetic diction with *badiʿ*. *Badiʿ* eventually found its way, via *sajʿ*, into prose, where it provided epistolographers with a vehicle parallel in both workmanship and function to the *qasida*; its more ludicrous applications were mocked in Hamadhani's *maqamat*, while on the pen of Tawhidi it reveals itself capable of effects as diverse as lampoon and mystical rapture. But *badiʿ* did not dominate prose as it did poetry; naturalistic prose which reproduces the rhythms of conversation, paints scenes, analyses relationships, is found in the stories – cast in the interchangeable forms of 'reminiscences' and exemplar – of Tanukhi (d.994) and in the acute political observation of the historian Miskawayh (d.1030).

Late ʿAbbasid poetry

The late ʿAbbasid period, in parallel with the growth of scholastic philosophy, also saw the flowering and formalization of mysticism and mystical poetry, which drew on all the devices made available by *badiʿ* and by the proliferation of poetic genres; one such genre which reached its peak during this period was strophic lyrical verse with multiple rhymes; archaic in origin, it developed contemporaneously with formal (that is, monorhyme) poetry. In Spain and the Maghrib the *muwashshah* (in classical Arabic) and the *zajal* (in colloquial Arabic) enjoyed critical esteem, though not of the same order as that accorded to 'formal' poetry; the *muwashshah* later had considerable vogue in Egypt and Syria. We also have records of genuinely popular, as opposed to 'informal', lyric poetry for this and earlier periods.

Later Arabic literature

Little studied, the succeeding periods of Arabic literature are often dismissed as an 'age of decadence'; but they saw the consolidation of at least two major forms. Popular prose epics, first referred to in the twelfth century, though much older in origin, recount the knightly adventures of tribal heroes and heroines in their encounters with Muslim and pagan rulers and Crusaders, in semi-classical Arabic laced with borrowings from 'high' literature in the shape of verse inserts and *sajʿ*. *The Thousand and One Nights* (*ʾAlf layla wa layla*), which seem to have crystallized in their present form in Mamluk Egypt, go back at least to pre-Islamic Persia but are, despite their ancestry, a more thoroughly Islamicized folk-form than the epic, reminiscent in many ways of ʿAbbasid homiletic narratives. Post-ʿAbbasid historiography* produced not only the work of the historical philosopher Ibn Khaldun (d.1406), but also many of the great biographical dictionaries and local chronicles, containing much material from earlier sources, on which modern research relies; besides their documentary value, they are of interest to narratologists.

Classical Arabic literature, with its characteristic capacity to explore and develop the implications of form and formulas and its reliance on a highly practised audience, might seem to have little in common with modern Arabic writing, which draws on Western models; but it is at least arguable that its influence persists in some areas, such as the tendency in recent prose to present character serially and to depict the individual as a nexus of external relationships. Both of these are devices reminiscent of the Hamadhanian *maqama* and legacies of a complex of intellectual traditions which underlay the civilization of 'classical' (ʿAbbasid) Islam and still inform major aspects of popular culture.

JA

Further reading

G. J. H. van Gelder, *Beyond the Line* (Leiden, 1982) (poetic criticism)
H. A. R. Gibb, *Arabic Literature* (Oxford, 1963)
A. Hamori, *On the Art of Medieval Arabic Literature* (Princeton, 1974)
Sir Charles Lyall, *Translations of Ancient Arabic Poetry* (London, 1885)

Modern Arabic literature

Modern Arabic literature has developed out of the encounter in the nineteenth and twentieth centuries between the older indigenous literary traditions and Western culture and literature; in this it resembles other modern non-Western literatures. In the early nineteenth century, when the West began its economic, political and cultural penetration of the Arab world, Arabic literary activity flowed in two channels. The poetry and prose forms of medieval Arabic literature still retained their prestige but, except in Iraq, had lost their vitality. Literary creativity found an outlet in popular, often oral, poetry and prose.

Revival in prose

The first signs of literary revival occurred in prose. In Egypt the government-sponsored programme of translations of European technical and scientific manuals begun by Muhammad ʿAli* required a new, efficient prose style and a vocabulary capable of conveying modern scientific information. In Syria and Lebanon Christians who had had direct contact with the West undertook a revival of classical Arabic, adapting it to the needs of their contemporaries and forging a language to express modern concepts simply, directly and precisely; this prose became the medium of the press which rapidly developed after 1860 in Beirut and then Cairo. The rise of the press* was of incalculable importance in stimulating literary activity; in the nineteenth century, and also later, it was mainly through cultural magazines, weeklies and even daily papers that writers succeeded in reaching an audience for the first time and creating a public for new literary forms.

Development of modern poetry

In poetry, where the hold of tradition was far stronger, the revival began with a return to the great masters of the ʿAbbasid period, following whose example poets learned to compose vigorous, effective and linguistically correct poetry. A number of the most famous modern Arab poets wrote in this neo-classical style, among them the Egyptian Ahmad Shawqi (1869–1932) and the Iraqi Maʿruf al-Rusafi (1875–1945); these poets and their contemporaries in Egypt, Iraq and Syria succeeded in re-establishing poetry as a vehicle for expressing the concerns of public life, especially the awakening national consciousness. The precursor of a new approach to poetry, the Syro-Egyptian Khalil Mutran (1872–1949), deserves mention for his introduction of the genre of the narrative poem into Arabic literature. While the next generation of poets from the 1920s onwards looked to European Romantics and Symbolists for their models, Syro-Lebanese immigrants to North America (known with their South American colleagues as the *mahjar* poets) embarked on radical experiments in prose poetry, into which they integrated a new responsiveness to nature and a visionary stance. Jibran Kahlil Dibran (1883–1931) (also known in English as Khalil Gibran) is the most famous of this group. The *mahjar* had a limited influence, however, and it was only in the 1940s that formal changes which have since gained wide acceptance were introduced by the Iraqis Badr Shakir al-Sayyab (1926–64) and Nazik al-Malaʾika (b.1923). The free verse form they developed retains the verse foot of classical Arabic metrics but uses it in lines of unequal length, while rhyme is employed irregularly. This and other innovations emancipated Arabic poetry from what poets had come to experience as the strait-jacket of traditional form. Tone and subject matter changed too; since the Second World War Arabic poetry has spoken increasingly of alienation and rebellion, frustration, the rejection of social and political injustice and the search for new values. It tends to reflect the poet's subjectivity and often betrays an explicit political commitment, as with the Egyptian Salah ʿAbd al-Sabur (1931–82), the Iraqi ʿAbd al-Wahhab al-Bayyati (b.1926) and the poets of the Palestinian resistance, best-known of whom is Mahmud Darwish (b.1941). Symbolism and other literary movements have enriched contemporary Arabic poetry, and the use of myth and extended imagery has become widespread. Extreme intellectualism and even obscurity have marred the later work of some leading poets, but a reaction against this can be expected. Arabic poetry now exhibits a range of possibilities in form, theme, diction and imagery unparalleled in earlier periods.

Development of prose

The beginning of the revival in prose literature saw an attempt by a few writers to adapt the *maqama** form to modern themes but this proved unworkable. Although the press published translations and adaptations of European novels and short stories, fiction not clad in rhymed prose was for long dismissed as mere entertainment. Jurji Zaydan's (1861–1914) historical novels with their didactic aim and al-Manfaluti's (1876–1924) extremely sentimental short stories did much to acclimatize these new genres in Arabic, and the appearance of *Zaynab* by the Egyptian M. H. Haykal (1913) and the early short stories of the *mahjar* writer Mikhaʾil Nuʿayma (from 1913 on) mark the beginning of the Arabic novel and short story respectively. In Egypt the inter-war period saw the publication of novels on the theme of the relationship between the intellectual and society, short stories exploring individual psychology and social injustice, and the autobiographies of some prominent intellectuals, such as Taha Husayn's three-volume *The Days* (1926, 1939, 1972). Since the forties fiction has become generally recognized as a serious literary form in the Arab world. Trends have emerged, such as socialist realism (in Egypt, Iraq and to some extent Syria during the 1950s and 60s), existentialism (especially in Lebanon), and a more philosophical and abstract mode, as represented in the later work of the leading Egyptian novelist, Najib al-Mahfuz (b.1911). The use of experimental techniques was pioneered in the 1960s especially by the Syrian surrealist Zakariyya Tamir (b.1931), and younger writers are also turning to the indigenous Arabic narrative heritage for themes and forms through which to criticize contemporary society indirectly or expose its absurdity. The need to choose between literary Arabic and dialect, a problem which bedevilled fiction (and even more drama) in the early days, seems now to pose less of a dilemma, the purist stance which rejected the use of dialect under any circumstances yielding to a more flexible attitude.

Drama

Drama, another import from the West, first established itself in Egypt, where Tawfiq al-Hakim* (b.1898) demonstrated its possibilities for exploring philosophical and contemporary themes. After the revolution of 1952 a number of gifted writers emerged, treating contemporary and historical subjects in a variety of modes. In other Arab countries drama has developed more recently; probably the most accomplished dramatist is the Syrian Sa'd Allah Wannus (b.1941), who applies avant-garde techniques to subjects drawn from Arab history and folklore.

Literary criticism, an indispensable aid to the development of literature, has acquired recognition as a serious scholarly activity, and at least one journal, the Egyptian *Fusul*, is entirely devoted to it.

The elite forms of literature were for long a male preserve, but since the 1940s women have made an important contribution, first in poetry and then as writers of the novel and short story.

North Africa and other regions

Since the 1960s, areas of the Arab world which had not previously contributed significantly to literary developments have begun to produce writers whose reputation has spread beyond their own country. Sudan, remote from traditional centres of Arab culture, has witnessed the emergence of poets, critics and a writer of novels and short stories, al-Tayyib Salih, who is internationally known. North Africa was for long dominated by French culture, although even in the colonial period Tunisia produced one of the greatest Romantic poets in Arabic, Abu'l-Qasim al-Shabbi (1909–34). Now both Tunisia and Morocco can boast a significant number of writers in Arabic, especially of fiction; Tunis is also a centre of drama. The Arabian peninsula, too, is beginning to make its voice heard as a new generation adopts the forms current among fellow Arab writers. Each of these regional traditions, however, retains its own specific flavour, and thus the spectrum of modern Arabic literature is becoming increasingly varied.

HK

Further reading

Roger Allen, *The Arabic Novel: an historical and critical introduction* (Manchester, 1982).
M. M. Badawi, *A Critical Introduction to Modern Arabic Poetry* (Cambridge, 1975)
I. J. Boullata, tr., *Modern Arabic Poets* (London, 1976)
D. Johnson Davies, tr., *Modern Arabic Short Stories* (London, 1976)
S. K. Jayyusi, *Trends and Movements in Modern Arabic Poetry* (Leiden, 1977), 2 vols.
M. Manzaloui, ed., *Arabic Writing Today: the short story* (Cairo, 1968)

Note: A number of translations of modern Arabic prose and poetry have appeared, especially in Heinemann's Arab Authors Series

Classical Turkish literature

The Ottoman period: folk and court traditions

The Oghuz* Turks entering Asia Minor between the ninth and thirteenth centuries brought with them a rich oral literature whose origins lay in the nomadic and shamanistic culture of Central Asia, but which already bore the imprint of the Islamic faith they had embraced. It continued to flourish among the masses, largely ignored by intellectuals until this century.

Using a Turkish reasonably free of borrowings, the folk literature perpetuates the old Turkic traditions of genre, metre, rhyme and embellishment. Strong in both prose and poetry, it serves as a source of entertainment, but is at the same time a vehicle for religious teaching and a safety valve for the outpouring of personal or collective emotions. It boasts a large corpus of proverbs and riddles. Myths and fables, legends, tales and epic narratives capture the life of the Oghuz from Central Asia to the Middle East and Turkey-in-Europe, reflecting age-old beliefs and customs as well as more recent accretions. The *Book of Dede Korkut*, a collection of chivalrous epic tales, and the adventures of the hero-bandit Köroglu, are the best known.

The Turks have a special predilection for short anecdotes. Structured with the utmost economy of expression and giving full force to the punchline, these may depict a social type, such as the Bektashi dervish or a single figure such as the, reputedly, thirteenth-century Nasreddin Hoca. They are filled with folk wisdom and well-directed jibes at human foibles and official iniquities. Moral and social issues are also dealt with dramatically through the medium of puppets (*kukla*), shadow plays (*karagöz*), and the *Orta oyunu* ('Theatre in the round') folk-theatre, as well as in the presentations of story-tellers (*meddah*).

Popular poetry

Folk poetry, usually sung to musical accompaniment, is a vehicle for both secular and religious expression. The metre of it, like that of English poetry, is syllabic; the Turks call it *parmak hesabı*, 'finger-count'. Rhyme is bound by no rigorous rules, often being replaced by assonance. The main genres of folk poetry are the *mani*, or four lines of seven syllables, rhyming AABA or ABCB, or of five lines rhyming ABACA; and the *koşma*, with many variants on the basic form, which has three stanzas, each of five lines of eleven syllables, rhyming ABAB CCCB DDDB.

Some of it, composed by unknown poets, is part of the true folkloric tradition. The rest is attributed to known poets, many of them wandering minstrels (*aşık*). Yunus Emre (d.1321), schooled in both folk and scholarly traditions, the paramount figure of Turkish mystic humanism, used colloquial Turkish to express his impassioned oneness with the Divine. Many poets felt his influence, but none achieved his force and lyricism. Later religious poets include the founder of the Bayrami order, Hacı Bayram Veli (d.1429) and his disciple Eşrefoglu Rumi (d.1469); the Bektashis Kaygusuz Abdal (fifteenth century) and Hasan Dede (fifteenth–sixteenth century); and Pir Sultan Abdal (sixteenth century) of Sivas, whose lines vibrate with social and political protest.

Popular among both sedentary and nomadic groups and frequently found with the armies on campaign, the wandering minstrels sing of love and heroism, bemoan protracted absence from home, and often blend longing for the beloved they left behind with nostalgic description of the natural beauty of their homeland. In their elegies (*ağit*), love mingles with sorrow, and heroic defiance heightens the satire with which they belittle their enemies. Most famous are Köroğlu and Öksüz Dede (sixteenth century), Kayıkçı Kul Mustafa and Karacaoğlan (seventeenth century), Aşık Ömer and Gevheri (eighteenth century), Dertli, Bayburtlu Zihni, Erzurumlu Emrah, Seyrani and Dadaloğlu (nineteenth century), and in this century Aşık Veysel (d.1973).

The beginnings of written literature

As for a written literature in Oghuz Turkish, it is uncertain when and where this began. The Seljuks of Rum adhered to Persian culture and patronized Persian literature. A written literature in Oghuz Turkish developed in Anatolia, therefore, only with the post-Mongol rise of the Oghuz *beyliks**. Court patronage sustained it. First the Germiyans and other *beylik* leaders, then Ottoman sultans, princes and statesmen gathered scholars and poets round them; and, in addition to the Ottoman capitals of Bursa, Edirne, and Constantinople*, several provincial towns became centres of learning and culture. Arabic continued to be used among the *medrese**-educated class for religious writing, and many Ottomans composed poetry in Persian. At the same time, the new Turkish literature was based on Arabo-Persian tradition, adopting its genres, themes, metre and rhyme systems, symbolism and metaphor. It was strongest in poetry, with verse the accepted medium for all kinds of writing. The metrical system was *aruz* (the Arabic *ʿarūd*), which was quite unlike the 'finger-count' of folk poetry, being based on the variation between long and short syllables, as in Latin prosody.

Initially the literary language remained close to the spoken. Lack of long vowels, however, made it difficult to write Turkish poetry in the quantitative *aruz* metre, and derogators claimed that it lacked refinement of expression. In spite, therefore, of some attempts to maintain the integrity of Turkish, extensive borrowings were made from Arabic and Persian (the Arabic mostly via Persian). The resulting literary language was comprehensible only to a limited circle, reinforcing a dichotomy between folk (*halk*) and court (*divan*) literature. Though 'court literature' is a fair equivalent of the Turkish *divan edebiyatı*, it is not a literal translation, *divan* being used here not in its sense of 'court' but in the sense of 'the collected works of a classical poet'. Since members of the mystic orders and other religious denominations were among the few who used both styles, scholars frequently place them in a third category, designated religious (*tekke*).

Powerful religious currents influenced early court literature, and poets experimented with most verse forms, at first producing translations and adaptations, the latter sometimes incorporating additions of special Turkish interest. A general didacticism contrasts with the élan of poets like Yunus Emre, Nesimî (d. *c.*1409) and Kadı Burhaneddin (d.1398), the last two including Turkish *tuyugs* in their *divans*. Important works of the early fifteenth century include Süleyman Celebi's *Mevlit* (Birthsong of the Prophet), and Şeyhî's satirical *Harname* (Book of the Ass).

The flowering of poetry

The fifteenth and sixteenth centuries brought poetry to its peak. Abstraction, mystic symbolism and conventional metaphors restricted freedom of expression, and artistic perfection rated higher than originality. Yet great vitality and freshness was achieved by the leading poets: Aşık Paşa (d.1494), Mesihî (d.1512), Necatî (d.1509), Zatî (d.1546), Hayalî (d.1557) and Bakî (d.1600), master of the *gazel* and author of a moving elegy on Süleyman I. Fuzulî (d.1556) usually is ranked superior to all. His masterpiece is a *mesnevi* that carries the story of Leylâ and Mecnun to new heights of human and mystic love. The only important *mesnevi* subsequently was *Hüsn ü Aşk* by Seyh Galip (d.1799).

Nef'î (d.1635) is known for his biting satire, and represents the neo-Persianism fashionable in the seventeenth century. This movement took *divan* poetry to new extremes of aesthetic preciosity that blinded Ottomans, for the time being, to the possibility of new directions. Nedim (d.1730) brought a breath of light-heartedness with *şarkıs* (songs, mainly love poems) that epitomize the mood of the Tulip Age, and Nabi's *Hayriye* (1701), a *mesnevi* (poem in rhymed couplets) giving counsel to his son Ebülhayr, includes vivid scenes of an Ottoman society at its point of decline. Neither poet attracted a strong following, and *divan* literature waited a century before meeting a real challenge.

Development of prose

As for prose, it was regarded as secondary to verse as a vehicle of expression and was little used at first. Subsequently, rhymed prose (*seci*, Ar. *sajʿ*) was developed. Like poetry, this was taken to extravagant limits by writers like Veysî (d.1628) and Nergisî (d.1634). Outstanding works exist, however, in several fields. The most important is historiography, and names include Aşıkpaşazade (d.1502), Neşrî (fifteenth century), Lütfî Paşa (d.1563), Âlî (d.1599), Peçevî (d. *c.*1649), Silâhtar Mehmet (d.1724) and Naîmâ (d.1716). In geography and travel literature we may mention *Seyahat-Name* (Travel Book) of Evliya Çelebi (d.1682) and *Cihannüma* (World View), an encyclopaedic compilation of geographical knowledge by Kâtip Çelebi (or Hacı Halifi; d.1657). He also prepared a bibliography of Arabic, Persian and Turkish works by his contemporaries, *Keşfü 'z-Zünun* . . . (Survey of Thoughts . . .), still invaluable to scholars. Among biographies of poets the best-known are the sixteenth-century works of Sehi, Latifî, Aşik Çelebi and Kınalızade Hasan Çelebi. Later there are several unique treatises (*risale*) and reports on the state of the Empire and modernization by Koçi Bey (seventeenth century), Yirmisekiz Mehmet Çelebi (d. 1732), and Ibrahim Müteferrika (d. 1748).

Modern Turkish literature

The challenge to court literature came around 1860 with a movement led by Şinasi (1826–71), Namık Kemal (1840–88) and Ziya Paşa (1825–80). Known as *Tanzimatçılar* (men of the *tanzimat*) or the *Tasvir-i Efkâr* School (from the journal that Şinasi helped to found), these men were products of the modernization process begun a century earlier, therefore familiar with European literature and ideology. Not subscribing to the principle of art for art's sake, they sought to make literature a vital social and political force. Working first through translation and adaption, especially from the French, the school introduced Western-style poetry and short stories. Şinasi produced the first modern drama, Namık Kemal the first real novel, and both were active journalists. They wrote 'for the people', teaching the concepts of freedom, justice, fatherland, nation, sovereignty and constitution. Such activism brought them, and other Young Ottomans, years of exile in Europe, from where their writing was smuggled into the Ottoman Empire. Younger members of the group, such as Abdülhak Hâmit Tarhan (1852–1937), Recaizade Mahmut Ekrem (1847–1914) and Sami Paşazade Sezai (1860–1936) applied artistic aims more vigorously, introducing additional European genres.

The reformers believed that literature should use a language the people could understand, and they effected some simplification of Turkish. The process was reversed in the nineties, however, with new emphasis on artistic perfection by Tevfik Fikret (1867–1915), Cenap Şahabettin (1870–1934), Halit Ziya Uşaklıgil (1866–1945) and others. Grouped round the journal *Servet-i Fünun* (Treasure of Science), this generation was under the censorship of the Abdülhamid regime, but bitter poems such as *Sis* (Fog) by Tevfik Fikret, circulated underground.

The new literature raised the question of national identity. Influenced by French romanticism, Namık Kemal's *Vatan* (Fatherland) and other historical plays by Abdülhak Hâmit highlight Muslim allegiance. Some writers referred to Ottomanism, but few demonstrated feelings of Turkishness until, in 1898, Mehmet Emin Yurdakul (1869–1944) published poems in the folk syllabic metre and proclaimed, 'I am a Turk'.

The search for national identity and language reform have continued in this century, their paths often merging. From 1932 onward, the Turkish Language Society waged a campaign 'to free Turkish from the yoke of Arabic and Turkish', to such effect that fewer and fewer Turks could read, without special training, the Turkish of fifty years before, quite apart from the fact that the replacement in 1928 of the Arabo-Persian alphabet by the Latin alphabet had put Ottoman literature out of popular reach. The campaign was ended in 1980, but the changes already introduced were irreversible. Nevertheless, the continuity of literature was maintained by writers schooled in the older language, side by side with younger writers who took their models from English and French literature.

Many writers, including the Pan-Turkist Ziya Gökalp (1875–1924), have taken themes from the old Turkic material. Many have equated Turkishness with use of the syllabic metre. Moreover, the desire to stand as one nation has made the villager and the 'little man' of the town important figures in all genres.

Modern short stories and novels reflect the Turks' ancient love for story-telling, and both genres have produced masters. The novel has developed from romanticism to stream-of-consciousness writing, and Halide Edip Adıvar (1844–1964), Yakup Kadri Karaosmanoğlu (1889–1974) and Reşat Nuri Güntekin (1892–1956) were popular writers. Yaşar Kemal (b.1922) is famed worldwide for his novels about life in south-east Turkey, and Adalet Ağaoğlu (b.1929) is gaining great attention with her novels analysing Turkish life in the light of her own experiences. The first short stories were weakly constructed and ponderous. Those of Ömer Seyfeddin (1884–1920), however, marked a great development. Sait Faik Abasıyanık (1907–54) concentrated on city life while Kemal Tahir (1910–73), Orhan Kemal (1914–71) and Samim Kocagöz (b.1916) – in addition to Yaşar Kemal – portrayed village life. The greatest and most admired recent writer of short stories was Haldun Taner (1916–86). Aziz Nesin (b.1915) is the master of satire.

The short-lived *Fecr-i Âti* (Dawn of the Future; 1908) was the last School to follow the old style of poetry. Ahmet Haşim (1884–1933) the great twentieth-century symbolist, one of its members, continued to use *aruz* in his colourful poems. So, too, did Yahya Kemal Beyatlı (1885–1933), a neo-classicist whose nostalgic verses reflect both Ottoman and French influence, while Mehmet Âkif Ersoy (1873–1936), the 'Poet of Islam', coupled *aruz* with everyday Turkish.

Two outstanding contemporary poets have been *sui generis* figures: Nazım Hikmet Ran (1902–63) and Fazıl Hüsnü Dağlarca (b.1914). The former's earliest poems were in syllabic metre. Later, while in Russia, he fell under the influence of Mayakovsky and turned to free verse. Written in colloquial Turkish, his verse often reflects his Marxist attachments and is filled with protest. His best works are vital and full of musicality. They include his monumental *Memleketimden İnsan Manzaraları* (Human Landscapes from my Country) and touching poems about his family. Dağlarca too is a protestor. Like many other writers, he took his early inspiration from the War of Independence, then turned his critical eye to the national causes of other nations, demanding action on their behalf.

For the rest, some Turkish poet has always caught the mood of a new movement – from free verse and poetic realism to surrealism and obscurantism – and found it matched his own. We may mention Orhan Veli Kanık (1914–50), Oktay Rifat (b.1914) and Melih Cevdet Anday (b.1915), Salih Birsel (b.1919), İlhan Berk (b.1916), Edip Cansever (b.1928) and Asaf Çelebi (1907–58). Drama also has turned to the West for much of its technique, and many foreign plays are performed in Turkish theatres. Turkish playwrights' main strength, however, continues to be that they take many of their themes from their local environment.

KB

Mosque interior, Turkey

Further reading

E. J. W. Gibb, *A History of Ottoman Poetry* (London, 1900–9), 6 vols.
T. S. Halman, *The Humanist Poetry of Yunus Emre* (Istanbul, 1976)
T. S. Halman, ed., *Contemporary Turkish Literature: fiction and poetry* (London, 1982)
S. Huri, tr. with introduction by Alessio Bombaci, *Leyla and Mejnun of Fuzuli* (London, 1970)
G. Lewis, *The Book of Dede Korkut* (Harmondsworth, 1974)
G. Lewis, *The Present State of the Turkish Language* (London, 1987)
N. Menemencioglu, ed. in collaboration with Fahir Iz, *The Penguin Book of Turkish Verse* (Harmondsworth, 1978)
Review of National Literatures, vol. IV/1 (Spring 1973), *Turkey: From Empire to Nation*. Special editor, T. S. Halman
W. S. Walker and A. E. Uysal, *Tales Alive in Turkey* (Cambridge, Mass., 1966)

Classical Persian literature

Persian, in the broadest sense of the word, includes the language of the Achaemenian* cuneiform and the Pahlavi* texts of the Zoroastrians*, as well as the language of present-day Iran. In terms of time and geographical dispersion, therefore, it has a long and complex history. It has served, in some stages in its history, as the main literary medium at courts as widespread as those in the Indian sub-continent and Anatolia. It has influenced, and itself come under the influence of, other cultures and languages of the region, notably Arabic and Turkish. But in spite of the vicissitudes of its history, it has developed a cohesive and yet malleable tradition capable of producing masterpieces as diverse as Firdawsi's epic, *Shah-Name* (*The Book of Kings*) and Hafiz's lyrical poetry.

Old Iranian, from which Modern Persian is ultimately derived, belongs to the Indo-Iranian branch of the Indo-European languages. It includes two major languages, Old Persian* and Avestan*, the latter containing the earliest religious texts of the Zoroastrians. The cuneiform of the Achaemenians is all the written evidence we have in Old Persian although its cultural legacy is not limited to it. Evidence from Zoroastrian religious literature as well as external information from Greek historians points to the existence of a tradition of oral heroic poetry which survived into later periods and proved of crucial importance in the formation of Persian literature after the rise of Islam.

The sources available for the study of Middle Persian*, the language of the Sasanian* court (*c.*225–651) are more substantial but no less problematic. The Middle Persian language itself survived among communities of Zoroastrians in Iran in the three centuries after the Arab invasion (the first half of the seventh century). But, as a community on the defensive, their main concern was the preservation of the old religion and their output was mainly religious and didactic. Nevertheless, the existence of a strong tradition of oral poetry and a general literature of entertainment is beyond dispute, although its significance can be studied (apart from a few isolated texts) only through its refraction in the later literature in Arabic and Persian. Its heritage provided the poets and writers of Islamic Iran with a strong sense of the past and with a wealth of ideals and images of the ceremonial life at the Sasanian court; and a tradition which could be influenced but not submerged by Arabic, the new dominant cultural language.

Influence of the Arabs and Arabic

The Arab conquest of Iran brought not only a new language with its own sacred text, but also, if more gradually, new notions of aesthetic excellence. The effect of these imports and their ready assimilation may at first suggest a complete break with the past, at least as far as the form and content of Persian poetry are concerned. There may seem to be a clear line dividing the unrhymed accentual versification of pre-Islamic poetry in Middle Persian and the quantitive prosody of Classical Persian poetry, with its regular rhymes and distinct forms such as the *qasida** (pl. *qasa'id*) and the *masnavi*. But recent research has considerably altered this view. The discovery of the Manichaean hymn cycles in Parthian, the analysis of fragments of Middle and Early Persian quoted in later texts, as well as a better understanding of the transmission of oral poetry and its survival after Islam, have all helped to show new lines of enquiry and possible transitional phases. On the other hand, a reappraisal of the Persian metres and poetical forms has shown radical differences in Persian and Arabic prosody, to the extent that some recent research has even denied the existence of any links between the prosody of the two languages.

Patronage of the Samanids and Ghaznavids

Unlike technical questions of prosody, the broader subjects of forms and themes in poetry and prose cannot be isolated from their historical context. Much of the surviving medieval literature in Persian was written under the patronage of rulers and their high officials. The first great centre of patronage was the Samanid court (mid-ninth century to the end of the tenth century) in Khorasan and Transoxiana. Their geographical location, away from the possible cultural domination of Baghdad, their pride in their Persian descent, and perhaps most important of all the survival of many Persian landowning families with a strong attachment to their pre-Islamic past, were to prove crucial in the creation of a Persian literary world in which poets, scholars and translators could flourish.

The syncretic nature of the Samanid* literary output can be seen in the surviving prose and poetry of the period. The most celebrated poet of the time is Rudaki (d.940–1), remembered for the ballad-like simplicity of his diction and the balance between melancholy and fortitude in the *ubi sunt* motif which runs through many of his poems. Much of his poetry is lost, including (apart from a few fragments) a verse translation from the Arabic version of the Indian fable of *Kalila wa Dimna*. In prose, too, much of the remaining evidence is in translation, including that of Tabari's monumental *Commentary* on the Qur'an and his *History*. The latter illustrates the way the history of Iran itself was then more accessible through Arabic, and how complex, therefore, the systems of cultural borrowing were.

The Samanid era is often depicted as a Golden Age of decorum, innate taste and munificence. Their successors, the Ghaznavids*, descendants of their Turkish slave guard, have fared less well. Later chronicles hint at their capriciousness and frown at their lineage. Yet the same critics praise the magnificence of their courts and the number of poets in their entourage. The court of Mahmud of Ghazna (998–1030) can be regarded as the culmination of the Samanid endeavours.

The most important poetic form closely associated with Mahmud's court – although examples survive from the Samanid era – is the *qasida*. It is a poem in monorhyme which can vary greatly in length but contains distinct thematic divisions. Beginning with what can loosely be defined as a descriptive prelude, depicting a scene or an action (for example, a paradisaic landscape, the spring festival, a town in mourning, a dialogue between lovers), it moves through a short transitional link to the other main part, the encomium of the patron. The poem ends with a prayer for the patron's wellbeing, coupled perhaps with a request for some favour on behalf of the poet. Although the *qasida* was also used to express religious and didactic ideas (as in the case of Sana'i and Nasir-i Khusrau), the main models for it remained the three great Ghaznavid court poets Unsuri, Farrukhi, and Manuchihri. The *qasida* maintained its popularity (apart from a relative decline in the Mongol period) to the present century.

The other major poetic form with extant examples from the Samanid and Ghaznavid era is the *masnavi*, the most flexible of all the poetic forms. Each hemistich rhymes with its counterpart and the rhyme changes for each line. Freed, therefore, from the constraints of monorhyme, it is ideally suited to long poems on a wide range of subjects (one of the earliest is a versified treatise on medicine). It is also the form used for narrative poetry, including its first masterpiece, Firdawsi's *Shah-Name*.

Although completed in the time of Mahmud, both in style and outlook the *Shah-Name* belongs to the Samanid age. It narrates the legendary history of Iran from Kayomarth, the first mythical king, to the end of the Sasanian era, drawing on both oral and written traditions. The note of apology, detectable in some near-contemporary works describing the same pre-Islamic myths, is absent; nor are there any traces of that favourite *topos* of the Ghaznavid *qasida*, the comparison and praise of the present ruler at the expense of past heroes. In spite of its formidable length, the work is held together by its vision of history and its ability to transcend the limitations of a 'national' epic. The linear chronicle of dynasties is counterbalanced in the middle section of the book by the interlacing of heroic episodes with strong thematic contents. The aesthetic pleasure aimed at, therefore, is the synoptic one enjoyed by an informed audience already conversant with the whole work and able to detect the same theme being treated from different perspectives in different episodes.

Limitations of space allow us only a brief reference to Persian prose, but this is not to deny its intrinsic value and its contribution to a better understanding of Persian culture in general and poetry in particular. Medieval prose manuals like the *Qabus-Name* (1082–3) and the *Chahar Maqala* (1155–7), both of which have been translated into English, provide the best preface to medieval lyric poetry and the function of the poet in relation to his audience. The best introduction to Ghaznavid court life and bureaucracy, and, more obliquely, to Firdawsi's *Shah-Name*, is Baihaqi's *Tarikh-i Mas'udi* (History), where a skilful juxtaposition of styles depicts the very society from which Firdawsi, with his idealization of a pre-Islamic Iran, attempts to distance himself. Both works are concerned with man in society (but in different representational modes), and both introduce a personal voice at crucial stages as an effective means of framing and commenting on their themes.

The Seljuk period

The extant volumes of Baihaqi (d.1077) end in 1040, the year of an important battle marking the supremacy of the Seljuks over the Ghaznavids. The period between 1040 and the Mongol invasion of Iran in 1220 is the most creatively productive phase in the history of Persian literature. It saw the geographical expansion of Persian culture into India and westward into Anatolia. There was a gradual rise of local styles in western Iran, reducing for the first time the hitherto all-powerful eastern cultural dominance. Most important of all, the growing cultural importance of the Sufi* orders as well as the intellectual impact of Isma'ili* propaganda contributed to changes in the function of poetry and the position of the poet in society. These aspects of the age are reflected in the works of the Azerbaijani poet Nizami (d. *c.*1209) and the Sufi poet 'Attar (d. *c.*1220) from Khorasan. The latter mentions no patrons and makes frequent use of the *topos* of impatience with mere (eulogistic) poetry, a sentiment already expressed by the Isma'ili poet Nasir-i Khusrau and the first great mystic poet, Sana'i. 'Attar's narrative poems are often spiritual quests, depicting the mystic way by an allegorical technique which manages to unify and propel the argument without appearing cumbersome or forced.

Although Nizami had patrons, the dedicatory passages are overshadowed by extensive descriptions of the process of poetic inspiration. Unlike 'Attar and Rumi, it is the ordered imagination rather than selfless spontaneity which he sees as the hallmark of a great poet. Like the *qasa'id* of his contemporary Azerbaijani poet Khaqani (d.1199), Nizami's narrative poems are avowedly literary artefacts in which selected sources are exploited for their very literalness and 'made strange' by new interpretations.

There are examples of the *ruba'i* and the *ghazal* poetical forms from earlier centuries, but they become increasingly popular in the eleventh and twelfth centuries, although the *ghazal* can be said to have reached its artistic apogee in the later centuries, in the Mongol and Timurid era, in the works of Rumi, Sadi and Hafiz.

FitzGerald's *Rubaiyat of Omar Khayyam* has made the *ruba'i* familiar in the West. As a short poem of only four hemistichs, with either all, or all save one rhyming together (AAAA or AABA), it is well suited to express an epigram or a single motif, like the *carpe diem* theme so frequent in Khayyam (d.1122). It is often difficult to establish the authorship of a *ruba'i*, and this is true not only of Khayyam, but of most other early examples, including those of Baba Tahir Uryan (*c.*eleventh century), whose quatrains, composed in dialect form, have a close affinity with folk poetry. The *ruba'i* is also used in Sufi discourses and other types of prose literature almost as an extended proverb or anecdote to emphasize an argument or to round it off.

The first two hemistichs of the *ghazal* rhyme together and thereafter the same rhyme occurs at the end of every line. Gradually it became a convention for the poet to mention his *nom de plume* in the final couplet. Ranging from five to about fifteen lines, the *ghazal* describes a variety of sacred or profane themes or exploits the multiplicity of semantic levels produced by the fusion of the two.

The Mongols and the Timurids

The last great classical poets, Rumi (d.1273), Sa'di (d.1292) and Hafiz (d.1390) belong to the turbulent times which began with the Mongol invasion of Khorasan in 1220. But their poetry can be regarded as the culmination of the literary experiments of the pre-Mongol period. Here again the interaction between prose and poetry should be emphasized. The figurative language of the visionary recitals of Suhravardi (executed in 1191), the meditations on the nature of mystic love in the works of Ahmad al-Ghazali* (d.1126) and Ruzbahan Baqli (d.1209) and 'Ayn al-Qudat Hamadhani's speculations on Qur'anic exegesis and the limits of language, as well as being models of imaginative prose can serve as a preface to Hafiz's own richly textured poetic diction.

This figurative language, relying both on symbolic focal images and allegorical techniques, fell victim to the excessively exegetical approach to poetry which became dominant in the late Timurid period. This attitude could be described as a perversion of the inner reality and outer surface dichotomy (*batin/zahir*) into a crude binary division of the esoteric versus the obvious. Illustrations of this approach can be found in both the prose and poetry of Jami (d.1492) as well as in the many imitations of Nizami's narrative poems which failed to grasp the structural subtleties of his poetry. Vestiges of this ultimately sterile critical attitude have survived to the present day.

The period from the Safavids to the earlier Qajars

It has been said of the Safavids* (1501–1722) that their painters were good poets and their poets bad painters. The origins and the time-span of the dominant style of the period, called the Indian style and highly prized at the Moghul court in India, are matters of dispute.

The style has been consistently castigated by Iranian scholars for over-indulgence in fanciful aetiology in its metaphors, for its langorously sensual diction, and for producing arid stretches of trite word-play enlivened only occasionally by a striking single line. This harsh view can be retraced to the late eighteenth century and the proponents of the 'Literary Return' movement (or 'The Return School') who advocated a return to what they saw as the more harmonious poetry of the Ghaznavid and Seljuk times. Recently, some critics have objected to the crude notions of naturalism inherent in these strictures and have attempted a more favourable reappraisal in terms of the style's own 'baroque' aesthetics. Further studies may show that the Indian style is not as homogenous as both its advocates and adversaries have assumed and that more discrimination is needed in distinguishing the characteristics of a great poet like Sa'ib (d.1677) from that of his contemporaries. A distinction also exists between this style and the more simple, vigorous language of the religious poetry of the Safavid era, a genre which was very much at home in the Shiʿi state. It is the dirges (*marthiya*) of Muhtasham of Kashan (d.1587), lamenting the martyrdom of Imam Husayn which, printed on strips of black cloth, drape the streets of modern Tehran in the month of mourning. The tradition continued into the Qajar era, as exemplified in the poems of Vassal (d.1846).

The conservative aims of the Literary Return movement dominate the cultural life of the early Qajar* period. Indeed, Fath ʿAli Shah's reign (1797–1834) can be regarded as the Indian summer of the traditional court patronage, with a large circle of poets praising the King in *qasa'id* and *masnavis*. The poet Saba (d.1822), for example, described the war with Russia in his *Shahanshah-Name*, in the manner of Firdawsi. In prose too, although the writings of Abu'l-Qasim Farahani (*Qa'im-maqam*) exploit the immediacy of the epistolary genre without losing the sense of decorum, they are essentially refinements of past styles rather than new beginnings.

Modern Persian literature

The long reign of Nasir al-Din Shah (1848–96) is usually associated with the gradual emergence of modern literature in Iran although, as in the case of most periodizations, many elements are traceable to earlier origins and some key figures defy categorization. A poet like Qa'ani (d.1854) can be regarded as a traditionalist, but his contemporary panegyrist Yaghma (d.1859) presents more of a problem. His religious poetry, couched in a colloquial language, is reminiscent of the later political ballads (*tasnifs*) of ʿArif (d.1934) in the Constitutional Period. And Yaghma's prose, with its suppression of Arabic loan words, was part of a gradual trend which later became enmeshed in the wider concepts of nationalism in the last decades of the nineteenth century.

A brief reference must be made here to institutional factors relevant to the development of modern literature and political consciousness. A polytechnic (Dar al-Funun) was founded in Tehran in 1852 with a modern curriculum taught by Europeans and Iranians. There was a gradual rise in the number of students educated abroad, and a more sudden increase in the number of scientific and literary translations into Persian, partly as a response to the growth of secular education. Most important of all, the creation of printing presses and newspapers brought new ways of more immediate mass communication as well as new expectations.

Against this background, literature became more concerned with social and political issues and with the search for the causes of the relative backwardness of the country. Among the themes of this diagnosis were foreign manipulation of Iranian interests and the archaic rigidity of the state and its arbitrary exercise of power: themes on which the Constitutional movement as a whole was conceptualized. The creators of this literature were a generation of poets and writers who remained influential in later years, notably Nasim-i Shumal (Ashrafuddin Gilani, 1871–1933), ʿAli Akbar Dihkhuda (1880–1956) and Muhammad Taqi Bahar (1886–1951).

Influence of newspapers

The writers mentioned above were all active journalists, and although Bahar and Dihkhuda later produced monumental works of scholarship in stylistics and lexicography, it is their contribution to newspapers* and periodicals of different periods (for example, *Sur-i Israfil*, 1907–9 and *Nau-Bahar*, 1921–51) which are also of great importance for the development of literature. The study of the rise and fall of newspapers and journals, both inside Iran and abroad, in the context of the alternating phases of relative freedom and strict censorship, is one of the most instructive ways of approaching the literary history of modern Iran.

Several of the historical novels which became a predominant feature of post-Constitutional prose also had their beginnings as newspaper instalments. Their episodic nature can thus be related both to the manner of their publication and to possible influences of the popular tales of adventure still enjoying a wide circulation in the Qajar era (for example, *Amir Arsalan*, written during the reign of Nasir al-Din Shah). In spite of the scholarly apparatus which sometimes accompanied these historical novels, their view of history was essentially naively sentimental.

Although such earlier historical novelists as Muhammad Baqir Khusravi and San'atizada Kirmani have their modern counterparts, and the genre has always had a public, its full potentials have not been exploited except, significantly, by a fusion with the *novella* (as in the contemporary writer Gulshiri's *Shazda Ihtijab*). For it was the short story which, from the early twenties, became the main literary medium. Jamalzada's collection of short stories, *Yeki bud yeki nabud* (Once Upon A Time) and its preface, published in 1921, are regarded as a literary milestone, although such earlier works as *Siyahat-Name-i Ibrahim Beg* by Zain al-ʿAbadin Maragha'i (d.1910), Dihkhuda's *Charand-u-parand*, and the Persian translation of Morier's *The Adventures of Hajji Baba of Isfahan* should be noted in this context.

Once Upon A Time and its preface contain the over-simplifications and contradictions of a period piece by a mediocre liberal thinker. His forced superimposition of proverbs and folklore has been noted by critics and can be contrasted with the more varied and imaginative works of other contemporary writers, notably Sadigh Hidayat (1903–51) and later novelists, including Sadiq Chubak (b.1916). Hidayat's *Buf-i Kur* (The Blind Owl) draws on the peculiarly indeterminate world of 'popular', 'folk' and 'classical' imagery of Persian literature, where neat divisions between high and low, and polite and popular, taken from other cultures and other times, do not apply.

The poet ʿAli Isfandiyari (Nima Yushij, 1897–1960) is regarded as the first truly modern Persian poet. Although the gulf between the poetry of the early Qajar court and the political verse of the twentieth century is a wide one, it was Nima's experiments with prosody in the twenties and his critical writings which finally brought a break with tradition both in form and content, and led to a debate which was widely echoed in later literary circles and periodicals. Most modern poets, including Shamlu (A. Bamdad) and Akhavan-i Saless (M. Umid) acknowledge his influence on their poetry.

Literature and the Revolution

The decades between the *coup d'état* of 1953 and the revolution of 1979 form a distinct phase. A sense of despair pervades collections of poems like Akhavan's *Winter*. Because of censorship, a range of symbols is created to hint at political pressures. Short stories, like Al-i Ahmad's (1923–69) *The School Principal*, which makes a school epitomize the weaknesses of a whole society, and polemical essays, like his *Plagued by the West*, attack the establishment as morally corrupt and servile. The image was not new, but the concept of a complacent elite was broadened and greater stress was placed on its philistine consumerism and on its alienation from its own traditional roots.

Since the fall of the Shah, some intellectuals have settled abroad and published works expressing their sense of anger and betrayal at the turn of events. Many have remained at home, writing as they had done prior to the revolution and publishing works already begun. The long novel *Kalidar* by Dawlatabadi, a vast panorama of tribal and village life in Khorasan, is an example of this continuity. A more immediate outcome of the revolution are the writings of a young generation of its active supporters, the so-called *maktabi* literature, with its themes of martyrdom, trust in the Divine will, and its pan-Islamic aspirations.

MAs

Further reading

A. J. Arberry, *Classical Persian Literature* (London, 1958)
E. G. Browne, *A Literary History of Persia.* 4 vols. (Cambridge, 1902–24)
The Cambridge History of Iran (Cambridge, 1968–86); most volumes contain chapters on literature
H. Kamshad, *Modern Persian Prose Literature* (Cambridge, 1966)
J. Rypka, *History of Iranian Literature*, (Dordrecht, 1968)

Note: A great number of important classical and modern texts, including many of the works mentioned in the article, have been translated into English. Among recent translations, Davis and Darbandi's translation of Attar's *The Conference of the Birds* (Harmondsworth, 1984) deserves to be singled out.

Medieval Hebrew literature

The Muslims exerted a strong influence in practically every sphere of Jewish literary creativity in medieval times: philosophy, poetry, grammar, historiography, and to some extent even in the field of Jewish law. The Arabic language*, and the study of that language by Muslim grammarians, were themselves potent forces for change and development in Jewish milieux, because they opened up new philosophical vistas and enabled Jews to study their own traditions with hitherto unknown systematic objectivity. The foremost Jewish philosophers all wrote in Arabic (in the Hebrew script) and the Hebrew* translations of their works, made for non-Arabic-speaking Jews in Europe, required a large expansion of Hebrew vocabulary in order to accommodate unfamiliar philosophical terminology. These new coinages, principally the work of the Ibn Tibbon family of translators in Provence, made a significant contribution to the development of modern Hebrew.

The influence of Arabic literature was crucial in the growth of a new Hebrew poetry in Muslim Spain* in the period AD 800–1200. After the great heights reached by biblical poetry the genre had practically disappeared from the Jewish scene. A tentative revival took place in Palestine with Eleazar Kallir (eighth–ninth century) and his contemporaries, but their poetry was entirely liturgical, and its style characterized by often obscure midrashic imagery and allusion, which renders it incomprehensible to an unschooled mind.

The Jewish discovery of Arabic secular poetry was revolutionary in its impact. The Jews of the western Caliphate*, whose vernacular was Arabic, were overwhelmed by the beauty and ingenuity of this poetry and resolved to copy it in Hebrew. This was a deliberate and methodical process of imitation, not a matter of vague, subconscious influence. Dunash Ben Labrat, who appears to have been born in Baghdad, but was educated in Fez and lived in Spain, was writing Hebrew poetry on Arabic models before 950. Moses ibn Ezra (*c.*1055–1135?) wrote a manual of Hebrew prosody, analysing in detail the themes, images and strophic forms of Arabic poetry and finding parallels in biblical Hebrew. For the first time since the biblical era Jews began to write poems on non-religious topics: poems of war, of wine, of love, of bereavement and parting, and of natural and urban description.

The poet's social position was also much influenced by Islamic culture. Poets sought wealthy patrons, often passing from one to another, and writing occasional poetry for them, marking significant events in their lives.

The Jews were impelled not only by a desire to produce something aesthetically pleasing, but also by a strong competitive element. Hebrew for the Jews (like Arabic for the Muslims) was a holy tongue, the language which God used to reveal his message to man. For Jewish poets of Muslim Spain it was important to demonstrate that their holy tongue could be used to the same effect as that of their masters. This explains why they wrote very little poetry in Arabic, although superscriptions are often in that language. It also led them to pursue a remarkable course in their choice of vocabulary. They used the language of the Bible and very little else. The vocabulary of later Hebrew – of Mishnah and Talmud, for example – hardly ever appears in their poetry. Practically every phrase has a biblical equivalent. The poems become an intricate mosaic of scriptural quotation and allusion, which gives their work an additional profound dimension, because for the Jew biblical references strike innumerable religious, ethical and historical chords which the poet consciously uses for intellectual and aesthetic ends. He is also able to create startling effects by using 'sacred' phrases to describe 'profane' objects or situations.

This competitive spirit may also be seen in the fact that while imitating the descriptions that Muslims lavished on the beautiful towns of Andalusia, the Jews reserved their praises for the Holy Land and Jerusalem.

Religious poetry

The secular poetry of the Jews in Spain was matched in profusion and intensity by their religious poetry. Here they were able to take advantage of the opportunities provided by Jewish tradition for private meditation within the structure of the statutory services to compose new poems (*piyyutim*) linked thematically to the liturgy. Although, in this field, the language and imagery tended to be more Jewish in inspiration, the forms (metres and strophic patterns) were based on Arabic models.

Foremost among the practitioners of this art were Samuel ibn Nagrela, called ha-Nagid (993–1055), wazir in the Muslim court at Granada, who excelled in writing war poetry; Solomon ben Judah ibn Gabirol (*c.*1020–57), renowned chiefly for his 'Keter Malkhut', a philosophical poem; and Judah ben Samuel Halevi (d.1141), whose 'Odes to Zion', expressing his deep love for the Holy Land, have left a deep impression on Jewish consciousness.

An Arabic genre, which had repercussions on the Jewish literary world beyond the confines of Andalusia, was the *maqama**. Hebrew stories in rhymed prose and in a 'precious' florid style were written not only in Spain but subsequently in Provence and in Italy.

Revival of Jewish historiography* was also to a great extent dependent on Arabic models. The Letter of Rabbi Sherira ben Hanina (987), head (*gaon*) of the Academy of Pumbeditha, Mesopotamia (modern Iraq), constructs a chain of rabbinic transmission from the earliest times to his own day, in order to justify the authority of the tradition. This is very much in the style of the Islamic *isnad**, and was copied and enlarged upon in Spain by Abraham Ibn Daoud (*c.*1110–80) in his *Sefer ha-Kabbalah*.

Judeo-Arabic

The vernacular of the Jews living in Muslim countries, from the earliest years of the Islamic conquest, was Arabic. In their written work they transliterated the language into Hebrew script, and also introduced Hebrew vocabulary. This form of Arabic, known as Judeo-Arabic, displays varieties in grammar, vocabulary and orthography which reflect the Arabic milieu in which the Jews found themselves. Judeo-Arabic is still used among Jews in the Maghrib. (Some communities, notably the Karaites, persisted, however, in the use of Arabic script.)

Hebrew grammar and lexicography received new impetus from Arabic models. Indeed, before the Islamic period Jews did not analyse their language in any systematic way. However, first in Judeo-Arabic and then in Hebrew, Jewish scholars soon applied to Hebrew the Semitic grammatical structure erected by Muslim scholars. Saadya Gaon (882–942), who lived in Egypt and Mesopotamia, was among the first to compose a Hebrew grammar, and he was followed by Judah Hayyum (tenth–eleventh century) of Fez; and his pupil, the most renowned of all early grammarians and lexicographers, Abu 'l-Walid Marwan (Jonah ibn Janah) (eleventh century), who lived in Spain, and whose work had great influence on all who came after him, not only in the field of linguistics but in the application of his theories to exposition of Bible and Talmud. These authors wrote in Judeo-Arabic. Menahem ibn Saruk (tenth century), born in Tortosa, wrote in Hebrew and his dictionary (*Mahberet*) had therefore an immediate influence on Jewish learning in non-Arabic speaking communities.

DG

Further reading

E. Ashtor, *The Jews of Moslem Spain* (Philadelphia, 1973–9)
D. Goldstein, *The Jewish Poets of Spain* (Harmondsworth, 1982)
S. Spiegel, 'On Medieval Hebrew Poetry', in L. Finklestein, ed., *The Jews, their History, Culture and Religion* (Philadelphia, 1949)

Modern Hebrew literature

The publication in 1850 in Berlin of a Hebrew weekly entitled *Kohelet* based broadly on the London *Tatler* marks not only the beginning of modern Hebrew literature but also of the Jewish movement of enlightenment (*Haskalah**), which was to be the chief inspiration for secular literature for the next 130 years. The German phase of the *Haskalah* introduced German Jews to a wide range of modern subjects, but as they acquired Western learning as opposed to traditional Jewish learning they quickly assimilated to the host culture and Hebrew was abandoned in favour of German. No Hebrew literature of any value was produced by the German *Haskalah*.

As the movement spread eastward into Austrian Galicia a number of satirical works were produced, notably by J. Perl (1773–1839) and I. Erter (1791–1851), which poured scorn, *inter alia*, on the superstitions of the recently formed Hasidic sect which had found numerous adherents in Galicia. It was only when the *Haskalah* reached Lithuania that a literature of any significance was generated: the poetry of J. L. Gordon (1830–92), A. D. Lebensohn (1794–1878) and his son, Micah (1828–52), marked a turning point in the development of a 'Europeanized' poetry dealing in part with nationalist and romantic themes. The quality of *Haskalah* poetry can be adduced from the fact that *The Penguin Book of Hebrew Verse* makes no mention of it.

The novel

The first Hebrew novel, *The Love of Zion*, set in the time of Hezekiah, was written in 1853 by A. Mapu (1808–67), a Lithuanian Jew. This work, the first novel in any language to treat a biblical theme, was the highest literary achievement of the early stages of the *Haskalah* and was the most finely crafted example of the early tendency of the new literature to restrict itself to purely biblical Hebrew. Mapu himself was later to argue that the emerging literature would have to throw off the shackles of the classical language and incorporate Mishnaic and medieval forms and vocabulary if it were adequately to mirror contemporary society. Mapu's first novel played a role in the development of early Zionist sentiments in its lyrical descriptions of the natural beauty of the Land of Israel (which Mapu had never seen). It was only with the novels of S. Y. Abramovitch (1836–1917), who wrote under the pen-name Mendele Mokher Seforim (Mendele the Bookseller), that Hebrew *belles-lettres* were to draw on the full resources of the Hebrew language, although rabbinic and publicistic literature had already done so. Mendele is considered, perhaps uniquely, to be the father of two modern literatures: modern Hebrew and Yiddish. His portrayal of the poverty, degradation and superstitious faith of the

Jewish masses of the Pale of Settlement (the area in which the Jews of Russia were permitted to reside) is masterly: for the first time in over a thousand years Hebrew was made to express the rhythm and earthiness of normal speech, even though Mendele can have had little occasion to hear Hebrew spoken.

Poetry

H. N. Bialik (1873–1934) did for Hebrew poetry what Mendele had done for prose. Using the full range of Hebrew literary sources he created a rich and extensive *oeuvre*, which expressed Jewish national aspirations as well as his own sense of identification with the problems posed by a Jewish way of life which was disintegrating under the pressures of Russian anti-Semitism, poverty and secularism. During his lifetime Bialik was considered the 'national' poet of the Jews of Central and Eastern Europe and his influence is felt in Hebrew poetry up to today. S. Tchernikhovsky (1875–1943), a Russian Jew, wrote outstanding poetry touching national as well as universal themes.

A wandering literature

One of the more remarkable aspects of Hebrew literature until the 1930s was its peripatetic nature. Its centre of production and to a certain extent its readership moved first from Germany to Galicia, then to Lithuania and towards the end of the nineteenth century moved on to the Black Sea city of Odessa. The First World War and the Russian Revolution had the effect of shifting the centre of Hebrew creativity from Russia; there were some attempts in the 1920s to create a Hebrew literature which could serve the purposes of the revolution, but they were short-lived and had no lasting significance. During the 1920s, Berlin became the centre not only of Hebrew literature but also of a more generalized Jewish culture, although most of the members of the Berlin group were refugees from Eastern Europe. The rise of Nazism brought an end to Jewish intellectual activity in Germany. From the 1930s to the present the only important centre of Hebrew literature has been Palestine/Israel.

From the 1890s to after the First World War Hebrew literature was dominated by the themes of disintegration of traditional Jewish life and the rootlessness which became the hallmark of that generation of Jewish intellectuals. By the turn of the century modern Hebrew literature had adopted all the genres of a modern literature and had become thoroughly European in form and conception in a way that almost all pre-*Haskalah* literature had not been. Even before the First World War, such avant-garde phenomena as 'stream of consciousness' had been introduced most effectively in the writing of Y. Brenner, who settled in Jaffa in 1909 and was killed by Arabs in 1921.

Literature in Palestine

In Palestine, Hebrew literature in a more or less European form first appeared in the 1880s and 1890s during the period of what is called in Zionist historiography the first *aliyah** (tide of immigration). The era of the early Zionist pioneers is vividly portrayed in the writing of M. Smilansky (1874–1953). In the 1880s and 1890s Palestine became the centre of the revival of Hebrew as a spoken language chiefly as a result of the activity of Eliezer Ben Yehudah (1858–1922), often called the reviver of the Hebrew language, and partly as a result of the linguistic diversity of the Jewish communities in Palestine which created the need for a common spoken language. The *Biluim*, a pioneering group of Russian Jews who settled in Palestine in 1882, and the settlers who followed them, became the keenest supporters of Ben Yehudah's attempt to revive Hebrew as a language of speech and it was in the schools of the early colonies that the phenomenon of spoken Hebrew developed most rapidly.

A parallel 'revival' of Hebrew had taken place over the previous 130 years as the language was required to address itself to a variety of modern concepts and topics. Nonetheless, the term 'revival' must be used with caution because Hebrew was never a dead language nor merely a language of prayer; it had a wide variety of functions as a written means of communication among oriental and European Jews alike, although until the beginning of the twentieth century it was rarely used for speech.

With the revival of spoken Hebrew in Palestine, Hebrew literature took on a new dimension. During the 1930s and 1940s the poetry of the older poets such as Bialik and the new generation of Palestine-based poets began to reflect and call upon colloquial Hebrew. The outstanding poets of this period, much influenced by the symbolist and imagist schools in Europe, were A. Shlonsky (1900–73), N. Alterman (1910–70) and Y. Lamdan (1899–1954).

Influence of Agnon

Since the 1920s Hebrew prose has been dominated by the writing of S. Y. Agnon (1888–1970), who was awarded the Nobel Prize for Literature in 1966. Agnon, who first settled in Palestine in 1909, dealt mainly with Jewish life in Galicia and Palestine/Israel. Although Agnon frequently adopted the innocent form of the Hasidic folk-tale and used a sort of rabbinic Hebrew with a resonance quite unlike that of any other Hebrew writer, he nonetheless was a thoroughgoing modernist. The dreamlike quality in much of his work has led many critics to compare him with Kafka. It has been argued that Agnon's influence has been so overwhelming that in some sense it has retarded the development of the Hebrew novel. The writing of his contemporary, H. Hazaz, for instance, certainly suffered both by its author's exposure to Agnon's work and by comparison with it.

After the Arab-Israeli War* in 1947–8, S. Yizhar (b.1918), the

Palestine-born great nephew of M. Smilansky, wrote a number of fine short stories which dealt sensitively with contemporary issues and marked a development in Hebrew prose style. Important contributions to the development of the Hebrew novel were made in the 1950s and later by M. Shamir (b.1921), B. Tammuz (b.1919), A. Meged (b.1920), D. Shahar (b.1926) and Y. Amihai (b.1924). From the next generation of prose writers A. B. Yehoshua (b.1936), A. Oz (b.1939), A. Apelfeld (b.1932), A. Kahana-Carmon (b.1931), Y. Ben Ner (b.1937) and H. Beer (b.1945) have made important contributions to Hebrew prose writing, while eschewing some of the primary codes of the so-called Palmach generation. Oz, Shahar and Apelfeld have acquired considerable reputations in translation.

Throughout the twentieth century Hebrew literature has been characterized by the peculiarity that it generated much better short stories than novels. Setting aside Agnon, whose Hebrew is *sui generis* and barely conforms to modern Hebrew, the conclusion may perhaps be drawn that the evolution of Hebrew in its modern guise is not yet complete, and whereas the language is able to sustain shorter genres it lacks the depth, colour and idiom to sustain a great novel.

Literature since the creation of Israel

The most important aspect of post-1948 Hebrew literature is undoubtedly its poetry. Y. Amihai, A. Gilboa (b.1917), H. Guri (b.1922), N. Zach (b.1930), T. Carmi (b.1925) and D. Pagis (b.1930) were responsible for the creation of new poetic idioms which rejected the formality and neo-romanticism of the Palestinian Hebrew writing of the previous generation. Since 1948, Hebrew poetry has increasingly been influenced by the understatement and irony typical of American and English post-war poetry. Of the younger generation of Israeli poets the most significant are D. Ravikovitch (b.1936) and M. Wieseltier (b.1941), whose work reflects the growing lexicon of Hebrew colloquialism. Israel* continues to produce a vast amount of poetry, a great deal of which bears comparison with the poetry of major contemporary literatures. Although much modern Hebrew poetry lacks either Jewish or specifically Israeli content, it is often marked by a fusion of the personal and national 'I'; this feature may help to account for the great popularity in Israel of Amihai, who more than any other has become the national poet of modern Israel.

TP

Further reading

T. Carmi, ed., *The Penguin Book of Hebrew Verse* (London, 1981)
S. Halkin, *Modern Hebrew Literature – Trends and Values* (New York, 1950)
D. Patterson, *The Hebrew Novel in Czarist Russia* (Edinburgh, 1964)
I. Rabinovich, *Major Trends in Modern Hebrew Fiction* (Chicago, 1968)
E. Silberschlag, *From Renaissance to Renaissance*. 2 vols. (New York, 1973–77)

Armenian literature

Of the rich oral lore of ancient Armenia*, only a few fragments survived the zealous suppression of pagan traditions after the proclamation of Christianity in Armenia, *c.*300. Momentous though the conversion was, its cultural impact was felt fully only after the invention of a native script, *c.*400, by a genius named Mashtots. Immediately, a group of translators rendered into Armenian,

One of the treasures of the Armenian Patriarchate, the illuminated Gospel of St Mark by Thoros Rosslin (AD 1265)

mainly from Greek and Syriac, a vast corpus of religious and secular texts, setting an illuminating example for posterity to emulate. At the same time, an original literature blossomed and shaped, out of piety and patriotism, a new national ethos which in many ways still dominates the Armenian self-image.

In the fifth to tenth centuries, historiography* was a main genre. Agathangelos, Eghishe and Movses Khorenatsi, the architects of the new Armenian tradition, blazed a trail for subsequent historians, most of whom wrote of Armenia under the Arabs. Poetry attained eloquent expression in religious hymns (*sharakan*). There was a keen interest in grammar, rhetoric and logic, but as the Armenian Church asserted its independence, homiletic writings proved of spiritual, as well as practical, significance. A towering figure was the poet Grigor Narekatsi (tenth century), whose *Book of Lamentations* has been held in reverence such as that accorded only to the Bible. Armenian aspirations for freedom were embodied in the oral national epic, *David of Sasun*, which seems to have acquired its basic outline during the Arab conquest of Armenia and the Mamluk onslaught on Cilicia.

After the tenth century, major shifts in Armenia and the neighbouring regions left their mark on Armenian letters. Classical Armenian was still employed in religious texts, but Middle Armenian gradually emerged as the vehicle for mundane concerns: social injustice and vices, emigration, love and women, and the theme of the rose and the nightingale. Riddles and fables gained popularity and elegies and histories lamented with alarm the retreat of Christendom, the arrival of invaders and the fall of Constantinople. Among some of the eminent names of the time were Frik, Nerses Shnorhali, Kostandin Erznkatsi (poets), and Aristakes Lastiverttsi and Kirakos Gandzaketsi (historians).

A platitude holds that the fifteenth to seventeenth centuries were a period of decline. But, notwithstanding the disastrous consequences of wars and ravages, the age was in effect one of transition. In a number of 'schools' (reminiscent of medieval Armenian 'universities'), scholars and scribes preserved the received tradition by recopying old manuscripts, long since vanished. Historiography was of lesser scope, but elaborate colophons developed into valuable sources. Historians and poets alike decried oppression and yearned for deliverance from Muslim domination. The spread of worldly poems relegated traditional religious poetry, now jejune and lacking its former spontaneity, into a secondary position. Though many writers were still torn between the temptations of this world and the mysteries of the next, Nahapet Kuchak (sixteenth century), in poems attributed to him, wrote in finely and frankly sensuous imagery. Humour, convivial poems (*Naghash Hovnatan*) and the songs of Armenian minstrels, whose art crystallized in the passionate poems of Sayat Nova (eighteenth century), marked the predominance of the secular spirit.

Nineteenth-century literature

In the nineteenth century, Western ideas flowed into Armenia principally, but not solely, through the Mekhitarists*, whose research and publications revived the Armenian past and fostered hopes for nationhood. The modern Eastern and Western dialects prevailed as the literary standards respectively for the Eastern Armenians, now under Russia, and the Western Armenians, under the Ottoman Empire. In the 1850s and 60s, journalism disseminated the new political concepts imported from Europe; and evanescent historical plays kindled pride which, allied with the poetry of Alishan, M. Beshiktashlian, P. Durian and R. Patkanian, generated a romantic patriotism. But it was in prose writings that the political aspects of the corporate Armenian self gained prominence. Kh. Abovian's novel, *Wounds of Armenia*, illustrated armed struggle and emphasized the importance of the mother-tongue. Raffi's historical novels promoted total devotion to national ideals as the ultimate goal to aspire to, providing a source of inspiration for the Armenian liberation movements. Social issues and problems were tackled in the comedies and satire of G. Sundukian, H. Baronian and, a little later, that of E. Odian. In the 1880s, A. Arpiarian, G. Zohrap, T. Kamsarakan, Erukhan and others took a closer look at Armenian social and political realities under Abdülhamid's regime.

By the turn of the twentieth century, a wide range of political, social, aesthetical and philosophical issues, from subjective poetry to the effects of the oil industry, and all the usual European genres had been incorporated into the Armenian literary tradition. At this period, Armenian literature flowered in the drama and prose of Shirvanzade, L. Shant, Tlkatintsi and R. Zardarian; and in the verse of A. Isahakian, H. Tumanian, V. Terian, M. Metzarents, V. Tekeyan, Siamanto and D. Varuzhan. The last two in particular sought spiritual fortitude in the pagan past, but others, notably K. Zarian, preferred the creation of a new spirit to resurrecting the old.

Modern literature influenced by the massacres

The chief glories of modern Western Armenian literature were put to death during the Armenian massacres of 1915. Dispersed in France, the USA and the Middle East, survivors (V. Tekeyan, H. Oshakan) and younger writers alike were haunted by the carnage which at once inspired and restricted their work. In the United States, Hamastegh, B. Nurikian and others captured their memories of Armenia and portrayed the remnants of a traditional society in the New World. The same theme found a more dramatic expression in the prose of V. Shushanian, Z. Orbuni, H. Zardarian and many others residing in France. Their literary experiments and the psychological insight they provided into the psyche of the uprooted proved refreshing and amounted, at the same time, to a rejection of what they perceived as parochialism in Armenian literature. Most outspoken and pessimistic was Sh. Shahnur who in his work, notably his novel, *Retreat Without Song*, buried traditional Armenian values with nihilism and predicted doom and gloom for the Armenian dispersion.

A more optimistic tone distinguishes the writers of the Middle East in general and Lebanon in particular. A. Zarukian, M. Ishkhan and Vahe Vahian are some of the leading authors whose personal experiences as orphans during the massacres and concern for Armenian identity dominate their literary output. With the threat of assimilation looming large, they have found a redeeming source of perseverance in patriotism, a sentiment they share with Soviet Armenian authors. Although the distances, ideological, cultural, geographical and otherwise, between the two literatures are considerable, in recent decades Mount Ararat has emerged as a common symbol of national aspirations.

KBB

The Middle East and the Western imagination

The Middle East has appeared as an exotic locale for innumerable European novels, operas, paintings and films. As such it is probably rivalled only by India in popularity. The image of the Middle East that has developed in Europe is an amalgam of many attitudes and impressions and of a long historical experience. The area first impinged on European consciousness during the Crusades and the image was intensified by centuries of contact with the Ottoman Empire, by the era of piracy in North Africa and by the first-hand accounts of traders and travellers, until all these experiences were incorporated into European art and literature. The resultant picture was, in general, based on one or more of three imagined aspects of the Middle East: its immutability, its exoticism and its disillusioning reality. Although the Middle East was known in European literature before 1700 (see Shakespeare, Cervantes, Marlowe, Milton), and although a number of works were written during the eighteenth century with Middle Eastern or pseudo-Middle Eastern backgrounds (see Montesquieu's *Lettres persanes* (1721), Beckford's oriental fantasy *Vathek* (1786), Mozart's *Die Entführung aus dem Serail* (1782)) it was not until the nineteenth century that the popularity of the Middle East really blossomed.

Nostalgia for the ancient past

The image of the unchanging, timeless Middle East was derived from its background of ancient civilizations and biblical heritage. It was the depository of wisdom and truth, the guardian of tradition and righteousness. Mozart had immortalized this vision as early as 1791 in *Die Zauberflöte*, where in ancient Egypt truth is found in the Temple of Wisdom. Goethe in his *West-Östliche Diwan* (1819) described the timeless East as 'pure', a place of escape where the poet could regain his inspiration. He saw himself as an imaginary traveller through Eastern lands where reality and poetic intention melded together. For some the Middle East was also a dreamed-of homeland, an inherited part of the European experience from which all civilization stemmed. To visit the area was to return to something already known. Goethe wrote of seeking the origins of the human race there; for Lamartine it was the 'patrie de mon imagination'; there Flaubert came upon his 'rêves oubliés'.

Others sought in an unchanging environment evidence of biblical history and visions of biblical characters. They looked for the pastoral life and biblical atmosphere in the villages. In the imagination 'Arab' dress was that of biblical characters. The artist David Wilkie believed that the Arabs looked 'as if they had never changed since the time of Abraham'. Artists and early photographers wanted the Middle East to resemble their vision and often rearranged nature to suit. Holman Hunt used Eastern faces to replace the typical European models of biblical paintings and based his work on an accurate archeological reconstruction of biblical scenes.

Odalisque à l'esclave by J. A. D. Ingres (1780–1867)

Mystery of the desert

The desert was another essential element of the European image of the unchanging Middle East – a place of adventure and cleanliness quite unlike anything in the West. The beduin was a symbol of natural hospitality unspoiled by life in the city. The desert was the site of the struggle between man and nature, desolate, parched, and bleached under an intense light. Isobel Burton yearned 'for the desert to recover the purity of [her] mind and the dignity of human nature'; for Gertrude Bell waking 'in the desert was like waking in the heart of an opal'. Other travellers have revelled in the challenge posed in crossing the 'pitiless wastes'. T. E. Lawrence has been an important cultural image in this century and if not everyone has read *The Seven Pillars of Wisdom* at least everyone knows of Lawrence of Arabia and his warriors riding out of the desert.

To the majority of Europeans the Middle East was not pure or immutable, corrupt or decadent – it was simply exotic, a place of derring-do, of voluptuous sensuality, of romantic atmosphere, where forbidden but desirable activities could take place. It was an image deriving from Montesquieu's imaginary descriptions of the East, from the translations of the *Thousand and One Nights*★.

In 1812 Lord Byron in his *Childe Harold* established the Middle East as a setting for romantic experience. By 1825 in Delacroix's early pictures and in Victor Hugo's lyrical poems, *Les Orientales*, the essentials of this romantic image were fixed, and they have persisted to this day. For Richard Burton, one of the most influential figures in transmitting this image, the Middle East was a place of freedom from the taboos of Victorian moral authority; for the French traveller Fromentin the East escaped all conventions and lay 'outside all disciplines'. On the whole the French view was incorrigibly more romantic than the British. Gérard de Nerval saw the Middle East as 'le pays des rêves et de l'illusion'; for Lamartine it was 'the land of prodigies'. Numerous novels, poems, operas, paintings, pantomimes and, later, films perpetuated this vision. Following on Byron, James Morier published *Hajji Baba of Isphahan* (1824), a picaresque tale in an exotic setting which had an immediate and lasting success. It is peopled with a host of 'typical' Middle Eastern characters, ranging from slave to holy man. Walter Scott based his *Talisman* (1825) on the romantic and idealized figure of Saladin, a 'generous and valiant enemy', written without first-hand experience and based on 'early recollections of the *Arabian Nights' Entertainment*'. Disraeli in 1840 wrote *Tancred*, an oriental tale full of exotic background, where his hero scents 'a spicy gale from the farthest of Arabia'.

On the stage a few nineteenth-century operas and plays used the Middle East as an exotic background (Boieldieu's *The Caliph of Baghdad*, Verdi's *Aida*) but it was only in this century that the play described as 'a summit of Oriental exoticism' was written. Flecker's *Hassan* is the perfect evocation of the European image; romantic disillusion, ill-starred love, camels sniffing the evening breeze, all set in medieval Baghdad and written in a language owing much to FitzGerald's *Omar Khayyam*. Lawrence described Flecker's particular sympathy for the Arab scene with its 'satins and silks, perfumes, sweet-meats, grocers and' – with a significant sting in the tail – 'Syrian boys'. It was the Western version of the East and this was underlined when that quintessential English romantic, Delius, added incidental music – on the face of it the height of absurdity; in practice a magical evening at the theatre. The advent of the cinema made easier the faking of Middle Eastern backgrounds, and the flying carpet and the figure of the 'sheik' became familiar to cinema audiences. *Lawrence of Arabia* was a popular success, as was Pasolini's realistic version of the *Arabian Nights*, filmed in Yemen where it was still possible to find the 'unchanging' East.

Rudolph Valentino as 'The Sheik'
Courtesy of Paramount Pictures Corporation

The sexual ethos

An integral part of the exoticism of the Middle East was its imagined sexual licence. Montesquieu and Lady Mary Wortley Montagu had described the delights of *harim* and Turkish baths and Ingres had immortalized them in several paintings, such as *La Grande Odalisque* in 1814 (the lithograph of which became widely popular) and *Le Bain Turc* in 1862. The nudes there, derived from antique sculpture, were given an exotic flavour and background, appealingly erotic and morally reprehensible. Middle Eastern women were seen as offering delights unavailable in the West. Théophile Gautier insisted that the first question to be asked of returning visitors was: 'And the women?' Although in fact men were not admitted to the *harim* and Flaubert complained of the lack of good brothels and dancers in Cairo, visitors still hoped to live out their dreams. Renoir glimpsed eyes 'half-seen through a veil', Nerval, 'the sparkle of the inquiring eyes of young girls', and members of a prurient European society flocked in particular to see the dancing of the *ʿalmahs*, a version of striptease put on canvas by Gérôme in his *Danse de l'almée* (1863), which one critic described as overtly titillating public sensibilities and too immoral to be shown to Parisians. (This same critic had already seen the dance itself in Cairo.) If pleasure remained largely vicarious, the myth of a pervasive Middle Eastern sensuality persisted.

Disappointment and revulsion

When visitors found the Middle East not to be as immutable and exotic as they had hoped they often reacted in a critical manner. They formed an opposite and negative image. The decay and neglect of biblical and other ancient sites caused inevitable disillusion. Some artists (for example, David Roberts) painted scenes of contemporary Egyptian life against a background of ancient Egypt, thereby implying criticism of the modern inhabitants, who failed to live up to the ideals of their ancestors. Roberts reported his melancholy thoughts on the 'mutability of human greatness', and others seeking the Bible saw instead the squabbling priests and the squalid streets of Jerusalem which blocked their wider vision. Some photographers and painters felt it their task to record the area before it fell into irremediable decay: 'Let us hasten if we wish to enjoy the sight', wrote the early photographer Bonfils.

Those who saw only the decay accused the Arabs of indolence and neglect. Their contempt was buttressed by widely held ideas of racial superiority which classified the Arabs not as unspoiled children of nature but as second-class members of the human race. There are countless examples of these ideas in the literature, from Chateaubriand – the Arab was 'civilized man fallen again into a savage state' – to John Buchan in this century – the Arabs are 'one part of the human race. It isn't ours, it isn't as good as ours' (*Greenmantle*). From this sense of superiority it was but a short step to assessing the exotic as something nasty. Each feature seemed to have its dark side. The romantic 'sheik' becomes lecherous, bloodthirsty, cruel and dishonest. The ruler, once admired, becomes a despot. In John Wilkie's portrait of Muhammad ʿAli* (1841), because they were seeking such characteristics, critics claimed to see force and despotism in the depiction of a rather placid old man. The desert, no longer purifying and uplifting, becomes a place of cruelty and suffering. Gautier read in Gérôme's painting *Les Recrues égyptiennes traversant le désert* (1857) confirmation of Middle Eastern fatalism (of the recruits) and contempt (of the officer); the harshness of the desert, 'l'implacabilité de la nature', was matched by the 'implacabilité du despotisme'. In another work by Gérôme, *Le Prisonnier du Nil* (1861), a critic found only 'implacable fatalism' and 'blatant cruelty'.

The erotic tale spills over into the pornographic Victorian novel and though some writers (Gautier, for instance) commented on the dignity of marriage in Islam, Muslim sexual relations in the Western view were degraded. The Arab man was believed to be lustful and dangerous. As late as 1985 one writer was still claiming that: 'As a lover the Arab male is generally violent and often cruel.' Such images naturally bred the conviction that it was Europe's moral duty to tame the wild Arab and to civilize the 'savage'.

DH

Further reading

S. J. Nasir, *The Arabs and the English* (London, 1979, 2nd edn.)
M. Rodinson, 'The Western Image and Western Studies of Islam', in J. Schacht and C. E. Bosworth, eds., *The Legacy of Islam* (Oxford, 1974)
E. W. Said, *Orientalism* (London, 1978)
S. Searight, *The British in the Middle East* (London, 1969)
M. A. Stevens, ed., *The Orientalists: Delacroix to Matisse. European painters in North Africa and the Middle East* (London, 1984)

Ancient Egyptian art and architecture

Ancient Egyptian monuments and works of art form the largest visible legacy from pre-classical times in the Middle East. The overpowering presence of the Giza pyramids outside Cairo has dominated classical, medieval, and to some extent modern perceptions of early Egypt, which has been seen as extremely ancient and dedicated to permanence; in the words of ʿUmara al-Yamani, cited by Maqrizi, they are monuments 'feared by time, yet everything else in our present world fears time' – an image that remains apt despite the contribution of their fine limestone casings to the building of medieval Cairo.

In other respects, the pyramids are almost mute witnesses to Egyptian art and society. The architectural complexes of which they were the climaxes are almost completely lost, as are the inscriptions, relief decoration and statuary that gave life and meaning to them. Egyptian art and architecture form an integrated system, whose basic organization was designed at the beginning of the dynastic period (*c.*3000 BC). Most works of art of all periods down to the Roman (first century BC to third century AD) fit within this system, which is a fundamental method of presenting official ideology. Although many inscriptions consist primarily or exclusively of text, the majority of preserved writing is on permanent monuments incorporated within an artistic and architectural context and should be interpreted with that in mind. Art was central to high culture; in times of prosperity, a very large proportion of the country's surplus wealth was used to create works of art.

Fresco in a tomb of the Valley of the Kings, Luxor (1050–1700 BC)

The Temple of Ramesses II, Abu Simbel

Architecture

The majority of known architecture is funerary, consisting of free-standing or rock-cut tombs sited on the edge of the Nile Valley between Cairo and Aswan. Within the valley are a number of temple complexes, principally of the New Kingdom (*c.*1500–1100 BC) and the Graeco-Roman period.

Mud brick, which survives less well than stone, was used for religious and secular structures from temples to private houses. The Egyptians were skilled and inventive in using mud brick, creating rich effects in panelled façades to palaces and tombs, difficult structural elements such as wide vaults and domes, and roof-top air scoops and clerestoried central living rooms that responded to the hot dry climate and have left a legacy visible in the country into modern times.

Most of the main monuments, however, are built of limestone or sandstone (with parts in granite and other hard stones). Their structural forms are simpler than those of mud brick. The earliest stone buildings in the region, the step pyramid complex of Djoser at Saqqara (*c.*2650 BC), imitate plant models, from reeds and flowers to tree trunks, for the forms of columns and decorative motifs, including the typically Egyptian cavetto cornice and torus moulding. Architectural design in stone is rectilinear: arches were not used until the late period (from the seventh century BC), and the only vaulting was corbelling, which was carved in New Kingdom temples (*c.*1530–1100 BC) to produce curved ceilings for sanctuaries. A highly distinctive stylistic feature is the batten on exterior walls, most of whose faces slope slightly back from the vertical.

The underground spaces of Djoser's step pyramid were decorated with reliefs and glazed tiles, and by the 4th dynasty (*c.*2575–2465 BC), the time of the great pyramids, some royal mortuary temples had a rich repertory of reliefs, whose subjects included the worship of the gods, the provisioning of the temple by its estates, and 'historical' events primarily showing the king's dominance of the world and maintenance of order.

Royal tomb complexes are the chief religious structures of the Old and Middle Kingdoms (*c.*2575–1650 BC), but from the New Kingdom on, temples of the gods were more important. New Kingdom temples in Thebes (modern Luxor and Karnak), Abydos and Lower Nubia, and Graeco-Roman structures in those places and at Dendara, Edfu, Kom Ombo and Philae are the principal remaining monuments. In their complete form, the temples were covered in painted reliefs and contained ritual equipment and many large and small statues. They were surrounded by service buildings and enclosed within massive mud-brick walls. The gods, whose dwellings the temples were, left them only at festivals, and priests alone could enter the dark spaces within. But despite this seclusion, temples had a central significance as symbolic, sanctified representations of the perfect world at creation. All their wall surfaces contributed to their meaning. Their reliefs – normally low raised relief within and sunk relief out of doors – show the King (in Graeco-Roman times the Ptolemy or Roman Emperor) offering to the gods and receiving benefits from them, and are organized into registers with sequences of scenes that summarize the stages of rituals or are arranged according to more abstract schemas. The world of the reliefs is almost exclusively divine and royal; its relation to humanity is indirect.

Mesopotamia: Neo-sumerian sculpture of Gudea of Lagash

Representational art: sculpture

The art that filled architectural spaces and decorated their surfaces was all designed on the same basic principles. As a result, Egyptian art has a stylistic unity that has been recognized since antiquity. The application of its principles is best seen in the canon of proportions, which provided a convenient means of accurately depicting objects, especially the human form, on square grids, while also facilitating the organization of artists working in groups.

In sculpture in the round, the products of these techniques are easily appreciated. Apart from a geometrical character which is basic to the system and was probably valued for its dignity, the human figure is depicted 'realistically'. Great mastery was achieved in stoneworking, in rendering the masses of the human form and of detail, and in the subtle modelling of faces and of the upper part of the body. Except from the Old Kingdom, most statues come from temples and show gods, kings, and human beings in repose, standing with the left foot forward or seated, singly or in small groups. They are idealized, with a concept of beauty not very different from that of the modern West. Transient or dynamic poses and the depiction of aged and careworn features are rare. Details of clothing and insignia indicate the identity of many gods and of the King, but in addition most statues are inscribed and their owners named; statue and inscription complement each other so that the statue is the last 'hieroglyph' of the text. Sculptures from colossi 15 metres high to figurines of a few centimetres are remarkably uniform in style, but small works, especially in wood, can be surprisingly free. This applies particularly to decorative figures such as unguent jars in the form of offering-bearers carrying pots.

Relief and painting

Egyptian principles of representation have more distinctive consequences in relief and painting, which are organized as systems conveying visual information rather than visual images, and do not record foreshortening or other perspective phenomena, which are largely restricted to Western or Western-influenced art. The pictorial surface is an area to be filled, seldom a space or a specific location, and there is no fixed point from which compositions should be viewed. Figures are related to one another by their actions and gestures or by overlapping, while relative size indicates relative importance, not distance. The chief method of organizing compositions is the register, a sequence of figures or separate scenes on a single base line. A set of registers fills a wall surface, while principal figures or scenes may be the height of several registers. The aim of a design is to fill a surface evenly and arrange it meaningfully, rather as is done in the layout of an illustrated book.

The human form is treated as a set of aspects unified by its outline (the composition of male and female figures differs slightly). For figures standing at rest, a profile head encloses a single, mostly enlarged, eye, and the shoulders are shown at full width, while a front profile joins the forward armpit to the waist. The hips and legs are again in profile. This construction retains proportional accuracy and allows figures to interact naturally on the pictorial surface, as well as being in harmony with Egyptian ideals of physical beauty. Because full faces are not shown, it does not address itself strongly to the viewer or suggest the third dimension. Similar compositional principles govern the representation of most objects. Any conventional form is necessarily a choice among many possibilities; once forms were devised, they mostly varied only in detail.

Private tombs of the Old to New Kingdoms have a wide range of scenes of 'daily life', such as agriculture, fishing, marsh pursuits and craftsmen, as well as some religious elements and, in the New Kingdom, figures of the King rewarding the tomb owner. Almost all scenes have identifying and descriptive text captions. Most Old Kingdom tombs at Giza and Saqqara are decorated in fine low relief, originally painted, while New Kingdom Theban tombs have more paintings, whose flexible medium encourages freer and livelier effects. Reliefs and sculpture of the late period (712–332 BC), scattered in the world's museums, include notable masterpieces but are much rarer than their predecessors.

Mesopotamia: detail of one of the reliefs decorating Ashurbanipat's palace at Mineveh representing a lion hunt

Mesopotamia: modern impression of a cylinder seal bearing the name of King Ur-namma of Ur

Minor arts

In prosperous periods, especially the central New Kingdom, vast numbers of decorative everyday and funerary objects were made. These followed the same representational principles as relief and painting, and because of the diagrammatic character of representation, depictions of items such as boxes and preserved pieces correspond closely to each other. Egyptian furniture is remarkably elegant and sophisticated, and several other genres, such as cosmetic equipment, were as highly developed. Art was thus not confined to temples and tombs but pervaded elite life as a whole. Some objects were, however, unartistic. Most pottery is plain and utilitarian, and painted wares are known only from one or two short periods. The reason for this is probably that the focus of elite interest in vessels was on stone – worked with astonishing virtuosity in the first two dynasties (*c.*2950–2650 BC) – and later metal.

The legacy of Egyptian art

Egyptian art may seem static and rigid, but within its representational system it evolved very greatly. Development tended to be uniform in direction within major periods, mostly moving toward greater complexity and richness, but artists often sought instruction in works of much earlier times than their own. This tension between continuity with the immediate past and innovation with a backward glance is not unique to Egypt; it is known from many long-running traditions. The only time of truly radical departures is the attempted religious 'revolution' of Akhenaten (*c.*1352–1335 BC), during which both the style and the subject matter of reliefs and statuary were transformed, while representational conventions also changed significantly; most of these innovations were soon rejected.

Egyptian artistic motifs, and typical objects like scarabs, were very influential in the ancient Near East, and in the first millennium BC Egyptian style had a profound effect on the art of Syria–Palestine, while Egyptian conventions as a whole (including writing) formed the point of departure for Meroitic art in northern Sudan*. Late period art spread to Greece and, through the Phoenicians, to much of the Mediterranean. 'Nilotic' motifs and genuine Egyptian objects were common in ancient Rome. With successive European revivals of interest in Egypt since the Renaissance, Egyptian motifs and forms have often been used in the West, most successfully in architecture and the decorative arts. Western artists have, however, often been blind to Egyptian representational conventions, the understanding of which began in the nineteenth century with the advent of facsimile recording and an increased awareness of cultural diversity. The attractiveness and apparent naturalness of Egyptian art often lead the viewer to overlook the fact that its principles have a logic of their own that is largely alien to that of Western art.

JB

Further reading

C. Aldred, *Egyptian Art in the Days of the Pharaohs, 3100–320 BC* (London, 1980)
A. Badawi, *A History of Egyptian Architecture*. 3 vols. Vol. 1, *Giza*; Vols. 2–3 (California, 1966–8); Vol. 4, forthcoming (Graz)
B. V. Bothmer, *Egyptian Sculpture of the Late Period, 700 BC to AD 100* (New York, 1969, rev. edn.)
J.-L. de Cenival, *Living Architecture: Egyptian* (London, 1964)
K. Lange and M. Hirmer, *Egypt: architecture, sculpture, painting* (London, 1968, 4th edn.)
H. Schäfer, tr. J. Baines, *Principles of Egyptian Art* (Oxford, 1974; rev. edn., Oxford, 1986)
W. S. Smith, *The Art and Architecture of Ancient Egypt*, rev. by W. K. Simpson (Harmondsworth, 1981, 3rd edn.)

Ancient Near Eastern art and architecture

The art of the Near East has been rediscovered thanks to excavations of the ancient ruin-mounds or *tells* which are a feature of the landscape and were formed by the superimposed debris of successive settlements built predominantly of mud brick. The objects found during these excavations are now housed in the national museums of the countries concerned but the British Museum (London), the Louvre (Paris), the University Museum (Philadelphia) and the Metropolitan Museum (New York) also have large collections.

Mesopotamia

The early settlers in the alluvial plains of the Tigris and the Euphrates used hand-made painted pottery of which the Halaf, Samarra and Ubaid are the most aesthetically pleasing; they also modelled distinctive figurines. Mud-brick architecture developed: circular buildings at Gawra, Arpachiyah and in the Hamrin; niched architecture at Gawra and in the south; and a distinctive T-shaped unit which could be combined to form elaborate buildings. Towards the middle of the fourth millennium BC, plain, wheel-made pottery appeared at Uruk in the south, together with monumental, elaborately niched architecture, sculpture in the round and writing on clay tablets which were sealed with cylindrically shaped seals bearing designs in *intaglio*. Cylinder seals were to be used for some 3000 years, not only in Mesopotamia but also, at certain periods, in adjacent countries and are our prime source for iconographical development.

During the earlier part of the third millennium, Sumerian art is remarkably homogeneous. Statues of worshippers are angular, with large staring eyes, but gradually become more rounded and wear distinctive, tufted skirts. Victory scenes are depicted on stelae and on votive plaques. A huge copper relief testifies to developing metallurgy as do the vessels and jewellery found in the Royal Cemetery at Ur. When the Akkadians united Mesopotamia, they created a court style best illustrated in their cylinder seals, sculpture in the round and Naram-Sin's victory stele. Little is known of their architecture since their capital has not been found. The statues of Gudea belong to the succeeding neo-Sumerian revival, and Ur-Nammu built a ziggurat at Ur: a huge, stepped, mud-brick structure supporting a shrine.

Towards 1800 BC temples at a number of sites (Ur, Larsa, Tell Haddad, Tell al-Rima and, in Syria, Tell Leilan) were decorated with elaborate mud-brick palm-trunks and barley-sugar columns. Hammurabi's Law Code* is carved on a huge diorite stele bearing a relief (Louvre). The succeeding Kassites were not innovative but their ziggurat at Aqar Quf still dominates the landscape and their boundary stones display divine symbols. Mitannian and Middle Assyrian art are best represented in cylinder seals and by the excavations at Nuzi, Assur and Kar Tukulti Ninurta.

The neo-Assyrians decorated their huge palaces at Nimrud (ninth–eighth centuries), Khorsabad (late eighth century) and Nineveh (seventh century) with stone reliefs depicting religious, hunting and military scenes. A distinctive feature of their palaces is the throne-room unit, whose huge doorways were protected by winged, human-headed bulls or lions. The Babylonians used reliefs of glazed mud brick in Nebuchadnezzar's throne-room and the Ishtar Gate at Babylon, but the ziggurat or 'Tower of Babel' no longer survives and opinions differ as to the location of the Hanging Gardens.

The caravan city of Hatra is predominantly Parthian but Greek influence is also attested. The palace at Ctesiphon, near Baghdad, was rebuilt by the Sasanians and is dominated by an enormous mud-brick arch.

Iran

The early pottery cultures of Iran remained isolated from each other, but Susa had close cultural as well as political links with Mesopotamia and its development parallels that of Uruk in the late fourth millennium BC and of Sumer in the third millennium, when Susa adopted the highly individual Proto-Elamite style. Fine bitumen vessels and terracotta heads have been found in second millennium contexts at Susa and there is an impressive ziggurat at Choga Zanbil. Settlements on the main trade-routes, such as Malyan, Siyalk, Yahya (where chlorite bowls were manufactured), and Shar-i Sokhta (which handled the lapis lazuli trade) also developed distinctive cultures.

The art of the late second millennium was marked by the influx of the Indo-Aryans, bringing grey pottery and advanced metal-working techniques, including iron technology. The graves at Marlik date to this period and so, probably, does the famous Hasanlu gold bowl. Luristan is renowned for its bronze standards, finials, weapons and horse-trappings, Amlash for its stylized, zoomorphic pots, Siyalk for distinctive painted, spouted vessels and Ziwiye for its eclectic goldwork and ivories. The Medians built a fort and temple at Nush-i Jan and the Achaemenid Persians established their capital first at Pasargadae and then at Persepolis and buried their kings nearby. Their art reflects their use of Babylonian, Egyptian and Ionian Greek craftsmen. Parthian jewellery, terracottas and a large bronze statue have survived but Parthian art is best represented outside Iran. Sasanian art is known from numerous rock-reliefs (such as Taq-i Bustan, Naqsh-i Rustam and Bishapur), palaces (including Bishapur, Qaleh-i Yazdagird and Firuzabad), textiles and metalwork.

Anatolia

Excavations at Çatal Hüyük have revealed a series of settlements going back to before 6500 BC, with well-planned houses, and shrines decorated with painted plaster reliefs incorporating horn-cores. Stone and clay figurines have been found here and at other sites such as Hacilar. At Troy and at Kültepe in the third millennium we have the prototypes of the Greek megaron and rich jewellery and vessels have been found at Troy and in the tombs at Alaca Hüyük.

In the second millennium BC, the houses of Assyrian merchants at Kültepe contained fine red-burnished vessels and clay tablets whose sealings show mixed Anatolian and Mesopotamian motifs. Palaces at Acem Hüyük and Maşat Hüyük foreshadow the Hittite architecture of Boğazköy and the reliefs at the rock-cut shrine of Yazilikaya, at Alaca Hüyük and at Malatya are the forerunners of those found at the neo-Hittite sites on the Syrian–Turkish border in the first millennium, notably at Sincirli and Carchemish. In the east the Urartians built fine ashlar citadels and temples and produced beautiful bronzework, while in the west the Phrygians used painted vessels and carved elaborate tomb façades and rock reliefs. The hill-top tumulus at Nemrut Dağ is decorated with monumental sculptures in a mixture of styles, where the Parthian king Antiochus (69–34 BC) is shown shaking hands with Greek gods.

Syria–Palestine

Sites on the Euphrates and Khabur rivers were linked to Mesopotamia by trade: Habuba Kebira and Brak were important Uruk-period sites, while Mari has produced sculpture similar to that of Early Dynastic Mesopotamia. The palace at Ebla was destroyed by the Akkadians, who also built a fort at Brak. In *c.* 1800 BC Shamsi-Adad united northern Syria and Mesopotamia and built numerous palaces and temples. The palace at Mari,which belongs to this period and boasts a fine range of wall paintings, was added to by Zimri-Lim. Alalakh was the summer residence of the kings of Aleppo in the eighteenth–seventeenth centuries and its palace and temple were rebuilt in the fifteenth century BC when Mitannian influence was strong. Neo-Hittite and Aramaean Kingdoms set up along the borders with Turkey in the early first millennium BC have produced reliefs and portal sculpture which probably influenced the Assyrians.

The coastal sites of Ugarit and Byblos go back to Neolithic times. They traded with the Aegean and Egypt, whose art strongly influenced that of the Levant, as demonstrated by the Phoenician ivories and bronze bowls of the ninth–eighth centuries BC. Further south there were citadels and temples at Hazor, Megiddo, Lachish and Ajjul, but most of the local population lived in small villages and their art is chiefly known from the contents of their rock-cut tombs. The Jerusalem of David was very small but part of Solomon's temple platform may survive.

DC

Further reading

E. Akurgal, *The Art of the Hittites* (London, 1962)
P. Amiet, *Art of the Ancient Near East* (New York, 1980)
H. Frankfort, *The Art and Architecture of the Ancient Orient* (London, 4th edn, 1979)
H. Klengel, *The Art of Ancient Syria* (London, 1972)
A. Moortgat, *The Art of Ancient Mesopotamia* (London, 1969)
E. Porada, *The Art of Ancient Iran* (London, 1965)

The Graeco-Roman heritage

The Arab conquerors of the Roman Near East found an urban civilization which had developed continuously since the Hellenistic period, with large and regularly planned cities, substantial villages and frontier fortresses. All had experienced considerable growth under the Romans and transformation in the Christian period of late antiquity (late third to early seventh century).

Remains of sites like Apamea, Jerash and Bostra give a clear picture of urban life. Cities occupied substantial sites – about 1.5 by 2 km for a middling-sized place like Apamea, while a large city like Antioch was about twice the size – and were distinguished by orthogonal plans with broad boulevards, monumental buildings of stone and a considerable space devoted to structures of public use. The main streets were lined with colonnades, adorned with arches and interrupted by open squares. They gave access to such universal structures as open colonnaded market-places, baths built on an imperial scale with a series of hot and cold rooms, temples often on a podium in a courtyard, and the theatre and stadium; provincial capitals would also have a palace for the governor. Behind and around these public buildings, symbols of the services which the city provided to its denizens, were dwellings ranging from palaces to small houses and usually constructed with well-cut stone.

The Temple of Jerash, Jordan

The Khazneh at Petra, Jordan

Influence of Christianity

The triumph of Christianity* brought visible changes. Although public works of the previous era were maintained, temples were abandoned and churches became prominent. Most were modest basilicas, but many cities erected splendid cathedrals and *martyria* on a variety of plans; notable examples adorned Apamea, Bostra and Jerusalem. The churches were typically paved with mosaics and decorated with cut marble and frescoes, much as were the more opulent civic and private structures. In general, the cities had a colourful appearance enhanced by exterior paintings and prominently displayed sculptures.

On the other hand, urban decay was also manifest. Late antique cities suffered from the rapacity of the central government, natural disasters and Persian invasions, especially in the sixth and early seventh centuries. As a result, parts of most cities lay in ruins, and open spaces became cluttered with small and poorly built structures, whether houses, shops or industrial installations. The reign of Justinian brought considerable rebuilding, especially evident in the churches, but the new work was rarely of the size or quality of the old. The degree of delapidation varied considerably: Bostra, for example, seems little affected, while Antioch lay largely in ruins.

The cities, nevertheless, would have impressed by their scale, and by the consistent use of stone for permanent, often monumental structures. These could serve as a model for the buildings of the conquerors, among which the Dome of the Rock* in Jerusalem and the Umayyad Mosque of Damascus* most clearly fit into the context of late antique urbanism.

Most of the population lived in small towns and villages, whose abundant remains give an idea of life in the countryside. Although the sites vary in size and quality of construction, they are all characterized by buildings of neatly cut stone and one or more churches. Some settlements had large dwellings, baths, and meeting houses among the houses, rarely arranged on the regular plans of the cities. Buildings were almost universally low and square, with little decoration; the unclassical forms reflect a fundamental difference between city and country. The prevalence of stone construction, however, attests to the high standard of living throughout the country. Unlike the cities, most of the small towns and villages appear to have flourished, even grown, in late antiquity, with construction continuing through the sixth century.

Sites on and near the frontier were usually surrounded with heavy fortification walls. Many formed part of the imperial defences which were constantly maintained and rebuilt. These, too, contained the normal complement of public buildings and churches. Many, though, were small forts, less than 100 m in length, containing barracks, chapels and open courtyards. Such structures served as a model for the Umayyad* palaces of the desert.

Roman North Africa

A similar pattern of settlement and buildings characterized Roman North Africa, with the exception of Egypt, which was dominated by one huge city, Alexandria, and by the large estates of the aristocracy. Virtually nothing has survived of either. Rural settlements there were less substantially constructed than those of Syria, making extensive use of mud brick. On the other hand, the country did contain impressive fortresses, as at Babylon (Cairo), as well as large fortified monasteries.

The Libyan sites of Apollonia, Cyrene and Leptis Magna show the typical rich variety of monumental public buildings and churches, but the first two, like much of the region, had suffered considerable decline before the Arabs arrived. Urban areas had contracted considerably and open spaces were built over with shoddy constructions. Apollonia, the provincial capital, forms a notable exception. Elsewhere, the insecurity of the time is attested by a large number of fortified farmhouses.

Transformation was even more drastic in the densely populated province of Ifriqiyya* (Tunisia), which under the Romans had been covered with a thriving network of cities. With the possible exception of the poorly known metropolis of Carthage*, the African cities had suffered drastic contraction under the Vandals and during the wars of Justinian's reconquest. Flourishing cities were deserted or reduced to small forts, and the country which the Arabs entered would have seemed impoverished and underpopulated.

Study of surviving monuments makes it possible to reconstruct the Graeco-Roman heritage, which universally featured complex and sophisticated cities, adorned with a variety of stone buildings and a rich decoration. The heritage was perhaps most dynamic in the countryside of the Near East, and still flourished in many of its cities, but increasing delapidation and abandonment would have greeted the Arabs as they moved west. In all areas, however, they would have found buildings, and styles of construction and decoration which were destined to have a considerable influence on their subsequent development.

CF

Further reading

I. Browning, *Jerash* (London, 1982)
H. C. Butler, *Ancient Architecture in Syria* (Leyden, 1907–20)
P. MacKendrick, *The North African Stones Speak* (University of North Carolina, 1980)
C. Mango, *Byzantine Architecture* (London, 1976)

Modern archaeology and the rediscovery of the past

Modern interest in the ancient world was slow to waken; in spite of Renaissance enthusiasm for classical Greece and Rome, little or nothing was known of the civilizations that had preceded them. In the eighteenth century European travellers in North Africa, the Levant and Persia often sketched and described the ancient ruins they encountered and by the end of the century curiosity had been aroused. In 1798 Napoleon's military expedition to Egypt was accompanied by a team of savants and draughtsmen who travelled up the Nile recording what they saw. Their discovery of the trilingual decree carved on the stele known as the Rosetta Stone proved the key to the language of the hieroglyphs, and Champollion's decipherment, completed in 1822, gave impetus to the study of the monuments; at last the stones could speak. At more or less the same time work was progressing on the cuneiform script: Grotefend first deciphered Old Persian at Persepolis, but it was not until Rawlinson in 1857 succeeded in copying the long trilingual texts of Behistun that inscriptions on the Assyrian sculptures found at Nimrud and Kuyunjik by Layard, and by Place at Khorsabad, could be read, and the thousands of tablets found by Loftus and de Sarzec in the mounds of southern Mesopotamia began to be understood, though some, in Sumerian, could not yet be read.

The great discoveries in Egypt

Between 1828 and 1845 serious scholars, Champollion, Rossellini and Lepsius, carried on the work of recording in Egypt, but there were other, less reputable ventures: Muhammad ʿAli* encouraged the presence of Europeans and agents of the great museums, and wealthy private collectors were commissioned to procure antiquities, often by dubious means involving the plundering of ancient sites. Salt, the English consul in Cairo, employed Giovanni Belzoni to remove large monuments, some of which went to the British Museum, others to the Louvre. Layard and Rassam sent hundreds of carved slabs from the palaces of Assyria to the British Museum, P. E. Botta those from Khorsabad to the Louvre; other antiquities found their way into private hands. The appointment of Mariette, who had been sent to collect manuscripts but stayed to excavate the Serapeum, marked a new era in Middle Eastern archaeology: in 1851 he established the first national museum at Bulaq in Cairo, and filled it with antiquities excavated under his direction; efforts were made by the Egyptian government to stop clandestine digging and the unauthorized export of antiquities. Mariette's successor Gaston Maspero encouraged properly conducted excavations by foreign missions; the first, sent by the new Egypt Exploration Fund of London, had as one of its field directors W. M. Flinders Petrie, who, by insisting on accurate recording and prompt publication, and on the importance of humble domestic artefacts such as pottery (hitherto discarded), set new standards for the excavator. By 1900 he had pushed back the story of Egypt to an age before the earliest dynasties.

At that time no other country of the Middle East had been systematically explored. In Turkey, following the excavation of the Greek cities – Pergamon, Ephesus, Priene, Halicarnassus – Schliemann and Dörpfeld between 1870 and 1890 revealed in the hill of Hissarlik a Bronze Age civilization far older than (as they believed it to be) the Homeric city Troy. Little was yet known of the early peoples of Anatolia, though Hugo Winckler in 1905 identified at Boğhazköy the site of the Hittite capital Hattusas. Great classical sites in North Africa, such as Volubilis, Carthage, Dougga and Timgad, 'the African Pompeii', were laid bare by the French. Pious enthusiasm prompted the search for biblical sites; the Palestine Exploration Fund, founded in 1865, carried out surveys and investigated the walls of Jerusalem, and Petrie, sent out by them in 1890, at Tall al-Hesy made the first stratified excavation of a *tall* (mound), dating each layer by pottery familiar to him in Egypt. In Iran, French archaeologists started their long exploration of the mounds of Susa, and in Mesopotamia the Germans began the great task of uncovering the city of Babylon.

Occupation and conservation

The First World War put a temporary stop to excavation; as the war came to an end it was clear that in those territories which had been part of the Turkish Empire, as already in Egypt, the occupying powers must take responsibility for the protection of ancient monuments in the territories under their Mandate; Departments of Antiquities were formed in Iraq, Palestine, Syria and Lebanon, museums were built and laws promulgated restricting excavation to authorized expeditions and preventing the illegal export of antiquities. The 1920s and 1930s saw the unfolding of many new pages in the record of the past. Excavation at Boğhazköy produced thousands of tablets in the Hittite language; other Hittite cities were dug. Blegen at Troy linked Schliemann's discoveries with those of the unfolding Mycenaean world. At Byblos a city of great antiquity was found by French archaeologists, important for its links with Egypt. Further north on the site of ancient Ugarit (modern Ras Shamra) near Latakia, Claude Schaeffer in 1929 found one of the most important Late Bronze Age sites in the Levant, from which tablets in an alphabetic script and a hitherto unknown language threw new light on Canaanite mythology and ritual. Tall al-Hariri (ancient Mari) in Iraq also produced many thousands of tablets, illuminating the diplomatic history of the second millennium BC. Leonard Woolley's discovery of royal burials with rich goldwork at Ur of the Chaldees made headline news in 1927; even more sensational had been the discovery in Egypt a few years earlier of the intact tomb of one of the wealthiest of the pharaohs, Tutankhamun.

Recent research and restoration

In the years since 1945, the frontiers of knowledge have been pushed still further back and new techniques enable the archaeologist to extract hitherto unhoped-for information from what he finds. Scientific tests can establish the date of pottery, wood and bone and a computer analyses his results. The excavations of Kathleen Kenyon at Jericho and J. Mellaart in southern Turkey have revealed impressive town remains dating to as early as 6500 BC. Governments

Entrance to the ruins of Babylon, Iraq

of the countries now independent of Western control have their own antiquities services and conduct their own excavations; many of their archaeologists have trained in the universities of Europe and America. Ancient sites are tourist attractions, so consolidation and restoration of monuments are part of the official programme; the Iraq government has restored Hatra, the ziggurat at Ur and the Ishtar Gate in Babylon; rebuilding is in progress at Persepolis, in Tyre, in Ephesus and Sardis. New museums are being built; the Gulf states have museums of the most modern design and equipment. In recent years the building of irrigation dams and hydroelectric projects on the Tigris in Iraq, on the Euphrates at Tabqa in Syria and on the upper Euphrates in south-east Turkey has called for international cooperation in urgent rescue excavations in the areas to be submerged. The greatest of these, under the aegis of UNESCO, was the campaign to rescue the sites and monuments of Nubia before the completion of the Aswan High Dam*; this operation involved some fifty different teams of many nationalities, and the removal to safety of large temples. The recovery of the ancient past has become the concern of all the world.

MSD

Further reading

C. W. Ceram, *Narrow Pass, Black Mountain. The discovery of the Hittite Empire* (London, 1957)
M. S. Drower, *Flinders Petrie: a life in archaeology* (London, 1985)
K. M. Kenyon, *Archaeology in the Holy Land* (London, 1960)
S. Lloyd, *Foundations in the Dust: the story of Mesopotamian Exploration* (London, 1980, rev. edn.)
H. V. F. Winstone, *uncovering the Ancient World* (London, 1985)

A Byzantine courtesan, Damascus

Islamic art and architecture

Islamic art poses formidable problems of definition. In certain media, such as architecture and calligraphy, it is primarily a religious phenomenon. In other fields, such as pottery, metalwork, carpets and painting, its main emphasis is frankly secular. Thus when the word 'Islamic' is used to describe the visual arts, it is as well to remember that it cloaks a built-in ambiguity. A convenient alternative definition, and one which is sufficiently uncontentious for the present purpose, would emphasize its application to that medieval culture and society which was united by the Muslim faith. That will be the definition employed in this essay.

Some such general term is required for quite another reason: the enormous span of Islamic art in space and time. That great span could easily be used to justify numerous subdivisions of the material according to geographical or chronological criteria. Yet such subdivisions would serve only to blur the perception that Islamic art is not a mere concept, an abstraction, but is recognizably an entity, even if that entity defies easy definition. Geographically, Islamic art extends from Spain in the west to Indonesia in the east, and flourished from the seventh to the seventeenth century; yet, despite all the odds conjured up by these facts, it has a cachet as instantly recognizable as that of Chinese art. That cachet is most apparent in Islamic decoration, which displays well-nigh unequalled resource and virtuosity. Here, if anywhere, must be sought the key to what makes Islamic art Islamic. The answer seems to lie in the means of expression which Islamic artists selected for preference and in the underlying reasons for their choice.

It is important to be aware of the fact that Islamic art expresses itself in a choice of media which may seem idiosyncratic to Western eyes. The splendour of the great Islamic religious buildings has

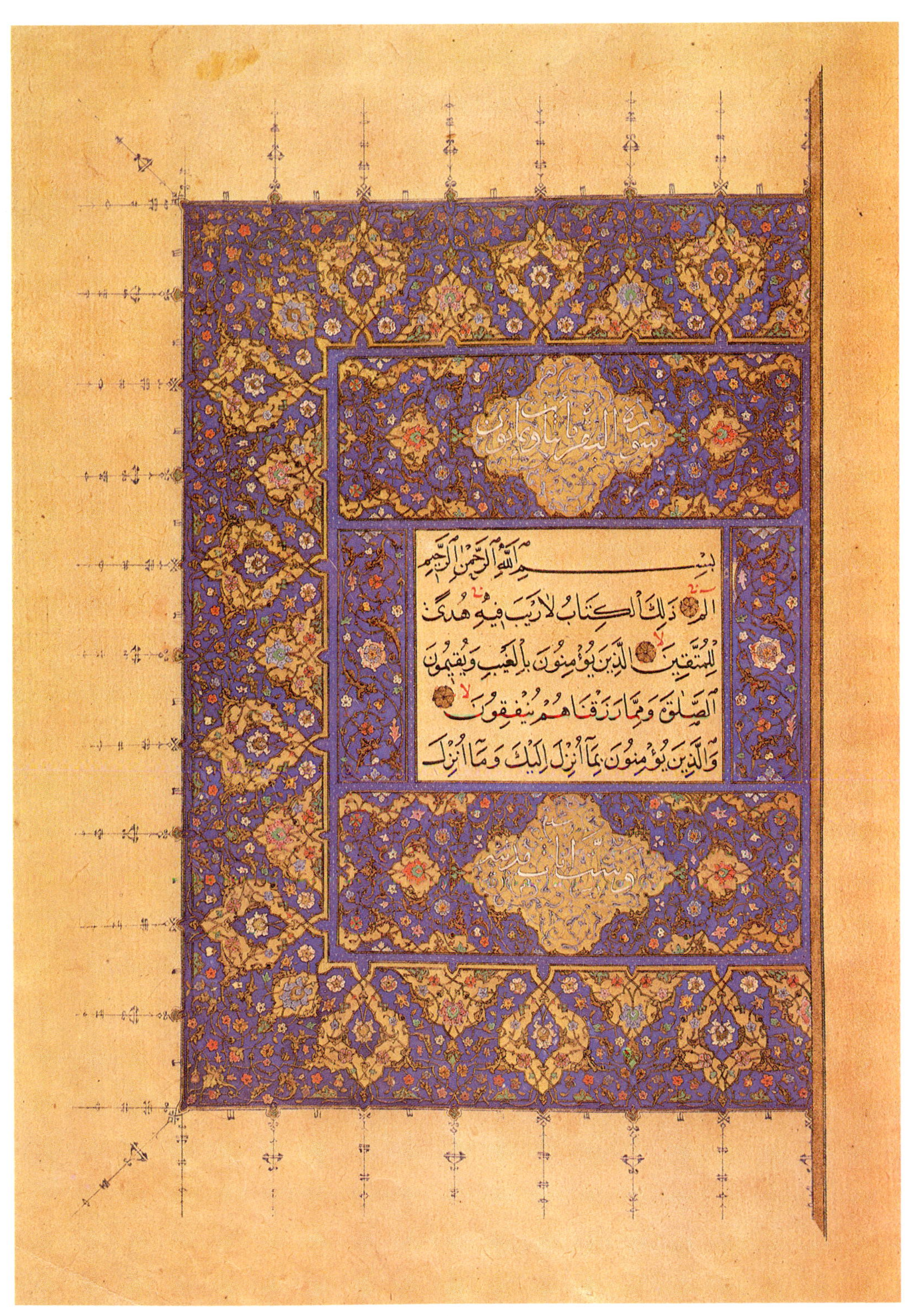

An illuminated page from the Qur'an; example of *naskhi* script tended to obscure the importance of the so-called 'minor arts' which achieve a major status under Islam. Their secondary importance in the European tradition is betrayed by the slightly dismissive term 'decorative arts'. In the medieval Islamic world, where easel and panel painting were unknown and fresco painting and figural sculpture of negligible importance, the priorities were necessarily different from those which reigned in contemporary Europe. Nor was the difference confined to the choice of media. Islamic art offers the choice paradox of a tradition saturated with religious associations yet virtually devoid of a developed religious iconography. This paradox deserves closer study.

The importance of ornament

Much has been made of the Islamic ban on the representation of living figures in a religious context – a ban, incidentally, which, despite popular belief to the contrary, is totally inoperative in secular art. Again, contrary to popular belief, the ban does not originate from the Qur'an*; the idea surfaces repeatedly in the *hadith**, the sayings attributed to Muhammad*, though only collected systematically in the early ninth century and therefore apt at times to incorporate much later ideas. It is a ban, moreover, which was repeatedly broken in areas under Iranian Shiʿi* or Turkish dominion. Nevertheless, its general validity in Islamic religious architecture is not seriously subject to question, and it turned that architecture in a decisively new direction.

This reluctance to depict living creatures in a religious context had one crucial consequence: it directed the imaginative energy of the artist towards geometric, vegetal and epigraphic ornament. Such ornament becomes of primary, not secondary, importance since in addition to its intrinsic meaning it also takes on the role which in other cultures is reserved for figural images. It thus acquires a unique intensity. In the case of geometric and vegetal themes, the lack of a single exclusive or, at any rate, principal meaning fostered a certain ambivalence which may well have enriched their impact – witness the numerous symbolic and mystical interpretations of such ornament generated by modern observers. The virtuosity and complexity of geometric ornament testify to the strong mathematical bias of much Islamic architecture and design, and some have professed to recognize the influence of Pythagoras and Euclid in such work; its affinity with certain structural forms encountered in the natural world, such as crystals, has also been remarked. As for vegetal ornament, the key innovation here is the ubiquitous and aptly named arabesque, a distant relation of the classical acanthus and vine-scroll yet subtly different from both of them. Propelled as it is to centre stage, the arabesque naturally enough takes on a complexity for which there was no need when vegetal ornament remained in the background or was restricted to a few well-defined locations.

Epigraphy

The third major area of Islamic ornament was writing, and this alone was wholly original. Numerous varieties of Arabic script – a script also used for the other major Islamic languages – were developed, many of them decorative in the extreme and not readily legible. Often they are set too far from the ground to be deciphered. These considerations suggest that inscriptions had a symbolic function independent of what the words actually said. For the most part such illegible inscriptions are of religious content; historical inscriptions are normally placed where they can be read. Qur'anic texts predominated in religious buildings, and, given that most educated (and many uneducated) Muslims knew large sections of the holy text by heart, and needed only the trigger of a word or two in order to recognize a passage, it seems at least possible that these inscriptions functioned as the Muslim equivalent of sacred images. It is only logical that with these sacred associations calligraphy was accorded special reverence and took pride of place among ornamental motifs.

Mingling of the genres of ornament

These, then, are the principal expressions of Islamic ornament. Though each is of its nature very different from the others, they have a surprising amount in common. Each lends itself to a remarkable range of reduction and expansion, alike suitable as a muted background theme on a tiny scale – for example as a decorative border – and as the principal theme of a huge composition – for example the exterior of a dome. They can be equally effective from a distance of a metre or of a kilometre. Such extraordinary flexibility has other side-effects. It means that the three genres mingle easily and do not need to be kept apart. Moreover, it predisposes the artist to experiment not only with scale but also with colour, with texture, with media and with levels of design. This in turn opens the door to a wide range of interactions not only within each genre – geometric, vegetal and epigraphic – but also between one genre and another. Hence the popularity of vegetal scrolls which are little more than concentric circles, or of geometric networks with vegetal or epigraphic infill. It is perhaps inscriptions, however, that best exemplify this capacity of the various genres to borrow freely from each other, to such an extent sometimes that the boundaries between them become blurred. It is standard practice for Arabic letters to emerge as if with difficulty from a ground of scrolling floral ornament. Inscriptions often create patterns like geometric forms, as in the type of Kufic apparently derived from Chinese seal script. In other styles the letters are foliated or floriated.

This free-wheeling approach to categories of ornament also helps to account for the magisterial skill with which different levels are played off against each other. The more elaborate Persian carpets, where successive designs are superimposed upon each other to create a composition of polyphonic complexity, epitomize a further consequence of the flexibility of so much Islamic design – its inherent ambiguity. Variations in colour or texture can create the same ambiguity, allowing a pattern or design to operate in different but interdependent ways, like positive and negative film. This allows the artist to make the most of a given idea or motif. The selfsame motif looks different when it is executed in a different colour, texture or material. Inscriptions can be superimposed freely upon each other without loss of legibility simply by altering the type of script, the size of the letters or the colour in which they are executed.

It should be clear from these remarks that the role of abstract ornament, and the scale on which it was used, was profoundly different in Islamic art *vis-à-vis* European art. Any definition of Islamic ornament in particular, and by extension of Islamic art in general, which sets out to characterize it on the basis of what it is not, by so doing brands itself as the work of an outsider. Such negative definitions are typical of the Eurocentric approach which marks most modern historians of Islamic art. Equally characteristic of that approach in popular belief (though not among professional art historians) is the notion that Islamic ornament changed comparatively little after its first appearance in the early Middle Ages. A brief glance at the pre-eminent role allotted to ornament in Islamic art should be enough to scotch such a theory. It is this evolving ornament, as much as any other single feature, that provides the unifying element in the otherwise bewilderingly diverse mosaic of local artistic traditions in the Islamic world.

Historical development

So much for generalities. How do they mesh into a chronological framework? The evolution of Islamic art falls naturally into three distinct phases. The first, a period of primal unity encompassing the entire Islamic world, was roughly co-extensive with the political authority exercised by the Umayyad* and early ʿAbbasid* Caliphs, and dates from *c*.660–*c*.950. The second and much longer phase represents the Islamic Middle Ages, ending around 1500 and witnessing the rise of distinctive local traditions corresponding to new political and ethnic groupings. The third of these epochs, covering principally the sixteenth and seventeenth centuries, coincides with the partition of the Islamic world into three great Empires – Ottoman*, Safavid* and Mughal – and the gradual infiltration of that world by European influences. In the visual arts these influences – such as classical detailing in architecture or modelling and perspective in painting – were inimical to the spirit of the Islamic tradition and their ready acceptance boded its downfall.

The early period

Islamic art had a late start. The reason is not far to seek. In the early decades of the Muslim state, the burgeoning new Empire was ruled from the Hijaz*, an environment in which the visual arts had little part to play. With the transfer of the capital from Medina to Damascus in Syria, at the behest of the Umayyad dynasty* in 661 (see History), the stage was set for the appearance of an art worthy of this new world power. This Umayyad art, whose major surviving examples are concentrated in the Levant and were indeed produced in the immediate orbit of the Umayyad court, owes little but the impetus of the new faith to the Arabs. Its patrons were well aware of the need to make appropriate contact with their subjects in this as in other fields, and readily appreciated the propaganda dimension of splendid buildings and of symbolic images. Their use of art as an instrument of policy is well documented in their coinage, delicately poised between East and West. Throughout their reign the Umayyads drew freely on the established artistic traditions of Byzantium* and Sasanian* Persia, adapting and transforming them to their own purposes with a remarkable lack of inhibition. The period 661–750 witnessed a gradual erosion of classical influences in favour of those derived from ancient Near Eastern art*. Thus the earliest great Islamic building, the Dome of the Rock* in Jerusalem (completed *c*.691), could easily be mistaken for an early Christian *martyrium*; but less than a generation later the Great Mosque of Damascus* (completed *c*.712–15), while employing the standard component parts of a Christian basilica, reshuffles them in a completely unexpected way to create a brand new building type. Graeco-Roman architectural detailing and glittering glass mosaics cannot diminish the impact of this new way of seeing. The country palaces built later in the period take even more liberties with classical forms, using the shell of Roman frontier forts but clothing them inside and out with decorative themes of Persian origin (as at Khirbat al-Mafjar and Mshatta, both early 740s). Such eclecticism remained a constant of Islamic art.

The fall of the Umayyads in 750 led to the eclipse of Syria and a shift in the political centre of gravity to Mesopotamia (see History). In the visual arts the effect was decisively to replace the lingering Romano-Byzantine influences by Persian ones. This was exemplified by the new capital of the ʿAbbasid Caliphate* at Baghdad (founded in 762). In this concentric circular design, housing for the citizens occupied the outer perimeter while the Caliph's palace, oriented to the four points of the compass and dominating the Friday Mosque beside it, was located at the dead centre of the city and girdled by a largely empty precinct. This powerful symbol of cosmic dominion and royal absolutism owed little to the Graeco-Roman world but had a long pedigree in the ancient Near East. This concept of the palace-city was perpetuated in the following century at Samarra, with its numerous sprawling official residences moulded by remorselessly axial planning. They were rendered independent of the outside world by integrating gardens, domestic housing, military and administrative quarters and a royal compound within a single but vast walled enclosure. It was at Samarra that Islamic art came of age, and from that centre it spread virtually throughout the entire Muslim world.

The setting of the city on an inland waterway with easy access to the Persian Gulf opened Samarra, like Baghdad before it, to influences from India and China as well as Persia, and thus gave Islamic art much wider horizons than it had previously possessed. The new aesthetic is perhaps best expressed by the wall decoration most fashionable in Samarra: painted stucco, both carved and moulded, using geometric and rigorously stylized vegetal motifs, and capable (like wallpaper) of indefinite extension. Its abstraction and its even patterning fitted it for any number of architectural contexts, and the 'Samarran style' soon penetrated the minor arts too. From the ninth century onwards, the gradual spread of Turkish hegemony throughout most of the Muslim world – a process whose early stages are, appropriately enough, inextricably linked with Samarra – brought to Islamic art a fondness for equally stylized animal motifs characteristic of the nomads of the Eurasian steppe.

The later periods

As the power of the ʿAbbasid Caliphs waned, new political groupings generated five distinctive regional styles: Moorish, Syro-Egyptian, Turkish, Persian and Indo-Muslim. In Spain* the establishment of an anti-ʿAbbasid state – and finally Caliphate – by scions of the Umayyad house gave Syrian art a new lease of life there. Though adopted in a deliberately retrospective spirit, it nevertheless inspired a distinctive style which, with the unchallenged cultural supremacy of Andalusia behind it, spread throughout north-west Africa. This style was marked by an extreme, mannered finesse of ornament in which lobed and horseshoe arches played a major role. The major mosques show developed hierarchies of decorative elements and some, such as the Great Mosques of Cordoba and Qayrawan, even incorporate esoteric references to the great Muslim buildings of Jerusalem. Others employ gigantic minarets, apparently as symbols of power (Seville, Rabat, Marrakesh, all twelfth century).

The Syro-Egyptian tradition at first flourished principally in Cairo (mosques of Ibn Tulun, 876–9; al-Azhar*, begun 970; and al-Hakim, *c.*1002–3), but under the Ayyubids* (1171–1250) and the Mamluks* (1250–1517) its orbit extended to include major building programmes in Jerusalem, Tripoli, Damascus and Aleppo. This was an essentially urban architecture with much emphasis on exterior carved stone façades (often Mecca-oriented), perhaps to compensate for interiors whose often cramped and irregular sites tended to inhibit the free unfolding of extensive spatial units. Mosques took second place in this tradition to buildings of lesser scale and narrower function – *madrasas*, mausoleums, *ribats* and *khanqahs* – often planned as joint foundations combined in various ways.

The very notion of Turkish architecture as a separate entity is somewhat misleading when applied to the period before *c.*1200, since Anatolia was part of a wider political grouping centred on Iran and Iraq. The very late start of this local tradition is also noteworthy, though the explosion of building activity in the thirteenth century under the patronage of the Seljuk* Sultans, which resulted in hundreds of fine stone tombs, *madrasas** and caravansarais being built, is ample recompense. Turkish architects, at first greatly influenced by the neighbouring Arab and Persian styles, later responded energetically to the challenge of Haghia Sophia, the greatest of Byzantine churches, by perfecting the Ottoman type of mosque. This is Islamic architecture at its most Western, with its great central dome, visually (but not structurally) shored up by tiers of half-domes and its slender pencil-shaped minarets at the corners. Courtyards are not an afterthought but are fully integrated into the ensemble, often in a proportional relationship to the rest of the mosque, and the façades reveal parsimonious decoration, its location precisely calibrated and not suffered to impair the powerful architectural statement of the exterior as a whole. This style spread, probably by blueprint, throughout the Ottoman domains.

In Persian and Central Asia a strong indigenous tradition favoured domed square chambers with a highly articulated zone of transition on squinches. The ready availability and cheapness of brick, whether fired or unfired, predisposed Islamic architects here in favour of daring and elaborate vaulting. For larger buildings, courtyards punctuated by *iwans* – large vaulted halls with a rectangular façade – disposed in cruciform fashion enjoyed enduring popularity. Thus the façade was transported inside the building. The strong cubic masses of Persian architecture were at first left plain and were thus of a formidable austerity. In time their surfaces were embellished by decorated brickwork, polychrome tiles and 'stalactite' vaulting.

Indo-Muslim architecture, like that of Turkey, had a late start, but thereafter flourished to such an extent that most of the surviving architecture of the medieval Islamic world is to be found in the subcontinent, a fact not sufficiently well known. Foreign influences are much stronger here than is the norm in Islamic architecture – Hindu and Jain sculptural and structural traditions, as well as Buddhist domical forms, constantly recur. Exceptional scale was a consistent feature of the Indo-Islamic style, and is exemplified in the tallest of Islamic minarets – the Qutb Minar of *c.*1193; the most celebrated of Islamic tombs – the Taj Mahal of *c.*1635; and in the great Mughal palace-forts at Delhi, Agra and Lahore. The setting of many of these structures in spacious gardens illusionistically increased their size still further. Detailing of local inspiration, especially in marble, red sandstone and even semi-precious stones, was grafted onto forms which for all their non-Islamic veneer were basically Persian in origin.

Types of Islamic building

The major Islamic building types are quickly enumerated. Chief among them is the mosque, of which there are two types: the *jami*ʿ*, in which the whole community celebrates the Friday prayer, and the *masjid**, intended principally for normal daily worship. In the absence of municipal institutions, both types of mosque double as community centres with a wide range of political, administrative, legal, teaching, military, social and welfare functions. In its primitive form the mosque derived from Muhammad's house in Medina, which featured a walled open courtyard with a long narrow roofed area at one end facing Mecca. This essential schema persisted in most later mosques, though the covered sanctuary (*musalla*) increased very substantially in size and by degrees acquired various types of articulation, such as a gabled façade, one or more domes over the *mihrab** area, an axial *iwan*, a wider central aisle (thus creating the T-shape so popular in Maghribi mosques) and further domes at the centre of the façade and at its rear corners. These features were often combined to assert an axial emphasis and thus evoke princely associations. Numerous local traditions, already briefly analysed above, diversified the primitive schema, often beyond recognition. The lack of formal liturgy allowed mosque architecture to dispense with furniture and kept the interior of the mosque austerely empty. A *mihrab* to emphasize the direction of prayer, a *minbar*, or pulpit, for the *khutba** (part sermon and part bidding prayer) and a minaret, a tall tower for the call to prayer itself, sufficed.

Other characteristic Muslim buildings include the caravansarai, a kind of wayside inn often built in chains along the major trade and pilgrimage routes to accommodate travellers and their beasts; the *madrasa* or theological college, at first built principally to encourage the spread of Sunni orthodoxy; the multi-domed *hammam* or bath; and the *ribat*, a fortified residential building strategically placed along the Islamic frontiers and intended to house warriors for the faith. Palaces are often administrative and military centres as well as lavishly appointed royal homes. Mausoleums abound, often functioning not only as secular memorials but also as centres of local piety and pilgrimage. These various building types differ considerably from one area to the next, but they do normally share a predilection for domes, usually carried on squinches; lengthy arcades with pointed or horseshoe arches; complex, especially stalactite, vaulting; and open courtyards as an integral part of the design – though of course few baths and tombs share this last feature. The large expanses of flat wall surfaces which characterize these buildings are frequently clothed in carved stucco, polychrome tilework or inlaid marble, all applied with an acute sensitivity to texture and colour. Often the material of construction, whether stone or brick, is used for ornament too. The essential plainness of the façades in Ottoman architecture is the exception that proves the rule of this inherent decorative bias.

Fourteenth–fifteenth century pottery, Amman

The minor arts

Pottery

The minor arts, which occasionally borrowed from China and in turn influenced Europe, reach prominence – for reasons still insufficiently explored – only in ʿAbbasid times. Statistically most Islamic pottery is monochrome, utilitarian and undistinguished, but the glazed wares, especially lustre, often display technical virtuosity of a high order. The accent was less on shape or body (as in China) than on decoration. The extraordinarily varied themes of this repertoire are still largely unstudied, but frequently borrow from other media (such as metalwork, textiles and the art of the book), from pre-Islamic artistic traditions and from folk art. The relative cheapness of most fine pottery made this the most popular of the minor arts, and archaeological evidence indicates that in Iran at least pottery was displayed on walls. The major centres were successively Mesopotamia, Egypt, Iran, Andalusia and Turkey, whose 'Iznik ware' spread well beyond the frontiers of the Muslim world.

Metalwork

Islamic metalwork, being much more expensive in time and materials, was necessarily directed at a more exalted class of patron. Most of the surviving early Islamic pieces are silver dishes and ewers of Iranian origin; their courtly and animal themes display strong Sasanian influence. The eleventh century witnessed an increasingly severe silver shortage, which eventually resulted in the primacy of bronze and brass as the materials of high-quality metalwork, though silver continued in use alongside copper and niello for inlay work of polychrome splendour. In addition to great technical diversity – engraving, casting, repoussé and inlay were among the methods used – the range of Islamic metalwork encompassed remarkably diversified shapes, including in its depictions of animals the major expression of three-dimensional sculpture in Islam. The iconography favoured cycles of scenes depicting courtly pursuits framed by benedictory inscriptions of somewhat stereotyped content. The heyday of this metalwork was in Iran and the Arab Near East from the twelfth to fourteenth centuries; under the Mamluks of Egypt and Syria the repertoire changed yet again, emphasizing heraldic blazons and densely packed stately inscriptions proclaiming the titulature of the military aristocrats for whom such pieces were made.

Textiles

Islamic textiles fall naturally into two groups: silks and carpets. The silks served mainly ceremonial and funerary purposes; textiles of lesser value were the norm for everyday costume. Literary sources prove beyond doubt that textiles constituted the most significant artisanal industry of the medieval Islamic world, though few of the superabundant literary references can be matched with surviving textiles. Their ceremonial uses included wall-hangings, robes of honour distributed as official gifts, coverings for thrones and other items of furniture and – most significant of all – *tiraz* fabrics in which official inscriptions formed the main if not the only ornament. The textiles with figural designs betray marked dependence on Sasanian and Byzantine prototypes, with much the same emphasis on royal and hybrid beasts depicted in roundels in heraldic fashion – affronted, addorsed, rampant, passant or regardant. These themes, though most commonly encountered in Iran, permeated the whole Islamic world; their golden age was *c.*800–*c.*1200.

Carpets, by contrast, despite their ancient and distinguished pedigree in the Near East, do not survive from this early period. The first Islamic examples known so far are Anatolian rug fragments with rather simple geometric designs; these date perhaps from the thirteenth century. Much more complex and chromatically subtler carpets of geometric design were produced in the later Mamluk period, but the best source for early Near Eastern carpets remains contemporary Western painting, in which such rugs were carefully displayed as luxury objects. Timurid book-painting similarly offers the best clue to contemporary Persian carpets. Thereafter Anatolia and Iran dominate the history of carpets. Iconographically, Safavid carpets of the sixteenth century, in which hunting scenes and floral motifs of a complex symbolism abound, afford the richest field for enquiry. A single example must suffice. The Ardabil carpet, signed by Maqsud of Kashan and dated 1539–40, invokes the age-old equation of floor with ceiling design and, by extension, the heavens. Mosque lamps 'hang' from a central lobed medallion, itself set like a great planet amidst a revolving galaxy. Sombre blue and red tones predominate. Such compositions are rarely explicit. The quartered designs of garden carpets could be read as references to the seasons, the cosmos or paradise itself. In Anatolian carpets the folk element is much more pronounced.

Book-painting

Despite the absence of easel painting and the rarity of frescoes and mosaics, book-painting always, it seems, had a place in the Islamic world. But its high cost ensured that it was never truly popular. Rather was it a court art fostered by connoisseurs for their private gratification. The early history of the art is lost, so that the style of the earliest substantial body of material to survive – thirteenth-century Arab painting – is assured rather than experimental. It owes much to Byzantine and Jacobite art, and in its love of silhouette and its genre quality reflects the influence of the shadow theatre. It delights in animal fables, scientific treatises and the picaresque humour of the *maqamat**. The mature Iranian tradition, by contrast, which influenced both Indian and Turkish painting, favoured scenes from epic and lyric poetry, especially the *Shah-Name** of Firdawsi and the *Khamsa* of Nizami. The repeated illustration of a very few texts encouraged the growth of iconographic cycles rather as in Christian art. Perspective, modelling and all the paraphernalia of naturalism are conspicuously absent. Instead the artists strive to recreate a fairy-tale world of jewelled colours and tiny figures set in toy landscapes. This pervasively conceptual and two-dimensional approach maintained itself for a good four centuries, drawing freely on Chinese ideas and motifs but remaining unresponsive to those from Europe until the later seventeenth century. Indian painting, by contrast, though initially dependent on Iran, soon adopted – under European tutelage operative principally through the medium of engravings – a much more naturalistic approach, a rarity in Islamic art. The eager patronage of the Mughal emperors Akbar and Jahangir fostered large-scale experiments in history and narrative painting as well as lovingly detailed studies of animals, flowers and, above all, the personalities of the court. Turkish painting, like that of Muslim India, is a late starter and is heavily indebted to Iranian influences. Its emphases, however, are markedly different: religious and historical narratives, including the major Ottoman campaigns; festivals and crowd scenes; and highly stylized academic studies of Chinese elements (such as dragons and *chi'lins*), vegetal motifs (for instance, *saz* painting) and other themes set as exercises.

Calligraphy

Chief among the arts of the book, and indeed among all the arts, was calligraphy. Its unique prestige derived from its religious associations: it was God who taught man to write. The role of inscriptions as a substitute for religious iconography ensured their wide dispersion throughout the Islamic world. Nowhere was fine writing more important than in the copying of the Qur'an*. God had made His revelations in Arabic and thus the actual written words of the Qur'an gradually acquired a sacred character. To copy a Qur'an was an act of merit; in fact many rulers regularly did so themselves. Unlike painters, calligraphers enjoyed a very high status, and their art always enjoyed a special prestige in the Islamic world. Many early Qur'ans must have run into many volumes, for there are often no more than three lines per page, the sacred text encased like a relic in a welter of ornamentation. The variety of abstract ornament and the striking colour harmonies of these illuminated Qur'ans suggest that the artists were in no way cramped by the lack of figural decoration. Early Islamic epigraphy, like Qur'ans of the period before *c.*1200, uses the script loosely called Kufic*, a style named after Kufa in Mesopotamia, one of the first cultural centres of Islam. It is characterized by angularity, stiffness and an emphasis on the vertical strokes of letters; gradually the addition of curves and flourishes complicated the original simplicity of the script. In later, cursive hands the dimensions, swells and curves were all subject to a strict canon devised by masters who laid down detailed laws on questions of distances between letters, width of margins and so on. The subdivisions of these cursive hands are too many to enumerate but *naskh*, *thulth* and *nastaʿliq* are of major importance.

The Muslim city

The principal setting within which the arts of Islam flourished was the city. Given the remarkable variety of Muslim cities, generalizations are especially perilous. The lack of formal municipal institutions in the Islamic world precluded the development of such structures as law courts and town halls. It was typically the mosque which, among its many other functions, fulfilled the judicial and communal needs of Muslims. Cities built by fiat according to a pre-ordained symmetrical plan were always exceptional. In the early centuries of Islam this was reflected in the models chosen for such cities – Graeco-Roman for the Umayyad city of ʿAnjar in the Lebanon, ancient Near Eastern for ʿAbbasid Baghdad. The nucleus of most medieval cities was a spacious Friday Mosque with the palace of the ruler (itself also the centre of administration) beside it. By degrees it became the norm for the royal seat to be fortified – a veritable castle. The recurrent use of certain architectural modules – long blank walls, inner courtyards, vaulted alleys, domed chambers – and of certain materials such as mud brick, tilework or ashlar masonry, ensured that medieval Islamic cities had a powerful visual unity. This transcended the social or economic divisions of the city into quarters and bazaars. The absence of wheeled traffic, which tended to encourage narrow winding alleys rather than straight and broad arterial roads, was a further factor inhibiting symmetrical subdivisions of the city and favouring a dense urban fabric. There is no equivalent of the park or of the Roman forum, but wider spaces within the city walls would often be found in the great religious shrine complexes, most lavishly exemplified by the *külliyes* of the Ottoman world.

The conflict between orthodoxy and custom

Finally, what of the role of the visual arts in the Islamic world? The obvious utilitarian function of most Muslim architecture provided its own justification. For example, if trade were to prosper, caravansarais would have to be built. The very nature of Islamic culture created a need for a wide range of religious buildings whose functions embraced much of the secular sphere too: communal assembly, the process of the law, teaching, and the care of the sick. Calligraphy, by virtue of its built-in association with the Qur'an, was practised and honoured throughout the Muslim world. Yet, with these exceptions, virtually all Islamic art was subject to a continual tension between the pull of strict orthodoxy and that of fashion and custom. Christianity, Hinduism, Buddhism and many other faiths have traditionally used figural art for religious purposes. With minor exceptions, Islam has not done so. More than that, Islamic theology tended to regard figural art as not wholly respectable, though there are many shades of opinion on this matter. However, the sheer weight of evidence in the form of the architecture, minor arts and painting which survive from the medieval period allows only one conclusion: the theological lobby failed in its implicit attempt to outlaw the non-religious visual arts. That lobby may well have gained widespread support across Islamic society, and indeed the dearth of certain types of art and architecture at some periods and in specific areas of the Islamic world suggests that on occasion these proscriptions won the day. Thus the division between the secular and the religious sphere was in practice fully operative in the field of the visual arts, even if in theory no such division existed. Yet these remarks should not be construed to mean that much medieval Islamic art could fairly be termed 'popular'. Quite the contrary. With the admittedly major exception of glazed ceramics, most medieval Islamic art that has survived was produced for at least relatively wealthy patrons and often for royalty. Most book-painting, for example, was created for the enjoyment of a mere handful of people. Folk art as expressed in clothes, rugs, simple utensils or wall-paintings has virtually disappeared. Thus the medieval Islamic art which survives gives little clue to the attitudes, beliefs and tastes of the silent majority of the people in that vanished world.

RH

Islamic architecture in the modern world

The relevance of the Islamic tradition of architecture to urbanization in the contemporary Islamic world has only recently been recognized. On the whole, interest in 'Islamic architecture' has been carried on in isolation from architectural production within the changing urban environment; this has given rise to urgent problems, most evidently in cities with a legacy of Islamic architectural achievement.

The oil boom which began after the Arab-Israeli War* of 1973 resulted in the investment of a large proportion of the newly acquired capital in the development of city centres. Whether in large planning projects or in construction, the models which were followed were those of the modern Western style, linked with a certain definition of 'development'. As the Western-style quarters and towns were being constructed, in response to a demand for 'modernity' and 'development', the interest in Islamic architecture started to increase. The main reason for this was the rising awareness of the need to give a certain 'Islamic' or national identity to buildings of a new style which would otherwise stamp the new urban centres with anonymity.

Until then, Islamic architecture had been mainly a subject of academic research related to archaeology or art history rather than to the living architecture or art of the Islamic world. It was along this line that it was approached by orientalists, art historians, archaeologists and others in Europe and the United States, as the wealth of publications on the subject shows. In the Islamic countries themselves, however, Islamic art and architecture had less priority; efforts to mobilize resources for research and documentation, or for the rehabilitation of the monuments and the 'Islamic' quarters of cities, were eclectic and slight in relation to the dimensions of the task. Such efforts have been directed towards public events – exhibitions, prestigious conferences, and occasional publications – but Islamic art and architecture have not been regarded as a necessary part of the architectural education, of which the curriculum is usually constructed according to the conceptions of the 'modern' or 'international' school.

Islamic versus modern architecture

In order to understand the problem, it is necessary to attempt some definition of the word 'Islamic'; only in this way will it be possible to avoid the confusion which may result from a loose and abstract use of the term as related to architecture.

'Islamic architecture', in its strict sense, should refer to buildings of a certain kind which grew up in Islamic cities during the period which extended from the rise of Islam to the Ottoman* and Safavid* periods. Such buildings include religious structures (mosques, *zawiyas*, *takiyyas*, *madrasas*), centres of power and administration (palaces and courts), and public commercial structures (*suqs*, *khans*, *wikalas*). Surrounding such buildings, and forming the urban fabric, are 'domestic' buildings, and these can scarcely be called 'Islamic' except by general reference to the pattern of town-planning; the style of such buildings changes according to geographical location, climatic conditions and local context. Terms such as 'traditional' or 'indigenous' or 'local' would be more appropriate than 'Islamic' for these parts of the urban and rural architectural fabric.

The justification for making this distinction is that the monumental structures were influenced by religion and state ideology, and shared unified concepts of design from one country to another in the Islamic world. It is true that patterns of town-planning also had certain common features – narrow winding streets, closed vistas, a well-defined relationship between the public and private, the religious and domestic, exterior and interior space – but local techniques, the availability of materials, and traditions of building design gave rise to wide local variations. The courtyard house, for example, has been traced as far back as the fifth millennium BC in northern Iraq, and cannot strictly be called 'Islamic'. Even within the Islamic period, there are great differences between a courtyard house in Baghdad and one, for example, in Muharraq in Bahrain.

The National Commercial Bank's headquarters building in Jidda, Saudi Arabia

The house of Haddad (Umar ibn Hasan Shaykh al-Kaf) in the Bil-Majaff quarter in Terim, South Yemen, built entirely of mud brick

The contemporary state of the traditional urban fabric

What remains of Islamic architecture is for the most part fragmented, decrepit and dilapidated. Some parts of it have been well researched and documented, but conservation on a comprehensive scale and on the level of rehabilitation of an area, rather than simple preservation of a monument, is still at the primary stage. This is true of most countries of the Middle East, from the Gulf to Egypt, where Cairo has the largest number of Islamic monuments surviving in a single city. By exception, Morocco and Tunisia have succeeded in maintaining and conserving larger portions of the urban fabric, and continue to be actively engaged in area rehabilitation projects; the reconstruction of the Hafsiyya quarter in Tunis, completed in 1977, was the first large-scale renovation project of its kind. Complete quarters which continue to maintain their original function can be found in both countries, for example Fez in Morocco and Sidi Bou Said in Tunisia. For the most part, however, the larger residential sections of Islamic towns have been subject to a cumulative process of neglect and deterioration on every level; this is equally true of the old quarters of Cairo and San'‘a. The collapse of the infrastructure (roads, sewers, water or electricity supply) and superstructure (buildings in urgent need of structural repairs or maintenance) both emphasize that these sections are the new slums, and the contemporary domain of squalor. Capital has been invested not in these quarters but in the newly developed urban centres constructed to cater for the new service economy.

The modern style

It is in these new centres and towns that there is to be found the modern architecture which has grown up in the colonial and post-colonial periods. In simple terms, two phases can be distinguished: first, the period of transformation, from the Islamic and traditional to the ‘colonial’ style, and secondly the adoption or development of the modern international style.

Colonial architecture was the product of an era of transition in concepts of architectural planning. Eventually a new style was established which was a hybrid, a mixture of an Islamic and local style with an outward expression dependent upon European neo-classical forms and concepts of design. There were wide variations from one country to another, because of the differing origins of the borrowed style and varying combinations of classicist architectural elements with local building techniques. This was a style employed equally by the local elite in their residential houses (see photographs of houses in Terim and Baghdad) and by colonial officials in the public offices or centres of power. The style was developed and formalized by foreign architects and engineering companies. As a consequence, new planning methods were adopted and used in newly constructed urban centres which gradually replaced those of the traditional cities. New suburbs were also created, isolated in location, planning and structure from the old centres and not related to them.

The 1950s and 1960s saw the spread of modern architectural structures fashioned after the *Bauhaus*. A considerable number of architects had returned from studying in the United States and Europe and contributed to the formation and development of the contemporary urban fabric. Their way of building was marked by complete abandonment of the inherited concepts of planning and design, and of local building materials and techniques. By their choice of the ‘modern technology’ of building, both residential and public quarters and centres of various kinds of public activity came to be housed in prototype concrete structures which were taken directly, in form and related function, from the international style; hardly any consideration was given to the need to adapt to special environmental, climatic, social or economic conditions. The Islamic local architectural culture was ignored as the product of an archaic period and society.

Modern technology seemed to promise solutions to architects and planners which were expedient and efficient. High-rise buildings, glazed façades and open-plan spaces exposed to the exterior replaced the local introverted house and street plans. The distinction between delicacy of space articulation and the architectural nuances seen in courtyards, patios, arcades, meandering narrow streets, vaulted pathways, closed vistas, articulated window openings covered with claustra-work or latticed screens – to name a few of the features of traditional and Islamic architecture – were eliminated in the process. Architecture was no longer the craft of building and the creative process of design, as related to cultural and socio-economic factors proper to the environment. Instead, it became a profession which was restricted by a construction industry and by common concepts of design and planning; whether in Tokyo or Jidda, the architectural product was the same.

National architectural initiatives: Hasan Fathy

An early attempt to challenge the dominant stream of modern architectural and planning practice was made by the Egyptian architect Hasan Fathy in the 1940s. In 1948 he completed the construction of 'New Gourna' village in Upper Egypt. The village was built in mud brick by master-masons from Aswan. Fathy employed and developed the design concepts indigenous to Egyptian rural architecture, and principles of town-planning which related to the environmental and social context. Once completed, however, the prospective inhabitants turned out to be unwilling to occupy it. Their former dwellings, on the archaeological site of Old Gourna, had provided them with an economic subsistence based upon the antique trade. Fathy's project sprang from the government's endeavour to evacuate the archaeological site and resettle the inhabitants in agriculture and grazing. Markets were built for agricultural products and cattle. Fathy also included artisanal craft centres in his plan, and trained a large number of the inhabitants in building *in situ* throughout the process of construction. Prior to building, a comprehensive social survey was conducted so that each house could be designed according to the individual needs of a family. The cooperation which the architect received from the population at the various stages of designing and building the village did not, however, signify their genuine endorsement of the project. In due course they flooded the new village twice in order to impede their removal to it from Old Gourna.

In the short term, perhaps this cast doubt on the structure of the new village, the success of the project, and the realization of Fathy's architectural dream. In the long term, however, the experience has been extremely fruitful in more than one way. In his book, *Gourna, the Tale of Two Villages* (later reprinted as *Architecture for the Poor*), Fathy used the experiment in order to illustrate in detail the principles and methods of his architectural theory. The most important principle is the need to establish a national modern discipline of architectural and planning policy for social housing. Moreover, he has had an influence on contemporary architectural thought and practice by establishing the need to recognize and reassess the principles of Islamic architecture and town-planning, the local technology and the use of local materials. In calling for a scientific understanding of the local architectural language, by his extensive research, teaching and practice, he has set a precedent; he has challenged the credibility of modern Western practice for the long-term development of the urban and rural fabric of the Third World. His major contribution lies not only in the buildings he has designed and built, nor in his architectural theories, writings and sayings, but also in laying the foundation for a new school of architectural thought. Whether on the level of planning policies or architectural solutions, Fathy defined the problems and underlined the possibilities available for developing a progressive architecture, one that not only draws from and relates to the heritage of the past but can respond creatively to the aspirations of community development.

Contemporary Islamic architecture

The production of an architecture which is both contemporary and Islamic in concept is a complex problem. The aspiration to revive the language of the Islamic architecture of the past has not been fulfilled except by an eclectic use of its vocabulary. In most cases, the failure has been due to a lack of understanding of the delicate relationship between the principles of architectural design and town-planning on the one hand and the local technology of building production on the other. As a consequence, modern concepts of design and planning have been used, and on to the main concrete structure have been grafted 'copies' of Islamic or traditional architectural elements (arches, stalactites, geometrical patterns) or spaces (courtyards, arcades, niches). Little has been done to redefine what a contemporary Islamic town would be on a socio-economic, cultural or functional level. There is today a large amount of architectural production which has experimented on these lines, but whether it can be regarded as 'modern Islamic' depends on the formulation of national criteria. Individual projects (whether an airport, a bank or a mosque) cannot by themselves go further than introducing an innovative style or a subjective interpretation of what can be vaguely called 'contemporary Islamic' architecture. (The work of the Egyptian architect ʿAbd al-Wahid Wakil provides perhaps the only exception to this. His residential villas, mosques and some public buildings in Saudi Arabia and Egypt provide a successful interpretation of a 'modern traditional' style.) Continuity of the style, however, can only be assured if it succeeds in creating a movement in which architecture is an integral aspect of a national planning process, widely accepted.

'Regional modernism'

Among the pioneer researchers during the early 1960s for an architectural style which would employ major traditional elements within the framework of modern building design and technology were the Iraqi architects Qahtan ʿAwni and Rifʿat Chadirji. Whether in the use of baked bricks or ceramic facing, arch forms, courtyards, arcades, niches or articulated openings, their buildings, although conforming to modern construction technology, marked a clear breakthrough in design concept and style (for example, the Mustansiriyya University designed by ʿAwni). The work of both architects set a trend which has influenced the modern architectural style not only in Iraq but elsewhere. With them may be coupled the name of Muhammad Makkiyya; the renovation of the Khalani Mosque in Baghdad is a prominent example of his work.

The Agha Khan Architectural Award

In late 1976, Karim Agha Khan established the Agha Khan Award for Architecture. 'I am convinced', he stated, 'that there is no such thing as one type of Muslim environment or one type of Muslim building. Each region of the Islamic world must create its own architectural solution.' In the most constructive effort of its kind, the issue of Islamic architecture was to be actively and seriously faced by a foundation set up with the aim of recognizing and encouraging architectural projects which contributed to the future physical environment of the Islamic world. Its aim was defined as being 'to nurture a heightened awareness of Islamic culture within the architectural profession, related to disciplines and society, while encouraging architecture appropriate to the twentieth century'.

Awards were announced in 1980 and 1983, and it is intended to announce them every three years; in 1980, a special Chairman's Award was made to Hasan Fathy. In addition, a series of international seminars have been held in a large number of cities, from Beijing in China to Dakar in Senegal. Issues discussed at these seminars have included the main themes of conservation, housing, changing rural habitats, development and urban metamorphosis, the contemporary African city, and other relevant topics. Another activity of the project is the collection of data on Islamic architecture, so as to form the basis of a permanent archive of past and contemporary architecture. Moreover, an Agha Khan Islamic Architecture Programme has been set up simultaneously at Harvard University and Massachusetts Institute of Technology, in order to carry out research, hold seminars and encourage postgraduate study. Over the last decade, the Agha Khan Architectural Award has contributed, on the national and international levels, to bringing about a change of attitude towards architectural thought and design in the Islamic world. The challenge which the Agha Khan described as being 'fundamental and unique' still persists, however, and the identity of a credible and contemporary Islamic architecture can only emerge through an attempt to define the socio-economic and cultural forces which underlie that challenge.

SSD

Hasan Fathy, the Egyptian architect

Further reading

J. L. Abu-Lughod, *Cairo: 1001 Years of the City Victorious* (Princeton, 1971)

J. L. Abu-Lughod, *Rabat: urban apartheid in Morocco* (Princeton, 1980)

S. Cantacuzino, ed., *Architecture in Continuity: building in the Islamic World today* (New York, 1985)

R. Chadirji, *Towards a Regionalized Architecture* (London, 1986)

H. Fathy, *Architecture for the Poor* (Chicago, 1973)

R. Holod and D. Rastorfer, eds., *Architecture and Community: building in the Islamic World today* (New York, 1983)

Mimar, quarterly magazine on Architecture in Development, ed. H. Khan, Singapore

Gardens

Gardens of the Middle East can be seen on both a real and a symbolic level, although their function has probably always been the same – to provide water and shade. The archetypal layout of the garden derives from Persia, its antecedents being in the Mesopotamian basin and in ancient Egypt. Documentary evidence is scant for the former, although we know that the ziggurat (the artificial hill dominated by a temple surrounded by a sacred grove of trees) was made up of terraces planted with shrubs, trees and vineyards. According to writers such as Strabo and Diodorus Siculus, the Hanging Gardens of Babylon, attributed to the reign of Semiramis (614–810 BC), were of the ziggurat type.

This restored Qajar pavilion in Shiraz, the Bagh-i-Iram, became the royal pavilion for the spring and summer visits of the Shah and Shahbanu

More is known about early Egyptian gardens due to surviving paintings and inscriptions. Egypt's greatest asset was the annual flooding of the Nile, whose fertile silt ensured a reliable, luxuriant growth of crops. The gardens were surrounded by fences of reed, thorn, and later, bricks. The Egyptians cultivated vegetables, pot herbs and trees as well as vines which were often trained on pergolas. Their produce included peaches, figs, melons, radishes, onions, chicory, date palms and incense-bearing trees. Temple gardens were centres of horticulture, also growing medicinal herbs much as the monasteries of Europe did in the Middle Ages. Exotic plants were imported from abroad and each temple had its own sacred species. Royal gardens and those of rich officials appear to have been innovative in garden design: tree-shaded brick walls surrounded an area which was laid out in rectangles with plots for trees, vegetables and fruit, and with pools and canals containing water-lilies, rushes, fish and waterfowl.

Influence of the Persian garden

The art of landscape gardening as it later appeared in Europe is thought to have its origins in Persia. The oldest Persian garden it is possible to reconstruct was built by Cyrus the Great at Pasargadae, *c.*546 BC. The plan is a formal geometric structure whose layout, defining the purpose of the garden, is a carved stone watercourse with trees and shrubs planted symmetrically in plots. This layout established the essential elements of the later Islamic garden. A pavilion, usually porticoed, was an integral part of the design, and pools and canals were incorporated into a rectangular layout with plots containing groves of shady and fruit-bearing trees. The two most important trees were the plane and the cypress, while the fruit cultivated included grapes, peaches, pomegranates, pears, dates and figs. For the Persian, the rose came to be the flower *par excellence*, while the jasmine was favoured for its sweet smell.

With the Arab conquests of the seventh century and the establishment of the ʿAbbasid* dynasty in Baghdad after AD 750 came a widening of the scope of Persian artistic ideas. The ʿAbbasid rulers were strongly influenced by Persian culture, and the traditional architectural and garden complex of Persia came to be adopted. The ideal of the Arabs, a desert people, was the green oasis, shade and water, elements which already existed in the Persian garden.

Nothing remains of Baghdad, the first ʿAbbasid capital, but we do have important archaeological evidence of the layout of the palace complex at Samarra, which became the capital of the Empire for some forty-five years from AD 833. The Jawsaq al-Khagani, as the palace was known, was built beside the Tigris. It consisted of numerous courts surrounded by walls, huge rectangular pools, and canals which are thought to have been bordered by flowers.

A symbol for paradise

Mention should be made of our word 'paradise'. Xenophon, while fighting with Greek mercenaries in Persia in 401 BC, heard the word *pairidaeza* used to mean a walled garden: he rendered the Old Persian into Greek *paradeisoi*, and is thus credited with introducing the word. The Qur'an* gave the garden an added significance for Muslims. The vision of paradise as a garden is one of the most ancient concepts in the Middle East and the Qur'an makes abundant references to the nature of this ideal garden which is usually termed *janna*. It is a place of shade and plenty, abundant gushing water, lush fruit and shade-bearing trees, where those in paradise are attended by youths dressed in green silk, the sacred colour of Islam, and by dark-eyed maidens (*huriya*: houri). Eden (*ʿadn*) and paradise (*firdaws*) are referred to as idealized gardens, as is also Iram, although with some caution. Iram is usually identified with the luxuriant Ma'rib* of the ancient Sabaeans* in the Yemen, a desert area made abundantly fertile by the construction of a huge dam, which one day burst, flooding the whole region. Numerous legends arose; Mar'ib is symbolic of desert potential as well as a reminder that God's abundance should not be taken for granted.

The four rivers of paradise mentioned in the Bible and the Qur'an constitute a basic plan for the earthly garden. The number eight is significant, denoting the eight gates of paradise (see gardens mentioned in *Sura* 55 of the Qur'an), representing four rivers. The octagon form is frequently adopted for garden pools and pavilions. Many Persian gardens came to be called Hasht Bihesht ('eight paradises'). Water is always a main consideration in these gardens as is evident by the many *qanawat* (sing. *qanat**), canals, fountains, pools and tanks, and the complicated irrigation systems.

Islamic literature abounds with garden imagery – flowers, trees, nightingales, pavilions, fruit, falling leaves, faded blooms and the changing seasons provide a rich field for poets such as Hafiz* and Saʿdi*. The triliteral roots of most Arabic words further invite mystical interpretation. *Laleh* (a tulip), for example, contains the consonants used for 'Allah' and 'hilal' (the crescent moon) which is a symbol of Islam.

Gardens in India

India inherited the archetypal Islamic garden directly from Persia. Known as *charbagh* (*chahar bagh*: four gardens), the layout of a formal walled garden consisted of intersecting watercourses representing the four rivers flowing out of paradise, forming four plots of cultivable land. The term *chahar bagh* appears to have been prevalent by Timurid* times. The design of such gardens can be seen in surviving miniatures and probably derived from the influence of Babur (1483–1530), whose Bagh-i Wafa, Garden of Fidelity, near Jalalabad in present-day Afghanistan, was of this quadripartite form. From the time of Babur, Mughal India inherited a rich tradition of garden art which reached perfection in the gardens laid out by Jahangir and Shah Jihan in Kashmir. The garden tomb, of which the Taj Mahal is the most obvious example, is said to derive from Mongol and Tartar tradition. Garden tombs were built as places of pleasure to be enjoyed during the owner's lifetime, and placed under the guardianship of holy men on his death.

Gardens in Spain

Andalusia too, inherited the Persian garden. Excavations at sites such as Madinat al-Zahra, outside Cordoba, have revealed gardens of quadripartite form with vast pools to mirror the architecture of palace and pavilion. The Alcazar at Seville (twelfth century) has also yielded remains of similar gardens, with the added feature of sunken flowerbeds which were stuccoed and painted round the sides to provide colour in winter, an idea unique to Spain*. In the thirteenth-century Patio de la Acequia of the Generalife, Granada, tiles have been found which seem to indicate the use of containers in which small plants or trees could be planted or bedded out in warm weather, a method later common to non-Muslim European gardens.

A feature of interest still to be seen in the Generalife (*jinan al-ʿarif*, gardens of the overseer) is the 'water stairway', akin to the *chadar* of Mughal India whereby water descended to lower levels. Its ripples could be seen as a sculpted pattern on the chute. The Alhambra's Palace of the Lions consists of two gardens, a courtyard and a splendid central fountain bearing lion supports standing at the convergence of eleventh-century water axials, and a lower terraced garden with sweeping views of the landscape: a reminder of the great care with which Islamic sites were chosen.

Among plants known to have existed in Spain of the eleventh and twelfth century are the myrtle, jasmine, narcissus, water-lily, almond, poppy, lavender and carnation. Trees and shrubs include thyme, mint, lemon, cypress, basil, willow, quince and fig. Detailed plant lists were compiled by al-Himyari, a Spanish Muslim, Ibn Bassal and Ibn al-ʿAwwam. An Arab garden would be assumed to contain flowers, fruit and vegetables laid out in plots always with groupings of one kind adjacent to another.

An extension of the ideas used in Persia for 'pleasure parks', as well as the horticulturally orientated gardens of Spain, is found in the *agdals* of Morocco (the word is Berber, and in the twelfth century came to denote a huge area bordering on a royal residence and surrounded by fortified walls). From an area for pasturing flocks and camping troops, it developed to take on certain features of the Persian park and was embellished with fountains, water-courses, gardens and pavilions. The *riyad* or interior courtyard of a Maghribi palace or prosperous house, on the other hand, appears to have its origins in both East and West. Its porticoed surround is a legacy from the Graeco-Roman peristyle, while the actual courtyard, with intersecting paths and/or canals with decorative fountains and interspersed with plots containing fruit trees and flowers, is reminiscent of the traditional Persian layout as depicted on the Persian 'garden carpets'.

SE

Further reading

S. Crowe, S. Haywood, S. Jellicoe and G. Patterson, *The Gardens of Mughal India* (London, 1972)
B. Macdougall, and R. Ettinghausen, eds., *The Islamic Garden* (Washington, 1976) (With articles by A. Schimmel, W. L. Hanaway, Jr., R. Pinder-Wilson, J. Dickies and S. Jellicoe)
D. N. Wilber, *Persian Gardens and Garden Pavilions* (Rutland, Vermont and Tokyo, 1962)

Cuisine

Among the least well known facets of Middle Eastern culture is its art of cooking or cuisine, overshadowed as it is in today's popular mind by the cuisines of recognized international stature such as the Chinese, Indian, French or Italian. Yet, were one to conjure up a medieval library of world literature written prior to AD 1400, the cookery section (while admittedly minuscule compared with that containing theological tomes) would be overwhelmingly dominated by culinary manuscripts in Arabic. For the period from roughly 800 to 1400 (by which date certain European cooking traditions had just begun to find their way into print), the Arab-Muslim world was the major literary source of recipes which ranged in provenance from modern-day Iran to Spain.

This medieval corpus of culinary knowledge formed a part of any sophisticated urbanite's cultural awareness. As a Muslim, he took to heart God's injunction in the Qur'an to 'eat of the good things I have provided for you'. On the other hand, gastronomic concerns together with the necessary cooking technology were clearly inherited from ancient centres of civilization, especially Mesopotamia, although the content of this pre-Islamic cuisine has yet to be recovered in detail.

The earliest extant Arabic culinary manuscript, dating from late tenth-century ʿAbbasid Iraq, enables us to perceive certain of these ancient influences, notably the oven (*tannur*, from the Akkadian *tinuru*), and a kind of prepared seasoning called *murri nabati*. More particularly, the same work reveals how a group of individuals who lived in Baghdad during the first half of the ninth century helped create a culinary *nouvelle vague* and thus establish the ʿAbbasid capital as the gastronomic 'navel of the universe'. This generation of like-minded epicures were men of many talents and interests, the leading figure among them being a prince of the ruling family, Ibrahim (d.857), the son of Caliph al-Mahdi and half brother of the famous Harun al-Rashid. As depicted in the surviving fragments of their cookery books, the ʿAbbasid high-cooking tradition (or cuisine) was a phenomenon of some complexity. While understandably emerging within an urban milieu, it was not essentially urban in origin. Cities, and especially imperial ones like Baghdad (and later Cairo) are political, economic and cultural centres of attraction which, like magnets, draw toward them persons from widely scattered parts of the imperial domains. These individuals bring to the metropolis their own local or regional cooking traditions which, informally at first, are placed in a common and increasing pool of culinary knowledge from which others can share. A wealthy and powerful court also plays an important role in establishing a new cuisine, by dominating a rich and stable agricultural hinterland and by stimulating even more extensive commercial networks to distant

Lunchtime in Manakha, North Yemen

regions. The court and the metropolitan markets therefore are assured a ready supply of every imaginable food commodity. The court, moreover, sets fashions of life-style eagerly emulated by other segments of the urban population. Then, once the original element of the cuisine (the collective oral, regional cooking traditions) is captured in written form, the recipe both 'fixes' that tradition and itself becomes subject to further experimentation and elaboration. In this second, more formal stage, peasant fare appears greatly transformed upon the merchant's table, and the urban cuisine reaches toward maturity.

The influence of Ibrahim ibn al-Mahdi and his generation of gastronomes extended well beyond the heartland of the Empire, Iraq, and throughout the ninth and tenth centuries. A later, thirteenth-century cookery book, pays tribute to the master by including a dish called simply Ibrahimiyya. The thirteenth century seems to mark the literary apex of the high-cooking tradition, at least so far as the Arabic evidence permits us to see; by the end of that century all of the manuscripts now extant were in circulation and are of Iraqi, Syrian, Egyptian(?) and Moroccan–Andalusian origin. The extant Persian and Turkish works stem from the seventeenth and eighteenth centuries.

In the period between the later Middle Ages and the present day (*c.*1500 onwards) long-established cooking styles survived largely unchanged in this, the most conservative realm of human culture. Some shifts, however, occurred as well. Both the high, written and the local, oral cooking traditions were perhaps disturbed only by the periodic unavailability of a traditional food or the introduction of a new one. For example, a number of food plants had been introduced into the Middle East from India in the pre- and early-Islamic period and slowly they were diffused westward. Among these plants some are found in the earliest-known recipes: rice, egg-plant, spinach and sugar cane. One vegetable is known to have spread in the opposite direction. The tomato entered Spain from the New World perhaps as late as the sixteenth century, and from there it gradually spread eastwards to become a notable feature of all circum-Mediterranean cooking traditions.

In the case of rice, however, it is impossible to judge how quickly it became the staple base of all cooking traditions; its first appearance in a recipe is for a delicately flavoured dish cooked with milk and smoked meat. New strains of existing cereal foods such as wheat and barley (and new cereal plants such as sorghum and millet) were also introduced in this same process. The ubiquitous flat bread loaf (Arabic *khubz*, Persian *nan*) was of great antiquity; it could be made leavened or unleavened, roasted or baked from the finest wheat flour to the lowly 'secondary' grain, the acorn. Prepared for immediate consumption, bread was used at mealtimes as a utensil for conveying morsels of food to the mouth, or even as a 'plate' when eaten together with a variety of fillings purchased from street vendors.

Glimpses of certain rural cooking traditions which survived the centuries can be found in the accounts of the more perceptive European travellers to the Middle East in the nineteenth and early twentieth centuries. Doughty, Burckhardt and Musil each provides many valuable vignettes of nomadic food traditions. Whereas these traditions perhaps remain the least changed of all, other rural practices among the settled peasantry may have also been affected over time by, for example, major migrations of communities of a different ethnic origin: consider the Turkish migrations into Anatolia and the Arab throughout North Africa. The true nature of the resulting culinary exchanges is, however, imperceptible, owing to the lack of documentation.

In areas too where the vitality of urban life declined, the city's high-cooking tradition likewise suffered and took on more the character of its immediate rural hinterland. Nevertheless, it has been generally the case throughout the Islamic period that the basic dichotomy in the culinary culture has been between town and country; that where neighbouring towns within a region may be renowned for different specialities, the cuisines of widely separated major cities could share similar features in common. Thus today a cuisine is scarcely contained within the boundaries of the modern nation state. The most appropriate metaphorical description of the contemporary Middle Eastern gastronomic scene is not of a melting-pot but rather of an intricate geometrically patterned mosaic with three (or four) dominant shades of the same colour, the shades representing somewhat different geo-historical culinary traditions. These are the Persian, the Arab, the Turkish (or simply Turko-Arab) and the Maghribi (North African).

The preparation of stews

Common to each of the older traditions is a basic stew preparation which today is found under various names such as *yakhni*, *khurish* and *tajin*; certain Turkish *pilavs* may be included as well. Meat and vegetables or fruits (dried or fresh) or nuts or some combination thereof are cooked slowly together and then served alone as a main dish or else 'with' rice, or 'over' it. In the classical cuisine these dishes were often named after a particular ingredient highlighted in it. Thus *basaliyya*, an onion dish, was meat browned in oil, then simmered in stock with fresh coriander and cinnamon bark; fresh chopped onions were then added seasoned with cumin, coriander, pepper and cinnamon. A bitter taste could be imparted by using lemon juice or vinegar. The combinations of such stews were endless. A sampling of these dishes would include *saljamiyya* (a turnip dish), *isfanakhiyya* (a spinach dish), *rutabiyya* (a date dish) and *fustaqiyya* (a pistachio dish).

Two points about the stew preparation are worth noting, as they reflect the endurance of medieval cooking customs to the present day. First, the preferred meat throughout the Middle East was mutton, with kid's meat and lamb close second choice. In medieval times custom was supported by the opinions of physicians, who claimed that beef was not beneficial to sound bodily health. Muslim and Jewish practices converged in the ritual slaughter of animals

Spread of Lebanese mezze

and the prohibition of pig's flesh, but otherwise Muslim dietary laws were very relaxed and open. Secondly, the principle of 'meat substitution' was employed in stew preparations. Poultry, which was also widely enjoyed, could be substituted for meat in almost any of these dishes. A modern North African practice combines meat and poultry in the same dish to fine effect.

Stews also illustrate the fundamental rural–urban dichotomy in the cooking culture. Simply expressed, the urban cuisine was characterized by the wider range and higher cost of ingredients and the complexity of their preparation. A village stew was a modest meal, more likely to be made with rice or other cereal (like cracked wheat, *burghul*), together with a vegetable and occasionally with meat, and seasoned with whatever was available locally in addition to the commonplace flavouring of salt. The nomad's stew was less pretentious still, despite the fact that meat was considered a luxury. The meat could be boiled in camel's milk and cracked wheat and served on a large tray with meat around the edges; a bowl of melted animal fat placed in the middle was for dipping morsels of meat in before eating. Geohistorical influences may also be seen in certain contemporary stew preparations. A sweet-sour flavour, achieved by combining vinegar with sugar or honey or dried/fresh fruit with almonds, is Persian in origin. This flavour was found typically in the classical dish *zirbaj* and may be seen today in some North African *tajins*. The classic North African stew is made with couscous, a special type of semolina preparation, for which there are recipes dating from the thirteenth century. The dish is of Berber origin, adopted and adapted by the Arabs and, as the staple in the North African diet, couscous characterizes the Maghribi cooking tradition. The basic procedure is to steam the grain over a stew of meat and vegetables. The combination of chickpeas and raisins, found in some versions of this stew, may also be Persian in origin. Finally, in some classical stews one detects the influence of the early Arab tradition, possibly that of central Arabia in the time of the Prophet Muhammad. These are meat dishes cooked with onion and other seasonings, but particularly with milk or milk products such as *masl*, dried or cooked whey, which gives its name to the dish *masliyya*. Another famous preparation was *madira*. These two dishes bear a family resemblance to the nomad's stew of the present day, although in their medieval form they reflect the sophistication of an urban cuisine. Meat dishes cooked in milk or yoghurt remain favourites today in much of the Middle East, among them *laban immuh*, implying young meat cooked in its own mother's milk. In the relatively more recent Turkish cooking tradition, meat and vegetables tend to be treated as separate entities each honoured in its own fashion. Thus the seemingly infinite variety of ways of preparing vegetables, whether stuffed, pickled, as cold side dishes or in salads, may owe as much to the Turkish tradition as to any other. Consider as representative the famous egg-plant dish *imam bayildi*, 'the fainting imam'. The classical cuisine as reflected in the medieval cookery books featured relatively few dishes in which vegetables appear on their own; marinated or pickled vegetables, however, are present as well as a cold dish (*bawarid*) which could be made from vegetables, meat or fish.

Fish dishes of much variety and delicacy have always been enjoyed, and not only by those who inhabited the coastal regions or the great river valleys. Early recipes call for salted fish which could be prepared at some time and distance from their point of origin. Most commonly the fish was first fried (after desalting, where necessary), and then placed in a sour sauce made from vinegar and other ingredients. One delicious thirteenth-century preparation was fried fish served in milk and garlic sprinkled with cumin, coriander and cinnamon; curiously, to modern Arab taste this combination is regarded as an abomination to be avoided.

One consumable which was strictly deemed an abomination religiously was the intoxicating beverage. While the modern tolerance of alcoholic consumption or the degree of social abstinence of it varies considerably across the breadth of the Middle East, there are extant medieval recipes for several kinds of wine and beer both licit and illicit.

It is not possible here to cover the entire range of food resources used in the several geohistorical cooking traditions. Every region within each tradition fully exploits the resources available, from pulses to fruit and from plant leaves to its root, from one season to the next. Moreover, it is worth remarking that the customs of food preparation and consumption reveal little waste. Almost every part of an animal or bird would appear in some dish or other, for example, from the tail fat of a sheep to its offal including the eyes and testicles. Most dishes, where there are leftovers, can be served the next day either reheated or cold, the taste enhanced in subtle ways in the interval.

The cooking oils (chiefly olive and sesame), the herbs and spices lend to a dish this delayed quality of enhanced flavour. The immensely wide spice spectrum of the urban cuisine comprising both indigenous and imported ingredients is the main realm of the cook's creative ingenuity. Proportions and amounts of spices are only exceptionally mentioned in the medieval recipes. The creative manipulation of the spice spectrum was perhaps the major contribution the Arab world made to European culinary customs. The intended object in the former tradition was to achieve a balance between 'pungent' and 'aromatic' seasonings in any given dish, together with an overall harmony among the several dishes comprising an entire meal. These features of balance of flavour and harmony of texture may have been the origin of the contemporary *mezza*, that kaleidoscope of hors d'oeuvres, a meal of miniatures: the primary meaning of the root of the word *mezza* is to impart a taste half-way between sweet and sour.

Alcohol

Finally, it might be thought that the Islamic prohibition of the alcoholic beverage would have meant its absence from the table. Yet even in the earliest extant recipe collection there are preparations for wine (*nabidh*), both licit (that is, unfermented) and illegal, and for a kind of barley beer (*fuqqa*) which was decidedly *haram*. Drinking sessions were commonly held after the evening meal, combined, in more refined and affluent circles, with poetry recitations, music and dancing girls. Avoidance of alcohol was, nevertheless, far more prevalent in medieval urban societies than it is today.

In any event, for more than a millennium the urban culinary culture of the Middle East has displayed that quality for which the eighteenth-century French philosopher of the kitchen, Brillat-Savarin, coined the term 'gourmandism': without excess, an impassioned, reasoned and habitual preference for everything which gratifies the organ of taste.

DW

Further reading

Claudia Roden, *A New Book of Middle Eastern Food* (London, 1985)

Muhammad ʿAbduh, a popular singer from Saudi Arabia

Islamic musical theory

Until recently all music in the Middle East was transmitted aurally. Theorists quickly developed efficient techniques of notation, but practising musicians were generally unaware of them, and the examples of notated music that survive are, with the important exception of two substantial seventeenth-century Turkish collections, far too few and unrepresentative to be in any way comparable to the vast array of scores which have been the central concern of Western historical musicology.

There can thus be nothing equivalent to, say, analyses of madrigal technique or the development of sonata form. Certain inferences can reasonably be drawn from contemporary practice, and valuable information gleaned from iconographic representations of musical activity; but our chief source for the history of music in the Middle East is undoubtedly the written word. Here mention may be made in particular of polemics on the contentious issue of the legal admissibility of music within Islam; of general literary works incidentally providing information of a biographical and sociological nature; and of theoretical treatises, the most important source of all. But the theorist is neither historian nor reporter: his bias is towards the speculative and abstract, and the relationship between theoretical structures and the realities of practice is often complex. In the Islamic codification of the sciences, as in medieval Europe, music is a branch of mathematics.

Greek influence

The initial, crucial phase in the development of a theoretical literature took place during the first century of the ʿAbbasid* Caliphate. Already in the growth of a more precise technology for art-music one may detect the elaboration of indigenous technical criteria; but the decisive impulse towards the formal articulation of a theory was to come from exposure to Greek ideas as they became increasingly available through translation. Two main strands may be noted. One, broadly Aristotelian, is marked by scientific rigour and emphasizes especially the mathematical expression and manipulation of various (ideal) interval sizes; the other embraces a neo-Platonic concern with cosmology and numerology. Both are represented in the several short treatises by the first major theorist, the philosopher al-Kindi*, but later they tend to be elaborated separately. The mathematical approach is pursued in a much more highly developed and extensive fashion by the other great philosopher-theorists, al-Farabi* (d.950) and Ibn Sina (Avicenna*) (d.1037), while cosmological affiliations are stressed by the *Ikhwan al-safa* (tenth-century Brothers of Purity).

Within the theoretical literature as a whole the topic that receives the most detailed treatment is the analysis of intervals, scales, and the melodic modes related to them. If indebtedness to Greek ideas is here particularly obvious, such ideas are not merely repeated, but developed and refined, for instance in the elaboration and classification of types of tetrachord (that is, the various ways in which the interval of a fourth, say from *do* to *fa*, may be subdivided for melodic use). The most extensive and abstract working out of such material is to be found in Farabi and Ibn Sina, but they do at the same time provide a certain amount of information about melodic modes in actual use. Ibn Sina, for example, is the earliest writer to describe the mode *rast*, still important today.

The Systematists

The next important group of theorists, known collectively as the Systematist school, dates from the thirteenth to fifteenth centuries. Written in Persian as well as Arabic, their fairly homogeneous treatises probably relate to an urban art-music exhibiting considerable uniformity over a wide area stretching from Egypt to eastern Persia. The analysis of scale devised by the first author of this group, Safi al-Din (d.1294), combines clarity with symmetry, and while the opportunity it offered for abstract transformations was by no means ignored it was also used to record with greater fidelity than hitherto the intricacies of the modal system of the period.

With the analysis of rhythm, the shift from system building to the provision of factual information is rather more marked. Here the conceptual model is provided by what was for the Arabs the sister science of prosody, so that the subdivisions of a rhythmic cycle tend to be represented in the same way as metric feet. With Farabi, followed to a certain extent by Ibn Sina, we are confronted by a comprehensive, and complicated, set of possible structures, only some of which are noted as occurring in practice. But with the Systematist school such theorizing is effectively abandoned, and in its place one finds a descriptive catalogue, including variants, of the rhythmic cycles then in use, some of which were extremely long and complex.

Other important areas of general concern are forms of composition, and instruments. Of particular value here are the works of ʿAbd al-Qadir al-Maraghi (d.1435), for they contain not only a full inventory of instrumental and vocal forms, but also an extensive descriptive catalogue of instruments (including exotica from beyond the Islamic cultural domain). Further areas of practice are illuminated by al-Hasan al-Katib (late tenth century), who deploys a rich vocabulary of technical terms concerned with vocal and instrumental technique, and also deals with such matters as performance etiquette.

Influence of cosmology

Alongside the Systematist treatises, representing the tradition of mathematical analysis and scholarly precision, one may find a number of shorter works in which the alternative interest in cosmology finds expression. With Kindi this had been articulated mainly in terms of fourfold sets (such as the humours and elements) relatable to the four strings of the lute; the main focus of attention now is a main set of twelve modes (plus a subsidiary set of six), relatable in the first instance to the signs of the Zodiac. After the fifteenth century the mathematical tradition fades away, and cosmology prevails, although sometimes tempered by a concern to provide a note-by-note description of the basic melodic outline of the modes. The culmination of this latter trend may be seen in the important Turkish treatise (*c.*1700) of Demetrius Cantemir (1673-1723), which effectively excludes cosmology, covers mode, rhythm, and form, and has appended to it a notated collection of some 350 pieces from the late seventeenth-century Turkish instrumental repertoire.

Modern theory, particularly in Turkey, may be considered in part a re-exploration of the major areas of concern of the great ʿAbbasid theorists. Forms are defined, rhythmic cycles listed at length with their variant percussion patterns and, most characteristically of all, there is an almost obsessive concern with intonation and the definition of interval sizes.

OW

Music in Middle Eastern societies

The Middle East, including the Arab world, Turkey and Iran, has widely shared musical characteristics. Cultural exchange has existed in this area throughout history. For over a millennium, individual musical traditions have been shaped by a social matrix in which Islamic beliefs, institutions and attitudes have played a major role. Musical diversity in this large area results from migrations as well as from differences in local histories, indigenous socio-political hierarchies and cultural values. Among the significant factors have also been the demographic and cultural exposures to adjacent areas, including sub-Saharan Africa, and central and south Asia.

Middle Eastern music history is difficult to reconstruct. With some exceptions, music has been passed on aurally, without recourse to notation. Historical information comes largely from biographical and literary accounts, archaeological artefacts, and extant pictorial depictions. In the twentieth century, Western scholars such as Hans Hickmann, Eric Werner, Egon Wellesz and Henry George Farmer have researched the musical cultures of ancient Egypt, Mesopotamia, the Holy Land, Byzantium and medieval Islam. Their studies generally provide information about musical scales, instruments, functions of music, and the position of music in cosmological systems. Certain works have dealt at length with actual repertoires, particularly in the case of Byzantine music, where an ecclesiastical system of neumes, or notational signs, had been utilized. This system is still used in its modern form in Eastern Orthodox churches. Further contributions, including the writings of Curt Sachs (1881–1959), have presented theories of diffusion of musical instruments within broad areas encompassing Sumeria, Pharaonic Egypt and ancient Greece.

Early links with the West

The history of performance practice in medieval Islam has been a topic of study for several well-known scholars. Interest in the area was usually combined with a desire to ascertain the nature of the musical contact between the Latin West and the Islamic world during the Middle Ages, particularly at the time of the Crusades (eleventh to thirteenth centuries). Julian Ribera attempted to demonstrate significant Arabian influence through his musical interpretations of the 'Cantigas de Santa Maria', which were prepared for King Alfonso X in thirteenth-century Spain. Henry George Farmer, a prolific British Arabist and music historian, argued for extensive Arabian influence over medieval Europe, and wrote several works on Arabian music history, primarily from the rise of Islam until the thirteenth century AD. Another historian was Baron Rudolphe d'Erlanger, who translated musical treatises by major medieval music theorists, including Farabi, Ibn Sina and Safi al-Din into French. In addition, he presented extensive discussions of theory and practice in modern Arab music.

Although medieval theorists tend to follow a speculative approach, focusing on music as a scientific discipline, they furnish clues about music as a practical art. Such clues become meaningful in light of information offered by major literary sources, such as *Kitab al-aghani* by Abu'l-Faraj al-Isfahani (d.967). This multi-volume work provides us with miscellaneous information about the inner court circles of tenth-century Baghdad, including descriptions of social customs, musical events, biographical information on artists, and occasionally song texts with indications of the appropriate rhythmic patterns and melodic modes. Musical attitudes are expressed in various writings by religious legists and Sufis*.

Court music

During the Middle Ages, court music incorporated diverse ethnic influences, Persian, Syrian and others. The legacy of Arabia was prominent, especially in the areas of song texts, and the adoption of sung Arabian genres such as the *qasida* or 'poem'. Extant song texts testify to the emphasis placed on vocal music, and on the central role of poetry in music. Singers were typically accompanied, or accompanied themselves, on the *ʿud* (short-necked lute), an instrument of great popularity. Among the recognized *ʿud* virtuosi were: Mansur Zalzal (d.*c*.800), who made contributions to both theory and performance technique; Ishaq al-Mawsili (d.849), also an accomplished singer; and Zaryab (d.*c*.850). Zaryab was a prolific performer, composer and music teacher who lived in al-Andalus (Andalusia), medieval Moorish Spain. He is also known for his compilation of the medieval *nawba* repertoire, which consisted of twenty-four 'suites' or multi-sectional compositions, each associated with a different hour of the day.

Descriptions of performance ambience present medieval court music as an intimate art, characterized by spontaneity and direct audience participation, mannerisms common in traditional performances of the present-day Middle East. Impromptu performances described in medieval writings indicate that improvisation played an important role in musical practices.

Importance of melody

Theorists' interest in pitch and tuning systems, in addition to literary descriptions of performance practice, further point toward the central position of melody, and the likely complexity of the sung or instrumentally produced melodic line. Often referred to in specific terms, melodic ornaments appear to have contributed significantly to the craft of singing. As in today's Arab, Turkish and Iranian traditions, the melodic material was conceived modally. In *Kitab al-aghani*, reference to the melodic mode to be used with listed texts was made through *asabiʿ* indications, or corresponding fingering sequences on the neck of the *ʿud*. In vocal music, the selection of *awzan*, or rhythmic modes, was influenced by the poetic metre of the text, as well as by the ethos, or aesthetic effect of each mode.

Tonality

Intonation appears to have changed from one epoch to another. During the early centuries of Islam, theorists indicate a wide acceptance of the diatonic system of Pythagorean half and whole steps. This system may have followed, or overlapped with, others such as one based on quarter-tones, and attributed by Farabi to pre-Islamic Arabia. From the tenth to the thirteenth centuries, we encounter a strong tendency among theorists to incorporate microtones within their diatonic scalar matrices, perhaps a phenomenon reflecting acceptance of such intervals in the area of performance. Farabi speaks of a low Persian third at a ratio of 294 cents, and another (neutral) third, roughly at 350 cents introduced by the *ʿud* player Mansur Zalzal. (In modern European tuning, a semitone is equal to 100 cents, or pitch units.) Later, Safi al-Din presented a system of melodic modes based on scales of Pythagorean diatonic semitones, whole tones, and microtones. These microtones consisted of whole steps minus a small interval called a comma, or 24 cents. They provided the possibility of systematically accounting for microtonality in the modal practice of his time.

The musician in society

In Middle Eastern history, performing musicians varied in their social roles and degree of prestige. In the early decades of Islam, secular music was a commodity offered typically by the *qaynat*, or female slave entertainers, whose rank in society was very low. Later on, particularly during the ʿAbbasid period, artistic life featured highly regarded celebrities, some of whom came from distinguished family backgrounds. Among these artists were Ishaq al-Mawsili and the Amir Ibrahim al-Mahdi. Some musicians were generously remunerated by the ruling Caliphs, many of whom were known for their particular fondness for music.

Genres permitted by Islam

The attitude of Islam toward music, often described as one of suspicion and denigration, was not expressed as such in the Qur'an. Strictures against music and musicians appeared in the *hadith*. Prohibitions and negative sentiments were usually directed against music-making as a secular activity, particularly the more accessible forms of entertainment. That exempted religious expressions, which were considered outside the domain of 'music' *per se*. In this group were the call to prayer, or *adhan**, and the highly revered Qur'anic chanting which, in its most elaborate form, is known as *tajwid*. The various moral stances against music-making also appear to have excluded folk and ritual musical genres, such as wedding music, work songs and songs for religious holy days. Meanwhile, the liberal attitudes toward secular music during the Golden Age of Islam were enhanced by the cosmopolitan cultural life of large cities such as Baghdad, Cordoba and Seville. Court affluence and the emulation and assimilation of the cultural and humanistic legacies of conquered civilizations contributed to the growing interest in the arts among the rulers.

Sufism

A further development was the spread of Islamic mysticism since the thirteenth century. Sufi* orders gradually dominated social, cultural and artistic life throughout the Islamic world, and exerted a profound impact upon music. Islamic mysticism generally followed a spiritual path aimed at direct experience of the Divine, through *samaʿ* (literally 'auditioning') or mystical music and dance. The Sufis also practised *dhikr* (literally 'remembrance'), which refers to the rhythmic reiteration of God's name, *Allah*, or of religious formulas such as *La ilah illa Allah* (literally, 'There is no god but God'). The practice usually occurs with rhythmic body movement and chanting. The use of percussion instruments and the *nay*, or reed flute, was and is still common among some Sufi orders, particularly the Mevlevis, who are also known as the 'whirling dervishes' in reference to their dance movements.

In the Middle East, Pakistan and North India, some of the foremost poets and musicians were either members of Sufi orders, or directly influenced by Sufi teachings. During the Ottoman period (fifteenth to early twentieth centuries) the Mevlevi order functioned as a primary institution of musical learning. Mevlevi composers, such as Dede Efendi (1777–1845), composed pieces for the Mevlevi ritual and instrumental works played as secular music in the courts. The Mevlevi order also included music theorists, such as the Rumanian Prince Demetrius Cantemir (1673–1723), and others who devised indigenous systems for notating Ottoman classical compositions.

The Shiʿa–Sunni divide

The post-medieval era witnessed political and cultural separation between Persia, which declared Shiʿism as its official religion during the Safavid* dynasty (1501–1772), and the largely Sunni Ottoman world. In both cultures, music continued to flourish under the auspices of local patrons. Secular genres connected with the courts coexisted and interacted with religious expressions, particularly Sufi music. Military and ceremonial music were represented by ensembles such as the Persian *naqqare khane*, which incorporated trumpets, double-reed instruments and kettle-drums, and the illustrious *mehter* bands connected with the Janissary army of Ottoman Turkey. As shown by historical accounts, such as the Turkish Evliya Çelebi's* (1611–82) travelogue *Seyahatname*, throughout the Ottoman world professional musicians of various specializations were, like members of other professions, grouped into guilds, each with its own patron saint and guildmaster. The formal guild system remained in vogue until it gradually came to an end in the early twentieth century.

Contacts with the West

In Middle Eastern music, Westernization essentially began during the early nineteenth century, through direct contacts with Europe. The Napoleonic conquest of Egypt (1798–1801, see Modern History), a tangible demonstration of Europe's military might, generated a growing trend of military, technological and cultural borrowing from the West. In Egypt, the founder of the Khedival dynasty, Muhammad ʿAli* (1805–48), brought in French military advisers to train his army. Among them were band directors, who taught Western notation and Western band instruments in Egyptian military schools. In Turkey, the dissolution of the traditional Janissary army in the early nineteenth century under Sultan Mahmud II (1808–39) was accompanied by deliberate attempts to Westernize military music. The invitation by the Sultan of the Italian composer Giuseppe Donizetti to Istanbul led to the adoption of European military band instruments and musical notation. Similarly, several European music teachers were invited to Persia during the nineteenth century. Among them was Alfred J. B.

A girl playing the *qanun* at Cairo's Institute of Islamic Music

Lemaire (1842–1909), who established an academy for instruction on military-band instruments and training local music administrators.

Among the musical borrowings from the West was the European conservatory tradition. Music was increasingly accepted as an artistic discipline and pedagogical system to be taught methodically, through notation. Musical Westernization also emerged through the adoption of Western keyboard instruments and through direct contact with European performing ensembles. The performances of Verdi's *Rigoletto* (1869) and *Aida* (1871) at the Cairo Opera House, during the reign of Khedive Isma'il (1863–79) were followed in subsequent years with performances by various musical and theatrical groups which visited Cairo and other Middle Eastern cities. Western missionaries also introduced European and American tunes into the Arabic Protestant hymnal, a practice begun during the second half of the nineteenth century.

General characteristics

In the Middle East today, music appears in a wide variety of contexts. Different styles often represent different ethnic and religious groups. Music also serves basic functions cross-culturally. Qur'anic chant, the call to prayer and, to some extent, Sufi *dhikr* practices are almost universal throughout the Islamic world and among Muslim sects in Eastern Europe. Social and religious events, manual work and life-cycle occasions are generally connected with music and dance. Throughout the Middle East, open-air festivities, for example weddings, typically feature ensembles consisting of double-reed wind instruments and percussion. Also in many rural communities, music for social entertainment is presented by a bard or poet-singer such as the Anatolian *aşik*, who sings while accompanying himself on the *saz*, or long-necked lute, and the Arab beduin *shaʿir*, who accompanies himself on the *rababa*, a single-string fiddle comparable in overall form and function to the *gusle* of Yugoslavia and the *masinqo* of Ethiopia.

In the Middle East, many musical categories are based on literary genres. The Arabic *qasida*, the *muwashshah*, a literary form originated in Moorish Spain, the Turkish *ghazal* (literally 'love poetry') and the Persian *avaz* (literally 'voice') are cases in point. The structure of vocal performance is influenced by the textual phrasing. Usually, the musical melismas coincide with the vowels, and the musical cadences match the rhyme endings and final syllables of the individual poetic verses.

Lyrical song texts are prevalent. Although there are some narrative forms, such as the sung epic of Abu Zayd al-Hilali now popular in Egypt, many song texts deal with stylized sentimental themes, including symbolic mystical love. Abstract non-programmatic music is also typical. Examples are Turkey's extensive repertoire of classical instrumental music, and the modal improvisations found in various Middle Eastern traditions.

Texture

Generally speaking, the music lacks elaborate polyphony of the type found in Central Africa and Western Europe. Instead, the focus is on a complex melody, characterized by intricate ornamentation. Solo unaccompanied performances, such as the Turkish *taksim* (instrumental improvisation) are quite common. An instrument may also produce a melody and a drone, as with the *arghul* or double clarinet (drone and a chanter) of Egypt. When voices or instruments play together, as in the *pishdaramad* of Iran, the *peşrev* of Turkey, and the *dulab* of the Arab world, the parts are essentially in unison or octaves, but also in characteristic heterophony. This texture occurs when all instruments or voices play essentially the same melody, but each simultaneously produces its own rendition of ornaments and subtle rhythmic and melodic nuances. In a vocal improvisation such as the Egyptian *mawwal* and the Iranian *avaz*, the accompanying instruments may heterophonically follow the vocal phrases by reinterpreting them and imitating their overall contour and motivic content. When a solo instrument takes a leading role, as for example in the *çiftetelli*, a Turkish dance-related genre, the accompanying instrumental ensemble may maintain an ostinato, a constantly repeated melodic and rhythmic pattern.

Melody and mode
What further contributes to the distinctive quality of Middle Eastern melody is the predominance of microtonality, or the inclusion of intervals divisible into distances other than tones and semitones. Middle Eastern folk-traditions generally have their distinct patterns of intonation. In the urban styles the tuning systems are related to the melodic theories and scalar divisions of the Islamic Middle Ages. The ancient Greek concepts of tetrachord and octave species are still treated as theoretical foundations. Pythagorean intervals containing microtonal subdivisions have been used by Persian, Turkish and Syrian theorists to explain intervals in their own respective musical traditions. In Egypt, as in other Middle Eastern countries, performances normally feature intricate pitch patterns and fluctuations. Yet many local theorists, some inspired by Western equal temperament, have resorted to fitting Arab intonation into a rigid matrix of twenty-four equal quarter-tones per octave.

In major traditions, modality is recognized as the basis of melody. In North Africa, Egypt, the Levant, Iraq, Turkey, Iran and Central Asia there are specific concepts that refer to melodic modes. These traditions feature different numbers of modes, each with its own name, tonic (or central note), scale, notes of emphasis, patterns of melodic progression and, in some cases, stock motifs. The modes are used as a basis for either improvisations or precomposed vocal and instrumental genres. Although they may have similar or shared historical origins, the present modal systems of the Middle East differ in matters of nomenclature, details of intonation, and overall application.

The Arab modal system of Egypt and the east Mediterranean is based on a few dozen *maqamat* (singular *maqam*, or 'melodic mode') that are theoretically illustrated in terms of one or two octave scales. In an instrumental improvisation in a particular *maqam*, the performer often begins somewhere around the tonic and gradually ascends, reaching a tonal climax around, or higher than, the upper tonic. Before concluding on the tonic, the improvisation may introduce accidental notes and momentarily shift to other related modes. In the process the melodic material appears in the form of phrases, each ending with a *qafla*, a somewhat stylized cadential motif, followed by a short pause.

In Turkish classical music, modality is represented by almost a hundred *makams*. Each has its own name, scale and characteristics. These characteristics are articulated under the epithet of *seyir*, which means 'path' and actually refers to theoretical descriptions of the modal content and realization. Turkish *makam*-theory indicates the intervals in terms of small Pythagorean pitch units called *commas*, each roughly equivalent to one-ninth of a whole tone.

In Persian classical music the modal system is based on twelve *dastgas*, each of which in some ways operates like an Arab *maqam* or Turkish *makam*. However, the *dastga* system differs from its Turko-Arab counterpart in the systematic and structured nature of modulation which it incorporates. Each *dastga* has its own set of *gushes* or subsidiary modes. Consisting of dozens of individual sections, the *gushes* are based on narrower scalar patterns, sometimes as small as a few notes. They may also acquire their individual character from the rhythmic motifs they feature. In a typical *avaz* or in an improvised instrumental rendition, a musician presents a full exposé of the *dastga* proper in a section called *daramad*. Then he may select a number of *gushes* from the *radif*, or full order of prescribed inner modulations. In between these modulations he may present a *forud*, a brief 'descent', thus momentarily returning to the original mode, or *dastga* proper.

Rhythm
In Middle Eastern music, the concept of melodic mode is paralleled by the modal treatment of rhythm. Especially in Turkey and the Arab world, there are numerous systematically conceived metric patterns, listed in theoretical books and applied by composers and performers. In urban traditions, metric compositions such as the Mevlevi *selam* (a religious choral piece) are based on metric cycles. Rendered on percussion instruments such as the Mevlevi *kudüm* (a pair of small kettledrums), or the Egyptian *tabla* (a small, goblet-shaped drum), a metric pattern is theoretically conceived in terms of rests and beats of different timbres. In the Arab system of *iqaʿat* (metric modes), the word *dumm* refers to a low-pitched accentuated drumbeat, while the word *takk* refers to a high-pitched percussive sound played on the perimeter of a drum head. In practice, an Arab percussionist observes the number of beats, which could range from two to sixteen or more, and the basic places of emphasis. However, he provides highly ornate renditions of each pattern using a wide vocabulary of nuances, timbres and rhythmic subdivisions.

Form
Improvisatory genres are, as a rule, non-strophic, in other words, featuring constant creation of essentially new musical material. We also encounter wide occurrence of strophic forms in which a melodic verse or stanza is repeated with or without a refrain. As illustrated by the laments of Turkey and heroic songs of the beduin nomads of Syria and Jordan, the verse repeats are seldom exact. Instead the folk singers present a series of variations, rendered through rhythmic flexibility, vowel elongations and ornamentation.

In urban traditions other forms may be found. In the Iranian *tasnif*, a precomposed vocal genre, the sections usually follow the order of the *dastga* in terms of prescribed inner modes. In the Turkish *peşrev*, a refrain alternates with verses, each with a differing melodic and, usually, modal content. Irregular forms are illustrated by the modern Egyptian *ughniya* or 'song', which often presents a sequence of musical segments varying in rhythm, mode and stylistic flavour. Examples are some of the film songs of Muhammad ʿAbd al-Wahhab.

In various parts of the Middle East, musical performances are presented in multi-sectional or compound formats. Resembling a suite in structure, such formats exist in the musical traditions of North Africa, Egypt, the Levant, Iraq, Turkey, Iran and Central Asia. The names as well as the details and contents of each form vary from one tradition to another. A single compound-form performance is a medley of pieces differing in rhythm and style of performing. These pieces may be soloistic or for the entire ensemble, instrumental or vocal, improvised or precomposed. In general, the total medley is in one melodic mode, or closely related modes. The rhythmic patterns used are usually varied and tend to proceed from slow and stately to more animated, as in the *fasil* of Turkey and the *nawba* of Morocco. In the latter, where rhythmic patterns define structural divisions, the main part consists of five vocal sections or 'movements', each known by the name *mizan*, which means 'balance', 'measuring scale' or 'rhythmic mode'. In turn, each section is divided into two parts, a slow one called *muwassaʿ* (literally 'broad'), and a fast one called *insiraf* (literally 'departure'). A compound-form performance typically begins with a precomposed instrumental introduction by the ensemble. Examples are the *pishdaramad*, before a *dastga* performance by the ensemble, the *peşrev* at the beginning of a *fasil*, and the *bughya*, a non-metric instrumental passage played by the ensemble at the beginning of a *nawba*.

Instruments

Certain instrument types are widely shared. Double-reed instruments (the *ghayta* of Morocco, the *zukra* of Tunisia, the *mizmar* of Egypt, the *zurna* of Turkey) are commonly played out of doors in public festivities. Fiddles such as the folk *rabab* of Morocco, the *rababa* of Egypt (a two-stringed spike-fiddle made from a coconut shell) and the beduin *rababa* (a single-stringed quadrilateral fiddle), are generally connected with vocal music and with self-accompanied singers. Reed instruments are similarly prevalent. Examples are the various end-blown flutes such as the classical Persian *ney*, the Turkish *ney*, the urban Arab *nay*, and their folk counterparts, such as the North African *qasaba* (literally 'reed') and the Palestinian *shabbaba*. Clarinet types made from reed are also widely prevalent in rural areas. Examples include double clarinets such as the *mijwiz* or *mitbiq* of the east Mediterranean and Iraq respectively, the *zummara* of Egypt, and the *maqruna* of Tunisia and Libya. Also predominant are certain types of percussion instruments. These include various kinds of double-headed drums (such as the *tabl* of Egypt and the *davul* of Turkey), frame drums of various sizes, and goblet-shaped single-sided drums (such as the *tabla* of Egypt and the *dombak* of Iran).

In urban traditions, melodic instruments tend to have comparable ranges and compatible technical capabilities. On the other hand, they feature a variety of timbres and manners of performing. These instruments suit both soloistic and heterophonic ensemble playing. Among the widely distributed urban instruments are the *ʿud*, a short-necked fretless lute, the *qanun*, a plucked zither, the *nay* and the violin, which are commonly played throughout Turkey and the Arab world.

Illustrating variety within Middle Eastern music are instrumental-vocal groups associated with particular regions and styles. In

Shibli Hamid, a rababa player and poet-singer from southern Syria

Morocco, where the influence of sub-Saharan Africa is felt in the areas of folk rituals, rhythm, and musical instruments, the *qinnawa* musicians use metal clackers and skin-covered long-necked lutes. In the Arabian Gulf, which has been exposed to cultural, commercial and material influences from Africa, Iran, India and South-East Asia, we encounter a rich variety of styles and instrumental ensembles. In the *tanbura* genre of the Gulf, dancing is accompanied by a large lyre similar to the ones found in Sudan and East Africa, and by several cylindrical drums. The *tanbura* ritual, like some others in the area, is associated with spirit possession. The repertoire of the Gulf pearl-fishers presents polyrhythmic clapping, a high-pitched leading vocal part, a low-pitched drone by a chorus, and a percussion part played on clay pots.

In Turkey, the traditional Mevlevi ensemble, which accompanies dance, consists of singers, a number of *ney* players (including a leading performer), *kudüm*, and a pair of large brass cymbals. The ensemble may also include other melody instruments such as the *tanbur*, a long-necked fretted lute.

Iran's distinct modal style and vocal ornaments are complemented by a distinctive set of classical instruments, some having close counterparts in Iraq and Central Asia. Persian classical instruments include the *santur*, a zither with metal strings struck by thin wood hammers, the *tar*, a long-necked fretted lute with a double-belly covered with skin, the *setar*, a small, long-necked lute, the *kamanche*, a four-stringed spike-fiddle, the *ney* and the *dombak*.

Recent trends

Eastern musical cultures have been increasingly exposed to Western musical concepts, techniques and instruments. Musical genres, including some that were popular in pre-First World War Cairo, have either changed considerably or disappeared in favour of more modern and recently developed compositions. Urban ensembles have generally expanded in size, many incorporating instruments such as the cello and the double bass. Some older compositions are presented in modern renditions. Iranian *tasnifs* have been played on native and European instruments and rendered in polyphonic textures. Recently established folkloristic ensembles present modernized and formally staged arrangements of indigenous folksongs and dances. Other ensembles use American rock and jazz-band instruments and perform a synthesis of Middle Eastern and Western musical elements. In some of the cities there are symphonic and chamber ensembles and local Western-trained composers and performers. Mass technology, radio, sound recording and film have promoted Western musical influence, as well as accelerating musical exchange among various rural and urban communities throughout the area.

AJR

Further reading

S. Sadie, ed., *The New Grove Dictionary of Music and Musicians*, 19 vols. (London and New York, 1980)
M. A. Saleh, 'A Documentation of the Ethnic Dance Traditions of the Arab Republic of Egypt', Ph.D. dissertation, New York University, New York, 1979
K. Signell, *Makam: modal practice in Turkish art music* (Seattle, 1977)
O. Wright, *The Modal System of Arab and Persian Music, A.D. 1250–1300* (London, 1978)

Music in Israel

The Holy Land has always been a melting-pot of races, nations, creeds, cultures and languages. Archaeology and written sources indicate that its earliest musical traditions were influenced by the Greeks, Phoenicians, Mesopotamians and Egyptians. Liturgical and secular chants, and the playing of drums, cymbals, lutes, lyres, harps, pipes, trumpets and the *shofar* (ram's horn, the only biblical instrument extant), were essential ingredients in religious and social life.

Instrumental music, associated in the rabbinical mind with conviviality, was generally regarded as inappropriate to a people who had lost their geographical and religious centre. However, song was encouraged as a suitable medium for prayer. So, the cantillations and psalms of the earlier Temple epoch evolved and generated new styles: prayer modes, fixed chants, table songs and choral music. All were subjected to varying degrees of acculturation, depending on the environments in which the Ashkenazi, Sephardi and Oriental Jewish communities had settled. But even from the earliest days of the Christian era, small numbers of Jews trickled back into Palestine*. The first Hebrew song-book to be published in the Near East appeared in 1587. It contained Palestinian synagogue hymns and melodies of Arabic, Greek, Turkish and Spanish origin.

Modern Palestine

The early Jewish pioneers escaping *en masse* from the pogroms of Eastern Europe in the 1880s would have been bewildered by the music of the indigenous beduin, fellah, Druze, Christian Arab, Samaritan and Circassian communities. New models had to be created if Yiddish prototypes were to be reconciled with the instrumental music, songs and dances of west Asia. Recently arrived composers were encouraged to set texts which extolled the virtues of physical labour and self-sacrifice. Love of nature enjoyed a renaissance after centuries of submersion in the urban ethos of the ghetto. There was also a swing toward a more secular, socialist, Zionist interpretation of the Bible. Modern Hebrew became

An old man blowing a shofar

another potent factor. Although 'minor keys' remained popular, the 'augmented 2nd' was largely rejected during this period as being too evocative of the Diaspora and its traumas.

Tel Aviv, the first modern Jewish city in the region, came into being in 1909. The following year saw the establishment of its first music school; a second was founded in 1914. Four years later, an Institute of Music was opened in Jerusalem; and in 1924 a similar institute was founded in Haifa. In the same year, the acknowledged 'Father of Hebrew Song', Joel Engel, emigrated from Russia and settled in Tel Aviv.

Between the First and Second World Wars, many professional performers, conductors, composers, teachers and historians arrived in the country. In 1923 the Russian-born conductor Golinkin introduced Verdi's *La Traviata* in Hebrew translation, the first opera to be produced in Palestine. By 1927 the Palestine Opera had presented some twenty operas from the standard repertoire. In the same year the Institute for New Music was set up in Jerusalem.

The rise of Nazism caused a second mass immigration in the 1930s, this time including Jews from Central and Western Europe. In 1933 Emil Hauser established the Jerusalem String Quartet and the Palestine Conservatoire of Music and Drama. This was later to become one of the two highly prestigious Rubin Academies of Music in Jerusalem and Tel Aviv. In April 1936 the Palestine Broadcasting Service began operating; and the Jerusalem Symphony Orchestra was founded under its auspices ten years later. In December 1936 Toscanini conducted the first concert of the Palestine Symphony Orchestra – forerunner of the Israel Philharmonic; and in 1941 Eytan Lustig established the Tel Aviv Philharmonic Choir. Two years later the first annual Festival of Music and Dance was organized at Kibbutz ʿEn Gev, where a concert hall seating 2000 was later built. In 1945 the first Music Teachers' Training School was opened in Tel Aviv. The recording of music on the spot began when the record company Hed Arzi was formed the following year.

Modern Israel

The *Hatikva* (The Hope), a poem by Imber set to a melody based on a Rumanian folk-song, had been firmly established as the Zionist National Hymn since 1907, and became the Israeli National Anthem in 1948. The 1948 Arab-Israeli War brought forth a flood of songs about patriotism and yearning for peace. The Palestine Broadcasting Service was split into the Arabic *Ramallah* and the Hebrew *Kol Yisraʾel* (Voice of Israel); later a further station, *Kol Zion Lagolah*, began to broadcast Israeli and Arabic music to the outside world. The music department of the General Labour Federation encouraged music in settlements throughout the country. Children from deprived backgrounds were helped to integrate socially and to acquire a basic musical knowledge. In the *kibbutzim* music societies sprang up, and orchestras, bands, choirs, festivals of song and dance were organized on a large scale. In 1949 Peter Gradenwitz founded Israeli Music Publications, in association with the Israeli Association of Composers, to produce books on musical biography, theory, and sheet music of works by composers from the twelfth to twentieth centuries who utilized Jewish subjects.

The establishment of the new state precipitated the third and greatest 'ingathering of exiles', largely from nearby Arab lands. Folk-trios, duos, and solo singers accompanying themselves on guitar or piano, became popular. Musical comedy influenced, and was influenced by, the growth of the theatre* (groups such as Habima and Ohel). Jazz was pioneered in the 1950s by the American-born Melvin Keller. In the classical domain, two complementary trends arose: (a) a reassessment of cantillation and cantorial song and their active use in cantatas and oratorios; and (b) a significant change in the cultural climate leading to experimentation with new techniques such as serialism and electronics. Different admixtures of Jewish and non-Jewish, Western and Oriental, art and folk elements gradually crystallized into seven main 'schools' of composition: 'East European', 'Central European', 'Eastern Mediterranean', 'East–West Synthesis', 'New Ways', 'Light Music and Popular Song', and the 'Younger Generation'.

In 1950 the Research Institute for Oriental and Jewish Music was set up so that the increasing wealth of ethnic materials could be recorded, transcribed and studied. In the same year a City Symphony Orchestra was established in Haifa. In 1951 the Israel Philharmonic Orchestra (IPO) undertook a tour of North America, its first visit abroad. The following year saw the first *zimriyya* (choir festival), which has since attracted Jewish and non-Jewish choirs from many countries. In 1958 the Israel Opera and the Israel National Symphony Youth Orchestra Gadna-Matan were founded. The latter won first prize at competitions in Holland in 1958, 1962 and 1966. The triennial International Harp Contest was first held in Jerusalem in 1959. Meanwhile two auditoria, each holding 3000, were opened: the Mann, home of the IPO, in Tel Aviv in 1957, and the Binyanei ha'Uma in Jerusalem in 1959.

The Song Festival held on the night of Israeli Independence Day in 1960 became an annual competition for songs in the folk idiom. The Israel Festival, founded in 1961 by the Government Tourist Corporation, has put on performances of music and drama annually in Tel Aviv, Jerusalem, and the amphitheatre at Caesarea, and over the years has absorbed many smaller festivals, including the Rubinstein International Piano Master Competition which began in 1974. The Israel Music Institute was established in 1962, further to publish works by Israeli composers. Research activities expanded enormously during the decade. In 1960 Josef Tal inaugurated the Israel Centre for Electronic Music at the Hebrew University, Jerusalem, for composers, analysts, and ethnomusicologists; and in 1965 Israel Adler established a music department in the same university. Similar departments were opened in Tel Aviv University the following year, and at Bar-Ilan University in 1970. The Jewish National and University Library in Jerusalem currently holds one of the largest corpora of Jewish music materials in the world; and sizeable collections are kept at the Central Music Library, Tel Aviv, and the Haifa Music Museum (AMLI Library). The latter also displays traditional instruments from Europe, Africa and Asia, as does the Rubin Academy, Jerusalem.

The Jerusalem Music Centre was conceived by Isaac Stern and established in the city's artists' quarter in 1973. Master classes held by internationally acclaimed musicians are recorded on tape, cassette, and video-cassette, and preserved for future generations of teachers and pupils.

The 1967 Arab-Israeli War* and the 1973 War generated a stream of songs, of which the best known is *Yerushalayim Shel Zahav* ('Jerusalem of Gold') by Naomi Shemer. Television arrived in Israel in 1968. So pervasive has the Western influence been that Israel was able to win the Eurovision Song Contest in 1978 and 1979, and to come second in 1982 and 1983. Noteworthy among the numerous musical events of 1985 were the Israel Festival, comprising hundreds of performers from Europe, the Americas and the Far East; the fifth international Israel Jazz Festival; the second World Harp Congress; and a joint concert by the Israel Philharmonic and New York Philharmonic Orchestras, conducted by Zubin Mehta, musical director of both.

AK

Further reading

William Elias, *The Music of Israel* (Tel Aviv, in prep.)
P. Gradenwitz, *Music and Musicians in Israel* (Tel Aviv, 1978, 3rd edn.)
Zvi Keren, *Contemporary Israeli Music: its sources and stylistic development* (Israel, 1980)

Dance

The tradition of dance in the Middle East and North Africa is one of richness and diversity. With numerous countries and regions represented, dance incorporates a wide variety of styles and functions. Dance movements are connected with social, religious, therapeutic and nationalistic activities, and include recognized dance genres (*raqs* in Arabic), and categories not conceived of as being dance proper.

Throughout the history of the region, dance has been a major form of cultural expression. There are references to it in the Bible, and pictorial depictions and sculptures which attest to its extensive role in ancient Mesopotamia and Egypt. After the coming of Islam, dance continued to occupy a central place in the life of courts, whether those of medieval Muslim rulers or of the Ottomans and Persians, as an entertainment performed by skilled artists, and also at every level of society. The Islamic dance tradition is less well documented, however, than that of music, which was regarded as a speculative science and discussed in numerous theoretical treatises. Moreover, traditional attitudes towards dance as a secular practice and a profession were largely negative, perhaps because of its supposed link with immorality.

Today, there are considerable differences in movement detail between broad regions: the Moroccan Berber dances of the Atlas Mountains, for example, are very different from those of Iran or Anatolia. Within a region, choreographic variants often coincide with ethnic or other differences. In Turkey, for example, dances are identified with localities such as Erzurum, Bitlis, Ankara, and the Black Sea area; in Iran, dances differ from one tribe or group to the other: Qashqai, Luri, Bandari, Bakhtiyari and others. Even within the same community, dances may differ in terms of gender association as well as symbolic significance.

Dance and music have a primary social function. At weddings, birthdays, circumcisions, festivals, and informal gatherings, various collective and individual dances are performed. Examples of these are the Moroccan *shaykhat* dances performed in moving line formations by women, the Algerian Awlad Na'il dances presented by several professional female dancers, the Egyptian *ghawazi* dances performed usually by two or three women with an orchestra of male accompanists, and the solo *raqs sharqi* (literally 'eastern dance', but mis-named 'belly dance' by Westerners). In a wide area ranging from Kurdish communities in Eastern Turkey and Northern Iraq to the eastern Mediterranean shores of the Levant, line dances are common; an example is the *dabka* (literally 'stomping' dance) of Jordan, Lebanon and neighbouring Arab communities. Among some beduin tribes, there are certain dances where two lines of dancers face one another. Occasionally, dancing may take the form of animal performances, for example the bear and the monkey dances of Anatolia and the Levant, and the horse dances of Egypt.

Stylized war dances also exist in a wide variety of forms. Performed by men, they may feature two duelling performers or lines of dancers. War dancers use real or symbolic weapons. For example, curved daggers are used in certain parts of the Arabian peninsula; frame drums, swords, and occasionally rifles are held in the *'arda*, a line dance of Saudi Arabia, Qatar and other Gulf States; swords and shields appear in Lebanon, Syria and Anatolia; and long bamboo sticks are wielded by Egyptian performers of the *tahtib* dance.

The religious function of dance is shown in the practices of some Sufi brotherhoods, for whom dance and music enhance mystical experience. Sufi dances may be accompanied by vocal or instrumental music or both. They exist in a variety of forms and styles throughout the Middle East and North Africa. For some orders, such as the Mevlevis or 'Whirling Dervishes', dance movements, hand gestures and dance attire all have cosmic and spiritual significance; during the Mevlevi *sama'*, or ceremony, each dancer spins counterclockwise around the *shaykh*, symbolizing the rotation of the planets around the sun. In some Egyptian Sufi brotherhoods, the performance of *dhikr* involves several rows of dancers. In the *hadra* ritual of the 'Isawiyya order in the Maghrib, the dervishes dance in front of accompanying musicians and reach a state of trance during which they may characterize by their movements lions or other animals.

Dance may also have a therapeutic function. The *zar*, a healing trance dance, used in order to propitiate spirits in people possessed by them, is found in North Africa, the Nile Valley, and certain parts of the Arabian peninsula and the Gulf. In certain Moroccan festivals, the goatskin-garbed *Bu Jlud* performs frantic dances which impart to those present the supernatural powers of an untamed spirit of nature.

In recent times Middle Eastern dance cultures have shown the influence of the West and its modern technology. Since the late nineteenth century, dances have appeared in theatrical productions, and later in films. The Egyptian cinema, which produced its first talking film in 1932, has been an influential medium for the presentation of traditional and newly choreographed dances. With the appearance of national folk ensembles in practically all Middle Eastern countries, many folk dances have been stylized and formally staged. Many regional dance repertoires, which were originally ritualistic, have been 'festivalized'. Unlike the typical traditional folk performances, the newly created dances have choreographies which have been set in advance and allow for little or no improvisation. Typically, the dancers are professionally trained young men and women from middle-class families. Many modern dances are programmatic and present a repertoire ranging from comic skits to historical dramatizations. These dances are manifestations of a nationalistic spirit and often show Eastern European, Western balletic and modern dance influences. In some cities, Western ballet is taught in officially sponsored schools and academies, and popular Western dances, including modern disco, are now widespread throughout the region.

BTR

Further reading

M. And, *A Pictorial History of Turkish Dancing* (Ankara, 1976)
Arabesque: A Magazine of International Dance (New York)
I. Friedlander, *The Whirling Dervishes* (New York, 1975)

Theatre

The theatre in the Arab world, Turkey and Iran

Drama, as it is known in the West, did not appear in the Middle East until the mid-nineteenth century when *The Miser*, the first play in Arabic, was performed in Beirut. Certain basic dramatic forms had existed in the Arab regions from the time of the Pharaohs but none had developed into a complete dramatic narrative. Among these were the ritual Pharaonic 'passion' or religious plays; the succession dramas acted by incoming pharaonic rulers; to some extent the *zar* ceremonies and, most importantly, the *ta'ziya* rites attached to the Shi'a practice of *'ashura*.

Non-ritualistic forms included the *maqama* (assembly), a primarily literary form which came into being in the eleventh century and gradually developed dramatic elements of character and dialogue based on a skeleton plot (see Arabic Literature). With time, another more popular, less literary form appeared as expressed in the art of the *hakawati* or story-teller, who assumed a series of roles while recounting popular tales.

More theatrical than the *hakawati* were the *khayal al-zill* or shadow plays – and the similar hand-puppet shows – which date from around the end of the tenth century in Egypt and are thought to have been imported originally from the Far East. These had a linear narrative which followed the adventures of the 'hero' Karakoz from one situation to another. An array of social types was included in the script, which was usually sketchy and depended on improvisation by performers. The emphasis was on the comic, including slapstick, which often gave way to vulgarity, but there were also moral and satirical preoccupations.

From the shadow play, which involved acting through puppets, a crude form of live comic theatre ultimately evolved. This became known as *fusul mudhika* (comic scenes) and was performed by itinerant groups in Egypt from around the mid-eighteenth century. None of these could be classified as a forerunner to drama in Arabic but as theatre developed they became an important reference for those seeking to develop a legitimate form of Arab theatre.

A Cairo poster of Umm Kulthum

Theatre in Egypt

Although it was a Lebanese, Marun Naqqash, who staged the first play in Arabic, the main theatrical developments were to take place in Egypt. The Egyptians had been exposed to European drama as early as 1798, when French troupes visited Egypt in the wake of Napoleon's invasion. Under the Khedive Isma'il other foreign troupes were invited to perform in Cairo and it was in this relatively liberal atmosphere that drama began to take root in the Arab world.

Naqqash staged just three plays. The first, *The Miser*, is said to have been inspired by Molière, but it was extensively adapted by Naqqash to give it an appropriately Arab tone. The second, *Abu'l-Hasan, the Fool*, was again influenced by Molière, but took its main inspiration from *The Thousand and One Nights*, and, in a way, could be classified as the first real attempt at Arab drama. The third, *Impudent and Envious One*, seems to have been taken mainly from European sources. All three were written in a mixture of dramatic poetry and rhymed prose and included music and songs in order to cater to popular taste. In many ways they set the guidelines for others to follow.

Like Naqqash in *Abu'l-Hasan*, the Syrian playwright Ahmad Abu Khalil al-Qabbani (who, due to opposition at home, worked mainly in Egypt), saw fit to use Arab sources for his plays. These included stories from the *Arabian Nights*, folk-tales and historical themes. Like Naqqash, he was anxious to teach through his plays and his choice of popular themes was useful in this. His strict adherence to classical Arabic text, however, probably restricted his appeal.

The first attempt to simplify dramatic language was made by the Egyptian writer Ya'qub Sanu' (popularly referred to as the Molière of Egypt), when he introduced colloquial speech into his plays. Though Sanu''s works show borrowings from Molière and the influence of the Commedia dell' Arte, the tradition of the shadow theatre features strongly. This can be recognized primarily in the witty repartee, the slapstick comedy and the underlying social message; and also in stock characters such as the talkative Egyptian maid and the Nubian servant, which were classic shadow theatre types. These plays provide something of a transition between the early crude forms of entertainment and the first attempts at Arab drama.

Overall, however, the early dramatists relied heavily on Western models and the main tendency was towards adaptations and translations of Western works. In the hands of translators like 'Uthman Jalal, these turned out to be quite innovative and thoroughly Arab in expression.

Music and song became basic prerequisites, often dominating a play at the expense of the text and sometimes having little relation to it. The singer-stars proved the biggest draw for a production; when music was excluded, the play failed to attract an audience. During the early 1920s a number of key figures came to the fore as actor-producers. They were to play a major role in the development of theatre in Egypt for the next three decades. They included George Abyad, the first Egyptian to receive theatrical training overseas. He went on to become the leading tragic actor in the country.

Yusuf Wahbi also studied abroad and returned to Egypt to form the Ramses Theatre Group, which became an unofficial training ground for Egyptian actors. Though Wahbi's famous melodramas could be dismissed today as rhetorical tear-jerkers, they were immensely popular and thoroughly professional in their presentation. So, too, were ʿAli al-Kassar's lively revues with their mandatory love-song duets and slapstick routines.

In the meantime, new serious playwrights started to make their mark. In 1927, Ahmad Shawqi's *Fall of Cleopatra*, a verse-drama, received much critical acclaim. It is still highly rated by today's standards and was recently performed by the Egyptian National Theatre. Muhammad Taymur's comedies were quickly recognized for their ability to capture the Egyptian personality. Working sometimes in collaboration with the leading composer of the time, Sayyid Darwish, he produced a series of immensely well-received plays. Tawfiq al-Hakim, the most prolific of Egyptian playwrights, had also begun writing. His *People of the Cave* was chosen for the opening of the National Theatre in 1935, which was a landmark in the history of Egyptian theatre.

Theatre was now beginning to play a key role in Egyptian cultural life and critical debates on its development were well under way. The problem of language, colloquial versus classical, caused heated discussion. There was a growing desire to get away from European models and to define a more appropriate Arab form. As time went on writers tried to bring serious theatre down from an elitist position to a level accessible to all. Theatre was starting to be considered as education and entertainment and new social and political themes were introduced. When Nasser came to power in Egypt in 1952, the boom years for theatre were just beginning, and with the weight of the state behind it, it flourished.

Throughout the 1950s and 60s, state, private and commercial theatre developed side by side, with the National Theatre attracting the cream of the talent. Plays by Yusuf Idris, Alfred Farag, Saʿd al-Din Wahba, Nuʿman ʿAshur and ʿAbd al-Rahman Sharqawi were performed there. Several key themes were introduced, which reflected a growing maturity on the part of the playwrights and the audiences alike. The gap between popular and fine art was being reduced and colloquial language, a more appropriate form of speech through which to consider the plight of the ordinary man, became an accepted form.

Society was in flux and the fate of the individual became a main preoccupation. Often it was the case of the little man, confronted by faceless authority. Man was portrayed as weak but honest, authority as cruel and powerful. A cry for respect of the individual faced with sudden change was raised in works like Mikha'il Ruman's *The New Arrival* or ʿAshur's *The Doghry Family*, both written in the mid-1960s.

While some writers like Wahba, Ruman or ʿAshur aimed at social realism, others like Farag and Idris resorted to myth and allegory, preferring to use historical allusion or some imaginary setting where actuality and fantasy, past and present blended into one. Tawfiq al-Hakim moved freely from one form to another, drawing variously on historical, religious, fictional and factual sources, writing in both classical and colloquial Arabic, and using the comic, the tragic, the absurd and even the surreal, in a catalogue of approaches that mirror the experiments of the time.

Also during this time, prompted by the writings of Dr ʿAli al-Rʿai, there were serious experiments to achieve a more recognizable Arab form of theatre. A major proponent of the idea was Yusuf Idris, whose *Al-Farafir* (1964) deliberately exploited the Karakoz traditions by incorporating comedy, music and dance and presenting a series of characters derived directly from the shadow-play stereotypes. The play itself examined the human predicament through the tensions of a master–servant relationship, the servant, Flipflap, enjoying the role of wise fool.

Meanwhile, other writers turned to historical sources. Alfred Farag, for example, focused on the *fusul mudhika* and began working from the descriptions of plays given by the English traveller E. W. Lane during time spent in Egypt between 1820 and 1830.

The Egyptian defeat in the 1967 War against Israel, which sent shock waves across the Arab world, had a profound effect on the playwrights and instigated a series of bitter and critical works reflecting feelings of anger and dismay. ʿAli Salim's *Ballad on the Passage* was written in commemoration of the dead. Alfred Faraj's *al-Zir Salem*, adapted from a folk-tale about warring tribes, spoke about the reunification of the Arab nation. Rashad Rushdi's *My Country, oh my Country* portrayed a leader isolated from his people and betrayed by his aides. Najib Srur's *Say it to the Eye of the Sun* was a cry of outrage against the defeat.

Critics generally agree that at this time theatre in Egypt was showing a new maturity. More writers were producing, competent actors were emerging from the National Drama School, and both state and private theatre were providing an impressive choice of plays. The 1970s looked like continuing along the same lines when progress was halted by the strict imposition of censorship laws introduced by President Sadat* in February 1973. The day the laws came into effect three out of four theatres were forced to stop production on the spot and reorganize their programmes. The political bite was taken out of theatre and it became harder to produce relevant contemporary works. Some playwrights left Egypt, preferring to work in exile. Many of those remaining do not expect to see their work performed unless the laws are relaxed.

Nowhere else in the region did theatre develop along the strong and specific lines of Egypt.

Theatre in Turkey

The developments in Egypt were in some ways mirrored in Turkey where, in the very early stages at least, the patterns were similar. Here too, the shadow theatre played an important role in entertainment from around the twelfth century; while the *orta oyunu* (theatre in the round) can be compared with the *fusul mudhika*. The Turkish *meddah* or story-teller played a role equivalent to that of the *hakawati*.

The first original plays in Turkish were produced just before the turn of this century. They were mainly melodramas. By 1910, Muhsin Ertegrul, the colossus of early Turkish theatre, had established the Istanbul Municipal Theatre and embarked upon a career which was to make his name synonymous with the evolution of Turkish theatre. His adaptations of Shakespeare are performed to this day. His devotion to theatre was to be the inspiration for aspiring young dramatists.

Though there were many attempts to establish a recognizable form of Turkish theatre, the real breakthrough came during the 1960s when a more liberal constitution was introduced. Turkish theatre now entered into what is nostalgically referred to as its Golden Age, during which all kinds of theatre thrived and theatre-going picked up in the cities and at the regional level. Of all the plays produced during this time, Haldun Taner's *The Ballad of ʿAli from Keshan* stands out as the best piece of authentic Turkish epic theatre.

With each new political turn, however, theatre has suffered. The optimism of the sixties gave way to the repression of the seventies, with tight censorship laws and a concurrent decline in the quality of works being produced. Today, with the exception of the productions from places like the Ankara Arts Theatre and the Friendship Theatre in Istanbul, the level of theatre has basically been reduced to that of cheap musical and even burlesque.

Theatre elsewhere

It was not until the late 1940s and early 50s that the movement really started to take shape in Iraq and Syria. Initially, criticism against the old regime and the fight for independence fired the imagination of the writers, who often found themselves in conflict with the authorities. With independence, state-supported theatre functioned in tandem with private groups and the two gained ground. In both countries, however, it was the talents of the exceptional few that made the main impact.

In Syria, writers like Saʿdallah Wannus and Muhammad Maghut, and the satirist Durayd Lahham, stand out among the rest. In Iraq it is Yusuf al-ʿAyni and Qasim Muhammad and actor-director Sami ʿAbd al-Hamid. In Morocco, Tayyib al-Siddiqi's unique theatrical approach dominates the scene. In Tunis it is the work of director Munsef Sweisi and the experiments of the New Theatre Group. In Algeria it is Katib Yasin.

In Lebanon, where every type of theatre once flourished, certain individuals still struggle to keep theatre alive despite the war. Some, like Nabih Abu'l-Husn, have used the war theme for propaganda purposes. Others, like Yaʿqub Shadrawi, remain on the political fringes working hard to maintain an active theatrical life.

One group making headway is Roger ʿAssaf's Hakawati troupe, which, as the name implies, seeks to revive the ancient art of story-telling as a base for theatre. Materials for the plays are collected during social gatherings and impromptu rehearsals where the local participants exchange ideas with the actors, sing songs, tell jokes and recount tales. These spontaneous forms are then interwoven into a narrative. ʿAssaf's two recent works, *Tales from the Year of 1936*, which recalls the struggle of south Lebanon against the French, and *Days of al-Khiyam*, which recounts the forced migration of south Lebanese to Beirut in face of Israeli aggression, were well received at recent Damascus theatre festivals.

Similar praise was accorded there to Tayyib al-Siddiqi's plays, which draw upon classical and contemporary Arabic literary sources for their text and incorporate these with a range of popular folkloric ideas. Siddiqi basically eschews formal theatre and creates lively and colourful spectacles with lavish costume, lighting and props, a mixture of ritual and burlesque based on a solid literary foundation, with some political undertones. Together with leading Lebanese actress Nidal Ashqar, Siddiqi has also organized an Arab actors' company, the first such pan-Arab venture, which brings together the talents of a dozen leading Arab players. Their first production, *1001 Nights in Suq Ukaz*, bears all the hallmarks of Siddiqi's work and reflects Ashqar's preoccupation with popular traditions as a theatrical base.

Working along similar lines, the Jerusalem-based Hakawati troupe produces plays which are a curious but inspired mixture of mime, pantomime, slapstick, and serious political and social comment. This was conceived as an itinerant form of theatre which must have as much appeal to the village elder as to the city dweller. It also assumes the responsibility of preserver of tradition and heritage, which under Occupation are gradually being eroded. In many ways it resembles the idea of the *fusul mudhika*, in others it is as powerful and innovative as Brecht.

It is in the work of groups like the above that the quest for that illusive form of Arab theatre, that writers have been discussing for the last century, may lie. In the meantime, all forms of drama continue to be explored: Arabized Shakespeare, adaptations from Lorca, reinterpretations of Beckett, as well as original works in

Arabic, some of which will not be staged until the overall political situation improves.

Attendance at the theatre remains surprisingly high, in spite of television and video. In Iraq, for example, new theatres have recently been opened in various parts of the country and are doing well. In the Gulf, theatre complexes have been built and state support for theatre groups is generous. Training and production here take place largely under the experienced eye of theatre exiles from other Arab countries. Nascent talents are being nurtured among budding playwrights who concentrate on social themes, such as the impact of oil on society and the changing face of the Gulf.

Theatre festivals still take place, on a sporadic basis, in Damascus, Carthage, Cairo and recently in Baghdad. Where politics do not interfere, they attract a largely pan-Arab participation. Nevertheless, though some optimism over the spirit of survival might be in order, there is deep pessimism, especially among the old guard, about the intellectual decline of theatre in face of censorship, war and the Islamic backlash. As Yusuf Idris put it in a recent interview: 'These rulers are very well aware of the role of true writers and they try to eradicate them.'

MA

(For Bibliography see under Cinema)

Cinema

Cinema arrived in the Middle East at about the same time as in the United States and Europe, and took root quickly in the main cities of Egypt and Turkey. By 1895 audiences in Cairo and Istanbul were as fascinated by films such as Lumière's *Moving Train* as Westerners were. Within two years, the men from Pathé were much in demand as they plied their trade across the region. By the early 1900s Egyptian magazines were already discussing film-making techniques and the first proper cinemas were being built.

By 1917, some eighty cinemas had opened in Egypt and a small studio had been established in Alexandria, which began by producing 30–40 minute documentaries. In the same year, the first Egyptian comedy, *Why Does the Sea Laugh?* was released. It was later exported to Lebanon, marking the beginning of Egypt's domination of the film industry throughout the Arab world.

In Turkey, a documentary produced in 1914, *The Demise of the Russian Monument in Ayestefanis*, ushered in the Turkish film industry. It was slower to develop than in Egypt and distribution was limited to Turkey because of the language barrier, but with time it grew into a substantial commercial enterprise.

Meral Orhonsoy plays Emine in Yilmaz Güney's 1982 film *Yol*

Egyptian cinema

Egypt's first full-length feature, *Layla*, produced by its star, stage actress 'Aziza Amir, was screened in 1927 and set the tone for many future films. It is a melodramatic story of a young peasant woman abandoned in pregnancy by her beduin lover and driven from her home by shame. She heads for Cairo where, after losing the baby, she embarks on a sad life of deprivation and desperation. *Layla* was a great success, as was its rival, *Kiss in the Desert*. The money-making potential of film-making was quickly recognized by both the state and private investors. Government played a part in organizing export and distribution and looked forward to a substantial tax revenue from cinema receipts. Private investors saw fit to pour money into studios, the most important of which, Studio Misr, was established in 1934. Between the late 1930s and early 1940s over a hundred production companies were formed and some twenty features a year were being released.

With the introduction of sound in the early 1930s, music became an essential component of the Egyptian film as it had been of theatre. The leading theatrical stars inevitably drifted over to the new medium. Comedies featuring Najib al-Rihani and the melodramas of Yusuf Wahbi were adapted for the screen. Top singers like Muhammad ʿAbd al-Wahhab and Umm Kulthum starred time and again in stories written around their songs.

There was also an early attempt to produce something more serious. In 1934 actress-producer Assia Daghia presented the first historical film, *Queen Shagar al-Durr*, set in the Middle Ages and filmed in and around the Azhar quarter of Cairo.

But the turning point came in 1940 when Kamal Salim gave Egyptian audiences their first taste of neo-realism with *Determination*, which dealt with the everyday problems of ordinary Egyptians through the story of a hard-working young man seeking stable employment with the government. The film was shot largely on location in Cairo's streets and alleys and incorporated many aspects of daily life in the city. It was well liked.

By the mid-1940s Egypt was producing over fifty films a year, many of which were exported to other parts of the Arab world. The Egyptian cinema industry thrived on a staple commercial fare of musical, comedy and melodrama. The screenplays were largely indistinguishable from each other: boy meets girl, loses her and finds her again, the action being punctuated by song and dance routines. Another variation was that the rich boy falls in love with the poor girl (or vice versa) and must overcome family opposition to their marriage.

More committed directors like Salah Abu Sayf and Yusuf Shahin, who were pioneers in establishing a socio-political cinema, were at the beginning of their careers and were yet to make an impact.

Turkish cinema

The story was similar in Turkey where, for almost two decades, cinema had been dominated by the work of Muhsin Ertegrul, a committed thespian whose theatrical ideas were transferred onto film. His monopoly of Turkish cinema remained virtually unbroken until the mid-1940s, when younger directors were returning from film studies overseas.

Like Kamal Salim in Egypt, Lutfi Akad turned the tide of cinema in Turkey with *Death of a Whore* (1949), followed by *In the Name of the Law*, both of which were neo-realistic in style and carried a social message. Akad, along with directors like Metin Erksan, Memduh Un, Atif Yilmaz, Ertem Gorec and Halit Refig, instigated a 'new wave' cinema which dealt with social discrimination, injustice, the problems of urban migration, the deprivations of rural life and the oppressive nature of tradition. But they were in the minority. Tax concessions granted to producers in 1948 had opened the floodgates for all manner of productions, primarily melodramas, musicals and romances, and what was eventually to evolve into the soft-porn genre. Annual production was creeping up to the one-hundred mark.

Cinema to the present day

Developments in Egypt continued to run roughly parallel, though annual production never exceeded seventy films during the peak period of the 1950s. This was at the beginning of Nasser's regime, when government instigated changes in the way the film industry was organized. During this period, a number of prestige films were produced, including Yusuf Shahin's *Cairo Station*, a brooding microcosmic view of the capital as represented by the comings and goings at Cairo's main railway station; Salah Abu Sayf's *Between the Sky and the Earth*, a psychological suspense story in which fourteen people from different social backgrounds find themselves stuck in an elevator without hope of immediate help because it is a holiday; and Tawfiq Salih's *Idiots' Alley*, a study of life among Cairo's poor.

New directors like Kamal Shaykh and Henri Barakat were entering the scene, as were the actors and actresses who were to dominate the screen for years to come. Faten Hamama and her then husband, ʿUmar Sharif, became the darlings of the screen, along with Hind Rustum and Suʿad Husni. A hierarchy of stars following a rigid system of front-liners, runners-up and minor players was established. Though the names may change the system endures.

As with theatre, the 1960s marked something of a turning point for Egyptian film-makers, most specifically because of the 1967 defeat by the Israelis. A new, more serious tone of political questioning was introduced into the films. Working with the country's leading writers, directors turned their focus onto a society in flux and exposed confusion, bitterness and corruption. Shahin's *The Sparrow*, written in collaboration with Lutfi al-Khuli, presented an unflattering view of society in Egypt on the eve of the 1967 War. Produced in 1973, it was suppressed in Egypt until 1975. ʿAli Badrakhan's *Karnak*, based on a novel by Najib Mahfuz, showed society in a state of demoralization and deterioration on the eve of the June War (1967).

The October War of 1973 also became an important theme as evidenced by films like Hasan al-Din Mustafa's *The Bullet is Still in my Pocket* and Nadir Galal's *Budur*.

But not all the important films were political. Saʿid Marzuk's *I Want a Solution* (1974) was a daring indictment of the divorce laws and the status of women in Egypt. ʿAtif Salim's *The Grandson* (1978) took a satirical look at modern living in Egypt and especially at the problems of overpopulation. Salah Abu Sayf's *The Water-carrier is Dead* (1977) treated the subject of death with compassion and delicacy. Shadi ʿAbd al-Salam's *The Mummy*, which dealt with ancient and modern life in Upper Egypt, received international acclaim. Kamal Shaykh's *Rising to the Bottom*, starring Heba Salim, retraced the true story of a girl who decides to sell herself for money, while Kamal Salah al-Din's *A Girl Different from Others* (1978) examined the life of a young woman seeking liberation from the confining barriers of Egyptian society.

Similar developments were taking place in Turkey, with committed new directors starting to produce socio-political films of a high calibre. At the forefront of the group was Yilmaz Güney, a well-educated actor turned producer-director, whose own colourful story of imprisonment and dramatic escape into exile captured the imagination of film fans. Güney and his colleagues Şerif Goren and Zeki Okten formed a formidable team and were the natural successors to Akad. Güney made his directorial debut with *Umut* (The Hope), a highly polished socio-political work which many critics considered the first authentic Turkish film of professional quality. Together and separately Güney, Goren and Okten produced a series of meaningful films with outspoken ideas and underlying political comment. Though thoroughly Turkish in context, these films have enjoyed a growing success in the West. Among them are Güney's *The Herd* (1978), a moving chronicle about the erosion of tribal existence and the difficulties of adjustment to urban ways; and *The Way* (winner of the 1982 Palme d'Or at Cannes), a powerful story about the shocks and disappointments awaiting five men on home leave from prison.

These films set new precedents for Turkish film-makers and other directors responded. Ali Ozgenturk's *The Horse* took up the theme of urban migration, highlighting the sufferings of a villager trying to make his way in the city in order to provide an education for his son. Erden Kiral's *A Season at Hakkari* recounts the experiences of an urban intellectual sent into internal exile in a remote part of Hakkari province. The film won four international awards, but because of its critical nature has not yet been shown in Turkey.

Threats to the industry

Outspoken film-makers like these are finding it increasingly difficult to raise funds. With rising costs, diminishing audiences and competition from video films to contend with, producers in Egypt and Turkey are feeling the pinch. From over two hundred films a year in the 1970s, production in Turkey dropped to eighty in the mid-1980s. In Egypt, an average of forty-five films a year are produced, but many are of lamentable quality. The industry is dominated by a handful of producers who have their eye as much on the video market as on the cinemas. The films are pre-sold with video rights and less and less attention is given to quality. If a film fails to earn the expected amount in the cinema, it is immediately withdrawn and replaced by another which may attract a bigger audience in an effort to realize profits. Cinema audiences in Cairo have suddenly and somewhat inexplicably started to fall.

As in Turkey, it is hard for serious directors to assemble the necessary funds under such circumstances. Having done so, like their Turkish colleagues, they sometimes come unstuck at the hands of the censor before the film is released. The most serious film-makers in Egypt are usually politically oriented and must tread carefully. Saʿid Marzuk's *To Save What is Possible to Save*, which is said to be critical of prevailing political influences in Egypt, was banned at the beginning of 1986. ʿAtif al-Tayyib's *The Innocent*, the story of a prison guard who realizes he has been duped into applying torture by his superiors, was also suppressed.

Corruption in high places appears to be a taboo subject, though it can be shown lower down the scale, as in Ahmad's Yahya's *The Smoke does not leave the Room*. This traces the career of a poor man who, initially shocked by the decadence and debauchery of his upper-class friends, uses his knowledge of their practices to climb up the social ladder and achieve power. Among other things he participates in drug dealing and, for the first time, smoking hashish appears in an Egyptian film without any kind of moral admonition.

While films at the more popular level celebrate the benefits of the *Infitah* (the late President Sadat's 'open door' economic policy) with rags-to-riches stories of the good guys doing well while remaining good guys, the other side of the story comes out in films like ʿAli Badrakhan's *People at the Top*, which looks at the corruption and greed the policy has encouraged in the sea ports.

ʿAtif al-Tayyib's *The Bus Driver* shows how the new-found materialism is undermining traditionally strong family ties. So, too, does Henri Barakat's *The Night of Fatma's Arrest*. Khayri Bishara's *House Boat 70* reveals corruption and bribery at factory level as people struggle to make money.

Despite all the difficulties facing it, however, the Egyptian film industry remains dominant throughout the region. The export market to other Arab countries is still lucrative (despite the boycott imposed at the time of Camp David*) and there has never been any real competition. Elsewhere in the Middle East, developments in cinema have been sporadic.

Algerian cinema

In Algeria, Syria and Iraq there have been well-intentioned attempts by the state to lay the foundations of a film industry. Of the three, Algeria is the success story. In the last two decades over fifty high-standard feature films and innumerable documentaries have been produced there under the aegis of the Algerian National Institute of Cinema.

At first the themes concentrated purely on the liberation struggle. Later, in the early 1970s, other issues such as urban migration and the role of women started to predominate. Muhammad Salim Riyad's *Wind from the South*, Assia Djebar's *Nouba of the Women of Mount Chenoua*, Sayid ʿAli Mazef's *Layla and the Others*, and, more recently, ʿAli Ghanem's *A Wife for my Son* all condemn the treatment of women in Algeria.

In the mid-1970s, Merzan Allouache's *Omar Gatlato* broke new ground with its exposure of the bored, aimless existence of contemporary urban youth. The recently released *The Roof*, a black comedy about a young couple who cannot find anywhere to live, takes a satirical view of urban pressures. The destruction of the rural life-style is another theme that has been developed over the years, most notably in Muhammad Bouamari's works, such as *The Coalman*, in which a man leaves his village in search of work but, unable to cope with urban pressure, returns home to find that everything there has changed. His *Heritage* tells the story of peasants returning to their lands after the war only to find their village destroyed and their livelihoods gone for ever. Lamine Merbah's *Uprooted* shows a group of peasants dispossessed by the French and forced to move to the city.

Algerian cinema has gained the respect of Arab and European critics alike, in terms of both content and quality. Muhammad Lakhdar Hamina's *The Oracle Winds* set the standard as a Cannes prizewinner in 1966. His *Chronicle of the Hot Years* gained the Palme d'Or award in Cannes in 1975. Both films look back to Algeria's past, the first recounting the story of a mother's search for her son, imprisoned in a French concentration camp during the Algerian war of independence; the second examines the causes which precipitated the independence struggle. Though his *Wind of Sand*, an epic production about survival in a desert village, failed to have the same impact as his previous films, it was still a moving and powerful work which prompted discussion in Europe.

Due to institutional changes in the Cinema Organization, production has fallen back in Algeria during the 1980s. Even so, some interesting films have been released. Ibrahim Tsaki's *Story of an Encounter* is a symbolic tale about two deaf-mute children, an American and an Algerian, who communicate through a world of make-believe. They meet and play against the arid backdrop of the Algerian oilfields where their cultures share mutual dependence. Mazyan Yala's *Song of Autumn* traces life on a disputed farm at the beginning of the Algerian War and is a study of individual and group behaviour.

Iranian cinema: new inhibitions

While Algerian cinema blossomed as a result of the revolution, the story in Iran, at least until now, has been rather different, and a once-promising industry has, for the moment, disappeared under the wave of change.

Until 1979, cinema-going in Iranian cities was a popular pastime. The first Iranian feature film had been made in 1948 and over the years production had increased to around a hundred films a year – mainly low-budget, lightweight works, action stories, comedies and so on. By the beginning of the seventies, an estimated 70 million cinema tickets a year were being sold and a new wave of young directors was beginning to emerge.

Overseas-trained and with a healthy streak of liberalism which often brought them into conflict with the authorities, these young film-makers soon discovered ways in which to draw on the history and heritage of their native land to produce poetic, allegorical works with a message, which often only just slithered through the censor's grip.

The first film in this group to establish itself both at home and abroad was Daryush Mehrju'i's award-winning *The Cow*, a sad tale about rural poverty. This was followed by Bahram Beiza'i's *Downpour*, a realistic and at the same time humorous account of life in Tehran's slums; and by Mehrju'i's *The Postman*, which dealt with the effects of colonialism and industrialization. Shortly after came *The Mina Cycle*, which many considered to be Mehrju'i's most important film. This exposed the blood trade in Iran's hospitals from which, at physical cost, the poor eked out extra cash.

It was never easy for the new wave of directors to get productions off the ground for, although their work was having an impact abroad, at home producers were more interested in satisfying popular tastes with cheap productions. Nevertheless, during the fertile period of the seventies, several more films of note were made and received overseas distribution. Among them, Khusraw Haritash's *The Guardian* (1976) represents an astute statement on social change taking place in Iran during the last years under the Shah, focusing in particular on the growing conflicts caused by the generation gap.

In 1977, ʿAbbas Kiya Rustami's *The Report*, a chronicle of life in the urban environment, was praised for its insight and understanding of the problems of adjusting to contemporary pressures. The same year, Bahram Beiza'i's *The Crow* tackled the subject of identity and the search for roots on a universal as well as an Irani level.

At this time, Bahman Farmanara's *Prince Ehtejab* was released. This was a complex film dealing with life under the Qajar Dynasty in which historical, social, psychological and mystical threads were skilfully interwoven. His later *Tall Shadows in the Wind*, a sociological tale with mystical overtones, about a group of superstitious villagers spellbound by the presence of a giant scarecrow, was one of the last films to come out of Iran as the revolution took a hold. It was highly acclaimed by international critics.

Film-making in Iran now fulfils a mainly educational role concentrating primarily on documentaries about the revolution and the Gulf War. It is as yet impossible to put these works into context, and it is a matter of conjecture whether, as in the case of Algerian cinema, they could form the basis of a new national cinema in the future.

Those film-makers remaining in the country who have tried to produce more secular or neutral works do so by treading an extremely cautious path. There are also Iranian directors working in exile whose films are obviously never seen in Iran. The most successful of these films, Parvis Sayyad's *The Mission*, which deals with people caught up in political or social events beyond their control, was well received in the United States and Europe, but remains an unknown quantity in Iran.

New energy in North Africa

Though production elsewhere is falling, in Morocco, Tunisia and Lebanon more films have been made in recent years than ever before. This is partly due to the drive and energy of young film-makers who received their training in Europe and established enough contacts to persuade European backers to enter into co-productions.

In Tunisia, the example was set by Ridha Behi's immensely successful *Hyena's Sun*, which shows how Tunisian society is being undermined at the expense of tourism development. His recent *The Angels* takes a closer look at Tunisian society and the stultifying, sometimes destructive nature of traditional attitudes. Nasir Khemir's first film, *Markers in the Desert*, weaves myth and reality together in an allegorical tale where past and present meet in a remote desert village.

Nasir Katari's *The Ambassadors*, which was shot in France and deals with the insoluble problems facing North African immigrants there, introduces one of the preoccupations of Maghribi cinema. Mahmud ibn Mahmud's *The Crossing* takes up the theme with an ironic tale about a visa-less immigrant who must keep on sailing from shore to shore, unable to embark anywhere because his papers are not in order. Lotfi Essid's *What Shall we Do on Sunday?* looks at the bleak daily existence of immigrants. Abdalkarim Bahloul's *Tea with Mint* highlights the problems of adjustment to the European way of life.

Increase of films in Lebanon

Co-productions have acted like a life-saving transfusion for film-makers in Beirut, who, in spite of an apparently endless civil war, have stepped up production and put together an unusual chronicle on the war seen from a variety of angles. Even in the commercial sector, film-making is on the increase, with some sixteen features produced in 1985.

Marun Baghdadi's *Little Wars*, shot on a shoe-string budget with technical help and equipment from the United States, concentrates on the lives of four young people – each with a different political leaning – at the outbreak of the war. Their personal struggles mirror the major conflict taking place around them.

In Burhan ʿAlawiyya's *The Encounter*, war hovers in the background as two young people struggle to come to terms with what it has done to their lives. A Shiʿi boy from the south manages to make contact with his Christian girl friend in the east by telephone during a lull in the fighting. Their plans to meet are continuously frustrated by renewed fighting so they exchange their feelings by cassette tapes. When the opportunity to meet presents itself they do not seize it, recognizing that war has changed their relationship. A second film by ʿAlawiyya, *Letter in a Time of War*, concentrates on the fate of Lebanon's Shiʿa population, but it was not as well received as *The Encounter*. A more successful film on the same subject is Roger Assaf's *Maʿraka*, which shows how the villagers of Maʿraka resisted the Israeli occupation in the south.

Rafiq Hajjar's *Bomb Shelter*, in which a group of people from different political factions find themselves cornered in a shelter by a sniper outside, provides a revealing study of prevailing attitudes in Lebanon. His *Explosion*, which examines the factors leading to the war and its effect on the lives of a young couple (a Christian and a Muslim) seemed to lack the incisiveness of the first.

Jocelyn Saʿb's recently released *The Sweet Love of Adolescence* has received critical praise in Europe. It tells the story of a 14-year-old girl, who was born in the war and has had to develop survival techniques to live through it. Inevitably her youth has been cut short as a result. The effect of the war on the young women of Lebanon is also touched upon in Hayni Srur's rather rambling *Layla and the Wolves*, a chronicle of the Arab woman betrayed by war and revolution.

When making these co-productions, the Arab film-makers obviously have their eye as much on the European as the domestic market and for the most part their films do well in European film festivals and on the art circuit.

The pioneering steps taken by directors like Lakhdar Hamina, Yilmaz Güney and Yusuf Shahin (whose recent big-budget French co-production *Adieu Bonaparte* did better in France than at home) set an example for the younger generation by proving that Middle Eastern cinema could have an impact on the international scene. It gave them new hopes and incentives.

The world of international film-making has also had a magnetic effect on a new breed of Arab producer, who is providing financial backing for European or American productions. Among these are Mustafa Akkad, director-producer of the Arab epics *Muhammad the Messenger* and *ʿUmar Mukhtar*. Now Hollywood-based, Akkad is turning out feature films for the American market.

Working from Tunisia, Tarek Ben Ammar has proved adept at attracting major Western film projects to his studios and has acted as producer on prestige productions like Zeffirelli's *La Traviata*.

The Jordanian Mu'in Nabulsi is making his debut as a producer on a new British film, *Claudia's Story*. What is heartening about film-making in the Middle East and North Africa is that although quantity may be on the decrease, quality seems to be improving and the results are showing in European film festivals. The annual Arab Film Week in Paris is an important showcase for film-makers from the region. A growing body of critical literature on their work is coming out of France. With this comes the vital exposure the better directors need to enable them to continue working; all of which must give encouragement to an industry threatened by shrinking audiences, competition from video and political obstacles.

MA

Further reading

F. Abdel-Wahab, *Modern Egyptian Drama, an Anthology* (Minneapolis and Chicago, 1974)
P. Cowie, ed., *International Film Guide* (London, 1974–1986 edns.)
M. Khan, *An Introduction to Egyptian Cinema* (London, 1969)
M. al-Khozai, *The Development of Early Arabic Drama* (London, 1984)
J. M. Landau, *Studies in Arab Theatre and Cinema* (Philadelphia, 1958)
M. Manzalaoui, *Arabic Writing Today: the drama* (Cairo, 1977)
H. Salman, S. Hartog and D. Wilson, *Algerian Cinema* (London, 1976)

Israeli theatre and cinema

Theatre

With five major companies, some twenty busy auditoria and a reported 50 per cent of the adult population attending at least one live performance each year, Israeli theatre is thriving. The main companies (the Habimah National Theatre and the Cameri Theatre in Tel Aviv, the Khan Theatre in Jerusalem and the Haifa and Beer-Sheba Municipal Theatres) are all generously supported by central and local government. There is a flourishing if down-market commercial sector embracing shows in immigrant languages (Yiddish, Russian, Romanian, English) as well as in Hebrew and in the past ten years an increasing number of ad-hoc and 'fringe' companies have started to make their presence felt, especially in the Greater Tel Aviv area and in the tourist and entertainment centres of Jaffa and Jerusalem. The size of the country enables most companies to tour without the need for an overnight stay, and the repertory system operated by all the major companies leads to frequent exchanges of productions, enabling audiences in large cities as well as small settlements to see the best of the season without undue effort. Actors and directors find employment with considerable ease and most of them remain attached to the same company for many years. There are a number of festivals around the year, with the Jerusalem Festival bringing in small-scale companies from around the world, while the Acre Festival provides a constantly enlarging platform for local alternative and experimental theatre.

Yet all this frantic activity covers a typical Middle Eastern crisis of identity: Israeli theatre as a cultural phenomenon is constantly torn between imported European and American productions (plays, directors, designers, sometimes even an entire West End set are brought in lock, stock and barrel) and the home-grown variety. For the generation of theatre builders active at independence, with its roots in the Russia of the 1920s (Vakhtangov's Moscow Habimah company settled in the 'little Tel Aviv' of the 20s via a few years in the United States) or in the Central European traditions embodied above all by the luminous yet intense figure of the actor-director-manager Yosef Milo, who was responsible in one way or another for founding all the other main theatres between 1944 and the early 1970s, it seemed natural to look west for both models and material. For their followers, the people in charge of theatres today, most of whom are English or American trained, it again felt right to adopt a West End or Broadway-oriented outlook. Yet, despite a repertory dominated by imported plays and directors (statistically, under 10 per cent of the repertory since Independence has been made up of original plays) it is to the poorer, simpler, sometimes naive Israeli play that the public at large genuinely warms. In the early years, plays like *He Walked in the Fields* by Moshe Shamir (1948, directed by Milo) or Nathan Shaham's *They will Arrive Tomorrow* (1950) – both dealing in idealized terms with the War of Independence – overshadowed in the public memory real achievements in producing major classics, such as Milo's landmark productions of *Richard III* and *The Caucasian Chalk Circle*. In later years, playwrights such as Hanokh Levin, Nissim Aloni and Yehoshua Sobol proved extremely successful, while the original output grew constantly: 167 original plays were performed between 1948 and 1970, and almost double that number since.

Among these, Hanokh Levin's brand of writing stands out as the most controversial yet the most successful. Rooted in the great Jewish tradition of social satire, Levin's best plays cut Israeli society and its myths to the quick. In his early revues (*You and I and the Next War* (1968), *Queen of the Bathtub* (1969)), Levin slaughters most Israeli sacred cows: the military, the elders' blind preoccupation with their 'sabra' heirs, and above all the great Israeli pastime of self-congratulation, with a ferociousness rarely encountered in the otherwise conformist Israeli society. His later, full-length plays (*Hefetz*, *Yakobi and Leidenthal*, *Vardalleh's Youth*, *Shitz*, *The Rubber Merchants* and above all *The Suitcase Packers*, seen in a memorable production by the British/Israeli director Mike Alfreds in Tel Aviv in 1984 and in London in 1985) turn inwards, onto the greatest Israeli institution of all: the hallowed lower-middle-class family. Family relationships, parental worship for the young, male aggression and weakness, loneliness and alienation in the midst of a frantic and inquisitive society, all are exposed to the author's bitter loathing to shudderingly comic effect.

If Hanokh Levin is the master satirist of the *shkhuna* (neighbourhood) microcosm, Nissim Aloni is concerned with major themes brought to the stage in experimental, modernistic forms. The most 'universal' playwright in Hebrew, Aloni draws consciously on European traditions (the Absurd, Symbolism and Expressionism) with a sovereign disregard for anything specifically Israeli. *The King's Clothes* (1961) is an allegory based on the Andersen story. *The American Princess* (1963) is a virtuoso piece for two characters and a set of disembodied, pre-recorded voices. *Napoleon – Live or Dead* (1970) is another allegory about the illusions of power and ambition. Central to all Aloni's writing, the Oedipus myth is given an explicit modern treatment in *Eddie King* (1975). Aloni's most accomplished play, *The Gypsies of Jaffa* (1971) is set in a nightclub in which gypsies tell fortunes while Death – the central theme of the play – hovers. With *The Gypsies of Jaffa* Aloni seems to have assimilated the European influences (Maeterlinck, de Ghelderode, Jarry, Ionesco have been quoted) into an essentially Israeli modern idiom, at once anarchic and highly charged with symbolism, colloquial yet pointed in its use of language.

A similar attempt, but from a social realist angle, with documentarist leanings, is to be found in Yehoshua Sobol's plays. His recent *The Night of the 20* (1976) (about the failure of the socialist/kibbutznik ideal of collective and personal freedom as experienced by a group of young immigrants in the 1920s) and *Jewish Spirit* (1983) (about a pre-existentialist philosopher as a symbol of Jewish self-loathing) were among the greatest successes of recent years.

Levin, Aloni and to a lesser extent Sobol write in a determinedly non-naturalistic manner, inviting strong visual elements in production and a style of acting in which characters are drawn with thick, cartoon-like lines, a style bordering on the grotesque. Most Israeli actors fall in with ease with this type of acting and they share with their audiences a love of parody, slapstick and non-verbal humour. Unfortunately, when it comes to staging classics (Shakespeare, Chekhov and Brecht are regularly attempted) these skills prove insufficient, and the general levels of production and acting are poorer than the Western models they emulate.

The Israeli school of acting, led by the main drama and film academy at 'Beit Zvi' in Ramath-Gan, under the immensely energetic and ever expanding figure of Gershom Bilu, its principal, strives to improve standards through a methodical, determined effort to train the new generation of actors in the classical, realistic tradition, and has thus become the originator and focus of much that is positive in today's Israeli theatre. Above all, Bilu's achievement in publishing for the past five years a series of simply printed play-scripts, with hundreds of titles to its credit, has created for the first time a pool of classical material in translation (remarkably, major poets like Nathan Alterman and Ted Carmi had been drafted over the years by different theatres to translate Molière, Shakespeare and even Farquhar) available to all and constantly enlarging the dramatic repertory. The effect of all this activity is still to penetrate the theatrical establishment and in the meantime the split in perception what constitutes 'good theatre' between public and practitioners tends to deepen. This tendency is exacerbated by the critical community, who are largely academically based and academically minded. Israeli critics tend to expand their reviews beyond the scope of topical notices in popular newspapers into the realm of essays positing what the Israeli theatre 'ought to be' and constantly pitching its achievements against Western models. They tend to create an artificial ideal of the nation's theatre against which the living, breathing variety has very little chance of measuring up. Israeli playwrights and directors, torn between critical onslaughts and the often contradictory demands of the audiences, find themselves increasingly unsure of their self-image. This leads to wildly disparate standards of writing and production, through which some achievements of note occasionally emerge.

VM

Further reading

G. Abrahamson, *Modern Hebrew Drama* (London, 1979)
M. Kahansky, *The Hebrew Theatre – Its first 50 years* (New York, 1969)

The cinema in Jewish Palestine and Israel

Among the implements of twentieth-century Europe the Jewish settlers brought with them to Palestine was the magic movie camera. At first, somewhat non-professional newsreels and propaganda films for the Zionist cause were produced, but a new immigrant from the USSR, Natan Axelrod, produced the first feature film shot in Palestine, the Hebrew-language *Oded Hanoded* (*Oded the Wanderer*), in 1933. He also established the first professional newsreel company, Carmel Films. Another pioneer, Baruch Agadati, also produced newsreels. After the Second World War a number of dramas and documentaries were made dealing with the Holocaust and the movement of illegal immigration of Jewish refugees from Europe to Palestine, notably Herbert Klein's *My Father's House* and *The Illegals*, both based on stories by the Jewish American writer Meyer Levin.

After the establishment of the state of Israel in 1948, two film studios, Geva and Herzliya, were built, mostly to cater for the government's information services. In 1955 the first feature film of note was produced in the new state: *Hill 24 Does not Answer*, directed by the British director Thorold Dickinson, and telling the tale of a detachment of Jewish soldiers in the bloody battle for Jerusalem. Few other features were produced in the 1950s, but a long line of major Hollywood productions filmed in Israel and dealing with the 1948 War of Independence was inaugurated by

Otto Preminger's *Exodus* (1959). The indigenous film industry, however, tiring of heroic sagas and myth-making, began to produce films which more closely reflected the strains and schisms of a new social order in works such as the humorist Ephrayim Kishon's *Salah* (1964), starring the then local actor, Hayim Topol, as an 'oriental' immigrant from the Arab countries who battles the mostly European bureaucracy for a place in the sun. Other directors, Menahem Golan and Uri Zohar, reflected the life and dramas of modern Israel in films like *Fortuna* (Golan, 1966) and *Three Days and a Child* (Zohar, 1967). A spate of low budget, 'oriental' melodramas for the eastern communities erupted in the 1970s with tear-jerkers like *Nurit* and *Sarit*, directed by Persian immigrant George Ovadia. Many local low-grade comedies were also produced. But, from 1969, a newly formed Israel Film Centre, and later, a fund for quality films, also made possible the production of a new line of thoughtful, 'social conscience' dramas, with new directors more eager to challenge (as far as their sponsors would allow) the prevailing ethos of nationalism and self congratulation: Yehuda (Judd) Ne'eman, with *Paratroopers* and *Fellow Traveller*; Danny Waxman with *Khamsin*, a tale of forbidden love between an Israeli-Jewish girl and an Arab labourer; Uri Barabash with *Beyond the Walls*, a savage tale of Jews and Arabs in prison; Yaki Yosha with *The Vulture*, a bitter tale of the exploited myth of the hero; Rafi Bukaee with *Avanti Popolo*, a black comedy of the 1967 War. Also of note are Yitshak (Tsepel) Yeshurun's *Noa is 17*, a fine study of schisms in the *kibbutz* movement of the early 1950s, and David Perlov's *Diary*, a deceptively private series of films reflecting the liberal-minded intellectual's place in an increasingly shrill and warlike society which, to many, has lost sight of the individual vision which motivated its progenitors. It is increasingly likely that the dissident voice will continue to be heard in this medium, in a culture whose monolithic image is belied by the challenge of diversity.

SL

The philosophical tradition

It is generally accepted that philosophy entered the medieval Islamic world over the period 800–1000, along with the translation of Greek works into Arabic. It is worth noting, however, that even before Greek philosophy made its official appearance in the Islamic world there existed a body of religious, legal and theological disputes both within Islam and between the faiths in the Middle East which incorporated aspects of philosophical methodology. The arrival of the ʿAbbasids*, the move of the capital of the Islamic Empire to Baghdad, and the integration of Syria, Egypt and Iran, with their long history of Greek cultural and scientific traditions, into the Empire, led to the transmission, initially with official backing, of Greek texts dealing with medicine*, astronomy*, geometry and philosophy in Arabic. Although the original translators were Christian, there were no major Christian philosophers in the Islamic period. The first important thinker was al-Farabi (873–950), who wrote commentaries on Aristotle and developed a philosophy which was heavily influenced but by no means dominated by aspects of neo-Platonism.

Neo-Platonism was a strong influence on philosophy at this time because of the nature of Greek texts which were available in translation. Farabi accordingly accepts a view of God's relationship to the world being by way of emanation, and an account of happiness as related to intellectual achievement, with an Aristotelian emphasis upon different types of happiness, social and intellectual, leading to different sorts of perfection. Islam is seen as reconciling these different paths to happiness and perfection, and the perfect state should be run by a prophetically inspired ruler who embodies divine law in civil law. Ibn Sina* (Avicenna, 980–1037) built upon Farabi's foundations a much broader theory which, like the work of his predecessor, did not stop at an eclectic synthesis of different views but was genuinely creative. An important aspect of the state of philosophy after Ibn Sina's contribution was that it seemed to challenge the ordinary interpretation of basic religious principles: belief in creation out of nothing, individual immortality and God's knowledge of particulars. He also provided a general account of the structure of the universe and its motion which seemed to ignore God. Although God plays the role of unmoved mover and appears to get the mechanism going, the philosophers' arguments for the world's eternity, and their insistence upon God following certain principles of construction when He creates, pose problems for the orthodox believer who expects God's existence to make some difference to the nature of the world.

This demand for a bigger role for God and Islam in philosophy was taken up and brilliantly expounded by al-Ghazali* (1057–1111), who argued that the philosophers influenced by Ibn Sina not only

Astrological maps (Libra, Leo, Scorpio, Virgo), thirteenth century AD, Turkey

fell foul of the principles of Islam but also went wrong in the reasoning by which they arrived at their impious conclusions. This onslaught was in turn attacked by Ibn Rushd* (Averroes, 1126–98), who agreed with many of Ghazali's criticisms of Ibn Sina, but argued that Aristotle's approach to these issues could be defended with confidence and at the same time reconciled with religion. As well as writing a large number of commentaries on Aristotle, Ibn Rushd produced a series of works in which he argued that the truths of reason and of revelation must coincide, and moreover that the study of philosophy is required by Islam of those capable of undertaking it. No-one after Ibn Rushd equalled his ability for philosophical creativity within the Greek tradition, and that way of doing philosophy largely died out with him in the Muslim community. There existed a parallel development of philosophy in the Jewish community of the Middle East, culminating in the work of Musa ibn Maymun (Maimonides, 1135–1204), which continued for a little longer than in the Muslim community, but which also largely petered out after attacks by the religious establishment.

The development of philosophy by way of mysticism and theology did continue, however. Both Ibn Sina and Ghazali wrote mystical works, the latter clearly identifying with the Sufi* movement, and these Persians were followed by many others, ranging from Suhravardi* (1155–91) to Mulla Sadra (1571–1640). It is worth distinguishing however, the sort of philosophy which was in the Greek tradition, and of which the name in Arabic – *falsafa* – betrays its Greek origins, from *hikma* or wisdom, the kind of knowledge to which mystical philosophy aspired by way of moral discipline, Sufi practices and instruction, personal spiritual and intellectual effort, and divine illumination. *Falsafa* did not altogether disappear from the Middle East, however, and something of it was incorporated in *kalam* (theological disputation), because of the interest shown by some theologians in the use of logic to help in establishing more securely theological and legal positions. In modern times there has been a revival of interest in the study of *falsafa*, although it is regarded with suspicion by some of those who think of themselves as very orthodox in matters of doctrine and law. Western philosophy is also studied today in Muslim countries, and has had an influence on some modern thinkers and writers, such as Taha Husayn.

What are the main characteristics of *falsafa*? First, there existed an interest in Aristotle and other Greek thinkers because of the great conceptual power of their philosophies. Demonstrative reasoning, the use of valid arguments with certain premises, was strictly distinguished from other forms of reasoning which are incapable of resulting in universally true conclusions. Dialectical or theological reasoning was regarded as capable of defending a religious or legal principle, but not of establishing it as certain in the first place. Religion was regarded as logically secondary to philosophy, as a means of representing to a wider and less sophisticated audience what implications philosophical truths have for human behaviour and belief. Similarly, the philosophers were concerned to demonstrate the rational basis of the desirable forms of political association in Muslim communities. They felt compelled by the demands of intellectual honesty to follow their arguments through to the very end, thus frequently embroiling themselves in controversy with the authority represented by their legal and theological contemporaries.

OL

Further reading

M. Fakhry, *A History of Islamic Philosophy* (New York, 1983)
G. Hourani, *Reason and Tradition in Islamic Ethics* (Cambridge, 1985)
O. Leaman, *An Introduction to Medieval Islamic Philosophy* (Cambridge, 1985)

Mathematics, physics and astronomy

The first appearance of serious scientific activities of any magnitude within the Islamic world can be approximately dated to the latter part of the eighth century AD. These activities were ushered in by a two-pronged translation process: translations of Sanskrit texts on mathematical astronomy, and Greek texts on nearly every branch of the classical scientific heritage. In view of subsequent developments the Hellenistic tradition proved to be by far the more important of the two.

The complex process by which most of the Greek texts dealing with the exact sciences were translated into Arabic, between the end of the eighth century and the third quarter of the ninth, is still, however, very poorly understood. One cannot yet explain how the best of the Greek scientific texts, such as Euclid's *Elements*, Ptolemy's *Almagest* and *Optics*, Apollonius' *Conics*, Diophantus' *Arithmetica*, which were all but forgotten in the Greek-speaking Byzantine world, were efficiently resuscitated and professionally translated into Arabic within a relatively short period.

Creativity, not imitation

What we know for certain is that this translation activity was accompanied from its very inception by an unprecedented creative scientific production, whose very magnitude is also difficult to explain. Moreover, this combined process of translation and original writing was in no sense a passive activity, for the scientists who were engaged in it were at the same time developing their own methods of criticism and reaction to this Hellenistic heritage, which they could now read in their own language. Early results were double-checked and corrected, and new methods were devised to avoid the pitfalls of the Hellenistic methods. This phenomenon is nowhere better illustrated than in the case of the *Almagest* translations, and the activities that they generated by way of correcting the Ptolemaic parameters through devising, for example, new methods for observations, which would give far more secure results than their Ptolemaic counterparts.

This flourish of scientific activities, translations, original writings, new observations, and new methodological approaches, set the stage for the birth of a genuinely Islamic scientific culture, which, in certain disciplines, continued to be productive until the fourteenth and fifteenth century. It was this culture that was passed on to medieval Europe, when Europeans who had also begun to seek the classical scientific tradition realized that this Hellenistic heritage was mainly available in an Arabic form.

Important as these translation activities were, they should be considered as only one part of the Islamic scientific tradition. For the original achievements of the scientists who produced this tradition encompassed every scientific discipline known in medieval times, and went far beyond the contour lines of the classical scientific tradition. In mathematics, for example, whole disciplines, such as algebra and trigonometry, were created almost from scratch. New concepts, such as negative and real numbers, decimal fractions, trigonometric identities, generalizations of solutions and algorithms in the theory of equations and in mathematical geography, and theory of combinatorial mathematics, were all introduced and pursued by these same scientists. From the perspective of medieval Europe, probably the most impressive innovation, which was introduced by the Islamic scientific tradition, was the incorporation of the decimal system within arithmetic. The designation 'Arabic numerals' is a vivid reminder of the impact that this innovation had on Europe.

Developments in optics

In optics, on the other hand, the works of Ibn al-Haytham (d.1038) and his commentator Kamal al-Din al-Farisi (d.1320) revolutionized classical optics in every sense of the word. Not only did they reverse the classical theory of vision – by introducing the intromission theory of light as opposed to the extramission – but furthermore they went on to describe in mathematical language the observable physical phenomena. Ibn al-Haytham's book on optics was the most comprehensive study of direct and indirect vision – that is, vision along straight lines (theory of reflection), or bent lines (refraction) – before the time of Kepler. And even the elusive rainbow of the classical tradition was given a mathematical treatment by Farisi, which correctly analysed the scientific reasons for its occurrence. The importance of Haytham's book for medieval Europe cannot be overemphasized, for it became the standard book on the subject. That of Farisi, on the other hand, was not known in the Latin West.

Developments in astronomy

It is in the field of astronomy, however, that we find the greatest advances. After noting and correcting the discrepancies between their observations and the inherited values from the Hellenistic tradition, scientists working within the Islamic domain initiated a deeper investigation of the philosophical foundations of the subject matter of astronomy in terms of its relationship to the real world and with regard to its inner consistency as a mathematical–physical system. As early as the first half of the eleventh century the same Ibn al-Haytham, among others, devoted a special treatise to the criticism of the inherited Hellenistic astronomical tradition. Astronomers of the next two centuries took this criticism seriously, and added to it their own criticism as well.

In Andalusia, Jabir Ibn Aflah (fl.1100), Ibn Rushd (Averroes*) and al-Bitruji (fl.1200) all had something to say about the defects of the inherited astronomy. Bitruji went so far as to propose a new set of mathematical models in an attempt to replace Ptolemaic astronomy altogether. However, despite the philosophical justification, the inability of the newly proposed models accurately to predict positions of the planets rendered this new astronomy useless for all practical purposes. Nevertheless the impact of this Andalusian school on medieval European astronomy has to be measured in terms of the questions that it raised and the methods that it introduced. The philosophical doubts raised against Ptolemaic astronomy made it impossible for any self-respecting astronomer, especially someone like Copernicus, to continue to operate within the assumptions of Ptolemaic astronomy. New techniques, on the other hand, like the use of modern trigonometric functions, instead of the chord functions used by Ptolemy, introduced the subject of trigonometry (fully developed within the Islamic scientific tradition) into medieval Europe.

An alternative astronomy

In the eastern part of the Muslim world, beginning sometime towards the middle of the thirteenth century and continuing at least through the middle of the fifteenth century, a far more sophisticated programme of research was undertaken in an attempt to define an alternative astronomy that was both physically and mathematically consistent. The works of ʿUrdi (d.1266), Tusi (d.1274), Shirazi (d.1311), and Ibn al-Shatir (d.1375) are all attempts in that regard. Modern research has revealed that the results developed by these astronomers (now known as the Maragha astronomers after the Ilkhanid Observatory that was established in the city of Maragha in north-west Iran in 1259, and with which the first three astronomers were affiliated) were technically identical to those reached by Copernicus some two centuries later. In the most recent work on the mathematical astronomy of Copernicus, Copernicus is depicted as the last of the Maragha astronomers. However, we have yet to discover the method by which these results would have reached Copernicus.

GS

Further reading

E. S. Kennedy *et al.*, *Studies in the Islamic Exact Sciences* (Beirut, 1983)
ʿAbd al-Hamid Sabra, 'The Scientific Enterprise', in B. Lewis, ed., *The World of Islam* (London, 1980), published in the USA as: *Islam and the Arab World*

Chemistry and alchemy

Chemistry and alchemy in the Islamic world form the one scientific field which can claim not only a great deal of originality, but also the parenthood of that process which led to the modern science of chemistry. No other natural science in Islam can make this claim so directly and so confidently. At the same time, Islamic alchemical activity can be treated as a unique discipline in that many of its fundamental traits are non-Greek.

It is strange, therefore, that in recent years research in this field has almost come to a halt, and, in particular, the early history of Islamic alchemy still remains largely wrapped in darkness, with many basic questions left unresolved or abandoned. Thus, much of what is sketched below should be received with caution; the sketch is tentative and is open to revision as and when new material comes to light and research revives.

Alchemy

Alchemy is defined in Arabic literature by several authors, and it is not difficult to glean from these characterizations that the theme of this science is the transmutation of base metals into noble ones. Thus, strictly speaking, mineralogy, metallurgy, the technical chemistry of the craftsman, the concerns of the apothecary, the practical science of preparing synthetic perfumes and artificial jewels, are all outside the field of alchemy despite obvious points of mutual contact. Some of these related disciplines are to be subsumed under the heading of chemistry.

Alchemy differs from these more technically oriented professions because of its distinct philosophical foundations, which include two constituent parts, a theory of matter and a cosmology. The former is derived from Aristotle and runs roughly like this: all substances are composed of one and the same prime matter which, upon uniting with the Corporeal and Specific Forms, gives rise to individual bodies. The simplest manifestation of this process produces the four elements fire, air, water and earth, which are distinguished from one another by their qualities. The primary qualities are four: heat, cold, moisture and dryness. Some alchemists, such as Jabir ibn Hayyan (see below), looked upon these qualities as real material constituents.

Metals are produced by such a union of prime matter with a specific form. All varieties of them (*anwaʿ*) belong to one single species (*jins*). They are differentiated only in accidents (*aʿrad*) which can be proper (*dhatiyya*) or occasional (*ʿaradiyya*). But, as experience confirms, these accidents are not stable but changeable. Thus transmutation is possible. There are many ways of carrying out this transmutation, but the most important is the method of elixir (*al-iksir*).

An astrolabe

The other element, namely, the cosmology of the alchemist, seems to have been derived from non-Greek sources. One such source is the *Kitab sirr al-khaliqa wa san'at al-tabi'a* (Book of the secret of creation and the art of nature) attributed to Balinas, probably compiled before the eighth century. In this work is found that short enigmatic text known in Latin as *Tabula smaragdina* which was immensely influential throughout the later Middle Ages and post-Renaissance periods. The *Tabula* indicates the belief that there is a correspondence between celestial and terrestrial affairs, and between inner and outer worlds; and that the manifold forms in which matter occurs have but a single origin. This unity in diversity implies transmutation, and accommodates astrology. Also, the efforts to refine matter are thus rendered inseparable from the purification of the soul. In this way the natural philosophy of alchemy aimed not only at teaching transmutation, but also the whole connection of the world.

This is the theoretical framework of alchemy, which distinguishes it from other chemical sciences. Not all those who studied chemistry accepted this theoretical framework. Thus Kindi (800–67) compiled a valuable work on technical chemistry – *Kitab kimya al-' itr wa'l-tas'idat* (Book of Perfumes, Chemistry and Distillations) – but vehemently condemned all attempts to fabricate noble metals. Likewise, Ibn Sina had much to say about the physical chemistry of metals in his *Kitab al-shifa* (Book of Remedy), but censured the alchemists and wrote a work against astrology.

But – strange as it may seem – the major contributions of Islam to our science of chemistry come not from the chemists but from the alchemists. One contribution is the theory that all metals (in some cases all substances) are composed of sulphur and mercury existing in various proportions. It was this idea – unknown to the Greek alchemists and original to Islam – which led to the celebrated phlogiston theory of modern chemistry. Another is the introduction of sal ammoniac in the repertoire of chemistry. Of this substance the Greek alchemists seem to have had no knowledge. Two varieties of sal ammoniac (*nushadir*) were distinguished: natural (*al-hajar*) and derived (*mustanbat*) – ammonium chloride and ammonium carbonate. The latter was obtained by the dry distillation of hair and other animal substances. Again the use of organic materials, both plant and animal, in addition to the inorganic, was a significant innovation of the Islamic alchemist.

Jabir ibn Hayyan

The two most important alchemists are Jabir ibn Hayyan and Ibn Zakariyya al-Razi. The former is supposed to have lived *c.*722–*c.*813, and there exists a huge corpus that passes under his name. Doubts had been expressed as early as the tenth century as to the authenticity of the corpus, and some even doubt that he ever existed at all. But there is sufficient evidence for the historicity of Jabir, though much of the Jabirian corpus seems to be the work of later authors, probably a group of early Isma'ilis. Perhaps the most interesting part of the corpus is the collection entitled *Kutub al-mawazin* (Books of Balances) in which the author attempts to reduce all forms of human knowledge to a system of quantity and measure, thus conferring upon them the character of an exact science.

If Jabir is the first alchemist, then he is the pioneer of all that is important in alchemy. It is also said that he gave the recipe of nitric acid in his *Sunduq al-hikma* (The Chest of Wisdom). At least three Jabirian treatises were translated into Latin.

Abu Bakr Muhammad ibn Zakariyya al-Razi

Razi is recognized as one of the greatest physicians of Islam. In his books we find for the first time a systematic classification of carefully observed facts regarding chemical substances, reactions and apparatus described in an unambiguous language. It is also clear that in his experiments he managed to produce mineral acids, but without recognizing them as pure isolated substances. He was also familiar with caustic soda and glycerol. In one book, Razi for the first time distinguishes between smallpox and measles.

Another prominent alchemist is Maslama ibn Ahmad al-Majriti (d.1007), to whom is ascribed an important alchemical treatise, the *Rutbat al-hakim* (The Sage's Step), and the relatively well-known work, the *Ghayat al-hakim* (The Aim of the Wise), known in Latin as *Picatrix*. The former contains precise instructions for the preparation of gold and silver by cupellation. It is clear, however, that the *Rutbat* as well as the *Ghayat* was edited and perhaps enlarged from an original writing of the author.

In the same period we have Muhammad ibn Umayl al-Tamimi (*c*.900–60), whose well-known work was the *Kitab al-ma' al-waraqi wa'l-ard al-nujumiyya* (Silver Water and Starry Earth), known in Latin as *Tabula chemica*. Another of his works, the *Risalat al-shams ila'l-hilal* (Epistle of the Sun to the Crescent Moon), was also known in Latin. The last important name is that of ʿAli ibn Aydamur al-Jildaki, who lived in the first half of the fourteenth century. He is perhaps the only later alchemist to have taken Jabir's theory of *mizan* (balance) seriously. In a sense he is also a historian of chemistry.

SNH

Further reading

E. J. Holmyard, *Alchemy* (London, 1957)
J. Needham, *Science and Civilization in China*, vol 5, pt 4 (Cambridge, 1980)

Engineering

The technologies that had sustained the ancient civilizations of the Middle East and the Mediterranean were given new impetus by the advent of Islam and were expanded and developed in the ensuing centuries. From the outset, large urban communities were a feature of Islamic life. A thriving agriculture, supported in every stage of the production chain by the contributions of engineers and craftsmen, provided for the needs of those communities.

In many regions of the Muslim world irrigation was (and remains) the most important type of public works undertaking. In Iraq, for example, the existing Sasanid system in central Iraq was greatly extended to supply the great city of Baghdad, and in the south of the country a completely new network of canals was constructed for the newly founded city of Basra. Arabic methods of irrigation were introduced to the Iberian peninsula, particularly in the province of Valencia and in the valley of the Guadalquivir. The excavation and maintenance of canal systems and their associated hydraulic works depended upon the skills of surveyors, engineers, craftsmen and managers. The administration of irrigation was assigned to large, well-organized departments. In the tenth century, for example, the chief of irrigation of Merv in Khorasan had 10,000 men under his control, divided into sections each with its appropriate tasks. There was even a team of divers responsible for the underwater maintenance of dams and dikes. A treatise written in Iraq in the eleventh century demonstrates that the techniques of surveying, quantity surveying and subcontracting were essentially the same then as they are today. In some regions, notably Iran, water for irrigation and domestic uses was – and still is – provided by *qanawat* (sing. *qanat*), the underground conduits which conduct the water from aquifers to the supply points. The detection of the aquifers and the surveying and excavation of the conduits are a specialized application of the difficult and dangerous profession of mining.

Irrigation involves other techniques besides the excavation of canals or *qanawat*. Canals must be bridged, but bridges were of course also built over natural obstacles, and a number of fine Islamic bridges of masonry or burnt bricks have survived over the centuries. Dams are an essential part of nearly all irrigation systems – to divert the water from rivers into canals and to impound water for storage. Dams were also built to provide additional power for water-wheels and mills. In the twelfth century the dam at Cordoba in Spain incorporated three mill-houses each containing four mills. Until recently these three mill-houses still functioned. The Muslims made several innovations in the design of dams, later copied in Christian Europe. These included the introduction of de-silting sluices and the careful design of the air faces of the dams to dissipate the energy of the water and so protect the foundations. These improvements are undoubtedly responsible for the survival of many Muslim dams into modern times.

Water-raising machines were in widespread use in the Muslim world, the two commonest being the water-driven wheel, or noria, and the machine driven by an animal through a pair of gears, usually called the *saqiya*. These machines are still in use today; in terms of efficiency, durability and ease of construction and upkeep they are in many circumstances superior to motor-driven pumps.

Muslim engineers also designed special pumps to suit particular hydraulic conditions. Jazari, writing in 1206, describes a water-driven piston pump with twin cylinders and true suction pipes, the earliest-known example of such a machine. Another of his machines incorporates a crank, the first example of the non-manual use of this important mechanism. Writing about the year 1560, Taqi al-Din describes a remarkable six-cylinder water-driven pump.

Water power was widely used in the Muslim world. Various methods were used to increase the power delivered to the water-wheels including, as we have seen, the use of dams to provide a greater head of water. Wheels were mounted on the piers of bridges to take advantage of the increased flow due to the channelling of the water. Ship-mills were a common expedient, not only to make use of the increased rate of flow in midstream, but also to avoid the problems caused by the lowering of water levels in the dry season. In the tenth century very large ship-mills were moored along the upper reaches of the Tigris and Euphrates, for processing the grains of Upper Mesopotamia to meet the needs of Baghdad. Each was capable of producing about ten tonnes of flour in 24 hours. At Basra there were tidal mills in the tenth century, about a century before the first mention of this technique in Europe. Apart from corn-milling, water power was used for a variety of industrial purposes including paper-making, rice-husking, the crushing of ores, the fulling of cloth and the crushing of sugar-cane. Windmills with vertical axles were known in Central Asia in the seventh century and later spread to other parts of the Muslim world. They were used mainly for corn-milling, but also for other industrial purposes.

Much of our knowledge of mechanical technology in Islam comes from a few precious treatises, prominent among which are those of the Banu (sons of) Musa, written about AD 850, and Jazari. The range of devices described includes trick vessels and automata, water-clocks, fountains and water-raising machines. The apparent triviality of some of these devices should not be allowed to obscure the fact that they incorporate a number of techniques and components that were later to enter the vocabulary of European engineers. These include feed-back control systems, the closed-loop principle, automatic cut-off mechanisms, complex gear-trains and the casting of metals in closed mould-boxes with green sand. It can therefore be said that Muslim engineers were successful in two main fields: first in providing for the needs of the population and meeting the demands of a thriving commerce; and secondly in introducing new ideas that were to be of great significance in the development of modern engineering.

DRH

Further reading

D. R. Hill, *A History of Engineering in Classical and Medieval Times* (London, 1984)

al-Jazari, *The Book of Knowledge of Ingenious Mechanical Devices*, tr. D. R. Hill (London, 1974)

Medicine and biology

In Arabic medicine the continuity of the cultural traditions of the Middle East before and after Islam is very pronounced. Medicine in medieval Islam was based on the Greek system of Hippocrates and Galen, that is, on the same medical tradition which had existed in the Middle East for centuries before Islam. To be sure, there were significant new developments: Arabic became the scientific language instead of Greek, and the vigorous development of Islamic civilization nurtured a renaissance in medicine as it did in the other ancient sciences. It produced a group of physicians, including Razi and Ibn Sina (Avicenna), whose scientific influence lasted until the rise of modern medicine in the last two centuries, and whose influence on folk medicine is still evident today.

Influence of Greek and Sanskrit

The translation of the Greek sources into Arabic was accomplished early, and much of the credit goes to Hunayn ibn Ishaq (fl.808–73) and his associates who firmly established Arabic as an exact and flexible language of the medical sciences. Thanks to their efforts, Islam had access to more of Galen's work in Arabic than we have in the original Greek today. Hippocrates, Galen and Aristotle were commonplace names in medieval Arabic literature, as much part of the culture as anything else in it.

The medieval Muslims became acquainted with other medical traditions, for example the Sanskrit Indian, but their theories of medicine remained strongly in the Greek tradition. The first systematic Arabic medical book, *The Paradise of Wisdom* (*Firdaws al-hikma*) of ʿAli ibn Rabban al-Tabari (d.861, a contemporary of Hunayn who apparently worked without benefit of his translations), contained a detailed description of the Indian medical system based on the Sanskrit books of Caraka, Susruta, Vagbhata and Madhavakara. Yet Tabari put the Indian material in an appendix at the end of a book whose main body consisted purely of the medicine of Hippocrates and Galen and the natural philosophy of Aristotle. Later physicians showed even less interest in the Indian theories of medicine and their adoption of specific medications from India had no bearing on medical theory.

Razi

The generation after Tabari produced one of the towering figures of Arabic medicine, Abu Bakr Muhammad ibn Zakariyya al-Razi* (d.932). Razi was born about the middle of the ninth century in Rayy in Persia, where he became the chief physician at its hospital, and later administered the great hospital in Baghdad which he helped found. He was a philosopher who held radically independent points of view, a brilliant clinician and a prolific author. Ibn al-Nadim's *Fihrist*, the tenth-century survey of Arabic culture, listed about 140 works by him, the most important of which is the *Hawi* (*Liber Continens*). This was a posthumous collection of Razi's voluminous private notes, put together rather hastily by his students. Nevertheless, later physicians had no doubt about its scientific value. The *Hawi* quickly became the standard reference work of Arabic medicine and remained so for centuries. Even in fourteenth-century Spain, at the other end of the Arabic-speaking world, it was still a primary source for medical authors such as Ibn al-Khatib (d.1374).

But the *Hawi*, given its confusing arrangement, its bulk and expense, was never available beyond the limited circles of distinguished physicians and the libraries of the very rich. There remained a need for more concisely and elegantly written medical textbooks. ʿAli ibn ʿAbbas al-Majusi (d.994), the distinguished physician of the generation that followed Razi, said as much in justifying his own book, and in *Kamil al-sinaʿa al-tibbiyya* he produced one of the two most impressive medieval medical works, the other being Ibn Sina's *Canon* (*Al-qanun fiʾl-tibb*).

Ibn Sina

Abu ʿAli al-Husayn ibn Sina (980–1037), or Avicenna*, was born near Bukhara and died at the age of fifty-eight near Hamadan. He became the best-known scientist of the Islamic world and the most influential philosopher and physician of the Middle Ages. No one occupies a more important place in the history of medicine after its ancient Greek founders, and no other single medical work rivals the *Canon*'s wide and lasting influence. As a magisterial exposition of Galenic medicine (for it is Galen's ideas about anatomy, physiology, disease and treatment of disease that have the pride of place in the *Canon*, as they do in all of Arabic medicine) the *Canon* is not unique; Majusi's *Kamil al-sinaʿa*, in particular, rivals the *Canon* in size as well as in the clarity and authority of its exposition of Galenic medicine.

It is difficult to understand Ibn Sina's influence without recognizing the central role that he played in the history of medicine and natural philosophy. In his day natural philosophy and medicine overlapped, sharing a large area of the field that we call biology today. But they were two distinct traditions, each having its own literature and dominant authorities, namely Aristotle for philosophy and Hippocrates and Galen for medicine.

Galen had differed sharply with Aristotle on some questions, the most central of which was whether the powers that control animal life have one single source (the heart, as Aristotle believed) or three distinct sources (the brain, heart and liver, as Galen argued). He also forcefully challenged Aristotle's views on the male and female roles in sexual generation. These differences fuelled a fierce dispute between the followers of Aristotle and the followers of Galen for centuries.

Ibn Sina's response to Aristotle and Galen

Nowhere in medieval thought was the contest between Galen and Aristotle as dramatic as in the works of Ibn Sina, where the two great traditions intersected. More than anything else, it was Ibn Sina's success in bridging the Aristotelian–Galenic division that accounts for his later influence. He produced a potent synthesis which depended on accepting the new (post-Aristotle) Galenic evidence in anatomy and physiology, and equally on interpreting it so as to fit Aristotelian theory.

Ibn Sina's allegiance in matters of theory (that is, the domain of natural philosophy – what we would today call basic science) lay openly with Aristotle. Already in Book 1 of the *Canon* (written when he was thirty-five years old), he had taken his side in the theoretical controversies, with the ironical result that this most influential Galenic document of the Middle Ages was written by someone openly committed to the Aristotelian point of view. In the circumstances this was a difficult position to take, because all medical and biological discussion depended on anatomy, and Aristotle's anatomy was primitive compared to Galen's. For example, Aristotelian biology asserted that the heart was the origin, anatomically, of the arteries, veins and nerves. This view resulted from Aristotle's belief that the heart was the central location of the soul – the organizing principle of all the functions of the body, including digestion, sensation and movement. Galen, who was the beneficiary of centuries of anatomical discoveries after Aristotle, argued that the brain was the origin of the nerves, the liver of the veins, and the heart of the arteries only; and Galen's arguments were based on more accurate anatomical facts than had been available to Aristotle.

Ibn Sina's works

Ultimately Ibn Sina was able to deflect Galen's challenge only by rebuilding the Aristotelian system on the firmer basis of the new anatomy. In the *Canon* he did no more than recognize the problem, by stating often that a controversy exists between Galen and Aristotle and promising to resolve the dispute in his philosophical works. It was only towards the end of his life, in *Kitab al-hayawan* (Book of the Animals), the biological section of his *Kitab al-shifa* (Book of Remedy) (see also Chemistry and Alchemy), that he worked out his definitive solution.

The *Hayawan* is the last and largest part of the 'Physics' (*Tabiʿiyyat*) of the *Shifa*. The *Shifa* itself is highly original in conception, being the first all-inclusive work in philosophical literature. In it, Ibn Sina gave a detailed exposition of all the Greek, primarily Aristotelian sciences; his purpose was not simply to write a commentary on Aristotle, but to restate the Aristotelian theories convincingly.

The *Hayawan*'s organization follows the scheme of Aristotle's own 'Book of the Animals'. This was a translation of the three treatises, *Historia Animalium*, *Parts of Animals*, and *The Generation of Animals*. This Arabic translation, traditionally ascribed to Ibn al-Batriq, was especially poor, and in his *Hayawan* Ibn Sina provided a more accessible account of the Aristotelian biology in the form of clear summaries of the *Historia* and the *Generation*. But it was in the section which paralleled the *Parts of Animals* (that is, the treatise on anatomy) that Ibn Sina performed his radical solution: he simply discarded the original Aristotelian text and replaced it by new anatomical material. The new material consisted of the later anatomy of the Hellenistic physicians which Galen had inherited and elaborated, and Ibn Sina had already taught in the *Canon*. The substituted text included verbatim all the anatomy of uniform parts from Book 1 of the *Canon* and nine sections on the anatomy of the organs from Book 3.

The substitution of the new anatomy for the old carried out – with a vengeance – Ibn Sina's evident design to modernize Aristotle. Yet he managed to do so without sacrificing basic Aristotelian theory. For example, he kept true to Aristotle's idea that the heart is the origin of all the body's faculties by arguing that Galen's anatomical facts derived from dissection of the completely formed animal, where indeed the nerves appear to 'grow' from the brain and spinal cord, and the veins from the liver. Ibn Sina interpreted Aristotle to mean that the heart is the origin of all the organs and their faculties in embryological development, where it is the first organ to be formed by the soul, and all else is formed later through its agency.

The problem which Ibn Sina faced was a 'medieval' problem, namely that for medieval Aristotelians the master's anatomy was primitive and had enfeebled his whole biological system. His solution was to bring Aristotle's facts up to date, and to restate the original arguments on a firmer basis. Most medieval Aristotelians, East and West, attest to the success of Ibn Sina's solution, for they elected to view their biology through him, even though the original Aristotle was available to them in both Arabic and Latin. Ibn Sina's version was much less vulnerable to Galenic attack than the original.

Development towards modern medicine

However, Ibn Sina's solution shifted the direction of the medical and biological sciences towards modern medicine. The modern medical sciences developed from the sixteenth century onwards on the basis of new anatomical discoveries which finally helped overthrow the ancient Greek–Arabic medical system. It was Ibn Sina who, in the process of updating Aristotle, had changed the emphasis in biology. Aristotle, although emphasizing man, considered the whole animal kingdom as his subject. But the anatomy transplanted from the *Canon* was exclusively human anatomy, tending to shift the focus of biology from the living creation as a whole to man. Equally important is that Ibn Sina radically changed the original balance of Aristotle's biology by nearly doubling the space devoted to anatomy. Overall, Ibn Sina gave much greater importance to anatomy than it ever had before, and by so doing he prepared the way, quite inadvertently, for developments that in later centuries were to put an end to his authority together with that of Aristotle and Galen.

Ibn al-Nafis

These new developments are evident in the history of Arabic medicine itself, particularly in the work of Ibn al-Nafis (d.1288), 'the second Ibn Sina', whose focus on anatomy, following Ibn Sina's example, allowed him to make a major medical discovery, perfectly in line with modern understanding. One of Ibn al-Nafis' two most important books was in fact a *Commentary on the Anatomy of the Canon* (*Sharh tashrih al-qanun*), the other being a *Commentary on the Canon* (*Sharh al-qanun*). In these two works he studied the anatomy of the heart, rejected the received description of Galen and Ibn Sina, and described for the first time the minor or pulmonary circulation of the blood nearly three centuries before Michael Servetus (1556) and Rinaldo Colombo (1559). Ibn al-Nafis denied the existence of any passage between the right and left ventricles of the heart, and said flatly that the blood flows from the right ventricle to the left by way of the lungs.

The modern authority on Galenism as a medical system has noted how the first major assault on Galen in the sixteenth century 'did not arise over specific points of anatomy', but 'attempted an overthrow of the whole'. Here too, Ibn Sina in the *Hayawan* had prepared the ground by forcefully assaulting the whole: 'Let us then look at Galen's contradictions, and show that he did and said nothing well, that even when he thought he presented proof, he did not convince; and that he is extremely weak in the principles [of natural philosophy, that is, basic science], even though he is very productive in the branches of medicine.'

BM

Further reading

'Avicenna X. "Biology and medicine"', in the *Encyclopedia Iranica*
S. H. Nasr, *Islamic Science* (World of Islam Festival, London, 1976), chapter 8.
O. Temkin, *Galenism, Rise and Decline of a Medical Philosophy* (Ithaca and London, 1973)
M. Ullmann, *Islamic Medicine* (Edinburgh, 1978)

Historiography and geography

Al-Idrisi's map of the world

Historiography

Islamic historiography is immense in volume and wide-ranging in subject and style. It was among the very earliest Islamic sciences to achieve a unity of inspiration and purpose. The Qur'an's intense interest in the moral significance of the past, the eager quest for every detail of the life of the Prophet and of his Companions, the very early adoption of an era, the *hijri*, and the spectacular events of Islam's first century all combined to give historiography its impetus and its broad relevance to the Muslim community. History was quickly seen to be of use for both individual piety and for state administration. In the last half-century, this literature has been receiving increasing attention from Muslim and Western scholars but, where the pre-modern period is concerned, a considerable portion of it is still in manuscript form and largely unknown.

If we consider this literature within the various cultural contexts in which it has been produced, five dominant genres of historiography may be distinguished, arranged roughly in order of their appearance: (1) *hadith*, (2) *adab*, (3) *hikma*, (4) Sultanate or regional, and (5) nationalist. Some overlap is of course inevitable among these genres.

(1) *Hadith** is the earliest genre of historiography. It began in concert with the efforts of the early scholars to assemble and classify the *hadith* ('traditions') of Muhammad and of his Companions. When these traditions were finally systematized in the ninth and tenth centuries AD, this genre also attained maturity and began to surrender its dominance to others. In this genre, historical writing is almost indistinguishable from *hadith* in form. Historical reports are discrete, individual items, complete with their own chain of transmitters (*isnad*). The historian assembled this material under topics, such as *maghazi* (expeditions of the Prophet), *futuh* (conquests) or *ansab* (genealogy), but generally speaking did not pronounce on their veracity. Among the most important figures in this genre are Baladhuri (d.*c*.892) and Tabari (d.923).

Biographical literature, a byproduct of this genre, continued to thrive, however, reaching a high point of development between the fourteenth and eighteenth centuries in the *tabaqat*, or biographical dictionaries.

The *tabaqat* form a genre which is unique in world historiography before the nineteenth century. The genre was fully developed by the ninth century and has survived without interruption into the present. The *tabaqat* originated from two basic but distinct motives: to commemorate pious ancestors and to establish the trustworthiness of *hadith* transmitters. Eventually they were to become alphabetical dictionaries either of particular groups (such as poets, scholars) or of a cross-section of prominent (and some less prominent) figures of a particular century. A typical entry would list a person's full name and ancestry, place and date of birth and death, a list of teachers and works, and a biography which varied in length between a few lines and several pages. At their best, these entries were carefully written biographical essays, often reflecting the author's estimate of the character and accomplishment of an entry. The *tabaqat* contain abundant, readily quantifiable information on the society, economy and cultural life of various periods and regions, but this information has yet to be fully exploited by modern scholars. Among the more important authors of *tabaqat* works are Ibn Saʿd (d.845), Ibn Khallikan (d.1282), Subki (d.1370) and Sakhawi (d.1497).

(2) Historiography written under the influence of *adab*, or *belles-lettres*, began to appear in the ninth century. Here, history writing becomes continuous narrative, the historian comes forward, so to speak, as a conscious author, the subject-matter expands to include pre- and non-Islamic countries and nations, and other Islamic sciences such as geography and the natural sciences make their influence felt in subject-matter and treatment. The historian is not solely a moralist; he is also a political adviser and a literateur. Ibn Qutayba (d.889) and Masʿudi (d.956) may be taken as foremost practitioners of this genre.

(3) Historiography written under the influence of *hikma*, or wisdom, accounts for a small proportion of Islamic historians who sought to apply rational rigour to historical writing and attempted systematic reflection on the patterns and meaning of history. They may be said to have prepared the way for Ibn Khaldun (d.1406), who is by common consent the most profound historical thinker of classical Islam. Some of the more important figures in this genre are Maqdisi (fl.*c.*966), Biruni (d.*c.*1050) and Ibn Miskawayh (d.1030).

(4) Sultanate or regional historiography, usually annalistic in form, appears between the eleventh and thirteenth centuries, continuing right up to the nineteenth century. This is where the Persian and Turkish contribution is most significant, helped by the highly developed secretarial and bureaucratic traditions of these two cultures. Ths genre accompanies and records the rise of the Islamic Sultanates: Mamluk*, Ottoman*, Safavid*. The size of these annals is often massive, the spirit is encyclopaedic, the style sometimes rhetorical. The ruler and his court are central to events and frequent use is made of official documents. The typical historian of this genre was a state secretary, critical of individual rulers but loyal to dynasties, and generally less interested in pan-Islamic history than his predecessors. Regional histories and biographies proliferated and reached a high degree of focalization, reflecting increasing rank and class differentiation in government and society under the Sultanates and decreasing contacts among Islamic scholars. Among the major figures of this genre are Ibn al-Athir (d.1234), Ibn Taghribirdi (d.1469), Juvayni (d.1283), Rashid al-Din (d.1318), and Iskandar Munshi (d.*c.*1632).

(5) The wars of the Sultanates in the sixteenth to eighteenth centuries intensified proto-nationalist sentiments among some Islamic historians – the Safavids are a good example. Nationalist historiography in the stricter sense became the dominant genre in the nineteenth and twentieth centuries. The influence of European nationalist historiography has produced historians whose works have more in common with other contemporary nationalist historians than with their own Islamic predecessors. Even when historians write from a Marxist or positivist standpoint, the focus is the origins and history of the national state. The tendency to neglect pan-Islamic history has continued, accompanied by a revival of interest in the pre-Islamic past, although there have been some important studies of Islamic cultural history, especially of the early period.

The classical Muslim historian was once most typically an *ʿalim* or state bureaucrat and a private person with a limited audience of peers. Now historians are either academics or journalists, more public persons, and often called upon to justify the relevance of the past to present political issues. History in contemporary Muslim nation-states of the Middle East has a vivid immediacy and is widely used in political discourse and the polemics of reform. The influence of ideology has tended to single out certain historical periods to the neglect of others, and works on the meaning or theory of history are few. However, the works of modern Muslim historians are increasingly seen to be indispensable to non-Muslim historians of Islamic history, and much valuable work is being done on the critical editing of Islamic historical manuscripts by Muslim academies and individual scholars.

TK

Further reading

A. Duri, *The Rise of Historical Writing Among the Arabs* (Princeton, 1983)
T. Khalidi, *Islamic Historiography: the histories of Masʿudi* (Albany, 1975)
B. Lewis and P. M. Holt, ed. *Historians of the Middle East* (London, 1962)
M. Mahdi, *Ibn Khaldun's Philosophy of History* (Chicago, 1964)
F. Rosenthal, *A History of Muslim Historiography* (Leiden, 1968)

The Muslim geographers

Islamic geography began in the ninth century, probably under the influence of *adab*, or *belles-lettres*, a discipline which encouraged the pursuit of polymathy. A network of commercial routes within Muslim territory led to a sharper awareness of the differences among peoples and regions. From its earliest beginnings, Islamic geography was in the main ethnographic, with much information on the customs and economy of Muslim and non-Muslim societies. But history and literature were also considered to be necessary auxiliaries of geography, as were astronomy and mathematics. Climatic determinism was a widespread belief and an interest in world ethnography led to early formulations of 'race' theories.

The classical Muslim geographers were better informed than were the Greeks regarding the geography of Asia and Africa. There was greater accuracy in cartography and the measurement of distances. Maps were first used in the geographical works of the tenth century, gaining thereafter in exactitude and range. Many early geographers were state employees and wrote for the guidance of the secretarial class, making use of the archives of the *barid*, or state postal service. However, geography was also nurtured by trade. The commercial products of the various regions and countries, together with estimates of their natural resources, taxation and occasional population figures, became regular themes in the geographical texts of the tenth century. A little later travel accounts appear, in which one finds the most detailed information anywhere on the topography and social customs of Muslim and non-Muslim cities and regions. Concurrently, geography also embraced the literature of *ʿajaʾib*, or wonders, of creation, which, apart from their entertainment value and their invitation to the pious to contemplate the manifold works of God, throw light on the classical Islamic notions of science. Among the geographers of this early period one may cite Yaʿqubi (d.897), Ibn Khurdadhbih (d.*c*.912), al-Istakhri (d.*c*.950), Qazvini (d.1308), Abuʾl-Fida (d.1321) and Ibn Battuta (d.1355).

Three other genres of geographical literature achieved maturity between the thirteenth and sixteenth centuries: the *ziyarat*, or pilgrimage guide books, the geographical dictionaries and the *khitat*, or historical topographies, this last being a fusion of history and geography. The first genre may have been stimulated by the Sufi renaissance of the twelfth century, the attempt to hold the Muslim world together by nurturing piety towards a network of holy sites, culminating in Mecca. The geographical dictionaries were voluminous, alphabetically arranged compendia of the geographical, historical and literary lore of the cities, towns and villages of the Muslim world and beyond. The *khitat* genre was a detailed survey of the streets, quarters and types of buildings of the various Muslim cities, a tribute perhaps to the efficiency of the bureaucratic methods of the Islamic Sultanates. The *khitat*, like the dictionaries, also included historical, biographical and literary materials. Among the geographers of these three later genres, one might include Harawi (d.1173), Yaqut (d.1229) and Maqrizi (d.1442).

Between the sixteenth and eighteenth centuries, the Ottomans produced the most original works in Islamic geography. The Ottoman dominions in Europe, Asia and Africa and their naval power in the Mediterranean resulted in maps, cosmographies and books of travel which revived the comprehensive range, ethnographic interests and literary elegance of the earliest Islamic geographical literature. At their best, these works were plain in style, well-structured, and recorded the personal observations of travellers and seamen. In the rest of the Islamic world, pilgrimage accounts enjoyed wide popularity. These were often the product of Sufis, whose piety created a sacred geography of saintly shrines, perhaps in response to the ravages of the countryside by governments and nomads. Among the geographers and pilgrims of this period may be included Piri Reis (d.1554), ʿAli Reis (d.1562), Hajji Khalifa (d.1657), Evliya Çelebi (d.1682) and Nabulusi (d.1730).

Two classical genres endured into modern times: historical topographies and travel accounts. Nationalism and the encounter with the West provided the new cultural context for works which largely preserved the classical format but were motivated by a concern to familiarize their readers with the national landscape and with a fascinating but menacing Europe. Geography, in tandem with history, is a regular part of all school curricula in the contemporary Islamic countries of the Middle East. In universities and higher academies the most notable contribution so far has been in the field of cartography and urban geography.

TK

Further reading

Nafis Ahmad, *The Muslim Contribution to Geography* (Lahore, 1947)
S. M. Ahmad, 'Djughrafiya', *Encyclopaedia of Islam*, 2nd edn., Vol. 2
A. Miquel, *La Géographie humaine du monde musulmane* (Paris, 1967)

Part V
THE COUNTRIES

The Muhammad ʿAli Mosque, Cairo, seen through the Rifaʿi Mosque

Introduction: history since 1939

The Second World War, 1939–45

When war broke out in September 1939, most of the countries of the Middle East and North Africa were under European rule or control. Great Britain held the Mandate* for Palestine* and Transjordan*, ruled Cyprus* as a colony, Aden* also as a colony with a surrounding protectorate, and Sudan* as a condominium with Egypt*, and had privileged treaty arrangements with Egypt, Iraq, and the small states of eastern Arabia. France had the Mandate for Syria and Lebanon and protectorates over Tunisia and Morocco, ruled Mauritania* as a colony and Algeria as an integral part of France. Italy ruled Libya as a colony and had recently conquered Ethiopia, and Spain had a protectorate over the northern part of Morocco and also held an area of the Western Sahara to the south of Morocco. Turkey, Iran, Afghanistan*, Saudi Arabia* and Yemen* were fully independent, but Britain had predominant influence in Iran, Afghanistan and Saudi Arabia. Of the countries in the region, Turkey, Syria and Lebanon were republics, but the others had monarchs: the Sultan of Morocco, the Bey of Tunisia, the King of Egypt, the King of Iraq and the Amir of Transjordan (both belonging to the Hashimite dynasty), King ʿAbd al-ʿAziz (Ibn Saʿud)*, the founder of Saudi Arabia, the Imam of Yemen, the rulers of the small principalities of southern and eastern Arabia, Riza Shah*, founder of the Pahlavi dynasty in Iran, and the King of Afghanistan.

It seemed probable that the region would be drawn into the European conflict, because Italy was closely aligned with Germany and had ambitions to extend its influence in the eastern and southern Mediterranean. Britain and France maintained a strong position, both in order to prevent possible attacks by Italy or Germany, and to protect the communications which passed through North Africa to French possessions further south, and through the Mediterranean and the Suez Canal to British and French territories further east.

The threat that the war would spread in the Mediterranean became imminent when France capitulated and Italy entered the conflict in June 1940. The frontiers lying between the British and Italian zones of control – the western desert between Libya and Egypt, and the frontier between Sudan and Ethiopia – became areas of active warfare. British forces moved into Ethiopia, and ended Italian rule there by 1941. From Egypt, which did not enter the war officially but was the most important base of British operations in the region, British and Commonwealth forces advanced far into Cyrenaica, the eastern part of Libya. Early in 1941, however, a German army, which had been sent to reinforce the Italians, made a successful counter-attack against British forces, which had been weakened by the need to send help to the Greeks, who were facing an Italian invasion and a threat from Germany.

The situation in the countries under French control remained ambiguous for a time. After some hesitation, the French authorities in Syria and Lebanon and in North Africa accepted the authority of the Vichy government in France. In spring 1941 a new threat appeared when German armies occupied Yugoslavia and Greece. The possibility that Germany would send help to the government of Iraq, which had fallen into the hands of a group of politicians and officers who wished to loosen the British hold, led to a brief British campaign in May 1941, which reasserted control of the country under a more compliant government. In the next month, the fear that Germany might extend its influence in Syria and Lebanon led to a military occupation by British and Commonwealth forces, with help from the Free French (those who had decided to continue the war under the leadership of de Gaulle).

The strategic position was transformed in 1941 by two events, the German invasion of Russia in June and the entry of the United States into the war in December. The rapid German victories in Russia appeared to pose a new danger to the British position in the Middle East, that of an attack from the north. Turkey, however, was able to remain neutral, and a joint Anglo-Russian occupation of Iran opened up a line by which British and American supplies could reach Russia. In spite of the war with Russia, German forces in Libya remained strong, and in July 1942 were able to drive British forces back almost to the Delta. By October, however, the British forces had been strengthened, in spite of the activities of German and Italian naval and air forces in the Mediterranean, and were able to win the decisive battle of Alamein and occupy the whole of Libya. In November, Anglo-American forces landed in Morocco and Algeria, and an attack from both east and west on the last German position in Tunisia* ended with the occupation of Tunis in May 1943. At this point the region ceased to be among the main theatres of warfare, although it continued to be important as providing bases from which operations in Sicily, Italy and the Balkans were mounted.

The countries of the Middle East which were formally independent did not enter the war officially until near its end, when there was a rush to declare war so as to become founder-members of the United Nations, but their governments and societies were affected in many ways by the fact that most of them were under military occupation and served as bases or battle-grounds. Economically, occupation by armies led to large-scale expenditure, and some countries accumulated sterling balances. On the other hand, problems of transport and the difficulties of communication through the Mediterranean led to shortages of imported goods and disrupted the export of local products. From 1941 an effort was made to improve the situation through planning for the region as a whole; the Middle East Supply Centre, set up in Cairo by the British with American cooperation, supervised the distribution of scarce goods and encouraged local production. There was no famine, and some classes in society profited from the situation.

The events and changes of the war had effects upon the political feelings and aspirations of the peoples of the region. The independent states were mainly concerned to preserve their independence. Turkey succeeded in doing this, but in Iran Riza Shah was deposed after the Anglo-Russian occupation, and his son and successor, Muhammad Riza, had little freedom of action. Saudi Arabia became more dependent than before upon Britain, which gave an annual subsidy in place of the revenues lost by the virtual cessation of the annual pilgrimage to Mecca; by the end of the war, however, British influence was being replaced by American, as the oilfields*, for which an American company had the concession, began to be brought into production.

For the countries under European control, the war offered both new dangers and the possibility of improving their position. The propaganda put forward by the competing states, particularly through the new medium of radio broadcasting, encouraged hopes of a change. Nationalist feelings were swayed by hostility towards the European powers who were in occupation, and also by doubts about the probable outcome of the war. Two nationalist movements were inescapably on the British or Anglo-American side: the Zionists* in Palestine* had everything to fear from a German victory, and the Sanusi* of Cyrenaica had been engaged in resistance to the Italians for many years. In Egypt, however, such friendly feelings as had been aroused by the Anglo-Egyptian Treaty of 1936 had grown weaker, and governments in the early years of the war were inclined towards sympathy with Italy; but a British ultimatum to King Faruq* in February 1942 brought to power the main nationalist party, the Wafd*, which held steadily to the British alliance during the critical years. Dismissed by Faruq in 1944, it began once more to press for a wider measure of independence than the treaty had granted.

In Palestine, the Arab revolt against British policy had been suppressed by 1939, and in the White Paper of that year the British government had come nearer to accepting Arab demands than before, but there was a general fear, among Palestinian Arabs and their supporters, that if there was an Anglo-American victory Jewish immigration would resume and end in the creation of a Jewish state. In Syria and Lebanon, the British and Free French agreed at the time of the occupation that the two countries would be given independence but French influence would remain paramount. Anglo-French disagreements about how this should be brought about, and skilful use of them by local leaders, led to a crisis in Lebanon in 1943 and another in Syria in 1945, and then to a process of negotiation which ended in total British and French withdrawal by the end of 1945, and the unrestricted independence of both countries.

A certain part in these events was played by a new organization of Arab states. The movement for unity of the Arab countries had existed ever since the dissolution of the Ottoman Empire* at the end of the First World War, and now Egypt began to take the lead in it, with some encouragement in general terms from the British government. Two conferences, at Alexandria and Cairo in 1944 and 1945 respectively, led to the creation of the League of Arab States (Arab League*). For a time this seemed likely to strengthen the position of the Arab countries in the world.

For the moment, the Arab countries of North Africa lay outside the movement for unity. In Libya, the war led to the end of Italian rule and the creation of British and French military administrations. In the countries ruled by France, the war did not bring any immediate change. French control remained, but France was weaker than before 1940, the presence of British and American armies offered new opportunities, and the fact that many thousands of North African soldiers had fought in the reconstituted French army was a source of potential strength. The most articulate and best organized of the nationalist movements, the Neo-Destour party in Tunisia, emerged from the war united, and not compromised by association with Germany and Italy at the moment when they seemed to be in the ascendant. In Morocco, the Sultan, Muhammad V, emerged as the champion of the national cause and an ally of the Istiqlal, the nationalist party, and he received some expression of sympathy from President Roosevelt during the allied conference at

Jamal Abd al-Nasir (Nasser) and Anwar al-Sadat

Casablanca in 1943. In Algeria prospects were less hopeful. The main nationalist group issued a manifesto of demands in 1943 but met with no adequate response. In May 1945 nationalist disturbances were repressed by the French army supported by the *colons*, the European settlers, in a way which was to have far-reaching consequences.

National independence, 1945–55

By the time the war ended, great changes had taken place in the relations of the great powers with each other and with the nations of the Middle East and North Africa. Italy had lost Libya and Ethiopia. France had come out on the victorious side, but in a weakened form and with grave internal problems; it had lost its position in Syria and Lebanon, and was facing difficulties in its attempt to restore its rule in Indo-China. Britain ended the war in control of all it had held before, and also of the Italian colony of Libya. The efforts of war, however, had weakened it economically, and the Labour government which came to power in 1945 had ideas on empire which differed from those of its predecessors; the withdrawal from India in 1947 was to have repercussions on the British position in the Middle East. The war had increased the military and economic power of the United States and given it interests in all parts of the world, and the USSR too, although weakened by its great losses, had emerged as a world power whose interests had to be taken into account. Within a few months of the end of the war it became clear that the war-time alliance was at an end, and there began a new period of tension and hostility between the USA and the USSR, each with its allies and clients.

Some of the effects of these changes in the structure of power became clear soon after the war ended. Both in Turkey and in Iran the USSR put forward claims, in Turkey to a revision of the north-eastern frontier, in Iran to an oil concession; this latter claim was supported by Russia's military presence in the north of the country, and by the creation of a pro-Soviet autonomous regime in Azerbaijan. In response, the USA extended its military protection to Turkey, under the 'Truman Doctrine', and Britain and America both gave diplomatic support to Iran. In the event, the Iranian government refused to ratify an agreement about an oil concession, Russian and British forces withdrew from the country, and the regime in Azerbaijan came to an end.

Agreement was also reached on the future of Libya, after negotiations in which both Italy and the USSR put forward claims. It was decided by the United Nations that Libya should become an independent kingdom by the end of 1951, with the leader of the Sanusi becoming king as Idris I. The new regime made an agreement by which Britain and the USA could use bases.

The fate of Palestine was also decided at the United Nations, but with more difficulty. The end of the war saw a revival of political activity there. The Arabs, supported by the Arab League, demanded an end to Jewish immigration and the carrying out of the provisions of the White Paper, by which Palestine would become an independent state with an Arab majority; the Jews demanded that the doors be opened to what was left of European Jewry, and a Jewish state be created in part at least of Palestine. They found considerable support among Jews in Europe and America, and governments moved by the fate of Jews in Europe. The British government was not willing to carry out a policy which would have to be imposed by force on either of the parties, but was no longer free to act without regard to the American government, on which it was dependent financially, and which wanted Jews in the refugee camps of Europe to be allowed to enter Palestine. The USSR also showed a certain interest in the problem, as offering a way to weaken the British presence in the Middle East.

Between 1945 and 1947 attempts were made to find a policy on which British and Americans could agree, against a background of increasing Jewish military activity in Palestine itself. Finally in 1947 Britain handed the problem over to the United Nations. A special committee (UNSCOP) recommended by a majority that the country should be divided into Jewish and Arab states, on terms favourable to the Jews, while Jerusalem should have a special regime. This was opposed by the Arab states but accepted by the Zionists and a majority of the United Nations, including the USA and USSR. Britain declared itself unwilling to carry the plan out, and announced its decision to withdraw from the country by May 1948. In the next months there was a rapid decline of British authority and growing conflict between Jews and Arabs, in which the better-organized Jewish community gained the upper hand.

On the day the withdrawal was completed the Jews proclaimed the independence of the State of Israel*, and this was recognized by the USA and USSR. At the same time the Arab states intervened militarily; there followed some months of fighting interrupted by truces, by the end of which Israel had occupied more territory than had been allotted to it by the decision of the United Nations. By early 1949 Israel and the neighbouring Arab states had signed armistice agreements, the effect of which was that Israel held the greater part of Palestine, and most of the rest was in the hands of Transjordan (which had changed its name to Jordan*). Egypt held a strip of land around Gaza*, and Jerusalem was divided between Israel and Jordan, although this was not recognized by the United Nations. In the course of the fighting some two-thirds of the Arab population was displaced, partly through the confusion and panic caused by war and partly by the actions of the Israeli army. They took refuge mainly in Jordan, Gaza, Syria and Lebanon. In subsequent negotiations the Israeli government showed itself unwilling to allow most of them to return, preoccupied as it was by the task of absorbing a large number of Jewish immigrants; a special UN agency (UNRWA*) was set up to look after the Arab refugees. In 1951 King ʿAbd Allah of Jordan, who was accused by many Palestinians of having been too ready to reach an agreement with Israel, was assassinated.

The armistices did not serve as a basis for peace treaties, and the problem of Palestine was to remain in one form or another, but for the next few years it was overshadowed by others. The way in which Britain had withdrawn from Palestine was generally regarded as a defeat for British policy, but the British position in the Middle East remained strong. The USSR was preoccupied in other parts of the world, and the USA, having taken over responsibility for the defence of Turkey, was prepared to leave the Arab countries as a sphere of British influence, apart from its special relationship with Saudi Arabia. During the next few years, Britain was able to reassert its position as the most important external power in the region, by means of adjustments to its relations with a number of states.

The process was comparatively simple in regard to two states with which Britain had privileged relations. In 1955 an Anglo-Iraqi agreement ended the British occupation of air bases, and a similar agreement was made with Jordan in 1957. An agreement with Egypt was more difficult to make. The treaty of 1936 had left two questions outstanding, that of the British base in the Suez Canal Zone, and that of the future of Sudan, which was ruled jointly by Britain and Egypt but over which Egypt had claims. Negotiations on both these matters came to nothing; the withdrawal from India had not diminished the importance of Egypt for Britain, both as a base in the event of conflict with the USSR and because British control of Egypt and the surrounding countries was thought to give it a certain power of independent action in world affairs. In 1951–2 there was a period of conflict in the Canal Zone. This led to an outbreak of violence against British establishments in Cairo, and this in turn was one of the events leading to a *coup d'état*: in July 1952 a group of army officers seized power, deposed King Faruq and dissolved the political parties. Negotiations with Britain were resumed, and the situation was altered by the success of the new regime in making an agreement with the main parties in Sudan. In 1953 it was agreed that Sudan should become independent after a period of transition under international supervision, and another agreement in 1954 provided for British withdrawal from the base in the Canal Zone, which could, however, be reactivated if there were an attack upon Egypt, another Arab country, or Turkey. Sudan duly became independent in 1956; soon, however, it was troubled by the outbreak of a revolt in its southern provinces, which were neither Arab nor Muslim, and this was to continue intermittently for many years.

Iran: the Musaddiq episode

An equally grave challenge to the British position came further east, in Iran. The joint Anglo-Russian occupation during the war had strengthened nationalist feeling, and this was mainly directed against Britain, because of the paramount influence which it derived from the control of the production and export of the oil of the south-eastern regions by the Anglo-Iranian Oil Company, in which the British government held 51 per cent of the shares. The deposition of Riza Shah had left a vacuum of power which his son did not yet have the personal ascendancy to fill. In 1951 Muhammad Musaddiq*, a politician of strong nationalist convictions, became prime minister with the support of a coalition of forces. His aim was to strengthen the unity and independence of the country by creating a strong executive power and reasserting Iranian control of its oil resources. The oil industry was nationalized, and this brought about a direct collision with the British government, which organized an international boycott of Iranian oil. Negotiations for a settlement, into which the American government was drawn, had no result, because the interests and views of the two sides were too far apart. The conflict, and its effects upon the Iranian economy, tended to dissolve the coalition on which Musaddiq's power was based, and in 1953 he was overthrown by a coup organized by his opponents, with active support from the British and American intelligence services. The Shah, who had left the country, was restored, and an agreement was reached by which the operations of the oil industry were to be shared between a new national company and an international consortium.

In the meantime France was trying, in a similar way but with more difficulty, to restore its position in North Africa. In both Tunisia and Morocco nationalism had a new strength and unity; in Tunisia it was organized by the Neo-Destour Party and the confederation of trade unions, and in Morocco by a combination of the Sultan and the Istiqlal Party. French governments were too weak, and the military and settler lobbies too strong, to make possible an agreement which the nationalists would accept, but economic difficulties and the war in Indo-China made it impossible to reimpose French authority by force. Some years of tension and repression culminated in a crisis in which Moroccan tribes, encouraged by the local French authorities, forced the deposition and exile of the Sultan in 1953. In Tunisia, too, the leader of the Neo-Destour Party, Habib Bourguiba*, was arrested and held in detention in France. By 1954 both countries were in open revolt, which only ended when a new French prime minister, Mendès-France, faced with an even more serious problem in Indo-China, was able to bring about a reversal of policy. The Sultan was brought back from exile, and an agreement was made by which Morocco became independent in 1956; the Sultan took the title of King. In the same year, Tunisia became independent too; the dynasty of Beys was brought to an end and Bourguiba became the first president of the Republic.

The problem of Algeria was more intractable. The repression of

1945 was one of the factors which strengthened the demand of Algerian Muslims for a change in their status, although some of them still wished for equal rights within France rather than separation from it. The central government made some attempts at reform in 1947; Algerian Muslims were given representation in the French parliament and a larger share in local affairs. The strength of the *colons*, however, both in local government and in Paris, prevented the changes having much effect. In these circumstances, Algerian Muslim opinion moved in the direction of a complete break with the past. From the existing nationalist parties there emerged a secret organization, formed largely of men who had served in the French army, and convinced that change could only be brought about through armed struggle. In November 1954 there took place the first violent incidents which were to open a long war for independence.

Popular nationalism, 1955–67

The conflicts and agreements between European imperial powers and nationalist movements might have appeared to be continuing the political processes of the pre-war period, in a situation where relationships of power had changed. Beneath the surface, however, fundamental changes were taking place in the countries of the region and their place in the world.

There was a rapid growth of population*, caused mainly by improvements in public health*, and a change also in its distribution; by the 1960s, a larger proportion lived in the cities, particularly in the capitals. Immigrants in the cities needed work and social services. They had access to the new media – the daily press, radio and cinema – and were more aware of political processes than those who lived in villages. Such social changes* were expressed in a new kind of political discourse and activity. It began to be widely accepted that the task of government was to initiate economic development and improve social welfare, and to create a more stable and unified nation able to stand up to the challenges of the modern world. This would involve greater control by government over society, a wider intervention by it in social and economic life, and the mobilization of popular support on a larger scale than had been necessary for governments of a different kind.

In some of the countries of the region, attempts were made to carry out politics of development and mobilization within a system of representative institutions. Lebanon and Israel remained parliamentary republics throughout the 1950s and 1960s. So too did Turkey, apart from an interlude of military rule in 1960–1. In Syria, representative government alternated with periods of military dictatorship until the mid-60s, and in Sudan, too, there was a period of military rule between 1958 and 1964, but representative government before and after it.

In most countries, however, effective power was concentrated in the hands of small, self-perpetuating groups, although the forms of constitutional government inherited or copied from those of Europe might continue to exist. Such regimes took two main forms. On the one side stood monarchies claiming legitimacy on their own terms: the Hashimite Kingdom of Jordan, and that of Iraq until 1958; the Kingdoms of Saudi Arabia and Yemen and the principalities of the Gulf; the Kingdoms of Libya and Morocco. In Iran, the Shah increased his hold over power after the crisis of 1951–3, and in Afghanistan a member of the ruling family, Daud Khan*, held power as prime minister. Apart from Yemen, the monarchical governments were by this time committed to new policies of economic growth. In Iran and Iraq, revenues from oil production made possible large-scale works of construction; other countries were in receipt of foreign aid from the USA or Europe, and Afghanistan also received aid from the USSR. Such governments did not, however, try to make basic changes in the structure of wealth and social power; the Shah began a reform of the system of landownership, but economic growth gave new opportunities for acquiring wealth.

There was a second kind of regime, however, that of a strong, centralizing government dominated by one man or a small group, and attempting to combine economic growth with a certain redistribution of ownership and wealth. The general policies of such regimes laid emphasis upon the creation of industries, the redistribution of land among smallholders linked by cooperatives, mass education, and the social emancipation of women. In Tunisia, such were the ideas and policies of Bourguiba* and the Parti Socialiste Destourien*, who continued to dominate the life of the country just as they had led the movement for independence. The land which had belonged to the European *colons* was taken over, and a policy of agrarian reform was adopted. For a time there was an attempt at state control of economic life, but by the end of the 1960s there was a reaction against this.

In some other countries, however, the older politicians and parties were displaced by new groups dominated by army officers, mainly of a younger generation and from humbler origins, claiming to stand for the interests of the nation as a whole as against those of particular factions or classes, and ruling in unequal partnership with the 'technocrats', without whom no modern government could be carried on. The archetype of such regimes was that of Egypt, where the revolution of 1952 had led by 1954 to the domination of one of the officers, Jamal ʿAbd al-Nasir (Nasser*). Having begun by expropriating the land of the royal family and limiting the size of other landholdings, the regime moved in the direction of control of economic life by the state, in order to create industries, extend cultivation, and generate hydro-electric power; its most important enterprise was the construction of the High Dam on the Nile at Aswan*. By the early 1960s this policy was being described in socialist terms. Nasser used all the means of modern publicity to project his own personality and ideas upon the people not only of his own country but of the other Arab countries. Through the mass media he appealed to peoples over the heads of their governments, in the name of Arab nationalism and 'Arab socialism', and for a time he seemed to embody a new conception of a united and reformed Arab nation.

Part of his appeal lay in his claim to be pursuing a certain line of foreign policy. The 1950s were a period of great tension in the relations between the USA and USSR and their respective allies. There was pressure on the independent states of Asia and Africa to join the Western system of defence against the real or supposed threat of Russian expansion, and to give facilities for military installations, and there were some attempts, too, by the USSR to secure allies or well-wishers. Some Middle Eastern states had no hesitation about joining the Western alliance. Turkey became a member of NATO, and Iran and Iraq, too, looked to the West for support against their northern neighbour; the most prominent Iraqi politician, Nuri al-Saʿid, was a strong advocate of a pro-Western policy. Israel hoped for Western support in the event of attack from Arab states, and Saudi Arabia, Tunisia and Morocco also had pro-Western inclinations. Afghanistan, on the other hand, fell more under Russian influence after the British withdrawal from India. Some of the newly independent states, however, were more inclined towards neutralism, a middle stance between the two superpowers, without commitment to either of them. The movement of 'non-alignment' was first given formal expression at the Bandung Conference in 1954, and Nasser became one of its main spokesmen.

The tension between monarchist regimes committed to free enterprise and private ownership and republics with ideas of radical social change, the tension also between pro-Western and neutralist states, the claim of Nasser to speak in the name of the 'Arab nation', and the continuing hostility between Israel and its Arab neighbours, all combined to produce a series of crises. The first of them concerned the Western idea of a Middle Eastern defence alliance. In 1955, states which supported this idea – Turkey, Iran, Iraq and Pakistan – formed the Baghdad Pact*, to which Britain adhered and the USA gave support. This was strongly opposed by Egypt and some other states, both out of their belief in non-alignment and because it appeared to challenge Egypt's predominance in the Arab world. The relations of Egypt with the USA and Britain grew worse in 1955, when Nasser broke the Western monopoly of arms supply to the Middle East by buying arms from Czechoslovakia. Next year, Britain and the USA withdrew their offer of financial support for the High Dam project, and Nasser responded by nationalizing the Suez Canal Company, in which British and French interests were dominant.

This precipitated an international crisis. There were negotiations between Egypt and the countries most concerned with the free use of the canal, but Britain, France and Israel also engaged in secret discussions which showed an identity of interest in ending Nasser's regime. In October, 1956, Israel invaded Egypt, and Britain and France immediately sent an ultimatum to both countries, of which the ostensible aim was to separate the two armies but the real purpose was to provide a pretext for overthrowing Nasser. When Egypt refused the ultimatum, British and French forces landed in the Canal Zone. The plan miscarried, however, because of strong opposition from all sides, and in particular from the USA and also the USSR, since neither of them could allow Britain and France to act in the Middle East as if they were still paramount there.

7000 French and British troops landed at Port Said on 5th November 1956 in response to Nasser's decision to nationalize the Suez Canal

The crisis ended with the withdrawal of British, French and Israeli forces, and an agreement to set up a UN force along the frontier between Israel and Egypt. The repercussions of the affair continued, however. Nasser's regime moved closer to the USSR, which gave military aid and also financial and technical assistance to build the High Dam; this new relationship with the USSR was one of the reasons for Egypt's move in the direction of socialism. Nasser's prestige and influence in the Arab countries increased, as the events of the next few years were to show.

In 1958, at a moment when the political situation in Syria was precarious, some politicians with radical tendencies, and certain army officers, persuaded Nasser to agree to a union between Egypt and Syria, with the name of the United Arab Republic*. This was widely believed to be the first step towards a broader Arab unity, but in the event the union collapsed in 1961, mainly because of the unequal balance of power between the two countries. A coup by Syrian officers restored the independence of the country, and after a few years power fell into the hands of members of a radical Arab nationalist party, the Baʿth*, with strong support in the army. In 1958 there also took place a military revolution in Iraq. The King and most members of his family were killed, as also was Nuri al-Saʿid. A military regime with socialist tendencies took over, to be replaced a few years later by one with Arab nationalist and Baʿthist ideas.

In the south-western corner of Arabia, the success of Nasserism was one of the causes of a revolution in Yemen, which hitherto had remained almost untouched by the changes in the outside world under the conservative rule of the Zaydi Imams*. In 1962, after the death of an Imam who had ruled for a long time, his successor was deposed and a republic proclaimed, of which the rulers had strong Nasserist sympathies. Civil war soon broke out, however, with Saudi Arabia supporting the monarchist opposition and Nasser drawn into giving military help to the Republic; there was an indecisive struggle which was to continue until the withdrawal of Egyptian forces in 1968.

While these events were disturbing the Middle East, the Algerian revolt against French rule was affecting the whole of North Africa. The insurrection which had broken out in 1954 became a national revolution supported by the greater part of the Muslim population. In addition to guerrilla forces and their supporters inside the country, there were military forces in Morocco and Tunisia, political offices there and in Egypt, and support throughout Asia and Africa; in 1958 a provisional government was established in Tunis. Attempts by the weak French governments of the period either to suppress the revolt or to reach agreement with the nationalists failed, because of the strength of the *colons* and their allies. In 1956 local French military governments were able to arrest one of the main leaders of the revolt, Ben Bella*, while on a flight from Morocco to Tunisia, and in the same year French participation in the attack on Egypt was mainly the result of a belief that it was Egyptian help which kept the revolution going.

In 1958 the frustration of the *colons* and the army with the failure of the French government sparked off a political crisis which ended with the coming to office of de Gaulle as president of the Republic, with increased powers under a new constitution. In spite of doubts and deliberate ambiguities, de Gaulle's policy soon emerged as being one of maintaining France's position in Algeria so far as possible, while preparing French public opinion for an agreement with the nationalists. It took some years to do this, and a potential military revolt had to be crushed in 1961, but finally agreement was reached in 1962; power was transferred to the provisional government, the French army was withdrawn, and Algeria became an independent republic. It was a costly victory; hundreds of thousands of the Muslim population had been killed, and even more had been displaced. The French army had had heavy losses during the war, and after independence the vast majority of the European population left for France, leaving their homes and property. Many thousands of Algerians who had supported French rule were killed or forced into exile.

The Suez crisis of 1956, the Iraqi Revolution of 1958, and the end of the Algerian War in 1962 marked the virtual end of European rule in the region. De Gaulle's policy was one of transforming the French Empire into an association of independent states; among others, Mauritania became independent in 1960. Britain still had a position of power in Aden, the Gulf and Cyprus. In the colony and protectorate of Aden*, the British had created a federation of local rulers in 1959, but unrest, encouraged by Egyptian propaganda and the example of Yemen, led to an explosion of violence. Faced with a growing revolt, the British withdrew in 1968; the local rulers were deposed by the nationalists, who created the People's Democratic Republic of Yemen* (commonly known as South Yemen, to distinguish it from the other Republic, now known as North Yemen); the new government was strongly inclined towards the USSR and its economic system. Further east, there were two kinds of revolt against the Sultan of ʿUman (Oman*), who ruled under British protection: a movement in favour of an alternative ruler, the Ibadi* Imam, and one in the west of the country encouraged by South Yemen. These movements were ended with British help; also with British support, the very conservative ruler was replaced by his son, who was more fully aware of the need to open the country to the modern world. Elsewhere in the Gulf, British withdrawal took place with less difficulty. Kuwait became fully independent in 1961, and in the late 1960s a review of British strategic policy ended in a decision to withdraw from positions of strength east of Suez. The withdrawal from the Gulf was completed by 1971 without political disturbances; the small principalities became independent, and six of them came together to form the United Arab Emirates (UAE*), while Qatar* and Bahrain* remained separate states.

In Cyprus*, too, British rule came to an end. The movement for union with Greece, which had always been strong among the Greek majority in the island, turned into an armed insurrection. This was opposed by the Turkish minority, with support from Turkey. After several years of mingled repression and negotiation, agreement was finally reached in 1959; Cyprus would not be united with Greece, but would become an independent republic, with safeguards for the position of the Turkish population. The arrangement was to be guaranteed by Greece, Turkey and Great Britain, which was to retain sovereignty over two military bases.

At the same time as Britain and France were withdrawing from the vestiges of their Empires, the oil companies, the largest and most powerful Western enterprises in the region, were trying to reach new agreements with the countries where they extracted oil. Oil was already being exported from Iran, Iraq and Bahrain before the beginning of the Second World War. The oilwells of Saudi

Arabia came into large-scale production by the end of the war, and those of Kuwait soon afterwards. By the 1960s large deposits had also been discovered and were being exploited in Qatar, the UAE, Oman, Libya and Algeria. The oil and natural gas of the Middle East and North Africa were providing Europe, Asia and Africa with a large proportion of what it consumed, and by the 1980s they formed some 60 per cent of the known reserves of the world. The agreements made by the companies with the host countries during the period of British and French predominance had been favourable to the companies. A small proportion of the profits was paid to the governments of the host countries, and the greater part went to the companies, and to the governments of the countries in which they paid taxes. The first major change in this system came in 1950, when the American company which had the concession for Saudi Arabia made a new agreement by which company and government would share the profits on an equal basis. The Iranian crisis of 1951–3 underlined the need for change, and in subsequent years the other main producing countries acquired a predominant share in the companies to which they had given concessions. In the 1970s they went further and took over the companies completely, beginning with Algeria in 1971. Some of the governments, however, still had partnership agreements of one kind or another with foreign companies whose help they needed in exploring and developing new fields.

From Nasserism to the *infitah* 1967–78

By the mid-1960s Nasser and 'Nasserism' seemed to be at the height of their influence. In 1967, however, the political and strategic balance was suddenly changed by a new outbreak of war between Israel and its Arab neighbours. The situation had remained uneasily stable for a number of years after 1956, but two new factors gradually entered in. One of them was a revival of Palestinian nationalist activity. For the first fifteen years or so after the war of 1948, the 'Palestine problem' had mainly been one which concerned Israel, the Arab states, and their patrons among the external powers. The Palestinians themselves, disoriented by the loss of their homes and the scattering of their communities, and deprived of power and effective leadership, had played little part. The shock of dispossession, however, had formed them into a separate nation, and by the mid-1960s there was appearing a new generation, inspired by Nasserism, the Algerian Revolution, and similar movements elsewhere in the world. In 1964 the Palestine Liberation Organization (PLO*) was created, and in 1968 it fell under the control of Fatah*, the largest of several groups dedicated to direct confrontation with Israel, with Yasir ʿArafat* as its leader.

Another change had been in the strength of Israel. Under the rule of the Labour Party, led for most of the period between 1948 and 1963 by David Ben Gurion, the state had coped with the problems of mass immigration, much of it from Middle Eastern and North African countries; American aid on a large scale had made possible economic growth and the creation of effective armed forces; with French help the country had also acquired a nuclear capacity.

By the middle of the 1960s Nasser was under pressure to show himself to be still the leader of the Arabs. In 1967 a crisis suddenly blew up over a real or supposed threat by Israel to Syria, where a more radical wing of the Baʿth Party had taken over, and the prevention by Egypt of Israeli ships entering the Gulf of ʿAqaba. Nasser requested the withdrawal of the UN forces on the frontier, and Israel took this as a threat to its security. An attempt by the USA to work out a compromise was ended on 5 June by a sudden Israeli attack upon Egypt and Syria, and then upon Jordan when it entered the war on the side of Egypt. In a brief war of six days Israel showed its complete superiority in the air, and occupied the whole of Sinai as far as the Suez Canal, the Jawlan (Golan) district in southern Syria, and all Jordanian territory west of the Jordan, including the Jordanian part of Jerusalem.

The war ended quickly, with a cease-fire in accordance with a United Nations resolution (Resolution 242), but it did not lead to negotiations or peace. The hostility between Israel and its Arab neighbours entered a new phase. Israel acquired a new status as a military power, and was henceforward to receive increased aid from the USA as a potentially valuable ally, but it also had new problems; in the territories which it had acquired, it now had a large Palestinian population under its rule, and also began to create Jewish settlements. Palestinian nationalism increased in strength, and received financial and political support from the Arab states. Nasser remained the most powerful Arab leader, but had lost the prestige given by success, and did not recover it before his death in 1970.

Frustration with Arab failure and weakness was one of the factors which led to a number of changes of regime in 1969 and 1970. These changes did not affect all countries. Saudi Arabia remained under the strong rule of Faysal*, who had become King in 1964 when his elder brother, who had succeeded their father ʿAbd al-ʿAziz* in 1953, had shown himself incapable of dealing with the new problems created by the coming of wealth from oil production and the opening of a traditional society to the modern world. In Morocco, King Hasan*, who succeeded his father in 1963, strengthened his personal domination as against the Istiqlal and other more radical parties. In Tunisia, Bourguiba* remained in control of party, government and country. In Libya, however, a group of officers, with Qadhafi* as the most prominent figure, deposed the King; in Algeria Ben Bella was replaced by another soldier, Boumedienne*, who set on foot a policy of rapid industrialization; in Sudan, officers led by Nimeiri* overturned the constitutional government; in Syria, power passed into the hands of the military wing of the Baʿth Party, with Hafiz al-Asad* as the dominant figure from 1970; and a similar process took place in Iraq, although a member of the civilian wing, Saddam Husayn*, emerged as the most powerful leader.

A change seemed likely to take place in Jordan too, where King Husayn*, who had succeeded his grandfather ʿAbd Allah in 1951, had to contend with an upsurge of nationalist feeling and activity among the Palestinians who formed the larger part of the population of his Kingdom. The organizations which controlled the PLO wished to make Jordan the base from which they could carry on the struggle against Israel and give support to the Palestinians under Israel occupation. A strong reaction by the government and army led to the expulsion of the Palestinian armed groups. They moved out of Jordan into southern Lebanon, and henceforward Husayn was unchallenged as ruler of Jordan. He still had to take Palestinian nationalism into account, however; it was a main aim of his policy to restore Jordanian rule over the West Bank*, and this did not appear possible without some agreement with the PLO, which the Arab states agreed in 1974 to regard as the sole representative of the Palestinian people.

The situation was once more changed suddenly in 1973, when Syria and Egypt, both of which had strengthened their armed forces with Russian help, launched an attack upon Israeli positions in the occupied territories. Egyptian forces crossed the Suez Canal, but the Israeli army, with American arms, was able to strike back and make its own crossing of the canal. At the same time a Syrian advance in the Jawlan (Golan) was checked by an Israeli counter-attack. The aim of Anwar al-Sadat*, Nasser's successor, was political rather than military: to demonstrate the dangers of the situation and the need for a political settlement. The danger became clear when the conflict threatened to lead to a confrontation of the two superpowers, neither of which could allow its clients to be defeated. A cease-fire was arranged. In the next two years Sadat reversed Nasser's policies. Even before the war of 1973* he had asked for the withdrawal of Russian military advisers, and now he severed the link with the USSR and drew closer to the USA, which took the lead in negotiating agreements for Israeli withdrawal from some of the Egyptian and Syrian lands it had occupied in 1967.

Both the Egyptian government and the US government under

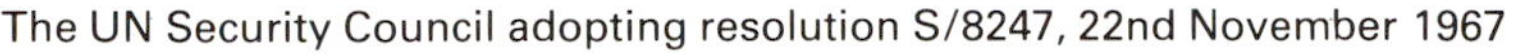
The UN Security Council adopting resolution S/8247, 22nd November 1967

Carter, who became president in 1976, wished to go further. Sadat was convinced that Israel, with American backing, could not be defeated in war, and his aim was to make Egypt as valuable an ally for America as was Israel, and induce the USA to follow a more even-handed policy which would make possible a lasting compromise; the USA for its part wished to exclude Russian influence from the Middle East. Negotiations began under American auspices, but once more the situation changed when, in November 1977, Sadat suddenly flew to Jerusalem to make a direct appeal for peace. There ensued a long process of bargaining between Egypt, Israel and the USA, which ended in the Camp David Agreements* of 1978. One of them set out the basis of a peace treaty between Israel and Egypt; this was signed in March 1979. The other suggested the main lines of a settlement of the conflict as a whole. The inhabitants of the West Bank and Gaza* would be given autonomy under an elected self-governing authority; after a transitional period of five years, there should be negotiations to determine the final status of the West Bank and Gaza, in which Egypt, Israel, Jordan, and representatives of the Palestinians should take part.

The consequences of these events were far-reaching. They brought immediate economic benefits to Egypt, which became a recipient of direct aid on almost the same scale as that given to Israel. This aid was given to strengthen both the armed forces and the economy, and it had implications. Egypt virtually abandoned its non-aligned stand and took a strongly pro-Western one, and its economic policy changed from one of state socialism to one of encouraging private enterprise and foreign investment. This new policy, first announced formally in 1974, was known as that of *infitah** ('opening up').

The increase of American influence and the turning away from socialism to private enterprise were processes which affected other countries of the region as well as Egypt. In the midst of the war of 1973, the Arab oil-producing countries* imposed an embargo on the export of oil to countries believed to be too favourable to Israel. Soon afterwards, the organization of the most important oil-exporting states, OPEC*, taking advantage of the increased demand for oil, raised prices by more than 100 per cent. As a result, there was a vast and sudden increase in their revenues: in Iran, from 5.6 billion dollars in 1973 to 20.5 in 1975, in Saudi Arabia from 7.2bn in 1973 to 27.0 in 1975, and then to 76.0 in 1982.

These states were, therefore, able to embark on large-scale projects of capital expenditure; they strengthened their armed forces, created a modern infrastructure of communications, established petrochemical and other industries, encouraged agriculture* to a rather lesser extent, and expanded their systems of education* and public health*. In Iran, Iraq and Algeria, population and resources were large enough to absorb all or most of the revenues, but other countries, such as Kuwait, Saudi Arabia and Libya, were not able to use all their revenues in these ways; part of the surplus was given in loans or grants to other states which did not have revenues from oil, and part was invested in Western countries.

The inflow of wealth had effects upon individuals as well as governments. Members of ruling families, officials, contractors, importers and others profited from it, and so did migrants from poorer countries who came to work in the richer ones. By the early 1980s there may have been as many as six million migrants from other countries in Saudi Arabia, the Gulf states, and Libya; the largest numbers came from Egypt, Yemen and Jordan, with an increasing number from India, Pakistan and South-East Asia.

One of the results of these changes was to strengthen the economic ties of most states of the region with the USA and Western Europe. Governments and individuals invested there; capital goods for development, modern armaments, and technical assistance for large-scale projects of construction came mainly from there, as did the goods for consumption which those who had become rich demanded. Governments which had oil resources looked for the most part to the West as the final guardians of their wealth, their independence, and the stability of their regimes.

The events which followed the war of 1973 had another chain of consequences, however. They increased the tension between those states with a pro-Western orientation and those which wished to pursue a neutralist policy. Sadat's policy aroused strong opposition both inside Egypt and outside. No other Arab state followed his policy of making peace with Israel, and Egypt was expelled from the Arab League, but several of them were no less inclined towards the West – Morocco, Tunisia, Jordan, Sudan, Saudi Arabia and Oman; King Faysal of Saudi Arabia tried to use his personal ascendancy to persuade the USA to moderate its support for Israel, until he was assassinated in 1975. On the other side stood those countries which wished to follow a more neutral policy, suspicious of the USA and looking to the USSR as a counter-balance to American predominance. The more or less permanent members of this group were Syria, Libya and Algeria, together with the PLO. Iraq balanced between its neutralist principles and its economic interests; South Yemen was more inclined to the USSR; so too was Afghanistan, after a *coup d'état* in 1973 led to the deposition of the King and the appointment of Da'ud Khan as president.

The way in which the Camp David Agreements were carried out strengthened the position of their opponents. The agreements had not been made with an Israeli government dominated by the Labour Party, which had held the ascendancy since 1948. The changing structure of the Israeli population, the growing military strength of Israel, the unconditional support of the USA, and the comparative failure of the economic policies of the government had all combined to bring about a change in the political scene. The election of 1977 had brought to power a coalition of nationalist groups with

Menachem Begin as prime minister, and it was this government which made the agreements with Sadat and carried them out in its own way. The withdrawal from Sinai took place, but on matters concerning the Palestinians and the future of the West Bank the government showed itself unwilling to make any real concessions. The creation of Jewish settlements continued, and no steps were taken towards self-government. Israel, in fact, had made a separate peace with Egypt, and the result was to increase opposition to Sadat's policies, widen the rift between the different Arab camps, and strengthen support for the PLO.

These developments had disastrous effects upon Lebanon*, a small, weak country with a liberal economy over which the government had limited control, and with a system of power-sharing which held together a number of religious communities. Over the last generation the balance of population had moved in favour of the Muslims, and this led to a demand for a change in the political system. At the same time, the prosperity generated by the flow of money from the oil-exporting countries into the banking and service sections of the Lebanese economy was producing greater and more visible inequalities of wealth. Another kind of instability was created by the attempt of the PLO to use southern Lebanon as a base from which to carry on the struggle with Israel; they received support from the Palestinian refugee population and some of the political leaders, but were opposed by others, and laid southern Lebanon open to the danger of Israeli reprisals. Civil war* broke out in 1975, with militias drawn mainly from the largest Christian community, the Maronites*, fighting a combination of Muslim, left-wing and Palestinian forces. External powers were drawn into the conflict; Israel gave aid to the Maronites, and Syria at first supported the other side, and then changed its position so as to ensure that neither side should be predominant and its own influence should be decisive. The war was fought savagely; by late 1976 an uneasy balance had been established, with the Maronites controlling much of the north, Syria the east, the PLO the south, Beirut divided, and the government almost powerless. It was an uneasy situation, however; the power of the Palestinians in the south was seen as a threat by Israel, which retaliated against attacks across the frontier, crossed it in 1978 in a brief invasion, and gave support to a local militia. The presence of a UN peace-keeping force was not able to stabilize the situation.

In the far west of the Arab world, a conflict had meanwhile erupted which set neighbouring states against each other. Under pressure from Morocco*, Spain withdrew in 1976 from its colony in the Western Sahara*, which was sparsely populated but had valuable deposits of phosphates. The territory was divided between Morocco and Mauritania, but both of them found themselves faced with opposition from a movement for independence among the inhabitants (Polisario) with support from Algeria. In 1979 Mauritania renounced its share, which Morocco took over, but the revolt continued, draining the resources of Morocco and embittering its relations with Algeria and some other African states.

Although standing outside the Arab world with its political tensions, Iran* was deeply affected in various ways by the dominant processes of this period, the increase in revenue from oil and the assertion of American influence. By the 1970s the Shah was in full control of the country, having defeated the last serious attempt to challenge his power in the early 1960s. He had already started on large projects of economic and social change. After 1973 the funds at his disposal increased rapidly, and so did the pace of economic change. This led to dislocation, as the country's infrastructure was not adequate to the rapid growth, and also to vast and obvious social inequalities. At the same time, a decision was made by the US government under President Nixon to give Iran whatever it asked for in the way of armaments, as the defender of Western interests in the Gulf area and against a possible Russian expansion. There took place a rapid increase of expenditure on the armed forces, and the Shah began to exert some influence over the Gulf area. The USA also helped to create an efficient and repressive security service, Savak.

Turkey stood somewhat apart from the processes which were taking place among its neighbours to the east and south; it was only involved in the Arab–Israeli conflict in marginal ways, and did not have the problems and opportunities created by wealth from the production of oil; it was part of the Western alliance and a member of NATO. It had had a constitutional government, with alternations of power between different parties, since 1950, with a brief interregnum in 1960–1. Its political problems were those of Western European rather than Middle Eastern countries, problems of economic policy and greater or less control by the government over the economy. From the end of the 1960s there was an increase in political violence caused by extreme parties of the right and left. The main parties which contended for power were the Republican Peoples Party under Ecevit and the Justice Party under Demirel, but others had emerged, with extreme nationalist or Islamic ideas. In 1971 the army intervened once more. Martial law remained in force until 1973, when constitutional rule was restored, but with continuing influence for the army. By this time the policy of economic growth with the help of US aid, which had been followed since the 1950s, was in trouble; foreign indebtedness, inflation and unemployment all increased, and the next few years were a period of economic crisis, weak governments and violence in the streets.

At the same time, Turkey was plunged into an international crisis over Cyprus*. The agreement by which the island had become an independent state with safeguards for the Turkish minority had not worked well. Relations between Greeks and Turks deteriorated, and the two groups looked for support to Greece and Turkey respectively. In 1974 a Greek military group seized power and proclaimed the union of Cyprus with Greece. They were encouraged by the military junta which was then in power in Greece, but Turkey reacted immediately by sending an army, which seized control of the northern part of Cyprus where the Turks mainly lived. Cyprus was divided *de facto* into two states, and a large part of the Greek population was dispossessed. There followed a period of tension not only between the two parts of the island but between Greece and Turkey, and agreement had not been reached by 1986.

Social change and the Iranian Revolution, 1979–86

The rapid increase of population* continued throughout the 1960s and 1970s; that of Egypt had grown from 19m in 1947 to over 40m by 1980, that of Turkey from 21m in 1950 to 40m by 1980, that of Iran from 19m in 1950 to 40m by 1980, that of Algeria from some 10m at the moment of independence to 19m twenty years later. The proportion of the population which cultivated the land had shrunk and most countries were by now net importers of food. The numbers of those who lived in cities had increased rapidly; in some countries a majority were living in the larger urban centres by 1980. The largest cities had grown with special rapidity: Cairo from 2m in 1947 to 10m or so by the 1980s, and Istanbul, Tehran, Baghdad, Damascus, Beirut, Algiers and Casablanca to a similar extent. In most countries more than 50 per cent of the population was under twenty years of age.

The vast mass of unskilled or semi-skilled workers, torn from their roots in the village, and, in the case of the migrants, living far from their homes, found themselves in an alien and divided urban world. There was a division between the mass of the population and those who reaped the main immediate profits from the new wealth generated by revenues from oil and economic growth; this sector included those who belonged to the ruling groups or were connected with them, those who possessed the higher skills which were needed by governments and enterprises of a new kind, and those who had useful connections with the Western economies. As is inevitable in a process of rapid economic growth, the gap between rich and poor grew wider, and it was a difference not only of wealth but also in ways of life. The wealthy and educated lived in much the same way as their counterparts in Europe and America, in modern offices and houses filled with imported consumer goods, in new quarters where women could move more freely, sending their sons and daughters to study abroad. The centre of power in the cities had moved from the old sector to the new, where the external signs of the Islamic social order were no longer visible or dominant. The poorer dwellers in the city were shut out of this new life; however quickly schools, hospitals and social services were expanded, they could not keep pace with the growth and movement of population. They were more aware of their position than before, because of the new media of communication; this was the age of rapid transport, and of television and radio. At all levels of society there was also a division between the generations: the older one which had been brought up in the age of secularizing nationalism and the struggle for independence, and the new one which was facing the problems of a different world.

The new means of communication were also means by which the urban masses could be mobilized for action, by parties or leaders wishing to overthrow the existing order. In addition to those who spoke in the name of nationalism or socialism, there were the voices of those who condemned the whole path of progress along which Asian and African communities had been trying to move during the last generations: the path of remaking themselves in the image of Western Europe and North America. Those who thought in this way wished, before it was too late, to reinforce the foundations of the society which they had inherited, the moral system and doctrines derived from revealed religion. These ideas were particularly strong among those elements of the urban population who were educated, but not to the point where they could profit from economic growth, and who were still conscious of their roots in the traditional society. They included women as well as men, turning their backs upon what they regarded as the illusory freedom of Western women.

Such movements existed all over the Middle East. Even in Turkey, which seemed in so many ways to stand aloof from the other countries of the Middle East, there appeared organizations which challenged the political consensus on which the Republic had rested since the time of Atatürk*: secularism, openness to European civilization, a free-enterprise economy, and membership of the Western alliance. Extremist organizations, nationalist, Islamic and left-wing, had been growing in strength throughout the 1970s, and the army took over once more in 1980. Its declared aim was to restore law and order, but this led it to suppress the existing political parties and limit freedom of speech and teaching. As in previous coups, the balance gradually moved back in favour of representative government, and by 1986 the political parties, in more or less disguised forms, were once more taking part in elections and government, in uneasy symbiosis with the military.

In Israel there was a revival of orthodox Judaism*, usually but not necessarily linked with an uncompromising nationalism. In the Arab countries, great influence was exercised by movements of which the society of the Muslim Brothers (*Ikhwan**) in Egypt was the prototype. This began as a movement of moral renewal, but soon developed ideas of social and political reform; Islam, if properly understood, offered, it believed, a middle way, a valid alternative to capitalism and communism. The movement became a political force in Egypt in the 1930s; suppressed under Nasser*, it revived under Sadat, and gave rise to more extreme groups which aimed at overturning the existing order by violent means. In 1981 one such group assassinated Sadat*, in protest against the political and economic policies with which he was associated. A similar group took over the Great Mosque at Mecca in 1979, in revolt against the corruption into which wealth had led the once austere regime of the Saʿudi family, but was defeated. In Syria, the Muslim Brothers gained much support among the Sunni* Muslim majority, which was alienated from the government by the power held by the ʿAlawi* community, to which Asad himself belonged; an attempt by the Brothers to raise a revolt in the city of Hama was suppressed with much bloodshed in 1982. The Brothers were also powerful in Sudan.

In Iran, the Islamic movement took a different form and had more far-reaching consequences. The population of Iran consists mostly of Shiʿi* Muslims, and the Shiʿi scholars and teachers have preserved their independence and their position as spokesmen of society more than those of Sunni countries. Most of them stood to some extent in opposition to the absolute rule of the Shah* and the direction in which he was taking the country. They called, not, as did the Muslim Brothers, for a return to the real or imagined Islam of the early centuries, but for a reassertion of the developed system of doctrine and law of which they were the guardians. By the late 1970s there was growing discontent with the power of the Shah and the way in which he was using it; this was articulated by a number of movements, but the men of religion emerged as the only leaders who could serve as a unifying force for all of them.

In 1978 the discontent began to take the form of a popular rising against the Shah, calling for the restoration of constitutional government. A number of groups took part in this: the nationalists who had supported Musaddiq*, the communists of the Tudeh Party, and an Islamic revolutionary group, the Mujahidin*. The leading role was taken by a man of religion, Ruhallah Khumayni (Khomeini*), in exile first in Iraq and then in France but communicating with his followers in various ways. The Shah proved unable either to crush the movement by force or to make the necessary concessions to it, the US government did not support him wholeheartedly, and the army was unwilling to fire upon the vast demonstrations which filled the streets of Tehran. Finally, the Shah left the country in January 1979, and Khomeini returned in triumph.

The events of the next few months showed that what had happened was more than a change of regime. Within the coalition of forces which had made the revolution, a struggle for power soon broke out, and it ended with the triumph of the religious party. Iran became an Islamic Republic, with a new constitution which gave supreme power to Khomeini as chief jurisconsult (*faqih**). An attempt was made to restore the rule of Islamic law; the system of education was changed; traditional dress and modes of behaviour were imposed upon women; a large number of supporters of the old regime or opponents of the new one were executed or forced to leave the country.

Khomeini returning to Tehran to a triumphant welcome, 27th January 1979

In external affairs the new government devoted itself to spreading its version of Islam in other countries, and opposing those it regarded as enemies of Islam. In November 1979, the hostility aroused by American support of the Shah's rule led to the occupation of the US embassy in Tehran and the taking of hostages by supporters of the new regime. This opened a long conflict with the US government which had repercussions on American domestic politics, and was not ended until January 1980.

Almost at the same time, a graver and more lasting problem arose. The Iraqi regime had strengthened itself throughout the 1970s; its economic growth was rapid and its international position appeared to be strong. In 1980 it launched an invasion of Iran, partly in order to win back concessions it had made to Iran at the time of the Shah's greatest strength, and also to prevent the danger of Khomeini's ideas spreading among the Shiʿis who formed the major part of the Iraqi population. After initial successes, the Iraqi armies met with fierce resistance, as Iranian national feeling and Islamic conviction came together to support the regime. The struggle became almost a personal contest between Khomeini and Saddam Husayn. As it went on, there was a danger that it would draw in the other countries of the Gulf, which gave some support to Iraq, and affect the export of oil. By 1986 Iran appeared to be in the better position. It occupied some Iraqi territory, but it was not yet possible to say whether it would be able to achieve a victory, or how long the war would last (see Iran–Iraq War).

To the east of Iran, in Afghanistan*, a conflict of another kind broke out at almost the same time. In 1978 a military coup

Behind mocking posters of President Carter and the Shah, Islamic guards watched the US Embassy in Tehran where 60 US hostages were guarded by students

overthrew and killed Daud Khan, and replaced his rule by that of a single party, carrying out a policy of land reform and state socialism, and looking to the USSR for support. A year later, dissensions within the ruling group led to a Russian military occupation; a government of communist inclinations took power. It made some attempt to broaden its support, but could not prevent the outbreak of armed resistance to it, expressing itself in Islamic terms, and receiving help from the USA and Pakistan, where a large number of Afghans took refuge. By the end of 1986 indirect negotiations between the Russian, Afghani and Pakistani governments seemed to be reaching the point where a Russian withdrawal might be possible, on condition that a government friendly to the USSR remained in power.

Both the Iranian Revolution and the Russian occupation of Afghanistan played a part in the movement of American public opinion which brought Reagan to the presidency at the beginning of 1981. The new American administration soon began to depart from the line of policy laid down by its predecessors, that of striving for an accommodation with the USSR. Its policy was that of building up American armaments and America's system of alliances. A determined effort was made to strengthen its allies in the Middle East, Egypt, Oman, and above all Israel, with which an understanding on strategic cooperation was reached, by which Israel was given extensive military aid and provided facilities for the strategic purposes of the USA.

Strengthened by this, and by the separate peace with Egypt, the right-wing government of which Begin was the head was now able to try to destroy Palestinian nationalism once and for all. Internally, a policy was followed of planting Jewish settlements on the West Bank and taking measures designed to induce the Arab population to leave; externally, an attempt was made to crush the PLO in its stronghold in Beirut and southern Lebanon, and to instal a new, pro-Israeli regime in Lebanon. In the south, after some disturbed years, there was a cease-fire in 1981 which was more or less observed, but in June 1982 the Israeli government seized the opportunity given by an attempt to assassinate its ambassador in London, and launched a large-scale invasion of Lebanon. It soon became clear that the aim was to occupy not only southern Lebanon but the western part of Beirut where the PLO were in the ascendant. The southern half of Lebanon was occupied, Syria agreed to a cease-fire after a short confrontation with the Israelis, and west Beirut was besieged. An agreement negotiated by the US government permitted the leaders and armed forces of the PLO to leave Lebanon for other Arab countries without the Israeli army entering west Beirut; a short time afterwards, however, the assassination of the new, pro-Israeli president of Lebanon gave Israel the pretext for sending its army into west Beirut. A large-scale massacre of Palestinians and Muslim Lebanese by Maronite allies of Israel compelled US intervention to set a limit to Israeli actions. The Israeli army was obliged to withdraw from Beirut, and a mixed force of Americans, French, British and Italians took over the maintenance of peace and order.

Installed in Lebanon as keeper of the peace, the US government soon found itself involved in the politics of the country. It helped to negotiate an agreement by which Israel would withdraw its forces from Lebanon in exchange for concessions which would leave it in virtual control of the government and country. This ran counter to the interests of important parts of the population and of the Syrians, and there ensued some months of conflict between the Lebanese army, backed by the USA, and the opposition, backed by Syria. Attacks upon American and French military posts led finally to the evacuation of the multilateral peace-keeping force, and then to the withdrawal of the Lebanese government from its agreement with

Israel. In the course of this struggle, a new and important factor in the Lebanese political scene emerged. The Israeli invasion and the Palestinian withdrawal stirred into action the Shiʿi population, who formed a majority in the south, and left a vacuum for them to fill. From 1984 they dominated west Beirut as well as the south, from which they actively opposed the Israeli presence. As they grew stronger, however, a split appeared between the more secularist element and those who followed the lead of Khomeini.

The repercussions of the Lebanese War upon Israel were no less far-reaching. The losses incurred, the discredit of the massacre for which the army had some responsibility, the failure of the agreement with Lebanon, and the growth of Shiʿi opposition in the south, all gave rise to a certain, although not universal, revulsion in Israel. In the elections of 1984 the right-wing alliance lost part of its ascendancy to the Labour Party, and a fragile coalition was put together, which carried out an incomplete unilateral withdrawal from southern Lebanon, and tried to improve relations with some Arab countries and the Palestinians on the West Bank, but with limited success; the other wing of the coalition was opposed to concessions, the Arab states were unwilling to enter into negotiations except within an international framework, and the US government was reluctant to use its power in order to make possible an effective effort for peace.

The effect of the war upon the PLO was even greater. It had lost the position in Lebanon from which it could carry on an independent political and military policy, and henceforward had to operate as an organization in exile, living on the sufferance of Arab governments unwilling to allow it too much freedom of action. Its position grew worse when its relations with its main supporter, Syria, deteriorated in a way which split the movement. Arab states now found themselves in a dilemma: they could scarcely enter a process of negotiation without the support of the PLO, but the PLO was too disunited to be able to follow a clear line of policy which would involve an ultimate recognition of Israel and some kind of link between Jordan and the West Bank.

The Iranian Revolution, the resurgence of Islamic feeling which was encouraged by it, the war between Iraq and Iran, the war in Lebanon, and the continuation of the Arab–Israeli conflict, all had effects on the internal stability of the surrounding Arab countries, and to these another factor was added in the mid-1980s: the crisis in the oil industry, because of an excess of supply over demand and a consequent fall in prices. This had repercussions not only in the oil-exporting countries, of which the revenues and the projects of development were mainly dependent on the sale of oil, but also in other countries to which migrant workers sent back remittances or the richer countries gave loans or grants.

The disturbances of the region did not shake the hold of King Husayn over Jordan or that of the rulers of Saudi Arabia and the Gulf states; the danger of an extension of the war between Iraq and Iran led them to form the Gulf Cooperation Council* in 1981, in order to coordinate their policies in regard to defence and economic policies. North Yemen continued to be ruled by military regimes, with some attempts at giving them a constitutional basis, and South Yemen continued to follow a Marxist line, although with some violent upheavals. In Syria, Asad maintained himself in power in the face of an economic situation which was growing worse. So too did Sadat's successor in Egypt, Husni Mubarak*, against two kinds of challenge, that of the popular Islamic forces, and that of those who wished representative government to be restored and were uneasy about Egypt's isolation from the Arab world; some tentative steps were taken towards restoring the system of political parties and elections. In Sudan, a more dramatic step was taken. Nimeiri attempted to restore the strict rule of Islamic law*; in the south, this led to a revival of the civil war, and in the north, his policies, together with the worsening economic situation, led in 1985 to a sudden upsurge of protest by political parties, the overturning of the regime by a military coup, and the restoration of parliamentary government.

The countries of North Africa were not so directly affected by the events of the Middle East, but had their own causes of disturbance: the rule of Qadhafi* in Libya, following a policy of popular socialism with an Islamic colouring, and giving help to revolutionary movements in neighbouring countries; and the continuing problem of the western Sahara*, which affected relations between Morocco and Algeria. In spite of these problems, and of an undercurrent of Islamic opposition, the regimes managed to remain in power. In Tunisia there was a move towards recognizing political parties and therefore differences of political opinion, but the domination of Bourguiba remained unshaken, although uncertainty about the succession to him was a factor of instability. In Algeria, the coming to power of Chadli Bendjedid* after the death of Boumedienne* in 1979 led to a change of economic policy, with greater emphasis on free enterprise, agriculture and the production of consumer goods. In Morocco, the Western Saharan problem helped to create a certain rapprochement between the king and the parties which had been in opposition, and thus to make possible a certain liberalization.

As the 1980s drew towards their end, an observer of events in the Middle East and North Africa might have been tempted to ask whether these regions existed in any except a purely geographical sense. There were, indeed, ways in which the different countries of the region seemed to be drawing closer together. Easier travel, the movement of workers, the circulation of books and newspapers, and the expansion of television were tending to create a common culture among those who spoke and read Arabic, and the Iranian Revolution had given encouragement to those, in all Muslim countries, who wished to reform the social order on the basis of Islamic principles. Such factors, however, seemed to add a new dimension to the political fragmentation of the region. The distance which had always existed between Arabs, Persians and Turks had grown no narrower; the enmity between Israel and its Arab neighbours was still bitter; most Arab regimes, even if they claimed legitimacy in similar terms, looked at each other with suspicion, if not hostility. The rapid economic growth made possible by the rise in the price of oil in the 1970s had widened the gap between rich and poor, skilled and unskilled, and the depression of the 1980s shook the economies and societies of countries which depended, directly or indirectly, upon the profits of oil production.

The place of most states of the region in the international order was by no means assured. The idea of the 'Third World', of a bloc of developing neutral states, had grown weaker as the age of empires came to an end. With the development of modern technology, the gap between technically advanced states and the rest of the world was wider. The great European states, and Europe as a whole, were no longer able to create their own world-order; the USSR had been almost excluded from the Middle East, and had not had much success in its efforts to restore its presence; and the vast power of the USA was not, or so it seemed, being used in accordance with any very clear and consistent policy.

AHH

Further reading

L. C. Brown, *International Politics and the Middle East* (London, 1984)
W. M. Hale, *The Political and Economic Development of Modern Turkey* (London, 1981)
A. Horne, *A Savage War of Peace: Algeria 1954–1962* (London, 1977)
N. Keddie, *Roots of Revolution* (New Haven, 1981)
W. F. Knapp, *North-West Africa* (London, 1977, 3rd edn.)
W. R. Louis, *The British Empire in the Middle East 1945–1951* (Oxford, 1984)
P. Mansfield, *The Arabs* (London, 1985, 3rd edn.)
E. Mortimer, *Faith and Power* (London, 1982)
M. Rodinson, *Israel and the Arabs* (London, 1982, 2nd edn.)
J. Waterbury, *The Egypt of Nasser and Sadat* (Princeton, 1983)
R. Wilson, *The Economies of the Middle East* (London, 1979)

Afghanistan

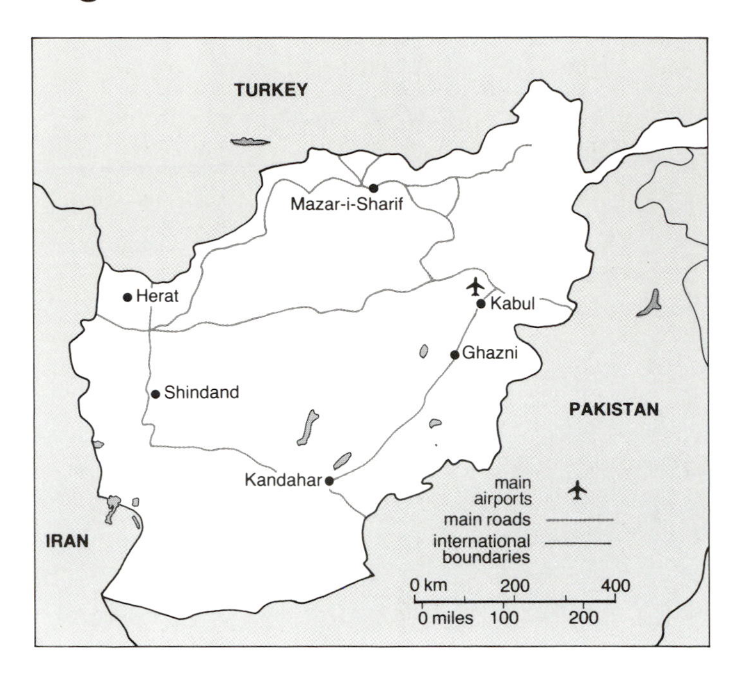

Geography and topography

The geographic zones of Afghanistan show great diversity. In general there are hot dry summers and bitterly cold winters, with heavy snowfalls in mountain areas. Mountains and deserts account for 75 per cent of the total area, dominated by the Hindu Kush mountain system and the Himalayas. Much of the land is semi-desert, with stony deserts in many regions and sandy deserts in the south-west. Only a few small forests are left, in the south-east. Four main river systems exist; the Amu Darya, Hari Rud, Hilmand-Arghandab and Kabul rivers.

Passes through the natural mountain barriers have allowed access through to the rich sub-continent of India for Afghan traders, migrants or invading armies. Afghanistan's fertile regions are often separated from each other by mountains or desert, and communications are poorly developed. Many of its 18,000 villages are cut off for almost half the year by winter snowdrifts, and most are far from roads. Only 13 per cent of the land area is cultivated, with 10 per cent more used as pasture lands for large flocks of sheep and goats. By far the largest city is the capital, Kabul, followed by Kandahar, Herat, Mazar-i-Sharif and Kunduz.

Peoples

The peoples of Afghanistan reflect the fact that it borders on Central Asia as well as Iran and the sub-continent. The largest single ethnic group, hitherto dominant in Afghan politics, are the Pushtun*.

Official title	The Democratic Republic of Afghanistan
Area	650,000 sq. km
Population	14.8 million (of which some 3.8 million are in exile)
Government and constitution	A new constitution was ratified by the National Assembly (Loya Jirgah) in April 1985. According to this, the People's Democratic Party of Afghanistan is the nation's guiding force. Elections to the Loya Jirgah are based on secret, free and equal votes. Head of State is the President of the Revolutionary Council and the Council of Ministers is the supreme executive organ of state power
Currency	1 afghani = 100 puls; US $1 = 50.60 afghanis
Languages	Persian (Dari) and Pashto are the two main languages and the mother tongues of 80 per cent of the population. Turkic and Mongolian dialects are also spoken
Religion	Although most Afghanis are Sunni Muslims, groups such as the Hazara are Shi'i
Climate	Temperatures are extreme. Lowland temperatures in July can reach 49°C, while winter temperatures on the high plateau areas can drop to −26°C. In the drier areas of the west, annual rainfall varies between 100–150 mm but reaches 250–400 mm in the east

They have in common a tribal culture and the Pashto language*, but are divided into many tribes and clans. The Persian-speaking Tajik are the second largest ethnic group. Uzbek, Turkoman, Hazara, Aimaq, Baluchi and Nuristani are also represented.

The complexity of ethnic groups and sub-groups in Afghanistan has made observers compare it to a 'living museum' of races, or describe it as an empire rather than a nation. Most of the ethnic groups continue on across the Afghan borders into other states; the Pushtun (also known as Pathan) in Pakistan, the Uzbek, Tajik and Turkoman in Soviet Central Asia, and the Baluchi in Pakistan and Iran.

Religions

Islam* is the religion of the overwhelming majority. Some 80 per cent are Sunni* Muslims, with about 19 per cent Shi'a* – most of whom are Twelver* or 'Imami' Shi'i, together with scattered Isma'ili* communities. In the towns there are tiny trading communities of Hindus, Sikhs and Jews.

History up to 1939

It was the decay of two mighty Empires, the Safavid* based in Iran and the Mughal based in India, which provided the opportunity in 1747 for an Afghan chieftain, Ahmad Shah Durrani, to seize control of lands bordering on Central Asia.

From the mid-eighteenth century a separate, independent Afghan political identity began to emerge. It was based on the dominance of the Pushtun over other ethnic groups, and the overall kingship of the Durrani royal family. Although the large Afghan Empire proved ephemeral, Afghanistan nevertheless retained its independence. Twice invaded by British Indian armies (1839–42 and 1878–80), it became a buffer state between the two expanding Empires of Russia in Central Asia and of Britain in India.

Under the 'iron Amir' 'Abd al-Rahman (1880–1901) a process of internal consolidation took place; opposition was firmly crushed, rebellious Pushtun tribes forcibly removed to colonize northern regions, and for the first time a central government structure was created. In economic development, education and infrastructure, though, Afghanistan remained very backward compared to its neighbours. A sign of its semi-dependent status was Britain's monopoly of the state's foreign relations, which lasted until after the third Anglo-Afghan War of 1919.

A sharp setback for what little degree of progress there had been in the social field occurred in the disastrous reign of King Amanullah (1919–29). Attempts to force through far-reaching social changes on the model of Kemal Atatürk's* Turkey foundered against strong opposition. Civil war led to anarchy and the fall of Amanullah, and with it any prospect of reform. A Tajik adventurer named Habibullah seized power briefly in 1929, only to be ousted by a cadet branch of the Durrani royal family.

King Nadir Shah (1929–33) had strong backing from Pushtun tribesmen from North-West Frontier Province in British India. His victorious tribal army sacked Kabul in payment for their services, inaugurating a grim cycle of violence and repression which led to Nadir Shah's assassination in 1933. It was Nadir Shah's brothers who effectively ruled the country for the next two decades in the name of the young heir King Zahir Shah (1933–73). One of the royal uncles, Shah Mahmud, briefly flirted with democracy by allowing in 1949 the election of independent liberals as well as tame nominees into the so-called 'liberal parliament'. The experiment did not flourish, and ended in imprisonment for the most active and outspoken liberals.

History since the Second World War

Unlike its neighbour Iran, Afghanistan was not directly touched by the Second World War. British and Soviet war aims did not require invasion, but their combined pressure did result in the expulsion from Kabul of the influential German colony. It was rather the partition of India in 1947 which deeply affected Afghanistan. With British withdrawal from India, the long dormant issue was revived of Kabul's claims to the Pushtun and Baluchi lands across the border – the Durand Line or tribal belt demarcated in 1893. Kabul demanded a plebiscite. What it got was a *fait accompli*.

As successor state to British rule in this part of united India, the new state of Pakistan inherited the bitter resentment of Afghan rulers over the inclusion of these disputed lands into Pakistan. The issue of 'Pushtunistan' became a festering sore in relations between the two states, hindering their cooperation for mutual economic benefit. Ruling circles in Kabul fed irredentist hopes for separation of the Pushtun lands from the new state of Pakistan, and for landlocked Afghanistan's thereby gaining a port on the Indian Ocean. This sterile rivalry caused periodic confrontation with Pakistan and, in particular, disruption of Afghan traditional trade routes via the port of Karachi.

Relations with the Soviet Union

Popularly associated with the Pushtunistan cause, and rightly so, was the forceful prime minister from 1953–63, Prince Muhammad Daud Khan. A key member of the royal family, Daud guided Afghanistan into closer relations with the USSR. The periodic disruption of trade routes via Pakistan made the alternative land route across the USSR increasingly relied upon over the next decades.

Until 1953 Kabul had maintained a cautious, suspicious attitude towards its mighty northern neighbour. Under Daud, however, close links in all areas rapidly developed. With the benefit of hindsight, the most significant were in the military field, with Soviet agreements to equip (from 1956) and to train (from 1961) the Afghan army and air force. These Soviet–Afghan military links only came about, in fact, after Afghan failure to obtain US arms without strings attached, and on attractive loan terms. Afghanistan's decision to refuse to become a member of the Baghdad Pact* (later CENTO) was meant to keep the country independent and a full member of the non-aligned movement. In practice, however, it gave the Russians great potential influence.

The USA, West Germany and other traditional Western aid-givers found they had a keen rival in the Soviet Union. In the Cold War climate of the time their competition for the goodwill of this strategically placed state led to an abundance of foreign-aid offers. The scale of Soviet aid showed the considerable importance attached to Afghanistan in Moscow. Within just two years of the first small loan, Soviet leaders Khrushchev and Bulganin visited Kabul (1955), agreeing terms for a loan for the then enormous sum of $100 million.

Among the infrastructure projects assured by this loan were some of great strategic interest to Moscow; a highway from the Soviet border to Kabul, port facilities on the Amu Darya river border and also a new military airport at Bagram. Particularly favoured in Soviet-directed development plans was the half of Afghanistan north of the Hindu Kush, throughout which there was soon a virtual monopoly of projects established by Soviet aid.

A new stage in bilateral relations was reached after the discovery of large reserves of natural gas in Jowzjan Province, close to the Soviet border. In 1968 Soviet engineers completed a gas pipeline, by which low-priced Afghan gas was exported to Central Asian industrial centres. Gas exports steadily grew in volume in the 1970s, with gas constituting the largest single export item. By 1985 annual gas production was claimed to be 2400m m^3. But even in 1985, only 3 per cent of gas production was being utilized for Afghan needs, all the rest serving the needs of the Soviet economy.

Already by the mid-1960s, competition in the aid field between the USA and the USSR had passed its peak. However, the overall dominance of the Russians before 1978 was somewhat obscured by the aid activity of many other states, notably West Germany, France, China and India. Already by 1972 the USSR was by far the largest creditor of this poor state, with $900m committed between 1957 and 1972, 60 per cent of all civil aid. Unlike the USA and most Western aid-donors, the USSR only rarely gave grants, and its loans built up heavy annual interest charges.

Soviet soldiers, on leave from the war in Afghanistan, being welcomed in the town of Kushka, the Soviet Republic of Turkmenistan, 18th October 1986

Political liberalization

A new liberal constitution introduced in 1964 under King Zahir Shah ushered in 'New Democracy', a system of elected parliamentary democracy. It came after the dismissal of the authoritarian Prime Minister Daud. The next decade saw unprecedented liberalization in the political arena. Parties came into the open and a lively, relatively free political press came into being in Kabul. Out of this ephemeral press freedom from 1964 emerged some small political groupings which gained a following in the educated elite; left-wing weekly newspapers coexisted with liberal and nationalist ones. In some cases, the names of weeklies were adopted for those political parties – more properly, factions around politicians – still banned in theory under the 'New Democracy'.

To contemporary observers, the trend was far from plain. From 1964 there was an increasing polarization of Afghan politics, and growing influence of left-wing circles, impatient to remedy what they claimed were the corrupt ways of a tired regime. The influence and communist leadership of the small left-wing parties were alike underestimated. Even less remarked was the steady underground growth of fundamentalist Muslim ideology in the same key areas of potential influence – the high schools and university in the capital as well as among junior officers of the armed forces.

The eponymous weeklies *Parcham* and *Khalq* were produced by two distinct and rival wings of the newly founded Peoples' Democratic Party of Afghanistan (PDPA). The Parcham (Banner) faction tended to draw its support more from the Persian-speaking, young urban elite, while Khalq (People) attracted mainly Pushtuns of more humble rural background. At odds with both was the more extreme (and so-called Maoist) group Shula-i-Jawed (Eternal Flame), with wide appeal among the ethnic minorities, many of whose educated members felt discriminated against by the Pushtun-dominated royal establishment. However, the lingering appeal of ultra-nationalist Pushtun ideas among the educated youth was plain from the success of the weekly, and party, *Afghan Mellat* (Afghan Nation).

The 1964 Constitution failed to give rapid progress or stability, nor were five successive prime ministers in just one decade able to go far in imposing enlightened democratic ways in a cynical environment. The democratic experiment lost momentum, though it had modest success in some areas. The nature of King Zahir Shah was, after all, against the experiment, for he was too spineless to intervene decisively in support of capable, honest prime ministers like Muhammad Hashim Maywandwal and Nur Ahmad Etemadi in the crises they periodically faced. Much of the blame for the faulty working of the new constitution often fell on the King's son-in-law General Abdul Wali, rather than on the weak Zahir Shah. The regime itself was discredited in the country for its gross mishandling of foreign relief aid at a time of drought, which resulted in a terrible famine in 1972, killing up to 100,000 Afghans.

Muhammad Daud Khan

A cousin and contemporary of King Zahir Shah, Muhammad Daud was groomed for power from early youth. He was a forceful prime minister from 1953 to 1963, deliberately reshaping Afghanistan's foreign policy. Daud, like other members of the royal family, was banned from politics under the 'New Democracy' for the next decade. By a military coup in 1973, Daud seized power and declared a Republic with himself as president. The new regime proved unpopular and quite unable to resolve the country's problems, economic as well as political. President Daud was killed, together with most of his family, resisting a communist-led coup in Kabul in April 1978.

Fall of the monarchy

A sudden military coup in 1973 during the absence abroad of Zahir Shah abolished the monarchy and proclaimed a Republic under former prime minister Daud Khan. Daud returned to power an older but not a wiser man. As president he failed to grapple with the needs of the changing times, relying on brute force to crush dissent. In spite of the participation, both in the army coup and in the new cabinet, of left-wing PDPA members, and Daud's own reputation in Western circles as 'the Red Prince', the Republic proved neither radical nor particularly Soviet-oriented.

Under Daud there were few signs of change in foreign policy or social reforms. Afghanistan as a non-aligned state maintained cordial aid links not only with the USSR, China and the traditionally important Western states, but increasingly, too, with the conservative oil-rich Muslim states, notably Iran and Saudi Arabia, from which large-scale development funds were confidently expected. Among Daud's early backers who were disillusioned were many Parchamis.

This reaction against Daud's Republic, as well as direct Soviet pressure, probably explains the reunion of the two rival PDPA factions, Khalq and Parcham, in 1977. It was a fragile kind of unity, but it helped produce the 'Saur' (April) Revolution, another military coup on 27 April 1978, by which the PDPA finally came to power in Kabul. PDPA leaders arrested by Daud's police after the discovery of a plot were released by junior officers of the army and air force.

It was the Khalq faction which won out in 1978, through its numerical superiority over Parcham. The new president, Nur Muhammad Taraki, was a pedestrian Marxist writer, a figurehead ruler for the much abler Hafizullah Amin. Leaders of the Parcham faction were forced into exile or imprisoned after June 1978. Khalq tried to move fast to expand its narrow base of support, but a misconceived and brutally executed programme of reforms, an extraordinary personality cult around the unlikely figure of Taraki, together with purges of opponents, frightened away potential sympathizers. Khalq militants showed they had little understanding of, and even less sympathy with, traditional Afghan society. They rode roughshod over conservative customs, alienating the rural poor as well as landlords and *mullas* (Muslim clergy). A popular uprising and mutiny in the army garrison of Herat in March 1979 unnerved the frail PDPA regime, and was the signal for risings in many other provinces.

The Soviet investment of money, men and prestige was steadily rising in Afghanistan. Immediately after the Saur Revolution a series of new major agreements was signed between Kabul and Moscow, while economic ties with East European states of the Comecon bloc multiplied. By 1979 the Kabul regime was more than ever dependent on the USSR, which was providing alone over half its loans and aid. In the military and technical spheres, too, the place of Soviet officers and officials rapidly grew, as they took over from capable, trained Afghans arrested in purges or dismissed from their posts. As guerrilla resistance spread in the summer of 1979 through many of the country's twenty-eight provinces, and army units defected with their weapons, Russia airlifted military equipment, new warplanes and military 'advisers', including pilots and army officers on active service.

At the same time, hitherto cordial links with important non-communist states were deteriorating. After the shooting in bizarre circumstances in Kabul of US ambassador Adolph Dubs in February 1979, Washington froze its aid, pulled out Peace Corps volunteers and failed to appoint a new ambassador. All prospect of Iranian cooperation in developing infrastructure by alternative trade routes via Iran disappeared with the chaos of the Islamic Revolution. It was Iran as well as Pakistan which was blamed by the Taraki/Amin government for organizing uprisings in the Afghan provinces from the spring of 1979.

The troubles besetting the Taraki regime were, at this stage at least, almost entirely home-grown; spontaneous uprisings in many rural areas by tribes of the well-armed Pushtun borderlands, and by Tajik, Hazara and other hardy ethnic groups north of the Hindu Kush, were, however, joined by activists of initially tiny Afghan exile parties based in Peshawar, capital of Pakistan's North-West Frontier. The parties' expanding influence inside Afghanistan alarmed the Taraki regime. The ideology of Muslim Fundamentalism blended with nationalism, justifying resistance as *jihad** against a communist, alien regime. Crucial to this growth in influence of obscure exile leaders was the freedom to organize from Peshawar granted by the military government of Pakistan, and authority given them over rapidly increasing numbers of Afghan refugees.

Even so, the Soviet-backed PDPA regime could probably have held on to power indefinitely, for it had some support in the armed forces and from youth elements in the capital. Its enemies were many, but localized, disunited, untrained and poorly armed. With secret-police prisons, and full coercive powers of the state, the party was strong.

The murder of Taraki

It was at this juncture that the top leaders of Khalq fell out. Favoured by the Russians, Taraki nevertheless lost out and was murdered. When Hafizullah Amin formally replaced his 'Great Teacher' in September 1979, he blamed on Taraki the murders, arrests and disappearances carried out by the PDPA regime. There are a number of clues, but still some dark areas, as to why the Russians felt it necessary to intervene by invading Afghanistan at the end of 1979. Amin was too independent, a nationalist rather than a pliant tool, erratic, brutal and ultimately unreliable. Soviet advisers in Kabul may well have felt that Amin's regime was too unpopular for protests to be a serious nuisance. There may, too, have been apprehension about imminent chaos along the sensitive Soviet borders in Central Asia, through civil war.

The Soviet invasion

What had been largely ignored until the invasion were the precise terms of the Treaty of Friendship and Cooperation signed in 1978 between Afghanistan and the USSR. It had serious implications for the independence of this small land, for by the treaty the USSR was committed to giving military assistance if so requested by the Afghan government. The sending of the 'limited military contingents' into Afghanistan was justified by this treaty, according to Soviet spokesmen, though they found it hard to explain who or what represented the Afghan government in December 1979, if not Amin's regime, which the Russians replaced by that of Babrak Karmal.

The Soviet invasion itself was carefully planned and brilliantly executed. Only minimal and ineffectual resistance by Afghan army units appears to have taken place in the last days of 1979. The force of some 85,000 Soviet troops (rising to 120,000 by 1983) was anyway larger than the demoralized Afghan army, spread out around the country. Moreover, well-placed Soviet advisers in Afghan army bases apparently helped deceive pro-Amin units as to the significance of the operation until a bridgehead in Kabul airport and essential installations were assured.

International repercussions to the invasion were swift and fierce, expressed in resolutions before the UN Islamic Conference, the EEC and other bodies. Inside Afghanistan, popular reaction was also not slow to show itself. In the first months of 1980, large-scale civil demonstrations took place in Kabul, Kandahar, Herat and other cities, in protest at the presence of Soviet troops. A general strike in the capital in February 1980 was accompanied by mass civil disturbances, put down by troops with heavy loss of life. At night through the winter, scores of thousands of Afghans in the cities gathered on their flat roofs to cry, 'Allahu akbar' (God is great), to show their defiance of the Soviet invasion and the Karmal regime imposed by foreign troops.

The Soviet invasion marked a watershed; what had been a localized civil war became after 1980 – gradually and unevenly in the different regions – a national guerrilla resistance. All the Afghan opposition parties based in exile gained in prestige, and soon in influence inside Afghanistan. The six major parties attracted large-scale funds and modern arms from foreign backers in the USA, China and the Gulf states of Saudi Arabia and Kuwait. All such aid was channelled through Pakistan, whose unpopular military regime under General Zia ul-Haq suddenly found favour with many governments. Foreign interest or help for the Afghan opposition had been very restricted until 1980, with Afghan Mujahidin in general inadequately armed and dependent on captured weapons or those turned over by deserters. The Soviet military presence in Afghanistan alarmed especially the states of the region, stirring their concern on strategic grounds as well as, in some cases, claims of 'Islamic solidarity', or sympathy with a justified Islamic struggle. In this way Soviet allegations of massive foreign intervention in Afghanistan – advanced to justify the invasion – have proved a self-fulfilling prophecy.

Pages from a book of political strip-cartoons produced by the Afghan Resistance

Babrak Karmal

Born in 1929 into a prominent family, Karmal began his career in politics as a student activist at Kabul University in 1949. He was one of seven full members of the PDPA in 1965, and was elected to parliament in the first elections held under the 1964 Constitution, where Karmal was an eloquent left-wing critic of the regime. One of the best-known leaders of the Parcham faction of the PDPA, Karmal was briefly appointed as deputy prime minister after the Saur Revolution in April 1978, but was forced into exile in Czechoslovakia in July.

Karmal returned to Afghanistan only at the beginning of 1980, after the Soviet invasion. He replaced his old rival Hafizullah Amin as president and general secretary of the PDPA Central Committee.

Afghan refugee children attend camp school in North West Frontier Province, Pakistan

Pakistan and Iran, the two key neighbour states, were sucked steadily deeper into the Afghan problem from 1980. They received a massive number of refugees (2.5m and at least 1m respectively) generated by bombardments, air raids and deliberate sweeps by Soviet-led forces to clear strategically sensitive areas of their population. In the case of both host countries, Afghan parties were permitted to organize the large refugee communities and recruit Mujahidin from the refugee camps strung along the Afghan borders. In the case of Iran, though, official relations with the larger, Sunni-dominated exile parties were far from easy, and the limited aid given to the Afghan resistance seems to have gone mainly to Shi'a groups based in central Afghanistan (Hazarajat).

The guerrilla war

Most observers had predicted early on that the Russians with all their military muscle would rapidly crush the Afghan rebels. The most surprising lessons of the guerrilla war have been the tenacity of Afghan Mujahidin in the face of overwhelming odds, and the inability of Soviet-led forces to exploit to the full their total command of the air. The demoralization of the Afghan army, standing at 80,000 in 1978, resulted in the number of effective troops dwindling to less than one-third of this by 1982. Only press-gangs in the towns and extensions of conscription to wider groups of males kept up numbers, with desertion remaining a constant problem. In these circumstances, the Afghan army was bound to remain a junior partner – not always reliable, either – to the Soviet army in anti-guerrilla operations.

Politics today

In 1985 there was evidence of the growing use of elite troops, Soviet commando or *Spetznaz* units, in well-planned ambushes or raids against guerrillas. Soviet military advisers have also trained a considerable force of Afghan gendarmerie and tribal militia units, which have a growing role in counter-insurgency operations. However, even the escalating warfare seen in 1985–6, with the largest forces of Soviet–Kabul government troops yet deployed, seems to have failed in its goal of crushing the strongholds of the resistance.

The fighting in the summer of 1985 in the key strategic province of Paktya provided a significant example of the changing face of the warfare. Paktya controls access into the heart of Afghanistan from the Pakistan border, while its terrain is unusually favourable to

Afghan Mujahidin in the Parwan Province north of Kabul

large-scale anti-guerrilla sweeps, involving an entire Soviet division. For the first time in this war, Mujahidin fought a conventional battle of positions, digging in with trenches and using very effectively light artillery, in the siege of the garrison town of Khost. It confirmed doubts that the Soviet–Afghan forces can win this war without a massive increase in troops, and inevitably, too, in casualties.

Many centres of Afghan resistance are still poorly armed, with little or no military training for volunteers for *jihad*. Overall, the level of guerrilla ability remains strikingly uneven, and some of the best guerrilla commanders have lost their lives in heavy fighting.

But in spite of these problems, morale is very high, and inside Afghanistan, the outstanding commanders have attracted general support, regardless often of party or tribal rivalries which still plague the resistance in some regions. Many of the emergent leaders are young and well educated, like Commander Massoud in the Panjshir Valley (north of Kabul), and more interested in regaining independence than in pursuing the narrow aims of party leaders based in exile.

Although the supply of foreign weapons via Pakistan has become crucial in some border areas to the success of the resistance, it is far from essential. Even with very limited weapons or other aid from outside, some able commanders have created guerrilla strongholds, as in Herat (on the Iranian border with Khorasan), where Mujahidin led by Isma'il Khan were still in control of much of the city after six years of struggle. Afghanistan's second city is much battered by frequent Soviet air raids, but most of Herat remains outside government control in 1986. Even in the capital, Kabul, a night-time curfew imposed in 1978 is still in force, a testimony to the difficulties the regime has in ensuring security.

Kabul

It is the capital, though, which is the vital constituency for the Karmal regime. Its population has probably doubled to 1.5m since the war began, because of the influx of rural families from ruined villages. Kabul may now account for 15 per cent of those Afghans left in the country, among them many children. More than ever Kabul is the centre of an education drive, since schools in the provinces are mostly burned or abandoned. Education has a high political content, and even in the 10–14 age group, Young Pioneers groups have been organized. Also on the Soviet model – and directly organized by Soviet, Czech and East German advisers – are special classes designed to attract Afghan youth to such activities as vocational courses or literacy classes, linked to instruction in 'political ideas', or pro-regime propaganda.

At the higher level of Kabul University and the Polytechnic, the combination of war crisis, arrests, defections and the constant threat of military conscription have depleted the ranks of Afghan teachers and students alike. Partly for this reason, many thousands of Afghan students left for higher studies in the USSR and other socialist states. The strong existing links of Kabul University with Western universities in the USA, France and West Germany were ruptured in 1980.

The Afghan capital is a haven of peace, relatively speaking, for ordinary Afghans keen to escape the dangers and privations of the anti-guerrilla war. Much of Kabul's food and fuel needs have to be satisfied from the USSR, across long communication lines. The USSR has built a bridge across the Amu Darya (Oxus) frontier, and is proceeding – albeit painfully and slowly – with railway construction across the Hindu Kush. This poorly developed land's infrastructure is steadily being integrated into that of Soviet Central Asia, where its economic and political future may well lie.

Support for the resistance

It is, however, very difficult to predict the outcome of the Afghan struggle. Efforts mounted by the UN to reach a peace settlement seem to have foundered so far, mainly on a timetable and precise conditions for a withdrawal of Soviet troops. Even if agreement is reached at Geneva, or between the superpowers on the future of Afghanistan, it must remain uncertain how the Afghan people react to a dictated settlement. Afghanistan's traditional society is certainly in crisis, but the resistance does appear to enjoy general support from the Afghan population. It relies upon the rural population for practical help of all kinds, which largely explains the ability of the Mujahidin to fight on.

Even Kabul, protected as it is by large Soviet and Afghan army

Afghan refugees in a Pakistani camp

posts, still experiences frequent guerrilla attacks mounted often with the help of collaborators in the capital. One sign of the ambivalent loyalties of many Afghans is the regular circulation in the cities of clandestine opposition newsletters (*shab-name* or 'night letters'), really only possible under curfew conditions by extensive cooperation between army officers, civil servants and PDPA activists. The struggle for Afghanistan still clearly has elements of a civil war, with families divided in sympathies as well as in exile, and uncertain about their future. The war is far from over.

Economy and society today

A sharp decline in most sectors of the economy has taken place since 1978. Agriculture*, the backbone of Afghanistan's economy, has been badly hit by the war, though unevenly. The exodus of millions of villagers as refugees has greatly reduced the rural workforce – but also the number of mouths to feed. Destruction of crops, livestock and the *qanats* (the fragile water irrigation system) has been serious in many areas and some farmers have turned to a subsistence economy instead of growing cash crops. Many rural areas are outside the control of the Kabul government, and lack of state-produced fertilizer has reduced crop yields. However, some important traditional exports like raisins have had record crops in recent years. Foreign trade links have grown rapidly with the USSR and other Comecon states, but trade is still maintained with many other countries, too.

Afghan industry is weakly developed, and shortages of raw materials, electricity and of a skilled workforce have closed down enterprises around the country, although Afghanistan's considerable mineral assets have been prospected and some are being exploited in spite of war-time disruption. The natural gas industry centred in Jowzjan province, close to the Soviet border, accounts for most of the state revenues, with 97 per cent of the 2.6 bn cu metres annual production of gas piped to the USSR. The country's weak and damaged infrastructure is also receiving attention, with emphasis on the energy sector, which is being expanded with Soviet and Czechoslovak technical help and loans.

Afghan society is highly traditional. Almost 90 per cent of its 15m people were living in isolated rural communities in 1978, with distinctive ethnic and tribal cultural traditions. The war has broken down many barriers between rival tribes and ethnic groups, forcing them to cooperate and spreading a new consciousness of a common Afghan nationality. Nationalism and Islam have proved a potent mixture, being the inspiration for the stubborn guerrilla resistance to Soviet domination and a Soviet-backed Marxist regime in Kabul.

The pattern of traditional, pre-1978 Afghan society has altered dramatically and for good. Much of the development over three decades of rural clinics and schools has been destroyed in the war. The country was still very underdeveloped and poor compared with its neighbours, even before 1978, with a low rate of literacy even for young males and a high mortality rate for babies. There is now among many Afghans, refugees as well as villagers and town-dwellers, a backlash against most forms of secular and modern civilization, and an intense suspicion of state schools – with reason – as a means of political indoctrination by the Marxist regime.

AH

General (Dr) Najibullah

President Babrak Karmal was suddenly replaced as head of the ruling PDPA in May 1986 by the much younger Dr Najibullah. Born in 1947 in a wealthy Pushtun family of Paktya, Najibullah was a senior member of the Parcham faction of the PDPA, and like Karmal was sent away to an Afghan embassy abroad soon after the Saur Revolution in 1978. Returning from the USSR in 1980, after the Soviet intervention, Najibullah was made head of Khad, the Afghan secret police, which has had a key role in the anti-guerrilla war. Khad is a state within the state, with a large budget, KGB training, and an extensive network of agents and informers. Najibullah at once showed himself a more energetic and dynamic leader than the ailing Karmal, flying to the provincial towns and making fiery speeches promising victory against the counter-revolution. He also spoke of concessions – free elections, a new constitution and peace. However, tensions and gunfights in the capital as well as provincial centres showed there was hostility even within the PDPA to Najibullah's appointment, and there was no serious prospect of the new leader rapidly healing the deep factional rifts within the ruling Marxist party.

Further reading

L. Adamec, *Afghanistan's Foreign Affairs to the Mid-Twentieth Century: relations with the USSR, Germany and Britain* (Tucson, Arizona 1974)
A. Arnold, *Afghanistan's Two-Party Communism. Parcham and Khalq* (Stanford, California, 1983)
H. S. Bradsher, *Afghanistan and the Soviet Union* (Durham, NC, 1985)
L. Dupree, *Afghanistan* (Princeton, 1980)
V. Gregorian, *The Emergence of Modern Afghanistan: politics of reform and modernization, 1880–1946* (Stanford, 1969)
A. Hyman, *Afghanistan under Soviet Domination 1964–83* (London, 1984)
O. Roy, *Islam and Resistance in Afghanistan* (Cambridge, 1986)

Algeria

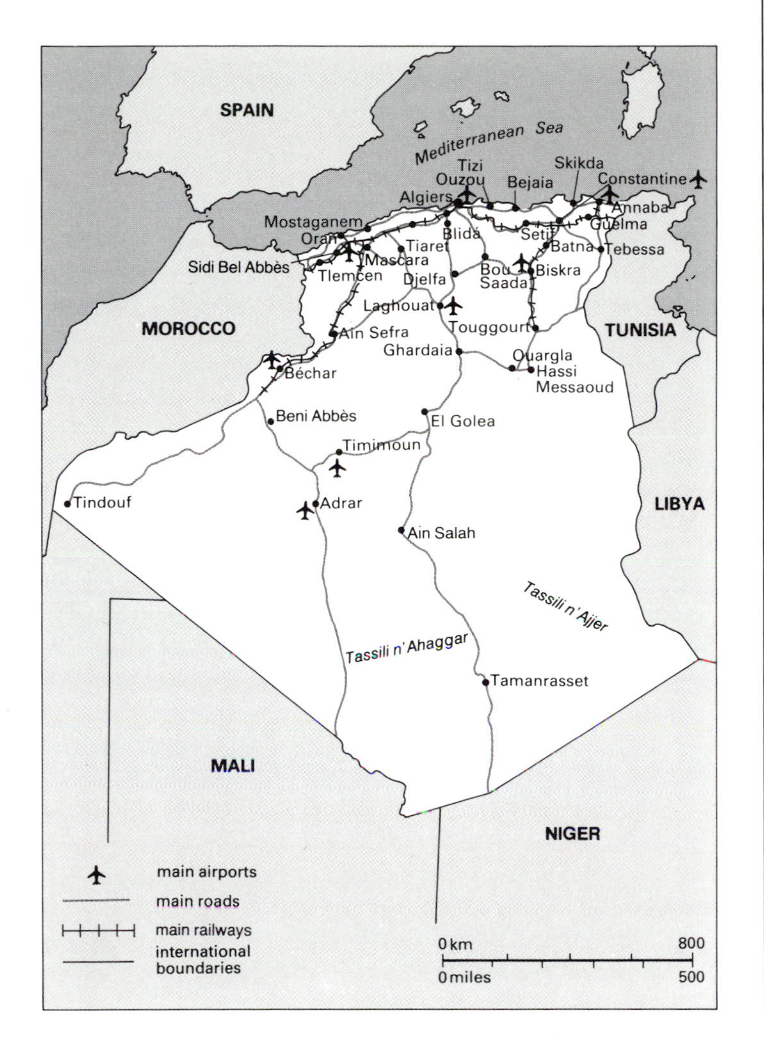

Official title	The Democratic and Popular Republic of Algeria
Area	2,381,741 sq. km
Population (1984)	21.56 million
Government and constitution	Algeria is, in principle, a one-party state ruled by the National Liberation Front (FLN), but power is concentrated in the officer corps of the armed forces and the administrative elite. The armed forces provide a fifth of the delegates at the regular five-yearly Party Congress which elects the 160-member FLN Central Committee and the general secretary, who is automatically the FLN nominee for the presidency of the Republic, subject to endorsement by popular vote.
Currency	1 Algerian dinar = 100 centimes; US $1 = 4.90 dinars
Language	Arabic (official). Berber and French are also spoken
Religion	Islam is the official religion of the state. Most Algerians are Sunni Muslims. There is also a small Christian community, mostly of European descent
Climate	Temperate on the coast, varying to hot and dry in the south. In Algiers (altitude 59 m) the hottest month is August, with temperature ranges between 22 and 29°C (average daily minimum and maximum); and the coldest month is January, with temperatures ranging between 9 and 15°C. The driest month is July, with 1 mm average rainfall and the wettest month is December with 140 mm average rainfall

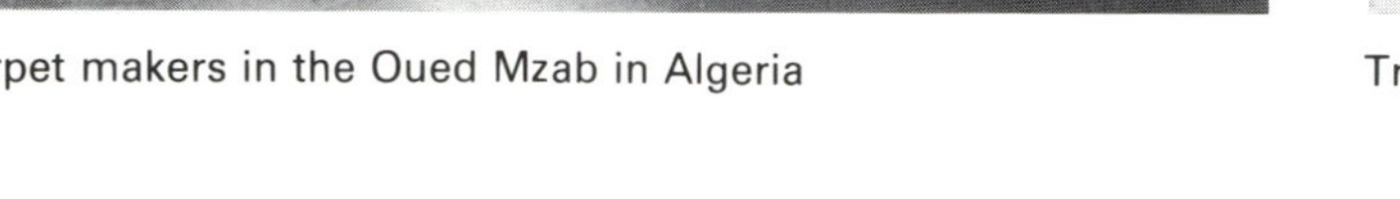

Carpet makers in the Oued Mzab in Algeria

Traditional fairground swings, 1958

Geography and topography

Four-fifths of Algeria is desert. The remaining fifth, the north, varies in depth along the 1000 km coastline from between 250 km in the west to 350 in the east and contains 92 per cent of the population. It is divided into two zones, the Tell, which is Mediterranean in climate and ecology, and the High Plateaux of the interior, which have a continental climate characterized by low rainfall and extremes of temperature. The Tell is dominated by the coastal Atlas, notably the Ouarsenis range, the Jurjura (Mount Lalla Khadidja, 2308 m) and the Aurès massif (Jebel Chélia, 2326 m). There are three small coastal plains, at Oran in the west, Algiers (the Mitidja) in the centre and Annaba in the east. The principal river is the Chélif, which rises in the Tell Atlas and flows west to reach the sea near Mostaganem. To the south, the thinly populated High Plateaux stretch from Morocco to the Tunisian frontier and form the pastoral zone of the economy. They are themselves spanned by a belt of salt-marsh basins, the *chotts*, and are separated from the desert proper by the ranges of the Saharan Atlas, which also span the country from west to east. The Saharan region is varied, comprising vast sand deserts, immense stretches of rocky plateau and the dramatic mountains of the Tassili n'Ahaggar (Mount Tahat, 3031 m) and the Tassili n'Ajjer in the far south and south-east. As a result of a massive rural exodus since 1962, the urban population of Algeria is now approximately 45 per cent of the total. The principal towns are Algiers (1982 pop.: 2,165,000), Oran (1978 pop.: 680,000), Constantine (1978 pop.: 489,000), Blida (1978 pop.: 438,000), Setif (1978 pop.: 348,000), Sidi Bel Abbès (1978 pop.: 330,000), Annaba (1978 pop.: 306,000) and Tlemcen (1978 pop.: 281,000).

Peoples

The indigenous Berber* population of Algeria was largely Arabized following the Arab influx in the seventh and eleventh centuries, but a minority (about 20 per cent) have retained Berber speech and customs to this day. The principal Berberophone populations are the Kabyles near Algiers (*c.* 2.5m), the Chaouia of the Aurès and Sud-Constantinois (*c.* 1.2m), the Mzabis of the Mzab Valley in the northern Sahara (*c.* 100,000) and the Tuareg of the Ahaggar and Ajjer mountains (at most 25,000). Other much smaller Berberophone populations survive in parts of western Algeria and in certain Saharan oases. Ottoman rule* (1516–1830) introduced a Turkish element into the population which has since been assimilated, as has the Moorish element composed largely of refugees from Andalusia. Algeria also used to have a Jewish* community of long standing. This was assimilated into the European population during the colonial period and almost all of it left the country at independence. The large, if heterogeneous, European community established in the wake of the French* conquest numbered about a million by 1962. Nearly all of its members chose to retain French citizenship and left the country soon after independence. As a result of labour migration, there are about a million Algerians in Western Europe, over 700,000 of them in France.

Religions

Practically all Algerians are Sunni* Muslims of the Maliki* rite. The exceptions are a small band of Sunnis of the Hanafi* rite – a vestige of the Turkish period – and, more important, the Mzabis of the Sahara who have long adhered to the Ibadi* variant of Kharijism* and enjoy local religious autonomy. Following the European exodus, the Christian community has dwindled to a few thousand and most churches in Algeria have been demolished or converted into mosques since 1962. Official Islam is the heir to the reform movement led by Shaykh Abdelhamid Ben Badis and the Association of ʿUlama (doctors of religious law), whose combination of fundamentalist orthodoxy and modernism in opposition to the Sufi* orders and the traditional cult of the saints contributed to the growth of Algerian nationalism in the 1920s and 1930s. A dissident Islamic tendency has developed since the mid-1970s, however, inspired partly by the Muslim Brotherhood (*Ikhwan**) and partly by the Iranian Revolution.

History up to 1939

Northern Algeria acquired its present boundaries under the Turkish Regency (1516–1830), when it was nominally a province of the Ottoman Empire but in effect an autonomous state. The Turks formally unified Algeria (although large parts of the interior successfully resisted the central power), but failed to integrate it economically or politically. It was the socio-economic transformation initiated by French colonialism which laid the material basis for the subsequent national integration of Algeria.

The French conquest began in 1830 and quickly overthrew the Turkish state, but then faced unrelenting resistance from the indigenous population. From 1832 to 1847 this was led by the Amir ʿAbd al-Qadir, who for long periods controlled much of western and central Algeria. Following his capture in 1847, resistance continued in Kabylia until 1857 and major rebellions occurred in the Sud-Oranais in 1864 and in Kabylia and the Constantinois in 1871. In 1863 and 1873 the French enacted agrarian laws which made land a commodity and thus undermined the basis of tribal cohesion, and European settlers were encouraged to take advantage of the newly available land and consolidate the French presence. By 1900, over 2 million hectares of the best land in Algeria was in European ownership, most of it devoted to highly capitalized cereal crops and viticulture. From the 1920s onwards, however, many settlers sold up their holdings and moved to the coastal cities, progressively abandoning the hinterland to the Muslim population.

Early nationalism

The first stirrings of modern anti-colonialism were prompted by the conscription of Muslims during the First World War. By the mid-1920s, three main tendencies had developed: the movement of the French-educated *évolués*, seeking equal rights for Muslims within the framework of French rule; the cultural nationalism of Ben Badis and the Association of ʿUlama which, while not explicitly challenging the colonial order, strongly attacked the 'assimilationist' perspectives of the *évolués* from a nationalist standpoint; and, finally, the revolutionary populist nationalism of the Étoile Nord-Africaine (1926–36), based on the labour migrants in France, and its successor, the Parti du Peuple Algérien (PPA, 1937–54), both of which were led by the charismatic Messali Hadj and vigorously canvassed a separatist solution to the national question. The repeated failure of the first tendency to obtain significant reforms from French governments paralysed by the settler lobby strengthened the position of the separatist movement, despite the banning of the PPA in September 1939.

History since the Second World War

France's defeat in 1940 and the democratic principles proclaimed by the Allies encouraged the nationalist movement in its demand for the right of self-determination with which the former leader of the 'assimilationist' tendency, Farhat Abbas, associated himself from 1943 onwards. But liberated France proved determined to maintain Algeria as an integral part of the French Republic and on VE Day, 8 May 1945, an abortive rising instigated by the clandestine PPA in eastern Algeria was repressed with over 8000 Muslim deaths. Thereafter, the nationalist movement was divided between those favouring a legalist and electoralist strategy, notwithstanding systematic ballot-rigging by the colonial authorities, and those adhering, with Messali, to a revolutionary vision, despite the discovery and dismantling of the PPA's para-military Organisation Spéciale (OS) in 1950. It was in order to transcend this division that a handful of former OS activists launched the armed struggle on 1 November 1954, in the name of a new organization, the Front de Libération Nationale (FLN).

'La Question'; French soldiers preparing to interrogate an Algerian prisoner during 'Operation Bigeaud', March 1956

By mid-1958 the war had spread throughout northern Algeria and the FLN had absorbed or eliminated all other tendencies in Muslim politics, while the inability of successive French governments to resolve the crisis had led to the fall of the Fourth Republic and the return to power of General de Gaulle. It took de Gaulle three years to neutralize opposition to his policy within the French army, but serious negotiations with the Provisional Government of the Algerian Republic (GPRA), which the FLN had set up in Tunis in September 1958, finally got under way in 1961, leading to the Evian Agreements and a cease-fire on 18 March 1962. Bitter opposition to Algerian independence continued up to the last moment, however, in the campaign of terror mounted by the Organisation de l'Armée Secrète (OAS), led by diehard settlers and dissident army officers. When independence finally came on 3 July (officially 5 July) 1962, the polarization between Muslim and European communities was so extreme that most of the latter immediately fled the country, leaving its economy and infrastructure in chaos.

Ahmed Ben Bella

Born 25 December 1916 at Maghnia near the Moroccan border, the son of a poor peasant, Ahmed Ben Bella fought with the French forces in Europe from 1943 to 1945, attaining the rank of adjutant and distinguishing himself at Monte Cassino. On his return to Algeria in 1945 he joined the PPA and was elected a municipal councillor for Maghnia in 1947. As chief of the OS in the Oran region, he took part in a famous hold-up of the Oran post office in 1949. Overall chief of the OS from 1949, he was arrested in 1950 and sentenced to seven years in prison but escaped in 1952 and made his way to Cairo, where he played a leading role in the External Delegation of the FLN. He was captured with other FLN leaders in October 1956, and spent the rest of the war in prison. Victorious in the power struggle in 1962, he was a charismatic and imaginative president of Algeria, but his impulsiveness and individualism alienated many of his colleagues in government, in particular his Minister of Defence, Houari Boumedienne, who deposed him in a military coup on 19 June 1965. After fifteen years of imprisonment without trial, Ben Bella was released on President Chadli's instructions in 1980 and has since lived in exile. His recent political positions have appeared much less socialist and much more Islamic than in the past, but in May 1984 he founded the Mouvement pour la Démocratie en Algérie and in December 1985 he finally joined forces with Hocine Aït Ahmed on a common platform calling for a pluralist democratic regime in Algeria.

Ben Bella: emergence and eclipse

Independence also precipitated a power struggle within the FLN, from which Ahmed Ben Bella*, one of its founder members, eventually emerged victorious with the support of the 'army of the frontiers' in Tunisia and Morocco under Colonel Houari Boumedienne* at the expense of the GPRA and the exhausted guerrilla units of the interior. Ben Bella's election as Algeria's first president did not end the faction fighting, however, nor did the military coup by Boumedienne and his followers on 19 June 1965. It was only after the further, abortive, coup in December 1967 by army chief-of-staff Colonel Tahar Zbiri that the Boumedienne regime settled down and political stability returned to the country.

Building a nation

The next four years (1968–71) saw the construction of the state apparatus at national, regional and local level and the development of a vast public sector of the economy, at the expense of both foreign capital and the experiments in workers' self-management undertaken during the Ben Bella period. Instead, public corporations (*sociétés nationales*) on the French model were introduced, together with central planning of public investment. This phase culminated in the successful nationalization of Algeria's oil* and gas industry in 1971, whereupon Boumedienne unexpectedly embarked upon an audacious strategy of popular mobilization around a number of ambitious social reforms, notably the 'agrarian revolution', the introduction of a national health service and that of 'socialist management' in the public sector. The 'left turn' was finally consecrated in the distinctly socialist content of the National Charter, adopted by referendum after an unprecedented public debate in June 1976. It also occasioned the departure of Boumedienne's more conservative colleagues and, in particular, focused attention on the shortcomings of the party in the political system. Boumedienne sought to revitalize the FLN by recruiting new and explicitly socialist blood into its ranks, in order to enhance its capacity to mobilize the population and control the sprawling bureaucratic apparatus. The appointment of his close follower Colonel Mohamed Salah Yahiaoui to the new post of Coordinator of the Party in 1977 heralded a major campaign to this end, designed to climax with the holding of a party congress, the first since 1964, which would elect a central committee and a political bureau and adopt new statutes and so launch the party on its new role at the centre of Algerian political life. It was on the eve of this congress that Boumedienne fell ill. He died on 27 December 1978.

When the congress opened in late January 1979, the struggle for the succession had been resolved in favour of the senior ranking army officer, Colonel Chadli Bendjedid. Neither Yahiaoui on the left nor the more right-wing foreign minister Abdelaziz Bouteflika had secured sufficient military support to sustain his candidature. The army's choice was promptly endorsed by the congress, underlining the true balance of forces in Algerian politics.

Politics today

It took President Chadli several years to establish his authority fully. By July 1981, Yahiaoui, Bouteflika and other Boumedienne notables had been evicted from the regime, but the government also faced opposition from autonomous social movements, notably the Berberists in Kabylia and the radical Islamic movement. Resentment of the official refusal to recognize Berber language and culture exploded in a spectacular movement of strikes and demonstrations in Kabylia in March-April 1980, but the government managed to contain this unrest without making significant concessions to it. The Islamic radicals enjoyed a measure of official tolerance until late 1982, when the government clamped down on the movement, arresting many of its leaders.

Both power struggles and protest movements had developed in the context of a protracted debate within government circles over the economic development strategy pursued since 1965. By 1983, the new orientation was clear. With the world economic recession and falling oil prices, the government has retreated from the ambitious industrialization objectives of the Boumedienne period, adopting a more cautious hydrocarbons policy and an unprecedentedly positive attitude towards the private sector, while promising renewed attention to agriculture and water supply. Bureaucratic inefficiency is also being tackled in a new way: instead of subjecting the administration to greater party control, the government has fragmented the public corporations and state farms into a plethora of smaller enterprises, to facilitate proper accounting, encourage profitability and eliminate buck-passing. It has also launched a drive against corruption, with the State Audit Court investigating irregularities in the conduct of public companies and government departments.

Houari Boumedienne

Born August 1932 at Al-Hassainia (formerly Clauzel), near Guelma in eastern Algeria, Boumedienne's real name was Mohamed Ben Brahim Boukharrouba and he was the son of a small farmer of Kabyle origin. He received a traditional Arabo-Islamic education at Constantine and joined the PPA shortly before leaving in 1952 for Cairo, where he joined the FLN two years later. In 1955 he made his way to western Algeria, where he joined the guerrilla forces in *Wilaya* V (Oranie), assuming the *wilaya* command with the rank of colonel in October 1957. Chief of the western general staff at Oujda, Morocco, in September 1958, he was promoted chief of the unified general staff with his HQ at Ghardimaou in Tunisia in February 1960. In conflict with the provisional government, he supported Ben Bella in 1962 and became Minister of Defence and first vice-president of the Republic, before deposing Ben Bella in June 1965 and taking power as president of the Council of the Revolution. A rigidly self-effacing ruler at first, his unflamboyant but methodical approach to governing Algeria slowly won him public respect and by the mid-1970s he conspicuously dominated his regime, while orienting policy in an increasingly socialist direction. His sudden illness and death in December 1978 came as a major shock to the Algerian public, and while the state institutions he created survived the transition crisis without difficulty, his conception of Algerian socialism died with him.

Ben Bella with Boumedienne, shortly before the latter engineered a successful coup against him

Chadli Bendjedid

Born 14 April 1929 at Boutheldja, near Annaba in north-eastern Algeria, the son of a relatively prosperous farmer, Chadli joined the guerrilla forces of the FLN in 1955 and spent most of the war in the Tunisian frontier zone, attaining the rank of captain. From late 1962 onwards, he was in charge of the Fifth Military Region (Constantine) with the rank of commandant, before taking command of the Second Military Region (Oran) in June 1964, a post he retained until 1979. A member of Boumedienne's Council of the Revolution, 1965–77, promoted colonel in 1969, he was rumoured to be out of sympathy with Boumedienne's socialist policies in the 1970s. Apparently uninterested in ideology or doctrinal debate, conservative in his political instincts if also, reputedly, liberal and tolerant by personal inclination, Chadli's preferred role in government is that of arbiter and conciliator, leaving the advocacy of particular policies or projects to others.

Better relations with the West

Changes in foreign policy have reflected the 'new course' at home. In place of Boumedienne's radical anti-imperialist conception of non-alignment in the 1970s, Chadli's Algeria has sought better relations with the West and has distanced itself from the communist bloc. Algeria's mediation in the Iranian hostages affair led to improved relations with the United States, and in November 1983 Chadli became the first Algerian president to pay a state visit to France, although relations between the two countries have remained volatile. Algeria has also sought better relations with her neighbours, but the rhetoric of Maghribi unity has failed to persuade Morocco to negotiate a settlement of the Western Saharan question and Algeria remains the principal supporter of the Polisario Front. With Tunisia, a close entente has developed, at the expense of Algeria's former alliance with Qadhafi's* Libya. The Libyan–Moroccan treaty of August 1984 was badly received in Algiers and, while the polarization of the Maghrib into two hostile axes appears to have been arrested, tension in the region remains high.

Following the Fifth Party Congress in December 1983, Chadli's nomination for a second presidential term was confirmed by popular vote in January 1984. During the celebrations in 1984 of the thirtieth anniversary of the revolution, the government sought to heal old wounds by rehabilitating victims of war-time purges and awarding medals to anonymous war veterans and defeated political rivals alike. It also invited opponents in exile to return home on condition that they abandoned all political activity, and some of them did so. Among those who refused this offer was ex-President Ahmed Ben Bella, whom Chadli had released from his fifteen years' confinement in 1980 and who announced the formation of the 'Mouvement pour la Démocratie en Algérie' (MDA) in May 1984.

The following year was dominated by a lengthy public debate, held at the government's instigation, on the National Charter adopted in 1976. The purpose of this was to bring the charter up to date and into line with changes in government policy since 1979. A much revised text, in which new emphasis was placed on Islam, was finally adopted at an Extraordinary Party Congress in December, for subsequent submission to popular ratification. The debate took place against a background of renewed unrest. Six members of the security forces were killed in clashes with a small armed band of Islamic radicals in the mountains south of Algiers in August and October and heavy jail sentences were imposed in a trial of Berberists and human rights activists in December. Moves towards the unification of the *émigré* opposition were announced in London on 16 December 1985 by Ben Bella and Hocine Aït Ahmed, a co-founder with Ben Bella of the original FLN, who has been in exile since 1966.

The economy and society today

Algeria has small but high-quality oil deposits and vast natural gas reserves in the Sahara. Under Boumedienne, her economic strategy was 'to sow oil to reap industry', but since 1979 the government has slowed the rate of new capital formation and emphasized rather the need to achieve respectable productivity levels in the industries which have already been established. These include steel, mechanical engineering, chemicals, petrochemicals, cement, vehicle assembly, electrical goods and textiles, but hydrocarbons sales account for no less than 98 per cent of total export revenues. A policy of diversifying hydrocarbons sales away from oil towards natural gas and petroleum products, particularly condensate, has enabled revenues to be maintained despite falling oil prices, although disputes over volume and price terms have plagued gas contracts with American and West European customers in the last two years.

A major aim of the second five-year plan (1985–9) is to increase agricultural production in order to reduce Algeria's alarming food deficit. Much new investment in water supply, dams and irrigation is scheduled and private enterprise in agriculture is receiving strong encouragement, as it is in other sectors of the economy (light industry, services), in contrast with the severely socialist approach of the 1970s.

Official figures put unemployment at 16.9 per cent in May 1985 but the true percentage is almost certainly higher. The million-strong Algerian community in Western Europe is a subject of constant government concern, in view of the development of an

Central Algiers

anti-immigrant political movement in France. The new plan envisages the creation of a million new jobs by 1989 and it is hoped that this will enable many migrant workers to return home. The economic and social infrastructures are also due to receive much new investment in the plan, with 15.7 per cent of total investment being allocated to housing alone, reflecting the government's concern to deliver a better standard of living.

Algeria's population* is predominantly young and is still growing very fast, at over 3.2 per cent per annum. The government has at last begun, if timidly, to promote family planning and is also seeking to relocate industrial development in the interior, in order to ease the pressure on the coastal cities. Algeria's Islamic character has received fresh emphasis in government social policy in recent years, notably in the Family Code promulgated in 1984 despite opposition from an unofficial women's movement and, more broadly, the modernist wing of the intelligentsia. Arabization remains the centre-piece of cultural policy, together with the continued expansion of higher education, although emphasis on quality and standards in educational provision has begun to take precedence over quantitative growth. Official recognition continues to be denied to the Berber language, and this is likely to remain an extremely sore point in Algeria for some years to come. The two most popular Kabyle singers were jailed for three-year terms in late 1985.

HR

Further reading

I. Clegg, *Workers' Self-Management in Algeria* (London, 1971)
A. Horne, *A Savage War of Peace: Algeria 1954–1962* (London, 1977)
W. Knapp, *North West Africa, A Political and Economic Survey* (Oxford, 1977)
R. Lawless and A. Findlay, eds., *North Africa: contemporary politics and economic development* (London, 1984)
W. Quandt, *Revolution and Political Leadership: Algeria 1954–1968* (Cambridge, Mass. and London, 1969)

Bahrain

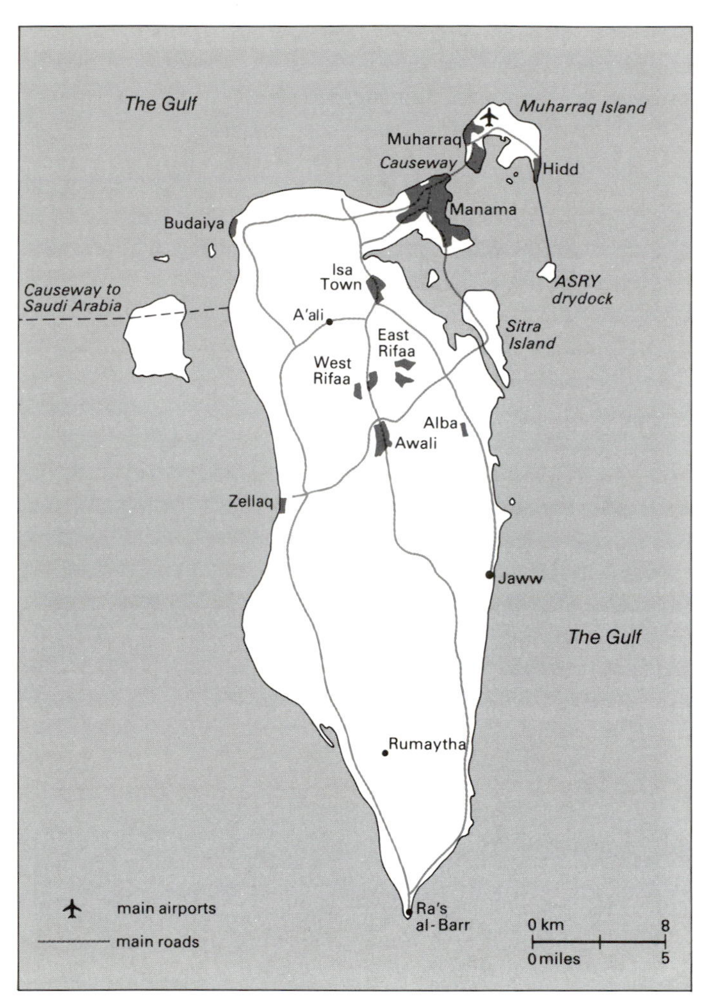

Official title	The State of Bahrain
Area	677.9 sq. km
Population	350,798 (1981 census)
Government and constitution	The Head of State, who appoints the cabinet, is the Amir. A National Assembly provided for by the 1973 constitution was dissolved by Amiri decree in August 1975
Currency	1 Bahrain dinar = 1000 fils; exchange rate fixed at US $1 = 376.0 fils since November 1980
Languages	Arabic (official), but English is widely spoken
Religion	Islam is the official religion of the state. The ruling family is Sunni although some 60 per cent of the population is Shi'i
Climate	Summer temperatures are hot, reaching 49°C in the shade, while the coldest winter month, January, sees temperatures ranging between 2.8°C and 28.3°C. Humidity can be extreme

Geography and topography

The state of Bahrain consists of an archipelago of thirty-three islands covering 678 km^2, of which only three, with a surface area of 539 km^2, are inhabited. For all practical purposes, however, Bahrain consists of the main island, Bahrain Island, which houses the major population concentration at Manama and which is linked to the second largest island of Muharraq by a causeway.

Bahrain is formed from a small limestone dome, rather like the neighbouring peninsula of Qatar. Erosion has formed a series of low-lying basins in the southern part of the island, separated by low limestone outcrops running either side of the limestone crest line. The northern section of the main island is dominated by its access to the sea through the coral reefs between Bahrain and Qatar. There are good artesian water supplies which have ensured the location of main population settlement in this part of the island.

Indeed, the relatively good access to underground water supplies – which are generated on the Arab peninsula and which pass through aquifer systems under the sea into the 'freshwater lens' system under the island – has traditionally made Bahrain one of the most fertile regions in the Gulf. The system breaks the surface in the northern part of the island, with one spring being as much as 10 m across. This access to underground water has compensated for the annual minimal rainfall of 70 mm.

Peoples

In 1983, the population* of Bahrain was estimated to be 400,000, with an annual growth rate of about 4.6 per cent – a growth level that it has maintained since 1978. As a result, 41 per cent of the Bahrain population is under 15 years of age. Of this overall population, about 67 per cent are native Bahrainis, while the rest are expatriates, mainly from the Indian subcontinent, Iran, Oman and the Far East.

According to the 1981 census, the economically active element of the population totalled 146,133 – 56 per cent of it being expatriate; the economically active expatriate male labour force totalled 74,348 – 51 per cent of the total. The total employed population was 137,892, including 123,221 males, of whom 73,917 were not Bahraini.

Religions

The majority of Bahrainis are Shi'i* Muslims, while the ruling groups are Sunni*. The concentration of Shi'is in Bahrain is the highest of any of the Arab Gulf states. In the overall population in 1981, 85 per cent were Muslim, 7.3 per cent Christian and the balance was made up from Asian religions.

History up to 1939

Within two years of the Prophet Muhammad's* death, Bahrain became a part of the Muslim world and has remained as such ever since. Given its closeness to Iran, it has always been open to influences from across the Gulf and, from 1603, was actually ruled by an Iranian Shi'i dynasty. In 1783, the dynasty's Arab governor of the island was overthrown by a local Sunni group from the 'Anaza tribal federation of the Najd – the same region and federation from which the Al Sa'ud* family, now the rulers of Saudi Arabia, originate. The conquerors of Bahrain, the al-Khalifa family of the 'Utab tribe, which had formed part of the 'Anaza federation, have remained in power ever since, although the sectarian difference between them and the majority of their subjects has always been a source of political weakness. A further problem, particularly in recent times, has been the long tradition of suzerainty or direct control exercised by Iran over the archipelago.

Treaties with Britain

Khalifa independence in Bahrain was short-lived, however. Partly because of piracy in and around the mouth of the Gulf and partly because of growing anxieties over its imperial role in India and over regional communications, Britain began to take an increasing interest in local affairs. In 1816, the British resident in Bushehr, just across the Gulf, paid an official visit to Bahrain and an initial treaty of friendship was signed between Britain and the ruler, Shaykh 'Abd Allah ibn Ahmad al-Khalifa. British influence intensified after the initial treaty was followed up by a peace treaty in 1820 – also signed by the ruler of Ras al-Khayma – which brought piracy from Bahrain to an end. Further treaties were signed in 1856 and 1861 which progressively limited the freedom of action of the Khalifa rulers of the island.

Two further treaties, in 1880 and 1892, virtually turned Bahrain into a British protectorate, since the Khalifa rulers abdicated the right to an independent foreign policy in 1880 and accepted British tutelage in 1892. The final stage in the institution of British control over Bahrain occurred in 1923, when the ruler, Shaykh 'Isa al-Khalifa, was deposed and Sir Charles Belgrave was appointed as adviser to the new ruler.

This situation persisted until 1971, although serious tensions had begun to appear long before. During the 1930s, oil revenue* began to produce major changes in Bahrain, as industrial and oil-industry-related activities began to create an industrial working class and as literacy began to improve. These developments also helped to spare Bahrain from the most extreme consequences of the collapse of its pearling industry, in the face of competition from Japanese cultured pearls which began to dominate world markets at the same time. Unsatisfied demands for a legislative assembly and for the removal of Sir Charles Belgrave were paralleled by the development of a trade union movement* which unsuccessfully attempted to organize strikes in 1938.

History since the Second World War

With the end of the Second World War and the growth of Arab nationalist sentiment throughout the Middle East – particularly after the Egyptian Revolution in 1952 – the situation in Bahrain became more acute. In the wake of sectarian riots in 1953, a Council for National Unity was formed which attempted to canalize Bahraini sentiment for independence and identity into the growing tide of Nasserist Arab nationalism*.

Civil strife

Massive demonstrations met the Franco-British intervention in the Suez War in November 1956 and, in their wake, the council was suppressed and the opposition dispersed. However, despite

Manama's commercial centre

attempts by the government to woo various commercial groups in the population and a change in ruler – with Shaykh ʿIsa ibn Salman coming to power in 1961 – the 1960s were punctuated by further disruption with a school-teachers' strike in 1962 and an oil-industry strike in 1965. The latter escalated into a general strike which, through the leftist-dominated Progressive Forces Front, began to articulate political demands – an end to the state of emergency instituted nine years before, the grant of trade union rights and the institution of a legislative assembly.

Under Saudi pressure, these demonstrations of dissatisfaction with the political dispensation in Bahrain were met with severe repression and widespread arrests. In the late 1960s, as South Yemen (the PDRY) achieved independence, the British regional military headquarters was moved from Aden* to Bahrain, although in 1968 Britain warned that it would pull out from the Gulf region. Bahrain's local reputation as a centre of radicalism led to it being excluded from the proposed Gulf federation that eventually became the UAE (United Arab Emirates)* and, as a result, the ruler began to consider compromise, with the appointment of a twelve-member advisory Council of State in 1970.

Independence

With the announcement that Britain would depart from Bahrain in August, the Council of State was transformed into a Council of Ministers, and plans were proposed for a new constitution which would permit a limited degree of popular participation. However, political tensions began to rise immediately after Britain left – largely as a result of the growing power of the left, now linked to the Popular Front for the Liberation of Oman and the Arab Gulf (PFLOAG), as well as to the nationalist Bahrain National Liberation Front (BNLF). General strikes in March and September 1972 forced an acceleration of the proposed constitutional changes and elections were held in December 1973, just six months after the draft constitution had been approved by Shaykh ʿIssa.

The elections were held on a restricted franchise of 30,000 for 30 seats in the proposed 42-member assembly and, while the PFLOAG decided to boycott the elections, the BNLF fought them in conjunction with the Bahrain Nationalist Movement as a single party – the Popular Bloc. It won 70 per cent of the vote and became the most powerful element in the assembly, where it called for radical change.

Tensions between the ruler – who was under considerable pressure from Riyadh to limit the growing radicalism of Bahraini politics – and the left, with its powerful base amongst oil-industry workers, came to a head in October 1974, when a new law on state security was promulgated. The assembly, under Popular Bloc pressure, refused to endorse the law and, in August 1975, the assembly was dissolved, as thirty leaders of the Popular Bloc and the PFLOAG were arrested.

The result of this action was to drive political opposition in Bahrain underground until the Iranian revolution in early 1979. Events in Iran soon found an echo in Bahrain, with its Shiʿi majority, even though the government attempted to suppress news of developments there. On 15 May 1979 there were massive demonstrations in Bahrain which were broken up by troops and 900 were arrested. Shiʿi leaders then issued a demand for Bahrain to be proclaimed an Islamic Republic, for the state security law to be reviewed, for the assembly to be reinstated and for measures to be taken to ease economic hardship. Despite assurances – which still have not been honoured – that the assembly would be reinstated, the government responded by suppressing all demonstrations in connection with the demands and by expelling a Shiʿi leader, Saʿid Hadi al-Mudarrisi. The tension had been worsened, not only by the growing alliance between the Bahraini secular left and Shiʿi militants, but also because it had become clear that military links with the USA – supposedly broken off in 1973 – had been intensified after 1977. During the early years of the Iranian Revolution, particularly in 1979–80, during the US embassy hostage crisis in Tehran, Bahrain became a major US staging point and this exacerbated tensions there.

Politics today

Since the Iranian Revolution, the political scene in Bahrain has been galvanized by new-found Shiʿi radicalism, in place of the radicalism of the secular left. There were rumours of an unsuccessful Shiʿi coup attempt in 1981, and in 1984 arms caches were found that were assumed to be part of yet another Shiʿi coup attempt. This sense of insecurity has been exacerbated by renewed Iranian hints over its long standing claim on the archipelago – even though this was formally abandoned in 1970. Bahrain has also been seriously concerned over the implications of the Gulf War. As a result, in 1981 it signed a formal defence agreement with Saudi Arabia – which has always made it clear that it would not tolerate radical political change in Bahrain – and became a founder member of the Gulf Cooperation Council* in the same year.

The economy and society today

Traditionally, Bahrain was one of the richest places in the Gulf, with a major pearling industry, boatbuilding, weaving and fishing. It was also a crucial entrepôt point for Saudi Arabia and Iran. These activities have either disappeared or been severely downgraded in recent years, although entrepôt trade is still important.

The modern Bahraini economy depends on its location as a communications and banking centre, with the additional benefit of a

Shaykh Isa ibn Khalifa of Bahrain

well-developed oil sector on which development has been based. Bahrain was the first Arab state to exploit oil after its discovery in the archipelago in 1932. However, given its very limited oil reserves – production has declined by 5–6 per cent per year since the 1970 peak of 76,000 barrels per day (b/d) from the Awali field and there seems little prospect of major new discoveries, despite a large-scale exploration programme in recent years – Bahrain depends on the export of refined petroleum products from the 250,000 b/d capacity Sitra refinery. Only 16 per cent of the input originates in Bahrain, the balance being imported from Saudi Arabia. Until 1984, this processing role meant that Bahrain managed to avoid the serious declines in its revenues that had typified other oil producers from 1981 onwards. Bahrain also has access to non-associated gas from the Khuff formation in the Gulf and this is used for industrial fuel purposes, petrochemical production and reinjection into the ageing oilfields. The oil and gas sectors are nationalized.

Manufacturing and industry in Bahrain are dominated by the Alba smelter, which produces aluminium from bauxite imported from Australia by utilizing Bahrain's cheap energy supplies. The smelter began operation in 1972 and is owned by the government (as the majority shareholder), Saudi Arabia, Kaiser Aluminium and a West German company, Beton. It has stimulated a series of processing industries which form part of Bahrain's diversified secondary industrial sector. This includes food processing, plastics, consumer durables and light engineering.

Bahrain is also a centre for integrated Gulf and Arab industry, with a methanol plant, an iron pelletizing plant (Aisoc) and the dry dock and ship repair yard (Asry). Asry began operations in 1977 and, after an initial period of success, has now seen its business go into decline as a result of the Gulf War. However, economic activity has been sustained by construction, which has avoided the decline that has faced this sector in other Gulf states. This is partly because of the massive causeway project now being built to link Saudi Arabia to the island, and due to open at the end of 1986. In addition, however, there are still several major housing schemes under way, including Madinat Hamad and a major new reclamation scheme which is due to start in 1987.

The most important aspect of Bahrain's economy is its role as a major Gulf telecommunications centre and banking* centre. Bahrain has an active offshore banking sector, with 77 units involved in 1984 and assets around the $63 billion mark. Five large banks dominate the domestic sector, controlling 80 per cent of local assets and the financial sector operates under the control of the Bahrain Monetary Authority. However, the sector now faces competition from increasing banking activity elsewhere in the Gulf and in Saudi Arabia, together with the growing depression in Arab financial sectors as a result of the downturn in oil prices. Nonetheless, even though Arab oil economies now face a difficult future, Bahrain's high degree of diversification means that it will probably survive the stresses ahead far better than other states in the region.

G.J.

Further reading

C. Belgrave, *The Pirate Coast* (London, 1966)
F. I. Khuri, *Tribe and State in Bahrain: the transformation of social and political authority in an Arab state* (Chicago, 1980)

Cyprus

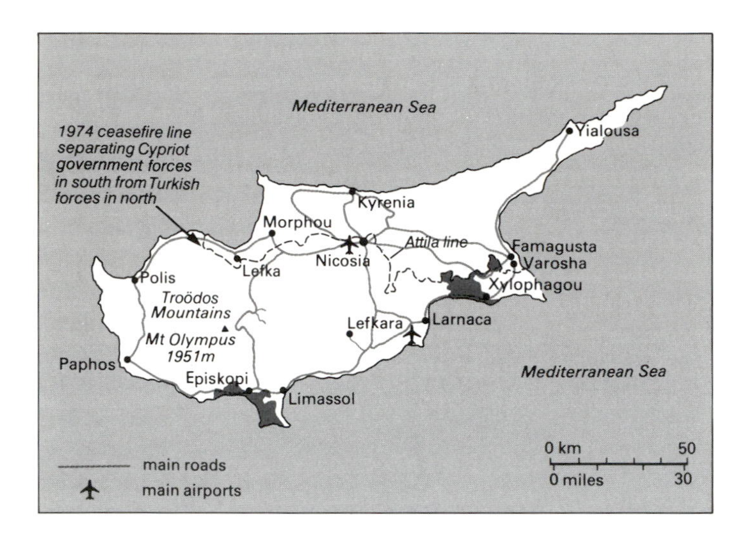

Official title	The Republic of Cyprus (south – internationally recognized); the Turkish Republic of North Cyprus (north – recognized only by Turkey)
Area	9251 sq. km
Population	657,000 (503,498 in the south; 153,239 in the north – 1982)
Government and constitution	A unitary multi-party Republic with a unicameral legislature (both north and south)
Currency	(south) 1 Cyprus pound = 1000 mils; US $1 = 1 CP; (north) 1 Turkish lira = 1000 kurus; US $1 = 689.0 liras
Languages	(south) Greek; (north) Turkish
Religion	(south) Greek Orthodox (majority) and several other Christian minority sects; (north) mainly Sunni Muslim
Climate	Mediterranean with hot dry summers and warm wet winters. Summer temperatures can reach 38°C while severe winter frosts may occur in the highlands

Geography and topography

Cyprus is the third largest and the most easterly island in the Mediterranean, with Turkey and Syria as its closest neighbours (70 and 100 km away respectively) and Greece being 400 km distant. Its land area is 9251 km^2 and the island is 222 km long and 95 km wide.

The topography of Cyprus is dominated by the Troödos Mountains – with Mount Olympos as the highest point at 1951 m – which occupy the southern half of the island. It is separated from the other major elevated feature, the Kyrenia range which runs parallel to the northern coastline, by the Mesaöria Plain. The plain has traditionally been the major agricultural area in Cyprus and contains the major town, Nicosia. All other major towns are located around the coast as a result of the mountainous nature of the interior, although a large number of villages are located on the southern flanks of the Troödos and around Mount Olympos, as well as in the Mesaöria Plain.

Although the island enjoys adequate rainfall – with an average of 500 mm per year to support cereoculture and citrus cultivation in the Mesaöria and arboriculture in the mountains – there are no perennial rivers or lakes. There are, however, many watercourses which are dry in summer, but which carry torrential runoff in winter, as a result of the winter rains. Attempts have been made to save this runoff through dams and there are three major irrigation projects under construction – the Southern Conveyor Project, the Vassilikos-Pendaskinos Project and the Khrysokhou Project.

Peoples

At the end of 1984, the population* of Cyprus was estimated to have reached 661,800, with the population growth rate being set at 1.3 per cent since 1982. This figure must, however, be treated with caution, for since 1974 the island has been divided into two zones by the so-called 'Attila line' as a result of the Turkish invasion of the island. The northern zone, which is occupied entirely by Cyprus' Turkish Cypriot population, together with more recent migrants from the Turkish mainland, does not provide statistics to the authorities in the south. General statistics for the island as a whole are, therefore, unreliable. Population densities are of the order of 71 per km^2 and 53 per cent of the population was urban-based in 1982.

In 1980, 80.7 per cent of the population was of Greek origin, with 18.7 per cent being of Turkish origin, the 0.6 per cent balance being composed of other Europeans and persons from the Middle East. As a result of the Turkish invasion in 1974, the Turkish Cypriot population occupies 38.5 per cent of the land area of Cyprus.

Religions

From a confessional point of view, 76.2 per cent of the population was Greek Orthodox and 18.7 per cent was Muslim. The balance was composed of adherents of other Christian denominations, mainly Armenian*, Maronite* and Roman Catholic.

History up to 1939

Although human occupation in Cyprus dates back to the Neolithic period, the island only became integrated into the complex patterns of Mediterranean civilization in the late Bronze Age. The earliest contacts seem to have been with Egypt, but Cyprus soon became closely involved in the interplay between the Aegean, Assyrian and Persian civilizations until it was integrated into Ptolemeic Egypt in about 300 BC.

Thereafter Cyprus fell under Roman and, later, Byzantine* control until its Arab occupation in 647 AD. For the next five hundred years, Cyprus was once again an outpost on the front line between two warring Empires, until, with the decline of the Byzantine Empire in the twelfth century it fell under Crusader control. With the collapse of the Crusader Kingdoms of Outremer, Cyprus became an independent state under the Lusignans in 1192, until it was handed over to the Venetian Republic in 1489.

In 1571, Cyprus was conquered by the Ottoman Turks*, who introduced Turkish settlers into the population, while permitting Christian society to continue. Within two centuries, however, desires for independence began to manifest themselves. These were stimulated by the Greek War for Independence in the early nineteenth century and by the decay of the Ottoman Empire. Increasingly, too, British influence in Istanbul mitigated the more extreme rigours of Ottoman rule and in 1878 Britain took over the administration of Cyprus from the Ottoman Empire.

Cyprus and Britain

British interest in Cyprus was a reflection of its imperial and strategic concerns, in that it was anxious to ensure that no other power could threaten its lines of communication via Egypt to India, or its control over the Mediterranean basin. Under British control, material conditions on the island were considerably improved. However, the growing demands of the Greek Cypriot population for autonomy, or unity with Greece (*enosis*), were ignored. By the end of the Second World War, however, these demands had become too powerful to be ignored any longer.

Rural view of central Cyprus

History since the Second World War

The movement for *enosis* found a charismatic leader in Bishop (later Archbishop) Makarios, who organized a plebiscite in 1947 which claimed a majority of 96 per cent in favour of *enosis*. The Greek government also took up the cause of *enosis*, although it was warned that too great a pressure on Britain might persuade the British government to insist on tripartite talks with both the Greek and Turkish governments over the issue – thereby blocking the demand for *enosis*, even if autonomy or independence were conceded instead. In 1955, as a guerrilla campaign waged by the Eoka organization under a former Greek army officer, Colonel Grivas, gathered pace, the British government did offer tripartite talks with Turkey and Greece. The Greek government – to Greek Cypriot consternation – accepted and, in 1957, the discussions were transferred to the UN, where the principle of the independence of Cyprus was established.

Further negotiations were opened between Greece and Turkey over Cypriot independence, in which the Greek authorities, in abandoning claims for *enosis*, were determined to prevent Turkey from claiming similar rights for its co-religionists on the island. In 1959, the Turkish, Greek and British governments drew up the Treaty of Zurich, which provided for Cypriot independence as a unitary state, while Britain retained sovereignty over two military

Archbishop Makarios, President of the Republic of Cyprus 1960–77

base areas at Akrotiri and Dekhelia – a total area of 260 km². Archbishop Makarios was forced to accept the arrangements, albeit with the greatest reluctance.

Independence

The new Cypriot constitution, which came into effect in 1960, as independence was proclaimed, attempted to provide for the interests of the two communities on the island. There was to be a Greek Cypriot president and a Turkish Cypriot vice-president, both elected by universal suffrage for five years and wielding executive power. They were to appoint a Council of Ministers consisting of seven Greek Cypriots and three Turkish Cypriots. All were to be responsible to a house of representatives, of which 70 per cent of the deputies were to be Greek Cypriots and 30 per cent Turkish, elected for a five-year term by universal suffrage.

These arrangements soon broke down, however. The basic problem was the way in which the difficulties created by the existence of two separate ethnic communities in the island could be resolved. Archbishop Makarios, the president, wanted to work towards complete integration of the two communities, while his vice-president, Dr Küçük, was anxious to preserve their separateness. Eventually, Makarios threatened to enforce his view by constitutional revision and, in November 1963, put forward new constitutional proposals to that effect. The initiative was immediately met with bitter intercommunal fighting and by a threat from the Turkish government to intervene if the proposals were introduced unilaterally by the Greek Cypriots. Calm was only restored in February 1964 when the UN sent in a peace-keeping force and a mediator. Although the mediator achieved little, the peace-keeping force did restore a tense peace between the two communities.

For the next ten years a state of uneasy truce was maintained, with many Turkish villages as virtual enclaves surrounded by UN units. After November 1967 conditions improved somewhat as negotiations began between both communities over a final resolution of the problems facing them. However, these dragged on inconclusively for the next seven years, since the Turkish negotiators looked towards a federal solution, with the forcible transfer of populations and a Turkish area in the north of the island, while the Greek side sought an integrative solution. At the same time, there was considerable economic integration and the isolation of the Turkish community was eased in other ways.

The 1974 Turkish invasion

This slow process of intercommunal negotiation was abruptly discontinued in early 1974, when Grivas, the old Eoka leader, attempted to overthrow the Makarios government with overt support from the right-wing military *junta* that was in power in Greece. The attempt failed, partly because Grivas died in January 1974. However, it was swiftly followed by a successful coup organized by the Greek-officered national guard which placed an old Eoka leader, Nicos Samson, as the new president of Cyprus.

Turkey* responded immediately with an invasion of the island in July 1974, rapidly taking control of Turkish occupied areas and eventually extending its control over 38.5 per cent of the island's land area. The island was *de facto* divided and 180,000 Greek Cypriots trapped in the Turkish-held areas fled southwards. This was matched by the northward displacement of 11,000 Turkish Cypriots from the new Greek Cypriot zone. The Turkish invasion also caused angry reactions in Athens, where popular disgust at the incompetence of the *junta* led to its downfall and to Greek encouragement for the return of Makarios in December 1974 to govern the new Greek Cypriot entity in the southern half of the island. The 'forcible exchange of populations', long proposed by the Turkish

Cypriot community, had effectively taken place – although there are still 1000 Greek Cypriots living in enclaves in the northern part of the island. Furthermore, the 115,000-strong Turkish Cypriot population had been joined by 27,000 Turkish troops (who still guarantee their security) and, in 1983, by 30,000 migrants from mainland Turkey.

The divided island

The divisions created in 1974 have hardened over the past twelve years. In 1975, a Turkish Cypriot federated state was proclaimed under Rauf Denktash and his leadership of the new state was confirmed in elections in the Turkish Cypriot zone in June 1976. In the south, the Makarios government was confirmed in power by elections in September 1976. Negotiations between the two sides were initiated as early as 1974 and the Greek Cypriots accepted that federation would have to be the eventual solution. However, they also insisted on a strong central government elected through proportional representation, while the Turkish Cypriots insisted that a weak central government should cede power in a bizonal system.

A breakthrough seemed possible in early 1977, when Makarios and Rauf Denktash met and laid down the four basic guidelines that would determine any future settlement. These required that Cyprus should be a non-aligned bi-communal federal Republic; that the territory for each community should allow for economic viability, while honouring as far as possible existing land-ownership patterns; that the central government should be provided with sufficient powers to safeguard national unity; and that freedom of movement and property would be ensured. Before further negotiations could take place, however, Archbishop Makarios died unexpectedly on 3 August 1977.

Politics today

Makarios's successor, Spyros Kyprianou, was confirmed as president in elections in February 1978. Negotiations with the Turkish Cypriot authorities did not proceed successfully, however, since neither side was able to compromise on its understanding of the nature of the eventual federation that was to be imposed. Even though pressure from the Greek lobby in Washington forced the USA to take an ever-greater interest in Cypriot affairs, and Greek Cypriot lobbying at the UN brought a series of UN-sponsored initiatives after 1982, there has been no significant change in the position of either side. The Turkish Cypriot state has evinced increasing irritation and in an unexpected, though well-signalled, move in November 1983 it proclaimed itself unilaterally independent as the Turkish Republic of North Cyprus (TRNC).

Further UN-sponsored negotiations were undertaken in 1984, without success, although hopes were briefly raised in January 1985 when Rauf Denktash and President Kyprianou met in New York. Once again, however, nothing came of the meeting. This failure created domestic problems for Kyprianou, when he faced a vote of censure in the House of Representatives on a motion moved by the Akel Communist Party – which had been a warm supporter of the president until he renounced his formal pact with it just before his meeting in New york – and the right-wing Rally Party of Glafcos Clerides. The president was left with support from his own party, Diko, and the socialist Edek party – a combined total of twelve seats to set against the twenty-three seats held by Rally and Akel. The result was that the house passed a motion requiring the president to sign the draft agreement drawn up by the UN for signature by himself and Denktash. The president refused to agree and called an election – one year before it was due – on 8 December 1985. To general surprise, his Diko Party won substantially increased representation, at the expense of the Akel which has traditionally dominated Cypriot politics. The president now looks forward to continued popular support for his hard line over negotiations with the TRNC and to a radical change in Cypriot voting patterns that will free him from his earlier dependence on Akel support for the presidency.

As far as a resolution to the wider issue of reunification of the island is concerned, however, there seems little prospect of significant compromise on either side. Denktash organized a referendum on a new constitution for the TRNC in May 1985, his own re-election as president of the TRNC in June 1985 and new parliamentary elections later in the same month, when his supporters won 37 per cent of the vote, a greater proportion than any other party. It is clear that he is now in a strong position to resist any pressure at compromise, whether from the UN or other states. The outlook is thus bleak. Even though the south is internationally considered to be the official government of Cyprus, it cannot force the north to accept its proposals, while the north, although only recognized by Turkey, is actively promoting its cause amongst states in the Muslim world. In short, the division of the island would now appear to be virtually permanent.

The economy and society today

The Cypriot economy has been based on the three pillars of agriculture, manufacturing and tourism, with the major emphasis in all sectors being placed on the role of the private sector. The major development emphasis has been to improve irrigation facilities and export crops for Europe; to increase contribution from manufacturing to exports, both to the EEC with which Cyprus has an association agreement, and to the Arab world as Lebanon ceased to be a significant exporter in the wake of the civil war; and to improve tourist facilities for European and, latterly, Arab tourism. These ventures have been controlled by a series of three five-year development plans since 1962.

The Turkish invasion in 1974 caused major economic disruption and this was corrected in the south by three emergency action plans. Nonetheless, the invasion resulted in the Greek Cypriot economy losing access to 60 per cent of the island's agricultural and manufacturing potential, as well as to 38.5 per cent of the land area. These involved 80 per cent of Cyprus's citrus plantations and 25 per cent of the industrial sector, mines and tourism. The Turkish sector retained control of 30 per cent of the water supplies and has continued to supply the south in return for free supplies of electricity. The major concern, however, was to house the 180,000 refugees and provide them with work. The emergency action plans were directed towards labour-intensive projects and towards export development. They depended in part on foreign aid, but more on native Cypriot energy and expertise.

The emergency plans were successful in overcoming the consequences of the invasion by the early 1980s. Cyprus introduced a fourth development plan, running from 1982 to 1986, designed to stabilize growth, reduce foreign debt, improve stagnating export performance and create a service sector in Cyprus to satisfy growing Middle Eastern demand. There is also a flourishing offshore sector, with over 3000 companies operating, including several offshore banking units.

In the north, economic progress has been less successful. A major problem has been a lack of expertise in managing the agricultural and manufacturing sector – much of it taken over from fleeing Greek Cypriots and put under the control of the *evkaf* (*waqf**) or Sanayii Holding, a state company – while the services sector has become the main absorber of manpower. Development plans have also been directed at improving the water supply – with a proposal for a water pipeline from Turkey, now in abeyance – and at reinvigorating the tourist sector. The problem is that, lacking international recognition, international tourism has passed the TRNC by. Foreign investment is now coming in, however. The London-based Polly Peck group has set up manufacturing and packing facilities on the island and has claimed satisfaction with its returns. But in the final analysis the north will not enjoy effective growth without wider international contacts and separation from the Turkish economy to which it is tied, and because of which it has suffered from the effects of inflation and austerity policies. The outlook for the north, economically at least, is therefore bleak.

GJ

Further reading

M. A. Attalides, *Cyprus and International Politics* (Nicosia, 1979)
G. S. Georghallides, *The Political and Administrative History of Cyprus* (London, 1979)
H. D. Purcell, *Cyprus* (Nicosia, 1969)

Djibouti

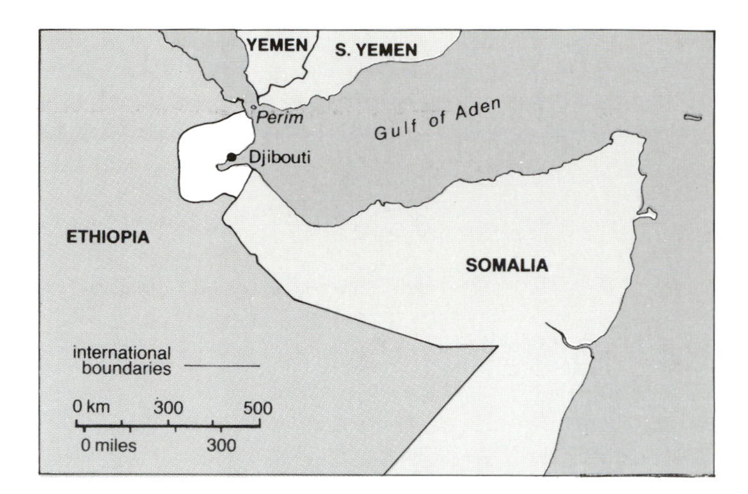

Geography and topography

This arid and barren country offers little arable land, with year-round growth found only in the northern range of high altitude.

Peoples

The Afar, who make up slightly more than half the population, live in the north while the Somali, the second largest group, live in the south. Both are traditionally nomadic peoples, Muslim and Cushitic-speaking. An estimated 25,000 refugees from Somalia and Ethiopia are also resident. The foreign community is primarily from France and works in the military and government. Up to half of the country's estimated population of 405,000 lives in the capital city of Djibouti.

Religion

Almost all Djiboutians are Sunni* Muslims of the Shafi'i* rite, in common with the people of Somalia.

History up to 1939

What is now the Republic of Djibouti came under French rule in 1863 when it became French Somaliland and later, the French Territory of the Afars and the Issas. In the early 1860s France developed the port city of Djibouti to provide a fuelling station on the Suez Canal route from Europe to the Indian Ocean and South East Asia. This was followed, in the late 1890s, by the construction of the Franco-Ethiopian railway to move Ethiopian goods to the French port. During that period the city grew to a population of several thousand, drawing large numbers of immigrants from Somalia*.

Official title	Republic of Djibouti
Area	23,200 sq. km
Population (1984)	405,000
Government and constitution	Djibouti is a one-party state led by the Rassemblement populaire pour le progrès (RPP), formed in March 1979 to replace the Ligue populaire africaine pour l'independance (LPAI) which was the official opposition party prior to independence in 1977. The first politbureau and central committee of the ruling party were elected in October 1979. The president, the party's sole candidate, serves a six-year term. Legislative elections were held in 1982 from a single list of RPP candidates. The head of state presides over a 65-seat Chamber of Deputies, serving five-year terms, and a 14-seat Council of Ministers. The last elections were held on 24 April 1987
Currency	1 Djibouti franc = 100 centimes; US $1 = 178 francs
Languages	Arabic, French (official); Somali and Afar are also spoken
Religion	Islam is the official religion of the state
Climate	High temperatures combined with heavy humidity during the rainy season. Between June and August temperature ranges from 30–40°C, with rainfall between November and March variable, the past decade's annual average being more than 200 mm

Politics today

Djibouti celebrated its tenth anniversary of independence from France on 27 June 1987. It followed the re-election of President Hasan Gouled Aptidon for a third six-year term in elections on 24 April. He was the sole candidate of the country's only legal party, the Rassemblement populaire pour le progrès.

Sixty-five deputies were also elected for five years to the National Assembly, their origins reflecting a traditional balance between the different ethnic groups and clans. The Issa, of Somali origin, make up almost half of the country's population of 405,000. The largest group is the Afar.

While official tallies showed the president receiving more than 90 per cent of the vote, murmurings of discontent are on the increase and national security to protect the government was increased in 1986–7. On 18 March a bomb exploded in a Djibouti café killing eleven people. Later that month a Tunisian national pleaded guilty to planting the bomb and said the action was in protest against the presence of French troops. Four of the five Frenchmen killed in the blast were from the 3000-strong army and navy garrison.

While Djibouti authorities suggested the bombing was the work of Tunisian terrorists linked to the Middle East, unofficial reports connected the incident with the exiled Mouvement national djiboutien pour l'instauration de la démocratie (MNID). The group went public in February 1986 in a communiqué which called for a government of national salvation, an end to the single-party system and the establishment of a constitution which provides for 'a true liberal democracy'.

The group was founded by the former commerce minister Aden Robleh Awaleh. In September 1986 he received a life sentence in absentia for his alleged part in a bombing in January of that year.

While the Horn of Africa remains one of the most conflict-prone regions in Africa, the Djibouti government has sought a mediator role in the hopes of reducing disruptions to trade and the flow of refugees from Ethiopia, as well as discouraging the support of its dissidents in neighbouring countries. To date President Hasan Gouled has had some success in this area.

The economy and society today

Djibouti has continued to receive favourable donor support for development and national infrastructure from both the West – led by France – and the Gulf – led by Saudi Arabia. In 1986 French aid totalled 60m French francs ($9.4m) and, under an agreement signed in January 1987, France gave 26.25 m French francs ($4.1 m) in budgetary aid.

Current development projects include the upgrading of Djibouti port, which will see the renovation of two quays and a loading area and extension of the container terminal. Total freight volume has fallen in recent years, mainly because of a 51 per cent fall in oil traffic. Container transshipments have increased, however, and port improvements are expected to bring further gains.

In other projects, the American firm Pool Intairdril has carried out the first of two geothermal drilling programmes. The work, funded by foreign aid, commenced in December 1986 after a surface exploration programme raised hopes that Djibouti has sufficient resources for the export of power to neighbouring countries. In May, however, results from the first two wells drilled showed inadequate water temperatures. Work on the final two wells of the $16.6m first phase commenced that same month.

Another project which will boost the important service sector is the $20m upgrading of the Ambouli international airport. The three-year project, expected to commence in 1987, is funded by Gulf donors.

CB

Egypt

Official title	The Arab Republic of Egypt
Area	1,002,000 sq. km
Population	51 million
Government and constitution	The People's Assembly is the legislative body and is elected for five years. The law governing its composition was altered in May 1979. The country's president is nominated by a minumum of two-thirds. He is then elected by popular referendum for a six-year term. He has executive authority and appoints one or more vice-presidents as well as all ministers including the prime minister.
Currency	1 Egyptian pound = 100 piastres; exchange rate (31 May 1986): US $1 = 70 piastres. (As of 31 December 1985 the premium rate relating to some imports and exports was $1 = £E 1.33 and the parallel or free market rate was $1 = £E 1.74)
Languages	Arabic (official); English and French are also widely spoken
Religions	About 90 per cent of Egyptians are Muslims, mainly Sunni. There are some 6 m Copts, who form the largest religious minority
Climate	Most of Egypt is arid with even Alexandria receiving only 200 mm of rain a year. Summer temperatures range between 38 and 43°C except on the Mediterranean coast where the maximum is 32°C. Winters are generally warm with occasional rain

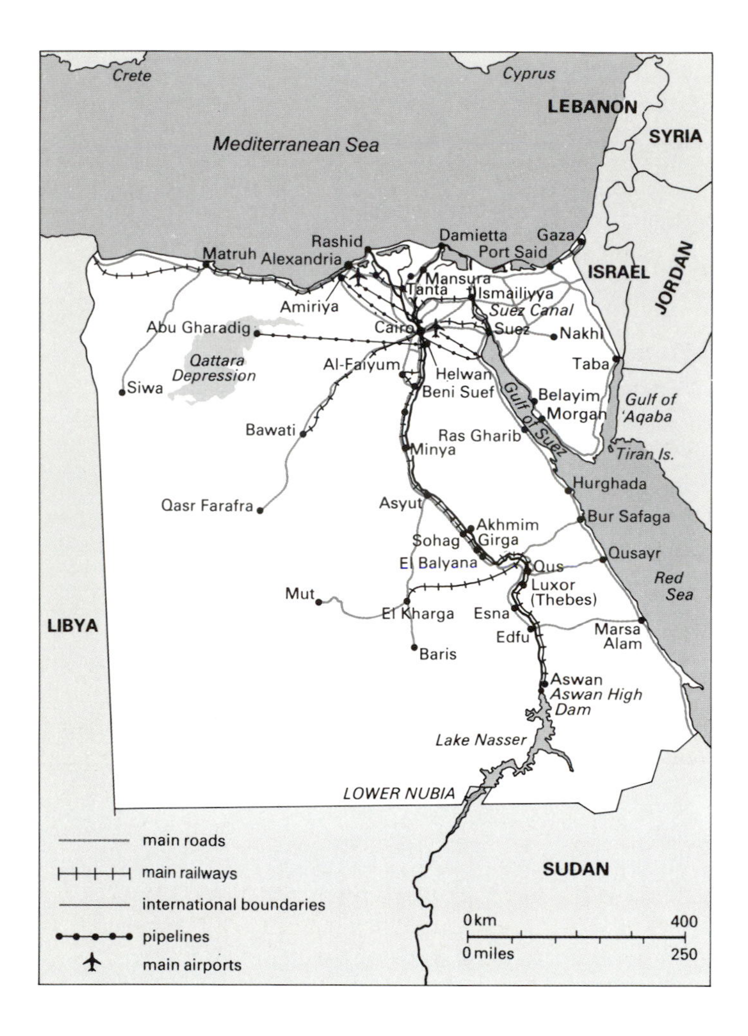

Geography and topography

Egypt covers almost 1 million km^2, made up of desert and the valley of the life-giving Nile. Only about 5 per cent of the total area is cultivable. The most populous and cultivated region is the Nile Delta, which fans out north of Cairo. To the south lies Upper Egypt, where the valley narrows to a ribbon stretching to Aswan and the artificial lake created by the High Dam. To the east and west of the Nile lie deserts, and further east Suez and the Sinai, bordering Israel, Jordan and Saudi Arabia. The climate is arid and hot, with very little rainfall. The seasons vary only slightly, with average temperatures ranging from just over 20°C in winter to 40°C in the height of summer.

Peoples

Egypt has been continuously inhabited for more than 8000 years. For millennia, the majority of the population has consisted of peasants. Islam* spread to Egypt as early as the seventh century AD and most Egyptians are Muslims. There is also an important Coptic Christian* minority, making up about 10 per cent of the total population of more than 50 million. There is still a small Jewish community, but most Egyptian Jews left after the creation of Israel in 1948. The Egyptians have been Arabic-speaking since the early Islamic conquests*.

History up to 1939

For centuries, until the 1952 Revolution, Egypt was governed by rulers of foreign origin. After the last dynasty of Pharaohs was conquered by Alexander the Great, Egypt was ruled by his successors, then as part of the Roman and Byzantine Empires, until the Arab Islamic conquest in 642. A succession of Arab dynasties followed. In 969, the Fatimids marked their conquest with the creation of a new capital city, al-Qahira, which has become the modern Cairo. In 1517, Egypt fell to the Ottoman Turks, who ruled the country from Constantinople/Istanbul for the next three centuries.

The French* invasion of Egypt under Napoleon Bonaparte and the short occupation (1798–1801) which followed exposed Egypt to Western ideas and technology (see Modern History). French withdrawal was followed by the foundation of a new dynasty under Muhammad ʿAli*, an officer from Kavala in Macedonia who led Albanian soldiers to Egypt in the nominal service of the Ottomans. Muhammad ʿAli held power from 1805 until his death in 1849, establishing virtual independence from Istanbul and initiating a process of modernization which reached its peak during the period of rule of his grandson, Khedive Ismaʿil. A negative legacy of Muhammad ʿAli's successors, Saʿid and Ismaʿil, was to saddle Egypt with an unmanageable foreign debt. The debt led to the assumption by Britain and France during the last quarter of the nineteenth century of a large degree of control over the economy. Ismaʿil was forced to abdicate in 1879; in 1882 British forces invaded Egypt to suppress a movement of opposition to the Khedive's rule and the growth of foreign control, led by an army officer, Ahmad ʿUrabi. In one form or another British control continued until 1936, when an Anglo-Egyptian Treaty gave Egypt a limited independence. Full independence was only secured after the last of the dynasty founded by Muhammad ʿAli, King Faruq, was overthrown by the nationalist 'Free Officers' Movement'.

History since the Second World War

Egypt emerged from the Second World War in a state of turmoil. The country witnessed a growing tide of agitation, directed mainly against the presence of British troops. The central demand from a wide array of political forces was for genuine independence, and the evacuation of British troops at least to the Suez Canal zone. King Faruq had been in power since 1936 – also the year of the Anglo-Egyptian Treaty, which had contained some concessions to Egyptian nationalist sentiments. The King was a largely ineffectual ruler, associated in many Egyptians' minds with a pleasure-seeking elite unable or unwilling to deal with the country's problems. Government and parliament were dominated by traditional politicians more or less committed to winning full independence from the British. The most important political party was the Wafd*, a moderate nationalist group formed by Saʿd Zaghlul who, in 1919, had tried to send a delegation (*wafd*) to plead Egypt's case at the Paris Peace Conference.

Opposition to the British was voiced more forcefully by other groups outside the established political circles. The *Ikhwan al-Muslimin* (Muslim Brothers*) in particular succeeded in fomenting unrest. The *Ikhwan**, founded in 1928 by Hasan al-Banna*, was dedicated to ridding Egypt of the British, as well as overthrowing King Faruq and his government, accusing him of neglecting the needs of the Muslim community.

Demands for radical change were also pressed by the Communist Party and the student-based movement, Misr al-Fatat. The defeat of Egyptian troops dispatched to Palestine in 1948 to attack the nascent Israeli state added to the discontent within Egypt. In late 1948, Prime Minister Mahmud Nuqrashi was assassinated by a member of the *Ikhwan*. Nuqrashi's successor, Ibrahim ʿAbd al-Hadi, ordered a clampdown on the *Ikhwan* and the other opposition groups, many of whose members were arrested. In February 1949, the *Ikhwan*'s leader, Hasan al-Banna, was assassinated: government agents were suspected of the act, but this was never proven. In 1950, the Wafd was elected to power, and the party's leader, Mustafa Nahhas, took over as prime minister. He pursued a strong anti-British line, abrogating the Anglo-Egyptian Treaty and giving limited backing to *Ikhwan* and leftist guerrilla activity against British forces in the Canal Zone. Clashes escalated through 1951 and early 1952. The most serious incident occurred on 25 January 1952 when British troops destroyed the police barracks in Ismaʿiliyya, killing fifty Egyptian policemen. The incident provoked riots in Cairo the next day. Buildings, including bastions of British life such as Shepheard's Hotel and the Turf Club, were burned and looted and a number of British and other foreigners were killed. After the riots, the King dismissed Nahhas, but was unable to restore coherent government.

Throughout this period, a group of young army officers had been meeting to consider if they could solve Egypt's problems by taking power themselves. These *dubbat al-ahrar* (Free Officers) had been drawn together in the 1940s under the leading inspiration of Jamal ʿAbd al-Nasir (Nasser)*. Most of the group's members had benefited from the 1936 decision by the army to open the officer corps to men from the middle and lower classes. Nasser, born in Upper Egypt on 15 January 1918, was elected chairman of the nine-member committee of the Free Officers' Movement in 1950.

The Revolution

The officers, believing that King Faruq was about to arrest them, launched their coup on 23 July 1952. The army and the capital fell into their hands with hardly a shot fired. The King went into exile three days later. The respected General Muhammad Najib was appointed commander-in-chief of the armed forces and chairman of the Revolutionary Command Council (RCC). The civilian politician ʿAli Mahir agreed to serve as prime minister. But disagreements soon surfaced about the extent of the army's role in the post-revolutionary government. The Free Officers had yet to formulate a coherent set of policies; they were agreed on the need to root out corruption in the army and political elite and on the need to effect the evacuation of British forces. The new government did have a clear idea about one area of economic policy: land reform. In September 1952, a law was passed limiting the size of an individual landholding. This ceiling on landownership was progressively lowered through the 1950s. The land reform was aimed at bettering the lot of the peasants, increasing agricultural production and making extra funds available for investment in industry. The RCC took no immediate measures against foreign interests in Egypt (mainly British and French) and it did its best to encourage private sector industrialists to invest. The main targets of the regime's early economic measures were the large landowners and merchants, who were seen to be holding back industrial development.

In early 1954, Nasser himself took overall control. He ousted Najib, and on 18 April became prime minister. His chief internal opponents were the *Ikhwan*, a member of which fired a number of shots at Nasser at a public rally in Alexandria on 26 October 1954. While consolidating his hold on power in Egypt, Nasser became more and more embroiled in international issues. He came to the attention of the wider Arab world when he opposed Arab participation in the Baghdad Pact*, a pro-Western alliance of Middle Eastern states. In April 1955, Nasser received much acclaim as co-founder of the non-aligned movement at the conference at Bandung in Indonesia. In September 1955, he announced the signing of a weapons agreement with Czechoslovakia. Earlier attempts to buy weapons from Britain, the United States and France had been made conditional on Cairo making various political concessions. Nasser denied that the Czech agreement meant Egypt had fallen into the Soviet Union's sphere of influence. However, relations with the West became worse after the US, on 19 July 1956, withdrew its offer of finance for the construction of the Aswan High Dam*. In retaliation for the increasingly hostile stance of the West, Nasser, elected president one month previously, took his most dramatic decision to date: on 26 July 1956 he announced the nationalization of the Suez Canal* Company.

The Suez crisis

Britain and France resolved to use force to restore their former control over the canal. They joined forces with Israel, which was seeking an opportunity to cut Nasser down to size and to punish Egypt for allowing Palestinian guerrillas to attack Israel from the Egyptian-administered Gaza Strip. Israeli forces invaded Sinai on 29 October 1956, reaching the canal two days later. According to a prearranged plan, British and French forces landed in the Canal Zone, ostensibly to separate the Egyptian and Israeli armies. The Anglo-French action received widespread international condemnation. Under pressure from Washington, Britain, France and Israel agreed to a UN-supervised cease-fire on 6 November, and the attacking forces withdrew in late 1956 and early 1957. Egypt agreed to compensate the shareholders of the Suez Canal Company. The canal was declared open to all ships, except those of Israel. The UN Emergency Force (UNEF) was deployed in Sinai and in the Gulf of ʿAqaba, where its task was to keep the peace and ensure free access of Israeli shipping to Eilat.

After the Suez affair, Nasser stepped up attempts to unify the Arab world. In January 1958, Egypt formed the United Arab Republic (UAR) with Syria*. However, other Arab states refused to join the union, and in 1961 it collapsed when Syria withdrew. One state which did join was North Yemen*. In 1962, Egyptian troops were sent to intervene in the North Yemeni civil war on the side of the army against the Saʿudi-backed followers of the religious dynasty which had ruled previously. Egyptian troops remained in Yemen for most of the decade, without achieving a clear-cut victory. The intervention also contributed to Egypt's woeful performance in the June 1967 War with Israel.

Through the late 1950s, Nasser moved towards setting up a one-party state, with greater state control over the economy. In 1960, the Misr Group – the largest consortium of private sector companies – was nationalized, the first of a series of steps towards establishing a socialist system. The regime's new orientation was formalized in the 1962 Charter of National Action. The charter called for setting up the Arab Socialist Union (ASU), the most ambitious attempt since 1952 to create a mass political party to legitimize the regime and act as a forum for political debate. The public sector henceforth would play the central role in industrialization. But private companies still controlled a number of manufacturing concerns, and the private sector remained dominant in domestic trade, tourism and recreational activities.

Egypt received assistance from the Soviet Union, in particular, in the effort to industrialize. In 1958, Soviet aid was pledged for the construction of the Aswan High Dam and hydroelectric plant. The first stage of the dam was completed in 1964 in a ceremony attended by the Soviet leader Nikita Khrushchev. Despite the large scale of Soviet economic and military aid, Egypt's relations with Moscow were never entirely smooth. Disagreements arose about numerous issues, including Nasser's treatment of communists, the extent of Egypt's commitment to socialism, and the pace of weapons deliveries.

The 1967 War

In the mid-1960s, Egypt and Nasser faced a number of serious setbacks after the period of relative success in the years since the revolution. On the economic front, industrial progress was hampered by balance-of-payments deficits. Tension with Israel* began to escalate with the upsurge in Palestinian* guerrilla activity and increasing deliveries of American weapons to Tel Aviv. In May 1967 Nasser ordered the UNEF peace-keeping force out of Sinai and closed the Tiran Straits to Israeli shipping. These actions were taken, ostensibly, in light of information from the Soviet Union that Israel was about to invade Syria. Nasser appeared to be trying to warn Israel that Egypt was ready to go to the help of Syria in the event of an invasion. The crisis intensified, and on 5 June Israel launched a series of devastating raids on Egyptian air bases. Israeli troops swept through Sinai, and a cease-fire was declared along the Suez Canal on 8 June. During the war, Israel also occupied the Syrian Golan Heights and the Jordanian-controlled West Bank. On 9 June, faced with the enormity of the defeat, Nasser announced his resignation. However, he agreed to continue as president after crowds of Egyptians demonstrated in the streets demanding that he do so.

The aftermath of defeat

Nasser's first action was to purge the armed forces of commanders accused of negligence and corruption. The Soviet Union helped replace destroyed military equipment. Nasser started work on long-term plans to restore the strategic balance with Israel. These plans culminated in the October 1973 War. From March 1969 until August 1970 hostilities with Israel continued along the Suez Canal in the 'war of attrition'.

Sadat

Nasser died of a heart attack on 28 September 1970. He was succeeded by Anwar al-Sadat*, a fellow Free Officer. Sadat had been named vice-president in December 1969, but had yet to occupy any office of great significance. Sadat's first task was to consolidate his own position. He then had to deal with the profound economic and political problems he had inherited. In May 1971 he arrested a group of political rivals, led by ASU president ʿAli Sabri, accused of plotting to take power with Soviet backing. The same month, Sadat signed a friendship treaty with the Soviet Union, but relations with Moscow became increasingly strained. In July 1972, Sadat ordered all Soviet military experts to leave the country – there were about 15,000.

The 1973 War

Sadat promised decisive action to end the Israeli occupation of Sinai in 1971 and 1972. On 6 October 1973, to the surprise of Israel and the rest of the world, that decisive action was taken. Egyptian troops poured over the Suez Canal and broke through Israeli defences on the waterway's east bank. Simultaneously, Syrian forces pushed through Israeli lines on the Golan Heights. Egypt was unable to

President Sadat in the year he died

protect its initial advantage, and by 20 October Israeli counter-attackers had succeeded in surrounding the Egyptian Third Army on the west bank of the canal. A UN-backed cease-fire went into force on 22 October. The war was by no means a victory for Egypt, but it gave an important morale-boost to the Egyptians and the Arab world, while it established Sadat as a major statesman. After the war, Sadat set about negotiating for the return of Sinai and the realization of a lasting peace in the region. This marked a big shift in Egypt's political alignment, from the Soviet Union to the US, which Sadat saw as more influential because of Washington's close ties with Israel.

With US mediation, Sadat signed two disengagement agreements with Israel in January 1974 and September 1975. According to the second agreement, Israel handed back the Sinai oilfields. Sadat's decision to court Washington resulted in 1974 in the start of a large programme of US military and economic aid. By 1985 the total US aid allocation had reached $2300m a year.

The Open-door Policy

The shift in foreign policy was mirrored by a change in economic orientation. In 1974, Sadat announced a policy of *infitah* (opening)* to foreign investment. The key instrument was Law 43 of June 1974, which included a provision for setting up joint-venture companies, with the local partner holding at least 51 per cent. The *infitah* was the final, dramatically presented move in a trend dating back to 1968, when balance-of-payments problems forced Egypt into relaxing some of the restrictions in force on the movement of capital. The *infitah* failed to realize the hoped-for increase in productive investment. Foreign companies tended to concentrate on the oil sector and banking*. The foreign banks directed most of their business to import finance. Despite Arab and US aid, Egypt's economic problems worsened; external debt increased, and government finances fell heavily into deficit. In January 1977, a draft budget was announced including drastic cuts in food subsidies and increases in the prices of unsubsidized goods. This austerity package provoked widespread rioting by the Egyptian poor, protesting against what was seen as an unjustified attack on their already low standard of living.

The Camp David Accords

The economic crisis was soon overshadowed by Sadat's dramatic initiative on the Arab–Israeli conflict*. On 9 November, he announced before the People's Assembly (parliament) that he was ready to go to Israel to try to achieve peace in the Middle East. Events moved fast thereafter. Sadat addressed the Israeli Knesset (parliament) on 21 November and, after a series of negotiations between Egyptian and Israeli officials, Sadat signed the Camp David Accords* with Israel and the US on 17 September 1978. The accords consisted of two agreements, one covering the return of Sinai to Egyptian sovereignty, the other proposing a solution to the problem of the West Bank. Formalized in a peace treaty signed in Washington on 26 March 1979, the Camp David Accords were denounced by the Arab League* as capitulation. Arab states cut diplomatic ties with Egypt, the Arab League headquarters was moved from Cairo to Tunis, and Arab aid was cut off.

Internal politics

Sadat proclaimed throughout his rule that he intended to make Egypt's political system more democratic. He allowed political parties to operate, subject to some restrictions. In July 1978, he announced the abolition of the ASU, which was merged into the newly formed National Democratic Party (NDP). This party, headed by Sadat, regularly swept the board at elections, and the experiment in liberalization only had very limited success. The most effective opposition to Sadat was being organized outside established structures. Sadat's rule saw the appearance of numerous clandestine groups professing various means to achieve a more truly Islamic society. The traditional *Ikhwan** also re-emerged.

The assassination of Sadat

In 1981, clashes erupted in parts of Cairo between Muslims and Copts. Sadat blamed the disturbances on agitators, and proceeded to arrest about 1500 people, including prominent journalists and authors. The clampdown came amid frustration about Sadat's foreign policy. Egypt had failed to extract any substantial concessions from Israel on the Palestinian question, and the new US administration under President Ronald Reagan showed no inclination to help Sadat out of his predicament. On 6 October 1981, Sadat was killed by a group of soldiers passing in front of his reviewing stand at a military parade marking the anniversary of the 1973 War. The soldiers, led by Khalid al-Islambuli, belonged to the Jihad group, Islamic activists favouring violence to achieve their goals. Despite Sadat's violent end, power passed relatively smoothly to Husni Mubarak*, appointed vice-president in 1975.

Politics today

Mubarak

Mubarak resolved to approach Egypt's problems in a measured fashion, in contrast to Sadat's more flamboyant style. One of his first actions was to crack down on corruption among the elite, who had enriched themselves through the *infitah*. Mubarak also tried to adopt a more balanced foreign policy. In 1984, he re-established diplomatic relations with the Soviet Union, broken off by Sadat in 1981. He succeeded in improving Egypt's ties with the Arab world, notably through restoring relations with Jordan in 1984. Mubarak's top priority was the economy, but his efforts at economic reform made slow progress. By the mid-1980s Egypt was having difficulty servicing its foreign debt as oil revenues declined and the balance of payments fell heavily into deficit. Mubarak had failed to make a

President Sadat and his entourage sprawling among chairs as his assassins spray the reviewing-stand with machine-gun fire

significant personal impact on Egypt, but he did not face any well-organized opposition proposing an alternative leadership.

Mubarak determined to make Egyptian politics more democratic. The need for a more responsive political system was apparent, particularly in light of the numbers of young Egyptians attracted by Islamic movements. These movements ranged from traditionalists calling for the application of *shari'a** (Islamic law) to underground groups rejecting the modern world and believing in the violent overthrow of the state. Mubarak also wanted Egypt's economic problems to be debated as widely as possible so that reforms could be seen to be democratically approved, rather than imposed from above.

The 1984 'free' elections

Mubarak set great store by the first general election to be held under his rule, in May 1984. The election was to be the most free since the revolution, and he clearly hoped that the People's Assembly would, for the first time, have a substantial opposition to create the right climate for genuine debate. To give the electoral process credibility, Mubarak authorized all political parties to take part, except the Muslim Brothers* and communists. The Wafd*, which had been the biggest political party in the pre-revolution period, was allowed to reconstitute itself. However, the election rules said that any party obtaining less than 8 per cent of the vote had to transfer its votes to the party polling the highest number. This was clearly to the advantage of the government party, still the NDP. The election attracted a very low turnout – only 20 per cent of the registered electors. The NDP took more than 85 per cent of the seats. Of the opposition parties only the Wafd did well enough to qualify for seats: it won 57. The election proved a great disappointment for Mubarak, although the Wafd has given more substance to parliamentary debates by providing at least some opposition to the government.

Mubarak received credit in the first few years of his rule for his caution and his willingness to canvass a wide range of views before embarking on a new policy. But, by 1985, he and his mainly technocratic governments began to be seen as indecisive, and incapable of dealing with Egypt's problems. In October 1985, Mubarak was badly embarrassed by the US, when American jets intercepted an Egyptian airliner carrying Palestinians involved in the hijacking of an Italian cruise-ship. Mubarak had decided to hand the Palestinians to the Palestine Liberation Organization (PLO)* in Tunis. The US action aroused a growing tide of feeling that Egypt had become too subservient to the US. This anti-American feeling is linked with the sense of frustration about Egypt's peace treaty with Israel. Despite the restoration of relations with Jordan in 1984, Egypt is still isolated in the Arab world and has been unable to take advantage of the Israeli peace treaty to achieve anything for the Palestinians. In the mid-1980s Egypt's economic problems deepened, and Mubarak hinted that he might be forced to revert to a more authoritarian style of rule in the face of growing opposition being expressed in newspapers and street demonstrations. The armed forces continued to be an important centre of power, as they had been to varying degrees since the Free Officers took power in 1952.

The economy and society today

Egypt today remains a predominantly agricultural country. The Nile Valley – although only a fraction of Egypt's total area – contains some of the most fertile land in the world. Egypt also has a long tradition of industry, dating back originally to the efforts of Muhammad 'Ali* to modernize the country in the early nineteenth century. In recent years, however, Egypt has become increasingly dependent on the remitted earnings of migrant workers, oil revenues, Suez Canal dues and tourism. The growth in agricultural output is failing to keep pace with the population increase, and the country's industries tend to be inefficient and uncompetitive on the world market.

By the end of the nineteenth century, much of Egypt's cultivable land was given over to cotton, whose local long-staple strains are the best in the world. In the 1920s and 1930s, Egyptian industry grew dramatically, dominated by Tala't Harb's Misr Group. Egypt was able during this period to take advantage of the depression in Europe and America, and big strides were made, particularly in light industries geared to import-substitution. The 1952 Revolution was the culmination of a long political crisis, but economic factors also played an important role. It was felt that further strides towards industrial growth would depend on Egypt's agricultural wealth being better utilized. This required reducing the power of the landlords, who tended to invest their surpluses in property rather than in industry. In the event, little of the surplus taken from the country by the state in the years after the revolution was invested in industry. The big push towards industrialization came in the 1960s, after the decision to nationalize the Misr Group and other private sector companies.

Much of the industrial growth in the 1960s was achieved thanks to generous credits from the Soviet Union. However, the scale of expenditure on capital equipment left its mark on the balance of payments, and by the end of the decade Egypt's trade account fell heavily into deficit. The 1967 War was an added blow to the economy because it resulted in the closure of the Suez Canal, an important source of services income. The 1960s also saw the introduction of a social welfare system, based on subsidizing consumer goods. The government also guaranteed employment to university graduates, a policy which resulted in the massive inflation of the bureaucracy.

Development of the open-door policy
In the early 1970s, Egypt began to relax restrictions on the private sector and to encourage foreign investment. The most important piece of legislation in this regard was Law 43 of 1974, which allowed the establishment of joint ventures as long as the foreign partner did not hold more than 49 per cent of the equity. The *infitah*, or 'open-door' policy of the 1970s attracted foreign banks and oil companies in particular. But it also resulted in a rise in imports, while exposing Egypt more directly to worldwide inflation. Because much of the economy remained state-controlled and subject to administered prices, the *infitah* failed to bring in substantial foreign investment in sectors other than oil* and banking*: the foreign investor had to set the advantages of cheap labour and tax holidays against problems of access to local markets, higher energy costs than were available to the public sector, and above all bureaucratic obstacles. Imported and domestic inflation contributed to the escalation of the subsidies bill, while Egypt's external debt began to increase towards the end of the 1970s.

Many Egyptian business people took advantage of the *infitah* to amass large fortunes, usually through imports, while the living standards of the majority of the population did not appreciably improve. This aspect of the *infitah* sharpened social conflicts, and was a factor in provoking the January 1977 riots in protest against proposed cuts in food subsidies. President Mubarak, on taking power after Sadat's assassination, took action against a number of business people involved in corruption. He also tried to introduce measures to direct foreign and private sector investment towards productive activities, rather than to services and consumer goods imports.

In the early 1980s, Egypt benefited from rising oil prices and increased oil output. The economy was also boosted by the increasing sums sent home by migrant workers. Remittances, which by 1983 had become the largest single source of foreign exchange, were almost sufficient to cover the rising trade deficit. About $2000m a year in civilian and military aid from the US helped keep the overall balance of payments in the black. However, the subsidies bill continued to rise, the performance of industry and agriculture remained disappointing, and the state-dominated banking system proved inadequate. The rise in remittances spawned a thriving black market, operating at more competitive exchange rates than the fixed official rates. By 1986, the black market was handling at least $3000m a year, most of this being spent directly on private sector imports. As the world oil market weakened in late 1985, Egypt was forced to cut the price of its exported oil, with revenues dipping from almost $3000m in 1982 to below $1500m in 1986. The fall in oil revenues made it more and more difficult to service Egypt's external debt, which totalled more than $30,000m by the end of 1985. Egypt was forced to start negotiating with the International Monetary Fund (IMF) about financial assistance, the price of which was radical reform, in particular to the subsidies system and the exchange rate. Successive governments under Mubarak tried to institute reforms, but at too slow a pace to satisfy the IMF. Efforts were also made to improve the quality of education* and steps were taken to try to tackle one of Egypt's most serious problems, housing, which had been largely neglected through the 1960s and 1970s. However, Egypt can look forward to the last part of the century with little optimism. The problem of dealing with the financing gap seems certain to continue to be acute, while the overall performance of the economy is set to remain sluggish, with persistent problems of resource allocation and sorting out price differentials. One of the most difficult problems is the 2.7 per cent annual increase in population*. In 1986, the population reached 50 million; by the end of the century it will exceed 70 million.

DB

Further reading

M. Heikal, *The Road to Ramadan* (London, 1975)
D. Hirst and I. Beeson, *Sadat* (London, 1981)
D. Hopwood, *Egypt: Politics and Society 1945–1984* (2nd ed. London, 1985)
R. Stephens, *Nasser: a political biography* (London, 1971)
P. J. Vatikiotis, *The History of Egypt* (London, 1985)
J. Waterbury, *The Egypt of Nasser and Sadat* (Princeton, 1983)

Iran

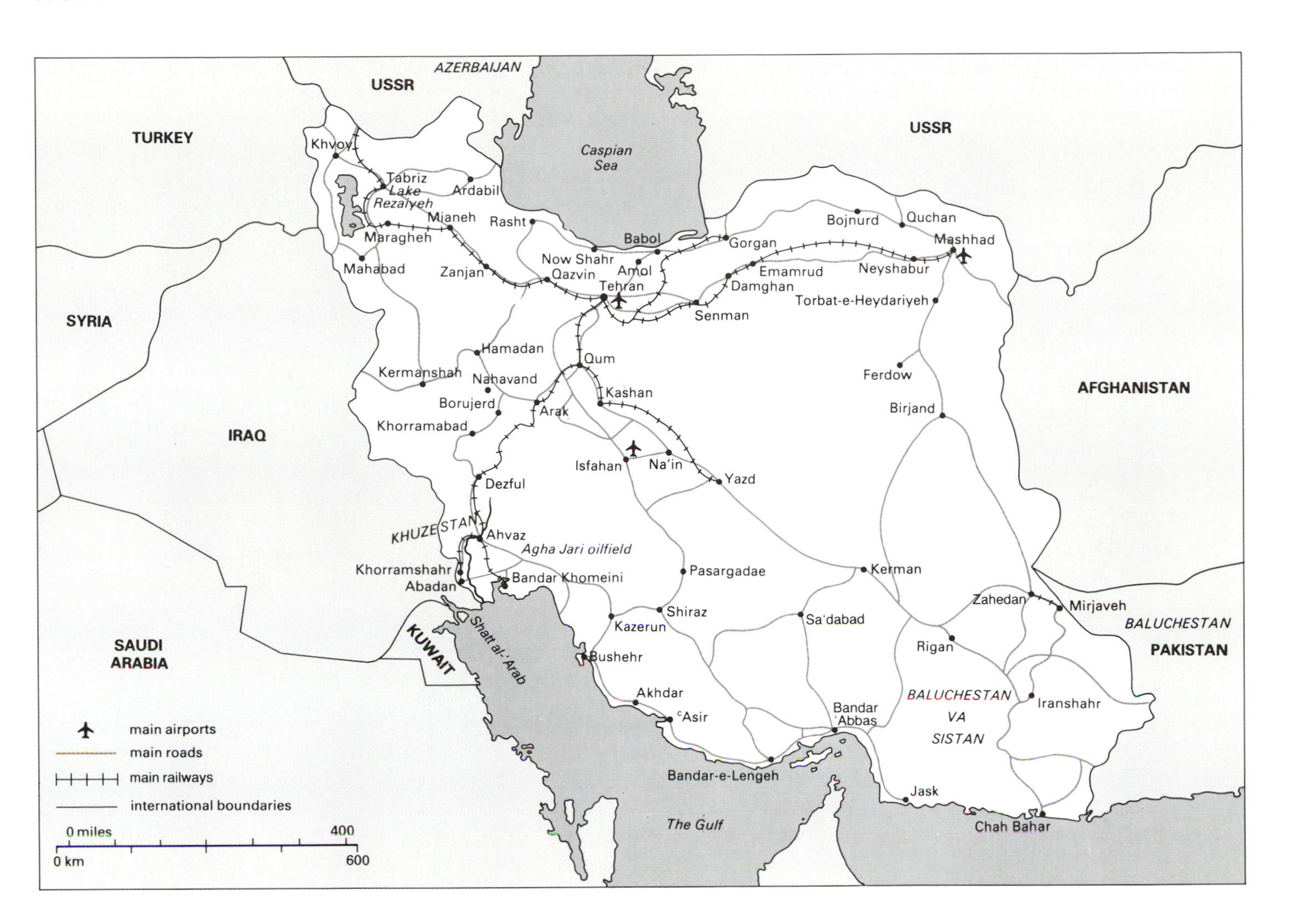

Geography and topography

Iran is bounded on the north by the Transcaucasian and Turkistan territories of the Soviet Union and by the Caspian Sea lying between them. On the east it is bounded by Afghanistan and Pakistan, on the west by Iraq and Turkey and on the south by the Gulf and the Indian Ocean. It consists of a plateau surrounded on almost every side by mountains. Of these the Zagros Mountains extend from the north-west to the eastern part of the Gulf and from there eastwards into Baluchistan. Along the southern edge of the Caspian Sea are the narrower but equally high Elburz Mountains. The interior of Iran is covered partly by a salt swamp called *kavir* and partly by a region of loose stones or sand called *dasht*, while most of the country's cultivation is on stretches of land around the foothills of the mountain ranges. Most of the *kavir* is too desolate and dangerous for exploration. Iran's climate ranges from as high as 55°C in the summer in the interior to as low as −20°C in some areas in the winter. The Caspian Sea area, the most densely populated in the country, is hot and humid while most of the country is arid.

Peoples

The population of Iran is made up of various ethnic groups of whom those who speak Persian, in the north and centre of the country, form the majority. Nomadic tribes such as the Bakhtiaris are almost certainly of Kurdish stock while the Qashqai are Turkic. Smaller

Official title	The Islamic Republic of Iran
Area	1,648,000 sq. km
Population	44.8 million (1985 estimate)
Government and constitution	An amended constitution stating that the form of government would be an Islamic Republic was approved by referendum on 2–3 December 1979. An Islamic Assembly (Majlis) is popularly elected. A president is elected separately for a four-year term and appoints the prime minister with Majlis approval. The 270-member Majlis holds legislative power and is elected for a four-year term. The Ayatollah Khomeini is regarded as the spiritual guide of the nation as the *Vali-i-faqih* (see *Vilayat-i-faqih* under Iran)
Currency	1 rial = 100 dinars; US $1 =IR 80.70
Languages	The official language is Farsi; Kurdish, Baluchi and Turkic are also spoken
Religion	The majority are Shiʿi Muslims, but there are some Sunnis and there are small Christian, Jewish and Zoroastrian communities
Climate	The summer is extremely hot with temperatures of over 55°C recorded. The winters are cold with temperatures of −20°C common in many areas. Most of Iran is dry, although the Caspian shore is hot and humid

groups such as Circassians and Georgians are found in the northern provinces of Azerbaijan and the Caspian while Baluchi groups exist in the south. Kurdish dialects are spoken in the north and the central Zagros Mountains.

Religion

Most of Iran submitted to Islam after defeats by the Arab Muslim armies in the seventh century AD. Persian influence became increasingly felt after the transfer by the ʿAbbasids* of the capital to Baghdad in 750 AD. Until the foundation of the Safavid* Empire in the sixteenth century most of the population of present-day Iran was Sunni*. However the principal weapon used by Ismaʿil Safavi in his struggle to wrest control from the Ottomans in the west was to foster a sense of national identity by adopting Shiʿi Islam. Shiʿism has been the official sect of Islam in Iran since then.

Iran was transformed from a monarchy into an Islamic Republic in 1979, following a year-long revolutionary movement against Shah Muhammad Riza Pahlavi. The end of the Shah's 37-year-old reign came spectacularly and suddenly. The religious revolution which brought about the collapse of his formidable monarchy was like no other popular rising before it. It was not a traditional revolution and seemed an anachronism in the twentieth century. Despite chaos, bloodshed and a devastating war with Iraq, however, the Islamic Republic not only survived but became a force within the region and within the Muslim world beyond.

The Shiʿis* of Iran, in contrast with the Sunnis* who predominate in most other Muslim countries, had always tended to reject secular authority, and had revolted against unjust kings and foreign domination at the turn of the century. However, they had also shown distaste for government. In 1905–7, having succeeded in imposing a constitution on absolute monarchy, they had withdrawn, leaving the field to their secular, Western-oriented allies of convenience. This reluctance for political involvement was to be reflected in the Mosque's passive role during the Westernizing rule of Riza Shah in the 1920s and 1930s. Even during the Allied occupation of the Second World War the Shiʿi leadership kept a low profile. Not until the nationalist turmoil of the late 1940s and early 1950s was the Mosque again to be involved in politics, drawn into them by its more maverick members.

History up to 1939

The first Persian empire, the Achaemenid Empire, was founded by Cyrus, under whom Babylon was taken in 529 BC and in 525 BC his successor Cambyses took Egypt. This period of conquests was continued by Darius. The empire was finally defeated by Alexander in 331 BC. A power struggle following Alexander's death led to the creation of the Seleucid Empire. The next great empire, that of the Sasanians, lasted until it was defeated by the Arabs at the battle of

Qadisiya in 637 AD. Muslim rule reached its zenith with the ʿAbbasid Empire in which Persian rather than Arabian influences were increasingly felt. Pressure from Turkish tribes contributed to the disintegration of ʿAbbasid power and the emergence of empires such as that of the Seljuks. The sixteenth century saw the emergence of the Safavids under whom art and architecture flourished. The late eighteenth century saw the rise of the Qajars, who transferred the capital from Isfahan to Tehran. The latter part of the nineteenth century saw increasing influence by Russia in the north of the country and by Britain in the south. During the First World War Iran was essentially pro-Turkish although remaining nominally neutral and, following the country's state of economic chaos at the end of the war, British advisors were sent to help reorganize the economy.

The tottering Qajar* dynasty which had ruled Iran since the late eighteenth century was overthrown by Riza Khan (Riza Shah*), a military officer in the Russian-modelled Cossack Brigade. Staging a coup in February 1921 with the help of some British officials, Riza Shah spent five years consolidating his position as strongman – ultimately overthrowing the Qajars in late 1925 and crowning himself the first Pahlavi Shah in early 1926.

A strong nationalist in the mould of Turkey's Kemal Atatürk*, Riza Shah embarked on a determined drive to modernize and secularize Iran. He was a natural leader with a powerful personality, but he was also an illiterate and a man of crude methods. The modernization programme he instituted amounted more to Westernization and blind imitation than the long-overdue reforms which many had hoped for. This created much resentment and, in trying to curb the influence of the clergy who had dominated most aspects of Iranian society, he chose the kind of physical methods which compounded the resentment.

Riza Shah's most lasting reforms included the secularization of the legal system, education and bureaucracy, the centralization of the administration and the creation of a disciplined army. At the same time he tried to industrialize the country by building factories and a transnational railway. Apart from the textile industry, many of these schemes were ill-conceived and wasteful. For example, the railway trunk line, which took a decade to build at heavy cost to the population, was more a showpiece to symbolize Iran's entry into the twentieth century than a boon to the economy. The southern terminal serviced an obscure Gulf port, while the northern section ended in rich agricultural lands Riza Shah had seized by force.

Perhaps more deleterious were Riza Shah's dealings with the clergy and their traditionalist followers, who made up the bulk of the population. In trying to secularize and modernize society, an impatient Riza Shah banned the wearing of traditional clothes in public. Religious leaders were forced to shed their cloaks and turbans. Women were ordered to cast off the *chadur* (veil) and don Western dress. Men, in turn, had to wear Western suits, ties and brimmed hats. The new rules were enforced by the police and the military and this often led to violent confrontations – particularly in 1935 in Iran's second most holy city of Mashhad. The social consequences of this forced modernization were to be felt long after Riza Shah was deposed by Allied occupation forces in the Second World War.

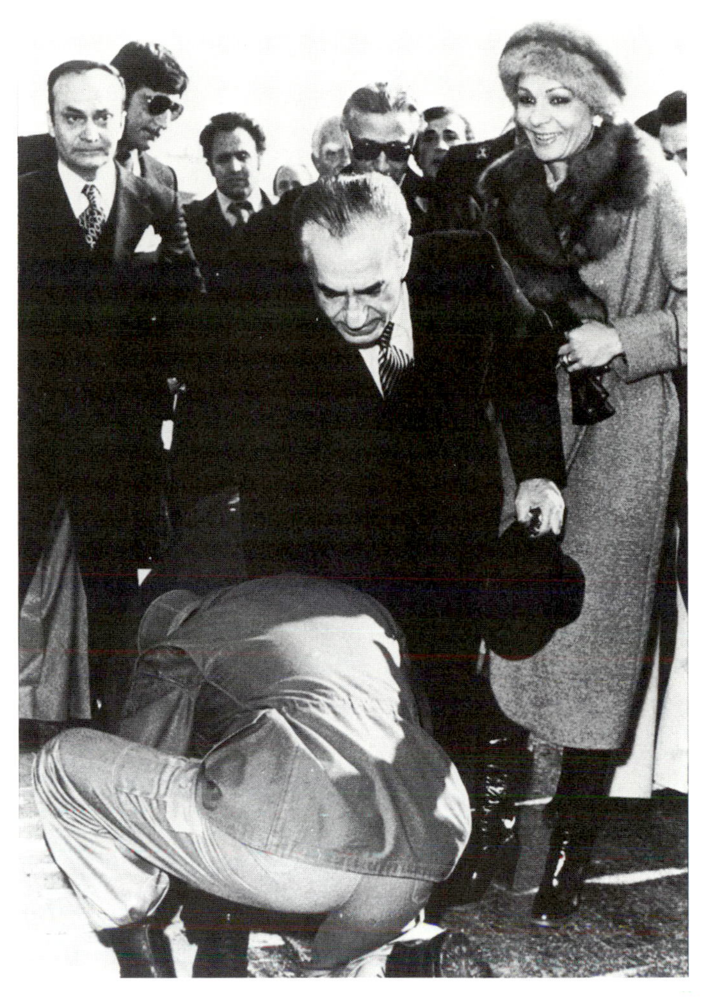

A soldier kneeling to kiss the Shah's feet as a last homage before he departs for exile on 16th January 1979

In the first half of his reign, Riza Shah was seen by many as a saviour of a disintegrating country. His strength of leadership and nationalism were welcomed after the succession of weak and corrupt Qajar rulers. The second half of his rule, however, was better remembered for its brutality, arbitrariness and corruption. Few mourned his forced abdication in 1941 but few also disagreed that he was one of the more impressive and exceptional Iranian leaders of the last two centuries.

History since the Second World War

From August 1941 to spring 1946 Iran was an occupied country, used as a route for Western supplies to the Soviet Union. From September 1941 Riza Shah's 21-year-old son Muhammad Riza was Shah, an uncertain man who lacked his exiled father's will to power. The occupation fuelled a nationalist movement which burst open once the foreign troops had left. The Soviet Union withdrew reluctantly, but Britain's timely departure barely reduced its control (through the Anglo-Iranian Oil Company) of Iran's economic and political life. Iran's confrontation with Britain came to a head with the nationalization of the oil industry* in March 1951.

The Musaddiq period

The nationalization movement was led by Muhammad Musaddiq*, an ageing but popular politician who became prime minister in 1951 on a wave of nationalist fervour. He was helped by Ayatollah Kashani, a radical religious leader who became a member of parliament in 1951. However, the Musaddiq movement came to an inglorious end in August 1953 in a coup engineered by the US Central Intelligence Agency (CIA), British Intelligence and Iranian officers. The Shah, who had fled to Rome at the height of the coup, returned within days to consolidate his powers with the help of the military, of Savak (*Sazman-i amniyat va ittilaʿat-i kishvar*), a secret police modelled on the CIA, and of Washington. For the next quarter-century the Shah created a highly unstable dictatorship. By the end of the 1950s economic mismanagement and extravagant military spending presented the Shah with a new crisis. Opposition, led by remnants of the Musaddiq movement such as Mehdi Bazargan, Allahyar Salah and Shapur Bakhtiar, surfaced once again. The Shah tried to take the initiative with half-hearted reforms aimed at Iran's feudal village life. In 1961, with a reformist John F. Kennedy in the White House, he felt under such pressure that he appointed ʿAli Amini, an able and ambitious reformist and a one-time US ambassador in Washington, as prime minister.

By mid-1962, however, the Shah had visited and mollified Kennedy and was soon able to replace the prime minister with Asad Allah ʿAlam, a childhood friend who proceeded to undo most of Amini's reforms. Faced with continuing secular opposition but unable to silence it for fear of Washington's disapproval, he announced a 'White Revolution' in January 1963, involving the redistribution of lands and the vote for women. A referendum was held in which 99.9 per cent were said to have voted in favour. This shifted the focus from secular dissidents seeking Western-style democratic reforms to religious zealots opposing an ostensibly modernizing monarch. This equation was easier for the Shah to solve, providing a lesson which he would try to apply again in 1978.

The first challenge from Khomeini

A radical religious leader called Ruhallah Khumayni (Khomeini)* emerged from the quietist clergy to challenge reforms seen merely as an attempt to consolidate the Shah's power. Khomeini was arrested on 4 June 1963 and hundreds of protesters who took to the streets the following day to demand his release were killed. The massacre reflected less the Shah's resolve than that of ʿAlam and hardline military commanders such as Ghulam ʿAli Uvaysi (Oveissi). Khomeini's conservative colleagues, such as Ayatollah Kazim Shariʿatmadari, appeared to desert him, leaving the Shah free to deal with the 'fanatics' in the streets. Released within a year, Khomeini was back on the offensive in late 1964 when the Shah pushed through legislation granting US military personnel immunity from local laws. Khomeini was rearrested and exiled in November to Turkey, from where he moved to Najaf in Iraq, the second holiest site after Mecca for the Shiʿis, where he was to remain in relative obscurity until the crisis of 1978.

In the last half of the 1960s and in the early 1970s the Shah and Iran enjoyed exceptional stability and prosperity, albeit at high cost in human rights. Reflecting this continuity was the 1965–77 tenure of Prime Minister Amir ʿAbbas Huvayda (Hoveyda).

US encouragement and the 1970's economic boom

With the 1969 inauguration of President Richard Nixon, the Shah found a friend in the White House who, unlike Kennedy, would not keep him on a short leash. In May 1972 Nixon visited Tehran and gave him *carte blanche* to America's non-nuclear armoury. After the 1973 Arab-Israeli War* and the fourfold increase in oil prices, the Shah was presented with the financial means – about $20,000m in annual revenues – to fulfil his highest ambitions. He aimed to put Iran among the top economic and military giants of the world in half a generation. The result was massive spending, starting in 1974. Imports and spending went up more than fourfold, straining Iran's inadequate infrastructure, overheating the economy, producing raging inflation and creating shortages of food and consumer goods. Large-scale development and the promises of riches sparked a massive exodus from the villages to the cities, crippling agriculture and creating unforeseen new social problems. Europeans, Americans, Japanese and half a million people from the neighbouring region poured into Iran. Westerners took the best jobs and housing, creating resentment and housing shortages. The sudden changes and the influx of Western ways produced a culture shock.

The seeds of crisis

The changes were so sudden and disruptive that the Shah and his bureaucrats soon lost control of the economy and society. The Shah

October 1977, the Shah organized a reception at the Gulestan Palace to celebrate his 58th birthday. To his right stands his loyal prime minister, Amir ʿAbbas Hoveyda

made matters worse by trying to mobilize the population through a one-party system – the Rastakhiz Party – and instituting anti-corruption and anti-profiteering campaigns. The creation of the Rastakhiz Party angered nearly everyone, while the arbitrary crack-downs against economic crimes alienated those in the business community who supported him most. Reduced oil revenues, meanwhile, brought about wrenching cutbacks in the economy. This general atmosphere was aggravated by breakdowns in the over-strained electric power system which plunged Tehran and other cities into darkness and crippled industries.

Perhaps worse than the apparent disintegration of Iran's physical infrastructure and its administration was the cultural dislocation that the Iranian people underwent in the 1970s. It seemed to many that their traditions were being destroyed and their country was being turned over to the West and recast in the image of America.

Political emergence of the Mosque

The main beneficiary of the cultural backlash provoked by the boom years of the 1970s was the Mosque. Young women abandoned Western dress for the *hijab* (head covering), and angry young men and women sought sanctuary in tradition and religion. Even less religious critics sought the Mosque's relative protection from the Shah's repression. Shiʿi leaders, who are dependent on donations from the faithful, first criticized violations of Islamic rules, then tackled economic issues and finally challenged the whole system. Well before the start of the revolution in 1978, some sort of social explosion seemed inevitable.

The revolution

The first signs of trouble were the open-protest letters from secular nationalist dissidents in mid-1977. Responding to popular discontent, they had calculated that the election to the US presidency of Jimmy Carter, a self-proclaimed champion of human rights, would so shake the Shah's self-confidence that he would not dare arrest them. They were right.

To prevent a repetition of his problems with Kennedy in the early 1960s, the Shah embarked on a 'liberalization' campaign. Indeed, the open letters served him well as long as the authors could be controlled. However, mounting economic problems – highlighted by the most serious power blackouts yet – forced him to dismiss Hoveyda in the summer of 1977 and replace him with Jamshid Amuzegar, a US-educated technocrat well-liked in Washington. The dissidents, meanwhile, pressed home their advantage with public gatherings – the first such open protests – under the guise of poetry readings and literary lectures. The pace of events was mainly dictated by the Shah's scheduled visit to Washington in mid-November. Before the visit, radical students and politicians of the Musaddiq era seemed to hold the initiative, with the Shah showing uncharacteristic restraint. The riot police were used sparingly. After returning from Washington, however, where he had received some reassurances from Carter, he used massive force to silence the opposition within a few days. When Carter paid a return visit at the turn of the year Iran did, indeed, seem an 'island of peace and stability' as the US president chose to describe it.

However, in late 1977 the mysterious death in Najaf of Khomeini's eldest son, Mustafa, touched off demonstrations by theology students. On 6 January 1978, a Shah-approved article in the local press insulting Khomeini provoked the religious community. When theology students in Qum took to the streets to demand a retraction, police opened fire, killing at least six people.

Days of mourning

The religious reaction to the killings forced moderate leaders such as Shariʿatmadari to declare a '40th-day' of national mourning, a minimum response from a conservative religious hierarchy who did not want to upset the status quo but had to take some action to buy time and cool tempers.

The 40th day after a killing is a particularly emotional date on the Shiʿi calendar because of the tradition of mourning for Shiʿi martyrs in the early days of Islam. The Shah was now being compared with the oppressors of those days and his victims with the martyrs, particularly Imam Husayn and his seventy-two companions, who were massacred in Karbala, now in Iraq.

Violent 40th-day incidents between mourners and troops followed, first in Tabriz, then in Yazd. Hundreds died and the rioting and burning of public buildings which ensued in Tabriz resembled an uprising. The refusal of protesters to be intimidated and the adverse public reaction ensured that any tough response from the regime would now hurt the regime more than the protesters. With the third round of 40th-day mourning celebrations centring on Tehran, and with the Shah forced to exercise restraint in his own capital, the cycle of violence was finally broken in mid-May. During the three-month hiatus that followed, the religious hierarchy tried to win enough royal concessions to defuse the crisis.

The Shah, in turn, had neither the heart nor the will for the massive crackdown that would now have been necessary to silence the opposition. He was less willing than in 1963 to give his more hardline subordinates a free hand; indeed, having reached heights of megalomania and surrounded himself with sycophants, he had no one left to turn to for advice. An important consideration was the reaction a crackdown would have in the West. Throughout the crisis he had reiterated his 1977 pledge to liberalize and widen his regime's popular base, a theme echoed by his allies in Washington. The kind of crackdown he was now considering would make nonsense of his whole strategy. Yet he was unwilling to make real concessions that would reduce his powers.

In the event, he neither cracked down nor made real concessions. In 1978 he dismissed the ageing Savak chief Niʿmat Allah Nasiri and announced a limited purge of senior security officials associated with the worst excesses of the regime. Failing to mollify the public, the purges unintentionally panicked the security organizations, crippling their effectiveness at a time when they were most needed.

The Abadan cinema burning

On 19 August 1978, when an Abadan cinema burned down with 477 people locked inside, the regime immediately blamed the religious fanatics but the public finger pointed towards the Shah. The outrage through Iran was so intense that Shariʿatmadari secretly appealed to the Shah to act. The Shah responded by changing governments; in place of Amuzegar – who, ironically, bore no responsibility for the political system – the Shah appointed on 27 August Jaʿafar Sharif-Emami. An old and faithful friend, Sharif-Emami was given a mandate to continue liberalization and to prepare the country for 'free' elections in June 1979.

Concessions – but too few, too late

Not only were these moves too late but both the choice of prime minister and later events made matters worse. One of Sharif-Emami's first tasks was to make 'concessions' to the religious community by banning gambling, imposing restrictions on the consumption of alcohol and vowing to combat corruption. However, given the fact that Sharif-Emami had for years run the Shah's Pahlavi Foundation (whose assets included Iran's first grand casinos), his promises were ridiculed.

The only real concession was to allow the press greater freedom. Earlier, this might have been a key to the Shah's salvation, but all it did now was to expose to an avid audience the royal dirty linen, thus confirming the worst accusations of the Shah's opponents.

The Jaleh Square massacre

Whatever credibility Sharif-Emami or the Shah had left was shattered on 8 September at Tehran's Jaleh Square, when troops opened fire on peaceful demonstrators, killing hundreds, perhaps over one thousand. The massacre, known as 'Black Friday', further polarized the two sides, horrified even the Shah's middle-class supporters, made any collaboration with conservative religious leaders like Shariʿatmadari impossible and, in hindsight, marked the beginning of the end of the Shah's rule.

After 'Black Friday' the Shah found his options extremely limited. His harsh measures had backfired, while his pledges of liberalization were derided. Further concessions that did not include immediate elections and the Shah's departure, or at least temporary exile, seemed unlikely to satisfy the opposition. Roaming the palace, often tearfully, even in the presence of foreign visitors, the Shah seemed to have lost all capacity for decision. It was later revealed that he had been suffering from a rare form of cancer since 1974; but the Shah's main problem was not physical.

Beset by advice from all sides and unable to make up his mind, he came increasingly to rely on the Americans to save him as they had done in 1953. The American and British ambassadors of 1978 draw a picture of a helpless Shah constantly seeking advice and support from Washington and London. At one stage even a startled Soviet ambassador found himself being asked to offer a solution.

Tehran's day of anarchy

By November 1978 the Shah, actively considering leaving the country, warned the US ambassador that he might abdicate. Instead, he was persuaded by the hardliners to fight back, arrest 10–20,000 dissidents and break the back of the opposition. The groundwork for the crackdown was laid by *agent provocateur* security men who fanned out through the streets of Tehran on 4–5 November, setting fire to banks, government buildings and cars. In response to the chaos the Shah formed a military government on 6 November. However, once again his nerve failed and, instead of the tough Oveissi, the new military prime minister chosen to supervise the crackdown was Ghulamriza Azhari, a scholarly general without the necessary ruthlessness.

The military was unable to impose its will on the demonstrators and oil-industry strikers although it did for a few weeks succeed in forcing enough workers back to work to raise production to reasonable levels. The demonstrators, however, quickly returned to the streets. Troops armed with submachine guns responded by sometimes shooting wildly into the crowds, sometimes looking the other way. This was a reflection of the uncertainty at the top as well as of the psychological toll on soldiers called upon to shoot down their fellow citizens. The Shah's trump card, the army, could no longer be relied upon.

Khomeini's demands from France

In Neauphle-le-Château, a village near Paris where Khomeini had been forced to move from Najaf in October, the Ayatollah was insisting that the Shah had to go. The demand articulated such widespread feeling that neither the moderate religious leaders nor the dissidents dared contradict it. Indeed, since the Abadan cinema fire and, in particular, since Black Friday, Khomeini had become the undisputed leader of the protest movement. All the other potential leaders, having compromised with the Shah at some stage in the previous decades, were tainted.

The Ayatollah Khomeini during his brief exile in France

In December, two extraordinary demonstrations dispelled any remaining doubts about the Shah's fate. Starting in early December and coinciding with the start of the religious month of Muharram, demonstrators added a new tactic to the street marches. Going onto their roof-tops at night they shouted 'Allahu akbar' (God is great) and 'Khumayni rahbar' (Khomeini is leader). All the disoriented troops could do was to shoot into the air, adding to the drama of the occasion.

The departure of the Shah

Then, on 10 and 11 December (Tasuʿa and Ashura) – the anniversary of the day of Imam Husayn's martyrdom – between two and four million people marched through the streets of Tehran calling for the removal of the Shah, the return of Khomeini and the establishment of an Islamic Republic. Similar demonstrations took place in other cities. The extraordinary size of the demonstrations and the discipline and control of the opposition left no room for doubt even in Washington that the Shah had to go. Things having been left until too late, however, the choice of alternative governments had narrowed. Ultimately, in late December, only Shapur Bakhtiar, one of the senior figures in the secular National Front of Musaddiq, could be found to serve and justify the Shah's departure. The Shah finally left on 16 January 1979, having installed Bakhtiar as his prime minister.

The return of Khomeini

An ambitious politician, Bakhtiar did not see himself merely as a front and tried to prevent Khomeini from returning to take over the direct leadership of the movement. But Khomeini eventually flew back to Tehran on 1 February to a riotous welcome by millions. Basing himself in the poorer section of Tehran, Khomeini appointed his own provisional prime minister, Mehdi Bazargan, a colleague of Bakhtiar in Musaddiq's days but with deep roots in the religious community. In the ensuing confrontation, Khomeini's forces ruled supreme in the streets and were now also wooing away military commanders. Within a week of Khomeini's return it became evident that the Shah's establishment would very soon collapse or wither away.

Revolution – the final showdown

Behind-the-scenes negotiations with the military were, however, aborted by rebellious air-force technicians at the Dawshan Tapeh air base east of Tehran on the night of 9 February. Imperial guards (the Javidan) rushed down from the palace but failed to quell the rebellion. The following morning, when the guards returned, civilians had joined the rebels, erecting barricades and making molotov cocktails (petrol bombs). On the afternoon of 10 February, the military declared a curfew. Khomeini ordered the people to

As the nation awaited the return of Khomeini, a soldier places a flower against the Ayatollah's portrait

On 20th January 1979, four days after the Shah's departure, hundreds of thousands congregated around the Shahyad (now Azadi) memorial to agitate for Khomeini's return

The 20th January demonstrations

Khomeini's triumphant arrival from France at Tehran's international airport, 1st February 1979

ignore it. Going onto the offensive, the revolutionaries – armed with weapons obtained from the rebel base – then started attacking police stations and army bases in and around Tehran. By noon the following day, 11 February, they had captured most of the police stations and army bases. Similar battles were raging in other cities. Meeting in emergency session late that morning, senior military commanders decided that the only way of preserving what was left of the army was to declare neutrality and recall all soldiers back to their barracks. It was, however, too late. The revolutionaries hardly paused in their head-long victorious drive, capturing the Shah's last bastion, the palace, by noon the following day.

It had been one of the more unusual revolutions recorded in history. Certainly, neither the French nor Soviet revolutions had involved such large sections of the population; nor had they seen an unarmed people defying troops for a whole year – at first every forty days, then almost daily as they marched in the streets offering their bodies in sacrifice until their tormenters cracked.

Post-revolution

On the afternoon of 12 February and on the following day an eerie calm descended on Tehran and most other cities. Good cheer was the order of the day. Members of the Shah's regime, such as the former Savak chief Nasiri, Hoveyda and hundreds of agents and secret police, were taken to Khomeini's headquarters to await trial. Those familiar with the Shah's regime and the street killings of the previous year had expected the blood of retribution to flow in the streets; but it did not.

Then, on 14 February, the US Embassy was attacked and that night mysterious gunfire broke the silence of Tehran. Panicky revolutionaries rushed from one apparently besieged television station to another and to threatened power plants and other vital installations, often ending up shooting each other. It was not clear who was responsible for the gunfight. Some thought it was the extremists, perhaps the leftists, others thought it was the work of Savak agents and counter-revolutionaries. The revolution, until then so orderly, seemed to be disintegrating.

On the following day the first executions took place after summary trials. They were of Nasiri and three others and, it was later revealed, were aimed at bringing home to the counter-revolutionaries the reality of the revolution. The executions totalled about 600 – not all political – in the first six months. Their summary nature instilled fear and insecurity in many people and brought calls from moderates in Iran and from around the world for a halt. But once released, the urge for revenge was so strong that all those who had the power to moderate it discovered that the price in lost credibility was too high.

Khomeini was no exception. Five weeks and forty-nine executions after the revolution, he called a halt to summary punishment. Within three weeks, however, he had to admit defeat, giving the go-ahead for the execution of more than thirty former officials, including Hoveyda, in the space of a few days. Within another two weeks, the execution toll rose to 150. In the weeks and months that followed, Khomeini, often at Bazargan's urging, tried at least twice more to stop the killings. Each time he had to give way to the radicals, in the process surrendering some more of his authority.

The liberals, nationalists and leftists had little or no quarrel with the Westernization that had taken place under the Shah. Steeped in Western traditions, they refused to concede that the leaders of the Mosque had any role to play in running the country. It was, perhaps, true that Khomeini had led the revolution but he and his colleagues, they said, should now retire to the mosques and let the politicians take care of the country.

The Islamic Republic

These differences came out into the open, and onto the streets, over the 1 April 1979 referendum, which sanctioned the declaration of the 'Islamic Republic of Iran' and over the Islamic constitution of December. Ironically, the latter was modelled on the Western and principally French presidential parliamentary system. There was only one key difference, enshrined in the provision granting ultimate authority to a collegially elected spiritual leader or guide (*Vilayet-i-faqih**). For the moment this referred to Khomeini until his death or incapacitation.

These disagreements were to lead to a political explosion in June 1981 and prolonged bloodshed that verged on civil war. In both the short and long terms the Mosque prevailed. The liberals and leftists were to charge that the Mosque had 'hijacked' the revolution. In truth, events developed as much, if not more, by accident than by design. Khomeini had, despite his rhetoric, initially given the leading role to liberals such as Bazargan and his Musaddiqist ministers. He himself had spent the first year after the revolution in the holy city of Qum. Indeed, had the liberals shown themselves capable of governing, it may be that Khomeini would have merely returned to the role of spiritual guide.

The hostage crisis

As it transpired, events evolved through a fitful process of trial and error. It did not help that these issues were being resolved in an atmosphere of intense crisis precipitated by the seizure of the US embassy in Tehran on 4 November 1979 and by neighbouring Iraq's 22 September 1980 invasion of Khuzestan and other border provinces (see Iran–Iraq War).

The seizure of the embassy and of some fifty diplomat hostages was the signal for the so-called Second Revolution. Ostensibly aimed at US interference and Washington's decision in October to admit the ailing Shah for medical treatment, it was in fact aimed mainly at pro-Western forces within Iran that were hostile to the religious and cultural aspirations of the people and intent on renewing the old dependence on the US. This trend had been symbolized by the 2 November meeting in Algiers between Bazargan and President Carter's national security adviser Zbigniew Brzezinski, a former hardline supporter of the Shah and an advocate of forceful measures against the revolutionary movement. Pictures and television films of Bazargan and Foreign Minister Ebrahim Yazdi shaking hands with the revolution's biggest symbolic enemy abroad brought all the pent-up frustrations of Muslim radicals to a head. Unable to strike back directly at Bazargan himself, who was, after all, Khomeini's chosen man, they struck at the next most obvious target, the sprawling US embassy compound in central Tehran.

The militant Muslim students who took over the embassy

apparently planned a protest sit-in, but after thousands of demonstrators rallied to their support at the embassy gates and Khomeini backed their demand for the return of the Shah to face justice, the students decided to stay for a showdown. Within two days, on 6 November, Bazargan and his cabinet of liberal ministers were forced to resign and hand over power to the Islamic Revolutionary Council, which had been operating as a parallel government ever since February.

The US hostage crisis lasted 444 days. Washington retaliated by freezing over $10 billion in Iranian assets abroad on 14 November; and on 25 April 1980 it attempted a military rescue mission which was aborted when two US aircraft collided in the Tabas Desert, killing eight American commandos. The hostages were released on 20 January 1981, following prolonged negotiations in Algiers.

The crisis had a severe diplomatic and financial effect on Iran. The radicals, however, argued that these losses did not negate the much greater political and psychological benefits. The Western connection had been weakened and, whatever the morality of the hostage-taking, Iranians had stood up to a superpower and shed their debilitating inferiority complex.

Iranian troops preparing for battle with Iraq, 1980

*The Iran–Iraq War**

On 22 September 1980, Iraq* invaded Khuzestan (containing the oilfields and the giant Abadan refinery), Ilam, Kermanshahan and Kurdestan Provinces. After initial successes, however, the Iraqi forces became bogged down in siege warfare. Iran went on the offensive in September 1981 and in the following year recaptured most of the occupied territories. Later Iranian offensives were less decisive but by late 1985 Iraq was almost entirely on the defensive and Iran seemed determined to continue pressing for the downfall of the Iraqi regime.

Iraq, helped by its rich Arab allies and France and the Soviet Union, had superior weaponry. Iran's strength lay in the commitment and fervour of its Revolutionary Guards (Pasdaran), volunteers (*basij*) and regular army. Khomeini and his supporters described the fight as one between the spiritual and material worlds, giving the war near-mythical dimensions. If Iran won, the Islamic movement would clearly assume an entirely new international dimension.

Rift between Mosque and secular forces

The conflict between religious and secular forces within Iran itself, partly fuelled by the war with Iraq and partly by the hostage crisis, was to lead to a direct clash and much bloodshed in June 1981. On 25 January 1980, Abu'l-Hasan Bani Sadr had been elected president of the Islamic Republic. A previously obscure Islamic economist who had spent the fifteen years before the revolution in exile in France, he was viewed as Khomeini's favourite for the office and won the popular vote with a 75 per cent majority. A modernist educated in the Western tradition, the 46-year-old president started his term with high expectations all round. His prestige was further enhanced when Khomeini transferred to him his functions as supreme commander-in-chief of the armed forces and gave him a mandate to run the government. Within weeks, however, Bani Sadr had impaled himself on the hostage issue and all but destroyed his authority.

Shariʿatmadari and the Tabriz revolt

The differences which had been building up since early 1979 between the traditionalists and modernist Muslims had been inchoate and sporadic. At first, near the middle of 1979, secular and leftist forces challenged Khomeini's vision of the new Iran with street demonstrations on issues such as press and political freedoms and then the rights of women. Later in 1979, soon after the seizure of the US embassy, secular forces joined modernists as well as outright counter-revolutionaries in a grand alliance under the banner of Ayatollah Shariʿatmadari and made the boldest challenge yet to Khomeini. Although Shariʿatmadari had now grudgingly reconciled himself to the revolution, he remained an object of exploitation by opportunists and counter-revolutionaries. He had lost prestige during the revolution because of his record of collaboration with the Shah's regime. Nevertheless, he still commanded a large following, particularly among the 13m Azerbaijanis of his home province. Those who opposed Khomeini had an ideal vehicle in the mild-mannered Ayatollah. Thus, the Muslim Peoples Republican Party (MPRP), created with his blessing, tried to take over Tabriz in December soon after the seizure of the US embassy. For a while they succeeded, seizing the radio and TV station and other key buildings. But they overplayed their hand by trying to spark off a revolt in Qum itself.

Shariʿatmadari, Khomeini and most of the religious hierarchy were based in Qum. Khomeini's supporters struck back, executing four of the leaders of the Tabriz revolt. Khomeini himself went to see Shariʿatmadari, who was reportedly presented with evidence that counter-revolutionaries were using him to overthrow the whole religious leadership. Shariʿatmadari then ordered the MPRP's offices closed; the revolt collapsed and nothing more was heard of the party again. Some two years later Shariʿatmadari was himself placed under house arrest after becoming involved in another coup attempt.

In the debate between traditionalists and modernists, an emerging theme had been whether 'doctrine' or 'expertise' should take precedence. The modernists and secular groups argued that the main criterion in deciding who ran the country should be expertise. The traditionalists stressed the importance of doctrine, or ideological commitment.

The Mujahidin-i-khalq

Under Bani Sadr, the debate took clear shape with the president becoming the focus for all those who thought the religious leaders should withdraw to their mosques and leave the running of the country to the 'experts', the professional politicians and the Western-educated technocrats. Ranged with the president were the middle classes, the modernists, the secular forces and, ultimately (and most importantly), the Mujahidin-i-khalq Organization (MKO). The Mujahidin were a Muslim guerrilla organization which had been fighting the Shah since the late 1960s. An offshoot of the Freedom Movement of Iran set up in the early 1960s by Bazargan, the Mujahidin rejected the peaceful methods of their elders for the violent overthrow of the Shah. Their inspiration came from leftist guerrilla organizations in other countries and from ʿAli Shariʿati, a modernist Muslim whose writings had captured the imaginations of young Iranians in the 60s and 70s and who died a premature death in exile in England just before the revolution.

The Mujahidin's sole surviving leader in prison, Masʿud Rajavi, was freed just before the revolution. Hailed as a hero, he went on to become one of the more popular leaders in post-revolutionary Iran. His movement, made up of young boys and girls, in turn became a major political force. The Mujahidin, initially declaring themselves supporters of Khomeini, increasingly became critics while retaining their underground network. On the side of Khomeini and the traditionalists were the ordinary masses of the faithful, particularly in the rural areas and among the city poor. On the national political front the traditionalist line was led by former Khomeini students such as Muhammad Beheshti, a highly intelligent, multilingual scholar, Hashimi Rafsanjani, a tough and politically astute middle-level religious leader, and many others, including religious scholars such as ʿAli Khamenei and Musavi Ardebili.

The Islamic Republican Party

Their vehicle in the coming battle was the Islamic Republican Party (IRP), set up at the turn of the revolution by Beheshti, Rafsanjani and Khamenei. With the presidency of Bani Sadr, the traditionalists, who had so far been tilting in all directions, finally found their target. Bani Sadr chose to make the hostage issue the first priority of his administration. Most Iranian politicians saw a confrontation with the militant students in charge of the US embassy as political suicide. Bani Sadr, however, was apparently unwilling to be president of a nation branded as an outlaw in the West. Moreover, the students represented a rival power centre and an obstacle to good government.

Whatever his motives, Bani Sadr's crusade on behalf of the hostages set him not only against the students but also against the country's anti-Western forces, not to mention Khomeini. Another fatal mistake was Bani Sadr's packing of the presidential office and other organizations with Western-trained technocrats who did not hide their disdain for the 'reactionary' and 'incompetent' religious leaders. The IRP, which had failed to create a popular base, exploited Bani Sadr's miscalculations, gained Khomeini's ear and captured about 60 seats in the two-round Majlis elections of 14 March and 9 May 1980. The remaining members of the 270-seat Majlis (with over 50 seats unfilled for months) were potential Bani Sadr supporters but so provocative were Bani Sadr's tactics that his sympathizers sided with the IRP on key votes. The president further burnt his bridges with the Majlis by staying away after members did not rise to honour him on his first visit.

When a prime minister, Muhammad ʿAli Rajaʿi, was imposed on him in August, Bani Sadr publicly described him as 'incompetent' and refused to acknowledge his presence. He then refused to approve Rajaʿi's cabinet list, leaving half the government departments leaderless. By September, Bani Sadr was a spent force. He seemed fated to disappear into obscurity, but the Iraqi invasion of September gave him a new lease of life.

Opposition and violence

It was against this backdrop that the political crisis now resumed with even greater ferocity. Both sides were now fighting each other as well as the Iraqi invaders. Bani Sadr himself set the tone and pace of the crisis – alleging torture in the prisons and accusing his enemies of opportunism, cynicism and other crimes. He seemed to be seeking a showdown, but every time he brought the situation to the boil he would back off.

In the period leading to June 1981 street clashes took place between supporters of both sides and included, to an increasing extent, the Mujahidin. Khomeini, repeatedly drawn into the confrontation, unexpectedly tended to side with the elected president, Bani Sadr. Although he appeared to be increasingly despairing of Bani Sadr's erratic behaviour, he seemed equally suspicious of Beheshti and his colleagues' motives.

With the war with Iraq at an apparent standstill and with food rationing and shortages and other economic troubles, the first half of 1981 saw an unprecedented level of frustration and public dissatisfaction, which was also rubbing off on Khomeini himself. As had happened to Shariʿatmadari, the president now became a focus for all doubters and dissidents. Chief among his new allies were the besieged Mujahidin whom Bani Sadr had once dismissed as *munafiqin* (hypocrites) and whom he now gratefully welcomed.

Bani Sadr was apparently influenced by weekly polls taken by his aides which invariably placed him at the top of the popularity chart. Underlying this popularity was the public assumption that he and his allies were fighting allegedly unprincipled conspirators such as Beheshti, not Khomeini. The implication was that if they challenged Khomeini directly they would lose support. Bani Sadr's final, fatal move was a speech he gave at the Shiraz air-force base calling for resistance against dictatorship. This was tantamount to threatening a military coup. Two days later, on 10 June, Khomeini stripped him of his title as supreme commander-in-chief of the armed forces. The Majlis, in turn, moved to impeach him.

The Mujahidin now rallied openly to Bani Sadr's cause. On 20 June, the day of the Majlis' impeachment vote, the Mujahidin called on their supporters to take to the streets.

These moves were the most open challenge yet to Khomeini and an unmistakable attempt to overthrow the religious establishment. The authorities reacted swiftly and violently, sending revolutionary guards and Muslim toughs into the streets to prevent the demonstrations at all costs. Armed with chains and sticks, they broke up the crowd near central Ferdowsi Square. Serious fighting then ensued between the guerrillas and the revolutionary guards in which up to twenty people died, including several revolutionary guards. Some of the Mujahidin were summarily executed.

On 21 June the Majlis voted 177 to 1, with 11 abstentions and 20 others absent, to impeach Bani Sadr, and on the following day Khomeini dismissed him from office. But that was not enough to settle the question. As sporadic Mujahidin demonstrations continued and as Bani Sadr issued further calls for a mass uprising from a secret hideout, the authorities reacted with unprecedented violence, which included summary executions in the streets. In a week of clashes more than fifty opponents of the religious leadership were killed in the streets and in the prisons. Although the chances of the Mujahidin being able to overthrow Khomeini were small, there were indications that the IRP leaders – who had never commanded the kind of popularity which the Mujahidin and Bani Sadr enjoyed – were so nervous that they over-reacted to the challenge. The large numbers of executions and killings were backfiring and creating a new wave of sympathy for the Mujahidin.

On 28 June a powerful bomb destroyed the IRP headquarters in south-east Tehran, where the IRP leaders were holding urgent discussions. Among the more than seventy people killed were Beheshti and other key party functionaries as well as a minister and about a dozen members of parliament. It was a devastating blow which stunned the establishment and the whole country. It was never discovered who the bombers were. The finger pointed as much at opportunist counter-revolutionaries, such as the royalists or groups in the military, as at the Mujahidin. In the event, the Mujahidin neither claimed nor refused to disclaim responsibility for the massacre, ending up carrying the blame in the public mind.

After the explosion the authorities' crackdown against the Mujahidin and all potential enemies intensified. Thousands were imprisoned and at least a hundred were executed within two weeks, a toll that rose to nine hundred by late August. On 30 August the mysterious bombers struck again, this time killing President Rajaʿi – who had been elected on 24 July to replace Bani Sadr – and his prime minister Muhammad Javad Bahonar. Unlike Beheshti, Rajaʿi commanded wide sympathy and affection from the general public and the reaction against the Mujahidin was intense. Both the Mujahidin leader Rajavi and Bani Sadr had, meanwhile, escaped to France, seemingly abandoning their followers and thus further undercutting their credibility.

The 'executions' and assassinations of leading officials by the Mujahidin were to continue for some time. Between 2000 and 3000 of the government's supporters were killed in the next year or two. Executions of Mujahidin supporters and leftists, meanwhile, increased to about the same number. In the process, the authorities set up a repressive machinery that would prove difficult to dismantle. The threat from the Mujahidin had been essentially defused in late 1981. The main danger now lay in the government's own behaviour and the effects of the repression on the general public.

There was evidence that in late 1981 and during most of 1982 torture, described officially as 'punishment', was practised in the prisons. This mostly took the form of beatings on the soles of the feet and psychological torture such as prolonged periods of blindfolding, isolation and mock executions. The opposition's accusations of even more widespread and vicious forms of torture, the execution of 50,000 and the imprisonment of 120,000 by 1985, are generally considered to have been grossly exaggerated. However, even the more reliable figures of about 4000 executed and 20,000 imprisoned were enough to cause widespread unease throughout the country.

Stability returns

In December 1983, Khomeini stepped in to signal the official end of the crisis touched off by the June 1981 confrontation, by establishing strict guidelines for the security and prison authorities. But it took more than another year to purge extremist officials who had risen to the top and to dismantle most of the repressive machinery erected in late 1981. By 1985 the political and social atmosphere and sense of public security had much improved.

A measure of the Republic's own improving stability was the long tenures of the president and prime minister who followed Rajaʿi and Bahonar. The former was Khamenei and the latter Husayn Musavi, a former journalist and member of the IRP. Leader of the Majlis since the mid-1980 elections was Rafsanjani, who emerged as one of the most powerful and influential personalities of the Republic. On the political front, the Islamic Republic that had emerged from years of anarchy and internal and external wars seemed to have securely established itself by 1985. Certainly, all its internal enemies were in disarray. In Paris, the opposition front set up by the Mujahidin gradually lost Bani Sadr and many of its other allies. It was not so much the executions that had broken the Mujahidin's back but their own mistakes and contradictions. Rajavi's escape from Iran in July 1981 had had a devastating effect on the majority of his followers and his later open deals with Iraq (the 'enemy') destroyed the last remnants of public sympathy in Iran for his movement.

The Islamic Republic still faced dangers from bombers and assassins, but the only real challenges were posed by the Gulf War, the economy and the authorities' ability to build a new Islamic order.

The economy and society today

The war had played havoc with the economy. Revenues from oil* exports – the principal foreign-exchange earner – had dropped dramatically in 1980 and 1981. There were shortages of consumer goods and food and a nationwide rationing system had to be established. Industrial output fell to an all-time low, perhaps down to 30 per cent of capacity. Inflation was rampant.

By late 1982, however, oil exports were back at a reasonable level, helping to fill the foreign-exchange coffers, thus permitting the

Islamic Government in Iran

The institutions of the Islamic Republic in Iran are based on Khomeini's theory of the *Vilayet-i faqih* (the Jurisconsult's trusteeship). Khomeini believes that, in the absence of the Twelfth Imam (see Twelver Shiʿa), it is the duty of the clergy, as the trustees of the Prophet, to establish a just social system for the implementation of Islamic laws. In Khomeini's view a just and learned jurisconsult with administrative abilities has the same authority as the Prophet Muhammad in administering society.

Khomeini's theory was first delivered as a series of lectures in Najaf in 1969. After the revolution it was perfected and incorporated into the constitution of the Islamic Republic through four institutions within which Khomeini enjoys the supreme position as *Vali-i faqih* (the Guardian Jurisconsult) or leader (*rahbar*). These four institutions are as follows:

(1) *The Council of Leadership*. In the absence of a charismatic leader such as Khomeini, a council of three to five leaders must be formed. It is the duty of an elected body of eighty-three expert theologians to elect, advise or dismiss the leader of the Council of Leadership.

(2) The Legislature. The legislature is subdivided into a Council of Guardians and an Islamic Assembly (Majlis). The council is a body of twelve theologians and jurists apointed for six years. Six are appointed by the leader and six by the Supreme Judicial Council and the Majlis. The council vets all legislature to ensure its compliance with Islam and the constitution. The Majlis is a 270-seat parliament, elected for four years. It has five non-Muslim seats set aside for Jews, Zoroastrians and Assyrians, with two seats for Armenians.

(3) The Executive. This comprises the president and the Council of Ministers. The president is elected for four years. His election must be approved by the leader to whom he is second in rank. The president co-ordinates the executive, the legislature and the judiciary and appoints the prime minister with Majlis approval. The Council of Ministers is appointed by the prime minister with the approval of the Majlis and the president.

(4) The Judiciary. The Supreme Judicial Council is Iran's highest judicial authority. It is composed of a chief justice and a state prosecutor, both appointed by the leader, and three judges appointed by the judicial bench for five years.

MBM

import of vital raw materials for industry. In 1983, there was even an economic mini-boom with imports and government expenditure rising to an all-time high. So much so, indeed, that there was a renewed bout of inflationary pressure driving prices sky-high.

The government had taken the easy way of relying on maximum oil income. In the process, charged some critics, it had missed a unique opportunity to use the emergency of war to mobilize the public in the cause of a much-needed economic revolution. Under intense Majlis pressure starting in late 1983, the government was forced to lower its sights and concentrate on keeping inflation under control. Imports were reduced to about $16,000m a year by 1985, almost one-third below the 1983 level. According to Bank Markazi (Central Bank) figures in the year ending 20 March 1983, there was a surplus of $6552m; this had become a deficit of $115m by the first half of 1984. According to some Western estimates the deficit for the whole of 1983/4 was $800m and for 1984/5 $4500m. They quoted a surplus of $1300m in 1985/6 and projected a deficit of $1800m for the year ending 20 March 1987. Inflation dropped from a high of over 40 per cent to well under 10 per cent by late 1985. However, industrial output also dropped and business activity slowed down. Considering the circumstances and pressures, the Republic's ability to hold the economy together was generally creditable. What was troublesome was the apparent lack of vision and boldness at the top in dealing with the fundamental issues and challenges thrown up by the revolution.

The Foreign Minister Ali Akbar Velayati

With the revolution, the properties of many people and officials associated with the old order had been confiscated. These included hundreds of industries, businesses and farms. The banks were nationalized and, in line with Islamic requirements, interest was abolished. The new Islamic banking* system was officially inaugurated in early 1984 in a surprisingly smooth changeover.

That, however, was about the only ideologically and structurally fundamental innovation that the Islamic Republic could claim. Most other issues came up against an inability to reconcile Islam's concern for the sanctity of property and the revolution's requirements for redistribution of wealth. Left unresolved, these issues placed the Islamic Republic in a legislative limbo. For example, the Islamic constitution clearly states that all foreign trade is the responsibility of the state. Yet, seven years after the revolution, the issue was still unresolved. Similarly, the status of many industries and businesses was left in confusion because the government did not quite know what to do with them. Some confiscated properties were returned, others were kept. Some 20 per cent of Iran's prime agricultural land area was affected by ownership disputes. In 1979, one set of revolutionary bodies began redistributing agricultural and some urban lands, while another set, along with the courts, tended to side with the previous property owners. The latter were unable to enforce their decisions against revolutionary resistance, while the former were having legal obstacles thrown in their way.

Some sections of the population, particularly the urban middle classes, ignored or rejected the Islamic way of life and its values. This was most noticeable in the hostility to restrictions on entertainment and music and to the wearing by women of the *hijab* (veil). Persistent violations of these restrictions resulted in Muslim zealots sporadically taking to the streets to enforce the rules. This concentration on what outsiders judged to be the more superficial aspects of Islam was partly the result of irreversible changes in Iranian society in the preceding decades and partly the result of the Republic's failure to provide a convincing model.

Disappointingly, also, there was no spectacular progress on the cultural front. This was, perhaps, the most important long-term issue in view of the revolution's aspirations towards undoing the Westernization of the previous decades and erecting a new Islamic structure. The arts, cinema and theatre presented a relatively bleak landscape.

Iraqi prisoners of the Zulfiqar Brigade listen to President Khamenei at the 1984 celebrations of the start of the war

The degree of change and innovation possible under war-time conditions was, of course, open to debate. Inevitably, the necessary freedom of experimentation was bound to be discouraged. As it was, many found the free-wheeling Majlis and its raucous deputies an unusual phenomenon in war-time. Equally striking was the world of publishing, where the authorities tolerated a surprising latitude of freedom. Most of the newspapers and periodicals were on the tame side, but when it came to books all sorts of views were allowed circulation, short of blasphemy and direct calls for the overthrow of Khomeini or the Republic. Some opponents of the system were allowed to air most of their criticisms, and even Marxist books were openly available in the thousands of bookshops that sprang up after the revolution.

Indeed, the freedoms experienced in book publishing and some other aspects of life drew attention to a much-ignored attribute of the authorities. If intolerance, fanaticism, repression and other shortcomings were a reality, so was the religious leaders' concern for caution, accommodation and order. The revolution had seen many unhappy days, bloodshed and ugly deeds committed in the name of religion and the people, but the basic trend had always been towards accommodation. Indeed, so accommodating were the authorities in general that they stood in danger of a backlash from their radical followers. The harsher forms of Islamic punishment, such as the cutting off of limbs for third-time theft and the stoning of adulterers, were observed only exceptionally, while the Christian minorities were openly allowed to ignore the ban on alcohol. After 1983 there were frequent flare-ups by radicals accusing the authorities of not being revolutionary enough in enforcing Islamic principles and in purging ideologically suspect officials and bureaucrats. Within a wider context the government was being accused of favouring technocrats over committed Muslims and sacrificing ideology to efficiency. The issue of the government's ideological soundness and its propensity towards pragmatism was, however implausible abroad, serious enough within Iran potentially to pose the most serious long-term threat to the Republic's stability.

In the meantime, the war was dictating much of the pace and nature of the social, cultural, political and economic evolution of the young Islamic Republic. Some also saw the unifying role of the war as the main bond holding the Republic together, arguing that with peace and/or the death of Khomeini the establishment would disintegrate. Such an eventuality, however, seemed very unlikely. As far as Khomeini's role was concerned, the institutional framework created in the first seven years – including the late 1985 selection of Ayatollah Husayn ʿAli Montazeri as his successor – gave every appearance of being deep-rooted and stable enough to survive his death. As far as the role of the war was concerned, a victorious end would provide an immeasurable boost to the Republic's self-confidence and future; only a defeat or a peace through a humiliating compromise could threaten the leadership of the Republic. Defeat in the war did not seem a real prospect. As for compromise, despite more than five years of bloody fighting there was no reason to doubt the leadership's and military's pledge to carry on until the other side cracked.

VP

Further reading

P. Avery, *Modern Iran* (London, 1965)
S. Bakhash, *The reign of the Ayatollahs* (London, 1985)
D. Hiro, *Iran Under the Ayatollahs* (London, 1985)
N. Keddie, *Iran: religion, politics and society* (London, 1980)
R. Mottahedeh, *The Mantle of the Prophet: learning and power in modern Iran* (London, 1985)
A. Parsons, *The Pride and the Fall: Iran 1974–79* (London, 1984)

Iraq

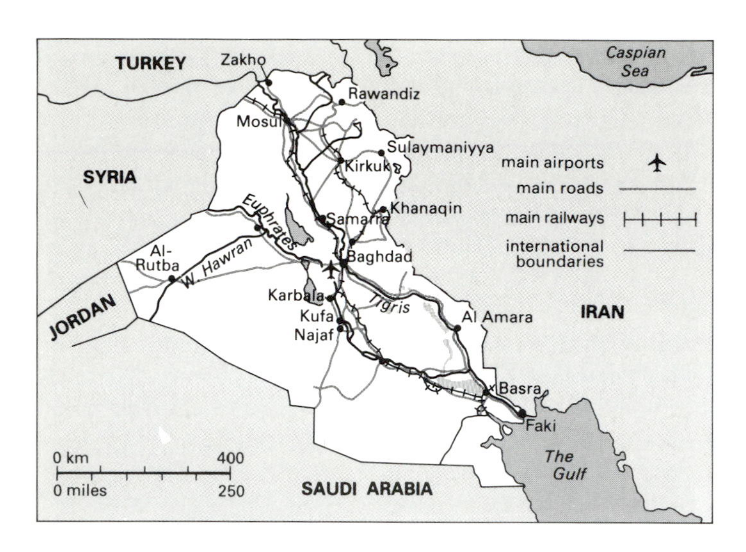

Official title	The Iraqi Republic
Area	447,964 sq. km, including 3522 sq. km of Iraq's half share of the Iraq/Saudi Arabia Neutral Zone
Population	15.21 million (1984)
Government and constitution	The Ba'th Party took power on 30 July 1968. Power is vested in a president and a Revolutionary Command Council (RCC), which elects the president and vice-president by a two-thirds majority. A National Assembly and a Kurdish legislative council were elected in June and September 1980 respectively. Elections for the second National Assembly were held on 20 October 1984
Currency	1 Iraqi dinar = 1000 fils; US $1 = 310.86 fils
Languages	Arabic (79 per cent); Kurdish (16 per cent); Persian (3 per cent); Turkish (2 per cent)
Religion	Some 90 per cent of the population is Muslim of whom some 40 per cent are Sunni and 60 per cent are Shi'i. There are also several Christian sects
Climate	Summers are extremely hot with temperatures in the shade reaching 43°C. Winters can be extremely cold with frost in the north

Geography and topography

In comparison with most other Arab countries, Iraq is relatively well endowed with natural and human resources. Under normal circumstances, its oil wealth would be sufficient to facilitate the development of its considerable agricultural and industrial potential, and its population of about 15 million is, given the land area, neither unmanageably large, as in Egypt, nor impracticably small and scattered as in Libya or Saudi Arabia.

Iraq has a land area of 448,500 km^2, about half of which consists of mountains and deserts. The cultivable area forms about one-sixth of the whole, some 75,000 km^2, of which only about two-thirds is actually under cultivation. This area is declining each year (as is agricultural production generally), due partly to inefficient irrigation practices but also as a consequence of large-scale rural-to-urban migration. The country is completely landlocked except for a 40-km-wide outlet at the head of the Gulf; the southern part of the country below Baghdad consists either of desert or of the fertile alluvial plains of the Tigris and Euphrates. In the north and north-east, on the borders with Iran and Turkey, are substantial mountain ranges.

Peoples

The population is divided along both racial and religious lines: about 75 per cent are Arabs, 18 per cent Kurds, and the remaining 7 per cent Assyrians, Turcomans, Armenians, Persians and a number of smaller ethnic groups. Some 90 per cent of the population is Muslim, the remaining 10 per cent consisting of a variety of Christian sects and the Yazidi and Sabaean communities which are only to be found in Iraq. The 1977 census showed that some 65 per cent of the population lives in cities and 35 per cent in the countryside, a complete reversal of the figures thirty years earlier, showing the very considerable rural-to-urban migration which has taken place since the Second World War.

Religions

The Arab Muslims are divided into the Sunni* and (Ja'fari) Shi'i* sects, the Shi'is forming the largest single religious community in the country as a whole. However, since most Shi'is are poor peasants or recent migrants to the cities from the countryside, they have never wielded political power commensurate with their numbers. In general terms, the rulers of Iraq are now, as they have been since the time of the British Mandate, the Sunni Arabs of the cities. The Kurds*, who are mostly Sunni Muslims, inhabit the mountainous north and north-east of the country. For most of this century the Kurdish population has been at loggerheads with the central government in Baghdad.

History up to 1939

The state of Iraq was created in 1920, out of the three former Ottoman* provinces of Basra, Baghdad and Mosul. British forces invaded the southern part of the country in November 1914, and by the end of the war were in effective control of almost all of the territory that forms the modern state. By the Treaty of San Remo (25 April 1920), Britain was awarded the Mandate for Iraq under the auspices of the League of Nations; a year later, Britain imported a King, Faysal*, the son of Sharif Husayn* of Mecca, and set up what purported to be a democratic system of government, with a constitution and a bicameral legislature. However, behind every Iraqi minister stood a British adviser whose advice had to be taken, and ultimate authority lay in the hands of the British high commissioner and the commander of the Royal Air Force. Political power lay in the hands of a small urban clique, in an uneasy alliance with powerful tribal leaders. In the words of a visiting British cabinet minister in 1925: 'If the writ of King Faisal runs effectively throughout his kingdom it is entirely due to British aeroplanes. If the aeroplanes were removed tomorrow, the whole structure would inevitably fall to pieces.'

The situation changed little in 1932, when Iraq became formally independent, and even the succession of *coups d'état* beginning in 1936 which brought the armed forces more directly into politics did not change the basic political configuration of the country. Real power still lay in the hands of the British embassy, the court and the professional politicians, most of whom saw office simply as a means of personal enrichment. British interests in Iraq were twofold. First, in terms of the imperial thinking of the inter-war period, Iraq occupied a vital strategic position on the route to India, and was an important military base and communications centre. Secondly, it had substantial oilfields, over which a concession had been given to an Anglo-Franco-American consortium, the Iraq Petroleum Company, in 1925. It was considered essential that control over access to these oilfields should remain in British hands, although large-scale exploitation did not take place until after 1945.

In 1941, there was a brief attempt at resistance to Britain, but this was put down by a second British occupation, which lasted until 1945. For the next thirteen years a series of 'musical-chair' cabinets came to power, in which the same key figures occupied all the important portfolios. Headed by the veteran pro-British politician Nuri al-Saʿid, this group, together with the monarchy, was to be swept away by the revolution of 1958.

History since the Second World War

Before, and indeed long after the revolution, Iraq exhibited many of the characteristics of a dependent and underdeveloped economy. In 1957–8, some 2000 individuals out of a rural population of nearly four million owned nearly two-thirds of the country's agricultural land. Industry was tiny; outside the oil industry*, which employed about 15,000 workers, only 90,000 individuals were engaged in production. However, the numbers of those being educated had increased fivefold since the 1930s, and by 1950 there were some 175,000 children in school. The expansion of the educational system* and of the army provided important career opportunities for people from relatively poor families. These individuals, whose own backgrounds had contributed to their sense of the need for greater social justice, thus had fairly prestigious employment but no political power. The new intelligentsia, and the petty bourgeoisie in general, were destined to play a vital part in the events of the next decades; although divided ideologically, the clandestine opposition was united in its hostility to the monarchy and the British presence.

The revolution of 1958

On the eve of the revolution, therefore, Iraq presented the spectacle of a highly politicized society, dominated by a corrupt and ageing clique entirely dependent on the political and military support of Britain. In July 1958 a revolt began in the army, and developed into a revolution in which the old political order was overthrown and a number of fundamental social and economic changes took place. The new government was headed by the Free Officers under Brigadier ʿAbd al-Karim al-Qasim*, although the cabinets contained a mixture of military and civilian members. However, those who came to power did not share a common vision or political ideology, and for a variety of reasons Qasim was unable to establish a mass base for his rule. Major political differences soon developed, especially between the communists, who had been at the forefront of opposition to the monarchy since the foundation of the Communist Party in 1934, and those who can be broadly labelled Arab nationalists.

These differences were symbolized by the clashes which took place around the issue of whether or not Iraq should join the United Arab Republic of Egypt and Syria. The nationalists advocated joining the union both out of conviction and as a means of controlling the communists, and the communists opposed it both because they understood its implications for their own future and because they saw it as essentially irrelevant to the task of constructing a new social and economic order. For his part, Qasim had no desire to defer to Nasser*, and was thus on the same side of the political divide as the communists without sharing their political views.

During the crucial years between 1958 and 1963 there were fierce verbal and physical battles between the supporters of these two viewpoints over how radical the revolution should be. Eventually an alliance of nationalists and Baʿthists* seized power in February 1963, and instigated a reign of terror against the left and the Communist Party in particular until November, when the Baʿthist faction was pushed out of the alliance. There followed five years of confused and indecisive politics, during which a series of military governments came to power, preaching, but not practising, vague ideas of Arab unity and generally becoming bogged down by a costly and apparently fruitless war against the Kurdish minority in the north. Political parties remained illegal, but the intensity of political persecution diminished.

Rulers of Iraq

1920	British Mandate
1921	Faysal ibn Husayn
1933	Ghazi
1939	Faysal II
1958	ʿAbd al-Karim al-Qasim
1963	ʿAbd al-Salam Muhammad ʿArif
1966	ʿAbd al-Rahman Muhammad ʿArif
1968	Ahmad Hasan al-Bakr
1979	Saddam Husayn al-Takriti

Iraq since 1968

On 17 July 1968 a group of Baʿthist officers under Ahmad Hasan al-Bakr organized another military coup, and succeeded in taking over the government some two weeks later. In the course of the 1960s the political situation in the Arab world had changed markedly. In particular, the ignominious defeat of the Arab armies by Israel* in 1967 had shown the hollowness of Arab nationalist claims; Iraq itself had not been able to send more than a token force to the front because the regime's crack troops had to stay at home to guard it against a coup. The United States now became widely identified with Israel, and it was clear that Israel's military and economic strength depended very largely on American support. Thus any Arab regime which wished to give itself a 'revolutionary' or 'progressive' image had to present itself as opposed to the West in general and the United States in particular.

In this atmosphere, the Iraq government's approaches to the Soviet Union for technical aid for the oil industry undoubtedly enhanced its image at home. An agreement was signed in June 1969 promising Soviet assistance to start production in North Rumayla, a major oilfield whose exploitation was essential if Iraq was to develop an independent oil policy. At the end of the same year, the Baʿth government, represented by Saddam Husayn, the vice-chairman of the Revolutionary Command Council (RCC), began to make cautious overtures to the Kurdish leader Mulla Mustafa Barzani, which led to the conclusion of the Manifesto on Kurdish Autonomy of 11 March 1970.

The Imam ʿAli Shrine, Najaf, Iraq

The Kurds

Very briefly, the Kurds* had been offered a form of limited autonomy within Iraq by the British authorities in the 1920s. This arrangement proved unacceptable and resulted in constant conflict between successive Iraqi governments and the Kurds, led first by Shaykh Mahmud Barzinji and subsequently by Mulla Mustafa Barzani. In 1946, after the collapse of the short-lived Kurdish Republic of Mahabad, Barzani and his closest supporters left Iraq for twelve years of exile in the Soviet Union. After the 1958

Kurdish guerillas firing at the Iranian army barracks, 23rd March 1979

Revolution, Qasim invited Barzani to return to Iraq, where he immediately assumed the leadership of the Kurdish movement, although, like any other nationalist grouping, 'the Kurds' by no means represented a unified body of political opinion. Furthermore, while Qasim himself may have been prepared to grant a form of autonomy to the Kurds, there were powerful pressures from Arab nationalist and other quarters to prevent this happening. In 1961 Barzani and his followers grew impatient at Qasim's continuing inability to deliver, and fighting broke out, which continued intermittently until the opening of negotiations between the Kurds and the Baʿth at the end of 1969.

Although the proclamation of the March Manifesto proved to be a ruse on the Baʿth's part to buy itself time until it was in a position to recast its Kurdish policy more to its own advantage, the general political atmosphere of the early 1970s gave grounds for optimism. At the end of 1971, the Baʿth issued its National Action Charter, which put forward a distinctly 'socialist' social and economic programme and a few weeks later announced the opening of negotiations with the Iraq Petroleum Company (IPC). In April 1972, a few days after the signature of a 15-year Iraqi–Soviet friendship treaty, the first consignment of North Rumayla oil left Fao; on 1 June the government announced the nationalization of IPC. No step taken by any Iraqi government since the 1958 Revolution was greeted with such universal enthusiasm, and the Baʿth was able to live off the moral capital it generated by this action for many years.

Conversely, of course, such policies aroused a wave of hostility to the Baʿth, both in the West and in the more conservative states in the Gulf. One consequence of this was that when it became clear that the Baʿth's promises on Kurdish autonomy were not going to be fulfilled, Iran became more closely involved in the affairs of Iraqi Kurdistan in an attempt to weaken the regime in Baghdad, supplying Barzani with quantities of money and sophisticated weapons. Thus the Baʿth could present itself as the victim of conspiracies masterminded by 'Western imperialism' and carried out by its agents. In such circumstances, and in spite of the Baʿth's previous anti-communist record, the Communist Party felt that it could not do less than give the regime its support: communist ministers were appointed to the cabinet in May 1972 and a National Patriotic Front, in which the communists agreed to act as a junior partner, was formed in July 1973.

Nationalization of the oil industry

Although the nationalization of IPC had been a calculated risk, the calculation soon paid off. Major deals were quickly concluded with energy ministries in several Western countries, and with IPC's French participant company, Compagnie Française de Pétroles; quite fortuitously, all marketing problems were solved for good in the wake of the fourth Arab–Israeli War* in October 1973. By this time, however, the Baʿth's inability or unwillingness to implement the March Manifesto on Kurdish Autonomy had pushed Barzani further into the arms of the Shah, and a major conflict between government forces and the Kurds broke out in the spring of 1974. In the bitter fighting which followed, Barzani attracted the support of the vast majority of the Kurdish movement, including those who had long entertained doubts about the 'feudal' and 'reactionary' style of his leadership and the propriety of his Iranian and American contacts.

By the beginning of 1975 the stalemate familiar from previous confrontations between the Kurds and the government had begun once more, and Iraqi military expenditure escalated sharply. However, this time Barzani and his forces were totally dependent on

Iranian support, to the extent that if the Shah could be convinced to stop supporting the Kurds their resistance would collapse. As early as October 1974 King Husayn of Jordan arranged preliminary meetings between representatives of Iraq and Iran, which paved the way for the Algiers Agreement, signed between the two countries in March 1975. Within hours of the agreement the Iranians withdrew their heavy artillery and closed the border, so that the Kurds could not regroup in or attack from Iran. The resistance collapsed, and Barzani went into exile, dying in the United States in 1979.

For the Baʿth, the agreement meant the settlement of the Kurdish question on its own terms as well as the 'final' resolution of a frontier dispute which had bedevilled relations between the two countries since the 1930s. For obvious reasons, it was widely welcomed by Iraq's neighbours in the Arabian peninsula as a vital stage in the slow but perceptible process of Iraq's integration into the moderate camp in the Arab world. Perhaps most significantly, the cessation of hostilities with both Iran and the Kurds meant that the Baʿth was no longer so dependent on the Soviet Union or the communists, and could now begin to edge away from both. Hence, over the period between 1975 and 1979 the Iraqi regime gradually moved into the general orbit of the West on a global level and towards the moderate Arab states on a regional level. Another important characteristic of Iraqi politics in the years before the Iranian Revolution and the outbreak of the war with Iran was the growing diversion of power away from the Baʿth Party and the RCC and its concentration in the hands of Saddam Husayn and a few particularly trusted subordinates.

The effects of oil wealth

After the war of October 1973 oil prices rose spectacularly; Iraq's revenues increased from $575m in 1972 to $5700m in 1974. This sudden acquisition of wealth meant that the state itself was now the principal focus and agent of economic activity and capital accumulation, and of course the Baʿth government had only the most minimal public accountability. In the course of the 1970s huge sums were spent on welfare and infrastructural projects, and increases in wages and salaries together with the new employment opportunities helped to bring about rapid and visible improvements in living standards for the population as a whole.

The combination of the new oil money and the 'settlement' of the Kurdish question gave a major boost to the Baʿth's confidence, and it now began to work even more systematically towards the creation of a political system over which it had exclusive control. The Baʿth Party itself was transformed into an instrument of the leadership, and it came increasingly to resemble a national rally in which adulation of itself and its leaders came to take the place of whatever ideological discourse may have existed formerly. Naturally this process met with considerable opposition from the communists, supposedly the Baʿth's partners in the National Progressive Front, especially as it was accompanied by the arrest and 'disappearance' of a number of communists. In May 1976, twelve communists were executed, allegedly for carrying out political activities in the army, and in July 1978 the RCC enacted a blanket decree making non-Baʿthist political activity illegal and punishable by death for all former members of the armed forces. In the context of universal conscription, the decree applied to all adult males.

Understandably, the Kurdish resistance took some time to recover after the Algiers Agreement. A strip of territory running parallel to the borders with Iran and Turkey was turned into a *cordon sanitaire* and completely evacuated of its population; the inhabitants were rounded up in trucks and taken to southern Iraq, or resettled in specially constructed villages surrounded by barbed wire and fortified posts. Although divided internally, the Kurdish organizations had rallied sufficiently by the beginning of 1977 to mount guerrilla operations in the area, in which they were joined by the communists in 1979.

Status of the Shiʿi population

Another growing threat to the Baʿth regime emerged in the course of the 1970s in the form of opposition from sections of the Shiʿi population. The Shiʿis have always been under-represented in Iraqi politics, for historical reasons and also because most Shiʿis lived in or were recent migrants from the countryside. In general, the spread of secularism in the Middle East had served to lessen the influence of the Shiʿi clergy in the holy cities of Karbala and Najaf, and had also made the religious professions less attractive, trends which were further influenced by the spread of modern education and the burgeoning of career opportunities in government service.

In addition, migration from the countryside brought the new migrants (who came very largely from the Shiʿi south) into contact with the secular political currents in the cities. Partly because Arab nationalism has definite Sunni connotations, the ideas of Nasserism current in the late 1950s and early 1960s were generally unattractive to the Shiʿis, most of whom felt themselves to be more Iraqi than Arab. Baʿthism, though more avowedly secular, also has obvious aspirations towards Arab unity. Thus it was almost inevitable that most secularized politically articulate Shiʿis should be attracted to communism, especially in the period between 1958 and 1961 when the influence of the Iraqi Communist Party was at its height.

In 1958 an association of Najafi *ʿulama* was founded, specifically to combat 'atheism', and its members became the nucleus of al-Daʿwa al-Islamiyya, founded some ten years later. A leading member of al-Daʿwa, Ayatollah Muhammad Baqir al-Sadr, formulated a theory of the Islamic polity very similar to that of Ayatollah Khomeini*, although the two do not appear to have been in particularly close contact during the latter's exile in Najaf between

1964 and 1978. In general, this view amounted to a denunciation of the various un-Islamic regimes ruling in the Muslim world, and their replacement, through revolution, by a social and political order based on Islamic principles. The growing popularity of such views began to cause the Baʿth considerable alarm, since al-Daʿwa now seemed more concerned to combat secularism and the growing encroachment of the state into every sphere of life than specifically to oppose communism, presumably because the latter no longer represented a realistic threat.

There had already been unrest in the holy cities in the early 1970s; five *ʿulama* were apparently executed in December 1974. In February 1977, on the occasion of the Muharram celebrations, there were large anti-government demonstrations in Karbala and Najaf, after which several *ʿulama* were executed and others sentenced to life imprisonment. By the autumn of 1978, when it became obvious that the days of the Iranian regime were numbered, al-Daʿwa members began to attack Iraqi police posts and Baʿth Party offices, and generally made no secret of their support for the Iranian Revolution. In response, the Baʿth launched a fierce campaign against al-Daʿwa; Baqir al-Sadr was interrogated in Baghdad in the spring of 1979, and when he refused to disclaim his support for the Iranian Revolution he was put under house arrest in July, and executed in April 1980. The regime's ruthlessness seems to have been effective to the extent that no major Shiʿi demonstrations took place after July 1979. The war with Iran has pre-empted the possibility of any effective reformation of the movement within Iraq by creating a situation in which the idea of a Shiʿi polity has become synonymous with treason, as well as profoundly unattractive to the majority of Iraqis, both Shiʿis and non-Shiʿis.

In the latter part of the 1970s the regime gradually moved away from the Soviet Union and aligned itself more closely with Jordan and the states of the Arabian peninsula. At the Tripoli and Baghdad summit meetings in December 1977 and November 1978 Iraq successfully headed off attempts by more radical Arab states to take effective sanctions against Egypt for Sadat's actions in 1977.

Internally, it was clear that it was only a matter of time before Saddam Husayn took over full powers from Ahmad Hasan al-Bakr, whose close contacts with senior army officers had been invaluable in consolidating the regime in its first few years, but had now become somewhat redundant. In October 1977 Bakr handed over the defence ministry to his son-in-law, ʿAdnan Khayr Allah Tulfa, who is also Saddam Husayn's brother-in-law. At the same time the Baʿthist People's Militia was built up as a counterweight to the regular army. These changes were accompanied by an increasing struggle for power within the RCC, which had been enlarged to twenty-two members in January 1977.

On 16 July 1979 Bakr appeared on television to announce his resignation, and the immediate succession of Saddam Husayn to the presidency. Twelve days later a 'plot' to overthrow the regime was uncovered, involving members of the RCC. Five of them, and seventeen others, were executed within a few days by Saddam Husayn and the remaining members of the leadership. The fact that even those who had been closest to the leader could fall so suddenly and fatally from favour showed that no opposition whatever, whether inside or outside the party, would be tolerated.

Almost from its inception it was clear that the Iranian Revolution was going to prove a severe test for the Iraqi regime. In the first place, the Algiers Agreement now went into abeyance, and it seemed most likely that the 'Kurdish question' might resurrect itself. Saddam Husayn was well aware of the encouragement which the fall of the Shah might give to his own domestic enemies, although these fears proved to be largely unfounded. It was also the case that the apparent confusion in Iran and above all what was assumed to be the state of chaos existing in the Iranian armed forces seemed to present him with a unique opportunity to pre-empt a possible Shiʿi uprising in Iraq, to fulfil his ambitions to become a major Arab statesman, and to make Iraq into a substantial regional power. The defeat of the Iranian Revolution would enable him to emerge as the defender of the Arab nation, and the undisputed master of the Gulf. In addition, the fall of the Shah had been a severe blow for the United States, and the overthrow of Khomeini and the restoration of 'normality' to the region would be greatly in its interests as well, especially if this could be achieved with no direct intervention on its part.

*Iran–Iraq War**

In such circumstances, it is easy to see how the temptation to launch a war against Iran became almost irresistible, especially as Iran was widely regarded as being far too feeble to put up an effective resistance. The war is essentially a clash of personalities and ambitions on the part of the leaders of the two states, with a seemingly endless toll of loss and devastation endured by their populations. Saddam Husayn responded to Khomeini's threat to export the Islamic Revolution to Iraq by attempting to impose upon Iran a regime more compatible with his own ambitions. More elaborate theories may well be put forward, but the real reasons, with all their tragic consequences, are simple and prosaic enough.

The consequences of the war for Iraq

Iraq's failure to win an immediate victory over Iran, and the long duration of the war, greatly weakened the political and economic capacity of the regime. The devastation caused by the war, the defeats sustained by the army, and the high casualty rate at the front – an estimated 200,000 killed and wounded, over one per cent of the entire population – amounted to a great loss of face for the Baʿth Party and for Saddam Husayn, and the regime was only able to

In September 1982 Iraqi tank troops were preparing to invade Iran

maintain itself in power by skilful use of propaganda, playing on Iraqi fears of the possible installation of an Islamic Republic in Iraq, and by the utter ruthlessness of the security forces. Economically, Iraq will be in debt to its neighbours for the foreseeable future, and the combination of the damage to the physical infrastructure and the sharp fall in oil prices since 1984 means that the regime will have far less resources at its disposal to attract domestic support than it did in the 1970s.

The economy and society today

Iraq's principal natural resource is oil. Pipelines connect the oilfields with the Mediterranean (through Turkey and Syria), the Gulf, and, most recently, following the closure of those to the Gulf and across Syria, with the Red Sea across Saudi Arabia. Apart from oil, Iraq's main industries are petrochemicals, cement and construction materials, and the processing of animal and vegetable products. The petrochemical industry is located close to the area where the primary products originate, around the southern oilfields near Basra and Zubayr. Most other large industries are located around the three major centres of Baghdad, Mosul and Basra, where nearly half the population lives.

Foreign trade plays a crucial role in the economy. Oil exports brought in about 98 per cent of all foreign earnings immediately before the outbreak of the war with Iran. Other exports have traditionally included dates and cement, and it is likely that petrochemicals, iron, steel and aluminium will figure more prominently in the future. After the Iranian Revolution in 1978–79, when Iraq was the second most valuable market in the Middle East after Saudi Arabia, its main trading partners were France, Italy, West

Baʿthism (See also Syria)

Baʿthism* is a form of pan-Arabism, the notion that the 'Arab nation' is a single entity stretching from Morocco to Iraq, which has been divided artificially by colonialism, imperialism and (since 1948) Zionism*. The basic ideology of Baʿthism and its slogans 'Unity, Freedom, Socialism' and 'One Arab Nation with an Eternal Mission' were elaborated by the Syrian Christian writer Michel ʿAflaq in Damascus in the 1940s and 1950s. In 1953, ʿAflaq and his colleague Salah al-Din Bitar joined forces with Akram Hawrani, the founder and organizer of the Arab Socialist Party, a step which gave the Baʿth (the Arab Baʿth Socialist Party) an organizational base in Syria. According to ʿAflaq, Arab society could only be revitalized and liberated through Arab unity; the Baʿth Party was to be the standard bearer and vanguard of the new Arab nation. Baʿthism is vague, romantic and mystical, and makes constant reference to an idealized Arab past which has little to do with historical reality. It stresses the primacy of national/ethnic identity, and rejects the notion of antagonistic social classes; once the Arabs are liberated and united it is claimed, social conflicts within particular states (or 'regions of the Arab nation', in Baʿthist parlance) will somehow disappear. There is no indication in Baʿthist writings of how political power is to be achieved, nor how the liberated 'Arab nation' should be governed, nor how it is to interact with the non-Arab world. In Baʿthist rhetoric words and phrases like socialism, democracy, and the toiling masses can be and regularly are made to fit almost any day-to-day contingency, since their meaning is taken as self-evident and never defined.

In contrast to the success it achieved in Syria, where Arab nationalism had always drawn supporters, Baʿthism was slow to take root in pre-revolutionary Iraq, partly because the heterogeneous nature of the Iraqi population (Kurds, Sunni Arabs, Shiʿi Arabs) meant that pan-Arab nationalism itself had not attracted a particularly widespread following there before Nasser's rise to power, and partly because the Communist Party had played a vital part in the opposition to the monarchy since the end of the Second World War. However, in 1957, the Iraqi Baʿth Party (which had less than 300 members in 1955) joined the National Front with the communists and other parties, and welcomed and supported the revolution of 1958.

In the heady atmosphere of the period immediately after the revolution, the main polarization of political forces came to be between the communists on the one hand, and the nationalists and Baʿthists on the other. The main point at issue was how far the revolution should actually go, with the communists' opponents using the issue of union with Egypt and Syria as a rallying cry to create a diversion from the profound socio-political changes which they feared the communists were planning. Qasim, who had no desire to defer to Nasser, thus found himself almost fortuitously aligned with the communists, but tried to distance himself from them as their influence grew. After the failure of the attempt on Qasim's life which it organized in November 1959, the Baʿth went underground and split into a number of small groups. Although nominally a branch of the founding organization in Damascus, the Iraqi and Syrian parties had become separate entities in practice long before the formal split between them, which occurred in 1966; all efforts at reconciling the two have foundered, including the most recent attempt in 1979.

The Iraqi Baʿth first came to power in a short-lived coalition with the Nasserists/nationalists, after a military coup in February 1963; their ten months in power saw some of the most terrible violence hitherto experienced in the post-war Middle East, bloody acts of revenge against the communists and the left. In November, the Baʿthists were edged out of the coalition by their nationalist partners; after some five years in the political wilderness they returned to power after a further military coup in July 1968, and have been in government ever since. Since the middle 1970s the Baʿth Party has ceased to be an elite organization in the sense that entry is no longer subject to strict controls, and membership is now almost obligatory for those who do not wish to arouse suspicions of their loyalty to the regime. It is difficult to assess the Baʿth's role as a political party since Saddam Husayn's advent to power in July 1979; its functions seem to be restricted to applauding the actions of the leadership and acting as an arm of the state security services, and it no longer acts – if, indeed, it ever did – as a forum for political discussion, criticism or debate.

A bridge straddling the Tigris, central Baghdad

Germany, the United Kingdom, Brazil, Turkey and Japan; the main imports were foodstuffs, machinery, capital equipment and motor vehicles.

As a result of extensive nationalization in the 1960s and 1970s, and particularly after the nationalization of the Iraq Petroleum Company (IPC) in 1972, the 'commanding heights' of the economy are controlled by the state; in addition to those working directly for the state bureaucracy (662,000, around one-fifth of the economically active population in 1978) nearly two-thirds of those working in enterprises employing more than ten people are working in state organizations. However, although the state controls the bulk of very large enterprises, the private sector maintains a sizeable involvement in manufacturing and construction. In general, the greater involvement of the state in the economy has had the effect of promoting rather than limiting the interests of the private sector.

Iraq has undergone a major economic and social transformation since the 1960s, particularly following the spectacular oil-price rises after 1973. The population doubled between the censuses of 1957 and 1977, and the flow of migration from the countryside greatly accelerated. The fact that far fewer people work on the land, together with the spread of better living and working conditions in the country as a whole, has made Iraq a net importer of food since the 1960s. Like the population, the economy has also expanded very rapidly, if the abnormal conditions since 1980 are discounted, and the foundations of a heavy industrial sector and of a modern transport, power and communications infrastructure have been laid.

PS

Further reading

H. Batatu, *The Old Social Classes and the Revolutionary Movements of Iraq: a study of Iraq's old landed and commercial classes, and of its Communists, Baʿthists and Free Officers* (Princeton, 1978)

M. Farouk-Sluglett and P. Sluglett, *Iraq since 1958: from revolution to dictatorship* (London, 1987)

M. Khadduri, *Independent Iraq 1932–1958; a study in Iraqi politics* (London, 2nd edn, 1960)

P. Marr, *The Modern History of Iraq* (Boulder and London, 1985)

P. Sluglett, *Britain in Iraq 1914–1932* (London, 1976)

Israel

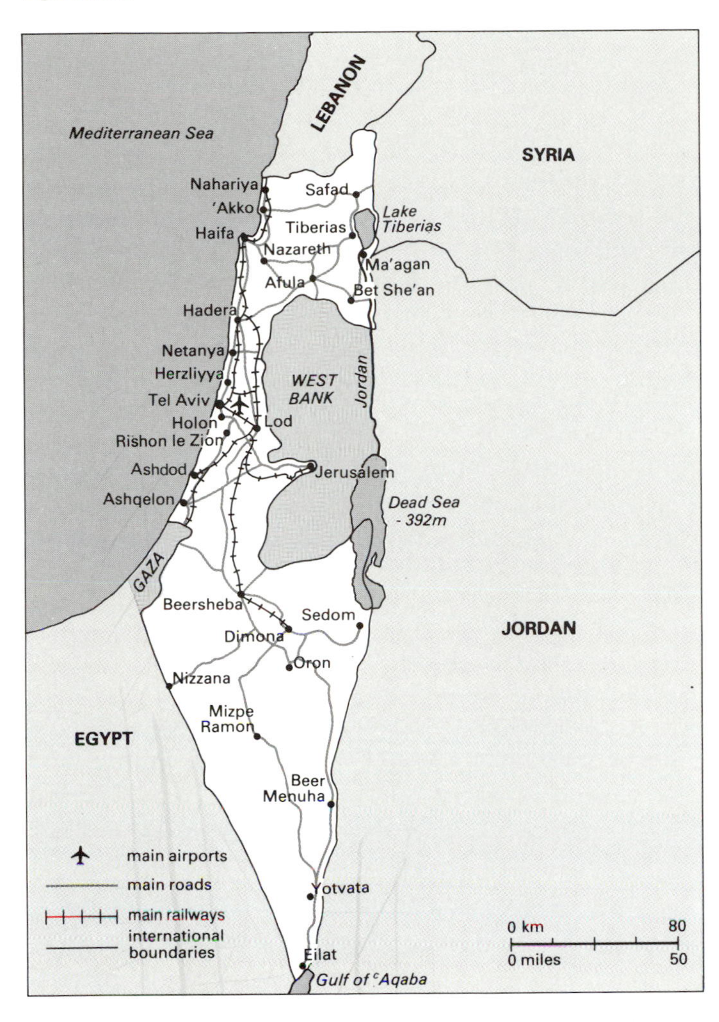

Official title	The State of Israel (Medinat Yisraʿel)
Area	20,770 sq. km. Includes 70 sq. km of East Jerusalem, annexed in June 1967, and inland lakes. Does not include West Bank, Gaza Strip or Golan Heights
Population	4.275 million
Government and constitution	A parliamentary democracy. There is no written constitution, but a series of Basic Laws defining the organs of government and their powers. A unicameral legislature, the Knesset, is elected by proportional representation for a four-year term. It consists of 120 members (MKs). The Head of State is the president, elected for a renewable five-year term by the Knesset. The prime minister and the government require the confidence of a majority of the Knesset, which alone can call a new election before term. A Supreme Court heads the independent judiciary
Currency	1 new Israeli shekel = 100 agorot 1.5 new Israeli shekels = US $1
Languages	Hebrew, Arabic
Religions	There is no established religion. The four main religions, Judaism, Islam, Christianity and Druzism are recognized and endowed with judicial powers
Climate	Israel enjoys hot, dry summers when temperatures range between 32°C and 38°C. Winters are usually mild and sometimes rainy. Snow sometimes falls on the hills. Rainfall reaches 1000 mm a year in parts of Galilee, but less than 250 mm a year in the Negev

Geography and topography

Israel lies at the eastern extremity of the Mediterranean. It has borders with Lebanon, Syria, Jordan and Egypt. Israel's recognized borders as delineated in the armistice agreements of 1949 encompass a total area, including inland lakes, of 20,700 km^2.

In 1967 Israel annexed east Jerusalem (70 km^2) and in 1981 it applied Israeli law to the Syrian Golan Heights (1176 km^2). Since 1967 it has militarily occupied the West Bank formerly under Jordanian sovereignty (5879 km^2) and the Gaza Strip, formerly under Egyptian administration (378 km^2).

The country falls into four main regions of considerable topographic variety. The densely populated coastal plain of the Mediterranean extends from the Lebanese border in the north to the Gaza Strip. To the east of the plain the Galilee hill range reaches its peak at some 1200 metres, rolls down through the fertile Yizre'el (Esdraelon) Valley to the Samarian Hills which peak at about 960 m, and then southward to the Judaean Hills rising to 750 m. To the east of the hill range is the deep Jordan Rift Valley, following the river from its sources in the north through the Sea of Galilee down to the lowest point on the earth's surface at the Dead Sea, 392 m below sea level. The southern region, the Negev Desert, covers more than half of the country's territory, from the Judaean Desert at the Dead Sea down to the port of Eilat on the Gulf of ʿAqaba, Israel's outlet to the Red Sea.

Peoples

The peoples of Israel are mainly Jews and Arabs. Including those who live in the occupied territories there are some $3\frac{1}{2}$ million Jews.

The Jews* derive largely from the waves of immigrants that came from Europe before 1948, and the mass immigration from both Europe and the Middle East after the establishment of the state in 1948. Some half-million Jews immigrated to Palestine* between 1882 and 1948, the great majority of them from Eastern Europe. About 1,750,000 have immigrated since the establishment of the state, including virtually the entire Jewish populations of Yemen and Iraq and a large part of those of North Africa. Poland, Russia, Rumania and Morocco are the countries of birth of the largest number of Jewish immigrants. The Jews from the Middle East are more fertile than the European immigrants and they and their offspring born in Israel now make up a majority of the Jewish population. In addition to the large masses of European and oriental immigrants came many small exotic communities of Jews, such as the Kurdish, Bukharan and Berber Jews, Cochinese Jews, Bene Israel from Bombay and Beta Israel from Ethiopia.

The Arabs total some three-quarters of a million, including the residents of east Jerusalem who have declined Israeli citizenship. Apart from these people, who were incorporated within Israel when Jerusalem was annexed in 1967, the Arabs are those who remained in the country after the war of 1948, and their offspring born in Israel. They are for the most part indigenous to the region. Approximately three-quarters of the Arabs are Muslims, the rest are Christians* and Druze*. There is also a dwindling beduin population, estimated in 1985 at about 46,000.

There are an estimated 787,000 Arabs on the West Bank*, being those who remained there after the war of 1967 as well as refugees from the Israeli side of the border who came in 1948. The half-million Arabs of the Gaza Strip* are mostly refugees from the war of 1948. About 20,000 Arabs, mainly Druze, live in the Golan Heights occupied since 1967 and brought under Israeli law in 1981.

Religions

For historical and ideological reasons Israel regards itself as the Jewish state, in the sense of belonging to the worldwide Jewish people. From this perspective Israel sometimes purports to speak and act on behalf of Jews elsewhere. However, there is no established religion. Except for the link with foreign Jewry made concrete in law by the offer of citizenship on special terms to Jews who immigrate, all religions are equal in law. While the Jewish Sabbath and festivals are public holidays, the rights of non-Jews to observe their own day of rest and holy days are guaranteed by law.

Personal status and all the rights and issues associated with it are in the jurisdiction of religious courts, Jewish, Sunni* Muslim and Christian. Muslim *shariʿa** courts operate alongside rabbinical courts and those of the recognized Christian denominations applying canon law: these are the Greek Catholic, Greek Orthodox, Roman Catholic, Maronite and Protestant. The Druze also have religious autonomy, exercised in their own courts of law.

Only orthodox Judaism is recognized in Israel. There are some minor ritual differences, and some more considerable differences in attitudes to religion, between European (Ashkenazi) and oriental (Sephardi) Jews. Each of these main branches of Jewry has its own chief rabbi at the head of the Supreme Rabbinical Council. Small ancient communities which do not accept rabbinical authority are the Karaites* and the Samaritans*.

History up to 1939

The state of Israel arose out of the collapse of Jewish life in Eastern Europe during the nineteenth century. About three-quarters of the world's ten million Jews a century ago lived in Eastern Europe, where they were caught up in the national and social ferment of the deteriorating old imperial regimes.

Severe persecution and impoverishment of the Jews coincided with a breakdown of orthodox tradition and authority within the Jewish community. At the same time, in Western Europe, secular anti-semitism took a good deal of the joy out of the new freedom the Jews had experienced since Napoleon.

An anti-semitic *cause célèbre*, the Dreyfus Affair, resulted in Theodor Herzl*, a Viennese Jew who worked as a journalist in Paris, reaching the conclusion that anti-semitism was endemic, and that only if they obtained a Jewish state in which they were a majority could the Jews expect to survive in dignity. Educated Jews in Eastern Europe had come to the same conclusion, with the additional proviso that only the holy land of Jewish prayerful aspiration would qualify for statehood.

The birth of Zionism

Thus was born political Zionism*, the concept of a return of the Jews to the land of their ancient tradition in quest of political independence. A Jewish population in dispersion was considered an archaic form of association. Zionism supplied a secular national rationale for Jewish identity, with a programme for its reconstruction, on the assumption that both orthodox religion and social assimilation were untenable adjustments in the modern world. By means of political self-help the Jews would become a normal territorial nation like all others.

Herzl in 1897 founded the international Zionist Organization to mobilize Jewish support, while he engaged in personal diplomacy in the capitals of Europe seeking a charter for a Jewish state. The statesmen were lukewarm and so were the Jews. Zionism proved unable to match the appeal of socialism or emigration to the United States, nor could it overcome fierce opposition by the religious leaders.

Before Herzl published his political tract, *Der Judenstaat* (The Jewish State) in 1896, a wave of settlers (the first *aliyah**) came from Eastern Europe to Palestine seeking personal fulfilment through a return to the soil of the holy land. Between 1882 and the end of the century some 25,000 had come, matching in number the old Jewish community that had lived there for centuries immersed in divine worship. These first settlers were saved from bankruptcy by Baron Edmond de Rothschild.

The most important contribution of the first *aliyah* to Zionism was the Hebrew revival, which ensured the establishment of modern Hebrew as the language of instruction in schools and eventually as the universal language of the Yishuv (a collective term to denote the Jewish population of the land).

A second wave of immigrants (the second *aliyah*) numbering over 50,000, of whom half remained in the country, came to Palestine between 1904 and 1914. These new settlers were imbued with Herzl's political vision, but they thought that practical economic efforts in Palestine, especially in establishing Jews in agriculture, were essential to prepare the way for mass immigration and independence. They saw themselves as the pioneering vanguard of the national movement that would build a Jewish state.

The second *aliyah*, which included David Ben-Gurion and other youngsters who rose to leadership of the movement, together with the third wave which came after the First World War, are properly regarded as the founding fathers of the Jewish state. The practical Zionists who came between 1919 and 1923 included young enthusiasts who were inspired by both the Balfour Declaration* and the Bolshevik Revolution.

The Zionists, led by Chaim Weizmann, were a minority among the Jews abroad. In the Balfour Declaration Weizmann secured the charter that had eluded Herzl. Knowing that in general the Jews were not attracted to Palestine, Weizmann put aside the goal of statehood, and concentrated the energies of the Zionist Movement and the Jewish Agency on assisting the practical Zionists, with the help of Britain, to establish a 'national home' in Palestine.

Waves of Jewish immigration (rounded figures)

Period	Immigrants
1882–1903	25,000
1904–14	35,000
1919–31	130,000
1932–38	210,000
1939–48	180,000
1948–51	690,000
1952–64	520,000
1965–85	540,000

Chaim Weizmann taking the presidential oath in the Knesset

Among the institutions which enabled the settlers to prevail over the Arab majority in the struggle for the future of Palestine were those of the general labour organization, the Histadrut. Influenced by socialism, the Zionist pioneers integrated their social, economic, military and political sinews in a tightly woven web of power, which in effect laid the basis for the partition of the country.

The best-known socialist innovation was the *kibbutz*, a communal settlement which pooled all energies in the service of the community. This and other forms of cooperative organization associated with the Histadrut, including schools and hospitals as well as entrepreneurial companies in industry, construction, transport and banking, financed by Zionist sympathizers abroad but controlled by the workers, created in effect a self-governed Jewish society in a high state of mobilization. By the mid-30s, Ben Gurion, a fanatical visionary gifted in political organization, came to the leadership of the Yishuv through control of the Histadrut of which he was the main architect.

In the 1920s the British administration provided protection for the Zionists as its Mandate required, but it was unable to reduce the hostility of the Arabs to the revolutionary Jewish incursion upon their patrimony. By the mid-30s the Mandate began to come unstuck as Jewish immigration increased and violence grew with it. The Peel Report of 1937 for the first time brought partition into official view as a possible solution.

As Hitler's shadow spread across Europe in the 1930s the pace of Jewish immigration stepped up, adding thousands from Central

Europe to the influx from Poland. By 1939 the Jews in Palestine numbered close to half a million, nearly a third of the population.

History since the Second World War

Following the Arab rebellion of 1936 Britain imposed severe restrictions on immigration. The Zionists managed to bring thousands into the country illegally, but millions of Europe's Jews were doomed as the Nazis took over the continent during the early years of the Second World War.

Hitler's holocaust annihilated the six million Jews in Central and Eastern Europe on whose behalf the Zionist programme had been conceived, and who were the designated human reservoir for the Jewish national renaissance. When the facts of the holocaust began to be known in 1942, rescue was still thought possible. The Zionists were galvanized to work explicitly for a Jewish state, a goal which they had previously regarded as unrealistic and unlikely to attract support. Now the energies of American Jewry were mustered in the cause, and Jews throughout the world gave their support to Zionism.

When at the end of the war it became known that European Jewry had perished, and that Jewish statehood had in effect become a posthumous solution, the drive for statehood was undiminished, for it now seemed imperative to the Zionists that Jews in future should have a haven of free immigration.

In the meantime the Yishuv had acquired a political dynamism of its own, impelling it to claim national independence in the interest of the settlers, who had no wish to become merely another minority Jewish community tolerated by its host society.

The Jews of Palestine set their sights on the succession to British rule when they realized that the British administration was no longer working in favour of Zionism. Since the administration crushed the Arab rebellion of 1936 the Jews had become stronger relative to the Arab majority. After the Second World War the Jewish underground militia, the Haganah, continued illegally to bring in survivors from Europe. While the Haganah acquired arms and trained for battle, the dissident Jewish organizations, Irgun and Lehi, mounted a campaign of terror to undermine the administration and hasten its collapse.

Britain gradually lost control, unable to contain the tide of Jewish pressure within the country and abroad, and called in the United Nations Organization. On 29 November 1947, the General Assembly resolved to partition Palestine (see Arab–Israeli Conflict and The Palestinians), to allow for the establishment of a Jewish state and an Arab state within the territory.

The creation of Israel and the 1948 War

On 14 May 1948 Israel was formally declared independent. In the war of 1948*, which is known in Israel as its War of Independence, the land under Israeli control was increased by a third over that allocated to the Jewish state in the partition plan. The armistice agreements concluded with its neighbours one by one in 1949 confirmed Israel's boundaries, with minor adjustments, on the basis of the military status quo. As a result of the fighting a large proportion of the Arab population left.

Within two years of the last battle Israel doubled its Jewish population through mass immigration. Some 325,000 survivors of Europe's horror camps were brought in, as well as a similar number from the Middle East. The great majority of newcomers were destitute on arrival. Throughout the 1950s and 1960s immigration continued, now in the main from North Africa, until the Jewish population redoubled to 2.6m by 1969. Thereafter the main source of immigration was the Soviet Union.

The absorption of masses of propertyless immigrants was first made possible by injections of capital from West Germany under the Reparations Agreement of 1952, through the sale of Israel Bonds, and by raising Jewish donations in the United States. After 1967 large-scale private investment from abroad, as well as loans and gifts from the United States government, helped to sustain the rapid growth and development of the economy. Transport and construction, modern agriculture with extended irrigation, basic industries and manufactures, were all quickly developed on a scale commensurate with the expanding labour force. In recent years science-based industries have proliferated, while military industries have become one of the country's biggest employers and exporters.

In January 1949 elections were held to the first Knesset. The electoral system and political parties were carried over from the Yishuv, and they proved adaptable and effective in establishing representative democracy in the state, notwithstanding the need to induct masses of immigrants.

The Labour group of parties maintained its control of government by entering into an alliance with the mainstream religious parties, which endured until its electoral defeat in the ninth general election of 1977. Labour obtained broad support from its partners on economic and social policies as well as foreign affairs, in return for which it undertook to honour the status quo on religious issues and to give due regard to religious sensibilities in public life.

Ben-Gurion

David Ben-Gurion dominated Labour's approach to all major issues. His vision shaped the society and moulded its political personality. He took risks with a decisiveness and will that exceeded the capacities of his colleagues.

Ben-Gurion was sure that the Arabs would not accept the existence of a Jewish state in their midst unless and until they concluded that it was too powerful to destroy. He therefore adopted an intimidatory approach to the Arab world. He considered that

David Ben-Gurion

Israel's master-politician, statesman.
1886 Born in Plonsk (Poland), David Gruen, educated privately in Hebrew
1903 Joined Po'ale Zion (socialist Zionists)
1906 Settled in Palestine
1907–11 Labourer, journalist
1911–14 Student, Constantinople
1915–20 Zionist speaker, organizer, USA and UK
1920–33 Architect and leader of Histadrut (labour movement)
1933–5 Member, Palestine Zionist Executive and Jewish Agency Executive
1935–48 Chairman, Palestine Zionist and Jewish Agency Executive, i.e. political leader of the Yishuv
1948–53 Prime minister and minister of defence
1953 Retired to Kibbutz Sedeh Boker, in the Negev, hoping to inspire young people to go south and settle the desert
1955 Returned as minister of defence in Sharett government
1955–63 Prime minister and minister of defence
1963 Retired from government, in conflict with his own party
1965 Formed Rafi Party
1969 Formed State List Party
1970 Retired from Knesset
December 1973 Died, buried at Sedeh Boker. His home in Tel Aviv is maintained as a museum

David Ben-Gurion, Israel's first prime minister

Israel's survival would depend on maintaining a qualitative edge over its enemies in education, science and industry as well as military prowess. He regarded the army as the pinnacle of national pride, and placed its interests and its morale above all else as a symbol of national regeneration.

Ben-Gurion quickly foiled the conciliatory approach to the Arabs favoured by Moshe Sharett, Israel's first foreign minister. Fearing an increase in Egypt's military potential, Ben-Gurion responded to Egyptian provocations by launching the Sinai War of 1956*. However, Ben-Gurion did not favour extending Israel's territory and ruling over a hostile Arab population. He withdrew from the Gaza Strip under American pressure in 1957, and later, in the aftermath of the 1967 War*, from his retirement, he called upon his successors to withdraw from the conquered territories. His old colleagues, thinking he was out of touch and that he had lost his judgement, ignored his advice.

Concerned to forge a coherent secular national identity for a people drawn from disparate sources, made up largely of refugees without Zionist commitment, Ben-Gurion had elaborated an ideology that drew heavily upon the historical mystique of the Bible for inspiration. By placing the state, the Bible as history and the army at the centre of public consciousness Ben-Gurion in effect speeded the displacement of socialist and liberal objectives from the national ideology, and prepared the way for a tide of populist chauvinism and religious nationalism that was generated by the intoxication of conquest.

Its heavy losses in the war of October 1973*, in which Israel was caught napping, sapped morale. The war made possible eventual peace with Egypt, but damaged the reputation of the labour leaders.

From 1967–77, under successive Labour governments led by Levi Eshkol, Golda Meir and Yitzhak Rabin, Israel encouraged Jewish settlement in parts of the occupied territories, including the Sinai peninsula, that were regarded as important for security. Israel's policy followed the unofficial Allon Plan, in offering to negotiate peace on the basis of returning some of the territories to Arab sovereignty while retaining some to meet Israel's strategic requirements. There were no Arabs willing to make peace on these terms, although as a result of the war of 1973 Israel and Egypt were able to agree on staged Israeli withdrawals from parts of Sinai.

The Begin era

Menachem Begin's accession to office in 1977 brought about a change in Israel's policy. Begin made it clear that his government had an absolute commitment to retaining Judaea and Samaria (the West Bank) in perpetuity, but that Sinai did not have comparable ideological significance for Israel. Egypt and Israel could now make peace, with the help of the United States. In accordance with the treaty drawn up in March 1979 (see Egypt: the Camp David Accords), Israel in April 1982 withdrew from Sinai except for a disputed strip of land on the border at Taba, near Eilat.

Under the terms of the treaty Israel and Egypt undertook to create the machinery of autonomy for the population of the West Bank and Gaza, while deferring the issue of sovereignty. Begin stalled on this and brought the discussions to a standstill, thereby causing the resignation of his Foreign Minister, Moshe Dayan, who favoured self-rule for the West Bank, and eventually also of his Defence Minister Ezer Weizmann, who felt that Begin was needlessly squandering Egyptian goodwill.

In 1980 Israel passed a law establishing Jerusalem as its undivided capital for all time, and in 1981 it applied Israeli law to the Golan Heights.

During Begin's period of office the movement of Jewish religious nationalists to place a ring of settlements around the Arab centres of population on the West Bank ran out of steam. The number of Jews settled on the West Bank after eighteen years of occupation was no more than 50,000.

Seeking to counter Palestinian resistance to the occupation and the heightening of Palestinian national consciousness, which undermined Israel's control of the territories, Defence Minister Sharon and Begin, together with the chief-of-staff, General Eitan, resolved to invade Lebanon to extirpate the PLO from its territorial base. The resulting war of 1982 and the occupation of Lebanon that followed it failed to achieve its objectives (see Lebanese Civil War). It was the most unpopular war in Israel's history, whose costs in blood brought Israel's morale to its lowest point, and the expense of which brought the economy to the brink of collapse.

Begin resigned from government in August 1983, a broken man, tormented by the failure of his military adventure and haunted by the guile of Ariel Sharon, who had drawn him out of his depth into the Lebanese quagmire. Yitzhak Shamir carried on as prime minister, but he lacked Begin's popularity in the street and was unable to carry the right-wing coalition (Likud) to a third election victory.

The general election of July 1984 to the eleventh Knesset resulted in a stalemate between the two major parties, Labour and Likud. Neither was able to muster sufficient support among the small parties to form a coalition government. The big two in September 1984 therefore joined in a national unity government, with the novel formula of a rotating premiership. Labour took first turn and Shimon Peres became prime minister with a two-year lease.

President Sadat of Egypt, President Carter and Israel's Prime Minister Begin joining hands as the Camp David agreements were sealed

The government succeeded in imposing Draconian measures of restraint and sacrifice, to bring runaway inflation down to a manageable double-digit rate by the end of 1985. Peres was also able in June 1985 to withdraw the bulk of the army from the expensive occupation of Lebanon.

Politics today

A record fifteen parties obtained representation in the eleventh Knesset elected in July 1984. In forming a unity government the two largest parties agreed upon joint action to save the economy from collapse, while agreeing to differ on other issues. The implication was that any major initiative led by either party, in areas other than economic policy, such as peace talks or changes in the administration of the West Bank, could result in the fall of the government.

Although Labour and Likud enjoyed a two-thirds majority in the Knesset between them, and did not depend upon the votes of the smaller parties to sustain them in power, the influence of the religious parties increased. This was because of the fragility of the government involving the undertaking by Prime Minister Peres to exchange places with Foreign Minister Shamir of the Likud in October 1986. Both large parties were anxious to cultivate the religious groups in case the government fell and a new election necessitated the formation of a conventional coalition.

The most divisive issues in Israeli politics are those relating to the West Bank and those concerning religious claims. Since 1977 the

Political parties in Israel

Israel's political parties evolved during the forty years before statehood. In the absence of sovereignty the parties elaborated detailed blueprints for the organization of a future Jewish state. But they did not stop at ideology. In competition for the allegiance of new immigrants, the political parties delivered services such as employment (especially in the public service), housing, health insurance and a host of social and cultural amenities. The parties thereby acquired a central role in the social and political life of the new state in 1948.

After statehood the political parties adapted to competing through the electoral system for control of the government. A pure form of proportional representation was adopted, enabling the multi-party system to continue unchanged. Mass immigration gave continued relevance to the old pattern of induction through material services rendered, so that the doubling and tripling of the population was effected without incurring instability.

Over the years the political parties have undergone many changes of name as new alliances were formed to replace old electoral bonds. In spite of this, and continual fragmentation, the basic pattern of three ideological 'camps' persists: socialist, nationalist and religious.

Left of centre:

The Israel Labour Party, heir to Ben-Gurion's *Mapai*. Originally socialist, but increasingly pragmatic and technocratic. The largest party in the 11th Knesset elected in 1984. Incorporates *Yahad*, the group led by the popular General Ezer Weizmann.

Mapam, a classical Marxist party. Withdrew from the Labour Alignment when the Labour Party formed a national government with Likud in 1984.

Citizens' Rights Movement, a libertarian group attracting many intellectuals, oriented towards Jewish–Arab peace and equality, and against religious coercion.

Shinui (Change), reformist, social-democratic, the rump of the Democratic Movement for Change which brought about Labour's defeat in 1977, but it quickly dwindled and dissolved.

Democratic List for Peace and Equality, largely Arab, communist.

Progressive List for Peace, Jews and Arabs for Palestinian self-determination.

Right-wing:

Likud, the nationalist bloc, combining the populist Herut, founded by Menahem Begin, with the Liberal Party in an uneasy alliance. Approximately equal to Labour in electoral appeal, came to power in 1977 after 29 years in political opposition.

Tehiya (Resurrection), hard-line nationalists led by nuclear physicist Yuval Ne'eman and General Eitan, who was chief of staff in the invasion of Lebanon in 1982.

Religious:

National Religious Front (*Mizrahi*), for long the mainstream religious party, split into fragments in 1984.

Aguda, hard-line orthodox but not nationalist, founded early in the century to combat secular Zionism.

Shas (Sephardi orthodox), seeks to stem the tide of secularization within the oriental Jewish population, broke away from Aguda in 1984.

Morasha, religious ultra-nationalists, replaced Mizrahi in 1984.

Kach, anti-Arab racists led by Rabbi Meir Kahane, claim religious cover for their anti-democratic beliefs.

Israel's prime ministers

1948–53	David Ben-Gurion (1886–1973)
1954–5	Moshe Sharett (1894–1965)
1955–63	David Ben-Gurion (1886–1973)
1963–9	Levi Eshkol (1895–1969)
1969–74	Golda Meir (1898–1978)
1974–7	Yitzhak Rabin (b. 1922)
1977–83	Menachem Begin (b. 1913)
1983–4	Yitzhak Shamir (b. 1915)
1984–6	Shimon Peres (b. 1923)
1986–	Yitzhak Shamir

religious parties have shown greater rapport with the nationalist Likud than with their old socialist partners. This reflected an increase in nationalist sentiment within the religious fold, but it appears that this may have subsided and that direct favours to religious interests may count for more in the future when these parties decide whom to support.

Israel's political parties fall into three main camps, differentiated by ideology and the interests they serve. The Labour camp includes socialists of varied hue from Marxists to social-democratic technocrats. Labour's appeal is strongest among veteran Israelis of European origin, the middle classes, and the more affluent workers. The Likud camp combines nationalist populism and economic liberalism to appeal mainly to Israelis from the Middle East with less seniority in the country, the poor and less affluent workers, and the young. The religious camp, fragmented in recent years into many small groups including separate Ashkenazi and Sephardi lists, represents various degrees of orthodoxy and theocratic aspiration.

The three main camps are flanked on the left and right respectively by communists supported by Arab voters, and hard-line secular nationalists in *Tehiya* allied with religious zealots.

The Labour Party and its camp followers are divided within themselves on the issues arising from the occupation. The majority considers that the status quo provides better security than any available alternative. A minority in the Labour camp, many of these in the left-wing Mapam, which bolted the Labour alignment when the Labour Party joined in government with Likud, advocate withdrawal from the occupied territories in return for peace. In the absence of an authoritative Arab peace initiative they are likely to remain a minority. As long as concrete peace prospects such as were generated by the Sadat* initiative are not injected into Israeli politics from the Arab side, the whole issue loses relevance, and apathy reigns outside the salons of the intellectuals.

Labour's approach has been formed by security considerations rather than ideological first principles. The Likud, by contrast, on the basis of historical claims that have always held absolute ideological force in that camp, is unwilling to contemplate peace on any other terms than continued Israeli control of the West Bank and Gaza Strip.

The politics of religion are extremely complex. Apart from competitive material interests pursued by the religious parties, the camp tends to unite on broad ideological claims which crystallize very often in the issue: Who is a Jew? The perennial battle with the secularist majority on this issue reflects a deeper struggle for strategic positions on the more important issue: What is a Jew?, which for the longer term may be of fundamental significance in the determination of the balance between secular and religious values in the national ethos, and equally for the future of relations between Israel and the Jewish diaspora.

The economy and society today

As a result of immigration from all corners of the globe, Israel's social and cultural configuration is extraordinarily diverse. At the end of 1985 the population comprised 3,525,000 Jews, of whom 60 per cent were born in Israel, and 750,000 Arabs, including the residents of east Jerusalem. There were also some 1.3m Arabs under Israeli military occupation.

About 87 per cent of the Jews and 64 per cent of the Arabs live in the cities. The largest conurbation is the commercial and cultural centre, Tel Aviv, with well over a million living within its metropolitan area. Haifa, which has the largest concentration of heavy industry, with its environs exceeds half a million. Jerusalem, the nation's capital and seat of government, which grew rapidly after its unification in 1967, approaches the half-million mark. The largest Arab urban centres within the pre-1967 boundaries are Acre and Nazareth. Of the rural Jews, 116,000 live in a *kibbutz*, and 155,000 in a *moshav*, a less rigorous form of cooperative settlement.

The rapid growth of population, from 800,000 in 1948 to over 4.25m in 1985, accompanied by a constant inflow of capital from abroad in aid and investment, stimulated steady economic expansion and development. At the same time, the burden of military spending and debt service resulted in chronic inflation. Unilateral transfers from abroad, including US government grants and loans, and Jewish donations and purchases of bonds which regularly amount to several hundred million dollars per year, offset the budget deficit and also make good the annual deficit in the balance of foreign trade.

As a result of firm government measures to control inflation, real standards of living were reduced by up to a quarter in 1985, bringing standards at the end of the year to about the average that prevailed in 1980. Even so, per capita GNP at around $5000 per annum exceeds that of several advanced industrial countries. However, owing to military expenditure ranging from a quarter of the total to more than a third in some years, the average real standard of living resembles those of the less affluent countries of the Mediterranean.

Israel is poor in natural resources and has to import all its energy requirements. Modern high-yield agriculture renders the country self-sufficient in basic foodstuffs and contributes significantly to exports. Israel has a developed industrial base resembling those of Europe in diversity and level of technology, comprising about a third of the economy. A considerable portion of industry, and exports, consists of electronics and military arms. Israel has become a world-class centre of the diamond cutting and polishing industry. In 1985 exports of gems amounted to a finished value of $1.2 billion. Israel's largest trading partners are the EEC and the United States, with each of which it has a free-trade agreement.

Within Jewish society there prevails a relatively equalitarian ethos, which has not precluded the occurrence of stratification. The

The Tel-Aviv shoreline

conventional hierarchies of occupation and income are overlaid by specific factors like seniority of citizenship and regard for the culture of the region of birth of immigrants. Those from the Middle East are the more recent arrivals in the country, and their cultural background is not so well regarded as that of their European or Western counterparts. This has exacerbated a social cleavage due to economic stratification, in which the Ashkenazi community has enjoyed greater advantages than the Sephardi. However, this ethnic cleavage has not resulted in the political explosion that many observers predicted. Prominent members of the Sephardi population in recent years have included the president, the chief-of-staff, the head of the labour movement, the chairman of the Knesset, as well as many government ministers and local officials.

Conscription to military service has been perhaps the greatest engine of social integration and national cohesion. By the same token, apart from the Druze, Arab citizens precluded from service are that much more alienated.

The Arab minority in Israel has adapted to the circumstances of life as a minority with some uneasiness, sharpened in recent years by the subjection of their brethren on the West Bank and Gaza to military occupation. Arab resentment of the dual society which is developing on unequal terms between the two peoples is matched by great concern among Israeli liberals about its effects on the Jewish state.

NL

Further reading

B. Avishai, *The Tragedy of Zionism: revolution and democracy in the land of Israel* (New York, 1985)
S. N. Eisenstadt, *The Transformation of Israeli Society* (London, 1985)
H. Fisch, *The Zionist Revolution* (London, 1978)
R. J. Isaac, *Israel Divided: ideological politics in the Jewish State* (Baltimore, 1976)
C. S. Liebman and E. Don-Yehiya, *Civil Religion in Israel* (Los Angeles, 1983)
N. Lucas, *The Modern History of Israel* (London, 1975)
R. F. Nyrop, ed., *Israel: a country study* (Washington, 1979)
Y. Peri, *Between Battles and Ballots: Israeli military in politics* (Cambridge, 1983)

Jordan

Official title	The Hashimite Kingdom of Jordan
Area	97,740 sq. km, including 5880 sq. km of the occupied West Bank of Jordan
Population	2.49 million (East Bank only, 1983: 3.15 million, both Banks, 1983 estimate)
Government and constitution	A monarchy. The King is Head of State and approves and promulgates laws. He orders the holding of elections and appoints the prime minister, the president and members of the senate. The Council of Ministers is responsible to the House of Representatives
Currency	1 Jordanian dinar = 1000 fils; US $1 = 339.2 fils
Language	Arabic (official). English is the second language
Religion	At least 80 per cent of the population is Sunni Muslim and there is a Christian minority of about 6 per cent
Climate	Summers are hot with temperatures reaching 49°C. Winters are short but cold and often wet

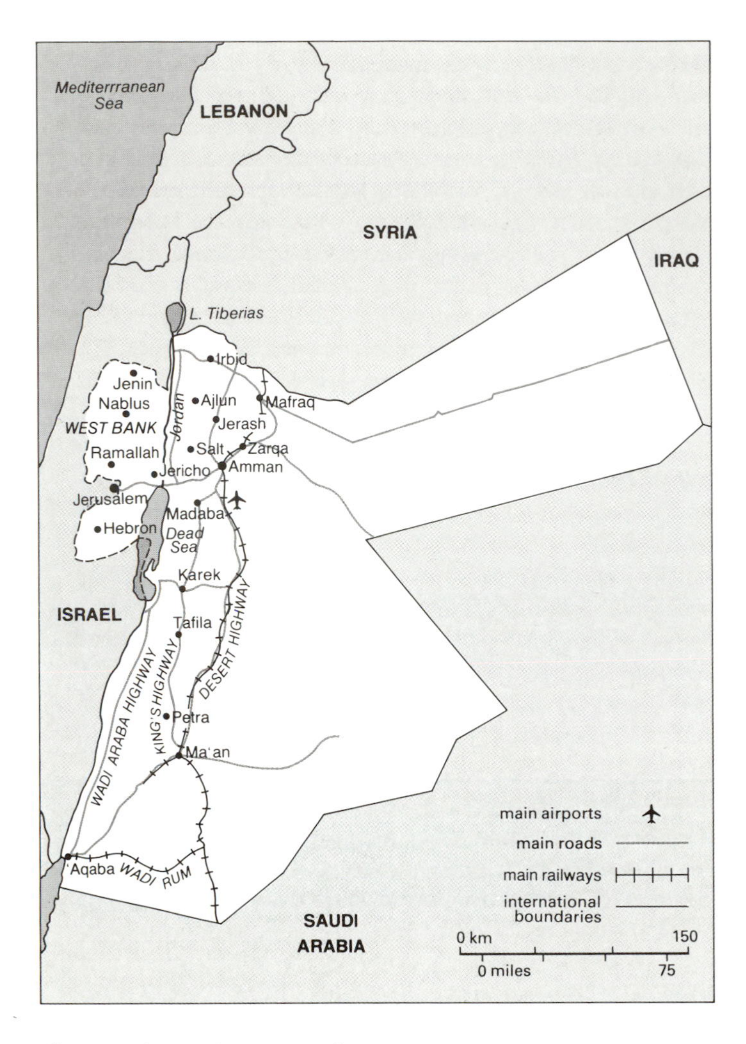

Geography and topography

The East Bank of Jordan is bounded to the west by the Great Rift, which runs along the Jordan Valley and the Dead Sea and down through the Gulf of ʿAqaba. In the north and centre of the country, the land rises steeply to the east to a line of precipitous hills some 3500 feet above sea level. Beyond these is the central plateau region which stretches from the Syrian border down to the town of Maʿan. South of Maʿan the area is mountainous, sloping down to Jordan's only port of ʿAqaba on the Red Sea. To the east of the country is the vast expanse of the Syrian Desert.

Peoples

The most important distinction in Jordan is between Palestinians and Transjordanians, a term which is usually used to refer to those who lived in east Jordan before 1948. Following the first (1948) Arab–Israeli War*, some 100,000 Palestinian refugees fled to the East Bank. A further 310,000 arrived after the 1967 War. Together with the general demographic drift to the east, it is estimated that about 60 per cent of the population of the East Bank today is Palestinian* in origin. The proportion is even higher in the thriving cities of Amman and Zarqa, though East Bankers form a majority in the outlying towns such as Irbid, Kerak and Maʿan. However, the term 'East Banker' does not represent a homogenous group. Before 1948, Jordan was made up of peasants, beduin tribesmen, most of whom are not settled, and townsmen, many of whom were of Palestinian or Syrian origin. There is also a small but politically significant minority of Circassians and Chechens, who came to Jordan towards the end of the last century.

Religions

A large majority of both East Bankers and Palestinians are Sunni. However, there are small groups of Druze in the north, while the Chechen community is Shiʿi*. Approximately 6 per cent of the population is Christian, encompassing Transjordanians and Palestinians alike. The largest group is the Greek Orthodox, which forms nearly two-thirds of the Christians in Jordan. Almost one-third are Greek Catholics, the balance being made up of Roman Catholics, Protestants, Armenians and Syrian Orthodox.

History up to 1939

The area which is now Jordan became largely Muslim after AD 636, when the Byzantine forces of the Emperor Heraclius were defeated by the Arab armies of Khalid ibn al-Walid at the Battle of Yarmuk in northern Jordan. Then followed Umayyad* and ʿAbbasid* rule and a short period of Seljuk* rule in the late eleventh century. Parts of Jordan were then included in the Latin Kingdom established by the Crusaders* in Jerusalem in 1099. After their defeat at the Battle of Hittin in 1187, crusader rule was replaced by that of Saladin*. After an ensuing period of Mamluk* rule, the 400-year rule of the Ottomans began. Much of this period was one of stagnation for the region.

The First World War and the Mandates

From the beginning of the sixteenth century Transjordan, the area east of the Jordan river, was part of the Ottoman vilayet of Damascus and remained a romantic backwater until the First World War. It was included in the area of British influence allocated under the Sykes–Picot agreement of May 1916. A year after ʿAqaba was captured by the Arab army of Prince Faysal ibn Husayn in July 1917, Amman was captured. However, when the General Syrian Congress in Damascus declared the independence of Syria with Faysal as King, France and Britain denounced the decision. The San Remo Conference of the following month awarded the Palestine Mandate* to Britain, and Syria proper fell to the French who forced Faysal to leave Damascus. In December 1920 the British and French agreed to include the area of Transjordan within the Palestine Mandate. In April 1921 ʿAbd Allah, Faysal's brother, was officially recognized as *de facto* ruler of Transjordan. The final draft of the Palestine Mandate confirmed by the Council of the League of

A view of Wadi Rumm from Ra's al-Naqb

Nations in July 1922 gave the mandatory power considerable latitude in its administration of the territory east of the Jordan River. On 15 May 1923 Britain formally recognized Transjordan as an independent state under the rule of the Amir ʿAbd Allah but under British tutelage and supported by a British subsidy. The Arab Legion, a small but elite armed force numbering a little over 1000 men, was built up by Peake Pasha, and in 1931 the Desert Patrol, commanded by Colonel Glubb (later Glubb Pasha), was formed to bring civil order to the rural areas and to secure the allegiance of the beduin to the state. In 1928 Britain signed a treaty giving the new state further independence, although reserving financial policy and foreign relations to the advice of a British Resident. In April the same year a constitution was promulgated. The Second World War delayed the achievement of full independence, which was at least nominally achieved by the Treaty of London on 22 March 1946. On 25 May 1946 ʿAbd Allah was proclaimed King and a new constitution was promulgated; the name of the state was changed to Jordan.

History since the Second World War

Following the slow pace of development in the 1920s and 1930s, the country was to face a period of rapid political change after the end of the Second World War. In March 1946, Britain granted Transjordan independence in recognition of its loyal support during the war. Two months later ʿAbd Allah was crowned King of the Hashimite Kingdom of Jordan. However, Britain's special position continued to be enshrined in a treaty which allowed it to maintain troops in Jordan. The United States and the USSR refused to recognize the Kingdom on this basis, which prompted Britain to go through the largely cosmetic procedure of renegotiating the treaty in 1948.

Jordan took part in the first Arab–Israeli War of 1948, fighting alongside the sorely uncoordinated forces of its neighbouring Arab states. The Jordanian army, although small, fought with distinction, especially in resisting ferocious assaults on east Jerusalem. At the end of the hostilities, the army was also left in occupation of most of the area of east Palestine allocated to the Arabs under the United Nations partition. This area, popularly known as the West Bank*, was formally incorporated into the Kingdom in April 1950.

Although it realized part of King ʿAbd Allah's dream of Arab unity under the Hashimite throne, the acquisition of the West Bank had severe economic and political consequences. The influx of some 400,000 refugees swamped Jordan's modest economy, causing chronic unemployment. The UN Relief and Works Agency for Palestinian Refugees (UNRWA)* was set up in 1949 to cater for them (see Palestinians). It also completely changed the internal political complexion of the Kingdom where the previous style of government, a benevolent patriarchy, was no longer workable. The Palestinian conflict eventually cost ʿAbd Allah his life: he was assassinated on the steps of al-Aqsa Mosque in Jerusalem on 20 July 1951.

The short reign of ʿAbd Allah's son and successor, King Talal, saw the introduction in 1952 of a new constitution in keeping with the more democratic trends of the day. The chief reforms enshrined in the new document were to make the cabinet accountable to parliament, which comprised an elected 40-man chamber of deputies and a 20-strong senate appointed by the King; however, the monarch still retained considerable power, such as the ability to choose and dismiss the prime minister at will. Talal stepped down after a few months due to mental illness in favour of his teenage son Husayn.

King Husayn

The first two decades of King Husayn's* reign were punctuated by bouts of civil disorder which threatened the Hashimite regime and the existence of the Jordanian state. In the mid-1950s, the King's inexperience and naivety seemed to exacerbate the turmoil. But by the end of the decade he had proved to be a courageous and tenacious leader, and had earned the respect of a large majority of his subjects.

Husayn's reign began with a series of blows to his prestige, notably with the reversal of his initial policy of liberalization and his failure, amid widespread demonstrations throughout the Kingdom, to take Jordan into the British-sponsored Baghdad Pact* in 1955. Egged on by the radical Arab nationalist states of Syria and Egypt, the riots continued, especially on the West Bank where resentment at Israeli raids often spilt over against the King. Husayn swayed with the breeze for a time by dismissing his British chief of staff

King Husayn

General Glubb, allowing free elections in 1956 to return a radical parliament, and choosing a pan-Arab nationalist premier. During its brief term, this administration negotiated an end to the Anglo-Jordanian Treaty.

Almost from the beginning, a trial of political strength ensued between the government and the palace over the former's increasingly radical policies, ending in Husayn outmanoeuvring his prime minister, the National Socialist Party's Sulayman Nabulsi. Amid evidence of an attempted *coup d'état*, the young King, backed by the East Bank tribes, initiated a clampdown. Amongst a number of draconian steps, this included a purge of nationalists and extremists and the proscription of political parties – a ban which is still in force today.

In the wake of such insecurity, King Husayn turned to the United States which, in return for his adherence to the Eisenhower Doctrine, replaced Britain as Jordan's chief source of foreign aid. Periods of instability returned from time to time, notably in 1958 after the bloody overthrow of Husayn's cousin, King Faysal II, in Iraq. In 1963 more coup attempts were uncovered. But by the mid-1960s Jordan's future appeared more secure.

The 1967 War

The relative calm of this period was shattered by the third Arab–Israeli War* of 1967 in which Jordan actively participated with Egypt and Syria. The crushing defeat experienced by the Arabs was shared by Jordan, which lost the entire West Bank, including Arab Jerusalem. It is the restoration of this land and in particular the holy city which has dominated Hashimite diplomacy ever since.

The débâcle of 1967 disabused the Palestinians of the notion that the Arab states were capable of fighting their cause for them. The Palestine Liberation Organization*, which had hitherto been an extension of Egyptian foreign policy, was radicalized and militarized, launching guerrilla raids against Israel from Jordanian territory. As the power of the *fida'iyyin* (commandos; 'those who sacrifice themselves') grew, they increasingly began to challenge both the army and the state in the Kingdom. Eventually, at the bidding of leading East Bankers, King Husayn reluctantly ordered the army to move against the PLO. A short but bloody civil war took place from September 1970 in the wake of which the organization's leadership fled abroad.

After being verbally vilified by Arab governments for attacking the guerrillas, Jordan was reconciled with its frontline neighbours three years later. Even so, the Kingdom did not participate in the 1973 war with Israel, reflecting King Husayn's belief that only a negotiated peace could result in a just and durable peace settlement, and illustrating Jordanian fears of Israeli military might. However, Jordan did send troops and equipment to the Syrian front in an expression of Arab unity.

Children in Irbid, northern Jordan

King Husayn tangled again with the PLO, although this time over the diplomatic table, in October 1974 at the Arab heads of state summit in Rabat. Challenged by successful PLO lobbying, he accepted a resolution which recognized the PLO as the 'sole legitimate representative' of the Palestinian people. But Husayn has at no time given up his claim to the West Bank, which is still occupied Jordanian territory. In response to the resolution, the King prorogued parliament, with its ex-officio West Bank representation, only restoring it to a legislative function at the beginning of 1984.

The Rabat summit resolution gave a fillip to the Jordanian nationalist movement. Reasoning that if the PLO represents the Palestinians Jordan should be a state for the Jordanians, the nationalists have demanded a larger share of appointments. Consequently, the decade from 1974 has seen East Bankers increasingly coming to occupy a greater proportion of the posts in the bureaucracy and the services. In 1979 there was a rapprochement between King Husayn and the PLO, and ʿArafat* made several visits to Amman.

Politics today

Domestic politics

The position of King Husayn at the head of the Jordanian state has been more secure in the 1980s than at any other time during his reign. He enjoys the loyalty of the vast majority of Jordanians, regardless of their ethnic background, and the respect of even more. He is extremely powerful internally, yet by hiving off responsibility for the day-to-day administration of his Kingdom he avoids being tarnished by the policies of individual governments. His rule is patriarchal but far from autocratic, and most of the country's constitution is carefully observed. While his own position is comparatively strong, question marks inevitably exist about the degreee to which the monarchy has become institutionalized.

The cabinet is the most important institution in governing the country, and the prime minister, who selects his own ministers, tends to dominate it. Although personal competence is increasingly important in the appointment of ministers, the cabinet tends to be a carefully constructed mosaic which reflects the tribal, ethnic and confessional balance in the country.

Since its recall in 1984, parliament has re-emerged as an important debating chamber and watchdog on government policy. In particular, members have been vocal about corruption and civil rights. The constitution was amended to enable by-elections to be held on the East Bank to replace those deputies who had died since the last national poll in 1967. The election, which was not subject to government manipulation, was successful, although campaigning was restricted. The lower house then similarly voted to fill the gaps in the West Bank's representation, a popular election being impossible due to the occupation of the area by Israel.

In the by-elections, Muslim fundamentalist candidates did proportionately well. The results reflected a more religious outlook among Jordanians, but were not themselves evidence of a radicalized, populist Islamic movement capable of challenging the political order. The leftist and pan-Arab traditions of the 1950s attracted a negligible following, suggesting a more conservative direction in the political debate.

One of 40 000 refugees in Baqa'a camp near Amman carrying water after weeks of winter snow and rain storms

The Palestine problem

In foreign affairs much of the King's energies are concentrated on the question of Palestine (see Arab–Israeli conflict*, Palestinians*), both because of the large number of Palestinians living in the Kingdom and the need to salvage Hashimite pride by effecting the return of Arab rule of the territories lost in 1967. Knowing that the Arabs are not strong enough to inflict a military defeat on an Israeli state backed by the United States, the King is a strong advocate of a negotiated peace.

King Husayn sees the United States as the key to a settlement, as only Washington has real influence over its client. However, Israel's influence on the US has consistently stymied the King's various peace strategies and has left Jordan seriously under-equipped militarily because of Congressional obstruction to the sale of advanced weaponry to Jordan. He also appreciates the need for support from the Palestinian constituency and from Jordan's fellow Arab states.

A manifestation of the King's search for peace was the 11 February 1985 agreement with the PLO, which enshrined the idea of the exchange of 'land for peace'. While the agreement improved the King's credentials with the Palestinians, a new wave of international terrorism in 1985 damaged the pretensions of the PLO to a seat at the negotiating table. After nearly twenty years of diplomacy, many Jordanians privately doubt whether Israel will ever voluntarily give back the West Bank.

Regional relations

The lessons of the 1950s have shown Jordan the risks of being at serious odds with Egypt, Syria and Iraq, especially all at once. Jordan broke off links with Egypt when President Sadat* began unilateral peace talks with Israel in 1978. Arab disunity and the death of Sadat, however, enabled Jordan to re-establish diplomatic relations with Egypt in September 1983. Amman's attempt to obtain the readmission of Egypt to the Arab League*, and so increase the bargaining power of the moderate Arabs at the expense of Israel, has so far failed.

Jordan improved relations with Syria in the autumn of 1985. Bad blood nearly led to war between the two states in 1980. Since then

Damascus had frequently sanctioned attacks on Jordanian representatives abroad. The future course of the rapprochement depends on the issue of ʿArafat's leadership of the PLO and support for Iraq.

Jordan has been a forthright supporter of Iraq in its war against Syria's ally, Iran (see Iran–Iraq War). Although King Husayn may have regretted his commitment to Baghdad after Iraq failed to secure the expected sweeping victory in 1980, Jordan prospered from an Iraqi economic boom in the early years of the war. The 1980 Arab summit in Amman, aimed at ushering in a decade of Arab development inspired by the Iraqis, saw the beginning of Iraqi loans to Jordan in exchange for Iraqi use of Jordanian facilities as an alternative supply route. Although relations have cooled somewhat, Iraq is retaining Jordan's loyalty with the prospect of more prosperity after the war ends.

Ironically, Jordan's key friend in the region is its old dynastic rival, Saudi Arabia*. As the recession has increasingly affected Jordan, the payment of an annual Saudi JD130 million in grants has softened the blow. The remittances of the many thousands of Jordanians working in Saudi Arabia (see Population and Migration) and aid from Saudi banks and government agencies have also helped. In addition, Saudi Arabia is of major strategic importance as the pipeline running west to the refinery at Zarqa is Jordan's only permanent line of crude-oil supply.

Foreign policy

Throughout its short history the Kingdom of Jordan has remained friendly with the West. Despite its formal non-alignment, it retains intimate bonds with Britain and close political ties with the US. This goodwill now extends to the European Economic Community. France, like Britain, is a significant supplier of military equipment to Jordan, while West Germany has been an active provider of aid. Commercial links with Europe have both reflected and boosted the political support given to King Husayn. In its recent history, Jordan has always sought at least civil relations with the Soviet Union because of the influence Moscow has over both Syria and the Communist Party in the Kingdom. Jordan has also bought small consignments of weapons from the Soviet Union, although this has been of only symbolic significance for King Husayn to demonstrate that he is not wholly dependent on the US.

The economy and society today

Given the scarcity of natural resources and with a small indigenous market, the economy of Jordan is closely tied to those of its neighbours. Consequently, it benefited greatly from the spinoffs of the oil-price boom in the 1970s, but in the mid-1980s it shared the general regional recession.

Given its precarious economic state, the Kingdom has concentrated on developing commercial acumen. It has a highly educated population, and has some 350,000 of its nationals working in the oil-rich Arab countries. In 1984, these expatriates remitted through official channels some JD475 million – the largest single contribution to the balance of payments. Jordan also possesses a dynamic and resourceful private sector.

The decade of prosperity made Jordan a regional entrepôt. Judicious government spending has established an efficient infrastructural system, including prestigious projects such as the port of ʿAqaba and the new Queen Alia international airport. Free zones have also been set up near the city of Zarqa and in ʿAqaba, and the Kingdom's first industrial estate has been opened to the south of the capital. In the private sphere, the banking and finance sectors have become far more sophisticated and efficacious, but close supervision has avoided the disasters which have befallen finance houses and stock markets elsewhere in the region.

However, the effects of the rapid growth, which saw real Gross Domestic Product increase between 1975 and 1983 by an average annual rate of 13.9 per cent, were not always desirable. With the urban economy, based primarily on the services sector, experiencing a boom, rural workers flocked to the cities. This placed an enormous burden upon urban social resources such as housing and education. The growth of Amman was particularly rapid, and by 1983 nearly 45 per cent of the country's population was resident in the capital.

Nor has the boom left Jordan with a strong industrial base. With easy profits from land speculation and construction, remarkably little capital was invested in medium-sized industrial ventures. Consequently, the Kingdom has some small-scale factories engaged in manufacturing, which exist alongside the handful of large capital-intensive concerns. These giants, in which the public sector has a majority stake, produce cement and fertilizer and extract Jordan's most marketable natural resources, potash and phosphates.

The decline of agriculture since the loss of the West Bank has been severe. Despite the introduction of new technology and the extension of irrigation in the Jordan Valley, the contribution of agriculture to the GDP fell from 9.7 per cent in 1974 to 5.6 per cent ten years later. This means that the Kingdom spends JD100 million on the importation of grain, meat and fruit every year. The strategic and economic implications of these figures, and the need to stem rural drift, have put agriculture at the very top of the plan's development list.

Even if the problems of agriculture can be eased, the country's structural deficit on the balance of trade, which in 1984 stood at over JD310 million, looks set to continue. Oil imports from Saudi Arabia form the largest single component of the deficit at around JD200 million. Efforts are being made to prospect for commercially exploitable oil reserves and foreign companies are being invited in to search for oil. So far, however, only two wells in the Azraq Basin producing modest quantities of oil have been found.

So far, the Kingdom has coped adequately with its change of economic fortunes. However, as Arab aid has slowed right down, Jordan has started to borrow on the Eurodollar market and to run down the level of its foreign currency reserves which had been such a source of pride.

Another fear is that significant numbers of its expatriates will come home as the economic health of Gulf economies continues to deteriorate. This would reduce remittances as well as exacerbating an unemployment rate which in 1985 was believed to be near to 8 per cent. With over 50 per cent of the population under the age of 15 and an increasing proportion of women seeking work, doubts surround the ability of the economy to be able to absorb many of the newcomers into the job market, with all its attendant political implications. It would be ironic if Jordan's manpower, the Kingdom's most valuable export, should end up as a burden to the economy.

PJR

Further reading

N. Aruri, *Jordan: a study in political development 1921–1965* (The Hague, 1972)
P. Gubser, *Jordan: crossroads of Middle Eastern events* (London, 1983)
King Hussein, *Uneasy Lies the Head* (London, 1962)
M. P. Mazur, *Economic Growth and Development in Jordan* (London, 1979)
P. J. Vatikiotis, *Politics and the Military in Jordan* (London, 1967)

Kuwait

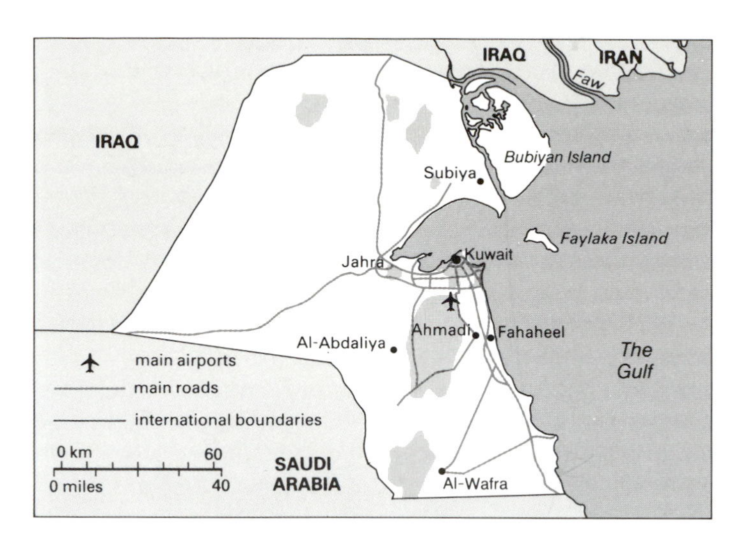

Geography and topography

The state of Kuwait is located at the head of the Gulf, close to the Shatt al-ʿArab estuary which marks the frontier between Iraq and Iran. It covers 17,818 km^2, including 2590 km^2 taken from the former neutral zone now shared with Saudi Arabia, and includes nine offshore islands, the most important of which are Warba and Bubiyan (both uninhabited), and Faylaka. Kuwait enjoys a common border with Iraq, which has not been properly demarcated, and, to the south, lies Saudi Arabia, where the old neutral zone jointly controlled by the two neighbours has now been divided between them.

Geologically, Kuwait forms part of the Arabian peninsula tectonic plate. This tilts downwards towards the east before it merges into the Gulf, partly because of the accumulation of silt from the rivers entering the Gulf and partly because the Arabian plate is being forced under the Iranian and Asian plates by expansions in the Red Sea floor.

Only 2 per cent of Kuwait's land area – about 3600 hectares in 1981 – is given over to agriculture and only 10 per cent could be converted to agricultural use, of which, moreover, 85 per cent is only suitable for pastoral purposes. The reason for this is not only the poor quality of desert soils but the lack of adequate water resources. Kuwait lies in the semi-arid zone and enjoys only about 150 mm of rainfall annually. There is virtually no surface water and what there is is saline.

Peoples

According to the 1985 census, Kuwait's population totalled almost 1.7 m, of whom 40.1 per cent were Kuwaiti citizens. In the previous

Official title	The State of Kuwait
Area	17,818 sq. km
Population	1,695,128 (1985 census)
Government and constitution	A constitutional monarchy with a single parliamentary house, the National Assembly. The Amir exercises executive power through a Council of Ministers and appoints and dismisses ministers, including the prime minister. The New Assembly was elected on 23 February 1981 and new legislative elections took place on 20 February 1985
Currency	1 Kuwaiti dinar = 1000 fils; US $1 = 295.6 fils
Languages	Arabic is the official language but English is widely spoken
Religion	60–70 per cent of the population are Sunni Muslims and some 30 per cent are Shi'i. There are also small Christian minorities
Climate	Summer temperatures are hot, reaching 49°C in the shade, while the coldest winter month, January, sees temperatures ranging between 2.8°C and 28.3°C

census in 1980, Kuwait's population had been 1.4m, with 41.7 per cent being Kuwaiti citizens.

History up to 1939

The eighteenth century

Kuwait's existence as an independent state really dates from the early eighteenth century, when in 1710 the 'Utab, a member of the 'Anaza tribal confederation in northern and central Arabia, took over control of Kuwait – until then an obscure fishing village. Kuwait had been passed by in the development of the Gulf because it could not contribute to the major patterns of trade from the south Iraqi port of Basra through the Gulf to the East. Although the Kuwait region had been under the nominal control of the Ottoman Empire* since the late sixteenth century, the 'Utab were able to develop the port of Kuwait as a terminus for trade from Syria and the Levant and thus create a commercial significance for the town. In 1760, the 'Utab in charge of Kuwait split, with the Khalifa fraction migrating to Bahrain and the Sabah fraction creating the Amirate of Kuwait that has lasted – formally at least – until the modern period.

Within a few years, however, Kuwait came to the attention of another major power in the region – Britain. In 1776, the East India Company set up a base in the Gulf, thus signalling the development of British interest in the region, partly for commercial advantage and partly because the Gulf was seen increasingly as part of the geographic complex that controlled access to British India from Europe. For the next century, however, British direct interest in Kuwait was fitful, thus mirroring the Ottoman attitude which, provided its nominal sovereignty was recognized, allowed the Sabah rulers virtually total freedom of action. This situation only changed towards the end of the nineteenth century, as the result of two separate developments – the Ottoman desire to reassert its authority over al-Hasa and British fears over proposals to integrate Kuwait into the Berlin–Baghdad railway project.

British relations with Kuwait

Britain, at the time, was concerned about developments in the Gulf. First of all, there had been rumours that Russia might establish a coaling station at the mouth of the Gulf and seek a railway concession to link Kuwait with Tripoli in Lebanon. It was feared in London that the Ottoman authorities would have been sympathetic to such a request because of Istanbul's irritation over the British occupation of Egypt in 1882. Secondly, even though the Russian project turned out to be a myth, there was a far more worrying possibility – that German interests, which had already been encouraged by the Ottoman Empire as a counterpart to British interests in the region, would attempt to extend the projected Berlin–Baghdad railway to Kuwait because it offered better harbour facilities than did Basra. It was this that persuaded the British government to react sympathetically towards overtures from the Amir of Kuwait in 1899, whereas two years earlier it had rejected them. Under the terms of the agreement signed between Britain and the Kuwaiti leader in 1899, Shaykh Mubarak was to obtain an annual subvention in return for agreeing not to alienate any portion of his territories to a foreign power.

Britain was most unwilling to grant Kuwait the protected status its ruler sought after 1901. However, in return for a series of exclusive economic concessions in Kuwait in the first decade of the twentieth century and to reassure the ruler over the territorial integrity of his state and over the security of his personal possessions in Iraq, Britain eventually accepted that Kuwait was to be 'an independent government under British protection' under the terms of the 3 November 1914 agreement.

This agreement came after the outbreak of the First World War, which had impeded the ratification of an earlier agreement in July 1913, whereby the Ottoman Empire had recognized the independent status of Kuwait. Kuwait attempted to consolidate its hold on territories in the north-west Gulf, but was confronted by the expansionist power of the Saudi rulers of al-Hasa. In 1920 the Saudis advanced to besiege Kuwait City but were forced to withdraw through British intervention. Through the 1922 Treaty of Ugair which Britain negotiated with Ibn Sa'ud on Kuwait's behalf, Kuwait lost to the Saudis two-thirds of the territory it had been allotted under the unratified 1913 Anglo-Turkish agreement, but had its borders with Iraq guaranteed.

Pearl-fishing, which had been a mainstay of the local economy and on which much of the initial mercantile wealth had been based, in addition to that derived from the re-export trade within the Gulf, began to decay in the early 1930s because of competition from Japanese cultured pearls, while the world depression caused its own remote echoes in the region. At the same time oil prospecting began, with the US and the British creating the Kuwait Oil Company (KOC) for the purpose. Oil was discovered in 1938 in the Burgan field – then the largest in the world – but exploitation was delayed by the Second World War. Eventually, production began in 1946, reaching 1.83m barrels per day (b/d) by 1962.

History since the Second World War

The population make-up of Kuwait began to alter as oil wealth flowed in, particularly after the Iranian oil supply was temporarily interrupted during the Musaddiq* crisis between 1951 and 1953. Palestinians began to move to Kuwait as demand for labour rose, as did – in lesser numbers – Egyptians. At the same time and partly as the consequence of the increasing prominence of immigrants in Kuwaiti life, the rising tide of Arab nationalism*, particularly after the Egyptian Revolution in 1952, began to make itself felt. This, in turn, led to demands for changes in the political structures inside Kuwait and in the relations between Kuwait and Britain.

Independence

The Franco-British role in the 1956 Suez war and the collapse of the pro-British monarchy in Iraq in 1958 intensified Arab nationalist sentiment in Kuwait which was represented in the National Cultural Club led by Ahmad Khatib. A majority of the more conservative elements among the ruling family and the merchants also accepted that the link with Britain was outdated and the Amir 'Abd Allah Salim began negotiations with Britain to abrogate the 1899 treaty and to achieve Kuwaiti independence. He also announced his intention to hold elections to a constituent Assembly to draft a constitution.

An independent Kuwait came into being in June 1961 and immediately faced a threat to its existence from Iraq, where the Qasim government laid claim to Kuwait on the grounds of its prior integration into the Ottoman province of Basra. British forces were sent back, ostensibly to defend Kuwait against this Iraqi threat, only to be withdrawn as the Arab League took over responsibility for defending Kuwait from what soon turned out to be an empty Iraqi threat.

Controlled democracy

The new constitution, promulgated in November 1962, provided for a 50-seat Assembly, elected by a franchise limited to about 10 per cent of the Kuwaiti population – non-Kuwaitis had no electoral rights. Ministers, to be appointed by the Amir, had automatic membership of the Assembly, while formal political parties were disallowed. The Assembly itself was denied effective executive power, although it was to be granted a role in choosing the Amir.

In spite of these limitations, elections for the Assembly were held in January 1963 and at four-yearly intervals thereafter. Despite the fact that the government took great care to ensure that the complexion of the Assembly should be as favourable as possible, it came to articulate the views of the major elements in Kuwaiti society (except for the numerically dominant immigrant groups): the tribes, the merchants and businessmen, and politically committed professional groups. The ability of the ruler to control the make-up of the Assembly depended on his ability to ensure cooperation from the 5000-strong merchant community, dominated by the fifteen leading families, and from the major tribes in the state – the 'Ujman and the 'Awazim. Nonetheless, although such cooperation was usually forthcoming, external events increasingly improved the electoral chances of the Arab nationalist group led by Ahmad Khatib.

The development of the Assembly – the first political instrument of its kind in the Arabian peninsula – was mirrored by the growth of the press*. Here, however, immigrant journalists dominated the sector and, by the 1970s, the consequent radical criticism of Gulf politics had found its echo in the Assembly, where the opposition was still led by Dr Khatib. This was particularly true over major issues such as the Palestinian problem and the Lebanese civil war*. At the same time, the 1973 War* between Israel and the frontline Arab states led to calls in the Assembly for a limitation of Kuwaiti oil production and the nationalization of the Kuwaiti oil industry, as well as further liberalization of press controls.

These developments disturbed both the Amir's government and the rulers of neighbouring Saudi Arabia which, as the ultimate guarantor of Kuwaiti independence, took a considerable interest in the domestic political scene. As a result, on the ground that the Assembly had maliciously wasted time, Amir Jabir al-Sabah suspended it in August 1976 and, at the same time, suspended parts of the constitution. A year later, the Assembly was dissolved and autocratic rule was restored to Kuwait.

*The Iranian Revolution**

The collapse of the Pahlavi regime in Iran in February 1979 caused considerable nervousness in Kuwait, both because of the sizeable Shi'a minority inside Kuwait and because of the evident hostility of the new Khomeini* regime in Tehran towards the Arab Gulf states.

This nervousness was intensified when the Gulf War broke out in September 1980, since Kuwait's northern border is only 20 km away from the Shatt al-ʿArab and the Iranian border (see Iran–Iraq War). Furthermore, Iraq, which has not accepted the legitimacy of the existing border between it and Kuwait, began to apply pressure for access to the Kuwaiti islands of Warba and Bubiyan as sites for Iraqi naval bases. After a border incident in 1983, a border agreement was patched up in November 1984.

However, Kuwait has continued to be subject to considerable pressure from Iran, despite the ongoing tensions with Iraq. Iran, angry that Kuwait, together with Saudi Arabia, has consistently provided financial aid to Iraq, either in terms of direct subventions of up to $5bn, or as counterpart oil sales of 125,000 b/d, has repeatedly voiced its displeasure with Kuwaiti policy. As a result of these tensions, not only has shipping bound for Kuwait regularly been attacked by Iran in the past two years, but Kuwait was also the scene of suicide bombings against French and US property in December 1983, the hijacking of a Kuwaiti airliner to Tehran in December 1984, and an attempt on the life of the Amir and the bombings of cafés in Kuwait city in mid-1985. Kuwait has responded to this by constantly seeking greater security for itself through collective Gulf action in the Gulf Cooperation Council*, created by Arab Gulf states in 1980 in response to the perceived threat of the Gulf War to regional stability. Kuwait has also attempted to maintain a balance between the superpowers, being the only Gulf state until 1985 to enjoy formal diplomatic relations with the Soviet Union, and, despite its unabashedly capitalist economy, taking a firm stand against the USA over its support for Israel in the Arab–Israeli dispute*.

Kuwait's National Assembly in session

Domestically, the Kuwaiti authorities initially responded to the Iranian Revolution with a show of firmness. This action was undertaken, not only because the revolution had been greeted with enthusiasm by the Shiʿi minority, but also because of the welcome it received from the large Palestinian population in Kuwait as a result of the initially close relations between the PLO and the revolutionary regime in Tehran. The initial official response was further to restrict press freedom and to ban public meetings as well as public discussion of political issues. Attention was then directed to the implicit threat offered by Kuwait's growing Shiʿi minority, swollen by migrants during the 1970s. This was a particularly crucial consideration because of the role played by Shiʿis in the armed forces and because of the open support voiced by Shiʿi notables for the Iranian Revolution in 1979. A programme of expulsions of non-Kuwaiti Shiʿis was initiated, with 20,000 being expelled by early 1980. Further waves of expulsions followed after the bombings in Kuwait in 1983 and 1985.

The Amir eventually accepted, however, that demands voiced in 1979 by thirty former parliamentary deputies for a restoration of the Assembly might well help to restore domestic stability. As a result, the Assembly was reconstituted in 1981 and, in elections in February 1985, the Islamic fundamentalist groups that had appeared to be a considerable threat in 1981 lost significant support to Arab nationalist groups. The Assembly suffers, as before, from its relative lack of power, but it does serve as an effective medium for voicing criticism of government policy. It opposed the provision of Kuwaiti aid to the frontline states – Jordan, the PLO and Syria – in 1984 and 1985. Similar opposition appeared in 1985 to government proposals to cut back on the cost of Kuwait's immense and comprehensive welfare system. It has also reacted vigorously to government attempts to hush up some of the more embarrassing scandals associated with the unofficial Suq al-Manakh stock-market crash in 1982, which involved debts of KD 27bn and 29,000 post-dated and dishonoured cheques.

The economy and society today

Since the end of the Second World War, Kuwait's economy has been based on oil*, with reserves set at 90 billion barrels at the end of 1984, the third largest reserves in the non-communist world and, at current rates of production, sufficient to last for about 250 years. The oil industry, which accounts for 50 per cent of Kuwait's Gross Domestic Product and over 90 per cent of its visible export earnings, has been nationalized since 1975 and is organized in five subsidiaries under the overall control of the Kuwait Petroleum Corporation. In addition to crude oil and associated gas production, Kuwait operates three refineries, with a combined capacity set to reach 650,000 b/d by the end of 1986, and petrochemical and fertilizer plants.

Other directly productive sectors – particularly in agriculture* and fishing – have been insignificant, given Kuwait's natural resource restraints, and the re-exporting trade in the Gulf has collapsed since the start of the Gulf War. The other major economic sectors have been industry and financial services. Success here has been mixed. The industrial sector, which is directed mainly towards construction and consumer industry, has suffered from the fact that it is largely dependent on government expenditure, which itself is oil-dependent and has been increasingly depressed in recent years. The financial services sector has suffered severely from the collapse of the Suq al-Manakh stock-market, which has severely undermined regional confidence. So far, despite considerable official and private effort, the adverse economic climate in the Gulf has made it extremely difficult to effectively revive Kuwait's developing financial institutions.

In two areas, however, Kuwait can report considerable success. The government has pursued a consistent policy of foreign investment since the early 1970s and income from this source is said to have been of the order of 85 per cent of oil revenues in 1985. Furthermore, 10 per cent of all government revenues are placed in a special investment fund, according to legislation drawn up in 1976 – the Reserve Fund for Future Generations. Kuwait is also a large-scale foreign-aid donor – one of the most generous in the world, with grants totalling $1.3bn in 1982 – 4.9 per cent of GDPK. The other area of economic success has been Kuwait's policy of turning its oil industry into a vertically integrated operation, with the purchase of distribution networks in Europe and oil-operating companies in the USA. It has been the first Middle Eastern oil producer to do this.

Kuwait, like other oil producers, now faces a difficult and uncertain future as oil prices fall dramatically. Already, the government has announced cutbacks in expenditure and tighter patterns of economic management have been introduced. However, given its reserves of around $77bn – half of it in liquid form – and its careful overseas diversification, Kuwait is far better set than most Middle Eastern states to cope with the problems it faces. Furthermore, the cautious liberalization of political life, coupled with the government's ruthless determination to eliminate what it sees as foreign-based subversion, should guarantee domestic peace in the medium term. However, the immigrant majority of the population, excluded from the political, social and economic benefits enjoyed by Kuwaitis themselves, represents a significant political danger that the government will now have to address.

GJ

Further reading

J. Bulloch, *The Gulf* (London, 1984)
D. Hiro, *Inside the Middle East* (London, 1982)
A. al-Moosa and K. S. McLachlan, *Immigrant Labour in Kuwait* (London, 1985)
R. Shaw, *Kuwait* (London, 1976)

Lebanon

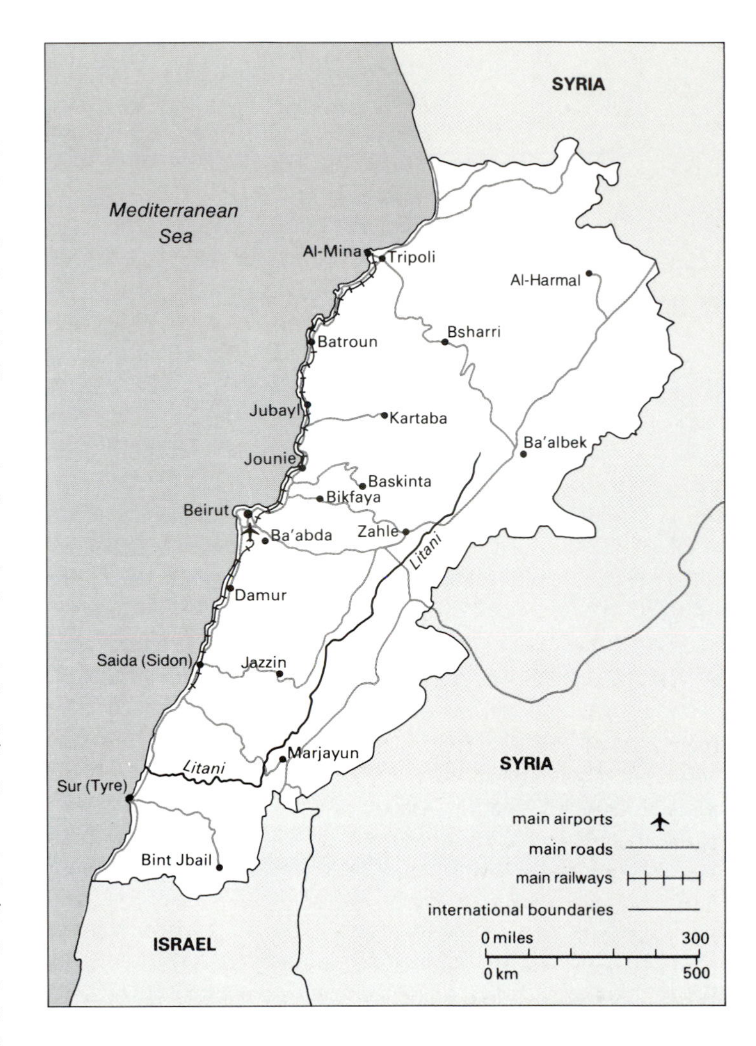

Geography and topography

Lebanon's 10.452 km^2 are dominated by the mountain range running north to south up the middle of the country. The limestone Mount Lebanon range rises from the Mediterranean coast to a maximum height of 3556 m above the northern Akkar Plain. The range continues south, tapering off in the hilly stretch of country along Israel's northern border. To the east of the mountain range lies the fertile Biqaʿ (Bekaa) Plain, where most of Lebanon's agriculture is based.

Peoples and religions

Before the modern-day borders of Greater Lebanon were drawn in 1920, Lebanon was thought of as consisting primarily of the central

Official title	The Republic of Lebanon
Area	10,452 sq. km
Population	3 million (1984 UN estimate)
Government and constitution	Since 1960 Lebanon has had a single chamber parliament with 99 members. The president, who is elected for a single six-year term, is traditionally a Maronite Christian. The prime minister, who is chosen by the president, is traditionally a Sunni Muslim
Currency	1 Lebanese pound = 100 piastres; US $1 = £L 32.40
Language	Although Arabic is the principal language, French is for many Lebanese a first language and English is widely spoken
Religion	1983 estimates are as follows: Shiʿi Muslims: 1.2 m; Sunni Muslims: 750,000; Christians 1.5 m; Druze: 250,000
Climate	Coastal lowlands fairly hot in summer and warm in winter. However, there is heavy winter snowfall in the hills from December to May

mountain range. The main peoples of the mountain are the Maronite* Catholics, based in the north but also living in many parts of the south, and the Druze*, with their base in the southern part of the range, known as the Shuf. The Maronites emerged as a sect in the sixth or seventh century AD, settling in their present heartland after the arrival of the Muslim armies from the Arabian peninsula in the 630s. The Druze trace their origins as a distinct sect to the eleventh century. Their beliefs are a mystical offshoot of Shiʿa Islam combined with features of other religions, including a belief in reincarnation. There are some 200,000 Druze in Lebanon today.

Both Druzes and Maronites have powerful attachments to their traditional regions, and their respective communities are marked by a strong sense of internal solidarity. The Sunni* Muslims – more closely identified with the wider Arab world – have their traditional base in the coastal cities of Beirut, Tripoli and Sidon. The Shiʿi* Muslims come mainly from the south of the country and the northern part of the Biqaʿ, regions only incorporated into Lebanon after 1920. Originally the third largest group after the Maronites and the Sunnis, the Shiʿis are now clearly the largest, accounting for about one-third of Lebanon's total population of an estimated 2.5–3 million. Besides the Maronites, Lebanon contains a number of other Christian sects, notably the Greek Orthodox and Greek Catholic, as well as Armenians* of various Christian denominations. Estimates for 1984 put the total Christian population at 1.5m.

Lebanon became the host country for a large number of Palestinians* – most of whom are Sunni Muslims – after the creation of Israel* in 1948. The Palestinians number up to 400,000, a figure normally included in the higher estimates of Lebanon's population. Population statistics in Lebanon are imprecise because there has not been an official census since 1932; as political power has been divided up on a sectarian basis, the question of population growth has been a highly charged issue.

History up to 1939

After being part of succeeding Muslim states, Mount Lebanon came under the sway of the Ottoman Empire* in 1516. The people of the mountain enjoyed a measure of autonomy for the next 300 years under local princes, owing ultimate allegiance to the Ottomans. For most of this period, the Druze, with their well-organized fighting forces and core of powerful landlords, were the dominant force. But gradually the Maronites, more numerous and quicker to take advantage of growing commercial ties with Europe, emerged as the leading group. The shift of power between the Druze and Maronites occurred against a backdrop of conflicting involvement of foreign powers in Lebanese affairs. The power of the Janbulat (Jumblat) and other Druze families expanded during the eighteenth century but began to wane during the nineteenth. But decisive changes in mountain politics took place as a result of the turbulent events between the Egyptian invasion in 1832 and the imposition of a new provincial administration by the great powers of the day in 1861.

The Egyptian expedition was dispatched by Muhammad ʿAli* as part of an effort to expand his own power at the expense of the Ottomans, to whom he was nominally subject. The Egyptian move was supported by Amir Bashir, the then ruler of the Shihab dynasty which had held sway in Mount Lebanon since 1697. The Shihabs were originally Sunni Muslim, allied to the Druze, but in later years some had converted to Maronite Christianity. By allying himself with the Egyptians, Bashir alienated the Druze, who objected to increased conscription and higher taxes. Bashir was ousted and the Egyptians forced out of Lebanon when European troops intervened to restore Ottoman rule. A system of cantonal rule – known as the *qa'imaqamiyya* – was imposed, but this failed to satisfy either Druze or Maronites. Serious intercommunal fighting broke out in 1859–60, resulting in heavy losses for the Maronites, who suffered about 11,000 killed. The new system which went into force in 1861 – the *mutasarifiyya* – was based on overall rule by a non-Lebanese Christian appointed by the Ottomans, with a provincial administrative council. The system produced stability and economic prosperity, with raw-silk exports flourishing and Lebanon's ports developing into important staging centres of European trade with the Arab world.

The Qadeesha Valley, Lebanon

Lebanon was badly affected by the First World War and particularly by famine. After the war, an expanded Lebanon, with the same borders as exist today, was placed by the League of Nations under the French Mandate* for Syria and Lebanon and the frontiers of the previous *mutasarifiyya* were enlarged. In 1926, a constitution was drawn up under French auspices by a committee of which the Lebanese banker Michel Chiha was an important member, elaborating the division of power on the basis of religious confession. A Lebanese president was elected by a chamber of deputies to exercise office under French supervision. A precedent for the future was set in 1937 when the Maronite president Emile Edde appointed a Sunni Muslim to be prime minister. Henceforth, all presidents would be Maronites and all prime ministers Sunnis.

History since the Second World War

Lebanon was accorded full independence in 1943 after the Vichy French had been ousted by a British-led force. Bishara al-Khuri was elected president in the summer of 1943 after working out a National Pact with Sunni leaders. The pact – an unwritten agreement – served as a supplement to the 1926 Constitution. It formalized the division of the presidency and premiership between Maronites and Sunnis, adding the stipulation that the speaker of the chamber of deputies should be a Shiʿi, the commander of the army a Maronite and the chief-of-staff a Druze. The pact also endorsed the principle that all state bodies – the legislature, executive, civil service and army – should be staffed according to a ratio of six Christians to five Muslims.

In 1949, Khuri pushed through parliament a special dispensation allowing him to stay on as president after his first six-year term had ended. But he soon lost the backing of his supporters when, reacting to a failed coup attempt by the Parti Populaire Syrien (PPS), he moved to suppress all paramilitary organizations. These included the Maronite-dominated Phalanges Libanaises (commonly referred to as the Kata'ib) led by Pierre al-Jumayyil (Gemayel), as well as the PPS, which was campaigning for a Greater Syria. Khuri also came up against the newly formed political party of Druze leader Kemal Jumblat, the Progressive Socialist Party (PSP). Khuri's Sunni prime minister Riyad al-Sulh was assassinated by the PPS in 1951, provoking a string of cabinet crises, and Khuri eventually resigned the following year after army commander Fu'ad Shihab refused the president's request to send in troops to break a general strike inspired by Jumblat. On 18 September, Kamil Shamʿun (Camille Chamoun) was elected president.

Chamoun aligned Lebanon closely with Western interests in what was becoming an increasingly turbulent region. In 1957 he announced acceptance of the Eisenhower Doctrine, which allowed Washington's allies to call in US troops in the face of outside threats. This move put Chamoun at loggerheads with two of the region's most powerful states – Egypt and Syria. It also increased tensions with the mainly Sunni supporters of Egypt's President Nasser* and with traditional opponents, notably Jumblat.

Tensions mounted after the early 1958 merger of Egypt and Syria into the United Arab Republic*. Local Nasserites agitated for Lebanon to be brought into the union, while Jumblat took the opportunity of stepping up his opposition to Chamoun. The situation degraded into open civil war by the summer of 1958. With the July overthrow of the pro-Western monarchy in Iraq, the events in Lebanon began to appear to a worried Washington as part of a general upheaval in the region, seriously threatening US interests. At Chamoun's invitation, US marines landed in Beirut on 15 July, while British troops were deployed in Jordan* against the possibility that events in Iraq might spill over and threaten yet another pro-Western regime in the Middle East. The US intervention helped calm the crisis in Lebanon, and Chamoun was persuaded to drop his plans to stand for election again after his term ran out in September. Fu'ad Shihab, who, as in the lesser crisis of 1952, had insisted on keeping the army neutral, was prevailed upon to stand for the presidency. He was elected by a large majority, and was to become the most successful of modern Lebanon's heads of state.

Shihabism

The new president elaborated a set of policies – to become known as Shihabism – aimed at increasing the powers of the state in the face of the entrenched influence of the various traditional leaders who had reduced politics and administration to an endless bout of factionalism serving particular interests rather than the general good. On the political front, Shihab set up a formidable internal intelligence network, the Deuxième Bureau, which kept a close watch on traditional politicians and radical opposition alike. Shihab also reckoned that Lebanon's economy, although flourishing, was in danger of becoming too dominated by the service sector, in particular the banks. He sought to regulate the banking system, creating a new central bank (Banque du Liban) in 1959, and moved to increase public investment in industry, while improving public provision of education, health and infrastructure services. He also tried to tighten up fiscal administration, notably by pursuing tax-evaders.

The Palestinians

In 1964, Shihab departed at the end of his term. He was succeeded by Charles Hilu (Helou), who subscribed to most of Shihab's policies. But the attempts to strengthen the Lebanese state as an autonomous entity standing above factional rivalries was not wholly successful; nor were Shihab and Helou able to build up industry as a sufficient counterweight to the dominance of the services sector in the economy. But the failure of Shihabism to set Lebanon on a more stable political and economic course is attributable as much to external as internal factors. The June 1967 Arab–Israeli War* marked a major new turning point for the region, with ultimately disastrous consequences for Lebanon. The war galvanized support for the Palestinian guerrilla organizations who were able to operate with most freedom in Jordan and Lebanon. In 1969, Palestinians* in Lebanon's refugee camps clashed with Lebanese security forces. The Palestinians demanded to be entitled to take care of their own security in the camps and to be able to launch guerrilla operations against Israel across the Lebanese border. Under pressure from the large, mainly Muslim, body of support for the Palestinians, the Lebanese government in October 1969 signed the Cairo Agreement with the Palestine Liberation Organization (PLO)*, endorsing most of the Palestinians' demands. Palestinian strength in Lebanon was increased when many guerrillas moved to Lebanon after the September 1970 civil war in Jordan.

The Cairo Agreement was bitterly opposed by the rivals to the Shihabists in the Maronite community, who felt the president had given in too easily on an issue of Lebanese sovereignty. The Shihabist candidate at the 1970 elections – Elias Sarkis – was defeated by one vote by Sulayman Faranjiyya (Frangieh), whose presidency marked a return to power for the traditional factional and communal leaders. Through the early 1970s clashes with the Palestinians persisted, culminating in a heavy round of fighting in 1973 between the PLO and the Lebanese army. Lebanese social tensions were also rising in the early 1970s. The Shihabist effort to spread the benefits of Lebanon's economic success in the services sector had not paid off. Agriculture had declined, and few regional development schemes had got off the ground. More and more people from rural areas were migrating to the capital, moving into poor districts, often next to Palestinian refugee camps. Heavy Israeli retaliation for Palestinian attacks had proved an additional spur, driving mainly Shiʿi southerners to seek shelter in the capital.

By 1975, the fragile Lebanese polity was starting to fall apart as a result of a welter of diverse pressures. The growing strength of the Palestinian guerrillas had prompted the Maronite organizations to seek to boost their own military power. The Maronites were concerned about the links between the PLO and the cluster of left-wing and Muslim groups which were to become known as the Lebanese National Movement (LNM). The LNM, under the leadership of Kemal Jumblat, was pressing for reform of the political system to end Christian dominance and ultimately abolish confessionalism. The LNM argued that an improvement of the Muslims' economic lot was impossible while the Christians dominated the political structure. The left-Muslim alliance also proclaimed unreserved support for the PLO. The Maronites feared that political reforms would destroy the existing guarantees of Christian security and they also resented the freedom of action enjoyed by the PLO, and incidents between Palestinian guerrillas and Maronite militiamen became more and more frequent around Palestinian refugee camps sited in Christian areas.

As the Syrians advanced towards Bhamdoun in an effort to push the Palestinians towards southern Lebanon, Palestinian Fatah guerillas were firing at them with a 50 cal. machine gun

Radical Maronite leaders believed that it was important to reduce the Palestinians' power before PLO military might could be combined with Muslim superiority in numbers to threaten Christian privileges and security. The Maronites also gambled on receiving support from outside forces – Arab states, Israel and the West – in the task of cutting the PLO down to size.

The civil war

Tensions started to increase in early 1975. In February, a prominent Sunni Muslim politician, Maʿruf Saʿd, was assassinated in Sidon as he led a march to protest against a new fishing project planned by Camille Chamoun. The killing sparked off a round of fighting between the army and local Muslim militias, backed by PLO guerrillas. On 13 April, Maronite militias killed twenty-seven Palestinians passing through the Christian ʿAyn al-Rummana quarter of Beirut. The incident followed an attack by unknown gunmen earlier in the day on Kata'ib leader Pierre Gemayel. Fighting broke out between Palestinians and the Kata'ib in ʿAyn al-Rummana and around the Palestinian camps in Christian east Beirut. The political crisis caused by the fighting was briefly resolved by the formation of a new cabinet at the end of June by the new prime minister Rashid Karami. At the same time, a cease-fire agreement was signed between the commander of the army and PLO chairman Yasir ʿArafat. But in September, heavy fighting broke out again, and by the end of 1975 Lebanon was in the throes of all-out civil war. Attempts at inter-Lebanese political dialogue came to nothing, as the Maronites pressed for army intervention to restore security and the LNM, viewing the army as biased in favour of the Christians, insisted that political reform should come first. ʿArafat kept the bulk of the PLO's fighters out of the conflict, but the PLO was active in arming and training LNM militiamen. The main beneficiaries of PLO help were the Sunni, Nasserite Murabitun and Amal, the Shiʿi movement, growing in strength under the leadership of Musa Sadr. Amal (*afwaj al-muqawama al-lubnaniyya* – the masses of the Lebanese resistance; the acronym also means 'hope') was set up in 1974 as a mass-based movement with a strong religious flavour, pressing for reforms to ensure social and economic justice for the Shiʿis. Amal remained independent of the LNM, with which it competed for the loyalty of the predominantly Shiʿi urban poor.

Escalation

The fighting took on a more destructive turn in September 1975. Four days of Kata'ib bombardments reduced the central market area of Beirut to rubble. The LNM, spearheaded by the Murabitun, hit back, fighting heavy battles with the Kata'ib in west Beirut's hotel district. On 6 December – 'Black Saturday' – the first massacre of the war occurred when Kata'ib militiamen avenged the killing of four of their comrades by murdering more than seventy Muslims on the basis of the religious affiliation marked on their identity cards. In early 1976, the Kata'ib – now allied with other Maronite groups, notably Chamoun's National Liberal Party with its Tigers militia wing – moved against the Palestinian refugee camps in Christian east Beirut. The attacks on the camps increased the pressure on ʿArafat from radical PLO groups to commit Palestinian forces to fighting directly in the civil war. The Kata'ib onslaught culminated in a full-scale attack on the Karantina and Maslakh slums in east Beirut. The attack resulted in a mass exodus of these areas' mainly Shiʿi population to west Beirut. In retaliation, the LNM, with substantial support from mainstream PLO units, attacked the Maronite town of Damur between Beirut and Sidon. This ferocious attack led to the almost total evacuation of Damur, whose inhabitants were transported by sea and helicopter to east Beirut.

The escalation of the war in January impelled Syria to step up its mediation efforts. Pro-Syrian PLO military units were sent into Lebanon to be used as a counterweight against ʿArafat's fighters. Syria also tried to defuse political tensions by helping draft a compromise package of political reforms, unveiled by President Frangieh on 14 February. The package offered the Muslims equal representation in parliament, but otherwise fell far short of the changes sought by the LNM. On 11 March, Brigadier ʿAziz al-Ahdab occupied Beirut's television station and demanded Frangieh's resignation. This was taken as a signal for a move on the presidential palace by units of Ahmad al-Khatib's Lebanese Arab Army, which had recently split from the regular army. This move was blocked by pro-Syrian PLO units, which were playing an increasing role in checking LNM efforts to secure an outright military victory over the Maronites.

The Syrian intervention

On 8 May, under Syrian prompting, the Chamber of Deputies elected Elias Sarkis to become the next president when Frangieh's term ran out in September. By this stage relations between the LNM and Syria had badly deteriorated: Damascus was adamant that the LNM and the PLO should not secure the outright victory that by mid-1976 looked to be within their grasp. On 1 June, Syrian troops invaded, and by the end of September the LNM and PLO had been subdued. In the meantime the Maronite forces took advantage of the Syrian action against the LNM and PLO to attack Palestinian and Muslim enclaves in east Beirut. In early August, the mainly Shiʿi Nabʿa quarter fell. On 12 August, after a three-month siege, the Palestinian Tal al-Zaʿtar camp fell. More than a thousand of the camp's inhabitants were massacred during its evacuation.

The civil war's illusory end

The civil war formally came to an end after the 16–18 October Arab summit meeting in Riyadh, which called for the formation of an Arab Deterrent Force (ADF) to keep the peace. The ADF was predominantly Syrian, with a few contingents from other Arab countries. The civil war left about 30,000 people killed, thousands more maimed and hundreds of thousands displaced. The productive sectors of the economy were devastated, but Lebanon's traditional reliance on services meant that a fairly rapid recovery was possible in the years after the war's formal end. However, the entry of the ADF did not succeed in abating the domestic and external tensions affecting Lebanon.

First Israeli invasion

In March 1977, the LNM suffered a heavy blow with the assassination of Kemal Jumblat. But the main focus now turned to the south where the LNM and PLO became involved in a series of clashes with Israeli-backed, mainly Christian militias in the border area. After a Palestinian guerrilla raid on Israel in March 1978, Israeli forces invaded south Lebanon on 14 March, occupying the entire area south of the Litani River, with the exception of Tyre. UN Security Council resolutions 425 and 426 called on the Israelis to withdraw and to hand over control of the border region to the UN Interim Force in Lebanon (UNIFIL)*. The Israelis did pull back, but they handed over a border strip in what should have been the UNIFIL zone to the Christian militias led by Major Saʿd Haddad*.

Tensions were also growing between the ADF and the Maronite

militias. Bashir al-Jumayyil (Gemayel), the younger son of the Kata'ib's leader, had emerged in 1976 as head of the party's military wing. His powers were extended with the decision in August 1976 to unify all Maronite fighting groups under the single command of the Lebanese Forces (LF). Bashir Gemayel turned the LF into a formidable power base for his own political ambitions. In 1978, the LF moved to free Christian areas from ADF control, succeeding by the end of that year in removing Syrian forces from east Beirut. In June 1978, Gemayel eliminated one of his rivals as leader of the new generation of Maronites – Tony Frangieh, son of the former president. Tony was killed by an LF strike force on 13 June.

Abortive attempts to rebuild
The government, led by economist Salim al-Huss under the somewhat weak stewardship of Sarkis, tried to rebuild the economy and bring into being a national army fit to take over the role of the ADF and UNIFIL. In 1977, the Council for Development and Reconstruction (CDR) was formed to administer projects to repair schools, water supplies, hospitals and other parts of Lebanon's shattered infrastructure. But these efforts were thwarted because of the continual outbreaks of fighting. There were two principal fronts: the south, where the newly elected Likud* government in Israel announced a policy of preventive raids against the PLO, and the Maronite heartland, where Bashir Gemayel was consolidating his power under the slogan of liberating Lebanon from Syrian and PLO control. In 1979 and 1980 there were repeated Israeli bombardments of south Lebanon and incursions against PLO positions. The PLO moved heavy artillery into the region, responding to Israeli pressure by shelling northern Israel. Relations between the PLO and local Shiʿi villagers worsened. The Shiʿi Amal movement grew stronger, despite the mysterious disappearance of its founder Musa Sadr in 1978. In east Beirut, Bashir Gemayel crushed his last remaining rival, the militias of Camille Chamoun's National Liberal Party. This move, in June 1980, left Gemayel the dominant Maronite figure, policing east Beirut and its hinterland and controlling the region's sources of revenue: illegal ports and taxation, the proceeds of which went to the LF rather than the state.

In early 1981, Bashir Gemayel was ready to challenge Syria directly. The LF made a bid for control of Zahle, a mainly Greek Catholic town in the solidly Syrian-controlled Biqaʿ. From April to mid-June, Syria laid siege to Zahle, while Beirut saw heavy artillery duels between the LF and ADF. In the midst of the fighting Syria deployed SAM anti-aircraft missiles in the Biqaʿ after Israel shot down two Syrian helicopters outside Zahle. No sooner had the Zahle crisis abated than the PLO–Israel conflict erupted again. On 10 July Israel began a series of raids on south Lebanon, culminating in an air attack on the PLO headquarters in Beirut on 17 July. The PLO retaliated with a heavy bombardment of northern Israel. The US mediated a cease-fire on 24 July. But this proved only a brief respite, and Israel launched a full-scale invasion of Lebanon* on 6 June 1982 with the aim of crushing the PLO as a military and political force.

The second Israeli invasion: assassination of Gemayel: Sabra and Shatila massacres
The invasion caused devastating damage, leaving about 20,000 dead. But after the final 12 August cease-fire, which resulted in the withdrawal of PLO fighters, there was hope that Lebanon could make a new start. Bashir Gemayel was elected the new president and pledged to act as a leader of all the Lebanese, not just his own powerful faction. Gemayel was assassinated on 14 September, nine days before he was due to be inaugurated as president. After the killing, Israeli forces moved into west Beirut, delegating the job of subduing the Palestinian refugee camps to the LF. The LF proceeded to massacre hundreds of Palestinians in the Sabra and Shatila camps.

Bashir Gemayel's elder brother Amin took over as president. Ambitious plans for economic reconstruction were drawn up in 1983 by the CDR, but once again the chance of carrying out these plans was thwarted because of political tensions. Under the protection of the Israelis, the LF had moved into the Shuf region to reassert the Maronite presence in a locality which had become an almost exclusively Druze fiefdom. When Israel withdrew from the Shuf in September 1983, fierce battles erupted as the Druze moved to expel the LF. The Druze were prominent in the alliance of pro-Syrian groups opposed to the 17 May 1983 agreement on an Israeli withdrawal. The agreement, mediated by the US, covered an Israeli withdrawal in return for the establishment of relations between Beirut and Tel Aviv. Syria was not consulted, and worked to undermine the agreement. American troops, the main contingent of the four-nation multinational force in Beirut to keep the peace in the wake of the ADF's withdrawal in 1982, came under increasing attack from Amal, the Druze and shadowy sabotage squads. The US embassy was blown up in April 1983, and on 23 October suicide bombers blew up the American and French barracks in Beirut. The multinational force departed in early 1984. In February, Gemayel's hold on west Beirut was smashed when Shiʿi militias expelled the army. The focus then shifted to south Lebanon, where the occupying Israeli forces came under constant attack from local guerrillas. Israel pulled out of Sidon in February 1985, and by midsummer had withdrawn to the border strip south of the UNIFIL zone. With the Israelis' departure, hopes once more rose that the Lebanese could work out a lasting settlement, under discreet Syrian patronage. Conflicts broke out within the LF: on one side was Elie Hubayqa (Hobeika), who favoured cooperating with Syria to work out a new political system giving greater representation to the Muslims; on the

After the massacre at the Shatila Camp, 20th September 1982

other was Samir Geagea, at the head of a strong body of Maronite opinion which objected to Hobeika's tough measures to keep control, and reckoned he was betraying Christian interests. Hobeika signed a comprehensive peace and reform agreement in Damascus at the end of 1985 with Druze leader Walid Jumblat (the son of Kemal, who had been assasinated) and Amal leader Nabih Berri. The reform package was to start with the election of a new expanded parliament, wth equal Christian and Muslim representation, to debate proposed constitutional changes to give more power to the Muslims. In early 1986, Geagea, with Gemayel's tacit support, ousted Hobeika, and the agreement suffered a grievous setback. Lebanon entered the second decade of civil war with nothing solved, the population demoralized and the economy in ruins. No end of the war was in sight, even to the optimist.

Presidents of Lebanon

1926	Charles Debbas
1934	Habib Sa'd
1936	Emile Edde
1941	Alfred Naccache
1943	Ayyub Tabet
1943	Petro Trad
1943	Bishara Khuri
1952	Camille Chamoun
1958	Gen. Fouad Chehab
1964	Charles Helou
1970	Sulayman Frangieh
1976	Elias Sarkis
1982	Amin Gemayel

Politics today

The institutions set up at independence remained precariously intact even after ten years of civil war. But the real arena for politics is the rivalry between the various militias. The Shi'is have become clearly the largest group, but they remain relatively weak. Amal has a mass following, but limited military power. It is supported by funds from the urban Shi'i middle class, but is still poorer than other movements which have their own sources of revenue from exclusively controlled regions. Amal is challenged by the Hizbullah* (Party of God), a more consciously religious Shi'i militia movement, supported by Iran. The Maronites, despite the late-1985 split, are still a formidable block, thanks to the LF's tight discipline and economic self-sufficiency. The Druze, although small numerically, have copied the LF in creating a strong autonomous base.

With the prolongation of the civil war, politics tended to become more and more fragmented: political power reverted to smaller and smaller units as the credibility of the state continued to erode. One solution proposed over the years has been partition or cantonization, formalizing the *de facto* divisions of the country. But for partition to succeed it would need to be part of an overall agreement, with a strong central apparatus to mediate between the various constituent parts. Lebanon's fate has been bound up with external powers and events for hundreds of years, and there is unlikely to be peace in Lebanon until the Middle East enjoys peace.

The economy and society today

Lebanon's economy survived the 1975–6 civil war and the troubled period up to the 1982 Israeli invasion. One of the reasons for this was that, as a services centre, Beirut reaped some of the benefits from the economic boom in the Arab countries. The civil war also tended to be localized: when fighting was heavy in one region, another region could still be prospering. But the Israeli invasion, and the subsequent occupation of south Lebanon, proved too heavy a blow for the economy to withstand. The chief indicator of the economy's health – the local currency – collapsed in 1984–5 after holding remarkably steady since 1975. In 1986, the pound settled at $1 = £Leb.20; until 1984, the rate had averaged about $1 = £Leb.4. In 1983 and 1984, the government started to have serious balance-of-payments problems for almost the first time in Lebanon's history. This was mainly because the president had made large weapons purchases from the US and France in an ill-fated effort to boost the army's strength. The balance of payments returned to surplus in 1985, mainly because the weapons purchases had stopped and imports had fallen because of the pound's depreciation. Inflation soared, and large sections of the Lebanese population suffered increasing hardship. The banking* system continues to operate, thanks largely to many banks' decision to expand overseas. The banks have also subsisted on a diet of treasury bills issued to cover the state's huge budget deficits. State revenues have dwindled to close to zero because of militia control of ports and customs collection.

Lebanese society has been traumatized by years of unremitting conflict. The talents and well-educated skills that had created Beirut's prosperity in the 1950s and 60s are fast disappearing into exile or oblivion. A new generation has grown up with experience of little other than war and destruction. The Lebanese characteristics of flamboyance and style have come up against a wave of intolerant Islamic fundamentalism which has taken root among the slum-dwelling Shiʿis who have had little respite from the war.

The Museum crossing on the Green Line (The Damascus Road) that divides West from East Beirut

Effects of civil war on society

Breaking down barriers based on religious affiliation was one of the great slogans of the civil war. But the protracted, unresolved conflict succeeded only in cementing these barriers. Ten years of civil war left Lebanon's different communities firmly entrenched behind confessional barricades, but deprived of the relative security which existed before the war when the traditional leaders were stronger.

But the most lasting effect of the war has been on the economy. Lebanon in the mid-1980s was starting to feel the effects of acute poverty. The collapse of the Lebanese pound had a devastating impact on living standards. Since the bulk of the country's food is imported, the decline in the currency's value was reflected in soaring retail prices. Lebanon's rich have largely departed; the increasing ranks of the poor have grown poorer.

DB

Further reading

L. Binder, ed., *Politics in Lebanon* (New York, 1966)
H. Cobban, *The Making of Modern Lebanon* (London, 1985)
D. C. Gordon, *Lebanon: the fragmented nation* (London, 1983)
P. K. Hitti, *Lebanon in History* (London, 1957)
M. Hudson, *The Precarious Republic: political modernization in Lebanon* (New York, 1968)
W. R. Polk, *The Opening of South Lebanon, 1788–1840* (Cambridge, Mass., 1963)
I. Rabinovich, *The War for Lebanon 1970–1983* (Ithaca, NY and London, 1984)
J. C. Randal, *Going All the Way: Christian warlords, Israeli adventures, and the war in Lebanon* (New York, 1983)
K. S. Salibi, *The Modern History of Lebanon* (London, 1977 edn.)
K. S. Salibi, *Crossroads to Civil War: Lebanon 1958–1976* (Delmar, NY, 1976)
Z. Schiff and E. Yaʿari, *Israel's Lebanon War* (New York, 1984)

Lebanese political factions and militias

Socialist and Nasserist groups

Communist Party of Lebanon (CPL)
One of the oldest communist parties in the Middle East, the CPL was established in 1925. It played a major role in the 1975–6 civil war as part of the Lebanese National Movement (LNM). More recently it has been active as part of the anti-Israeli front, the Lebanese National Resistance in southern Lebanon, and was allied with the Druze* and the PLO* against Amal* in West Beirut in 1987. Led by George Hawi, a Christian, it is estimated to have a membership of 1000–2000.

Progressive Socialist Party (PSP)
The PSP was founded by Kemal Jumblat, the Druze leader in 1949 and after his assassination in 1977 has been led by his son Walid Jumblat. It was the major cross-confessional party in the LNM. Although the bulk of its military strength has always come from within the Druze community, recently significant numbers of Sunnis have joined the party. The PSP's military wing is sometimes known as the People's Army, a body which was strengthened by Libyan and Syrian arms and tanks after it gained hold of the Shuf in 1983. The People's Army is reputed to have around 3000–4000 soldiers.

Organisation of Communist Action (OCA)
The OCA was founded in 1971 by those who left the Communist Party and other Arab radical groups. It was active in the 1975–6 civil war as part of the LNM and later as part of the LNR. Its leaders include Muhsin Ibrahim (a Shi'i) and Fawwaz Tarablusi (a Christian).

Lebanese National Movement (LNM)
The LNM was the broad umbrella organization which spanned the religious divide in the 1975–6 civil war; it consisted of organizations such as the OCA from the left to the Shi'a Movement for the Deprived. It was led by Kemal Jumblat but fell into disarray when the Syrians intervened in 1976.

Lebanese National Resistance (LNR)
LNR is a coalition of mainly left-wing organizations which was formed to fight the Israeli occupation after 1982. It is active mainly in southern Lebanon.

Syrian Social National Party (SSNP)
SSNP was formed in 1932 to fight for the establishment of a 'Syrian' state to include Lebanon, Syria and other countries. It is considered one of the most established non-sectarian organizations and tends to attract non-Maronite Christian elements mainly, but also a few Muslims as well as Kurds* and Armenians*. It played a major role in the LNM and later the LNR. It is active in the north, Beirut, and the fringes of the mountain and recruits from the urban and rural population. Its main leader during the 1975–6 civil war was In'am Ra'd, a Christian.

The Murabitun
Formed in 1969, Murabitun has pan-Arab Nasserist politics and is led by Ibrahim Qulaylat. It was the main Sunni organization until its military strength was demolished by Amal when it took over West Beirut in 1986.

Tripoli Nasserists
These are organized under the October 24 Movement which was also founded in 1969, consisting mainly of Sunnis and now practically defunct.

Sidon Nasserists
These were grouped under the Popular Nasserist Organization (also known as the Popular Resistance of Ma'ruf Sa'd) formed in 1958. They were mainly Sunnis and led by Mustafa Sa'd during the 1975–6 civil war.

Shi'i and Sunni groups

Movement of the Deprived/Amal
This movement is a Shi'i organization which was set up by Musa Sadr in the early 1970s with support coming mainly from the poor Shi'i population in the south and the Biqa'. Its militia fought along with other organizations under the LNM in the 1975–6 civil war. After the disappearance of Musa Sadr in 1978 during a trip to Libya Nabih Berri became the leader of the organization which was mainly referred to as Amal (Hope). Under Berri, Amal has become the mainstream Shi'i organization but it has lost support in recent years for its too compromising stance towards Syria and the Christians. Amal's fighting forces, which are estimated at around 4000 paid militia, were equipped by Syria in 1986 with Soviet-built T-54 tanks as well as armoured personnel carriers, and transformed into regular forces. The Sixth Brigade of the Lebanese Army operates in conjunction with Amal's soldiers. Its main area of activity has been West Beirut and the south, particularly around Sidon.

Islamic Amal
There was a radical split from Amal in 1982, when Nabih Berri joined the Karami government. It was led by Husayn Musawi and is known to be based in Baalbeck. It was rumoured to have been responsible for the US and French compound bombings at the time; little independent activity has been reported by this organization more recently.

Hizbullah (Hizb Allah: Party of God)
The Hizbullah is a shadowy umbrella organization of radical Shi'is who have links with Iran. It is led by Shaykh Muhammad Husayn Fadl Allah and Shaykh Ibrahim al-Amin. The Hizbullah surfaced after the TWA hijacking in 1985. The recent kidnappings claimed by Islamic Jihad and other previously unknown groups are thought to operate from within this umbrella organization. Hizbullah's stronghold is South Beirut, but it has also been gaining in power in southern Lebanon and retains its strength in the Biqa'. Although the Hizbullah is a Shi'i organization which aims at setting up an Islamic State in Lebanon, there has been recent evidence of joint fronts with Sunnis in Tripoli, Sidon and Beirut.

Tawhid
This is a radical Sunni movement led by Shaykh Sa'id Sha'ban, and based in Tripoli. Their forces were badly beaten by the Syrian army during their security operation conducted in Trippoli in early 1986. Shaykh Sha'ban is rumoured to have links with Iran and Tawhid has also fought alongside the PLO.

Christian groups

Kata'ib
This party was founded in the 1930s by Pierre Gemayel, the father of Bashir and Amin Gemayel, and was modelled after European fascist organizations. It has always represented the dominant Maronite trends. The Phalange is its military wing, which has now been absorbed into the Lebanese Forces.

Lebanese Forces (LF)
This is the military wing of the Lebanese Front, which is a coalition of Maronite leaders dominated by the Kata'ib. The LF is now led by Samir Geagea, who seized control from Elie Hobeika in January 1986 in rejection of the Syrian sponsored peace pact signed by Hobeika in December 1985. Geagea has sought to turn the 7000 or so militia into a regular army of 5000 through a military training academy in Ghosta in the north-eastern hills of Beirut. The forces have been armed by Israel for several years now.

Zgharta Liberation Army (ZLA)
This militia was set up by the Frangieh family and was most active in the early seventies. The Frangieh stronghold is in Zgharta in northern Lebanon and they are known to have some links with Syria.

National Liberal Party (NLP)
NLP was associated with ex-President Camille Chamoun. Its militia, the 'Tigers', was crushed by the Phalange in 1980.

South Lebanon Army (SLA)
The SLA is an Israeli-funded army operating in southern Lebanon. It was established in 1978 after Israel's first invasion up to the Litani River. Led by Major Sa'd Haddad until his death in 1985, it has been considerably weakened since the Israeli withdrawal in 1985.

MT

Libya

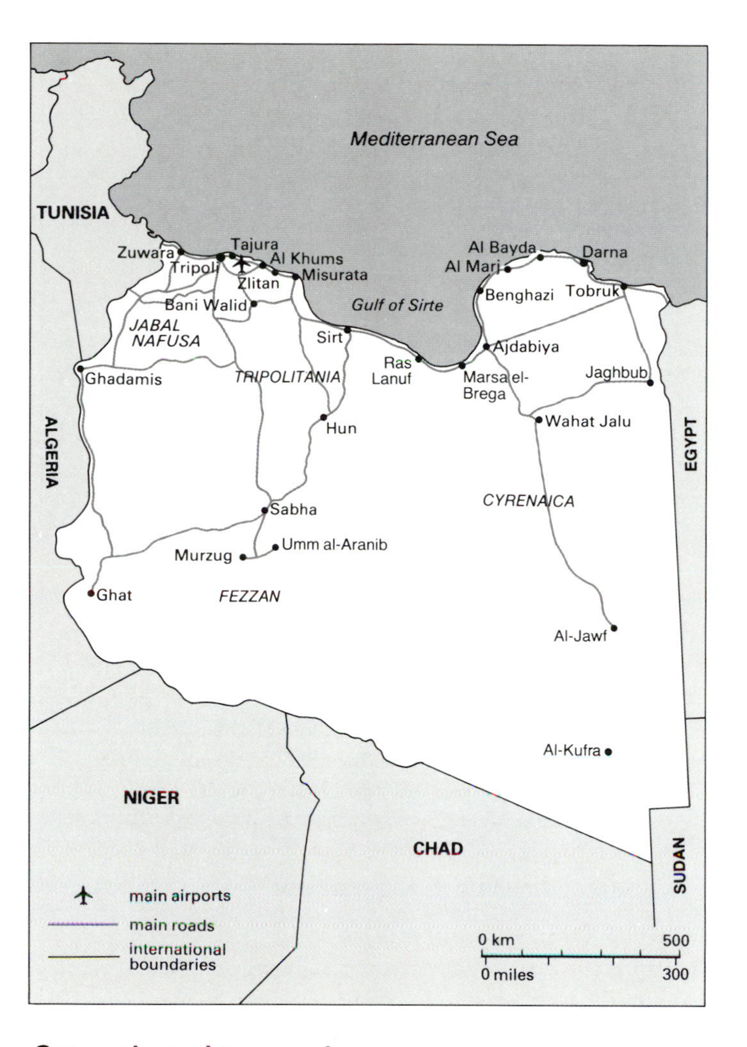

Official title	The Libyan Socialist People's Arab Jamahiriyya (renamed April 1986 as Great Libyan Jamahiriyya)
Area	1,775,500 sq. km
Population	3.6 million (1984 census)
Government and constitution	A direct popular democracy, expressed through basic popular congresses and popular committees in the General People's Congress, which elects the General Popular Secretariat (cabinet) and which embodies Libyan sovereignty in the People's Authority
Currency	1 Libyan dinar = 1000 dirhams; US $1 = 335.9 dirhams
Languages	Arabic. English and Italian are also widely spoken
Religion	Islam. Most Libyans are Sunni Muslims
Climate	Temperatures vary, with summer temperatures reaching 49°C in the south and cold winter temperatures sometimes bringing light snow. In most of Libya annual rainfall is 200 mm or less, but in the hills of Tripolitania and Cyrenaica it may reach 400–500 mm

Geography and topography

Libya, with a surface area of 1,759,540 km^2, is the fourth largest country in Africa. Located on the southern shores of the Mediterranean, its coastline is punctured by the deep indentation of the Gulf of Sirte, 450 km wide and 200 km deep, to which Libya lays claim as a historic bay, according to a 1973 declaration, with a closing line along the 32°20′ line of latitude. This claim is not recognized by any other riparian or, indeed, maritime state.

Apart from two narrow coastal strips, the Jafara Plain in Tripolitania and the Jabal al-Akhdar in Cyrenaica and the oasis complexes of the Fezzan, most of Libya is desert. The UN Development Programme has described 94.6 per cent of Libya's land area as 'wasteland'. Of the remainder, only 1.4 per cent is arable, of which only 0.1 per cent is actually irrigated. Much of the irrigated area – located in the Jafara Plain and the Jabal al-Akhdar – is now saline, as the result of the over-exploitation of the underground aquifers that collect rainwater runoff, and sea water has been reported to have penetrated as far as 20 km inland in the Tripoli region.

Peoples

In 1985, the Libyan population was estimated to total 3.78m, compared to an official figure in 1980 of 3.245m of which 2.803m were Libyan nationals. In 1982, it was estimated that Libyan nationals formed 82.4 per cent of the total population. The balance consisted of migrant workers. The total number of foreigners in Libya in 1983, according to the Secretariat of Planning, reached 569,000, with Egyptians topping the list at 174,000, followed by Tunisians (74,000), Turks (45,000) and Pakistanis (24,000). Amongst Europeans in Libya, there were 15,000 Italians, 13,000 Yugoslavs, 11,000 Britons and 10,000 Poles. These foreigners contributed to a total workforce of over 900,000. In recent years, however, the number of foreigners in Libya has fallen, as Libyan economic fortunes have declined from 1980 onwards. After mass expulsions in August 1985, involving over 30,000 Tunisians and about the same number of Egyptians, together with large numbers from Sahelian countries such as Mali, Mauritania, Chad and Niger it is believed that the total of foreign workers in Libya has fallen to about 200,000.

The annual growth rate of the Libyan population is one of the highest in the world, at 3.9 per cent, according to official sources. It is expected to reach 4.4m by 1990 and 6.5m by the year 2000. In 1980, 53.8 per cent were urban-based, a percentage that has certainly increased since then. As a result of the high population growth rate, a very high proportion of the Libyan population is very young. In 1980 46.6 per cent were under fifteen years of age, while 25.1 per cent were between fifteen and twenty-nine years old. Sunni* Muslims form 97 per cent of the total population.

History up to 1939

The origins of Libya extend back into prehistory with the Capsian culture throughout what is now North Africa and extending into the Sahara – then fertile and temperate but already undergoing the processes of desiccation and desertification that have produced the modern desert. The pressure of the Libyan tribes on the complex civilization of Egypt produced a growing intermingling of polities and races in the Nile Delta and in 935 BC a Libyan dynasty was established in Egypt under Sheshonq – the twenty-second dynasty of the New Kingdom, the Sheshonnaq dynasty.

As Egyptian power declined, Phoenicians began to settle along the Libyan coast, to be followed in the fourth century BC by Greeks in Cyrenaica. Inland, an indigenous civilization, the Garamantean, developed. In the mid-third century BC, the Punic Wars began and, with the collapse of Carthage in 146 BC, Libya gradually became integrated into the Roman Empire. This lasted until the mid-fifth century AD and, in the latter part of the Roman period, the indigenous Berber* population of Libya was largely Christianized, a conversion that lasted throughout the Vandal occupation and the Byzantine* reconquest in 533.

The Arab and Ottoman periods

Between 643 and 667, Libya was exposed to a new occupation, that of the newly Islamized Arabs from Egypt. Although Arabization/Islamization was to be a slow process, by the twelfth century Libya was, to all intents and purposes, an Arabophone Muslim country in which all vestiges of Christianity had disappeared. The Arab occupation also changed the political nature of the country, in that the old Roman provincial system disappeared and political control became split, with Cyrenaica tending to depend on Egypt and Tripolitania on Tunisia (Ifriqiyya). At the same time, the earlier Mediterranean dimension of Libya under the Romans and Byzantines was replaced by a linkage into the Middle East in which Libya became a means of transit from North Africa to Egypt and Arabia. At the same time, Tripoli became a terminal point for trans-Saharan trade which then filtered into Europe.

The Mediterranean began to reassert itself, however, after the *Reconquista* in Spain which was completed in 1492. Although there had been an isolated period in the early twelfth century in which Norman occupation of coastal towns such as Tripoli had served a commercial purpose in allowing the Normans to tap the trans-Saharan trade directly, this had been ended by the Almohads*. Now, however, as corsairing became an ever more important means of resistance to growing Christian domination of the Mediterranean basin, Tripoli became an important corsairing port.

This development coincided with another – the extension of Ottoman* control into the central and western Mediterranean. Spain had extended its control over a series of North African ports in the wake of the *Reconquista*, occupying Tripoli in 1510. In 1530, the town and castle were given to the Order of the Knights of St John at Jerusalem, at the same time as they took up residence in Malta. In 1551, the town was taken from the Knights by Dragut, by that time a commander in the Ottoman navy. Tripolitania once again became integrated into a unitary administration that – nominally at least – eventually covered Cyrenaica and the Fezzan. Nonetheless, it was the Mediterranean dimension that dominated Ottoman political horizons henceforth.

Direct Ottoman rule soon broke down, however, to be replaced by autonomous administrations paying only lip service to the Ottoman link. In 1711, Ahman Qaramanli established a virtually independent dynasty which lasted until 1835, when, in the wake of implicit British and French threats to take over control of Libya, the Ottoman Empire re-established its authority there. The Ottoman administration had to confront the threat of French penetration into southern Libya at the end of the nineteenth century. It also faced the problem of the growth of Sanusi* influence, particularly in Cyrenaica and the south, where the Sanusi religious order provided a political infrastructure and integration that bypassed the ineffective Ottoman alternative. In the end, however, Ottoman Libya fell prey to Italian imperial ambitions, with the Italian occupation of the old Ottoman province in 1911.

The colonial period and independence

The Italian occupation of Libya – the 'fourth shore' of fascist ideology with its dream of recreating the Roman Empire in Africa – proved to be far more difficult than anticipated. The major problem was to overcome the fierce resistance waged by the nomadic tribes to Italian occupation under the leadership, initially, of the Sanusi order until 1927 and thereafter by the Libyan resistance hero, ʿUmar al-Mukhtar. It was only in 1932 that full colonial control was achieved and that Italy could begin to build up its colony of settlement in the more fertile regions of the Jabal al-Akhdar and the Jafara plain. Much of the colonization was handled by large companies created for the purpose and most of the peasantry settled in Libya came from the impoverished *mezzogiorno* in the south of Italy. By the Second World War there were 100,000 Italians in Libya, out of a population then estimated at one million. The administration also paid considerable attention to building up an adequate infrastructure and, despite fascist boasts to the contrary, the indigenous Libyan population – decimated by the long war – was accorded a secondary place in the colonial scheme of things.

The Second World War, however, brought Italian ambitions to a full stop. Once the British Eighth Army had pushed the Italian army and the Afrika Corps back from the Egyptian border to the Tunisian border and the Free French Army of General Leclerc had forced its way northwards through the Fezzan from Chad, Libya was put under joint British–French military administration for the duration of hostilities. Britain took control of Cyrenaica and Tripolitania, while France administered the Fezzan.

History since the Second World War

The French and British presence in Libya at the end of the war was to have a profound effect on the way in which Libyan independence was achieved. First of all, it meant that the three Libyan provinces – Cyrenaica, Tripolitania and the Fezzan – all acquired a sense of uniqueness, for each of them was separately administered. Secondly, it affected proposals for a post-war settlement in Libya. In Cyrenaica the Sanusi, under British influence, sought control of the region for Sayyid Idris, the leader of the order who had migrated to Egypt during the Italian period. In Tripolitania, political groups based in Tripoli tried to persuade Britain to guarantee independence in return for their acceptance of Idris's suzerainty. In the Fezzan, the French administration, based on the Awlad Sayf al-Nasr, agitated for union with Algeria or Tunisia. Italy, after the war, attempted to regain control of Tripolitania through the Bevin–Sforza Plan. There was even a proposal for a Soviet UN Mandate over Libya. In 1949, however, the UN called for Libyan independence to be achieved by the beginning of 1952.

The solution for Libya, as organized by the UN commissioner, Adrien Pelt, in 1951, provided for a federal monarchy under Sayyid Idris al-Sanusi. In effect, this was, for Britain at least, the best solution, since the new King was closely allied to British interests through his long residence in Egypt in the pre-war period and his sponsorship, during the war, of the Cyrenaican Defence Force, which joined British forces in the Western Desert campaigns as a Libyan contribution to the Allied defence effort. The newly independent state accepted a US and a UK military presence and close alignment with Western strategic interests – at a time when Nasserism was beginning to sweep through the Middle East. It was, however, a solution that could not last, given the new structures and ideas being articulated in the Middle East. Particularist sentiment in the individual provinces that made up the federal structure, combined with resentment against the renewed Sanusi dominance and the strongly pro-Western policies of the royal government, ensured that it became increasingly unpopular.

Development of the oil industry

Nonetheless, the royalist period was to be one of rapid change. The development of the oil industry*, with oil exports beginning in 1961, meant that Libya, from being one of the poorest countries in the world, had sudden access to wealth. In 1963, Libya joined Opec*. By 1964, oil exports had reached 800,000 barrels a day (b/d). However, in the wake of the influx of revenues came corruption and social dislocation, as Libyans began to move into the cities. The government was slow to wake up to the need for a radical restructuring of Libyan society and the growing discontent found increasing expression, particularly in Tripolitania, through Arab nationalism* and Nasserism, with a concomitant dislike of Libya's official pro-Western stance. Popular anger reached a peak in 1967, when the government failed to make a strong stand over the issue of the 1967 Arab–Israeli War*. Thereafter, it was merely a matter of time before the monarchy was overthrown.

The revolution

The coup, when it occurred two years later, came – as might have been expected – from the army. However, it did not involve the senior officer corps which had been expected, and which had expected, to replace the King. Instead, it involved junior officers in what was to prove to be a typical Nasserist-style revolution. It was led by a 28-year-old signals captain who had long been recognized as an outspoken and fervent Nasserist – Muʿammar Qadhafi* – and had been organized through a clandestine Free Officers Movement inside the army which had been carefully constructed over the preceding five years. Although the initial government was civilian, it was soon replaced by a military Revolutionary Command Council (RCC). The Nasserist and Arab nationalist nature of the regime was underlined when, in 1971, a single political party – the Arab Socialist Union – was created as a means of radicalizing Libyan society. At the same time, the traditional power of the old rural and urban elites – the Sanusi in Cyrenaica, the mercantile groups in Tripolitania, Berber groups in the Jabal Nafusa, tribal groups in the Fezzan – was undercut and new administrative structures were introduced.

The struggle for union

The new regime showed its radicalism in two other directions. First of all, as befitted an Arab nationalist regime, it sought to unify the

Colonel Qadhafi

Arab world – particularly in the wake of the death of President Nasser*. In December 1969, Libya, Egypt and Sudan planned a political union which was to prove abortive, although Syria announced its willingness to join in 1970. A further attempt at union was made in April 1971 with Egypt and Syria, but this, too, failed. Egypt and Libya tried again in August 1972, but President Sadat* proved reluctant and, after the 1973 war, over which Libya was not consulted (to Qadhafi's chagrin), the attempt was abandoned. A further attempt in 1974 to create a unity agreement with Tunisia after a meeting between Qadhafi and President Bourguiba* collapsed within a few days, while proposed unions with Syria in 1980 and Chad in 1981 have had little effect. The one plan for unity that has had some significance has been that with Morocco, signed in September 1984 and in reality a riposte to Algerian plans to organize political unity within the Maghrib from which both Libya and Morocco were to be excluded. At the same time as these attempts at Arab unity progressed, Libya also became an outspoken supporter of the Palestinian cause, rejecting any idea of a compromise. This attitude has been maintained ever since and has led Libya to take the lead in resisting developments such as the Camp David Accords* on peace between Israel and Egypt or joint Jordanian–Palestinian attempts to negotiate a solution to the dispute.

Secondly, the new Libyan authorities confronted what they saw as the legacies of a colonial past. One of the first moves was to insist on the departure of British forces from al-Adhm airbase close to Tobruk and of US forces from Wheelus Field, just to the east of Tripoli. Then, in a series of moves that was to presage similar changes in the relationship between Opec countries and the international oil companies, Libya first forced up prices and then obliged the companies to enter into participation agreements. By 1974, Libya controlled directly about 60 per cent of its oil industry. However, Libya still does not control the totality, with some 25 per cent of the sector still being controlled by foreign companies. Finally, in a move in part designed to express Libya's new-found independence from Western influence, relations were opened with the Soviet Union in 1973. Since then, the Soviet Union has become Libya's major arms supplier, having provided up to $14bn worth of arms – on a strictly cash basis – over the past twelve years.

Despite these radical changes in the foreign policy field, domestic developments inside Libya did not keep pace and, in 1973, a distinct quickening in the demand for change became apparent. In a famous speech in the coastal town of Zuwara, Colonel Qadhafi called for a cultural revolution in Libya – in reality a demand for cultural conformity. At the same time 'popular' committees began to appear as a device for further radicalizing certain aspects of Libyan life. Then, in the mid-1970s, Qadhafi began to put himself forward as a Third World political theorist, with his political vision being embodied in the famous *Green Book*.

The consequent political changes were hastened by an abortive coup against the Qadhafi regime in August 1975, led by a member of the RCC, ʿUmar Mahayshi. As a result, in 1976, the old Nasserist structures were swept away, to be replaced by direct popular democracy. A general national congress was called together to oversee these changes and was transformed into the General People's Congress in March 1977, when the 'People's Authority' – the enabling instrument of direct popular democracy – was proclaimed. Colonel Qadhafi and his remaining four collaborators from the old RCC stepped down from formal power in order to devote themselves to 'revolutionary agitation'.

These developments removed two of the major sources of opposition to the Qadhafi regime – intellectuals who were forced out in 1973, and former political figures. They also confirmed a vocal and growing body of opposition amongst students, particularly those studying abroad. The third main strand of opposition – the private business sector – was removed in 1978, when all economic activity was collectivized and personal wealth was strictly limited. By 1980, there was a significant opposition abroad, although it was fragmented and quarrelsome. Nonetheless, the Qadhafi regime found it to be a threat.

The answer to this problem and to the growing indigenous disenchantment with the direct popular democratic system was the revolutionary committee movement, which first began to appear in 1978. In February 1980, the revolutionary committees were recruited for the purpose of destroying opposition, both at home and abroad. The movement has, over the past six years, been responsible for scores of murders worldwide. Its activities have led to at least one very public coup attempt against the regime in May 1984. Libya has also incurred considerable hostility in Europe and the USA for its support of Palestinian radicalism, particularly the extremist groups which have been engaged in terrorism. This has been intensified by Libya's closeness to radical regimes such as Syria and South Yemen and, most recently, Iran.

Today, despite its revolutionary and radical pretensions, the Qadhafi regime suffers from considerable unpopularity inside the Middle East and is distrusted by radical and moderate alike for its unpredictability in foreign relations. Domestically, the exigencies of revolutionary government have disaffected much of the Libyan population. These tendencies have been intensified by the collapse of Opec oil revenues since 1981, particularly during 1986. Libya in 1986 enjoyed oil revenues of as little as $4bn, compared with the 1980 level of $21bn. This is a crucial component in undermining the stability of the regime, since virtually all consumer goods have to be imported, including 70 per cent of all food. Against this, however, is the implacable hostility that Libya has aroused in the USA, culminating in the raids on Tripoli and Benghazi in early April 1986 which, paradoxically, have increased the survival potential of the regime.

The economy and society today

The Libyan economy is totally dominated by its dependence on oil, which forms the totality of its exports. Libyan crude is sweet and light and this has made it much desired in Europe. Increasingly Libya is looking to the export of refined products from its new 220,000 b/d export refinery at Ras Lanuf and to exports of basic petrochemicals. The Libyan oil industry was based on joint ventures between the Libyan National Oil Company (LNOC) and independent companies Occidental, Conoco, Amerada Hess, Marathon, Grace, Agip. The oil majors have ceased operations in Libya – Shell in the early 1970s, BP after nationalization in 1971, Exxon in 1980 and Mobil in 1982. Their activities have been taken over either by LNOC or by special Libyan companies created for the purpose. In mid 1986 Reagan forced many of the independent companies to leave Libya.

Oil revenues have been devoted to development through a series of plans stretching back to the monarchy. In recent years, however, the collapse of oil revenues has prevented effective planning, and development has increasingly been devoted to single projects which have been identified as having an export potential – the Misurata steel plant, the Zuwara aluminium smelter, the Ras Lanuf refinery and petrochemical complex and the Sirte fertilizer complex – or to the Great Man-made River. This is a scheme to bring fossil water* from underground reserves in the Sahara to the coast, where it will be used for domestic and industrial purposes, as well as for reviving agriculture which has been increasingly restricted by salinity in the fertile littoral regions. One purpose of these developments is to reduce Libyan dependence on imported food – 70 per cent of all food is imported.

The Libyan economy is hampered, not only by the collapse of oil revenues, but also by its dependence on external inputs. The most significant issue in this respect has been the dependence on foreign labour – which reached 46 per cent of the total labour force in 1982 but which has fallen significantly since then. Nonetheless, the role of foreign labour is crucial in two respects – in providing the vital technological skills needed for a modern economy and in satisfying the need for bulk labour in areas in which Libyans themselves are not prepared to act. Despite attempts to reduce this dependence, the structure of the Libyan economy is such that it is unlikely that it can ever be removed altogether, particularly given the declining efficiency and popularity of the regime.

Social structures in Libya have undergone profound and radical change over the past thirty-five years since independence in 1951. At the end of the colonial period, the traditional dominance of the Cyrenaican tribes and of the Sanusi religious order was reaffirmed by the creation of the monarchy under Idris al-Sanusi. This occurred at the expense of the merchant classes of Tripoli – who had traditionally dominated political power and economic life in western Libya – and of the old trading centres in the Fezzan, and of transhumants and sedentary peasants in areas such as Sirtica, the Jabal Nafusa or the Jabal al-Akhdar. Since Qadhafi's 1 September 1969 Revolution, these alignments have gone. First, the dominance of the Cyrenaican tribes and the Sanusi was destroyed by the revolution itself. Then, after 1973, the dominant intellectual role of Tripoli was destroyed. After 1978, the power of the private mercantile sector was eliminated through nationalization of the means of production.

Over all of this was the idea of direct popular democracy as expressed through the 'state of the masses' – the *jamahiriyya*. This obliges all Libyans to participate in a series of popular congresses which, in theory, govern all aspects of Libyan political life. It also appoints or arranges the elections for members of the popular committees that handle daily life and organization. The congresses, convened on a locational or vocational level, mandate representatives to regional congresses and to the General People's Congress. The latter body decides (at meetings organized at least twice a year) on issues of national importance and embodies, in theory, supreme and sovereign political power. However, its members are all mandated from the basic popular congresses and thus express, at a national level, local will – as direct popular democracy should.

In this structure Qadhafi and his close collaborators play no formal part. However, they are charged with 'agitation' for the revolution that the Colonel has decreed. The problem is that some Libyans are not aware of the inherent and absolute moral and political benefits of the *jamahiri* system and become dissidents, either in Libya or abroad. To the Colonel, the perfection of the political system he has defined means that opposition to it must be reactionary and malicious. Thus, such opposition – as a political and moral obligation – must be eliminated. Since February 1980, this has taken concrete form through the revolutionary committee movement. This clandestine movement, created in 1979, is under the personal control of Qadhafi – unlike the popular committee movement. It has become particularly important in galvanizing the popular committees and in organizing a grotesque series of murders, both in Libya and abroad, of dissidents. Most recently, its

A Libyan army camp for women soldiers

members have been given full executive power in various industrial and productive sectors to ginger up sagging production levels and industrial morale.

However, neither the popular congresses nor the revolutionary committees are the real controllers of power in Libya. In fact, ultimate control of power is informal. It is still the prerogative of Qadhafi and his old collaborators from the days of the revolution – Major Abdesslam Jalloud; Abu Bakr Yunis Jabir, the commander of the armed forces; Mustafa al-Kharoubi; and al-Khawaldi al-Hamaidi. Beyond this small group, there is also the role played by Qadhafi's own relations and tribal links. Many members of Qadhafi's family and tribe (Qadhadhfa) have important roles in the power structure and some, such as Ahmad Qadhafi Adhm, Mohamed Masʿudi, Khalifa Khanash or, until his death, Hassan Ishkal, have been involved in the small ruling group around Colonel Qadhafi himself. Thus, outside the formal structures of direct democracy, or the clandestine pressure of the revolutionary committees, real power resides in a small coterie linked to Qadhafi by personal or kin ties.

Most Libyans have experienced radical changes in life-style during the past two decades, largely as a result of sudden national access to oil wealth. Despite the limitations placed on personal wealth, most people have seen their personal situation change radically for the better. They have also moved into urban areas, particularly around the two major cities of Benghazi and Tripoli. This has meant that Libya has changed from being one of the poorest societies in the world, with a largely rural-based population at independence in 1951, to being a predominantly urban-based society today, in which most nationals are employed in the service sector, while more menial activities are carried out by foreigners.

GJ

Further reading

J. A. Allen, *Libya, the Experience of Oil* (London, 1981)
R. First, *Libya, the Elusive Revolution* (London, 1974)
J. Wright, *Libya* (London, 1969)
J. Wright, *Libya, a Modern History* (London, 1982)

Mauritania

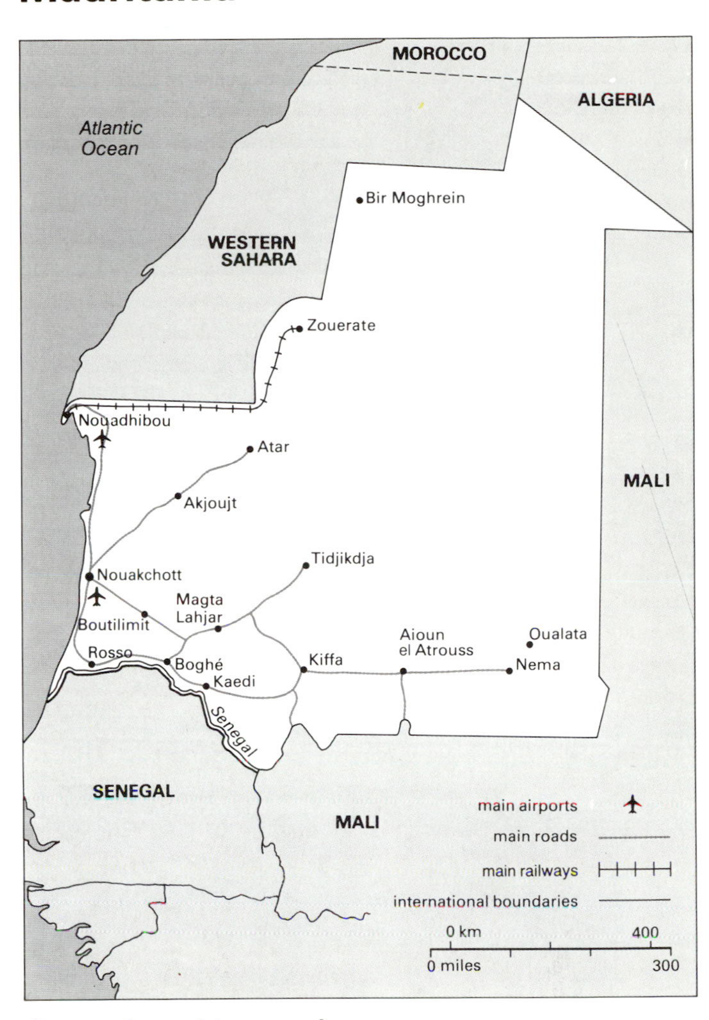

Geography and topography

Covering a million square kilometres of Saharan wasteland, fringed only by an Atlantic shoreline and the marginally fertile right bank of the Senegal River in the south, the modern state of Mauritania has assumed its boundaries and separate identity in the course of the twentieth century. Previously known as *turab al-baydan* (land of the whites) or to the Arab world as Shinqit (after the Amirate based at Chinguetti), Mauritania's sandy wastes and rocky plateaus have defied all but the most respectful economic and political mastery. Since the Sahara ceased to support vegetation this western region has been a lost and lonely expanse of pure desert with very few water sources and supporting only the hardiest of people and animals – a situation scarcely changed today.

Whereas in the purely Saharan northern half of the country the rainfall never exceeds 100 mm in a year, the southern strip manages

Official title	The Republic of Mauritania
Area	1 million sq. km
Population	1.83 million (1984)
Government and constitution	Since independence in 1960 Mauritania has been controlled by the *Parti du Peuple Mauritanien* which controlled all seats in the National Assembly. However, the PPM regime was displaced in 1978 by a military coup which gave control of the government and army to the Military Committee of National Salvation.
Currency	US $1 = Ouguiya (UM) 77.09
Language	Arabic and French
Religion	Almost all Mauritanians are Sunni Muslims
Climate	Mauritania has an arid, desert climate with temperatures ranging from freezing point at night in winter to daytime temperatures of 50°C in summer.

an average 600 mm a year, sufficient in a good year to grow millet and sorghum and to support sheep, goats and cattle. Since the 1960s Saharan conditions are thought to have moved south by as much as 200 km. In 1983 the rainfall over the whole country reached only 27 per cent of the average for the thirty years between 1941 and 1970.

Peoples

The population of Mauritania in the 1980s has sharply changed its pattern of life since independence in 1960, when over 80 per cent of the people were nomadic, with sedentary farmers in the south forming the remainder. There were no large towns. Now 75 per cent of the people are settled, many of them in shanty towns on the edge of the capital Nouakchott, which only came into existence at independence.

Ethnically the people of Mauritania may be divided into those of Berber, Arab or Negro stock, although the parallel social and cultural divisions often confuse the distinctions. The concept of 'white Moors' and 'black Moors' is now becoming outdated, largely as a result of the enormous social changes of recent years. Formerly the nomadic 'white' Moorish tribes, known collectively as Sanhaja or Zenaga, formed the majority in the desert areas but they were joined increasingly from the thirteenth century onwards by Arab nomads*, the Bani Hasan, who gave the area its Hasaniya dialect of Arabic and who also assumed supremacy, remaining as warriors after disarming the Berber tribes in 1674. Both Berber and Arab groups kept slaves, of mainly Negro origin. When they acquired their freedom they became known as *haratin*, and form the group still known as 'black Moors'. Separate from these formerly nomadic people were the settled African populations of the south who presently make up around 25 per cent of the population. The pure-blooded nomadic Fulani or Peulh form about 66 per cent of the population but the sedentary Tukolor (or Tekrur), also of Fulani origin, make up 15 per cent. The other African peoples include the Wolof and Soninke (Sarakolle).

Religion

Islam is almost universal in Mauritania, and since independence the country has been a full Islamic Republic. Since the Arabs first brought Islam to the Moroccan coast in 680, the region of Mauritania has felt the influence of the Qur'an, at first taking to it half-heartedly until in 1035 ʿAbd Allah ibn Yasin laid the basis of the Almoravid* Empire that controlled Morocco* and southern Spain for a hundred years until 1150. This period also introduced Islam to the African populations, including the Fulani and Soninke. Chinguetti was founded as a monastic centre in 1262.

History up to 1939

The earliest inhabitants of Mauritania are thought to have been a Berber* people known as the Bafur, whose descendants adopted a nomadic existence based on the use of camels, and profited from control of trading links between the Atlas mountains and the Niger and Senegal basins. In the south-west of modern Mauritania, stretching into Mali, the Ghana Empire began to flourish from this trade and from its control of the gold supply from regions to the south. Ghana, controlled by a Soninke aristocracy, reached the height of its power in 960 but was eclipsed following the rise of the Almoravid Empire in 1050.

Although the Moors founded Marrakesh, their native region of Mauritania had little potential to develop politically or economically and fell prey to warring tribal factions impossible to control, pacify or unify. Zenaga resistance to the arrival of tribes of the Bani Hasan reached a pitch in the seventeenth century, when a thirty-year war was waged between the two sides, resulting in a symbolic subjugation to the Bani Hasan. Marginal allegiance was shown to the Sharifian Kingdom of Morocco, which undertook occasional expeditions to Tindouf, Toudeni and Timbuktu, but there was no automatic authority granted to the Moroccan Sultan.

The French first arrived at St Louis at the mouth of the Senegal River in 1626 but did not attempt to control the region until the mid-nineteenth century, meeting immediate resistance both from the Tukolor under al-Hadj ʿUmar and in Trarza until 1858. Governor Faidherbe of Senegal tried in the 1860s to gain the allegiance of various tribes but French protection over the region was only first agreed between Governor Coppolani and Amir Ahmad Salloum in

1902. A northern religious leader, Ma al-ʿAynayn, then raised an army against the French which continued to fight until defeated in 1910. Further sporadic resistance was not suppressed until 1932.

History since the Second World War

Mauritania achieved independence with the rest of the French Empire in 1960, although its political life was limited at the outset to participation by a very few personalities. Mokhtar Ould Daddah asserted his rule by establishing a single party, the Parti du peuple mauritanien (PPM), in order to ensure against internal squabbling and to defend the country against Moroccan expansionism, which continues to cast a shadow over the country. Some elements among the Moorish population have favoured union with Morocco while the southern, African, population fears and has resisted Arab domination. Throughout its early years most Arab states refused to recognize Mauritania as a sovereign nation. Morocco did not recognize it until 1969.

The decolonization of the Spanish Sahara in 1975/6 provoked further difficulties when both Morocco and Mauritania claimed the territory as their own. The solution found by Spain, of sharing the territory between the two claimants, proved almost disastrous for Mauritania, which subsequently had to bear the brunt of attacks by the Polisario independence movement in Western Sahara*. The Mauritanian army was expanded from 1500 to 12,000 in 1976 and later to 17,000 but could not defend its new borders effectively. The crisis ended the political career of Ould Daddah, who was overthrown by the military in July 1978.

Although there have been changes of leadership since 1978, the Military Committee of National Salvation has retained its control of army and government, responding pragmatically to the demands of a strategic and economic crisis worsened by severe drought. The first chairman of this committee, Lt-Col. Moustapha Ould Salek, tried to maintain Mauritania's claim to the Western Sahara but he was replaced in July 1979 by Lt-Co. Mohamed Haidalla, who renounced the claim and tried to make peace with both the Polisario and Morocco. Haidalla was increasingly drawn towards recognition of the Polisario's rights in Western Sahara but he too was replaced in December 1984 by Lt-Col. Maawiya Ould Sid Ahmed Taya, who has reopened the dialogue with Morocco.

The economy today

Since independence the economy has been transformed from being purely rural to a dependence on earnings from iron ore. Drought, the falling demand for iron ore and the effects of Polisario attacks on iron-ore trains have all contributed to stagnation since the 1970s. In the 1980s the government looked towards the fishing industry as a new source of foreign exchange and revenue, but the overall economic outlook remains very uncertain. The loss of pasture and agricultural land has created a big urban population dependent on food aid.

Fish exports totalled $130m in 1985, only slightly less than the iron ore produced by the state mining company SNIM. Mining is set to continue. The guelbs mining project is now coming on stream with a capacity of 6m tonnes of high-grade iron ore per year, expandable to 30m tonnes per year, while the older mine at Kidia d'Idjil, which produced 7m tonnes in 1983, will be depleted by the 1990s. There are also plans to bring a new copper mine into production in 1987.

RS

Further reading

A. G. Gerteiny, *Mauritania* (London and New York, 1967)
R. M. Westebbe, *The Economy of Mauritania* (New York, 1971)

Morocco

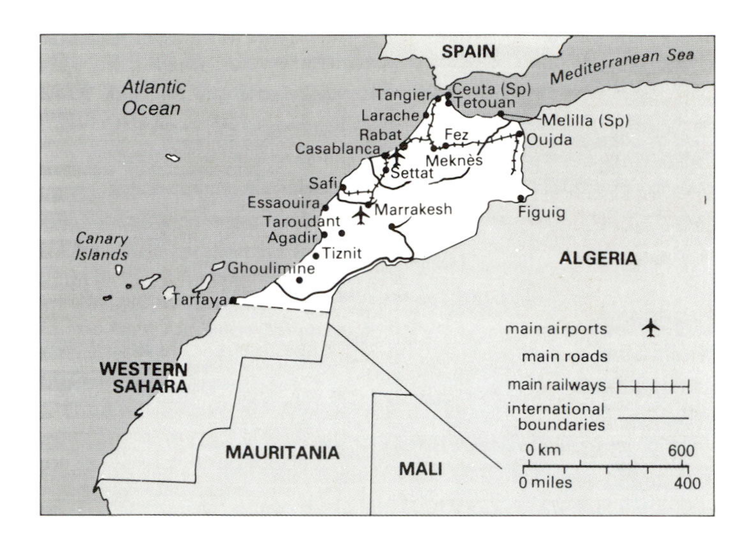

Official title	The Kingdom of Morocco
Area	458,730 sq. km
Population	20.4 million (1982 census)
Government and constitution	A constitutional monarchy with one legislative house. A multi-party democracy, but the King appoints ministers
Currency	1 Moroccan dirham (Dh) = 100 centimes; US $1 = 9.39 dirhams
Languages	Arabic is the most widely spoken. French is also widely spoken as a second language. Some 45 per cent of Moroccans speak the Berber dialects of Tarift, Tamazight and Tashilhait
Religion	Most of the population is Sunni Muslim. However, there is still an established Jewish minority in the cities and the Catholic community of 30,000 predominates among Christian sects
Climate	The northern and central regions enjoy warm, wet winters and hot, dry summers, while semi-arid to desert conditions prevail in the south

Geography and topography

Morocco's location in north-west Africa, with coastlines facing both the Atlantic and the Mediterranean, provides it with unique advantages amongst the states of North Africa. Its climate, for instance, is governed by the fact that it is open to the Atlantic trade winds and also benefits from the rain-bearing wind systems in the Mediterranean. This factor, combined with Morocco's mountain systems, has meant that the country enjoys a relatively good distribution of rainfall for agricultural purposes and well-developed river systems that support irrigation wherever rainfall is inadequate.

Geographically, Morocco is dominated by its fertile coastal plains which are isolated from the African interior and the Sahara Desert by the Atlas Mountain ranges. Only to the south, as Morocco merges into the Western Sahara*, does the desert extend to the coast and the Atlantic Ocean. In the north, the Mediterranean coastline from the Straits of Gibraltar to the Spanish enclave of Melilla is dominated by the rugged mountains of the Rif, while inland the plains shade into the high plateaus which act as a piedmont to the Atlas Mountains, with the Middle Atlas thrusting northwards towards the Rif and separated from it only by the Taza Gap. To the south, the Anti-Atlas range breaks away southwards from the High Atlas range, to form the Souss Valley.

The rainfall patterns governed by the mountain ranges and the wind systems have created river systems draining into the Mediterranean and the Atlantic, together with endoreic systems in the Sahara – all of which are critical to the agricultural sector as sources of irrigation and to the growing urban population for potable water supply. The Muluwaya River drains into the Mediterranean; the Lukkus, Sebu, Bu Regreg, Um Er-Rbia, the Tensift, the Sus and the Draa rivers all drain into the Atlantic; while the Ziz and the Gheris rivers vanish into the Sahara after watering the Tafilelt. These rivers now support thirty-four dams providing water for irrigation, as the result of plans designed to double the irrigated agricultural area from the traditional level of 500,000 hectares, out of a total cultivated area of about 7m hectares. Most of the cultivated area, however, depends on rainfall which ideally comes during October and November and again during February and March. The rainfed areas support extensive cereoculture on the plains and arboriculture in the mountains and piedmont areas.

Peoples

The Moroccan population* now numbers just under 23m according to 1985 estimates. The September 1982 census identified a population of 20.4m and the current annual population growth rate is of the order of 3.33 per cent. This will mean that Morocco's population will top 40m by the end of the century. Foreigners resident in Morocco number about 60,000 (61,935 according to the 1982 census) and about one million Moroccans are resident abroad, mainly in Europe, as migrant workers.

A shop on the market square, Agadir

ments have been active through the Front Progressiste since 1973 and are regularly purged by the authorities, while an organized fundamentalist opposition, involving up to twenty different groups, has been operative since 1979. However, the opposition, both legitimate and clandestine, has now been effectively muzzled.

The economy today

Ever since independence, the monarchy has sought to operate a liberal economic system, in which state investment partners the private sector with development guided by a series of five- and three-year plans. The economy depends heavily on external markets, mainly in the EEC, with phosphates, fertilizers and phosphoric acid – about 40 per cent of the total – and agricultural exports (mainly citrus) providing the bulk of export revenues, although manufactures, particularly textiles, have become increasingly important in recent years. However, Morocco's burgeoning population and stagnant agriculture have meant that, since 1968, cereals have had to be imported. Furthermore, apart from small coal deposits and some hydroelectricity, all energy must be imported and represents about 30 per cent of imports. These two considerations have meant that the chronic trade deficit has had to be balanced by invisibles – mainly tourism and migrant remittances.

In 1974, Morocco, which was then the largest exporter of phosphates in the world, decided to use its quasi-monopoly power to quadruple phosphate prices – as Opec had done with oil prices. This backfired, as previously uneconomic Florida deposits became economically viable again and, in 1976, phosphate prices collapsed. By then Morocco had embarked on elaborate development plans and had to borrow to compensate for the unexpected falls in export revenues. This led to a massive foreign debt, totalling $12bn by 1983, when the government had to call for IMF help. Since then, Morocco has undertaken the sorts of austerity policies favoured by the IMF, with trade liberalization, decreases in public sector expenditure, particularly on consumer subsidies, and encouragement to private sector investment. This has been sustained, despite serious riots in June 1981, during a previous attempt at domestic economic austerity, and in January 1984.

Morocco has rescheduled its foreign debt – in September 1983, September 1985 and in July 1987 – and is expected to continue this process until the 1990s. The Sahara War has been an added burden on the economy, but here much of the strain has been taken by aid from Saudi Arabia, Kuwait, the USA and France. Nonetheless, the war continues to be a drag on economic revival. However, the fact that agriculture has recently benefited from exceptionally good harvests and that oil prices have collapsed means that the pressure on Morocco's balance of payments in the future will be considerably eased. This, combined with the fact that the economy has already been largely restructured, suggests that the economic outlook for Morocco is reasonably good.

GJ

Further reading

J. Abun-Nasr, *A History of the Maghrib* (Cambridge, 1975)
G. Blake and A. Drysdale, *The Middle East and North Africa, a Political Geography* (London, 1985)
K. Dwyer, *Moroccan Dialogues* (Johns Hopkins, 1982)
W. Knapp, *North West Africa, a Political and Economic Survey* (London, 1977)
A. Laroui, *A History of the Maghrib* (Princeton, 1978)
M. Morsy, *North Africa 1800–1900* (London, 1985)
H. Munson, *The House of Si Abdullah* (Princeton, 1982)
R. Nyrop, *Morocco, a Country Study* (The American University, 1979)

Oman

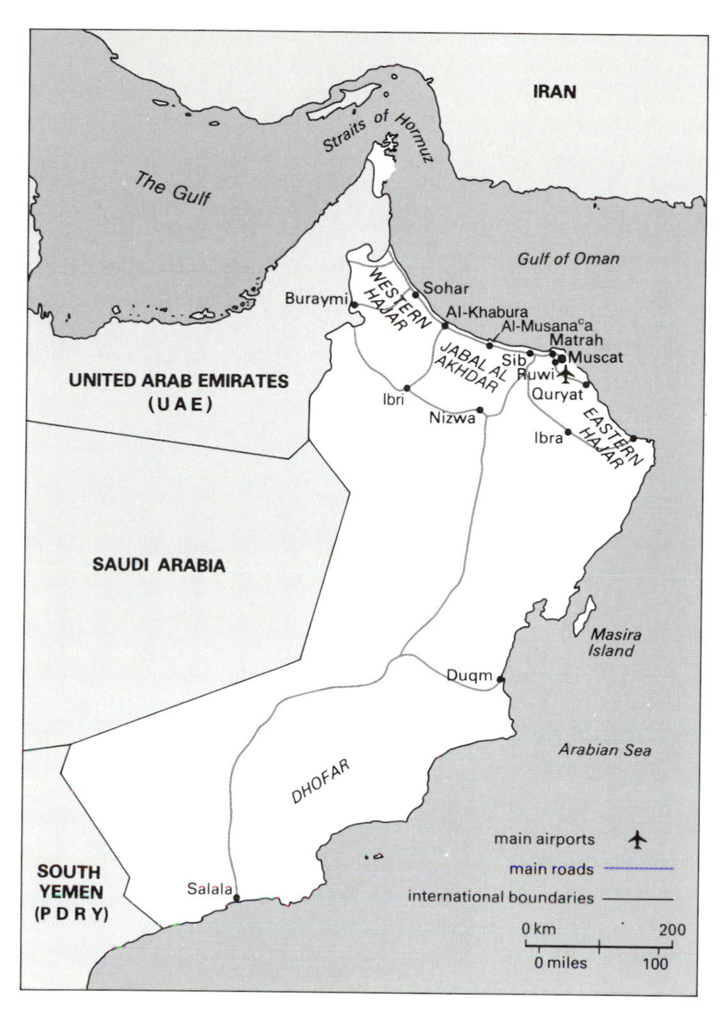

Official title	The Sultanate of Oman
Area	300,000 sq. km
Population	2 million (1985 estimate)
Government and constitution	The Sultan is assisted by an appointed cabinet but enjoys absolute power and legislates by decree. In 1981 a Consultative Assembly containing 45 nominated members, of which 17 were government officials, was established. The Assembly meets four times a year and its members are nominated for two-year terms
Currency	1 Omani rial = 1000 baiza; US $1 = 384.5 baiza (January 1986 fixed exchange rate)
Language	Arabic. English is widely spoken in the capital area
Religion	Islam. Some 75 per cent are Ibadi Muslims and some 25 per cent are Sunnis
Climate	Temperatures in Muscat vary between 20°C and 43°C. The mean annual rainfall in Muscat is 100 mm, while rainfall in the highlands is heavier. Dhofar is the only region in Arabia to experience a summer monsoon

Geography and topography

For centuries Oman has been the gateway to the Gulf, the first stop on the long merchant routes from India and Africa. The towering cliffs of Musandam overlooking the Straits of Hormuz were once a pirate's haven, but now guard the narrow channel through which most of the Gulf's oil is exported.

Oman's dramatic mountain scenery and fierce summer heat present an austere, forbidding landscape. The Omanis are a seafaring people, independent tribesmen who have never been colonized. The Omani Empire once encompassed parts of Africa and the Indian subcontinent, but wars and the advent of steam ships killed its maritime trade and the country lapsed into a century of obscurity from which it only recently emerged.

With an area of 271,949 km^2 and a population of around one million, Oman is the second largest country on the Arabian peninsula. The country is divided into five main geographical regions: the Batina Plain and Hajar Mountains in the north; the Naj Desert; Dhofar in the south; and Musandam, the rocky peninsula which is divided from the rest of Oman by a 70-km strip of the UAE. The main areas of population are the northern coast and the southern Salala plain, which only in 1982 were linked by a surfaced road.

In the north rainfall is erratic and years of drought are common. Vegetation is sparse except where cultivated date plantations form an oasis in the desert. In the mountains the ancient *aflaj* system of irrigation is used, which taps groundwater and channels it to the villages. On the Batina well water is used. The Salala Plain is the only part of Arabia touched by a monsoon, and for three months a heavy mist hangs over the countryside, turning the hills to verdant grasslands during October.

Peoples

Oman has been inhabited since prehistoric times. Legend has it that the first Arabs came to Oman from Yemen around the second century AD, when Azd tribesmen fled after the collapse of the great Marib Dam. Later a second wave of Arab immigrants – the Nizari or Adnani – moved southwards from Iraq.

Matrah Harbour

The Omanis were settled people with an aristocracy drawn from the townspeople (*hadar*). Tribal politics played a large part in Oman's history, and there was frequent conflict between the people of the coast and the interior, and between the two main tribal groups, the Hinawi and the Ghafiri. The beduin were a minority and took no part in running the country, although the ancient nomadic traditions were highly respected. There are six main beduin tribes – the largest are the Duru, Harasis and Wahiba – who between them divide the desert territory. Oil* has now dramatically changed their lives as most of the oilfields lie in beduin country, but many still follow the traditional life-style for at least part of the year.

Oman's population now has a cosmopolitan flavour, a result partly of its colonizing past, and partly of the 300,000 expatriates helping to develop the modern economy.

Religions

The majority of Omanis are Ibadi* Muslims, belonging to a movement which emerged in Basra in the early days of Islam. The Ibadi ideal was to return to the pure Islamic state as under the Prophet, but its adherents believed in elected leadership and appointed an Imam who had both spiritual and temporal responsibility. Despite its orthodoxy, Ibadism is receptive to change and technological innovation, and Omani women are encouraged to play a full part in their country's economic progress.

History up to 1939

In prehistoric times Oman's climate was probably wetter than it is today. Relics of a petrified forest have been found in the southern desert, and traces of Stone Age man dating from 30,000 BC. There is archaeological evidence of settled communities in northern Oman from about 3000 BC, farming by flood irrigation, with evidence of primitive copper smelting. By 2000 BC copper had developed into a major industry, and Magan, the city that exported copper to Mesopotamia*, is now proved to be almost certainly linked with Sohar in northern Oman.

By about 1000 BC Omani seamen were regularly sailing the monsoon sea routes to India and Africa, but in the fourth century BC Persian forces invaded and imposed suzerainty on northern Oman for 1200 years. The commercial focus shifted to Dhofar, based on the frankincense trade. The incense is made from the sap of the mughur tree, which grows only in Dhofar, the Hadramaut and Somalia, and was much prized by civilizations of the eastern Mediterranean. The incense was carried by camel train to Mecca, and thence northwards, and brought riches to Dhofar, but the trade gradually declined with early waves of Arab immigration.

Gradually the Persians were forced to give the Arab tribes local autonomy. In 630 AD envoys from Medina converted the Arabs to Islam, and they in turn called on the Persians to embrace the new religion. When they refused the Julanda leaders attacked Rustaq, and the Persians eventually sued for peace.

For the next three centuries the country entered a period of prosperity. Trade flourished and by the ninth century AD Omani ships regularly sailed to the East Indies and China. New Persian attacks and internecine warfare ended this golden age, but by the fifteenth century Muscat was again a major anchorage and entrepôt.

In 1507 the Portuguese captain Alfonso Albuquerque found Muscat a 'populous town with elegant houses'. He promptly subjugated it, and for the next 150 years the Portuguese occupied the coastal towns, though they interfered little with internal affairs. Several times they repelled Turkish attacks, but Portuguese influence in the Gulf was waning, and they were finally ousted in 1650 by the powerful Yaʿariba leader Sultan ibn Sayf.

Sultan rebuilt the power of the government and developed foreign trade. He built the great fort at Nizwa, and his son the palace at Jabrin, both still standing today. Wars between the Ghafiri and Hinawi factions again provided an opening for Persian invasion in 1743, but this time their domination was short, and they were

Omani girls at the Seeb camel race

dislodged by the governor of Sohar, Ahmad ibn Saʿid, who was elected Imam in 1749. He was the founder of the Al Bu Saʿid dynasty that rules today.

In 1800 Oman signed a major treaty with Britain under which a British representative was to reside in Muscat, and in the same year Wahhabi* forces from Saudi Arabia took Buraymi.

Zanzibar had been occupied by Oman since 1730, and in the nineteenth century trade began to flourish. In the 1830s Sultan Saʿid ibn Sultan built a new capital and moved to Zanzibar. On his death in 1856 the sucession was disputed between his sons, and Oman and Zanzibar were divided again, each now having Omani rulers. Unfortunately, many ships of the Omani navy and merchant fleet were in Zanzibar at the time and the compensation payments agreed with Oman were soon discontinued. Steam ships and internal warfare spelled the end of the Omani maritime trade.

In the 1860s Buraymi was recaptured from the Wahhabis. In 1879 a leading Shaykh of Dhofar invited the Sultan to take over the province. Although Muscat and Dhofar had been loosely associated at certain periods in their history, Sultan Turki now took over the administration in Dhofar, creating the basis of Oman as it is today.

Fighting in the north continued. For several decades rival tribes squabbled over the leadership, and on two occasions British warships intervened on the side of the Sultan. Finally in 1920 peace was made between the Imam of the interior and Sultan Taymur ibn Faysal. The British political agent, Ronald Wingate, mediated between the two factions and a treaty was signed at Sib.

The first oil concessions were also granted in the 1920s, and several expeditions into the interior took place, but exploration was difficult and dangerous because there were no maps or roads and the tribesmen were often far from friendly. In 1932 the reluctant Sultan Taymur abdicated in favour of his son Saʿid ibn Taymur, but there was no money in the coffers and the country relapsed into a period of extreme poverty.

History since the Second World War

The Second World War barely touched Oman. Oil was found in the early 1950s in the south at Marmul, but it was heavy and uneconomic to produce. In 1950 the Saudis again occupied Buraymi, and in 1954 the old disputes between the interior and the coast were awakened when the new Imam of the Ibadis, Ghalib ibn ʿAli, set out to create an independent state in the interior. In 1955 the Sultan advanced on Buraymi with a force of 9000 tribesmen on camels, backed by the Trucial Oman scouts, and the Saudis withdrew. He then went on to subdue the interior. In 1957 fighting broke out again when Ghalib's younger brother Talib returned from military training overseas, but the rebel forces were finally routed from their Jabal Akhdar retreat by British SAS troops.

Sultan Qabus

In 1965 a communist-backed uprising took place in Dhofar, where the tribesmen rebelled against the country's backwardness, and when in 1967 Sultan Saʿid's dream of oil production came true it was too late for the old man to adapt and bring about the modern development that his country needed. In 1970 he was overthrown by his son, Qabus, whose early military training in Sandhurst and the British army had been followed by six years under house arrest in Salala. The young Sultan took over a country that had only twelve hospital beds, 10 km of tarmac roads, and three primary schools. Radios and spectacles were banned, civilians were not allowed to drive, and a curfew was imposed in Muscat each night.

Qabus faced two immediate problems, developing the country from scratch and coping with a civil war in the south. British forces again played a vital role in quelling the insurgents, who were supported by South Yemen*, but the new Sultan sought to show that his desire to improve living standards had removed the *raison d'être* of the war. Rapid development and a 'hearts and minds' campaign in Dhofar soon won over the rebels and by 1975 the disturbances had been quelled.

The Sultan also set about developing the country. One of the first contracts in 1971 was for the building of six schools and hospitals in the interior. Contractors faced immense difficulties as there were no local supplies and the villages were virtually inaccessible. In Sur all the equipment had to be shipped by dhow, and because there were no port facilities it had to be manhandled onto the shore.

Gradually a modern administration was set up. Exiles returned from abroad and with their education and wider experience played an important part in the new government. In 1970 the Omani riyal was introduced, replacing several other currencies then in use. In 1973 it was pegged to the US dollar at a rate of RO 0.345, and held its value until it was devalued by 10 per cent early in 1986.

Meanwhile new oilfields were opened up, but in comparison to major oil producers the fields were small. The area round Fahud in northern Oman was developed first. The fields produced light crude, but production peaked at 370,000 barrels a day in 1976 and everyone predicted that Oman's oil would run out in a decade. It seemed the boom had been and gone.

By 1980 the oil price had risen sufficiently to make production of heavy oil from Marmul economic, and production was boosted again. Since then continuing finds of new reservoirs in the desert have transformed the future outlook, and by 1985 production was running close to 500,000 barrels a day. The lion's share of oil is produced by the state oil company, Petroleum Development Oman.

Politics today

Oman now plays a full part in international affairs. Sultan Qabus is head of state and prime minister. He heads the Cabinet of Ministers, and authorizes laws and royal decrees, which become law as soon as they are published in the official gazette. The administration also includes the Governorate of the Capital and nine specialized councils including defence, water and finance. The regions are divided into forty-one *wilayas* (provinces) headed by a *wali* (governor).

Sultan Qabus's style as head of state is to temper authority with consultation. In 1981 he set up the State Consultative Council, with fifty-five nominated delegates, including ten government appointments and others representing the regions and private sector.

Oman was one of the prime movers in the establishment in 1981 of the Gulf Cooperation Council (GCC)* whose six member states are Saudi Arabia, Bahrain, the UAE, Kuwait, Qatar and Oman. In November 1985 Oman hosted the summit meeting of GCC heads of state, and a few days later celebrated its fifteenth National Day.

Oman has followed a non-aligned foreign policy, and its close ties with Britain have broadened to include many other countries. In 1982 Oman held joint military operations with the US, and is also extending friendship to the eastern bloc, having recently opened diplomatic relations with its former adversary South Yemen, and with the Soviet Union.

The economy today

Economic planning is on a five-year basis. At the beginning of 1986 the country entered its third five-year plan, which aims to develop the private sector and social services. Overall spending of RO 9250 ($24,057) is forecast against revenues of RO 8656m ($$22,276m), compared with spending in the second five-year plan of RO 7360m ($19,141m) and revenues of RO 6950m ($26,722m). An annual growth rate of 4 per cent is predicted and the deficits will be made up from international borrowing, state reserves, or increasing non-oil receipts, but the policy is not to increase oil production. Oman has an enviable credit rating and should have no difficulty borrowing funds as needed.

Despite the government's strenuous efforts to diversify, oil will dominate the economy for many years to come. In 1984 oil revenue was RO 1292m ($3360m), some 84 per cent of national income. In 1984 the country's first oil refinery at Mina al-Fahal was opened, making Oman self-sufficient in refined oil products. A second refinery is planned at Salala.

In 1984 Oman became the first significant exporter in the Arabian peninsula of a mineral other than oil or gas. The Sohar copper mine has reopened sites exploited by the Sumerians 5000 years ago. Excavation began in 1979 and in 1984 Omani copper was recognized in the London Metal Exchange. In 1985 the state-owned Oman Mining Company exported about 14,000 tonnes of electrolytic refined copper. At present extraction rates the deposits of some 11m tonnes of ore will have a life of eleven to twelve years, and the hope is now to develop downstream industries.

Oman has a free economy and offers investment incentives to new firms. To encourage small to medium-sized industry a fully serviced industrial area was built at Rusayl 15 km from Sib airport, and has been so successful that others are now planned.

Rapid change in the last fifteen years has brought dramatic improvements to the standards of living and health of the Omanis, and has produced few signs of social stress. Oman's increasing sophistication, and growing tensions in the region have brought it into the international limelight in a way that would have been impossible only a few decades ago.

AB

Further reading

J. Whelan, ed., *Oman: a MEED Practical Guide* (London, 1984, 2nd edn.)
D. Hawley, *Oman and its Renaissance* (London, 1983, 3rd edn.)
W. Thesiger, *Arabian Sands* (London, 1977)

Qatar

Official title	The State of Qatar
Area	11,437 sq. km
Population	257,081 (1982 estimate)
Government and constitution	Executive power is with the Amir who appoints the Council of Ministers. An appointed 30-member Advisory Council assists the Amir. A provisional constitution was adopted on 2 April 1970
Currency	1 Qatar riyal = 100 dirhams; US $1 = 3.640 riyals
Language	Arabic. English is widely spoken
Religion	Almost all Qataris are Sunni Muslims, mostly of the Unitarian (Wahhabi*) sect
Climate	Hot and humid in summer. Summer temperatures reach 44°C from July to September. Winter temperatures range between 10°C and 20°C. Some rain falls in winter

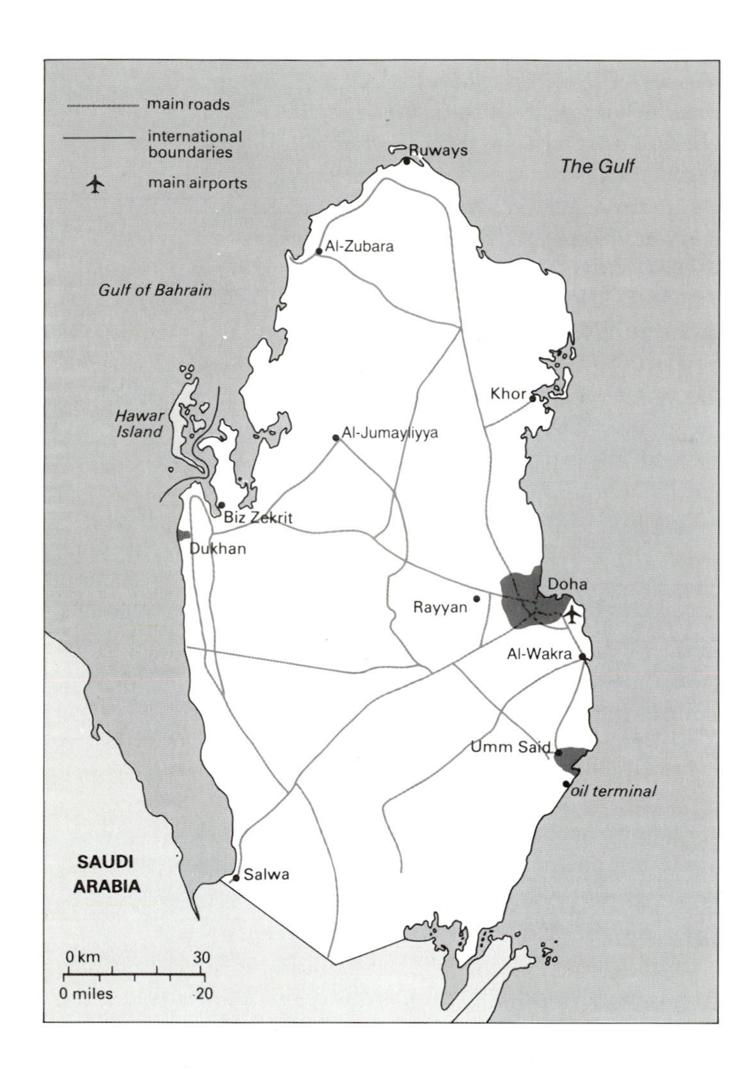

Geography and topography

The State of Qatar is a peninsula projecting northward from the Arabian peninsula into the Gulf. Its area of 180 km by 85 km is mainly desert. Qatar's climate is hot and humid in the summer with temperatures reaching 44°C between July and September. Winter temperatures range between 10° and 20°. Some 50 per cent of the state's water supply is from desalination. The capital is Doha and the main towns are Umm Saʿid, al-Khawr, al-Wakra and Dukhan.

Peoples

About one-third of the population is Qatari. There are also substantial numbers of people from other Arab countries. Most of the expatriate population comes from India, Pakistan and Bangladesh.

Religion

Islam is the official religion and most Qataris belong to the Sunni* sect although a few are Shiʿis.

History until 1939

Archaeological finds date human presence in Qatar to about 4000 BC. But historical documentation of the small peninsula is scarce. In the eighth century AD, at the time of the ʿAbbasid Empire, the Arabian Gulf coast became an important trading centre. Apart from trading, the families and tribes along Qatar's coastline lived by pearl-fishing and herding in the desert.

The peninsula's inhospitable terrain and climate made it unattractive to exploitation and conquest during the years of European rivalry for the area. For most of the time until the early nineteenth century it was dominated by the Khalifa family from nearby Bahrain. In 1872 Qatar became part of the Ottoman Empire*. By the time Britain came to dominate the area in the early twentieth century, the Thani family had become the dominant force on the peninsula. The protection treaties of 1916 and 1934 were signed between Britain and Shaykh ʿAbd Allah al-Thani, and recognized his offspring as his successors.

History since the Second World War

The Second World War delayed the development of Qatar's oilfields. A concession had been awarded to the Anglo-Persian Oil Company in 1935 but it was not until 1949 that commercial production began at the onshore Dukhan field on the western side of the peninsula. Oil wealth has provided the basis for the peninsula's development ever since.

Qatar was a prime mover in the discussions of the Gulf states to form a federation following the announcement of British withdrawal from the area in 1968. Disagreements led to Qatar's decision to go it alone, however, and on 1 September 1971 it became a fully independent state. Five months later Shaykh Khalifa Ibn Hamad al-Thani, Crown Prince and prime minister, deposed Shaykh Ahmad al-Thani, the ruler since November 1960, in a bloodless coup and with the support of the rest of the family.

In the fifteen years since independence, Qatar has become one of the world's wealthy states. Like its neighbours it has rapidly developed its infrastructure and attempted to become less dependent on oil for its economic well-being. The government has taken control of the oilfields from foreign companies. It is a member of most international organizations, such as the UN and its affiliates. It is also a member of both OPEC* and the GCC*.

Politics today

Absolute power over all the country's affairs rests in the hands of the Amir. He is advised by a council of ministers, which he appoints mainly from within the Thani family. There is little open political debate, and opinions and grievances are dealt with informally by word of mouth. The stability of the regime was mildly shaken in mid-1983 by the discovery of an arms cache outside Doha and reports of an alleged plot to overthrow the government.

The economy and society today

Qatar's transition from a simple economy reliant on pearl-fishing and trading to a simple economy reliant on oil has been rapid. Since 1949 when oil was first exported from the onshore Dukhan field hydrocarbons have accounted for more than three-quarters of the government revenues and more than 90 per cent of the country's exports. Nearly all economic activity is generated by the Amir and his advisers. Economic planning is based on the annual budget and the overall strategy has been rapid but conservative development.

Qatar is one of the Gulf region's smaller oil producers. Its reserves of about 4000 million barrels are expected to last forty years at present consumption rates. Oil exports have allowed the economy to grow at a rapid rate since 1960. Although it does not work to development plans there has been an obvious pattern of development. Housing, roads, hospitals, schools, offices and other basic infrastructure have been provided by the government. The government's budget has not fallen below $1700m since 1978 and in 1981 was as high as $4050m. Assuming a population of 250,000, this represents about $16,000 a person.

Qatar General Petroleum Corporation (QGPC), the government's oil company, has been the instigator behind efforts to create some form of alternative to oil for the country's revenue. Refining capacity has been expanded from 600 barrels a day (b/d) in 1953 to about 62,000 b/d in 1984. Industrial development has included the establishment of the Qatar Fertilizer Company (Qafco), which produces ammonia and urea, in 1969. The Qatar Steel Company (Qasco) began commercial operations in 1978, while the Qatar Petrochemical Company (Qapco), which produces ethylene and some derivatives, was set up in 1980.

As well as oil Qatar is also sitting on the world's single largest gas reservoir. Lying off the north-east coast, the North Field covers an area of about 6000 km^2 and has estimated recoverable reserves of 150 million million cubic feet of natural gas – nearly 4 per cent of the world total – and reserves that are probably more than double that. The reserves were discovered in 1971 by the Shell group. Gas for commercial use, mainly as feedstock for power stations and local industries, is unlikely to be pumped ashore before 1988. Future plans include supplying gas to other Gulf countries and to Europe, or in liquefied form to the Far East.

An inhospitable climate has made agricultural development slow and costly. It shares with its neighbours the burden of limited water resources. While some efforts have been made to encourage this sector it still accounts for little more than 1 per cent of the country's Gross Domestic Product; and nearly all the country's food is still imported. Qatar's main trading partners are Japan, Britain, the United States, West Germany, Italy and France.

Most of Qatar's infrastructure is now in place. The waves of foreign workers pouring in to build houses, hospitals, schools and roads have now slowed to a trickle. The hydrocarbons sector continues to employ large numbers of people, the construction sector less so. Leisure and services, including retailing and finance, continue to attract foreigners. And in contrast to the early settlers who lived on the peninsula's west coast, three-quarters of the population now live in and around Doha.

TO

Further reading

J. Bulloch, *The Gulf: a portrait of Kuwait, Qatar, Bahrain and the UAE* (London, 1984)
J. Moorehead, *In Defiance of the Elements: a personal view* (London, 1977)
J. Whelan, ed., *Qatar: a MEED Practical Guide* (London, 1983)
R. Said Zahlan, *The Creation of Qatar* (London, 1979)

Saudi Arabia

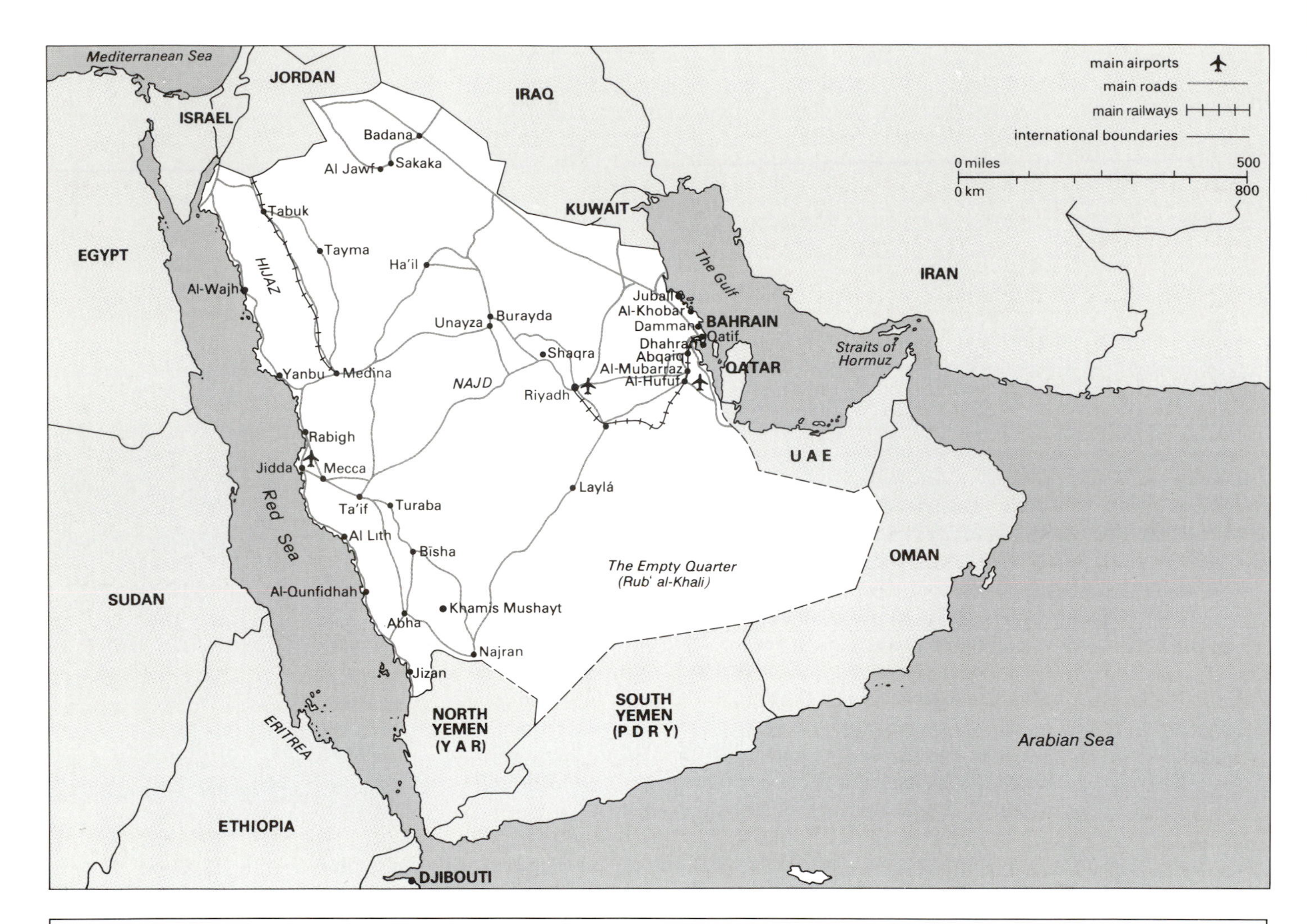

Official title	The Kingdom of Saudi Arabia
Area	2,150,000 sq. km
Population	9 million (1987 estimate)
Government and constitution	A monarchy with a Council of Ministers. The constitution is Islamic, based upon the Qur'an and the *hadith* (sayings) of the Prophet Muhammad. However, a reform programme, covering a new constitution, an independent judiciary and a modern judicial system was established in 1962 and is still under way
Currency	1 Saudi riyal (SR) = 20 qursh = 100 hallalas; US $1 = SR 3.65
Languages	Arabic. English is also widely spoken in business and government circles. Various other languages, such as Urdu and Filipino, are spoken by guest workers
Religion	(Sunni) Islam; about 5 per cent of the population, mostly concentrated in the Eastern (Hasa) Province, is Shi'i
Climate	Maximum temperatures are 38°C in summer. The winter minimum is 13°C

Geography and topography

Saudi Arabia is a parched, mainly barren land covering an area of 2,150,000 km^2, equivalent to the United States east of the Mississippi. On the western coast is the Tihama plain, a hot region with a stifling, humid coast, which receives virtually no rainfall. The southern part of the plain, which runs through the province of Jizan and along the coast of Yemen, resembles the drier parts of East Africa, with some African flora and fauna – acacia trees and weaver birds – and a population of African descent which in places still lives in beehive-shaped huts.

From 24–120 km inland from the coast rises a steep escarpment, running the whole length of the Kingdom and getting broader and higher towards the south. In the centre of the escarpment is the mountain resort town of Ta'if, where the government moves in the summer, and in the south, where the range broadens to become a high hilly plateau, is the populous province of ʿAsir.

The Najd

On its eastern side the mountain range descends gradually; the topography of the Kingdom slopes downwards with few interruptions the whole way to the Persian Gulf. The area between the mountains and the Tuwayq escarpment, which is the one point where the land does rise slightly, is bleak, monotonous and almost uninhabited. At Tuwayq begins the plateau of the Najd, which is physically and culturally the centre of the Kingdom; it is the home of the royal family and of the strict unitarian creed which the family has adopted. The Najd is a relatively populous region, traditionally having many small oases and mud-brick villages, whose people have always outnumbered the bedouin. The region receives some winter rainfall and the strata beneath it contain enormous quantities of fresh water.

The area around the town of Kharj, south of Riyadh, is now an important wheat grower, and 300 miles north of the capital the province of Qasim is an even bigger and more prosperous farming area. It is mainly Qasim that has made the Kingdom self-sufficient in wheat and poultry in the last seven years. On the northern borders of the Najd, including the Shammar Mountains and part of the Nafud sand sea, is the province of Ha'il, which until its final defeat in 1922 was the home of the house of Saʿud's longstanding rival, the Rashid family.

Eastern Province

The Najd ends on the eastern side in a thin line of sand dunes, the Dahna, which curves east and south from the Najd, through Qasim and the Eastern Province to the vast sand sea of the Rubʿ al-Khali, the Empty Quarter. This uninhabited desert, where not a drop of rain may fall for a decade, covers a quarter of the Kingdom.

Beyond the Dahna, on the eastern side of the Kingdom, the land reaches sea level. In the north is gravel desert, further south, around Dhahran, Abqayq and Hufuf, where the biggest oilfields lie, is an undulating topography with rocky outcrops. The Eastern Province contains the Kingdom's two biggest oases – one on the coast around the towns of Qatif, Sayhat and Safwa, and the other, known as al-Hasa (which used to be the name of the entire region) near Hufuf. The oases are known for their production of dates and vegetables. Farming here is a traditional activity, whereas in the centre of the Kingdom it is a new commercial enterprise depending on modern technology.

Fourteen provinces

For administrative purposes Saudi Arabia is divided either into three regions or fourteen provinces. Some government agencies divide their operations between the centre, east and west/south-west; others operate according to provinces. The major provinces are Mecca, which apart from the Holy City embraces Jidda and Ta'if, Riyadh, which covers the Najd south of Qasim, and the Eastern Province. Apart from those names mentioned earlier, the other provinces are: Juf, Qurayyat al-Milh and Northern Frontiers bordering Jordan and Iraq, Tabuk in the northern Hijaz, Medina to the south of it, al-Baha, a tiny mountainous province just north of ʿAsir, and Najran, a wild and beautiful area containing the rugged eastern edge of the mountain plateau and the southern part of the Empty Quarter.

Peoples and religions

Najdis

The people who dominate Saudi Arabia politically and culturally are the Najdis. Although the Najd proper covers a fairly limited area, the Najdis in a cultural sense are thought of as the desert and small village people of all parts of the Kingdom. They are of pure Arabian blood and rough, independent and aloof temperament; the sense of superiority for which they are known derives from their survival (before oil) in a harsh and desperately poor environment and from their having conquered the rest of the Kingdom.

In the first thirty years of this century and earlier, the main division in Najdi society was the tribe – major names, working from north-west to south-east, being Bani ʿAtiyya, ʿAnayza (the tribe of Al Saʿud), Ruwala, Shammar, Billi, Juhayna, Harb, Mutayr, ʿUtayba, Subay, Bani Khalid, Ajman, Dawasir, Qahtan, Shahran, Yam and Murra.

Since 1930, when King ʿAbd al-ʿAziz crushed the Ikhwan rebellion, and the beginning of regular oil exports after the Second World War, the tribes have ceased to be of much political significance, but it is still very important socially whether a man can claim honestly

Jidda

that he has a tribal ancestry (in any tribe) or whether his tribal origin has been lost. Najdis whose families forgot their tribal roots, through members being killed in war or famine or through long settlement in a village where the support of a tribe was not necessary, do not have the prestige of those with a proper genealogy. The two groups do not intermarry. Most of the famous Najdi merchant families in the west and east of the Kingdom are established in these parts because their ancestors left the Najd, in time of famine, to escape the stigma and disadvantage of having no tribe.

The Najdis' cultural dominance is reinforced by their being the devotees of the puritanical creed known in Saudi Arabia as Unitarianism and in the West, wrongly, as Wahhabism*, after the name of its founder. The Unitarians – *muwahiddun* – trace their origins from 1745 when Muhammad ibn Saʿud, a chieftain in the village of Diriyya just north of Riyadh, became the patron of an ardent religious revivalist, Shaykh (teacher) Muhammad ibn ʿAbd al-Wahhab. The preacher, who held to the views of the strict Hanbali* school of Islamic jurisprudence, was seeking to cleanse society of corrupt and mystical practices which had grown up since the time of the Prophet. These included the veneration of saints and the practice of going on pilgrimages to their tombs, ideas which Muhammad ibn ʿAbd al-Wahhab regarded as being tantamount to polytheism. To this day the *muwahiddun* bury their dead, including the Kings, in unmarked graves in the desert. The Shiʿis*, who of all Muslim sects are the most concerned with saints and tombs, they regard as heretics of the most undesirable sort.

Since the time of the alliance between the teacher and Muhammad ibn Saʿud the propagation of the unitarian creed has been the theoretical *raison d'être* of the Saudi state. The descendants of Muhammad ibn ʿAbd al-Wahhab, known as the Al al-Shaykh (the 'family of the teacher') have been steadfast allies of the Saʿuds and now occupy numerous ministerial and judicial positions in the government.

Hijazis

Much the most important group of people in the Kingdom outside Najdi society are the Hijazis, the urban people of Jidda, Mecca, Ta'if, Medina, Yanbuʿ, Wajh and the other towns of the central and northern parts of the Tihama plain and the mountains in the west of the Kingdom. The Hijazis are a mixture of races – people from the desert who have settled in the towns and the descendants of pilgrims who stayed in Arabia. Medina is known for its families descended from Syrians, Turks, Egyptians and central Asians, Mecca for its communities from India and South-East Asia. Jidda is a totally polyglot city with many families from the Hadhramaut, in what is now Southern Yemen, some from Africa and a few from Iran.

From a doctrinal point of view there is no religious difference between the Najdis and Hijazis, because the unitarian creed of the Najdis, after all, is Sunni Islam stripped of its inessentials. The courts of the Hijaz since the conquest of the region in 1925–6 follow Hanbali interpretations of *shariʿa* law; earlier under the Hashimites and the Ottoman Empire the judges were trained in the Hanafi* school. The fact that the Hijaz contains the two holiest Muslim cities, Mecca and Medina, gives Saudi Arabia added prestige in its own eyes and internationally but it is not of great significance in the context of cultural differences between regions within the Kingdom. The only obvious religious distinction between the Hijaz and the Najd today is that the Hijazi mosques are more decorated and the Hijazi muezzins more tuneful.

In other ways Hijazi–Najdi differences are more important. The Hijazis are a softer people than the men of the interior, more humorous and tolerant, less austere and less gravelly of voice. In the early days of oil, having had far more contact with the outside world, they were much better educated and more sophisticated than the Najdis and so came to dominate the civil service. They were well-liked by King Faysal (1964–75), who from the mid-1920s until after the Second World War was his father's viceroy in the Hijaz. Now, although King Fahd enjoys staying in the Hijaz and spends much of his time there, the tenor of Saudi society and government is much more Najdi. The Najdis are now as well-educated as their western neighbours and they seem sometimes to have taken delight in pushing them aside as they have furthered their own interests in the administration. Riyadh now is the capital of the Kingdom in every sense, whereas until the early 1980s the Foreign Ministry, the embassies, the central bank (the Saudi Arabian Monetary Agency), most of the foreign banks and the headquarters of almost all the big merchant houses were in Jidda. The rivalry between the two peoples is fairly visible – one notices the different tones of Hijazi and Najdi newspapers and becomes aware that certain parts of the administration are almost exclusively Hijazi and others Najdi – but it is not a matter that affects the Kingdom's stability in any way.

Shiʿis

The only other Saudi peoples of significance are the inhabitants of the ʿAsir plateau and the Shiʿis. The ʿAsiris are racially akin to the Yemenis, but unlike the people of the northern part of North Yemen they are religiously orthodox. Their views of political and religious matters are very much like those of the Hijazis.

The Shiʿis are less numerous than the other groups in Saudi society and very much separate from them. Almost all of them live in the Eastern Province, particularly in the oases of Qatif–Sayhat–Safwu, which is entirely Shiʿi, and Al-Hasa, which is about half Shiʿi. A small number live in Medina, which is the only significant oasis in the western part of the Kingdom and is important to the Shiʿis because it contains the graves of several members of the Prophet's family and four of the twelve Imams, the early leaders of the sect. The total number of Shiʿis in the Kingdom is thought to be 350,000 to 400,000, which compares with a Saudi population in the Eastern Province of about a million and a total Saudi (as opposed to immigrant) population of some seven million.

In the Eastern Province the Shiʿis work in the date gardens – it is often said that they have an affinity with water and agriculture – and they make up a large part, about half, of the labour force of the oil-producing company, ARAMCO. A few of them own quite large businesses. Their relations with the Najdi people of the province are good – Shiʿi and Sunni businesses employ people of each other's sect, there are Shiʿi–Sunni friendships and even one or two mixed business partnerships. However, the view of the Shiʿis held by the royal family and the religious establishment of central Arabia is much more hostile – they are regarded by many as heretics and madmen – and the Shiʿis in turn fear their rulers. There are no Shiʿis in the National Guard, which is one of the forces responsible for internal security, and there are no more than three or four in important positions in the government.

In 1953 the Shiʿis in ARAMCO were involved in a major strike, which was suppressed violently, and in November 1979 and February 1980 there were riots, stimulated partly by Iranian propaganda, in the town of Qatif. After the riots King Khalid (1975–82) twice visited the Eastern Province to meet Shiʿi notables, and in due course a new governor of Qatif town and a new commander of the National Guard in the region were appointed. In 1985 Prince Muhammad ibn Fahd, the second son of King Fahd, was made governor of the Eastern Province, replacing ʿAbd al-Muhsin Bin Jaluwi, whose family had ruled the province since it was incorporated in the Saudi domains in 1913. Prince Muhammad and his deputy, Prince Fahd ibn Salman, the eldest son of the governor of Riyadh, have been much more active than their predecessor and have shown themselves more interested in the welfare of all the peoples of their province. The series of administrative changes has been accompanied since 1980 by much greater government spending on the development of Qatif and Al-Hasa. One result is that the region is now regarded much less as being potentially unstable than it was at the end of the 1970s.

History up to 1939

Early history of the Saʿud family

The proselytising state that Muhammad ibn Saʿud and Muhammad ibn ʿAbd al-Wahhab founded in the 1740s expanded steadily in the later eighteenth century. In 1801 the *muwahiddun* sacked the Shiʿi town of Karbala in Mesopotamia and in 1806 they seized Mecca and Medina from the Ottomans. This spurred the Sultan to ask his viceroy in Egypt, Muhammad ʿAli*, to invade Najd and after a slow campaign of seven years the viceroy's son, Ibrahim Pasha, took Diriyya in 1818 and destroyed it. The Saʿudi Amir, ʿAbd Allah, the great grandson of Muhammad ibn Saʿud, was taken to Istanbul and executed. The Wahhabi pirates of the Persian Gulf and Indian Ocean were destroyed by the British at Ra's al-Khayma in 1819.

Before long Saʿudi power rose again, under the rule of Turki (1824–34), a cousin of the dead ʿAbd Allah, and then, after Turki's assassination and a turbulent period marked by rebellion within the family, under Turki's son, Faysal. During the main period of Faysal's rule (1843–65) the Saʿuds extended their authority north to the Jebel Shammar and south to Oman.

On Faysal's death there was another collapse of Saʿudi power when his sons, ʿAbd Allah and Saʿud engaged in twenty-five years' of civil war, resulting in 1871 in the loss of the Hasa province to the Turks and in 1887 in the capture of Riyadh by Muhammad ibn Rashid, the chief of the Shammar tribe, who ruled in Ha'il. Faysal's third son, ʿAbd al-Rahman, served briefly as the Rashids' governor of Riyadh and then fled with his family and followers to Kuwait.

ʿAbd al-ʿAziz

It was from this exile that the modern Saudi state began. The man responsible was ʿAbd al-ʿAziz ibn ʿAbd al-Rahman ibn Faysal, later known as Ibn Saʿud, who was one of the great Arab leaders of this century. He was a man of impressive physical stature and good looks, a master of desert diplomacy – in the course of which he married numerous wives and sired some eighty children – and a

Overlooked by a portrait of King ʿAbd al-ʿAziz, King Fahd (right) talks to the UAE president Shaykh Zayed ibn Nahayan, during the GCC summit held in Riyadh, December 1987

leader with the capacity to inspire his men to love him. He also had an extraordinary breadth of vision and foresight. He recognized the limitations of his own position and the strength of foreign powers, which his isolated predecessors had failed to do, and he was able to restrain his more chauvinist followers, who would have offended the governments and oil companies with which he dealt, and so he was able to use the foreigners to his advantage. ʿAbd al-ʿAziz ruled the Saudi state from 1902 until his death in 1953.

ʿAbd al-ʿAziz's campaigns began in the winter of 1901–2, when he took a group of followers from Kuwait and, in a surprise attack which has become a legend in Saudi Arabia, seized Riyadh from its Rashidi governor. The new Amir of Najd fought the Rashids for much of the next twenty years but he did not finally subdue them and capture Ha'il until 1922. Meanwhile he took the Hasa province from the Turks in 1913, installing as governor the fearsome ʿAbd Allah ibn Jaluwi, who ruled his subjects with an iron hand. In the First World War, ʿAbd al-ʿAziz, like the Sharif Husayn of Mecca, sided with the British, though his relations with the Sharif were poor – the latter had captured one of his brothers in 1912 – and he did not participate in the Arab Revolt of 1916–18.

The Ikhwan

During this period there emerged in the Saudi territories a fanatical warrior brotherhood known as the Ikhwan, which was sponsored partly by ʿAbd al-ʿAziz but more, it seems, through the proselytizing vigour of a few chiefs. The Ikhwan, who established themselves in small puritanical settlements, set out to regenerate in their strictest form the slightly softened *muwahiddun* ideals.

The Ikhwan soon came into conflict with the Sharif's forces in the lands of the ʿUtayba tribe between Ta'if and Riyadh. In 1919 they virtually wiped out a Hashimite army at Turaba. Five years later, when ʿAbd al-ʿAziz's patience with the eccentric and arrogant Sharif was exhausted by Husayn's declaring himself Caliph of all the Muslims, the Ikhwan were unleashed on the Hijaz. Taʿif was sacked and Jidda and Medina were taken by siege in 1925 and 1926. To avoid embittering the inhabitants of his new and relatively rich and prosperous territories, ʿAbd al-ʿAziz promptly sent the Ikhwan back to the Najd and established a fairly liberal form of Saudi rule through the vice-regency of his son Faysal. It was after the capture of Jidda that ʿAbd al-ʿAziz adopted the title of King of Najd and the Hijaz.

The years 1929–30 saw a rebellion by the Ikhwan, who sensed, rightly, that the growing organization of the Saudi state would force an end to the old form of tribal life, with its raids, shifting alliances and intermittent pursuit of richer or less godly tribes beyond the borders of the state. Using forces made up of tribal segments that were not affiliated to the Ikhwan, ʿAbd al-ʿAziz defeated the rebels at Sibilla. Faysal Darwish, the chief of the Mutayr and greatest of the Ikhwan leaders, surrendered to the British in Kuwait, was returned to his King and imprisoned.

Two years after the rebellion, in 1932, ʿAbd al-ʿAziz consolidated his territories into the Kingdom of Saudi Arabia. In 1934 he finished his territorial acquisitions with a brief war against Yemen which was won by his son Faysal. This confirmed his control of ʿAsir, Najran and Jizan, which the Ikhwan had seized in 1924.

Discovery of oil

The 1930s, which were uneventful years in the political sense, saw the beginnings of the development of Saudi Arabia's oil. A concession agreement with Standard Oil of California was signed in 1933, and in 1938 commercial quantities of oil were discovered in the famous 'Dammam No 7' well. During the early 1940s the exploration teams discovered the Abqayq field, which was bigger than any field ever found in the USA. Coming at a time when America realized that it was about to change from being an exporter to an importer of oil, Abqayq and other big discoveries stimulated considerable American interest in the Kingdom. Lend-lease aid was granted towards the end of the Second World War and scarce steel was made available for the construction of pipelines and a refinery. In 1945 Saudi oil production began in earnest. Standard of California (now known as Chevron), which had joined with Texaco in all its overseas operations in 1936, sold shares in its concession to Standard of New Jersey (now Exon) and Mobil in 1948, creating the Arabian American Oil Company, ARAMCO.

A few months before the end of the Second World War King ʿAbd al-ʿAziz met both President Roosevelt and Winston Churchill in Egypt, one on a destroyer in the Great Bitter Lakes, the other on dry land. In both meetings he was concerned mainly with preventing the creation of the state of Israel, and the leaders of the two powers were talking to him because he was the foremost Arab leader and the head of the only truly independent Arab state (apart from Yemen). They hoped he would use his influence to moderate the Arab position on Palestine. What is significant is not what came out of the meetings, which was little, but that they took place. Because the Kingdom has never played a noisy role in Arab politics it is often forgotten that it has always been able to deal independently with the great powers. The Saudis have none of the social and political complexes that are associated with the peoples of countries that were once colonies and they have no inherited colonial structure of government. The fact that they seem to view the world differently from everyone else and run their affairs in a very individualistic fashion is a reflection of their independent past.

History since the Second World War

King Saʿud

King ʿAbd al-ʿAziz died in 1953 and was succeeded by Saʿud, the eldest of his surviving sons. Saʿud was a generous and well-meaning man, but he was weak, found difficulty in applying himself to the tasks of government and had no understanding of the modern world. The waste, confusion and corruption that had marked the last years of his father's reign continued under Saʿud. Both men viewed money in the manner of a tribal chief: when they had it they gave it away without stint, believing that to save it would be mean and dishonourable. They had no conception of spending in an organized fashion.

The two major projects carried out in the early 1950s were Tapline, the oil pipe that was built to the Mediterranean to supply oil for the reconstruction of Europe, and the Riyadh–Dammam railway. Both of these were built under the supervision of ARAMCO. The principal project of King Saʿud's reign, and his most obvious monument, was the original set of ministry buildings in Riyadh. It was only with Saʿud's accession that Saudi government was made into a more or less modern shape, with the appointment of a Council of Ministers to replace the small group of a single minister, ʿAbd Allah Sulayman who controlled the exchequer, and a team of 'secretaries' and ambassadors, which had served King ʿAbd al-ʿAziz.

Crisis of 1958–64

In due course the disorganization of Saʿud's administration brought the Kingdom to the verge of bankruptcy. The riyal was devalued and the government had to borrow from the International Monetary Fund – a humiliating experience which has caused it to eschew borrowing ever since. Prince Faysal, the next in line to the throne, was appointed finance minister in 1958 and with surprising speed restored both the budget and balance of payments to order. Impressed by the apparent simplicity of the exercise, Saʿud again took control of the Kingdom's revenues and again brought financial chaos. His maladministration was made more dangerous by the fact that this was the era in which the influence of Jamal Abd al-Nasir (Nasser*), the president of Egypt, and republican and nationalist ideas were at their strongest. Cairo beamed propaganda at Saudi Arabia daily and on one occasion parachuted arms to imagined rebels in the mountains north of Jidda. A few of Saʿud's younger brothers formed themselves into a group called the Free Princes to press for radical reform, and one of them, Talal, went to Lebanon and Egypt and declared himself to be a republican. He was joined by two of his brothers. There were cases of Saudi air-force officers defecting to Egypt. In 1963 the Kingdom's situation was made yet more precarious by the outbreak of the Yemeni civil war, which involved Egypt sending troops to help the republicans and Saudi Arabia giving financial support to the royalists.

It was widely thought outside the Kingdom in the years from 1958 to 1964 that the Saudi monarchy was doomed. In 1962, however, Saʿud was prevailed upon by his family to bring Prince Faysal back into the government as prime minister. At this time Faysal appointed his brothers Fahd minister of the interior; ʿAbd Allah, commander of the National Guard; Sultan, minister of defence and aviation; and Salman, governor of the province of Riyadh. These men have remained at the centre of the Kingdom's government – the last three of them occupying the same positions – ever since.

Saʿud remained King for a further two years, which were marked by a power struggle between him and Faysal and agonized debates within the royal family. Finally, in 1964, he was persuaded to go into voluntary exile. He died in Athens in 1969.

King Faysal

The new King, Faysal, had far more experience of the modern world and countries outside Arabia than either his father or his elder brother. He had been to Europe and America on several occasions, starting with an official visit to Britain in 1919, when he was fourteen. As King he had a definite view of how his country should develop: he wanted slowly to modernize it in the physical and intellectual sense while seeing that it retained its traditional social and religious values. This has been the guiding philosophy of Saudi government ever since. It explains many of the inconsistencies and illogicalities that so much frustrate foreigners in the Kingdom, as well as the 'two steps forward, one step back' approach to social change that marked the reigns of King Faysal and King Khalid. Given that Saudi Arabia remains an extraordinarily conservative and religious society and that the family unit is as strong as ever, the policy must be counted a remarkable success.

King Faysal with the British publisher Robert Maxwell

King Faysal was austere, upright and strict. He had an obsession with communism and was inclined to think that any opposition must be subversive. Many of those who incurred his displeasure were thrown into prison. Under his rule, however, Saudi Arabia changed from seeming to be on the brink of revolution to being as stable as any country in the Middle East. The Yemeni civil war became gradually less of a threat, though the Egyptian air force bombed the oasis of Najran, and in 1967, after the disastrous Egyptian defeat at the hands of Israel, the Saudi government paid for the repatriation of the Egyptian forces in Yemen. The Egyptian defeat, the subsidies which the Kingdom and the other Gulf oil producers paid to the front-line states from 1967 onwards and the more conservative climate of Arab politics from the early 1970s took away the radical threat that had been so dangerous a decade earlier.

During his reign King Faysal began the development of a modern infrastructure, a health service and an educational system. He introduced television and education for girls, both innovations which provoked violent protests. The Kingdom's development prospects were improved hugely towards the end of his reign by the increases in the price of oil. After some relatively small rises in 1970–2, the first for well over a decade, the price multiplied four times in the autumn of 1973. The second of the two big price rises of this period was caused by the shortage that followed the use of the oil weapon, a combination of production cuts and an embargo on the export of Arab oil to the United States that was intended to force American policy in the Middle East to be less slanted to the Israeli cause. The fact that the weapon could be used effectively was due entirely to King Faysal's exasperation with the lack of American response to Arab warnings and his conversion during the course of 1973 to the idea that oil could be used as a political weapon. After production had been restored to normal in the early spring of 1974, a further large increase in revenue came about in the course of the next two years from the gradual takeover of ARAMCO by the state and huge increases in the volume of Saudi production.

King Khalid

King Faysal's reign ended on 25 March 1975, when a deranged nephew shot him in revenge for the death of his brother, a religious zealot, in the riots that had accompanied the introduction of television ten years earlier. The succession passed smoothly to the Crown Prince, Khalid bin ʿAbd al-ʿAziz, a sensible, devout man of unselfconscious piety; he carried with him a pocket Qur'an, to which he referred often. It was expected at the time of his accession that King Khalid would play little active role in government. His relatively modern-minded brother, Fahd, who became Crown Prince, moved from being minister of the interior to first deputy prime minister, and a highly able technocrat Cabinet (known in the Kingdom as the Ph.Ds' Cabinet) was appointed to support him. But in practice, although it was Fahd who masterminded the vast development push that began in 1975, Khalid took an active interest in what was happening and approved, or occasionally annulled, major decisions. He was very much more liberal with dissenters than his brother Faysal had been – during his reign the Saudi prisons were emptied of their not very great number of political prisoners. Also in 1981 and 1982 Khalid was responsible for the reinstatement of the reputation of King Sa'ud, who for seventeen years had been a 'non-person', a character who was never mentioned in any official speech or publication. The new dictum was that Sa'ud had been good but misguided; Riyadh University was renamed King Sa'ud University and the former King's portrait began to appear alongside the other monarchs' portraits in government offices.

King Khalid's reign was a period of extraordinary prosperity, in which the non-oil gross national product grew by up to 30 per cent a year. It saw some notable episodes of waste and greed, but was much more remarkable for a series of enormous projects and some monumental triumphs of organization. Three years before Khalid's accession there had been no telexes in the Kingdom outside the government, ARAMCO and the Saudi Arabian Monetary Agency; the road network in 1975 was patchy, there was only one top-class international hotel and the telephone system was small and inefficient. By the end of his reign Saudi Arabia had multiplied its capacity in all of these facilities many times. It had solved the biggest port bottlenecks ever seen – at times there had been over a hundred ships waiting to unload at Jidda. In the space of three years – 1976–9 – it had changed its internal air transport system from near chaos to well-organized routine. With the help of the nationalized ARAMCO it had virtually completed the master gas system in the Eastern Province, which was said to be the most expensive project ever undertaken anywhere.

With only one exception (1978) in every year of King Khalid's reign the Kingdom earned a large budget surplus which was invested by SAMA abroad. Its surplus was greatly increased in 1979–80 by the second oil-price explosion, caused by the revolution in Iran. In 1981, which stands as a record year, the government's oil revenues ran to $113bn, from crude exports of 9.1m barrels a day.

The major disturbance of the reign was the uprising in November 1979 of Juhayman Muhammad al-'Utaybi, a religious zealot who led an occupation of the Grand Mosque in Mecca on the eve of the Muslim New Year of 1400. It took the authorities an embarrassingly long time to flush Juhayman's followers out of the labyrinthine cellars and passages of the mosque and, at the time, given the recent revolution in Iran and the oubreak of rioting in Qatif that occurred while the battle of the mosque was still in progress, it was thought that the uprising might be the forerunner of many violent outbreaks. But soon afterwards thoughtful Saudis were saying that the appearance of strange holy men was an episodic phenomenon in Muslim societies and that the uprising should be seen in this context. Judging from the peace that has prevailed in the Kingdom since it seems that their interpretation was right.

King Khalid died of a heart attack in June 1982 and was succeeded by the Crown Prince, Fahd. Almost from the moment Fahd came to power there began to be signs of a recession, caused by a rapid fall in demand for OPEC oil, the brunt of which was borne by Saudi Arabia. While King Khalid ruled in what has since seemed a rich, confident golden age, King Fahd has had the misfortune to preside over a much poorer Kingdom in an increasingly violent Middle East.

Politics and society today

At the beginning of his reign King Fahd spoke on several occasions about three major political changes which he said were to be introduced in the near future. They were: a Majlis al-Shura, an appointed consultative assembly; a statute of government, which would be a secular constitution supplementing *shari'a* law, which is the country's official constitution; and a reorganization of the government of the fourteen provinces, involving the governors being given greater authority over the development of their territories; and, possibly, a reorganization of provincial boundaries. In a typically Saudi way there has been some *de facto* change in the economic role of the provincial governors – without anything being said about it – but on the other matters there has been no movement at all. One reason has been the innate conservatism of the royal family, another that in troubled times King Fahd has not wanted to introduce radical reforms.

The Sa'ud family

Officially there are no politics in Saudi Arabia. There are no political parties or trade unions and there is no organized opposition or political debate; the very concepts are most un-Saudi and would be irrelevant in the Kingdom. The country is ruled by the King and the most senior and/or able members of the Sa'ud family. The most important of these form a group known as the Al Fahd (the family of Fahd), which is made up of the King's full brothers and sisters with their spouses and children. The King's brothers, the offspring of King 'Abd al-'Aziz and Hassa bint Ahmad Sudayri – a wife whom the great King married twice – are well-educated, by the standards of Saudi Arabia before the 1960s, and able. In order of age they are: Sultan, the minister of defence and aviation and second in line of succession, 'Abd al-Rahman, the deputy minister of defence, Na'if, the minister of the interior, Turki, the former deputy minister of defence, Salman, the governor of the province of Riyadh and Ahmad, the deputy minister of the interior. Members of the younger generation include the governor and deputy governor of the Eastern Province, Muhammad ibn Fahd and Fahd ibn Salman; the deputy head of external intelligence, Sa'ud ibn Fahd; the Arab world's first astronaut, Sultan ibn Salman; the president of the Organization of Youth Welfare, Faysal ibn Fahd; the Saudi ambassador in Washington, Bandar ibn Sultan; and the head of the Royal Commission for Jubayl and Yanbu, 'Abd Allah ibn Faysal ibn Turki, a son of one of the King's sisters.

Two other prominent families in government are the Al al-Shaykh, the descendants of Muhammad ibn 'Abd al-Wahhab, who have in their ranks three ministers and numerous members of the judiciary, and the Sudayris, who are longstanding allies of the Sa'uds, coming originally from the Dawasir tribe. The Sudayris govern several of the frontier or near frontier provinces – Najran and Jizan in the south and Juf and Qurayyat in the north – and one of their number, Turki ibn Khalid, is the minister in charge of the civil service.

'Ulama

The royal family is influenced in its policies by the members of the religious establishment, the *'ulama*, who make their views felt in meetings with the royal family and in their sermons – though if their comments and criticisms become too strident they are prevented from preaching. In answer to those who argue that there should be reform in Saudi Arabia, for example through the government allowing a freer press and letting women work or drive cars, members of the royal family argue that they cannot act because the *'ulama* would object. It is said that they would be shocked by what they might read in the papers and by the danger that the granting of unnecessary rights to women would pose for the family, and they would rouse the people against the reforms in their sermons. Cynics outside the Al Sa'ud say that the *'ulama* are beholden to the royal family financially and are closely supervised by it, and that the reason for the lack of change is the Sa'uds' own conservatism.

What nobody denies is that the government is concerned about the challenge of populist Islam, which has its adherents as much outside the ranks of the *'ulama* as within them. (Throughout the Arab world a distinction has to be made between the official Islam of the religious establishments and the new populist or fundamentalist Islam, which seeks to reorganize society on religious lines.) The upsurge of populist Islam must be a relatively small threat to the state in a rich, yet austere and conformist society such as Saudi Arabia, but it has nevertheless prompted the government to build more mosques and increase the amount of religious instruction in schools. King Fahd, whose speeches are full of references to Islam, announced in 1986 that he was to be known as the Custodian of the Two Holy Harams, Mecca and Medina.

A further influence on the policies of the government is the business community, which has regular contact with ministers, many of whom come from the big merchant families. There are also numerous princes in business, many of them in joint ventures with people from outside the royal family, and these royal entrepreneurs lobby more senior princes on their own behalf, and indirectly on behalf of the business community as a whole. In recent years there have been three formal meetings of businessmen and ministers, including senior princes: at Dammam in 1984, Riyadh in 1985 and Abha, the capital of 'Asir, in 1987.

Majlis

Ordinary Saudis have access to the royal family through the *majlis* (council chambers) of its members. All of the provincial governors, the minister of the interior and his deputy – Prince Na'if and Prince Ahmad, Crown Prince 'Abd Allah and Prince Sultan – receive up to two or three hundred of their subjects every day. The King receives people less regularly and after a filtering process, and the less important princes receive visitors in small numbers – the people who come to them are those who consider that they have some special connection that makes the prince worth petitioning.

People come to the *majlis* because they want the princes' help in arbitrating disputes or dealing with the bureaucracy. Or they may want financial help, which might be for a daughter's dowry or a trip to London for medical treatment. Medical treatment abroad can be arranged, where necessary, by the Ministry of Health, which will always pay for the patient to be accompanied by a member of his or her family, but many of the simple Najdi constituents of the royal family dislike dealing with the foreign or Hijazi officials in the bureaucracy and prefer to take their case to a prince. (The prince may also be less strict than the Ministry in deciding which illnesses do not warrant treatment abroad.)

Many visitors to *majlis*, especially in the provinces, go simply because they want to join in the general conversation, hear other people's news and eat a good meal.

The bourgeoisie

The system of *majlis* works very well for the lower strata of Saudi society but it is not relevant to the Saudi middle class, which is growing bigger every year as more people come out of secondary and university education. The bourgeoisie does not need to petition – and the idea itself is embarrassing to it. Nor are professionals and businessmen interested simply in joining general discussions, which might verge on politics. Inasmuch as they would like a say in the way the Kingdom is governed they would like to have it through some sort of democratic institution, which would allow serious debate and might have some limited authority.

But it should not be thought that there is any clamour for democracy in Saudi Arabia; many middle-class families, who have been slightly shaken by the way their lives have been transformed since 1973, are now less certain about the desirability of change than they were five years ago. The interest in political innovation is moderated by the extraordinary conformism of Saudi society – young Saudis who appear quite radical when studying abroad seem happily to accept the traditional pattern of family life when they return home. The climate of conservatism is deepened by the fact that most articulate Saudis come from families that are very well off.

The economy today

For ten years after the oil-price explosion of 1973 Saudi Arabia's economic development was guided, very roughly, by the Second and Third Plans. These amounted to little more than general statements of objectives followed by enormous lists of projects. The lists were greatly altered and expanded as the plans proceeded; sometimes allocations for particular types of projects were increased in the middle of the budget year. On other occasions administrative delays and physical bottlenecks prevented the government from spending as much as it intended.

The Second Plan

The Second Plan, which ran from 1975 to 1980 and budgeted expenditure (current and capital) at $149 billion, concentrated on the development of the Kingdom's physical infrastructure – ports, airports (there are now twenty-five in the country), telecommunications, power stations, roads, desalination plants, the national airline (Saudia), schools and hospitals. It also provided for the construction

The 'City Center' building, Jidda

of basic facilities – including huge ports and desalination plants – at two entirely new industrial cities, Jubayl and Yanbu', and established a Royal Commission to oversee the work. ARAMCO in the same period oversaw the construction of the Master Gas System, which cost over $10bn, a unified electricity grid in the Eastern Province and an enormous expansion of the Kingdom's oil-production capacity, which by 1980 was about 12m barrels a day. Huge sums were lent interest-free for the construction of housing, apartment blocks and offices by the Real Estate Development Fund. A similar institution, the Saudi Industrial Development Fund, lent at the rate of 2 per cent to the private sector for the construction of light industrial plants. The response of Saudi businessmen to this opportunity was much greater than had been expected, though the plants they built were almost all quite simple. Most of them manufactured building materials.

The Third Plan

The Third Plan, which ran from 1980 to 1985, continued and largely finished the Kingdom's infrastructural development. It saw the construction of two huge new airports at Riyadh and Jidda and a big expansion in the number of state hospitals. The new feature of the plan was the creation of petrochemical and refining industries at Jubayl and Yanbu' – in all about a dozen plants were built at a cost of roughly $1bn each. The most extraordinary development during the plan was the rapid expansion of Saudi agriculture, assisted by subsidies and interest-free loans from the Saudi Arabian Agricultural Bank and a government policy of buying wheat through the Grain Silos and Flour Mills Organization for $1,000 a tonne, about six times the world price. From the time work on the Plan started it was decided that there should be some emphasis on the development of the provinces and agricultural incentives were part of this design, but nobody expected the response that came from the private sector. By 1985 Saudi Arabia was producing more wheat than it could consume, and production has not decreased since in response to the government almost halving its purchase price. The Kingdom has also become self-sufficient in chickens and eggs, and it produces most of the fresh milk that it needs. The latest area of expansion is in fruit and vegetables. In the province of Qasim and around the oasis of Kharj, south of Riyadh, agriculture is by far the most conspicuous economic activity.

Recession

Since the Third Plan ended, in March 1985, the Saudi economy has been badly affected by recession. It was in the summer of 1985 that oil exports sank to little more than 1m b/d, a level not seen since the early 1960s. This prompted the government to start concluding net-back deals, which tied its receipts to the amount its customers received for their products in the market, and it was this, in turn, which led to the halving of oil prices at the beginning of 1986. Saudi government revenues from all sources, including foreign investments, sales of liquified gas and tariffs in 1986 were about a third of what they were at their peak in 1981.

This drop in income has made the Fourth Plan, which was never properly published, a mainly irrelevant document. The original intention was that it should encompass current and development spending of a trillion (million million) riyals (about $280 billion) to be divided between five annual budgets of 200bn riyals each – figures which give a good indication of the very generalized nature of Saudi planning. The emphasis of the Plan, which still gives a guide to current Saudi policies, was to be on developing Saudi manpower and encouraging the private sector to take up the running in the Kingdom's industrial development – in particular by building intermediate industrial plants downstream from the basic industries at Jubayl and Yanbu'.

The most direct effect of the decline in government revenues has been felt by the construction industry, which would have entered a period of decline even without the recession because by 1983 most of the big projects that could be built in the Kingdom had been built. Many small contractors have ceased operating and a few bigger ones have gone bankrupt or, in the case of foreign firms, left the Kingdom. Suppliers of construction equipment have found themselves with unsaleable stock in their warehouses, and more than a million labourers, out of a foreign workforce that was about three million in 1983, may have gone home. Rents have fallen by at least a half and land has become almost unsaleable. Even though the government, partly for political reasons, has largely maintained its spending on subsidies (on gasoline, electricity, water and basic foodstuffs), and has made fairly minor reductions in the salaries of its employees, the effects of the fall in project spending are felt in all parts of the economy. For example, the fact that there are a million fewer mouths to feed – equivalent to a drop of 10 per cent in the population – has entailed smaller turnovers for foodstuffs importers and the bankruptcy of many small supermarkets.

One of the most serious effects of the recession has been a banking crisis caused by the inability of contractors and other businesses to earn sufficient income to service their loans and their reluctance to repay them from capital held abroad. During 1985 and most of 1986 the banks found themselves virtually unable to pursue their debts because of the Saudi courts' refusal to acknowlege the legality of interest payments and their consequent habit of deducting both interest due and interest already paid from whatever sums the banks claimed were owed to them. In late 1986 and early 1987 there were signs that the courts were slightly modifying this position and the government at the beginning of 1987 announced that it was going to take banking disputes out of the jurisdiction of the *shari'a* courts at least in the first instance and put them under the authority of a central bank committee.

The principal benefits of the recession, apart from a slowing of the rate of social change, have been a big decline in industrial construction and operating costs, which should make more, and more sophisticated, industries competitive in Saudi Arabia, and a change in young Saudis' expectations. Whereas during the boom years people had very high income expectations and were not prepared to do skilled manual and clerical jobs, there are now many applicants for this type of work. Unskilled labour, though, remains totally unacceptable to Saudis.

In spite of these changes, which augur well for the development of Saudi Arabia as a partly diversified industrial and service economy in the future, Saudi Arabia remains for the time being an economy that is driven by government spending. Private sector companies, apart from the banks and importers of consumer goods, do little business with other private sector institutions. They look to the government for their livelihood, and they watch the oil market for signs that the government's fortunes are going to improve. It is an article of faith among Saudis, in government and in business, that in the early 1990s the oil market will turn decisively upwards, mainly because by that time production from virtually all sources of oil outside the Gulf will be declining. Then Saudi Arabia, with proven reserves of some 160 billion barrels, equivalent to a quarter of the proven reserves of the whole world in the mid-1980s, will once again enjoy all the income it could hope for, though whether this will assist or hinder the development of the diversified economy it wants is an open question.

MF

Further reading

M. Field, *The Merchants* (London, 1984)
D. Holden and R. Johns, *The House of Saud* (London, 1982)
R. Lacey, *The Kingdom* (London, 1982)
D. Long, *Saudi Arabia* (Washington, 1976)
T. Mostyn, *Saudi Arabia: a MEED Practical Guide* (London, 1983)
W. Quandt, *Saudi Arabia in the Nineteen Eighties: foreign policy, security and oil* (Washington, 1981)

Somalia

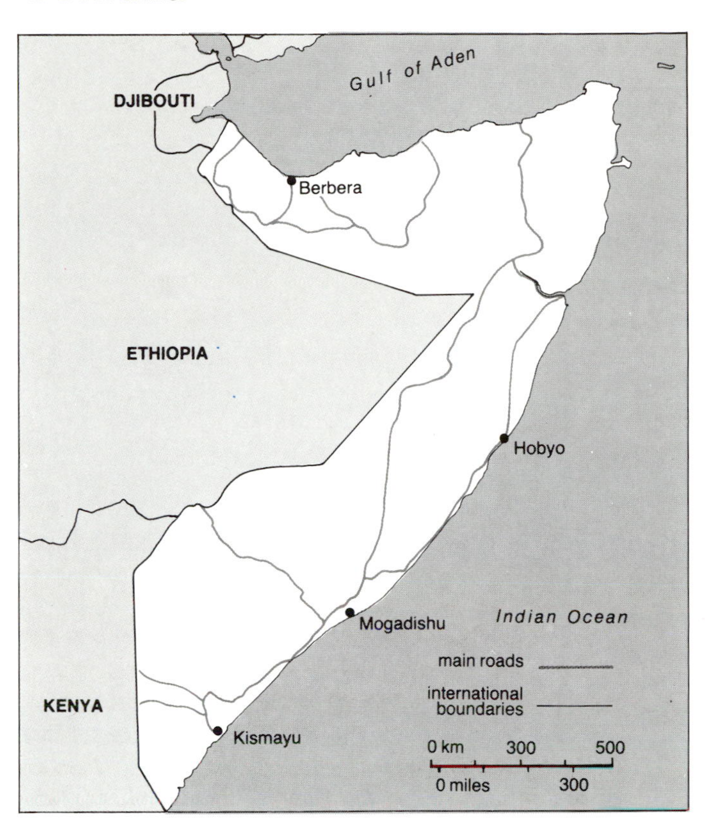

Official title	Somali Democratic Republic
Area	637,657 sq. km
Population	5.8 million (1985) (official census count)
Government and constitution	Executive power is with the President who is elected every seven years. The only legal political party is the Somali Revolutionary Socialist Party (SRSP), founded in 1976
Currency	1 Somali shilling (So. sh.) = 100 centesimi; US $1 = So.sh. 99 (Dec 1987)
Language	Somali, a language of the Cushitic group. Arabic is also widely spoken
Religion	Almost all Somalis are Sunni Muslims
Climate	Semi-arid in the south and north, to arid in the central rangelands. Rainfall is bimodal, with an annual mean of from 200 to 500mm.

Geography and topography

Forming the Horn of Africa, Somalia has a coastline with the Gulf of Aden to the north and with the Indian Ocean to the east and south. Ethiopia lies to the west, Djibouti to the north-west and Kenya to the south-west. Somalia's landscape is mainly of rolling bushland, rising in altitude from the Indian Ocean coast towards the west. In the north a range of largely treeless mountains rising to over 2400m lies parallel to the Gulf of Aden coast. The economy of Somalia was traditionally pastoral but agricultural development is expanding, primarily in the south, and especially through irrigation from the only two perennial rivers, the Jubba and the Shabeelle, both of which rise in the highlands of Ethiopia.

Peoples

Many ethnic Somalis live outside the borders of the Somali Democratic Republic. As much as 10 per cent of the population of the Republic consists of refugees from strife over political demarcations. The most recent population estimate for the capital, Mogadishu (Muqdisho), was 500,000. Other principal towns are Hargeisa and Kismayu with populations of over 70,000 and Berbera with a population of 65,000. Somalia's total population in 1986 was officially estimated at 5.69 milion, though other estimates have ranged up to 8 million. In addition, however, some 2 million Somalis live in the Ogaden region of Ethiopia, 500,000 in northern Kenya, 100,000 in Djibouti and several thousands in the Arabian peninsula (see Languages and Peoples).

Religion

Mogadishu appears to have been an Arab trading post since before the tenth century AD. Almost all Somalis are Sunni Muslims, the religion having been introduced into the north of Somalia during the early expansion of Islam.

History up to 1939

Between the seventh and twelfth centuries Muslim traders established trading posts along the Somali coast, fought the Christian Ethiopians of the interior and organized themselves into Muslim Sultanates. From ports such as Mogadishu and Berbera they exported slaves, ostrich feathers and valuable gums. Between the tenth and fifteenth centuries the nomadic Somalis themselves adopted Islam and fought for the various Sultanates, spreading Somali dominion south as far as present-day Kenya.

From the turn of the twentieth century Somalis fought colonial wars with the British, the Ethiopians and the Italians. Principally in order to defend its trade route to Aden, Britain had established a protectorate over the northern regions of Somalia in 1886, while France extended its dominion in the region by control of the Afars and Issas, now Djibouti*. In order to prevent France from extending its foothold, Britain encouraged the Italians to establish a colony in southern Somalia. From Italian Somaliland, the Italians were to conquer Ethiopia in 1936, and occupied British Somaliland during 1940–1. However, after the defeat of Italian forces in the region, both Somalilands were placed under British military administration up to 1950. It was during the war, in 1943, that the Somali Youth League (SYL) was founded, which was soon to become the country's most important nationalist party.

History since the Second World War

After the Second World War the Italians returned to Somalia under a United Nations mandate to prepare the country for independence in 1960. The British protectorate had already reverted to civilian rule and, following negotiations with both Italy and Britain, a united Somalia achieved full independence on 1 July 1960. The SYL joined with the two major parties of the north to form the new Somali Republic and the prinicipal Somali clans united under the government of the new prime minister, Dr Abdirashi Ali Shirmarke of the Darod clan.

Differences of outlook between the British and Italian regions were somewhat offset by a common Somali identity as well as by united support by all the clans for irredentist claims in neighbouring countries such as Kenya and Ethiopia, where large numbers of ethnic Somalis lived. In the first elections since independence, in 1964, the SYL won most of the seats in the new National Assembly. However, internal problems came once again to the fore after the government agreed to drop its claims on Somali communities in neighbouring countries.

In the 1969 election the SYL won a landslide victory but in October of that year President Muhammad Haji Ibrahim Egal was assassinated and a week later the army seized control of the country in a bloodless coup. The new head of state was the president of the newly formed Supreme Revolutionary Council, Maj.-Gen. Muhammad Siad Barre. Barre's policies have been based on a form of 'scientific socialism' adapted to local conditions but he has stressed that the principles of Islam and of socialism are the same. In 1974 Somalia was elected a member of the Arab League.

In mid-1977 the Western Somali Liberation Front (WSLF), aimed at 'liberating' the largely Somali-inhabited Ogaden region of Ethiopia, was formed with apparent Somali military support. Backed also by various guerrilla groups, the WSLF managed to drive the Ethiopians out of the region and by November had surrounded the Ethiopian city of Harar. In that month Somalia cancelled its treaty of friendship with the USSR and broke off diplomatic relations with Cuba; but promises of support from the West were half-hearted while with Cuban and Soviet support Ethiopia managed in 1978 to take back most of the region captured. Since then periods of fierce border fighting between the countries have taken place, particularly in 1982 and 1984. Relations with countries such as Kenya have, however, considerably improved. Despite a car accident in May 1986 in which he was seriously injured, Barre appears to have retained army support and to have remained in firm control of the country.

The economy and society today

Somalia's principal exports are of live animals, skins, clarified butter and canned meat and bananas, although the livestock sector, which traditionally represents 80 per cent of export trade, and the production of bananas was severely hit by the drought of the mid-1970s. Since 1972 emphasis has been placed on fishing, an industry originally set up with Soviet assistance to diversify away from drought-threatened cultivation. Somalia has had to look to the International Monetary Fund for various standby loans; negotiations for a new loan in 1984 broke down because of the government's reluctance to devalue the Somali shilling.

Shortly after the revolution which brought Siad Barre to power, the Somali language, written in Roman rather than Arabic characters, was adopted in place of English, Arabic or Italian as the country's official language. Meanwhile the government's rural development campaign virtually coincided with the drought of 1972 in which at least 18,000 people died. With the help of a Soviet airlift, some 140,000 people were relocated mainly in farming settlements of the south. The Ogaden War of 1978 saw the creation of a severe refugee problem. Today some 750,000 refugees are estimated to be housed in nearly 40 Somali refugee camps.

The Somalis are principally nomadic herdsmen who, because of competition for vital resources, tend to be individualistic and to indulge in intertribal feuds. The townspeople of the coast, for long exposed to Islamic traditions and contacts with foreign traders, are highly organized orthodox Muslims who have traditionally played the role of middlemen between the Arab world and the nomads of the interior. The traditional basis of Somali society is the *rer*, a large self-contained kinship group which consists of several families claiming a common descent from a male ancestor. The system is patriarchal with the *rer* dominated by a chief chosen by a group of elders.

TM

Further reading

M. Ayoob, *The Horn of Africa: regional conflict and super-power involvement* (Canberra, 1978)
P. Contini, *The Somali Republic: an experiment in legal integration* (1969)
I. M. Lewis, *Modern History of Somalia: nation and state in the Horn of Africa* (London)

Sudan

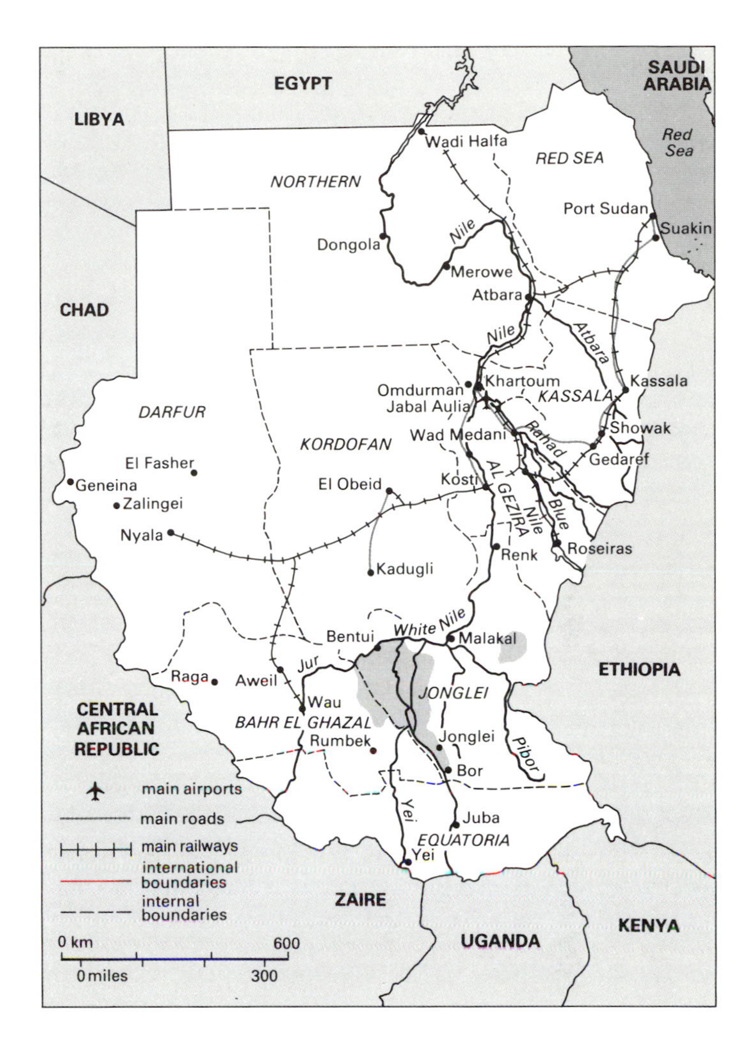

Geography and topography

Sudan is the largest country in Africa and the ninth largest in the world. It stretches more than 2000 km from the northern deserts of Upper Egypt to the equatorial forests of Uganda and Zaire. From east to west it spans 1760 km at its widest point. Sudan is as large as the United States east of the Mississippi River, and is larger than the combined area of the twelve EEC nations.

Within its vast area Sudan has considerable physical and climatic variety. There are tropical forests, swamplands, savannah scrublands and mountain ranges, as well as large tracts of partial and total desert. The country can be described as an amphitheatre, since it is surrounded to the south, east and west by mountain ranges. The waters of the Ethiopian Plateau and the Nile–Congo watershed collect on the broad Sudanese flood-plain and then flow north

Official title	The Republic of Sudan
Area	2,505,813 sq. km
Population	21.55 million (mid-1985 estimate)
Government and constitutiion	A transitional constitution was approved in October 1985 following the 6 April 1985 coup and the constitution of April 1973 was suspended
Currency	1 Sudanese pound = 100 piastres; US $1 = £S 2.50
Languages	The official language, spoken by about 60 per cent of the population, is Arabic but English is the lingua franca of the south. Some 115 languages, mostly in the south, are spoken, 26 of them by more than 100,000 people
Religions	70 per cent of the population is Muslim, 26 per cent Animist and 4 per cent Christian. The north is essentially Muslim and the south essentially Animist/Christian
Climate	The north has high average temperatures ranging from 35°C in summer to 20°C in winter, and little rainfall. Annual rainfall ranges from 25 mm in the northern desert area to 1200 mm in the Equatorial south. The principal feature of the southern climate is the northwards movement of the inter-tropical rain belt during the summer and its retreat during the autumn

towards Egypt. The White and Blue Nile Rivers converge at Khartoum and continue their journey to the Mediterranean as the River Nile.

Peoples

Sudan's peoples are as diverse as the country's physical characteristics. There are 19 major ethnic groups and a further 597 subgroups. The Arabs form the largest group and represent about 60 per cent of the total, followed by the Dinka (12 per cent), Beja (7 per cent), and groups of West African origin (6 per cent). The Southern Region, which is a partially self-governing African area, contains about 25 per cent of the total population. For centuries there has been interbreeding in Sudan between the predominantly Arab northerners and the negroid African southerners. There are very few areas and tribes that have been unaffected by this, although ethnic and tribal divisions remain important obstacles to national unity.

Two of the most important features of Sudan's demography are the great variations in population density and its mobility. Although no exact figures are available, it is estimated that the population totals about 21.5m with an annual growth rate of 2.8 per cent. The average population density is about 8.8 per km^2, although this varies substantially from the sparsely populated desert areas to the demographic and agricultural heartland to the south of Khartoum. Following rapid rural–urban migration in recent years, the capital, which incorporates the 'Three Towns' of Khartoum, Khartoum North and Omdurman, now has a population of 1.5m–2.0m.

The Sudanese population is highly mobile. Almost 2.2m people, or 10 per cent of the population, are still entirely nomadic. In addition, almost a million herdsmen practise transhumance, following the northward movement of the summer rains in search of new pastures. Besides increasing rural–urban migration, there are also about 500,000 seasonal workers who migrate between the major irrigated agricultural schemes. During the past decade there have also been increasing numbers of refugees from Ethiopia, Chad and Uganda, who cross the frontiers at will depending on the conditions in their own country. As a result of the recent catastrophic drought and famine, the number of refugees still total over 1m.

Suakin

A Nuba village

Religion

Despite the fact that Islam is Sudan's official religion, only about 70 per cent of the population are Muslims. In the north there are significant pockets of non-Muslims in the Nuba Mountains, the Red Sea Hills and parts of Darfur in western Sudan. Southern Sudan, which contains about a quarter of the national population, is predominantly animist, following a wide variety of tribal religions. Although they are politically influential because of their missionary education, Christians only make up about 15 per cent of the southern population, or 4 per cent of the national total.

History up to 1939

Although there were a number of historically important regional civilizations such as Meroe, which is believed to be the cradle of iron-working in Africa, and Kush, Sudan did not exist as a single entity until the end of the nineteenth century. Even following the Egyptian conquest in 1822 and during the Mahdiyya between 1885 and 1898, large areas of current-day southern Sudan were outside central control. For centuries Sudan exported gold, exotic products and, above all, slaves. The ancient Egyptians, Greeks, Romans, Ottoman Turks and their Egyptian Khedives all recognized central and southern Sudan as an important source of slaves.

In 1820 Muhammad ʿAli* of Egypt decided to invade the region, and within two years most of northern and central Sudan was overcome. Khartoum was developed as the military and administrative capital of Turco-Egyptian Sudan. One of the principal attractions of the region to Egypt was as a source of gold, slaves and mainly press-ganged soldiers for its new professional army.

During the nineteenth century, southern Sudan was 'opened up', first by slavers and then by European missionaries. This process was curtailed when a Sudanese rebellion against the Turco-Egyptian administration, led by the Mahdi, finally triumphed when General Gordon was killed at the siege of Khartoum in 1884. The Mahdist state was finally defeated in 1898 at the battle of Omdurman, and was replaced by the Anglo-Egyptian Condominium which continued until independence.

Although the British-dominated administration was both efficient and well-intentioned, its policy towards southern Sudan was, in hindsight, very damaging to Sudanese national unity. It was decided in 1922 that the south should eventually become part of a federation of East African states. During the next twenty-five years contact between the north and south was discouraged. Northern merchants and Muslim preachers were prohibited from entering the region, the teaching of English was encouraged and of Arabic forbidden. At the same time many of the missionary teachers in southern Sudan revived memories of slavery and kindled a fear and hatred of the Muslim northerners.

History since the Second World War

Even before the war there had been a growing tide of Sudanese nationalism* in the north, including the White Flag League which began in 1923. During the Second World War the Sudan Defence Force fought with the British against the Italians in Ethiopia. From 1945 onwards the future of the Sudan was a matter of dispute between the two partners in the Condominium. Egypt claimed that the Sudan should be united with it under the Egyptian crown, while Britain wanted it to remain separate and eventually to become an independent state. It was not until the Egyptian revolution of 1952 that the impasse was broken. The Egyptian monarchy was ended, and the new republican government made an agreement with the main parties in the northern Sudan, recognizing the right of the country to independent existence. In January 1954 power was officially transferred to Sudanese hands when the first parliament was opened, with Isma'il al-Azhari as the country's first prime minister. Following a transitional period, Sudan achieved full independence on 1 January 1956.

During the period between the end of the Second World War and independence in 1956, the policy of separating northern and southern Sudan was therefore reversed. The British authorities tried to integrate the southern provinces with the rest of Sudan. By the time of independence in 1956 this had not been entirely successful, and there was still considerable antagonism between them. The southerners were scared of Muslim domination and the northerners despised the non-Muslim southerners, adopting a racialist attitude towards them.

During the transitional period between January 1954 and independence in January 1956 the south was largely ignored in the drive towards Sudanization. Resentment was fuelled by the fact that no southerner was taken into the civil service, and northerners replaced the British officers in charge of the army units in the south.

Just before independence in August 1955, the Torit garrison's soldiers mutinied after being ordered to Khartoum without their weapons to take part in a military parade. This minor incident was the spark which ignited a civil war which lasted for seventeen years and which resulted directly and indirectly in the deaths of over 500,000 people. Although their methods varied, almost all the governments from independence until 1969 sought to subjugate the south through force. Except for one brief period in 1964, dialogue was never contemplated.

The period from independence until the revolution of May 1969 was dominated by two parties which were, and are now again, the political expressions of two very powerful families and their religious sects or *tariqas*. The Umma Party (the Nation) is the political expression of the Ansar, who are the followers of the Mahdi's descendants. The Mahdi family leads both the Ansar sect and the Umma Party. Sadiq al-Mahdi, who became prime minister in 1986 and had also briefly held office in the mid-1960s, is the great-grandson of the Mahdi. He is now generally recognized as being the political and spiritual leader of the movement, despite previous family disputes and rivalries.

The Khatmiyya sect, which is led by the Mirghani family, has always favoured a closer relationship with Egypt. Consequently its political party was originally known as the National Unionist Party (NUP), and it sought unity with Egypt. The unionists have been far less united than the Umma Party and went through a complicated series of division, coalitions and name changes. The Democratic Unionist Party (DUP) which is in the current coalition government is the dominant wing of the movement.

The 1956–69 period can be broadly divided into four. There were two periods of multi-party democracy between 1956 and 1958 and between 1965 and 1969, in which there were five coalition governments. They were dominated by the Umma Party and National Unionist Party, which respectively owed their support to the powerful Ansar and Khatmiyya Islamic sects. Unfortunately they seemed more concerned with maintaining power than in resolving the civil war and other political and economic problems.

The two periods were separated by six years of military rule between November 1958 and late 1964. This was brought to an end by the widely supported and popular October Revolution, which followed student demonstrations against the military government. The broad-based coalition, which held power between October 1964 and the elections in May 1965, was the only true government of national unity and was the only period in which a political settlement was sought to the civil war.

On 25 May 1969 there was a bloodless junior officers' coup, which was led by Colonel Ja'afar Muhammad al-Numayri (Nimeiri)*. His regime lasted for almost sixteen years until the 1985 April Revolution, which was modelled on the 1964 October Revolution. The Nimeiri era can be broadly divided into three periods: the radical years which lasted until July 1971, the period of general optimism during the 1970s, and the decline into political and economic bankruptcy.

Until an attempted communist coup in July 1971, Nimeiri and his Revolutionary Command Council (RCC) steered Sudan sharply to the left. The traditional parties were purged and there was a major nationalization programme, which led to the withdrawal of expatriate businesses and personnel. Although Nimeiri had promised a political settlement to the civil war when he came to power, it reached its most savage intensity during this period while he attempted to consolidate his position in northern Sudan. Policy differences with his hardline communist supporters eventually led to the attempted coup, which was only foiled with Libya's assistance – a fact that Qadhafi* never forgot.

There was an immediate change in policy direction after the attempted coup. The communists were purged and the new Sudanese Socialist Union (SSU), which was the only legal political party, soon became socialist only in name. Following a referendum in late 1971, Nimeiri was elected president and assumed increasing powers as the RCC diminished in importance.

Having secured his position in northern Sudan, Nimeiri turned his attention to the civil war in the south. Following complex and difficult negotiations with the Anya-Nya guerrilla movement, the Addis Ababa Agreement was signed on 3 March 1972. It created the Southern Region as an autonomous area within a united Sudan. The three southern provinces were to be administered by the regional government, known as the Higher Executive Council, from the southern capital of Juba. The agreement was a monumental achievement for the country as a whole and especially for President

Nimeiri. After seventeen years of war, which had resulted in about 500,000 deaths and had severely hindered political and economic development, an equitable and just political solution had been found. In 1972 it seemed that Sudan could act as a model for other heterogeneous countries in Africa.

Following the peace settlement, Nimeiri turned his attention to the economy. There was an over-ambitious plan to turn Sudan into the 'breadbasket of the Arab world'. By combining Arab finance and Western technology with Sudanese land, water and human resources it was hoped to produce a major food surplus which could be exported to the rest of the Middle East. A wide variety of indigenous and exdogenous factors turned the dream into a nightmare. Sudan became trapped in a spiral of external debt, from which it is now unable to extract itself.

In 1975 and 1976 there were coup attempts, led by exiled Umma and NUP leaders, which very nearly succeeded in overthrowing Nimeiri. Following secret negotiations, a policy of 'national reconciliation' led in 1977 to the return of most of the exiles, who subsequently joined the SSU. One of their preconditions was a greater role for Islam in Sudan, which also coincided with the Islamic revival in the Middle East following the Iranian Revolution. Faced with this new challenge, President Nimeiri became increasingly autocratic, despotic and unpredictable. He played groups and individuals against each other in a very skilful policy of divide and rule.

Despite his previous success in the south, Nimeiri allowed a second civil war to develop. The southerners had a number of major grievances which eventually led to the formation of the Sudanese Peoples' Liberation Army (SPLA). The regional government in Juba had proved unworkable and had become a byword in mismanagement and corruption. The smaller Equatorial tribes also resented the domination of the numerically and politically powerful Dinka. Nimeiri therefore decided to redivide the Southern Region into the original three provinces. The Dinka and their allies considered that this was a ploy to weaken the south at the expense of the central government. At the same time they accused Khartoum of planning to steal southern water resources, and the crude oil which had been found in the region. Following the mutiny of three southern garrisons, the SPLA was created in the summer of 1983. The initially small and insignificant guerrilla army received a major

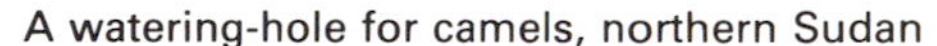
A watering-hole for camels, northern Sudan

fillip following the introduction of Islamic *shari'a* law in September 1983, which was universally unpopular in the south.

This marked the beginning of the end for President Nimeiri. It was assumed that, like everything else in Sudan, the application of *shari'a* law would be lax and tolerant. After a few months of uncertainty a five-month State of Emergency was introduced in April 1984. During this period *shari'a* law was rigorously applied; there were floggings, over fifty amputations and a number of executions.

Even when the State of Emergency was lifted in September 1984, it was obvious that it was only a matter of time before Nimeiri was overthrown. It was thought that the situation was getting better until a respected septuagenarian opposition politician was hanged for alleged heresy in January 1985. The spark for the revolution came when, at the insistence of the International Monetary Fund (IMF), Nimeiri removed food-price subsidies. As Nimeiri flew to the United States to see the Reagan Administration, riots against the price rises led to political demonstrations and strikes. In a carbon copy of the 1964 October Revolution, the army eventually surrendered to the will of the people and on 6 April 1985, President Nimeiri's sixteen-year rule was ended.

Politics today

A Transitional Military Council (TMC), and a non-party civilian government replaced Nimeiri. They ran the country until the promised elections took place in April 1986. During this period they had to deal with five major problems; the civil war in the south, the role of Islam in Sudanese society, the continuing effects of the catastrophic drought and famine, the realignment of Sudan's foreign policy, and the crippling debt crisis.

Little or nothing was achieved on any of these issues during the transitional year and they remained severe problems for the new party-political civilian government. This was a grand coalition of the Umma Party and the Democratic Unionist Parties, which won 162 of the 301 seats in the election, together with a number of other minor parties. The government was led by Sadiq al-Mahdi.

Responsibility for the famine is still largely being left to the international community because Sudan does not have the economic and administrative resources to cope with the problem. While almost all the political parties believe that Nimeiri's implementation of *shari'a* law was barbaric and un-Islamic, few are publicly prepared to advocate its total abolition. Since the abolition of *shari'a* law is one of the SPLA's absolute preconditions for any political settlement to the civil war, this is likely to hinder peace talks. The attitude of Ethiopia, which provides considerable assistance but does not control the SPLA, is also important. Ultimately, however, a political settlement is the only solution, since neither the national army nor the SPLA can win a decisive military victory.

Under Nimeiri the country had moved progressively further into Washington's orbit and had assumed the role of a Western bastion separating pro-Soviet Libya and Ethiopia. Since the April Revolution, the TMC and the civilian governments have sought to balance Sudan's foreign relations. This led to a rapprochement with some of the radical Arab states, including Libya. Fearing Libyan influence in Sudan, the United States put pressure on Khartoum to loosen its ties with Tripoli. This interference has angered the Sudanese government and people and has fuelled anti-American sentiment.

Sudan's relations with the rest of the Arab world are now generally much better than they were under President Nimeiri. Sudan has sought to return to the Arab fold after having been largely ostracized because of its general support for Egypt's Camp David Accords* with Israel, and the 1985 exodus of Ethiopian Falasha Jews to Israel via Sudan. Both the transitional administration and the new civilian government have stressed Sudan's support for the Palestinian cause and for a peaceful settlement to the Gulf War. Besides the rapprochement with Libya and the other radical Arab states, the government has also tried to mend fences with the moderate Arab countries. Sudan's relations with Egypt have, however, become rather strained because of two principal issues. After having had a very close relationship, Egypt is naturally worried by Sudan's recent rapprochement with Libya, which it considers to be a destabilizing influence in the region. At the same

An aerial view of Port Sudan

time Egypt's refusal to extradite ex-President Nimeiri of Sudan has also strained bilateral relations.

The economy today

One of the forms of pressure which Washington is applying is through its role as a major aid donor and adviser. Sudan is bankrupt in all but name, with external debts of over $13,000m. Although it could not meet the target, the 1985/6 budget set aside over half the total government expenditure for servicing its foreign debts. It has had to reschedule its debt repayments three times but the IMF and some of Sudan's major creditors, including the United States, have made further rescheduling conditional upon an economic austerity programme. Besides further currency devaluations, salary freezes and tax increases, the package includes the removal of all price subsidies. Since this led to the overthrow of President Nimeiri, the government is naturally reluctant to comply in full with these measures. In reality, however, continuous rescheduling will not resolve Sudan's debt crisis. This can only be achieved if its creditors write off a proportion of its debts and thereby remove part of the burden. Until that happens, the rest of the economy will remain largely irrelevant.

Sudan has an overwhelmingly agricultural economy. The irrigated areas produce the cotton and other export crops, while the mechanized and traditional rainfed areas supply the country with food. Besides cotton, in normal years Sudan's most important exports are livestock, gum arabic, sesame, sorghum and groundnuts. Oil has been discovered by Chevron in southern and central Sudan, which could produce about 250,000 barrels a day over an eighteen-year period. There were plans to construct a 1405 km oil-export pipeline from the main Unity field to Port Sudan. These have now been shelved because of the resumption of the civil war in southern Sudan. There are now doubts whether Chevron will remain in Sudan unless there is an early settlement to the war. Even if it was completed and oil was exported, however, it would only provide partial economic relief. In the forseeable future Sudan will remain a predominantly agricultural country. At the moment a solution to the war and the debt crisis are the two most important issues facing Sudan.

CG

A cane harvester on the Kenana sugar project

Further reading

M. O. Beshir, *The Southern Sudan: background to conflict* (London and New York, 1968)
Y. F. Hassan, *The Arabs and the Sudan* (Edinburgh, 1967)
P. M. Holt, *The Mahdist State in the Sudan: 1881–98* (Oxford, 1970)

Syria

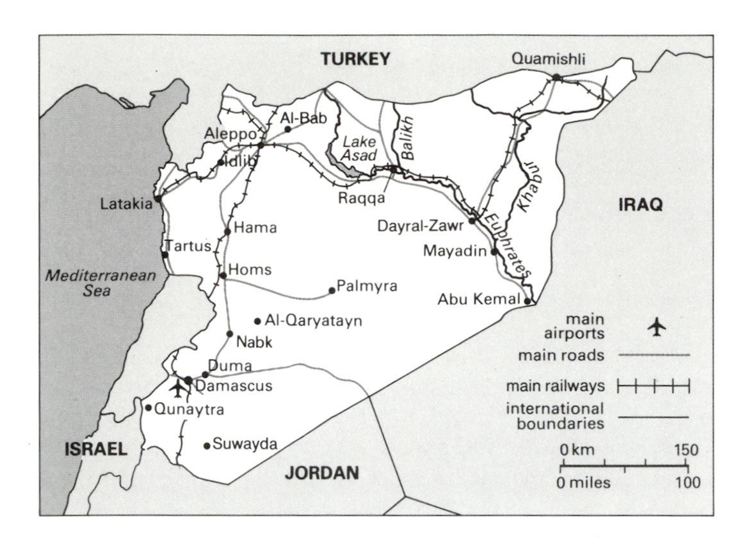

The Umayyad Mosque, Damascus

Official title	The Syrian Arab Republic
Area	185,180 sq. km (including Golan Heights)
Population	10.27 million (1985 estimate)
Government and constitution	The new constitution endorsed by a national referendum in 1973 defines Syria as a socialist popular democracy with a pre-planned socialist economy. The president can appoint and dismiss the vice-president, the prime minister and all government ministers
Currency	1 Syrian pound = 100 piastres; US $1 = £S3.93
Language	Arabic (85–90 per cent), with Kurdish, Armenian, Turkic and Syriac minorities
Religion	Sunni Muslim (70 per cent) with ʿAlawi (12 per cent), Druze, Ismaʿili and numerous Christian (15 per cent) minorities
Climate	The Mediterranean coast is humid; central and eastern Syria have summer temperatures reaching as high as 43°C and reasonably cold winters with some frosts. Rainfall is fairly abundant in the west

Geography and topography

Syria is topographically varied. Broadly speaking, its western edges are mountainous. The Jabal al-Ansariya range, whose highest peaks reach elevations of 1500 m, parallels the narrow Mediterranean coastal plain. To its south, the even loftier Anti-Lebanon Mountains, exceeding 2500 m in places, straddle the boundary with Lebanon. The country's highest point, Mount Hermon (2814 m), is in the south-west. Much of the rest of the country to the east of these mountains consists of a plateau, which is generally 300 to 800 m above sea level. This is intersected by a line of low mountains between the Jabal Druze in the south-west and the Euphrates River in the north-east.

Syria's surface configuration influences its climate. The coastal region experiences mild winters and warm but humid summers because of the moderating effect of the Mediterranean. It is also fully exposed to the moisture-bearing winds from the west, which bring heavy rain between November and March. Areas immediately to the east of the Jabal al-Ansariya and Anti-Lebanon Mountains, by contrast, are blocked off from the moderating effects of the ocean and lie within a rain shadow. Thus, winter temperatures are much lower, especially in the north, and summer temperatures are much hotter. From the standpoint of human habitation, the sharp decrease in rainfall from west to east and north to south is far more significant. Roughly one-third of Syria lies within a zone of transitional, semi-arid steppe and about 60 per cent has a true desert climate. Most of the country receives less than 250 mm of rain annually, and much of it gets less than 100 mm. Away from the coast, precipitation also becomes increasingly undependable.

Syria's settlement pattern is largely determined by the availability of water and the potential for agriculture. The great majority of Syrians live within 100 km of the coast. All of the largest cities are here: Damascus, Aleppo, Latakia, Homs, Hama and Tartus. Another belt of settlement extends through northern Syria, corresponding with the Euphrates River and its two main tributaries, the Khabur and Balikh. Inland from this so-called 'fertile crescent' rimming the western and northern periphery, population is sparse, consisting largely of nomads who exploit an agriculturally unusable environment.

Peoples

Syria has a rapidly growing population. In 1946, it had only 2.8m people. By 1985, it had an estimated 10.3m. At the current annual growth rate of 3.9 per cent, the population will double in only eighteen years. In addition, some 48 per cent of Syrians are under 15 years old – and yet to have their children. Syria's population is also rapidly urbanizing. In 1960, 37 per cent of all Syrians lived in towns. By 1985, some 50 per cent did. Because cities are expanding through both natural population increase and immigration from rural areas, their growth rates greatly exceed that of the population as a whole. Damascus may double in size in just ten years. As long as acute regional disparities in the standard of living persist, urbanization will continue at a rapid rate.

Historically, Syria has been a strategic land bridge between Mesopotamian and Nile Valley civilizations, as well as a link between Europe, Asia and Africa. Ideas and people, no less than conquering armies, have repeatedly passed through it, bestowing on it a rich cultural heritage and making it a place of intense interaction. The cultural diversity of the population today reflects this legacy.

After armies from the Arabian peninsula brought Islam to the Levant in the seventh century, Syrians gradually converted to the new faith and adopted the Arabic language. Although a majority of the population today is Muslim and Arabic-speaking, Syria's cultural map is one of the region's most variegated. Precise statistics are unavailable, but the best estimate is that 85–90 per cent of Syrians speak Arabic as their first language. The Kurds* constitute the largest linguistic minority and are thought to make up 9 per cent of the population. Other language minorities include the Armenians* (2–3 per cent) and small numbers of Turkomans* and Circassians*.

Religion

At least 85 per cent of Syrians are Muslim. Most of these – some 70 per cent of the total population – are Sunni*. Sunni Islam transcends linguistic divisions: most Arabs, and almost all Kurds, Turkomans and Circassians, belong to this branch of Islam. Another 15 per cent of the population belong to three splinter Shi'i* sects: the 'Alawis*, who are concentrated in the mountainous interior of coastal Latakia and Tartus provinces and comprise 12 per cent of the population, the Druze*, who are located largely in the Jabal Druze region in the south-west and account for 3 per cent of the population, and the Isma'ilis*, who are found mainly in central Syria. The 'Alawis have played a prominent, and controversial, role in Syria's political life since 1963 because of their over-representation within the armed forces and Ba'th* Party. With the exception of a tiny Jewish community in Damascus, the remaining 15 per cent of Syria's population belong to ten Christian denominations, the largest of which is the Greek Orthodox. Generally, the Christians are concentrated in Aleppo and Damascus, where they have been active in trade and the professions.

History up to 1939

Ancient Syria, a region extending east from the Mediterranean coast, was divided into a number of distinct regions. The north was linked with Mesopotamia* by major trade routes along the Euphrates and Khabur Valleys. During the early part of the second millennium BC the region that was then Syria formed part of the Assyrian Kingdom which was overthrown by Hammurabi of Babylon in 1759 BC. Later, the Persian Achaemenid Empire was to absorb Syria and Palestine until they were conquered by Alexander the Great* in 333 BC and fell under Hellenistic cultural domination. In 312 Seleucus 1 Nicator founded a Greek dynasty in Babylon which came to rule the eastern parts of Alexander's Empire from the Syrian coast to the foothills of the Pamirs for two centuries. Cities such as Antioch (Antakya), now part of Turkey, were founded during this period. In 64 BC Syria was made a Roman province by Pompey. The policy of the early Roman Empire towards Parthia centred on a strong mobile army in Syria. During the first two centuries AD transcontinental trade increased as the Roman Empire increased in wealth. Much of the trade from the Silk Route from China passed through the Syrian desert to towns such as Damascus and Antioch. At the same time the area saw the emergence of Christianity. Antioch was the town where the Christians first received the name of their religion.

At the end of the sixth century AD came the struggle between the Byzantine and Persian Empires and the victory of the Persians who ravaged the entire region for a quarter of a century. When the Arab armies appeared from the Hijaz in the seventh century the two great empires were exhausted and Syria, Iraq and northern Mesopotamia were quickly conquered. The Umayyads* established their capital in Damascus but after the ʿAbbasid* revolution of 749 the capital was moved to Baghdad. Soon, however, various dynasties were to rule Syria: the Tulunids (864–905), the Ikhshidids (935–69) and the Fatimids* (969–1171). Control of the region by the Seljuks*, who defeated the Byzantines in 1071, was never to be strong, with the Fatimids continuing to rule most of the coastal cities while Shiʿi schismatics and Christians ruled the Syrian and Lebanese highlands. From the first Crusade in 1099, the Crusaders were to establish principalities along the coast. Saladin* ruled Syria from 1183 but after his death rival Ayyubid* dynasties ruled the Syrian cities. The Mamluks* took control after their defeat of the Mongols in 1259.

From the beginning of the sixteenth century onwards Safavids*, Mamluks and Ottomans* fought over eastern Anatolia, eventually provoking the Ottoman Sultan Selim's invasion of Syria in 1516. Ottoman rule was to continue in Syria until the First World War with the Ottoman defeat by the Allied armies and Amir Faysal of Mecca's entry into Damascus in October 1918. The mandate* established by France during the inter-war period was highly unpopular among Syria's Muslim majority and led to a major national rising in 1925–7. However, negotiations on a treaty with France took place between 1936 and 1939 and full independence was finally granted in 1946.

History since the Second World War

In the first decade and a half after independence, Syria earned a reputation as the most ungovernable, turbulent country in the region. There were three *coups d'état* in 1949 alone. In part, this instability resulted from the humiliating Arab defeat in the 1948–9 war with Israel, which discredited the traditional ruling elite. In a deeper sense, Syria's political problems resulted from the perceived illegitimacy of the state itself, which many Syrians viewed as a colonial artefact and as an obstacle to achieving Arab unity. To the extent that Syrians identified with a space called Syria, it was a Greater Syria that encompassed Lebanon, Jordan and Palestine. The preoccupation with Arab unity ensured that Syria would get caught up in the vortex of regional disputes and rivalries. Throughout the 1950s, Egypt and Iraq actively competed to bring Syria into their sphere of influence, backing rival factions within the country in the process. The intrusion of the Cold War into the region in the 1950s was also deeply disruptive. Syria's neutralism and arms purchases from the Eastern bloc caused apprehension in the United States and encouraged external interference. Finally, Syria was wracked by a series of complicated and bitter power struggles, which reflected the deep regional, sectarian, class and ideological cleavages within the country. The most important of these was waged between a landowning and urban mercantile elite and a rising class that saw the urgent need for reform and modernization. The pan-Arab, secularist, socialist Baʿth Party was the best organized and most forceful advocate of change. It won growing support in the 1950s, especially in the heavily politicized but multifactioned officer corps and among minorities and peasants.

Union with Egypt

So severe were Syria's internal political problems that full union with Egypt*, which the Baʿth Party engineered in 1958, seemed to offer the only solution. In effect, Syria voluntarily ceased to exist. The union failed to live up to expectations, however, and Egyptian domination and misrule were soon resented. Socialist reforms, though supported by many segments of the population, aroused the opposition of Syria's business class. In 1961, Syria seceded from the United Arab Republic after a coup which temporarily restored the traditional elite to power. Paradoxically, the unionist experiment helped to define Syria's national identity.

The Baʿth

The Baʿth's* ascent to power in 1963 as a result of a military coup was a major turning point in Syria's political history. Land reform and nationalization of major sectors of the economy fundamentally altered the distribution of wealth and power and ensured that the traditional ruling class would not easily be able to mount a challenge to the new order. Socially, the new rulers were quite unlike those they replaced: a disproportionate number were young officers from rural areas or small towns in remote provinces, particularly Latakia and Tartus. ʿAlawis and, to a lesser extent, other minorities were heavily over-represented. Many Sunnis from Damascus and Aleppo, who had traditionally monopolized political power, resented the newcomers, who increasingly exploited sectarian and kinship ties to strengthen their hold over the armed forces and the Baʿth Party and thereby consolidate the regime. The officer corps was purged and an 'ideological army' created. Within a relatively short time an authoritarian one-party state, within which real power lay with the military, was established.

Although Syria has lived under continuous Baʿthi rule for over twenty years and enjoyed relative stability since 1963, the regime has changed course several times because of intra-party disputes. Between 1963 and 1966 a power struggle was conducted between the more conservative, veteran Baʿthis who had guided the party since its formation, and younger members from the provinces who wanted the party to adopt more radical policies. The latter, referred to usually as the neo-Baʿth, emerged victorious as a result of a 1966 coup engineered by the unpopular Salah Jadid.

Hafiz al-Asad

A second 'corrective' coup in 1970 brought Jadid's arch-rival, Hafiz al-Asad*, to power. Asad moved the regime sharply back to the centre and broadened its base of support. A pragmatist, he liberalized the economy and ended Syria's regional isolation, mending relations with conservative Arab neighbours. This positioned Syria to take advantage of the post-1972 oil-price explosion in the Arabian peninsula and ushered in a period of sustained, rapid economic growth. During much of the 1970s, GDP grew at an annual rate of 8 per cent and real income climbed significantly. In addition, the army, which performed poorly in the 1967 war* with Israel and bore responsibility for the loss of the Golan Heights, was rebuilt along more professional lines, enabling it to restore some of its lustre in the 1973 war*. By 1975, President Asad's popularity was at its peak.

Intervention in Lebanon

The regime lost some of its political capital during the Lebanese civil war*, in which it intervened militarily in 1976 to prevent a leftist Muslim-Palestinian victory over the rightist Christians. Many Sunnis felt the action tarnished the regime's Arab nationalist credentials and raised new doubts about the ʿAlawis' Muslim credentials. The regime's subsequent efforts to bring the Christians to heel improved its image only marginally. Syria's involvement in Lebanon also proved to be expensive, doubly so because certain Arab countries demonstrated their disapproval by cutting back the aid upon which Syria was so dependent. By the end of the 1970s, Syria's economy showed signs of stress.

The fundamentalist challenge

Discontent also mounted as a result of widespread corruption, nepotism, and sectarianism within the elite. In 1976, Muslim fundamentalist organizations began a wave of bombings and assassinations directed at prominent ʿAlawis. During the next six years, these attacks took the lives of several hundred ʿAlawis, polarized Syrians along sectarian lines, and provoked the regime to clamp down hard on all opponents, which only aggravated the situation. Increasingly, the regime relied for its security on a heavily ʿAlawi palace guard commanded by the president's brother, Rifʿat al-Asad. In 1980, large-scale strikes and civil disturbances erupted in Aleppo and Hama, causing the regime to send in the army. However, this did not destroy the opposition. In 1982, a large insurrection broke out in Hama, traditionally a stronghold of religious conservatism and opposition to the regime. The regime's response was brutal: some 12,000 troops sealed the city off and pummelled it into submission. In two weeks, some 5000 to 10,000 civilians were killed and large sections of the city were demolished.

Hafiz al-Asad

President Asad, November 1977

Born in Qardaha in north-west Syria in 1928, Asad is a member of the minority ʿAlawi* sect of Islam. He was educated at the Syrian military academy and is married with several children. From 1966–70 he was a member of the inter-Arab and regional command of the Baʿth Party and minister of defence. In 1970 he led a *coup d'état* against the regime of Salah Jadid and was elected, in the following year, as president of the Syrian Arab Republic. Following the 1973 Arab–Israeli War* he negotiated a partial withdrawal of Israeli troops from Syrian territory with Henry Kissinger. In 1976 he sent Syrian troops into Lebanon, a move which was to be repeated in early 1987. In 1982 he put down an Islamic extremist uprising in Hama at an estimated cost of 5–10,000 lives. Since the self-imposed exile of his brother and vice-president Rifʿat al-Asad, he has been Syria's undisputed leader.

The water wheels of Hama

Since then, the opposition has not posed a serious threat to the regime.

Late in 1983 new doubts about the regime's political future were raised after President Asad had a serious heart attack. The president's illness prompted his would-be successors, notably his unpopular younger brother, to jockey for position. Confrontations between pro- and anti-Rifʿat factions forced the recovering president to send his brother into temporary exile. By 1985, the president was well enough to be re-elected for another seven-year term.

The wars with Israel
No single issue has dominated Syria's political life so much as the dispute with Israel (see Arab–Israeli conflict). The two countries have fought wars in 1948, 1967, 1973 and 1982. As long as the Golan Heights remain occupied the prospects for peace are remote. Syria is currently the only Arab state offering any credible military challenge to Israel. In 1967 it had 80,000 men in uniform; today, it has 225,000 and perhaps the best equipped armed forces in the Third World as a result of the Soviet Union's support. Syria's military expenditures have been a significant economic burden, however. In 1985 the military budget accounted for over 50 per cent of non-development outlays and 30 per cent of total government spending. Syria could not maintain its current level of military preparedness without substantial aid – variously put at between $800m and $2.3bn in 1983 – from Saudi Arabia, Libya, Iran, and other countries. The flow of aid has not been reliable, however, particularly since oil revenues* began to decline in the main donor countries in the early 1980s.

Regional relationships
Syria's regional relationships have been volatile and shaped by geopolitical perceptions, ideology, and the continuing need for external assistance. As the self-proclaimed guardian of pan-Arab ideals, it has invariably explained its foreign policy in terms of the interests of the Arab nation as a whole, although its neighbours, with whom it has often been on poor terms, remain unconvinced about the purity of its motives. Under Asad, Syria has emerged as one of the region's leading powers and its influence is felt far beyond its borders. Significantly, it is directly and actively involved in the future of the Palestinians, of Lebanon, and of the territories occupied by Israel in 1967 – three of the region's key problems. One of Syria's overriding foreign policy goals has been to demonstrate that none of these problems can be satisfactorily solved without its participation and consent. Widespread recognition that Syria is indeed a key player gives it considerable leverage, which it has adeptly exploited. In addition, Syria has great influence potentially over the outcome of the war between Iran, which it supports, and Iraq, whose rival Baʿthi regime has been Syria's most consistent foe. Nevertheless, Syria's regional activism has not been without its risks and costs, and in the mid-1980s Syria had few real friends in the area except Iran and Libya.

The economy and society today
Syria's economy has undergone profound structural change in the past quarter-century. Until fairly recently, Syria remained essentially an agricultural country. In 1963, the agricultural sector employed over 60 per cent of the labour force and contributed 30 per cent to the GDP. By 1982, the commercial, manufacturing and mining sectors dominated the economy while agriculture employed only 30 per cent of workers and contributed less than 17 per cent of GDP. The role of the state in the economy has also grown significantly and the public sector currently accounts for three-fifths of GDP. Despite the regime's professed socialism and close political ties with the Eastern bloc, Syria's main trading partner has been the European Economic Community.

Less than one-third of Syria is actually cultivated because of unfavourable environmental conditions in much of the country. Along the coast agriculture is rainfed, but in the interior dry farming methods must be used. Only 9 per cent of the cultivable land is irrigated, with the result that production of wheat and barley, which accounts for roughly two-thirds of the cultivated area and represents local consumption, fluctuates dramatically. Cotton is by far the main cash crop, as well as the basis for Syria's textile industry. Until the mid-1970s it was Syria's main export, accounting for 33 per cent of export earnings. By 1983, cotton exports brought in $173m, or some 9 per cent only of total earnings. Other crops include sugar-beet, tobacco, olives, citrus fruits and vegetables. Livestock, particularly sheep and goats, form an important additional component of the rural economy.

Historically, landownership patterns in Syria were grossly

inequitable, and most peasants worked as share-croppers on large estates owned by absentee urban landlords. Less than 1 per cent of the rural population controlled over one-third of all farmland and 70 per cent owned no land at all by the late 1950s. Landholding patterns have been drastically altered since 1958, when the government first made modest attempts to limit landownership. The Baʿth Party embarked on a more radical land reform programme after seizing power in 1963; within four years the regime had expropriated 1.4m hectares of land. Whereas farm properties measuring 2–25 hectares accounted for 30 per cent of cultivated land in 1959, such farms represented over 90 per cent of all farmland by the mid-1970s.

Further increases in Syria's agricultural production partly depend on continued irrigation development. Considerable expansion of the irrigated area has already occurred in the Ghab region of the Orontes. Currently, projects associated with the Euphrates Dam, which was completed in 1973, are receiving most attention. It was originally hoped that the dam would enable an additional 640,000 hectares to be irrigated by the turn of the century. Technical and environmental constraints make this extremely unlikely, however.

Oil revenues

Since the mid-1970s, Syria's major export has been petroleum. In 1983, oil exports were worth $1323.5m, or 69 per cent of total exports. Nevertheless, Syria is not a major producer by Middle Eastern standards (output in 1984 averaged only 161,000 barrels daily, compared with 4.5m barrels daily in Saudi Arabia). Despite a sizeable discovery recently near Dayr al-Zawr, its reserves are small. In addition, Syria's oil is generally high in sulphur; the portion reserved for domestic consumption must be blended with imported light crude, which currently comes from Iran, before being refined at Homs. Syria, thus, is only a small net exporter. However, without this net self-sufficiency in oil, Syria's balance of payments problems would be far worse than they currently are. Falling prices and declining exports because of reduced global demand since the early 1980s have had a serious economic impact. Moreover, Syria may soon become a net importer of oil as reserves are depleted and production falls. Syria is also a significant producer of phosphates, which are mined in the Khnayfis region. Output expanded from 800,000 tonnes in 1978 to 1.5m tonnes in 1984. The government hopes, perhaps unrealistically, to triple production by 1988 and to produce as much as Morocco by 2000.

Industry

Syria's industrial sector barely existed half a century ago. Many of the earliest industries processed local agricultural raw materials and foodstuffs or produced a small range of light consumer goods. In the 1970s, the government embarked on a policy of rapid industrialization*, allocating almost one-half of all public investments in the 1971–5 development plan to this sector. Priority was given to establishing heavy industries, such as fertilizers, chemicals, cement, and iron and steel. In addition, assembly plants began turning out such diverse products as refrigerators, television sets, furniture and telephones. As a result of this drive, industrial output grew by 13.6 per cent annually in the 1970s. The 1981–5 development plan projected a 15.3 per cent annual growth rate in the industrial sector, which accounted for 17 per cent of GDP by 1983. Since the 1960s, the building of a national transportation infrastructure has been another development priority. Today, Syria has an integrated rail and road network and modern ports at Latakia and Tartus.

Syria's accomplishments since independence have been considerable. Dramatic improvements have been made in the standard of living and quality of life, particularly in rural areas. Despite weaknesses in the economy, gains will continue. Syrians feel proud of their country's stature within the Middle East. Nevertheless, the future is not altogether bright. Syria's military commitments are a huge economic burden and have caused the country to become overdependent on external assistance. Moreover, these commitments will not end soon. A solution to the Arab–Israeli conflict* does not appear imminent and Syria will not find it easy to extricate itself from the Lebanese morass. The ʿAlawi complexion of the current regime is another serious problem. Sectarian tensions are close to the surface and could easily be ignited with disastrous consequences. Finally, President Asad, who has been in power for over seventeen years, has no obvious successor.

AD

Further reading

J. F. Devlin, *Syria: modern state in an ancient land* (Boulder, 1983)
R. F. Nyrop, ed., *Syria: a country study* (Washington, DC, 1979)
T. Petran, *Syria* (New York, 1972)
I. Rabinovich, *Syria Under the Baʿth, 1963–1966: the army–party symbiosis* (Jerusalem, 1972)
N. van Dam, *The Struggle for Power in Syria: sectarianism, regionalism and tribalism in politics, 1961–1980* (London, 1981, 2nd edn.)

Tunisia

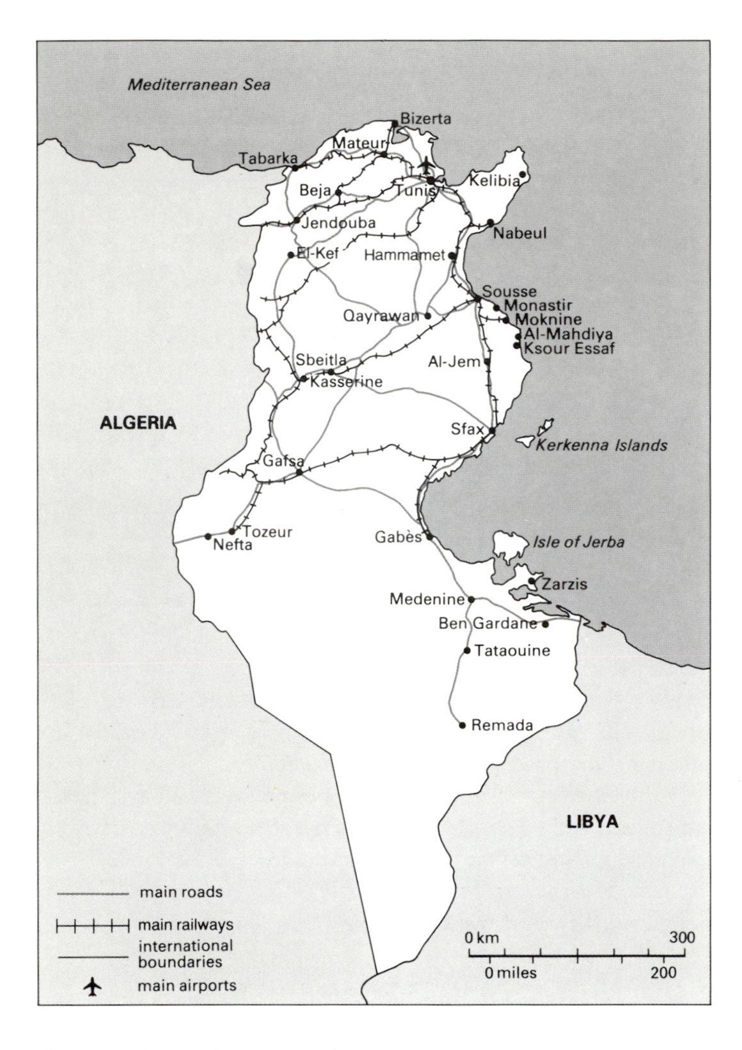

Official title	The Republic of Tunisia
Area	154,530 sq. km
Population	7 million
Government and constitution	According to the 1959 constitution, the president of the Republic is Head of State and Head of the Executive. He is also commander-in-chief of the army. The National Assembly, which is elected every five years, exercises legislative power. There are several political parties, although one – Le Parti Socialiste Destourien (PSD) – dominates
Currency	1 Tunisian dinar = 1000 millimes; US $1 = 775 millimes
Languages	Arabic and French. Various Berber dialects are also spoken
Religion	Most Tunisians are Sunni Muslims. Minority religions include Jews (approximately 20,000), and Christians
Climate	Dry, hot summers and warm, wet winters. Average rainfall over most of northern Tunisia ranges between 40 and 100 cm a year. The south is mostly desert and only enjoys about 20 cm a year

Geography and topography

Tunisia is located on the south Mediterranean shore with Algeria and Libya as neighbours.

Northern Tunisia, which runs along the eastward extension of the coastline from the Algerian border to Nabeul on the southern coast of the Cap Bon peninsula, consists of a mountainous coastal region which is bisected by the Majarda river valley – Tunisia's only perennial river. Around the coastal cities of Bizerta and Tunis are two small plains. The region as a whole is Tunisia's most populous area and receives the highest level of rainfall – between 1000 and 1500 mm – which is particularly intense close to the Algerian border. The climate here is typically Mediterranean with dry hot summers and wet winters in which rainfall tends to be concentrated into the November–December and February–March periods.

The north is separated from central Tunisia by an extension of the Atlas range of mountains which shades off southwards into the steppe region, an arid plains area with scanty vegetation cover that slopes down to the coastal Sahil plain. Rainfall south of the Dorsale falls off progressively, thus rendering much of the region semi-arid.

Southern Tunisia consists of an extension of the Sahara desert, with the arid coastal plain forming the western limit of the Jafara plain, cut off from the desert proper by the Jabal Nafusa and the Matmata Mountains. Rainfall here is below 100 mm and population is concentrated in a series of palm oases, mainly located along the coast and the line of the chotts.

Peoples

Tunisia has a population of just over 7 million people. According to the last census, held on 30 March 1984, the population totalled 6,966,173 and has been growing at 2.5 per cent per year since 1975. In 1982, 42 per cent of the population were under 15 years of age and a further 27 per cent were between 15 and 29 years old. In 1980, 97.9 per cent of the total population were characterized as being ethnically Arab, 1.5 per cent as Berber, while most of the rest are French and Italian.

In 1984, 52.8 per cent lived in an urban location, wtih much of the population being located on the Mediterranean coast between Tunis and Sfax. There has been a conscious effort by government to reduce urban drift – a problem that has also seriously affected other countries in North Africa – and Tunis has, as a result, only grown at 0.9 per cent since 1975. Its population in 1984 was 596,654. Sfax, the second largest city, grew at 1.7 per cent during the same period to 231,911. However, governmental attempts to curb urban drift have proved less successful in other areas. Two municipalities neighbouring Tunis – Ariana and Ben Arous – have experienced dramatic growth rates of 8.4 per cent and 7.6 per cent per annum. Gabès and, to a lesser extent Gafsa – both in the south of Tunisia which is relatively underdeveloped – have been the objects of government-sponsored development plans and have thus undergone considerable population growth.

The Roman theatre at Dougga

History up to 1939

Tunisia first developed an independent identity as a result of the Phoenician settlement of Carthage, founded, according to convention, in 814 BC. The Carthaginian Empire, based close to the modern city of Tunis, dominated the western Mediterranean until crushed by Rome as a result of the Punic Wars (264–146 BC). In the mid-fifth century AD, the Roman Empire in Africa collapsed under the weight of Vandal invasion from Spain in 429. By 533, Byzantine armies had recovered the area for Roman rule, but the Byzantine presence proved very unpopular.

In 800, the North African tradition of independent political existence began with the development of the Aghlabid dynasty in Tunisia. This was replaced by the Fatimids* a century later and, in the wake of the Fatimid takeover of Egypt in 969, a new period of North African independence began under the Zirids. Over the next one hundred years, migration and other factors changed the cultural and linguistic map of Tunisia.

In the mid-twelfth century the Almohads* occupied Tunisia. As Almohad power declined, the governorship became hereditary and the Hafsid dynasty developed. By the sixteenth century, Muslim corsairs in the region allied with the Ottoman* Empire, both to remove Hafsid authority and to push back European penetration. In 1534, the Hafsids were forced out of Tunis by Khayr al-Din Barbarossa. They only returned as the result of Spanish military help and Ottoman power was permanently established in 1574.

Despite the formal links thus created with the Ottoman Empire based in Istanbul, real power soon devolved onto the local military hierarchy of Deys and Beys. Little by little, the Beys came to symbolize absolute temporal authority and in 1705 a hereditary dynasty – which lasted until Tunisia gained independence from France in 1956 – was founded by Husayn Bey. Under the Husaynids, Tunisia gradually abandoned its role as one of the corsairing Barbary states in favour of commerce and, in the early nineteenth century, under the influence of Ahmad Bey, Tunisia became one of the first Middle Eastern states to attempt a thoroughgoing programme of modernization.

By the nineteenth century the European powers, led by France and Britain, had taken over control of the Mediterranean and, as a result of the Napoleonic wars, had come to dominate trade. The result was that the newly modernized Tunisia, staggering under the weight of the modernization programme and inadequate tax revenues, was unable to resist European commercial and diplomatic penetration. By 1868, Tunisia was bankrupt and saw its finances taken over by an international financial commission. At the Congress of Berlin in 1878, Britain accepted French intentions over Tunisia, in return for being granted a free hand over Cyprus. Finally, on the pretext of threats to Algeria from the border Khumir tribes, French forces invaded in April 1881.

The new French authorities instituted a protectorate over Tunisia by virtue of two treaties. As was to be the case in Morocco some decades later, France soon took over the administration, although officially the Bey and his government continued to rule, and allowed settler colonization to develop.

In 1908 a political group called the Young Tunisians was formed. The new group was soon drawn into wider issues, involving relations between the French administration and the mass of Tunisians. As a result, in the wake of the First World War in which 60,000 Tunisians served, a new political party was founded by ʿAbd al-ʿAziz al-Thaʿlibi. The new party took its inspiration and its name from the original Tunisian constitution of 1861 – the Destour. It looked towards the gradualist adaptation of French policy in Tunisia into a real acceptance that there was a sovereign Tunisian state with which France should collaborate, not dominate.

However, after the French Resident-General had banned the Destour in 1933, a political alternative to it appeared in the following year. The new elite, led by Habib Bourguiba*, a lawyer, formed a new and radical political party, the Neo-Destour. It looked towards independence for Tunisia, although prepared to accept close links with France. Its support came from a wide cross-section of Tunisian society and it was very efficiently organized.

Apart from the problems caused by the nascent nationalist movement, the decade leading up to the Second World War was one of growing confrontation between Italy and France over Tunisia. Not only had Italians been in a majority in the settler population up to 1921 – when all Europeans born in Tunisia were obliged to take French nationality – but fascist Italy also began to cast eyes on Tunisia from its colony in neighbouring Libya. In 1935, Mussolini negotiated concessions over Libya's southern border with French-occupied Chad against Italian concessions in Tunisia. Two years later, however, he put himself forward as a protector of Tunisian Muslims against French colonial control.

The result of these moves was that Tunisians willingly rallied to France in the early days of the war. However, with the Vichy armistice, Tunisia became a forward base for Axis troops in Libya and, with the Anglo-French occupation of Morocco and Algeria in November 1942, Tunisia itself was occupied by German forces. In May 1943 fighting ended and Tunisia came under the control of de Gaulle's Free French.

History since the Second World War

The nationalist movement under Bourguiba had resisted Vichy and German blandishments in order to support an Allied victory. With the end of the war, however, the Gaullist authorities threatened the nationalist movement anew and Bourguiba sought refuge in Egypt, while a Tunisian trade union movement began to form inside Tunisia itself, as a populist arm for the independence struggle.

By 1955, in the face of armed resistance throughout North Africa, the French government had come to accept that wide-ranging reforms were necessary and autonomy, virtually amounting to independence except for control of foreign affairs and defence, was granted in June. On 20 March 1956, the nationalist movement under Bourguiba took effective power of an independent Tunisia and, within eighteen months, the Bey had been deposed, to be replaced by a Republic dominated by the Neo-Destour as the single official party, together with the trade union movement, the Union Générale des Travailleurs Tunisiens (UGTT).

Tensions developed with France, however, over the single remaining French military base on Tunisian soil at Bizerta, after the French bombing of the Tunisian border village of Saqiyat Sidi Yusuf, as a result of Tunisian assistance to the Algerian nationalists. After armed incidents in 1961, the base was eventually evacuated by October 1963. French-controlled land in Tunisia was nationalized in 1964, a move which caused French economic reprisals, but these were eventually removed.

The first fourteen years of independent Tunisia were dominated by the process of adapting to a single party political system and of finding an effective means of economic development. The Neo-Destour – renamed the Destourian Socialist Party (DSP) in 1963 – had to ensure that Tunisian society as a whole would accept its lead. This was achieved by a moderate policy towards the private economic sector. At the same time, long-term economic planning was instituted and a cooperative movement was developed in the public sector, particularly in agriculture.

Towards the end of the 1960s, these tensions began to increase and led in 1968 to the first major defection from the party since the expulsion of Ben Youssef in 1956. Ahmed Mestiri, then in charge of the defence portfolio, resigned because of his dissatisfaction with party policy. Bourguiba, however, moved towards even more radical policies, with an extension of the cooperative system in 1969, under the guidance of Ahmed Ben Salah. Now all privately held land was to be cooperativized, as were commercial establishments. By September 1970 it was clear that these reforms were widely unpopular and they were suddenly abandoned, while the minister who had inspired them, Ben Salah, was dismissed.

By the start of the 1970s, Tunisia had become a mixed economy, in which the private sector enjoyed pride of place. Politically, the pro-Western orientation had been strengthened by the development of a new governmental team headed by Hedi Nouira, which sought to avoid linkage with the radicalism of North Africa or the Arab world.

Relations with Libya* became tense after 1974, as the hasty and ill-conceived Treaty of Unity, signed by Colonel Qadhafi* and President Bourguiba under the influence of the Arab nationalist Tunisian foreign minister, Mohamed Masmoudi, was rejected by the prime minister a few days after it was signed. With Algeria relations were cordial but not close, as Algeria became involved in the Western Saharan issue. In the Middle East, President Bourguiba's realism over the Arab–Israeli conflict* as early as the mid-1960s created considerable reserves.

In domestic terms, however, tensions began to mount in 1971. Student unrest was mirrored by growing pressures inside the DSP for reform. These culminated in the 1974 party congress, where Bourguiba reasserted his authority and was later elected president-for-life. Nonetheless, political coercion had by then become a commonplace of Tunisian life, with a major party purge in 1974 and the beginning of political trials, as demands for greater democracy began to surface both inside and outside the DSP. Tensions were worsened by growing economic stagnation and popular unrest. The UGTT, as the embodiment of workers' aspirations, began increasingly to act independently from the DSP and, in January 1978, there were widespread riots during a general strike.

By the 1980s, Tunisia's growing economic problems were acute and were mirrored by deepening political tensions. National Assembly elections in 1981 were held against the background of renewed demands for a democratization of Tunisian political life – from Islamists in the Islamic Trend Movement, although many of its activists, including the group's leaders, Shaykh Mourou and Rachid Ghannouchi, were imprisoned; from a new social democratic trend led by Ahmed Mestiri; from the Tunisian Communist Party under Mohamed Harmel; and from the Ben Salahists, particularly the breakaway Movement for Popular Unity. The trade union movement, the UGTT, was also anxious to break its links with the DSP. In the event, the 1981 elections were marked by widespread accusations of fraud and the DSP maintained its dominant role in the Assembly. Political tensions heightened subsequently and, in the wake of serious riots in January 1984, the government of Mohamed Mzali (Hedi Nouira retired from politics after a stroke in 1980) made overtures to the Islamists and the social democrats, while the communists became a legally permitted political party.

Politics today

The January 1984 riots marked a watershed for the Bourguiba regime. They signalled the onset of a major political role for the Islamists, as well as warning of the dangers of economic austerity. They also underlined the stagnation of the government which has been hamstrung by the fact that the president's advanced age has meant that political life has been dominated by the succession question. They finally served warning on the trade union movement that there was an alternative organizational centre through which proletarian discontent could be voiced.

The result has been that considerable attention has been paid to political infighting in Tunis over the succession. Although the prime minister is the immediate successor, his continued role as president will have to be put to the test of a referendum and there was much jockeying for power in this respect during 1984 and 1985. In this, the president has contributed to a significant degree. At the same time, the UGTT has endeavoured to distance itself from the DSP and, at the end of 1985, there was a full-scale confrontation between the government and the UGTT to ensure the latter's continued role within the DSP. The outcome, although initially a success for the government, is still uncertain.

These domestic problems have been further complicated by regional complications. Tunisia's anxieties over Libya were finally assuaged in March 1983 when Algeria offered a twenty-year treaty of fraternity and concord. This, however, meant a cooling of relations with Morocco, since the treaty also represented an Algerian attempt to construct a regional alliance which would pressure Morocco into compromise over the Western Sahara* issue. With Libya, relations have continued to be stormy, particularly after the expulsion of over 30,000 Tunisian workers in August 1985. Tunisia has also been dragged into the wider context of the Middle East, after the Israeli attack on the PLO headquarters just outside Tunis in October 1985. Tunisia has been the centre for the PLO since 1982, when it was expelled from Lebanon* by the Israeli invasion, and has housed the headquarters of the Arab League* since Egypt* signed the Camp David Accords* and made peace with Israel*.

The economy and society today

The Tunisian economy today has a relatively well diversified structure, with dependence on mineral exports – phosphates and oil – balanced by a growing manufacturing sector which is partly devoted to export production for foreign multinationals based in Europe. The agricultural sector is a source of considerable worry, since production growth rates are low and its foreign markets are restricted. In many respects, Tunisia is heavily dependent on the EEC*, particularly for the absorption of its agricultural excesses – citrus and olive oil – and as a preferential market for its industrial products, particularly textiles. The chronic foreign trade deficit is countered by invisible earnings from tourism and workers' remittances.

The economy has been increasingly dominated by the private sector since the collapse of the cooperative experiment in 1970. The state maintains control, however, of communications and heavy industry. There has been considerable effort in recent years to expand processing of primary materials, particularly phosphates around Gafsa and Gabès, and oil and gas production plays an important role in exports. Tunisia also obtains rent from the TransMed gas pipeline from Algeria to Italy. Economic development is controlled by a series of five-year plans which attempt to stimulate job creation as well as controlling sectoral economic growth and getting overall objectives for the economy. Today, the state controls about 20 per cent of employment, compared with almost 80 per cent at the end of the 1960s.

At the end of the 1970s, the government decided to avoid the dangers associated with over-rapid development financed by foreign loans, with a consequent growth in external debt. It also sought to restructure the economy by stimulating investment through a reduction of recurrent expenditure on subsidies. To this end, plans were made to introduce austerity policies, of which part was to involve the reduction of consumer subsidies. The IMF approved the plans. However, these measures led directly to the 1984 riots. Since then, the government has moved more carefully over the issue of consumer subsidies. Nonetheless, there has been a continued austerity policy and, in 1985, in response to IMF and World Bank wishes, the Tunisian dinar was allowed to devalue. The future for the economy has worsened, however, as a result of the decline in oil prices during 1986 and there is now little hope of an early improvement, although government policies should ensure that there is no catastrophic decline.

Tunisian society has been profoundly marked by its colonial and post-colonial experience. From 1881 until 1956 it was a French Protectorate, in which, in theory, the French authorities collaborated with the government of the Bey to modernize the country. In reality, however, political and economic control passed into French hands and a large Italian and French-dominated settler community grew up during the first half of the twentieth century.

The first decade of independence saw an unsuccessful and socially divisive experiment in the collectivization of the economy. This ended with the removal from power of the minister primarily responsible, Ahmad Bin Salah. Thereafter, under the guidance initially of the prime minister, Hedi Nouira, and, after his departure from power through illness at the end of the 1970s, under that of the new prime minister, Mohamed Mzali, Tunisia turned towards a mixed liberal economic path. This has caused increasing disparities of wealth between the small middle class and the far larger base – disparities which have caused at least two major social eruptions, in January 1978 and Janary 1984.

Another profound change has been the political and social cast imparted to Tunisia by President Bourguiba – now president-for-life and in his eighties. Habib Bourguiba was determined to reconstruct Tunisia as far as possible in the frame of a synthesis of European and Muslim values. He tried to eliminate the rigid observance of Ramadan, on the grounds that Tunisia was engaged in a battle against poverty and underdevelopment and that Tunisians were thus excused on religio-legal grounds from observing the fast. He also introduced far-sighted and moderate legislation on the role of women in Tunisian society. At the same time, President Bourguiba attempted to inject a degree of moderation and realism into Arab attitudes over the Arab–Israeli conflict – an attempt that had earned him much obloquy in the Arab world.

Many of these moves have been opposed and Tunisia has developed in recent years one of the most widespread Islamist movements in North Africa and the Middle East. This movement is exemplified by the Islamic Trend Movement and is characterized, however, by its moderation and by its desire to participate in formal Tunisian political life. The extremist trend, characterized by the Islamic Liberation Party and other splinter groups, has only been active inside Tunisia's armed forces. There has also been a growing demand for political pluralism in recent years – to which the government has only reluctantly and grudgingly responded since 1983.

Another area of profound change for Tunisian society has been the role played by migration in the formation of social attitudes. Tunisians have not only been involved in migration to France, but in recent years migration to the Middle East, particularly to Libya, has played a crucial role in the economy of the southern part of the country. In addition, political disaffection in the south of Tunisia has often been linked to political agitation by the Libyan regime, with which relations have often been tense since the abortive attempt at union between the two countries in 1974. In January 1980, this tension broke out into active accusations in the wake of the Gafsa revolt and this was repeated in August 1985, as over 30,000 Tunisian workers were expelled from Libya for ostensibly economic reasons – although the timing of the move, at least, was dictated by political considerations.

GJ

Further reading

J. Anthony, *About Tunisia* (London, 1961)
W. Knapp, *Tunisia* (London, 1972)
A. Sylvester, *Tunisia* (London, 1969)

Turkey

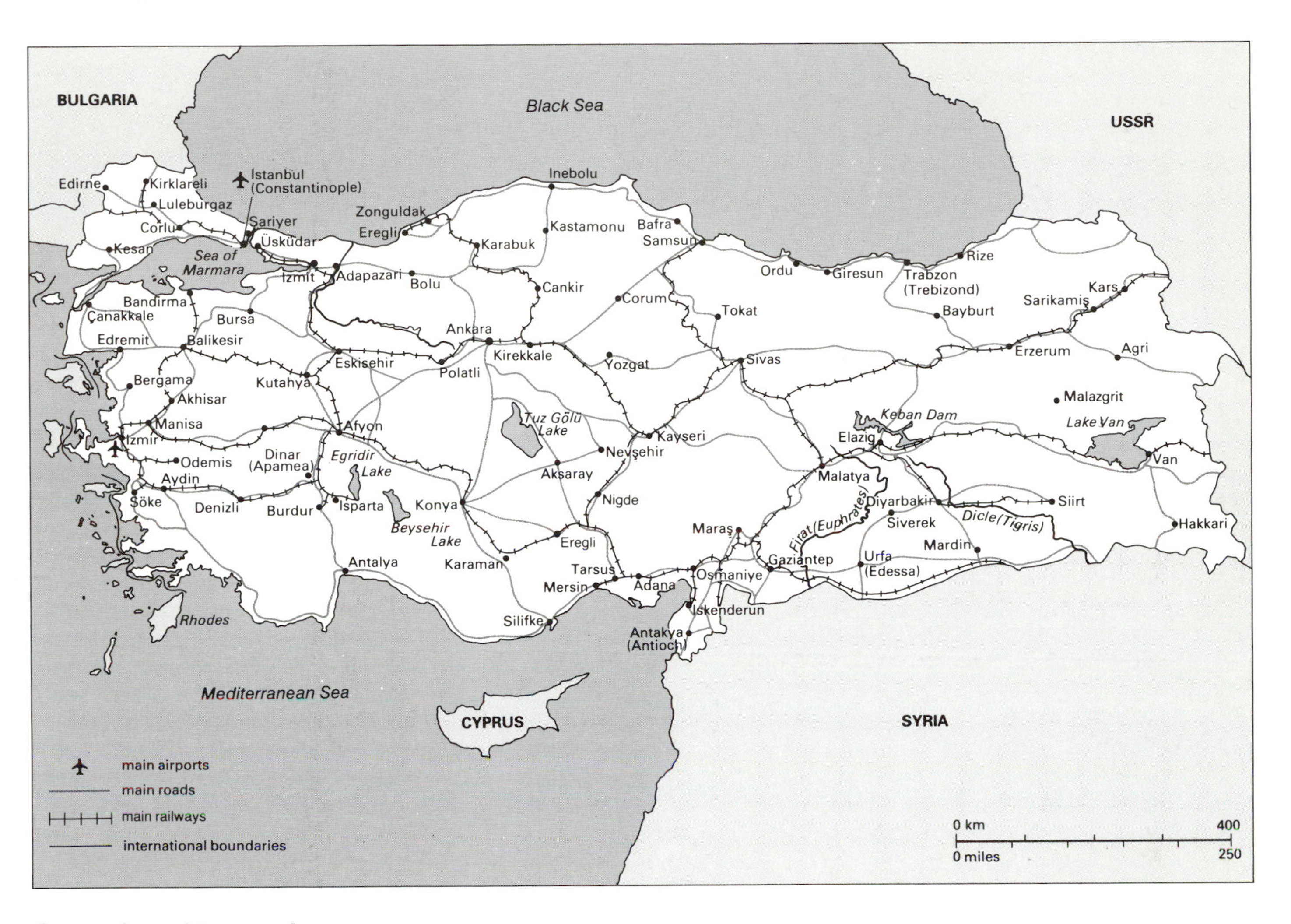

Geography and topography

The Republic of Turkey extends over the peninsula of Asia Minor in western Asia (with adjoining areas, which are geographically part of northern Syria and northern Mesopotamia), and over eastern Thrace in the Balkans. Turkey-in-Asia, known as Anatolia (*Anadolu* from the Greek *Anatole* – the east) covers some 756,000 km^2, and is separated from Turkey-in-Europe (*Trakya*), which has an area of some 24,000 km^2, by the Turkish Straits, consisting, from north to south, of the Strait of the Bosporus, the Sea of Marmara, and the Dardanelles. The Straits are controlled by Turkey, which administers the provisions of the international Montreux Convention of 1936. The two Aegean islands of Imbros and Tenedos at the western entrance to the Dardanelles belong to Turkey.

The territory of the Republic is roughly in the shape of a rectangle (situated between 42° and 36°N and 25°40′ and 44°48′E), measuring 550 km from north to south, and 1565 km from east to west at its widest points. It is bounded on the north by the Black Sea, on the north-east and east by the USSR (for 610 km) and Iran (454 km), on the south by Iraq (331 km), Syria (877 km), and the Mediterranean Sea, and on the west by Bulgaria (269 km), Greece (212 km) and the Aegean Sea.

Mountain ranges, rising from west to east, extend along the shores of the Black Sea (Pontic Alps), and the Mediterranean (Taurus), meeting in a maze of mountains in the east, where the Tigris (523 km long in Turkish territory), and the Euphrates (971 km long in Turkey) have their headwaters. Between the

Official title	The Turkish Republic
Area	779,452 sq. km of which Turkey in Europe is 23,764 sq. km
Population	51.4 million
Government and constitution	A national referendum approved a draft constitution in September 1982. The 400-member National Assembly exercises legislative power. The National Assembly elects the president for a seven-year term. The president exercises executive power, and appoints the prime minister. Political parties were dissolved in 1981 prior to the creation of a Consultative Assembly. Elections were held in November 1983 and political parties were allowed to form subject to strict rules
Currency	1 Turkish lira = 100 kurus; US $1 = 684.83 lira
Languages	Turkish is the official language. Kurdish is spoken by over 3 million people. Caucasian dialects, Greek and Armenian are spoken by minorities
Religion	Some 99 per cent of the population are, mostly Sunni, Muslims. There are Christian and Jewish minorities. Turkey is a secular state and Islam ceased to be its official religion in 1982
Climate	Turkey experiences wide climatic extremes. Winter temperatures can fall to −40°C in the east while summer temperatures exceed 30°C, even reaching 50°C in some areas

northern and southern ranges, the plateau is dotted with extinct volcanoes, the highest being Ararat (5137 m high), on the borders of the Armenian Soviet Socialist Republic. The average altitude of Turkey is 1130 m. There are several lakes on the Anatolian plateau, the largest being the salt lake of Van (3713 km^2) in the east.

Peoples

Turkey's population of 51.4m (in 1985) is predominantly Turkish-speaking. While the ethnic origins of the Turkish-speakers vary, and while many of them are refugees or descendants of refugees (from the Balkans, from which more than a million refugees came since 1923; from Russian-ruled territories, whence more than a million Turkic-speakers, Circassians and others migrated in the nineteenth century), there is a strong shared feeling of Turkish national identity, based on religion, language and community of interest.

Speakers of Kurdish* dialects constitute the largest linguistic minority. In the 1965 census (after which linguistic statistics were not published) some 2,400,000 people declared Kurdish (and the western Kurdish, Zaza dialect) to be their mother-tongue. Another 365,000 people (mainly in the south-east) gave Arabic as their mother-tongue. Other minority languages (Serbian, Bulgarian and Greek, spoken by Balkan refugees; Circassian, Laz etc.) are disappearing.

Religions

More than 99 per cent of Turkey's population is Muslim. Non-Muslims, numerous before the First World War, are now restricted to a handful of Syrian Christians in the south-east, and Armenians, Greeks and Jews in Istanbul. The majority of Muslims are Sunni*, with a sizeable, but uncounted minority of Shiʿis* (known in Turkey as 'Alevi') of Turkoman stock, mainly in central Anatolia. The Sunnis are predominantly of the Hanafi* rite, with Shafiʿis* in the south-east. Religious brotherhoods (Mevlevi, Bektaşi, Nakşibendi, Nurcu, Süleymancı, Ticani etc.), banned by the republican government, maintain a shadowy existence. The constitution bans the use of religion for political purposes.

History up to 1939

The history of Turkey, although not of the land which it occupies, can be said to start in 1071, when the Seljuk Sultan Alp Arslan defeated the Byzantine Emperor Romanus Diogenes in the battle of Malazgirt, north of Lake Van, and began the Turkish conquest of Anatolia. The Seljuk Sultanate of Rum, centred on Konya, which arose after the first conquest, was destroyed by the Mongols in the thirteenth century. But the Mongol invasion resulted in the migration to Anatolia of more people of Turkish stock, and it was at that time that the land became known to Europeans as 'Turkey'. With the breakdown of central authority, a number of Muslim principalities emerged on the embattled western frontier. One of these, ruled by Amir Osman (ʿUthman) on the Bithynian march, grew at the expense of the Byzantine Empire to the west and of its Muslim neighbours to the east and south. The reign of Osman is believed to have started in 1280. In 1345 his descendants crossed into Europe; by the end of the century they had conquered most of the Balkans. Constantinople (modern Istanbul) fell in 1453 to Sultan Mehmed II and became the Ottoman capital. In the east, Ottoman rule in western Anatolia was extended roughly to Turkey's present eastern borders in the sixteenth century by Sultan Selim I, who also conquered the Arab Near East and Egypt. Through subsequent Ottoman conquests and retreats, the whole of the present territory of Turkey remained under Ottoman rule until after the end of the nineteenth century. The land was inhabited by a majority of Muslims, mainly Turkish-speaking, with large minorities of Greeks and Armenians, minorities whose economic importance increased in the nineteenth century. However, the number of Muslims grew as refugees flooded in from lost territories. The Ottoman Empire was finally defeated in the First World War. In 1918 most of its territory was occupied by the armies of the Allies, who decided on its dismemberment in the Treaty of Sèvres*, which the last Sultan's government signed in 1920. The treaty was never carried out. Turkish national resistance had already started in Anatolia. From 19 May 1919 onwards it was organized and led by Mustafa Kemal* Pasha (later called Atatürk, the 'father of the Turks'), a Turkish general who had distinguished himself in the war. Mustafa Kemal and his commanders defeated the troops of the short-lived Armenian Republic in the east, secured the withdrawal of the French occupation troops in the south, and finally defeated the invading Greeks in the west on 30 August 1922. On 23 April 1920 the foundations of modern Turkey were laid when the Grand National Assembly (GNA) met in Ankara and constituted itself as the *de facto* government of the country. After the nationalist victory, which was recognized by the Allies in the Treaty of Lausanne, signed on 24 July 1923, the GNA proclaimed the Republic of Turkey. The proclamation of the Republic on 29 October 1923 determined the form of the Turkish national state which arose from the ruins of the Ottoman Empire, the last Sultan having fled from Istanbul a year earlier after siding with the Allies against the nationalists.

The new Turkish Republic was nationally homogeneous, since most of the Armenians had been deported, or had fled or perished during the war, and the remaining Greeks (outside Istanbul) left in the exchange of populations decided at Lausanne. The Republic was also desperately poor and short of skills. Mustafa Kemal ruled the country as president of the Republic until his death in 1938. He completed the westernization of institutions which Ottoman modernizers had begun in the nineteenth century. Government was secularized, laws imported wholesale from Western Europe, Islam disestablished, dervish orders were banned, the Latin alphabet replaced the Arabic script, European forms of dress were imposed, while European political and economic privileges were eliminated. In form, Turkey became a liberal parliamentary democracy. In fact, it was ruled by a single-party nationalist regime. However, the Republican People's Party (RPP), which Mustafa Kemal had formed, enjoyed a large measure of support among the elite of officers and civil servants, and, therefore, had little difficulty in controlling discontent among the traditionally minded masses. Socially, the RPP fostered the rise of a Turkish Muslim commercial class, by the use of liberal, albeit nationalist, economic policies and, after the 1929 economic crisis, by expanding the public sector as an interim measure.

Mustafa Kemal had won the Turkish War of Independence not only on the battlefield, but also through a foreign policy which divided his enemies. He enlisted Soviet help against the Allies before making his peace with them. After Lausanne, Turkey became by and large territorially contented, losing one claim (on Mosul in 1926), but winning another (on Hatay, formerly the *sanjak* of Alexandretta, in 1939). It therefore sided with the defenders of the status quo, which it sought to support by joining the Balkan Entente in the west and the Saadabad Pact in the east. Thanks to a prudent foreign policy, Atatürk inaugurated the longest period of peace which Turkey has ever known. The population, estimated at

Republic Day parade, Ankara

12.5m in 1923 reached 17m in 1938. The first factories (textiles, cement, sugar and finally iron and steel) were built; the railway network was extended. Atatürk's prudent foreign policy was continued by his successor Ismet Inönü, who kept Turkey out of the Second World War, until a purely formal declaration of war with Germany on 23 February 1945, which allowed Turkey to become a founding member of the United Nations.

History since the Second World War

The post-war history of Turkey was profoundly influenced by the Soviet decision, communicated on 19 March 1945, to denounce the Turkish–Soviet Treaty of Neutrality and Non-Aggression of 1925 and to propose a new treaty. On 7 June the USSR stipulated two conditions for a new treaty: the cession of (some or all of) the territory which Turkey had regained from Russia in eastern Anatolia in 1921, and the establishment of Soviet bases in the Turkish Straits. In resisting these claims Turkey sought and received United States support under the Truman Doctrine, the Marshall Plan and, finally, the North Atlantic Treaty Organization (NATO). The signature of a military assistance agreement with the United States on 12 July 1947, and of an economic cooperation agreement on 4 July 1948 (by virtue of which Turkey became a member of the Organization of European Economic Cooperation, and then of its successor the Organization of Economic Cooperation and Development), the decision on 26 July 1950 to send a Turkish brigade to Korea, Turkey's admission to the Council of Europe in the same year, and its accession to NATO on 15 February 1952 placed Turkey within the Western system. The formal retraction of Soviet territorial claims on 30 May 1953 did not affect the development of Turkish links with the West. Turkey was a founder member of the Baghdad Pact in 1955, and of its successor, the Central Treaty Organization, which had its headquarters in Ankara from its inception in 1959 until its dissolution in 1979. On 12 September 1963, Turkey signed an association agreement with the European Economic Community (EEC), prompting Professor Walter Hallstein, president of the European Commission, to declare: 'Turkey is part of Europe'. On 14 April 1987 Turkey applied for full membership of the EEC.

The question of Cyprus

However, both in Europe and in NATO, Turkey's position was complicated by its decision, announced formally in April 1954, to have a say in the future of Cyprus*, were the status of the island as a British colony to be disturbed. The beginning of the terrorist campaign by the Greek Cypriot EOKA organization on 1 April 1955, therefore, brought Turkey into the conflict. Turkey took part in the conference on Cyprus held in London in September 1955, whose failure coincided with an outbreak of anti-Greek riots in Istanbul. In response to the Greek demand for the union of Cyprus with Greece through the process of self-determination, Turkey at first opposed the demand for the partition of the island between the Greek and Turkish communities, and ultimately for its partition into parts of metropolitan Greece and Turkey respectively. However, on 11 February 1959, Turkey and Greece reached agreement on an independent Cyprus, to be ruled jointly by its Greek and Turkish inhabitants. Britain accepted the agreement, and the Republic of Cyprus came into being on 16 August 1960.

Turkey acquired the right to station a small contingent on the island and to intervene in order to restore its constitution if it were violated. It was, therefore, immediately involved when Greek Cypriots attacked the Turkish community on 21 December 1963. The breakdown of the Cyprus settlement influenced Turkey's relations not only with Greece but also with the United States when, on 5 June 1964, the US warned Turkey against a military intervention in Cyprus. A second Turkish threat of intervention was warded off by the United States in 1967, this time by agreement. But when Turkish troops finally landed in Cyprus on 20 July 1974, after the island's president, Archbishop Makarios, had been overthrown by a coup organized from Athens, Turkey's foreign relations were deeply affected. As a protest against the unauthorized use of weapons supplied under US military assistance the US Congress imposed an arms embargo on Turkey between 1975 and 1979. The persistence of the Cyprus dispute made it impossible to resolve disagreements which had emerged with Greece on other subjects: the delimitation of the continental shelf under the Aegean Sea, as also of territorial waters and air space, the control of flights over the Aegean, and the arming by Greece of Aegean islands demilitarized after the First and Second World Wars. Tension with Greece led to the virtual disappearance of the Greek community in Istanbul and to the exercise of pressure against the Turkish minority in Greek western Thrace. After Greece had become a full member of the EEC on 1 January 1981, Turko-Greek disputes were reflected inside the EEC, as had already happened inside NATO.

Foreign relations

The Cyprus dispute encouraged Turkey to seek new friends and to improve relations with its adversaries. A visit by the Turkish foreign minister to Moscow in October 1964 was followed in 1967 by an agreement under which Turkey began to receive Soviet economic aid and, generally, by the development of more normal relations. Turkish relations with the Arab states, which had languished after the creation of the Turkish Republic, and which had been affected by the establishment of full diplomatic relations with Israel in 1952, and by Turkey's participation in Western-backed defence schemes, began to revive. However, they did not acquire much substance until after 1973, when the wealth brought to some Arab states by the sudden increase in the price of oil made it possible for Turkey to trade with them and led to a significant reorientation of Turkish foreign trade. In 1984, 37 per cent of Turkey's exports went to Middle Eastern and North African countries, from which Turkey received 33 per cent of its imports (almost exclusively in oil). The building of the pipeline between Kirkuk and Yumurtalık (near Iskenderun in Turkey), the agreement made in 1984 to build a second oil pipeline from Iraq, and plans for oil and gas lines from Iran and even from as far afield as the Persian Gulf, provided new physical links between Turkey and its Muslim neighbours, which received many of their Western imports by road through Turkey, particularly after the outbreak of the Gulf War.

But while Turkey adapted its foreign policy to changing world circumstances, it continued to see its national interest in continued membership of the Western system. Its membership of NATO was supplemented by Defence and Economic Cooperation Agreements with the United States (under which Turkey received American military and economic aid in exchange for military facilities afforded to the Americans for NATO purposes), by the association agreement with the EEC (within which a special relationship developed with the Federal German Republic, home for a million or so Turkish migrant workers and source of much military aid), and, particularly after 1980, by the growing integration of the Turkish economy in the free world trading system, and the influx of Western tourists.

Internal politics

Turkey's internal political, economic and social development since the Second World War reflected, even if it did not derive from, its foreign policy options. The process of liberalizing a disciplined, single-party regime was smoothly directed by President Ismet Inönü. On 7 January 1946, a number of dissidents from the ruling Republican People's Party (RPP) formed the Democrat Party (DP), which expressed widely felt discontent against the largely secularized elite of serving and retired civil servants and military officers, entrenched in power as the agents of Kemalist policies. The Democrat Party achieved some representation in the National Assembly in the dubiously conducted elections held on 21 July 1946, and won an absolute majority (with 53 per cent of the poll, but 86 per cent of the seats) in the first genuinely free elections of 14 May 1950. Voting in all subsequent Turkish elections has been free (whatever the constraint on political parties), and the RPP never again won an absolute majority, the DP being returned to power in 1954 (with 57 per cent of the poll) and in 1957 (with 47 per cent).

Democratic rule

The ten years of Democrat rule (1950–60) transformed Turkey. As roads were built, at first largely with American help and under American guidance, the countryside was opened up. Political participation increased in a population which, under the impact of modern medicine, grew from 21m in 1950 to 28m in 1960. The area under cultivation increased by half; the production of cereals doubled; the national income grew at an annual rate of over 6 per cent (thus nearly doubling during the decade), while industrial growth averaged more than 8 per cent. Physically, dams and roads symbolized the rule of the Democrat Party under its President Celâl Bayar and Prime Minister Adnan Menderes. Politically and socially, the party organization emerged as a rival to the civil service as a source of power and patronage. The semi-literate, semi-Westernized Democrat Party ward chairman symbolized the new regime to the old elite, which complained of violations of the Kemalist canon of enlightened secularism. But although religious feeling was expressed more freely, mosques were built in prodigious numbers, and traditional culture was allowed some place in public policy, particularly in education, the secular character of the state was preserved. In economic policy too, although liberalization was advocated by Western experts and proclaimed by the government, the public sector continued to account for roughly half the economy.

However, Adnan Menderes's march 'to a sunny horizon' encountered problems: inflation rose from 3 per cent in 1951 to a peak of 20 per cent in 1957, and the external current account deficit from $50m in 1950 to a peak of $177m in 1955 and 1956. Western, largely American, aid and credits had underwritten the Democrats' expansionist policies, but when Turkey's foreign debts reached a billion dollars in 1957, the West began to apply pressure for restraint. In August 1958, Menderes agreed, devalued the currency and restricted credits, at much cost to his popularity. As discontent grew, particularly in the armed forces (whose status and salaries had been eroded) and in the universities, and as the opposition led by Ismet Inönü began to campaign vigorously, claiming that Kemalism was in danger, Menderes sought to restrict political freedoms.

The 1960 army coup

This provided the justification for the military coup of 27 May 1960, organized by junior officers, but taken over by the military high command and supported by the 'enlightened' elite. The Democrats were overthrown, Menderes and two of his ministers were hanged, his party was dissolved and its leaders removed from the political scene. A new constitution, liberal in tone but designed above all to check the power of an elected parliamentary majority, was approved by referendum, and the military handed over power to parliament after the elections held on 15 October 1961.

The titular head of the *junta*, General Cemal Gürsel, became president and Ismet Inönü returned to power as head of a coalition government, since his RPP had won only 35 per cent of the votes. But the clock could not be put back. The supporters of the Democrats transferred their allegiance to the new Justice Party (JP), founded by a general, but taken over by Süleyman Demirel, a civilian politician who had risen to fame at a young age as the planner of the Democrats' dam-building programe. In 1965 the Justice Party won an absolute majority in the Assembly, with 53 per cent of the popular vote, and economic expansion resumed, although in a more disciplined way, bringing with it increased social and political mobility.

Dissent

Mobility created tensions. The 1961 Constitution granted autonomy to the universities and broadcasting, and guaranteed the freedom of the press. Trade unions grew stronger, and in 1963 they acquired the right to strike, under a law prepared by Ismet Inönü's minister of labour, Bülent Ecevit. Privileged enclaves were thus created, within which radicalism could develop. The disappointment felt by the elite at the electoral victory of the Justice Party, and the fear that their gains after the 1960 coup would be undone, encouraged the search for radical solutions.

Marxist influences, which had earlier been confined to a small group of mainly upper-class intellectuals, began to spread. An avowedly Marxist and anti-American Turkish Workers Party was formed in 1961. Electorally it made little impression, but its views found a growing echo among university students. Turkey's dependence on the United States had begun to produce a nationalist reaction as early as the mid-1950s, when disagreements had arisen on the amount of American aid. In the early 1960s, the provision of aid began to be coordinated by a special consortium of the OECD, but the restraint urged by the United States on Turkey in the Cyprus dispute fed anti-American feeling, which was also stirred up by agitation over the status of US military personnel and the issue of foreign mining rights. When Turkish student agitation started in the spring of 1968 following the events in France, it immediately assumed an anti-American character. On 16 July 1968, one student was killed when the Istanbul riot police broke into a student hostel of the Istanbul Technical University, which had been used as the headquarters for attacks on sailors of the visiting US Sixth Fleet. Left-wing agitation immediately produced a right-wing backlash, equally nationalist in character, which found its expression in the Nationalist Action Party, led by Colonel Alpaslan Türkeş, one of the conspirators in the 1960 coup, and in the Islamic fundamentalist National Salvation Party (NSP) of Necmettin Erbakan. In 1969, attacks on the Americans were accompanied by clashes between rival right-wing and left-wing factions. Agitation spread in 1970, when the trade union movement split between moderates and Marxists, and increased in 1971 when the death-roll of students killed rose to twenty, and five Americans were kidnapped.

After appealing vainly to politicians to cooperate in re-establishing law and order, the high command of the armed forces staged the 'coup by memorandum' of 12 March 1971. Demirel was forced to resign as prime minister, and parliament was prevailed upon to accept a number of coalition governments. Constitutional rights were restricted, while martial law authorities succeeded in suppressing terrorism. However, the effect of the military intervention was short-lived. The elections of 14 October 1973 ushered in a period of turbulence under weak coalition or minority governments. The RPP moved to the left, under its new leader Bülent Ecevit who had ousted the octogenarian Ismet Inönü in 1972. Its electoral showing improved to 33 per cent in 1973, and to 41 per cent in 1977, its best result in free elections. However, it never achieved an absolute majority. The right wing fragmented: the moderate Justice Party dropped to 30 per cent in 1973, rising to 37 per cent in 1977, while the radical right won 15 per cent of the vote in both elections (with the fundamentalist National Salvation Party achieving its best result in 1973 with 12 per cent, falling to 9 per cent in 1977).

After an interregnum, Ecevit's RPP formed a coalition with the fundamentalist NSP. The government lasted from 25 January to 17 November 1974, and was responsible for ordering the Turkish landings in Cyprus. After another interregnum, Demirel returned to power at the head of a right-wing coalition, which included Islamic and quasi-fascist radicals, under the name of the Nationalist Front. The Nationalist Front held office until the general elections of 5 June 1977, and then, with increasing difficulty, from 21 July to 31 December 1977, when twelve JP deputies defected to the RPP. Violent clashes between right-wing and left-wing militants had in the meantime increased, the worst incident occurring in Istanbul, when a May Day rally organized by Marxist trade unions came under attack by dissidents and thirty people were killed. Nor did violence subside when Ecevit assumed power at the head of a coalition of his RPP and JP dissidents. In provincial Anatolia, the feud between left and right turned into a battle between minority Shiʿis (Alevis) and Sunnis. On 26 December, after 104 people had been killed in Kahramanmaraş when Sunnis attacked the Alevi community, parliament declared martial law in thirteen of the country's sixty-seven provinces.

Economic decline

Political instability and violence were accompanied by economic mismanagement. The Turkish economy had grown strongly after the introduction of the first five-year plan in 1963: the Gross National Product increased at an annual rate of 6.7 per cent between 1963 and 1967, and of 7.1 per cent during the second quinquennium, 1968 to 1972. But growth policies were pursued even after the 1973 first oil crisis. During the third plan period, from 1973 to 1977, annual growth rates averaged 6.5 per cent, at the cost of increasing inflation and growing foreign indebtedness. Prices which had increased by only 50 per cent between 1963 and 1970 rose by 1979 to over twelve times the 1963 level. The external current account balance, which was manageable until 1973 (when there was actually a surplus, thanks to the remittances of Turkish emigrants), then deteriorated rapidly. In 1977 there was a record deficit of $3.4bn. The stabilization programme introduced by the Ecevit government in February 1978 proved inadequate: a lack of foreign exchange led to shortages, the rise of a black market, and the closure of factories which could not procure foreign raw materials and equipment. The aim of Turkish planners since 1963 had been to increase the country's self-sufficiency through industrial development. In fact, by the end of the 1970s, Turkey was more dependent than ever on foreign supplies for its new industries, as well as for oil. The GNP, which had grown by only 3 per cent in 1978, actually decreased slightly in 1979 and 1980.

Economic hardship and violence sapped confidence in Ecevit and his government, which had been billed as a reformist social-democratic administration. On 14 October 1979, the JP won all five by-elections for vacant seats. Ecevit resigned two days later, to be succeeded once again by Demirel at the head of a minority government on 12 November. On 24 January 1980, Demirel took decisive action to liberalize, and cure, the Turkish economy which subsequently resumed its growth. But, in spite of martial law in large tracts of the country, he could not check political violence, which claimed some 2000 lives during his ten months in office. Moreover his chances of survival in parliament were slim. The crisis was ended on 12 September 1980 by the high command of the armed forces which took over the government as the National Security Council, under the chief of the general staff, General Kenan Evren.

Military rule: peace at a price

Turkey remained under military rule for three years. During this time, terrorism was largely suppressed through the arrest of over 30,000 people; a new constitution was prepared and approved by 91 per cent of the electorate in a referendum held on 7 November 1982; the old political parties were dissolved and their leaders banned from politics for ten years; institutions were reformed, with privileges and autonomies reduced; and the economy revived. The approval of the constitution brought with it the automatic election of Evren as civilian president of the Republic for a seven-year term.

The parliamentary elections held on 6 November 1983 were contested by three parties, whose founders and candidates had been approved by the military. They were won by the new Motherland Party (MP), led by Turgut Özal, who had been head of the State Planning Organization under Demirel, and was retained by the military as deputy prime minister in charge of the economy until his resignation in June 1982. The Motherland Party won 42 per cent of the poll, which gave it an absolute majority of 211 out of the 400 seats in the new single-chamber parliament. The Nationalist Democracy Party, which had been groomed by the military as the vehicle for moderate right-wing opinion, obtained 23 per cent, and the Populist Party, designed to appeal to the old RPP vote, 30 per cent. The National Security Council dissolved itself, and Özal took over as prime minister on 13 December 1983. His authority was reinforced by the results of local government elections on 25 March 1984, when the MP obtained 41 per cent of the vote, while the Right Path Party, known to represent Demirel, won only 13 per cent. However, on the left, the Populist Party achieved only 9 per cent, 23 per cent of the electorate voting for the new Party of Social Democracy, led by Professor Erdal Inönü, son of Ismet Inönü. The two parties merged in November 1985, under the Social Democrat leader, Professor Endal Inönu. A few days later, Ecevit's wife, Rahşan, formed her own party of the Democratic Left.

Politics today

At the beginning of 1986, the political scene had not yet settled down after the military intervention of 1980. Özal's Motherland Party was the main vehicle of right-wing opinion, represented earlier by the Democrat and then by the Justice Party, but its future was not yet assured. On the left, the Social Democratic Populist Party was the strongest contender for the old RPP vote, while being more moderate than the RPP had been under Ecevit. A pious Muslim, but loyal to the Kemalist secularist republic, Özal was liberal in politics and economics, while being culturally conservative. He represented the large mass of Turks who felt at home in the Kemalist republic and wanted to see it advance to the level of liberal, prosperous West European societies, while preserving its distinctive cultural heritage, based on Islam. The heirs of the Kemalist elite, who represented the left, shared with President Kenan Evren the wish to see 'the religion of Islam, outside state and worldly affairs, as a system of belief bringing peace and contentment to men'. The political debate centred partly on the danger of religious reaction (as it had since the 1920s), but largely on the merits of a free economy and the threat which it posed to social solidarity. Marxism and Islamic fundamentalism, both banned by the constitution, survived on the fringes. It was generally assumed that the mass of the people had been shocked by the violence of the 1970s into a rejection of extremes. However, the campaign of violence launched by the Kurdish Workers Party (PKK) in south-eastern Turkey raised the question whether the majority of Kurdish-speakers would remain content to be treated as Turks, or whether a significant number of them could be persuaded to espouse Kurdish nationalism.

The economy and society today

By 1985, the population of Turkey had grown to 51.4m. Roughly half lived in towns, some in shanties (which were, however, no worse than many village houses), but increasingly in apartment blocks. Most households had both radio and television, and many video equipment. While television (broadcast in colour on two channels) was the main medium of social communication, there was a vigorous press, centred on Istanbul but printed simultaneously in several towns, with the top daily circulation approaching one million copies. Education*, available universally at the primary level, was a national preoccupation, with keen competition for entry to the better schools and places in the twenty-seven state universities. The literacy rate increased to 72 per cent. The Turkish language continued to adopt Turkish neologisms, replacing words of Arabic and Persian origin, and thus to grow away from its Islamic past. It was estimated that the number of words of Turkish origin in current use had doubled in the last fifty years to some 75 to 80 per cent. But while nationalism was the dominant ideology, knowledge of the outside world increased and was derived partly from Turkish emigrants (in West Germany, elsewhere in Europe, but also the oil-producing Arab states), and largely from television (which relied mainly on Western programmes). Living on the frontier between the Islamic Near East and Christian Europe, Turkish society was increasingly influenced by modern mass culture, and animated by an ethic of achievement, which stimulated mobility. The population continued to move from the countryside to the cities (with an estimated 6m inhabitants in greater Istanbul), from the east to the west and from the interior to the coast. Between 1980 and 1985 it grew at the annual rate of 28 per thousand.

High demographic growth was one difference between Turkey and developed countries. Another was the fact that at $1100 (in 1985), the Gross National Product per person was the lowest in the OECD. However, at an estimated 5 per cent in 1985, the growth rate was the highest. With some 60 per cent of the labour force engaged in agriculture (which, however, accounted for only 21 per cent of GNP in 1984), Turkey had the advantage of being self-sufficient in food, with a surplus for export. However, agricultural products accounted for only a quarter of the $7.1bn of goods which Turkey exported in 1984, the rest being made up largely by processed and manufactured goods (among which textiles made up another quarter). In 1984, foreign trade accounted for 36 per cent of GNP, thus showing the integration of Turkey in the world economic system. Also in 1984, Turkish construction firms had contracts worth $14bn in Arab countries.

In spite of the rapid development of the country's hydroelectric resources, Turkey continued to suffer from a lack of domestic energy sources. In 1984, some 40 per cent of the import bill went on crude oil. However, the situation should improve with the commissioning of new dams, the construction of thermal power stations, and as the nuclear energy generation programme gets under way (and, probably marginally, as new domestic deposits of oil and natural gas are discovered). In the meantime, the Turkish economy is able to meet the cost of imported fuel. The main economic problems in 1985 were inflation (of about 40 per cent) and unemployment. In 1984 there were some 850,000 registered unemployed, while the labour surplus (including underemployment in agriculture) was estimated at some 3 million people. However, hardship was mitigated by the traditional solidarity of the extended family.

A Bedouin woman and child

While good economic management should succeed in reducing inflation, the full absorption of the growing labour force is not practicable in the foreseeable future. But in the long run Turkish economic prospects are good, provided political stability is preserved. Unlike the position in some neighbouring Muslim countries, the Turkish economy has advanced on a broad front, and the growth in the acquisition and dissemination of skills should guarantee further development.

AM

Further reading

R. H. Davison, *Turkey: a short history* (Beverley, UK, 1981, 2nd edn.)
C. H. Dodd, *Democracy and Development in Turkey* (Hull, 1979)
C. H. Dodd, *The Crisis of Turkish Democracy* (Hull, 1983)
W. R. Hale, *The Political and Economic Development of Turkey* (London, 1981)
Lord Kinross, *Atatürk: the rebirth of a nation* (London, 1971, 5th edn.)
G. Lewis, *Modern Turkey* (London, 1974, 4th edn.)
A. Mango, *Turkey* (London, 1968)
A. Mango, *Discovering Turkey* (London, 1971)
S. J. Shaw, *History of the Ottoman Empire and Modern Turkey*, 2 vols. (Cambridge, 1976–7)

The United Arab Emirates

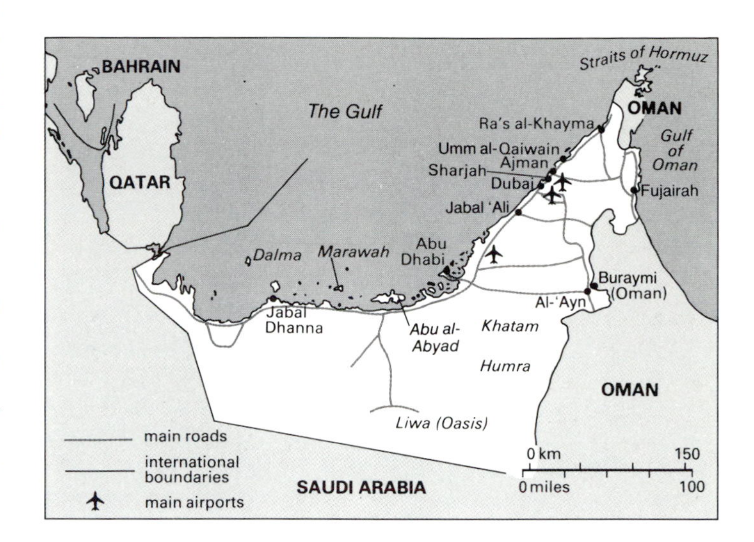

Official title	The United Arab Emirates (UAE)
Area	83,600 sq. km (77,700 sq. km excluding islands)
Population	1.6 million (December 1985 estimate)
Government and constitution	The UAE is a federation of seven states whose rulers form its highest authority, the Supreme Council. The present ruler of Abu Dhabi is president of the UAE while the present ruler of Dubai is prime minister of the Federation
Currency	1 UAE dirham (Dh) = 100 fils; US $1 = Dh 3.671
Languages	Arabic is the official language but English is widely spoken throughout the Emirates; languages such as Persian and Urdu are also spoken, particularly in Dubai
Religion	Most UAE nationals are Sunni Muslims but there is a small minority of Shi'is
Climate	Coastal areas are very hot and humid in summer but mild in winter. The interior has a typically desert climate. However, Ra's al-Khayma is more temperate, with 150 mm average annual rainfall

Geography and topography

The United Arab Emirates (UAE) has a long coastline in relation to its overall size. With 750 km inside the Gulf* and another 75 km on the Gulf of Oman*, providing direct access to the Indian Ocean, it occupies a strategically important position on either side of the Straits of Hormuz. Because these two coasts, on either side of the Musandam peninsula, are separated by the rugged highlands of the Hajar mountain range, communication from east to west of the UAE was, until recently, easier by sea than by land. This factor, combined with the extreme shallowness of this part of the Gulf, the historic local importance of pearling and fishing and the arid nature of the interior, explains why most important settlements in the country have developed along the coastal sands. Behind the coast lies the uncultivable *sabkha* saltmarsh, which extends deep into the interior and then disappears under the sand desert which covers four-fifths of the country's land area. Pockets of cultivation do occur, in the wadi channels which dissect the steep mountain slopes or around the oases at Liwa, Al-ʿAyn and Dhayd. Traditionally, however, parts of these fertile areas have belonged to landlords from the coast.

A young Abu Dhabi girl dancing the Zar

Peoples

The country which is today identified as the UAE has been inhabited for some 6000 years. Archaeological excavation, which only began in earnest in the 1960s, has unearthed evidence of settlements at Ghalila in Ra's al-Khayma and at Umm al-Nar and Al-ʿAyn in Abu Dhabi, dating back to the third and fourth millennia BC. These communities apparently lived above subsistence level and traded overseas from ports like centuries-old Julfar in Ra's al-Khayma and Jumayra in Dubai. The present nationals of the UAE are, for the most part, descendents of two main tribal groupings, the Qawasim and the Bani Yas, which both grew to importance in the eighteenth century, occupying two topographically different areas. The Qawasim built up a power base as traders and seafarers, inhabiting the mountains and wadis of Ra's al-Khayma and Sharja in the north and coming to dominate most tribes of the Musandam peninsula, with the exception of the fiercely independent Shihuh. The Bani Yas, meanwhile, held sway over the sandy desert areas that are now Abu Dhabi and Dubai. The Bani Yas were a confederated tribe comprising over twenty subsections, some beduin and some settled. It was when one subsection, the Al Bu Falasa, seceded to the fishing village of Dubai in 1833 that the modern Emirate of Dubai was founded. Today the names of those tribes and subsections live on among the Emirates' prominent families, being borne by the ruling al-Nahyan, al-Qasimi, al-Sharqi and others and by those with family names such as Mazruʿi, Suwaydi and Zahiri. In the case of the ruling families, first names are also known to have been handed down across five or six generations.

Religions

Little is recorded about religions in this part of the Gulf before Islam came to Oman in 630 AD, although different influences may have been exerted by animism, the religions of Persia and Christianity, which had become established in Oman and Bahrain. Significantly, however, when Islam took hold, different schools (*madhabs*) were adhered to by different tribes. While all were Sunni* Muslims, the majority of tribes coming under the authority of the Qawasim followed Ibn Hanbal (Hanbali*), the Bani Yas followed the Maliki* school and some tribes in Sharja were Shafiʿi*. These distinctions were superimposed upon the age-old division between the Ghafiri and Hinawi factions – the Ghafiri being those tribes who migrated from the north-western part of the Arabian peninsula and the Hinawi having come from Yemen. In the Emirates, broadly speaking, the Qawasim are identified as Ghafiri and the Bani Yas and others as Hinawi. It was not until much later that Shiʿi* Islam and Hinduism came to the UAE, with the arrival in Dubai of Persian and Hindu merchants attracted by the growth of the pearling industry.

History up to 1939

The identities of the Qawasim and the Bani Yas are central to an understanding of why the UAE was known until 1971 as the Trucial States. The truces, signed in the nineteenth century between the rulers of the region and Britain, put a stop to what contemporary Europeans saw as piracy. The first was signed between the Qawasim and Britain in Bandar ʿAbbas in 1806. The Qawasim were to respect the East India Company's flag and possessions, in exchange for which they were allowed to frequent ports from 'Surat to Bengal'. Britain's first formal treaty with the Gulf states was the 1820 General Treaty of Peace for the Cessation of Plunder and Piracy. In 1835 the Shaykhs of Sharja, Dubai, ʿAjman and Abu Dhabi bound themselves to an inviolable truce, pledging not to retaliate against aggression but to report it to the British. This undertaking was renewed at intervals until, in 1853, a 'Perpetual Maritime Truce' was signed, calling a halt to all hostilities at sea. A major side effect of these treaties, in curbing the power of the Qawasim, was to allow the rise of the Bani Yas. By the start of the twentieth century, meetings of the Trucial Shaykhs were presided over by the Shaykh of Abu Dhabi.

Throughout the nineteenth century Britain's interest in the Trucial States had stemmed from its concern to police the sea route to India, abolish the slave trade and control the acquisition of arms. In 1892 it signed 'exclusive' agreements with their rulers stipulating that they should not enter into any agreement with any power other than Britain nor cede, sell or mortgage any part of their territory to another power. It was not until 1939 that, as a result of mounting interest in oil and civil aviation, Britain appointed a political officer to reside in Sharja.

The Iraq Petroleum Company had started looking for oil in the Trucial States in 1935. Its subsidiary, Petroleum Development Trucial Coast, obtained concessions from the Shaykhs of Dubai, Sharja, Ra's al-Khayma and Kalba (at that stage an independent Shaykhdom) in 1938. Shaykh Shakhbut, nervous about the implications of awarding an oil concession for Abu Dhabi, finally gave way in 1939. Hostilities that year between Dubai and Sharja threatened to endanger the search for oil and the activities of Imperial Airways. However, 1939 also saw the outbreak of the Second World War and brought oil exploration to a temporary halt. After the war, oilfield development efforts in the Gulf concentrated initially on Kuwait and Qatar where discoveries had already been made.

Shaykh Shakbut, with Shaykh Zayed to his right

History since the Second World War

When, in the 1950s, exploration fully resumed in the Trucial States, it was again hindered by internal feuding and this time Britain assumed a more active role. It established the Trucial Oman Levies, a force originally intended to keep the peace but substantially expanded in response to the Buraymi dispute in 1952, in which the Saudis attempted to enforce a claim over the oasis based on events that had taken place 150 years before. The Levies evicted the Saudis from Buraymi and an armistice was signed with Britain. Likewise in 1952 the Trucial States Council was set up, under the chairmanship of the British political agent, to bring the rulers closer together. The council had no formal constitution but generally met twice a year. At that stage money for economic development, including the agricultural station set up at Digdaga in Ra's al-Khayma in 1955, came from Britain. Oil was not discovered in the Emirates until 1958. It was found in Abu Dhabi first, offshore at Umm al-Shayf, and then, two years later, at the Bab field onshore.

The creation of the UAE

The prelude to the creation of the UAE as such began during the latter half of the 1960s and culminated in the founding of the federation in December 1971. The transition from British tutelage to complete autonomy hinged on the British Labour government's determination to reduce defence spending by liquidating all British military bases east of Suez. Just as Britain was busy building a base in Sharja, moves were afoot in London to withdraw from the Gulf. The final announcement was made in 1968. Shaykh Zayid of Abu Dhabi and Shaykh Rashid of Dubai reacted promptly by agreeing to merge their two Shaykhdoms and a federation comprising all seven Trucial States, as well as Qatar and Bahrain, began to be discussed.

On the joint initiative of Zayid and Rashid a meeting of all nine rulers was held within a matter of weeks. Zayid stressed that 'Abu Dhabi's oil and all its resources and potentialities' were at the service of all the Emirates. There were immediate problems, however. Qatar, anxious to get the situation under control, proposed that the five smaller emirates (Sharja, Ra's al-Khayma, Fujayra, Umm al-Quwayn and ʿAjman) should themselves group together into a single larger Emirate before joining the federation, which would then have five fairly evenly sized members instead of nine disparate ones. Shocked by this suggestion, hopeful that the British decision

Dubai Creek in the 1950s

to withdraw might anyway be reversed by a Conservative government, unnerved by the daunting task of drawing up a constitution and fearful at the reactions of Iran and Saudi Arabia which were still pressing territorial claims, the nine rulers failed to form a federation as planned.

The formation of the UAE was a last-minute decision in July 1971, which was only reached after Abu Dhabi had prepared for the worst by setting up its own cabinet and consultative committee. Even then the federation was a six-member affair from which Ra's al-Khayma remained aloof. Its reason for doing so among other factors lay in some offshore islands which Iran, having given up its claim of Bahrain, was now vehemently claiming as its own. Just as Britain reneged on its treaties with the Trucial States by withdrawing from the area, leaving Abu Dhabi with the Buraymi dispute unresolved, so too it failed to intervene over the islands of Abu Musa and the Tunbs. Sharja managed, on its own initiative, to reach a reasonable agreement with Iran whereby it retained sovereignty over part of Abu Musa, took a share in any future oil revenues and won a promise of Iranian aid. With the Tunbs and Ra's al-Khayma, in contrast, it was not so simple. On the eve of the British withdrawal Iran occupied the two tiny scarcely populated islands by force and several people were killed. Iraq severed diplomatic ties with Iran and Britain in protest, while Libya nationalized British Petroleum's interests in Libya. Ra's al-Khayma for its part simply stayed outside the newly proclaimed UAE for two months, finally joining in February 1972.

As is obvious from the history of the UAE's seven members before their new entity was formed, the federation was not immediately destined to become anything more than a loose and fluid association of independent Shaykhdoms whose shared past was one of antagonisms, unfulfilled ambitions and unresolved border disputes. The catalyst which helped to create the federation was external, not internal, and the act of surrendering independence to some federal authority was one which most Shaykhs failed even to contemplate, let alone implement. The UAE was founded on the basis of a provisional constitution, renewable every five years, and internal politics since its formation have been dominated by issues related to succession, internal boundaries and periodic calls for political reform.

Traumas of succession

The succession issue, already complicated by the absence of a law of primogeniture, is complicated still further by the overlay of federal and local government structures. The transfer of power by palace coup has always been a fact of life in the Emirates. Shaykh Ahmad, the former ruler of Umm al-Quwayn, came to power when his father was murdered in 1929. Shaykh Saqr of Ra's al-Khayma deposed his uncle in 1948. Shaykh Zayid deposed his brother, Shaykh Shakhbut, in 1966 and Shaykh Sultan of Sharja came to power after his brother had been murdered by a previously deposed ruler in 1972. Of ten Abu Dhabi rulers between 1818 and the present day, five were killed and two deposed. Only in Dubai have all eight rulers in that time had their tenure terminated by natural death. In many cases a ruler's close relations represent his greatest threat. Conse-

The balcony of the palace of the ruler of Fujayra

quently it is they – sons, brothers, cousins and uncles – who wield political power in a network of interest groups that also includes other tribes, merchant families, religious leaders and influential expatriates. Because there are benefits for them in this system, these groups all have a vested interest in the survival of shaykhly rule. But which Shaykh? In the early 1980s the succession issue came to the fore in Dubai, where Shaykh Rashid fell seriously ill in 1981, leaving three sons to govern as a triumvirate. Officially, Shaykh Rashid's eldest son, Maktum, was groomed to take over as ruler of Dubai and prime minister of the UAE, while Shaykh Zayid's eldest son, Khalifa, was appointed Crown Prince of Abu Dhabi and seen as the next president of the UAE. History suggested, however, that things might not work out as planned.

Politics today

Despite widespread acceptance of the shaykhly system of government, through the *majlis*, the Emirates have experienced isolated incidents of political protest. One major example occurred with the so-called Dubai Reform Movement of 1938, in which a split within the ruling family, arising from dissatisfaction with the ruler, Sa'id ibn Maktum, errupted into violence, sparked off on one occasion by a dispute over taxi-service rights. As the feud developed, Shaykh Sa'id's opponents formulated specific demands for a budget, civil list, a police service, proper health care and sanitation and the abolition of monopolies over ferries and other services held by the ruler, his wife and son. Although very few of these demands were conceded, a representative council was established which, for a limited period, took its duties quite seriously. Matters came to a head when the council tried to fix the ruler's income. He reacted with a show of strength and many council members fled to Sharja, but not without having influenced the attitudes of Dubai citizens and of Shaykh Rashid, who acted on Shaykh Sa'id's behalf before becoming ruler himself in 1958.

Calls for accountability on the part of the Shaykhs have surfaced on various occasions since then but without any positive result. In 1979, during a time of turmoil in the Gulf and lack of political direction in the UAE, the appointed parliament, the 40-member Federal National Council, issued a memorandum appealing for tighter federal control combined with more equitable distribution of wealth and improved living standards for all, on the grounds that 'economic and social justice is a pillar of internal stability'. Such calls came to be repeated as economic recession took hold in the mid-1980s and the December 1986 deadline for a decision on the federation's constitution approached. With concern mounting that the provisional constitution, due to expire on that date, would simply be renewed for a third time, UAE nationals in professions such as law, accountancy and education pressed for wider consultation on the constitution. They also sought elections to the Federal National Council, introduction of taxation and implementation of a coherent federal development plan.

Tribal fragmentation

Whatever the basis of a future constitution, the individual Emirates can be relied upon to cling to their separate identities and borders. These internal borders are an aspect of today's UAE that cannot be overlooked. The potential for disagreement as to their demarcation can be gauged from the fact that tiny 'Ajman consists of four discrete territories, one of which is jointly administered with Oman. Fujayra consists of four portions, including one jointly administered with Sharja. Sharja itself lays claim to an additional five separate areas. This situation, which reflects the traditional division of tribes between beduin and settled populations as well as the extent of internal migration over the years, came to light in the late 1930s when the search for oil prompted the first attempts to define each ruler's territorial claims. Because of the economic implications of boundary locations, border disputes have been critical in shaping relations among Emirates within the federation just as they have featured so prominently in relations with the two most powerful neighbours, Saudi Arabia and Iran. The Buraymi dispute with Saudi Arabia, for example, though finally settled in 1974, threatened for a time to deprive Abu Dhabi of some of its key onshore oilfields. Abu Dhabi itself was at war with Dubai between 1945 and 1948, during which time Shaykh Shakhbut maintained that his Emirate extended as far north as Jabal 'Ali. Dubai and Sharja, meanwhile, having gone to war in 1939, were again at loggerheads in the late 1970s. That situation was exacerbated by major oil discoveries on either side of the disputed border in 1980–1. A settlement was finally reached in May 1985 but similar situations could yet recur with other emirates.

Abu Dhabi

The economy and society today

Clearly, the UAE underwent no fundamental transformation when its name changed from the Trucial States in 1971. Nor did it when oil revenues soared in 1974. These revenues paid for outward signs of modernization but, when viewed in perspective, brought fewer profound changes than might be assumed. Indeed, there are strong parallels between the pearling boom which took place in the Emirates in the late nineteenth and early twentieth centuries and the 1970s oil boom. It was the pearling industry in its heyday which made Dubai a focal point for trade and immigration long before the advent of oil. When pearling collapsed in the 1930s as a result of world recession and the arrival of the Japanese cultured pearl, the intricate network of debt relationships that existed between pearl divers and boat owners was pushed to breaking point; only those with diversified sources of income – camels, dates and fish – survived. Already, long before the onset of the oil era and the latest surge in migrant labour, societies in the Emirates' larger towns were conscious of divisions between local tribal, migrant Persian and British-protected Indian communities.

The oil boom

One main influence of the oil boom, which was to reinforce Abu Dhabi's dominant position in the federation, may prove transient too. Abu Dhabi was the only member of the UAE with an established oil industry when the UAE was formed in 1971. Oil was found in Dubai in 1966 but not exported until 1969. That picture is somewhat different now that the oil boom has come and gone. Abu Dhabi, with enough oil to last another hundred years, has cooperated with other members of the Organization of Petroleum Exporting Countries (OPEC)* to protect joint interests and, in doing so, cut its oil output again and again – from a peak of 1.65m barrels a day (b/d) in 1977 to a mere 700,000 b/d in 1985. Dubai, in contrast, ignoring OPEC directives, has sustained its production at 360,000 b/d for several years. The gap between its output and Abu

Dhabi's has consequently narrowed. At the same time Dubai has exploited its historic role as an entrepôt to establish two massive ports (Port Rashid and Jabal ʿAli), an aluminium smelter, a dry dock large enough to take supertankers bigger than have ever been built, and a free zone for assembly and manufacture of goods destined for Asia, Africa and the Middle East. These projects have grown while Abu Dhabi's plans for industrialization at Ruways have had to be scaled down. Ruways today consists mainly of a gas processing plant and fertilizer factory. Simultaneously, new oil and gas discoveries have been made in Dubai, Sharja and Ra's al-Khayma. These serve to enhance the Emirates' financial independence from Abu Dhabi and to convince the three remaining Emirates that they could find oil too. Eventually, Abu Dhabi, as a prospective oil exporter of the twenty-first century, can expect to regain leverage over the other Emirates. In the meantime the fluctuations that have characterized the Emirates over the past 200 years are set to go on.

The weight of immigration

The immigration phenomenon also has its ups and downs. The Emirates' population doubled between 1975 and 1983, by which time UAE nationals accounted for fewer than 20 per cent of the total and feared they would represent a mere 12 per cent by 1990. This fear was not new. It had been uppermost in the mind of Shaykh Shakhbut when he held out against granting the oil concession. The latest wave of immigration may have peaked in 1983, however. Since then a fear of alien cultures, dislike of mixed marriages, resentment against the scale of public spending required to provide social services for immigrants' dependents and concern at the way remittances drain the balance of payments, have all contributed to the drive to reduce the expatriate workforce. Yet the UAE's migrant community is still remarkable for two basic reasons. The first is the preponderance of Indians and Pakistanis, who together make up nearly 45 per cent of the total population, with Iranians comprising another 16 per cent. The second is the preponderance of males. At the time of the 1980 census, the UAE had more than twice as many males as females.

The problem of diversification

When the pearling industry collapsed it was diversification which counted. Most Gulf states are acutely aware that the same applies in the face of a fickle market for oil. But attempts in the UAE to develop manufacturing capacity and agriculture have been badly hindered by lack of coordination among the seven member states and the prevalence of rivalry, leading to duplication. By 1986, the absence of a central licensing authority for industry had left the UAE with the capacity to produce three times as much cement as the domestic market consumed. The absence of controls on water drilling had likewise resulted in unrestrained exploitation of aquifers and a startling drop in the water table. This realization, compounded by the technical difficulties encountered in early experiments in covered agriculture on Abu Dhabi's Sadiyat Island, as well as sudden unmarketable seasonal surpluses of certain vegetables in 1983, demonstrated that money alone could not buy food security and that policies had to be more carefully thought out. Surging oil revenues in the 1970s cushioned the UAE against the effects of a mismanaged economy. In the latter half of the 1980s it has sometimes looked as though the revenues were receding, leaving few viable alternative sources of income in their wake.

NS

Further reading

M. M. ʿAbdullah, *The Modern History of the United Arab Emirates* (London, 1978)
K. G. Fenelon, *The United Arab Emirates* (London, 1976, 2nd edn.)
D. Hawley, *The Trucial States* (London, 1970)
F. Heard-Bey, *From Trucial States to United Arab Emirates* (London, 1982)
ʿAli M. Khalifa, *The United Arab Emirates: unity in fragmentation* (Colorado, 1979)
T. Mostyn, ed., *UAE, A MEED Practical Guide* (London, 1983)
R. Said Zahlan, *The Origins of the United Arab Emirates* (London, 1978)
N. Sakr, *The United Arab Emirates to the 1990s* (London, 1986)

West Bank and Gaza

WEST BANK	
Area	3,402 sq. km
Population	*c*.700,000
Currency	The Jordanian dinar (see Jordan) and Israeli shekel (see Israel)
Language	Arabic
Religion	Most Palestinians are Sunni Muslim but there is a large Christian minority
Climate	As Jordan
GAZA	
Area	224 sq. km
Population	450,000–500,000
Currency	The Israeli shekel
Language	Arabic
Religion	As in the West Bank
Climate	As Israel

The Arab–Israeli War* of June 1967 was as great a disaster for the Palestinian* people as had been the previous wars of 1948 and 1956. In 1948 some 726,000 Palestinians had been made homeless refugees and the State of Israel was declared on 78 per cent of Palestinian territory. In 1967 a new refugee problem emerged. By December 1967 an estimated 247,000 Palestinians had crossed the River Jordan into the Hashimite Kingdom of Jordan*, whilst another 11,000 sought refuge in Gaza. Of greater significance, however, is the fact that with the war of 1967 the Palestinian people experienced a kind of political eclipse as, with the Israeli military occupation of the West Bank and Gaza, their entire ancestral homeland was transformed into an Israeli settler society. Within three weeks of the 1967 War* Israel illegally annexed East Jerusalem and placed the rest of the West Bank and Gaza under Israeli military occupation.

The Israeli military occupation of the West Bank and Gaza in 1967 is the last chapter of a series of foreign occupations, throughout the present century, in a land which has been inhabited for more than 1300 years by Palestinian Arabs. The end of 400 years of Ottoman* rule during the First World War was followed by 30 years of British rule. On the same day the British Mandate* ended, on 15 May 1948, the State of Israel was declared in Palestine. The successive occupations differed in character and objective. The expropriation of revenue in the form of tax collection exemplified the Ottoman rule, while the British occupation was rationalized by a League of Nations Mandate to promote the 'well-being and development of peoples not yet able to stand by themselves under the strenuous conditions of the modern world'. Britain, however, added in 1917 the Balfour Declaration* with the promise of assisting in the establishment of a 'National Home' for the Jews. Thus, with the establishment of the State of Israel in 1948 it was to be expected that the Israeli military occupation of the remaining Palestinian territories in 1967 would differ significantly from that of the Ottoman and British occupations of the land of Palestine. This is reflected in the 'Homeland Doctrine', supported by successive Israeli governments, which states that the territories occupied since 1967 form part of the natural boundaries of the State of Israel and are not occupied within the meaning of international law.

Legal sovereignty of the region

It was the 1978 Camp David Accords* between Egypt and Israel, and their peace agreement in the following year, both under the sponsorship of the United States, which placed the issue of the legal sovereignty of the West Bank and Gaza on the international agenda. Nevertheless, the then Israeli prime minister Menahem Begin*, and his successors to the present day, limited this issue by addressing themselves to the 'autonomy' of the Palestinian Arabs in the occupied territories and excluding the land. Thus, by April 1985, the Israeli authorities had ensured control over 40 per cent of the land of the West Bank and 31 per cent of the Gaza Strip. The significance of these figures is highlighted when it is noted that in 1947 the Jews possessed less than 10 per cent of the total land of Mandatory Palestine and in 1983 they possessed 85 per cent of the total area.

With regard to the occupied territories, this massive expropriation of Palestinian land has permitted the creation of two spatially segregated regions, ethnically divided, separate and unequal. The Israeli region, encompassing the entire eastern third and a considerable part of the western side of the West Bank, and almost the whole of the southern half of the Gaza Strip, is designed for the exclusive use of Israelis. Only Israeli planning and implementation processes operate, based on Israeli standards, interests and national priorities. The Palestinian regions are characterized by stagnation and an almost universal absence of physical expansion. This is due to the successive military orders which prohibit building, road networks which fragment and dissect Palestinian settlements, and an overall Israeli policy which is aimed at the prevention of the expansion of Palestinian townships and villages.

Expropriations of Palestinian land

The methods employed by the Israelis to expropriate Palestinian land are numerous, but regardless of the precise legal context by which they were acquired they irrevocably became Israeli patrimony. Practically no Palestinian who has challenged the expropriation process has received a favourable judgement in the Israeli

Palestinians who have just fled to east Jordan across the Allenby Bridge, 1967

courts. This is primarily due to the fact that much of the expropriation is carried out through a series of military orders issued by the military commander. For example, in 1984–5 Military Order 1091 altered the definition of 'government property', retroactively, and included in that definition all 'declared state land' claimed and seized since 1979. 'State land' in the West Bank and Gaza invariably means land which Palestinians have occupied for centuries but have never registered under ther names because of the nature of the Ottoman land tenure system (see Ways of Life). Thus, its incorporation into the category 'government property' not only alienates it permanently from its rightful owners, but the reliance on military orders renders it inconceivable that the Palestinian owner would succeed in challenging the decision.

The Palestinian municipalities

Palestinians in the West Bank and Gaza are not only unable to seek justice through the judicial system, but they are also effectively disenfranchised in their own towns. Twenty-five Palestinian towns have municipal status, but since 1981 most of these municipalities are administered by Israeli officers. This is due to the fact that the Israeli state views independent Palestinian municipalities as a threat to their long-term objectives in the occupied territories. Thus, when the town of Dura, in the Hebron district, petitioned the Israeli High Court of Justice and demanded municipal elections, the high court rejected their petition on the grounds that the military commander of the occupied territories viewed municipal elections as a framework for national struggle and an instrument for the Palestine

Liberation Organization (PLO) to undertake subversive activities. Similarly, the military commander is in a position to ban all forms of Palestinian institutional activity or political organization which he deems to be a 'security' risk. Thus, Palestinians in the West Bank and Gaza are denied all forms of political expression and many forms of social and cultural expression. Trade unions, universities, cultural centres, etc. are constantly harassed or closed for lengthy periods and their officials are regularly imprisoned, administratively detained, placed under house arrest or deported.

Movement of labour to the Israeli economy

It is within such a form of military occupation that the Palestinians in the West Bank and Gaza have attempted to sustain an independent identity and their struggle for self-determination. A cornerstone of this struggle is the economic structure of the occupied territories which ultimately may determine the extent to which Palestinians are able to remain on their land. Although agriculture used to constitute the primary form of economic activity, the expropriation of land by the Israelis and the restrictions imposed on the use of water resources has pushed it into second place after transportation, which represents 27 per cent, and commerce and private services, which represent 36 per cent of the economy respectively. They are followed by construction (16 per cent), public services (14 per cent) and industry (7 per cent). Given the low level of productive economic activity it is not surprising that 90 per cent of all imports in the occupied territories are from Israel, and 84 per cent of those are in the form of manufactured goods.

This extensive reliance on Israel has also brought a dramatically high rate of inflation which has further undermined the viability of the West Bank and Gaza economy. This has contributed to an increase in unemployment and a movement of Palestinian labour from the occupied territories to the Israeli economy. In Gaza, for example, almost half of the working population is employed in Israel, and predominantly in low-status and low-pay jobs and occupations. The construction industry in Israel absorbs 48 per cent of all West Bank and Gaza workers. This vulnerability has pushed most Palestinians to seek formal education as a means of increasing their chances to obtain a job, and especially through temporary migration to the Arab oil-producing states. Thus, the West Bank and Gaza have five accredited degree-granting universities, seven teachers' training colleges, and two commercial colleges. Illiteracy rates are some of the lowest in the Third World; in 1984 they were 12 per cent for males and 37 per cent for females.

An improvement in literacy figures and an expansion of formal education constitute the only areas where Palestinians in the West Bank and Gaza have been able to achieve some form of 'self-determination' and development. Otherwise the overall political and economic situation has compounded their feelings of despair, thus enhancing the violent nature of their struggle for true self-determination. In the first poll conducted in the occupied territories since 1967, 93 per cent supported the PLO, 81 per cent rejected the UN Resolution 242, and 60.7 per cent were in favour of the armed struggle as the most effective means of solving their predicament. Of particular significance, only 3 per cent favoured a confederation with the Hashimite Kingdom of Jordan. It can be concluded, therefore, that nineteen years of Israeli military occupation have contributed to the steadfastness of the Palestinians in the West Bank and Gaza, and enhanced their sense of independent identity and desire for self-determination.

PG

Further reading

N. Aruri, ed., *Occupation: Israel over Palestine* (London, 1984)
M. Benvenisti, *The West Bank Data Project* (Washington, 1984)
H. Z. Nuseibeh, *Palestine and the United Nations* (London, 1981)
S. Roy, *The Gaza Strip Survey* (Jerusalem, 1986)
E. W. Said, *The Question of Palestine* (London, 1980)

The Western Sahara

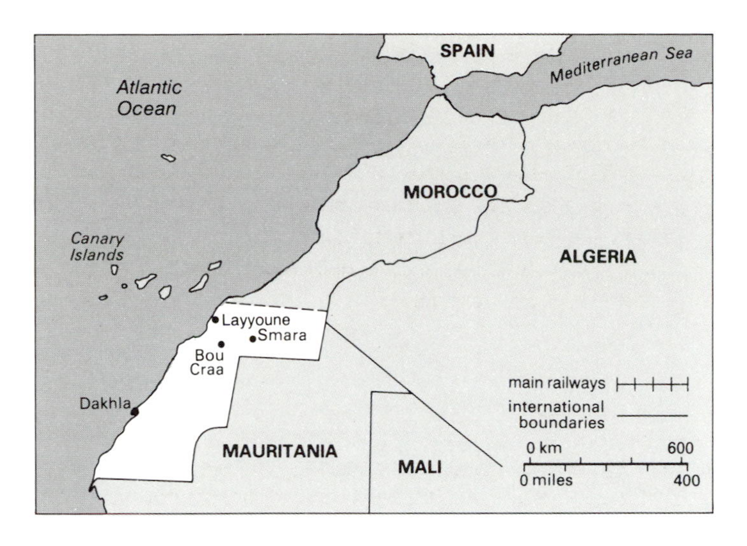

Official title	Sovereignty over the region is disputed
Area	252,120 sq. km
Population	250,000 (estimated)
Government and constitution	The region is under *de facto* Moroccan control but this is contested by the Polisario Front
Currency	As Morocco
Language	Arabic, and Berber dialects. Some Spanish is also spoken
Religion	Almost all the population is Sunni Muslim
Climate	The region has an arid, desert climate and the temperatures can range from freezing point at night in winter to a daytime temperature of 50°C in summer

Geography and topography

The Western Sahara is located on the north-west Atlantic coast of Africa, between Morocco* and Mauritania*, with Algeria forming its north-eastern border. It covers an area of 252,120 km^2. Until 1976 the area formed the Spanish colony of the Spanish Sahara, and was then jointly occupied by Morocco and Mauritania until 1979, when Mauritania withdrew and Morocco occupied the zone it had controlled. Sovereignty over the area is contested by an indigenous Saharan independence movement, the Polisario Front, which was founded in 1973 and which now acts as the political arm of the Saharan government in exile, the Saharan Arab Democratic Republic (SADR). The SADR's claim is recognized by 63 countries.

The Western Sahara lies at the extreme western edge of one of the world's greatest deserts, the Sahara, and is squarely placed in the region's most arid zone, with average annual rainfall below 100 mm. Topologically, the region consists of a flat plateau rising towards the east and, in the north-east, running into the Draa Mountains and the Jabal Warksis. The northern third of the territory is dominated by wide and shallow valleys linked to an endoreic river system flowing east to west into the Atlantic – the Saqiyat al-Hamra – which reaches the coast by the major town in the region, ʿAyun.

Peoples

The traditional social structure of the population of the Sahara was complex and typical of a society in which centralized authority was remote or non-existant. The sparse resource base and the harsh environment ensured that communal life was tribally organized, and power was diffused through a system of segmentary opposition. Tribes were either warlike and egalitarian in social structure – such as the Reguibat, the Oulad Dlim or the Tekna – or pacific and hierarchical, with claims to religious status, as was the case with the Ahl Ma al-ʿAynayn in Smara. There was also a very small population of sub-Saharan African origin, as a result of slave trading over the centuries. This, as elsewhere in the Sahara, was largely sedentary in life-style. The typical life-style, however, was pastoral and nomadic*, with the range of nomadic migration ranging into what are today adjacent countries, such as Morocco, Algeria, Mali and Mauritania. All claim Arab descent, although it is evident that the vast majority are ethnically Berber. Linguistically, however, the Western Sahara tribes are Arabophone, all speaking variants of Hasaniyya Arabic.

Population size is extremely difficult to determine. Although some sources speak of population sizes of up to 200,000 at the start of the century, the first population statistics that are generally accepted as reliable are those of the Spanish authorities, who claimed in 1974 that there was a population of 74,000 in the then Spanish Sahara. However, this ignored a population of Saharans, variously estimated at between 20,000 and 40,000, who had migrated into southern Morocco in the wake of combined French and Spanish military operations in 1960. The SADR has, until recently, argued that the true population of the region is of the order of 700,000, allowing for nomadic migration, although this figure has now been reduced to about 250,000.

History up to 1939

The colonial period

In the early stages of colonial rule in North Africa the colonial states took little interest in the Western Sahara. It was only when European traders began to cast envious eyes on the region that European powers, particularly Spain, began to consider occupying the area. A formal claim to the Western Sahara was made by Spain in 1884, in the wake of decisions taken at the Conference of Madrid four years earlier. However, no real attempt was made to make good the claim on the ground.

Indeed, under Ma al-ʿAynayn, the Saharan populations, particularly in the north of the territory, began to take considerable interest and alarm in the increasingly obvious European intentions over Morocco. Under Ma al-ʿAynayn's leadership support began to be given to the ineffectual resistance offered by Moulay ʿAbd al-ʿAziz and Moulay ʿAbd al-Hafidh – the last two independent Moroccan Sultans – to French and Spanish pressure. When, eventually, sultanic resistance collapsed in 1912, Ma al-ʿAynayn's son, al-Hiba, proclaimed himself Sultan in a final and doomed attempt to save Marrakesh from French occupation. The Saharan resistance was forced back into the Sahara, however, from where it continued to cooperate with southern Moroccan tribal resistance until 1934. Spain only decided to make its claim to the area effective as the result of prodding from the French colonial administrations in Algeria and Mauritania, and as it began to pacify its southern Moroccan province of Tarfaya, which lay just to the north of the Saqiyat al-Hamra.

History since the Second World War

Spanish control over areas outside the major urban settlements of Layyoune, Smara and Villa Cisneros (Dakhla) was at best intermittant, however, until the end of the Second World War. Then, as Spain began to recover from the effects of its own civil war and the allied blockade applied to its North African possessions for long periods during the Second World War, a concerted attempt was made to sedentarize the Western Saharan tribes. This had a radical effect on local society and limited educational and economic benefits also began to appear, as Spain sought ways to integrate the territory. At the same time, however, it became evident that Morocco would lay claim to the region, once it had obtained independence.

After this occurred in 1956, external military pressure on the Spanish colony began. Buoyed by the ideological arguments of the nationalist movement, Istiqlal, it was organized by the Moroccan Army of Liberation – a guerrilla organization that had developed in the latter years of French colonial occupation and which the newly independent Moroccan monarchy was anxious to divert from internal Moroccan affairs. The actions were abetted by large numbers of northern Reguibat tribesmen. Eventually, a combined French and Spanish military operation in 1958 liquidated the resistance and restored Spanish control. The Reguibat involved were forced into exile in southern Morocco.

In the aftermath of this Moroccan-inspired attempt to force Spain to relinquish control of the Western Sahara, two separate initiatives to achieve the same end developed. On the one hand, the UN took up the issue as one of decolonization in 1964. On the other hand, an indigenous movement for independence from Spanish control began to emerge in 1967 and took the modern form of the Polisario Front in 1973. However, from 1974 onwards, Morocco began to press for the return of the Sahara to its sovereignty, on the grounds that the region had been an integral part of the precolonial Moroccan state, while Spain pushed for a referendum to provide for complete independence or complete integration in Spain.

After the issue was referred to the International Court for Justice at the Hague – which provided an ambiguous evaluation of Morocco's claims – Morocco organized the famous 'Green March' of 350,000 volunteers into the edge of the Sahara at the start of November 1975. Spain, then in the throes of the succession to the Caudillo – Generalissimo Franco – acquiesced in the Moroccan takeover, in which Mauritania also participated, with a tripartite agreement over the future administration of the territory being signed by the three countries in February 1976.

The post-Spanish era

The immediate aftermath of the Moroccan–Mauritanian occupation of the Western Sahara saw large numbers of Saharans fleeing eastwards to refugee camps hastily created around the Algerian border town of Tindouf, while Algeria proclaimed its opposition to the Moroccan–Mauritanian move and sought a defensive alliance with Libya, signed at Hassi Messaoud in November 1975. The constellation of regional forces created then has lasted, with only two major changes, until now. Mauritania was forced out of the Sahara in 1979 by the military actions of the Polisario Front, while Libya, in June 1983, switched its allegiance to Morocco for reasons of regional and international political alignments. This was codified in September 1984 by the Arab–African Union, a treaty of confederation drawn up between Morocco and Libya to counter the Treaty of Fraternity and Concord signed between Algeria and Tunisia in March 1983, to which Mauritania adhered in December 1983. Morocco and Libya have not been able to join this particular arrangement because of their border problems with Algeria and their attitudes over the Sahara.

Over the past ten years, the Polisario Front has organized the refugees – who now number 165,000, according to the Algerian government and the UN High Commissioner for Refugees – into a series of camps around Tindouf. After a series of initial military victories against Morocco up to 1980, a new Moroccan strategy of constructing defensive walls with sophisticated protective devices has forced the Polisario Front to abandon military activities in two-thirds of the territory of the Western Sahara. The region south of Dakhla was integrated into the Moroccan defensive system in early 1987. However, from a diplomatic point of view, the SADR, with Algerian help, has rallied Third World opinion and now looks towards the developed world and the Middle East for further support. Algeria believes – and the SADR accepts – that, in the end, only diplomatic pressure will force Morocco to compromise on the Saharan issue. In any case, in the current economic climate, Algeria cannot afford the military expenditure and strategic dangers that would be involved in outright victory.

The future

Morocco, on the other hand, is confident that its support in Europe, the USA and the Middle East will not wane, particularly given its close links with the West's strategic requirements. It has, as a result, abandoned – since November 1984 – the Organization of African Unity as a forum in which a solution to the Western Saharan issue can be found. Instead, Morocco has turned to the UN, where a unilateral proposal for a referendum on the Western Sahara was made in October 1975 and, in April 1986 and May 1987, indirect negotiations through UN auspices, over the way in which such a referendum could be organized so as to satisfy UN requirements were undertaken by the UN secretary-general. It is difficult to see, however, how any successful referendum can take place, given Morocco's refusal to withdraw or abandon its claims to sovereignty and the SADR's inability to abandon its *own* claim without destroying the integrity of its own efforts over the past ten years.

The economy and society today

Quite apart from the increase in population in the Sahara from whatever source – despite the emigrations of Saharans to Tindouf – Morocco has made major investments in the Western Sahara. By the end of 1985, Dh6 billion ($630m) had been spent on development there, involving housing in major urban centres, roads, ports, airports, education, health and commerce. The economy is increasingly integrated into that of Morocco and the region is now administered from the southern Moroccan town of Gwilimin. Military expenditure runs at about $600m–$700m annually, covered partly by aid from Saudi Arabia, France and the USA, and a five-year programme of modernization of Morocco's armed forces – at a cost of $1bn – began in 1985. Against this background it seems most unlikely that Morocco will abandon its Saharan claim.

GJ

North Yemen

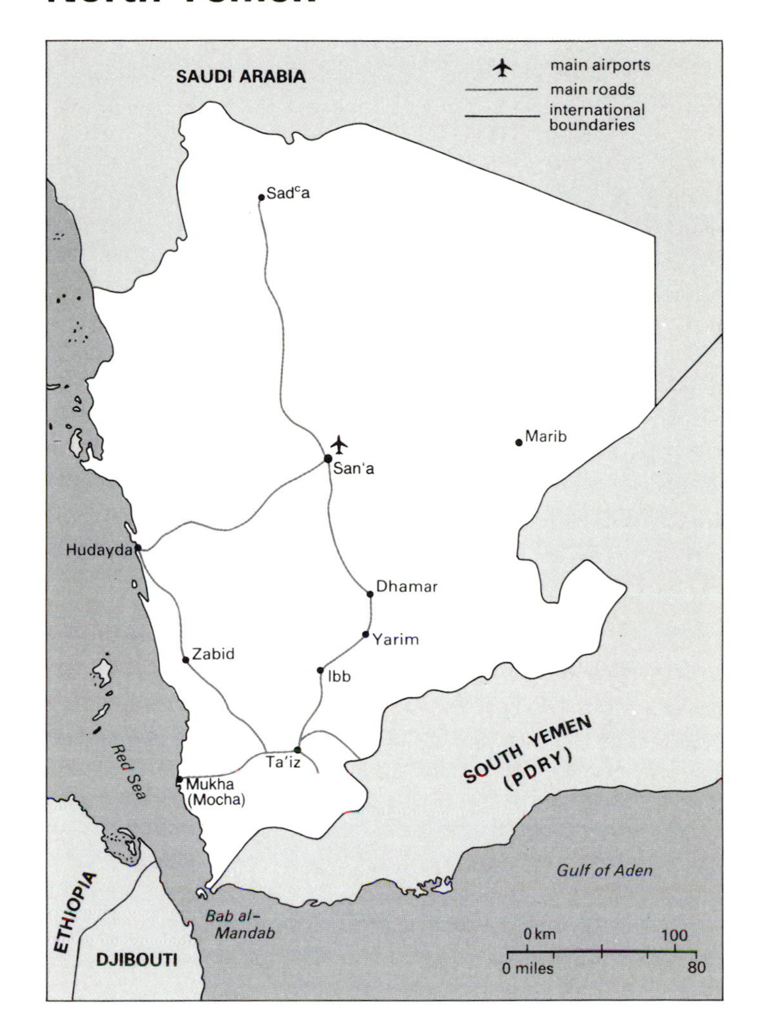

Geography and topography

North Yemen, also known as 'the Yemen', lies in the south-west corner of the Arabian peninsula. It is bounded in the west by the Red Sea, on the south and south-east by South Yemen, and on the east and north by Saudi Arabia. Its area comprises 118,400 km^2, including some offshore islands, and it is divided into two main geographical zones: the coastal plain, or Tihama, and the highlands. Its major cities are Sanᶜa, the capital, and Ta'iz, both in the interior, and Hudayda, the major port. The total population, in 1986, was estimated at 9.4m. While the coastal plain is damp and generally dry, the interior enjoys considerable rainfall, of between 400 and 800 mm annually, and supports a substantial cultivated area.

Official title	The Yemen Arab Republic
Area	200,000 sq. km
Population	9.4 million
Government and constitution	A provisional constitution was published in 1974 by the military Command Council. In February 1978 a 99-member Constituent People's Assembly was appointed by the MCC. Political parties are banned. A General People's Congress, comprising 700 elected and 300 appointed representatives, agreed in August 1982 on a new National Charter. The GPC meets every two years and is re-elected every four years
Currency	1 Yemeni rial (YR) = 100 fils; US $1 = YR 7.24 (December 1985)
Language	Arabic
Religion	Most North Yemenis are Muslims. Some 50 per cent are Zaydi Muslims and 50 per cent Shafi'i Sunnis
Climate	The highlands experience warm, temperate and rainy summers and cool, fairly dry winters with some frost. Up to 900 mm of rain may fall on the highlands of the interior, while the coast usually receives only 130 mm

History up to 1939

North Yemen was the site of major ancient civilizations in the pre-Islamic period, those of Saba and Himyar, and in the sixth century AD there were short Ethiopian and Iranian occupations. The armies of Islam conquered Yemen in 631 AD, and during much of the subsequent centuries the area was ruled by quasi-independent Arab rulers. In 1517 the Ottomans* captured Yemen for the first time, but departed again in 1636. Power then fell into the hands of Yemeni Imams*, who, basing themselves on the Zaydi* tribes of the north, ruled much of south-west Arabia until the return of the Ottomans in the middle of the nineteenth century.

The north until 1962: Imamate and revolt

The modern state of North Yemen acquired independence in 1918, with the departure of the Ottoman forces at the end of the First World War. The Turkish occupation of the north, dating from the 1870s, had never been complete, and in the Zaydi areas the traditional leader, the Imam, had retained an element of political and spiritual power. Imam Muhammad (1891–1904), leader of the Hamid al-Din family, organized substantial opposition to the Ottomans, and this was continued by his son Imam Yahya (1904–48). Under the Treaty of Da'an of 1911 the Ottomans conceded some administrative and financial powers to the Imams; when the Ottomans were forced to withdraw at the end of the First World War, the Imams imposed their rule on the entire country.

History since the Second World War

Imam Yahya sought to consolidate his power by traditional means, and to insulate the country from outside pressures and contacts. The economy stagnated, emigration grew, and the merchants were alienated from the regime. Through a system of tribal alliances and hostages, Yahya controlled the population. But opposition amongst merchants, intellectuals and religious personnel grew into the Free Yemenis, a nationalist movement based in exile which challenged the rule of the Hamid al-Din. In 1948 the Free Yemenis succeeded in killing Imam Yahya, but their uprising was then defeated by Yayha's son Imam Ahmad (1948–62). Another uprising in 1955 was also crushed. However, the economic and social crisis of the country was increasing, and more and more Yemenis were provoked by the contrast between the impoverished autocracy that ruled their country and political and economic development outside. On the death of Imam Ahmad, in 1962, a group of nationalist officers seized power in San'a on 26 September, deposed the Hamid al-Din family, and proclaimed the Yemen Arab Republic (YAR).

Despite the attempts of the Imams to insulate their domain from external pressures, the impact of the outside world had been felt more and more in the Imamate. The initial establishment of the independent state after 1918 brought the Imamate into conflict over territory with Saudi Arabia*, and in 1934 led to an outright war between the two monarchies. The Saudi victory, enshrined in the Treaty of Ta'if of 1934, forced the Imams to accept Saudi control of three provinces formerly claimed by San'a – 'Asir, Najran and Jizan. Later in the decade North Yemen was the site of competition for influence between the Italians, based across the sea in Ethiopia, and the British in South Yemen. During the 1950s and early 1960s, as Britain had begun to merge the Sultanates and Emirates of the south into a single federation, clashes over border and tribal influence took place between the Imam and Britain. Searching for an external counterweight, Imam Ahmad turned to Egypt*, the USSR and China for support. In 1958 North Yemen joined with Egypt and Syria* in the Union of Arab States. But in the end it was political influences from Arab nationalist Egypt that encouraged the opposition within the army to seize power, in September 1962. A combination of socio-economic and political tensions, aggravated from without, provided the context in which the 1962 Revolution broke out.

The Yemen Arab Republic: civil war and consolidation

The proclamation of the Yemen Arab Republic (YAR) in September 1962 did not lead to a peaceful transition in the north. Instead, for the following eight years, North Yemen was rent by a civil war between republican forces, based in the major cities, and royalists, under the leadership of the Hamid al-Din family: although it was initially believed that he had died in the military uprising, Badr, Ahmad's son and now Imam, escaped to the mountains and there rallied a tribal opposition. Within weeks this Yemeni civil war had acquired an international character. Egyptian forces were despatched by Nasser* to support the embattled Republic, while Saudi Arabia, alarmed by the sudden emergence of a nationalist Republic on its south-eastern flank, provided military, financial and logistical support for the royalists. Britain, Israel and Iran at times provided supplementary aid to the royalist forces.

The civil war raged during 1963 and 1964 without either side gaining an upper hand. A number of Yemeni politicians sought to bring peace by constituting a 'third force' between republicans and royalists, and in 1965 Nasser met with King Faysal* of Saudi Arabia to discuss a compromise. Egyptian forces then took a less forward role in the war, and in late 1967, after the Israeli victory in the June war*, Egyptian forces were withdrawn altogether. The royalists, although themselves divided and weakened, then made one last effort to win victory and laid siege to Sanʿa in a historic 70-day

The village of ʿIbb

assault. In early 1968, with the siege a failure, pressure for a compromise built up, and in 1970 a coalition government, comprising personnel from both camps, was established under the premiership of Muhsin al-ʿAyni. The Hamid al-Din family itself was not permitted to return to the country, but the civil war between royalists and republicans was over and many royalists were incorporated into the Republic.

This termination of the civil war did not, however, bring peace in North Yemen. Conflicts within the government, and between it and the tribes, continued to aggravate the political situation. In 1974 the head of state, Qadi al-Iryani, was deposed by an army officer, Ibrahim al-Hamdi, who tried to reform the state machinery and strengthen central government. Hamdi himself was assassinated in October 1977, by what were believed to be dissident conservative officers opposed to his policies, and President al-Ghashmi, Hamdi's successor, was slain in June 1978 by a bomb sent from South Yemen. At the same time, radical republicans, including Baʿthists* and members of the Movement of Arab Nationalists opposed to the 1970 compromise, continued a low-level guerrilla resistance in the early 1970s. In 1976, they formed themselves into the National Democratic Front (NDF) and, after the death of Hamdi, became involved in substantial guerrilla conflict with the central government. The regime of President ʿAbd Allah Salih, who succeeded Ghashmi, has proven more stable: this former artillery officer from south of Sanʿa, born in 1942, has forged a stronger administration and army, and created the elements of a nationwide political system in the General People's Congress.

A merchant chewing qat in Sanaʿa suq

After some years of fighting between the central army and the NDF, a cease-fire was introduced in mid-1982. Thus, after twenty years of civil conflict, the YAR was at peace. Since the end of the civil war in 1970, the YAR has maintained close relations with Saudi Arabia and has received substantial economic aid from that state. The YAR has, however, sought to pursue a middle path in Arab politics, espousing neither the conservative nor the radical 'rejectionist' currents, and it has been consistently supportive of the PLO. Relations with Western countries have generally been good, and the YAR has received considerable sums of economic aid from the West. At the same time, the post-1970 governments have maintained the relations earlier established with the USSR and China. The majority of the YAR's military equipment still comes from the Soviet Union, and in 1984 the YAR signed a 20-year Treaty of Friendship and Cooperation with Moscow.

The most important issue in the YAR's foreign policy, apart from relations with Saudi Arabia, has been that of relations with South Yemen (PDRY)*. The nationalists opposing Britain in the south were closely allied to the republicans in the north during the 1960s, but hopes of unification after the independence of the south in 1967 were not realized, and each of the two Yemeni states became aligned with exiled opposition elements from the other. In 1972 and in 1979 the YAR and the People's Democratic Republic of Yemen (PDRY) fought short border wars, yet after each war agreements were reached on eventual unity of the two states. Yemeni unity remains a popular aspiration and official policy in both Yemens, but the obstacles to it are enormous, given the separate and variant character of the two states. In practice, the unity process may amount to coexistence and some coordination in economics and foreign policy.

Politics today

Since 1962 the central instrument of power in the YAR has been the army, and, with the exception of the years between 1967 and 1974, the head of state has been an army officer. President ʿAli ʿAbd Allah Salih, who came to power in 1978, was re-elected president in 1983 for a five-year term. He has significantly expanded the armed forces with the help of Saudi Arabia, the USSR and the USA, and has at the same time developed a network of political support inside the armed forces and administration, as well as through the General People's Congress. The latter, a surrogate national assembly, has 700 elected and 300 nominated members, and first met in 1982. Its Standing Committee, with 50 elected and 25 nominated members, encompasses a range of political opinion, and the congress has local branches in much of the civil administration. These branches meet to discuss the policies of the government and to discuss the National Pact, a broad political programme first proclaimed by the government in 1980.

The economy and society today

The YAR, with a 1986 population of 9.4m, remains a predominantly rural society. In the mid-80s, 85 per cent of the population lived in the countryside, and agriculture accounted for 80 per cent of GDP. The greatest source of change has lain in the increasing integration of the YAR economy with that of the oil-producing states, particularly Saudi Arabia, and the mixed blessings this has brought. Up to one million Yemenis were believed to be working abroad in the early 1980s and their remittances, at $1.2bn or more per annum, provided the great majority of the YAR's foreign-exchange earnings. Per capita income rose significantly, as did the availability of consumer goods in town and country. However, this income boom was accompanied by considerable inflation, especially in land prices, and by a neglect of indigenous productive resources, most particularly in agriculture. Production of the mild narcotic qat, consumed each day by much of the adult male population, displaced production of foods and the traditional cash export, coffee. As a result, the YAR came to rely increasingly on food imports. The YAR experienced an enormous balance-of-trade gap, with exports in 1983 at $204m accounting for only 12 per cent of imports, at $1.521m. In October 1983 the government imposed stricter import controls in the face of these disequilibria, and an expected fall in both remittances and official aid from the oil-producing states. One new source of hope was the discovery in 1984 of significant reserves of oil in the Marib region, near the border with Saudi Arabia and South Yemen.

FH

Further reading

M. Jenner, *Yemen Rediscovered* (London, 1983)
J. Peterson, *Yemen, the Search for a Modern State* (London, 1982)
B. Pridham, *Contemporary Yemen: politics and historical background* (Beckenham, 1984)
R. Stookey, *Yemen: the politics of the Yemen Arab Republic* (Boulder, 1978)
M. Wenner, *Modern Yemen, 1918–1966* (Baltimore, 1968)
World Bank, *Yemen Arab Republic, Development of a Traditional Economy* (Washington, 1979)

South Yemen

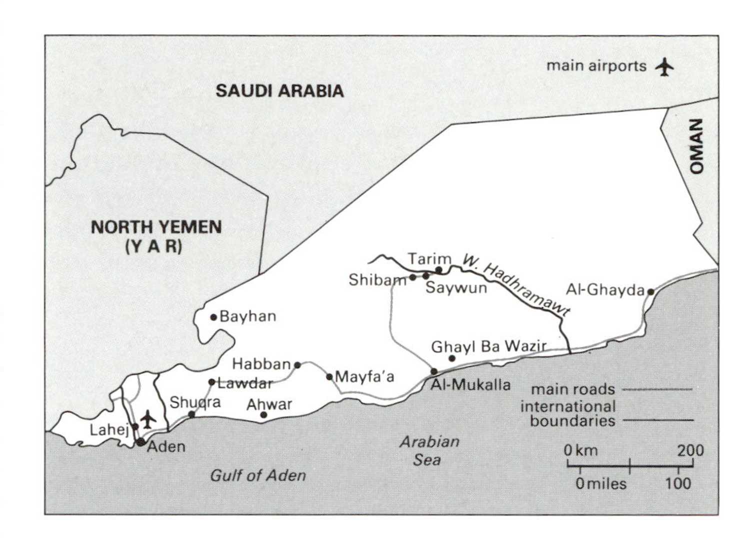

Geography and topography

South Yemen, known officially as 'the People's Democratic Republic of Yemen' (PDRY) and, under colonial rule, as 'South Arabia', lies in the southern part of the Arabian peninsula. It is bounded on the south by the Indian Ocean, on the north-west by North Yemen*, on the north by Saudi Arabia, and on the north-east by Oman*. Its total area of c. 180,000 km^2 comprises the mainland territories and some substantial offshore islands – Socotra, 350 km to the south, and Perim, at the south end of the Red Sea. Aden*, the capital and site of a substantial natural port, is by far the largest city. South Yemen includes a coastal plain, running from between 6.5 and 65 km into the interior, and a larger block of mountains and highland plateaus. The country has very low and irregular rainfall, and only about 0.2 per cent of it is cultivated. It is without significant natural resources, apart from fish and some small findings of petroleum and gold.

Peoples

Aden has a long history of contact with the outside world, and was a flourishing city in medieval times. Aden itself, and the interior areas, were throughout much of recorded history part of the political system ruling North Yemen, and it was only in the eighteenth century that a distinct entity arose in the south, with the breakaway of the Sultan of Lahej from rule by the Yemeni Imams*. In the east of South Yemen, the region known as Hadramaut had a distinct history, with separate Sultanates based on the coast and in the fertile Hadramaut Valley of the interior, building autonomous economic and political ties with India and South-East Asia. Up to

Official title	The People's Democratic Republic of Yemen
Area	336,869 sq. km
Population	2.294 million (mid-1985 estimate)
Government and constitution	A Supreme People's Council took over legislative power after the adoption of the new constitution in 1970. In 1978 general elections took place for a 111-member council which elected a Presidium, whose chairman became Head of State. In 1979 a commission from both Yemens was appointed to draw up a constitution for a unified state. There is one political party, the Yemen Socialist Party
Currency	1 Yemeni dinar = 1000 fils; US $1 = 345.4 fils
Language	Arabic
Religion	The majority of the population are Muslims
Climate	Temperatures are high throughout the country, mean figures ranging from 25°C in January to 32°C in June occurring in Aden. Summer temperatures can reach 38°C. Aden receives about 125 mm of rain a year between December and March, while during the summer up to 760 mm a year may fall in the highlands to the north of Aden

300,000 Hadramis lived in Singapore and Indonesia in the early part of the twentieth century, and this link provided substantial flows of wealth into the Hadramaut region. It was only under colonial rule that the Hadramaut was in practice brought under the same administrative and economic system as the rest of South Yemen.

History up to 1939

The area now called South Yemen, or the People's Democratic Republic of Yemen, was created as a result of military and administrative expansion from Aden, the Indian Ocean port seized by Britain in 1839. Aden was part of Britain's imperial communications but the hinterland had almost no importance, economic or strategic. The Ottoman Turks moved troops to the outskirts of Aden during the First World War, and it was not until the 1930s that the whole territory was brought under colonial control. Even then, the prevailing system was one of 'indirect rule': Aden was a colony, ruled directly by Britain, but in the twenty-three Sultanates and Shaykhdoms of the interior a measure of local administerative power was left in the hands of traditional rulers, 'protected' and financed by Britain.

History since the Second World War

In the 1950s, the British began to envisage the creation of a single political entity in the region, then known as 'South Arabia', and in 1959 a Federation of South Arabia, encompassing some of the hinterland rulers, was created. By 1963, it had been expanded to include Aden and the remaining Sultanates. But within the federation, tension between Adeni merchants and the tribal rulers of the interior was considerable, and from the 1950s onwards colonial policy as a whole came under increasing challenge from a nationalist movement, in Aden and the hinterland. The movement in Aden, in part influenced by exiled members of the Free Yemenis from North Yemen, was led by the Aden Trades Union Congress (ATUC), an organization encompassing many of the labourers, clerks and others who had found employment in the boom conditions through which Aden was passing. The ATUC, and its political associate, the People's Socialist Party, opposed the federation, which they saw as preparing the way for an undemocratic, tribal-based South Arabian state.

The opposition in the south initially took the form of strikes and demonstrations, but the situation sharpened in late 1962 after the proclamation of the Republic in the north. By October 1963, guerrilla warfare under the leadership of the newly founded National Liberation Front (NLF) had begun in the mountains of Radfan, north of Aden. The following four years were marked by widespread bloodshed and changes of political fortune. The British at first tried to defeat the resistance and save the federation. The nationalist guerrillas kept up their pressure against Britain and the federal rulers, and by 1965 substantial fighting was taking place in Aden as well as the countryside. Then, in February 1966, the British Labour government announced that it would not maintain the military base in Aden and would grant independence in two years. But, despite the prospect of an imminent British withdrawal, the nationalist movement was divided between the more radical NLF and a more cautious grouping backed by Egypt and based in Aden, the Front for the Liberation of Occupied South Yemen (FLOSY).

In 1967 the crisis came to a head. As British forces began to withdraw from the hinterland from June onwards, NLF forces took power, ousted the local rulers and seized their property. By September the NLF controlled most of the hinterland states. In October and early November, FLOSY and the NLF fought for supremacy in Aden, and in mid-November Britain agreed to negotiate with the

NLF as the representative of the South Yemen population. The federation had collapsed, and FLOSY was defeated. On 30 November 1967 South Yemen became independent under the control of the NLF.

The PDRY: socialism in a harsh environment

The triumph of the NLF in November 1967 was followed by a long economic crisis from which the country only began to emerge in the mid-1970s. Independence coincided with the ending of the three main sources of income: the direct British subsidy to the federal government, income from Aden's role as a large military base, and the bunkering and passenger services associated with the passage of large passenger ships, the last as a result of the closure of the Suez Canal* after the Arab–Israeli War*. Many thousands left the country and the new government had to cut back substantially on expenditures. Only in the latter part of the 1970s, with increased aid from Eastern bloc, Arab and multilateral sources, and an increased inflow of emigrants' remittances, did economic growth recommence.

This economic crisis was accompanied by political conflicts. Until 1973 opponents of the new regime, acting from North Yemen and Saudi Arabia, sought to overthrow the NLF. In September 1972, war between the two Yemens broke out, and in 1969 and 1973 there were clashes with Saudi Arabia. The NLF itself was divided, and the first president, Qahtan al-Shaʿbi, was overthrown in 1969 by a radical wing who wanted more far-reaching social reforms and an alliance with the Soviet bloc. They introduced a wide-reaching land reform, nationalized virtually all foreign enterprises, and established a system of centralized planning.

Even after 1969, however, factional differences continued to divide the NLF. In 1978 President Salim Rubayyi ʿAli attempted to assert his power by mobilizing military units against a majority of the Central Committee and was subsequently executed together with some of his associates. His chief opponent, ʿAbd al-Fattah Ismaʿil, was then president until 1980, when he resigned and went into exile in the USSR following disputes over economic management and foreign policy. The fourth post-independence president, ʿAli Nasir Muhammad, born in 1941 in the hinterland area of Dathina, was not in the end able to preserve greater unity in the party. In 1978 the ruling party had been renamed the Yemeni Socialist Party (YSP), and at its Third Congress, in October 1985, supporters of both the preceding presidents, together with ʿAbd al-Fattah Ismaʿil himself, had been integrated into the party apparatuses. Although ʿAli Nasir Muhammad appeared to have consolidated power and have broad support for his economic policies, he was ousted in January 1986 after a two-week-long outburst of fighting between different factions in the regime, which left many thousands killed and caused substantial damage in Aden.

The new president, Haydar Abu Bakr al-ʿAttas, had been prime minister under ʿAli Nasir but accused the former president of trying to kill his rivals within the party leadership.

The regime is committed to an ideology of 'scientific socialism', and has developed close links with the Soviet bloc. The Soviet armed forces maintain facilities in the PDRY and in 1979 the USSR signed a twenty-year Treaty of Friendship and Cooperation with the USSR, and acquired observer status with Comecon*. At the same time, the PDRY has continued to play an active part in Arab politics, and has been energetic, along with Algeria, in trying to preserve the unity of the Palestinian movement. The emphasis in the initial post-independence years on supporting opposition movements elsewhere in the peninsula, particularly in the YAR and Oman, has given way to the search for accommodation with these states. However, revolutions elsewhere, especially those in Ethiopia and Iran, have given the PDRY new opportunities to find allies in the region. Relations with the West have been poor. Relations with the USA were broken off in 1969, by South Yemen, and only France and Sweden have provided significant economic aid.

Politics today

Power in the PDRY lies with the ruling YSP, which comprises the radicalized continuation of the NLF, together with two smaller groupings, a Baʿthist* and a Communist Party, which merged with

Girl soldiers at the 1980 May Day parade in Aden's Khormaksar

the front in 1975. Membership of the YSP is estimated to be around 26,000. The YSP is governed by its Political Bureau of around a dozen members, and a larger Central Committee. It controls a number of mass organizations, whose membership is broader than that of the YSP itself. These include: the General Union of Yemeni Workers, the General Union of Yemeni Women, the Peasants Union, the Yemeni Youth Union, and the Vanguard Organization for younger children. Under the constitution, first promulgated in 1970 and published in a revised version in 1978, the legislature is the 111-member Supreme People's Council, a body that includes a minority of members not from the YSP. The chairman of the presidium of the Supreme People's Council is president of the PDRY. The Supreme People's Council nominates the prime minister and the Council of Ministers.

The economy and society today

Since independence, the state has taken an increasing role in managing the economy. Planning began in 1971–4 with a three-year development programme, and this was followed by five-year plans, the most recent being the 1981–5 second five-year plan with a planned investment of $1.5bn. In agriculture, production is divided between about 60 collective farms and about 50 state farms; in industry the state sector is the largest, followed by the mixed and the private sector. Average annual growth of GDP in the 1970s was 2.7 per cent, but the South Yemeni economy has continued to experience severe problems. Much of the growth has been due to state investment in infrastructure and construction, and production in agriculture, fisheries and industry has remained disappointing. The use and productivity of labour is low, and the PDRY has experienced a substantial balance-of-payments deficit, with 1983 imports, at $1010m, more than double exports at $449m. Workers' remittances, running in 1983 at $451m, and foreign aid made up the difference. Of total foreign aid of $785m disbursed from independence to the end of 1982, $270m came from the USSR, $133m from China and $210m from Arab sources.

FH

Further reading

F. Halliday, *Arabia without Sultans* (London, 1974)
J. Kostiner, *The Struggle for South Yemen* (London, 1984)
H. Lackner, *PDR Yemen, Outpost of Socialist Development in Arabia* (London, 1985)
M. Molyneux, *State Policies and the Position of Women Workers in the People's Democratic Republic of Yemen* (Geneva, 1982)
R. Stookey, *South Yemen, A Marxist Republic in Arabia* (London, 1982)
World Bank, *People's Democratic Republic of Yemen, A Review of Economic and Social Development* (Washington, 1979)

Peoples without a country

Armenians

There are between 6 and 7 million Armenians in the world today. Rather less than half of them are scattered in various countries in America, Western Europe and the Middle East. The most important Middle Eastern communities are those in Lebanon, Syria and Iran. Western Armenia, the area of eastern Turkey today that was the homeland of hundreds of thousands of Armenians until 1915 and to which Armenian nationalist aspirations were directed until 1920, is no more. Nor do Armenians now live in Cilicia (southern central Turkey today), even though it was the nation's second homeland. The Armenians who survived from those lands are all emigrants or refugees (many of whom have prospered) in other countries. In that sense, Armenians are a people without a country. However, one important Armenian homeland has persisted to the present, and that is the Armenian Soviet Socialist Republic (population, 3.3 m; capital, Erevan). It is only one-tenth of the size of the whole of historic Armenia – the land called Arminiyya by the Muslim geographers – but it plays a large role in the consciousness of many Armenians throughout the world.

Armenians have lived in their highlands since at least the sixth century BC; their presence is recorded in an inscription of King Darius at Behistun, Iran. Their language is an independent member of the Indo-European family, and is written in a script invented in AD 404. They are proud of being members of the oldest Christian nation; their Church has been independent from the sixth century, and is correctly known as the Armenian Apostolic (not Armenian Orthodox or Armenian Gregorian) Church. The Church is headed by the catholicos; historical circumstances have meant that, since 1441, there have been two catholicoses. Today one of them, the Catholicos of All Armenians, resides in Echmiadzin, Armenian SSR, while the Catholicos of the Great House of Cilicia lives in Antilyas, Lebanon. In the ancient and medieval period Armenia enjoyed long periods of autonomy within the orbit of the dominant regional great power (whether Eastern or Western); sometimes, as under the Bagratid monarchy (886–1045) the country achieved actual independence, recognized by both Emperor and Caliph.

It was after the collapse of the Bagratids that Armenian sovereignty re-emerged in Cilicia, which was initially a Byzantine principality and later an independent Armenian monarchy which lasted from 1198 to 1375. A number of Armenians adopted the Catholic faith when their ruling family married into the Crusader family of the Lusignans, giving us the origin of the Armenian Catholics today.

Turkish and Russian Armenia

In 1461 the Ottoman Sultan ordered the Armenian bishop of Bursa to order and regularize the affairs of the Armenian community in the Empire. Recent research has shown that the changes he made, and the powers he was given, were less far-reaching than was believed when the subject was first written about in Europe in the last century; but nevertheless the creation of the Armenian Patriarchate of Constantinople, which grew to have great power within the community, dates from this time. Armenia itself was not conquered by the Ottoman* Turks until early in the sixteenth century. Succeeding Sultans introduced Kurds* into the country, to act as Sunni* guards along the frontier with Shiʿi* Iran, not to oppress the native Armenians. In the course of Ottoman–Safavid warfare, Shah ʿAbbas of Persia deported the prosperous Armenian community of Julfa, a town in the marches between the two imperial powers, to create a trading colony, New Julfa, just outside his capital Isfahan, whose inhabitants would act as merchants throughout his realm. Here they flourished for a hundred years. They played an important part in the international trade in Persian silk. Armenian merchants were to be found in all the towns along the silk route through Anatolia to the Mediterranean ports. Some moved eastwards, to form communities in India and Burma. Some families went north to Moscow, and it was a Julfa family that created the Lazarev Institute (1815), which acted as a college for studying Eastern peoples.

From the time of Peter the Great, Russia had sought an outlet to the south, more for the sake of trade than territorial expansion. To this end she sponsored the causes of the Christian peoples of the Caucasus. In the early nineteenth century, war with Iran (Persia) yielded to her large tracts of Transcaucasia, and in the process Persia ceased to be of significance in the political fortunes of the region. Recent research has shown that the change of rulers did not bring any immediate material benefit for Armenians; but Russia brought stability and the possibility of modernization and development. From 1828 to 1840 the Tsar created an *Armyanskaya oblast* (Armenian district) out of the former Persian Khanates of Erevan and Nakhichevan. Armenian nationalists saw this as a step towards regaining their old autonomy.

Armenian nationalism grew slowly and indirectly. The first nationalist thinkers were traders in Calcutta and Madras; one of the latter established a printing press in Echmiadzin in 1771. Other important centres were the Catholic Armenian Mkhitarist seminaries of S. Lazzaro (Venice) and Vienna. Writers and thinkers emerged later in Moscow, New Nakhichevan, and Tiflis. They made possible the flowering of Armenian political and literary talent in the late nineteenth century in the Caucasus.

There was a rather different picture for Ottoman Armenians. In the capital, Armenians rose to high positions in the fields of government finance, imperial architecture and the early Ottoman theatre. The *tanzimat** played an important part in freeing the Armenian spirit within Istanbul, in a period which culminated with the 'National Constitution' of the Armenian community of the Empire (1860; ratified by the Ottoman government in 1863). But in the countryside the reforms had little or no impact; there the level of administration remained rudimentary and often brutal, and harsh living conditions exacerbated tensions and hostilities between Armenians, Kurds and Turkomans. Among the Armenians secret political societies grew up, principally three (the Armenakans – later Ramkavars – the Hunchaks and the Dashnaks) dedicated first to self-help and later to revolution. In 1894 there was a rising among the mountaineer Armenians of Sasun, which Sultan ʿAbd al-Hamid crushed with ferocity. Government assaults on Armenians throughout the Empire followed.

It was in this period that large-scale Armenian emigration to the New World began; the emigrants went, as did other subjects of the Sultan, both in order to escape from an oppressive government, particularly after the massacres of 1894–5, and in search of a freer, more prosperous life. In the late 1890s, the annual rate of Armenian immigration into the United States was 2500.

Pressure was also being exerted on Russian Armenians at the time. They became suspect in the eyes of the Tsar because of the prevalence of revolutionary and socialist ideas among them, even though their revolutionary sentiments were all directed across the frontier into Ottoman domains. A campaign against Armenians led to the seizure of the Church by the regime, and the occupation by soldiers of the monastery of Echmiadzin (1903). Government agents incited the Azerbaijani Tatars to attack Armenians in various locations; the disturbances culminated in widespread arson and murder in Baku (1905). Despite serious losses, the overall picture for Armenians was of successful self-defence, when measured against events across the frontier ten years earlier.

Armenian Dashnaks played an active part in planning the Constitutional or Young Turk Revolution of 1908, and initially thereafter their position improved greatly within the Turkish Empire. Thousands of Ottoman Armenians returned home. But by 1912 even the most ardent Armenian supporters of the Committee of Union and Progress (CUP) had grown disillusioned by the Turkish refusal to treat them as equals, exemplified by the CUP refusal to discuss the return of lands taken during the massacres of 1894–5. The growth of pan-Turkism within the CUP, and the inclusion in its politbureau of men of uncompromisingly nationalist outlook, was another indicator of the way policy was moving. Nevertheless Armenians continued to work within the Ottoman system to improve their lot, and a number of them fought commendably in the Ottoman armies in the Balkan Wars (1912–13).

The First World War and its aftermath

The outbreak of the First World War found most Armenians in a position which can probably be best described as loyally neutral. Large numbers enlisted; however, some fled east and joined the volunteer regiments which were being formed by the Russian government in Tiflis. In March 1915 those who had enlisted were disarmed, forced into labour battalions, and harshly treated. In April many of Istanbul's leading Armenians were taken into the interior and murdered.

Something more disastrous followed. By order of the government, hundreds of thousands of Armenians were deported from all centres of Armenian population in central and eastern Anatolia. They were sent in the direction of Syria and Mesopotamia. A large proportion of them died: very many men were killed on the spot, and women, children and the old died on the way, from exhaustion, desert heat, and lack of food and water. There is no doubt that local officials, gendarmerie units, and organized bands of irregulars took part in attacks on them, but the Ottoman army appears not to have been involved. Armenians remain convinced that the attacks took place on orders from the central government. This has been denied by successive Turkish governments, but eye-witness reports by relief workers, foreign consuls and some Ottoman soldiers support the Armenian viewpoint. According to Turkish estimates, the number of those who died was 5–600,000; German sources give an estimate of between 1 and 1.1 million; Armenians put the number at 1.5 million.

After the Russian Revolution, eastern (Russian) Armenia proclaimed its independence amid unpromising circumstances (May 1918). But with the ending of the war the Republic's situation improved, and in the succeeding two years Armenians experienced a genuine independence. Despite high hopes engendered by worldwide public support and favourable comments from statesmen, Armenia received no assistance except food aid. Allied delays in producing the Turkish treaty (the Treaty of Sèvres*) meant that by the time it was signed it could not be implemented. The rise of the Turkish nationalist movement, and establishment of a new Turkish army out of the Ottoman 15th Army Corps, led to an assault on Armenia in September 1920 and the collapse of the Republic of Armenia; at the same time, there was pressure on the Republic from the Bolsheviks in Azerbaijan to the east. Turkey took land in excess of Mustafa Kemal's* maximalist 'National Pact'. The Armenian government handed over power peacefully to the Bolsheviks on 2 December (however, communists today hold that Bolshevik rule began with an uprising a few days earlier).

The Armenian diaspora

In 1921 the French, keen for concessions from the new Turkey, withdrew from Cilicia, and Armenians from this territory, as well as many from western Armenia, became scattered throughout the Middle East, mostly in Syria and Lebanon. Armenians were not strangers to the Arab world: the Armenian Patriarchate of Jerusalem was of considerable antiquity, and the first and last governors of the privileged Ottoman district of Lebanon, Da'ud Pasha (1861–8) and Ohannes Pasha Kuyumjian (1921–5), were both Catholic Armenians. In Lebanon Armenians were offered citizenship in 1924; they gained their first parliamentary deputy in 1934, and their first government minister in 1958.

Scattered as they are throughout many countries, the Armenians continue to exist as an entity. There are various reasons for this. One is their Church. Although some Armenians are Catholics and some are Protestants, the vast majority of them belong to the Armenian Apostolic Church, a truly national church which has been at the centre of their life since it was established. Most Armenians have a feeling for their tradition and culture. There are organizations caring for the welfare of Armenians wherever they may be.

Wherever there are Armenians, they have their own political life, dominated by the same three parties. The Ramkavars (to use the western Armenian form of the name) are democratic liberals, whose party attracts conservative merchants and liberal intellectuals; they oppose political adventurism and support Soviet Armenia as being the alternative to obliteration; the Hunchaks have been consistently socialist since their foundation in 1887, and support Soviet Armenia on most issues; and the Tashnags, members of the Armenian Revolutionary Federation, are basically nationalist, with a socialist tinge. They have often been critical of Soviet Armenia, but less so in recent years.

It was because of the failure of these parties to pursue the Armenian cause in any meaningful way – even to obtain worldwide acknowledgement of the true nature of the massacre of 1915 – that a terrorist element emerged from 1975 from within the Armenian diaspora. The targets of the two or three groups who constitute this element have been Turkish diplomats abroad, national airline personnel and offices, and residents from locations within Turkey. Their tactics have on occasion led to splits within their organizations, and widespread revulsion at their tactics appears to have made them reconsider their methods and aims. Their emergence has made the traditional Armenian parties adopt a less complacent attitude to the furtherance of the Armenian cause.

Soviet Armenia is a land of magnetic interest to many Armenians, and many are very supportive of it; they see it as the part of the ancient homeland which has survived. Since 1956 the Soviet authorities have shown themselves to be responsive to this mood, and the country has flourished economically and culturally. The dissident movement within the country is more opposed to Soviet policies in the neighbouring territories of Karabagh and Nakhichevan (claimed by Armenian nationalists) than to communist rule *per se*. Despite the usual Soviet strictures on religion, the Armenian Church is unofficially well respected, and the part that it played in the struggles of the nation is acknowledged. A number of Armenians from the worldwide diaspora settled in Armenia in 1946–7, when there was a chance that Armenia would regain Kars and Ardahan, districts taken by Turkey in 1920.

Despite their preoccupation with Armenian affairs, Armenians from California to Singapore have identified strongly with their adoptive countries. In the Middle East, the Arab countries have shown hospitality and tolerance in absorbing a non-Muslim, non-Arabic-speaking people. However, Armenians are concerned about maintaining their own culture and schools in the face of any tendencies towards national streamlining that may occur; and the major preoccupations remain what they feel to be the war crime perpetrated by the Turks earlier in the century, and their determination to gain acknowledgement, and perhaps recompense, for it.

CJW

Further reading

R. G. Hovannisian, *The Republic of Armenia*, Vol. I, 1918–1919 (Los Angeles, 1917), Vol. II, 1919–1920 (Los Angeles, 1983)
K. M. Krikorian, *Armenians in the Service of the Ottoman Empire, 1860–1908* (London, 1987)
D. M. Lang, *Armenia: cradle of civilization* (London, 1971)
A. Nassibian, *Britain and the Armenian Question, 1915–1923* (London, 1980)
S. Der Nersessian, *The Armenians* (London and New York, 1969)
Permanent People's Tribunal, *A Crime of Silence: the Armenian genocide* (London, 1985)
C.J. Walker, *Armenia: the survival of a nation* (London, 1980)

Kurds

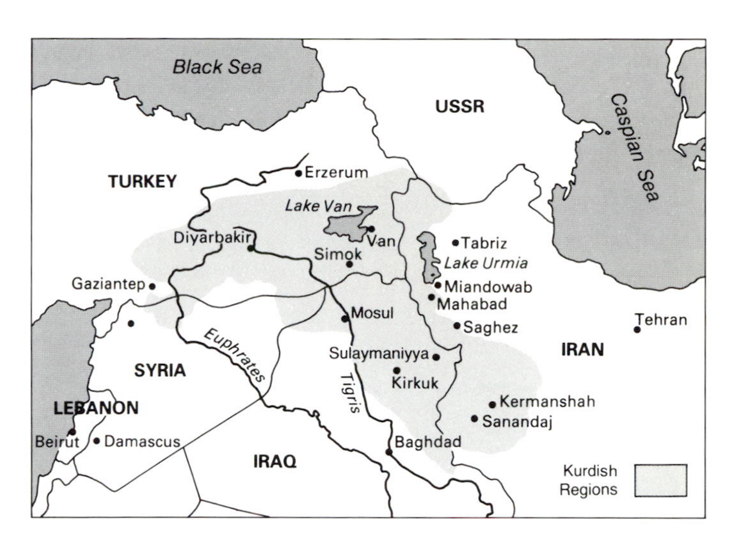

Although Kurds are to be found in Syria, Lebanon, the Soviet Union and Khorasan (in eastern Iran), the main concentration lives in the mountains where Iraq, Iran and Turkey meet. Originally the Kurds lived in the rugged and inaccessible Zagros range. From the fourteenth century onwards some Kurds moved northwards, spreading out over the eastern part of Anatolia, as far north as Mount Ararat. Since the sixteenth century the term 'Kurdistan' has been used to describe the predominantly Kurdish areas.

The Kurds are probably the descendants of Indo-European tribes settling amongst the indigenous inhabitants of the Zagros Mountains about 4000 years ago. Amongst these antecedents were the Karduchoi (Kardu or Gutu), who gave the Greek General Xenophon's Ten Thousand such a mauling during their famous retreat to the Black Sea in 400 BC. Kurds popularly believe in their descent from the Medes. By the beginning of the Arab period (seventh century AD), the ethnic term 'Kurd' was applied to the amalgam of Iranian or Iranicized tribes, some indigenous and some Armenian communities inhabiting the Zagros Mountains. Undoubtedly during the Islamic period the Kurds absorbed local Christian and Jewish communities, besides intermarrying (amongst the notable families at any rate) with Arabs and Turks.

Because the Kurds are found as minorities in six nation states, any estimate of their numbers is bound to be controversial. Governments tend to minimize and Kurds to maximize their numbers. The tabulated figures are based on percentage estimates applied to 1980 population figures.

Unlike the Arabs, Turks and Iranians, the Kurds have not yet evolved a single systematized written and spoken language. To this

Country	% of population	No. of Kurds
Turkey	19	8,455,000
Iran	10	3,701,000
Iraq	23	3,105,000
Syria	8	734,000
USSR	—	265,000
Lebanon	—	60,000
Estimated total Kurdish population		16,320,000

day Kurds are divided into two main dialect groups. Communication between members of these two groups is very difficult without some knowledge of the other dialect. They are: (1) Kurmanji, spoken northwards as far as the USSR from a line drawn roughly from Mosul across to Urmiya; (2) Sorani (or Kurdi), spoken roughly southwards from Urmiya to Khanaqin in the south on both sides of the Iran/Iraq border. In Iraq the Kurds are thus divided between the two major dialect groups. All Turkey is Kurmanji-speaking except for Dersim, an area lying between Diyarbakr, Sivas and Erzerum where a local sub-dialect, Zaza, is predominantly spoken. Three other sub-dialects exist in Iran between Kermanshah and Sanadaj: Leki, Gurani and Kermanshahi.

Almost all the Kurds are Sunni* Muslims. However, north-west of Diyarbakr some are Shiʿis and are mainly Zaza-speaking (though the two are not coterminous). Around Kermanshah and Khanaqin several tribes are Ithnaʿashari Shiʿi *(the 'established' faith of Iran). Two other religions exist, both considered Islamic 'deviations': *Ahl-i Haqq* (People of the Truth) in south-east Kurdistan, and the more widely followed Yazidi religion, a synthesis of elements of all the major and many minor religions of the Middle East. Yazidis are found mainly in Jabal Sinjar in north-western Iraq, although their main shrine, Shaykh ʿAdi, is 30 km east of Mosul. Both sects are small. Some Christians and Jews, whilst retaining their faith, can be considered part of the Kurdish culture. Many Sunni Kurds are loyal to one of two religious brotherhoods, the Naqshbandiyya* and the Qadiriyya*. Many villages profess specific loyalty to one or other of these, although such loyalties are currently on the wane.

Kurdish society today

Kurdish society is essentially tribal, and derives from the largely nomadic or semi-nomadic existence of most Kurds up to the end of the nineteenth century. The basis of tribal loyalty amongst the Kurds is a mixture of kin and territorial identity. However, many Kurds living on the plains or foothills of north Iraq, and also on the Anatolian plateau, are not tribal in any sense, and are socially more akin to their Arab or Turkish peasant neighbours. In any case, even in the mountains Kurdish tribalism is far from homogeneous, and is now in a period of disintegration even though tribal ties are still very strong. The complexity of relationship changes from tribe to tribe, although it is possible to say that differences in organization tend to be those of degree rather than kind, roughly conforming to the following divisions: tribal confederation, tribe and sub-tribe. The relationships within the confederation are not immutable and can be severed in response to political or economic change. Through prowess or skill a chief may detach tribes or sub-tribes from neighbouring confederations and establish a new grouping loyal to himself.

The confederations were largely artificial creations by government in the sixteenth century. There was an important interplay between confederations and government between the sixteenth and nineteenth centuries, with the latter confirming chiefs, or playing off one against another. Confederation chiefs were often government appointees and of no blood relationship to the tribes under them. For the tribes this had the advantage of impartiality in settling internal disputes, and frequently useful connections and contacts with a wider political world. Most of the confederate chiefs were of part-Arab origin, frequently claiming descent from the Prophet, and were consequently held in high esteem. They often intermarried with neighbouring Arab, Iranian or Turkish notable families, thus securing economic or political advantage for their confederation.

However, below the paramount chief a chief (or agha) at village or village-group level could wield considerable power. This, traditionally, was for several reasons: he was arbiter of water and land allocation each year, issues of extreme sensitivity; he decided when and where seasonal migration of livestock should occur; his guest-house controlled all contacts with the outside world; only he married outside the village (in careful alliance), and only he was polygamous (with consequently a very high proportion of villagers closely related to him). This last point in particular explains the strength of loyalty even under a despotic agha. With the collapse of the political strength of the confederations in the nineteenth century, the growth of a market economy and the registration of erstwhile tribal lands in the agha's name in the twentieth century, these aghas became stronger, since they dealt directly with government and since their position as landlords could be upheld by state law. By the 1960s in Iranian Kurdistan, for example, 78 per cent of land was registered as privately owned and only 2 per cent still registered as tribal, effectively a complete reversal of the state of affairs a century earlier. As a consequence, most tribespeople have now become a landless proletariat. With mechanization of agriculture many are now seasonal migrants to the cities and elsewhere where they can find work. Others have migrated permanently to the larger cities of the Middle East. Even so, tribal loyalties are still strong.

History

The history of the Kurds has been dominated by a complicated relationship with government and by internal divisions. Until the sixteenth century the mountains were the scene of recurrent revolts against government. These revolts were evidence of the disturbance of the delicate balance of coexistence which had evolved, and normally prevailed, between people of the mountain and those of the plain. The mountains were also the source of some of the best troops in the Islamic army. Saladin* himself was the son of a Kurdish general, but although he spoke Kurdish he never lived in Kurdistan.

After the battle of Chaldiran* in 1514, when the Ottomans* pushed back the Safavids* from eastern Anatolia, Kurdish tribes were used on both sides to police the border, and the hereditary rights of noble Kurdish families to paramountcy of confederations was recognized by government. The system worked happily until the nineteenth century, when both the Ottomans and Qajars (Iran) extended direct administration in the area. This triggered a series of unsuccessful revolts until the end of the century, which demonstrated the difficulty Kurdish leaders had in working together.

The destruction of the political power of the old confederate chiefs produced internal disorder in Kurdistan, since government was unable to replace the arbitrational role of the paramounts. The void was filled by the rapidly growing religious brotherhoods, the Qadiriyya and Naqshbandiyya, from roughly 1830 onwards. The shaykhs of these orders became immensely powerful, some acquiring control of village lands and combining secular with religious power.

Towards the end of the nineteenth century, Western political thought penetrated the cities of the Ottoman Empire and began to affect the thinking of urban intellectual and notable Kurd families. The idea of a 'Kurdish nation' began to take root. Neither government nor traditionally minded aghas and shaykhs welcomed this development, since the growth of nationalist feeling was likely to challenge their authority.

When Ottoman Turkey was defeated, some Kurdish nationalists hoped for an independent state and the Treaty of Sèvres* (1920) actually provided for this possibility (Article 64). It was the nearest the Kurds have ever got to a substantial state of their own.

Kurds in Turkey

The Treaty of Sèvres proved a dead letter. Mustafa Kemal Atatürk* led a successful war in Anatolia to establish a Turkish state. Kurds supported him, in the belief they were fighting for the 'Muslim Fatherland'. In 1922, however, Atatürk suppressed the Sultanate, and two years later suppressed the Caliphate, thus removing the two bases of belief in this concept. At the same time he proscribed Kurdish schools, associations and publications in an attempt to suppress Kurdish identity. Repression of the Kurds triggered revolts in Turkish Kurdistan in 1925 in the areas of Elazig, Kharput and Diyarbakr, in 1927–30 around Mount Ararat, and 1937–8 in Dersim. These rebellions were put down with utmost ferocity. Tens or hundreds of thousands died. Perhaps a million were forcibly displaced over this period, villages razed, young men forcibly conscripted in an attempt to assimilate them under duress. Aghas and shaykhs were deliberately exiled in order to remove the foci of Kurdish social solidarity.

By the 1950s it was generally believed that the Kurds had bowed to the inevitable. Aghas and shaykhs were able to return to their villages and many rapidly became essential to local government, a large percentage of them becoming landlords of previously communal lands. Despite some easing of the lot of Kurds, the extreme poverty led to the migration of much of the male working population. In the towns and cities some Kurds were deeply influenced by leftist thinking. By the seventies some were actively fighting alongside Turkish leftists against rightists in eastern Anatolia. Specifically Kurdish parties were formed, of which the Kurdish Socialist Party of Turkey (TKSP) and the Kurdish Workers Party (PKK) are the most notable. Their own implacable hostility each to each, expressed in frequent armed clashes, illustrates the quarrelsome nature of Kurdish politics even between leftist parties. In reaction to their experience of government brutality all Kurdish parties in Turkey are secessionist. The Turkish government has reacted vigorously, executing a number of those caught in guerrilla operations. Even those who have done no more than claim to be Kurdish have been sentenced to years of imprisonment with hard labour. In the words of the government, 'no Turk may describe himself as a Kurd'. Recent government efforts to develop the region may reconcile the majority of Kurds to government policy but this assumption must be open to question.

Kurds in Iran

Unlike Turkey, which is about 80 per cent Turkish, Iran is composed of several substantial communities, of whom the Kurds are but one. As a result Tehran has been reluctant to concede any kind of autonomous status to the Kurds. When Riza Khan* seized control of Iran in 1921 he dealt ruthlessly with rebel Kurd chiefs. But he also won widespread loyalty amongst other chiefs by transferring tribal lands to their personal ownership. Many chiefs were thus absorbed into the Iranian establishment, and became dependent on government goodwill for the sale of agricultural produce. The Kurdish community was allowed to express itself culturally, a distinctly better situation than in Turkey.

During the Second World War Soviet and British troops occupied western Iran. Kurds in the Soviet sector were encouraged to secede, and those in Mahabad* responded by declaring an independent Republic in January 1946. It enjoyed only limited support outside the town itself. Many chiefs were more worried about selling their tobacco crop to government. Others feared the dangers to their own status implicit in the new Republic. In Mahabad a Kurdish Democratic Party of Iran (KDPI) was formed. The revolt was only viable because of the fortuitous arrival of the Iraqi Kurd Mulla Mustafa Barzani with 3000 fighters. But when the Soviet troops suddenly withdrew from neighbouring Azerbaijan in May 1946 the Mahabad Republic found itself on its own. An Iranian force with Kurdish tribesmen hostile to Mahabad in the van reoccupied Mahabad at the turn of the year. The leaders of the revolt were hanged. Barzani withdrew to the USSR. Suppression of Kurdish areas followed. The security service Savak's* network of informers drove all activity by KDPI and by other Kurd nationalists underground. Nevertheless, KDPI was slowly able to build a substantial following, particularly from 1973 under its able socialist secretary-general, ʿAbd al-Rahman Qasimlu.

Following the Islamic Revolution of 1979, KDPI and Komala (the Revolutionary Kurdish Toilers Party) hoped to achieve an autonomy agreement with Tehran. They seized Kurdish areas from the Shah's troops and were strongly placed. But negotiations led by Qasimlu and a Sunni Kurdish shaykh of leftist persuasion, ʿIzz al-Din Husayni, ended in failure and fighting. Despite the heavy commitment of Iranian troops against Iraq from summer 1980, the Kurds were unable to resist army advances into Kurdistan. By 1985 only a small enclave in Hawraman was still held, thanks to assistance from the Iraqi side of the border.

Kurdish nationalists protecting the Sananaj Mosque from the Iranian forces

Kurds in Iraq

In 1918 the British army had occupied all of present-day Iraq. Three main groups of Kurds existed: those north and east of Mosul who, for obvious linguistic reasons, had closest ties with Kurds inside the new Turkish border; those around and to the east of Kirkuk; those around Sulaymaniyya, the largest solely Kurdish town, and the 'capital' of the Sorani dialect. Sulaymaniyya was thus the most influential centre of the Kurds, but it was resented by others.

When Britain decided to encourage Kurdish incorporation in the new Iraqi kingdom, the Kurds of Mosul and Kirkuk favoured inclusion, the Kirkuk Kurds more because of their fear of subordination to Sulaymaniyya in any Kurdish entity than on account of any enthusiasm for the Iraqi kingdom. Sulaymaniyya was decidedly hostile, reflecting a growing national consciousness. When Britain made Iraq independent by treaty in 1932, the guarantees Britain had given the Kurds were not transferred to the new Iraqi state. Undoubtedly the government feared that any concessions to Kurdish claims for special treatment would trigger claims amongst the much larger Shiʿi community of southern Iraq. The lack of confidence gave way to revolts, put down with British airpower.

In the mid-thirties Mulla Mustafa Barzani, a man from a family that combined religious and secular local leadership, emerged as a new leader for Kurd separatist feeling. Although he was driven out of Iraq in 1945 he was able to return in 1958, following ʿAbd al-Karim al-Qasim's* overthrow of the Hashimite monarchy. Barzani helped Qasim get rid of opponents of the new regime and in return obtained Qasim's help to strengthen his position locally against rival tribal chiefs, many of whom had benefited from his exile. He was also able to reassert his leadership of the Iraqi KDP, clashing badly with other leaders of KDP. Barzani soon broke with Qasim and was able to continue a war against successive governments intermittently until the Baʿth* regime in 1970 offered to hammer out an autonomy agreement. Negotiations failed, due largely to bad faith on both sides. A particular and recurrent bone of contention was the question of oil-rich Kirkuk. Kurdish nationalists claim it is Kurdish and should be within any autonomous region. War was resumed in April 1974 after Barzani's rejection of the autonomy law introduced by the Baʿth. The Iraqi army attacked with far greater vigour than the KDP had expected. Government troops, as usual, were supported by a considerable number of Kurds, reflecting traditional patterns of internal rivalries amongst Kurds and the ambiguous and complex relationship between the Kurds and government. As the KDP was driven up to the border, Iran came strongly to its aid. Only fear of all-out war between Iran and Iraq persuaded the Baʿth to negotiate with Tehran. In March 1975 Iraq ceded the *thalweg* demarcation of the Shatt al-ʿArab watercourse to Iran, and Iran cut off supplies to the KDP. Within a week the Kurdish revolt had collapsed. The Baʿth embarked on a programme of resettling thousands of Kurds elsewhere in Iraq, an issue which has continued to cause deep bitterness.

In 1976 Barzani's arch-rival and enemy from the sixties, Jalal Talabani, formed the Patriotic Union of Kurdistan (PUK) and continued the struggle. Although Barzani himself died in 1979 his sons Idris and Masʿud rallied KDP forces with the help of the new Islamic regime in Tehran in 1979. In the sixties Barzani had helped the Shah root out Iranian Kurdish activists, hanging some and handing others over. Once again bitter conflict ensued between KDPI fighting in Iran and Tehran's Iraqi KDP allies. KDPI worked in cooperation with PUK. Both felt that fighting should not occur between Kurdish parties. Although PUK and KDP failed to cooperate, partly because of PUK's abortive attempt to negotiate a new deal with the Baʿth, they had by mid-1985 achieved considerable success in establishing a swathe of Kurdish-controlled land along the border areas. What remains questionable is their ability to hold the land if Iraq and Iran cease hostilities. KDP and PUK's heartlands roughly reflect the linguistic divide between Kurmanji and Sorani. As in Iran, neither KDP nor PUK demands more than autonomy within the state. Nevertheless their demands outstrip what the government is willing to concede, and they are weakened by ideological, tribal and territorial rivalries which dog the footsteps of Kurdish nationalism. Meanwhile the government is still able to call on Kurdish irregulars, some, but by no means all, unwillingly.

Kurds elsewhere

Most Kurds in Syria* are there as a result of Turkish repression in the 1920s, and are settled along the border in the Jazira. Although there was persecution during the sixties and early seventies, this has now abated. The Kurds in Lebanon* arrived from Syria in the sixties in response to the building boom. They provided the cheap labour, living in shanties. Some of them were the first victims of Christian militia attacks in the Lebanese civil war. In the USSR the Kurds are one of a hundred recognized minorities, and are allowed full cultural expression. There are an estimated 350,000 migrant Kurdish workers in Western Europe, the vast majority from Turkey.

DMcD

Further reading

M. van Bruinessen, *Agha, Shaikh and State* (Utrecht, 1978)
G. Chaliand, *People without a Country* (London, 1980)
E. Ghareeb, *The Kurdish Question in Iraq* (Syracuse, 1981)
A. R. Ghassemlou, *The Kurds and Kurdistan* (London and Prague, 1965)
D. Kinane, *The Kurds and Kurdistan* (London, 1964)
D. McDowall, *The Kurds*. Minority Rights Group Report No. 23 (London, 1985)

Palestinians

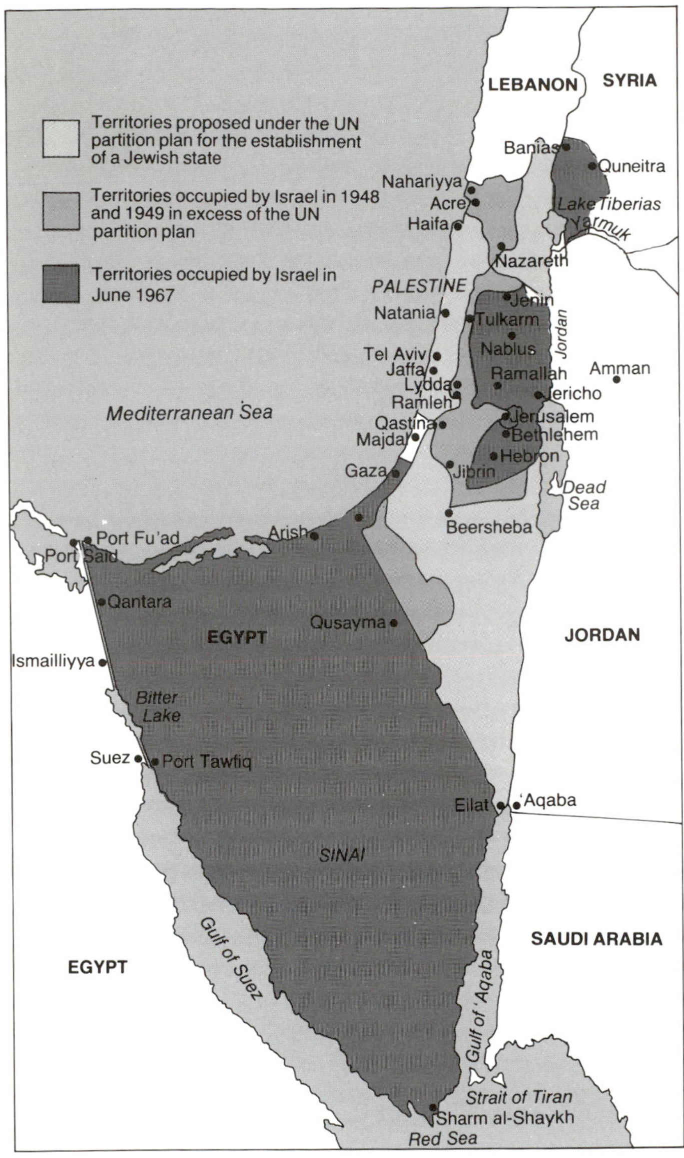

At the end of the first Arab–Israeli War* in 1948 an estimated one million residents of the former state of Palestine were registered for relief with the international charitable organizations set up to assist the homeless and the refugees. Although this number decreased somewhat at the end of 1949, as some of the refugees found accommodation with relatives and as the organizations tightened their criteria for assistance, the natural increase in the population as a whole, combined with the succession of wars in the area, led to a dramatic rise in the refugee population. By the autumn of 1982, after the Israeli invasion of Lebanon, the total number of Palestinian refugees was thought to have reached some two million, out of a total Palestinian population of just over four million.

The largest number of refugees is concentrated in the East Bank of Jordan, where they number more than 1.1m. Other communities of refugees, ranging in size from about 200,000 to 350,000, exist in Syria, Lebanon (400,000) and Kuwait, with smaller groups in Saudi Arabia, Egypt, Iraq, Qatar, the United Arab Emirates, Oman and Cyprus. An estimated 165,000 refugees live in Europe and North America.

Apart from the Palestinian refugees and their descendants now living outside what was Palestine, there are 1.8m Palestinians still resident in those areas of the country that came under Israeli control. These include 700,000 in the West Bank*, some of whom live in refugee camps as well. Another 480,000 Palestinians are concentrated in the tiny Gaza Strip, where they consist both of indigenous residents and those who fled from the Israeli occupation of the Palestinian coastal areas in 1948. Within Israel itself, there are some 530,000 Palestinians concentrated mainly in the Galilee, the Triangle and Haifa, as well as in parts of the Negev Desert.

Although it is almost forty years since Palestine itself disappeared from the map, the majority of those who have continued to live in Israel and in the Israeli-occupied territories, as well as those who have been forced to flee to other lands, continue to identify themselves as Palestinians and, with few exceptions, support the Palestine Liberation Organization (PLO)* – the body set up in 1964 to further Palestinians' claims to an independent state of their own.

Origins of the Palestine problem

The exodus of refugees began shortly after the United Nations General Assembly issued a resolution in 1947 ordering the partition of Mandate Palestine into two independent states, one for the Jews and the other for the Arabs. At first the exodus consisted mainly of middle-class urban Palestinians anxious to avoid the sporadic fighting which broke out between units of the Haganah – the underground Israeli army – and Palestinian irregulars. However, as the fighting spread to other parts of Palestine, particularly the Galilee, the exodus became general. Most sought refuge in those Arab territories closest to them: inhabitants of Haifa left for neighbouring Lebanon, along with the peasants of the Galilee. Others from the cities of Jaffa and Ramleh fled south to Egypt and the Gaza Strip. The declaration of the State of Israel on 14 May 1948, and the subsequent entry of the Arab Legion and of other Arab armies and irregulars from Syria, Egypt and Iraq, led to an escalation of the conflict. By the autumn of that year, hundreds of thousands of refugees were living in orchards, barns and caves, convents, army barracks and other places of shelter provided by charitable organizations.

Gradually, makeshift camps were set up in the West Bank and

Gaza Strip as well as in the neighbouring countries of Lebanon, Syria and Transjordan. Designed to be temporary, the camps have continued to house Palestinian refugees decades after the establishment of the State of Israel. Despite calls by the United Nations for their repatriation and compensation, Israel has refused to readmit the refugees pending a full-scale settlement of the Arab–Israeli conflict, and recognition by the neighbouring Arab states of Israel's right to exist. The Israeli occupation of the West Bank and of the Gaza Strip during the June 1967 war*, as well as the subsequent invasion of Lebanon* in June 1982, added further to the numbers of Palestinians who lost their homes or who were forced to seek refuge in areas outside Israeli control.

Over the years since 1948, however, large numbers of the Palestinian population have managed to become self-supporting and to avoid life in the camps, where they had been dependent on charity organized by institutions such as the International Red Cross and the United Nations Relief and Works Agency (UNRWA)*. Thus, although the number of refugees registered for relief rose from 1 million in 1949 to just over 1.8 million in 1979, the percentage of the total Palestinian population on relief dropped during the same period from 76.7 per cent to just over 41 per cent. The evidence available suggests that they achieved this self-sufficiency primarily by taking up jobs as casual labourers in agriculture, construction and industry, by opening up new businesses of their own and by pursuing advanced careers in the professions and technical trades in the neighbouring host countries as well as in more distant places of exile such as Kuwait, Saudi Arabia and the Gulf States, Europe and the United States.

The Jaramana Camp in 1967

The peasantry

During the Mandate* years, the peasantry made up more than two-thirds of the population of the country. Despite attempts by the British mandatory authorities to survey the land and to set up a system of private landownership, much of the countryside was still cultivated according to the *musha'* system, whereby those who planted the seed and harvested the crop were granted, in effect, rights to the arable land. However, the sale of land to the new Jewish immigrants, combined with the increasing tendency of the large landowners along the coast to plant cash crops such as citrus, had already deprived many of the peasants and share-croppers of these rights. By the mid-1930s, large numbers were forced to find work in the growing cities or by working as casual labourers on the larger, privately owned estates.

Although the outbreak of the Second World War and the increase in world demand for agricultural produce from the Mediterranean benefited those peasants who still had land to cultivate, by 1948 the standard of living of the peasantry as a whole had declined as more and more families were forced to find subsistence from fewer and fewer acres. And even this oppression paled into insignificance compared with the loss of their country in 1948. Without their rights to the land, the peasants found themselves unable to support themselves and their families, and while some managed to rescue a few farm animals or tools, these were of little use in the neighbouring host countries of refuge where arable land was also scarce and where unemployment was already extremely high in the agricultural sector.

Confined, for the most part, to the camps set up by UNRWA, the generation of peasants affected by the initial dispersion in 1948 never fully recovered from the loss of their land. Only by the late 1950s and early 1960s were their sons and daughters able to find some new employment, primarily as workers in UNRWA-run workshops or as casual labourers in the growing towns of Beirut, Amman and Damascus, where the need for labour in the building trades and in small-scale industries such as food processing and textiles had grown along with the rise in population occasioned both by the influx of Palestinian refugees and by the rapid urbanization of the area as a whole.

By the late 1960s still other avenues of employment had opened up in Saudi Arabia, Kuwait and the Gulf states, where the nationalization of the oilfields and the huge rise in oil prices in the early 1970s created a boom in construction and in industry. Palestinians were particularly valued as foremen on building sites and in warehouse and distribution centres – as well as in factories – where their knowledge of both English and Arabic made them ideal intermediaries between the expatriate Western supervisors and the less skilled indigenous workers.

By the early 1980s, however, the decline in oil prices and the

Temporary shelters replaced tents at UNWRA's Baqaʿa refugee camp in east Jordan in late 1968

ensuing recession in Saudi Arabia, Kuwait and the Gulf states had severely reduced the need for immigrant labour. Palestinians, who were seen as political activists, were particularly affected, especially as it was feared that their militancy could give rise to discontent among the local population and among other Arab immigrants. In Lebanon, ten years of civil war, too, had culminated in the establishment of a coalition of militias that was almost universally hostile to the Palestinians living in the camps around Tripoli in the north and in southern Lebanon, near the coastal cities of Sidon and Tyre, as well as in Beirut (see Lebanese Civil War). The devastation of the camps, the massacres of Sabra and Shatila in 1982 and the subsequent fighting with the Lebanese Shiʿis* left the peasant refugees more insecure than ever, subject always to expulsion and to the denial of their rights either to a home or to a livelihood.

The bourgeoisie

Unlike the peasantry, the Palestinian bourgeoisie often found it possible to recoup some of their wealth in exile. Many had grown prosperous during the Second World War, when the huge rise in British military expenditure in the country led to an increase in the demand for construction projects, banking and insurance, trade and other commercial services, as well as in exports of citrus fruits and other food crops. Some of their wealth had been invested in interest-bearing bank deposits, in shares, government bonds, commodity stocks and other forms of financial paper that had become available as Palestine was integrated into the world market. Most of this was transferrable to their places of exile. So, too, were the business contacts and enterprises they had established or helped establish in Palestine, and this mobility enabled a sizeable number to re-start their lives in the host countries where they sought refuge.

Well-known companies, such as Middle East Airlines and the Arabia Insurance Company, for example, opened offices in Lebanon in 1948. By the end of the 1950s, when they had experienced an impressive growth in their profits, their shareholders included some of the wealthiest Palestinians in the Arab world. Two banks*, founded by Palestinians – the Arab Bank and Intra Bank – played a key role in the development of Jordan and Lebanon respectively. Today the Arab Bank is one of the largest in the Middle East, with branches and affiliates in London, Geneva and the United States. Arab Bank's auditors, Saba and Co., moved their offices to Beirut and Amman and from there expanded their operations throughout the Middle East. Some of their former employees now run successful accountancy and other firms of their own.

Palestinian construction companies like CCC also benefited from the rapid development of the oil states in the Gulf. CCC's Palestinian founders, Hasib Sabbagh, Muhammad Kamel ʿAbd al-Rahman and Saʿid Tawfiq Khuri, started with only $3m in capital, but by 1967 were doing business worth $18m a year, a figure that rose to an estimated $60m a year by the early 1970s, thanks to the contracts they obtained in the Gulf states, Libya and Nigeria.

However, in retrospect it is clear that the rise of a new Palestinian bourgeoisie in exile was possible only in those states of the Middle East where the local bourgeoisies were in their infancy. In Lebanon the domination of the Palestinian bankers, financiers, merchants and industrialists was quickly challenged by the Maronites*, who feared the loss of their own hegemony in the country. Intra Bank, which at the time controlled huge sections of the economy – in tourism, transport, trade and communications as well as in banking – encountered a liquidity problem in 1966 and, although its assets outnumbered its liabilities, was liquidated later that year. Thousands of Palestinians lost their life's savings, while the bank's assets in the US, Europe and the Middle East were divided up among the governments of Lebanon, Kuwait, Qatar and a number of US, British and West German banks.

Elsewhere in the Middle East, the advent of new regimes in the late 1960s and the imposition of restrictions on immigration and on Palestinian residents severely limited the opportunities available to Palestinian entrepreneurs. Measures enacted by the Saudi Arabian government in the late 1950s meant that by the mid-1960s local Saudis were being given preference in government contracts, as well as in access to huge government subsidies designed to expand their role in industry and commerce.

In Kuwait, nationalization laws were passed that required Palestinian and other foreign firms to grant majority ownership to local Kuwaiti citizens. As a result, the Palestinians were often left with the job of running their own companies, but with their potential profits and decision-making powers severely reduced.

The advent of a republican regime in Libya in September 1969 meant that Palestinian consultants and advisers were no longer able to repatriate their profits and earnings to other countries, or to their families abroad, just as earlier, in 1958, the overthrow of the pro-British regime in Iraq had led to the introduction of a socialist economy designed to limit the role of private enterprise, particularly of companies run by non-Iraqis. By the late 1970s, Palestinians who wanted to start companies, or to expand existing ones, found the going particularly tough. While some managed to move their companies to Amman, Cairo, Cyprus or London to avoid the restrictions, the rising competition posed by the local bourgeoisies, plus the economic decline which followed a few years later, meant that many were finding it necessary to keep a low profile or to give more privileges to their local partners. The turmoil in Lebanon, the outbreak of the Gulf War and other regional political and military disturbances also added to the problems they faced. Many concluded that the only way they could ensure their economic viability was by establishing a state of their own, in their original homeland.

The professionals

The successes encountered by the Palestinian bourgeoisie in the 1960s and early to mid-1970s, however, also gave rise to a new class of professionals within Palestinian society. Palestinians who had entered training institutes, colleges and universities while still refugees advanced into jobs throughout the Arab world, where their skills as engineers, architects, journalists, doctors and academics were in short supply. Many brought their families with them to their new places of exile in Saudi Arabia, Kuwait and the Gulf states, as well as to places further afield such as London, Boston and Sao Paulo.

However, although Palestinians as a whole continued to experience one of the highest education* ratios in the Arab world, their access to jobs dwindled as oil revenues fell and as fears of terrorism arose within the Gulf and elsewhere. Palestinians without a passport, no matter how good their qualifications, found it difficult to obtain immigration visas, while others were given only temporary work permits. By the mid-1980s, education and emigration were no longer the golden ticket to a new life in the diaspora that they had been for an older generation now reaching middle age. Young Palestinians in their teens, twenties and thirties found themselves once again confined to the camps or permanently disbarred from professional and social advancement in their host countries.

Within the occupied territories, severe Israeli restrictions on Palestinian universities, combined with the rise of militantly anti-Palestinian forces within the Israeli government, removed the possibility of higher education for many. This, combined with the decline of job opportunities in the Arab world, meant that for many the future appeared to hold very little, if any, hope of escape.

Conclusion

For most Palestinians, the rise of the PLO* in the late 1960s and the diplomatic successes achieved by Yasir ʿArafat* in the 1970s provided a ray of hope and a central focus for their aspirations. Palestinians of peasant origin viewed the guerrilla organizations as their own, for, unlike their more prosperous compatriots, they placed a greater emphasis on action and on 'return'. Unable to prosper in exile, they welcomed the more militant stance taken by the PLO in the 1970s as a sign that at last something was being done about their problems, in their name, and by their own leaders. However, the bourgeoisie, too, welcomed the PLO, especially ʿArafat and Fatah*, the main guerrilla body. Unlike the Marxist movements within the PLO, Fatah eschewed polemics involving capitalism versus socialism and sought to remain outside the conflicts and rivalries that divided the Arab regimes. Even the remnants of the aristocracy at times rallied behind ʿArafat and the PLO, especially in the aftermath of the 1967 War*, when the Israeli occupation of the West Bank and Gaza destroyed their last remaining claim on power and on social and economic privilege.

Gradually, however, the splits within the PLO took their toll. While many of the refugees on the West Bank and in Gaza still continue to give support to ʿArafat and to Fatah, others, particularly in Syria, Lebanon and Jordan, support the more militant guerrilla bodies which have called for a halt to diplomatic negotiations and a resumption of revolutionary activity, both within the Arab world and in Europe. This in turn has led to a renewal of support by certain elements within the bourgeoisie and within the old ruling families for the policies of King Husayn of Jordan, the erstwhile ruler of the West Bank before its occupation by the Israelis. Convinced that time is running out, these elements within Palestinian society fear that a more militant approach puts at risk the achievements they have gained since the loss of their homeland in

1948. The agreement, however, of the more militant organizations such as the Popular Front for the Liberation of Palestine*, to bring Fatah* back into the PLO* at the meeting of the Palestinian National Council (PNC*) in Algiers in April 1987, appeared to herald a new era of unity that was expected to intensify PLO demands for negotiations on its own terms and to lead to more intense confrontation with the Israeli authorities in the occupied West Bank* and Gaza Strip.

PAS

Further reading

D. Gilmour, *Dispossessed: the ordeal of the Palestinians 1917–1980* (London, 1980)

S. Graham-Brown, *Palestinians and their Society 1880–1946: a photographic essay* (London, 1980)

R. Sayegh, *Palestinians: from peasants to revolutionaries* (London, 1979)

P. A. Smith, *Palestine and the Palestinians 1876–1983* (London and New York, 1984)

F. Turki, *The Disinherited: journal of a Palestinian exile* (New York, 1972)

Palestinian groups

The Palestine Liberation Organization (PLO)

The PLO and its military wing, the Palestine Liberation Army (PLA), were founded in 1964. The Palestine National Council (PNC) is the supreme governing institution of the PLO, while the 14-member Palestine Executive Committee (PEC) is responsible for daily affairs. The Palestine National Liberation Movement (PNLM or Fatah) joined the PNC in 1968 and in 1969 all the guerrilla organizations joined the PNC. The PLO is funded by annual contributions from Arab countries (Saudi Arabia is the biggest donor), by aid from other friendly countries and by a 3–6 per cent levy on all Palestinians. The PLO has offices in all Arab countries, and in countries such as the USA, the USSR, France, Great Britain, China, Cuba, Yugoslavia and Switzerland, although it does not enjoy official recognition in all of these countries. The October 1974 Arab Summit in Rabat affirmed the right of the Palestinian people to establish an independent national authority under the leadership of the PLO in its role as the sole legitimate representative of the Palestinian people. The PLO became a full member of the Arab League* in September 1976. The chairman of the PLO, which has been based in Tunis since the Egyptian–Israeli Peace Treaty in 1979, is Yasir ʿArafat, who replaced Yahya Hammuda in 1968. The PLO's first chairman was Ahmad Shuqayri (1964–7).

The Central Council of the Palestine Resistance Movement (CCPRM) was founded in 1970 and represents all the guerrilla groups, of which the most important are the following:

Fatah (The PNLM)

The biggest single Palestinian movement, Fatah was created in 1957 and is headed by Yasir ʿArafat. Its secretary-general is Faruq Qaddumi. Ten members of its Central Committee were expelled in November 1983 for their part in the revolt against Yasir ʿArafat.

Popular Front for the Liberation of Palestine (PFLP)

Founded in 1967, the Marxist–Leninist PFLP is headed by Dr George Habash and is based in Damascus.

Popular Front for the Liberation of Palestine – General Command (PFLP–GC)

This group, which split from the PFLP, is headed by Ahmad Jibril and is based in Damascus. It is pro-Syrian.

Democratic Front for the Liberation of Palestine (DFLP)
The DFLP, which split from the PFLP in 1969, is headed by Na'if Hawatmeh and is based in Damascus.

Saiqa (Vanguard of the Popular Liberation War)
Founded in 1967, Saiqa is headed by ʿIsam al-Qadi and is Syrian-backed.

Arab Liberation Front (ALF)
Founded in 1969, the ALF is headed by ʿAbd al-Rahim Ahmad and backed by Iraq.

Palestine Liberation Front (PLF)
The PLF split from the PFLP-GC in April 1977. It then split into two factions in 1983. One faction, based in Tunis, is nominally loyal to Yasir ʿArafat. The other faction belongs to the Syrian-based National Salvation Front.

Other groups include the extremist 'Black June' headed by Sabri Khalil al-Banna (Abu Nidal), and 'Black September'. The 'Rejectionist Front' consists of parties who reject any settlement which involves the recognition of Israel.

Palestinian organizations

Palestine National Council (PNC)
The 379-member PNC represents the guerrilla groups and other PLO bodies, trade and student unions, and Palestinians from throughout the diaspora. It meets yearly. Until Egypt's peace treaty with Israel the PNC met in Cairo. Since then it has met in Damascus, Algiers and Amman. In November 1984 it moved its headquarters from Damascus to Amman.

The Palestine Liberation Army (PLA)
Founded in 1964, the PLA has 16,000 men who are dispersed throughout the Middle East. Its commander-in-chief is Yasir ʿArafat and its military commander is Khalil al-Wazir (Abu Jihad).

The Palestine National Fund (PNF)
The PNF moved from Damascus to Amman in November 1984. It is financed by a contribution of 3–6 per cent of the income of every Palestinian but also receives aid from Arab and other countries.

Palestine Red Crescent
Founded in 1969, the Palestine Red Crescent operated seven hospitals, several emergency centres and clinics and 150 ambulances until the Israeli invasion of Lebanon in June 1982. By the following year it continued to function in Lebanon in areas under Lebanese and Syrian control but not in areas under Israeli control.

Palestine Research Centre
Founded in 1965, the centre has a library and archives and publishes magazines and books on questions relating to Palestine. It moved from Beirut to Cyprus in 1983.

Source: The Middle East and North Africa 1987, Europa Publications Limited, London.

Part VI
INTER-STATE RELATIONS

Signing the Camp David Agreements: President Sadat, President Carter and Prime Minister Begin

The Great Powers in the Middle East

In the aftermath of the Second World War Britain appeared as the paramount power in the Middle East region. It had fought virtually alone against the Axis in the Middle East; it retained military bases in Egypt and Palestine; it was politically dominant throughout the region, including the Gulf and South Arabia, and it controlled the oil resources of Iran. Britain gave some encouragement to the foundation of the Arab League* in 1945 and helped to exclude France from the Levant by securing the independence of Syria and Lebanon. But the facade of British power concealed a substantial weakness. Exhausted by the war and with an anti-imperialist Labour government in office, Britain began a process of abandoning much of its role in countries such as Greece, Turkey, Iran and Saudi Arabia to the United States which, with the announcement in March 1947 of the Truman Doctrine for aid to Greece and Turkey, was for the first time beginning to act as a great power in the region. In 1947 Britain decided to abandon its Palestine Mandate and hand over responsibility to the UN. The granting of independence to India in 1947 began to undermine the basis of Britain's great power status in the Middle East, though it continued to regard itself as a paramount power in much of the Arab world until the 1956 Suez crisis.

Britain shared with the US an apprehension of a Soviet threat to the Middle East but the two powers often differed in their approach. After Egypt's refusal to join an anti-Soviet Middle East Defence Organization, the US concentrated on strengthening the 'northern tier' of anti-communist states – Turkey, Iran and Pakistan. But in 1955 Britain joined with these three states and Iraq to form what became the Baghdad Pact*. While the US remained outside, although lending support, Britain made the Baghdad Pact the focus of its policies and attempted, against strong Egyptian opposition, to extend the alliance to other Arab states.

In 1950 Britain, France and the US issued a Tripartite Declaration on Palestine, rationing arms supplies and freezing armistice lines on Israel's periphery. This helped to keep the peace for five years. But France's interest in the Middle East was primarily related to North Africa where, with the granting of independence to Tunisia and Morocco, France concentrated on suppressing the Algerian revolt. Seeing this as backed by the pan-Arab movement led by Nasser's* Egypt France entered a close military alliance with Israel. Opposition to Egypt's role in the Arab world also became the hallmark of Britain's Middle East policy, leading to Anglo-French collusion in Israel's invasion of Egypt in 1956.

From the aftermath of the Suez War the US and USSR became the predominant outside powers in the Middle East. Britain's remaining important Arab ally was destroyed in the Iraqi 1958 Revolution. For a further decade Britain exercised direct control in the Gulf and South Arabia until its final withdrawal. With Algerian independence in 1962 France began to repair its damaged relations with the Arab states but henceforth, like Britain, its interests in the Arab world became almost exclusively commercial and cultural.

Policies of the super powers

Soviet intervention in the Middle East as rival great power to the US dates from 1954 when it began supporting the growing neutralism of Nasser's Egypt. In general it has pursued the policy of supporting popular national leaders rather than local communist parties. The Suez War enabled it greatly to extend its influence as it became the principal supplier of arms and economic aid to three key Arab states – Egypt, Syria and Iraq. Even pro-western Arab regimes have been happy to see the USSR act as a counterweight to overwhelming US support for Israel. Soviet influence reached a high point in the 1960s but with the death of Nasser in 1970, Egypt, followed by the Sudan, left the pro-Soviet camp.

The US position in the Middle East has been more solidly based although it has also suffered reverses – notably in the overthrow of the Shah of Iran in 1979. In the 1980s US Middle East policy is founded on various related concerns: the preservation of pro-Western regimes, the diminution of Soviet influence, the protection of oil supplies and other economic interests and, by no means the least important, the security of the State of Israel. A settlement of the Palestine problem is considered desirable but is not given precedence. There is frequent disagreement on the relative importance of these considerations between Congress and the administration and also within the different organs of the State Department. In general it is Congress which takes the more pro-Israeli line and the difference is especially reflected in the question of requests for US arms supplies from moderate and pro-Western Arab states such as Saudi Arabia and Jordan.

US and Israeli interests

Domestic political pressures have always influenced Middle East policy in Israel's favour but these have never been so powerful as during President Reagan's terms of office. Despite US disapproval of some of Israel's actions in Lebanon, a US–Israeli strategic understanding was reached in 1983, US aid to Israel – at one third of all US foreign aid – has reached record levels and the US veto is frequently used to prevent UN condemnation of Israel's actions.

The argument that US and other Western interests in the Middle East can best be protected by Israel receives powerful support in Washington and it can be argued that the oil recession of the 1980s has reduced the strategic importance of the Arab states. Nevertheless there is still a majority view in the State Department that the US must show some balance in providing support for pro-Western Arab regimes. US aid to Egypt, Sudan, Morocco and Tunisia is substantial and relations with the Arab Gulf states are close. Although the idea of a land-based Rapid Deployment Force for Middle East defence has not developed because of the Arabs' refusal to have US forces stationed on their soil, the US has repeatedly made clear that it would intervene against any Soviet or Iranian attempts to cut communications in the Gulf or the Indian Ocean.

At the same time the US has never finally abandoned attempts to achieve a settlement of the Palestinian problem through negotiation in order to follow up on the US success of the Camp David Agreements* and the Egyptian–Israeli Treaty. The difficulty is that the Arab states suspect that the US will ultimately always endorse the Israeli view and will never accept the principle of Palestinian self-determination. In the mid-1980s there is also a strong awareness that the Middle East is low in Washington's scale of priorities. If, in spite of this, the Arabs refuse to abandon all hope of the US taking what they would regard as an equitable stand on the Middle East it is because they recognize that the US is the most powerful external factor in the Middle East equation and the only one capable of influencing Israel. In its extreme form this was the late President Sadat's* view that 'the US holds 99 per cent of the cards in the Middle East'. Thus even radical Arab regimes such as those in Syria, Iraq and Algeria have never ceased to have dealings with the US and only the marginal exceptions of Libya and the PDRY (South Yemen) have been totally hostile. Iran's Islamic Republic, which is not directly concerned in the Arab–Israeli problem, can afford to continue to dub the US the Great Satan but in the mid-1980s there are signs that this may not be permanent, just as the US has to acknowledge that as a major Middle East power Iran cannot merely be isolated.

Iranian students and Western journalists mingling outside the besieged US Embassy, Tehran, 7th November 1979

Soviet policies

This unavoidable preponderance of the US role in the Middle East helps to explain why the Soviet Union has been unable fully to exploit with the Arabs either the extreme US partiality for Israel or US policy failures such as its intervention in Lebanon in 1983. Moreover, Arab conservative regimes' fears of a Soviet threat have greatly increased since the Soviet invasion of Afghanistan and the establishment of a Marxist regime in Ethiopia. The USSR's close relationship with the PDRY and Libya has brought some strategic advantages but has also alarmed the Arab neighbours of these two states. The fact that Middle Easterners generally regard Western technology as superior to the Soviet equivalent is also a factor. Even Soviet hopes aroused by the advent to power in Iran of an extreme anti-US regime have been disappointed, as this has been equally hostile to Moscow.

Since the early 1970s the USSR has been unable to recover its former superpower parity with the US in the Middle East. After the 1973 war* the US Secretary of State Dr Kissinger successfully excluded the Soviet Union from his peace diplomacy. President Carter was more willing to accept a Soviet role and a high point was reached with the US–Soviet agreement on a joint approach to a Middle East peace settlement of 1 October 1977. However, this was soon bypassed by President Sadat's visit to Jerusalem, leading to the Camp David Agreements, which again excluded the Soviet Union.

The USSR still has some important assets. In Syria it has a powerful Arab ally which has partially replaced the loss of influence in Egypt. By the mid-1980s it was apparent that any attempt to exclude both Syria and the USSR from the peace process was futile. The desire of many Soviet Jews to emigrate from the USSR could also be used as a bargaining factor. Soviet diplomacy scored a success with the establishment of relations with the UAE and Oman in 1985, although Moscow's conciliatory policy towards the conservative Arab oil states is continually at risk through its ties with the unstable Marxist regime in the PDRY.

The return of the USSR to a position of parity with the US in Middle East affairs depends largely on the state of Soviet–US relations. A *sine qua non* would be the restoration of Soviet–Israeli diplomatic relations, but even then the US would have to conclude that nothing could be achieved towards a Middle East settlement without full Soviet participation. The Reagan–Gorbachov summit meeting in November 1985 bore little on the Middle East although the Soviet leader reaffirmed the view that 'nothing can be done without us'. But there were signs that the Soviet Union, like the US, was not placing high priority on its relations with the Arab countries. It was much more concerned with the 'northern tier' states on its borders – Turkey, Iran and Afghanistan, and the potential effect of the Iranian Revolution on its own growing Muslim population. For both the US and the USSR this scale of priorities would only change in the event of a renewed Middle East crisis or conflict in which they could not avoid direct involvement.

Relations with the EEC

While the eleven members of the EEC collectively could have a potential great-power status in the Middle East, they have consistently failed to achieve the necessary unity of purpose. Differences of views on the Arab–Israeli problem have been exacerbated by a certain Anglo-French rivalry over the Middle East. The EEC Venice declaration of 1980 gave clear support for Palestinian self-determination but there has been no effective follow-up despite consistent encouragement from the Arab states for Europe to play a bigger role in the Middle East to balance US partiality towards Israel. The attitude of Israel is significant. The bulk of its foreign trade is with Europe but it looks to the US for diplomatic, military and financial support. Britain and France are major arms suppliers to key Arab states such as Iraq and Saudi Arabia, while Japan plays a role in the Middle East commensurate with its status as an economic superpower. Yet none of these states exerts influence in the Middle East comparable to that of the US and the Soviet Union and this situation is unlikely to change in the forseeable future.

Relations with Asia

In recent times the Arab states have given considerable importance to their relations with the three major Asian powers – India, China and Japan. With India and China the political aspect has taken priority. Egypt's President Nasser* established a relationship with the Indian Premier Nehru soon after the 1952 Revolution and thereafter Egypt was associated with India among the leaders of the non-aligned movement. Egypt and India cooperated in arms manufacture and India generally took a pro-Arab stance on the Palestine problem (in spite of the similar close relations between the Arabs and Pakistan).

Nasser first encountered the Chinese Premier Chou En-Lai at the 1955 Bandoeng Conference and in May 1956, to the outrage of the US, he recognized the Peking regime. His main motive was that, if the Soviet Union subscribed to a UN arms embargo on the Middle East, China might be an alternative source of weapons. However, although Nasser, like most Arab leaders, admired China's efforts to develop as an independent rival to the superpowers, with the growing rift between China and the USSR he felt bound to regard Soviet political, military and economic support for the Arabs as more important, and relations with Peking cooled. Arab states hostile to the USSR, on the other hand, have generally been more favourable towards China, which has recently extended its economic relations with the Arab world, including the Gulf states.

For decades the Arabs have admired Japan as an Asian state which has achieved economic superpower status and they have welcomed Japanese investment and expertise – especially as it has appeared to be politically disinterested. Japanese economic involvement in the Arab world is extensive. Japan has sometimes associated itself with EEC policy declarations on the Middle East but has undertaken no political initiatives of its own.

PM

Further reading

R. Allen, *Imperialism and Nationalism in the Fertile Crescent* (London, 1974)
M. Heikal, *Sphinx and Commissar: the rise and fall of Soviet influence in the Middle East* (London, 1978)
W. Z. Laqueur, *Confrontation, the Middle East War and World Politics* (London, 1974)
E. Monroe, *Britain's Moment in the Middle East 1914–1971* (London, 2nd rev. edn., 1981)
W. R. Polk, *The United States and the Arab World* (Cambridge, Mass., 1965)

International Islamic movements and institutions

A major setback to the Muslim sense of universalism was the abolition of the Caliphate* in 1924. Although the reality had diverged from the ideal almost from the very beginning of the Islamic era and territorial and political pluralism had long been entrenched, Muslims sustained the view that they constituted one community (*umma*)*. This was the social corollary of *tawhid**, the doctrine of God's absolute indivisibility, and the political corollary of the supreme Prophethood of Muhammad*.

Yet, durable as it has been, the idea of pan-Islam has time and again crashed headlong into the political ambition of several willing contenders for its leadership. This was apparent immediately after the Turkish Grand National Assembly, in March 1924, struck its radical blow at Islamic tradition. The caliphal mantle having unceremoniously been cast aside, international conferences were convened to advance the institutional and political cooperation of Muslims. But they displayed only the aspiration of the convenor either to succeed to the Caliphate himself – Sharif Husayn* at a conference in Mecca in 1924, King Fu'ad* at Cairo in 1926 – or to solidify his power and influence – King ʿAbd al-ʿAziz* at Mecca in 1926 and the Mufti Amin al-Husayni at Jerusalem in 1931.

In addition to the personal and dynastic rivalries, these conferences foundered on the nearly insurmountable difficulty of designing a blueprint of Islamic unity now that even a general framework, such as the Ottoman Empire* represented, no longer existed. While by no means novel, this difficulty was compounded by a certain petulance between the Arabs and the other Muslims. For example, at the Mecca Conference of 1926 several delegates, Indians, Turks and Russians among them, attempted – unsuccessfully – to set fixed charges for the pilgrimage and to hold the Saʿudis, the new guardians of the Holy Places, accountable for their revenues to the Muslim world at large. At the Jerusalem Conference, delegates agreed that an international Islamic university should be created and attached to the al-Aqsa Mosque, but could not agree on the subjects to be taught, including the desirability of secular subjects; its relationship with al-Azhar University; or the language of instruction. Shawkat ʿAli, leader of the Khilafat movement in India and mainstay of Muslim international conferences, irritated the Egyptians in particular with his implicit denigration of the venerable al-Azhar, and upset the Arabs in general with his proposition that Arabic was not the sole Islamic language.

However, the Jerusalem Conference was a notable success in raising the awareness of Muslims worldwide of the extent to which Jews and Zionist organizations were purchasing land in Palestine. Here was the beginning of the process that today has put Palestine –

Prayers to celebrate the Korban Bayram feast at the mosque at Kütahya, Turkey

'the Holy Land' – at the top of the Islamic as well as Arab political agenda. The beginning was modest nonetheless, and although a small secretariat had been established in 1931, funding proved elusive and nothing came of it. Other political leaders suspected Amin al-Husayni's intentions, but, more significantly, to the emerging middle-class professionals, intelligentsia and businessmen of the Fertile Crescent, the revival of the Caliphate increasingly seemed an obsession of the traditional *ʿulama*; in fact, they had constituted the bulk of delegates to the international conferences between 1924 and 1931. For members of the new middle class, rather, the real struggle was anti-colonial and nationalist.

The Muslim Brotherhood

In this atmosphere, Hasan al-Banna*, a school-teacher, in 1928 founded the Muslim Brotherhood (*Ikhwan al-Muslimun*) in Egypt and soon attracted many thousands of supporters from all classes, with well-educated and middle-class members particularly prominent. Like the international conferences, the Brotherhood drew inspiration from Islamic reformers such as al-Afghani*, ʿAbduh* and Rida*, but, unlike the conferences, it was rooted in the particular fortunes of one country. Indeed, the British occupation since 1882 brought home the twin dangers of Western imperialism: moral distortions on the one hand, and political and social injustices on the other. To fight against the British was thus to fight for Egypt as well as for Islam, and these Muslim activists, almost in spite of themselves, became committed nationalists.

Full participation in Egyptian politics in the 1930s and 1940s led the Brotherhood to a natural extension of its activities into the Sudan, over which there was officially an Anglo-Egyptian condominium; and to automatic sympathy with the Palestinian Arabs, who likewise appeared victims of a nefarious British imperialism. By 1948 when the Brotherhood sent volunteers to Palestine to stop the creation of the State of Israel, it had already begun to put down roots outside of Egypt itself and come to terms – long before, in fact – with another idea, Arab nationalism*, towards which devout Muslims were ambivalent. It did seem, for all the reasons of interconnected history and language which ʿAbd al-Rahman al-Bazzaz was to offer in a 1952 book, that Arabism and Islam were complementary.

But 1952 brought the Egyptian Revolution, ushering in an era of great turmoil in the entire Middle East. Two consequences ensued from the emergence of ʿAbd al-Nasir (Nasser)* as the undisputed power in Egypt by 1954, and as the principal Arab leader and ideologue soon thereafter.

First, the Muslim Brotherhood, despite having initially supported the Free Officers, quickly, and often violently, opposed Nasser's secular and socialist policies at home and abroad, which were couched in the name of Arabism. Whereas Brotherhood intellectuals had previously criticized the concept of one-state nationalism (despite the reality of accepting it) and yet had come to terms with, if not endorsed, the concept of Arab nationalism, the latter, too, began to appear less palatable the more it became synonymous with Nasserism. Sayyid Qutb*, for example, changed his view, announcing that Arabism's historical role had been completed and that the world stage was reserved for Islam. Greater accent was placed on the need to realize the Islamic *umma*.

In practical terms, the repression and eventual proscribing of the Brotherhood fragmented its leadership and sent many key people into exile abroad, particularly in Saudi Arabia, Jordan, Sudan, Syria and Iraq. If local Brotherhood groups had not previously existed in these countries, they now took shape as well-developed organizations with their own hierarchies, finances and publications. Saʿid Ramadan set up a kind of coordinating centre at Geneva, and between the various groups exchanges of visits, literature and ideas have occurred. But these groups have become caught up in the local contexts in which they operate, much as al-Banna's Muslim Brotherhood was part of the Egyptian political landscape, regardless of its broader interest in Palestine.

The ironical result of the confrontation with Nasser was not to have made the Brotherhood more national than transnational; it was always both. Rather, the irony was to have reinvigorated the idea of pan-Islam while at the same time helping to enhance the separateness of the groups dedicated to it.

The response from Saudi Arabia

The second consequence of Nasser's ascendancy was an ideological counter-crusade in the name of Islam by the conservative Saudi monarchy. The Egyptian president had denounced this throne as 'feudal' and tied to the Western imperialists, and flushed with the 'victories' at Suez (1956) and Baghdad (1958), he seemed, from the Saudi perspective, to be distinctly menacing. Egyptian intervention in the Yemeni civil war and the defection of several princes to Nasser's cause made the threat very real. Military battle with the Egyptians was joined, but so too was ideological battle. As guardians of the Holy Places, the Saudis relied on Islam to counter the appeal – to young Saudis as well as others – of pan-Arabism.

To this end, in 1962 they inspired the convocation of delegates from forty-three countries in Mecca to form a new organization, the Muslim World League (*Rabitat al-ʿalam al-islami*). It functioned at first as a propaganda forum for the Saudis but, recently, it has been a proponent of Islamic educational work (*daʿwa*). In late 1965, King Faysal* launched a more direct initiative, calling for an alliance of all Muslims. He travelled to Iran, Jordan and other countries to stimulate support for an 'Islamic summit' of Muslim heads-of-state, but the political climate proved to be uncongenial.

Nasser's power hindered the emergence of an institutionalized, international Islamic movement, and his weakness, as a result of the catastrophic losses in the 1967 War* with Israel, allowed events to take their course. The defeat had been so traumatic – it was *the* disaster, *al-nakba* – that it set into motion a process of re-examination so intense and broad that when a deranged tourist set the al-Aqsa Mosque alight in 1969, the outrage was instant and the assumption universal that, in one way or another, Israel was responsible. Twenty-five states assembled at the resulting Rabat summit meeting in September 1969.

The emergence of Islamic organizations

Its most notable achievement was the call for a foreign ministers' conference, which in fact took place in March of the following year. From this meeting we can date the process by which the most important contemporary Islamic movement was given concrete form. Plans had been circulating for decades, notably advanced by the World Muslim Congress (*Mu'tamar al-ʿalam al-islami*), which is based in Karachi and, putatively, claims descent from Amin al-Husayni's 1931 conference and its decision to establish a secretariat. In the event, in 1970 the foreign ministers of the Muslim countries did agree, over the objections of the representatives of then-Nasserist Egypt, Libya and the Sudan, to establish a permanent secretariat. Jidda was chosen as its home (pending the 'liberation' of Jerusalem); and Tunku ʿAbd al-Rahman, the first prime minister of Malaysia, became the first secretary-general of the new organization, the Organisation of the Islamic Conference (OIC; *Munazzamat al-mu'tamar al-islami*).

It differs from all other previous conferences in several ways: it is a grouping of states, not individuals or even unofficial national delegations, and is properly labelled an intergovernmental organization; a mechanism of regular consultation among members – heads of state summit meetings, foreign ministers' conferences, meetings of specialized agencies and standing committees – is well-established; and members make regular budgetary contributions to sustain an ever-growing list of activities.

This degree of institutionalization, which earlier conferences notably failed to develop, was due, in part, to the political ascendancy of Saudi Arabia in the aftermath of the 1967 War; and, in part, to the great wealth which the Muslim states of the Persian Gulf acquired as a result of the fourfold increase in oil prices in 1973. But too much can be made of the impact of the 'oil revolution', and it is perhaps fairer to say that while the newly generated wealth augmented the means, the disposition towards greater coordinated activity among Muslims already existed – a manifestation of the Islamic revival that has been apparent since the late 1960s.

But, like any international organization, the OIC is sustained by the belief of its members that it is a useful organization. It has in fact had an impact as a definable bloc within the Non-Aligned Movement (NAM) and the United Nations (UN). It was responsible, for example, for the censure which the UN General Assembly imposed on Israel as a result of its 'basic law' making united Jerusalem the eternal capital of Israel. Moreover, individual states, such as Saudi Arabia, Pakistan and Malaysia, have found the OIC particularly useful because it magnifies their voice in world counsels. Pakistan has found it a sympathetic audience in its continuing contest with India, and the Malaysian government maintains that, for the advancement of its foreign policy goals, it is the most important international forum after the Association of South-East Asian Nations (ASEAN).

As this suggests, member states are less concerned with creating the conditions of a structured and universal Islamic community than with advancing their own interests within a broad and vaguely defined community. The charter acknowledges that 'solidarity', not unity, is the goal, and one of its core principles is 'respect of the sovereignty, independence and territorial integrity of each member State'. In practice, even solidarity has often been elusive. The Algerians, for example, have generally given higher priority to the NAM than to the OIC, while the opposite is true of the Libyans. Although all member states objected to the Soviet invasion of Afghanistan, those also members of the Arab Steadfastness Front (Syria, the People's Democratic Republic of Yemen, Algeria, Libya, and the Palestine Liberation Organization) were hesitant to have the OIC condemn the Soviet Union outright. Moreover, Malaysia and Indonesia – out of deference to their allies in ASEAN – have urged the OIC to moderate its position on the Muslim minorities of the Philippines and Thailand, whereas Libya has agitated for a strong response, including the imposition of sanctions. Finally, the Iran–Iraq War* and the failure of OIC efforts to mediate an end to it have been a painful – and embarrassing – reminder of the limits of Islamic solidarity.

Despite these problems, the OIC has expanded into a broad network. Forty-five states are currently members, and of its five secretaries-general to date, two have been from the Arab world, and one each from South-East Asia, Africa and South Asia. Several specialized agencies have been set up to deal with particular tasks, such as the overtly political al-Quds Committee charged with advancing the liberation of Jerusalem, and the more prosaic Committee for Scientific and Technical Cooperation. One of the more interesting bodies to develop is the World Islamic Jurisprudence Academy (*Majmaʿ al-fiqh al-islami al-ʿalami*), a convocation of *ʿulama* from around the Muslim world who are charged with determining Islamic solutions to contemporary problems through the exercise of independent judgement (*ijtihad**).

Islamic banking*

The most important affiliated organization is the Islamic Development Bank (IDB), which, since its opening in 1975, has been dedicated to advancing the economic development of members through its lending, equity participation, foreign trade financing and leasing operations. These activities must be seen in the light of the growing insistence throughout the Muslim world that banking procedures fully conform to the *sharīʿa**. In principle this translates into a prohibition on usury (*riba**), and, in practice, into the charge of a carefully calculated service fee (generally not exceeding 3 per cent) on loans. Close cooperative relations have been established with Islamic banks in several countries, such as the Dubai Islamic Bank and the Islamic Bank of Jordan; the IDB may have equity in these banks or engage in joint financing of various projects. The idea of greater economic integration, particularly the creation of a free-trade zone and of an Islamic Common Market, have been mooted since the late 1970s, and, in principle, agreed. Yet the fact remains that for most Muslim states, the major import and export trading partners are, not other Muslim states, but the industrialized giants.

This pattern of the development of institutions but little substantive integration is somewhat reflected on the regional level. In November 1980 delegates from sixteen Asian states met in Kuala Lumpur to launch a new coordinating body, the Regional Islamic Daʿwah Council of South-East Asia and the Pacific (RISEAP). Funded principally by the Saudi and Malaysian governments, it has set up an Islamic training centre, publishes a regular magazine and produces books on Islam in the thirteen languages used in the area. Over sixty *daʿwa* groups have become members, and, although RISEAP is too diffuse and too self-consciously apolitical to become a powerful bloc, it has the potential of making its members more aware of each other, and of Muslims in the Middle East and elsewhere. Like the other larger organizations, RISEAP will not radically shift allegiances. But, like them, in a small and often imperceptible way, it is gradually helping to make the abstract notion of Islamic community more concrete for Muslims.

JP

Further reading

A. Dawisha, ed., *Islam in Foreign Policy* (Cambridge, 1983)
M. Kramer, *Islam Assembled: the advent of the Muslim Congresses* (New York, 1985)
R. P. Mitchell, *The Society of the Muslim Brothers* (London, 1969)
J. H. Proctor, ed., *Islam and International Relations* (London, 1965)

Inter-Arab relations

In the fifth decade of the Arab League's* existence certain elements in relations between the Arab states remain constant but there have also been significant changes with permanent consequences. The shared experience of colonial occupation or domination remains, with a feeling that the Arab world has been artificially divided, although this is a diminishing force and the growth of a territorial nationalism in individual Arab states is discernible. The Palestine question is still a major focus of Arab attention, affecting all inter-Arab relationships to varying degrees. At the same time the Arab world has become politically more complex and diffuse. The seven founding members of the League, which were the only independent Arab states at the time, have increased to twenty-one, with the Palestine Liberation Organization* accepted as a full member, together with Somalia and Djibuti which are not strictly speaking Arab states. The Maghrib or western half of the Arab world, which was formerly marginal, has become more integrated into Arab politics – a trend that has been enhanced by Libya, which belongs both to the Maghrib and the Mashriq, or eastern half, and by the transfer in 1979 of the Arab League headquarters to Tunis and the appointment of a Tunisian secretary-general of the League.

The oil boom of the 1970s and early 1980s greatly enhanced an existing trend which was increasing the importance and influence of the Gulf oil states headed by Saudi Arabia. The recession of the 1980s has scarcely reversed this trend because the relative economic power of the Gulf states remains substantial. Another important trend has been created by the large-scale and unprecedented shift in Arab population between the Arab states. The first wave was of Palestinians, with some Lebanese and Syrians, in the 1950s, to be followed by a flood of Egyptians in the 1960s and 1970s who went westwards to Algeria and Libya and eastwards to the Arabian peninsula and later to Iraq. Tunisians, a substantial part of the Sudanese elite, and most recently a new Lebanese diaspora have also found employment in other Arab states. The paradoxical consequence has been that while the Arab world, with the possible exception of Qadhafi's Libya, has abandoned the concept of the political merging of the Arab states along the lines of the Syrian–Egyptian union of 1958–61, and although a sense of national sovereignty has grown among most Arab citizens, from another aspect the Arab world has become more united.

Arabic: a factor for unity

The possibility which seemed real even thirty years ago that the different Arabic dialects would become virtually separate languages has disappeared as the Egyptian and the Syrian/Lebanese/Palestinian dialects have become universally familiar through the movements of population and the influence of radio, television, cinema and the press. A standard 'modern' written Arabic has developed and a large range of Arabic newspapers and periodicals, many of them printed in London and Paris, are published for immediate distribution throughout the Arab world. At the same time the approach to Arab unity has become more practical and less Utopian. Some pan-Arab institutions, which may or may not be organs of the Arab League, are active especially in the field of banking, finance and the provision of aid. The single most important example of the new approach to Arab unity has been the establishment in 1981 of the Gulf Cooperation Council (GCC)* of six Arab Gulf states. Its successful development offers the prospect that various Arab regional confederations – the Arabian peninsula, the Nile Valley, the Maghrib and Greater Syria – might lead by degrees to a wider Arab political union.

However, apart from the establishment of the GCC, and in spite of their greater cultural cohesion, the Arab states in the mid-1980s are politically more disunited than at any time in the past. Since 1980 the Iran–Iraq War has provided a new disruptive factor. Although the majority of Arab states support Iraq, with varying degrees of enthusiasm, Syria is a notable exception, followed by Libya, the PDRY and to a lesser extent Algeria.

The ostracization of Egypt

But the greatest impact on relationships between the Arab states in recent years resulted from President Sadat's* unexpected initiative in negotiating directly with Israel, which led to the Camp David Agreements of 1978 and the Israeli–Egyptian Treaty of 1979. The other Arab states, with marginal exceptions, agreed to boycott Egypt economically and politically and the Arab League headquarters was moved to Tunis. The boycott was never total and Egypt under President Mubarak* has gradually improved its links whether officially or unofficially with most Arab states. Diplomatic and commercial relations were restored with Jordan in 1984, while the improved relationship with Iraq only falls short of full diplomatic ties. In January 1984 Egypt was asked to return to the Islamic Conference Organization (ICO). However, Egypt has failed in its ultimate aim of returning to the Arab League, the obstacle being the treaty with Israel which Egypt, despite its freezing of relations with Israel after the invasion of Lebanon, has shown no sign of being willing to renounce. It is unlikely that countries such as Saudi Arabia would reopen their embassies in Cairo, still less agree to the return there of the League's headquarters, as long as an Israeli embassy remains. The strongest single obstacle to the return of Egypt to the Arab fold has been the Syrian veto and the standing Arab League practice that such important decisions must be unanimous.

Influence moves to Syria

Egypt's absence from pan-Arab diplomacy and the downgrading of Cairo's status as the most important Arab capital have changed the climate of inter-Arab relations. Arab leaders, including those who are opposed to Egypt's present regime, feel that the Arab voice in the world at large has been weakened. In some respects Egypt's central role as a regional power has been assumed by Syria. As a result of large-scale rearmament with Soviet assistance since the 1982 Lebanese war, Syria's operational armed forces are larger than those of Egypt, and Syria is the major Arab power confronting Israel. The Syrian role in Lebanon, backed by President Asad's* skilled diplomacy, has gained the country a dominant regional position which is seen by many as aspiring towards a Greater Syria concept which would include Syrian control over the Palestinian liberation movement. However, there are also weaknesses in the Syrian position. Its expanded armed forces still do not match the strength of the Israelis. Prolonged and intensive efforts by Syria to influence the conflicting parties in Lebanon to reach a compromise settlement which would preserve the country's unity under Syrian protection have been unsuccessful. Finally, although Syria has helped to weaken Yasir ʿArafat's* leadership of the PLO there is little indication that Palestinians either inside or outside the Israeli-occupied territories are prepared to accept Syrian sponsorship or follow the leadership of the pro-Syrian splinter groups from the PLO. Also, a rapprochement with Jordan after several years of hostility does not mean Jordan's acceptance of Syrian hegemony.

The position of the PLO within the Arab world in the mid-1980s has been weakened but has not finally collapsed (see The Arab–Israeli Problem). Most Palestinians still see no alternative and the majority of Arab states, including Egypt, Iraq and Saudi Arabia, continue to accept the formula adopted at the Arab summit in Rabat in 1974 that the PLO is the 'sole, legitimate representative of the Palestinian people'. A crucial factor in the PLO's future is the attitude of Jordan. If King Husayn were formally to reject the Rabat formula and claim to represent Palestinian interests the PLO position would be further undermined, but it is by no means certain that Jordan would be able to carry this through successfully. Moreover Syria, although hostile to ʿArafat's leadership, would not accept his replacement by a Jordanian nominee.

Syro-Iraqi relations

A constantly disturbing feature in inter-Arab relations in the 1970s and 1980s was the hostile rivalry between the Baʿthist* regimes in Iraq and Syria. Relations between Damascus and Baghdad were consistently bad throughout the period with only brief periods of remission. The differences are not ideological but rather reflect the territorial nationalism which has developed in the Arab states since independence; and there is a strong element of personal antagonism between Presidents Asad and Saddam Husayn. The most striking consequence has been Syrian support for Iran in the Gulf War, which is clearly strategic rather than ideological in view of President Asad's well-demonstrated hostility towards Islamic militants in Syria.

The Gulf Cooperation Council

The Iran–Iraq War has reduced Iraq's potential influence as a major regional power. It also provided the catalyst for the establishment in 1981 of the GCC* from which Iraq is excluded. This confederal organization with headquarters in Riyadh and a Kuwaiti secretary-general aims at close cooperation in the political and military fields and gradual moves towards a full common market of the six states. Its success has been facilitated by the similarity of the social and political systems of the members.

Saudi Arabia has a naturally dominant position in the GCC but it also plays a crucial role in the wider Arab world. It sees itself as the natural mediator and prefers to use quiet behind-the-scenes methods to settle or alleviate inter-Arab disputes. It constantly refuses to take sides. A typical product of Saudi diplomacy was the Fez Plan of the 1982 Arab summit meeting outlining Arab terms for a Middle East peace settlement which secured an Arab consensus. The lack of results from this initiative has not deterred Saudi Arabia from pursuing its efforts.

The presence in southern Yemen of a Marxist-dominated regime is a cause of concern to the GCC states. The Yemen Arab Republic (YAR) in North Yemen tries to maintain a balance between its close ties with Saudi Arabia and those with its fellow Yemenis to the south. These are frequently disturbed, although the aspiration towards unification of the two Yemens is never eliminated. There was satisfaction among the GCC states with the establishment in 1983 of relations between the PDRY (South Yemen) and Oman after years in which the former had supported a rebellion in southern Oman, but the future of the PDRY was placed in jeopardy by the brief and bloody civil war in early 1986, which raised the possibility that it would become an increased focus of instability in the peninsula.

Libya – a disruptive element

Libya has been a disruptive element in inter-Arab relations since Colonel Qadhafi's coup in 1969 and is likely to remain so while he is in power. His pursuit of his own highly individual Arab–Islamic nationalism has brought him into conflict with almost every Arab regime at some point, including Libya's Egyptian, Sudanese and Tunisian neighbours, and his relations have rarely been easy even with those radical and anti-Western Arab states with which he shares some common objectives. But the sudden shifts in Libyan policies create new alliances as well as disputes. An outstanding example was the Oujda Agreement with Morocco of 1983, which jeopardized Libya's relations with Algeria. But it was typical that this new alignment was placed in question by a meeting between Colonel Qadhafi and the Algerian president in February 1986.

Rifts in North Africa

Hostility between Algeria and Morocco is an outstanding factor in Arab Maghrib politics – bearing some analogy with that between Syria and Iraq in the Mashriq. Here there is again a strong element of territorial rivalry, although in this case there are also ideological differences between the pro-Western Moroccan monarchy and the socialist and non-aligned Algerian Republic. Moreover there is a specific long-running dispute over the former Spanish Sahara, which was ceded by Spain to Morocco and Mauritania in 1975, but which the Polisario Front declared independent as the Sahara Arab Democratic Republic (SADR) in 1976. With nearly all Moroccan political groups supporting the Moroccan claim and Algeria supporting the SADR, which by 1986 had been recognized by sixty-three countries, there is little prospect of this dispute being easily resolved.

Militant Islam in its fundamentalist form is regarded as a threat to varying degrees by all existing Arab governments, but until it wins control of an Arab state, as it has of Iran, it is not a factor in inter-Arab relations. However, the varying Arab reactions towards the Islamic Republic in Iran are an important cause of dissension between the Arabs. It will remain as long as Iran attempts to export its revolution.

PM

Further reading

F. Ajami, *The Arab Predicament* (Cambridge, 1981)
Europa Publications, *The Middle East and North Africa* (London, annually, 1948–)
M. Halpern, *The Politics of Social Change in the Middle East* (Princeton, 1963)
M. H. Kerr, *The Arab Cold War* (New York, 1971, 3rd edn.)
P. Mansfield, *The Arabs* (London, 1985, 2nd edn.)
P. Mansfield, *The Middle East: a political and economic survey* (Oxford, 1980, 5th edn.)
P. Seale, *The Struggle for Syria: a study of post-war Arab politics 1945–1958* (London, 1965)

The Arab League

Algeria	Oman
Bahrain	Palestine Liberation Organization
Djibouti	Qatar
Egypt	Saudi Arabia
Iraq	Somalia
Jordan	Sudan
Kuwait	Syria
Lebanon	Tunisia
Libya	United Arab Emirates
Mauritania	Yemen Arab Republic
Morocco	Yemen People's Democratic Republic

Founded in March 1945, the League of Arab States (Arab League) was established to encourage Arab cooperation and unity. The League's seven founder members were Egypt, Lebanon, Iraq, Syria, Transjordan (later Jordan), Yemen (later the Yemen Arab Republic – North Yemen) and Saudi Arabia. Since then a further fourteen Arab states have joined, plus Palestine which is considered an independent state and is represented by the Palestine Liberation Organization (PLO)* at League meetings.

The Pact of the League of Arab States, dated 22 March 1945, is the League's founding charter. The Council is the Arab League's supreme authority. The Council, in which each member state has one vote, usually meets in March and September at foreign minister level. The Council has sixteen committees, including the political committee and committees dealing with communications, health, information and social affairs. The secretary-general is appointed by a two-thirds majority of council members and holds the rank of ambassador.

The League's headquarters and the offices of its specialist agencies were established in Egypt. Its first three secretaries-general, ʿAbd al-Rahman ʿAzzam Pasha (1945–52), ʿAbd al-Khaliq Hassuna (1952–72) and Mahmud Riyad (1972–9) were all Egyptians and Egypt dominated the League until its rift with its Arab neighbours following the Camp David Accords* of 1978 and its peace treaty with Israel* on 26 March 1979. On the day after the peace treaty the Arab League Council in Baghdad expelled Egypt from the League and its headquarters was moved to Tunis. The League's agencies were also relocated. The Arab Organization for Education, Culture and Science (Alesco) moved to Tunis while the Arab Organization for Administrative Science moved to Amman and the Arab Labour Organization to Iraq. Mahmud Riyad resigned in March 1979 and Chedli Klibi, then Tunisia's information minister, was appointed the new secretary-general.

A period of decline

Disunity among the Arab ranks and failures to make any progress on the issue of Palestine weakened the League's influence. The Arab summit meeting scheduled to be held in Riyadh in November 1983 was postponed until April 1984 but divisions within the PLO and among Arab countries as well as the Iran–Iraq War led to the cancellation of the 1984 summit. The summit that was eventually convened on 7 August 1985 was boycotted by Libya, Syria, South Yemen, Lebanon and Algeria. Saudi Arabia was represented by the deputy prime minister, Crown Prince ʿAbd Allah, rather than by King Fahd.

The League was more positive in purely technical affairs and in 1985 two satellites were launched by the Arab Satellite Communications Organization (Asco – but better known as Arabsat*), a League agency based in Riyadh. The European Ariane rocket launched the first Arabsat satellite in February from French Guyana and the second was launched by the US space shuttle in June. Both satellites were built by France's Aerospatiale, which also built a third to be kept in reserve. The satellites are intended to improve telephone, telex, television, radio and data transmission services throughout the Arab world.

The Cooperation Council for the Arab States of the Gulf

The organization, better known as the Gulf Cooperation Council (GCC), was established on 25 May 1981 by Bahrain, Kuwait, Oman, Qatar, Saudi Arabia and the United Arab Emirates (UAE). The GCC's Supreme Council comprises heads of member states and meets annually. The president is a member of each state, according to an alphabetical rota system. The Supreme Council appoints the secretary-general on the recommendation of the Ministerial Council for a renewable three-year term. Each member state contributes in equal proportions towards the budget of the Secretariat. The secretary-general in 1986 was the Kuwaiti ʿAbd Allah Yaʿqub Bishara. The Ministerial Council, consisting of foreign ministers of member states, meets every three months.

The GCC provides for cooperation among member states in the fields of economics, industry, agriculture, transport and communications, energy, defence and external relations. In 1983 the GCC founded the Gulf Investment Corporation.

The Arab–Israeli problem today

Some four decades after the establishment of the State of Israel* in 1948, the conflict between Israel and its Arab neighbours was still a matter of major concern to the peoples and rulers of the region, as well as far further afield. The Egyptian–Israeli peace treaty of 1979 (see Egypt and Israel) succeeded in defusing the immediate military situation between Israel and its largest Arab neighbour. But the developments of the years which followed – in particular, Israel's 1982 invasion of Lebanon, the military build-up which continued in both Israel and Syria, and the recurring cycles of intercommunal violence in the Israeli-occupied West Bank and Gaza* – showed that considerable parts of the Arab–Israeli problem still awaited a solution.

No-one was more aware of this fact than the Israelis (and those living under their rule), and their immediate Arab neighbours. By July 1985, annual defence expenditures in Israel were estimated to have risen to $3.62bn, out of a total Gross Domestic Product (GDP) of around $25bn. At that stage, one out of every thirty Israelis was serving in the regular forces, and three times that number performing periodic duty in the reserves. In Syria, annual military spending was roughly equivalent ($3.312bn), out of a GDP which stood at only around $20bn; and one out of every twenty-seven Syrians was serving in the regular forces. Meanwhile, in the years following the conclusion of the Egyptian–Israeli peace, both Israel and Syria considerably strengthened the military dimension of their relations with their respective superpower sponsors. This development drastically increased the possibility that the USA and the USSR might become drawn into any future hostilities between them.

Israel and Syria were also paying a heavy social and political price for the continuation of hostilities. In Israel, the failure to resolve the Arab–Israeli problem was considered by many to be a major factor promoting the rise of the ultra-nationalist and religious fundamentalist right wing. This Israeli 'new right' gained its first serious political foothold in the country during the premiership of the Likud bloc's Menahem Begin* (1977–83). While Begin was concluding his negotiations for the peace treaty with Egypt, members of the Gush Emunim and other 'new right' parties mounted a show of force indicating that, although they might in the end agree to the dismantling of Jewish settlements in Sinai prior to its return to Egypt, they would strongly resist any similar moves in the West Bank*, which they considered to be the heartland of 'Eretz Israel' (the land of Israel). From 1979 onwards, and even after the arrival of the Labour–Likud National Unity government in 1984, the 'new right' was able to sustain sufficient pressure on the Israeli government to prevent it from launching any serious bid to open negotiations concerning the West Bank and Gaza. At the social level, meanwhile, 'new right' heroes such as Rabbi Meir Kahane or Ariel Sharon were, for a period, increasingly successful in winning the hearts and minds of young Israelis away from the attachment to socialist and secularist ideals proclaimed by many of the early Zionist pioneers, and toward their own more rigidly fundamentalist or nationalist agendas.

The role of Syria

In Syria, President Hafiz al-Asad* continued, despite some ill-health, to lead a regime dominated by members of his own ʿAlawi* Muslim sect, which constituted only about 12 per cent of the national population (see Syria). On several occasions since Asad's 1970 seizure of power, this sectarian imbalance had led to an explosion of resentment from his country's majority Sunni* Muslim population. But by the mid-1980s, the ʿAlawis' grip on power seemed firmer than it had been at the beginning of the decade; and Asad had achieved much of this acceptance – which extended a good deal beyond Syria's national boundaries – by virtue of the perceived seriousness of his bid to achieve strategic parity with Israel.

Israel's two other Arab neighbours, Lebanon and Jordan, were certainly directly affected by the rise in Syrian confidence in the mid-1980s, as well as by other aspects of the continuing Arab–Israeli dispute. Hardest hit of any of the Arab states was Lebanon*, which lost around 100,000 of its population of three million, and saw its society, economy and much of its political system shattered by the decade of violence which started in 1975 (see Lebanon). While internal, intra-Lebanese tensions contributed in great part to this violence, it was also endowed with a considerable (and equally deadly) Israeli–Arab component. This component was particularly noticeable during Israel's 1982 invasion of the country, which resulted in some 17,000 to 20,000 Lebanese and Palestinian deaths, and during the thirty months which followed the invasion, which witnessed the growth of an unexpectedly successful armed Lebanese movement in resistance to the Israelis' continued presence there.

The role of King Husayn

If the Syrians were able to take advantage of (as well as foster) the strength of this anti-Israeli movement in Lebanon, then they were also able to profit from the seeming inability of Jordan's pro-Western King Husayn* to move towards any acceptable peace process with Israel. Husayn, whose population included a clear majority of Palestinians, had invested most of his hopes for regional stability in the peace process which US President Ronald Reagan launched in September 1982, when he reiterated American opposition to any Israeli annexation of the occupied territories, and openly advocated 'self-government by the Palestinians of the West Bank and Gaza in association with Jordan'. The 'Reagan peace plan' – the first ever to be spelled out for the region in such detail by a US president – met with the blunt opposition of Israeli premier Begin, but when Labour's Shimon Peres* came into office in 1984 he evinced more interest than Begin had in pursuing the options indicated in the plan. In February 1985, King Husayn reached an agreement with the PLO leadership which gave him the Palestinian support he needed to proceed in his exploration of the Reagan plan. There followed a few months of low-level US–Israeli and US–Jordanian diplomacy, but by mid-1986 it appeared that the US administration had little interest in pursuing its own peace plan. For his part Husayn indicated his new understanding of the regional facts of life by moving closer towards Syria's Asad, who had bitterly opposed the Reagan plan throughout.

Egypt's relationship with Israel

As for Egypt*, the conclusion of the 1979 peace treaty had by no means resolved all of that country's longstanding differences with Israel. The assassination of President Anwar Sadat* in October 1981 by a group of junior officers with Islamic fundamentalist leanings made it starkly evident that many groups among Egypt's large (50m) population remained strongly opposed to any dealings with 'the Zionist enemy'. When Israel invaded Lebanon the following year, the outrage of the Egyptians was so strong that Sadat's successor, President Husni Mubarak*, recalled the Egyptian ambassador from Israel, pending a complete Israeli withdrawal from Lebanon. The Israelis' failure to effect this, and their continued refusal to agree to arbitration of the major remaining Israeli–Egyptian border dispute over the resort area at Taba, led many Egyptians to resent the whole tenor of Israel's behaviour. Mubarak, meanwhile, tried to reconcile his government's continued pro-American stance with the Islamic, pan-Arab and anti-Israeli feelings of most of his people, by espousing the PLO's call to be included in negotiations over the West Bank and Gaza.

Egypt, with by far the largest population of any Arab country, was experiencing the same political pressures created throughout the Arab world by the new ideological tides of the 1980s. The form of Arab nationalism articulated by Egypt's Gamal ʿAbd al-Nasir (Nasser)* in the 1950s and early 1960s had been dealt a heavy blow by Israel's defeat of the Arab armies in 1967. With Nasserism on the wane, the intellectual current in many Arab capitals had swayed first in support of the idealistic young Palestinian guerrilla movement, and then – after that became quite rigidly institutionalized – it shifted again, in the direction of the kind of Islamic fundamentalism which scored a stunning, anti-Western victory in Iran in 1979. The outbreak, prolongation and lethal nature of the war which broke out between Iran and Iraq in 1980 clouded the issue for many Arabs in the anti-Western camp, since both states proclaimed their public opposition to 'Western imperialism'. Nevertheless, by the middle of the decade, and with the apparent cessation of American Middle East peace efforts, the tide amongst Arab intellectuals seemed set on an anti-US course. Even those Arab rulers who considered themselves firmly pro-Western (Mubarak, Husayn and several of the Arab rulers in the Gulf) were, in these circumstances, making moves towards bettering their relations with Moscow.

US and Soviet positions

By the mid-1980s, the superpowers' entanglement in the Arab–Israeli dispute seemed more firmly established than ever. Back in 1979, US President Jimmy Carter had won the diplomatic success represented in the Egyptian–Israeli peace treaty by presenting the US as a neutral intermediary between the two sides. Four years

Palestine and Israel: population figures

Population of Palestine (in thousands)

Date	Muslims	Christians	Jews	Total
c. 1850 (rough estimate)	c. 300	42	14	c. 356
1922 (census)	589	71	84	752
1931 (census)	760	89	175	1033
1946 (estimate)	1143	145	608	1912

Population of Israel (in thousands)

Date	Jews	Muslims	Christians	Druzes and others	Total
1950 (estimate)	1203	116	36	15	1370
1985 (estimate)*	3517	577	99	72	4266

* including parts of Jerusalem formerly under Jordanian rule.

Total population of Palestinians (in thousands)

WestBank*	707
Gaza Strip	451
Israel	657
Eastern Jordan	1148
Syria	223
Lebanon	358
Kuwait	300
Saudi Arabia	137
Other Arab countries	202
United States	105
Other countries	140
Total*	4428

* including parts of Jerusalem formerly under Jordanian rule.
Sources: A. Schölch, 'The demographic development of Palestine, 1850–1882', *International Journal of Middle East Studies*, 17 (1985), pp. 485–505; Government of Palestine, *Survey of Palestine* (1946), vol. 1, and *Supplement to Survey of Palestine* (1947); Central Bureau of Statistics, Israel, *Statistical Abstract of Israel* (1986); J. Tahir, 'An assessment of Palestinian human resources', *Journal of Palestine Studies* 14, iii (1985), p. 39.

later, however, President Ronald Reagan abandoned the last vestiges of such neutrality when his administration concluded a 'strategic agreement' with Israel, which reportedly included provisions for intelligence sharing, prepositioning of US military supplies in Israel, and some joint military exercises. By 1986, US government aid to Israel was running at $3.7bn per year, with all of this amount now given as an outright grant. (US aid to Egypt, whose officials had thought the 1979 treaty might bring them equal treatment, amounted to only around $2bn in fiscal 1986.) The pro-Israeli lobby in Washington meanwhile extolled Israel's virtues as a strategic asset for the US, though many in the Pentagon, looking beyond Israel to US commitments in the Gulf and the Indian Ocean, remained unconvinced by these arguments.

For their part, the USSR worked hard to realign their Middle Eastern assets in the aftermath of the 1979 treaty, which by virtue of its unilateral American sponsorship and its removal of Egypt from the list of states confronting Israel dealt a considerable blow to their position in the region. In 1980, the USSR was successful in persuading Syria's President Asad to conclude a formal Treaty of Friendship and Cooperation with it. The treaty called for 'continued cooperation in the military field', as well as mutual consultations on threats to the security of either party, or indeed 'violations of peace and security in the whole world'.

Much of this treaty seemed a dead letter, however, until the second half of 1982. Then, in the aftermath of the Syrians' defeat by the Israelis in eastern Lebanon, the USSR stepped up considerably the quality and quantity of its arms shipments to Syria. (Most of these arms were paid for in hard cash, by the Saudis.) With the Syrian government now openly committed to achieving strategic parity with Israel, the likelihood of superpower involvement in any future confrontation between these two states seemed high indeed. The USSR, meanwhile, was explicit in its warnings of the importance it attached to the area. In 1984, prominent Soviet academician Yevgeny M. Primakov warned that 'The Middle East is experiencing a very grave period in its history. The persistent, destructive effect of US policies in this region . . . may even threaten universal peace.'

The continuation of the Arab–Israeli conflict thus had broad regional and geopolitical ramifications. Nevertheless, at its heart it remained a hard-fought dispute between the two peoples – Palestinians and Israelis – who each claimed title to the historic Holy Land.

HC

Further reading

D. Astor and V. Yorke, *Peace in the Middle East: superpowers and security guarantees* (London, 1978)
A. Dawisha and K. Dawisha, eds., *The Soviet Union in the Middle East: policies and perspectives* (London, 1982)
J. C. Hurewitz, *Middle East Politics: the military dimension* (New York and Washington, 1969)
M. H. Kerr, *The Arab Cold War* (London and New York, 3rd edn.)
W. Laqueur and B. Rubin, eds., *The Israel–Arab Reader: a documentary history of the Middle East conflict* (Harmondsworth and New York, 1984)
W. B. Quandt, *Decade of Decisions: American policy toward the Arab–Israeli conflict, 1967–1976* (Berkeley and London, 1977)

Palestine and Israel: important dates in the history of the problem

1882 First wave of Jewish immigration from Eastern Europe ('First Aliyah').

1896 Theodore Herzl publishes *The Jewish State*, proposing establishment of a Jewish state as a solution to the problem of European Jewry.

1897 First Zionist Congress in Basel (Switzerland) adopts resolution calling for 'a home in Palestine secured by public law'.

1904–14 Second wave of Jewish immigration ('Second Aliyah'). Creation of first collective settlements (*kibbutzim*).

1914 Entry of Ottoman Empire into the First World War leads to negotiations about future of lands ruled by the Empire, including Palestine:
(1) correspondence between Sharif Husayn of Mecca, on behalf of Arab nationalists, and Sir Henry McMahon, British High Commissioner in Egypt, on behalf of the British government, 1915–16: in return for Arab participation in the eastern campaigns, Britain would be willing to recognize Arab independence within certain limits. Whether Palestine was included in the area would later be a matter of controversy.
(2) agreement between Britain, France and Russia, 1916 ('Sykes–Picot Agreement'): Arab provinces of the Ottoman Empire to be divided into areas under British and French control and an Arab state or confederation with British or French priority.

Palestine to be placed under international administration.

(3) letter from Arthur Balfour, British foreign secretary, to Lord Rothschild, leading member of the British Jewish community, 2 November 1917:

> His Majesty's Government view with favour the establishment in Palestine of a national home for the Jewish people, and will use their best endeavours to facilitate the achievement of this object, it being clearly understood that nothing shall be done which may prejudice the civil and religious rights of existing non-Jewish communities in Palestine, or the rights and political status enjoyed by Jews in any other country.

1917–18 British and Allied occupation of Palestine and Syria: British military administration in Palestine, French in Lebanon and on Syrian coast, Arab in Syria under Amir Faysal, third son of Husayn.

1919 Treaty of Versailles: former provinces of Ottoman Empire to be placed under Mandate, i.e. temporary rule of European states to prepare for self-government.

1920 March: General Syrian Congress proclaims independence of Syria including Palestine, with Faysal as king.

April: San Remo Conference of Allies allocates Mandate for Palestine to Britain, for Syria and Lebanon to France.

July: France occupies Damascus and rest of Syria.

1921 Provisional arrangement by which areas east of river Jordan to be administered by ʿAbd Allah, second son of Husayn (later becomes permanent: ʿAbd Allah as Amir of Transjordan).

1921 Amin al-Husayni becomes Mufti of Jerusalem; later, as president of Supreme Muslim Council, to be leader of Arab opposition to policy of creating Jewish national home in Palestine.

1922 June: statement of policy by British colonial secretary, Winston Churchill: what is intended is 'not the imposition of a Jewish nationality upon the inhabitants of Palestine as a whole, but the further development of the existing Jewish community . . . in order that it may become a centre in which the Jewish people as a whole may take . . . an interest and a pride'; immigration to be allowed, but not so great as to exceed economic capacity of the country to absorb new arrivals.

July: Council of the League of Nations approves text of the Mandate: mandatory government required to further establishment of a Jewish national home in collaboration with an appropriate Jewish agency; to develop self-governing institutions; and safeguard civil and religious rights of all, irrespective of race and religion. Transjordan to be under the Mandate, but provisions relating to Jewish national home are not to extend to it.

1929 Establishment of Jewish Agency, including representatives of non-Zionist interests, as official body to cooperate with mandatory government in development of the national home.

August: serious disturbances, beginning in Jerusalem and spreading to other parts of the country.

1930 October: British statement of policy: immigration to be restricted, as no room for further settlement until further development of the country.

1931 February: letter from Ramsay Macdonald, British prime minister, to Chaim Weizmann, president of the Zionist Organization, modifying the statement of policy in direction more favourable to Zionist claims.

1933 Coming to power of Hitler in Germany leads to increase in Jewish immigration to Palestine.

1936 Arab general strike in protest against British policy, turning into rural rebellion. British government appoints Royal Commission to inquire into the problem ('Peel Commission'*).

1937 Report of Royal Commission recommends that Palestine be divided into Jewish state, Arab state, and an enclave to remain under mandate including Jerusalem, Bethlehem and a corridor to the sea: Arab part to be joined to Transjordan; exchange of populations, in the last resort compulsory.

Revival of Arab revolt, continuing until 1939.

1939 February–March: conference summoned by British government in London ('St James's Conference'): parallel discussions by British government with Zionist and other Jewish delegates, and with representatives of Palestinian Arabs and Arab governments. British proposals not accepted by either side.

May: British statement of policy ('White Paper'):

(1) Jewish immigration to be limited to 75,000 in next five years; no more after that unless the Arabs prepared to acquiesce in it.

(2) restrictions on sales of land to Jews.

(3) Palestine to become self-governing state with Arab majority.
Rejected by Jewish Agency on principle; rejected by Arabs on points of detail.

1942 May: Conference of American Zionist organizations adopts resolution 'that Palestine be established as a Jewish commonwealth'.

1945 Creation of League of Arab States (Arab League*).

1946 Appointment of Anglo-American Committee of enquiry regarding the problems of Jewish survivors of Nazi massacres in Europe, and Palestine.
April: report of Committee recommends immediate issue of 100,000 immigration certificates for Jewish survivors of the Nazi massacres in Europe: Palestine to be neither Arab nor Jewish state, but eventually state which guards the interests of Muslims, Jews and Christians; in the meantime, should continue under Mandate or trusteeship.
May: after treaty between Britain and Transjordan, Transjordan becomes Hashimite Kingdom of Jordan, with ʿAbd Allah as king.

1946–7 Unsuccessful British negotiations with United States, Arabs and Zionists; growing breach between British and American views on the question; strong resistance of Jewish community to British policy; actions by resistance organizations (Haganah, Irgun, 'Stern Gang').

1947 February: British government refers question of future of Mandate to United Nations.
August: report by United Nations Special Committee on Palestine (UNSCOP): majority recommends partition into Jewish and Arab states, with international administration for Jerusalem; minority prefers federal solution.
November: General Assembly of United Nations accepts majority recommendation, with some changes.
December: Britain announces decision to withdraw from Palestine by midnight 14/15 May.

1948 Early months: growth of Arab–Jewish fighting, in which Jews obtain upper hand: gradual British withdrawal.
14 May: British withdrawal completed. Jewish leaders proclaim establishment of State of Israel*: Chaim Weizmann as president, David Ben-Gurion* as prime minister. Armies of Egypt, Lebanon, Syria, Jordan and Iraq cross frontiers. First Arab–Israeli War. Israeli army occupies greater part of Palestine.
September: Bernadotte, appointed by United Nations as mediator, assassinated by Jewish extremists.

The Nahr al-Barid refugee camp near Tripoli, Lebanon, 1952

1949 Armistice agreements negotiated by Israel with Egypt, Lebanon, Jordan and Syria. As a result:
(1) Israel left in occupation of four-fifths of Palestine; the rest administered by Jordan (West Bank) and Egypt (Gaza Strip).
(2) agreed frontiers, but no formal peace or recognition of Israel by Arab states.
(3) Jerusalem divided de facto between Israel and Jordan.
(4) 700,000 or more Palestinian Arabs become refugees, through flight or expulsion.

1950 Creation of United Nations Relief and Works Agency (UNRWA) to assist Palestinian refugees.
April: Jordanian parliament votes for incorporation of the West Bank in Jordan.

1952 Military coup in Egypt*; ʿAbd al-Nasir (Nasser*) emerges as dominant figure.

1955 Growth of tension between Israel and Egypt: Israeli raid on Gaza; Egyptian purchase of arms from Eastern Bloc; activity of Arab guerrillas.

1956 After Egypt's nationalization of Suez Canal Company, secret Israeli–French–British agreement to depose Nasser's government.

	October: Second Arab–Israeli War. Israeli invasion of Sinai followed by Anglo-French attack on Suez Canal zone. British, French and Israelis obliged to withdraw under pressure from United States and United Nations. UN peace-keeping force established on Egyptian side of frontier with Israel.
1959–62	Creation of Fatah*, Palestinian resistance movement.
1964	Creation by Arab League of Palestinian Liberation Organization* (PLO).
1967	June: third Arab–Israeli War ('Six Day War'). Following growth of tension on frontiers, Nasser asks UN to withdraw peace-keeping force. Israelis make pre-emptive attack on Egypt; Jordan and Syria join in war. Israelis occupy Sinai, Gaza Strip, Jordanian part of Jerusalem, and Jawlan (Golan) in Syria. UN Resolution 242 calls for acknowledgement of independence and territorial integrity of all states; withdrawal of Israeli armed forced from regions occupied in the war; just settlement of refugee problem. Israel annexes Jordanian part of Jerusalem (formalized 1980), but not recognized by most states.
1969	Fatah and other resistance groups take control of PLO; Yasir ʿArafat* becomes chairman. November: Cairo agreement regulating activities of Palestinian resistance movements in Lebanon.
1969–70	'War of attrition' between Israel and Egypt in Canal zone.
1970–1	Fighting in Jordan between army and Palestinian resistance movements; Palestinians leave Jordan for Lebanon.
1970	Death of Nasser; succeeded by Anwar Sadat.
1973	October: Fourth Arab–Israeli War. ('Ramadan War': 'Yom Kippur War'). Egyptian forces cross Suez Canal into Sinai; Israelis cross Canal in opposite direction; Syrians attack simultaneously in Jawlan (Golan). Cease-fire and UN Resolution 338, calling for negotiations for just and durable peace.
1974–5	Disengagement agreements negotiated by Henry Kissinger, US Secretary of State, with Israelis, Syrians and Egyptians: partial Israeli withdrawals in Sinai and Jawlan (Golan).
1974	October: Arab Summit Conference in Rabat (Morocco) recognizes PLO as sole representative of Palestinian people. November: ʿArafat invited to address UN General Assembly.
1975–6	Lebanese civil war*. Supporters of existing political system, mainly Maronite Christians, against those wishing to change it, mainly Muslims, with PLO support. PLO becomes virtually dominant in west Beirut and much of south Lebanon. Syrian army in west Beirut, parts of north and east Lebanon.
1977	May: Israeli general election. Labour Party, dominant since creation of Israel, defeated by nationalist coalition (Likud). Menahem Begin* becomes prime minister. Large-scale Jewish settlement in West Bank begins. October: joint Russian–American declaration calling for settlement ensuring 'legitimate rights of Palestinians'. November: Sadat visits Jerusalem and addresses Knesset on need for peace and resolution of Palestinian problem.
1978	March: Israeli invasion of south Lebanon in retaliation for Palestinian attacks. UN calls for cease-fire and establishes peace-keeping force on frontier. Israel withdraws, leaving local forces under its control ('South Lebanon Army') in southern strip. September: negotiations between Sadat, Begin and Jimmy Carter, US president, lead to Camp David Agreements on framework for peace-treaty between Egypt and Israel and for autonomy of West Bank.
1979	May: Egyptian–Israeli peace agreement signed under US auspices. Egypt recognizes Israel; Israel to withdraw from Sinai (withdrawal completed 1982). Subsequent negotiations between US, Egypt and Israel on autonomy for West Bank have no result.
1980	June: EEC government leaders support Resolutions 242 and 338 and need for Palestinian 'homeland' ('Venice Declaration').
1981	July: after clashes between Palestinians and Israelis on Lebanese–Israeli frontier, US diplomat negotiates cease-fire agreement between PLO and Israel.
1982	June: following attempted assassination of Israeli ambassador in London, Israel invades Lebanon, in order to destroy political and military power of PLO and install regime favourable to peace and relations with Israel. Siege of Beirut. August: agreement negotiated by US diplomat: PLO forces to leave Beirut, also Syrian forces. PLO establishes new headquarters in Tunisia. September: after assassination of president-elect of Lebanon, Bashir al-Jumayyil (Gemayel*), Israeli

army occupies west Beirut; Maronite militiamen enter with it and massacre several hundred Palestinians (Sabra and Shatila camps). Under US pressure Israel withdraws from west Beirut; multinational force (US, British, French and Italian) sent to restore security.
September: Ronald Reagan, US president, puts forward plan for peace in the Middle East. Arab Summit Conference at Fez (Morocco) adopts plan for resolution of Palestine problem.

1983 February: report of Israeli committee of enquiry into Sabra and Shatila massacres leads to resignation of Ariel Sharon, minister of defence.
May: under US auspices, Lebanon and Israel sign agreement for Israeli withdrawal and future relations. Active resistance by Syria and Lebanese opposition groups.
September: Israeli army withdraws to south Lebanon.

1984 February: Shiʿi militia (Amal) takes control in west Beirut.
February: faced with strong resistance, US and other elements in multinational force are withdrawn.
May: Lebanese president abrogates agreement of 1983 with Israel.
October: Israeli general election with inconclusive result. Coalition government: Shimon Peres (Labour) as prime minister, Yitzhak Shamir (Likud) as foreign minister.
December: after crisis in relations between PLO and Syria, ʿArafat and Palestinian forces obliged to leave Tripoli, last stronghold in Lebanon.

1985 May: beginning of conflict between Amal and revived PLO forces in Beirut camps.
June: faced with opposition from Amal and other Shiʿi groups, Israeli forces withdraw from south Lebanon, but leaving 'South Lebanon Army'.
February: agreement between King Husayn of Jordan and PLO on attitude towards eventual peace-talks.
October: Israeli air force bombs PLO headquarters in Tunisia.

1986 October: change in Israeli government: Shamir becomes prime minister, Peres foreign minister. Split between them on negotiations with Arabs and future of West Bank.

TM/AHH

The Iran–Iraq War

This grim, terribly destructive war became by far the longest conventional war fought anywhere in the world since the Second World War. In terms of casualties, numbers of troops involved and economic damage to the two states' infrastructure, the Iran–Iraq War* has outweighed all other conflicts in the Middle East. Already in its first few years, the war had cost more lives than all Arab–Israeli wars together. It is a source of potential danger, of heavy costs – but also of profits – for states of the entire region and beyond too.

President Saddam Husayn's decision to invade Iran on 22 September 1980 at four border points, and to abrogate the Algiers Agreement of 1975 (granting Iran sovereignty over its half of the Shatt al-ʿArab), had some important goals; it was intended to right a national 'humiliation' for Iraq, to deter Iran's revolutionary regime from its hostile actions and propaganda aimed at Iraq's Shiʿis*, and possibly also to cut down to size and replace the rule of the clerics in Tehran, or even to annex Iran's oil-rich province of Khuzestan ('Arabistan'). In attempting this, Saddam Husayn seemed to have a good chance of enhancing his reputation in the Arab world. But the misconceived *Blitzkrieg* ran into difficulties by the end of October 1980, when Iran's armed forces in the Gulf sector put up fierce and successful resistance against Iraq's divisions. Instead of the rapid, crushing victory confidently anticipated in Baghdad, there was endless war.

In some obvious respects, this conflict resembled the First World War, with trench warfare, mass deaths in infantry charges and the use of chemical weapons (poison gas) by Iraq. Air and naval warfare in the Gulf quickly exposed the vulnerability of all the small neighbouring Gulf states to attacks by the more powerful forces of

Iranian 'al-Fajr-3' soldiers preparing for battle at Mehran, 30th July 1983

Iran or Iraq. Yet early fears of the international spread of fighting have not so far been fulfilled, in spite of several alarms; none of the neighbour states were directly engaged in the war, nor had the superpowers been drawn in.

The risk of superpower involvement in the Gulf War was there from the beginning, with the industrialized world's fears for the safety of its oil supplies from the Gulf region. Already in January 1980 – one month after the Soviet invasion of Afghanistan – an expansion to the Gulf of the Monroe Doctrine had been proclaimed (the so-called Carter Doctrine). Its explicit aim was to warn off Moscow from any move to gain control of the Gulf region, which was declared a 'vital interest' of the USA by President Carter.

Even without the hypothetical Soviet advance to the Gulf, the risk of outside powers' involvement in a Gulf War through a naval crisis did look serious. Both the USA and USSR maintained large naval forces in the Arabian Sea–Indian Ocean area, and there were also British and French units present. The USA was busy planning the deployment in a regional crisis of CENTCOM, the successor to the Rapid Deployment Force scheme of 1980. Foreign warships were being widely used in Gulf waters to escort shipping, against the threat of Iraqi or Iranian attacks. Periodic threats by Iran to blockade the Straits of Hormuz if its own vital oil installations were attacked naturally increased fears for the safety of this strategic passageway for oil tankers.

Another source of potential friction through oil has been the pipeline war between Iran and Iraq, which became almost as serious as the raids on each others' oil facilities in or soon after September 1980. Iraq's vital pipeline routes for oil exports through Turkey, Syria and Lebanon were cut by sabotage on many occasions. By April 1982 Iran succeeded in its manoeuvre to cut off Iraq's oil exports via Syria (amounting to some 400,000 b/d) when Syria refused to ship further oil and confiscated Iraqi oil stocks. Turkey managed to keep open its lucrative oil pipeline from Iraq, sending troops across the Iraqi border at one stage in order to crush Kurdish* guerrillas threatening the pipeline. Turkey has rapidly expanded trading links since 1980 with Iran and Iraq alike, being ideally placed to satisfy the civil needs of both war economies. This new reliance on Turkey as a major trading and industrial partner may well prove of long-term significance for both Iran and Iraq.

Other economic links have tended to continue along the lines established in peacetime, though, as far as Iran is concerned, a boycott by its traditional arms suppliers has resulted in tortuous dealings with middlemen and those few states willing to supply weapons – Libya, Syria, Israel and North Korea. The huge cost of modern warfare, and problems in oil exports, has meant that both combatant states exhausted as early as 1982 their large reserves of foreign currency, becoming heavily dependent on barter deals for their oil or credit.

Iraq's debts rose dramatically from 1982. Baghdad relied on France for arms credits – as well as for large civil contracts – then also on the USSR again, after Soviet arms exports to Iraq resumed in 1982. Iraq's ability to go on paying for guns and butter has come only from massive Arab financial support led by Saudi Arabia and Kuwait. Kuwait's 'loans' (which looked most unlikely to be repaid by Iraq) totalled $7bn by mid-1985. The conservative Gulf states had all become drawn in on the side of Iraq, reluctantly, and often against the better judgement of rulers. This was not so much the result of Iraq's ambitious economic diplomacy as the fear by Arab rulers of the consequences for their fragile states of an Iranian victory.

Implications for the region

Ever since the fall of the Shah, the Islamic revolutionary regime under Ayatollah Khomeini* has represented a deeply unsettling influence throughout the region, posing a direct threat to the stability of conservative Gulf states in particular. Although Iran failed to get its anticipated support from the Shiʿite majority of Iraq's population, the regime undoubtedly had admirers and sympathizers in plenty around the Gulf region, and indeed beyond. In all the Gulf states there was anxiety not only about Iran's wider offensive aims in this war, but at the possible response to Khomeini's repeated calls for revolution from three social groups: the Gulf's large Shiʿi* population – mainly of Iranian origin – Muslim fundamentalist circles and migrant labourers drawn from many lands.

The Baʿthist* regime in Iraq had become a natural ally of conservative Arab rulers, an Arab shield against Iran's Islamic Revolution. Costly though financial support for Iraq proved, and even if the war did not leave the Gulf states unscathed, at least they were not directly involved. The rich but militarily weak and disunited Gulf states had, in effect, bought time to improve their security and to develop a joint defence strategy, while the two major regional powers slogged it out.

The seriousness of the threat to the status quo led in 1981 to the formation of the Gulf Cooperation Council (GCC)*, together with bilateral security agreements between Saudi Arabia and some other Gulf states. Two events at the end of the year challenged the smug assumption that the Gulf states could somehow avoid being drawn into the war – an attack on Kuwaiti oil facilities by Iranian warplanes, and the discovery of an Iranian-inspired plot to overthrow the government of Bahrain*. Of all the small shaykhdoms in the lower Gulf, Bahrain was the most vulnerable, with its large Shiʿi majority and close links with Iran.

The relative distance from the battlefields of the UAE* has allowed their Shaykhs to be more detached than those of other member states of the GCC. It is a remarkable fact that mediation in the war by the UAE has been accepted by Tehran. Of the seven Emirates, it is Dubai which has had the greatest commercial as well as historical links with Iran, but Dubai's rival Abu Dhabi also felt ambivalent about Iraq's current role as champion of the Arab cause. It is, after all, Iraq quite as much as Iran which has in the past supported subversive groups in the UAE, while the big Iraqi exile colony in Abu Dhabi is composed mainly of opponents of the Baʿthist regime.

For the states of the region, there are grave implications of an outright victory in this war by either Iran or Iraq. Both states have claims which could be revived on the territory of their weaker Gulf neighbours, and the costs of this protracted war have bled their economies to a point where the accumulated wealth of oil-rich Gulf neighbours must look very tempting. Some observers believe that Iran and Iraq's rulers will realize before long that both have already lost, and that a meaningful 'victory' is no longer possible for either state.

In terms of political influence and prestige within the region, however, either Iran or Iraq will come out on top. The surprising resilience shown by Iran's armed forces, and the fact that they have moved the battlefields over into Iraq from the devastated cities of Khuzestan where the war began, probably gives such prestige as there is to Iran. How Iran or Iraq may seek to exploit such a limited victory as now seems likely at any peace settlement must be considered.

It is the Gulf states which look set to find huge sums of cash (from their shrinking oil revenues) to provide compensation for incalculable war damage in both Iran and Iraq. Being paymaster should, in theory at least, give Gulf states confidence in their independent future. Yet the course of this war showed up how difficult it is to translate financial backing into political influence; Kuwait and Saudi Arabia expended thousands of millions of dollars in aid to Syria as well as to Iraq in largely fruitless attempts to influence these key states' policies.

Implications of an Iranian victory

The prospect of a total victory achieving all Iran's stated war aims looked dim at the time of writing (1986). The replacement of Saddam Husayn's Baʿthist regime by an Iranian-backed Islamic revolutionary government remained a vision. Yet Iraq for its part seemed to have little chance of breaking the stalemate, even after a sharp increase in 1985 of effective Iraqi raids on Kharg Island and other Iranian oil installations, together with a renewal of the 'war of the cities' – air raids on many Iranian cities. What looked more likely was an eventual compromise peace settlement, made acceptable by mutual exhaustion.

If, however, a partial victory is achieved by Iran, some of the implications are clear. Iran's ambitions extend beyond the Gulf, to Palestine and the Lebanon where its Shiʿi acolytes are well entrenched. Iran's historical claim to Bahrain as its 'fourteenth province' could well be revived, and enforced. Kuwait would face probable military pressure or coup attempts mounted by Iran, a result of its strong support for Iraq, its massive wealth and its proximity. In the UAE existing tensions would grow sharply, possibly leading to its fragmentation. As for Saudi Arabia, an Iranian victory would immediately reduce its influence in the region, challenging Saudi leadership of the smaller Gulf states in particular. A blow would be struck at the Saudi regime's prestige and standing, but its firm alliance with the USA would almost certainly preclude any direct Iranian attacks on the Kingdom. The presence in Saudi Arabia, and in most of the Gulf states, of foreign military specialists and a large contingent of Pakistani troops would serve as a steadying factor in any crisis.

The impact of an Iranian victory over Iraq might be felt far beyond the Gulf. Speculation has mounted that Turkey has a contingency plan to occupy Iraq's northern oil fields feeding the Kirkuk–Yumurtalik pipeline, and to cover Turkey's own Kurdish problem borders. King Husayn* of Jordan, one of Iraq's firmest allies, could face a challenge from within by Palestinians as well as pro-Iranian elements. For Syria, the downfall of its rival Baʿthist regime in Iraq would satisfy the main goal of Asad's alliance with Iran, but this could mark also an end to their close relationship. Iran and Syria have different and to some extent opposed interests in Lebanon, and could soon come into conflict there.

An Iranian cleric waving a Qur'an at soldiers leaving for the front

Implications of an Iraqi victory

The implications of an Iraqi victory raise a less dramatic scenario. Iraq's struggle has become associated with defence of the status quo, of the established order. Baghdad is most unlikely to begin the dangerous game of 'reorganizing' Iran's provinces and absorbing Khuzestan after the chastening experience of this war. Iraq would strike hard at Kurdish KDP forces in exile in Iran, and try to establish firm control of the Kurdish borderlands, leaving a client regime in Tehran.

As far as Kuwait is concerned, there are real fears of Iraq's intentions. Iraq's reservations on Kuwait's independent status since 1961 still remain, while Iraq has solid strategic reasons to widen its narrow coastline on the Gulf, and to control or annexe Kuwait's island of Warba (close to Iraq's military port of Umm Qasr). Iraq would probably also wish to take over from Iran the Gulf islands of Abu Musa and the Tunbs.

In the final analysis, economic considerations would play a big part at a peace settlement. For a lasting peace, rulers in Baghdad and Tehran will have to realize that peace is in their interest. The wealth of the Gulf states will certainly be needed in order to meet the massive bill for wartime destruction. Much of this damage is irreversible, and some of Iran's ruined cities may be abandoned. Oil pollution in the Gulf has reached a critical level, causing serious damage to Bahrain, Qatar and Dubai and inland waters of Iraq, as well as threatening marine life, and with it the very future of what is one of the most fragile ecosystems in the world. Oil wealth alone will not suffice to repair the damage caused by the war.

AH

Iran–Iraq War: chronology of events

1980 *22 September*, Iraq invades Iran along 300-mile front.

1982 *Spring*, Iran launches successful counter-attack. *June*, Iraqi troops withdraw from Iranian territory. *July*, Iranians cross into Iraq.

1983 *October*, Iran attacks along northern border with Iraq, taking 270 square miles of Iraqi territory. Iraq increases missile attacks and bombing raids against Iranian towns and petroleum installations. Iraq threatens Kharg Island oil terminal with French Super Etendard aircraft. Iran threatens to block Straits of Hormuz.

1984 *February*, Iran attacks across marshlands around Majnun Islands near confluence of Tigris and Euphrates. Iraq regains some territory and establishes defence system of dams and embankments near Basra. *March*, USSR improves relations with Iraq, supplying two-thirds of Iraq's armaments. *November*, USA re-establishes full diplomatic relations with Iraq. *December*, Iraq renews attacks on Iranian shipping, especially tankers using Kharg Island terminal. Insurance rates soar.

1985 *February*, Iran builds floating export terminal at Sirri Island. *March*, Iran commits 50,000 troops to an offensive on southern front in the region of Hawiza marshes, east of the Tigris. Iranians cross Tigris, temporarily closing Baghdad–Basra main road. Iraqis repel attack with heavy losses on both sides. Iraq attacks over thirty Iranian towns. King Husayn of Jordan and President Mubarak of Egypt visit Baghdad to demonstrate support for the Iraqis. *April*, UN secretary-general visits Tehran and Baghdad. Iraq suspends attacks on two occasions but Iran does not respond and Iraqi raids recommence. *July*, toll of dead and wounded estimated at over half a million. Iran refuses to negotiate, insisting on removal of Iraqi regime, withdrawal of Iraqi troops and reparations. *July*, Iran launches offensives on southern front, in the region of the Hawiza marshes and in Kurdistan in the north. *August*, Iraq makes series of concentrated raids on Kharg Island, making about sixty by *December*.

1986 *January*, Iraq claims to have recaptured most of the Majnun Islands. *February* 9, Iran launches al-Fajr (Dawn) 8 offensive. 85,000 Iranian troops cross Shatt al-ʿArab waterway and occupy Iraqi port of Faw, threatening Iraq's only access to the Gulf. Meanwhile Iran begins operations along Faw–Basra road to divert Iraqi forces. *February*, Iraq extends its exclusion area for Iran to Kuwaiti coast. Both sides increase attacks on tankers and other commercial vessels. Iraq continues attacks on Kharg Island. Iraq launches counter-offensive on Faw in mid-*February*. Iran opens up second front in Kurdistan with its Wal-Fajr 9 offensive. End of *February*, UN Security Council calls for cease-fire. May, Iraq makes first armed incursions into Iran since 1982, occupying area around Mehran. Iraq bombs Tehran for the first time since *June* 1985. Meeting of Iraqi and Syrian foreign ministers scheduled for *June* to discuss reconciliation is cancelled by President Asad. *July*, Iran recaptures Mehran. By *August* Iraq had failed to dislodge 30,000 Iranian troops from region of Faw.

Further reading

H. Amirsadeghi, *The Security of the Persian Gulf* (London, 1981)
A. H. Cordesman, *The Gulf and the Search for Strategic Stability* (Boulder, 1984)
R. G. Darius, J. W. Amos and R. H. Magnus, eds., *Gulf Security into the 1980s. Perceptual and strategic dimensions* (Stanford, Cal., 1984)
L. G. Martin, *The Unstable Gulf: threats from within* (Lexington, Mass., 1984)
B. R. Pridham, ed., *The Arab Gulf and the West* (London, 1985)

The Lebanese civil war as an international problem

Lebanon is an international problem today largely as a consequence of the decision of an international body, the League of Nations, to place the area under a French Mandate* after the First World War. France's subsequent decision to establish Lebanon as a separate state with greatly enlarged borders produced the essential instability of modern Lebanon, polarizing the new country between those who benefited from the Mandate (i.e. France and its Lebanese allies) and those who felt that their interests had been ignored (i.e. Syria and the Lebanese Arab nationalists). This polarization, though frequently disguised by the complexity of events, was at the heart of the civil war that began in 1975. The outside actors for the most part changed, but they were recognizably the heirs of earlier powers: the League was succeeded by the United Nations, France's role was appropriated and then distorted by Israel* and the US, while Syria and the Palestine Liberation Organization (PLO)* could claim with some justification to be the heirs of the Arab nationalist tradition.

Beirutis inspecting their war-damaged apartment

During the first period of the war, which ended with the Riyadh summit of October 1976, Syria* was the only outside power prepared to use both diplomacy and force to end the conflict. Other countries played limited roles, trying to influence the fighting through arms supplies or surrogate forces inside Lebanon. A few, such as France and the Vatican, tried to mediate. Neither the US nor the Soviet Union made great efforts to find a solution, though the Americans encouraged Israel to send weapons to the Maronite militias and tacitly supported Syria's military intervention in 1976. Although the US became actively involved in Lebanon during President Reagan's first term, the Soviet Union never played an influential role in the conflict. In spite of its Treaty of Friendship and Cooperation with Syria, and its extensive supply of arms and technicians to the Damascus regime after 1982, the Moscow government appeared to have little influence over President Asad's Lebanese policies. Nor was it able to sway events in Lebanon itself, despite close relations with the local communists and Kemal Jumblat's* Nationalist Movement.

The role of Syria

Syria's efforts to end the fighting stemmed from its determination to prevent the civil war from provoking a further conflict between the Arabs and Israel. Its objective was to preserve as much as possible of the status quo and to prevent either side from achieving a decisive victory. By the spring of 1976, the Maronite militias had been defeated on most fronts and it seemed that the war would end either in a total victory for their opponents or in the partition of the country and the establishment of a tiny Maronite state in the central and northern regions of Mount Lebanon. The Syrians realized that either outcome would be disastrous for themselves: apart from anything else, a victory for Jumblat's radical Arab nationalists and their Palestinian allies would almost certainly lead to an Israeli invasion of southern Lebanon and probably to a general Middle Eastern war as well. Syria first tried to end the fighting with a series of constitutional reforms. When Jumblat rejected these and continued his offensive against the Maronites, the Damascus regime sent its army into Lebanon to stop him and force through its own compromise proposals.

Syria's military intervention turned Lebanon into a major problem for the Arab League*. Until then the member states had held differing and often ambivalent views of the conflict. Although publicly they supported the PLO, some of the conservative regimes were secretly aiding its Maronite opponents. But the Syrian rescue of the beleaguered Christians, accompanied by heavy casualties among the PLO, provoked unanimous criticism from the Arab world: at a meeting in Cairo shortly after the intervention, Arab foreign ministers called for the removal of Syrian troops and their substitution by a mixed Arab force. In the face of so much hostility (even from his ally the Soviet Union), Asad* withdrew his troops from the Lebanese coast, accepting a cease-fire and the arrival of Sudanese and Libyan units of an Arab peace-keeping force.

During the second half of 1976, however, Arab attitudes to the crisis changed. The war continued with fresh atrocities and renewed fighting between the Palestinians, the Lebanese militias and the Syrian forces. The Arab peace-keeping attempt had faded away, and there was reluctant agreement among the Arab countries that Syria was the only power willing and capable of imposing peace on Lebanon. At summit meetings in Riyadh and Cairo in October 1976, the Arab states tacitly agreed to Asad's solution, with only Iraq and Libya dissenting from the consensus. The 30,000 Syrian troops in Lebanon were renamed the Arab Deterrent Force (ADF) and given a smattering of troops from other countries for cosmetic effect. Moreover, the Arab League agreed to pay for the ADF without retaining any control, apparently, over its future use.

The Syrian intervention put a temporary end to the heavy fighting between the militias. But it did not produce a permanent solution to the conflict, because the major participants were still not interested in a compromise settlement based on the status quo ante and a handful of minor political reforms designed to give the Muslim sects a slightly greater influence in government. The Maronite forces were grateful for their unexpected rescue by the Syrians, whom they generally regarded as their enemies. But once the threat posed by Jumblat and the PLO had receded, they saw no further need to cooperate with Syria's policies for Lebanon. Instead, they turned increasingly for support to their principal arms supplier, Israel.

The role of Israel

Israel's politicians had been showing political and strategic interest in Lebanon ever since 1948, but it was not until after the 1967 War* that they decided to employ military force against their northern neighbour. The bombing raids against Lebanese villages and Palestinian refugee camps – as well as the attack on Beirut airport in 1968 – were explained as reprisals against the PLO, but their principal aim was to force the Lebanese government to take action against the guerrillas. As the structure and composition of Beirut governments made this virtually impossible, in the mid-1970s Israel stepped up its support for the Maronite militias: large quantities of weapons were landed in Lebanon, a considerable number of militiamen were taken to Israel for training, and assistance was provided to a rebel Lebanese officer, Saʿd Haddad*, who controlled an area of Lebanon directly north of the Israeli border.

The 1978 Israeli invasion

Israel's policy became more active and visible after 1977 when Menahem Begin's* Likud* replaced the Labour Party in government. In March 1978, following a PLO raid south of Haifa, an Israeli force of 25,000 crossed the Lebanese frontier and within a few days had captured all of Lebanon south of the Litani River. If the objective of the invasion was the declared one of destroying the PLO in the area, Israel failed because most of the guerrillas escaped northwards. But if the real aim was the undermining of Syrian influence in Lebanon, the invasion was a success: the fragile consensus between Syrians, Lebanese and Palestinians, embodied in the Shtura Agreement of July 1977, was destroyed, and Syria's credibility as an authoritative peacemaker went with it.

While the Lebanese conflict was being fought only by Arabs, the rest of the world did little to try to end it. But the Israeli invasion added an international dimension to the problem, and the UN Security Council promptly called 'upon Israel immediately to cease its military action against Lebanese territorial integrity and withdraw forthwith its forces from all Lebanese territory'. It also voted to set up a special UN force for southern Lebanon (UNIFIL)* 'for the purpose of confirming the withdrawal of Israeli forces, restoring international peace and security and assisting the government of Lebanon in ensuring the return of its effective authority in the area'. Unfortunately, UNIFIL's role was undermined within weeks of its establishment. During the final stage of the Israeli withdrawal, Begin handed over the last stretch of territory not to UNIFIL, as directed by the UN, but to Haddad. In subsequent years, the behaviour of Haddad and his militiamen – particularly the bombardments of units of UNIFIL and the Lebanese army – effectively prevented the Lebanese government from reasserting its authority in the south of the country. Nevertheless, UNIFIL enjoyed at least a partial success as a buffer force between the PLO and Israel.

The 1982 Israeli invasion

Israeli ministers made public their dissatisfaction with the results of the 1978 campaign and hinted strongly at a more ruthless invasion in the future. After various incidents with Syria, an air raid against Beirut and a cease-fire with the PLO arranged by the US in 1981, Israel invaded again in 1982. Its ambitions, as defined by government ministers, were much wider this time: to defeat the PLO and its Lebanese allies so heavily that a pro-Israeli Maronite regime would be set up in Beirut, while at the same time Palestinian nationalism would be so weakened that the annexation of the Occupied Territories (the West Bank* and the Gaza* Strip) could be achieved without difficulty.

Israel's invasion, during which it pushed UNIFIL aside, forced the Syrian army northwards, bombarded West Beirut and caused the PLO to leave the capital, finally persuaded the US to play a serious part in the unending crisis. The beginning of the civil war had coincided with the collapse of American-backed regimes in Cambodia and South Vietnam, and the country was in no mood for active involvement in Lebanon. Besides, the US saw little urgency in ending a war which had absorbed the Arab world and removed much of the pressure for an overall settlement of the Middle East conflict. Changes of policy in favour of more active participation and increased support for Israel came after Reagan's election in 1980. Whereas President Carter had condemned the first Israeli incursion into Lebanon, the Reagan administration largely approved of the second, far more devastating invasion. When the UN Security Council censured Israel for its invasion of West Beirut, the United States abstained. When Israel rejected the Americans' own suggestion that a UN force should be sent to Beirut to oversee the PLO evacuation, the administration accepted the Israeli view and agreed to commit its own troops to a new multinational force (MNF), to be composed of units from Italy, France and the US (Britain later added a small contingent to the other units).

The MNF withdrew from Lebanon shortly after the PLO had embarked, but returned in September 1982 after the massacres of Palestinian refugees by the Phalangists in Sabra and Shatila. Its objective was to help the Lebanese government reassert its 'sovereignty and authority over the Beirut area', although there was little guidance as to how it would achieve this or how long it would take. The role of the MNF was ambiguous and controversial from the beginning. The US claimed to be impartial, yet its support for Israel was well known and its partners in the MNF were all members of NATO. The marines were in Beirut to protect the civilian population from further massacres, but other American forces were in Lebanon to help train the Lebanese army. Moreover, the new regime in Beirut was headed by a Phalangist leader, Amin Gemayel, whose indecisive but pro-Maronite leadership alienated most sections of the Muslim population.

The US gradually became embroiled in Lebanon as an active military force. This was partly because it was not regarded by many Lebanese as a neutral or benevolent influence, and partly because of the lack of coherence in its own policy. The proclaimed American objective was the withdrawal of Israeli and Syrian forces from Lebanon, and officials spent many months negotiating an agreement. Eventually, after a personal intervention by the American secretary of state, Lebanon and Israel signed an agreement in May 1983 providing for the withdrawal of its forces if Syria simultaneously did likewise. But as the US had chosen not to involve Syria in the negotiations, Asad refused to be part of the plan. Reassured by the growing military support from the Soviet Union, the Damascus regime had no desire to accept terms which confirmed its own loss of influence in Lebanon. It thus denounced the agreement and threw its support behind a new Lebanese opposition group calling itself the National Salvation Front. In September 1983, after the Israelis had withdrawn from the Shuf mountains, fighting broke out between Phalangists and Druze supporters of the opposition. As the Druzes were victorious even after Lebanese army units had reinforced the Phalangists, the US decided to intervene itself. While American officers were sent to direct the defence of the small town of Suq al-Gharb, ships from the US navy bombarded Druze and Syrian positions nearby. The town was saved but American credibility as a mediator was finally destroyed.

Casualties among the MNF and the Israeli occupying troops increased during the autumn of 1983. Suicide lorries were driven into the compounds of the French and US peace-keeping units in Beirut, where they exploded killing 58 French soldiers and 241 US marines. Public opinion in Europe and the US reacted to the attacks with calls to bring the MNF out, and in February 1984 the American and British contingents withdrew, followed shortly by the Italian and French. Israeli public opinion was also demanding a withdrawal, and in January 1985 the government pulled back its troops from Sidon. By the summer all foreign troops had left Lebanon except the Syrians, though Israel still patrolled a narrow security zone inside the frontier, while the government tried to bring about a Lebanese settlement of the conflict in Beirut. Lebanon once more had been relegated from the status of an international problem to that of an intra-Arab dispute.

Of the three main foreign participants in the Lebanese conflict, only Syria appreciated that it was essentially an internal problem which had to be resolved by the Lebanese. Israel saw it as an extension of the Arab–Israeli conflict and exploited it as such. The US too saw it as part of the struggle between Israel and the Arabs, but also as an area where it had unspecified 'vital interests' from which Russian influence must be excluded. Syria, by contrast, tried to resolve the conflict so as to prevent it from provoking another Middle Eastern war. The Arab League, with reservations, backed this aim, and the UN sought to separate some of the contestants in the south. Yet in the terrible decade 1975–85, both the conciliators and those who tried to impose their own solutions failed.

DG

Further reading

G. Ball, *Error and Betrayal in Lebanon* (New York, 1984)
J. Bulloch, *Final Conflict* (London, 1983)
A. Dawisha, *Syria and the Lebanese Crisis* (London, 1980)
D. Gilmour, *Lebanon: the Fractured Country* (London, 1983)
W. Khalidi, *Conflict and Violence in Lebanon* (Cambridge, Mass., 1979)
J. Randal, *The Tragedy of Lebanon* (London, 1983)
Z. Schiff and E. Ha'ari, *Israel's Lebanon War* (London, 1984)

Index

Atlantic
Ocean
Mediterranea
Bizerta
Tunis
Annaba
Algiers
Constantine
Tangier
Oran
Sousse
Qayrawan
Biskra
Sfax
Gabès
Fes
Meknes
Rabat
Casablanca
Ghardaia
Ouargla
MOROCCO
Atlas Mountains
Marrakesh
Bechar
Tripoli
Benghazi
Tobruk
Sirte
ALGERIA
Ghadames
LIBYA
Libya
'Ayun
Ain Salah
Marzuq
WESTERN
SAHARA
Sahara
Hogar
Mountains
Tamanrasset
Zouerate
Nouradhibou
MAURITANIA
Nouakchott
El-Fas